S0-AIT-149

THE LETTERS OF
CHARLES DICKENS

AMATEUR COMPANY

Back Row: W. Telbin, G. or T. Evans, Shirley Brooks, M. Lemon Jnr, W. Jones, F. Evans Jnr, M. Stone, F. Berger, M. Lemon, A. Egg.
3rd Row: Albert Smith, Stanfield, Miss Evans, E. Pigott, Frances Dickinson, J. Luard
2nd Row: Keith, CD Jnr, Kate Dickens, Georgina Hogarth, Mary Dickens, Wilkie Collins, Helen Hogarth.
Front Row: Charles Dickens.

THE BRITISH ACADEMY

THE PILGRIM EDITION

The Letters of Charles Dickens

GENERAL EDITORS

†Madeline House Graham Storey Kathleen Tillotson

Volume Eight

1856–1858

EDITED BY

Graham Storey and Kathleen Tillotson

CLARENDON PRESS · OXFORD

1995

Oxford University Press, Walton Street, Oxford OX2 6DP
Oxford New York
Athens Auckland Bangkok Bombay
Calcutta Cape Town Dar es Salaam Delhi
Florence Hong Kong Istanbul Karachi
Kuala Lumpur Madras Madrid Melbourne
Mexico City Nairobi Paris Singapore
Taipei Tokyo Toronto
and associated companies in
Berlin Ibadan

Oxford is a trade mark of Oxford University Press

Published in the United States
by Oxford University Press Inc., New York

British Library Cataloguing in Publication Data
Data available

Library of Congress Cataloging-in-Publication Data
Data available
ISBN 0 19 812662 X

Typeset by Joshua Associates Ltd, Oxford
Printed in Great Britain
on acid-free paper by
Bookcraft Ltd.
Midsomer Norton, Bath

CONTENTS

LIST OF ILLUSTRATIONS vii

PREFACE ix

ACKNOWLEDGMENTS xix

BIOGRAPHICAL TABLE xxiii

ABBREVIATIONS AND SYMBOLS xxvii

The Letters 1856–1858 1

APPENDIXES

A Letter to *The Times*, 8 February 1856, from Thomas Carlyle, Charles Dickens and John Forster 729

B Draft Resolution concerning *Household Words*, February 1856 730

C Dickens's amended drafts for Miss Coutts's *Summary Account of Common Things*, 30 March and 7 April 1856 731

D Programme of events "In Remembrance" of Douglas Jerrold, June–July 1857 736

E Agreement between Shirley Brooks and Richard Bentley, 4 September 1857 738

F Letters and statements referring to the Separation 739

G Dickens's memoranda for his draft Will, 1858 750

H The reading tour, Autumn 1858 752

I Letters referring to the possible Colin Rae Brown slander action, October 1858 754

J Letters concerning *Household Words* between John Forster and Bradbury & Evans, November to December 1858 758

K Dickens's Reminiscences of Douglas Jerrold 762

CORRIGENDA 764

INDEX OF CORRESPONDENTS 765

INDEX OF NAMES AND PLACES 771

ILLUSTRATIONS

Amateur Company in *The Frozen Deep*,
12 July 1857 — *Frontispiece*

Dickens's "Personal" statement, *Household Words*,
12 June 1858 — p. 744

PREFACE

Since the publication of our seventh volume in 1993, the total of letters known to us has risen by 63, from 14,026 to 14,089. This volume contains 1,324 letters (including extracts and mentions). The texts of 467 have been transcribed from originals or photographs of originals. We have discovered six forgeries in this volume: *To* John Leech, 25 September 1856; *To* Wilkie Collins, 27 January 1857 and 21 November 1857 (derived from *To* Benjamin Webster, 21 November 1857); *To* W. M. Thackeray, 10 June 1857; *To* Sir Joseph Paxton, 23 December 1857; *To* T. C. Grattan, 24 April 1858. All appear to be by the "South Coast Forger".[1]

Dickens's chief work in this period was *Little Dorrit*, appearing monthly from January 1856 to June 1857. At the beginning of the year he was at first three, then two numbers ahead of the printers; at the end, he was writing the "two little words" of the final double number only on 10 May,[2] but sent the proof to Stanfield on 20 May and had the entire volume on 30 May. From the outset he had the confidence given by sales higher than for any of his previous monthly novels,[3] and his letters while writing in 1856 show little sign of strain or anxiety; the main lines had been planned, and crucial decisions taken by the autumn of 1855. There had been some months of uncertainty, but in October 1855 he altered the title from "Nobody's Fault"[4] to *Little Dorrit*, signalising a move away from a too narrowly topical response to the troubles in the Crimea. While it is still the most politically topical of his novels, specific commentary is broadened into satire, in the famous exposure of the Circumlocution Office, "How not to do it".[5] The narrative is set back in time—no railways, and the scenes in the long-abolished Marshalsea have their source in Dickens's childhood. But the Circumlocution Office is obviously dateless, as recognisable now as then. So is Lord Decimus, the leading Barnacle, both when seen in Parliament and as chief guest at Mr Merdle's dinner-party designed as a "Patriotic Conference", and clearly aimed at Palmerston.[6] For Mr Merdle himself Dickens drew on the rise and fall of John Sadleir; but as he says, he "already had the general idea of the Society business":[7] that is, an all-round attack on contemporary

[1] See Vol. I, Preface, p. xxix.

[2] *To* Collins, 11 May 57.

[3] *To* Bradbury & Evans, 2 Dec 55 (VII, 758 & *n*). In America *Harper's New Monthly Magazine* apparently purchased advance sheets and published the novel in instalments from Jan 56. As the whole magazine, of over 140 pp (2 cols), sold for 25 cents, they made a very good bargain. An account of Dickens's life and career, with many inaccuracies, accompanied the second instalment (Feb 56). Later in the same year, they lifted several pieces from *Household Words* without acknowledgment.

[4] But he reverted to it in "Nobody, Somebody, and Everybody" (*HW*, 30 Aug 56); though the war was over, the Commission of Enquiry into its mismanagement continued. See *To* Forster, 8–10 Aug, 56 and *fn*; CD also criticised the Report in "Stores for the First of April" (*HW*, 7 Mar 57).

[5] Bk I, Ch. 10 in No. III for Feb 56 (written Oct 55).

[6] Bk I, Ch. 34 in No. X and Bk II, Ch. 12 in No. XIII, the latter also a masterpiece of social satire.

[7] *To* Forster, 29–30 Mar 56.

society from several angles, as distinct from particular social abuses, and conducted with more animus than ever before.[1]

For the majority of these months of writing Dickens was resident in France, which perhaps made him more aware of what he disliked in England.[2] In Paris, he enjoyed the intervals of work by continuing to consort with writers, actors and artists, including his sittings to Ary Scheffer. He signed an agreement with Hachette et Cie for a complete translation of his novels,[3] which was completed a year later. As in 1855, some of his raciest letters, both to Forster and Wilkie Collins, describe theatre visits and dinner-parties.[4] Regular sallies across the Channel took care of his proofs and of *Household Words*, on which he kept his hand though contributing less of his own writing.[5] He entertained visitors from England, both in Paris and, still more, at Boulogne, now a favourite resort for holidaymakers with families. Though their residence was shortened[6] by a diphtheria scare, to the sorrow of their devoted landlord, the three schoolboy sons soon returned to continue their education.

During Wilkie Collins's visits they began work on their next play, designed for New Year, 1857; and for the latter part of the year its demands competed with those of *Little Dorrit*, so that by September he was falling behind. Although *The Frozen Deep* is mainly Collins's writing and never openly called a collaboration, it is clear both from letters and much surviving manuscript material[7] that Dickens was closely engaged in the writing as well as the production; at the rehearsal stage these can hardly be separated. Preparations were far more elaborate than for any previous Tavistock House play, with a large extension built out at the back of the house from the schoolroom, even "knocking down the drawing-room". The usual two nights of performance were extended to four (besides a pre-view) and the press were invited. One reason was to assist Collins's ambitions as a dramatist for the professional theatre,[8] but as always, the activity itself answered Dickens's deeper needs.[9] Before the end of October the script was complete (after some suggestions by Forster) and

[1] One result was that reviews were influenced by the political bias of the critic: see *To* Forster, 30 Jan, *fn*, and 5 May, and *To* Hollingshead, 27 July and *fn*. CD replied to James Fitzjames Stephen with justified sarcasm in "Curious Misprint in the Edinburgh Review".

[2] As is suggested in several *HW* articles; see "Insularities", "Why?" (19 Jan and 1 Mar 56); "Proposals for a National Jest-Book" (3 May); "Railway Dreaming" (10 May).

[3] See *To* Hachette, 14 Jan 56.

[4] See *To* Forster, 20 Jan for his meeting with George Sand, and *To* Collins, 13 and 22 Apr for her ridiculous version of *As You Like It*.

[5] The total for 1856–7, apart from the collaborated Christmas number and the "Lazy Tour", is about 14. For "Out of the Season", 28 June 56, see below, p. xvii.

[6] See *To* Mrs Dickens, 25 Aug and *fn*.

[7] Draft in Collins's hand heavily amended by Dickens; prompt book (with 3 different copyists), heavily amended both by Collins and Dickens (particularly in Act III), are in the Morgan Library (MA 81). They were edited by Robert L. Brannan, *Under the Management of Mr. Charles Dickens*, Cornell, 1966, with a useful Introduction and a text which does not claim precise accuracy. Only two facsimile pages are included; at p. 50 the copyist is a clerk, and at p. 51 the whole is in CD's hand. For the much revised Olympic version of 1866 see later vols.

[8] As is clear in 1855 over *The Lighthouse* (*To* Collins, 8 July 55, Vol. VII, pp. 669–70); declined then by Webster for the Adelphi. For its performance at the Olympic on 10 Aug 57 see *To* Emden, 20 Aug and *fn*.

[9] In the same way he had welcomed a change from writing to theatricals in 1848–9, 1851–2 and 1855.

Dickens had learnt his part during a 20-mile walk.[1] Richard Wardour, the tragic hero, in love with Clara, meets Frank Aldersley in the Arctic, his successful rival; he conceals his own identity and plots revenge upon Frank, but in the end magnanimously sacrifices his own life to save him for Clara's sake. The appeal of this romantic situation to Dickens lay simply in its strongly theatrical effect; at this stage it had no relation to his personal life and the emotion was independent of any object outside the play.

After the excitement had died down he returned to *Little Dorrit*, with "knitted brows" over the March number.[2] Many letters over the next three months mention his hard work; that it was eventually completed successfully and without too much stress or the breaking of other essential engagements[3] is a tribute to his stamina and command of his creative powers. Towards the end he moved to Gravesend for a week; this had the double advantage of comparative freedom to work on the big closing number[4] and nearness to Gad's Hill, now completely his own.

The family's new summer home was "inaugurated" by a party for Catherine's first visit on her birthday. June would have been a leisurely month, with the play receding into the past. But on 9 June news of the sudden death of Douglas Jerrold altered everything. His wide and varied popularity, as dramatist, *Punch* writer, editor of radical journals, called for commemoration. Dickens sprang into action. Before the date of the funeral he had assembled and planned a programme "In Remembrance" for June and July, copies being distributed on that very occasion.[5] A representative committee, with Arthur Smith as secretary, was named; family and friends in the casts of *The Frozen Deep* and accompanying farces were alerted,[6] to perform at the Gallery of Illustration. The hall with a small stage and large capacity was appropriate to semi-private performances, and especially to the genuinely private command performance before the Queen on 4 July.[7] The increasingly successful progress of this six weeks' programme, which also included Dickens's own reading of the *Carol* in a large hall, besides lectures, concerts and theatre performances of Jerrold's own plays, is demonstrated in the letters and notes, with one exception: a festive celebration[8] at a

[1] See *To* Collins, 26 Oct.

[2] *To* Macready, 28 Jan, and *To* Forster, ?9 Feb. Miss Wade's "History" was one problem, and he finished less than three weeks before publication. More exacting was the need to disentangle the threads of his plot (see *To* Macready, 28 Feb and *fn*).

[3] Except for joining Paxton at Coventry, as he had promised: see p. 320.

[4] See *To* G. F. Hudson, 11 Apr 57 and *fn* for the sources of Mrs Clennam's confession and reconciliation with Amy (Ch. 31).

[5] See *To* Cooke, 15 June 57, *fn*, and Appx D for a copy of the programme.

[6] All took part except Edward Hogarth and Mrs Wills: see *To* Collins, 16 June 57.

[7] A copy of the prompt book made by a professional calligrapher, with illuminated title pages, is in the Royal Library, Windsor.

[8] On 12 July; reported in the *Illustrated London News*, 18 July, no doubt by Lemon "... a capital group ... done by artistic hands ... the sun was powerful, the turf cool, and the champagne frozen-deeped ... everybody looked well; everybody was pleased." An original print is in the Tyrrell Collection, Dickens House. The setting was the garden of Albert Smith's home at North End Lodge, Fulham. An invitation card for Marcus Stone from "The Glaciers of Mont Blanc | requests ... to meet | The Icebergs of the Frozen Deep" is reproduced in Thomas Wright, *Life of Charles Dickens*, 1935, facing p. 253. Wright was mistaken in thinking that the host was Frederic Ouvry; the initials written in at foot of card are not "F.O.", but "T.O.", for "Turn Over" since directions for finding North End Lodge are on the other side. All the cast except Alfred Dickens were present; the "others" were Albert Smith and Miss Evans (i.e. Bessie).

party given to the cast and others, and photographed (see Frontispiece). Dickens enjoyed all the necessary activities,[1] and had the advantage of two bases, in city and country; but it was a crowded life; at Gad's Hill he entertained visitors, saw Andersen off at last, and helped with Walter's preparations for India. The youth was in London with his mother on 10 July (clearly to watch the play next day); on 19 July his father took him to Southampton and stayed overnight.

Dickens had to repeat his *Carol* reading (to an audience of over two thousand) and planned to do so in Manchester. The possibility of also taking the play there had been suggested[2] but was not finally settled until that occasion, 31 July. A final London performance followed on 8 Aug. Meanwhile, professional actresses for Manchester must be sought to replace the five amateurs. He wanted "the best" and first sought to persuade Mrs Compton, recalling how she had acted with him in 1851–2 and earlier; when she declined, or perhaps before, he invited Mrs George Vining, Ellen Sabine, Mrs Ternan and her two younger daughters, Maria and Ellen. He would certainly have seen Mrs Vining before, and could hardly have missed Mrs Ternan. He recalled Maria in her infant prodigy period. There is no certain evidence that he had seen Ellen Ternan. Whatever the situation, rehearsals were required which duly took place on 18–20 Aug in London.

Dickens and his family, including Catherine, were at Manchester from 20 to 25 August. The final scene of the play with Maria Ternan as heroine was an intense emotional experience;[3] no immediate letter describes it, but it must be implied in the "grim misery and restlessness"[4] soon after the excitement had subsided. This was clearly one reason for the journey to Cumberland; another, the convenience of going on to Doncaster[5] where he knew the Ternans were due to perform during Race Week. But the unexplored region itself attracted him[6] and the necessity of writing for *Household Words* was no mere excuse; there had been a long gap in his own contributions. Wilkie was the obvious companion; they would play the parts of "Two Idle Apprentices" (to their Muse) on a "lazy tour". In the writing, these roles were only partly maintained; in practice Dickens was far from idle. The week, which seems much longer, was packed with incident.

Before leaving London, Dickens wrote to Forster (but "no one else") of his unhappiness with Catherine, without blaming her. The same letter hints at the idea of public readings for pay. The latter subject did not surface again for some months, nor was actual separation[7] from Catherine proposed. But there are no letters to her

[1] One playgoer was surprised to find him helping to sell tickets (*CD by Pen and Pencil*, p. 188).

[2] See his cautious note on 25 July to Miss Coutts, who had evidently heard of it; he is "resolved" both to discuss (presumably with committee and cast) "engaging actresses" but also resolved, in the next sentence, "not to act there at all". On 27 July he told her merely that he was leaving on the 30th, "to read at Manchester". In *To* Frederick Hudson, before leaving town on 30 July, he had "made no arrangements to perform".

[3] See the vivid account in *To* Miss Coutts, 5 Sep; and more fully, still later, in *To* Mrs Watson, 7 Dec.

[4] *To* Collins, 29 Aug.

[5] See *To* The Angel Hotel, 3 Sep, before leaving London, booking rooms for himself and Collins from 13 Sep; the length of their stay was left uncertain.

[6] Dickens may also have recalled the romantic hero of Scott's *Guy Mannering*; see Chs 21–3 on the "upper part of Cumberland", the Solway coast, and (later) Allonby.

[7] Later (23 Oct) he wrote to de la Rue about Catherine in a "serio-comic" way.

during his fortnight's absence, in contrast to earlier travels when he always wrote to her as well as to Georgina.

The Doncaster visit added a chapter to the "Lazy Tour"; in its ulterior object it was apparently disappointing. Dickens left a day earlier than he planned,[1] and six months later recalled the "Doncaster unhappiness",[2] linked with "the last night of *The Frozen Deep*". A rational assumption is that his first strong interest had been in the Ternans as a courageous family group, and that he was attracted first to Maria. It seems likely that at Doncaster he met with discouragement, if not a rebuff, and was permitted only social encounters, such as the expedition to the country on the last Sunday. But when the Ternans returned to London in October for their theatrical engagements, Ellen was in the ascendant. Whether or not she knew it, his letter to Buckstone about her as "the young lady" in the Haymarket company shows his lasting concern for her.[3]

The next piece of writing may indirectly reflect his feelings. In October he began work on the Christmas Number, "The Perils of Certain English Prisoners".[4] Of this he thought very highly, partly because of its topical relevance to the Indian Mutiny. But he was long unable even to read the proofs of his last page, being overcome by weeping over the humble Gill's misplaced love for "my Lady".[5]

Otherwise, much of the autumn and early winter was occupied with impersonal routine and arrears of correspondence.[6] Dickens dealt with *Household Words* and other publishing matters, organised assistance to his old friend Marguerite Power, and fulfilled two promises of charity readings. He confessed himself very tired and went down with influenza in early December. No letter mentions Christmas celebrations at home, and New Year's Eve passed without any festivities. He kept his hand on the editing, but became increasingly restless, and uncertain whether to start a new book.[7] But by mid-March he had privately committed himself to the alternative plan of a reading tour in the autumn.[8] At the same time he had sounded Miss Coutts and Mrs Brown and was arguing the question with Forster. By the 9th April the matter was finally settled, and paid readings in London ran from 29 Apr to 22 July.

His immediate reason was to "do Something" strenuous to alleviate his unhappiness; other motives were the need for more money,[9] and perhaps above all, the prospect and stimulus of a still closer relation to a wider public. He may have foreseen the expense of Catherine's separate home, and would already hope to do more for the Ternans. The effect of these plans on his marriage is well summarized by Forster, when he says that "the one relief sought from the misery had but the effect

[1] See *To* Wills, 20 Sep, *fn*.

[2] *To* Collins, 21 Mar 58.

[3] *To* Buckstone, 13 Oct 57.

[4] Wilkie Collins's share, apart from general consultation, was confined to one chapter.

[5] *To* Lady Duff Gordon, 23 Jan 58; cf. references here to scaling mountains and killing dragons for the girl of his heart, and in Mrs Watson, 7 Dec, to his "Princess".

[6] Mostly from Tavistock House, but for his own writing, sometimes with Collins, he retreated to Gad's Hill, in spite of the winter.

[7] See *To* Forster, 27 and 30 Jan. Though Dickens does not say so, he was again attracted to the idea of a hero who renounces his love (see *To* Forster, 3 Feb; omitted from the *Life*).

[8] *To* Evans, 16 Mar.

[9] See *To* Cerjat, 7 July 58. He now had two homes to keep up, with considerable expenses for Gad's Hill.

of making desperate any hope of a better understanding"—clearly implying that Catherine was opposed to the whole reading project. Other "sorrowful misunderstandings" no doubt included Dickens's anger at her mistake in approaching Miss Coutts on behalf of her brother, Edward. She may have made some new discovery about Ellen.[1] In May the re-opening of Gad's Hill for the summer may have fixed the time for Dickens's decision to separate, made known to Miss Coutts at self-justifying length on 9 May.[2] Other old friends were told or had heard; Macready, for one, evidently expressed deep regret, and perhaps remonstrated in the light of his long knowledge and affection for them both.[3] The final stages are fully documented in the letters and notes. The "Personal" statement, however much Dickens was provoked by Mrs Hogarth and Helen (and incidentally Thackeray) ran counter to the advice Dickens had given to another only a few weeks before: "it would suggest to the public what they have no idea of" and its effect would be "exactly the reverse" of what was intended.[4] The wise counsel of Forster and Ouvry was disregarded. The statement raised more gossip and conjecture than it was supposed to allay. His one concession to his advisers had been to consult Delane and abide by his advice. On the face of it, this was a surprising choice; but besides being highly regarded as a great editor, a man openly consulted by statesmen, famous for his cool judgement, he was already a personal friend of Dickens, and recently in his confidence over a quite different matter.[5] On the other hand, however impartial, he still was editor of *The Times*, and that was where the statement first appeared, the day before a smaller public could read it in *Household Words*. The so-called "Violated letter" was bound to leak out, and Dickens's wish to have the "Personal" statement published in *Punch* marks the extremity of his irrational behaviour.

That his friendship with Forster was unaffected by their differences is evident, both in the testimony of the moving dedication of the Library edition and Forster's staunch support in the other battle of wills that was waged in the same months: the continued attempt to reform the Literary Fund. Its records in several letters, Minutes and pamphlets, and *Athenaeum* editorials, suggest that the reformers were right in principle though wrong in some details, and that Dickens's chief fault was his unwillingness to admit defeat.[6] The dispute seems to have made him no new enemies

[1] The much-repeated anecdote about a present of jewellery for Ellen, sent by the vendor to Catherine, might be dated in August 1857 at Manchester, or Christmas; but an even more likely occasion is Ellen's birthday on 3 Mar 58. If the article "Please to Leave your Umbrella" in *Household Words* on 1 May (XVII, 457) was related to an actual visit to Hampton Court, its date would be in the "fast-falling spring rain" of mid-March. Most of the piece is satirical, the writer's umbrella representing his own sensible views on art, justice, and politics, in contrast to those commonly held. In his comments on the Palace he adopts "the manner of the Sentimental Journeyer" (Sterne) and thinks (incongruously) of a "little reason" for good humour even in its melancholy setting. But he was clearly alone.

[2] See *fnn* on pp. 558–60. By 13 July, according to Crabb Robinson, who recorded a "very friendly chat" with Miss Coutts, she was "satisfied there has been nothing criminal—nothing beyond *incompatibilité d'humeur*—to require a separation, which should have been done quietly. Miss Coutts is friendly with both husband and wife." (*Henry Crabb Robinson on Books and Their Writers*, ed. E. J. Morley, 1938, II, 778).

[3] *To* Macready, 28 May; see also the letters to Leech and Mrs Gore.

[4] *To* Holman Hunt, 20 April 58.

[5] Letters in *The Times* from "Fallen Women".

[6] Crabb Robinson, who was present but did not vote, took this view, referring in his diary to Dickens's "bold, clever, but imprudent speech" (*op. cit.*, II, 758).

and the only opponent to attempt further retaliation in the following year was Thackeray.[1] But with him, relations were exacerbated by the "Garrick Club Affair" which broke out in July just when Dickens was convincing himself that he was happily settled at Gad's Hill. On this, modern scholars still take sides; but it is common ground that Edmund Yates was initially to blame. Neither Dickens nor Thackeray came out of it well, and many who read Thackeray's letters will think him the more gratuitously offensive. The affair rumbled on through 1859, and this quarrel would never be fully made up.

Much sadder was the long-lasting breach with that close friend and boon companion, Mark Lemon,[2] who acted for Catherine, and as editor of *Punch* was partly responsible for rejecting the "Personal" statement. With Evans, who shared that responsibility, and was another partisan, Dickens broke off all relations; but this was also complicated by the growing dispute with Bradbury & Evans over *Household Words*.[3]

At the end of July[4] there was an interval at Gad's Hill when several visitors were entertained. But the great reading tour[5] of England, Scotland, and Ireland started only ten days after the last London reading. Dickens and Arthur Smith had been preparing for it for some time, Dickens revising his chosen texts,[6] and his manager arranging the programme. Its extreme limits, north, west and east, were Aberdeen, Limerick and Hull; but because new requests kept coming in, towns had to be inserted in the list without regard to geographical or travelling considerations, and later, return visits made to satisfy demand.[7] By mid-October Dickens was giving eight readings in a week in five different towns, a feat never to be repeated. More often, he undertook extra travel so as to have a short break in London or at Gad's Hill; as this was impossible during the northern fortnight, his daughters joined him at Newcastle[8] and were with him throughout the Scottish tour. Their enjoyment was the only thing "without alloy"; both then and earlier he admitted great fatigue, and even reluctance, which nevertheless he believed did not affect the reading itself. The euphoria of meeting an audience never failed, especially from a gas-lit stage; he came to dislike his "morning" (3 p.m.) performances.

His longest absence from his family was from 17 August to 4 September, first in Liverpool and then in Ireland, and this produces many long and lively letters, giving his first impressions of a country and people new to him. The warmth of their

[1] At the Anniversary Dinner, normally a festive occasion, when controversy was avoided (see next vol.).

[2] They were reconciled at the time of Stanfield's death in May 1867, when they "embraced affectionately" at the grave (N, III, 781).

[3] A notice was served on them on 22 Dec to dissolve the partnership on 28 May 59; see *To* Wills, 20 Dec and *fnn*.

[4] In mid-July Dickens had seen Landor at the Forsters' on his way to what was to prove permanent exile from England: see *To* Georgina Hogarth, 29 Aug and *fnn*.

[5] It lasted from 1 Aug to 13 Nov and comprised at least 85 readings in over 40 different towns, which is twice the extent of the programme first proposed in *To* Evans, 16 Mar 58.

[6] For details see Philip Collins, *CD: The Public Readings*, Oxford, 1975, always indispensable; pp. 1–211 cover the current repertoire of readings. Some had been revised earlier, but new variations were constantly introduced.

[7] e.g. he read at Manchester on 18 Sep and again on 16 and 23 Oct, his visits separated by over a dozen others.

[8] See *To* Georgina Hogarth, 26 Sep, and *To* Forster, 10 Oct and *fnn*.

response at the readings and in casual conversations is especially emphasised. The five readings at Dublin were such a success that he would like to have continued; but to his surprise he did equally well at the apparently less promising towns, Belfast, Cork and "little Limerick". (Arthur Smith suffered from the roughness and confusion of the over-enthusiastic audiences in Belfast.)[1] A new and congenial friend was F. D. Finlay, editor of the *Northern Whig*; while a first meeting with Percy Fitzgerald, already a prolific contributor to *Household Words*, was the start of a long association.

All his audiences varied in their response to different readings, and occasionally he altered his programmes accordingly. The unexpectedly "rapturous audience" at Sunderland made him do "a vast number of new things in the Carol".[2] The experimental character of this first tour is also reflected in the tone of his letters reporting on it; the fullest and probably the frankest are to the family[3] and to Wills. To Forster he was somewhat more defensive, being anxious to convince him of his success (there is some evidence that family letters were lent for the *Life*). All letters emphasise the amount of money taken, and later, the extent of the profit (expenses were high) and this is confirmed by his accounts.

Dickens continued his correspondence on many other matters throughout his absence and in the intervals at home. These were often far from restful. Besides the "Violated letter", there was the business of organising Fanny Ternan's departure to Florence with her mother[4] in September, and the move of the two younger sisters to a milliner's house in Berners Street, evidently on his advice. When, in his absence, trouble arose there from the suspicious activity of a policeman, Wills, obviously completely in his confidence, was deputed to deal with it.[5] But it is clear that the apartments were retained until well into the following year and up to their mother's return.[6] No letter of November or December mentions any Ternan by name, but his delight over the brilliant performance of the young Marie Wilton in H. J. Byron's clever burlesque[7] at the Strand was accompanied by his appreciation of Maria's supporting part as a comic young soldier. Ellen, as the least gifted, continued in subordinate parts at the Haymarket; but she had one good part, as Mary, the farmer's niece, in *Used Up*, a favourite of Dickens's, who had acted in it with Mary Boyle in 1851, and with Emmeline Compton in 1852. This production he would wish to see.[8]

With his brother Frederick he had been long out of touch, but was unexpectedly appealed to by him when reading in Dublin.[9] Two months later, T. J. Thompson, in his capacity both as a friend of Dickens and Fred's brother-in-law, evidently offered to mediate between Fred and Anna.[10] His meeting with Fred was unsatisfactory;

[1] See *To* Mamie Dickens, 28 Aug.

[2] See *To* Wills, 24 Sep.

[3] To Katey as well as Georgina and Mamie; but hers have not survived (see Vol. 1, p. xxi).

[4] *To* Wills, 25 Oct, clearly implies that Dickens was paying for Fanny's further training as a singer.

[5] *To* Wills, *ibid.*

[6] See next vol.

[7] *The Maid and the Magpie*; see *To* Forster, 17 Dec and *fnn.*

[8] On 18 Nov: Malcolm Morley, *D*, May 1959, p. 115. Dickens was in London that week; no letters survive for 17–19 Nov.

[9] *To* Georgina Hogarth, 29 Aug.

[10] *To* Thompson, 25 Oct (from Hull), and *fn.*

later in the month Dickens thought there was some hope of staying the legal proceedings for a separation, but by the end of the year this had vanished.[1]

About Miss Coutts's Home for Homeless Women there is much less in this volume, mainly because she was so often away from London; but he took pains to advise her on her pamphlet about her prizes for "Common Things".[2] He was solicitous and sympathetic to the recently widowed Mrs Brown, recalling the anniversaries of Dr Brown's death and advising her about the Medical Exhibition in his memory at St George's.

Notwithstanding his many activities and preoccupations in these three years, Dickens more than maintained his regular tally of speeches, many in aid of charitable funds. Two alone call for comment. One was on behalf of the proposed Dramatic College which, by sheer misfortune, later proved to be yet another of the lost causes supported by him.[3] The other, outstanding in his whole career and remembered to this day, was the moving plea for the Hospital for Sick Children in Great Ormond Street.[4]

His active concern with *Household Words* continued throughout the three years, and letters to Wills contain many comments about contributors. The general standard was maintained by long-tested writers, notably Morley, who was joined in October 1856 on the salaried staff by Wilkie Collins. As Collins required some persuasion because of the anonymity, he had to be carefully approached through Wills,[5] to whom Dickens recommended him as "very suggestive . . . industrious and reliable", but also as "exceedingly quick to take my notions"—that is, likely to be co-operative and responsive to advice. This was sometimes necessary; but clearly *Household Words* drew much benefit from his contributions, comprising over forty articles, usually leads, besides *The Dead Secret* and two short serials.

As an editor, Dickens valued especially the "reliable", and found this in two more recently acquired contributors, James Payn (later a successful novelist and an editor himself), and John Hollingshead, an enterprising and very capable journalist. These, with Eliza Lynn and Harriet Parr (Holme Lee), the two regular women contributors, were responsible for the greatest number of articles and tales at a time when Dickens's own contributions had diminished in number and in the latter half of 1858 had almost disappeared. Those of earlier date he may have thought below his usual standard. When he was collecting "Reprinted Pieces" for the Library edition only one was thought worth including:[6] "Out of the Season", a personal account of his solitary holiday in Dover while he was finishing *Little Dorrit*.

In view of all that had happened since that summer, he might well have felt exhausted. In appearance he was ageing, and for the first but not the last time, looked older than his years. Yet, only a week after his arduous reading tour had

[1] *To* Thompson, 25 Oct, 8 and 22 Nov, and 27 Dec; for the five hearings of proceedings starting on 13 Jan 1859, see next vol.

[2] See Appx C and *fnn.*

[3] See *To* Kean, 1 and 22 July 58 and *fnn.*

[4] On 8 Feb 56, at the first Annual Dinner: see *To* Miss Coutts, 11 Feb and *fn.*

[5] *To* Wills, 16 and 18 Sep; his status was slightly different from Morley's.

[6] Many would be regarded as too topical; others represented a return to subjects previously treated (and included) such as "Well-Authenticated Rappings" (20 Feb 58), which is an attack on mediums, much cruder than "The Spirit Business" (7 May 55); "An Idea of Mine" (13 Mar 58), mocking conventional artists' models, overlaps with "The Ghost of Art".

ended, he wrote a story for the Christmas number so unusual and unexpected even to himself ("an odd idea ... so humourous") that he thought of withdrawing it for treatment at novel length. This must be "Going into Society", the tale of the hopes and disillusionment of Mr Chops the Dwarf, as told long after by a new kind of narrator, Toby Magsman the old showman, "a grizzled personage in velveteen". Though difficult to imagine expanded into a novel, it could be linked in Dickens's mind to the experiences of Pip, which developed on different lines when he returned to them in 1860.[1]

Further evidence of Dickens's resurging power as a writer is "New Year's Day", written in December. As he said, "the day itself is always potent"; it inspires a sequence of vivid and loving recollections of New Years in childhood and youth, mingling fact with fancy, but leading to joyous chronicles of Genoa in 1845 and Paris in winters as recent as 1856. Not an escape from the present to the happier past, but drawn from the timeless sources of the creative imagination.

GRAHAM STOREY
KATHLEEN TILLOTSON

[1] See *To* Wills, 25 Nov 58 and *fn*, citing Margaret Cardwell's Clarendon edition of *Great Expectations*. Additional "threads of association" are those of time and place; Mr Chops lived in the reign of George IV, and Magsman (who has a touch of Joe Gargery) is discovered in his humble caravan in sight of "misty marshes".

Introduction of Postal Codes

On 1 Jan 1857 the Post Office Department announced to the public that ten separate sorting offices were now established in London, and requested correspondents to observe their "Table of Districts", using the appropriate designation on envelopes and for their own addresses inside. These "initial letters" ("W.C." for "West Central", etc.) "should be legibly written on a separate line" and "end the address", which would help "to ensure a rapid and correct delivery". A long alphabetical list of addresses (*c.* 90 cols), with their designations, was given (*British Postal Guide*, Jan 1857); by April, a separate edition in large type with maps was available. Each quarterly issue of the *Guide* repeated the instructions, with the extra emphasis of heavy type; obviously the public took some time to follow them. Dickens's envelopes generally observed the requirement, but the first surviving letter with "W.C." added to his own address is 25 May 1857, and was not regular until he had a printed letterhead, which he first used on 16 March 1858. The practice is a trap for forgers who have occasionally used the district letters before their introduction.

ACKNOWLEDGMENTS

We are again deeply grateful to Christopher Dickens, owner of the copyright in Dickens's letters, for giving us permission to use unpublished materials; and to the Pilgrim Trustees for their generous initial grant which made this edition possible.

Our greatest obligation for this and future volumes is to the British Academy. It is now fourteen years since the Academy first allowed us annual grants and ten years since the edition was adopted as one of their official research projects. We are very grateful to the officers of the Academy and to the Fellows who are members of the relevant committees. To this valued assistance we owe the remuneration of Margaret Brown, and of Douglas Matthews, our experienced and co-operative indexer. We are also grateful for the Academy's generous contribution towards the cost of equipment, without which this volume would have required many more months of preparation time. This is the responsibility of Margaret Brown (and her assistant), whose other skills, long experience, resourcefulness and commitment to the edition have made her much more than a secretary.

The foundation of this volume, as of all others, past and to come, was firmly laid by the provision of texts and in many cases valuable material for annotation, for which our greatest debt is to Madeline House.

As in all our volumes, we are much indebted to Messrs Coutts & Co. Their archivist, Mrs Barbara Peters, who has continued and expanded the help initially given by her predecessor, has been particularly helpful in the facilities provided for access to the accounts. Dr David Parker of the Dickens House Museum and his staff have continued to be alert in collecting and passing on new letters and information and in answering queries.

We are also most grateful to Mr Brian Jenkins, Head of Special Collections, Cambridge University Library, for help with annotation in the early stages of this volume; we are only sorry that he was unable to continue because of his commitments to the Library. Professor K. J. Fielding was the first to investigate the Farrer–Ouvry Papers; his transcripts and published articles have been of valued assistance in this volume.

For their generous permission to use their important Dickens collections and their continuous help when it is asked for, we are again greatly indebted to libraries in the United States mentioned in our earlier volumes and especially to the following: the Houghton Library, Harvard University; the Henry E. Huntington Library and Sara S. Hodson; the Pierpont Morgan Library, New York, and Christine Helson, especially for help with the manuscripts of *The Frozen Deep*; New York Public Library; the Free Library of Philadelphia where Karen Lightner continues the tradition of generosity and prompt transmission of new letters; Princeton University Library (with the Robert H. Taylor Collection); the Research Centre of Texas at Austin; the Beinecke Library at Yale University and Vincent Giroud.

Among English libraries, our greatest debts, continuing and repeated, are to the Victoria & Albert Museum for access to manuscripts, letters, cuttings, and sketches in the Forster Collection, and to the accounts of Dickens's publishers; to the British Library, and to Cambridge University Library. In France, we are greatly indebted to Madame Janine Watrin, for her knowledge and generosity in answering questions. Unfortunately her book, on the friendship of Dickens and Ferdinand Beaucourt-Mutuel, *De Boulogne à Condette, Une Histoire d'amitié*, was published too late for Volume VII, when Dickens's increasing and steadily growing attachment to Boulogne and to Beaucourt-Mutuel first showed itself. It will be of still more help with future volumes.

To the following institutions we express our gratitude for permission to publish the letters they have recently made available to us:

British Dental Association and Mr Roger Farbey; Case Western Reserve University and Sue Hanson; Chicago University Library and Jonathan Walters; News International plc; Open University; Washington State University.

We are also grateful to the following owners who have kindly allowed us to see letters in their possession or have sent us photographs of them:

Mrs Paul Adams; Sr Stefano Anter; Mr John Brancher; Mr Maurice Canter; James Cummins; Miss G. M. Dawson; Mrs J. Felix-Davies; The Rev. Willard C. Grace; Mr Peter Harries of Boz Books; Mr Graham Heath; Mr David J. Holmes; Mr Michael Killick; Mr Brian Lake; Kevin MacDonnell (Rare Books); Dr Steven J. Pachuta; Mr John Pym; Mr Philip Rogers; Mr Thomas Shawn; Mr Michael Silverman; Dr C. van Steijnen; Mrs Ann Thwaite; Sr Carlos Ventura; Mr Robin Whitworth; Mr John Williams; Mr John Wilson; Mr Clive Woods (Falcon Books).

For help too varied to be specified we wish to record out grateful thanks to the following:

The Athenaeum and Miss Sarah Dodgson; Professor L. J. Austin; Dr Andrew Brown; Buffalo and Erie County Public Library and William H. Loos; Cape & Dalgleish and Mr David Horscroft; Mr Peter L. Caracciolo; Gaston Chappell; Mr Frank Collieson; Professor P. A. W. Collins; Companies House; Professor George Curry; Mr Edward Demery of Justerini & Brooks; Mr Michael Diamond; Dulwich College and Mr A. C. Hall; Dr E. Duncan-Jones; Sophie Dupré and Clive Farahar; Professor Angus Easson; Professor P. D. Edwards; Edinburgh Central Library and Miss Norma Armstrong; Edinburgh City Archives and Miss M. McBryde; Dr Simon Eliot; Messrs Farrer & Co and Mr R. A. Griffith; Miss Sybilla Jane Flower; Garrick Club Library and Mrs Enid M. Foster; Professor Elizabeth Gitter; Dr T. R. Gould, Hon. Archivist at St George's Hospital; Dr Donald Hawes; Mr B. C. Homer; Law Society and Mrs S. Arthur; Mr Raymond Lister; Gavin Littaur; Mrs Nathaniel Lloyd; Katharine Longley; Etrenne Lymbery; Professor Robert Martin; Manchester Central Public Library and Miss J. M. Ayton; Massachusetts Historical Society and Virginia H. Smith; Medway Area Archives and Mr Stephen M. Dixon; Mr Michael Meredith; Merton Civic Centre (Wimbledon) and Penny Parker; Mr Frank Miles; Professor Sylvère Monod; Professor Sidney P. & Dr Carolyn Moss; Mrs Virginia Murray; Pickering & Chatto Ltd and Kirsty Bain; Mr M. A. Pollak; Dr Mercedes Potau; Miss Eileen Power; Guildhall Museum, Rochester and Mr M. I. Moad; Mrs D. Rose; Royal Pharmaceutical Society of Great Britain and Kate Arnold-Foster; Royal Society for the Prevention of Cruelty to Animals and Miss Rita Mayes; Royal Theatrical Fund and Mr J. R. Coutts Smith; Professor F. S. Schwarzbach; Shakespeare Birthplace Centre and Mrs Marian Pringle; Professor

Michael Slater; Mr Frank D. Smith; Helen Smith; Mrs Margaret Smith; The Rev. M. Smith; Mr David Steel; Professor Garrett Stewart; Claire Tomalin; Walker Art Gallery and Miss Xanthe Brooke; Dr John Wells; West Yorkshire Archive Service and Mr W. J. Connor; Westminster School and John Field; Mrs Alison Young; Mr Vic Zoschak.

BIOGRAPHICAL TABLE

1856–1858

1856	1 Jan–29 Apr	Continued residence in Paris
	31 Jan	*Little Dorrit* No. III published; continued monthly to 30 June 1857
	4–10 Feb and 10–?18 Mar	In London
	12 Mar	Speaks at Annual General Meeting of Royal Literary Fund
	13 Mar	Presides at meeting of actors and actresses at Adelphi on Dulwich College
	14 Mar	Concludes purchase of Gad's Hill Place
	17 Mar	Speaks at Annual Dinner of Royal General Theatrical Fund
	29 Apr–2 May	At Dover
	3 May–6 June	In London
	5 June	Presides at Annual Dinner of Royal Hospital for Incurables
	7 June–3 Sep	At Boulogne (in London 30 June–3 July and 2–6 Aug)
	5–6 Oct	At Birmingham
	6 Dec	*Household Words* Christmas No., "The Wreck of the Golden Mary" with Wilkie Collins and others
1857	6, 8, 12, 14 Jan	Performances of Collins's *The Frozen Deep* (with a farce), at Tavistock House
	13 Feb	Takes possession of Gad's Hill
	11 Mar	Speaks at Annual General Meeting of Royal Literary Fund
	6 Apr	Speaks at Annual Dinner of Royal General Theatrical Fund
	7–15 Apr	At Gravesend
	21 May	Presides at Annual Dinner of Royal Hospital for Incurables
	25 May	Speaks at Annual Dinner of Royal Geographical Society (no record of speech)
	1 June–17 July	At Gad's Hill (with frequent visits to London)
	?12 June	Organiser of Fund in Remembrance of Douglas Jerrold

	30 June	Reads the *Carol* in St Martin's Hall for Jerrold Fund
	4 July	Performance of *The Frozen Deep* and farce, before the Queen at Gallery of Illustration
	11, 18, 25 July	Public performances of *The Frozen Deep* and farce at Gallery of Illustration
	24 July	Reads the *Carol* for Jerrold Fund in St Martin's Hall
	31 July	Reads the *Carol* for Jerrold Fund in Manchester
	8 Aug	Final public performance of *The Frozen Deep* and farce at Gallery of Illustration
	21, 22, 24 Aug	Performances of *The Frozen Deep* and *Uncle John* at the Free Trade Hall, Manchester
	7–21 Sep	Visits Cumberland (Wigton, Carlisle, and Allonby), Lancaster and Doncaster with Collins
	3–31 Oct	"The Lazy Tour of Two Idle Apprentices", by CD and Collins, published in *Household Words*
	5 Nov	Presides at Annual Dinner of Warehousemen and Clerks' Schools
	7 Dec	*Household Words* Christmas No., "The Perils of Certain English Prisoners", by CD and Collins
	15 Dec	Reads for Coventry Institute
	22 Dec	Reads for Chatham and Rochester Mechanics Institute
1858	19 Jan	Reads the *Carol* for Bristol Athenaeum
	9 Feb	Presides at first Annual Dinner of Hospital for Sick Children, Great Ormond Street
	10 Mar	Speaks at Annual General Meeting of Royal Literary Fund
	26 Mar	Reads the *Carol* for Edinburgh Philosophical Institution
	29 Mar	Speaks at Annual Dinner of Royal General Theatrical Fund
	15 Apr	Reads the *Carol* at St Martin's Hall for Hospital for Sick Children
	23 Apr	Speaks at Shakespeare Birthday Dinner at Garrick Club (no record of speech)
	29 Apr	First paid reading in St Martin's Hall; series of 17 continues until 22 July

1 May	Speaks at Royal Academy Banquet
8 May	Presides at Annual Dinner of Artists' Benevolent Fund
June–July	Divides time between Gad's Hill and London
1 June	Presides at first Annual Dinner of Playground and General Recreation Society
7 June	"Personal" statement about his separation published in *The Times* (repeated in *Household Words*, 12 June)
21 July	Speaks at Meeting for Foundation of Dramatic College
2 Aug–13 Nov	First reading tour (85 readings) in England, Ireland and Scotland; returning to Gad's Hill when possible
16 Aug	The "Violated Letter" published in *New York Tribune*; reprinted in English newspapers on 31 Aug
3 Dec	Gives prizes at Institutional Association of Lancashire and Cheshire at Manchester
4 Dec	Presentation and Dinner in his honour at Coventry
7 Dec	*Household Words* Christmas No., "A House to Let", by CD and Collins
24 Dec	First series of 8 Christmas readings in St Martin's Hall (continues until 10 Feb 59)
29 Dec	Reads for Chatham and Rochester Mechanics Institute

ABBREVIATIONS AND SYMBOLS

AYR	*All the Year Round*
CD	Used throughout this edition in all references to Charles Dickens and for his name in titles of books and articles.
CD as Editor	*Charles Dickens as Editor*, edited by R. C. Lehmann, 1912.
CD to WC	*Letters of Charles Dickens to Wilkie Collins. Selected by Miss Georgina Hogarth*, ed. Laurence Hutton, 1892.
D	*The Dickensian; a Magazine for Dickens Lovers*, The Dickens Fellowship, 1905–.
DAB	*Dictionary of American Biography.*
DNB	*Dictionary of National Biography.*
F, 1872–4	John Forster, *The Life of Charles Dickens*, 3 vols, 1872–4.
F	John Forster, *The Life of Charles Dickens*, edited by J. W. T. Ley, 1928. Our references are to this edition unless otherwise stated (text checked from F, 1872–4).
FC	The Forster Collection, Victoria & Albert Museum, London.
HW	*Household Words.*
Macready, *Diaries*	*The Diaries of William Charles Macready 1833–51*, edited by William Toynbee, 2 vols, 1912.
MDGH	*The Letters of Charles Dickens*, edited by his Sister-in-law and his Eldest Daughter. Vols I & II, 1880. Vol. III, 1882.
MDGH, 1882	*The Letters of Charles Dickens*, edited by his Sister-in-law and his Eldest Daughter, 2 vols, 1882.
MDGH, 1893	*The Letters of Charles Dickens*, edited by his Sister-in-law and his Eldest Daughter, 1 vol., 1893.
N	*The Letters of Charles Dickens*, edited by Walter Dexter, 3 vols, Nonesuch Press, 1938.
OED	*Oxford English Dictionary.*
To	"*To*" before a correspondent's name denotes a letter from Dickens.
[ ]	Square brackets in letter-headings enclose conjectural dates. In the text they denote words conjecturally supplied and breaks caused by damage to the MS. In footnotes they indicate editorial interpolations.
*	Asterisks in letter-headings denote letters which we believe to be hitherto unpublished. (Extracts from some of these have, however, appeared in Edgar Johnson, *Charles Dickens, his Tragedy & Triumph*, 2 vols, 1953, in later biographies and in sale-catalogues.)
†	Daggers in letter-headings denote letters of which we believe part to be hitherto unpublished.

To JOHN FORSTER,[1] [1 JANUARY 1856]

Extracts in F, VIII, iii, 65*n* and VII, v, 616–7. *Date:* first extract 1 Jan, according to Forster; second extract probably same letter; see notes below.

When in London Coutts[2] advised me not to sell out the money for Gad's Hill Place (the title of my estate, Sir, my place down in Kent) until the conveyance was settled and ready.[3]

On the entry into Paris of French troops from the Crimea,[4] *the Zouaves*[5] *pleased him most.* A remarkable body of men, wild, dangerous, and picturesque. Close-cropped head, red skull cap, Greek jacket, full red petticoat trowsers trimmed with yellow, and high white gaiters—the most sensible things for the purpose I know, and coming into use in the line. A man with such things on his legs is always free there, and ready for a muddy march; and might flounder through roads two feet deep in mud, and, simply by changing his gaiters (he has another pair in his haversack), be clean and comfortable and wholesome again, directly.[6] Plenty of beard and moustache, and the musket carried reverse wise with the stock over the shoulder, make up the sun-burnt Zouave. He strides like Bobadil,[7] smoking as he goes; and when he laughs (they were under my window for half-an-hour or so), plunges backward in the wildest way, as if he were going to throw a sommersault. They have a black dog belonging to the regiment, and, when they now marched along with their medals, this dog marched after the one non-commissioned officer he invariably follows with a profound conviction that he was decorated. I couldn't see whether he had a medal, his hair being long; but he was perfectly up to what had befallen his regiment; and I never saw anything so capital as his way of regarding

[1] John Forster (1812–76; *DNB*): see earlier vols. On 28 Dec 55 appointed Secretary to the Lunacy Commission at an annual salary of £800. He resigned from the *Examiner* immediately, but helped with editorial duties until his marriage, Sep 56. Published in the *Edinburgh Review* (No. 209, Jan 56) a critique of books by François Guizot (see Vol. V, p. 265*n*) on Commonwealth history, later reprinted with additions as "The Civil Wars and Oliver Cromwell" (*Historical and Biographical Essays*, 2 vols, 1858).

[2] Coutts & Co., CD's bankers, of 59 Strand.

[3] The purchase-money was not paid until 14 Mar: see *To* Georgina Hogarth, that day.

[4] On 29 Dec 55 the Imperial Guard marched with other line regiments from the Place de la Bastille to the Place Vendôme after their reception by the Emperor (*The Times*, 31 Dec 55). Henry Fielding Dickens "wore a French kepi and was held up in somebody's arms to cry 'Vive l'Empereur'" as he passed (*Recollections*, 1934, p. 8).

[5] The Zouaves of the Imperial Guard, formed in 1854 as the fourth regiment of a light infantry body originally raised in 1831 from the Kabyle tribe of Zouaoua. After the formation of the Tirailleurs algériens in 1838 as the corps for natives, it was composed of French soldiers, noted for their physique and dashing Oriental uniform. On this occasion they "were greeted with the greatest enthusiasm; their weather-beaten features, their faded uniforms, and their martial bearing, almost made the people frantic with gratitude and joy" (*Galignani's Messenger*, 1 Jan 56).

[6] CD praised the Zouaves' gaiters as suitable London wear in "Insularities", *HW*, 19 Jan 56, XIII, 1.

[7] The swaggering Captain in Ben Jonson's *Every Man in his Humour*. CD's part in the production by his Amateur Company, 1845, 1847–8, 1850.

the public. Whatever the regiment does, he is always in his place; and it was impossible to mistake the air of modest triumph which was now upon him. A small dog corporeally, but of a great mind. *On that night there was an illumination in honour of the army, when the* whole of Paris, bye streets and lanes and all sorts of out of the way places, was most brilliantly illuminated. It looked in the dark like Venice and Genoa rolled into one, and split up through the middle by the Corso at Rome in the carnival time.[1] The French people certainly do know how to honour their own countrymen, in a most marvellous way. *He was fairly lost in a mystery of amazement at where the money could come from that everybody was spending on the étrennes*[2] *they were giving to everybody else. All the famous shops on the Boulevards had been blockaded for more than a week.* There is now a line of wooden stalls, three miles long, on each side of that immense thoroughfare;[3] and wherever a retiring house or two admits of a double line, there it is. All sorts of objects from shoes and sabots, through porcelain and crystal, up to live fowls and rabbits which are played for at a sort of dwarf skittles (to their immense disturbance, as the ball rolls under them and shakes them off their shelves and perches whenever it is delivered by a vigorous hand), are on sale in this great Fair. And what you may get in the way of ornament for twopence, is astounding.

To W. H. WILLS,[4] 1 JANUARY 1856

MS Huntington Library.

Paris, First January 1856

My Dear Wills.

Many Happy New Years! And so, as Tiny Tim observed, &c[5]—

I return the Proofs.[6] As you observe in your note, they will want to be looked over, very carefully.

The Flag of England—Taboo.

Across the Street[7]—highly desirable to be postponed for the present. It is too manifestly a remnant from the Xmas No.[8] and would now come too near that story of Thomas's.[9]

Lead off the No. with the Guards and the Line.[10] With the new name I have given

[1] See *Pictures from Italy*, 1846, pp. 173—84, for CD's account of Rome at carnival time in 1845.

[2] New Year's gifts; word then more familiar to English readers.

[3] The line of the boulevards from the Madeleine to the Temple.

[4] William Henry Wills (1801–80; *DNB*), Assistant Editor of *HW*: see Vols I, p. 264*n* and VI, p. 14*n*.

[5] "God Bless Us, Every One!": the last words of *A Christmas Carol*.

[6] For *HW* No. 303, 12 Jan 56.

[7] No article appeared under this title.

[8] "The Holly Tree Inn", the *HW* Christmas Number for 1855.

[9] William Moy Thomas's "Dr. Graves of Warwick Street" (*HW*, 29 Dec 55, XII, 524), the narrative of an eighteenth-century murder. On 24 Nov 55 CD had complained to Wills that all the papers sent him for "The Holly Tree Inn" turned "on criminal actions and criminal trials" (Vol. VII, p. 753).

[10] 12 Jan 56, XII, 553. Its author, M. R. L. Meason (*b.* 1824), turned to journalism after an Army career and contributed both to *HW* and *AYR*.

it[1] (see to the proof, the punctuation, and slovenly composition here and there), it is the best thing we can do. [a]It has a distinct and appropriate purpose.[a]

Howitt,[2] all right. But take his German poetry out altogether, or make him render it in English also.[3]

Zoological Auction,[4] also licenced and returned herewith.

Ever Faithfully
CD.

I will write again in a day or two.

To JOHN FOWLER,[5] 2 JANUARY 1856

Extract in Sotheby's catalogue, July 1972; *MS* 1 p.; dated Paris, 49 Avenue des Champs Elysées, 2 Jan 56; *Address* (envelope MS Free Library of Philadelphia): L'Angleterre | John Fowler Esquire | 50 Occupation Road | Sheffield. PM Paris 2 Jan 56.

It gives me the greatest pleasure to learn from your letter that my reading[6] has been of solid advantage to your Institution.[7] *Fowler's kind remembrance of the actors*[8] *is particularly agreeable to him; CD is much interested to know that members were among the audience.*

I can answer your enquiry respecting the audience, in the warmest manner. It was an admirable one; I think I have not read to a better.

To MRS GASKELL,[9] 2 JANUARY 1856

MS Dickens House. *Address:* L'Angleterre | Mrs. Gaskell | Plymouth Grove | Manchester.

Paris, 49 Avenue des champs Elysées
Second January 1856

My Dear Mrs. Gaskell.

In case Household Words should not have spoken for itself in the notice that is

[1] The article, which contrasted an officer's life in the Guards with that in a line regiment, appeared as "Nob and Snob". CD used the word "snob" in the older sense of a lower-class person; cf. *Little Dorrit*, No. III, Ch. 10, where the Circumlocution Office exists "for the assistance of the nobs in keeping off the snobs".

[aa] Inserted as an afterthought.

[2] William Howitt's "The Land-Shark" (12 Jan 56, XII, 563), reprinted in his *Tallangetta, the Squatter's Home*, 2 vols, 1857.

[3] It was omitted.

[4] By the naturalist Francis Trevelyan Buckland (1826–80; *DNB*), 12 Jan 56, XII, 570. In Nov 55 all the animals in the Surrey Zoological Gardens were sold in preparation for the Surrey Garden Company scheme, with its new concert hall under the direction of Louis Jullien (1812–60; *DNB*). After the success of its inaugural festival, 15–19 July 56, the scheme was a financial disaster and collapsed in Apr 57.

[5] John Fowler, Hon. Secretary of the Sheffield Mechanics' Institute, established 1832. See earlier vols.

[6] Of the *Carol* at the Sheffield Mechanics' Hall on 22 Dec 55: see Vol. VII, p. 771 and *nn*.

[7] In Nov 55 the Institute had been in financial difficulty and was facing closure.

[8] The Amateurs who performed Bulwer Lytton's *Not so Bad as we Seem* in Sheffield on 30 Aug 52. Fowler was one of the Secretaries of the executive committee in charge of arrangements: see Vol. VI, p. 761, *n*.

[9] Elizabeth Cleghorn Gaskell (1810–65; *DNB*): see Vol. V, p. 539*n*.

now regularly appended to it,[1] or in case you should not have seen that notice, I think I may as well write to let you know that I waited on Madame Mohl[2] very shortly after she called here with your note. She fully explained its subject to me, and in the next No. we put to Press, I began an announcement that the writers in Household Words reserve the right of translation. On considering the matter it seemed to be best and strongest, to make the formality general and sweeping. It effectually preserves your right.[3]

I have been going on, hoping to see the end of the story you could not finish (which was not your fault or anybody's) in time for Christmas.[4] When will it be forthcoming, I wonder! You have not deserted it. You cannot be such an unnatural mother.

With kind remembrances from Mrs. Dickens and her sister and our united regards to Mr. Gaskell,[5]

Believe me | Very faithfully Yours
CHARLES DICKENS

To MESSRS HACHETTE ET CIE,[6] 2 JANUARY 1856

MS Librairie Hachette.

49 Champs Elysées | Mercredi Janvier 2, 1856

Messieurs.

Permettez-moi de vous faire savoir que je suis revenue à Paris,[7] et que je serai bien aise d'avoir l'honneur de vous entretenir, ou Lundi ou Mardi prochain, à deux heures.[8]

Recevez Messieurs l'assurance de ma consideration profonde.

Votre fidele
CHARLES DICKENS

Messrs. L. Hachette et Cie.

[1] A statement that "The Right of Translating Articles from Household Words is reserved by the Authors" appeared for the first time at the foot of the last page of *HW* No. 300, 22 Dec 55, and was continued in all subsequent issues. For the International Copyright Act of 1852, and CD's inclusion of such a statement on *Bleak House* No. 1, Mar 52, see Vol. VI, p. 23*n*.

[2] Née Mary Elizabeth Clarke (1793–1833; *DNB*), wife of the distinguished Orientalist Julius Mohl; no record of other meetings with CD; Mrs Gaskell stayed with her for a fortnight in Feb 55, when CD was also in Paris.

[3] For Mrs Gaskell's agreement with Hachette et Cie in 1855, see her letter to George Smith 29 Dec 56, *Letters*, ed. J. A. V. Chapple and A. Pollard, Manchester, 1966, p. 431). *Cranford*, which had appeared in *HW* Dec 51–May 53, and *Ruth* (1853) were published by Hachette in French translations in 1856.

[4] "The Poor Clare", 13, 20 and 27 Dec 56.

[5] The Rev. William Gaskell (1805–84; *DNB*), Unitarian minister: see Vol. VI, p. 545*n*.

[6] Publishers, 14 rue Pierre-Sarrazin: see Vol. VII, p. 759 and *n*. In a letter to CD of 10 Dec 55 the Head of the Office, Emile Templier, had proposed terms for a translated edn of his works and suggested a meeting for discussion.

[7] He had returned from London on 24 Dec.

[8] Precise date of meeting not known.

To LADY STRACEY,[1] 2 JANUARY 1856

Extract in Maggs catalogue No. 871 (1899); *MS* 1 p.; addressed Lady Stracey; dated Paris, 2 Jan 56.

We are passing the winter here, and though I make periodical flights to England they are merely for the transaction of business.

To EDMUND YATES,[2] 2 JANUARY 1856

MS University of Kentucky Library.

Paris, 49 Avenue des Champs Elysées
Wednesday Second January 1856.

My Dear Yates.

Supposing both Corsican Brothers to be available, I think I should prefer being Godfather[3] to the one who isn't Kean.[4] With this solitary stipulation, I very cordially respond to your proposal, and am happy to take my friendly and sponsorial seat at your fireside.

I will write you word when I purpose making another flight to London; for I must come and see my boy,[5] whether we fill the sparkling wine-cup (when I was in America, an Editor[6] wrote me a note of invitation begging me to come and "crush" that article with him), or not. I am but newly returned here, and hardly expect to be beckoned over for some weeks.

When you represent me at the Font and are renouncing, think that on Christmas Day I had seven sons in the Banquet Hall of this apartment—which would not make a very large warm bath—and renounce my example.

[1] Née Charlotte Denne (*d.* 1884), wife of Sir Henry Josias Stracey, 5th Bart, of Rackheath Hall, Norfolk, MP for East Norfolk 1855–7. No meeting with CD is recorded.

[2] Edmund Hodgson Yates (1831–94; *DNB*), journalist and novelist: see Vol. VII, p. 381*n*. At this time writing dramatic criticism for the *Daily News* and a column of personal gossip, "The Lounger at the Clubs", in the *Illustrated Times*. From Aug 55 edited the *Comic Times*, intended as a rival to *Punch* by Herbert Ingram, but discontinued by him after sixteen numbers. Its staff was unwilling to be disbanded and "formed [*itself*] into a kind of joint-stock company" to establish the *Train*, with Yates again as editor. The first issue, with contributions by Robert and William Brough and G. A. Sala, appeared on 1 Jan 56 and was praised in the *Examiner* by Forster. The first of Yates's four contributions to *HW* ("A Fearful Night", XIII, 424) appeared on 17 May 56.

[3] Yates's twin sons were born 27 Sep 55 and christened shortly after CD's letter of acceptance was received. CD's godson was named Charles Dickens Theodore Yates: for his christening present see *To* Williams & Clapham, 5 Feb. Yates's close friend, the novelist Frank Smedley (1818–64; *DNB*), was the other godfather.

[4] Charles John Kean (?1811–68; *DNB*): see Vol. I, p. 327*n*. As manager of the Princess's Theatre, had great success in Feb 52 with Dion Boucicault's *The Corsican Brothers; or the Vendetta*, adapted from Eugène Grange's and Zavier de Montepin's play *Les frères corses*, itself based on Dumas's story. Kean played both brothers.

[5] Charley. (But see p. 726.) Since Sep 55 working at the financial house of Baring Brothers (see Vol. VII, p. 508 and *n*).

[6] Thomas Ritchie (1778–1854), editor of the *Richmond Enquirer*, who took the chair at a "social supper" in CD's honour, 18 Mar 42: see Vol. VII, p. 457 and *n*.

Mrs. Dickens and Miss Hogarth unite with me in kind regards to yourself and Mrs. Yates[1]—as to whom I now consider myself with much pleasure, a sort of relation.

Very faithfully Yours

Edmund H Yates Esquire. CHARLES DICKENS

To W. H. WILLS, 3 AND 4 JANUARY 1856

MS Huntington Library.

49 Champs Elysées
Thursday Third January 1856 | (After Post time)

My Dear Wills.

H.W.[2]

I am sufficiently irritable—though, as you know, the most amiable of men!—to desire to avoid reading Miss Martineau's[3] vomit[4] of conceit,[5] unless I should feel myself positively obliged to do so. I have therefore put the precious packet by, without opening it. I will come to a decision upon Morley's[6] notice of it, when I see the Proof of his article.[7] But my present impression is, that I would rather (if only for the mortification it will cause her), not notice it at all. The Proof has not yet arrived.

You shall have a first paper[8] from me by Sunday's post, if you don't get it—to start[9]

[1] His wife Louisa Katharine Yates (*d.* 1900), daughter of the celebrated swordmaker James Wilkinson.

[2] Underlined with short double strokes.

[3] Harriet Martineau (1802–76; *DNB*): see Vol. VI, p. 45*n*. In the late summer of 1855 she was upset by Morley's *HW* articles on factory legislation (see Vol. VII, p. 655*n*), and replied to Wills's request for further contributions in an "abundantly plain-spoken" letter of refusal (copy dated 15 Sep 55 in Birmingham University Library).

[4] "outpouring" in *CD as Editor*, ed. R. C. Lehmann, 1912, p. 192, and in N, II, 720.

[5] *The Factory Controversy: a Warning Against Meddling Legislation* (Manchester) 1855. In Jan 54 Palmerston had renewed attempts to enforce Section 21 of the 1844 Factory Act, which demanded secure fencing of mill-shafts and gearing at all heights; but three Factory Inspectors' Circulars had been issued to little effect by Jan 55. The move supported by Morley (Apr–Sep 55), and opposed by a newly-formed National Association of Factory Occupiers, which published Harriet Martineau's pamphlet. She argued that the requirements of the law and the Inspectors' Circulars were unclear and contradictory: serious accidents were infrequent and caused by operatives' negligence, while fencing was itself dangerous. CD, "the humanity-monger", was accused of "pseudo-philanthropy" and "acts of unfairness and untruth"; the *HW* papers contained "unscrupulous statements, insolence, arrogance, and cant". (See P. W. J. Bartrip, "*HW* and the Factory Accident Controversy", *D*, LXXV [1979], 17–29.) She suggests that CD should confine himself to fiction, but does not approve of "Mrs Jellaby" or of *Hard Times*.

[6] Henry Morley (1822–94; *DNB*), prominent member of the *HW* staff since 1851: see Vol. VI, p. 79*n*. Appointed co-editor of the *Examiner* in 1856, "in charge of . . . the literary department, with all dramatic and art criticism" (H. S. Solly, *Life of Henry Morley*, 1898, p. 222).

[7] "Our Wicked Mis-Statements", *HW*, 19 Jan 56, XIII, 13.

[8] "Insularities", *HW*, 19 Jan 56, XIII, 1, on restrictive habits in English social and artistic life.

[9] A strip has been cut from bottom of first two pages of folded sheet: for a possible reason, see below. Probably 3–4 lines of text are missing.

BONBONS[1]

Mrs. Dickens has already sent to her sister[2] at Tavistock House,[3] instructions thereanent. It is to go back there.[4]

Poole's[5]

Quarter I have paid him. Enclosed is his proof of life. After you shall have sent me the receipt to sign, and after I shall have signed it, please pay the usual Paymaster General Order, to my account at Coutts's.[6]

Friday Afternoon

The Proof has arrived. I will read it and write to you about it, when I have done my article. Expect it on Monday morning. From 3 to 4 pages.

I send by this post a paper of White's.[7] I have not read it, but I know the design and it is a good subject.[8]

He wants an order on Lafitte's[9] for all we owe him, including Old Blois[10] *and* this paper—an order to pay Revd. James White so many pounds sterling. This will be as advantageous to him as gold. From the total he will be very much obliged if you will deduct the cost of [ ].[11]

—And if you will make a parcel of those books[12] and so send them to him, he will Ever Pray—&c.

Ever Faithfully
CD.

[1] Underlined with short double strokes.

[2] Helen Isabella Hogarth (1833–90), Catherine's youngest sister; married R. C. Roney *c.* 1867: lived at 10 Gloucester Terrace; later taught singing in London and at the Ladies' College, Cheltenham. Died in Liverpool.

[3] The Hogarth family lived there with Charley Dickens during CD's stay in Paris.

[4] Possibly referring to Miss Coutts's Twelfth Night cake, which would have "an accompanying box of bons-bons and Twelfth Night characters" (Mary Dickens, *My Father as I Recall him*, 1897), p. 43): see *To* Miss Coutts, 10 Jan. Charley returned to London before his birthday on 6 Jan, and the cake may have been sent after him.

[5] John Poole (1786–1872; *DNB*), miscellaneous writer: see Vol. VI, pp. 116 and *n*.

[6] CD's Account-book (MS Messrs Coutts) shows receipt of £23.16.1 on 16 Jan, presumably £25 less tax.

[7] The Rev. James White (1800–62; *DNB*), author: see Vol. IV, p. 504*n*. In Paris with his wife since Nov 55: see Vol. VII, p. 747 and *n*. The paper was "A King who *Could* Do Wrong", *HW*, 26 Jan 56, XIII, 37.

[8] Harsh prosecutions by James VI, extracted from Robert Pitcairn's *Criminal Trials in Scotland, 1829–33*.

[9] Thus in MS. Ferrère Laffitte, Bankers, 3 rue Laffitte, used by CD when in Paris.

[10] *HW*, 12 Jan 56, XII, 556.

[11] Two words may have completed the paragraph, and a further 3–4 lines are missing. Possibly they expressed irritation with White who was "in one of his fits of depression" a few days before: see Vol. VII, p. 774.

[12] A copy of Dr Richard Burns's *The Justice of the Peace and Parish Officer* for White: see Vol. VII, p. 772.

To GEORGE AUGUSTUS SALA,[1] 4 JANUARY 1856*

MS Private.

49 Champs Elysées | Friday Fourth January 1856

My Dear Mr. Sala.

I shall be at home on Tuesday from 12 to 1, and shall be happy to see you if that time will suit your convenience.[2]

Faithfully Yours

George A Sala Esquire. CHARLES DICKENS

To JOHN FORSTER, [6 JANUARY 1856]

Extracts in F, VIII, i, 624 and VII, v, 619*n*, 619 and 617*n*. *Date:* first two extracts dated 6 Jan, according to Forster; third and fourth extracts probably same letter (see notes below).

On Little Dorrit *he wrote* You know that they had sold 35,000 of number two on new year's day.[3]

I forget whether I have already told you that I have received a proposal from a responsible bookselling house here, for a complete edition, authorized by myself, of a French translation of all my books. The terms involve questions of space and amount of matter; but I should say, at a rough calculation, that I shall get about £300 by it—perhaps £50 more.[4]

The nightmare portrait is nearly done; and Scheffer[5] promises that an intermin-

[1] George Augustus Sala (1828–95; *DNB*), journalist: see Vols VI, p. 458*n* and VII, p. 392 and *n*. A valued but erratic contributor to *HW*; sometimes given advance payments for future articles.

[2] See *To* Wills, 10 Jan.

[3] *Little Dorrit*, No. II for Jan, was published 31 Dec 55: its first printing order was for 35,000 copies. 38,000 copies of No. I had been printed by the end of the year, and 69,608 copies of the two numbers sold or otherwise distributed (Bradbury & Evans Account Books, MS V & A). CD may therefore be accurate in saying that the entire first printing of No. II (or as many copies as had been stitched and wrapped) had sold out in its first two days: see Robert L. Patten, *CD and his Publishers* (Oxford), 1978, pp. 171–2 and 250–2. Tauchnitz was reproducing monthly numbers; his first issue carried the date 1855 and evidently reproduced No. I for December (published 30 Nov). His complete edition of the novel was in four successive vols of 1856–7 (Vols 350, 360, 380 and 390 of the "Collection"), but the unique survival in the Bibliothèque Nationale of a single defaced wrapper for 1855 shows that each monthly number was also issued separately, its circulation limited to Germany. No actual issue in numbers has been traced, though announced in Tauchnitz advertisements (as also for *Bleak House*, 1852–3). Copies of book-issues from the parts are in private collections and the Bodleian: see William B. Todd and Ann Bowden, *Tauchnitz Editions in English 1841–1955, a Bibliographical History* (New York, 1988), especially pp. 93–5 with illustrations of 1855 wrapper. (No such issues were known or recorded at the date of the Clarendon *Little Dorrit* [1979], which gives only the complete single volume, published May 57.)

[4] Emile Templier's letter of 10 Dec 55 had offered £20 per volume for works published before the 1851 reciprocal copyright agreement, and £40 per volume for later works. For the terms finally agreed with Hachette et Cie, see *To* Forster, 30 Jan and *n*.

[5] Ary Scheffer (1795–1858), artist: see Vol. VII, p. 727 and *n*. CD had found the sittings irksome with *Little Dorrit* on his mind, since they began in Nov 55: see Vol. VII, p. 758.

able sitting next Saturday,[1] beginning at 10 o'clock in the morning, shall finish it. It is a fine spirited head, painted at his very best, and with a very easy and natural appearance to it. But it does not look to me at all like, nor does it strike me that if I saw it in a gallery I should suppose myself to be the original.[2] It is always possible that I don't know my own face. It is going to be engraved here, in two sizes and ways—the mere head and the whole thing.[3]

We have wet weather here—and dark too for these latitudes—and oceans of mud. Although numbers of men are perpetually scooping and sweeping it away in this thoroughfare, it accumulates under the windows so fast, and in such sludgy masses, that to get across the road is to get half over one's shoes in the first outset of a walk.[4]

To W. H. WILLS, 6 JANUARY 1856

MS Huntington Library.

49 Champs Elysées, Sunday January Sixth 1856

My Dear Wills.

[a]I have read Morley's article,[5] and gone very carefully over that part of it which refers to Miss Martineau. Supposing the facts to be closely examined and verified, I think it should be printed, and should go into the opening of the next No.[6] [b]as I have arranged it in the enclosed proof.[b] I do not quite distinctly see how it is proved that the renunciation of the idea of paying the penalties dates from that Seventh of August beyond all doubt.[7] I should like it made clearer.

Miss Martineau, in this, is precisely what I always knew her to be, and have always impressed her upon you as being. I was so convinced that it was impossible that she *could* be anything else, having seen and heard her, that I am not in the least triumphant at her justifying my opinion. I do suppose that there never was such a wrong-headed woman born[b]—such a vain one—or such a Humbug.[b]

If you think any little thing I have put in, too hard, consult Forster. If you both think so, take it out. Not otherwise.[a8]

[1] The "next Saturday" after Sunday 6th Jan would be 12 Jan; but as Forster says it was "a fortnight" later, this must have been postponed.

[2] CD did not change his opinion. In 1858, reporting to W. P. Frith Scheffer's first impression of him as being "like a Dutch skipper", he added "As for the picture he did of me, I can only say that it is neither like me nor a Dutch skipper" (W. P. Frith, *My Autobiography and Reminiscences*, 1887, I, 310).

[3] Not traced.

[4] Cf. *To* Lemon, 7 Jan.

[aa] Omitted in MDGH.

[5] See 3 and 4 Jan and *fn*.

[6] It did not open the Number.

[bb] Inserted as an afterthought.

[7] In Mar 1855 a preliminary meeting of the National Association of Factory Occupiers resolved that a fund be set up to pay for the defence of any member prosecuted for failure to fence mill-gearing. In "More Grist to the Mill" (*HW*, 28 July 55, XI, 605) Morley pointed out the dubious legal position of the Association in protecting its members in their infringement of the law. The Association seems to have taken fright at the article, and produced a *Special Report* disclaiming any intention of paying damages. The Report was signed by the Chairman on 7 Aug, but the cover of the printed *Report* was dated July 1855 in an attempt, as Morley claimed, to persuade interested parties that it had been drawn up before the publication of his article.

[8] See Harry Stone (*Uncollected Writings of CD*, 1969, p. 550) for CD's probable alterations. While the factual arguments clearly derive from Morley's original, CD was concerned to set the tone for references to Miss

I should like Morley to do a Strike article, and to work into it the greater part of what is here.[1] But I cannot represent myself as holding the opinion that all strikes among this unhappy class of society who find it so difficult to get a peaceful hearing, are always necessarily wrong; because I don't think so. To open a discussion of the question by saying that the men are "*of course* entirely and painfully in the wrong", surely would be monstrous in any one. Shew them to be in the wrong here, but in the name of the Eternal Heavens shew why, upon the merits of this question.[2] Nor can I possibly adopt the representation that these men are wrong because, by throwing themselves out of work, they throw other people, possibly without their consent. If such a principle had anything in it, there would have been no civil war; no raising by Hampden of a troop of Horse, to the detriment of Buckinghamshire Agriculture; no self sacrifice in the political world. And O Good God when Morley treats of the suffering of wife and children, can he suppose that these mistaken men don't feel it in the depths of their hearts, and don't honestly and honorably—most devoutly and faithfully—believe—that for those very children when they shall have children, they are bearing all these miseries now!

I hear from Mrs. Fillonneau[3] that her husband[4] was obliged to leave town suddenly, before he could get your parcel. Consequently he has not brought it, and White's Sovereigns[5]—unless you have got them back again—are either lying out of circulation somewhere, or are being spent by somebody else.

I will write again on Tuesday. My article to begin the Vol.[6] enclosed.

Ever Faithfully

CD.

Martineau which, though pungent and deftly ironic, are scrupulously polite throughout, in contrast to the "personal invective" of "a pamphlet written in a passion" (*HW*, 19 Jan 56, XIII, 13). She considered the article "terribly false as to facts.... It will let tens of thousands of people know... that Dickens is distrusted on social subjects" (*Letters to Fanny Wedgewood*, ed. Elizabeth Sanders Arbuckle, Stanford, 1983, p. 145). A Bill which considerably reduced legal requirements on the fencing of mill-gearing was passed in May 56.

[1] In Morley's revised text of "The Manchester Strike" (*HW*, 2 Feb 56, XIII, 63) all the arguments he disliked were omitted, and emphasis placed on the moral that strikes could be avoided only by "the opening up of more and better opportunities of understanding one another, between man and master" (*HW*, 2 Feb 56, XIII, 65).

[2] The article says little specifically about the strike of minders and piecers in Manchester cotton-mills, begun on 14 Nov 55. The masters had given notice to reduce wages since trade was bad and their rates of pay higher than in surrounding districts. The men started to return on the reduced terms on 9 Jan, but many were still on strike when the article appeared on 2 Feb.

[3] Amelia Fillonneau, sister of CD's brother-in-law, Henry Austin: see Vols I, p. 18*n* and V, p. 9*n*.

[4] André Guillaume Fillonneau, agent and merchant, of 5 rue Gaillon, married Amelia Austin 15 July 37: see Vols I, p. 52*n* and IV, p. 497 and *n*.

[5] Wills had sent "gold" rather than an order on a bank, before White changed his mind: see *To* Wills, 3 and 4 Jan.

[6] *ibid.*, *fn.*

To F. BEAUCOURT-MUTUEL,[1] [?6 JANUARY 1856]

Mention in next.

Engaging the Villa Moulineaux for June.

To MARK LEMON,[2] 7 JANUARY 1856

Text from MDGH, I, 416–19.

49, Champs Elysees, Paris, Monday, Jan. 7th, 1856.

My dear Mark,

[a]I want to know how "Jack and the Beanstalk"[3] goes. I have a notion from a notice—a favourable notice, however—which I saw in *Galignani*, that Webster[4] has let down the comic business.[a5]

In a piece at the Ambigu,[6] called the "Rentrée à Paris,"[7] a mere scene in honour of the return of the troops from the Crimea the other day, there is a novelty which I think it worth letting you know of, as it is easily available, either for a serious or a comic interest—the introduction of a supposed electric telegraph. The scene is the railway terminus at Paris, with the electric telegraph office on the prompt side, and the clerks *with their backs to the audience*—much more real than if they were, as they infallibly would be, staring about the house—working the needles;[8] and the little bell perpetually ringing. There are assembled to greet the soldiers, all the easily and naturally imagined elements of interest—old veteran fathers, young children, agonised mothers, sisters and brothers, girl lovers—each impatient to know of his or her own object of solicitude. Enter to these a certain marquis, full of sympathy for all, who says "My friends, I am one of you. My brother has no commission yet. He is

[1] Ferdinand Beaucourt-Mutuel (1805–81): see Vol. VII, p. 104 and *n*. They had spent the summers of 1853–4 at his two villas in Boulogne.

[2] Mark Lemon (1809–70; *DNB*), playwright and editor of *Punch*: see Vol. III, p. 469*n*.

[aa] Omitted in MDGH 1882, 1893 and N.

[3] *Jack and the Beanstalk; or, Harlequin and Mother Goose at Home Again*, the Adelphi pantomime produced 26 Dec 55: "a decided novelty in its kind, being a mixture of the burlesque spectacle and the pantomime proper" (*The Times*, 27 Dec). The Burlesque was written by Lemon, "full of ... jocular allusions to the current talk of the day, sometimes very pointed and clever" (*Daily News*, 27 Dec.)

[4] Benjamin Nottingham Webster (1797–1882; *DNB*), actor, dramatist, and manager of the Adelphi Theatre.

[5] *Galignani* (2 Jan) reprinted the *Times* review, which thought the show "likely to have a good run", but found fault with "the pantomime proper". "Harlequin and Columbine tried one scrap of dialogue, but it was under difficulties.... Dancing and talking do not combine well, and both ladies were out of breath." The *Daily News* admired Madame Celeste, "the first female Harlequin we have seen.... The attire became her; she moved with much grace and lightness, and danced beautifully"; but the *Globe* (27 Dec) found this "a very questionable attraction", and Lemon was moved to defend her "generous motives, by some misunderstood and misrepresented" (*Illustrated London News*, 28 Feb).

[6] The Ambigu-Comique Theatre, Boulevard St Martin.

[7] "A popular play mixed with songs ... 100 seats are reserved each night for the brave soldiers of the army of the East" (*Le Moniteur*, 1 Jan). It ran 1–12 Jan.

[8] Presumably a representation of the system by which a magnetic needle was pivoted in the centre of a wire coil and intelligence transmitted by deflections to the right or left, in accordance with a pre-arranged code. For Sir Charles Wheatstone, its inventor, see Vol. VI, p. 574 & *n*.

a common soldier. I wait for him as well as all brothers and sisters here wait for *their* brothers. Tell me whom you are expecting." Then they all tell him. Then he goes into the telegraph-office, and sends a message down the line to know how long the troops will be. Bell rings. Answer handed out on slip of paper. "Delay on the line. Troops will not arrive for a quarter of an hour." General disappointment. "But we have this brave electric telegraph, my friends," says the marquis. "Give me your little messages, and I'll send them off." General rush round the marquis. Exclamations: "How's Henri?" "My love to Georges;" "Has Guillaume forgotten Elise?" "Is my son wounded?" "Is my brother promoted?" etc. etc. Marquis composes tumult. Sends message—such a regiment, such a company—"Elise's love to Georges." Little bell rings, slip of paper handed out—"Georges in ten minutes will embrace his Elise. Sends her a thousand kisses." Marquis sends message—such a regiment, such a company—"Is my son wounded?" Little bell rings. Slip of paper handed out—"No. He has not yet upon him those marks of bravery in the glorious service of his country which his dear old father bears" (father being lamed and invalided). Last of all, the widowed mother. Marquis sends message—such a regiment, such a company—"Is my only son safe?" Little bell rings. Slip of paper handed out—"He was first upon the heights of Alma." General cheer. Bell rings again, another slip of paper handed out. "He was made a sergeant at Inkermann." Another cheer. Bell rings again, another slip of paper handed out. "He was made colour-sergeant at Sebastopol." Another cheer. Bell rings again, another slip of paper handed out. "He was the first man who leaped with the French banner on the Malakhoff tower." Tremendous cheer. Bell rings again, another slip of paper handed out. "But he was struck down there by a musket-ball, and——Troops have proceeded. Will arive in half a minute after this." Mother abandons all hope; general commiseration; troops rush in, down a platform; son only wounded, and embraces her.

As I have said, and as you will see, this is available for any purpose. But done with equal distinction and rapidity, it is a tremendous effect, and got by the simplest means in the world. There is nothing in the piece, but it was impossible not to be moved and excited by the telegraph part of it.

I hope you have seen something of Stanny,[1] and have been to pantomimes with him, and have drunk to the absent Dick. I miss you, my dear old boy, at the play, woefully, and miss the walk home, and the partings at the corner of Tavistock Square. And when I go by myself, I come home stewing "Little Dorrit" in my head; and the best part of *my* play is (or ought to be) in Gordon Street.[2]

I have written to Beaucourt about taking that breezy house[3]—a little improved[4]—for the summer, and I hope you and yours will come there often and stay there long.[5] My present idea, if nothing should arise to unroot me sooner, is to stay here until the middle of May, then plant the family at Boulogne, and come with

[1] Clarkson Stanfield (1793–1867; *DNB*), marine and landscape painter: see Vol. I, p. 553*n*. Five of his pictures were in the 1855 Paris Exhibition.

[2] Lemon lived at No. 11, very close to Tavistock House.

[3] The Villa des Moulineaux, Boulogne, which CD had rented in Summer 1853: see Vol. VII, *passim*.

[4] See *To* Beard, 21 June.

[5] Lemon intended to visit: see 8 July. On 26 July Mrs Lemon gave birth to her daughter Kate.

Catherine and Georgy home for two or three weeks.[1] When I shall next run across I don't know, but I suppose next month.[2]

We are up to our knees in mud here. Literally in vehement despair, I walked down the avenue outside the Barrière de l'Étoile[3] here yesterday, and went straight on among the trees. I came back with top-boots of mud on. Nothing will cleanse the streets. Numbers of men and women are for ever scooping and sweeping in them, and they are always one lake of yellow mud. All my trousers go to the tailor's every day, and are ravelled out at the heels every night. Washing is awful.

Tell Mrs. Lemon,[4] with my love, that I have bought her some Eau d'Or,[5] in grateful remembrance of her knowing what it is, and crushing the tyrant of her existence by resolutely refusing to be put down when that monster would have silenced her.[6] You may imagine the loves and messages that are now being poured in upon me by all of them, so I will give none of them; though I am pretending to be very scrupulous about it, and am looking (I have no doubt) as if I were writing them down with the greatest care.

Ever affectionately

[CD]

To MADAME VIARDOT,[7] 7 JANUARY 1856*

MS Yale University Library.

49 Champs Elysées | 7 Janvier, 1856

Ma chère Madame Viardot

Samedi prochain me conviendra parfaitement.[8] Je serai charmé de vous revoir, et de faire connaissance avec cette dame illustre,[9] chez vous. Madame Dickens sera enchantée de m'accompagner.

Croyez-moi toujours, un des admirateurs de votre genie les plus sincères et les plus constants,

À Madame Viardot. CHARLES DICKENS

[1] CD preceded them to England by some two weeks on 29 Apr.

[2] He was in London 4–11 Feb.

[3] The Avenue de Neuilly.

[4] Née Nelly Romer (1801–90).

[5] The French equivalent of Danziger Goldwasser, a liqueur flavoured with aniseed and caraway, first made in 1598, later with gold dust or flakes added. In *Nicholas Nickleby*, Ch. 51, it is offered to Newman Noggs by Arthur Gride, who likes it "on account of its name".

[6] Perhaps when CD dined with the Lemons on 16 Dec 55.

[7] Pauline Viardot-Garcia (1821–1910), celebrated mezzo-soprano: see Vol. VII, p. 224*n*.

[8] Saturday was 12 Jan: Forster gives 10 Jan in error. But the date was changed to 13 Jan, at George Sand's request: see her *Correspondence*, ed. Georges Lubin, Vol. XIII, Paris, 1978, p. 495.

[9] George Sand, for many years a close friend of Mme Viardot. For CD's impressions, see *To* Collins, 19 Jan.

To MISS MARY BOYLE,[1] 8 JANUARY 1856

MS Morgan Library.

Paris, 49 Champs Elysées, | Tuesday Eighth January 1856.

My Dear Mary.

I am afraid you will think me an abandoned ruffian for not having acknowledged your more than welcome warm-hearted letter before now. But, as usual, I have been so occupied, and so glad to get up from my desk and wallow in the mud (at present about 6 feet deep here), that pleasure-correspondence is just the last thing in the world I have had leisure to take to. Business correspondence with all sorts of conditions of men—*and* women—O my Mary! is one of the Dragons I am perpetually fighting. And the more I throw it, the more it stands upon its hind-legs, rampant, and throws me.

Yes. On that bright cold morning when I left Peterboro',[2] I felt that the best thing I could do was to say that word that I would do anything in an honest way to avoid saying,[3] at one blow, and make off. I was so sorry to leave you all!—You can scarcely imagine what a chill and blank I felt on that Monday Evening at Rockingham.[4] It was so sad to me, and engendered a constraint so melancholy and peculiar, that I doubt if I were ever much more out of sorts in my life. Next morning, when it was light and sparkling out of doors, I felt more at home again. But when I came in from seeing poor dear Watson's grave, Mrs. Watson[5] asked me to go up in the Gallery—which I had last seen in the days of our merry Play.[6] We went up and walked into the bay-part he had made and was so fond of, and she looked out of one window and I looked out of another, and for the life of me I could not decide in my own breast whether I should console or distress her by going and taking her hand, and saying something of what was naturally in my mind. So I said nothing, and we came out again, and on the whole perhaps it was best; for I have no doubt we understood each other very well, without speaking a word.

Sheffield[7] was a tremendous success and an admirable Audience. They made me a present of table-cutlery after the reading was over,[8] and I came away by the Mail Train within three quarters of an hour—changing my dress and getting on my wrappers, partly in the Fly, partly at the Inn, partly on the Platform. When we got among the Lincolnshire fens, it began to snow. That changed to sleet, that changed to rain, the frost was all gone as we neared London, and the mud was all come. At two or three o'Clock in the morning, I stopped at Peterboro' again, and thought of you all, disconsolately. The Lady in the Refreshment Room was very hard upon me—harder even, than those fair enslavers usually are. She gave me a cup of tea, as if I were a hyæna, and she my cruel keeper with a strong dislike to me. I mingled my

[1] Mary Louisa Boyle (1810–90), miscellaneous writer: see Vol. V, p. 662*n*.

[2] On 19 Dec 55, after reading the *Carol* for the Mechanics' Institute the evening before: see Vol. VII, p. 766 and *n*.

[3] "My father had such an intense dislike for leave-taking that he always, when it was possible, shirked a farewell" (Mary Dickens, *My Father as I Recall him*, p. 118).

[4] On 17 Dec CD stayed at Rockingham Castle for the first time since the death of its owner, the Hon. Richard Watson (1800–52; see Vol. IV, p. 574*n*). For this visit, see Vol. VII, p. 766.

[5] Née Lavinia Jane Quin (1816–88): see Vol. IV, p. 574*n*.

[6] The private theatricals at Rockingham, Jan 51: see Vol. VI, p. 261 & n.

[7] His reading of the *Carol* at the Mechanics' Institute, 22 Dec 55: see Vol. VII, p. 771 and *n*.

[8] See Vol. VII, p. 770 and *n*.

tears with it; and had a petrified bun of enormous antiquity, in miserable meekness.[1]

It is clear to me that climates are gradually assimilating over a great part of the world, and that in the most miserable time of our year there is very little to choose between London and Paris—except that London is not so muddy. I have never seen dirtier or worse weather than we have had here, ever since I returned. In desperation I went outside the Barriers last Sunday on a headlong walk, and came back with top-boots of mud on, and my very eyebrows smeared with mud. Georgina is usually invisible during the walking time of the day. A turned-up nose may be seen in the midst of a heap of splashes—but nothing more.

I am setting to work again, and my horrible restlessness immediately assails me. It belongs to such times. As I was writing the preceding page[2] it suddenly came into my head that I would get up and go to Calais. I don't know why. The moment I got to Calais, I should want to come back here. The moment I got here, I should want to go somewhere else. But, as my friend The Boots says (see Xmas No. Household Words) "When you come to think what a game you've been up to ever since you was in your own cradle, and what a poor sort of a chap you are, and how its always Yesterday with you, or else Tomorrow, and never To Day—that's where it is."[3]

My dear Mary, could you favor me with the name and address of the Professor wot taught you writing? For, I want to improve myself. Many a hand have I seen, with Many characteristics of beauty in it—some, loopy; some, dashy; some, large; some, small; some, sloping to the right; some, sloping to the left; some, not sloping at all; but what I like in *your* hand Mary, is,—its plainness. It is like Print.[4] Them as runs, may read—just as well as if they stood still. *I* should have thought it was copperplate, if I hadn't a known you.

They send all sorts of messages from here, and so do I. With my best regards to Bedgy[5] and pardner[6] and the blessed babbies. When shall we meet again I wonder, and go somewhere! Ah!—

Believe me ever my dear Mary, yours truly and affectionately

(That doesn't look plain) JOE[7]

JOE[8]

[1] CD referred to the refreshment room lady ("Why does she feed me like a hyaena?") in "Why?", *HW*, 1 Mar 56, XIII, 145.

[2] CD here drew a pointing hand.

[3] On a later occasion, according to W. M. Wright, the words here quoted were recited by CD "feelingly and monotonous[ly]" (*CD: The Public Readings*, ed. Philip Collins, Oxford, 1975, p. 177).

[4] "Her handwriting had undoubted peculiarities" (*Mary Boyle her Book*, ed. Sir Courtenay Boyle, 1901, p. xii).

[5] Capt. Cavendish Spencer Boyle (1814–68): see Vol. VI, p. 174*n*. Miss Boyle's favourite brother and the youngest of six children, hence "the little Benjamin of the family" (*Mary Boyle her Book*, p. 4). He and his wife had attended the Peterborough reading.

[6] Rose Boyle (m. 1844): see Vol. VI, p. 666*n*.

[7] In script caps. CD's part in *Used Up* in the Rockingham Theatricals, 15 Jan 51: see Vol. VI, p. 262 & *n*.

[8] In printed caps.

To W. H. WILLS, 9 JANUARY 1856*

MS Huntington Library.

49 Champs Elysées | Wednesday Ninth January 1856

My Dear Wills. I write very hastily, in order that I may send the No.[1] back by this Post. It has come from the Printer's; and the same Post that brings it, brings no letter from you.

The No. is rather heavy. Look to Langthwaite,[2] to see that there is no covert Bawdry in it.[3] The Cattle Stealer[4] and the Roving Englishman[5] obviously dont do together. A change is wanted there.[6]

I send you for the following No. the Whitechapel case.[7] Ask Albert Smith[8] to call in at the office (after it is printed) and look at the Proof. It is perfectly accurate, except that the case is under-stated; but I shod. like him to see it, tell him.

You shall have another letter from me tomorrow, wherein I will tell you about Miss Coutts.[9]

Ever Faithfully
CD.

To MISS BURDETT COUTTS, 10 JANUARY 1856

MS Morgan Library.

49 Champs Elysées, Paris | Thursday Tenth January 1856

My Dear Miss Coutts.

The noble cake arrived in the best condition—was a great surprise—and was received with the loudest acclamations. I think Mrs. Dickens will have already thanked you for it,[10] but I cannot omit it from my note in reply to yours received yesterday.

I was very much pleased to receive that note, because I know its effect will be a great pleasure to Wills, and because I am certain of his deserving your confidence, and most zealously delicately and worthily acquitting himself of any function you entrust him with.[11] My experience of him is close and constant, and I cannot too

[1] Proofs of *HW*, No. 304, 19 Jan 56.

[2] *HW*, 19 Jan 56, XIII, 7: a story about a liberal-minded Italian widow living in a Cumberland village, by Eliza Lynn: see Vol. VII, p. 114*n*. She had been living in Paris since Nov 55, but returned to Brantwood in the spring to look after W. J. Linton's sick wife (who died in Dec 56) and their several children.

[3] See Vol. VII, p. x.

[4] "Ben Serraq", *HW*, 19 Jan 56, XIII, 4: a translation by Edmund S. Dixon of a tale from Charles Richard's *Algérie. Scènes des moeurs arabes*, 1850.

[5] E. C. Grenville Murray's "The Show Officer" (*ibid.*, XIII, 22) describes a passage from Galati to Sulina.

[6] The order of articles was changed, Dixon's article is placed second and Murray's is fifth.

[7] "A Nightly Scene in London", *HW*, 26 Jan 56, XIII, 25: see Vol. VII, p. 742 and *n*.

[8] Albert Richard Smith (1816–60; *DNB*), author and entertainer: see Vol. IV, p. 8*n*. Had been giving his illustrated lecture on "The Ascent of Mont Blanc" for the past three years at the Egyptian Hall, Piccadilly.

[9] Angela Georgina Burdett Coutts (1814–1906; *DNB*), later Baroness Burdett-Coutts.

[10] Catherine's affectionate letter of 9 Jan, sending love and sympathy to Mrs Brown, is in the Morgan Library.

[11] As part-time confidential secretary to Miss Coutts (Vol. VII, pp. 746–7). He was to hold the post until 1868.

highly commend him. I feel so much interested in hearing the arrangements you would prefer to make, that I put a strong constraint upon myself in not immediately coming to London. However, I shall try to force myself to write a No. of Little Dorrit first (I am just sitting down to one),[1] and that will hold me prisoner, if I submit, until early in next Month. Whenever I come to town, of course I shall come to you within a few hours.[2]

Next month reminds me of Walter.[3] Being fifteen next month, he will be able to go up for his examination next month twelvemonth. I found him so excessively deaf when he came over here, that I felt it necessary to have him examined by the Chief Surgeon (very famous in that way), of the Asylum for the Deaf and Dumb.[4] He found him to have an Ulcerated Tympanum, of a very aggravated and peculiar kind. He said it was of long standing, must have caused him great pain, and he should have thought must have forced itself on the attention of the Masters of his school.[5] He has greatly relieved and improved his patient, but says that his sense of hearing will never be quite delicate. To brush up the patient's French, I send him to a great school in the Faubourg St. Honoré,[6] two hours a day. An Omnibus comes round for the Pupils, every Morning—a private Omnibus belonging to the school—and the Driver blows a frightful whistle on the box, to announce himself.

I have made arrangements with a large bookselling-house in Paris here, for the publication of a French translation of the whole of my books. A volume will appear about once a month, and it will take a year and a half or two years to complete. It will be a pleasant thing to have done in one's lifetime. It is their venture, and they pay me three or four hundred pounds for it besides. The Portrait for which I have been sitting to Ary Scheffer, is just done.[7] He is a great painter, and of course it has great merit. I doubt if I should know it, myself—but it is always possible I may know other people's faces pretty well, without knowing my own.

I have omitted to say, in its proper place, that I had *not* communicated to Wills, what passed between you and me.[8] It did not seem to me quite decided, and I thought there was time enough: knowing that I could at any time tell him that I had had a reason for reserving it, and that he would be quite satisfied with that assurance.

There seem to be great misgivings here, that a pecuniary crisis[9] must come.

My kind love to Mrs. Browne,[10] whom I hope to find very much improved when I next see her.

Ever Dear Miss Coutts | Faithfully and affectionately Yours

CHARLES DICKENS

[1] No. V, probably finished before CD left for London on 4 Feb.

[2] He saw Miss Coutts on 8 Feb: see *To* Wills, that day.

[3] Walter Landor Dickens (1841–63), CD's second son: see Vols II, p. 205*n* and VII, p. 246*n*.

[4] Prosper Menière (1799–1862), surgeon at the Institution Royale des Sourde-muets de Paris. His *Mémoires sur les lésions de l'orielle interne*, 1861, gave the first description of aural vertigo, late known as Menière's Syndrome.

[5] Brackenbury and Wynne's School, Wimbledon.

[6] Probably the English Free School, 119 rue du Faubourg St Honoré, though intended for working class children. It was run under the patronage of the British Ambassador and the management of a Committee of English clergymen and other residents.

[7] CD expected this on 19 Jan but Scheffer was still not satisfied at the end of March.

[8] See *To* Wills, 10 Jan.

[9] CD was concerned about speculation on the Bourse: see *To* Forster, 20 April.

[10] Thus in MS. Mrs Brown, née Hannah Meredith (*d.* 1878), Miss Coutts's companion (see Vol. II, p. 168*n*), whose husband had died in Oct 55: see Vol. VII.

To SIR EDWIN LANDSEER,[1] 10 JANUARY 1856

MS University of Texas. *Address:* L'Angleterre. | Sir Edwin Landseer | &c &c &c | 1 St. John's Wood Road | London.

49 Champs Elysées, Paris | Thursday Tenth January 1856

My Dear Landseer.

I will not fail to report myself, when I next stand within view of the Village Church of St. Paul. My defection from the Blue Posts,[2] was caused by my having to read at Sheffield; which, I thought when you were here,[3] I had escaped. I was perpetually on Railroads, during the whole of my short Flight.

The Royal Couple[4] shall have my best attention. I will try to express you in the plainest manner, and to allow none of the interest of your argument—a most excellent one—to escape.[5]

What you say of Nos. 1 and 2, is a real delight to me. For, whenever I speak of men born by Nature to be writers if they had not highly distinguished themselves in some other Art (they are mighty few), I always instance you with your remarkable powers of observation and perception. My Lanny, there are some of your friends in Place-Regions[6] who will look mightily blue when they see No. 3.[7] Let me whisper *that* in your ear.

And now I come to the most portentous part of your letter. Seventy five times over, I read this Postcript:[8]

"What have you done with the Firs."

—what Firs, I asked myself? I have planted none here; I have no place to plant them in; I have purchased no Firs, sold no Firs, described no Firs, made no reference to any Firs whatsoever. I went to bed, partially delirious. In the dead of the night it came into my head that the Postcript must be:

"What have you done with the Tin."[9]

I done with the Tin?—*I*? Don't you know that Mr. Jacob Bell[10] took the business out of my hands? Don't you know, that in consequence of some difficulty respecting the attestation of your signature by the Consul[11] in your absence, he comes to me at the Household Words Office and says, says he, "I have therefore entrusted the matter

[1] Sir Edwin Landseer (1802–73; *DNB*), animal and child painter: see Vol. III, p. 298*n*.

[2] The Blue Posts Tavern, Cork Street, where "a good homely well-cooked English dinner may be had at a reasonable rate" (Peter Cunningham, *Hand Book of London*, new edn., 1850, p. 140).

[3] For the distribution of prizes at the Paris Art Exhibition on 15 Nov 55: see Vol. VII, p. 745 and *n*.

[4] The lion and lioness in the Zoological Gardens in Regent's Park.

[5] CD's "The Friend of the Lions" (*HW*, 2 Feb 56, XIII, 61) reports Landseer's complaints of their inadequate living area in the Zoo.

[6] Office-seekers.

[7] Published 31 Jan, *Little Dorrit*, No. III for Feb. introduced the Circumlocution Office in Ch. 10: see *To* Forster, 30 Jan.

[8] Thus in MS; no doubt Landseer's misspelling.

[9] The prize money awarded to Landseer, along with the Grande Medaille d'Honeur, at the Paris Exhibition: see Vol. VII, p. 745 and *n*.

[10] Jacob Bell (1810–59; *DNB*), pharmaceutical chemist and art collector: see Vol. VI, p. 99*n*. Acted for many years as Landseer's business manager. A letter from Landseer to an unknown correspondent, dated 18 Dec 55 and authorising CD to receive the prize money on his behalf, survives together with a covering explanatory letter to Bell (Sotheby catalogue, Feb 1978).

[11] Thomas Pickford, British Consul at Paris 1834–65.

to Mr. Redgrave,[1] who will get it done"? And now to be asked what *I* have done with the Tin—I the discarded one!—Ha ha ha!

(Here I broke off, put some straws in my hair, some more straws in my shoes, took a wisp in each hand, and went about the room, theatrically mad, repeating for two hours—"What have I—*I*—done with the Tin!)

Mrs. Dickens and Georgina send their kindest regards. They think you ought to come back and spend the—ha ha ha!—the Tin—*my* tin—the tin that I—ho ho ho!

Ever Heartily Yours

Sir Edwin Landseer. CHARLES DICKENS

To W. H. WILLS, 10 JANUARY 1856

MS Huntington Library.

49 Champs Elysées, Thursday January tenth 1856

My Dear Wills.

MISS COUTTS.[2]

I am happy to find from the enclosed letter[3] (which you are to read, after reading this), that I exercised a wise discretion in saying nothing to you of a conversation I had with Miss Coutts on the day after my arrival in town last time.[4] She then told me that she was under particular articles of agreement with her Partners in the Bank, never to associate herself with anyone, in any kind of engagement or business, who was connected with any House or Enterprize; and that she had doubted, since her interview with you, whether your position in respect to Household Words might not be construed in the Strand as coming within the line drawn. Observing my invariable custom of taking the perfectly independent course in any such matter, and of justifying no jealousy or suspicion, and of having nothing in common with anybody's intrigues or approaches towards her, I told her that if she had that doubt it was enough—that it was enough for me—that it would be enough for you—and that there was an end of it. She then begged me to explain it to you. But I thought I saw so distinctly that her mind was *not* made up and that there was a strong probability of her coming to an opposite conclusion, that I resolved to make no explanation to you for some little time. All this I now disclose to you in the strictest confidence—my confidence with her, being involved therein. You will see from her letter that she now contemplates the kind of relation I pointed out to you as desirable.[5] I have told her in reply, that I expect to be in town again about the 10th. of February, and that I shall then be very happy to pursue, and I hope settle, the subject with her.[6]

[1] Richard Redgrave (1804–88; *DNB*), genre and landscape painter; RA 1851. Responsible for the practical arrangements of the British section at the 1855 Paris Exhibition, suffering "many difficulties and discouragements": Landseer was one of "two or three painters who gave us infinite trouble by their procrastination . . . and never thought it worth while to offer me a word of thanks" (*A Memoir, compiled from his diary. By F. M. Redgrave*, 1891, pp. 116, 136).

[2] Underlined with short double strokes.

[3] From Miss Coutts, received by CD on 9 Jan.

[4] i.e., on 16 Dec 55.

[5] See Vol. VII, pp. 746–7.

[6] See 8 Feb.

ME.[1]

When you write next, will you enclose some stamps for cheques?

Is there any news of Gad's Hill Place?[2]

Will you send John[3] to Mr. Morgan, our family apothecary[4] (John knows his house near Russell Square), with a note asking him to call upon you at the Office at a certain time? When he comes, will you tell him that you have it in charge from me to beg him to charge his attendance medicines &c for Mrs. Hogarth[5] in her illness to my account, and just to say nothing at all about the matter to her, or her family, or any one else.

SALA.[1]

came here at 12 o'Clock on Tuesday, by appointment, at his solicitation.[6] It was the second appointment. On the first occasion he was 20 minutes behind his time (but I really believe by an accident), and of course I had gone out. He sat here *two hours*, telling me about his reputable friends at Erith,[7] and so forth. I had no suspicion that he was postponing a request for money and couldn't make up his mind to make it, until he at last stammered out a petition for £5.[8] I gave it him. Please place that sum to his debit and my credit.[9] He told me he had sent two articles to you.[10]

I derived the idea that he was living very queerly here, and not doing himself much good. He knew nothing, I observed, about the pieces at the Theatres; and suggested a strong flavor of the wine shop and the billiard table.[11] In Galignani, I see a quotation from the Leader, which, unless my memory deceives me (which I don't think it does), is a part of that article he wrote about the Young Man and his Uncle, and called, I think, Parisian Nights Entertainments.[12] You didn't give it back to him, did you? If you did, it was a mistake. I meant it to stand over, until Collins[13] should come here.

H.W.[1]

Forster does not think those two little poems[14] are otherwise than original. That is to

[1] Underlined with short double strokes.

[2] The delays in completing the sale were perhaps due in part to the position of the tenant, the Rev. Joseph Hindle: see *To* Miss Coutts, 9 Feb.

[3] John Thompson, CD's servant.

[4] Charles Morgan, surgeon, of 9 Bedford Place.

[5] Mrs George Hogarth (1793–1863). She had been very ill Nov–Dec 55, apparently with neuralgia.

[6] Sala's recollection, fifty years later, was different, more favourable to himself, and certainly inaccurate (*Things I have Seen and People I have Known*, 1894, I, 123–32).

[7] In Kent; his brother Charles Kerrison Sala lived there and was in poor health.

[8] Sala was "comically hard up" (*op. cit.*, I, 117) and wrote to Yates *c.* 11 Jan that he had been "utterly incapable of work" through "an incessant pain in my head that nearly drives me mad ... [CD] is most kind and jolly, and I think will do anything for me" (*Edmund Yates: his Recollections and Experiences*, 1884, I, 331–2).

[9] CD had been generous to Sala in the past (see Vol. VII, p. 392 and *n*), but was becoming more cautious over his fecklessness in money matters.

[10] Presumably "Beef", *HW*, 2 Feb 56, XIII, 49, and "Little Saint Zita", *HW*, 9 Feb 56, XIII, 91.

[11] He was drinking heavily, in debt to money-lenders, and behind with commitments both to *HW* and other periodicals. When his promised serials for Edmund Yates's *The Train* failed to materialise, an advertisement was placed in *The Times*, beginning "Bohemian, where art thou?" (Yates, *Recollections*, I, 328).

[12] Sala had given it to Yates, who published it in No. I of *The Train* (1 Jan); the *Leader* for 5 Jan quoted from it.

[13] William Wilkie Collins (1824–89; *DNB*), novelist: see Vol. VI, p. 310*n*.

[14] "A Shadow of George Herbert", *HW*, 26 Jan 56, XIII, 37, and "Sorrow and My Heart", *HW*, 9 Feb 56, XIII, 84, both obvious imitations of Herbert. No author given in *HW* Office book.

say, he cannot find them anywhere, though he has my general impression about them. Therefore get them back from him and insert them.

My head is necessarily so full of my own subjects, that I have not thought of that point to any advantage, though I have thought of it at various times. The Police Enquiry[1] was never done, though I spoke to you about it when you were here. Accounts of the constitution of foreign armies, especially as to their officering, and as to the officer's professional business being his professional pride and study and not a bore, are highly desirable.[2] An article on the prices of fares on Foreign Railways, on the cost of making them, on the public accommodation and the nature of the carriages &c—contrasting their law with our law, and their management with our management—would be highly desirable.[3] I suppose Dixon[4] could do it directly. Would it be possible to strike out a new man, to write popularly about the monstrous absurdity of our laws, and to compare them with the Code Napoleon? Or has Morley knowledge enough in that direction, or could he get it?[5] It is curious to observe here that Lord Campbell's[6] acts for making compensation to bodily-injured people, are mere shreds of the Code Napoleon. That business of the Duke of Northumberland[7] and his tenantry. Couldn't Sydney[8] do something about it?[9] It would be worth sending anybody to that recusant Farmer who leads the opposition.[10] Similarly, the Duke of Argyll, whom the papers drove out of his mind by agreeing to consider him a Phaenomonon, simply because he wasn't a born ass. Is there no Scotch source from whence we can get some information about that Island where he had the notice stuck upon the Church Door that "no tenant under £30 a year, was to be allowed to use spirits, at any marriage, christening, funeral, or other Gathering".[11] It would be a capital illustration of the monstrous nonsense of a Maine Law.[12] Life Assurance. Are proposals ever refused—if so, often—because of their suspicious character as engendering notions that the assured life may possibly be taken? I know of Policies being refused to be paid, on the ground that the person

[1] No such article appeared in 1856.

[2] As directed, M. R. L. Meason's "French and English Staff Officers", *HW*, 9 Feb 56, XIII, 84) compares their training and duties, greatly to England's disadvantage.

[3] No such article appeared.

[4] Edmund Saul Dixon (1809–93), historian, journalist and traveller. Prolific contributor to *HW* since 1852.

[5] Henry Morley's "Law and Order" (*HW*, 29 Mar 56, XIII, 241) argues on these lines.

[6] John, 1st Baron Campbell, Lord Chief Justice: see Vol. VII, p. 21*n*. 9 & 10 Vict. *c*. 93, known as Lord Campbell's Act, allowed representatives of a person killed by another's wrongful act, neglect or default to bring an action for damages. CD would have this in mind because of the Factory Act controversy.

[7] Algernon Percy, 4th Duke of Northumberland had introduced a new form of lease for his tenant farmers, specifying the course of cultivation to be followed on his land. The tenants had to sign or quit, and were subject to numerous penalties if they did not follow the prescribed rules.

[8] Thus in MS. Samuel Sidney, agricultural writer and contributor to *HW* on Australia: see Vol. VI, p. 27 and *n*.

[9] Sidney's "Feudal Fetters for Farmers" (*HW*, 8 Mar 56, XIII, 178).

[10] William Wetherell, of Kirkbridge, Yorkshire; "Mr. Netherwell" in the article.

[11] George Douglas Campbell, 8th Duke of Argyle (1823–1900; *DNB*), FRS. Succeeded to Dukedom 1847. A notice to this effect was posted in Tiree on 16 Nov 55. In his *Autobiography* (2 vols, 1906) Argyle wrote with great affection of early visits there, when the people were "as yet untainted by the passions of the demagogue and the ignorance of fools" (I, 133–47).

[12] The law prohibiting the sale and consumption of alcohol in Maine, passed in 1851; by 1855 twelve other states had followed suit.

was Murdered—and could insert an anecdote or two.[1] Poisoning. Can't Morley do something about the Sale of Poisons[2]—I suppose Miss Martineau's doctrine of never never never interfering with trade, is not a Gospel from Heaven in this case.

For a light article, suppose Thomas[3] went round, for a walk, to a number of the old coaching houses, and were to tell us what they are about now, and how they look. Those great stables down in Lad Lane whence the horses belonging to the Swan with two Necks, used to come up an inclined plane. What are *they* doing? The Golden Cross, the Belle Sauvage, the Houses in Goswell Street, the Peacock at Islington, what are they all about? How do they bear the little ricketty omnibuses and so forth? What on earth were the coaches made into? What comes into the Yard of the General Post Office now, at 5 o'Clock in the morning? What's up the yard of the Angel, St. Clements? *I* don't know. What's in the two Saracens' Heads? Any of the old brains at all?[4]

Mr. Paine[5] might do this, if Thomas couldn't. But Thomas would do it best.

—Your letter of yesterday has just arrived as I close this. Morley always wants a little screwing up and tightening. It is his habit to write in a loose way.

Certainly *not* the Burns at that price for White, I undertake to say. The Xmas Bills in the parcel, if you please. Ever Faithfully CD

To LOUIS HACHETTE,[6] 14 JANUARY 1856

MS Librairie Hachette. *Date:* misdated 1855 by CD.

49 Champs Elysées | Monday January 14, 1855

Dear Sir

I have read the agreement you have had the kindness to send me, and I return it enclosed.

When I wrote, hastily, the titles of my Romances,[7] I forgot Oliver Twist, which is distinctly one of them, which has always been so called and which is as widely known both in England and abroad as any book I have written.[8] Consequently the number of Romances is not nine, but ten.

As to Hard Times, and the Contes de Noel, they are comparatively short as separate books, and they form part of my Works as published in England, and no French

[1] No such article appeared.

[2] Morley's "Poison" (22 Mar 56, XIII, 220) urges legal restraints on the supply of drugs and poisons.

[3] William Moy Thomas, journalist and scholar: see Vol. VI, p. 738*n*. Contributed frequently to *HW* 1851–5, but not again until 1858.

[4] Almost all these coaching inns appear in CD's novels and letters. By this period many acted as railway receiving offices and omnibus stops. For a series on old inns in *AYR* see next vol.

[5] Thus in MS. James Payn, novelist and journalist: see Vol. VII, p. 72 and *n*; and see *To* Payn, 29 Sep 58.

[6] Louis Christophe François Hachette, founder and head of the firm: see Vol. VII, p. 759 and *n*.

[7] On 10 Jan CD had sent a list of nine of his novels in his suggested order of publication, beginning with *The Old Curiosity Shop* and ending with *Little Dorrit* (Jean Mistler, *La Librairie Hachette*, Paris, 1964, p. 156). Hachette then sent him a draft contract.

[8] Translations into eight European languages had appeared by 1846, including a French transl. in 1841. Published by Hachette in a transl. by Alfred Geradin, 1858.

translation could possibly be considered complete without them. I therefore suggest to you that they ought to form (as one Volume in all), part of the series of Romances,[1] and that it would be an absurdity to include them under the separate title of "Nouvelles"—Nor do I see how we can possibly include in our agreement, the titles of all the papers I have written in Household Words. If you call those "Nouvelles" (which I do not), there are many of them; but of opuscules *not* published in Household Words, there is only one large separate Volume. It is called "Sketches"[2] (Esquisses), and contains my juvenile productions. I do not think it would repay you to make any translations from that book.

I cannot say what Romances written by me have been translated in France,[3] and I wish to avoid embarrassing our agreement with any statement on that head. Your original letter containing nothing about it, I apprehend you will agree with me on the point.

It seems to me that there are only three essential points to be stated in the agreement.

First that I am the author of certain works, some of which appeared before the International Treaty; some of which have appeared since the International Treaty.[4]

Second. That the following are the dates of the publication of the said books, separately. Consequently that so many were published before the treaty, and that so many have been published since.

Third, that I cede to you the sole and exclusive right of making a translation authorized by me, of these books, into the French language, in consideration of so much money—so much for the books published before the Treaty, and so much for the books published since the Treaty—to be paid in monthly payments of a thousand francs each, commencing on the 1st. of April next.

The whole business would thus be settled in one plain agreement. I should greatly prefer this mode of proceeding, and I hope you will do me the favor to adopt it. Nothing is wanting on my part to render it complete, but a list of the dates of publication of all my books. On receiving your answer, I will write for it to my publishers in England, and obtain it within two days. I will then send it to you, you can alter the agreement in accordance with it, and we can discuss and conclude it here on any afternoon you please at 3 o'Clock.[5]

With the assurance of my high consideration, I am Dear Sir

Faithfully Yours
CHARLES DICKENS

A Monsieur L. Hachette.

[1] *Les temps difficiles*, transl. by William L. Hughes, and *Contes de Noel*, transl. by André de Goy and Mlle de Saint-Romain, appeared as separate vols in 1857.

[2] They were not included.

[3] Many translations had appeared since Mme Niboyet's *Aventures de Mr Pickwick*, 1838, some in Hachette's series "Bibliothèque des Chemins de fer". *Bleak House* and *Hard Times*, which appeared after the signing of the International Copyright Treaty, had not yet been translated.

[4] See *To* Mrs Gaskell, 2 Jan, *fn*.

[5] Under the contract signed 1 Feb Hachette agreed to publish translations of 11 novels, from *Pickwick Papers* to *Little Dorrit*, CD to receive 11,000 francs at the rate of 1,000 francs a month, beginning on 1 Apr 56; for articles, etc., he was to receive 500 francs. The financial terms had evidently been improved, since Templier's letter, on Hachette's behalf, of 10 Dec 55, offered only 500 francs for novels not protected by the International Copyright Treaty. In all, the edn ran to 28 vols, 1857–74 (Jean Mistler, *La Librarie Hachette*, pp. 156–62.

To SIR EDWIN LANDSEER, 14 JANUARY 1856

Extract in N, II, 728, and mention in next; dated Paris, 14 Jan 56; addressed Sir Edwin Landseer.

I have started the case of Mr. Sims, in what I hope is a pleasant little joke, that will amuse our personal friends and the public.[1] *Telling him to expect revise of CD's article.*

To W. H. WILLS, 14 JANUARY 1856

MS Huntington Library.

49 Champs Elysées, Paris | Monday Fourteenth January 1856

My Dear Wills.

H.W.[2]

I enclose the Proof of the Friend of the Lions. Will you have the corrections made at once, and then enclose a revise, by post, to Sir Edwin Landseer, 1 St. Johns Wood Road. I have told him that you will send it to him, and that he need not answer. He is not a ready writer.

I think I have a good idea for a series of Paris papers into which I can infuse a good deal of myself, if Collins comes here (as I think he will) for some time.

If Sala really has not sent those papers,[3] it is a very, very bad business. But he described one of them to me; and I shall still hope that they may turn out to have been on the road while we have been communicating about them.

POOLE.[2]

I enclose the document duly signed.[4] It is to go to my account at Coutts's, you observe; and *no* remittance is to be made to Paris.

BEGGING LETTERS[2]

I return three (see P.S); retaining Miss Walpole's[5] late of the St. James's Theatre. She has been a begging-letter-writer, within my knowledge, these fifteen years.

Mrs. Ramo Samee[6] is a case that there is no doubt about. John has been there once, and can do the needful again. Something like a couple of guineas, I should think would be the sum most useful to her. But if there were any hope (I fear there is not), of doing her any real good with more, I should not object to more.

The other two letters, I really cannot form a judgment upon. But I a little distrust "E. Martell"[5] who advertized in the Chronicle.[7] Do you think them worth enquiring into?

[1] In CD's "The Friend of the Lions" (see 10 Jan and *fn*) the author pretends to be painted "as a model for a Rat-catcher ... with an awful Bulldog much too near us". Perhaps a real Mr. Sims had proposed himself to Landseer as a model.

[2] Underlined by short double strokes.

[3] See 10 Jan and *fn*.

[4] For Poole's pension of £100 p.a.; paid to him through CD: see Vol. VI, p. 245.

[5] Not further identified.

[6] Ramo Samee and a friend, Ann Price, were charged at the Mansion House on 5 Mar with uttering counterfeit coin. As the coins were Prince of Wales medals and did not resemble genuine currency, the Lord Mayor regretfully discharged them, describing them as "living by plunder off the industrious classes".

[7] "To the Heart capable of feeling for another.—One of birth and education (widow) under the most bitter misery, prays immediate, though but temporary, AID—about £16" (*Morning Chronicle*, 5 Jan).

I bear such a long, long train, that I am never rich, and never was, and never shall be. But (Dixon[1] excepted), I always want to make some approach towards doing my duty, and I could give away £20 in all just now, to alleviate *real distress*—should be as happy to do that, as I should be the reverse in lazily purchasing false comfort for myself, under the specious name of charity.

MISS COUTTS.[2]

When you next see her, will you mention, if you remember it, that there was a sum she was to have paid to my account at the Bank, which I had laid out for her (I forget whether it was forty pounds or sixty, but I gave her the Memorandum) which was not entered in my book when I last saw it.[3] I have forgotten to mention it in writing to her; but I know she will prefer its being recalled to her recollection, in case there should have been any mistake.

I

think that's all at present.

Ever Faithfully
CD.

P.S. To save postage, I return no letter, but describe them.

1—Mrs. Ramo Samee lives at John knows where.

2—Mrs. or Miss Martell lives at 18 John Street, Holland Street, Blackfriars

3—Mrs. Mortlock[4]—poor woman, unable to pay her rent—husband ran away from her four years ago, and left her with two small children—lives at 8 Molyneux Street, Bryanston Square. Says she never wrote a begging letter before.

P.S.2.[5]

To MONSIEUR GALIMARD,[6] 15 JANUARY 1856*

MS Fales Collection, New York University Library.

49 Champs Elysées | Mardi Janvier 15, 1856

Monsieur

Permettez-moi de vous exprimer mes profonds regrets que la lettre que vous m'avez fait l'honneur de m'addresser, a eté le sujet d'une absurde meprise.

J'etais en Angleterre lorsque cette lettre arriva ici. Elle fut renvoyée à mon addresse à Londres. En attendant, je revins à Paris, et je ne l'ai que reçue en ce moment.

[1] Just possibly a reference to William Hepworth Dixon, who, as editor of the *Athenaeum*, had several times complained of pensions being given for poverty rather than merit.

[2] Underlined by short double strokes.

[3] See Vol. VII, p. 744. Probably the credit of £50 entered on 5 Apr as from Wills (presumably paid on Miss Coutts's behalf); Miss Coutts's next payment was of £90 on 9 June (CD's Account-book, MS Messrs Coutts).

[4] Not further identified.

[5] Space for *c.* six lines cut away.

[6] Nicolas Auguste Galimard (1813–80), French artist. Studied with his uncle Auguste Hesse and with Ingres; his exhibits at the Salons 1835–80 included lithographs and engravings. Specialised in religious painting, for which he was ridiculed as "le pou mystique" (mystical louse). His Leda was rejected by the jury of the 1855 Exhibition "pour cause d'indécence" not in the heroine's "attitude", but because of "un gland de chêne disposé d'une façon particulière entre les doigts de Leda".

Je suis desolé Monsieur d'avoir si longtemps paru indifférent a votre si flattante et si interessante invitation. Je vous prie d'agreer bien mes excuses, et l'assurance de ma plus haute consideration.

Je me manquerai pas (j'espere) d'avoir le plaisir de faire visite a votre atelier, ou Samedi ou Dimanche prochain.[1] Veuillez-bien accepter mes plus sincères remerçiements, et croyez-moi Monsieur

Votre fidele et obligé

À Monsieur Galimard CHARLES DICKENS

To [GEORGE] HOGARTH,[2] 15 JANUARY 1856

Extract in Anderson Auction Co. catalogue No. 1027 (April 1914); dated 15 Jan 56; addressed "My Dear Hogarth".

The Post-Delivery being late today, I have only time to empower you in so many words, to convey to Addison and Co.[3] my full permission to use the title "Little Dorrit" for the song[4] you desired. Mary[5] must add it to her Repertoire,[6]

To W. H. WILLS, [?15–16 JANUARY 1856]

Mention in *To* Wills, 19 Jan. *Date:* probably written soon after 14 Jan.

To E. F. PIGOTT,[7] 17 JANUARY 1856

Text from T. F. Madigan Autograph Bulletin, Jan 1926; *MS* 3 pp.; dated 17 Jan 56; addressed E. F. Pigott.

My Dear Pigott

I write hastily in answer to your welcome letter (the sight of your handwriting is the next best thing to the sight of your face, though I greatly prefer the latter), being in the midst of work.

I told the boys when they went back to Boulogne,[8] to ask Mr. Gibson to send me one of his prospectuses. As it has never arrived I suppose they forgot it, bowled it out

[1] Not recorded; Saturday unlikely in view of his long sitting for Scheffer.

[2] George Hogarth, music critic: see Vol. I, p. 54*n* and later vols.

[3] Robert Addison & Co., piano makers, music sellers and publishers, 210 Regent St and 47 King St, Golden Square.

[4] Music by Gerald Stanley, words by Henry Abrahams, published by Addison, Hollier & Lucas [1856]. CD's "kind permission" for use of title is acknowledged, and a passage from Ch. 7 in No. II, just published, is quoted (on the "pitiful look" at her father). The writer had little more to go on, but the song begins "Inspired with a holy love, | A father's lonely heart to cheer, | As some bright angel from above, | We welcome 'Little Dorrit' here", repeated as a slow and pathetic refrain. The second verse represents her sister and brother as "sadly pining".

[5] Mary ("Mamie") Dickens (1838–96), CD's eldest daughter.

[6] "As a child . . . I used to sing to my father a great deal, and in after years I used to play and sing to him constantly" (interview published in *The Young Man and the Young Woman*, Christmas No., 1895). For her solo in *The Lighthouse*, see Vol. VII, p. 920.

[7] Edward Frederick Smyth Pigott (1824–95), proprietor of the *Leader* 1852–8: see Vol. VII, p. 571*n*.

[8] Frank, Alfred and Sydney.

of their memories with a large cake they took back with them. However, I think I can give you the needful information.[1]

The address of the school is, "The Reverend Mr. Gibson, Rue d'Oratorie, Haute Ville, Boulogne Sur Mer". Mr. Gibson was formerly an Eton master.[2] His partner in the school is the Reverend W. Bewsher,[3] one of the Protestant clergymen of Boulogne. They take none but English boys, but French is the ordinary language of the boys lives, after they have been there three months. I pay for each of my boys £40. a year. This includes their French and Classical education (the latter as at Eton) and the usual branches of knowledge. Dancing, Fencing, German, Music, &c. are extra and duly set forth on a printed paper. It is a perfectly honorable establishment as to extras, and not a sharking one. An entrance fee of three guineas is substituted for the usual plate and fork business. After a certain age—I think 15—there is a rise in the annual payment. I do not remember how much, but it is not a large one. Two months vacation in the summer; none at Christmas unless the parents wish. I have three boys there, and they are very happy, and I have found nothing to object to.[4] One of them was ill there, and was thoroughly comfortable. Their manners are well looked after, and their clothes are reported to me by the domestic authorities as being particularly well kept. Mrs. Bewsher represents the domesticity of the establishment (Mr. Gibson is a widower) and there are an English lady housekeeper and an ancient French Griffin housekeeper. All these authorities I know, and their behaviour to the boys, and the behaviour of the boys to them is just what it should be.

We should all be sorry if you don't come to Paris—but I don't expect you. I am expecting to hear from Jollins as to his coming any day; and if he doesn't write soon, I'll put him in an article and avenge you.[5]

The family in these palatial rooms, is in consternation at the word "Drawn". Drawn Sir???

PLORN[6]

Mrs. Dickens thanks you very much for the Leader (so do I too, by the by), and begs me to say that it comes regularly. She and her sister and my daughters unite in kind remembrances. The PLORN sends his pity and forgiveness.

Ever, my dear Pigott | Very cordially your friend,

CHARLES DICKENS

[1] Pigott had probably enquired on behalf of his close friend G. H. Lewes, who was "anxious to remove" his two eldest sons "from their present school"; he decided in Apr to send them to Hofwyl School near Berne (*The George Eliot Letters*, ed. Gordon Haight, Vol. II, 1954, 235–6).

[2] The Rev. Matthew Gibson: see Vol. VII, p. 145 and *n*. Not an Assistant Master at Eton; presumably either a "Conduct" (Chaplain) or a private tutor.

[3] The Rev. James Bewsher (1802–79): see Vol. VII, p. 145*n*.

[4] CD retained his high opinion (see next vol.), but for Henry's dislike of it, see Vol. VII, p. 145*n*.

[5] In "The Cruise of the Tomtit" (*HW*, 22 Dec 55, XII, 490) Collins had given a comic and intimate account of the first of his many yachting trips with Pigott in Sep 55, calling himself "Jollins" and Pigott "Migott".

[6] CD's youngest son, Edward Bulwer Lytton (1852–1902): see Vol. VII, p. 87 and *n*.

To G. A. SALA, [?18 JANUARY 1856]

Mention in *To* Wills, 19 Jan. *Date:* shortly before that letter.

To WILKIE COLLINS, 19 JANUARY 1856†

MS Morgan Library.

49 Champs Elysées | Saturday Nineteenth January 1856

My Dear Collins

I had no idea you were so far on with your book,[1] and heartily congratulate you on being within sight of Land.

It is excessively pleasant to me to get your letter, as it opens a perspective of theatrical and other lounging evenings, and also of articles in Household Words. It will not be the first time that we shall have got on well in Paris,[2] and I hope it will not be by many a time the last.

I purpose coming over, early in February (as soon, in fact, as I shall have knocked out No. 5 of Little D.), and therefore we can return in a jovial manner together. As soon as I know my day of coming over, I will write to you again, and (as the Merchants—say Charley—would add) "communicate same" to you.

The Lodging, en garçon, shall be duly looked up, and I shall of course make a point of finding it close here. There will be no difficulty in that. I will have concluded the Treaty before starting for London,[3] and will take it by the month—both because that is the cheapest way, and because desirable places don't let for shorter terms.

I have been sitting to Scheffer to day—conceive this, if you please, with No. 5 upon my soul—4 hours!! I am so addle-headed and bored, that if you were here I should propose an instantaneous rush to the Trois frères.[4] Under existing circumstances I have no consolation. I *can't* go out with White—What the Devil's the good of *him*—

I think *the* Portrait[5] is the most astounding thing ever beheld upon this globe. It has been shrieked over by the United Family, as "O! The very Image!" I went down to the Entresol, the moment I opened it, and submitted it to the Plorn—then engaged, with a half franc musket, in capturing a Malakoff[6] of chairs. He looked at it very hard, and gave it as his opinion that it was Misser Higg[7]—We suppose him to have confounded the Colonel with Jollins.

The appalling generality as to the weakness of the Bean Stalk,[8] certain ominous praise in Galignani had prepared me for. But the terrific truth respecting the Wigs, is a point of detail so crushing that I have not held up my head since.

[1] *After Dark*, published in 2 vols, 15 Feb by Smith, Elder. It combined five pieces from *HW* with one new story and some linking passages.

[2] See Vol. VII, p. 721.

[3] The arrangements were left to Georgina: see *To* Catherine, 7 Feb.

[4] CD's favourite restaurant.

[5] Clearly of Collins, but untraced.

[6] The great stone tower, part of the defence-works of Sebastopol, stormed by the French.

[7] Augustus Leopold Egg, artist: see Vols V, p. 113*n* and VII, p. 322*n*.

[8] See *To* Lemon, 7 Jan and *n*.

I met Madame Georges Sand[1] the other day, at a dinner got up by Madame Viardot for that great purpose.[2] The human mind cannot conceive any one more astonishingly opposed to all my preconceptions. If I had been shown her in a state of repose and asked what I thought her to be, I should have said "The Queen's Monthly Nurse." Au reste, she has nothing of the Bas bleu[3] about her, and is very quiet and agreeable.

The way in which mysterious Frenchmen call and want to embrace me, suggests to any one who knows me intimately, such infamous lurking, slinking, getting behind doors, evading, lying—so much mean resort to craven flights, dastard subterfuge, and miserable poltroonery—on my part, that I merely suggest the arrival of cards like this

Forgues[4]
homme de lettres

or

Brouse[5]
Membre de l'Institut

or

Cregibus Patalanternois[5]
Ecole des Beaux Arts

—every five minutes. Books also arrive with, on the fly leaf,

Jaubaud[5]
Hommage a l'illustre Romancier d'Angleterre
Charles De Kean.

—and I then write letters of terrific empressement with assurances of all sorts of profound consideration—and never by any chance become visible to the naked eye.

At the Porte St. Martin they are doing the Orestes,[6] put into French Verse by Alexandre Dumas.[7] Really one of the absurdest things I ever saw. The scene of the Tomb, with all manner of classical females in black—with excessively unclassical behinds—grouping themselves—on the lid, and on the steps, and on each other, and in every conceivable aspect of obtrusive impossibility[8]—is just like the window of one of those artists in hair, who address the friends of deceased persons. Tomorrow

[1] George Sand (1804–76). CD writes "Georges". Adopted name of Lucile Aurore Dupin, by marriage la baronne Dudevant. In 1855 published *L'histoire de ma vie* (4 vols), her autobiography up to the end of her affaire with Frédéric Chopin and the 1848 Revolution. Later, spent much time at Nohant (her estate in the Berrichon countryside, inherited from her grandmother in 1821), writing plays, and novels of country and social life.

[2] See *To* Forster, 20 Jan.

[3] Blue-stocking. In 1844 Honoré Daumier caricatured les bas-bleus in forty plates in *Charivari* as physically repellent and morally perverse.

[4] Name enclosed in a drawn cloud. Paul Emile Durand Forgues (1813–83), journalist and critic: see Vol. III, p. 501 and *n*. Became editor of *Revue des Deux Mondes* and published there, Nov 55, in his series "Studies in English novels", an article praising Collins. For his article on CD, see 6 June and *fn*.

[5] Invented or distorted names. "Jaubaud" is written with a flourish underneath.

[6] *L'Orestie*, Dumas's adaptation of Aeschylus's *Oresteia*, ran 5–18 Jan. In a long review in *Galignani*, 13 Jan, the settings and acting were praised, though the whole fell "far short of the genuine sublimity" of the original; Dumas was greeted with "considerable applause". On 27 Jan *Galignani* described it as Dumas's "laborious resuscitation from the Greeks".

[7] Alexandre Dumas père (1802–70), novelist and dramatist.

[8] *Galignani* admired the women at Agamemnon's tomb, "whose attitudes were most graceful, and, it is said, faithful transcripts from the highest school of Grecian art".

week, a fête is coming off at the Jardin d'Hîver,[1] next door but one here, which I must certainly go to, and which I should think can hardly fail to attract all the Lorettes[2] in Paris. The fête of the company of the Folies Nouvelles![3]—The ladies of the Company are to keep stalls, and are to sell to Messieurs the Amateurs, Orange water and Lemonade. Paul leGrand[4] is to promenade among the Company, dresst as Pierrot—Kelm,[5] the big-faced comic Singer, is to do the like, dressed as "A Russian Cossack". The entertainments are to conclude with "la Polka des Betes feroces, par la Troupe entière des Folies Nouvelles". I wish, without invasion of the rights of British subjects, or risk of war, Doctor Cumming[6] could be seized by French Troops, brought over, and made to assist.

The appartement has not grown any bigger since you last had the joy of beholding me, and upon my honor and word I live in terror of asking Adelaide Kemble[7] to dinner (she lives near at hand), lest she should not be able to get in at the dining room door. I *think* (am not sure) the dining room would hold her, if she could be once pressed in; but I don't see my way to that. Nevertheless we manage our own family dinners very snugly there, and have good ones—as I think you will say every day at half past Five.

I have a notion that we may knock out a *series* of descriptions for H.W.[8] without much trouble. It is very difficult to get into the Catacombs, but my name is so well known here that I think I may succeed. I find that the Guillotine can be got set up in private—like Punch's Show. What do you think of *that* for an article? I find myself underlining words constantly. It is not my nature. It is mere imbecility after the four hours' sitting.

[1] As part of a series of "Fêtes de nuit", the *Folies Nouvelles* were announced for Sat and Sun, 26 and 27 Jan, with "Danseuses espagnoles, Trio d'enforces, Arlequin ravisseur, Joli regiment".

[2] "Ladies of pleasure."

[3] Opened as the *Folies-Concertantes* at 41 Boulevard du Temple in Feb 54 by the composer, conductor and singer Florimond Ronger Hervé (1825–92), who created the new genre of operette midway between opera-comique and vaudeville. The theatre was immensely popular and much used as a place of assignation by the demi-monde and upper classes until the latter were won over by Offenbach's *Parisiens* (opened July 55).

[4] Paul Legrand (1816–98), incomparable mime; inspired when young by the great pierrot Jean Deburau, joined the Funambules 1839 and gradually took over from his aging master. Based at the Folies Nouvelles 1853–62, he appeared in London 1848–9.

[5] Joseph Kelm (1807–81). Began career in 1839 as opera singer, but his physique and temperament led him to comedy. Known as "le joyeaux Jojo", the star of the Folies Nouvelles 1855–9; his comic songs such as "Le Sire de Framboisy" won him great fame.

[6] John Cumming, DD (1807–81; *DNB*), evangelical theologian and controversialist. From 1832 Presbyterian minister at the National Scottish Church in Covent Garden: his preaching was so popular that it had to be rebuilt in 1847–8 to hold 1000 people. A leading anti-Catholic agitator, he led the attacks on "papal agression" and Cardinal Wiseman in 1850. Much involved with philanthropic movements, including the Ragged School Union and the Metropolitan Sanitary Association (see Vol. VI, p. 18*n*). A strict sabbatarian (the point of CD's joke), he had in 1853 opposed the Sunday opening of the Crystal Palace for the benefit of working men. Attacked in *Westminster Review*, LXVI (Oct 55); unsigned, but in fact by Marian Evans.

[7] Adelaide Kemble (?1814–79; *DNB*), soprano: see Vol. II, p. 431 and *n*. She was passing the winter in Paris, and had been at the Viardot dinner with her husband Edward John Sartoris.

[8] This did not materialise. CD wrote nothing for *HW* between "Why?" (1 Mar 56, XIII, 145) and "Proposals for a National Jest Book" (3 May 56, XIII, 385).

All unite in kindest remembrances to you, your mother,[1] and brother.[2]

Ever Cordially

CD.

P.S. Beaucourt's Pipe has been purchased, engraved, and presented. Cost f.65.

To MESSRS. BRADBURY & EVANS,[3] 19 JANUARY 1856*

MS Bradbury, Agnew & Co. Ltd.

49 Champs Elysées, Paris

Saturday Night, Nineteenth January | 1856

My Dear B and E.

I am making an agreement with a French publishing house here, for a complete French translation of the whole of my books. Before I can complete it, I must have a list of the dates of their publication at home, severally and separately. Will you, at once, direct one of your people to prepare such a list of all the books you have published for me, and to go to Chapman's[4] and get a similar list from his books? The date of the original publication of Oliver Twist, I shall also want from Bentley's.[5] It will be well to distinguish (when the book has been a serial one) both the date of the publication of the first No. and the date of the publication of the completed book. The sooner I can have this list, the more acceptable and convenient it will be.

I hope to see you, early next month. I shall bring No. 5 over, please God, as soon as finished. You have no news, I take it for granted, concerning Little Dorrit.[6]

Great hopes of peace[7] here. I don't allow myself to be very sanguine thereof as yet though.

Ever Faithfully Yours

CHARLES DICKENS[8]

[1] Née Harriet Geddes (*d.* 1868), daughter of a retired Army captain, "A portionless bride", she married William Collins, landscape and figure painter, in 1822: his friend Sir David Wilkie found her "a nice woman, not particularly handsome, but accomplished and intelligent". After William's death she entertained her sons' friends freely, and "nothing could well exceed the jollity of these little dinners" (W. Holman Hunt, *Pre-Raphaelitism and the Pre-Raphaelite Brotherhood*, 1905, I, 309). But by 1855–6 Holman Hunt found in her "a spirit of humour now not unmixed with asperity" (*op. cit.*, II, 147), J. E. Millais referred to her often as his second mother, and reported in Apr 52 "one of the many parties held under [her] hospitable roof.... There were many lions—amongst others, the famous Dickens, who came for about half an hour and officiated as principal carver at supper" (*Life and Letters*, 1899, I, 163).

[2] Charles Allston Collins: see Vol. VI, p. 378*n*. Virtually gave up painting in 1855 and devoted himself to writing. Began contributing to *HW* in Feb 58.

[3] William Bradbury (?1800–69) and Frederick Mullett Evans (?1803–70), printers and publishers; CD's publishers since 1844: see Vols I, p. 397*n* and IV, p. 121 and *n*.

[4] Edward Chapman (1804–80), bookseller and publisher: see earlier vols.

[5] Richard Bentley (1794–1871), publisher: see Vol. I, p. 164*n*. Published edns of *Oliver Twist* up to 1840.

[6] i.e. sales of No. II: see *To* Georgina Hogarth, 8 Feb.

[7] An armistice was agreed on 26 Feb and the Peace of Paris signed on 30 Mar 56.

[8] About one third of second half of folded sheet torn away, probably containing a postscript.

To W. H. WILLS, 19 AND 20 JANUARY 1856

MS Huntington Library.

49 Champs Elysées Paris
Saturday Night, Nineteenth January 1856

My Dear Wills.

YOU[1]

have forgotten that I asked you to send, in the next letter you should write me, some stamps for cheques. I am demented for want of them.

H.W.[1]

The No.[2] did not arrive to day. Will come, I suppose, tomorrow.

Albert Smith has sent me a proof of his pamphlet about Hotels.[3] I, in my turn, have sent it to Sala, and suggested to him that he may write an article on the subject.[4] I have *begged him* to send it to me, here; thinking that may expedite him.

I[1]

report that White's parcel arrived safely.

Also that if B and E want to buy the collection of criticisms,[5] for themselves, they are heartily welcome. As to me, I don't want it.

MARK[1]

with his usual depth of diplomacy has made no mention to me of the Boots at the Adelphi.[6] Though I had a letter from him two days ago, with a deal about the Adelphi in it.

MUD[1]

at Paris, is 3 feet and 7/8 deep.

Sunday 20th.

The No. having arrived this morning, I have gone over it, and here it is. It wants careful correction (as usual) for pointing, avoidance of confusion in meaning, and making clear. I never saw such confused writers as we seem to vaccinate.

The Cricket Club paper[7] is desperately poor; but I have no Taboo to interpose.

BUCKSTONE.[8]

Does he ask whether I can recommend them to a chairman, or what they are to do for a chairman?[9] Have I anything to answer on that head?

Ever Faithfully
CD.

[1] Underlined with short double strokes.

[2] *HW*, No. 306, 2 Feb 56.

[3] *The English Hotel Nuisance*, 1856, praises continental hotels in contrast to old-fashioned, extortionate and uncomfortable English inns.

[4] "The Great Hotel Question", *HW*, 8 March 56, XIII, 172, and the two following numbers, countering Smith's rosy view: see 17 Feb.

[5] Untraced.

[6] *Boots at the Holly Tree Inn; or The Infant Elopement to Gretna Green*, adapted by Webster from the 1855 Christmas No. (third story) as a one-act farce. It opened on 4 Feb; CD saw it on 8 Feb (*To Webster*, 6 Feb).

[7] James Payn's "P.N.C.C.", *HW*, XIII, 58; an account of the disasters of being President of the Nettleton Cricket Club.

[8] Underlined with short double strokes. John Baldwin Buckstone, comic actor, dramatist, and manager of the Haymarket, 1853–76: see Vols I, p. 42*n* and VII, p. 581*n*.

[9] For the annual dinner on 17 Mar of the Royal General Theatrical Fund; Buckstone was Treasurer and CD a Trustee.

To JOHN FORSTER [20 JANUARY 1856]

Extracts in F, VII, v, 617*n*; VIII, ii, 639; VII, v, 619; VII, v, 608; VII, v, 613; VII, v, 613–14; VIII, ii, 636*n*. *Date:* first two extracts 20 Jan, according to Forster; third extract clearly same letter, and four others probably so (see below).

It is difficult to picture the change made in this place by the removal of the paving stones (too ready for barricades) and macadamisation. It suits neither the climate nor the soil. We are again in a sea of mud. One cannot cross the road of the Champs Elysées here, without being half over one's boots.

Again I am beset by my former notions of a book whereof the whole story shall be on the top of the Great St. Bernard.[1] As I accept and reject ideas for *Little Dorrit*, it perpetually comes back to me. Two or three years hence, perhaps you'll find me living with the Monks and the Dogs a whole winter—among the blinding snows that fall about that monastery. I have a serious idea that I shall do it, if I live.

Imagine me if you please with No. 5 on my head and hands, sitting to Scheffer yesterday four hours! At this stage of a story, no one can conceive how it distresses me.

At the Porte St. Martin he had attended a performance of Orestes *versified by Alexandre Dumas*. Nothing have I ever seen so weighty and so ridiculous. If I had not already learnt to tremble at the sight of classic drapery on the human form, I should have plumbed the utmost depths of terrified boredom in this achievement. The chorus is not preserved otherwise than that bits of it are taken out for characters to speak.[2] It is really so bad as to be almost good. Some of the Frenchified classical anguish struck me as so unspeakably ridiculous that it puts me on the broad grin as I write.

He had dined at the house of Madame Viardot.[3] I suppose it to be impossible to imagine anybody more unlike my preconceptions than the illustrious Sand. Just the kind of woman in appearance whom you might suppose to be the Queen's monthly nurse. Chubby, matronly, swarthy, black-eyed.[4] Nothing of the blue-stocking about her, except a little final way of settling all your opinions with hers, which I take to have been acquired in the country where she lives, and in the domination of a small circle.[5] A singularly ordinary woman in appearance and manner. The dinner was

[1] For similar restlessness before beginning a new book see Vols VI, p. 501 and VII, p. 428. His ascent and night spent at the hospice in Sep 46 are described in Vol. IV, pp. 618–20. For his use of this in *Little Dorrit*, see *To* Mrs Watson, 7 Oct.

[2] The lines of the Chorus in the three plays were divided between two old men, three young girls, and one Fate: "with considerable effect", according to *Galignani*, 13 Jan.

[3] On Saturday, 13 Jan.

[4] Anne Thackeray, who saw Sand at the theatre about this time, recorded that "Her black shiny hair shone like polished ebony, she had a heavy red face, marked brows, great dark eyes; there was something rather fierce, defiant and set in her appearance, powerful, sulky" (Lady Ritchie, *Chapters from Some Memoirs*, 1894, p. 211).

[5] She was said to be "very dictatorial" (Lady Ritchie, above, 212); but on CD's patronising remarks on her, Forster comments that he was "hardly the man to take fair measure of Madame Dudevant in meeting her thus. He was not familiar with her writings, and had no very special liking for such of them as he knew" (p. 613).

very good and remarkably unpretending. Ourselves, Madame and her son,[1] the Scheffers,[2] the Sartorises, and some Lady somebody (from the Crimea last) who wore a species of paletot and smoked. The Viardots have a house away in the new part of Paris,[3] which looks exactly as if they had moved into it last week and were going away next. Notwithstanding which, they have lived in it eight years. The opera the very last thing on earth you would associate with the family. Piano not even opened.[4] Her husband[5] is an extremely good fellow, and she is as natural as it is possible to be.

Emile de Girardin[6] *gave a banquet in his honour.*[7] No man unacquainted with my determination never to embellish or fancify such accounts, could believe in the description I shall let off when we meet, of dining at Emile Girardin's—of the three gorgeous drawing-rooms with ten thousand wax candles in golden sconces, terminating in a dining-room of unprecedented magnificence with two enormous transparent plate-glass doors in it, looking (across an antechamber full of clean plates) straight into the kitchen, with the cooks in their white paper caps dishing the dinner. From his seat in the midst of the table, the host (like a Giant in a Fairy story) beholds the kitchen, and the snow-white tables, and the profound order and silence there prevailing. Forth from the plate-glass doors issues the Banquet—the most wonderful feast ever tasted by mortal: at the present price of Truffles, that article alone costing (for eight people) at least five pounds. On the table are ground glass jugs of peculiar construction, laden with the finest growth of Champagne and the coolest ice. With the third course is issued Port Wine (previously unheard of in a good state on this continent), which would fetch two guineas a bottle at any sale. The dinner done, Oriental flowers in vases of golden cobweb are placed upon the board. With the ice is issued Brandy; buried for 100 years. To that succeeds Coffee, brought by the brother of one of the convives from the remotest East, in exchange for an equal quantity of Californian gold dust. The company being returned to the drawing-room—tables roll in by unseen agency, laden with Cigarettes from the Hareem of the Sultan, and with cool drinks in which the flavour of the Lemon arrived yesterday from Algeria, struggles voluptuously with the delicate Orange arrived this morning from Lisbon. That period past, and the guests reposing on Divans worked with many-coloured blossoms, big table rolls in, heavy with massive furniture of silver, and breathing incense in the form of a little present of Tea direct from China—table and all, I believe; but cannot swear to it, and am resolved to be

[1] Maurice Dudevant-Sand (1825–89), artist and writer. Closely involved with his mother's private theatricals at Nohant, he wrote and designed many marionette plays, and collaborated in her studies of comedia del'arte, published as *Masques et Buffons*, 2 vols, 1859.

[2] Ary Scheffer and his wife Sophia (*m.* 1850: see Vol. VII, pp. 727*n* and 753*n*). She had delicate health, and died in June 56.

[3] 23 Rue de Douai, built for them in 1848. The street ran off the Boulevard Montmartre, near the Barrière de Clichy.

[4] Mme Viardot played and sang often in private for friends; her devoted admirer Ivan Turgenev, among others, thought these her greatest performances. See April FitzLyon, *The Price of Genius: a Life of Pauline Viardot*, 1964, pp. 294, 301.

[5] Louis Viardot (1800–83), miscellaneous writer: see Vol. VII, p. 763.

[6] Emile de Girardin (1802–81), writer, journalist and politician; founded and owned the conservative *La Presse* 1836–56; elected to Chamber of Deputies five times; after initial support, turned violently against Napoleon III; published many social and political tracts.

[7] "Soon after" 13 Jan, according to Forster.

prosaic. All this time the host perpetually repeats "Ce petit dîner-ci n'est que pour faire la connaissance de Monsieur Dickens; il ne compte pas; ce n'est rien." And even now I have forgotten to set down half of it—in particular the item of a far larger plum pudding than ever was seen in England at Christmas time, served with a celestial sauce in colour like the orange blossom, and in substance like the blossom powdered and bathed in dew, and called in the carte (carte in a gold frame like a little fish-slice to be handed about) "Hommage à l'illustre écrivain d'Angleterre." That illustrious man staggered out at the last drawing-room door, speechless with wonder, finally; and even at that moment his host, holding to his lips a chalice set with precious stones and containing nectar distilled from the air that blew over the fields of beans in bloom for fifteen summers, remarked "Le diner que nous avons eu, mon cher, n'est rien—il ne compte pas—il a été tout-à-fait en famille—il faut dîner (en vérité, dîner) bientôt. Au plaisir! Au revoir! Au dîner!"

He wrote on one occasion[1] *of a youth who had fallen into a father's weaknesses without the possibility of having himself observed them for imitation.* It suggests the strangest consideration as to which of our own failings we are really responsible, and as to which of them we cannot quite reasonably hold ourselves to be so. What A. evidently derived from his father cannot in his case be derived from association and observation, but must be in the very principles of his individuality as a living creature.

To SIR JOSEPH OLLIFFE,[2] 20 JANUARY 1856

MS Mr Louis J. Heizmann.

49 Champs Elysées | Sunday Twentieth January 1856

My Dear Olliffe

I am vexed to reply that we can't. I have asked a friend here this evening. And as he is a Poet,[3] I mustn't put him off—or I would.

With kindest regards to Lady Olliffe[4]

Ever Faithfully Yours
CHARLES DICKENS

[1] See *To* Olliffe, 20 Jan; clearly the same person and almost certainly the Hon. Edward Robert Lytton, later first Earl of Lytton (1831–91; *DNB*), diplomat and poet: see Vol. VII, p. 694*n*. Published, under the pseudonym "Owen Meredith", *Clytemnestra*, the *Earl's Return*, the *Artist*, and other poems, 1855, followed by *The Wanderer*, 1857. Unpaid attaché at the Parish Embassy Aug 1854–Mar 1856. He had been brought up away from his father and was well known to Forster. In Forster's account of CD's many friends in Paris this winter, Robert Lytton is named (F, VII, v, 606).

[2] Sir Joseph Francis Olliffe (1808–69; *DNB*), physician to the British Embassy in Paris: see Vols V, p. 606*n* and VII.

[3] See last. Robert Lytton was CD's only friend in Paris who was a poet.

[4] Laura, daughter to Sir William Cubitt, civil engineer; married 1841: see Vols V, p. 655*n* and VII.

To MESSRS HACHETTE ET CIE, 25 JANUARY 1856

Extract in N, II, 735; dated 25 Jan 56.

You are mistaken in supposing me to have forgotten Master Humphrey's Clock. It is merely another name for the Old Curiosity Shop[1] and Barnaby Rudge;[2] which name has long been abandoned, and was never used for those books after their completion.

To FRANK STONE,[3] 27 JANUARY 1856*

MS Benoliel Collection.

49 Champs Elysées, Paris
Sunday Twenty Seventh January 1856

My Dear Middlesex.[4]

Your friend is misinformed—but in his misinformation there is just that grain of truth which hangs to the roots of these wonderful Bean Stalks. It became necessary, when I was last in town, that besides the usual Medical attendant[5] of the Home,[6] we should have another—able to look in constantly—with a particular object. I mentioned it to Miss Coutts, and she immediately, then and there, decided whom to have. There never, within my knowledge, was any delay, doubt, or discussion about it.

I hoped to have seen you when I was last in town—but I was perpetually on Railroads. There never was such a grinding and snorting week as I had. I hope however to be in town again within ten days or so, and then to Sparkle on you.

I am touched by your affectionate reference to my Little Dorrit. She is an immense success. There is a dash in No. 3 at the great system of abuse under which we live, that will flutter the Doves in the House of Commons Lobby, I flatter myself![7]

I hope you saw The Boots in the Xmas No. of Household Words?[8]

Having just laid down the Pen after a pretty long spell at my little friend,[9] I am in a state of imbecility, and am going out for a rush into the air

With kindest regards from all here to all in Russell House, Ever My Dear Pumpion[10]

Affectionately Yours
CHARLES DICKENS

[1] Published by Hachette as *Le Magasin d'Antiquités*, transl. by Alfred des Essarts, 2 vols, 1857.

[2] Transl. by M. Bonnemet, 2 vols, 1858.

[3] Frank Stone (1800–59; *DNB*), painter, CD's next-door neighbour in Tavistock Square: see Vol. I, p. 487*n*, and subsequent vols.

[4] Stone's part in *Not so Bad as we Seem*.

[5] Not discovered.

[6] The Home for Homeless Women, Shepherds Bush, opened Nov 47: see Vol. IV, pp. 552–6.

[7] Ch. 10.

[8] CD's three stories in "The Holly-Tree Inn", *HW*, 15 Dec 55.

[9] No. V, Chs 15–18, published 31 Mar, for Apr. He had been working on it throughout the previous week.

[10] For another nickname see Vol. VII, p. 425.

To JOHN FORSTER, [?27 JANUARY 1856]

Extract in F, VII, v, 617*n* and 607. *Date:* both probably from his usual weekend letter.

Three days ago the weather changed here in an hour, and we have had bright weather and hard frost ever since. All the mud disappeared with marvellous rapidity, and the sky became Italian. Taking advantage of such a happy change, I started off yesterday morning (for exercise and meditation) on a scheme I have taken into my head, to walk round the walls of Paris. It is a very odd walk, and will make a good description.[1] Yesterday I turned to the right when I got outside the Barrière de l'Étoile, walked round the wall till I came to the river, and then entered Paris beyond the site of the Bastille. To-day I mean to turn to the left when I get outside the Barrière, and see what becomes of that.

He wrote of the Théâtre Francais whimsically as a kind of tomb, where you went, as the Eastern people did in stories, to think of your unsuccessful loves and dead relations. There is a dreary classicality at that establishment calculated to freeze the marrow. Between ourselves, even one's best friends there are at times very aggravating. One tires of seeing a man, through any number of acts, remembering everything by patting his forehead with the flat of his hand, jerking out sentences by shaking himself, and piling them up in pyramids over his head with his right forefinger. And they have a generic small comedy-piece, where you see two sofas and three little tables, to which a man enters with his hat on, to talk to another man—and in respect of which you know exactly when he will get up from one sofa to sit on the other, and take his hat off one table to put it upon the other—which strikes one quite as ludicrously as a good farce. . . .[2] There seems to be a good piece at the Vaudeville, on the idea of the *Town and Country Mouse.*[3] It is too respectable and inoffensive for me to-night, but I hope to see it before I leave. . . . I have a horrible idea of making friends with Franconi, and sauntering when I am at work into their sawdust green-room.[4]

[1] For the articles he proposed to write with Collins.

[2] Forster notes that CD wrote a satirical account intended for *HW*, of one of these stock performances at the Théâtre Français, but destroyed it because it might have given pain to Régnier (F, VII, v, 607*n*).

[3] A one-Act operetta by Clairville and Montaugry, which opened on 24 Jan. A respectable country-girl dines with her foster-sister who had made her fortune "dans la galanterie". The dinner is interrupted by a lover, a poetaster and a creditor; the country-girl, finding the meal bought too highly, returns to her peaceful crust of bread. *Galignani's Messenger* described it as "A smart little affair . . . gaily written and pleasantly acted"; but Theophile Gautier, in the *Moniteur*, 28 Jan called it a complete flop ("Une chute complète").

[4] Now that he was free of his work on *Little Dorrit* Franconi's circus suited his mood, and was nearby in the Champs Elysées.

To W. H. WILLS, 28 JANUARY 1856

MS Huntington Library.

49 Champs Elysées | Monday Twenty Eighth January 1856

My Dear Wills

H.W.

This is a very shy No.[1] and White is a very bad first paper.[2] I suppose there is nothing else?[3]

My corrections (which are pretty numerous) are made in pencil, but I hope you will find them legible. The Rector Abroad, most relentlessly and ruthlessly Taboo.

In your Programme of the No. something called "The Russian Budget"[4] is in that place. Anyway, the Rector is out of the question.

GAD'S HILL.[5]

I must come to town sooner than I intended, because February is the short month, and I want to get back to my work. I think I shall come on Monday or Tuesday in next week. Will you tell Ouvry[6] therefore that I shall be glad to complete the purchase *at the end of next week*,[7] if he will make the arrangements accordingly.

MISS COUTTS[5]

I will write to, as soon as I can positively fix my day.

NO MORE[5]

at present.

From Yours ever faithfully

CD.

To JAMES BALLANTINE,[8] 29 JANUARY 1856

Extract in Merwin Sales catalogue No. 599 (1915); *MS* 1 p.; dated Paris, 29 Jan 56; addressed James Ballantine.

Expressing admiration and hearty sympathy *with his verses*.[9]

[1] No. 307, 9 Feb 56.

[2] "Two College Friends", XIII, 78 and 105; it did not open this or No. 308, 16 Feb.

[3] "The Sulina Mouth of the Danube" (XIII, 73), by Grenville Murray, opened the No.

[4] XIII, 88; a political "Chip" by the philosopher Arnold Ruge (1802–80), his only contribution.

[5] Underlined with short double strokes.

[6] Frederic Ouvry (1814–81; *DNB*), partner in Farrer, Ouvry, solicitors; CD's solicitor from 1856: see Vol. VII, p. 273*nn*.

[7] The purchase was not completed until 14 Mar.

[8] James Ballantine (1808–77; *DNB*), artist and writer. Author of several popular works, including *The Gaberlunzie's Wallet*, 1843, and *The Miller of Deanhaugh*, 1847. Head of the Edinburgh firm, Messrs Ballantine, glass-stainers; helped revive the art of glass-painting and executed the windows in the House of Lords.

[9] Ballantine's *Poems* are thus dedicated to CD: "Dear Friend, whose genial mind | And graphic pen | In joy and sorrow bind | Thy fellow-men, | Whose heart hath at its core | Humanity! | This gift—would it were more—I offer thee | James Ballantine. | Edinburgh, February 1856".

To WILKIE COLLINS, 30 JANUARY 1856

MS Morgan Library.

49 Champs Elysées | Thirtieth January 1856. Wednesday

My Dear Collins

I hope you are out of the wood, and holloaing.[1]

I purpose coming to town, either on Monday or Tuesday night, and returning (if convenient to you), on the following Sunday or Monday. I will write to you as soon as I arrive, and arrange for our devoting an early evening (I should like Wednesday next) to letting our united observation with extended view survey mankind from China to Peru.[2] On second thoughts, shall we appoint Wednesday now? Unless I hear from you to the contrary, I will expect you at Household Words, at 5 that day.

Ever Faithfully (working hard)

CD.

To JOHN FORSTER, [30 JANUARY 1856]

Extracts in F, VII, v, 615–16*n*; F, VII, v, 619*n* and F, VIII, i, 624. *Date:* 30 Jan, according to Forster.

It was cold this afternoon, as bright as Italy, and these Elysian Fields crowded with carriages, riders, and foot passengers. All the fountains were playing, all the Heavens shining. Just as I went out at 4 o'clock, several regiments that had passed out at the Barrière in the morning to exercise in the country, came marching back, in the straggling French manner, which is far more picturesque and real than anything you can imagine in that way. Alternately great storms of drums played, and then the most delicious and skilful bands, "Trovatore"[3] music, "Barber of Seville"[4] music, all sorts of music with well-marked melody and time. All bloused Paris (led by the Inimitable, and a poor cripple who works himself up and down all day in a big-wheeled car) went at quick march down the avenue, in a sort of hilarious dance. If the colours with the golden eagle on the top had only been unfurled, we should have followed them anywhere, in any cause—much as the children follow Punches in the better cause of Comedy. Napoleon on the top of the column seemed up to the whole thing, I thought.

I have arranged with the French bookselling house to receive, by monthly payments of £40, the sum of £440 for the right to translate all my books: that is, what they call my Romances, and what I call my Stories. This does not include the Christmas Books, *American Notes*, *Pictures from Italy*, or the *Sketches*; but they are to have the right to translate them for extra payments if they choose.[5] In consideration

[1] "Don't halloo till you are out of the wood" (proverb). In anticipation of his *After Dark* 2 vols, published by Smith, Elder, 6 Feb: consisting of his first five *HW* stories, 1852–5, with one further story and a chapter giving their setting as told by the narrator to his wife. Favourably reviewed in the *Examiner*, 1 Mar, along with three new novels.

[2] Cf. the first two lines of Samuel Johnson's poem, *The Vanity of Human Wishes*.

[3] First performed 1853.

[4] First performed 1816.

[5] See *To* Louis Hachette, 14 Jan and *fnn*. Presumably an extra payment was made for their publication of the Christmas Books.

of this venture as to the unprotected property, I cede them the right of translating all future Romances at a thousand francs (£40) each. Considering that I get so much for what is otherwise worth nothing, and get my books before so clever and important a people, I think this is not a bad move?

I have a grim pleasure upon me to-night in thinking that the Circumlocution Office sees the light, and in wondering what effect it will make.[1] But my head really stings with the visions of the book, and I am going, as we French say, to disembarrass[2] it by plunging out into some of the strange places I glide into of nights in these latitudes.

To [FRAU ALBERTI],[3] 31 JANUARY 1856

MS Messrs Maggs Bros.

49 Champs Elysées, Paris
Thursday Thirty First January 1856

My Dear and highly esteemed Correspondent.

My having been away from here, much occupied with Little Dorrit, has prevented my receiving and replying to your letter as soon as I could have wished. I believe I have never received a more delightful letter in my life, or one that has awakened within me a deeper sense of the loftiest responsibilities and triumphs of a writer. For the earnestness of your feeling towards me, I can never feel sufficiently proud or sufficiently grateful; and for the love you bear to my favorite book[4] (for your sympathy has truly divined that it *is* my favorite), I must love *you*—if I may—in return.

I gratefully accept the proposal you make to me.[5] To be associated in that way with the first production of so fervent a head and heart as yours must be, is a high grace and privilege. Whatever my deserts and claims to it may be, at least no man could possibly prize it more.

I write briefly, in order not to lose another Post. But I cannot refrain from adding that you do your English great injustice, if you suppose it to be anything

[1] On 5 Feb Anthony Trollope wrote, from Dublin, to the Editor of the *Athenaeum* (Hepworth Dixon), with an article on this No. of *Little Dorrit*, no doubt a criticism of Ch. 10 ("Concerning the whole Science of Government"). It was evidently rejected and has not survived: see *Letters of Anthony Trollope*, ed. N. John Hall (Stanford, 1983), I, p. 43 and *n*. He had already parodied CD as "Mr Popular Sentiment" in *The Warden*, published Jan 55, and in *The Three Clerks*, written in 1856, he inserted a long passage on the Civil Service (1st edn only), taken from the MS of his rejected *The New Zealander* (almost certainly written 1855–6), containing what reads like an attack on the Circumlocution Office: "Then comes the popular novelist, and, with his sledge hammer, gives it the last blow, and devotes every mother's son in the public offices to lasting ignominy and vile disgrace" (quoted in Bradford Booth, "Trollope and Little Dorrit", *The Trollopian*, 2 Mar 1948, 237–8.

[2] French "se debarrasser", to disencumber.

[3] Née Sophie Mödinger (1826–92), writer under the pen-name of Sophie Verena. Lived in Potsdam. Published several novels and tales, also children's stories and translations of Henry Mayhew and Mrs Craik.

[4] *David Copperfield*: see Vol. VI, p. 721.

[5] Her first book, *Else*, Berlin, 1856, is dedicated to CD: see 30 Apr.

less than a natural, eloquent, and charmingly unaffected expression of your feelings.

Dear Madam Ever believe me | Your faithful and affectionate
CHARLES DICKENS

As I cannot clearly read your adopted name, I have cut it from your letter to place on this envelope, that there may be no mistake.

To MISS BURDETT COUTTS, 3 FEBRUARY 1856*

MS Morgan Library. *Address:* Miss Burdett Coutts | Greenlands | Henley on Thames.

49 Champs Elysées, Paris | Sunday Third February 1856

My Dear Miss Coutts.

I purpose arriving in London tomorrow (Monday) night, and remaining through the week. Will you let me know where I shall find you, and what is the best time for seeing you—I mean, the best time in the day. I have a world of things to do, but of course the foremost among them all is to have a few minutes' glimpse of you.

We can then discuss Mr. Wills.[1]

If you will write to me at the Household Words office it will be best, as I shall be constantly there.

With love to Mrs. Brown

Ever Dear Miss Coutts | Most Faithfully Yours
CD.

To MISS BURDETT COUTTS, 5 FEBRUARY 1856*

MS Private (destroyed in Prestwick air-crash, Dec 1954). *Address:* Miss Burdett Coutts | Meadfoot House | Hesketh Crescent | Torquay | Devon.

HOUSEHOLD WORDS OFFICE,
Tuesday Fifth February 1856

My Dear Miss Coutts.

I will come to Stratton Street on Friday, between 2 and 4.

You will be glad, I know, to hear that Charley was presented with Five Pounds yesterday "for his punctuality" at Barings.[2]

With my kind love to Mrs. Brown

Ever Dear Miss Coutts | Most Faithfully Yours
CHARLES DICKENS

[1] See 10 Jan and *fn* and *To* Wills, 8 Feb.

[2] Baring Brothers, bankers: see Vol. VII, p. 709.

To PETER CUNNINGHAM,[1] 5 FEBRUARY 1856

Text from N, II, 739.

H.W. Office | Tuesday Fifth February 1856

My Dear Peter,

I return the curious book,[2] with many thanks.

Come and dine *here* next Thursday, my birthday, at half past five sharp, or expect the Vengeance of

Yours Ever
[CHARLES DICKENS]

To MRS CHARLES DICKENS, 5 FEBRUARY 1856

MS British Library. *Address* (envelope in Kitton's Dickens Ana, I, 147): La France | À Madame Charles Dickens | 49 Avenue des Champs Elysées | Paris. PM 6 Feb 56.

Tavistock House—I mean H.W. Office | Fifth February 1856

My Dearest Catherine. I have been so busy all day (commencing with having my tooth out), that this must be the shortest of notes or it will be too late for the Post.

I had a very agreeable journey—with two Glasgow men. We became great friends, dined together at Dover, and parted at London Bridge. The passage was very fine, though there was by no means an absence of motion; moreover, we had to go aboard in small boats. I felt so perfectly well, however, that I did not even take my Laudanum. They charged at the Dover Custom House, eight shillings duty on the Godfather-present.[3]

Charley looks well, and was, I am most happy to say, presented at Barings only yesterday, with Five Pounds "for his punctuality." I have not seen your mother. I saw your father this morning, and he was looking wonderfully well.

Anne[4] intends (John tells me) to come and wait on my Birthday.

Old Stone I saw for a few moments this morning. He had an ancient air upon him. The front court has also an ancient and deserted air;[5] our absence very perceptibly changing the whole place.

Best love to Georgy. And to Mamey, Katey, Walter, Harry, and the Noble Plorn. I found the faithful Mark in attendance at London Bridge; and he and his send all manner of Loves. I have not yet had leisure to see Forster.

Ever affectionately
CD.

[1] Peter Cunningham (1816–69; *DNB*), author and Chief Clerk in the Audit Office: see Vol. V, p. 285*n*.

[2] Unidentified.

[3] See next.

[4] Anne Cornelius, née Brown, Catherine's servant since 1839; married Edward Cornelius, 2 Sep 1855: see Vols II, p. 392*n* and VII, p. 693 and *nn*. See *To* Georgina Hogarth, 8 Feb and *fn*.

[5] J. B. Cardale, who occupied the house between CD's and Stone's, was responsible for the court's upkeep: see *To* Wills, 20 Apr.

To MESSRS WILLIAMS & CLAPHAM,[1] 5 FEBRUARY 1856*

MS Berg Collection.

Household Words Office
16 Wellington Street North, Strand | Fifth February 1856

Mr. Charles Dickens sends his compliments to Messrs. Williams and Clapham, and begs them to get the little French present sent with this, engraved with the Inscription over-leaf. Mr. Dickens would like to have it on the centre of the plate, and round the cup. In the place left for the purpose on the handle of the spoon, he wishes to have the child's initials C.D.T. Will Messrs. Williams and Clapham be so good as to have it done at once, and to send the case *here*.

Charles Dickens Theodore Yates
From his Godfather[2]
Charles Dickens.

To MRS WINTER,[3] 5 FEBRUARY 1856

MS Comtesse de Suzannet.

49 Champs Elysées, Paris[4] | Fifth February 1856

My Dear Mrs. Winter

It comes into my head that I have never acknowledged the little letter you wrote me on receipt of my books,[5] and which was accompanied by another pleasant letter from your other half.[6] Not that either required an answer, but that you may as well know that I received them, I send this short note.

My own writing so absorbs my time and attention, and my business correspondence is so very large, that the letters I write for pleasure are miraculously few. That they are also laudably short, let this sheet of paper witness.

With my regard to Mr. Winter and my love to little Ella,[7]

Believe me always | Faithfully Yours
CHARLES DICKENS

[1] Goldsmiths and jewellers, 13 and 14 Strand.

[2] See *To* Yates, 2 Jan.

[3] Maria Sarah Winter, née Beadnell (1810–86), CD's first love: see Vol. I, p. 16*n*; and, for her marriage to Henry Louis Winter in 1845 and CD's meeting her again in 1855, see Vol. VII, p. 532 and *n*.

[4] CD gave his Paris address, probably because he did not want Maria to know that he was in London.

[5] Eleven books, now in the Huntington Library, each inscribed (without date): "Charles Dickens | *To* Maria Winter. | In remembrance of old times." They consist of nearly all the first series of the Cheap edn, mostly not in their original issue; namely, *Sketches by Boz*, 1850 (1st issue), *American Notes*, 1850, *Old Curiosity Shop*, 1853, *Barnaby Rudge*, 1853, *Oliver Twist*, 1853, *Pickwick*, 1854, *Nickleby*, 1854, *Chuzzlewit*, 1855; and first editions of three more recent novels, *Dombey*, 1848, *Copperfield*, 1850, and *Bleak House*, 1853. A twelfth volume containing *Christmas Books* was separated from the set, the page of inscription removed but later restored: see *The A. Edward Newton Collection* (Parke-Bernet Catalogue, 18 Apr 1941). Its present location unknown.

[6] Henry Louis Winter (*d.* 1871), saw-mill manager: see Vol. VII, p. 533*n*.

[7] Ella Maria (1846–1915), the elder of Mrs Winter's two daughters: see Vol. VII, p. 533*n*.

To MRS CHAMBERS,[1] 6 FEBRUARY 1856

MS Free Library of Philadelphia.

Wednesday Sixth February | 1856.

Mr. Charles Dickens presents his Compliments to Mrs. Chambers, and begs to say that if the girl in question be brought by her mother, or some authorized person, tomorrow (Thursday) at One, to the Household Words office 16 Wellington Street North, Strand, Mr. Dickens will be happy to consider her case with a view to its fitness for admission into Miss Coutts's Home.

To C. W. DILKE,[2] 6 FEBRUARY 1856*

MS Churchill College, Cambridge.

Household Words Office | Sixth February 1856

My Dear Mr. Dilke

I should like to speak with you on the subject of the Literary Fund.[3] I will come over to your house for the purpose and with the hope of finding you at home, tomorrow (Thursday) at One.

Faithfully Yours always

Charles Wentworth Dilke Esquire. CHARLES DICKENS

To DR JOHN EPPS,[4] 6 FEBRUARY 1856

Mention in Noel Conway catalogue, ?1893; *MS* 1 p.; dated HW Office, 6 Feb 56; addressed Dr Epps.

Thanking Dr Epps for some books.[5]

To DOUGLAS JERROLD,[6] 6 FEBRUARY 1856[7]

Text from W. Blanchard Jerrold, *The Best of all Good Company. A Day with Charles Dickens*, 1872, p. 39, with corrections from MDGH, I, 427.

HOUSEHOLD WORDS OFFICE,
Sixth February 1856.

My dear Jerrold.

Buckstone has been with me to-day in a state of demi-semi-distraction, by reason

[1] Unidentified.

[2] Charles Wentworth Dilke (1789–1864; *DNB*), antiquary and critic: see Vols I, p. 127*n* and IV, p. 537*n*.

[3] Dilke had been an ally with Forster and CD in 1855 in attempts to reform the administration of the Fund: see Vol. VII, p. 353 and *n* and *To* Wills, 17 Feb (2nd letter) and *fn*.

[4] John Epps (1805–69; *DNB*), homoeopathic physician: see Vols IV, p. 473*n* and VII, p. 443*n*.

[5] Perhaps including Vol. I (Feb 56) of *Notes of New Truth* (*A Monthly Journal of Homoeopathy*), ed. by Epps.

[6] Douglas William Jerrold (1803–57; *DNB*), writer and wit: see Vol. I, p. 192*n*.

[7] Misdated 6 Mar in MDGH, I, 427 and N, II, 750.

of Macready's[1] dreading his asthma so much as to excuse himself (of necessity I know) from taking the chair for the fund[2] on the occasion of their next dinner.[3] I have promised to back Buckstone's entreaty to you to take it, and although I know that you have an objection which you once communicated to me, I still hold (as I did then) that it is a reason *for* and not against. Pray reconsider the point. Your position in connection with dramatic literature has always suggested to me[4] that there would be a great fitness and grace in your appearing in this post—am convinced that the public would regard it in that light—and I particularly ask you to reflect that we never can do battle with the lords[5] if we will not bestir[6] ourselves to go into places which they long monopolised. Now, pray discuss this matter with yourself once more. If you can come to a favourable conclusion, I shall be really delighted, and will of course come from Paris[7] to be by you; if you cannot come to a favourable conclusion, I shall be really sorry, though I of course most readily defer to your right to regard such a matter from your own point of view.

Ever faithfully yours
CHARLES DICKENS

Douglas Jerrold, Esq.

To DANIEL MACLISE,[8] 6 FEBRUARY 1856

Text from facsimile in Charles Hamilton catalogue No. 92 (Nov 1975).

[a]Household Words Office | Sixth February, 1845

My Dear Mac[a]

Äry Scheffer has been painting my Portrait in Paris, and means to send it to the Exhibition. He seems to me to be contemplating too broad a frame, and I have promised him (being over here for a few days) to ascertain the Academy's regulations in that regard.[9] Will you kindly tell me what width of frame, the laws of the Medes allow?

Ever affectionately
CHARLES DICKENS

[1] William Charles Macready: see Vol. I, p. 279 and *n*, and subsequent vols.

[2] The Royal General Theatrical Fund.

[3] The Anniversary dinner, held at the London Tavern, 17 Mar. For CD's speech as a Trustee, see *Speeches of CD*, ed. K. J. Fielding, Oxford, 1960 (reprinted 1988), pp. 220–2.

[4] Jerrold was a staunch Radical, implacably hostile to the Tories and the House of Lords; see Vol. v, p. 314 and *n*. CD anticipated an objection along these lines, although the aristocracy (apart from Bulwer Lytton) had little to do with the Fund, and Jerrold had proposed the Duke of Devonshire's health at a dinner for the Gardeners' Benevolent Fund on 9 June 51, when CD also spoke (*Speeches*, ed. K. J. Fielding, p. 133). Jerrold was not good at public speaking and disliked it. Ironically, Lord Tenterden (see *To* Webster, 9 June, *fn*) took the chair on 17 Mar, Jerrold having obviously declined, and the Marquis Townshend proposed his health.

[5] W. B. Jerrold reads, "with the love of the lords".

[6] MDGH and N read "bestow".

[7] Misread by Jerrold as "Dan's".

[8] Daniel Maclise, RA (?1806–70; *DNB*): see Vol. I, p. 201*n* and subsequent vols.

[aa] From N, II, 740.

[9] The Royal Academy set no restrictions for size of paintings, but warned that "excessive breadth in frames may prevent Pictures obtaining the situation they otherwise merit". The portrait was hung that May, unusually for a French painter.

To THE REV. EDWARD TAGART,[1] 6 FEBRUARY 1856

MS Mr Arthur Rogers.

Household Words Office | Wednesday Sixth February 1856

My Dear Mr. Tagart

We are passing the winter in Paris, and as I only make periodical rushes at this capital, I am but now in the receipt of your kind note. Let me heartily assure you that I reciprocate all its friendly feelings and expressions, with great cordiality.

I am afraid I may not be able to help the author of the book you have sent me; simply because I have no sort of association with, or control over, any Journal but this. It is only in exceptional cases that the plan of Household Words admits of books being made the subject of articles in its pages. They are never reviewed; and are described only when their objects have some direct present bearing on social advancement or convenience. If I find, however, that anything can be done in this instance (and I cannot determine that point without reading the book), it shall be done.

I left them all well in Paris. If they knew me to be writing to you they would all join me, I am sure, in kindest regard to Mrs. Tagart[2] and all your house.

Believe me | Always Faithfully Yours
[CHARLES DICKENS]

To BENJAMIN WEBSTER, 6 FEBRUARY 1856*

MS Free Library of Philadephia.

Household Words Office | Wednesday Sixth February 1856

My Dear Webster

I am sorry to say that I leave town on Sunday morning. If I had not made arrangements which involve the convenience of a friend who goes back with me,[3] I would certainly stay to have the pleasure of accepting your invitation.

On Friday evening I am coming to the Theatre[4] with Lemon. We can then, I hope, find an opportunity of talking over the Dulwich matter.[5] I think your movement (so far as I know it from him) to be an admirable one, based on common sense and justice, and undertaken in the becoming spirit of an artist who cares for his order.

Faithfully Yours always
CHARLES DICKENS

Benjamin Webster Esquire.

[1] The Rev. Edward Tagart (1804–58; *DNB*), Unitarian minister at Little Portland St Chapel: see Vol. III, p. 449*n*. His family had moved from Bayswater to Hampstead by 1850.

[2] Née Helen Bourne: see Vols III, p. 449*n* and VII, p. 364*n*.

[3] Collins's visit to Paris was postponed: see 12 Feb.

[4] To see Webster's *Boots at the Holly Tree Inn*: CD's response is not recorded. The scenery and acting were praised, especially Webster as Cobbs, the Boots. *The Times* (5 Feb) thought it "a perfect instance of a story placed upon a stage", but they and others noted that its reception was cool.

[5] See *To* Howes, 19 Mar, *fn*.

To MRS CHARLES DICKENS, 7 FEBRUARY 1856

MS British Library. *Address:* La France | À Madame Charles Dickens | 49 Avenue des champs Elysées | Paris.

Household Words Office | Thursday February Seventh 1856

My Dearest Catherine.

You will be glad, I know, to hear (and therefore I write to tell you) that Charley has been presented with another Five Pounds, and has had his salary raised Ten Pounds a year.

I have been perplexed by the non-arrival of any letter from Georgy, who was to have written to tell me what arrangement she had made for Collins. This failure rendered it impossible for me to tell him last night what had been done for him in the way of quarters,[1] and made me look rather foolish. I write in the middle of the day (the middle of my birthday by the bye), and even yesterday's foreign post is in, and yet I have no letter. I cannot conceive what she has been about.

You will have seen in the Times perhaps, that Scott Russell[2] is a bankrupt.[3] A hundred and eighty thousand pounds is stated to be the little amount of the debts of himself and Co.[4]

The weather is as vile here as need be. Chokingly warm, very wet, and miserably dark. Last night a violent wind blew from the West, besides. The streets are hideous to behold, and the ugliness of London is quite astonishing.

We purpose crossing to Boulogne on Sunday, if the weather should be reasonable, and coming on to Paris by the Train which leaves Boulogne at Mid Day on Monday. Let French[5] be at the station to receive us.

A certain Miss Holliday, or Haliday,[6] or some such name, sent to Tavistock House yesterday for Miss Barrow's[7] address. I knew nothing about it, of course. After that the same Unknown wrote a note addressed to you, again asking to have it. She might as well have asked Me for a map of the Moon.

Love to Georgy, and to Mamey, Katey, Walter, Harry, and the noble Plorn.

Ever affectionately

CD.

[1] See next.

[2] John Scott Russell (1808–82; *DNB*), civil engineer and shipbuilder: see Vol. VII, p. 351 and *n*.

[3] He was not personally made bankrupt, but the troubles over the *Great Eastern* which had begun in 1855 now reached a crisis. On 4 Feb his Shipbuilding Co. announced suspension of payment; the related Eastern Steam Navigation Co. took over the ship and imposed certain conditions on Russell's operations. His Co.'s affairs were liquidated; but in May work was resumed and by July he had come to terms with his creditors (for further details, see George S. Emmerson, *John Scott Russell*, 1977, Ch. 5).

[4] At the end of the week Russell discharged his employees, presumably still unable to pay them. According to the Sec. of the Co., "many unfounded reports were in circulation", of which the £180,000 was perhaps one (G. S. Emmerson, above).

[5] Charles French, CD's servant.

[6] Unidentified.

[7] No doubt his first cousin, Emily Elizabeth Barrow, who married George Frederick Lawrence, a clerk, in 1857; they had settled in America by Mar 58. See Katharine Longley, "Letters to the Editor", *D*, LXXXVIII (1992), 105.

To MISS GEORGINA HOGARTH, 7 FEBRUARY 1856

MS Dickens House.

Household Words | Seventh February 1856
(Just before dinner)

My Dear Georgy.

Your letters *both together*, have just come to hand. I have but a moment to reply. *Take the Pavilion.*[1] I have no doubt of its being the best place.

I will write you a real letter tomorrow.

Ever Affectionately
CD.

To MISS GEORGINA HOGARTH, 8 FEBRUARY 1856

MS Dickens House.

Household Words | Friday Eighth February, 1856

My Dear Georgy. I must write this at Railroad speed, for I have been at it all day, and have numbers of letters to cram into the next halfhour. I began the morning in the City for the Theatrical Fund—went on to Shepherd's Bush—came back to leave cards for Mr. Baring[2] and Mr. Bates[3]—ran across Piccadilly to Stratton Street—stayed there an hour—and shot off here. I have been in four cabs today at a cost of Thirteen Shillings. Am going to dine with Mark and Webster at ½ past 4, and finish the evening at the Adelphi.

The dinner was very successful. Charley was in great force, and floored Peter Cunningham and the Audit Office on a question about some bill transaction with Barings. The other guests were B, He,[4] Shirley Brooks,[5] Forster (in bad spirits I think)—and that's all. The dinner, admirable. I never had a better. All the wine, I sent down from Tavistock House. Anne waited, and looked well and happy—very much brighter and better altogether. It gave me great pleasure to see her so improved.[6] Just before dinner I got all the letters from home. They could not have arrived more opportunely.

The Godfather Present[7] looks charming now it is engraved, and John is just now going off to take it to Mrs. Yates. Tomorrow Wills and I are going to Gad's Hill. It will occupy the whole day, and will just leave me time to get home to dress for

[1] 63 Avenue des Champs Elysées, in the same grounds as CD's house. "Like a cottage in a ballet", as Collins reported to his mother (28 Feb; MS Morgan Library). During his illness he appreciated "the brightness and elegance of its little rooms" and the sympathetic portress, described in "Laid up in Two Lodgings. My Paris Lodging", *HW*, 7 June 56, XIII, 481.

[2] Thomas Baring: see Vol. VII, p. 638*n*; head of Baring Brothers, bankers; Conservative MP for Huntingdon since 1844; Chancellor of the Exchequer 1852 and 1858; formed celebrated collection of paintings.

[3] Joshua Bates, senior partner of Baring Brothers: see Vol. VII, p. 508*n*.

[4] i.e. F. M. Evans; CD's aspirated form of "E", mocking the Bradburys' Cockneyisms.

[5] (Charles William) Shirley Brooks, writer and editor of *Punch* 1870–4: see Vol. VII, p. 257*n*.

[6] Her daughter Catherine was born this summer.

[7] See *To* Williams & Clapham, 5 Feb.

dinner. I arranged with Miss Coutts concerning Wills this morning. He is to have Two Hundred a year—which I think very handsome.

I saw your mother yesterday for the first time. She looks rather better than usual, I think.

And that's about all I have to say, except that I have rescued Mark from a state of the deepest depression, and that the first No. of Little Dorrit has gone to 40,000, and the others are fast following.

My best love to Catherine, and to Mamey and Katey, and Walter, and Harry, and the Noble Plorn. I am grieved to hear about his black eye, and fear that I shall find it in the green and purple state on my return.

Ever affectionately
CHARLES DICKENS

To W. H. WILLS, 8 FEBRUARY 1856

MS Huntington Library.

H.W. Office | Friday Eighth February 1856

My Dear Wills. I think you may like to know the result of my talk with Miss Coutts, without waiting until tomorrow.

She asked me if I had thought of any precise acknowledgement for the services you rendered her, as she felt it very difficult to suggest an amount herself—much greater than she would have felt, if she had been able to place everything in your hands.[1] I said that whatever I might have thought, it seemed right that she should form her own opinion on the subject and suggest her own proposition. She then said, as there would be some little expences incurred now and then in going about, and as she wished her offer to include everything, what did I think of £200 a year? I replied that I thought it was handsome, and that I would communicate it to you.

I hope you approve? You will have a friend for life, who is worth having.

Ever Faithfully
CD.

To MRS WILLS,[2] 8 FEBRUARY 1856

MS Huntington Library.

H.W. Office | Friday Eighth February 1856

My Dear Mrs. Wills.

Pray accept my hearty thanks (and a halfpenny, or we shall quarrel)[3] for your welcome remembrance of me yesterday. It gave me the greatest pleasure, and the pretty knife shall be my constant companion.

Always My Dear Mrs. Wills | Very faithfully Yours

Mrs. Wills CD.

[1] It was understood that CD would continue to advise and act for Miss Coutts in many matters.

[2] Née Janet Chambers: see Vol. IV, p. 468*n*.

[3] Referring to the still common superstition that an outright gift of a knife or scissors cuts affection unless a small coin is given in return; when R. C. Lehmann edited *CD as Editor*, the coin was attached to the letter (p. 211).

To MRS EDMUND YATES, 8 FEBRUARY 1856*

MS Morgan Library.

Tavistock House | Friday Eighth February 1856.

My Dear Mrs. Yates.

Will you kindly present to my little Man, with my affectionate regard, the very extraordinarily-shaped box which accompanies this note?

And will you absolve me from any suspicion of neglecting my sponsorial duties in leaving you by 10 tomorrow night?[1] For I have to go elsewhere, after that time.

Very faithfully Yours

Mrs. Edmund Yates. CHARLES DICKENS

To MISS BURDETT COUTTS, 9 FEBRUARY 1856

MS Morgan Library. *Address:* Miss Burdett Coutts | 1 Stratton Street.

Household Words Office | Saturday Ninth February 1856

My Dear Miss Coutts.

First, as to Teignmouth,[2] Wills knows it very well. The soil is a red loam, and not naturally damp. But the town itself stands in a rent or gash made among great hills, by the mouth of the river,[3] and is certainly moist and low—decidedly *not* advisable for your purpose I should say.[4] On the other hand, if the house should not be in Teignmouth or in the valley of the river, but should be on the bold hills which rise about it, then the objection to it would be removed. The whole question turns upon the exact position of the house. If it be on the hills, good. If it be in the valley, bad. If it be in neither the one place nor the other, rather dubious.

Secondly, as to Wills himself. I have communicated to him the result of our conversation yesterday, and he is "gratified beyond expression". He says he considers it most generous, and is extremely anxious that I should express his sense of it to you in the most earnest and emphatic words I can employ.

Thirdly, as to Gad's Hill Place—which is the name of my house. If you mean in your kind note, the refusal of it *now*, I am sorry to say that it is not now available. As I told Mrs. Brown yesterday, the Rector[5] lives in it, and has lived in it for some years; and the object Wills and I have in view in going down there directly, is to ask him how and when it will suit his convenience to come out—as of course I wish to treat him with all handsome consideration. It is not now a furnished house, but my object is, as soon as I shall have got rid of the tenant, to make it clean and pretty in the papering and painting way, and then to furnish it in the most comfortable and cosey manner, and let it by the month whenever I can. Whenever I cannot, I shall use it for myself and make it a change for Charley from Saturday to Monday. When all this is done, I shall have a delight in taking you down to see it which I shall not try here to

[1] At the christening.

[2] On the Devon coast, 15 miles south of Exeter.

[3] The Teign.

[4] Miss Coutts was obviously thinking of renting a house there instead of at Torquay, from which she had just returned (see 5 Feb 56); but she rented Meadfoot House, 1 Hesketh Terrace, Torquay, the following spring.

[5] The Rev. Joseph Hindle: see *To* Miss Coutts, 12 Feb, *fn*.

express; and if you should like it so well as to think of ever occupying it as a little easy change, I shall be far more attached to the spot than ever. I think you will be very much pleased with it. It is old-fashioned, plain, and comfortable. On the summit of Gad's Hill, with a noble prospect at the side and behind, looking down into the Valley of the Medway. Lord Darnley's[1] Park of Cobham (a beautiful place with a noble walk through a wood) is close by it; and Rochester is within a mile or two. It is only an hour and a quarter from London by the Railway. To crown all, the sign of the Sir John Falstaff is over the way, and I used to look at it as a wonderful Mansion (which God knows it is not), when I was a very odd little child with the first faint shadows of all my books, in my head—I suppose.

Mr. Austin surveyed it for me, and was greatly struck by it. Large sums of money have been expended on it (for such a small place) at various times, and he found everything about the garden and so forth, in the best order. There is a very pretty garden, and a Shrubbery on the other side of the high road, at which the house looks. When I exhibit it to you with all my contrivances accomplished—of course some of them will be wonderfully ingenious—I will tell you what I paid for it.

With love to Mrs. Brown, who is looking immensely better.

Ever Dear Miss Coutts | Yours most faithfully and affecy.

CD.

To JOHN FORSTER, [9 FEBRUARY 1856]

Extract in F, VIII, iii, 651. *Date:* 9 Feb 56, according to Forster.

His first estimate for Gads Hill would have to be increased threefold. The changes absolutely necessary will take a thousand pounds; which sum I am always resolving to squeeze out of this, grind out of that, and wring out of the other; this, that, and the other generally all three declining to come up to the scratch for the purpose.

To JOHN LEECH,[2] 9 FEBRUARY 1856

MS Benoliel Collection. *Address:* John Leech Esquire | 32 Brunswick Square.

Household Words | Saturday Ninth February 1856

My Dear Leech.

My short stay, and my having been obliged to plan out each day before I left Paris, have not only prevented my having the pleasure (it would have been a great one to me), of dining with you, but even of getting round to Brunswick Square. Little Dorrits, Household Wordseses, Theatrical Funds, Shepherds Bushes, and miscellaneous affairs (taking me this very day to Rochester among other places) have so used me up and harried me about, that I have not had an hour's freedom. But I am coming to town again next month; and, if you'll have me, I will write from Paris before I leave, and propoge myself for a chop.

[1] John Stuart Bligh, 6th Earl of Darnley (1827–96): see later vols.

[2] John Leech (1817–64; *DNB*), comic artist: see Vol. III, p. 358*n*.

With kindest regards to Mrs. Leech[1] and the Darlings,[2]

Ever Faithfully

John Leech Esquire. CHARLES DICKENS

To GEORGE MOORE,[3] 11 FEBRUARY 1856†

MS Benoliel Collection.

49 Champs Elysées, Paris | Monday Eleventh February 1856

My Dear Sir

My friend Mr. Mark Lemon is so kind as to take charge of this letter for you, in behalf of a lady in whom we are both greatly interested. Her name is Horne, her husband is in Australia,[4] she has a remarkably good appearance, a good manner, great perseverance and strength of character, no fine notions of any kind whatsoever, and seeks to live by her own industry.[5] With this view she taught herself some two or three years since, a new art of preparing glass in imitation of marble.[6] She has worked at it until this time; but it does not seem to thrive, and she has written to me entreating my interest and remembrance.

Casting about in my head to whom I could represent her case, with any hope of obtaining her employment, it came into my thoughts that you might have in your great house[7] some means of suitably placing such a person and turning her qualities to account. I know her thoroughly well, and am most willing to become security for her in any responsible trust. I know her reliability and fidelity to be unimpeachable. She is barely thirty, though she looks a little older.

If you should have the means of helping me in this matter I should feel very heartily obliged; and if there should be anything more in reference to Mrs. Horne that you may desire to know, Mr. Lemon is as well acquainted with her history as I am, and will freely communicate it.

My Dear Sir | Faithfully Yours

George Moore Esquire. CHARLES DICKENS

[1] Née Ann Eaton; married 1843; see *ibid.*

[2] Their two surviving children, Ada Rose (1854–85) and John Charles Waddington ("Bouge" to the family), (1855–76). Leech was notably fond of small children; his son was "the main warmth and brightness of his life" (F. G. Kitton, *John Leech, Artist and Humorist*, 1884).

[3] George Moore (1806–76; *DNB*), businessman and philanthropist; partner in prosperous lace-house (see below); from 1844 devoted himself to philanthropy; his and CD's common interest in the Commercial Travellers' Schools, the Royal Hospital for Incurables and similar charities led to their friendship. Giving his toast as Chairman and Treasurer of the Commercial Travellers' Schools at the anniversary dinner on 30 Dec 54 (see Vol. VII, p. 499*n*), CD described him as "a synonym for integrity, enterprise, public spirit, and benevolence" (*Speeches*, ed. K.J. Fielding, p. 174). Declined office as Sheriff of London and refused six times to stand for Parliament.

[4] In Apr 57 he was appointed Commissioner for Water and Sewerage in Melbourne, at a salary of £400 *p.a.*; but post abolished at end of 1859.

[5] Mrs Richard Henry Horne, née Catherine Clare St George Foggo, in financial difficulties since her husband's emigration: see Vols. V, p. 389*n*, VI, pp. 678–9 and *nn* and VII, p. 396*n*.

[6] At the Ladies' Guild in Russell Square.

[7] Groucock, Copestake, Moore & Co., lace manufacturers and warehousemen, 5 Bow Churchyard, 62 Bread St and three other City addresses.

To WILKIE COLLINS, 12 FEBRUARY 1856

MS Morgan Library.

49 Champs Elysées, Paris | Tuesday Twelfth February 1856

My Dear Collins. I am delighted to receive your letter—which is just come to hand—and heartily congratulate you upon it. I have no doubt you will soon appear.[1] I would recommend you, unless the Boulogne Boat serves to a marvel, to come by the Calais route—the day Mail. Because in the winter there are no special trains on that Boulogne line in France, and waiting at Boulogne is a bore. The Pavilion[2] is all ready, and is a wonder. Upon my word it is the snuggest oddity I ever saw; the look-out from it, the most wonderful in the world.[3]

[a]I told them at home here that you had a touch of your "old complaint", and had turned back to consult your Doctor.[4] Thought it best, in case of any contretemps hereafter, with your mother on one hand and my people on the other.[a]

We[5] had a pleasant trip, and the best dinner at the Bang[6] I ever sat down to.

So, looking out for your next letter "advising self" of your coming, Ever Faithfully

CD.

To MISS BURDETT COUTTS, 12 FEBRUARY 1856

MS Morgan Library. *Address:* Miss Burdett Coutts | Stratton Street | Piccadilly | London.

49 Avenue des Champs Elysées, Paris
Tuesday Twelfth February 1856

My Dear Miss Coutts.

My Rector,[7] having lived in the house six and twenty years, has an ardent desire to stay there until Lady Day next year. I have of course acceded to his wish. In the meantime he purposes building a house for himself somewhere near, as there are very few indeed in that neighbourhood but Farms, and Farm-laborers' cottages. The only house thereabouts (except mine) that would suit you as a Retreat, is a very good one called the Hermitage. But it is in the occupation of the Owner and is not to be let.[8]

It has occurred to me that Tunbridge Wells might be a good place for your purpose. It is extremely healthy, very beautiful, very accessible, and has many pleasant

[1] He arrived on 27 Feb. His delay may have been due to a bout of the "rheumatic gout" which plagued him at intervals all year (but see Vol. VII, p. 585 and *n*); the tone of CD's letter suggests that he was with his mistress Caroline Graves. See William M. Clarke, *The Secret Life of Wilkie Collins*, 1988.

[2] See *To* Miss Hogarth, 7 Feb, *fn*.

[3] "The wonderfully gay view" over the Champs Elysées, "with its ever-changing human interest", described by Collins in "My Paris Lodging" (*HW*, XIII, 485).

[aa] Omitted in *CD to WC*, p. 45.

[4] Probably a humorous euphemism for Caroline Graves, here and on 13 Apr.

[5] Frederick Evans apparently crossed with him: see *To* Evans, 12 Feb.

[6] The Hotel des Bains, Boulogne.

[7] The Rev. Joseph Hindle (?1795–1874), Vicar of Higham 1829–74; educated at Sedbergh and St John's College, Cambridge; BA 1818; Fellow 1818–30; priest 1823; inherited the Lower Darwen estate, Lancs, from his brother John 1854; contributed generously to new Chapel-of-ease, Higham, and to National Schools.

[8] No doubt the Great Hermitage, Higham, home of J. N. Malleson.

houses that are let furnished by the month. Anywhere upon or near the Heath is a very fine situation, on light sand. If you should think well of it, Wills would be delighted to go down and look about for you. Or there is an excellent Hotel—The Calvary[1]—where you might be as private and as comfortable, almost, as in any hired house. If you don't think well of this, anywhere about Croydon, Dorking, or Guildford, is good, and particularly healthy.

Of course you will let me know where you go. I shall have to be in town about the Tenth of next month.

With my love to Mrs. Brown

Ever Dear Miss Coutts | Yours most Faithfully and affecy.

CD.

Mrs. Brown will immediately receive from Wills, the result of the London University enquiries.[2]

I forgot to speak to you about Mrs. Kenney,[3] 192 Faubourg St. Honoré. Perhaps it might be painful to her if I were to write to her, as she has not written to me. But the plain truth is, that I have no means of employing translators, and that I never do.

To F. M. EVANS, 12 FEBRUARY 1856

MS Rosenbach Foundation.

49 Champs Elysées, Paris | Tuesday Twelfth February 1856

My Dear Evans

I hope you had as good a passage home, as I had journey here. I was at dinner at a quarter past seven, comfortably. The weather changed some twenty miles out of Boulogne, and was bright and pleasant. The whole house I found in a jovial condition.

It occurs to me to say to you (and therefore I write so soon), that if it should be convenient to you, even to increase upon the £200 monthly payment,[4] it will suit me perfectly well. The circulation being so large, I do not care how much you pay in every month, or by how large[5] a sum you so diminish the half-yearly balance. It will be as useful to me in six large portions and a moderate lump, as in six small portions and a great lump. All that I care for, is, that it should always be the same appointed sum. I address this to you, as you are the currency man and as you spoke to me on the subject; but of course I refer the point to B and E. Let me know how you propose to proceed.

And be so good as to make up the last halfyear's account[6] with as little delay as you can, because, having this purchase to make[7] I am glad just now of all the money

[1] CD clearly meant the Calverley Park Hotel.

[2] Mrs Brown may have first considered funding a studentship at London University, in memory of her husband, before deciding on an Exhibition at St George's Hospital: see *To* Mrs Brown, 8 Aug 56 and *fn.*

[3] Perhaps A. Kenney, who translated J. P. Richter's *The Death of an Angel* from the German, 1839.

[4] From Feb 56 he received £250 per month, as against only £100 for Dec 55 and Jan 56 (Bradbury & Evans's Accounts, MS V & A).

[5] *Little Dorrit* No. III, published 31 Jan 56, sold 35,000 copies. For the large balance CD was owed in June 56, see *To* Evans, 8 Mar 57 and *fn.*

[6] For the half year ending Christmas 55.

[7] Of Gad's Hill Place.

I can get. I know that the usual time has not yet arrived, but you may perhaps be able to anticipate it a little, knowing my desire.

With regard and kind remembrance to B

Ever Faithfully Yours

F. M. Evans Esquire CHARLES DICKENS

To LORD GRANVILLE,[1] 12 FEBRUARY 1856

MS Mr D. Atherton.

49 Champs Elysées, Paris | Tuesday Twelfth February 1856

Mr. Charles Dickens regrets that his absence from England prevents his having the honor of accepting Lord Granville's invitation for Wednesday the Thirteenth. It has only reached him to-day, and he hopes Lord Granville will therefore do him the favor to excuse his delay in acknowledging it.

To MADAME JAQUET,[2] 12 FEBRUARY 1856

MS Berg Collection.

49 Avenue des Champs Elysées
Tuesday Twelfth February 1856

My Dear Madame Jaquet.

If I thought it possible that you *could* make a mistake, I should humbly submit to you that you achieve that miracle in supposing that it is my friends in Paris whom I treat with terrible rigor, and not myself. For, I assure you, I live under the delusion that when I am writing a book I deny myself a great deal that would be very pleasant to me and observe a seclusion that is not very consistent with my natural inclinations, simply because I have found by my experience that this habit is necessary to my Art, and that I cannot do my best without an entire devotion to it. I do not mean to say that on the evening when I hoped to have come to you, I was writing, or that I write half a dozen evenings in a year. But when I have been thus engaged all day, I cannot relieve my mind or prepare myself for the morrow, unless I am perfectly free from promises and engagements, and can wander about in my own queer way. At such times, hot rooms and society, worry me more than you can easily imagine—nothing but the open air will set me right.

This is the plain truth. I very rarely trouble any one by stating it; but I state it to you, because your kind note is so frank and friendly, and I felt so much sincere pleasure in seeing you again, and I always think so affectionately of the old days in Genoa and of your good father, that I am earnestly anxious you should understand me. If I could have gone anywhere on the night of your soirée, it would have been to

[1] Granville George Leveson-Gower, 2nd Earl Granville (1815–91; *DNB*), Liberal statesman: see Vol. VI, p. 463 and *n*. Leader of House of Lords 1855.

[2] Not further identified; but "the old days in Genoa" and "your good father" point to a married daughter of one of the friends he made when he spent Winter 1844 at the Palazzo Peschiere, Genoa: possibly Pierre-Edouard Alletz, the French Consul-general: see Vol. IV, pp. 164*n*, 180–1.

you; but my mind was so pre-occupied with my day's employment, that I could go nowhere with comfort but on a ten miles' ramble. From that, I came home quite rested and happy.

I should have written to you sooner, but for my having started for London very soon afterwards, and having only returned to Paris last night. Believe that my terrible rigor is one of the conditions on which I hold my success, and that I am with true regard

Very faithfully Yours

Madame Jaquet. CHARLES DICKENS

To W. H. WILLS, 12 FEBRUARY 1856

MS Huntington Library.

49 Avenue des Champs Elysées, Paris
Tuesday Twelfth February 1856

My Dear Wills.

I arrived here in the most brilliant and pleasant manner, to dinner yesterday.

H.W.[1]

It occurs to me that when you meet to return Forster's bills and note the end of that transaction, the future disposal of that share had better be arranged. What I propose to do with it, is, to divide it between you and me, equally, so long as we both live and you are the Sub-Editor of the Journal. That in the event of your death or your ceasing to be Sub Editor, the whole of it shall revert to me, in trust to bestow it or part of it upon any other Sub-Editor as I may think best and most to the advantage of the property. And that in the event of my death, the whole of it shall revert to the other proprietors, in trust to be similarly employed at their discretion.[2]

MY BIRTHDAY.[1]

Stanfield called at the office on Saturday as I was dressing to go out to dinner, and had not the least idea that I was in town. The note of invitation he received did not mention that I was coming, and had no signature to it. He addressed his answer to you at random, and called on Saturday to ask you if he had done right.

Faithfully Ever

CD.

[1] Underlined with short double strokes.

[2] In *CD as Editor*, p. 196, R. C. Lehmann records among Wills's papers an unsigned copy of a memorandum of Agreement of 22 Feb 54. It states that Forster had told his co-proprietors that he was unable henceforth to contribute literary articles to *HW*, as he had originally, in the Agreement of 28 Mar 50, agreed to do; but it was agreed, notwithstanding this, that he should retain his eighth share in *HW* on condition that, on 22 Feb 56, he should pay £1,100 to his co-proprietors; failing this, his share was to revert to the other proprietors. It is clear that Forster preferred relinquishing his one eighth share to making the payment of £1,100; and, in *CD as Editor*, pp. 196–7, Lehmann gives a further memorandum in CD's hand, undated but no doubt soon after 25 Feb 56, arranging the future disposal of that share: see Appx B.

To JOHN FORSTER, [13 FEBRUARY 1856]

Extract in F, VIII, iii, 650. *Date:* 13 Feb, according to Forster.

I was better pleased with Gadshill Place last Saturday, on going down there, even than I had prepared myself to be. The country, against every disadvantage of season, is beautiful; and the house is so old fashioned, cheerful, and comfortable, that it is really pleasant to look at. The good old Rector now there, has lived in it six and twenty years, so I have not the heart to turn him out. He is to remain till Lady-Day next year, when I shall go in, please God; make my alterations; furnish the house; and keep it for myself that summer.

To W. H. WILLS, 15 FEBRUARY 1856

MS Huntington Library.

49 Champs Elysées | Friday February Fifteenth 1856

My Dear Wills.

I enclose you the promised article for H.W.[1]

I have just received your letter, and am truly pleased to know that you are gratified by what I have done respecting the share. I hoped you would be; and in this, and in all other little ways in which I can ever testify my affection for you and my sense of the value of your friendship and support, I merely gratify myself by doing what you more than merit.

In haste | Ever Faithfully

CD.

To JOHN FORSTER, [17 FEBRUARY 1856]

Extracts in F, VII, iv, 597*n*, v, 609 and 611. *Date:* first extract 17 Feb, according to Forster; second and third extracts almost certainly same letter.

The picture he had given Forster of Napoleon[2] *had changed drearily in less than a year and a half.* I suppose mortal man out of bed never looked so ill and worn as the Emperor does just now. He passed close by me on horseback, as I was coming in at the door on Friday, and I never saw so haggard a face. Some English saluted him, and he lifted his hand to his hat as slowly, painfully, and laboriously, as if his arm were made of lead. I think he *must* be in pain.[3]

An uncommonly droll piece with an original comic idea in it has been in course of representation here. It is called *Les Cheveux de ma Femme*.[4] A man who is dotingly

[1] "Why?": see *To* Wills, 17 Feb (2nd letter) and *fn.*

[2] In Sep 1854: see Vol. VII, p. 412 and *n.*

[3] Napoleon III was examined in May 57 by Dr William Fergusson, Professor of Surgery, King's College, London, and found to be suffering from neuralgia, sciatica and dyspepsia (David Duff, *Eugénie and Napoleon*, 1978, p. 129). Fergusson reported to Lord Clarendon, the Foreign Secretary, the Emperor's "exhausted nervous system and diseased organs which ensue from such exhaustion" (Harolde Kurtz, *The Empress Eugénie*, 1964, p. 95).

[4] Performed at the Variétés; reviewed by *Galignani's Messenger* on Sun 10 Feb as a laughable trifle; the husband was highly comical.

fond of his wife, and who wishes to know whether she loved anybody else before they were married, cuts off a lock of her hair by stealth, and takes it to a great mesmeriser, who submits it to a clairvoyante who never was wrong. It is discovered that the owner of this hair has been up to the most frightful dissipations, insomuch that the clairvoyante can't mention half of them. The distracted husband goes home to reproach his wife, and she then reveals that she wears a wig, and takes it off.

Scribe[1] *had entertained him frequently; his dinners were very* handsome and pleasant; *as were all his belongings—a charming place in Paris, a fine estate in the country, capital carriage, handsome pair of horses,* all made, as he says, by his pen. *A guest at the first evening*[2] *was Auber,*[3] a stolid little elderly man, rather petulant in manner, *who told him he had once lived* at Stoke Noonton[4] *to study English, but had forgotten it all.* Louis Philippe had invited him to meet the Queen of England, and when L.P. presented him, the Queen said, "We are such old acquaintances through M. Auber's works, that an introduction is quite unnecessary."

To W. H. WILLS, 17 FEBRUARY 1856

MS Huntington Library.

49 Champs Elysées, Paris
Seventeenth February 1856. Sunday

My Dear Wills.

H.W.[5]

I will go over the proof[6] tonight, and write you what I think we had best do in respect of Collins's story,[7] tomorrow. At the same time I will return my Proof.

Pray take care that they always strike out that infernal dash which I myself have taken out five hundred times, between the heading In so many chapters, and the numbering of the chapter. I am vexed to see it in the last No. after all.

C.D.[5]

My agreement with the French booksellers for the complete translation, binds me to let them have a copy of everything I have written. Will you have, in the course of a week, a complete collection made of my papers in H.W.? (It would be no bad thing, while our people are about it to have it made in Duplicate, so that we may keep one at the office and regularly keep it up to the time); and when it is finished will you label it "From Mr. Charles Dickens's contributions to Household Words", and send it to B and E, to go into a parcel they are making for the said French booksellers? You will of course except all composite articles, and all such pièces de circonstance

[1] Augustin Eugène Scribe (1791–1861), prolific dramatist and librettist: see Vol. VI, p. 110*n*.

[2] Before Pichot's dinner on 23 Feb, according to Forster.

[3] Daniel François Esprit Auber (1782–1872), composer of instrumental music and *c.* 40 operas (librettos of many written by Scribe), including *Masaniello* and *Fra Diavolo*, besides *Manon Lescaut*; head of the Paris Conservatory 1842; musical director to Napoleon III 1857.

[4] i.e. Stoke Newington, then a village three miles north of the City.

[5] Underlined with short double strokes.

[6] No. 310, published 1 Mar.

[7] See next.

as the opening address[1] and the reference to the almanack.[2]

And will you ascertain from Augustus,[3] what Wine of mine has come to hand? There is some very precious champagne wandering about, somewhere.

Ever Faithfully
CD.

To W. H. WILLS, 17 FEBRUARY 1856

MS Huntington Library.

49 Champs Elysées
Sunday Night, Seventeenth February 1856

My Dear Wills.

On the principle that one XX number[4] is better than two X ones always, I would so re-arrange this No. as to begin with Why,[5] and get Collins (who, so far, is *admirable*) into the opening.[6] I have taken some things out of Sala,[7] where he is wrong. He has not been in Italy, I feel sure.

The Poem,[8] very good. But it is a remarkable thing, especially when that contrast is to be presented between the flourishing and the wasted Babylon, that the thriving City has not a single living figure in it![9] It is a very curious example of the incomplete way in which some writers seem to see their pictures.

Looking out of Window,[10] is so ridiculously printed in the huddling up of the Sentences, that I really cannot understand it. There appears to be a good idea in it, but I have become hopelessly confused by it and have given it up in despair.

The same remark applies to Far East,[11] which, in one place especially, I can't at all understand. Pray look to the Proof and the Copy.

Reverting to my article, *Why*,[12] I am not sure but that in a former article called A Few Conventionalities, I noticed the theatrical way of opening a letter.[13] Will you refer back? And if I did notice it, take that passage out.

I wish you would write, for 311, a temperate but strong article about the cost of

[1] CD's "A Preliminary Word", 30 Mar 50, I, 1–2.

[2] CD's "Our Almanac", 24 Nov 55, XII, 385, announcing the *HW* Almanac for 1856, published 22 Nov 55; reprinted in *D*, VII (Jan 1911), 16 and LVI (May 1960), 88. For the Almanacs of 1856–7 (by Henry Morley), see Vol. VII, p. 741*n*, and *To* Wills, 13 Nov 56 and *fnn.*

[3] His youngest brother, Augustus Newnham Dickens (1827–66): see Vol. I, p. 485*n*.

[4] Presumably "two-star".

[5] "Why?", by CD, the opening article of *HW* No. 310 (1 Mar, XIII, 145): an enquiry into English absurdities.

[6] Ch. 1 of the five instalments of Collins's "A Rogue's Life. Written by Himself" appeared in the same No. (III, 157), presumably in the space originally occupied by "Why?".

[7] "The Great Hotel Question", Ch. 3 (XIII, 148), an account of Italian hotels and a New York hotel.

[8] "A Vision of Old Babylon", by Edmund Ollier (XIII, 157).

[9] The description is entirely of buildings, gardens and fountains.

[10] By Morley (XIII, 166), a defence of looking out of the window ("the eye of the house").

[11] Also by Morley (XIII, 154); a notice of Paul B. Whittingham, *Notes on the late Expedition against the Russian Settlements in Eastern Siberia; and of a Visit to Japan* . . ., 1856.

[12] Underlined by short double strokes.

[13] In *HW*, 28 June 51, III, 312: "A stage-letter, before it can be read by the recipient, must be smartly rapped back, after being opened, with the knuckles of one hand" (p. 314).

administering the Literary Fund.[1] It will be the No. before the Annual Meeting.[2] I would recite the object and intention of the Institution, recite the monstrous expenditure, and plainly call upon the Subscribers to look into the thing at the next Annual Meeting on such a Day. If you are too busy to do it get Morley to do it; but let us have it in that No.[3] I will go carefully over it.

Ever Faithfully
CD.

[a]To Mr. Snow,[4] say it was a mistake of Mr. Carlyle's. We have made no investment in the Mitre office,[5] and I know nothing about it.[a]

To MISS BURDETT COUTTS, 19 FEBRUARY 1856

MS Morgan Library.

49 Champs Elysées | Tuesday Nineteenth February 1856

My Dear Miss Coutts.

Walter was born on 8th. of February 1841. His name (a mild one) is Walter Landor. Birthday, eighth of February eighteen hundred and forty one. Name, Walter Landor.[6] No vegetable designation, no flower, no beast, no terrors of any description.[7]

I don't know Dr. Sandwith.[8]

Your note finds me settling myself to Little Dorrit again,[9] and in the usual

[1] For CD's published report on proposed changes and the Special Meeting on 16 June 55, see Vol. VII, pp. 639*n* and 649*n*.

[2] Held on 12 Mar. On behalf of the "reformers" C. W. Dilke sent every member of the Fund an advance copy of the resolution he intended to propose at the Meeting, signed by CD, Forster, Dilke and his son, Lemon, Procter and Peter Cunningham; and by new supporters, including Forster's close friend, the Rev. Whitwell Elwin, and Hepworth Dixon (*Speeches*, ed. K. J. Fielding, p. 210). For the speech that CD made on behalf of the resolution, attacking the financial management of the Fund, and demanding reform, see pp. 210–14. He was preceded by Dilke and followed by Forster. The resolution was lost on an amendment moved by the publisher, John Murray, confiding the Fund's economy "to the consideration of the Committee", by 51 votes to 30 (p. 214). The *Literary Gazette*, once a strong supporter of reform, commented that the speeches of the three reformers "certainly did the cause more harm than any adversary could have done": the "vapid jaunty facetiousness" of CD's and Forster's speeches, "which is quite in place in the pages of 'Household Words', is very much out of place in addressing an assemblage of educated gentlemen" (15 Mar).

[3] "The Royal Literary Fund" (8 Mar 56, XIII, 169) was attributed solely to Morley in the Contributors Book, but was revised by CD who added the last two paragraphs himself (*Speeches*, p. 214*n*).

[aa] Written in a block to the right of the flourish of "CD".

[4] Possibly William Parker Snow (1817–95; *DNB*), explorer and writer, with whom CD had corresponded in Sep 47: see Vol. V, p. 159 and *n*.

[5] The Mitre Insurance Office, 23 Pall Mall: see Appx A.

[6] Miss Coutts no doubt needed this information for obtaining for him an East India Co. cadetship.

[7] Astrologically.

[8] No doubt Humphry Sandwith (1822–81; *DNB*), MRCS, Army physician; head of Army medical staff in Armenia 1855; in siege of Kars 1855; published his experiences there 1856.

[9] He was beginning No. VI, Chs 19–22, his chapter outlines for Ch. 20, "Moving in Society", and Ch. 21, "Mr. Merdle's Complaint", anticipating what he described to Forster (see 29–30 Mar) as "the Society business". Despite his "unsettlement", he completed writing the No. by 8 Mar.

wretchedness of such settlement—which is unsettlement. Prowling about the rooms, sitting down, getting up, stirring the fire, looking out of window, tearing my hair, sitting down to write, writing nothing, writing something and tearing it up, going out, coming in, a Monster to my family, a dread Phenomonon to myself, &c &c &c

With love to Mrs. Brown

Ever Dear Miss Coutts | Most Faithfully & affecYours

CD.

To GABRIEL LEGOUVÉ,[1] 20 FEBRUARY 1856*

MS M. Jean Paladilhe.

49 Champs Elysées | Mercredi Fevrier 20, 1856

Mon cher Monsieur

Je vous prie de veuiller bien accepter mes plus sincères et vives remerçiements pour votre aimable petite lettre, et votre noble Tragedie. J'ai lu Medée avec les plus profondes emotions, et je vous felicite d'avance, sur la triomphe qu'elle va achever.[2]

Croyez-moi, cher Monsieur | Votre fidele et obligé

À Monsieur Legouvé CHARLES DICKENS

To MESSRS. BRADBURY & EVANS, 24 FEBRUARY 1856

Text from N, II, 747.

49 Champs Elysées, Paris | Twenty-Fourth February 1856

My Dear B and E

I have only time before the going out of the Post, to acknowledge your note and the accounts,[3] and to say that all your arrangements are most convenient and satisfactory.

But, looking over the balance-sheet of the accounts, there seems to me to be a mistake in it, which will unnecessarily embarrass the present half-year. I take the profits on the 2 first Nos. to extend in this account, only to the last Day of 1855.[4] Then I think you should not charge to my debit in this account, £100 paid on the 1st. of January 1856. Would it not be best to alter the balance and the balance sheet, so as to put that hundred pounds into the half-year to which it belongs?

[1] Gabriel Jean Baptiste Ernest Wilfrid Legouvé (1807–1903), prolific playwright, poet and essayist, whom CD had met at the actor François Régnier's during his 1855–6 visit to Paris. Wrote three plays in collaboration with Eugène Scribe, including *Adrienne Lecouvreur*, 1849, which CD had seen and admired in Paris (F, VII, v, 612); wrote *Médée* 1856, for Mme Rachel, but she finally refused to play in it, leading to Court action; elected to French Academy 1855; many other successful plays 1855–77.

[2] The performance of his *Médée*, translated into Italian, by Adelaide Ristori; played throughout Europe with immense success. See *To* Forster, ?13 Apr 56 and *fn.*

[3] For the half-year ending 31 Jan 1855; the balance paid to CD was £865.9.7 (Bradbury & Evans's Accounts with CD, MS V & A), including the £100 debit below.

[4] The total profits on the first two Nos of *Little Dorrit* (73,000 sold) were £1,187.11.11, of which CD's three-quarter share was £890.13.11. (Bradbury & Evans's Accounts, above.)

If you think so, we can make the alteration in these figures when I come to town next month and bring the accounts with me.

Always Faithfully Yours
[CHARLES DICKENS]

To WILKIE COLLINS, 24 FEBRUARY 1856

MS Morgan Library.

49 Champs Elysées Paris
Sunday Twenty Fourth February 1856

My Dear Collins

The Post still coming in to day without any intelligence from you, I am getting quite uneasy. From day to day I have hoped to hear of your recovery, and have forborne to write, lest I should unintentionally make the time seem longer to you. But I am now so very anxious to know how you are, that I cannot hold my hand any longer. So pray let me know by return. And if you should unhappily be too unwell to write yourself, pray get your brother to represent you.

I cannot tell you how unfortunate I feel this to be, or how disconsolately I look at the uninhabited Pavilion[1]

To HENRY DAWKINS,[2] 24 FEBRUARY 1856

Catalogue mention in N, II, 748; *MS* 1 p.; dated 49 Champs Elysées, Paris, 24 Feb 56: addressed Henry Dawkins.

Regarding repairs at Tavistock House.

To JOHN FORSTER, [24 FEBRUARY 1856]

Extracts in F, VII, v, 620*n* and 611–12. *Date:* first extract 24 Feb, according to Forster; second extract just after 23 Feb (see below).

About the proposed edition by Hachette. It is rather appropriate that the French translation edition will pay my rent for the whole year, and travelling charges to boot.

Lamartine[3] *had expressed a strong desire to meet him again as "un des grands amis de son imagination."* He continues to be precisely as we formerly knew him,[4] both in appearance and manner; highly prepossessing, and with a sort of calm passion about him, very taking indeed. We talked of Defoe and Richardson, and of that wonderful genius for the minutest details in a narrative, which has given them so

[1] Bottom of page cut off; *CD to WC*, p. 46, followed by N, give the ending "Ever Faithfully, | C.D."; but more may be missing.

[2] No "Henry Dawkins" listed as builder; possibly of same firm as Thomas Dawkins, carpenter, 1 Desborough Terrace, Harrow Rd.

[3] Alphonse Marie Louis Prat de Lamartine (1790–1869), poet and Republican: see Vols IV, p. 171 and *nn* and VII, p. 70 and *n*.

[4] When Lamartine was in England in 1848; see also Vol. V, p. 259 and *n*.

much fame in France.[1] I found him frank and unaffected, and full of curious knowledge of the French common people. He informed the company at dinner that he had rarely met a foreigner who spoke French so easily as your inimitable correspondent, whereat your correspondent blushed modestly, and almost immediately afterwards so nearly choked himself with the bone of a fowl (which is still in his throat), that he sat in torture for ten minutes with a strong apprehension that he was going to make the good Pichot[2] famous by dying like the little Hunchback[3] at his table. Scribe and his wife were of the party, but had to go away at the ice-time because it was the first representation at the Opéra Comique of a new opera by Auber and himself, of which very great expectations have been formed.[4] It was very curious to see him—the author of 400 pieces[5]—getting nervous as the time approached, and pulling out his watch every minute. At last he dashed out as if he were going into what a friend of mine calls a plunge-bath. Whereat she rose and followed. She is the most extraordinary woman I ever beheld; for her eldest son must be thirty, and she has the figure of five-and-twenty, and is strikingly handsome. So graceful too, that her manner of rising, curtseying, laughing, and going out after him, was pleasanter than the pleasantest thing I have ever seen done on the stage.

To W. H. WILLS, 24 FEBRUARY 1856

MS Huntington Library.

49 Champs Elysées
Sunday Night Twenty Fourth February 1856 | after Post time

My Dear Wills.

I am perfectly confounded and amazed by receiving no letter from you concurrently with the proofs[6] from B and E. Cannot conceive what on earth is the matter.

The Roving Englishman—Taboo. It has all been done before, and better done. There is not the least pretence or excuse for thus doing it again.[7]

I have made an addition to the Royal Literary Fund[8]—but it is generally loose, and wants screwing up. Be tremendously particular as to all the facts. And try and make every sentence as plain as Cobbett.[9]

[1] Many translations of Richardson and *Robinson Crusoe* appeared in the 18th and early 19th centuries.

[2] Amédée Pichot (1795–1877), translator and editor of the *Revue Britannique* (which had a glowing review of No. III of *Little Dorrit* in its February issue): see Vol. VII, pp. 337*n* and 904*n*.

[3] In *The Arabian Nights*, transl. Jonathan Scott, 1811, II, 205, the little hunchback, one of the Sultan's buffoons, dies at the tailor's table, from choking on a fish-bone.

[4] *Manon Lescaut* opened on 23 Feb.

[5] Exaggerated, but his comedies were very numerous.

[6] Of *HW*, No. 311, published 8 Mar.

[7] E. C. Grenville Murray's latest article in his series was "The Sulina Mouth of the Danube" on 9 Feb (XIII, 73); no other appeared until "Messina", 15 Mar (XIII, 214). In the interval he had been to Constantinople.

[8] See *To* Wills, 17 Feb (2nd letter) and *fn.* The article shows many signs of CD's hand, with quotations from what was said at the meeting in 1855, and clearly he added the final paragraph which disclaimed anonymity.

[9] William Cobbett's *Rural Rides*, 1830, was in CD's library at his death.

Many other marks I have made in the other articles.

Ever Faithfully
CD.

Let me see a Revise of the Fund article, before the No. is worked.

To FERDINAND BEAUCOURT-MUTUEL, [FEBRUARY 1856]

Mention in *To* Beard, 21 June 56. *Date:* Feb 56, according to CD.

About their visit to the villa in June.

To GABRIEL LEGOUVÉ, 2 MARCH 1856*

MS M. Jean Paladilhe.

49 Champs Elysées | Dimanche Mars 2, 1856

Mon cher Monsieur

Je vous assure que j'ai ete desolé à cause de n'avoir pu assister a votre reception par l'Institute, Jeudi passé. Mais, en sortant de la porte de mon appartement, je reçus, par la poste, une lettre d'Angleterre contenant des "Proof-Sheets" qu'il me fallut corriger et retourner, absolument le meme jour. Ils m'occuperent jusqu'a la derniere moment; et le billet que vous avez-eu la bonté de m'envoyer, reste toujours sur ma table.

Permettez-moi de vous feliciter, avec la cordialité la plus sincère, sur votre si brillante reception. J'en ai lu dans les journaux avec le plus grand plaisir, et on me dit que votre addresse a charmée tout le monde et a ete accablée des louanges.

Votre tout devoué
CHARLES DICKENS

To W. H. WILLS, 2 MARCH 1856

MS Huntington Library.

49 Champs Elysées, Paris | Sunday March Second 1856

My Dear Wills. I have been so occupied with Little Dorrit, that I could not return you the Revise of No. 311,[1] in time for it to be of any use. I am sorry to see the Cold Water cure classed in Morley's article among the humbugs of the time.[2] Firstly, because I believe that in reason there is a good deal in it. Secondly, because you were at one of the great Malvern Doctors'[3] and my wife was at another's.[4] Perhaps this may have occurred to you and you may have taken it out.[5]

[1] Published 8 Mar 56.

[2] "One Cure More", *HW*, XIII, 191, deriding Dr Mathias Roth's *Handbook of the Movement-Cure* (published early Feb), particularly the "Positions, Movements, and Manipulation" of the title page, denounced as the "last extravagance of quackery".

[3] In 1854: see Vol. VII, pp. 309–10 and *nn.* Dr James Manby Gully's hydropathic establishment, set up in 1842.

[4] Dr James Wilson's (*d.* 1867), also set up in 1842; the two doctors had a brief partnership before practising on their own. For CD's "faith in Hydropathy" and the origins of the treatment, see Vol. IV, p. 28 and *n.* For Catherine Dickens's water-cure, 13 Mar–15 April 51, see Vol. VI, pp. 313*ff.*

[5] No explicit mention of the water-cure remains, but Wills had clearly modified the reference, at the end, where "mud-cures" are

The Gad's Hill purchase seems to me to be a sort of amateur Chancery Suit which will never be settled.

Will you tell John that Walter is coming home on Tuesday, and that I shall be glad if he will meet him at the London Bridge station on Tuesday night at 10.

If Johnson[1] has not yet acquitted himself of that selection-job,[2] the parcel (tell Bradbury and Evans) must come at once without it. The french booksellers are impatient for it, and worry me like sharp Dogs. Pray tell B and E to get it dispatched at once.

[a]You will see many yet stranger demonstrations in Stratton Street, of that same kind. She would do anything, conceivable or inconceivable, to make herself interesting to Miss Coutts, by keeping herself forcibly in Miss Coutts's attention. You must always be prepared for any eccentric turn that such a propensity may take, and must never shew (because that would pain Miss Coutts) that you wonder at it. Mrs. Brown has many excellent qualities; but, partly from her original character and partly from a long and strange disorder, has got to a morbid exaggeration of this propensity which nothing will ever subdue now. To be perfectly self possessed with her, quietly firm, calmly sensible, and thoroughly easy and natural, is to find the best way out of it.[a3]

Ever Faithfully
CD.

P.S. Your letter received, since I wrote the foregoing.

You remember my telling you sometime ago, that I greatly mistrusted Augustus's[4] affairs.

To the Gentleman who wants to play the Lighthouse,[5] please say that I am in Paris—that I have referred his request to Mr. Collins the Author of the piece—and that Mr. Collins, with every disposition to oblige him, would desire to keep the MS in his desk where it now lies.

[b]Polish Priest sends his benediction.[b]

To JOHN FORSTER, [?2 MARCH 1856]

Extracts in F, VII, v, 612 and 619, and XI, iii, 839. *Date:* first extract "a week later" than 23 Feb, according to Forster; second extract when "March had come"; third extract probably same letter.

He writes of Auber's opera as most charming. Delightful music, an excellent story, immense stage tact, capital scenic arrangements, and the most delightful little

derided (p. 192). CD himself had laughed at the water-cure in *Mr. Nightingale's Diary*.

[1] One of the *HW* Office staff for many years: see Vols IV to VII.

[2] See *To* Wills, 17 Feb.

[aa] Omitted in *CD as Editor* and N.

[3] For CD's adopting some of Mrs Brown's traits for Rosa Dartle in *Copperfield*, see Vols IV, p. 630 and *n* and VI, p. 28 and *n*.

[4] Name omitted in *CD as Editor*. CD's brother; he had married Harriet Lovell in 1848.

[5] Untraced; but unlikely to be Col. Waugh, who is named at 9 May 56. For Forgues's apparent wish to produce it, see *To* Collins, 13 Apr (postscript).

[bb] Omitted in *CD as Editor* and N. Perhaps a nickname for Collins.

prima donna ever seen or heard, in the person of Marie Cabel.[1] It is called *Manon Lescaut*—from the old romance[2]—and is charming throughout. She sings a laughing song in it which is received with madness, and which is the only real laughing song that ever was written. Auber told me that when it was first rehearsed, it made a great effect upon the orchestra; and that he could not have had a better compliment upon its freshness than the musical director paid him, in coming and clapping him on the shoulder with "Bravo, jeune homme! Cela promet bien!"[3]

Scheffer finished yesterday; and Collins, who has a good eye for pictures, says that there is no man living who could do the painting about the eyes. As a work of art I see in it spirit combined with perfect ease, and yet I don't see myself. And so I come to the conclusion that I never *do* see myself. I shall be very curious to know the effect of it upon you.

Lady Franklin[4] sent me the whole of that Richardson[5] memoir;[6] and I think Richardson's manly friendship, and love of Franklin, one of the noblest things I ever knew in my life.[7] It makes one's heart beat high, with a sort of sacred joy.

To MESSRS BRADBURY & EVANS, 3 MARCH 1856*

MS Free Library of Philadelphia.

49 Champs Elysées, Paris | Monday Third March 1856

My Dear B and E.[8]

If you will send up to Tavistock House on Wednesday Morning, your Messenger

[1] Née Marie Josephe Dreulette (1827–85), opera singer, married to, but separated from, Georges Cabu (known as Cabel), Professor of Singing; made her reputation in Brussels 1850; then great success at the Théâtre-Lyrique and the Opéra-Comique; created the heroine's part in *Manon Lescaut* and many other operas.

[2] The Abbé Prévost's novel, 1731.

[3] He was in his seventies.

[4] Widow of Sir John Franklin, Arctic explorer; née Jane Griffin: see Vol. VII, pp. 455*nn* and 473*n*.

[5] Sir John Richardson (1787–1865; *DNB*), FRS, Arctic explorer, surgeon and naturalist; MD 1817; physician (then Inspector) to the Royal Naval Hospital, Haslar, from 1838; accompanied Franklin on his polar expedition 1819 and his second expedition to the Mackenzie river 1825; Inspector of Hospitals 1840; knighted 1846; conducted two search expeditions for Franklin 1847 and 1849; awarded the Royal Geographical Society medal 1856. He married, as his second wife, Franklin's niece, Mary Booth; and as his third wife, Mary Fletcher, sister of CD's friend, the sculptor Angus Fletcher.

[6] Richardson's biographical account of Franklin first appeared in the 8th edn of the *Encyclopaedia Britannica*, Vol. X, published late Feb. Lady Franklin no doubt had an advance copy; Forster had evidently seen an extract in a review. Although called the "little memoir" in John MacIlraith's *Life of Richardson*, 1868, p. 251, it is over 9 cols long; from it Lady Franklin took the words for Franklin's statue: "they forged the last link of the North West Passage with their lives".

[7] Richardson praises, as one who served long under his command, Franklin's "calmness and unaffected piety" in "times of great difficulty and distress". Any appearance of "eulogy" in the Memoir comes from "a firm conviction of the truth of the statements he has made". Franklin, he ends, had no vindictive feeling: "while he defended his own honour, he would have delighted in showing any kindness in his power to his bitterest foe; and in emulation of that spirit the preceding pages have been penned".

[8] An unsuccessful attempt has been made to obliterate "B and E".

will find the greater part of No. 6 of Little Dorrit,[1] under cover for you. I will bring the last Chapter with me when I come—which I purpose doing, this day week. Walter is my avant-courier tomorrow.

Faithfully Yours always
CHARLES DICKENS

To WILKIE COLLINS, 3 MARCH 1856

MS Morgan Library.

Paris, Third March 1856.

The Humble Petition
of
Charles Dickens

A Distressed Foreigner

Sheweth

That your Petitioner has not been able to write one word to day, or to fashion forth the dimmest shade of the faintest Ghost of an idea.

That your Petitioner is therefore desirous of being taken out, and is not at all particular where.

That your Petitioner, being imbecile, says no more, But Will Ever &c—(whatever that may be).

To CLARKSON STANFIELD, 3 MARCH 1856*

MS National Maritime Museum.

49 Avenue des Champs Elysées, Paris
Monday Third March 1856

My Dear Stanny.

I am coming to town on the evening of this day week, and write beforehand (as we arranged), to let you know on what evening I shall be at liberty to dine somewhere with you and to see a Play.

Will you choose between Thursday the 13th. Friday the 14th. and Saturday the 15th. To meet, either day, at the Household Words Office at 5? Will you write me one line when you have chosen, *here*, that I may map out my time and engagements accordingly?

And will you let me know at the same time, whether you can come down to Gravesend and dine with me at Wate's Hotel on Sunday the 16th. Forster, and my boy Charley, and (I hope) Mark, are going down. We shall be very quiet and there will be no one else.

[1] Chs 19–22, published 30 Apr; Ch. 22, "A Puzzle", is the shortest, but needed delicate treatment as including the first hint of Amy's love for Clennam.

Catherine and Georgina send their loves to Mrs. Stanfield,[1] Mrs. George,[2] and all your house. I hope I may add mine.

To CHARLES KNIGHT,[3] 6 MARCH 1856

Extract in Alice M. Clowes, *Charles Knight, A Sketch by His Grand-daughter*, 1892, p. 134.

49, Champs Elysées, Paris. | Thursday, Sixth March, 1856.

My dear Knight,

Of *course* I shall be with you on Saturday.[4] Please God, at six o'clock, with his usual punctuality and his invariably pleasant face, the remarkable man will appear.[5]

My ladies will be here and must drink your health here; but they send all sorts of regards and kindest wishes to all your house, in which I cordially join.[6]

To CLARKSON STANFIELD, 6 MARCH 1856

MS Dickens House.

49 Champs Elysées, Paris | Thursday Sixth March 1856

My Dear Stanny.

Your note received with joy this morning. Let us say then, *Thursday*, Household Words, 5. Pray get yourself in to condition for Palm Sunday. The Railroad carriages are warm, and the ride short.

O think of Covent Garden being burnt down,[7] and you and I not there!

Ever affectionately
CHARLES DICKENS

Kindest loves from all to Mrs. Stanfield and all your house. I hear that you have painted the most wonderful picture ever seen.[8]

[1] Née Rebecca Adcock (1808–75), Stanfield's second wife: see Vol. IV, p. 116*n*.

[2] His daughter-in-law, wife of his second son by his second marriage, George Clarkson Stanfield, painter, pupil of his father, and exhibitor at RA and British Institution 1844–76. See Vol. VII, p. 464*n*.

[3] Charles Knight, author and publisher: see Vol. II, p. 231*n* and later vols.

[4] i.e. Saturday week, 15 Mar, Knight's 65th birthday: for CD and Catherine's regularly celebrating his birthday with him, see Vol. VI, p. 624 and *n*.

[5] The Knights lived at 8 Carlton Villas, Maida Hill.

[6] Text ends here.

[7] The theatre, sub-let to J. H. Anderson, conjurer, "The Wizard of the North", had been burnt down the previous night; the fire broke out in the carpenter's shop, between ceiling and roof, just before 5 a.m.; a Grand Carnival Gala and *bal masque* were just ending. For CD's description of the ruins to Macready, see 22 Mar.

[8] *The Abandoned*, a shipwreck, inspired by Washington Irving's story, "The Voyage" (*The Sketch Book of Geoffrey Crayon*, 1820, p. 9); one of two pictures he exhibited at RA this year. Illustrated in Pieter van der Merwe and Roger Took, *Clarkson Stanfield 1793–1867*, Tyne & Wear, 1979, p. 167. James Dafforne doubted whether "anyone ... could ever forget the appalling scene represented" (*Pictures by Stanfield*, 1873, p. 20); the *Art-Journal*, 1856 classed it as "among the most valuable works of one of the greatest artists of our age and country" (p. 164). Bought by Thomas Baring (see *To* Georgina Hogarth, 8 Feb 56, *fn*).

To W. H. WILLS, 6 MARCH 1856

MS Huntington Library.

49 Champs Elysées, Paris | Thursday March Sixth 1856

My Dear Wills.

C.G.T.[1]

I am deeply grieved that such a Fire should have come off in my absence. Am inconsolable.

I[2]

think I shall come to town in the night of Sunday; being so abominably used up as to the Calais Railway, that I feel desirous to be relieved from the contemplation of that enterprise by daylight. After brightening myself up in my usual beaming manner I will come down to the office; and—as I shall be dining out every day that week—if we dine together in peace at the Office *that* day (meaning Monday) it will perhaps be the usefullest thing we can do. Come and dine with me at Gravesend on the following Sunday. Forster and Charley are coming down to take a respectful look at the outside of the Giant Property.

MARK[2]

I understand, is helping the country to that noble representative, Mr. Herbert Ingram.[3] In case he should return before I come, will you tell him of the change in my arrangements (he supposes me to be due at London Bridge on Monday Night, which was my original intention), and that I am his, at Household Words at 8 on Monday Evening.

JOHN[2]

perhaps will come to the Station to receive me, at about 8 on Monday Morning. I purpose being there, unless it should blow Great Guns.

GAD'S HILL[2]

I suppose stands where it did?[4]

LITTLE DORRIT[2]

has completed her sixth; and that wonderful man the writer thereof is in that state of weary excitement which is a part of him at such periods.

Will you tear off, put in an envelope, address to my boot-makers Hall & Co.[5] Quadrant Regent Street, & send at once by John (he knows the place), t'other side.

Ever Faithfully

CD.

[1] Covent Garden Theatre. Underlined with short double strokes.

[2] Underlined with short double strokes..

[3] Herbert Ingram, co-founder of the *Illustrated London News*: see Vol. VII, p. 259*n*. Lemon, a close friend, was canvassing for him in Boston, Lincs, where he was elected Liberal MP on 7 Mar.

[4] Cf. *Macbeth*, IV, iii, 164: "Stands Scotland where it did?"

[5] Richard Hall: see Vol. VI, p. 655*n*.

To MISS GEORGINA HOGARTH, 11 MARCH 1856

MS Dickens House.

H.W. Office | Tuesday Eleventh March 1856

My Dear Georgy

[a]Madame de Bourgon[1] overlooks a point, which I think you may have overlooked too. She credits herself with the money to be paid by the Daughter Family,[2] but she does not remember that if the family do not suit us, we shall leave when our time is up in April. Therefore I will give her for the one month 300 francs, and not a farthing more if she won't take that.[a]

I have been in bed half the day with my cold: which is excessively violent. Consequently have to write in a great hurry, to save the Post.

Tell Catherine that I have the most prodigious, overwhelming, crushing, astounding, blinding, deafening, pulverizing, scarifying secret of which Forster is the hero, imaginable by the united efforts of the whole British population.[3] It is a thing of that kind, that after I knew it (from himself) this morning, I lay down flat, as if an Engine and Tender had fallen upon me.

Love to Catherine (not a word of Forster before any one else), and to Mamey, Katey, Harry, and the Noble Plorn. Tell Collins with my kind regard that Forster has just pronounced to me that "Collins is a decidedly clever fellow." I hope he is a better fellow in health, too.

Ever affectionately
CD.

To MISS GEORGINA HOGARTH, 14 MARCH 1856

MS Dickens House.

Household Words | Friday Fourteenth March 1856

My Dear Georgy.

[b]You did "quite right"[4] in rejecting that horrible old woman's conditions, and in closing the bargain upon absolute terms.[b] I am amazed to hear of the Snow (I don't know why, but it excited John this morning beyond measure); though we have had the same East wind here, and *the* cold and *my* cold have both been intense.

Yesterday evening, Webster, Mark, Stanny, and I, went to the Olympic, where the Wigans[5] ranged us in a row in a gorgeous and immense Private box, and where we saw Still Waters run deep.[6] I laughed (in a conspicuous corner) to that extent at

[aa] Omitted in MDGH.

[1] Presumably the owner of their apartment in 49 Champs Elysées.

[2] Unidentified.

[3] Forster's intended marriage: see *To* Mrs CD, 9 May and *fn* and *To* Hudson, 10 Oct and *fn*.

[bb] Omitted in MDGH.

[4] A favourite phrase of Forster's.

[5] Alfred Sydney Wigan (1814–78; *DNB*), actor, manager of the Olympic since Oct 53, and his wife Leonora, née Pincott (1805–84; *DNB*), actress, originally rope-dancer and performer on stilts; by now personal friends of CD, they had visited the Dickenses in France.

[6] By Tom Taylor, first performed at the Olympic 14 May 55; both Wigan, as the first John Mildmay, and his wife, as Mrs Hector Sternhold, were conspicuous successes in it.

Emery[1] when he received the dinner-company,[2] that the people were more amused by me than by the Piece. I don't think I ever saw anything meant to be funny, that struck me as so extraordinarily droll. I couldn't get over it at all. After the piece we went round, by Wigan's invitation, to drink with him. It being positively impossible to get Stanny off the stage, we stood in the Wing during the burlesque.[3] Mrs. Wigan [a]was great—amazing—in her Court-Circular conversation.[a] Seemed really glad, however, to see her old Manager;[4] and the company overwhelmed him with embraces. They had nearly all been at the Meeting in the morning.[5]

I have seen Charley only twice since I came to London, having regularly been in bed until mid-day. To my amazement my eye fell upon him at the Adelphi yesterday.[6]

This day I have paid the purchase money for Gad's Hill Place. After drawing the cheque, I turned round to give it to Wills (£1790), and said: "Now isn't it an extraordinary thing—Look at the Day—Friday![7] I have been nearly drawing it half a dozen times when the lawyers have not been ready, and here it comes round upon a Friday as a matter of course."

Kiss the noble Plorn a dozen times for me, and tell him I drank his health yesterday and wished him many happy returns of the day.[8] Also that I hope he will not have broken all his toys before I come back.

Ever affectionately

CD.

[a]This is the day of the Evans banquet—and I wish it was not, with all my heart.[a]

To MISS MARY BOYLE, 15 MARCH 1856*

MS Morgan Library.

OFFICE OF HOUSEHOLD WORDS,
Saturday Fifteenth March 1856

My Dear Mary

—A short reply, but better than none.

I cannot at present subscribe to the Hospital[9] because of other heavy claims. A

[1] Samuel Anderson Emery (1817–81; *DNB*); made his reputation in adaptations of CD as Jonas Chuzzlewit, Will Fern and Peerybingle; he later added Daniel Peggotty and Capt. Cuttle. He played Mr Potter, Mrs Mildmay's father.

[2] At the end of Act III. He has no conversation and simply repeats the first two guests' contradictory remarks about the weather with equal conviction.

[3] Planché's *The Discreet Princess; or, The Three Glass Distaffs*; it had been running since 26 Dec 55.

[aa] Omitted in MDGH.

[4] Mrs Wigan had been one of the professional actresses who performed with CD's Amateurs in July 47: see Vol. v, p. 126 and *n*.

[5] A meeting of actors and actresses at the Adelphi, chaired by CD, to prepare a memorial to the Charity Commissioners requesting the admission as foundation scholars of the children of actors and actresses to Dulwich College: for CD's speech, see *To* Howes, 19 Mar and *fn*; and, for the petition, *To* Lord Lyttelton, 9 June and *fn*, and *To* Webster, 15 June, *fn*.

[6] The programme was J. M. Morton's farce, *Betsy Baker*, followed by F. Moore's *That Blessed Baby*, both played by the Keeleys.

[7] CD's lucky day.

[8] His fourth birthday.

[9] Untraced.

promise to a dead sister[1] has been put before me this morning in an urgent form that I cannot resist. And it takes precedence of twenty public subscriptions at a blow.

However, I will not forget it.

I have a cold so unspeakably vile and oppressive, that I have been lying in bed half the day since I came to town, to get myself up for the other half. All night I snort and wheeze to that extent that, waking suddenly, I don't know which is the Inimitable Writer, and which the Engine that is always out of temper at the Nor' Western Station over the way.[2] A very large Mill, with a stupid old Brute of a horse in it, is always at work, making what appears to me to be either a cannon ball or a dutch cheese, in the centre of my head. Likewise, I weep continually in the most imbecile manner. Then it is my dear that I wish you were with me, occupying Tavistock House and forgetting mankind.

I have promised to go to the Theatrical Fund Dinner on Monday,[3] and am only waiting to get that over before returning to Paris. I think we shall be in town during the greater part of May, before we go to our queer little country place near Boulogne. Then I really shall hope to see you my Pet, and go to the Theatre with you, and have a good long talk.

My love to Bedgey and pardner.[4] And when you write to Mrs. Watson pray tell her that I wish she knew how much I think of her, and what a constant interest she is to me.

Ever My Dear Mary | Your loving

Joe.

To HERBERT FRY,[5] 15 MARCH 1856

MS National Portrait Gallery.

Tavistock House | Saturday Fifteenth March 1856

Dr. Sir.

I regret that you should have been at the trouble of seeking me in vain, owing to my being quite unacquainted with the nature of your business—to my being in town from Paris for a very few days—and to my having, in addition to many engagements, a cold so severe that it has been necessary for me, since my arrival, to keep my bed half the day, to prepare for the other half.

Nor can I have the pleasure of complying with your request.[6] I have but just now

[1] Fanny Burnett, who had died on 2 Sep 48: see *To* Burnett, 17 Mar.

[2] The London and North Western terminus at Euston Square.

[3] See *To* Jerrold, 6 Feb.

[4] Her brother, Capt. Cavendish Spencer Boyle ("Benjamin"), and his wife: see 8 Jan 56.

[5] Herbert Fry (1830–85), writer of guidebooks and other reference works, including *The Shilling Guide to the London Charities*, 1864–6; also a photographic publisher, at 8 York Place, City Rd. Secretary, Pall Mall Club 1872–7.

[6] For the series of *Photographic Portraits of Living Celebrities*, published in five-shilling monthly Nos from May 1856; photographs "executed by Maull and Polyblank" (presumably supervised by Fry) at their studio, 55 Gracechurch St, with biographical notices by Fry in first four Nos (Richard Owen, Macaulay, Robert Stephenson, J. A. Roebuck); after Aug 1856 the notices were by Edward Walford who continued the same series with 36 more Nos until Aug 1859 (see *To* Walford, 4 Oct 56 and *fnn*). At some later date, Fry also began another series, *The National Gallery of Photographic Portraits*, which ceased after 16 Nos, but was collected in 1858. CD appeared in neither. See *To* Fry, 4 Dec and *fn*; and *To* Watkins, 4 Nov 57 and *fn*.

finished sitting to a distinguished French painter, and have thoroughly made up my mind to sit no more.

Your faithful Servant

Herbert Fry Esquire. CHARLES DICKENS

To SIR EDWIN LANDSEER, 15 MARCH 1856*

MS Exeter University Library.

OFFICE OF HOUSEHOLD WORDS,
Saturday Fifteenth March 1856

My Dear Landseer

Will you meet me here (observe the address—opposite Vestris's Theatre[1] that once was), not later than halfpast 5 on Monday afternoon. I hope Stanny will go with us.

And bring the ticket in your pocket that I now enclose you.[2]

[a]"Shall we have Paxton?[3] Or will he bore us? Is there anybody I shall ask? Well then, we'll have Paxton. And he shall tell us how he hires his men."[a]

Ever Faithfully
CHARLES DICKENS

To HENRY BURNETT,[4] 17 MARCH 1856*

MS Robert H. Taylor Collection, Princeton University.

Tavistock House | Monday Seventeenth March 1856

My Dear Burnett.

I have read your account of your domestic sufferings, with great sympathy.

You will receive a letter by tomorrow's post, telling you at what bank at Manchester you will find remitted to you from Coutts's Bank in London, One Hundred and Five pounds.[5] That is to say, the one hundred you ask me for, and five as a little present to Charley[6] from his uncle and godfather.

I will not refuse the pictures, as you wish me to take them. But I will and do refuse the Engravings, because I hope the possession of them will be a pleasure to you. Pray keep them therefore.

I write a short note, being overwhelmed with business before going back to Paris.

[1] The Lyceum, in Wellington St, Strand; Mme Vestris (1797–1856) was a very successful manager, with her husband, 1847–55; her own last appearance was 26 July 54.

[2] Theatre not discovered.

[3] Sir Joseph Paxton (1801–65; *DNB*), gardener and architect; designer of the Crystal Palace; knighted 1851: see Vol. IV, p. 411*n*.

[aa] Probably a parody of one of Forster's pronouncements.

[4] Henry Burnett (1811–93), singer and music teacher; CD's brother-in-law: see Vol. 1, p. 342*n* and later vols.

[5] CD's Account-book (MS Messrs Coutts) shows £105 paid to Burnett on 19 Mar, remitted to Sir Benjamin Heywood, Bart, & Co, St Ann St, Manchester, by Masterman, Peters & Co., 35 Nicholas Lane, Lombard St.

[6] Charles Dickens Kneller Burnett, Burnett's second son, *b.* 12 Apr 41.

But I trust that your sister will recover,[1] and that the shadow of this great distress will soon pass away from your fireside.

With love to the boy, Believe me | Ever Faithfully

Henry Burnett Esquire CHARLES DICKENS

To THE REV. JOSEPH HINDLE, 17 MARCH 1856*

MS W. A. Foyle.

Tavistock House, London | Seventeenth March 1856.

Dear Sir

As I have now completed the purchase of Gad's Hill place, I beg to notify the fact to you, and to ask the favor of your paying the rent in future as it becomes due, to W. H. Wills Esquire Household Words Office 16 Wellington Street North, Strand.

I have the honor to be | Your faithful Servant

The Reverend Joseph Hindle. CHARLES DICKENS

To THE REV. CHARLES HOWES,[2] 19 MARCH 1856

Extract from owner's MS; dated Paris, Wednesday 19 Mar 56; addressed the Rev. Charles Howes.

Thanking him for his letter and explaining that he did not suppose all the inhabitants of Dulwich College to have the name of the founder.[3]

To W. C. MACREADY, 22 MARCH 1856

MS Yale University Library.

49 Champs Elysées, Paris
Saturday March Twenty Second, 1856

My Dear Macready

I want you—you being quite well again,[4] as I trust you are, and resolute to come to Paris—so to arrange your order of March as to let me know beforehand when you will come and how long you will stay. We owe Scribe and his wife a dinner, and I should like to pay the debt when you are with us. Ary Scheffer too, would be delighted to see you again. If I could arrange for a certain day, I would secure them. We cannot afford (you and I, I mean) to keep much company, because we shall want to look in at a Theatre or so, I dare say!—

It would suit my work best, if I could keep myself clear until Monday the 7th. of

[1] His sister kept house for him and had been seriously ill since 1849: see Vol. VI, p. 252 and *n.* Burnett obviously needed money for nursing and medical expenses.

[2] The Rev. Charles Howes, scholar, Trinity Hall, Cambridge, 1831; Fellow, Clare College 1835; MA 1838; Fellow and Chaplain, Dulwich College, 1842–58.

[3] Howes had obviously written about CD's speech at the Adelphi: see *To* Georgina Hogarth, 14 Mar and *fn.* He had referred to "some musty old men, in black gowns, all bearing the name of Alleyn" (Edward Alleyn, actor and founder of Dulwich College, 1613): *Speeches*, ed. K. J. Fielding, p. 215.

[4] See *To* Jerrold, 6 Feb.

April.[1] But in case that day should be too late for the beginning of your brief visit, with a reference to any other engagements you have in contemplation, then fix an earlier one, and I will make Little Dorrit curtsey to it. My recent visit to London and my having only just now come back, have thrown me a little behind-hand; but I hope to come up with a wet sail in a few days.

You should have seen the ruins of Covent Garden Theatre![2]—I went in, the moment I got to London—four days after the fire. Although the audience part, and the stage, were so tremendously burnt out that there was not a piece of wood half the size of a Lucifer Match, for the eye to rest on—though nothing whatever remained but bricks and smelted iron, lying on a great black desert—the Theatre still looked so wonderfully like its old self grown Gigantic, that I never saw so strange a sight. The wall dividing the Front from the stage still remained, and the iron pass-doors stood ajar, in an impossible and inaccessible frame. The arches that supported the stage were there, and the arches that supported the pit; and on the centre of the latter, lay something like a Titanic grape-vine that a hurricane had pulled up by the roots, twisted, and flung down there. This was the great chandelier. Gye[3] had kept the men's wardrobe at the top of the house, over the great entrance staircase. When the roof fell in, it came down bodily, and all that part of the ruin was like an old babylonic pavement—bright rags tesselating the black ground—sometimes in pieces so large that I could make out the dresses in the Trovatore.

I should run on for a couple of hours if I were to describe the spectacle as I saw it. Wherefore I will immediately muzzle myself. All here unite in kindest loves to dear Miss Macready,[4] to Katie,[5] Lillie,[6] Benvenuta,[7] my Godson,[8] and the noble Johnny.[9] We are charmed to hear such happy accounts of Willie[10] and Ned,[11] and send our loving remembrances to them in the next letters.

All Parisian Novelties you shall see and hear for yourself.

Ever My Dearest Macready | Your Affectionate friend

CHARLES DICKENS

Mr. F's Aunt sends her defiant respects.[12]

[1] See *To* Forster, 7 Apr.

[2] See *To* Stanfield, 6 Mar and *fn.*

[3] Frederick Gye, the younger, lessee and director of the Royal Italian Opera, Covent Garden, since Sep 1849; then, after its destruction by fire on 5 Mar 56, at the Lyceum: see Vol. VI, p. 364*n.*

[4] Macready's sister, Letitia Margaret (1794–1858), who lived with him.

[5] Catherine Frances Birch Macready (1834–69), Macready's second daughter.

[6] Lydia Jane (1843–58), Macready's fourth daughter.

[7] Cecilia Benvenuta, Macready's youngest daughter (*b.* 1847).

[8] Henry Frederick Bulwer Macready (1838–57).

[9] Jonathan Forster Christian Macready (*b.* 1850); became a surgeon.

[10] William Charles Macready (1832–71), Macready's eldest son; in Ceylon Civil Service since 1854: see Vols VI, p. 794 and *n*, and VII, p. 387 and *n.*

[11] Edward Nevil Bourne Macready (*b.* 1836), Macready's second son. Cadet at the East India Company's military academy, Addiscombe, 1853–4; then served in India (see *To* Macready, 10 July 57), where he became heavily in debt through gambling. He then went to Australia and became an actor, making his début at the Theatre Royal, Ballarat, Victoria, as Claude Melnotte in Bulwer Lytton's *The Lady of Lyons* (*Theatrical Journal*, XX, 1859, 399, quoting Bell's *Life in Victoria*).

[12] She had first appeared in Ch. 13 (No. IV, for Mar, published 29 Feb).

To JOHN FORSTER, [23 MARCH 1856]

Extracts in F, VII, v, 615 and 608; *Date:* first extract 23 Mar, according to Forster; second extract probably from same letter.

Emile Girardin was here yesterday, and he says that Peace is to be formally announced at Paris to-morrow amid general apathy.[1]

I was at the Porte St. Martin last night, where there is a rather good melodrama called *Sang Melé*,[2] in which one of the characters is an English Lord—Lord William Falkland[3]—who is called throughout the piece Milor Williams Fack Lorn, and is a hundred times described by others and described by himself as Williams. He is admirably played; but two English travelling ladies are beyond expression ridiculous, and there is something positively vicious in their utter want of truth. One "set," where the action of a whole act is supposed to take place in the great wooden verandah of a Swiss hotel overhanging a mountain ravine, is the best piece of stage carpentering I have seen in France. Next week we are to have at the Ambigu *Paradise Lost*, with the murder of Abel, and the Deluge. The wildest rumours are afloat as to the un-dressing of our first parents.[4]

To FRANK STONE, 23 MARCH 1856*

MS Benoliel Collection.

49 Champs Elysées, Paris
Sunday Twenty Third March, 1856

My Dear Stone.

A short note, because I have many to write, and proofs to overlook.

It seems to me that the best name for your charming picture, is,

The re-considered choice[5]

It helps at once to the story, and is unaffected and plain.

All here unite in kindest regard and remembrance to all Russell House.

Ever affectionately

Frank Stone Esquire CHARLES DICKENS

[1] The Treaty of Paris was not signed until 30 Mar. The war had "never in the least been popular" in France, says Forster (F, VII, v, 615). For CD's own disgust with the British Govt's handling of it, see Vol. VII, pp. 492–3 and *nn*; see also his satirical sketch, "Opinion", signed "J. Buzfuz" and dated 8 Jan 59, referring to portraits of the "Crimea Family" (G. Storey, "An Unpublished Satirical Sketch by Dickens", *D*, LXXIV [1978], 6).

[2] By M. E. Plouvier, reviewed by *Galignani* on 23 Mar as "A stirring drama." Maxime, the principal character, a quadroon, played by Charles Fechter (see later vols), is an appallingly treated slave, who wreaks a terrible vengeance on his master and finally, after a wretched but affluent life, in France, poisons himself. It had a warm reception, but was much too long. This was probably the first time CD had seen Fechter, whose acting was particularly praised.

[3] Maxime believes he has killed him and assumes his title; in fact, he has not and Falkland joins in pursuing him.

[4] See *To* Forster, 29–30 Mar and *fn*.

[5] Stone's only exhibit at RA—in fact entitled *Doubt*. "*Unheeded vows may heedfully be broken.*" (Proteus in *The Two Gentlemen of Verona*, II, vi, 11.)

To W. C. MACREADY, 27 MARCH 1856

MS Morgan Library.

49 Avenue des Champs Elysées, Paris
Thursday Night Twenty Seventh March | 1856 | (After Post time)

My Dearest Macready.

If I had had any idea of your coming (see how naturally I use the word when I am 300 miles off!) to London so soon, I would never have written one word about the jump over next week. I am vexed that I did so; but as I did, I will not now propose a change in the arrangements, as I know how methodical you tremendously old fellows are. That's your secret, I suspect. That's the way in which the blood of the Mirabels[1] mounts in your aged veins, even at your time of life.

How charmed I shall be to see you, and we all shall be, I will not attempt to say. On that expected Sunday you will lunch at Amiens, but not dine—because we shall wait dinner for you. And you will merely have to tell that driver in the glazed hat, to come straight here. When the Whites[2] left, I added their little apartment to this little apartment. Consequently, you shall have a snug bedroom (is it not waiting expressly for you?) overlooking the Champs Elysées. As to the arm chair in my heart, no man on Earth—but Good God you know all about it.

You will find us in the queerest of little rooms, all alone: except that the son of Collins the painter (who writes a good deal in Household Words), dines with us every day. Scheffer and Scribe shall be admitted for one evening, because they know how to appreciate you. The Emperor we will not ask unless you expressly wish it. It makes a fuss.

If you have no appointed hotel at Boulogne, go to the Hotel des Bains. There, demand "Marguerite", and tell her that I commended you to her especial care. It is the best house, within my experience, in France—Marguerite the best housekeeper in the world.

I shall charge at Little Dorrit tomorrow, with new spirits.[3] The sight of you is good for my boyish eyes, and the thought of you for my dawning mind. Give the enclosed loves a welcome, then send them on to Sherborne.

Ever Yours most affectionately and truly
CD.

To BENJAMIN WEBSTER, 27 MARCH 1856*

MS Brigham Young University.

49 Champs Elysées | Thursday Night
Twenty Seventh March 1856

My Dear Webster.

I am not at all surprised to find you in Paris today—because you said you were going away![4] Having administered this stab to your vital citadel, let me answer your note.

[1] No doubt Mirabel, the "wild goose" in Fletcher's *Wild Goose Chase*.

[2] The Rev. and Mrs James White.

[3] At No. VII: see 22 Mar and *To* Forster, 7 Apr and *fnn*.

[4] Webster was looking at Paris theatres in search of ideas for re-building his own Adelphi Theatre.

With pleasure as to the Odeon tomorrow night.[1] We shall find the man there, I dare say (perhaps you know that there *is* a man who goes to the stalls). Collins, objecting to be thrown upon the world for a dinner, suggests that we might dine together at one of the student houses on the other side of the water.[2] I think it a good notion, and, unless I hear from you to the contrary, shall expect to find you under the Obelisk on the Place de la Concorde at a quarter before 5. We shall want three arm chairs at the Theatre. Shall I take them or will you? If I am to take them, send me one line in the morning, and my servant shall be dispatched straightway. If I don't hear from you I shall conclude that you take them.

Always Faithfully Yours

Benjamin Webster Esquire. CHARLES DICKENS

To JOHN FORSTER, [?29–30 MARCH 1856]

Extracts in F, VII, v, 608–9; VIII, i, 625; VII, v, 619. *Date:* first extract later than 24 Mar (see below); second extract towards end of Mar (see below); third extract "at its close", according to Forster.

Rumours about Paradis Perdu *were at fever-pitch in London, and CD might have failed to get admission if Webster had not obtained a ticket for him. He went with Collins.*[3] We were rung in (out of the cafe below the Ambigu) at 8, and the play was over at half-past 1: the waits between the acts being very much longer than the acts themselves.[4] The house was crammed to excess in every part, and the galleries awful with Blouses, who again, during the whole of the waits, beat with the regularity of military drums the revolutionary tune of famous memory—Ça Ira! The play is a compound of *Paradise Lost* and Byron's *Cain*; and some of the controversies between the archangel and the devil, when the celestial power argues with the infernal in conversational French, as "Eh bien! Satan, crois-tu donc que notre Seigneur t'aurait exposé aux tourments que t'endures à présent, sans avoir prévu," &c. &c. are very ridiculous. All the supernatural personages are alarmingly natural (as theatre nature goes), and walk about in the stupidest way. Which has occasioned Collins and myself to institute a perquisition whether the French ever have shown any kind of idea of the supernatural; and to decide this rather in the negative. The people are very well dressed, and Eve very modestly. All Paris and the provinces had been ransacked for a woman who had brown hair that would fall to the calves of her legs—and she was found at last at the Odéon. There was nothing attractive until the 4th act, when there was a pretty good scene of the children of Cain dancing in, and desecrating, a temple, while Abel and his family were hammering hard at the Ark, outside, in all the pauses of the revel. The Deluge in the fifth act was up to about the mark of a drowning scene at the Adelphi; but it had one new feature. When the rain ceased, and the ark drove in on the great expanse of water, then lying waveless as

[1] To see *La Jeunesse*.

[2] On the Left Bank; bistros patronised by the Sorbonne students.

[3] On the first night, 24 Mar.

[4] "As a drama of course the thing is absurd", said *Galignani's Messenger*, 30 Mar, and described it as "contemptible"; "but the variety and beauty of the scenery and getting up will probably secure it a certain run". The tableaux of Pandemonium, the Garden of Eden, and the Deluge, were "received with applause". "Profane nonsense" was Forster's marginal note (F, 1872, III, 108).

the mists cleared and the sun broke out, numbers of bodies drifted up and down. These were all real men and boys, each separate, on a new kind of horizontal sloat.[1] They looked horrible and real. Altogether, a merely dull business; but I dare say it will go for a long while.

Of Little Dorrit, *No. VI, he wrote* I had the general idea of the Society business[2] before the Sadleir affair,[3] but I shaped Mr. Merdle himself out of that precious rascality. Society, the Circumlocution Office, and Mr. Gowan, are of course three parts of one idea and design. Mr. Merdle's complaint, which you find in the end to be fraud and forgery, came into my mind as the last drop in the silver cream-jug[4] on Hampstead-heath. I shall beg, when you have read the present number,[5] to inquire whether you consider "Bar" an instance, in reference to K F, of a suggested likeness in not many touches?[6]

I have not seen Scheffer since I came back but he told Catherine a few days ago that he was not satisfied with the likeness after all, and thought he must do more to it. My own impression of it, you remember?

To MISS BURDETT COUTTS, 30 MARCH 1856*

MS Morgan Library. *Address:* L'Angleterre. | Miss Burdett Coutts | Stratton Street | Piccadilly | London.

49 Champs Elysées, Paris | Sunday March Thirtieth, 1856

My Dear Miss Coutts.

I have gone over the paper[7] very carefully, and hope you will not find that I have made it—"too good"![8] My object has principally been, to state everything in its place and order; not often greatly changing your words, and never changing (I hope) your ideas. If I have misunderstood you anywhere, tell me and let me correct the mistake.

[1] Trap-door in stage.

[2] Introduced into Ch. 21 ("Mr. Merdle's Complaint", in No. VI, for May, published 30 Apr) as a major theme, in the description of the Society dinner-party given in Harley St by Mr and Mrs Merdle. In CD's number plans the word "Society" is three times repeated with triple underlining and includes "Fraud & Forgery bye and bye": see *Little Dorrit*, Clarendon edn, p. 812.

[3] John Sadleir (1814–56; *DNB*), Irish MP, Junior Lord of the Treasury 1853, financier and swindler, had poisoned himself on Hampstead Heath on the night of 16 Feb 56. The immediate cause was the collapse of the Tipperary Bank, in which he had an overdraft of £200,000; but a long history of forgery and fraudulent share-dealing was soon revealed. His suicide, like Merdle's, caused a sensation. CD refers to the suicide in "Nobody, Somebody, and Everybody", *HW*, 30 Aug 56, XIV, 145; for his use of it in *Little Dorrit*, see *To* Browne, 6 Mar 57 and *fn*. For H. P. Sucksmith's suggestion that the imaginative treatment of Merdle derives partly from Samuel Warren's "the Forger", *Passages from the Diary of a Late Physician*, 1830–7, see *ibid.*, p. xxvii.

[4] Found by the side of Sadleir's body.

[5] Forster would be reading the proofs at the end of the month.

[6] Forster virtually identifies "Bar" by reversing his initials to "KF": Sir Fitzroy Kelly, barrister (see Vol. VII, p. 230*n*). The "insinuating Jury-droop, and persuasive double-eye-glass" would have been at once recognized.

[7] The draft of her letter to the Rev. Harry Baber, Chaplain of the Whitelands Training Institution, given at pp. 6–11 of her *Summary Account of Common Things*, 1st edn, 1856.

[8] For CD's amended draft, see Appx C. See also *To* Miss Coutts, 8 Apr and *fnn*.

The mistress of your schools, I have left twice in blank as to her name. It looks, in your MS, like BUNGAY[1]—but I was afraid to write it.

The unfortunate Mrs. Cheadle appears to belong to nowhere. I have left a blank for the name of her School.[2]

I have also left a blank for the names of the eight Pupil Teachers, which certainly ought to go in there.[3]

I have written the close with an unsteady hand, because I faltered in going so near your heart.[4] But I hope it is what you would quietly say.

Pray let me know that you have received it; and if you would desire any change in it, send it back.

With loves to Mrs. Brown.

Ever most faithfully & affecy.
CD.

To W. H. WILLS, 1 APRIL 1856

MS Huntington Library.

49 Champs Elysées | First April 1856

My Dear Wills.

You will have seen by a letter from me received this morning, that we are all right. I think, in such a case as that of Collins's the right thing is to give £50.[5] I think it right, abstractedly, in the case of a careful and good writer on whom we can depend for Xmas Nos. and the like. But further, I know of offers for stories going about—to Collins himself for instance—which make it additionally desirable that we should not shave close in such a case.[6] I therefore tell him that you have paid in £50.

In great haste (at work) | Ever Faithfully
CD.

To MESSRS BRADBURY & EVANS, 4 APRIL 1856*

MS Dickens House.

Paris, 49 Champs Elysées | Friday Fourth April, 1856

My Dear B and E.

I send you enclosed £100 due from M. Tauchnitz to Household Words, to last

[1] Written in very large caps. In fact, Mrs Harriett "Bragg" (given in the pamphlet, p. 7), mistress of St Stephen's Schools, Westminster, who received a £4. prize.

[2] The Bayswater Schools, Paddington (given in the pamphlet, p. 8).

[3] Their names appear at the end of the letter (p. 18 of the pamphlet) as receiving ten-shilling prizes.

[4] The final paragraph, recounting William Brown's death the previous autumn. For further changes in it made by Miss Coutts, see 8 Apr, *fn*.

[5] For "A Rogue's Life".

[6] Perhaps offers from *Fraser's Magazine*, where Collins's "The Monkstones of Wincot Abbey" had appeared in Nov and Dec 55, or from Smith, Elder: see *To* Collins, 30 Jan, *fn*.

month.[1] I send it in a bill of M. Tauchnitz's for £50, and in a cheque of my own for £50.

All well.

Ever Faithfully Yours
CHARLES DICKENS

To GEORGE AUGUSTUS SALA, [?5–6 APRIL 1856]

Summary and extract from *Life and Adventures of G. A. Sala*, 1895, pp. 339 and 373. *Date:* see *To* Wills, 6 Apr.

Gladly accepting Sala's proposal that CD should send him to St Petersburg and Moscow, for him to write a series of descriptive essays about Russia and the Russians in HW.[2] You shall have the means of travelling in comfort and respectability.

To W. H. WILLS, 6 APRIL 1856

MS Huntington Library.

49 Champs Elysées, Paris | Sunday Sixth April, 1856

My Dear Wills.

[a]FIFTY POUNDS[3] IN ALL ITS ASPECTS[4]

all right.

SALA.[4]

I enclose my reply.[5] Need not repeat its terms, as you will open and read it for your own guidance. I wonder whether you anticipate its contents.[6] I shall be curious to know.

THE SIGN.[7]

I think not. I am doubtful, but I *think* not.[a]

CHRISTMAS.[2]

Collins and I have a mighty original notion (mine in the beginning) for another Play at Tavistock House. I purpose opening on Twelfth night, the theatrical season of that great establishment.[8] But now a tremendous question. Is

[1] For reprinting vols of *HW* which Tauchnitz had done since 1851. The present payment must have been for Vol. XII and represents B & E's share. After this Tauchnitz did not reprint complete vols but published a vol. of selections in Dec 56 with title *Novels and Tales reprinted from HW*.

[2] These appeared as "A Journey Due North", in 22 instalments, 4 Oct 56–14 Mar 57, XIV, 265–XV, 249.

[aa] Omitted by MDGH.

[3] Payment to Collins (see 1 Apr).

[4] Underlined with short double strokes.

[5] *To* Sala, 5–6 Apr. According to Sala, CD wrote "fully and warmly"; but he had lost the original letter (*Life and Adventures of G. A. Sala*, I, 27, 339).

[6] According to Sala, Wills proposed that he should travel direct to Cronstadt by sea, from Hull or another seaport in the North of England; but Sala preferred to go by Berlin and thence by land to St Petersburg; and CD accepted this (*ibid.*).

[7] Underlined with short double strokes. Probably a paper CD was rejecting.

[8] The first reference to the play which became *The Frozen Deep*, performed on Twelfth Night 1857; doubtless arising from his interest in the Arctic voyages.

MRS. WILLS![1]

game to do a Scotch Housekeeper, in a supposed country-house with Mary, Katey, Georgina &c. If she can screw her courage to saying Yes, that country house opens the piece in a singular way, and that Scotch housekeeper's part shall flow from the present pen. If she says No (but she won't),[2] no Scotch Housekeeper can be. The Tavistock House Season of 4 nights pauses for a reply. Scotch song (new and original) of Scotch Housekeeper, would pervade the piece.[3]

YOU[1]

had better pause for breath.

Ever Faithfully
CD.

POOLE.[1]

I have paid him his money. Here is the Proof of Life. If you will get the receipt for me to sign, the money can go to my account at Coutts's.

To JOHN FORSTER, [7 APRIL 1856]

Extracts in F, VIII, i, 625 and VII, v, 607. *Date:* first extract 7 Apr 56, according to Forster; second extract no doubt part of same letter.

There are some things in Flora in number seven[4] that seem to me to be extraordinarily droll, with something serious at the bottom of them after all.[5] Ah, well! was there *not* something very serious in it once?[6] I am glad to think of being in the country with the long summer mornings as I approach number ten,[7] where I have finally resolved to make Dorrit rich. It should be a very fine point in the story.... Nothing in Flora made me laugh so much as the confusion of ideas between gout flying upwards, and its soaring with Mr. F—— to another sphere.[8]

About a dreary theatrical experience. On Wednesday we went to the Odeon to see a new piece, in four acts and in verse, called *Michel Cervantes*.[9] I suppose such an infernal dose of ditch water never was concocted.[10] But there were certain passages, describing the suppression of public opinion in Madrid, which were received with a shout of savage application to France that made one stare again![11] And once more, here again, at every pause, steady, compact, regular as military drums, the Ça Ira!

[1] Underlined with short double strokes.

[2] Mrs Wills did play the housekeeper, Nurse Esther.

[3] "Wandering Willie" (a traditional song), is played on the piano several times in Act I, on Nurse Esther's appearances.

[4] Chs 23–5, published 31 May, for June. Forster would be reading proofs.

[5] Ch. 23 begins with the visit of Flora and Mr F's Aunt to Doyce and Clennam's factory; Flora is at her most flirtatious self with Clennam, but her genuine fondness for him is also apparent.

[6] His love for Maria Beadnell.

[7] Chs 33–6.

[8] From Flora's rambling recollections in Ch. 24.

[9] *Michel Cervantes*, by M. T. Muret; CD probably went on the first Wed of its run, 2 Apr.

[10] "Feeble in a dramatic point of view", wrote *Galignani's Messenger*, 6 Apr, and described the plot as "meagre and undramatic ... to say nothing of good taste or morals".

[11] *Galignani* found "Many passages of nervous masculine thought expressed in good round versification", which were warmly applauded.

To FRANCOIS RÉGNIER,[1] 7 APRIL 1856*

MS Comédie Francaise.

49 Champs Elysées | Monday 7 April, 1856

My Dear Régnier

Our friend Macready is staying here for a few days, and we hope very earnestly that you do not act—or at all events that you do not act in the first piece—on Friday next.[2] Because we wish to have the great pleasure of receiving Madame Regnier and yourself to dinner on that day à 6½ heures exactly. Pray tell me in reply, that you can come.

Always Very faithfully Yours

À Monsieur Régnier CHARLES DICKENS

To W. H. WILLS, 7 APRIL 1856*

MS Huntington Library.

Paris, Monday Seventh April 1856

My Dear Wills. I return the No.[3] after going over it carefully.

I should like the Sphynx[4] to stand over. She is so deserving of the name, that before Heaven I don't yet (though I have read it twice) understand what it means. Have you any idea?

Look carefully to my marks in the Aldershot paper.[5] Execrably written.

I think Whitehead's[6] name, Nemesis, one that had best stand.[7] Go carefully over the paper, and change inverted or obsolete language, as "I like him not",[8] &c.—Also, if people's eye-balls burst, or anything of that sort, apply some mild remedy.[9]

Observe that the town of B—— is always to be Battenham.[10]

Ever Faithfully

CD.

[1] François Joseph Philoclès Régnier (1807–85), French actor: see Vol. V, p. 8n.

[2] Régnier was free on 11 Apr.

[3] *HW*, No. 317, published 19 Apr 56.

[4] It did not appear under that title, but almost certainly became "A Summer Night's Dream", by James White, 3 May 56, XIII, 380. Paolina acts the part of a sibyl or "inspired pythoness".

[5] "Women at Aldershot", by Marianne Young, 19 Apr 56, XIII, 318; a description of the appalling conditions under which soldiers' wives and their children lived in the barracks.

[6] Charles Whitehead, novelist, dramatist and poet: see Vol. VII, p. 773 and *nn*.

[7] It appeared in two instalments (each of two chs), 19 and 26 Apr, XIII, 326 and 344.

[8] Wills clearly changed this to "I don't like him" (said by Meredith in Ch. 3).

[9] The horror of the face at the window and the secret grave-digging probably needed toning down.

[10] This was done.

To MISS BURDETT COUTTS, 8 APRIL 1856

MS Morgan Library.

Paris, Tuesday Eighth April, 1856

My Dear Miss Coutts.

I have gone over your draft received on Sunday, and have written it out again on the other side.[1] It is very slightly altered indeed.[2] It seems to me to be as plain and unaffected as possible, and to say what you wish to express, in few words. I quite felt what you explain relating to Mrs. Brown, and most heartily perceived and sympathized with your delicate and considerate intention. Nor have I the least doubt that it will be a great happiness to her.[3]

Mr. Macready has come to stay with us for a few days, and reports that as he passed through town he called in Stratton Street, hoping to see you. He was anxious to ask you what you thought about Young Warner,[4] and to say that he did not quite know whether he ought to have pursued the subject of his clothes—respecting which (I think he said, but he is at the Louvre, and I can't ask him), he had sent you some letter.

I have no doubt—please to observe particularly—NO DOUBT[5]—that my reading, and not your writing, is to blame (indeed I generally find it too plain) but the second name of Old Pierre[6] is an appalling mystery to me. I defy Mr. Wills to read it. I have got to this—old Pierre Mont—old Pierre Montle. I am now going out to the house you give me the direction to, to enquire vaguely whether le vieux Pierre Montle—and then I shall cough—lodges there. If I can get at him by these desperate means, you shall find the report on the other side.[7].

With kindest regard to Mrs. Brown,

Ever Dear Miss Coutts | Most Faithfully & affecy. Yours

CD.

To MISS MARGUERITE POWER,[8] 8 APRIL 1856

Extract in Anderson Galleries catalogue, Dec 1936. *MS* 1 p.; dated 49 Champs Elysées, 8 Apr 56; addressed "Doner" by catalogue, clearly in error.

Macready is here, and will be greatly pleased to see you and the marchioness.[9] Will you come, both of you, and dine with us on Friday at 1/2 past 6—on which occasion I have asked the Epicurians of La Dressa.[10] You know the beastly dimen-

[1] See Appx C.

[2] There are a number of verbal differences between the draft as corrected by CD and the printed text, but they do not change the sense. The para, "I return the papers ... more useful" (Appx C) is moved to the end of the letter in the printed text.

[3] The passage about Brown's death; in the printed text, "But it has pleased God ... my own" follows "great affliction".

[4] Son of the actress Mary Amelia Warner (1804–54; *DNB*), on whose death Miss Coutts had offered to pay her daughter's school-fees and Macready those of her son: see Vol. VII, pp. 116*n* and 122 and *n*.

[5] Written in very large cursive writing.

[6] Untraceable.

[7] CD has sketched a pointing hand.

[8] Marguerite Power (1815–67; *DNB*), Lady Blessington's niece, miscellaneous writer: see Vol. III, p. 340*n*.

[9] CD's nickname for Marguerite's sister, Ellen: see Vol. V, p. 128 and *n*.

[10] This must mean the Régniers; possibly a misreading in catalogue.

sions of our dining table (to say nothing of dining-room), and how we have had the cramp in this apartment for 6 months. I have told my trembling wife to write another note with this, and to rest assured that it will explain itself.

To BERNARD TAUCHNITZ, 8 APRIL 1856

Extract in Kurt Otto, *Der Verlag Bernhard Tauchnitz, 1837–1912*, Leipzig, 1912, p. 54.

Paris, 49, Champs Elysées, Tuesday, April 8th, 1856.

Having thus disposed of business, let me have the pleasure of adding that we all unite in kindest regards to Mrs. Tauchnitz and your family, and that we shall all remember our meeting here with great pleasure, and shall always look forward to a renewal of that friendship—somewhere.

To GABRIEL LEGOUVÉ, 9 APRIL 1856*

MS M. Jean Paladilhe.

Champs Elysées, 49. | Mercredi 9 Avril, 1856

Mon cher M. Legouvé

Vous devez être l'homme le plus heureux en tout Paris, ce matin!

J'aurai le grand plaisir de vous voir aujourdhui, mais, en attendant, je m'empresse de vous feliciter sur le triomphe que vous venez d'obtenir[1]—triomphe que vous ne partagez avec personne, car il me parait que la Ristori[2] ne jouera jamais aussi bien que vous ecrivez.

Votre tout devoué
CHARLES DICKENS

To THOMAS FRASER,[3] 10 APRIL 1856*

MS Berg Collection. *Address:* À Monsieur Fraser.

Champs Elysées, 49 | Thursday Tenth April, 1856

My Dear Fraser.

Will you have the kindness to let the two daughters of Mark Lemon[4] accompany you to London? They will cause you no trouble, as they are too young to require any gallantry. Both he and I will be very sensible of the kindness of your escort, and they shall be produced at the Station of the chemin de fer du Nord at the time you may appoint for your departure.

With kindest regard

Faithfully Yours always
CHARLES DICKENS

Thomas Fraser Esquire

[1] The performance of his *Médée*, transl. into Italian, and played by Ristori (see below), after Mme Rachel had refused to play the part.

[2] Adelaide Ristori (1822–1906), Italian actress; played in Italy until 1855; then throughout Europe; see *To* Forster, 13 Apr and *fn*; same year played Lady Macbeth and Italian tragedies in London with great success (see *To* Macready, 8 Aug and *fn*); played in America with equal success 1884–5.

[3] Thomas Fraser (?1804–69), special correspondent of the *Morning Chronicle* in Paris 1836–55: see Vol. I, p. 87*n*.

[4] See Vol. VII, p. 110 and *n*.

To ROBERT BROWNING,[1] 12 APRIL 1856*

MS Berg Collection. *Address:* Robert Browning Esquire.

Champs Elysées | Saturday Twelfth April, 1856

My Dear Browning

Macready found himself obliged, yesterday, to arrange to leave Paris early this morning: having letters that called him home. A torrent of commissions swept him away all day, and he was in a state of semi-distraction until dinner time. He made me solemnly promise to write this morning and make known to you and Mrs. Browning how it came to pass that he went away without repeating his visit.[2] In discharge of my conscience I write this note.

Always Very faithfully Yours

Robert Browning Esquire. CHARLES DICKENS

To WILKIE COLLINS, 13 APRIL 1856

MS Morgan Library.

Champs Elysées | Sunday April Thirteenth 1856

My Dear Collins.

We checked you off at the various points of your journey all day, but never dreamed of the half gale. You must have had an abominable passage with that convivial club! My soul sickens at the thought of it; and the smell seizes hold of the bridge of my nose exactly half way up, and won't let it go again.

Your porteress duly appeared with the small account and your note. I paid her immediately of course, and she departed rejoicing. The Pavilion looks very desolate, and nobody has taken it as yet. Macready left us at 7 yesterday morning, and I afterwards took a long country walk to get into train for work. It was a noble spring day, and the air most delightful. But I found the evening sufficiently dull, and indeed we all miss you very much.

[a]The "little Lemons" depart tomorrow, under the charge of an unhappy Englishman whom we have inveigled into taking them. You will be glad to hear that on the day of your departure, Lally began to transfer her Dinner Glares to Macready; and that Macready whenever he observed one of those terrible phenomena supposed it to mean that she wanted water, and instantly overwhelmed her with the largest Decanter.[a]

He went on Friday to the Rehearsal of Comme il vous plaira[3] which was produced last night.[4] His account of it was absolutely stunning. The speech of the Seven Ages, delivered as a Light Comedy joke—Jacques at the Court of the Reigning Duke instead of the banished one, and winding up the thing by *marrying Celia*—everything as wide of Shakespeare as possible, and confirming my previous impression that she knew just nothing at all about it. She was to have been here on Friday Even-

[1] Robert and Elizabeth Barrett Browning had been living in Paris since Oct 55; after a few months in England they returned to Florence in Oct 56.

[2] To 3 Rue du Colisée.

[aa] Omitted in *CD to WC* and N.

[3] Adapted from Shakespeare by George Sand.

[4] At the Français.

ing, but had "le migraine" (of which I think you have heard before), but Regnier said, as to the piece "La piece! Il n'y a point de piece"—tapped his forehead with great violence—and threw whatever liquid came out, into the air as an offéring to the offended Gods. Girardin said qu'il l'avait trouvé a la repetition, tres interessante, tres interessante, tres interessante—and said nothing more the whole evening. I dine at another of his prodigious banquets, tomorrow.

I am very anxious to know what your Doctor says. If he should fail to set you up by the 3rd. or 4th. of May for me, I shall consider him a Humbug. It occurs to me to mention that if you don't get settled early in May, the Hogarths will then leave Tavistock House to me and Charley, and you know how easily and amply it can accommodate you. Pray don't forget that it is available for your quarters. There will be two or three large airy bedrooms with nobody to occupy them, and the range of the whole sheeted house besides. The Pavilion of the Molyneaux I shall of course reserve for your summer occupation and work. Talking of which latter I am reminded to say that the Scotch Housekeeper is secured.[1]

You know exactly where I am sitting, what I am seeing, what I am hearing, what is going on around me in every way. I have not a scrap of news, except that Poole at the Français complained bitterly to Macready of your humble servant's neglect—which, considering that he would unquestionably be in some remote English workhouse but for me, I think characteristic. Macready's reply to him appears to have been. Er—really—er—no Poole!—er—must excuse me—host—um—friend—er—great affection—um—cannot permit—er—must therefore distinctly beg.

Miss Power had a story on Friday that they have done something to the Imperial Infant[2] which has paralyzed one of his arms. My information on the subject is not of a detailed nature, inasmuch as I am supposed to be unapproachable thereupon—as a flunkey question—and sternly to refuse to be enlightened. But I find Mrs. Dickens flying to the window whenever a fast carriage is heard, and then pretending to be so calmly looking towards the Ave de l'Etoile, that I know her to be on the watch for something from the Tuilleries. I am inclined to think that a carriage and four containing the Imperial and damaged infant is expected to go by, on some mission connected with the story.

All unite in kindest regard and best wishes for your speedily coming all right again.

Ever faithfully
CHARLES DICKENS

I enclose a letter from Forgues. The book of the Lighthouse accompanies it, which I will bring with me.

P.P.S. According to a highly illegible note I have from Forgues, it would seem that I ought to send you the book, with some idea of your sending it back to me to send to him.[3] The little Lemons therefore shall bring the book with them.

[1] Mrs Wills, who acted the Scottish Nurse in *The Frozen Deep*.

[2] Eugène Louis Jean Joseph Napoléon, the "Prince Imperial", *b.* 16 Mar 56, Napoleon III's only child; for his christening, see *To* Lemon, 15 June and *fnn*.

[3] See *To* Collins, 6 June and *fn*.

To W. H. WILLS, 13 APRIL 1856*

MS Berg Collection.

Champs Elysées | Sunday Night Thirteenth April, 1856

My Dear Wills.

H. W.[1]

I have gone over the No.[2] and return it. All up with everything[3] is loose, scrambling, and careless, for a first article. But I suppose you have nothing better?

Look to Nemesis for the same things as in the first part.

Love Memories, Taboo. If the authoress can do anything better—don't discourage her. But this really will not do.

So no more (most absurd title), I see nothing whatever in. I wish you would say to Morley that it is useless to pursue that subject without striking a blow. Wait until there is something to hit, and then in God's name hit it—hard. The article had best stand over until it can be made apropòs of something more—then added to and enlarged upon.[4]

The British Hadji would do as much towards shutting up Household Words for good and all, as most things could. Most decidedly, Taboo.

In No. 316,[5] in those articles which I did not see, I observe some things worth mentioning as requiring to be changed. Post to Australia.[6] 1st. column "to be interfering" is very awkward. Second column same article "the making a railway" is very bad English, and ought to be "the making of a Railway". Same column, "the only man *that* (instead of *whom*) they can trust" is bad too. Same article page 306 near the top, it ought to be "and our firm told the authorities that they would break down, or go ashore, and never get to Melbourne." The repetition of the three last words (used in the former part of the sentence), just makes the difference between the sense being plain at a glance, and being confused.[7]

I hope to send you an article of my own at the end of this coming week.[8]

"Stories from the State Trials" would make a very good subject, if you ever find anybody in hand, to whom to entrust it.

I mentioned to you sometime ago, that a monthly commentary on the Trials at the Central Criminal Court, with reference to the State of Education, the State of the Law, and the Vices of Society, would make a very remarkable set of papers. I think Collins would do it extremely well. He is now (unwell, and his family moving), at 24 Howland St. Fitzroy Square. Will you see him, mention the subject to him just as I state it, and ask him if he would like to undertake it regularly. In that case, cut out the best Reports for him from day to day. The Central Criminal Court is sitting

[1] Underlined by two short strokes.

[2] No. 318, published 26 Apr 56.

[3] By G. A. Sala, XIII, 337: a satirical account of Eugène Huzar's *La Fin du Monde par la Science*, 1855.

[4] Morley probably took the hint; he hits hard in "Flowers of British Legislation", 7 June, XIII, 490.

[5] Published 12 Apr.

[6] By E. M. Whitty (1827–60; *DNB*), journalist.

[7] CD presumably meant that alterations could be made for the vol.

[8] "Proposals for a National Jest-Book", 3 May 56, XIII, 361, a satire on the absurdities of politicians and institutions, including the Royal Literary Fund.

now. There are really few subjects more distinctly in the way of H.W. or more susceptible of interesting treatment with a great practical object.[1]

Faithfully Ever
CD.

To JOHN FORSTER, [13 APRIL 1856]

Extracts in F, VII, v, 612 and VIII, ii, 639. *Date:* just after Macready's visit (6–12 Apr).

CD and Macready had been to Ristori's performance as Médée[2] *together and pronounced it to be hopelessly bad.* In the day entertainments, and little melodrama theatres, of Italy, I have seen the same thing fifty times, only not at once so conventional and so exaggerated. The papers have all been in fits respecting the sublimity of the performance, and the genuineness of the applause—particularly of the bouquets; which were thrown on at the most preposterous times in the midst of agonizing scenes, so that the characters had to pick their way among them, and a certain stout gentleman who played King Creon was obliged to keep a wary eye, all night, on the proscenium boxes, and dodge them as they came down. Now Scribe, who dined here next day (and who follows on the Ristori side, being offended, as everybody has been, by the insolence of Rachel), could not resist the temptation of telling us, that, going round at the end of the first act to offer his congratulations, he met all the bouquets coming back in men's arms to be thrown on again in the second act. . . . By the bye, I see a fine actor lost in Scribe. In all his pieces he has everything done in his own way; and on that same night he was showing what Rachel did not do, and wouldn't do, in the last scene of Adrienne Lecouvreur, with extraordinary force and intensity.

Giving Forster a favourable report of Macready's enjoyment of his holiday; then, after recurring to his own old notion of going to settle in Australia, once he had finished Little Dorrit, *saying that perhaps Macready, if he could get into harness again, would not be the worse for some such troubles as were worrying himself.* It fills me with pity to think of him away in that lonely Sherborne place. I have always felt of myself that I must, please God, die in harness, but I have never felt it more strongly than in looking at, and thinking of, him. However strange it is to be never at rest, and never satisfied, and ever trying after something that is never reached, and to be always laden with plot and plan and care and worry, how clear it is that it must be, and that one is driven by an irresisitible might until the journey is worked out! It is much better to go on and fret, than to stop and fret. As to repose—for some men there's no such thing in this life. The foregoing has the appearance of a small sermon; but it is so often in my head in these days that it cannot help coming out. The old days—the old days! Shall I ever, I wonder, get the frame of mind back as it used to be then? Something of it perhaps—but never quite as it used to be. I find that the skeleton in my domestic closet is becoming a pretty big one.

[1] Collins did not pursue the subject, but CD's interest clearly encouraged Morley to write "Time's Sponge" (17 May), and "A Criminal Trial" (21 June).

[2] At the Théâtre Italien. *Galignani*, 13 Apr 56, described it as a triumph; Ristori's "effect on the public was immense; passage after passage was followed by shouts of applause". Many English and Italian celebrities were present, conspicuous from their hearty appreciation. The play ran until mid-May as a "continued unabated success" (*Galignani*, 4 May).

To W. H. WILLS, 15 APRIL 1856

Extracts in unidentified catalogue at Dickens House; dated Paris, 15 Apr 56; addressed W. H. Wills.

I do not wish personally to exert myself to get Sala's Letters.[1] Firstly, because I would rather not present him personally, except to people to whom I could unreservedly explain myself (and I know none such in America), and secondly because I very much doubt their doing him any service. His getting out anything for himself, is the best necessity he can be put to.... I do not think he can write *much* while in America.[2] Still if he writes an article or two occasionally.... I don't think they will involve him in any scrape.... If he should find the thing more difficult than he supposes ... then he had best stop ... and write home for instructions. Your letter of yesterday, has just arrived with the No.... but I clearly see that the British Hadji *is entirely out of the question.*[3] What! Five pages of Quotation from a Book!! I can't believe it, and yet I know the book and glance at the article and can't credit my eyes. What astonishing Lunacy! Pray look up something else, for this can't be.

To HENRY AUSTIN, 17 APRIL 1856*

MS Morgan Library.

Paris, 49 Champs Elysées
Thursday Seventeenth April, 1856.

My Dear Henry.

I will of course place my name and support at Southwood Smith's[4] disposal. Though I little thought ever to see myself in company with Lord Palmerston—whom I think, in his present place, one of the very worst signs of these times.

The word Testimonial has been so much abused, and has become so synonymous with Humbug, that I am fully persuaded it will damage Southwood Smith. It would be immeasurably better, to call it plainly, a Committee for offering a public acknowledgement to Doctor Southwood Smith, in recognition of the services he has rendered to the public health and comfort.[5] Something to that effect. Testimonial is a wet blanket, fifty feet thick.

I purpose coming to town at the end of the week after next—that is to say—about

[1] i.e. of introduction.

[2] Sala did not in fact go to America until 1864, when he went as special correspondent of the *Daily Telegraph*.

[3] See *To* Wills, 13 Apr.

[4] Thomas Southwood Smith, MD (1788–1861; *DNB*), sanitary reformer: see Vol. III, p. 303*n*.

[5] Smith had retired from professional practice in 1850 and as medical assistant of the General Board of Health 1854; his reports on quarantine (1845), cholera (1850), yellow fever (1852) and sanitary improvement (1854) were major contributions; but he was given only a modest pension. At a preliminary meeting held at Lord Shaftesbury's home on 7 May 56, it was resolved that, as "Recognition of the Public Services of Dr Southwood Smith", "a bust ... be executed in marble, and presented to some suitable institution, as an enduring memorial of his eminent services in the promotion of the Public Health" (Mrs C. L. Lewes, *Dr Southwood Smith: A Retrospect*, 1898, p. 164). The bust, by J. Hart, executed in 1856, was in 1872 presented to the National Portrait Gallery. CD was among 91 subscribers, headed by Lord Palmerston. For Southwood Smith's speech of thanks at a final meeting to tell him of the resolution, on 6 Dec 58, see Mrs Lewes, above, pp. 144–6.

the end of the present month—and staying there through May. We pass the summer at Boulogne, where you and Letitia[1] will arrange to come and see us (I hope) in the drollest of houses—quite a practical joke—in a really beautiful garden. As quaint a place as you will ever see.

Tuesday the 6th. of May, is our Household Words Audit. Will you come and dine at the office that day, at halfpast 5 sharp? If Yes, send your answer to Wills.

The Gad's Hill purchase is completed, and the (here I gasp)—the money—paid.[2] I have agreed to let the old Tory Rector stay there until next March. We will then dash in with our improvements and furnish the place. I purpose occupying it for that summer.

With Love from all, Ever affectionately

CD.

To JOHN FORSTER, [17 APRIL 1856]

Extracts in F, VII, v, 609–10*n*, 619–20*n*, and VIII, ii, 615. *Date:* first two extracts 17 Apr 56, according to Forster; third extract after Girardin's dinner on 14 Apr.

After seeing the Médecin des Enfants[3] *he writes* The low cry of excitement and expectation that goes round the house when any one of the great situations is felt to be coming, is very remarkable indeed. I suppose there has not been so great a success of the genuine and worthy kind (for the authors have really taken the French dramatic bull by the horns, and put the adulterous wife in the right position), for many years. When you come over and see it, you will say you never saw anything so admirably done. There is one actor, Bignon[4] (M. Delormel), who has a good deal of Macready in him; sometimes looks very like him; and who seems to me the perfection of manly good sense.

On Monday I am going to dine with all my translators at Hachette's, the bookseller who has made the bargain for the complete edition, and who began this week to pay his monthly £40 for the year.[5] I don't mean to go out any more. Please imagine me in the midst of my French dressers.

At Girardin's, his host again played Lucullus[6] *in the same style.* After dinner he asked me if I would come into another room and smoke a cigar? and on my saying Yes, coolly opened a drawer, containing about 5000 inestimable cigars in prodigious bundles—just as the Captain of the Robbers in *Ali Baba* might have gone to a corner of the cave for bales of brocade. A little man dined who was blacking shoes 8 years ago, and is now enormously rich—the richest man in Paris—having ascended

[1] CD's sister Letitia, Mrs Henry Austin (1816–93): see Vol. I, p. 34*n* and later vols.

[2] £1,790: see *To* Miss Hogarth, 14 Mar.

[3] *Le Médecin des Enfants*, by Anicet Bourgeois and Philippe Adolphus Dennery, first performed at the Gaîté Oct–Nov 55; published 1855; described by *Galignani's Messenger*, 4 Nov 55, as "a melodrama of much interest"; five long Acts; but the "intensity of latter scenes" produced a powerful sympathy in the audience.

[4] Eugène Bignon (1812–58), actor and dramatist; played at the Porte St Martin from 1851; d'Artagnan in *Les Mousquetaires* at the Gaîté; and Edmond Dantes in *Monte-Cristo*.

[5] See *To* Hachette, 14 Jan, *fn*.

[6] Lucius Licinius Lucullus, Roman consul 74 BC; famous as a generous patron.

with rapidity up the usual ladder of the Bourse. By merely observing that perhaps he might come down again, I clouded so many faces as to render it very clear to me that *everybody present* was at the same game for some stake or other!

To MRS WILLMORE,[1] 17 APRIL 1856

MS Huntington Library.

Champs Elysées, 49 | Thursday Seventeenth April, 1856

Dear Madam

I am extremely concerned to learn that you are enduring great anxiety on behalf of Mr. Wilmore,[2] but I beg to give you the most earnest and faithful assurance I can possibly convey in words, that your solicitude, though very natural, has no real foundation. It is absolutely impossible, in these times, that any accident of importance can have happened to any steamer leaving Calais, Boulogne, Dieppe, or Havre, so long ago as last Monday or Tuesday night, without the disaster being known in Paris by means of the Electric Telegraph, within a few hours of that time. Believe me, it cannot be. Delay may have arisen in the arrival of all the steamers at their respective destinations, and I have little doubt that is the case; but you may be sure that nothing of greater importance has occurred, and that nobody is the worse.[3]

I would on no account offer you this comfort, unless I were as fully convinced of its being true, as I am of my being really alive when I write this note. I have received no letters for two days, although I *know* that some must have been on their way to me from England, in the ordinary course, since Tuesday. Gales of wind will sometimes arise upon these coasts, which are nothing in themselves, but which prevent the steamers from getting into their ports, in consequence of the wind blowing sheer out of them. In that case, the Mails are stopped, and the passengers are prevented from getting ashore, and endure, for certain hours more or less, the great anxiety of knowing that their friends will be unhappy about them. To such an extent your husband deserves all the sympathy you can give him—but no further. And I have not a doubt that he is alive, and as merry as he can be without you, at this present writing. I shall hope to remind you, at our own house in London this winter, of the absolute confidence with which I sent you this assurance on his behalf. And I know it will be so plain to you, then, that you will not give me the slightest credit for having been such a common-place prophet.

Pray set your mind at ease. A few hours will certainly do so for you—but anticipate them with unquestioning cheerfulness.

Dear Madam | Very truly Yours
CHARLES DICKENS

[1] Wife of Graham Willmore (?1804–56), QC, to whom CD had written on 8 Feb 50; he lived at Taunton, Somerset: see Vol. VI, p. 33*n*.

[2] Thus in MS.

[3] CD was right; but Willmore died two months later (at Neuilly, near Paris, on 19 June).

To BERNHARD TAUCHNITZ, 18 APRIL 1856

Extract in Kurt Otto, *Der Verlag Bernhard Tauchnitz, 1837–1912*, p. 54.

Paris, 49, Champs Elysées, April 18th, 1856.

Leipzig is at present among my castles in the air, mes Châteaux en Espagne, but perhaps Germany and I may make a personal acquaintance yet.[1]

To THE SECRETARY, ROYAL ACADEMY,[2] [?19–20 APRIL 1856]

Mention in *To* Wills, 20 Apr 56. *Date:* close to that day.

To W. H. WILLS, 20 APRIL 1856

MS Brotherton Library, Leeds.

Paris, Sunday Twentieth April, 1856

My Dear Wills.

H.W.[3]

I enclose you what I think is a capital paper, with an odd and novel idea in it.[4] You must certainly alter the No. so as to make it the first article;[5] or some of the points of which it treats, will get out of date.[6] I cannot suggest how the No. is to be altered, inasmuch as I have not yet got it. In case of its coming by the Post to day, I will endeavour to return it by tomorrow's post.

I wish to see a Proof of the enclosed. But in case there should not be time, then ask Forster to correct it, by and with the MS.

You don't quite understand what I mean, I think, by Stories from the State Trials when you say your story is "almost one".[7] An admirable and picturesque book by Alexandre Dumas, called Crimes Celèbres,[8] expresses the idea in its execution.

SALA.[3]

I have no suggestion to offer on the subject of the credits, which seem to be well and carefully arranged. But I think that before he goes, you should draw up, and have legibly copied out, a Memorandum of all the arrangements made and all the understanding entered into, and should attach your signature on my behalf, and make him attach his. In that Memorandum you can state that the question of the partition

[1] CD never revisited Germany.

[2] John Prescott Knight (1803–81; *DNB*), portrait-painter; Professor of Perspective, RA, 1839–60; RA 1844; Secretary, RA, 1848–75; his best known painting *The Heroes of Waterloo* (*The Waterloo Banquet*), RA 1842.

[3] Underlined with short double strokes.

[4] "Proposals for a National Jest-Book": see *To* Wills, 13 Apr and *fn*.

[5] As it appeared, in No. 319, 3 May.

[6] A facetious article with references to the month of Apr, and other topical allusions.

[7] Wills must have referred to Ch. 9 of his story, "The Ninth of June", which describes a trial (*HW*, 7 June 56, XIII, 493, and the three following Nos). CD had seen what was probably the first draft of this serial in Apr 55: see Vol. VII, p. 591 and *n*.

[8] *Crimes Célèbres*, by Alexandre Dumas, père, Paris, 1839–40 (the 1841 edn in CD's library at his death: see Vol. VI, p. 569 and *n*); first transl. into English 1843; it contained vivid accounts of 10 celebrated crimes, beginning with "The Borgias" and ending with "Urban Grandier"; later edns included "Mary Stuart" (as victim) and other crimes.

of the copyright of the completed book, between Sala and H.W. is reserved until the book shall be producible.[1]

MACREADY'S DRAFT,[2] AND POOLE'S PENSION RECEIPT.[3]

I return, duly signed.

ROYAL ACADEMY DINNER.[3]

I have answered the invitation. But you tell me that the Dinner is on the "tenth of April", which is of course impossible. The tenth of May would be a week later than usual, and therefore I shall be glad if you will tell me on what day it really comes off.[4] Preserve the ticket, because it accredits one at the door, without reference to a book.

TAVISTOCK GROUND.[3]

I enclose a cheque in Mr. Cardale's[5] favor for £20.

The Tenantry

must be regaled on the Estate at Midsummer, I think, and have 15 per cent returned to them in a neat and appropriate.[6]

Ever Faithfully

CD.

To JOHN FORSTER, [?20 APRIL 1856]

Extract in F, VII, v, 615. *Date:* written "a few days later" than *To* Forster, 17 Apr 56, according to Forster.

If you were to see the steps of the Bourse at about 4 in the afternoon, and the crowd of blouses and patches among the speculators there assembled, all howling and haggard with speculation, you would stand aghast at the consideration of what must be going on. Concierges and people like that perpetually blow their brains out, or fly into the Seine, "à cause des pertes sur la Bourse." I hardly ever take up a French paper without lighting on such a paragraph. On the other hand, thoroughbred horses without end, and red velvet carriages with white kid harness on jet black horses, go by here all day long; and the pedestrians who turn to look at them, laugh, and say, "C'est la Bourse!"[7] Such crashes must be staved off every week as have not been seen since Law's[8] time.

To W. H. WILLS, [21 APRIL 1856]

Mention in N, II, 761.

[1] Either for Sala's later visit to Russia or the unfulfilled intention of visiting America: see *To* Wills, 15 Apr and *fn.*

[2] Probably connected with Macready's expenses in Paris.

[3] Underlined with short double strokes.

[4] It was held on 3 May and CD was present (*To* Mrs CD, 5 May).

[5] John Bate Cardale (1802–77; *DNB*), solicitor, CD's next-door neighbour in Tavistock Square: see Vol. VI, p. 482*n*.

[6] i.e. speech.

[7] "Type of the Empire" is Forster's marginal note (F, 1872, III, 119).

[8] John Law (1671–1829; *DNB*), Scottish financier settled in Paris; founder of the Banque Genérale, the first bank in France; Controller-general of French finance 1720; his "Mississippi scheme" collapsed the same year.

To WILKIE COLLINS, 22 APRIL 1856

MS Morgan Library.

Champs Elysées | Tuesday Twenty-Second April, 1856

My Dear Collins.

I have been quite taken aback by your account of your alarming seizure;[1] and have only become reassured again, firstly by the good fortune of your having left here and got so near your Doctor; secondly, by your hopefulness of now making head in the right direction. On the third or fourth I purpose being in town, and I need not say that I shall forthwith come to look after my old Patient.

On Sunday, to my infinite amazement, Townshend[2] appeared. He has changed his plans, and is staying in Paris a week, before going to Town for a couple of months. He dined here on Sunday, and placidly ate and drank in the most vigorous manner, and mildly laid out a terrific perspective of projects for carrying me off to the Theatre every night. But in the morning he found himself with dawnings of Bronchitis, and is now luxuriously laid up in lavender at his Hotel—confining himself entirely to precious stones,[3] chicken, and fragrant wines qualified with iced waters.

Last Friday, I took Mrs. Dickens, Georgina, and Mary and Katey, to dine at the Trois freres. [a]Mrs. Dickens nearly killed herself, but the others hardly did that justice to the dinner that I had expected.[a] We then Sir went off to the Français; to see Comme il vous plaira which is a kind of Theatrical Representation that I think might be got up, with great completeness, by the Patients in the Asylum for Idiots.[4] Dreariness is no word for it, vacancy is no word for it, gammon is no word for it, there *is* no word for it. Nobody has anything to do, but to sit upon as many grey stones as he can. When Jacques had sat upon seventy seven stones and forty two roots of trees (which was at the end of the second act), we came away. He had by that time been made violent love to by Celia, had shewn himself in every phase of his existence to be utterly unknown to Shakespeare, had made the speech about the Seven Ages out of its right place and apropos of nothing on earth, and had in all respects conducted himself like a brutalized, benighted, and besotted Beast.[5]

A wonderful dinner at Girardin's last Monday, with only one new (but appropriate) feature in it. When we went into the drawing room after the banquet, which had terminated in a flower pot out of a ballet being set before every guest, piled to the brim with the ruddiest fresh strawberries, he asked me if I would come into another room (a chamber of no account—rather like the last Scene in Gustavus) and smoke a Cigar? On my replying yes, he opened, with a key attached to his watch chain, a

[1] Collins had returned to London from Paris on 12 Apr, still ill, and took furnished lodgings at 22 Howland St, Fitzroy Sq. (described—and particularly his appalling landlady—in the second part of "Laid Up in Two Lodgings", *HW*, 14 June 56, XIII, 517); by June he had recovered sufficiently to go on a sailing trip in the Channel with Pigott and Pigott's brother (Collins *to* C. A. Collins, 26 June 56, quoted in Catherine Peters, *The King of Inventors*, 1991, p. 166).

[2] The Rev. Chauncy Hare Townshend (1798–1868; *DNB*), poet and antiquarian: see Vol. II, p. 110*n*.

[3] Of which Townshend had a major collection, bequeathed to the V & A.

[aa] Omitted in *CD to WC* and N.

[4] At Park House, Highgate and Essex Hall, Colchester: see Vol. VI, p. 172*n*.

[5] For Macready's similar description of the dress rehearsal, see *To* Collins, 13 Apr.

species of mahogany Cave, which appeared to me to extend under the Champs Elysées, and in which were piled about four hundred thousand inestimable and unattainable Cigars, in bundles or bales of about a thousand each.[1]

Yesterday I dined at the booksellers with the body of Translators[2] engaged on my new Edition—one of them a lady—young and pretty. (I hope by the bye, judging from the questions which they asked me and which I asked them, that it will be really well done.) Among them was an extremely able old Savant who occasionally expressed himself in a foreign tongue which I supposed to be Russian (I thought he had something to do with the Congress perhaps), but which my host told me when I came away, was English! We wallowed in an odd sort of dinner which would have been splashy[3] if it hadn't been too sticky. Salmon appeared late in the evening, and unforeseen creatures of the lobster species strayed in after the pudding. It was very hospitable and good natured though, and we all got on in the friendliest way. Please to imagine me, for three mortal hours, incessantly holding forth to the translators, and, among other things, addressing them in a neat and appropriate (French) speech. I came home quite light-headed.

On Saturday night, I paid three francs at the door of that place where we saw the wrestling,[4] and went in, at 11 o-Clock, to a Ball. Much the same as our own National Argyll Rooms.[5] Some pretty faces, but all of two classes—wicked and coldly calculating, or haggard and wretched in their worn beauty. Among the latter, was a woman of thirty or so, in an Indian shawl, who never stirred from a seat in a corner all the time I was there. Handsome, regardless, brooding, and yet with some nobler qualities in her forehead. I mean to walk about tonight, and look for her. I didn't speak to her there, but I have a fancy that I should like to know more about her. Never shall, I suppose.

Franconi's[6] I have been to again, of course. Nowhere else. I finished "that" No.[7] as soon as Macready went away, and have done something for Household Words next week, called Proposals for a National Jest Book, that I take rather kindly to. The first blank page of Little Dorrit No. 8[8] now eyes me on this desk with a pressing curiosity. It will get nothing out of me to day, I distinctly perceive.[9]—

[a]Townshend's Henri,[10] and Bully (the dog) have just been here—came in with a message at the double dash. Bully disconcerts me a good deal. He dined here on Sunday with his master, and got a young family of puppies out of each of the doors, fell into indecent transports with the claw of the round table, and was madly in love with Townshend's boots. All of which, Townshend seems to have no idea of, but merely says "Bul-ly!" when he is on his hind-legs like the sign of a public house. If he dines here again, I mean to have a trifle of camphor ready for him, and to try whether it has the effect upon him that it is said to have upon the Monks (with which piece of scientific knowledge I taunt Stanfield[11] when we go out together).[a]

[1] See *To* White, 17–22 Apr.

[2] Under the direction of Paul Lorain: see *To* Hachette, 17 Jan 57 and *fn*.

[3] Ostentatious (slang).

[4] Not discovered.

[5] At 7 1/2 Great Windmill St, virtually a high-class brothel.

[6] The equestrian entertainment put on by the Franconi troupe at the Cirque Olympique in the Boulevard du Temple: see Vol. VI, p. 117*n*.

[7] See *To* Forster, 7 Apr and *fnn*.

[8] Chs 26–9, published 30 June.

[9] He did not, apparently, begin the No. until 9 May (*To* Georgina, that day).

[aa] Omitted in *CD to WC* and N.

[10] Henri Foosters, Townshend's servant.

[11] As a Roman Catholic.

[a]That swearing of the Academy Carpenters is the best thing of its kind I ever heard of.[1] I suppose the oath to be administered by little Knight. It's my belief that the stout Porter now no more, wouldn't have taken it.—Our cook's going. Says she an't strong enought for [b]Boo Lone.[b] I don't know what there is particularly trying in that climate.—The Nice little Nurse who goes into all manner of shops without knowing one word of French, took some Lace to be mended the other day, and the Shopkeeper impressed with the idea that she had come to sell it, *would* give her money; with which she returned weeping, believing it (until explanation ensued) to be the price of shame. All send kindest regard. Ever Faithfully

CD.[a]

To [?THE REV. JAMES WHITE],[2] [?17–22 APRIL 1856]

MS (fragment) Mr L. Mastracci. *Date:* shortly after Girardin's dinner-party (14 Apr): see *To* Forster, 17 Apr.

above there is a conservatory which is like the South of France—only neither scorched nor dusty.

Think of this:

EMILE GIRARDIN[3]

gave another dinner the other day. We were about 15 or 18, and had every possible, impossible, conceivable, and inconceivable, dish—down to a little red flower pot for every guest, full of bright fresh strawberries. The only novelty was, that after dinner when we were in the Drawing Room, he asked me if I would go into another room and smoke a Cigar? On my replying Yes, he opened a species of mahogany cave with a key hanging on his watch chain, and shewed (as nearly as I could compute) about two hundred and fifty thousand inestimable and unattainable Cigars, tied up in bundles of about 1000 each.

ALL[3]

send their kindest loves to Mrs. White[4] and all the house. In which I heartily join.

Ever Faithfully
CHARLES DICKENS

To W. H. WILLS, 24 APRIL 1856*

MS Free Library of Philadelphia.

Paris, Thursday Twenty Fourth April, 1856

My Dear Wills.

I return you my Proof,[5] corrected.

[aa] Final paragraph of letter written very small and crowded into remaining piece of page. The stop and dash that occur twice are probably substitutes for new paragraphs for which there is no room.

[1] Allusion untraced.

[bb] Written very clear and larger than rest of letter.

[2] In view of the conclusion, may be to White.

[3] Underlined by short double strokes. This is the only known letter to another correspondent in which CD uses the sub-headings peculiar to letters to Wills.

[4] Née Rose Hill (1805–82): see Vol. v, p. 170*n*.

[5] Of "Proposals for a National Jest-Book."

I am very much disheartened by the last published No. of H.W.[1] which is—not to mince the matter—frightfully bad. No idea in it, no purpose, no appropriateness to or about anything, a mere hash-up of most indifferent magazine papers at chance-medley.[2]

Tomorrow morning I will go to work again and try to do another paper,[3] so that you may receive it on Monday Morning. It would be better not to begin a No. with your story,[4] under the circumstances, if it can possibly be avoided.

Ever Faithfully
CD.

To JOHN ROBERTSON,[5] 26 APRIL 1856*

MS Free Library of Philadelphia.

Paris, Saturday Evening Twenty Sixth April, 1856

Dear Sir.

I cannot estimate the length at which your proposed subject will have to be treated in Household Words, until your manner of treating it is before me. But I shall be glad to try it, and I think it promises well.[6] There is no objection to an article occupying four pages.[7]

Pray avoid anything like a fragmentary appearance. I think I rather observed it in one of the two papers you left with me. I need not tell *you* that it is never necessary to write "down" to the popular capacity; but that the great merit of plain, easy, flowing narrative, while it is acceptable to all readers, is particularly felt by a large and mixed audience.

I leave Paris immediately, and will myself give Mr Wills such instructions as shall ensure your sustaining no disappointment in reference to the request with which you close your note.[8]

Dear Sir
Faithfully Yours
CHARLES DICKENS

John Robertson Esquire.

[1] No. 318, which appeared as usual on 23 Apr.

[2] i.e. assembled at random. It contained Sala's "All up with Everything", an account of Eugène Huzar's book, which CD had already criticised (see *To* Wills, 13 Apr and *fn*); "Attraction and Repulsion" by E. S. Dixon, an account of a study of Algeria; the 2nd part of Whitehead's story, "Nemesis"; "Madame Freschon's" by Harriet Parr, an account of a French young ladies' school; and "The Marker", on billiard players, by James Payn. CD was probably most disheartened by their being no serious article of topical interest, or raising social issues.

[3] "Railway Dreaming", *HW*, 10 May 56, XIII, 385, on Paris and its institutions, including the Bourse and the Morgue.

[4] See *To* Wills, 20 Apr and *fn*. "The Ninth of June" did not appear until June; of its four instalments none began a number.

[5] John Robertson (?1811–75), journalist, living in Paris; frequent contributor to *HW* Oct 55–Apr 59: see Vol. VII, p. 705 and *n*.

[6] Coast Folk, the subject of four articles by Robertson: "Coast Folk", 21 June 56, XIII, 550; "Scotch Coast Folk", 5 July, XIII, 585; "Scotch Coast Folk. Footdee in the Last Century", 19 July, XIV, 16; and "English Coast Folk", 9 Aug, XIV, 81.

[7] All except the first occupied 4 or more pages.

[8] Clearly concerning payment; probably that his fee should be sent to Paris.

To W. H. WILLS, 27 APRIL 1856

MS Rosenbach Foundation.

Champs Elysées, Paris
Sunday Morning Twenty Seventh April, 1856

My Dear Wills.

H.W.[1]

I return the proof of No. 320,[2] and enclose a paper of my own with which to begin it.[3]

This will enable you to dispense in this No. either with Billeted at Boulogne,[4] or a Tale of a Pocket Archipelago.[5] They are both weak, and the latter (as a story) is really almost too blear-eyed to fall into the ranks.

Mr. Duthie's Sundays too, are washy in the last degree. There is really nothing whatever in them. And it is the diabolical property of colorless, shapeless, things of this nature, that they shut up good subjects and get no kind of point or effect out of them. I would as soon dine off an old glove, as read such pale literary boiled veal.[6]

Get Epidemics[7] as near the opening (the usual poetical place)[8] as you can, because it has a purpose in it.

In your list of the No. is a cabalistic word that looks like "Surnames". I have not received such an article.[9]

THE GUILD[1]

must certainly be first discussed by Forster, you, and me. Then it will be necessary (if we can see any course of action), to call a meeting.

MY ARRANGEMENTS[1]

are these.—The tent is striking here, and I can't work in the midst of the unsettled domesticity. The Hogarth family don't leave Tavistock House till next Saturday. And I cannot in the meantime bear the contemplation of their imbecility any more. (I think my constitution is already undermined by the sight of Hogarth at breakfast.) I am therefore going to leave here by the Mail, *next Tuesday Morning at 8* for Dover, where I shall stay at the Ship (working I hope in the mornings), until I come to town early on Saturday. The Ship Hotel, Dover, is consequently my address. I purpose arriving there to dinner on Tuesday, and no doubt shall either see or hear from you, then, or very soon afterwards.

Ever Faithfully
CD

P.S. Your letter just received. You make too much of my complaint[10]—that is, you take it too personally. I described the No. to you, just as I should describe it to

[1] Underlined with short double strokes.

[2] For 10 May 56.

[3] See *To* Wills, 24 Apr, *fn*.

[4] By Miss French; it appeared on 24 May (XIII, 442).

[5] A story by Bayle St John (1822–59: see Vol. V, p. 226*n*); it appeared on 14 June (XIII, 523).

[6] "More Sundays Abroad" (in Austria, Germany and France), by William Duthie (*HW* contributor since July 52), was nevertheless published in No. 320 (10 May 56, XIII, 400).

[7] By Eliza Lynn, an account of Southwood Smith's *Epidemics Considered with Relation to their Common Nature*, 10 May 56, XIII, 397.

[8] It is the fifth of seven items, following a short poem, "Dawn".

[9] Probably "Sundays".

[10] Of *HW*, No. 318, in *To* Wills, 24 Apr.

myself. Nothing more. It makes my visage very rueful, and my pen took the same expression. I have a way (perhaps you never observed it) of expressing myself in a strong manner. I beg to Sub to brighten up.

To MARK LEMON, 27 APRIL 1856

MS Benoliel Collection.

Paris, Sunday Twenty Seventh April, 1856

My Dear Mark. I dispatch this very short note, to let you know my movements.

As the Tents are striking here, and I can't work in the distracted apartments, I shall leave here, as I purpose, by the Day Mail on Tuesday morning, and dine at Dover.

As the Hogarths don't leave Tavistock House 'till Saturday, and as I cannot bear the contemplation of that family at breakfast any more, I think of remaining at Dover (working, I hope, in the mornings) until Saturday, when I shall come up early for the Academy Dinner.

Thus it is then, Sir (I stand with one leg bent, as delivering a Shakespearian message with this preface). From [a]and at[a] and after dinner time on Tuesday, the brightest and most intelligent of countenances will beam at

The Royal Ship Hotel, Dover.

On Sunday morning it will be found at Tavistock House, to let for the day. After which it will remain in that commodious Family Mansion throughout the month.

Kindest love from all

Ever affectionately

CD.

To AUGUSTUS TRACEY,[1] 27 APRIL 1856*

MS Texas University Library.

Paris, Champs Elysées 49

Sunday Twenty Seventh April, 1856

My Dear Jack.

I hope I enclose what you mean. Pray tell my friend Henry[2] with my regard that I am proud to be sponsor for him on his entrance into life, and feel gratified by his asking me to say my honest word for him.

This is but a fag-end of a rope to heave overboard to an old Salt floating about on the Hencoop of idleness; but if I were to pay out more, I should lose the post. So I won't yaw about like the dog-vane in a calm, but clap a stopper on and belay.[3]

[aa] inserted over caret.

[1] Lieut. Augustus Frederick Tracey RN (1798–1878), former Governor of the Westminster House of Correction, Tothill Fields: see Vol. II, p. 270*n*, and later vols; now living in Plymouth.

[2] Henry Elliott Tracey, Tracey's son by his first wife (*d.* 1845).

[3] Whole paragraph in nautical terms. A dog-vane is a small light vane, made of thread, cork and feathers.

Mrs. Dickens and Georgina unite with me in cordial messages to Mrs. Tracey,[1] and in best remembrances to Henry. So no more at present from yours ever

Edward Cuttle.

To JOHN FORSTER, [?26–7 APRIL 1856]

Extracts in F, VII, v, 620 and 621. *Date:* according to Forster, before he left Paris (29 Apr); Forster implies shortly before, and that both extracts are from same letter.

The murder over the way (the third or fourth event of that nature in the Champs Elysées since we have been here) seems to disclose the strangest state of things. The Duchess who is murdered lived alone in a great house which was always shut up, and passed her time entirely in the dark. In a little lodge outside lived a coachman (the murderer), and there had been a long succession of coachmen who had been unable to stay there, and upon whom, whenever they asked for their wages, she plunged out with an immense knife, by way of an immediate settlement. The coachman never had anything to do, for the coach hadn't been driven out for years; neither would she ever allow the horses to be taken out for exercise. Between the lodge and the house, is a miserable bit of garden, all overgrown with long rank grass, weeds, and nettles; and in this, the horses used to be taken out to swim—in a dead green vegetable sea, up to their haunches. On the day of the murder there was a great crowd, of course; and in the midst of it up comes the Duke her husband (from whom she was separated), and rings at the gate. The police open the grate. "C'est vrai donc," says the Duke, "que Madame la Duchesse n'est plus?"—"C'est trop vrai, Monseigneur."—"Tant mieux," says the Duke, and walks off deliberately, to the great satisfaction of the assemblage.[2]

An occurrence in England, three years earlier, and wildly improbable. B.[3] was with me the other day, and, among other things that he told me, described an extraordinary adventure in his life, at a place not a thousand miles from my "property" at Gadshill, three years ago. He lived at the tavern and was sketching one day when an open carriage came by with a gentleman and lady in it. He was sitting in the same place working at the same sketch, next day, when it came by again. So, another day, when the gentleman got out and introduced himself. Fond of art; lived at the great house yonder, which perhaps he knew; was an Oxford man and a Devonshire squire, but not resident on his estate, for domestic reasons; would be glad to see him to dinner to-morrow. He went, and found, among other things a very fine library. "At your disposition," said the Squire, to whom he had now described himself and his pursuits. "Use it for your writing and drawing. Nobody else uses it." He stayed in the house *six months*. The lady was a mistress, aged five-and-twenty, and very

[1] Née Marian Corydon, Tracey's second wife; married Nov 49.

[2] The murder of the Countess de Gaumont-Laforce, daughter-in-law of the Duke de Gaumont-Laforce, by her Wurtenberger groom, Antoine Baumann, described in gruesome detail in "Unhappiness in the Elysian Fields", by John Robertson, *HW*, 7 June 56, XIII, 502. She was a monster of avarice; Baumann (who strangled her with his hands, heated by brandy), confessed to the police at once; was tried on 15 Apr 56; and sentenced to life-imprisonment with hard labour.

[3] Probably someone living in Paris, but not identified; nor has his story been traced.

beautiful, drinking her life away. The Squire was drunken, and utterly depraved and wicked; but an excellent scholar, an admirable linguist, and a great theologian. Two other mad visitors stayed the six months. One, a man well known in Paris here, who goes about the world with a crimson silk stocking in his breast pocket, containing a tooth-brush and an immense quantity of ready money. The other, a college chum of the Squire's, now ruined; with an insatiate thirst for drink; who constantly got up in the middle of the night, crept down to the dining-room, and emptied all the decanters.... B. stayed on in the place, under a sort of devilish fascination to discover what might come of it.... Tea or coffee never seen in the house, and very seldom Water. Beer, champagne, and brandy, were the three drinkables. Breakfast: leg of mutton, champagne, beer, and brandy. Lunch: shoulder of mutton, champagne, beer, and brandy. Dinner: every conceivable dish (Squire's income, £7,000 a-year), champagne, beer, and brandy. The Squire had married a woman of the town from whom he was now separated, but by whom he had a daughter. The mother, to spite the father, had bred the daughter in every conceivable vice. Daughter, then 13, came from school once a month. Intensely coarse in talk, and always drunk. As they drove about the country in two open carriages, the drunken mistress would be perpetually tumbling out of one, and the drunken daughter perpetually tumbling out of the other. At last the drunken mistress drank her stomach away, and began to die on the sofa. Got worse and worse, and was always raving about Somebody's where she had once been a lodger, and perpetually shrieking that she would cut somebody else's heart out. At last she died on the sofa, and, after the funeral, the party broke up. A few months ago, B. met the man with the crimson silk stocking at Brighton, who told him that the Squire was dead "of a broken heart"; that the chum was dead of delirium tremens; and that the daughter was heiress to the fortune. He told me all this, which I fully believe to be true, without any embellishment—just in the off-hand way in which I have told it to you.

To MISS ELLEN CARROLL,[1] 28 APRIL 1856*

MS British Library. *Address:* À Mddle. Ellen Carroll | 40 Rue Laffitte | En Ville.

Champs Elysées | Twenty Eighth April, 1856

Madam.

Your letter reaches me when I am on the eve of quitting Paris, and am surrounded by many additions to my usual occupations. If I reply to you briefly, I beg you therefore to attribute my so doing to the heavy demands on my attention, and to no want of interest on my part in the confidence you entrust to me.

I regret to assure you that I am quite unable to advise you how to obtain employment in the way of translation. So far as I know, all the translations that are made from English into French, are made by French people. The kind of translations usually made from French into English, are made by English booksellers who (I assume) employ their own commissioned agents for this purpose. I am not in business-communication with any publisher of this kind, and, even if I were acquainted with your powers of translating freely and faithfully and could honestly commend them, I should be quite at a loss to whom to present to you.

[1] Not further identified.

I wish it were in my power to be as efficient towards you in this real working world, as you give me the gratification of informing me that I have been in that shadowy sphere in which much of my life is passed. But it would be cruel in me to disguise the truth, for the selfish pleasure of inspiring you with a false hope.

Your faithful Servant

Miss Carroll. CHARLES DICKENS

To MRS HANSEN,[1] 28 APRIL 1856*

MS Mr Alfred Palludan. *Address:* Affranchie | Mrs. Emmy Hansen | care of | Messrs A & N Hansen & Co. | Copenhagen.

Paris Champs Elysées 49 | Monday Twenty Eighth April 1856.

My Dear Mrs. Hansen.

I am afraid you will have begun, long ago, to think me unmindful of you, and uninterested in your good husband and your pretty child. But this is not the case. When I received your letter, I read it with great pleasure, and I have often thought of it since. Uncertainty, however, as to my summer arrangements has induced me to postpone writing to you from time to time, until I should see the way before me more clearly.

You know by this time, I hope, that I am busily engaged with a new book. I have been passing the winter in Paris, which I leave tomorrow morning. I shall remain in London during May, but not longer, as I design to pass the summer in a little country house at Boulogne Sur Mer. If you should pay a visit to England this year therefore (that is to say before October) I shall not be at my own house, but shall be living at

La Villa des Moulineaux
Boulogne Sur Mer

—and if you should come that way, it would gratify me very much to see you again and to become acquainted with your husband.

Pray give him my regard, and kiss your precious little daughter for me. And believe me as I truly am,

Your friend

Mrs. Hansen. CHARLES DICKENS

To THE SECRETARY,[2] EDINBURGH PHILOSOPHICAL INSTITUTION,[3] [OCTOBER 1855–28 APRIL 1856]

Mention in *To* Gordon, 2 May 56. *Date:* written from Paris, i.e. between Oct 55 and 29 Apr 56; more likely towards end of his visit.

[1] No doubt the former Emmely Gotschalk (also addressed as "Emmy"), a young Danish woman, to whom he had written several letters of advice in 1850–1. She was in London in Mar 54 (see Vol. VII, p. 291) and probably told CD of her coming marriage.

[2] Henry Bowie (1812–85), Secretary and cashier, Edinburgh Philosophical Institution, of Queen St, 1847 to his death; previously linen merchant in Edinburgh.

[3] Founded 1847.

To FRAU ALBERTI, 30 APRIL 1856

MS Mr Erich Lehmann.

Dover, England. | Wednesday Thirtieth April, 1856.

My Dear Correspondent.

While I was in Paris (which I only left yesterday), I received your book[1] and your charming letter, quite safely. I am grieved to say that I do not read German; but my eldest boy, who has been partly educated in Germany and knows the language well, has gone through your book at my side, and has enabled me to understand much of its pure idea, and fine, womanly, *true* sentiment. I am proud to be associated with it, and thank you more than ever.

It will take me a year from this time, to finish Little Dorrit. After that, I think I really shall begin (Please God) to make myself master of the German language. I lose so much pleasure by not knowing it, and I can learn a language with so little difficulty, that I often reproach myself for not having acquired it long ago. I am not so young as I am in the picture you have seen, for that was painted some fifteen years ago, and I am now 44.[2] It looks a good deal, on paper, I find; but I believe I am very young-looking still, and I know that I am a very active vigorous fellow, who never knew in his own experience what the word "fatigue" meant.

This is in answer to your first question. In reply to your second question whether I dictate, I answer with a smile that I can as soon imagine a painter dictating his pictures. No. I write every word of my books with my own hand, and do not write them very quickly either. I write with great care and pains (being passionately fond of my art, and thinking it worth any trouble), and persevere, and work hard. I am a great walker besides, and plunge into cold water every day in the dead of winter. When I was last in Switzerland, I found that I could climb as fast as the Swiss Guides. Few strangers think I look like one who passes so many hours alone in his own Study. You would be disappointed perhaps, to see me with a brown-red color in my face?

I very seldom write or talk about myself, but you express your interest so naturally and unaffectedly, that I feel I ought to describe myself in the same spirit.

It makes me sorry to find you describing your health as very delicate. You must remember that in all your literary aspiration, and whether thinking or writing, it is indispensably necessary to relieve that wear and tear of the mind by some other exertion that may be wholesomely set against it. Habitually, I have always had, besides great bodily exercise, some mental pursuit of a light kind with which to vary my labors as an Author. And I have found the result so salutary, that I strongly commend it to the fair friend in whom I am deeply interested.

I am now upon my way home, merely staying here a couple of days to have some walks on the high cliffs by the sea. During the summer, I shall be generally at a little French Country House among pleasant gardens near Boulogne Sur Mer. But that is only a few hours journey from London, and I shall receive my letters and papers from thence, two or three times a week. My best address therefore, is at my own house

[1] See 31 Jan 56 and *fn*.

[2] The *Nickleby* portrait by Maclise, frequently reproduced.

Tavistock House
London

—and there I shall always be delighted to hear from you. Perhaps I may see you there one day? If not, I must come to Potsdam after I have learnt German from your book.

Farewell. God bless you! Always believe me, with great regard,

Your affectionate

Miss Sophie Verena CHARLES DICKENS

To WILKIE COLLINS, 30 APRIL 1856

MS Morgan Library.

Ship Hotel, Dover | Thirtieth April, 1856.

My Dear Collins.

Wills brought me your letter this morning, and I am very much interested in knowing what o'Clock it is by the watch with the brass tail to it. You know I am not in the habit of making professions, but I have so strong an interest in you and so true a regard for you, that nothing can come amiss in the way of information as to your well-doing.

How I wish you were well now! For here I am in two of the most charming rooms (a third, a bedroom you could have occupied, close by), overlooking the sea in the gayest way. And here I shall be, for a change, till Saturday. And here we might have been, drinking confusion to Baronetcies, and resolving never to pluck a leaf from the Toady Tree[1] till this very small world shall have rolled us off! Never mind. All to come—in the fulness of the Arctic Seasons.

I take, as the people say in the Comedies of 80 years ago, "hugely" to the idea you have suggested to Wills. But you mustn't do anything, until you feel it a pleasure; from which sensation (and the disappearance of the East Wind until next winter) I shall date your coming round the corner with a great velocity.

On Saturday morning, I shall be in town about 11, and will come on to Howland Street[2] about 1. Many thanks for your bulletin academical which I have dispatched straightway to Ary Scheffer.

They were all blooming in Paris yesterday morning. I took the Plorn out in a cabriolet the day before, and his observations on Life in general were wonderful.

Ever Yours

CD.

[1] CD refers to his "The Toady Tree", *HW*, 26 May 55, XI, 385, on the Englishman's truckling to titles. Probably a mutual acquaintance had recently accepted a baronetcy.

[2] An extension of New Cavendish St, where Collins was born. He had taken lodgings at No. 34 on leaving his mother's home earlier that year; and Caroline Graves and her daughter Harriet were evidently living nearby: see William M. Clarke, *The Secret Life of Wilkie Collins*, p. 93.

To VISCOUNT RAYNHAM,[1] 30 APRIL 1856*

MS Texas University Library.

Dover, Wednesday Thirtieth April | 1856

Dear Lord Raynham

Although I am not so sanguine of the results of my advocacy as you are, I shall be happy to fulfil my promise and to preside at the First Dinner in behalf of the Hospital in which you are so humanly interested.[2]

Any day in May will suit me; the later in the month, the better.

After Saturday next, I shall be at my own house in town. If the Committee will have the goodness to let me know the appointed day as soon as they shall have fixed it, I shall feel obliged to them.

Faithfully Yours

The | Viscount Raynham CHARLES DICKENS

To J. T. GORDON,[3] 2 MAY 1856*

MS Berg Collection.

Dover, Second May 1856.

My Dear Gordon.

I am only now in the receipt of your letter, which has come to hand here, where I am pausing for a rest and a walk on my way home from Paris. It gives me great concern to hear of your having been so seriously ill. Wills, in some wonderful manner, has never communicated the intelligence; and I supposed you to be as robust as ever. Of course I should have written to Mrs. Gordon to enquire about you, if I had had the faintest suspicion of your having been ill.

Take care of yourself, and I dare say you will be the better in the long run for the attack.

I wrote from Paris to the Philosophical Institution, explaining that my work really makes such an expedition out of the question this year, but that I hope to be able to do what they want next year. I will come to you then, with the greatest pleasure.

They are all well at Paris, and would send all manner of messages if they knew me to be writing. They leave on Monday week, and we purpose remaining in Town through May. We then go to Boulogne for the summer.

Little Dorrit, has beaten all her predecessors, in circulation.[4]

[1] John Villiers Stuart Townshend (1831–99), who succeeded his father as 5th Marquis Townshend in 1863; Treasurer, Royal Hospital for Incurables; also of St George's Hospital, London; Liberal MP for Tamworth 1856–63.

[2] The Royal Hospital for Incurables. CD took the chair at its first Anniversary dinner on 5 May 56: for his speech, see *Speeches*, ed. K. J. Fielding, pp. 223–5.

[3] John Thomson Gordon (1813–65), advocate; sheriff of Midlothian since 1849: see Vols II, p. 314*n* and VI, p. 759.

[4] It was running at *c.* 35,000 a No., 1,000 more than *Bleak House* at the same period, and 13,000 more than *Copperfield*.

My love to Mrs. Gordon[1] and Master Charley and all. Poor Andrew![2] The Bulletin shall be forwarded to Paris.

Ever My Dear Gordon

Faithfully Yours
CHARLES DICKENS

J. T. Gordon Esquire

To MESSRS BRADBURY & EVANS, 3 MAY 1856*

MS University of Texas.

OFFICE OF HOUSEHOLD WORDS,
Saturday Third May 1856

My Dear B and E.

Will you send me round, Little Dorrit No. 6,[3] and a pull of No. 7.[4]

Faithfully Yours Ever
CHARLES DICKENS

To MESSRS COUTTS & CO., 3 MAY 1856*

MS Sr Francesco Pertile.

London, Third May, 1856.

Messrs. Coutts and Co.

Please to deliver to the Bearer, a New Cheque-Book for me, ————[5]

CHARLES DICKENS

To MARK LEMON, 4 MAY 1856

MS Benoliel Collection.

Tavistock House | Sunday Fourth May 1856

My Dear Mark

I am up to my eyes in dust!—I will be at home from and after 4.

Stanny couldn't come last night, having an appointment with Mrs. Stanfield.

Ever affecy.
CD.

[1] Mary, daughter of Professor John Wilson ("Christopher North"): see Vol. VI, p. 759 and *n*.

[2] Their eldest son, Andrew Rutherford Gordon, midshipman; Lieut RN 1861; retired as Lieut Apr 1870.

[3] Chs 19–22 for May, published 30 Apr.

[4] Chs 23–5 for June, published 31 May.

[5] Dash stretches to edge of page.

To MRS CHARLES DICKENS, 5 MAY 1856

Text from MDGH, I, 433–5.

Tavistock House, | Monday, Fifth May, 1856.

My Dear Catherine,

I did nothing at Dover (except for "Household Words"),[1] and have not begun "Little Dorrit," No. 8,[2] yet. But I took twenty-mile walks in the fresh air, and perhaps in the long run did better than if I had been at work. The report concerning Scheffer's portrait I had from Ward.[3] It is in the best place in the largest room,[4] but I find the *general* impression of the artists exactly mine. They almost all say that it wants something; that nobody could mistake whom it was meant for, but that it has something disappointing in it, etc. etc.[5] Stanfield likes it better than any of the other painters, I think. His own picture is magnificent.[6] And Frith,[7] in a "Little Child's Birthday Party,"[8] is quite delightful. There are many interesting pictures. When you see Scheffer, tell him from me that Eastlake,[9] in his speech at the dinner, referred to the portrait as "a contribution from a distinguished man of genius in France, worthy of himself and of his subject."

[a]I did the maddest thing last night, and am deeply penitent this morning. We stayed at Webster's till any hour, and they wanted me, at last, to make punch, which couldn't be done when the jug was brought, because (to Webster's burning indignation) there was only one lemon in the house. Hereupon I then and there besought the establishment in general to come and drink punch on Thursday night, after the play; on which occasion it will become necessary to furnish fully the table with some cold viands from Fortnum and Mason's. Mark has looked in since I began this note, to suggest that the great festival may come off at "Household Words" instead. I am inclined to think it a good idea, and that I shall transfer the locality to that business establishment. But I am at present distracted with doubts and torn by remorse.[a]

The school-room and dining-room I have brought into habitable condition and

[1] Presumably correcting the final proof of No. 320, including his own "Railway Dreaming", 10 May, XIII, 385. See next and *fn* for "Out of the Season".

[2] Chs 26–9, for July, published 30 June.

[3] Edward Matthew Ward (1816–79; *DNB*); historical and portrait painter: see Vols. VI, p. 337*n* and VII, *passim*.

[4] Of the RA; now in the National Portrait Gallery.

[5] The *Art Journal*, May 56, though highly praising most of Scheffer's work ("he is a school of poetic Art ... one of the magnates of the French School"), was critical of this portrait: "the features", it said in the introduction to its review, "want relief and roundness, and the colour of the flesh is entirely false"; and in the review itself: "It is extremely unassuming, but we think too highly glazed ... it is not, we think, a very striking resemblance."

[6] He exhibited two; but CD almost certainly refers to *The Abandoned*, hung in the main room, based on Washington Irving's description of a wrecked ship in "The Voyage" from his Sketch-book. The other was *A guarda costa riding out a gale, off Basque Provinces, Spain*.

[7] William Powell Frith (1819–1909; *DNB*): see Vol. III, p. 373*n*.

[8] Entitled *Many happy returns of the day*: "A taking picture", commented Ruskin, "much ... above Mr. Frith's former standard. Note the advancing Pre-Raphaelitism in the wreath of leaves round the child's head" (*Notes on Some of the Principal Pictures Exhibited in ... the Royal Academy* ..., No. II—1856, pp. 18–19).

[9] Sir Charles Lock Eastlake (1793–1865; *DNB*), FRS, President RA 1850–65: see Vol. VII, p. 95*n*.

[aa] Omitted in *Mr & Mrs CD* and N. This is difficult to explain; MDGH must have had a MS which does not survive and the omission in subsequent printed texts is mysterious and probably an error.

comfortable appearance. Charley and I breakfast at half-past eight, and meet again at dinner when he does not dine in the City, or has no engagement. He looks very well.

The audiences at Gye's are described to me as absolute marvels of coldness.[1] No signs of emotion can be hammered out of them. Panizzi[2] sat next me at the Academy dinner, and took it very ill that I disparaged———.[3] The amateurs[4] here are getting up another pantomime, but quarrel so violently among themselves that I doubt its ever getting on the stage. Webster expounded his scheme for rebuilding the Adelphi to Stanfield and myself last night, and I felt bound to tell him that I thought it wrong from beginning to end. This is all the theatrical news I know.

[a]I write by this post to Georgy. Love to Mamey, Katey, Harry, and the noble Plorn. I should be glad to see him here.[a]

Ever affectionately

CD

To MISS GEORGINA HOGARTH, 5 MAY 1856

MS Dickens House.

Tavistock House | Monday May Fifth 1856

My Dear Georgy.

You will not be much surprised to hear that I have done nothing yet (except for H.W.), and have only just settled down into a corner of the Schoolroom. The extent to which John and I wallowed in dust for four hours yesterday morning, getting books and papers put away, and making things neat and comfortable about us, you may faintly imagine. At 4 in the afternoon came Stanfield, to whom I no sooner described the notion of the new play than he immediately upset all my new arrangements by making a Proscenium of the chairs and planning the Scenery with walking-sticks. One of the least things he did, was getting on the top of the Long table and hanging over the bar in the middle window where that top sash opens, as if he had got a hinge in the middle of his body. He is immensely excited on the subject. Mark had a Farce ready for the managerial perusal—but it won't do.

[b]Catherine will tell you of a tremendous party that is coming off (with me for the unhappy host) next Thursday at half past ten in the evening.[5]

When I got out of the dust at last yesterday, I went up to Miss Coutts's. She was out, but Mrs. Brown was at home in company with Dr. Skey.[6] Mrs. Brown talking

[1] Since the destruction of Covent Garden by fire on 5 Mar (see *To* Macready, 22 Mar and *fn*), Gye had been directing Italian opera at the Lyceum.

[2] Anthony Panizzi, Principal Librarian of the British Museum since 1856: see Vol. VII, p. 642*n*.

[3] Name omitted in MDGH; perhaps Sir Robert Smirke (1781–1867; *DNB*), the architect, who was working closely with Panizzi on the new British Museum Reading Room.

[4] No doubt the Amateurs of the Fielding Club: see Vol. VII, p. 594*n*.

[aa] Omitted in *Mr & Mrs CD* and N.

[bb] Omitted in MDGH.

[5] See *To* Mrs CD, 5 May and *To* Georgina Hogarth, 9 May.

[6] Frederic Carpenter Skey (1798–1872; *DNB*), FRS, surgeon: see Vol. V, p. 241*n*; had travelled with Miss Coutts and Mrs Brown in 1855.

great nonsense about the French people and their morality, I felt it necessary to defend them; and I said that most reflective persons contemplating the two nations would observe, I thought, one strong leading difference between them; to wit, that in England people dismiss the mention of social evils and vices which do nevertheless exist among them; and that in France people do not dismiss the mention of the same things but habitually recognize their existence. After crying several times "Don't say that! Don't say that! It gives me such pain to hear you say anything that I can't agree in!" (to which I, as many times, replied "Oh! But I must say it, you know, when according to our national vanity and prejudice, you disparage an unquestionably great nation") she pulled out her pocket handkerchief and burst into showers upon showers of tears. Old Skey looked horribly frightened, and, having, as I conceive, caught about a third of the discussion, seemed to be in doubt what I had done. I remained, of course, quite composed and went on (and came off) as if nothing had happened.

I had a good dialogue with Mrs. Birmingham[1] at the Ship. Old Baron Brunow[2] was expected over for two days, and both she and Birmingham almost drove me wild by perpetually coming up with all manner of reports about the Baron, and about the wind deterring him, and Lord Cowley[3] deterring him, and I don't know who deterring him. When I went into breakfast on Friday morning, I found Mrs. Birmingham in the room with my letters, waiting to say "You will be glad to hear Sir, that the Baron left Calais at 7 this morning, and will be here at 9. You will be able to see the Boat Sir from your window." To which I replied with the greatest politeness and in the gentlest accents, "Mrs. Birmingham it becomes at last necessary for me to confess that I don't care a damn about the Baron, and that if he were sunk coming over, it would not make the least difference to me."—She said "*In*deed, Sir?" and went smiling away, rubbing her hands.[b]

I went to the Dover Theatre on Friday night, which was a miserable spectacle. The pit is boarded over, and it is a drinking and smoking place. It was "for the Benefit of Mrs. A. Green",[4] and the town had been very extensively placarded with "Don't forget Friday." I made out Four and ninepence (I am serious) in the house, when I went in. We may have warmed up, in the course of the evening, to twelve shillings. A Jew played the Grand Piano, Mrs. A. Green[4] sang no end of songs (with not a bad voice, poor creature), Mr. Green[4] sang comic songs fearfully, and danced clog hornpipes capitally, and a miserable woman, shivering in a shawl and bonnet, sat in the side boxes all the evening, nursing Master A. Green,[4] aged 7 months. It was a most forlorn business, and I should have contributed a sovereign to the Treasury if I had known how.[5]

I walked to Deal and back that day; and on the previous day walked over the

[1] Wife of John Birmingham, manager of the Royal Ship Family Hotel, Custom House Quay and Stroud St, Dover.

[2] Baron Ernst Philip Ivanovitch Brunnov (1797–1875), Russian Minister in London 1840–54 and 1861–74.

[3] Henry Richard Charles Wellesley, 1st Earl Cowley (1804–84; *DNB*), Ambassador in Paris 1852–67.

[4] Names omitted on each mention in MDGH.

[5] CD uses all these details at the end of "Out of the Season", *HW*, 28 June, XIII, 553, though without giving Dover as the watering-place; the family acting become the "Wedgingtons".

Downs towards Canterbury, in a gale of wind. It was better than still weather, after all, being wonderfully fresh and free.

If the Plorn were sitting at this schoolroom window in the corner, he would see more cats in an hour than he ever saw in his life. *I* never saw so many, I think, as I have seen since yesterday morning.

There is a painful picture of a great deal of merit (Egg has bought it) in the Exhibition, painted by the man who did those little Interiors of Forster's.[1] It is called the death of Chatterton.[2] The dead figure is a good deal like Arthur Stone; and I was touched on Saturday to see that tender old file standing before it, crying under his spectacles at the idea of seeing his son dead. It was a very tender manifestation of his gentle old boiling, bothering heart.[3]

This sums up my news, which is no news at all. Kiss the Plorn for me, and expound to him that I am always looking forward to meeting him again, among the birds and flowers in the garden on the side of the hill at Boulogne.

Ever affecy. CD.

[a]P.S. Your Boulogne boat will be in the afternoon (somewhere about 4) and you will not get to London before 11.[a]

To BENJAMIN WEBSTER, 5 MAY 1856

MS Mr and Mrs Donald F. Hyde.

Tavistock House | Monday Fifth May 1856

My Dear Webster.

From Dispatches I have received this morning, I conclude the proposed Wednesday's Gathering to be abandoned and off.

Thursday's appointment of course remains. Will you remind Madame Celeste[4] that I said Half past 10, last night; but that I had no need to say any time, in as much

[1] Henry Wallis (1830–1916), Pre-Raphaelite painter; exhibited in RA 1854–77 and in Old Water Colour Society. The painting shows the 17 year old poet Thomas Chatterton (1752–70; *DNB*), lying dead on his couch in his Holborn garret, having taken arsenic; Ruskin described it as "faultless and wonderful, a most noble example of the great school" (*Notes on . . . RA*, 1856, p. 26); the *Art Journal*, May 56 considered that "it exhibits marvellous power, and may be accepted as a safe augury of the artist's fame"; though it criticized the rich colours of Chatterton's dress, considering his poverty. It now hangs in the Tate. As a model Wallis used his close friend, the young George Meredith (see 10 May 56, *fn*) and two years later eloped with Meredith's wife to Capri, soon afterwards deserting her. Forster owned his painting, *In Shakespeare's House, Stratford-on-Avon*, exhibited with other similar pictures in RA 1854 (in FC).

[2] In fact, entitled simply *Chatterton*; with a quotation from Marlowe's *Dr Faustus*: "Cut is the branch that might have grown full straight, And burned is Apollo's laurel bough."

[3] Frank Stone's eldest son was Arthur Paul Stone (*b.* 1838); student of the Inner Temple June 57; later, barrister and law reporter.

[aa] Omitted in MDGH.

[4] Celeste Elliott, always known as Madame Celeste (?1814–82; *DNB*), actress and dancer: see Vol. VI, p. 120*n*.

as the Punch shall be in high condition as soon after the end of the first piece[1] as shall suit her convenience.

A horrible misgiving comes over me in the Easterly repentance of this morning, that I am engaged to Forster for next Sunday.

Faithfully Yours always
CHARLES DICKENS

To T. L. ALDRIDGE,[2] 6 MAY 1856*

MS Private.

Tavistock House, London | Sixth May 1856.

Mr. Charles Dickens presents his Compliments to Mr. Aldridge, and begs, in reply to Mr. Aldridge's note, to state that he has great pleasure in subscribing for five copies of the Original Poems.[3] Mr. Wills, Household Words office, will receive them, and pay the subscription.

To R. FRIEND,[4] 6 MAY 1856

Summary from Sotheby's catalogue, July 1982; *MS* 1 p.; dated Tavistock House, London, 6 May 56; addressed R. Friend.

Replying to his letter received that morning, he begs to assure him that his engagements make it impossible to accept the very welcome invitation of the Working Men's Institute.

To [?G. G.] LOWNE,[5] 6 MAY 1856*

MS Private.

Tavistock House | Sixth May, 1856.

Mr. Charles Dickens presents his compliments to Mr. Lowne, and begs to express

[1] At the Adelphi. *Like and Unlike*, adapted by Langford and W. J. Sorrell from the French play *L'Ange et Le Demon* and first produced 9 Apr. The performances of both Webster and Mme Celeste were praised in the *Globe*, 20 Apr; it was followed by J. S. Coyne's farce, *Urgent Private Affairs*, and J. E. Wilkes's farce, *How's Your Uncle?*

[2] T. L. Aldridge, an Oxford resident and, as the dedication page shows, a working man.

[3] *Fear-Nac-Flu, A Combat and other poems*, 1857; by two authors, T. L. Aldridge and G. Curtis, their contributions distinguished by "A" and "C"; dedicated "To the | Working Men of England ... fraternally inscribed | By Two of their Order." The title-poem by "A" is an admitted imitation of Scott's *Lady of the Lake*. Preface dated "Oxford, 1857"; the long list of subscribers, pp. 139–43, includes "Charles Dickens, Esq ... 5". The list contains senior figures in the University and many Oxford residents, including two other Aldridges.

[4] Probably Richard Friend, author of some priv. printed poems, to whom CD had written on 1 Oct 52 (Vol. VI, p. 767 and *n*); and perhaps related to the John Friend, also of Dover, of 5 Oct 55 (see Vol. VII, p. 716*n*).

[5] Perhaps George Gill Lowne, MRCS, of 35 Queen's Row, Walworth; for 30 years surgeon to Workhouse of St Mary, Newington and Superintendent of Pauper Lunatics there 1826–42.

his regret that he cannot have the gratification of complying with Mr. Lowne's request. He wishes to avoid sitting for any Portrait whatever. If he sat to the gentleman in question, that departure from his resolution would necessitate the fulfilment of conditional promises to others who have a prior claim upon him, and he must therefore unwillingly excuse himself.

To BENJAMIN WEBSTER, 7 MAY 1856

MS Houghton Library, Harvard.

Tavistock House | Wednesday May Seventh 1856.

My Dear Webster

An idea in the nature of an inspiration has occurred to me this morning, in connexion with the Punch project.

I was contemplating my dismantled Study, with the Carpet in the corner like an immense roly-poly pudding, and all the chairs upside down as if they had turned over like birds and died with their legs in the air, when it flashed upon me Why should I bring the ladies and you so far to a dreary house, when there is the Household Words office on your way home? I instantly changed the Venue, sent down certain bottles to Wellington Street, and shall expect you there instead. Pray tell Madame Celeste so, with my kind regard.

If there should be a small box disengaged tomorrow night, will you leave it for Stanfield and me?[1]

Faithfully Yours always
CHARLES DICKENS

To CLARKSON STANFIELD, 8 MAY 1856*

MS Yale University Library.

Tavistock House | Thursday Evening Eight May | 1856.

My Dear Stanny.

A knock-down blow!—I am desperately sorry, but there is no help for it, and I feel you do quite right.

Ever affectionately
CHARLES DICKENS

To MRS CHARLES DICKENS, 9 MAY 1856

MS British Library. *Address:* France | A Madame Charles Dickens | 49 Avenue des champs Elysées | Paris.

Household Words Office | Friday Ninth May 1856

My dearest Catherine

There has been such a Gale blowing for two days (it blew down one of the large

[1] See *To* Webster, 5 May and *fn.*

lilac trees in the front court), that I received your letter only this morning. No French Mail could get in yesterday.

I had no doubt that Hachette's payment would be made.

From what Georgy tells me, it appears to me that you will all require a new passport. I write by this post, to tell her what to do and how to get it.

The boat on Wednesday the 14th. (I have engaged to dine with the Emerson Tennents[1] that day at some unheard of hour—about 9, I think) leaves Boulogne at 5, 40. You leave Folkestone again, at 8,50, and arrive in London at 11,20. Some supper shall be ready at Tavistock House.

We have made a very different place of that establishment, by clearing out the dust on the first floor, where it lay an inch thick. We have swept and washed the Study and Drawing Room, opened the windows, aired the carpets, and purified every room from the roof to the hall. I have barely got to work yet, on Little Dorrit.

Maclise has given me the most wonderful account of Mrs. Colburn[2] on the occasion of the Richmond Dinner. "By God Sir the depreciation that has taken place in that woman is fearful! She has no blood Sir in her body—no color—no voice—is all scrunched and squeezed together—and seems to me in deep affliction—while Forster Sir is rampant and raging, and presenting a contrast beneath which you sink into the dust. She *may* come round again—*may* get fat—*may* get cheerful—*may* get a voice to articulate with, but by the blessed Star of Morning Sir she is now a sight to behold!"

Love to Mary, Katey, Harry, and the Noble Plorn.

Ever affectionately
CD.

To MISS GEORGINA HOGARTH, 9 MAY 1856

MS Dickens House.

Household Words Office | Friday Ninth May 1856.

My Dear Georgy. It appears to me that the whole party will necessarily require a new passport. In case this note should not arrive, through bad weather, in time to

[1] Sir James Emerson Tennent (1804–69; *DNB*), politician and author: see Vol. VI, p. 701*n*; and his wife, Letitia, daughter of a Belfast banker; married 1832.

[2] Née Eliza Crosbie, daughter of a RN captain; widow of the publisher Henry Colburn (*d.* 1855; *DNB*; see Vol. I, p. 170*n*); aged 37. She married Forster on 24 Sep. Maclise's joking account of her "depreciation" during the engagement is intended as a parody of Forster ("By God, Sir"). Richard Renton, her nephew, described her as "Petite, dainty in form and feature ... the most charming, the sweetest-natured woman it was possible to conceive" (Richard Renton, *John Forster and his Friendships*, 1912, p. 94). Despite Jane Carlyle's complaint that she "gabbles like a mill-clapper when she has any ideas" (given in James A. Davies, *John Forster: A Literary Life*, Leicester University Press, 1983, p. 109), a close friendship developed between the two. Davies quotes a telling letter to her from Jane Carlyle of 30 Oct 62: "Hang it! Why might not we go sometimes with a mutual carpet bag, and spend a day and night at some way-side Inn, when we feel to need 'a change' from our own comfortable homes, and men-of-genius Husbands!" (MS National Library of Scotland, *ibid.*, p. 110).

enable you to get one in Paris[1] on Saturday, you can go to that old ass of a Consul at Boulogne[2] and get it there; but it would be best done in Paris. I don't think the Embassy is the right place, but the Consul's office. The Consul is a Mr. Freeborn or Freeman,[3] I think, and you can instantly find out where his office is, by asking at Galignani's.[4]

The party came off here, last night, with great success. Cold collation of pigeon pie, collared red partridge,[5] ham, roast fowls, and lobster salads. One hot dish, consisting of a most immense heap of asparagus. Considerable quantities of punch were disposed of, and Charley and I got home at ½ past 2. I went to the Adelphi first, and saw a poor piece enough. On the previous night, went to Drury Lane to see "Mrs. Florence[6] in the Yankee Housekeeper".[7] A very quaint good thing. What was my amazement on coming here that day (Wednesday) to meet Stanfield, Forster and Maclise—to find Macready here! He had just come up by Railway, bringing Katey with him to stay at Fox's.[8] We improvised an admirable dinner here to his great delight, and he went back next day.

I am "going" to work furiously. Am only just beginning after all!

Ever affectionately

CD.

To LIEUT-COLONEL W. P. WAUGH,[9] 9 MAY 1856

MS Benoliel Collection.

Tavistock House | Friday Ninth May, 1856

Dear Colonel Waugh.

It is with great reluctance and regret that I express my inability to comply at present with the request so very agreeably and cordially preferred to me by Mrs. Waugh and yourself. It would give me real pleasure to return my cheerful assent to it, if I could do so at any moderate inconvenience and at the cost of any reasonable uneasiness. But I am so busy with my book just now, that to enter upon the getting-up of a Play with the attention and completeness that alone make that pursuit

[1] In London, passports for France were granted immediately on personal application at the French Consul's office and cost five shillings. No doubt the same regulations obtained at the British Consulate in Paris.

[2] Capt. William Hamilton, Rue de Boston, Consul since 1826: see Vol. VII, p. 430 and *n*.

[3] The British Consul in 1856 was Thomas Pickford. CD may have remembered one of his staff, with a name similar to the one he gives.

[4] At 224 Rue Rivoli.

[5] The red-legged or French partridge.

[6] Née Malvina Pray, Mrs Barney Williams's sister, wife of the American actor, William Jermyn Florence (1831–91; *DAB*); married 1853; his parts included Capt. Cuttle; they played together with great success for the first ten years of their marriage, mainly in Irish-American comedy.

[7] An Irish-American comedietta (author unknown) that ran for 50 nights from 28 Apr. Mrs Florence took the main part of Peg Ann Meritable Higginfluter and sang two new Yankee songs; her husband played O'Connor.

[8] The Rev. William Johnson Fox (1786–1864; *DNB*), Unitarian minister, preacher, journalist and radical MP; principal leader writer on *Daily News* 1846: see Vols I, p. 387*n*, IV, p. 411*n* and *passim*, and V, p. 621*n* (Vol. VI index has "William John" in error); wrote regular letters as "Publicola" for the *Weekly Dispatch* until 1861.

[9] Lt-Col. William Petrie Waugh, retired; for a charity performance by the amateurs in his home, Campden House, Kensington, managed by CD, on 10 July 55, see Vol. VII, pp. 669 and *nn*.

interesting to me, would be to undertake a painful labor. I honestly assure you that I have not the time for it, and that my thoughts are too much occupied.

I cannot easily tell you with what truthfulness I reciprocate your wish for our being better acquainted, or what a lively remembrance I always bear of your generous hospitality and your charming house and family. But the necessity I am often under of preserving a perfect command over my time, and of adapting all my habits to my Art, involves many little sacrifices of social enjoyment—of which I entreat you to accept these excuses as a notable specimen.

And in deed I have even a dramatic reason (in addition to the beckoning hand of Little Dorrit) for betaking myself resolutely to country quiet and country hours until the late Autumn. We have projects for another Play at home at Christmas time, and I must earn the leisure for that enjoyment in the future by diligent present work.

If we do not meet in the meanwhile, I shall hope to be so fortunate as to count you and Mrs. Waugh among the audience to our new piece. In any case I shall not lose you for the want of searching you out and giving you abundant notice.

It gives me great concern to learn that you are so unwell. But I know nobody whom the East wind has not blown into bed. Weather-wise people say it is to last until Midsummer; I have a kind of wicked joy in knowing that it is as bad in Paris, and that noses are as blue in the Champs Elysées as in Hyde Park. My family write me that it is black there too, and that the Sun gives in continually.

With kind compliments and regard to Mrs. Waugh, and best wishes for a better wind and your recovery,

Believe me | Dear Colonel Waugh | Very faithfully Yours

CHARLES DICKENS

I am vexed not to have been at my dismantled house when Mrs. Wrottesley[1] and your daughter called—but I am glad to have missed them too, when I think of the tremendous danger I should have fallen into, if I had seen them, of being utterly powerless to say No.[2]

To BENJAMIN WEBSTER, 9 MAY 1856*

MS British Library. *Address:* Private | Benjamin Webster Esquire | Theatre Royal Adelphi.

Tavistock House. | Friday Ninth May, 1856.

My Dear Webster.

I am afraid that I must stick to Lincolns Inn Fields. It was an old agreement when I was last in town. I should have been very glad to come to you on such an occasion, and if I *should* escape will come after dinner.

Head ache!—There is no such thing in my punch.

Ever Faithfully

CHARLES DICKENS

[1] The Hon. Mrs George Wrottesley, daughter-in-law of 2nd Baron Wrottesley (1798–1867; *DNB*), FRS, one of the founders of Royal Astronomical Society; she had acted in Charles Dance's *A Wonderful Woman* on 10 July 55: see Vol. VII, p. 667 and *n*.

[2] Written considerably larger than rest of letter.

To MRS JAMESON,[1] 10 MAY 1856

Extract in *A. Edward Newton Collection*, Parke-Bernet Catalogue, Apr 1941; addressed Mrs. Jameson; dated Tavistock House, 10 May 56.

you are perfectly right in supposing the article[2] to have been written by a lady. She is an officer's wife who knows camps well.[3]

To GEORGE MEREDITH,[4] 10 MAY 1856

MS Dickens House.

OFFICE OF HOUSEHOLD WORDS,
Saturday Tenth May 1856

Dear Sir

Allow me to thank you very cordially, for the book you have had the kindness to leave for me here inscribed with my name.[5] I take it home tonight to read, and shall not be unworthy to enter on its perusal, as one of the most constant and delighted readers of those "Arabian Entertainments" of older date that they have ever had, perhaps. A new Arabian Tale is charming to me in the promise it holds out, and I hope I may say that I know already you are not the man to disappoint me.

Dear Sir | Yours faithfully and obliged

George Meredith Esquire CHARLES DICKENS

To MISS BURDETT COUTTS, 12 MAY 1856*

MS Morgan Library. *Address:* Miss Burdett Coutts | Stratton Street | Piccadilly.

Tavistock House | Twelfth May 1856.

My Dear Miss Coutts

I have enquired about cleaners of pictures, and am assured that the most honest

[1] Mrs Anna Brownell Jameson, née Murphy, writer (1794–1860; *DNB*): see Vol. II, p. 243 and *n.* CD had met her at Macready's in 1841 and evidently maintained her acquaintance. They had many friends in common, including the Procters and Mrs Gaskell, who sought Mrs Jameson's advice on revising *North and South* in 1855. Her *Sacred and Legendary Art* and other works continued successful, with many revised editions; but her recent interest was more in public questions: e.g. *Sisters of Charity*, 1855. She lectured on *Communion of Labour . . . on the social employments of women* in Sep 1856 and attended meetings of the Social Science Association in 1859. After the death of her husband in Canada, his annual allowance ensured by their legal separation ceased, and in 1851 she received a Civil List pension and an annuity subscribed by her friends.

[2] "Women at Aldershot": see *To* Wills, 7 Apr, *fn.*

[3] Marianne Young, formerly Postans, miscellaneous writer, wife of Capt. Thomas Postans, of the Bombay Army; lived some years in India. Wrote several books about her experiences, including *Aldershot and All about it*, 1857, containing some detail from her article, above.

[4] George Meredith (1828–1909; *DNB*): see Vol. VI, p. 529*n.*

[5] *The Shaving of Shagpat: an Arabian Entertainment*, published 19 Dec 55 by Chapman & Hall, Meredith's first published fiction; he was still poor, struggling and unknown. Its close imitation of the style and narrative method of the *Arabian Nights* was misunderstood by some critics, but the book was praised by Marian Evans (anonymously) in both the *Westminster Review* and the *Leader*. Meredith had already sent a copy to Charles Kingsley.

and skilful of the craft is one Mr. Bentley of No. 128 Sloane Street.[1] When the fire took place down at Mr. Thomas Baring's country house,[2] in which several famous pictures were greatly damaged, he was employed to repair them; and acquired great celebrity by the dexterity he shewed. This is so distinct a recommendation, and the reference to Mr. Baring is so easy, that I do not confuse his name in this note with any others of the trade.

Ever Dear Miss Coutts | Most Faithfully Yours
CHARLES DICKENS

To MISS BURDETT COUTTS, 13 MAY 1856

MS Morgan Library.

Tavistock House | Tuesday Thirteenth May, 1856.

My Dear Miss Coutts.

I have indeed read this letter with great emotion.[3] If you had done nothing else in maintaining the Home—instead of having done so much that we know of, to which is to be added all the chance and bye-way Good that has sprung out of it in the lives of these women: which I believe to be enormous—what a great reward this case alone would be!

Unfortunately I was out last evening. I went to the Egyptian Hall,[4] and had left home for the Athenaeum before your note arrived. I will come to you on Thursday at half past four. I hope you got well out of the Animalculae—your account of which enjoyment in prospect, made me laugh heartily.

I am not without hope that in the winter nights when we are alone here, you and Mrs. Brown may be induced to take some interest in what I dare say you never saw—the growth of a play from the beginning. Mr. Collins and I have hammered out a curious idea for a new one, which he is to write, and which we purpose, please God, to bring out on Charley's birthday.[5] Mr. Stanfield has already been hanging out of the centre back-window of the schoolroom at the risk of his life, inventing wonderful effects and measuring the same. If you and O[6] were to come into the secret from the commencement, and see all the ways and means, and the gradual improvement of it, and the trials of patience to which my young people are submitted, and the general ingenuity and good humour, I think it would pass a few dark evenings pleasantly.

Ever Dear Miss Coutts | Most Faithfully Yours
CHARLES DICKENS

[1] William Bentley, listed as "artist".
[2] Norman Court, Stockbridge, Hants.
[3] Clearly from a former inmate of the Home, who had no doubt emigrated.
[4] In Piccadilly.
[5] Charley's 20th birthday and Twelfth Night.
[6] Mrs Brown.

To THOMAS JACKSON,[1] [?13–14 MAY 1856]

Mention in *To* Stanfield, 14 May 56. *Date:* no doubt written the same or previous day.

To CLARKSON STANFIELD, 14 MAY 1856*

MS Yale University Library.

Tavistock House | Fourteenth May, 1856.

My Dear Stanny.

I forget what Mr. Jackson's house is called.[2] Will you be so kind as to send him in the enclosed letter? It refers to the Canada Railway,[3] and an endeavour I am making to do something to help a sister and brother[4] to go out to Canada with some sort of light upon their way.

All this day have I been singing (without knowing a word of it), that song about the Devil's stitch in the sewn-up hammock.[5] I had no idea by the bye, that you were such a horrible deceiver as a story Forster told me last night proves you to be! "I assure you my dear boy", said he with that vigorous whisper which seems to go in at your ear and come out at the sole of your boot, "I assure you my dear boy, that not only was Stanny taken aback by the secret I imparted to him the other day,[6] but that he did sincerely and thoroughly believe that I was going to tell him I was about to turn Catholic! Now, there is no mistake whatever, about that Dickens. He was literally in expectation of that disclosure."

Oho! thinks I, looking at a rubicund countenance across the table, what a rosy impostor you are my boy![7]

Ever affectionately

CD.

To MISS BURDETT COUTTS, 16 MAY 1856*

MS Morgan Library. *Address:* Miss Burdett Coutts.

The Home | Friday Evening, Sixteenth May | 1856.

My Dear Miss Coutts.

Connor[8] will be here to see you at 12.

On looking into the cases, and consulting with Mrs. Marchmont,[9] I think that

[1] Thomas Jackson, Stanfield's near-neighbour in Hampstead; railway contractor and marble, stone and timber merchant: see Vol. VII, p. 634 and *n.*

[2] Mount Grove, Green Hill.

[3] The 1850s witnessed a massive railway boom in Canada: the Grand Trunk Railway was completed in 1853, followed by the Great Western and Northern. CD probably refers to one of these.

[4] Caroline Thompson and Frederick Maynard, whom Miss Coutts had helped after a full report of their case from CD: see Vol. VII, pp. 467–9 and Appx D.

[5] Untraced.

[6] His forthcoming marriage.

[7] Because CD had already told him this secret.

[8] Just possibly O'Connor, who wrote to CD about the Home on 2 Nov 54: see Vol. VII, p. 457 and *n.*

[9] Matron of the Home.

Beaver
Daley
Chalk
and
Jones

may now be sent abroad. I doubt if we should make much more of them by keeping them longer—we might make less. Jones has been here only about nine months, but is a strong hard working healthy girl—a little rough, and not very bright intellectually—whom it seems a sort of waste to keep here. She is commended as very truthful.

It occurs to me to night, that it would be a very good thing if I were to address a letter to the Inspectors on duty at the Chief Station Houses,[1] stating the objects of this place, and the good that might come of their recommending fit persons. I think they might hit some wretched cases at the very crisis of their fate. Will you think of this, before I see you on Sunday?

Ever Faithfully Yours
CD.

To VISCOUNT RAYNHAM, 16 MAY 1856

Extract in Maggs Bros catalogue No. 436 (1923); *MS* 2 pp.; dated Tavistock House, 16 May 56; addressed Lord Raynham.

Mentioning his plan of retiring to Boulogne for Country-ease and country work through the long summer holidays.

To DANIEL MACLISE, 17 MAY 1856*

MS Private.

Tavistock House | Seventeenth May 1856.

My Dear Mac.

Olliffe[2] and his wife are coming to dine here on Wednesday the 21st. at halfpast six. I know it would give them both pleasure, and do him good, to see you. Will you come? We shall have nobody else, for indeed we have only the dining room and schoolroom furnished.

Ever Faithfully
CD.

[1] There were six Station Houses in the City, each with an officer on duty day and night, and 18 further Metropolitan Police Stations, each with between four and 23 Inspectors.

[2] Olliffe had been a schoolfellow of Maclise's in Cork.

To THOMAS ROSS AND JOHN KENNY,[1] [19 MAY 1856]

Text from *The Times*, 20 May 1856.[2]

Tavistock-house, Monday, May 19, 1856.

Gentlemen,

I have received a letter signed by you, which I assume to be written mainly on behalf of what are called working men and their families, inviting me to attend a meeting in our parish vestry-hall, this evening, on the subject of the stoppage of the Sunday bands in the parks.[3] I thoroughly agree with you that those bands have afforded 'an innocent and healthful enjoyment on the Sunday afternoons, to which the people have a right;'[4] but I think it essential that the working people should of themselves, and by themselves, assert that right. They have been informed, on the high authority of their First Minister[5] (lately rather in want of House of Commons' votes, I am told) that they are almost indifferent to it. The correction of that mistake—if official omniscience can be mistaken—lies with themselves. In case it should be considered by the meeting (which I prefer for this reason not to attend) expedient to unite with other metropolitan parishes in forming a fund for the payment of such expenses as may be incurred in peaceably and numerously representing to the governing powers that the harmless recreation they have taken away is very much wanted, I beg to put down my name as a subscriber of 10*l.*,

and I am your faithful servant,

CHARLES DICKENS

To C. ROACH SMITH,[6] 19 MAY 1856

Mention in Catalogue of the Library of J. A. Clark, Sotheby, Wilkinson & Hodge, Apr 1895; dated 19 May 56; addressed C. Roach Smith; with envelope.

Accepting a book.[7]

[1] Names given in MDGH, 1893, p. 398. No doubt Thomas Ross, of Dixon & Ross, steel and copperplate printers, 4 St James's Place, Hampstead Rd, and John Kenny, printer, 5 Heathcot Court, 414 Strand, as representatives of working men (see below).

[2] The letter is headed: "MUSIC IN THE PARKS ON SUNDAYS | The following letter from Mr. Charles Dickens was read last night at a meeting held to consider the subject in the St. Pancras Vestry-hall."

[3] The Govt had stopped such music because of Church representations, led by the Archbishop of Canterbury. On 20 May a large meeting of residents in Westminster, chaired by Sir J. V. Shelley, MP, passed an almost unanimous motion for the ban to be lifted.

[4] CD had been concerned at attempts to restrict Sunday recreational facilities ever since his *Sunday Under Three Heads*, 1836 (see Vol. I, p. 154 and *n*), especially at the time of Lord Grosvenor's Sunday Trading (Metropolis) bill, withdrawn on 2 July 55, after the riots against it in Hyde Park on 24 June 55 (see Vol. VII, p. 666 and *nn*); and, for further comments on such restrictions see Sala's "Sunday Music", *HW*, 13 Oct 55, XII, 261 and William Duthie's "Some German Sundays", *HW*, 19 Apr 56, XIII, 320, and "More Sundays Abroad", *HW*, 10 May 56, XIII, 400.

[5] Lord Palmerston.

[6] Charles Roach Smith (1807–90; *DNB*), FSA, antiquary, collector and authority on Roman Britain, of Temple Place, Strood, near Rochester; sold his collection of Romano-British antiquities to British Museum this year; helped to found British Archaeological Association 1843; contributed to *Archaeologia and Numismatic Chronicle*; for some comments on CD, see his *Retrospections, Social and Archaeological*, 1883–91, II, 99; and W. R. Hughes, *A Week's Tramp in Dickens-Land*, 1891, pp. 231–6.

[7] Roach Smith's *Antiquities of Richborough, Reculver, and Lymne, in Kent*, 1850, inscribed

To MISS BURDETT COUTTS, 20 MAY 1856

MS Morgan Library.

Tavistock House | Tuesday Night Twentieth May | 1856.

My Dear Miss Coutts.

I have been very much interested in the pamphlet.[1] There is nothing in it that I see, demanding correction, except the paragraph which you pointed out to me and which I marked in Stratton Street.

Mrs. Thompson[2] has written me a letter, and I have seen her since its receipt. The lodging-letting does not succeed sufficiently well to be pursued. In June the notice she has given to quit her house, will expire. She will then, by the sale of her furniture and so forth, have from a hundred to a hundred and fifty pounds. With this sum, she desires nothing more than to emigrate to Canada along with her child,[3] *if* she can see any reasonably hopeful prospect of getting employment as a house-keeper, superintendent, attendant on children, companion, manager, any honest thing. She writes very well, is a good plain accountant, and generally neat and handy. Does any means of helping her, occur to you? I am trying among Canada Railway people, but I fear uselessly, as their schemes are in a bad way.[4] I should be very glad to hear from you on this, at your leisure.

You will have fine weather for the new house,[5] I hope, and will enjoy it. With kind regard to Mrs. Brown,

Ever Dear Miss Coutts | Most Faithfully Yours

CD.

To JOSHUA FIELD,[6] 21 MAY 1856

Text from N, II, 774.

Tavistock House | Twenty-First May 1856

Mr. Charles Dickens presents his compliments to Mr. Field, and begs to say that he has, at this time, reasons for declining to sign the enclosed requisition.[7] He does

to CD "with the Author's best respects. May 19, 1856" (*Catalogue of the Library of CD*, ed. J. H. Stonehouse, 1935, p. 102).

[1] See *To* Miss Coutts, 30 Mar and *fn.*

[2] Caroline Thompson.

[3] See Vol. VII, Appx D.

[4] See *To* Stanfield, 14 May and *fn.* The major opposition to the railway, to which CD may have been referring, came from the Hudson's Bay Co., which owned vast tracts of land in the West (see Pierre Berton, *The National Dream*, Toronto/Montreal, 1970, pp. 15–17).

[5] Prospect Hill, Reading, which Miss Coutts had rented.

[6] Joshua Field (1786–1863; *DNB*), FRS; of Balham House, Surrey; civil engineer, chairman South London Association, Patent Law Reform League: see Vol. VI, p. 180*n*; partner in Maudslay, Sons & Field, of Lambeth, which built the engines for the *Great Western*'s first crossing of the Atlantic 1838; one of founders of Institution of Civil Engineers 1817; President 1848.

[7] Probably about patents. There were complaints made in the Commons debate on Supply on 2 June 56 of the amounts paid under the Patent Law Amendment Act, to the Attorney and Solicitor Generals and their clerks for patents (over £21,800 that year). On the answer that £90,000 had been paid to the Exchequer for patents, thus leaving the public with the balance, one MP said he thought it "monstrous that the mechanical ingenuity of the country should be taxed to the amount of £90,000 a year."

so, without at all disputing (it is hardly necessary for him to remark), the general principle.[1]

To JOHN KENNY,[2] 21 MAY 1856

MS Dickens House.

Tavistock House | Twenty First May, 1856.

Sir.

I have received your letter of yesterday's date, with great interest and pleasure. It is particularly agreeable to me to learn that a Metropolitan Committee has been formed, and that a deputation requires permission to wait upon Lord Palmerston; because I am perfectly sure that the people of this City are only disparaged and placed at a disadvantage, when their moderate desires, their patience, good sense and good humour, fail to find adequate expression in high places.

I am inclined to think with you that Lord Palmerston is really favorable in this matter;[3] nevertheless he has a famous predecessor in the pages of Shakespeare, who did not get on particularly well by letting "I dare not" wait upon "I would."[4]

Faithfully Yours

Mr. John Kenny CHARLES DICKENS

To MISS BURDETT COUTTS, 22 MAY 1856*

MS Morgan Library. *Address:* Miss Burdett Coutts | Prospect Hill | Reading.

Tavistock House | Thursday Twenty Second May 1856.

My Dear Miss Coutts.

You remember Mrs. Matthews,[5] whom I told sometime since, as you and I agreed, that my friend could do nothing more for her? This morning's post brings me the enclosed letter. I do not send it with any idea of advocating her case, but merely because I hardly feel it right to answer it without having placed it before you.

With love to Mrs. Brown

Ever Dear Miss Coutts | Most Faithfully Yours

CD.

[1] Field had no doubt been reading *Little Dorrit*, No. V, in which Ch. 16, on Daniel Doyce, is very relevant to Patent Law Reform.

[2] See 19 May and *fn*.

[3] Palmerston, replying to a Question on 19 May, said he had told the Archbishop that he had no objection to military bands playing in the parks on Sunday afternoons; but he would not run counter to "the religious feelings of a large part of the community" and would therefore have the playing discontinued (Hansard, CCXLII [19 May 56], 326).

[4] Macbeth, reproached by Lady Macbeth, in I, ii, 44.

[5] Antonina Matthews, wife of a Yorkshire clergyman, whom Miss Coutts had been helping financially since May 1853: see Vol. VII, pp. 87–8 and *nn*.

To MARK LEMON, 22 MAY 1856

MS Benoliel Collection.

Tavistock House | Thursday Twenty Second May 1856.

My Dear Mark

Stanny does go with us tomorrow.

Ever Affecy.
CD.

To E. M. WARD, [23] MAY 1856

MS Mr A. R. Davis. *Date:* misdated by CD; Friday was 23 May.

Tavistock House | Friday Twenty Second May | 1856.

My Dear Ward

A new illustration of "Never Despair"![1] I *can* come on Monday, and shall be delighted to do so.

Very faithfully Yours
CHARLES DICKENS

E. M. Ward Esquire

To UNIDENTIFIED STAFF SURGEON, [?23] MAY 1856

Mention in *To* Miss Coutts, 27 May 56. *Date:* written a few days before.

To MARK LEMON, 26 MAY 1856

MS Brotherton Library, Leeds.

Tavistock House | Twenty Sixth May, 1856.

My Dear Mark.

Any time between 2 and 5 tomorrow (if you will appoint one in the course of the day), will suit me better. I shall not only have more leisure after my morning's work than before, but shall have a clearer power of attention.

The concluding paragraph of your note makes me all but lunatic with wonder.

Ever affecy.
CD.

To MISS BURDETT COUTTS, 27 MAY 1856

MS Morgan Library. *Address:* Miss Burdett Coutts | Prospect Hill | Reading.

Tavistock House | Twenty Seventh May 1856.

My Dear Miss Coutts.

I have made enquiries about the Staff Surgeon[2] who wanted the Fifty Pounds (as

[1] Letter endorsed by Ward, "Charles Dickens | In answer to invitation in which I despaired of his coming".

[2] Not further identified.

we agreed), and there is no doubt of his being a reality, and of his holding a responsible appointment, and of his representation being perfectly true.

I wrote to him to say that I was not rich and had a fearful number of claims upon me, and could not lend him such a sum. But that a friend of mine, generous and able in more cases than I should trust myself to mention, *might*—I by no means, said *would*—do so, if satisfied of his merits. That if, on this slight encouragement, he could send me any kind of corroboration, himself, I would shew it to that friend, but could give him no other assurance than that his confidence should be respected.

I enclose his reply, and its accompanying letters. Will you send them back to me with your decision?

Your letter from Oxford I received this morning. A beautiful place indeed! The journey down from Oxford to Reading, on the Thames, is more charming than one can describe in words. I rowed down last June, through miles upon miles of water lilies, lying on the water close together, like a fairy pavement.

I have held a Committee of One at the Bush, where all was going on thoroughly well. Mr. Illingworth's[1] case I will immediately see to.

With love to Mrs. Brown

Ever Dear Miss Coutts | Most Faithfully Yours

CD.

To THE DEAN OF ST. PAUL'S,[2] 27 MAY 1856

MS Free Library of Philadelphia.

Tavistock House | Tuesday Twenty Seventh May 1856.

My Dear Dean.

An odd idea has come into my head that a very striking idea of blazing London on Thursday night,[3] might be got from the top of St. Paul's, and might suggest a remarkable description. Could I be admitted (say with three companions for company) to the great outer gallery? I can understand the necessity of having no light, and perhaps of being kept there all night. I would willingly abide by any such conditions if so singular an experiment could be conceded to me. Also I should understand, of course, the design to be strictly private among the people concerned.

Can—and will—your authority help me in this matter? If so, I shall be very heartily obliged to you.

Very faithfully Yours always

The Very Reverend | The Dean of St. Paul's. CHARLES DICKENS

[1] The Rev. Edward Arthur Illingworth, chaplain to the Home: see Vol. V, p. 244*n*.

[2] The Very Rev. Henry Hart Milman, DD (1791–1868; *DNB*): see Vol. VI, p. 796*n*.

[3] See *To* Miss Coutts, 1 June. The illuminations were to celebrate the end of the Crimean War.

To THE DEAN OF ST PAUL'S, 29 MAY 1856

MS Mr D. C. L. Holland.

Tavistock House | Thursday Twenty Ninth May | 1856.

My Dear Dean.

I am very much obliged to you for your kind letter, and (remaining constant in my terrible purpose), will be with you tonight at 8. As I had only mentioned the matter to Mr. Lemon before hearing from you, I will bring only him.

Very faithfully Yours
CHARLES DICKENS

To F. M. EVANS, [?8–29 MAY 1856]

Mention in *To* Lemon, ?8–29 May 56. *Date:* written the same day.

To MARK LEMON, [?8–29 MAY 1856]

Text from *The Unpublished Letters of Dickens to Mark Lemon*, ed. Walter Dexter, 1927, p. 160. *Date:* May, according to N, II, 772, therefore any Thursday after 3 May.

Tavistock House | Thursday evening.

My Dear Mark,

If you like to transfer Evans to this mansion (and I leave a note at yours summoning him round here), I shall be delighted to see him.

Yours ever affectionately,
CHARLES DICKENS

To RICHARD MONCKTON MILNES,[1] 31 MAY 1856*

MS Trinity College, Cambridge.

Tavistock House | Thirty First May 1856

My Dear Mr Milnes

Allow me to have the pleasure of presenting to you, Mr Palfrey of Boston—the gentleman whose main object in visiting England, I have already explained to you.

Faithfully Yours

R. M. Milnes Esquire CHARLES DICKENS

[1] Richard Monckton Milnes, later 1st Baron Houghton (1809–85; *DNB*): see Vol. I, p. 508*n*.

To J. G. PALFREY,[1] 31 MAY 1856*

MS Houghton Library, Harvard. *Address:* — Palfrey Esquire | 19 Regent Street | St. James's.

Tavistock House | Saturday Thirty First May | 1856.

My Dear Sir

I owe you many apologies for this delay in pursuing the subject of our conversation at Mr. Grattan's[2] dinner. But my short present stay in London has been so constantly occupied by hard work at my desk every day—by the business consequent upon some months of absence—and by the necessity of going on several excursions into Kent—that I have hardly had an hour to call my own, since I saw you.

I enclose a note of introduction to Mr. Milnes, and have also made him acquainted with your object.[3] In October I shall return home to my usual settled abode, and, if you should not by that time have returned to yours, I hope you will give me the pleasure of that more favorable opportunity of improving your acquaintance.

My Dear Sir | Faithfully Yours
CHARLES DICKENS

— Palfrey Esquire.

To MISS BURDETT COUTTS, 1 JUNE 1856

MS Morgan Library. *Address:* Miss Burdett Coutts | Prospect Hill | Reading.

Tavistock House | Sunday First June 1856 | (Mid Winter)[4]

My Dear Miss Coutts. I have been so incessantly worked since the receipt of your last note, by Little Dorrit, Household Words, and business, that I have let two posts go by without answering it.

You will see by the enclosed that Mrs. Mathews[5] (who assuredly has a deadly perseverance), has written again.

What the Staff Surgeon wants, is a Loan of Fifty Pounds.

The letters of the Young La Touches[6] (which have naturally interested me very much), and the letter of Rhena Pollard[7] (ditto) I have returned under cover to you at Stratton Street. The two letters concerning the death of Harriet Tanner, I have

[1] John Gorham Palfrey (1796–1881; *DAB*), former Unitarian minister, later, liberal politician, editor and proprietor, *North American Review*, 1835–42, and regular contributor; best known for his *History of New England*, 4 vols, 1858–75 (5th posthumous, 1890). CD had met him in Boston in Feb 42: see Vol. IV, p. 22*n*.

[2] Thomas Colley Grattan (1792–1864; *DNB*), travel-writer and historical novelist, whom CD had met as British Consul in Boston in Jan 42: see Vol. III, pp. 15*n* and 342*n*. He obtained leave of absence in 1846 and returned to England, hoping for a consular post nearer home; none was available, and his son, formerly Vice-Consul at Boston, succeeded him there. Lived mainly in Europe until 1849, then in England, much occupied on his major work, *Civilized America*, 2 vols, 1859. A comprehensive historical survey, it includes his personal impressions, often severely critical, but fully documented and, as he says, "faithful and sincere."

[3] No doubt research for the English portions of his *History*.

[4] There was heavy rain every day from 27 May to 2 June. On 1 June the noon temperature was 56°F.

[5] Thus in MS: see 22 May 56 and *fn*.

[6] No doubt Willy La Touche, who had preceded Walter Dickens at Wimbledon School (see Vol. VII, p. 508 and *n*), and probably a brother.

[7] For her previous bad behaviour at the Home, see Vol. VII, pp. 237 and 274; she had subsequently had a good report and had probably emigrated.

returned for Mrs. Marchmont. There is a poor Mother, who enquired after her at the Home not long ago; and I think that for her satisfaction Mrs. Marchmont had best copy the passages that refer to the girl.[1]

The Schools Report,[2] I have also returned to Stratton Street.

You cannot imagine what a Wonderful sight Illuminated and Fireworked London was, from the top of St. Pauls.[3] I must try my hand at a description of it in Household Words.[4] In the next No. but one, by the bye, I wish you would read an opening paper of mine, with the rather alarming title of "The demeanour of Murderers".[5] It is a quiet protest against the newspaper descriptions of Mr. Palmer[6] in Court:[7] shewing why they are harmful to the public at large, and why they are, even in themselves, altogether blind and wrong. *I* think it rather a curious and serviceable essay!

I am writing in a great coat and a fur cap.

With my (cold and damp) love to Mrs. Brown

Ever Dear Miss Coutts | Most Faithfully Yours

CD.

To THE DUKE OF DEVONSHIRE,[8] 1 JUNE 1856

MS Devonshire Collections, Chatsworth.

Tavistock House | Sunday First June 1856

My Dear Duke of Devonshire

Allow me to thank you with all my heart, for your kind remembrance of me on Thursday night. My house were already engaged to go to Miss Coutts's, and I to—the top of St. Paul's, whence the sight was most wonderful! But seeing that your cards gave me leave to present some person not named, I conferred them on my excellent friend Doctor Elliotson[9] whom I found, with some Fireworkless little boys, in a desolate condition, and raised to the Seventh Heaven of happiness. You are so fond of making people happy, that I am sure you approve.

Always Your faithful and much obliged

The | Duke of Devonshire CHARLES DICKENS[10]

[1] Not further identified.

[2] On the prize-essays on "Common Things" inaugurated by Miss Coutts at Whitelands Training Institution: see 11 July and *fn*.

[3] On 29 May. The *Examiner*, 31 May, reported that "the vast town was a blaze of light, and the sky was illuminated with fires of every hue". There were illuminations in Hyde Park, St James's, Victoria Park (for the East End), and Primrose Hill; they were thought to have drawn *c.* two million spectators, including masses of visitors; "places" were very hard to obtain.

[4] None appeared.

[5] *HW*, 14 June 56, XIII, 505.

[6] Dr William Palmer, "the Rugeley poisoner" convicted of murder on 27 May: see *To* Forster, 15 Sep 57 and *fn*.

[7] The article attacks the Press's description of Palmer as self-possessed, cool and composed, as tending to show his innocence; CD argues that there is nothing in such qualities "but cruelty and insensibility" (p. 507).

[8] William George Spencer Cavendish, 6th Duke of Devonshire (1790–1858; *DNB*): see Vol. V, p. 272*n* and later vols.

[9] John Elliotson, MD (1791–1868; *DNB*), physician and mesmerist; for many years consulted by CD: see Vols I, p. 461*n* and II, p. 109*n*.

[10] The Duke replied the same day, saying what pleasure CD's letter had given him, "after two years of infirmity which did not afford much prospect of a renewed intercourse"; he was also pleased by "the grand and comprehensive view" CD must have had on Thursday;

To WILLIAM T. DYER,[1] 3 JUNE 1856

MS Private.

The Home, Shepherd's Bush | Third June 1856

Dear Sir

In answer to your note I beg to say that I have seen Dr. Waggett[2] on the case of the girl "Mason," and that the Matron of the Elizabeth Fry Refuge[3] will immediately receive a communication from this place empowering her to send the young woman here to be admitted.

Dear Sir | Faithfully yours

William T. Dyer Esquire CHARLES DICKENS

To HENRY BICKNELL,[4] 4 JUNE 1856

Mention in Parke-Bernet catalogue, Dec 1947; *MS* 1 p.; dated [London], 4 June 56; addressed Henry D. Bicknell.

Referring to an appointment.

To DR F. H. F. QUIN,[5] [?4–5 JUNE 1856][6]

Summary in John Wilson catalogue, June 1980; *MS* 1 p.; dated Saturday; addressed Dr F. H. F. Quin. *Date:* Just before 5 June 56: see below.

Explaining that Professor Fergusson[7] would find his place at table in the right hand corner near to Daniel[8] and Harvey.[9]

he had been about to complain of the disappearance of Flora in *Little Dorrit*, No. VI, since he had never been "more amused and excited" than he was by her and Clennam's meeting; but No. VII, Ch. 23, had amply repaired her loss; he ended by saying that, despite his "severe seizure" (his stroke on 3 June 54, which seriously affected his right side, but not his mind nor speech), his memory was wholly unimpaired, so that he could still enjoy the recollection of their "season of 1851" (CD's amateur company's performance at Devonshire House: Vol. VI, *passim*).

[1] William George Thistleton Dyer, surgeon, of 7 Berkeley St, Piccadilly; MRCS 1834; Medical attendant, Royal Masonic Institute for Boys; formerly Senior Surgeon, Blenheim St Dispensary; obviously a new member of the Home Committee (see *To* Miss Coutts, 15 Nov 56).

[2] John Waggett, of 4 Stanley Terrace, Kensington Park, Notting Hill; MRCS, MD (1842); formerly Hon. Surgeon, Kensington Dispensary.

[3] Established in Hackney, 1846, as a temporary home for destitute women on release from metropolitan prisons: see Vol. VII, p. 643 and *n*.

[4] Perhaps Henry Sanford Bicknell (?1818–80), at one time employed by the Crystal Palace Co: see Vol. V, p. 596*n*.

[5] Frederic Hervey Foster Quin, MD (1799–1878; *DNB*), leading homoeopathic physician: see Vol. I, p. 489*n*.

[6] The first anniversary dinner of the Royal Hospital for Incurables was on 5 June. CD took the chair (*Speeches*, ed. K. J. Fielding, pp. 222–5).

[7] William Fergusson (1808–88; *DNB*), FRS, FRCS Edin. 1829, London (Hon) 1844. Surgeon to King's College Hospital and Professor of Surgery, King's College, 1840; surgeon in ordinary to Prince Consort 1849, surgeon extraordinary to the Queen 1855. Bart 1866. The leading operator in London; author of *System of Practical Surgery*, 1842 (5 edns by 1870). Interested in the drama. Like many orthodox practitioners, on friendly terms with Quin despite different views on homoeopathy: see Edward Hamilton, *Memoir of Frederic Hervey Foster Quin MD*, 1879, pp. 101–6.

[8] John Bampfylde Daniell, MD, FRCP 1838; physician to Royal Pimlico Dispensary, London and lecturer at St George's School of Anatomy.

[9] William Harvey, FRCS 1853; surgeon to

To DANIEL MACLISE, [?EARLY JUNE 1856]

Extract in Maggs Bros catalogue, No. 258 (1910); *MS* 1 p.; addressed Daniel Maclise; dated Athenaeum. *Date:* perhaps referring to the same visit to Cremorne Gardens arranged with Lemon on 5 June.

My Dear Mac

I shall not order dinner till the manager returns on the chance of your being available for an al fresco entertainment at Cremorne.

To MARK LEMON, 5 JUNE 1856

Extract in N, II, 777; dated Tavistock House, 5 June 56.

I am delighted to find you in such force and coming up with so wet a sail,[1] Hooray! Certainly as to Webster . . . at six sharp, the notes of the cheerful Dick will be heard in the leafy groves of Cremorne.[2]

To FRANK STONE, [?3 MAY–6 JUNE 1856]*

MS Benoliel Collection. *Date:* before 2nd half of 1856 and when CD at Tavistock House; handwriting supports.

Tavistock House | Wednesday

My Dear Stone. As you know your Gardener, I think *you* had best propose the arrangement to him.[3] I find I am free for the front piece of ground[4] too.

Ever affecy.

CD.

To WILKIE COLLINS, 6 JUNE 1856

MS Morgan Library.

Tavistock House | Sixth June 1856

My Dear Collins

I have never seen anything about myself in Print, which has much correctness in it—any biographical account of myself, I mean. I do not supply such particulars when I am asked for them by editors and compilers, simply because I am asked for them every day. If you want to prime Forgues[5] you may tell him without fear of

Royal Dispensary for Diseases of the Ear since 1846; many publications.

[1] Possibly an allusion to Allan Cunningham's poem "A Wet Sheet and a Flowing Sea" (1825), which CD quotes several times in his letters.

[2] Cremorne Gardens, a popular place of entertainment in Chelsea, established 1845; closed for its notoriety 1877.

[3] See the payments in *To* Stone, 18 Feb 57 and *fn*.

[4] Which he had rented from his next-door neighbour, J. B. Cardale, since Oct 54.

[5] For his biographical sketch of CD in the Paris weekly journal, *L'Ami de la Maison*, Vol. II (1857), 6–8, "Biographies Contemporaines: XXVI. Charles Dickens"; signed "O.N." ("Old Nick", the pseudonym Forgues had used as literary and dramatic critic on *Le Commerce*) where it appeared between instalments of a translation into French of *The Lighthouse*.

being wrong, That I was born at Portsmouth on the 7th. of February 1812. That my father was in the Navy Pay office. That I was taken by him to Chatham when I was very young, and lived and was educated there till I was—12 or 13,[1] I suppose. That I was then put to a school near London,[2] where (as at the other place) I distinguished myself like a Brick. That I was put in the office of a Solicitor,[3] a friend of my father's,[4] and didn't much like it, and after a couple of years (as well as I can remember) applied myself with a celestial or diabolical energy to the study of such things as would qualify me to be a first-rate Parliamentary Reporter[5]—at that time a calling pursued by many clever men who were young at the Bar. That I made my debut in the Gallery (at about 18, I suppose), engaged on a Voluminous publication no longer in existence, called The Mirror of Parliament.[6] That when the Morning Chronicle was purchased by Sir John Easthope[7] and acquired a large circulation I was engaged there, and that I remained there until I had begun to publish Pickwick; when I found myself in a condition to relinquish that part of my labors.[8] That I left the reputation behind me of being the best and most rapid Reporter ever known,[9] and that I could do anything in that way under any sort of circumstances—and often did. (I dare say I am at this present writing, the best Short Hand Writer in the World.)

That I began, without any interest or introduction of any kind, to write fugitive pieces for the old Monthly Magazine,[10] when I was in the Gallery for the Mirror of Parliament. That my faculty for descriptive writing was seized upon, the moment I joined the Morning Chronicle, and that I was liberally paid there, and handsomely acknowledged, and wrote the greater part of the short descriptive "Sketches by Boz" in that paper.[11] That I had been a writer when I was a mere Baby, and always an Actor from the same age.

That I married the daughter of a Writer to the Signet in Edinburgh[12] who was the great friend and assistant of Scott, and who first made Lockhart[13] known to him.

And That here I am.[14]

[1] At the Rev. William Giles's School, Chatham, which CD attended Spring 1821–?Sep 1822, i.e. until he was 10.

[2] Wellington House Academy, Hampstead Rd: April 1825–Mar 1827.

[3] For his employment by Edward Blackmore, May 1827–Nov 1828, and then for a few months by Charles Molloy, see Vol. I, p. 35*n*.

[4] In fact, of his mother's.

[5] CD's maternal uncle, J. H. Barrow, claimed to have taught him the Gurney system of shorthand: see Vol. I, p. 33*n*.

[6] Founded and edited 1828–41 by J. H. Barrow: see Vol. I, p. 10*n*. CD probably joined the staff in 1831: see W. J. Carlton, "An Echo of the Copperfield Days", *D*, XLV (1949), 149.

[7] Sir John Easthope (1784–1865; *DNB*), bought the *Morning Chronicle* in 1834 and CD joined its staff that Aug.

[8] He published the first No. of *Pickwick*, 31 Mar 36, and left the *Morning Chronicle* that Nov.

[9] J. H. Barrow described him to Charles Knight as "the best reporter in the Gallery" (Vol. I, p. 33*n*).

[10] For the nine stories he published there, beginning with "A Dinner at Poplar Walk" (1 Dec 33), see Vol. I, p. 32*nn*.

[11] For first publication of individual sketches in the *Morning* and *Evening Chronicle*, see Vol. I, Appx F, pp. 692–4. *Sketches by Boz*, 1st Series was published by Macrone, 2 vols, 8 Feb 36; 2nd Series, 1 vol. Jan 37.

[12] George Hogarth.

[13] John Gibson Lockhart (1794–1854; *DNB*): see Vol. I, p. 325*n*.

[14] These facts about CD's early life are all reproduced by Forgues in *L'Ami de la Maison* (see above); for his article on CD in the *Revue Britannique* in Apr 43, see Vol. III, p. 501*n*. He lists here his novels and other works and ends his "biography" by attributing to CD "Une grande simplicité, une rare bonhomie, une noble cordialité d'acceuil"; closing with a

Finally, if you want any dates of publication of books, tell Wills and he'll get them for you.

This is the first time I ever set down even these particulars, and, glancing them over, I feel like a Wild Beast in a Caravan, describing himself in the keeper's absence.[1]

[a]With my kindest regard to Mrs. Glutch.[2]

Ever Faithfully
CD.

I made a Speech last night at the London Tavern,[3] at the end of which all the Company sat holding their napkins to their eyes with one hand, and putting the other into their pockets. A hundred people or so, contributed Nine Hundred Pounds, then and there.[a]

To PETER CUNNINGHAM, 6 JUNE 1856

MS Dickens House.

OFFICE OF HOUSEHOLD WORDS,
Friday Sixth June 1856

My Dear Cunningham

A most admirable Narrative[4] indeed!—With your leave I will take the other book[5] to Boulogne, and give it you back there.

Ever Faithfully
CHARLES DICKENS

To RICHARD MONCKTON MILNES, 6 JUNE 1856*

MS Trinity College, Cambridge.

Tavistock House | Sixth June 1856

My Dear Mr Milnes

Mr Palfrey's address is 19 Regent Street,[6] but I dare say he will have called upon you by this time.

reference to his 10–12 mile walks, sometimes alone, sometimes accompanied by Miss Hogarth.

[1] He had in fact given rather fuller particulars to Dr J. H. Kuenzel in ?July 38 (see Vol. I, pp. 403–4 and *nn*), as, with Forgues, perhaps being more ready to help a foreign writer. He also took the trouble to correct Shelton Mackenzie's errors in the *Durham Advertiser* (see Vol. I, p. 367 and *n*). He may also have given some help with the *Men of the Time* article of 1852 (see Vol. VI, p. 64*n*).

[aa] Omitted in MDGH and N.

[2] The name Collins gave to his actual landlady in "My London Lodgings", *HW*, 14 June 56, XIII, 517.

[3] See *To* Quin, 4–5 June.

[4] Cunningham's only publication in 1856 was Vol. I of his 9-vol. edn of Horace Walpole's letters in Nov; this includes over 80 pp. of introductory matter; the only part that might be called "narrative" is Walpole's own memoir of his life. Copy presented to CD on 17 Jan 57, inscribed "from his friend, The Editor" (*Catalogue of the Library of CD*, ed. J. H. Stonehouse, p. 116).

[5] Untraced.

[6] A private address; he no doubt had rooms there.

I was in the country on the day when you kindly asked me to meet Macaulay,[1] or I would have come with pleasure. Tomorrow morning we leave town for the Summer, to the end that I may write in a garden of peace, and swarm up and down all the hills near Boulogne.

Faithfully Yours

R. M. Milnes Esquire CHARLES DICKENS

To ALFRED HACHETTE,[2] 9 JUNE 1856

MS Librairie Hachette.

Villa des Moulineaux | Boulogne sur mer
Monday June Ninth, 1856

Dear Sir

I regret that in the great pressure of business occasioned by my leaving town, I was so much occupied that I was not at home on either of the two occasions when you called at my house.

On looking over your list, I find the following names of living authors now in England.

Ainsworth | Bulwer | Carlyle | D'Israeli | Lady Georgiana Fullerton[3] | Mrs. Gore | Jerrold | Miss Kavanagh[4] | Lewes | Macaulay | Thackeray | Warren[x5] | Mrs. Marsh | Miss Jewsbury[6] | Wilkie Collins

All these ladies and gentlemen, with the exception of the one name against which I have put a cross, I know.[7] Do you wish to have a letter of introduction to each? I do not quite understand from the letter I have received from your father, what service you wish me to render you. Neither do I understand what you wish to know from me in reference to authors who have long been dead. As Fielding, Smollett, Sterne, &c.

If you will explain what you require to know, I shall be happy to render you any assistance in my power. In the meantime I return your list,[8] with the addresses of several of the writers mentioned in it, written against their names.

Faithfully Yours

Monsieur Alfred Hachette CHARLES DICKENS

[1] Thomas Babington Macaulay (1800–59; *DNB*): see Vol. II, p. 279*n*.

[2] Alfred Hachette (1832–72), Louis Hachette's elder son, partner in Hachette et Cie. He was in London learning English, and, at his father's request, had left with CD the list of English authors referred to here.

[3] Née Leveson-Gower (1812–77), Lord Granville's daughter and niece of the Duke of Devonshire; had published three novels by 1856.

[4] Julia Kavanagh (1822–77; *DNB*); had published 6 novels by 1856; contributed to *HW* (27 July 50) and to *AYR*.

[5] Samuel Warren (1807–77; *DNB*), author of the highly successful *Ten Thousand a Year*, 1839; now Recorder of Hull (1852–74): see Vol. III, p. 412; and, for his patronizing and critical review of *American Notes*, pp. 412–13*n*.

[6] Geraldine Endsor Jewsbury (1812–80; *DNB*), novelist: see Vol. V, p. 510*n*. For other listed authors, see earlier vols.

[7] This is the first evidence that he personally knew Lady Georgiana Fullerton and Julia Kavanagh.

[8] Not with letter.

To LORD LYTTELTON,[1] [9 JUNE 1856]

Mention in Ogden Goelet Catalogue Jan 1935, dated 9 June 56; addressed Lord Lyttelton.

Requesting Lord Lyttelton to present a petition to the House of Lords about obtaining educational advantages for actors at Dulwich College.[2]

To BENJAMIN WEBSTER, 9 JUNE 1856

Mention in Sotheby catalogue Jan 1883; *MS* $1\frac{1}{4}$ pp.; dated 9 June 185[6]. *Address* (MS British Library): Angleterre. | Benjamin Webster Esquire | Theatre Royal Adelphi | London. PM 9 Juin 56.

Sending him notes of introduction to Lords Tenterden,[3] *Granville etc.*[4]

To HENRY AUSTIN, 11 JUNE 1856*

MS Morgan Library.

Villa des Moulineaux, Boulogne S/M
Wednesday Eleventh June 1856

My Dear Henry.

I very rarely mention any public case to Miss Coutts. Those are almost always instances of private distress in which I act for her.

Nor do I think it very likely that she would feel this claim strongly. Therefore if I were you, I would not individually address her on the subject. Let the Secretaries[5] do so, in the usual way. If she should then refer it to me, of course my good word shall not be wanting.

Will you put me down for £10, and I will either send it in the first parcel I send to town or bring it the first time I come.

Ever affectionately
CD.

[1] George William Lyttelton, 4th Baron Lyttelton, 2nd creation (1817–76; *DNB*), FRS; centre of intellectual life of Worcs from 1839; Principal, Queen's College, Birmingham, 1845; first President, Birmingham and Midland Institute 1853.

[2] See *To* Webster, 9 and 15 June and *fnn.* Obviously requesting an additional clause or amendment to the Dulwich College Bill, making a number of foundation scholarships available to the sons of actors and actresses; introduced by the Charity Commissioners to the House of Lords, the Bill received its third reading in the Lords on 14 July 57 and in the Commons on 16 July. A petition for the additional clause was presented to the Governors, but no evidence that it was discussed by them; and no special provision was made for actors' children (information kindly given by the Librarian & Archivist, Dulwich College).

[3] Charles Stuart Aubrey Abbott, 3rd Baron Tenterden (1834–82; *DNB*); joined Foreign Office 1854; Permanent Under-Secretary for Foreign Affairs 1873.

[4] Clearly to gain support for Webster's petition concerning Dulwich College; CD had asked Lord Lyttelton to present it to the House of Lords: see last and *To* Webster, 15 June 56.

[5] Of the Board of Health.

To JOHN FORSTER, [?11 JUNE 1856]

Extracts in F, VII, iv, 600. *Date:* He left London for Boulogne 7 June 56; Forster implies both extracts from same letter (see below).

He did not expect for another month to see land from the running sea of *Little Dorrit.*[1]

After dawdling about his garden for a few days[2] *with surprising industry in a French farmer garb of blue blouse, leathern belt, and military cap which he had mounted as* the only one for complete comfort, ... Now to work again—to work! The story lies before me, I hope, strong and clear.[3] Not to be easily told; but nothing of that sort *is*[4] to be easily done that I know of.

To MARK LEMON, 15 JUNE 1856

Text from MDGH, I, 439–40.

Villa des Moulineaux, Boulogne | Sunday, June 15th, 1856.

My dear old Boy

This place is beautiful—a burst of roses. Your friend Beaucourt (who *will not* put on his hat), has thinned the trees and greatly improved the garden. Upon my life, I believe there are at least twenty distinct smoking-spots expressly made in it.

And as soon as you can see your day in next month for coming over with Stanny and Webster, will you let them both know? I should not be very much surprised if I were to come over and fetch you, when I know what your day is. Indeed, I don't see how you could get across properly without me.

There is a fête here to-night in honour of the Imperial baptism,[5] and there will be another to-morrow.[6] The Plorn has put on two bits of ribbon (one pink and one blue), which he calls "companys," to celebrate the occasion. The fact that the receipts of the fêtes are to be given to the sufferers by the late floods[7] reminds me that you will find at the passport office a tin-box, condescendingly and considerately labelled in English:

FOR THE OVERFLOWINGS,

which the chief officer clearly believes to mean, for the sufferers from the inundations.

[1] He had not begun No. IX (Chs 30–2, for Aug, published 31 July 56). Forster mistakenly says he was leaving Paris for this visit to Boulogne.

[2] About four.

[3] Because he had already planned the Dorrits' sudden change from poverty to riches.

[4] Doubly underlined.

[5] The baptism took place in the Cathedral of Notre Dame on 14 June; followed by a Banquet in the Hôtel de Ville, attended by the Emperor and Empress.

[6] Both fêtes were reported in full in *L'Impartial* (19 June) and *La Colonne et l'Observateur* (22 June). They were held with the help of the Société de Bienfaisance and included balloon-flights, two public balls, illuminations and music; on the Sunday a statue was erected to the memory of Napoleon I, given by Mr Kent-Peron, an English resident of Boulogne, who also presented the city with a reservoir.

[7] There had been serious floods throughout France since the end of May, following continuous rain; the Saône had risen three feet and the Rhone six; Lyons had been particularly affected. *Galignani's Messenger* described the flooding as "a great calamity" on 9 June; 20/30,000 were homeless in S. France.

I observe more Mingles in the laundresses' shops, and one inscription, which looks like the name of a duet or chorus in a playbill, "Here they mingle."

Will you congratulate Mrs. Lemon, with our loves, on her gallant victory over the recreant cabman?

Walter has turned up, rather brilliant on the whole; and that (with shoals of remembrances and messages which I don't deliver) is all my present intelligence.

Ever affectionately
[CD]

To BENJAMIN WEBSTER, [15] JUNE 1856

MS University of Michigan. *Date:* Sunday was 15th.

Villa des Moulineaux, Boulogne
Sunday June Fourteenth 1856.

My Dear Webster.

When you have got your Dulwich petition[1] from the administrators of the Literary Fund, I shall be glad to hear from you, as I shall then immediately order in five hundred cart-loads of flints,[2] for the purpose of extracting New Milk from them.

You have taken some kind part in a certain Incledon[3] subscription. Will you pay a Guinea to it for me, and I will repay you when you come over here.

And I shall expect you to bring some of those plans and drawings with you, in order that we may sit (with Stanfield) in solemn council over the New Theatre,[4] and drink Success to it in some 1846 Champagne which is waiting in a cool corner for the purpose.

Always Faithfully Yours

Benjamin Webster Esquire CHARLES DICKENS

To JOHN FORSTER, [?16 JUNE 1856]

Extract in F, VII, iv, 600–1. *Date:* some days after he started work on ?11 June.

At work it became his habit to sit late, and then, putting off his usual walk until night, to lie down among the roses reading until after tea (middle-aged Love in a blouse and belt), *when he went down to the pier*. The said pier at evening is a phase of the place we never see, and which I hardly knew. But I never did behold such specimens of the youth of my country, male and female, as pervade that place. They are really, in

[1] The petition was one of several read at a Private Parliamentary sitting on 12 June 57; on 22 July 57 it was ordered by the Charity Commissioners that "all petitions relative to the Dulwich College Bill be referred to the Select Committee". Full details of the Bill, which provided for the dissolution of the existing Corporation and establishment of an upper and lower school, are given in William Young, *The History of Dulwich College*, 1889, I, 415–16.

[2] CD may have remembered the mill hand, Higgins, in *North and South*, Ch. 37 (published in *HW*, 30 Dec 55), saying "there'll be more chance o' getting milk out of a flint than there is hope of his getting to see Mr. Thornton."

[3] Charles Incledon (1791–1865; *DNB*), tenor; son of the more famous singer. Appeared at Drury Lane as an actor under John Braham in 1829; for many years lived in Vienna as an English teacher; died in France.

[4] The new Adelphi theatre.

their vulgarity and insolence, quite disheartening. One is so fearfully ashamed of them, and they contrast so very unfavourably with the natives.

To LADY JOHN RUSSELL,[1] 19 JUNE 1856*

MS Robert H. Taylor Collection, Princeton University Library.

Villa des Moulineaux, Boulogne
Thursday Nineteenth June 1856

Dear Lady John.

The date of the place where I am hard at work among the corn and Bean fields, affords the reason for my being so unfortunate as not to be able to dine at Pembroke Lodge[2] in compliance with your kind invitation. It is always so truly interesting to me, and always gives me so much genuine pleasure, to pass a few hours there, that I should have come over for the purpose but for having sworn fidelity to my desk (and Little Dorrit) at that time of the month.

Pray present my kind remembrance to Lord John[3] and Believe me always with much regard

Very faithfully Yours
CHARLES DICKENS

The | Lady John Russell.

To THOMAS BEARD, 21 JUNE 1856

MS Dickens House.

Villa des Moulineaux, Boulogne S/M.
Saturday June Twenty First 1856

My Dear Beard.

As I hope it may be pleasant to you in the midst of Baldwin[4] and Botheration (alliterative words for the same thing), to know how your holiday-quarters look, I scramble out of Little Dorrit's affairs to make a short report on the subject.

Beaucourt has grubbed up about half the trees that were here when we were here before, and has consequently improved the place remarkably. It is a great deal more free and fresh. Having had some months in which to prepare for us (for I wrote to him last February) he has also planted the garden with flowers in that ingenious manner that there is to be an uninterrupted succession of novelty during the whole of our Stay. Plants in pots, also abound in the greatest profusion. It is really very beautiful; and he is so charmed himself with what he has done, that he is perpetually flying out of that house at the top of the Hill, to look at it. Occasionally in the morning I find him lying down in the sandy paths, in order to get his nose and eyes on a level with the roses. I am inclined to doubt whether anybody else since Adam, has been so fond and proud of a garden.

[1] Née Frances Anna Maria Elliot, daughter of the 2nd Earl Minto, Russell's second wife; married 1841.

[2] The Russells' home in Richmond Park.

[3] Lord John Russell (1792–1878; *DNB*), now out of office.

[4] Edward Baldwin, proprietor of the *Daily Herald*.

Our Cook, growing infirm, has left us for a smaller family, and so arranged her departure as that we might have a Frenchwoman during our stay here. We have accordingly got a cook from the Prefect, of whom I think you will approve. She is at present (while we are alone), going gravely through her performances. She has an immense number: having been a fortnight at it, and showing no signs of exhaustion. I take my seat on the Bench every day at half past five, and try a new case. If I find any prevalent offence in the Calendar, I should say it was butter; but on the whole the state of the kitchen is highly gratifying. I have directed a cross and the word "Beard" to be put against several decisions in the filed records of the Court.

Bourgois, the wine merchant,[1] is in the best condition. I could get no such wines as his in Paris, for double the money at least. The dinner Bordeaux is remarkably good this time; and some light cool white wines, as Chablis and Sauterne, I have already in the most charming order. But the Cellar here is worth anything, and I would desire to have no better at Tavistock House. It is the only weak point of that Establishment.

(Talking of which, reminds me that there is an amazing cellar at Gad's Hill, and that my people were saying here the other night, Lord! Mr. Beard would be able again next year, after all these years, to come down again on a Saturday!)

Those unfortunate Cattermoles[2] are still with the more unfortunate Beaucourt, and I don't see how he is ever to get rid of them until they have died out. I was talking to him about them in the Avenue here the other evening, and he admitted, on being hard pressed, that Monsieur Cattermole "promises always, but that's all". They have an English nurse whom they can't discharge because they can't pay her her wages, and who, in consequence *will* stay, and *won't* work. One of the little boys is the Cook—"that poor Walter—cooks always," said Beaucourt. "They have broken nearly all the glass and china, and have nothing, or next to nothing, for use. That poor Vincent of the weak head[3]—that child afflicted—I have him to work in the garden with me, good infant (for it keeps his brain sounder), and he dines with us every day—lives with us—Madame Beaucourt has so much love and pity for that boy! I am desolated for them all."—"And for yourself, Beaucourt", said I, "you good fellow. Don't you say anything about yourself?"—"Ah Monsieur Dickens, pardon me, its not worth the trouble—its nothing—don't let us speak of it!"—and he pulled off his cap after we had shaken hands, and went backing up the Avenue, with such a generous, simple, amiable face, that I half expected to see him back himself straight into the Evening-Star (which was at the end of it), without going through the ceremony of dying first.

I do hope, and we do all hope, that you will take a good month this year. You want that period of relief and rest, I am sure, and I don't believe that your taking less, does you the least good with that rheumatic Bedlamite. On the contrary, I think he would care a great deal more about you if he had missed you more.

When I next come to town I will send you round a note, and propose a little

[1] F. Bourgois, of rue de l'Ecu, 50, Boulogne.

[2] The Rev. Richard Cattermole (?1795–1858; *DNB*), (the painter George Cattermole's brother), and his family; BD Christ's College, Cambridge 1831; author; Secretary, Royal Society of Literature, 1833–52; Vicar of Little Marlow, Bucks; he died in Boulogne.

[3] Vincent Cattermole, Richard Cattermole's son: see Vol. VII, p. 423 and *n*.

dinner at the Household Words office—in order that John may not grow rusty. In the meantime and ever, with kindest loves from all here to all your house

Ever My Dear Beard | Heartily Yours
CHARLES DICKENS

I have forgotten to mention the "Curaçoa and bis-kits", but they are all right.

To JOHN FORSTER, [22 JUNE 1856]

Extracts in F, XI, iii, 823 and VII, iv, 603. *Date:* first extract 22 June, according to Forster; description in second extract almost certainly same letter (cf. *To* Beard, 21 June).

I have had a story to hack and hew into some form for *Household Words*[1] this morning, which has taken me four hours of close attention. And I am perfectly addled by its horrible want of continuity after all,[2] and the dreadful spectacle I have made of the proofs—which look like an inky fishing-net.[3]

Replying to some questions about an English family,[4] *put to him by CD one day, he had only enlarged on their sacrifices and self-denials.* "Ah, that family, unfortunate!", he had answered. "And you, Monsieur Beaucourt", I said to him, "you are unfortunate too, God knows!" Upon which he said in the pleasantest way in the world, "Ah, Monsieur Dickens, thank you, don't speak of it!"—And backed himself down the avenue with his cap in his hand, as if he were going to back himself straight into the evening star, without the ceremony of dying first. I never did see such a gentle, kind heart.[5]

To W. H. WILLS, 22 JUNE 1856

Extracts in Retz & Storm catalogue No. 8[(aa)], and Anderson catalogue, Dec 1933; *MS* 2 pp.; dated Boulogne, 22 June 56; addressed W. H. Wills.

[a]I have had a tidy job with the Eric Walderthorn story, as you will see by the condition of the Proofs. The revise will want your particular attention, in consequence of my having cut them about so much.[a] The Mrs. Haydn[6] letter[7] may go straight to Miss Coutts. You can recommend her (she assisted Haydn in his lifetime), that all I

[1] Mrs J. C. Bateman's "Eric Walderthorn", the first of two instalments, 5 and 12 July 56, XIII, 590 and 606.

[2] These three chapters present a mysterious situation: Eric and Carl, driving by sleigh at night in Germany for the wedding of Eric's brother, rescue two sisters from wolves and recognise them from a meeting many years earlier.

[3] Examples of similar proofs survive (e.g. of his own "Foreigners' Portraits of Englishmen": see *Uncollected Writings of CD*, ed. Harry Stone, I, 145).

[4] See *To* Beard, 21 June and *fn*.

[5] Forster is evidently abbreviating a letter and conceals names, saying he is "necessarily silent" on Beaucourt's "touching traits", no doubt for the sake of Cattermoles still living in 1874.

[6] Mary Haydn, widow of Joseph Haydn (1793–1856; *DNB*), compiler of *Dictionary of Dates*, 1841: see Vol. II, p. 457*n*; and, for his help from the Royal Literary Fund in Jan 50, Vol. V, p. 685 and *n*.

[7] No doubt asking Miss Coutts for assistance; the Civil List pension of £25 *p.a.* granted to her husband in 1856 was continued to her.

know of her is unquestionably good. Sir John Forbes[1] perhaps you'll write to—say that I am visiting in the country, but that when I come to town you will shew me etc.[2] I would rather (between ourselves) not certify in this case[3] or any other, to the humbugs of the Circumlocution office,[4]

To BENJAMIN WEBSTER,[5] 29 JUNE 1856

MS British Library. *Address:* L'Angleterre. | Benjamin Webster Esquire | Theatre Royal Adelphi | London.

Boulogne | Sunday Twenty Ninth June 1856

My Dear Webster.

You know (I hope) that I would do a great deal for you, and that I have always a genuine and lively interest in the Profession. But I must decline to be examined before the Committee,[6] simply because I have no becoming and genuine locus standi as a witness there. It would merely be an obtrusion of myself and my name—which I detest, abominate, and abjure. Buckstone, as the Treasurer who always makes the statements concerning the General Theatrical Fund, is clearly the man to give evidence concerning it, if any be wanted. As to the other Funds,[7] I swear I know no more about them than the Committee itself. I am reluctant to say No, but I am obliged to say so, positively, both with a reference to myself and a reference to the case.

I don't know whether Mark's ill-looks[8] arise from any pimple in his memory, but I have begged him these ten or twelve days, to arrange with Stanfield and you about coming here, and he has not done it. I am not going to stand this, and therefore shall get hold of Stanfield forthwith (I write to him by this Post), and shall come and see The Flying Dutchman on Tuesday or Wednesday night. On which interesting occasion, you may expect to be refreshed with the sight of

Yours Ever
CD.

To CLARKSON STANFIELD, [29 JUNE 1856]

Mention in last.

[1] Sir John Forbes (1787–1861; *DNB*), MD, FRCS, physician and medical writer; for his giving CD a copy of his *A Physician's Holiday*, 2nd edn, 1850, see Vol. VI, p. 98*n*.

[2] Forbes may have given CD a copy of his *Sight Seeing in Germany and the Tyrol*, published late June 56.

[3] Perhaps being brought against Forbes or threatened by one of the impostors he had detected in his investigation of mesmerism; he had given the history of several in his *Illustrations of Modern Mesmerism from Personal Investigation*, 1845.

[4] A likely omission from the original letter is CD's comment on Harriet Parr's "Milverston Worthies": see *To* Wills, 12 July.

[5] Misdated 25 June in N.

[6] Presumably of the General Theatrical Fund. CD was a Trustee and often a speaker at anniversary dinners, but held no office.

[7] i.e. those of particular theatres, such as Drury Lane.

[8] For his illness, see *To* Lemon, 2 July.

To THOMAS BEARD, 1 JULY 1856

MS Dickens House. *Address:* Thomas Beard Esquire | Morning Herald Office | Shoe Lane.

H.W. Office | First July, 1856

My Dear Beard.

Will you come here tomorrow at 6 (no party) to eat Turtle and a steak.

Ever Heartily
CD.

To BENJAMIN WEBSTER, 1 JULY 1856*

MS Private.

H.W. Office | Tuesday First July 1856

My Dear Webster.

Here!—He *will* come and see the Dutchman[1]—and *will* come and see the Americans.[2] So I must come again. You know whom I mean by "he", of course. I refer to the old Salt.[3]

Will you leave us a Private Box (if you have one) at the top of the stairs?

Ever Faithfully
CD.

To HABLOT K. BROWNE,[4] 2 JULY 1856

Extract in D. C. Thomson, *Life and Labours of Hablot K. Browne*, 1884, p. 142, dated 2 July 56.

Saying that he was returning to Boulogne the next day and asking him to make "The Pensioner Entertainment"[5] illustration "as characteristic as ever you please, my little dear, but quiet."

[1] *The Flying Dutchman; Or, The Phantom Ship*, a nautical play by Edward Fitzball, music by G. H. B. Rodwell; first performed 1825; revived at the Adelphi, June 56, with both Webster and Mme Celeste. Performed 2 July.

[2] At the Adelphi: Mrs Barney Williams (see *To* Lemon, 2 July 56, *fn*) in the anonymous farce (first performed 30 June), *The Customs of the Country* and Barney Williams (see *To* Webster, 9 Dec 57, *fn*) in Buckstone's farce, *The Irish Lion*.

[3] Stanfield.

[4] Hablot Knight Browne, "Phiz" (1815–82; *DNB*), painter and illustrator: see Vol. 1, p. 163*n* and later vols.

[5] In Book 1, Ch. 31, No. IX, published 31 July; it shows William Dorrit "at home" in the Marshalsea, with Old Nandy taking his tea on a newspaper spread on the window-sill.

To MRS CHARLES DICKENS, 2 JULY 1856

MS British Library. *Address:* France | À Madame Charles Dickens | Villa des Moulineaux | Boulogne sur Mer.

H.W. Office | Tuesday[1] Second July, 1856

My Dearest Catherine.

I am coming home tomorrow (Thursday). The train leaves London at half past seven in the morning, and the boat will be due in Boulogne at about half past twelve. Stanny and Webster are to come on the 10th. and Peter[2] and his wife[3] on the 14th.

Love to Georgy. And to Mamey, Katey, Lotty,[4] Walter, Frank, Alfred, Harry, and the noble Plorn. Sydney—I forgot him— Sydney also. Tho' last, not least.

A modest Turtle repast comes off here this afternoon. Six is the hour, for Charley's convenience. Mark is ill at Brighton.

Ever affecy.
CD.

To MARK LEMON, 2 JULY 1856†

MS Berg Collection.

H. W. Office | Wednesday Second July, 1856

My Dear Mark

I am concerned to hear that you are ill—that you sit down before fires and shiver—and that you have stated times for doing so, like the demons in the Melo Dramas—and that you mean to take a week to get well in.

Make haste about it like a dear fellow, and keep up your spirits, because I have made a bargain with Stanny and Webster that they shall come to Boulogne tomorrow week, Thursday the 10th. and stay a week. And you know how much pleasure we shall all miss, if you are not among us—at least for some part of the time.

Wills has just told me that there is a letter from you, lying waiting for me at home at Boulogne. I go back tomorrow morning, and shall find it, no doubt.

Give my love to Mrs. Lemon, and tell her that the case of Eau d'Or[5] has at last been laid down on the stone floor at the basement of Tavistock House. When I next come to town the precious liqueur will have had ample time to recover, and I shall then send round these two bottles—which are to be a transitory remembrance of the great occasion when, calm in the strength and fortitude of Truth, she made her tyrant quail.

Mrs. Barney Williams[6] is very good—in some points extremely good—but I am afraid the pre-occupation of the Theatrical mind by the false Florence, is not favourable to the money return to Webster.[7]

[1] CD's error for Wednesday.

[2] Peter Cunningham.

[3] Née Zenobia Martin (*b.* 1816): see Vol. VI, p. 376*n*.

[4] Charlotte (?1838–59), second daughter of the Rev.James White: see Vol. VI, p. 30*n*.

[5] See *To* Lemon, 7 Jan.

[6] Née Maria Pray, American actress and singer, wife of Barney Williams, stage-name of Bernard Flaherty (1823–76; *DAB*). After their marriage in 1849, they played together, first in New York, and on tour in America, then in London 1855–9.

[7] Mrs William Jermyn Florence, who had been acting at Drury Lane with her Irish husband at intervals since Apr. Née Malvina Pray

If you find any unusually light appearance in the air at Brighton, it is a distant refraction (I have no doubt) of the gorgeous and shining surface of Tavistock House, now transcendantly painted. The Theatre partition[1] is put up, and is a work of such terrific solidity that I suppose it will be dug up, ages hence, from the ruins of London, by that Australian of Macaulay's who is to be impressed by its ashes.[2] I have wandered through the spectral Halls of the Tavistock Mansion, two nights, with feelings of the profoundest depression. I have breakfasted there, like a criminal in Pentonville (only not so well). It is more like Westminster Abbey by midnight than the lowest-spirited man—say you at present for example—can well imagine.

There has been a wonderful robbery at Folkestone, by the new Manager of the Pavilion,[3] who succeeded Giovannini. He had in keeping £16,000 of a foreigner's, and bolted with it, as he supposed, but in reality with only £1400 of it. The Frenchman had previously bolted with the whole, which was the property of his mother. With him to England the Frenchman brought a "lady", who was, all the time and at the same time, endeavouring to steal all the money from him and bolt with it herself. The details are amazing, and all the money (a few pounds excepted), has been got back.[4]

They will be full of sympathy and talk about you when I get home, and I shall tell them that I send their loves beforehand. They are all enclosed. The moment you feel Hearty, just write me that word by post. I shall be so delighted to receive it.

Ever my Dear boy | Your affectionate friend
CHARLES DICKENS.

To FREDERICK GYE, 4 JULY 1856†

MS Fales Collection, New York University Library.

Villa des Moulineaux, near Boulogne
Friday Fourth July, 1856.

My Dear Sir

As I was leaving town very early yesterday morning, your kind note came to my hands. Pray accept the thanks I had not time to send you in London, and with them the assurance that it will give me real pleasure, when I return to town for the winter, to improve the opportunity of knowing you which has now been presented to me. I have long been much interested in your enterprises, and shall be happy to add a personal regard to my public appreciation.

Faithfully Yours

Frederick Gye Esquire
CHARLES DICKENS

and sister of Mrs Barney Williams; as the *Yankee Housekeeper* (see *To* Georgina Hogarth, 9 May), and similar farces played by the Florences had also been performed by the Barney Williamses in New York, there was naturally some rivalry. Drury Lane was a much larger theatre, and the Florences had a two-month start. But the Barney Williamses' programme continued into the autumn, whereas Drury Lane closed in August.

[1] To create the "Tavistock House Theatre".

[2] In fact, a New Zealander, imagined as a traveller in some future age who "shall ... take his stand on a broken arch of London Bridge to sketch the ruins of St Paul's", when the Roman Catholic Church still exists ("Von Ranke", *Critical and Historical Essays Contributed to the Edinburgh Review*, 1843, III, 209).

[3] Mr Hastie, a Belgian: see *To* Miss Coutts, 5 July.

[4] No report found in local papers, since case presumably did not come to Court.

To [MISS HARRIET HANCOCK],[1] [?4] JULY 1856

MS (written on title-page of copy of Scott's *Rob Roy*) Fales Collection, New York University Library. *Date:* probably shortly after CD's return.

Boulogne, July 1856

H.H. | From | C.D.

This was my fictional companion on the railroad and steamboat coming over;[2] it shall be yours going back—

To HANS CHRISTIAN ANDERSEN,[3] 5 JULY 1856

MS Royal Library, Copenhagen.

Villa des Moulineaux, near Boulogne
Saturday Fifth July 1856

My Dear and worthy Hans.

I am extremely sorry that I cannot shew your friend Mr. Bille[4] the attention and interest that it would indeed be a great pleasure to me to testify to any friend of yours. But, I have left London for the summer, in order that I may work the more freely and pleasantly in the midst of a pretty garden here. You know, my dear fellow-labourer, what the distractions of a London life are, and what a relief it is to escape from them. You will not be surprised at my remaining away from it as long as I can, and not intending to return to London until late in October.

I cannot write to explain this to Mr. Bille, myself, because I have not received with your letter (which he left at my house in town), any card of his, and consequently I do not know his address. But when you next see him or communicate with him, pray do me the favor to tell him how glad I should have been to have tried to make his visit to London more domestic and agreeable, if I had been there. You have too much modesty to be able to tell him how delightedly and cordially I should have taken a hand that had been lately in your grasp—so I will tell him that, myself, when he comes again.[5]

And *you* my friend—when are *you* coming again? Nine years (as you say) have flown away since you were among us. In those nine years you have not faded out of the hearts of the English people, but have become even better known and more beloved by them than when you saw them for the first time. When Aladdin shall have come out of those caves of Science, to run a triumphant course on Earth and made us all wiser and better[6]—as I know he will—you ought to come for another visit. You ought to come to me for example, and stay in my house. We would all do our best to make you happy.

[1] Harriet Hancock, the recipient of five presents of books from CD 1854–70: see Vol. VII, pp. 377 and 685; but not further identified.

[2] CD returned to Boulogne on 3 July.

[3] Hans Christian Andersen (1805–75): see Vol. V, p. 47 and *n*; met CD in June–July 47 (see Vol. V, pp. 128 and 154 and *nn*).

[4] Carl Steen Andersen Bille, Danish journalist and writer; editor, *Dagbladet*, Copenhagen; author of *The Sleswig Question between Denmark and Germany*, transl. from German, 1872; his letters to Andersen published Copenhagen, 1877. See later vols.

[5] See *To* Jerdan, 21 July 57 and *fnn*.

[6] Presumably a modern adaptation of *Aladdin and his Wonderful Lamp*, but not discovered.

I am hard at work at Little Dorrit, and She will hold me prisoner for another nine or ten months. She is a wonderful favorite in England. The mention of my country's name reminds me to say that you now write English most admirably, and that this letter of yours now lying on my desk is a perfect Englishman's.

Mrs. Dickens wishes me to tell you that she would have been mortally offended if you had suspected her of forgetting you, and that you only do her justice in supposing that you live in her remembrance. Such of my children as you saw at Broadstairs by the sea, and especially my two daughters who are now young women, are very indignant at your dreaming of the possibility of their forgetting Hans Christian Andersen. They say that if you knew them half as well as they have for years and years known Tommelise,[1] and the ugly Duck,[2] you would know better. However, they send you their love and forgiveness.

My dear Andersen, I have had the heartiest pleasure in hearing from you again, and I assure you that I love and esteem you more than I could tell you on as much paper as would pave the whole road from here to Copenhagen.

Ever your affectionate friend

Hans Christian Andersen. CHARLES DICKENS

To MRS BROWN, 5 JULY 1856

MS Morgan Library. *Address:* L'Angleterre. | Mrs. Brown | Prospect Hill | Reading.

Villa des Moulineaux, Boulogne
Saturday Fifth July, 1856

My Dear Mrs. Brown

I owe you many thanks for your kind and interesting letter. I need not tell you that nothing in your account of that occasion[3] surprised me, great and high as the pleasure was, that I derived from it.

I meant to have written to you at once, but I was so busy with Little Dorrit that I could not detach myself from her for any pen and ink purpose. Then I had to go immediately to London, and purposed writing from there; but I found myself continually engaged, and had no peace until I came back here again, yesterday.

Walter and the three smaller boys have all come home with a Prize apiece. In honor of these achievements we have made rejoicings with five franc pieces, running matches, and cricket ditto. Besides the pretty gardens here, I have a field for them, in which they tear themselves to pieces all day long—immensely to their satisfaction, and the tailor's. Their bedrooms being in a little cottage in the garden, I have established (by way of a lesson in Common things)[4] a regular code of laws for the administration of that Institution. The washing arrangements and so forth are conducted on the strict principles of a man of War. Nothing is allowed to be out of its place. Each in his turn is appointed Keeper for the week, and I go out in solemn

[1] The story of the little girl who lived in a flower: entitled "Tommelise" in *Danish Fairy Legends and Tales*, 2nd enlarged edn, 1852 ("Little Totty" in 1st edn, *Tales and Fairy Stories*, 1852).

[2] It first appeared in English in Andersen's *Danish Story-Book*, transl. Charles Boner, 1846; as "The Ugly Duckling" in *Tales and Fairy Stories*, transl. Mme de Chatelain, 1852.

[3] Letter endorsed by Mrs Brown: "July 7th 1856 | answr. to mine re Whitelands": see next.

[4] See *To* Miss Coutts, 11 July and *fn*.

procession (Georgina and the Baby—as we call him—forming the rest of it), three times a day, on a tour of inspection. Meantime Charley seems to get on very well indeed in the City, and is coming here for a fortnight at the end of August.

Poor Mrs. Watson went to Southsea a few months ago, to see her second boy[1] through the Naval School before entering the service. There, he fell ill of Scarlet Fever. Having all her children with her, she was obliged to send the rest away into another house, and only to see them, day after day and week after week, from her own sick-room balcony. Nevertheless the little girl took the fever somehow, and then poor Mrs. Watson—all alone there, except for a servant—took it herself. The happy conclusion of the story is, that they are all now well again, and that we heard from her this morning. She has gone through a great deal of late years, but has a wonderful force of character.

Mrs. Dickens and Georgina and all the children send their loves. How beautiful the country now! We have Millions of roses here. And as I came from town yesterday the luxuriant hayfields were so beautiful that I felt as proud of them as if they were all mine.

Ever Dear Mrs. Brown | Affectionately Yours
CHARLES DICKENS

To [MISS BURDETT COUTTS], 5 JULY 1856

MS University of Texas.

Villa des Moulineaux, Boulogne
Saturday Fifth July, 1856

My Dear [Miss Coutts][2]

It seems as if months—not to say years—had passed since I wrote to you or heard from you. We have both been very busy, to account for it. I hope you generally liked what was done in the Papers about the Prizes?[3] There seems to have been a tardy and uneven distribution of the Summary, to the papers: of which I heard several complaints when I was in town.

This disaster of Itch[4] at the Home is a little unfortunate; but I have a strong hope that it will not spread in the least. The place being so extremely clean and well kept, there is every ground for feeling confident that it will not occasion much inconvenience.

[1] Edward Spencer Watson (1843–89); educated at Eton and Southsea Naval School; served as midshipman in Naval Brigade in Indian Mutiny at Cawnpore and as ADC to Capt. Sir William Peel at capture of Lucknow; then in 10th Hussars; JP Beds.

[2] Name erased; "Miss" distinguishable; clearly Miss Coutts.

[3] N reads "Pusies" in error. For the favourable *Times* leader on her *Summary Account*, see 11 July and *fn*. Miss Coutts had no doubt seen an advance copy of "Not Very Common Things", by Morley and Wills, *HW*, 26 July 56, XIV, 39, another very favourable account of her book (see *To* Miss Coutts, 11 July, *fn*). The *Examiner*, 28 June, had warmly welcomed Miss Coutts's visit on 14 June to the Whitelands Training Institution, Chelsea, to award her prizes. After "a kindly and sensible speech", she gave each successful mistress a copy of the Archbishop of Canterbury's *Commentary on the New Testament*, and each successful pupil another religious work.

[4] Scabies.

Louisa Cooper[1] (who, you remember, went to the Cape with Mrs. Boyle),[2] has been two or three times with Mrs. Marchmont, and the other day left a letter with her, addressed to me, describing her approaching want of a situation. She was only engaged by the lady who brought her home, for the Voyage and until she should be settled. She seems to have had a desperately hard place, with everything to do (mantua making[3] included) for 7 children, and to have rather overworked herself. She will leave on the 14th. and has no relations or friends except "the young man" to whom she is engaged, and who cannot marry (she says) until he finds a Gardener's place as a married man. Mrs. Marchmont is endeavouring to help her to a situation, but as yet without effect. Would you wish me to do anything in answer to the letter?

Going over to London the other day, I found the Pavilion at Folkestone in a state of amazing excitement about a robbery that had been committed there.[4] It would take three quarters of an hour to tell the story, but the following are the heads.

Chapter I

Frenchman arrives at Pavilion, with the small sum of £16,000 in a Courier's bag. Delivers same to Breach[5] the landlord, requesting him to "take care of it for him"—which he absurdly consents to do.

Chapter II

Breach the Landlord being summoned to Ireland, brings New manager of Hotel (a Belgian) to Frenchman, and says to Frenchman "Behold Mr. Hastie, my manager. If you want your money in my absence, he knows where it is, and has the key, and will duly deliver it up."

Chapter III

After two days, Frenchman does want that trifle of money. Asks for Mr. Hastie. Mr. Hastie gone to London. Just sent telegraph dispatch that he won't be back till tomorrow night. Frenchman alarmed, asks where is the key that locks up his money? Mr. Hastie has it. Frenchman more alarmed, insists on Housekeeper's breaking open the room. Room broken open, bag found cut open, Mr. Hastie having absconded with the contents, as he supposes—but in reality with only £1,400; there being several divisions in the bag, and several rolls of notes.

CHAPTER IV.[6]

All the Railroads and steamboats being telegraphed for apprehension of Hastie, going abroad—Hastie comes down *to Folkestone* by night Mail, disguised in an Italian coat, and feigning to be asleep with a pocket handkerchief over his face. Though everybody knows him on the line, gets to Folkestone unrecognized. Sharp Folkestone commissioner looks into carriage, says nothing, mounts the engine, goes to Dover, watches him as he gets out of carriage, makes sure he is the man, and takes him.

CHAPTER V.[6]

French Govt. telegraphs to English Govt. that the *Frenchman* stole the whole

[1] She had emigrated to Cape Town in Oct 54: see Vol. VII, p. 443 and *nn*.

[2] Not further identified; Louisa Cooper had accompanied her to the Cape; for Louisa's "very good" letter of thanks to Miss Coutts, see Vol. VII, p. 443 and *n*.

[3] A loose outer garment.

[4] See *To* Lemon, 2 July and *fn*.

[5] James G. Breach.

[6] Underlined with short double strokes.

£16,000 from his mother and sister; and wishes to know whether the English Govt. can issue a warrant and take him. English Govt. find it would be illegal without regular and formal proceedings, and can't do it. Consult with Police Commissioner, Scotland Yard. Scotland Yard says, send down Detective Saunders[1] who can speak French. Perhaps he may devise some scheme for getting back some of the money.

CHAPTER VI.[2]

Detective Saunders finds Frenchman at Folkestone. Says, This is a bad job, I'm going to take you into custody (which he could no more do than take you or me), have you got the money about you? If so, you had better avoid the inconvenience and indignity of being searched, as I must take it in charge in taking you. Frenchman immediately puts a hand in a pocket, and delivers it up. Detective Saunders says, That'll do. You're not as clever as I thought you. All I wanted was the money. Now you may go where you like.

CHAPTER VII.[2]

Frenchman discovered to have been all this time accompanied by a confidential friend[3] from Paris, *who was only biding his time to rob him of all the money*. Friend disappointed by the French Minister impounding it, including even the £1,400 (except a pound or two), which was taken by the Police out of Mr. Hastie's pocket at Dover. So, it seems as if it were enchanted money and nobody could keep it from the rightful owners.

THE END.[4]

On domestic matters I have merely to report that the Baby, with a nut-brown face and legs, will give any Suffolk baby[5] fifteen hundred out of two thousand and beat him easily. Our bird (the most wonderful ever known) having been perpetually waylaid by two ferocious and extra-cunning French Cats, one of the Cats has been shot, and one Man lies in wait behind bushes for the other, with his soul so set upon his murderous purpose that I expect him at least to blow his fingers off, at any hour of the day. He does nothing whatever but wait for the Cat. And all the boys (all home from School) encourage him from high places behind trees, and are monomaniacal on the subject; bringing in reports that they have "met the Cat down in the town", and that they "saw the Cat on the Pier", and believing the most unlikely and impossible things. Their rationality on other subjects is not affected, but they are all mad about this Cat. *I* feel my reason tottering when she is mentioned—and they never talk of anything else.

Ever Dear [Miss Coutts][5] | Most Faithfully Yours

CD.

[1] Frederick White Saunders, Commissioner's Office.

[2] Underlined with short double strokes.

[3] A "lady", according to *To* Lemon, 2 July.

[4] Underlined five times.

[5] See Vol. VII, p. 87*n*.

[6] Name erased; "Miss" distinguishable; clearly Miss Coutts.

To THE DUKE OF DEVONSHIRE, 5 JULY 1856

MS Devonshire Collections, Chatsworth.

Villa des Moulineaux, near Boulogne
Saturday Night Fifth July, 1856

My Dear Duke of Devonshire

From this place where I am writing my way through the Summer in the midst of rosy gardens and sea airs, I cannot forbear writing to tell you with what uncommon pleasure I received your interesting letter, and how sensible I always am of your kindness and generosity. You were always in the mind of my household during your illness;[1] and to have so beautiful and fresh and manly an assurance of your recovery from it, under your own hand, is a privilege and delight that I will say no more of!

I am so glad you like Flora. It came into my head one day that we have all had our Floras (mine is living, and extremely fat),[2] and that it was a half serious half ridiculous truth which had never been told. It is a wonderful gratification to find that everybody knows her. Indeed some people seem to think I have done them a personal injury, and that their individual Floras (God knows where they are or who) are each and all Little Dorrit's.

We were all grievously disappointed that you were ill when we played Mr Collins's "Lighthouse" at my house. If you had been well, I should have waited upon you with my humble petition that you would come and see it. And if you had come, I think you would have cried—which would have charmed me. I hope to produce another new play at home next Christmas, and if I can only persuade you to see it from a special arm-chair, and can only make you wretched, my satisfaction will be intense.

May I tell you, to beguile a moment, of a little "Tag"—or end of a piece—I saw in Paris this last winter, which struck me as the prettiest I had ever met with? The piece was not a new one, but a revival at the Vaudeville—les Memoires du Diable.[3] Admirably constructed, very interesting, and extremely well played. The plot is, that a certain M. Robin has come into possession of the papers of a deceased Lawyer, and finds some relating to the wrongful with-holding of an estate from a certain Baroness, and to certain other frauds (involving even the denial of her marriage to the deceased Baron, and the tarnishing of her good name), which are so very wicked, that he binds them up in a book, and labels them "Memoires du Diable". Armed with this knowledge he goes down to a desolate old château in the country, part of the wrested-away estate, from which the Baroness and her daughter are going to be ejected. He informs the mother that he can right her and restore her the property; but must have, as his reward, her daughter's hand in marriage. She replies "I cannot promise my daughter to a man of whom I know nothing. The gain would be an unspeakable happiness, but I resolutely decline the bargain". The daughter, however, has overheard all, and she comes forward and says "Do what you have promised my mother you can do, and I am yours". Then the piece goes on to its

[1] See *To* the Duke of Devonshire, 1 June, *fn.*

[2] i.e. Mrs Winter.

[3] By Etienne Arago and Paul Vermond (pseudonym of Eugène Grinot), first performed in 1842; loosely based on Frédéric Soulié's well-known novel of the same title, 1837–8. What follows is a much fuller version, but verbally close, of his description to Forster: see *To* Forster, 5 and 6 July.

development, in an admirable way, through the unmasking of all the hypocrites. Now M. Robin, partly through his knowledge of the secret ways of the old château (derived from the lawyer's papers), and partly through his going to a Masquerade as the Devil, the better to explode what he knows, on the hypocrites, is supposed by the servants at the château really to be the Devil. At the opening of the last act he suddenly appears there before the young lady, and she screams, but, recovering and laughing, says "You are not really the ——?"—"Oh dear no", he replies—"have no connexion with him. But these people down here are so frightened and absurd! See this little box on the table. I open it. Here's a little bell. They have a notion that whenever this bell rings, I shall appear. Very ignorant, is it not?"—"Very indeed", says she. "Well!" says M. Robin "If you should ever want me very much to appear, try the Bell—if only for a jest. Will you promise?" Yes, she promises, and the play goes on. At last he has righted the Baroness completely, and has only to hand her the last document, which proves her marriage and restores her good name. Then he says "Madame, in the progress of these endeavours I have learnt the happiness of doing good for its own sake. I made a mercenary bargain with you. I release you from it. I have done what I undertook to do. I wish you and your amiable daughter all happiness. Adieu. I take my leave!" Bows himself out. People on the stage astonished. Audience astonished. (I incensed.) The daughter is going to cry, when she looks at the box on the table, remembers the bell, runs to it and rings it, and he rushes back and takes her to his heart. Upon which we all cry with pleasure, and then laugh heartily.

This looks dreadfully long, and perhaps you know it already. If so, I will endeavour to make amends, with Flora in future numbers.

Mrs. Dickens and her sister beg to present their remembrances to your Grace and their congratulations on your recovery. I saw Paxton now and then when you were ill, and always received from him most encouraging accounts. I don't know how heavy he is going to be (I mean in the scale), but I begin to think Daniel Lambert[1] must have been in his family.

Ever Your Grace's faithful and obliged

The | Duke of Devonshire CHARLES DICKENS

To WASHINGTON IRVING,[2] 5 JULY 1856

Text from MDGH, III, 178–9.

Tavistock House, London, July 5th, 1856.[3]

My dear Irving,

If you knew how often I write to you individually and personally in my books, you would be no more surprised in seeing this note than you were in seeing me do my

[1] Paxton had become more portly. Daniel Lambert (1770–1809, *DNB*) was the fattest man of whom records exist.

[2] Washington Irving (1783–1859; *DAB*): see Vol. II, p. 55*n* and, for their meeting each other in New York in Feb 42 and Irving's clearly hostile attitude to CD after *American Notes* and *Chuzzlewit*, p. 70 and *n*. They had not met nor apparently corresponded since CD's American visit.

[3] According to N (II, 783), written at Boulogne on Tavistock House printed paper.

duty by that flowery julep (in what I dreamily apprehend to have been a former state of existence) at Baltimore.[1]

Will you let me present to you a cousin of mine, Mr. Barrow,[2] who is associated with a merchant's house in New York?[3] Of course he wants to see you, and know you. How can *I* wonder at that? How can anybody?

I had a long talk with Leslie[4] at the last Academy dinner (having previously been with him in Paris), and he told me that you were flourishing. I suppose you know that he wears a moustache—so do I for the matter of that, and a beard too—and that he looks like a portrait of Don Quixote.

Holland House[5] has four-and-twenty youthful pages in it now—twelve for my lord, and twelve for my lady; and no clergyman coils his leg up under his chair all dinner-time, and begins to uncurve it when the hostess goes.[6] No wheeled chair runs smoothly in with that beaming face in it; and ——'s[7] little cotton pocket-handkerchief helped to make (I believe) this very sheet of paper. A half-sad, half-ludicrous story of Rogers[8] is all I will sully it with. You know, I daresay, that for a year or so before his death he wandered, and lost himself like one of the Children in the Wood, grown up there and grown down again. He had Mrs. Procter[9] and Mrs. Carlyle[10] to breakfast with him one morning—only those two. Both excessively talkative, very quick and clever, and bent on entertaining him. When Mrs. Carlyle had flashed and shone before him for about three-quarters of an hour on one subject, he turned his poor old eyes on Mrs. Procter, and pointing to the brilliant discourser with his poor old finger, said (indignantly), "Who is *she*?" Upon this, Mrs. Procter, cutting in, delivered (it is her own story) a neat oration on the life and writings of Carlyle, and enlightened him in her happiest and airiest manner; all of which he heard, staring in the dreariest silence, and then said (indignantly, as before), "And who are *you*?"

Ever, my dear Irving, | Most affectionately and truly yours

[CHARLES DICKENS]

[1] Which they drank at their last dinner together on 23 Mar: see Vol. III, p. 166 and *n.*

[2] Name omitted in MDGH but given in N, II, 783. John Wylie Barrow (1828–85), son of Thomas Culliford Barrow: see Vol. VI, p. 656*n.*

[3] In 1867 he was a member of E. S. Jaffray & Co., importers, 350 Broadway.

[4] Charles Robert Leslie (1794–1859; *DNB*, *DAB*), painter: see Vol. II, p. 395 and *n.*

[5] For CD's first visit on 12 Aug 38, in the time of Lady Holland (1770–1845), famous hostess, wife of the 3rd Baron, see Vol. I, p. 415 and *n.* Now the property of their son, Henry Edward Fox, 4th and last Lord Holland (1802–59).

[6] The Rev. Sydney Smith (1771–1845; *DNB*), Canon of St Paul's, wit, and favoured member of the Holland House circle: see Vol. I, p. 431*n.*

[7] Unidentified.

[8] Samuel Rogers (1763–1855; *DNB*), the banker-poet; another member of the Holland House circle: see Vol. I, p. 602*n* and later vols.

[9] Née Anne Skepper, wife of Bryan Waller Procter.

[10] Jane Baillie Welsh Carlyle, née Welsh (1801–66; *DNB*): see Vol. IV, p. 32*n.*

To WALTER SAVAGE LANDOR,[1] 5 JULY 1856

Text from MDGH, I, 441–3.

Villa des Moulineaux, Boulogne,
Saturday Evening, July 5th, 1856.

My dear Landor,

I write to you so often in my books, and my writing of letters is usually so confined to the numbers that I *must* write, and in which I have no kind of satisfaction, that I am afraid to think how long it is since we exchanged a direct letter.[2] But talking to your namesake[3] this very day at dinner, it suddenly entered my head that I would come into my room here as soon as dinner should be over, and write, "My dear Landor, how are you?" for the pleasure of having the answer under your own hand. That you *do* write, and that pretty often, I know beforehand. Else why do I read *The Examiner*?[4]

We were in Paris from October to May (I perpetually flying between that city and London), and there we found out, by a blessed accident, that your godson was horribly deaf. I immediately consulted the principal physician of the Deaf and Dumb Institution[5] there (one of the best aurists in Europe), and he kept the boy for three months, and took unheard-of pains with him. He is now quite recovered, has done extremely well at school, has brought home a prize in triumph, and will be eligible to "go up" for his India examination soon after next Easter. Having a direct appointment, he will probably be sent out soon after he has passed,[6] and so will fall into that strange life "up the country," before he well knows he is alive, which indeed seems to be rather an advanced stage of knowledge.

And there in Paris, at the same time, I found Marguerite Power and Little Nelly, living with their mother and a pretty sister, in a very small, neat apartment, and working (as Marguerite told me) hard for a living. All that I saw of them filled me with respect, and revived the tenderest remembrances of Gore House.[7] They are coming to pass two or three weeks here for a country rest, next month. We had many long talks concerning Gore House, and all its bright associations; and I can honestly report that they hold no one in more gentle and affectionate remembrance than you. Marguerite is still handsome, though she had the smallpox two or three years ago, and bears the traces of it here and there, by daylight. Poor little Nelly (the quicker and more observant of the two) shows some little tokens of a broken-off marriage in a face too careworn for her years, but is a very winning and sensible creature.

We are expecting Mary Boyle too, shortly.

[1] Walter Savage Landor (1775–1864; *DNB*): see Vol. II, p. 23*n*. Still living in Bath.

[2] CD's last recorded letter to Landor was on 7 Jan 54 (Vol. VII, p. 239).

[3] Walter Landor Dickens.

[4] For Landor's frequent contributions to the *Examiner*, chiefly letters and poems, mostly during Forster's editorship, see R. H. Super, *W. S. Landor: A Biography*, 1957; one of his last letters, to the *Examiner*, 26 July 56, defended tyrannicide as a solution to Italy's problems (*ibid.*, p. 432). After Kossuth had become a regular contributor to the *Atlas*, Landor became a subscriber and contributed 29 letters and 7 poems during 1856.

[5] Prosper Menière: see *To* Miss Coutts, 10 Jan 56 and *fn*.

[6] For his sailing to India as a cadet on 20 July 57, see *To* Miss Coutts, that day.

[7] Before it was sold up in May 49: see Vol. V, p. 530 and *n*.

I have just been propounding to Forster if it is not a wonderful testimony to the homely force of truth, that one of the most popular books on earth has nothing in it to make anyone laugh or cry? Yet I think, with some confidence, that you never did either over any passage in "Robinson Crusoe." In particular, I took Friday's death as one of the least tender and (in the true sense) least sentimental things ever written. It is a book I read very much; and the wonder of its prodigious effect on me and everyone, and the admiration thereof, grows on me the more I observe this curious fact.[1]

Kate and Georgina send you their kindest loves, and smile approvingly on me from the next room, as I bend over my desk. My dear Landor, you see many I daresay, and hear from many I have no doubt, who love you heartily; but we silent people in the distance never forget you. Do not forget us, and let us exchange affection at least.

Ever your Admirer and Friend
[CHARLES DICKENS]

To JOHN FORSTER, [?5 AND 6 JULY 1856]

Extracts in F, VII, v, 611*n*, 610 and iv, 601–2. *Date:* first extract 5 July, same day as *To* Landor (see last); second extract doubtless same letter (cf. *To* Duke of Devonshire, 5 July); third extract 6 July, according to Forster.

You remember my saying to you some time ago how curious I thought it that *Robinson Crusoe*[2] should be the only instance of an universally popular book that could make no one laugh and could make no one cry. I have been reading it again just now, in the course of my numerous refreshings at those English wells, and I will venture to say that there is not in literature a more surprising instance of an utter want of tenderness and sentiment, than the death of Friday.[3] It is as heartless as *Gil Blas*,[2] in a very different and far more serious way. But the second part altogether will not bear enquiry. In the second part of *Don Quixote*[2] are some of the finest things. But the second part of *Robinson Crusoe* is perfectly contemptible, in the glaring defect that it exhibits the man who was 30 years on that desert island with no visible effect made on his character by that experience. De Foe's women too—Robinson Crusoe's wife for instance—are terrible dull commonplace fellows without breeches; and I have no doubt he was a precious dry and disagreeable article himself—I mean De Foe: not Robinson. Poor dear Goldsmith (I remember as I write) derived the same impression.[4]

[1] In his *Walter Savage Landor*, 1869, II, 460, Forster has a longer version of this opinion (one sentence and some phrases being identical with a conversation at Bath on Landor's birthday, 30 Jan 49). As reported by Forster, CD ends by attributing "the prodigious effect" of *Robinson Crusoe* to its "mere homely force and intensity of truth".

[2] All among the books the young *David Copperfield* read in the Rookery "in a little room upstairs" (taken from CD's fragment of autobiography: F, I, i, 5).

[3] See *To* Landor, 5 July and *fn*.

[4] CD may have been recalling, with his memory at fault, the *Bee*, No. 8, "Account of the Augustan Age", in which Goldsmith commented on the non-juror, Charles Leslie: "His stile and manner, both of which were illiberal, were imitated by Ridpath, De Foe, Dunton. . . ."

As I have no news, I may as well tell you about the tag that I thought so pretty to the *Memoires du Diable*; in which piece by the way, there is a most admirable part, most admirably played, in which a man says merely "Yes" or "No" all through the piece, until the last scene. A certain M. Robin has got hold of the papers of a deceased lawyer, concerning a certain estate which has been swindled away from its rightful owner, a Baron's widow, into other hands. They disclose so much roguery that he binds them up into a volume lettered "Memoires du Diable." The knowledge he derives from these papers not only enables him to unmask the hypocrites all through the piece (in an excellent manner), but induces him to propose to the Baroness that if he restores to her her estate and good name—for even her marriage to the deceased Baron is denied—she shall give him her daughter in marriage. The daughter herself, on hearing the offer, accepts it; and a part of the plot is, her going to a masked ball, to which he goes as the Devil, to see how she likes him (when she finds, of course, that she likes him very much). The country people about the Chateau in dispute, suppose him to be really the Devil, because of his strange knowledge, and his strange comings and goings; and he, being with this girl in one of its old rooms, in the beginning of the 3rd act, shews her a little coffer on the table with a bell in it. "They suppose," he tells her, "that whenever this bell is rung, I appear and obey the summons. Very ignorant, isn't it? But, if you ever want me particularly—very particularly—ring the little bell and try." The plot proceeds to its development. The wrong-doers are exposed; the missing document, proving the marriage, is found; everything is finished; they are all on the stage; and M. Robin hands the paper to the Baroness. "You are reinstated in your rights, Madame; you are happy; I will not hold you to a compact made when you didn't know me; I release your fair daughter; the pleasure of doing what I have done, is my sufficient reward; I kiss your hand and take my leave!" He backs himself courteously out; the piece seems concluded, everybody wonders, the girl (little Mdlle. Luther) stands amazed; when she suddenly remembers the little bell. In the prettiest way possible, she runs to the coffer on the table, takes out the little bell, rings it, and he comes rushing back and folds her to his heart. I never saw a prettier thing in my life. It made me laugh in that most delightful of ways, with the tears in my eyes; so that I can never forget it, and must go and see it again.

The only thing new in this garden is that war is raging against two particularly tigerish and fearful cats (from the mill, I suppose), which are always glaring in dark corners, after our wonderful little Dick.[1] Keeping the house open at all points, it is impossible to shut them out, and they hide themselves in the most terrific manner: hanging themselves up behind draperies, like bats, and tumbling out in the dead of night with frightful caterwaulings. Hereupon, French borrows Beaucourt's gun, loads the same to the muzzle, discharges it twice in vain and throws himself over with the recoil, exactly like a clown. But at last (while I was in town) he aims at the more amiable cat of the two, and shoots that animal dead. Insufferably elated by this victory, he is now engaged from morning to night in hiding behind bushes to get aim at the other. He does nothing else whatever. All the boys encourage him and watch for the enemy—on whose appearance they give an alarm which immediately serves

[1] A canary, tamed by Mamie Dickens; it survived until 1866, then aged 15, and was buried at Gad's Hill.

as a warning to the creature, who runs away. They are at this moment (ready dressed for church) all lying on their stomachs in various parts of the garden. Horrible whistles give notice to the gun what point it is to approach. I am afraid to go out, lest I should be shot. Mr. Plornish says his prayers at night in a whisper, lest the cat should overhear him and take offence. The tradesmen cry out as they come up the avenue, 'Me voici! C'est moi—boulanger—ne tirez pas, Monsieur Franche!' It is like living in a state of siege; and the wonderful manner in which the cat preserves the character of being the only person not much put out by the intensity of this monomania, is most ridiculous.

To BENJAMIN WEBSTER, 6 JULY 1856

Mention in Sotheby's catalogue, July 1883; *MS* 1 p.; dated 6 July 56; addressed Benjamin Webster.

To MARK LEMON, 8 JULY 1856*

MS Miss Phyllis Matthews. *Address:* Mark Lemon Esquire | Field Office.[1]

Villa des Moulineaux | Tuesday Eighth July 1856

My Dear Mark.

I hope that with your practical experience in Stage-Writing, you will not find much difficulty in making such additions to the accompanying notes as will sketch out a very funny piece. I should like to make it very compact too, so that everybody has to do with the plot. When we have thoroughly got the plot, we will divide the writing, and afterwards dovetail and finish up together.

It is quite a treat to think of a new farce.[2] We had so many happy hours with the old one.[3]

Pray let one of your disguises be something in the Cadger line in which you can sing Cupid's Garden.[4]

And we ought to think of something answering to the Combat or Hornpipe, to do together.[5]

Let me hear from you when you have thought a little about it.

"You are quite right my dear Lemon"[6] not to come, under the circumstances. I can't tell you how delighted I am to receive so good a report of you.

Loves from all my house to all yours. I write hastily, having been all the morning over the enclosed, and wanting a walk.

Ever Affectionately

CD.

[1] Lemon was the original editor of the *Field*, a sixpenny weekly, launched by Bradbury & Evans from the *Punch* office, partly through the influence of Surtees, and first published on 1 Jan 1853. He remained editor until the end of 1857. For several months in 1854 the proprietor was his friend Benjamin Webster.

[2] Nothing came of this plan; but see *To* Stone, 9 July.

[3] *Mr. Nightingale's Diary*, by CD and Lemon: see Vol. VI, p. 398 and *n*.

[4] i.e. disguised as a hawker or street seller, he could sing the ballad "As down in Cupid's garden with pleasure I did go", published by E. Hodges, 31 Dudley St, Seven Dials.

[5] A stock turn; cf. *Nickleby*, Ch. 22.

[6] Echoing Forster.

To W. C. MACREADY, 8 JULY 1856

MS Morgan Library.

Villa des Moulineaux, Boulogne
Tuesday Eighth July, 1856

My Dearest Macready

I perfectly agree with you in your appreciation of Katie's poem,[1] and shall be truly delighted to publish it in Household Words. It shall go into the very next No. we make up. We are a little in advance (to enable Wills to get a holiday); but, as I remember, the next No. made up, will be published in three weeks.

We are pained indeed to read your reference to my poor boy. God help him and his father! I trust he is not conscious of much suffering himself. If that be so, it is, in the midst of the distress, a great comfort.

Little Dorrit keeps me pretty busy, as you may suppose. The beginning of No. X[2]—the first line—now lies upon my desk. It would not be easy to increase upon the pains I take with her, anyhow.

We are expecting Stanfield on Thursday, and Peter Cunningham and his wife on Monday. I would we were expecting you! This is as pretty and odd a little French country house as could be found anywhere; and the gardens are most beautiful.

In Household Words next week, pray read The Diary of Anne Rodway.[3] (In two not long parts). It is by Collins, and I think possesses great merit, and real pathos.[4]

Being in town the other day, I saw Gye by accident, and told him, when he praised Ristori to me, that she was a very bad actress.[5] "Well!" said he. "*You* may say anything; but if anybody else had told me that, I should have stared". Nevertheless I derived an impression from his manner that she had not been a profitable speculation in respect of Money. That very same day, Stanfield and I dined alone together at the Garrick, and drank your health. We had had a ride by the river before dinner (of course he *would* go and look at boats), and had been talking of you. It was this day week by the bye.

I know of nothing of public interest that is new in France, except that I am changing my moustache into a beard.

We all send our most tender love to dearest Miss Macready and all the house. "The Hammy boy"[6] is particularly anxious to have his love sent to Misr Creedy.

Ever, My Dearest Macready

Most affectionately Yours
CHARLES DICKENS

[1] "The Shadow of the Hand", by Macready's daughter, Catherine; published in *HW* 26 July 56, XIV, 38.

[2] Ch. 33, published 31 Aug 56.

[3] By Wilkie Collins, 19 and 26 July, XIV, 1 and 30.

[4] The diarist's touching account of her friend and fellow-dressmaker, Mary Mallinson, found mysteriously dead, occupies most of Ch. 1; in Ch. 2 she eventually detects the killer, drawing the danger to herself, and he is tried and convicted of manslaughter.

[5] For CD and Macready's pronouncing her performance of Médée in Paris in Apr 56 as "hopelessly bad", see *To* Forster, 13 Apr.

[6] The four-year-old "Plorn".

To W. C. MACREADY, 9 [JULY][1] 1856*

MS Morgan Library. *Date:* Wednesday was the 9th in July; Macready's endorsement confirms.

Villa des Moulineaux, Boulogne
Wednesday Ninth June 1856

My Dearest Macready

This is merely a question relative to the Wine. I have got you a case of the 1846 Champagne (3 Doz). As I have bought a good deal during the last 3 years of the same man, I have it at my former price—that is to say, *on this side*, 4/7d. pr. bottle, though I believe it to be well worth nearly double the money now. How shall I get it to you? Shall I consign it to Wills, get him to have it cleared and then forwarded to you? Or is there anybody you would desire to employ for the purpose? If Wills—he will pay the duty and Custom House charges &c and you and I can balance the whole matter together, at any time. If anybody else—it will be equally easy.

Ever Most affectionately
CD.

To NATHANIEL POWELL,[2] 9 JULY 1856

MS Free Library of Philadelphia.

Villa des Moulineaux, Boulogne
Wednesday Ninth July, 1856

My Dear Sir

I remember that I have inadvertently omitted to reply to a question of yours relative to the cost of painting the names of our houses on the gate. It was something extremely small (I forget exactly what, and have not the bill here); and I will add it to the cost of painting the rails this year, when I receive and divide among us, Cubitt's account for that job.

It has several times been in my mind to mention to you that if you would like to share the garden in front with me as a resort for your children, I shall be happy to have it in the joint occupation of our two families, and have not the least desire to reserve it to myself. I pay your predecessor Mr. Cardale, £20 a year for it.

My Dear Sir | Faithfully Yours
Nathaniel Powell Esquire. CHARLES DICKENS

[1] Macready endorsed the letter "July 11", no doubt date of receipt.

[2] Nathaniel Powell (1813–73), wine merchant, CD's neighbour at Bedford House: see Vol. VII, p. 619*n*; and for the painting of the house-names, p. 630.

To FRANK STONE, 9 JULY 1856†

MS Benoliel Collection.

Villa des Moulineaux, Boulogne
Wednesday Ninth July 1856

My Dear Stone

Don't you think you might take a run over here, and stay with us a few days? The place is very much improved.

Have you the pattern of the Fishwoman's cap?[1] If you have *a* pattern, have you more than one pattern? And to doctor up your dresses, what color is principally required, do you think? With this information I may pick up such materials as we want, very cheaply here, in the course of the next two months.

I have got a capital part for you in the Farce—not a difficult one to learn, as you never say anything but "Yes" and "No". You are called, in the Dramatis Personae, an able bodied British Seaman, and you are never seen by mortal eye to do anything (except inopportunely producing a Mop), but stand about the Deck of the boat in Everybody's way, with your hair immensely touzled, one brace on, your hands in your pockets, and the bottoms of your trousers tucked up. Yet you are inextricably connected with the plot, and are the man whom everybody is enquiring after. I think it is a very whimsical idea and extremely droll. It made me laugh heartily when I jotted it all down yesterday.

Loves from all my house to all yours.

Ever Affecy.
CD.

To W. H. WILLS, 10 JULY 1856*

MS Rosenbach Foundation.

Boulogne, Thursday Tenth July 1856.

My Dear Wills.

All right as to H.W news, *except* that the part of Milverstone[2] you have put in, I never meant to go in at all.[3] I think the expression I used in my letter to you about that series was, that I approved of those parts which treated of "the town and its characters"[4]—something to that effect. You may have misunderstood me, or I may not have expressed myself clearly; but that is what I mean. Her opinions are worth nothing at all. I read this very paper, and unhesitatingly rejected it in my mind. It must not go in. Descriptions of the place and the people are what is wanted.

The No.[5] arrived by the post this morning, and I hope to go over it tonight and return it tomorrow.

[1] He had recently turned to realistic paintings of fisher-folk, examples being *Doubt* in RA, May 56 and *Bon Jour, Messieurs* in RA, May 57: see *To* Stone, 6 Apr 57 and *fn*.

[2] "Milverston Worthies", *HW*, 12, 19, 26 July and 2 Aug; XIII, 602, XIV, 13, 46 and 59, by Harriet Parr (1828–1900; *DNB*), novelist and regular contributor to *HW*: see Vol. VII, p. 687 and *n*.

[3] CD must have been looking at the proof of the third part, published 26 July; much shorter than the first two parts, which suggests a cut.

[4] Presented in each, without "opinions".

[5] No. 330, published 19 July.

ERIC WALDERTHORN[1]

is by Mrs. Bateman,[2] 7 Albion Terrace Folkestone. I think £15 will be enough for it—considering the trouble it cost me.[3]

ANNE RODWAY[1]

certainly pay Eighteen Guineas for. I doubt whether it would not be right (it is only another guinea) to make it £20. It is very specially good.

The Opal Ring[4] is by Miss Power, 5 Rue de Courçelles, Paris.

W.H.W.[1]

You were talking about running over here. Why don't you? And when are you going to take *your* holiday?

Ever Faithfully

CD.

P.S. I re-open this, after having put it in an envelope and written it some hours, to say that you had best give Collins £20—in a handsome note, stating that I had told you that I saw such great pains in his story and so much merit, that I wished to remove it from ordinary calculations. I have a floating idea in my mind that after Little Dorrit is finished (this is inviolably at present between you and me), he and I might do something in Household Words together.[5] He and I have talked so much within the last 3 or 4 years about Fiction-Writing, and I see him so ready to catch at what I have tried to prove right, and to avoid what I thought wrong, and altogether to go at it in the spirit I have fired him with, that the notion takes some shape with me. It may come to nothing—I may find it impracticable on closer scrutiny—but at present I have hope of it. The advance in any case is not a large one, and if I were asked, in reference to the claims of this little Diary, to say who else could have done that about the Dead Girl,[6] I confess I should find it very difficult (putting your conductor out of the question), to name the man.

I write this in the confidence of your knowing that I am not a Literary Bounderby, and not misunderstanding me. And I shall be very much interested in knowing how the fancy strikes you, of my chalking out a story with him, and saying "Leave me this character or situation, and let me give you such advice about that, and now let us see what is the strongest thing for H.W. that can be made of it."

P.P.S.[7] By Heaven!—no it isn't—I thought it was Friday!—

1 Underlined with short double strokes.

2 Mrs Jane Carr Bateman, novelist; author of *The Netherwoods of Otterpool*, 1858; *Forgiveness*, 1860, and three other novels.

3 For his revising and shortening the story, see 22 June and *fn*.

4 *HW*, 2 Aug, XIV, 62.

5 Their first collaboration in *HW* was the Christmas No., Dec 56.

6 See *To* Macready, 8 July, *fn*.

7 Necessary, since the next day would have been too late for the changes in Miss Parr's story.

To MISS BURDETT COUTTS, 11 JULY 1856

MS Morgan Library.

Boulogne, Villa des Moulineaux
Friday Eleventh July, 1856

My Dear Miss Coutts.

First, as to the Common Things.[1] I rather think that if I were you, I would *not* send to any more newspapers just now. The subject has been so well taken up by the best of them,[2] and the Times did it so much service by returning to it the other day in a Leader,[3] that I would not press it. I think by doing so you might bring out some ignorant caviller, and would not be likely to improve on its present position. I would beg Wills to send to the Quarterly[4] and Edinburgh,[4] if I were you; and there, for the present, I would leave it.

I thoroughly agree in that interesting part of your note which refers to the immense use, direct and indirect, of needlework.[5] Also as to the great difficulty of getting many men to understand them. And I think Shuttleworth[6] and the like would have gone on to the crack of doom, melting down all the thimbles in Great Britain and Ireland, and making medals of them to be given for a knowledge of Watersheds and Pre Adamite vegetation (both immensely comfortable to a laboring man with a large family and small income), if it hadn't been for you.[7]

It seems to me that Punch, which everybody sees, may be useful by just hitting the good nail neatly on the head, and there leaving it. I will say so much to Mr. Lemon, who may be safely trusted.[8]

I spell Harbor without the letter u, because the modern spelling of such words as "Harbor, arbor, parlor," &c. (modern within the last quarter of a century) discards that vowel, as belonging in that connexion to another sound—such as hour and

[1] See *To* Miss Coutts, 5 July and *fn*. "Prizes for Common Things" recently awarded by Miss Coutts, by examination among schoolmistresses and women pupil-teachers at the Whitelands Training Institution. The subjects were food, clothes and household arrangements generally. The scheme was described in her pamphlet, *A Summary Account of Prizes for Common Things Offered and Awarded by Miss Burdett Coutts, at the Whitelands Training Institution*, 1856.

[2] The movement was begun by Richard Dawes, Dean of Hereford, and inaugurated at a meeting at Winchester, Dec 53; Lord Ashburton spoke strongly in its support and offered prizes to teachers and pupil-teachers for essays on "the Knowledge of Common Things". In "School-Keeping", *HW*, 21 Jan 54, VIII, 499, Morley welcomed Ashburton's initiative.

[3] On 7 July. It praised Miss Coutts for her award of prizes, particularly as the first contestants had shown only a scanty knowledge of "common things" and on most of them were "curt, commonplace and incorrect." If Miss Coutts's prizes remedied this—particularly by the scant knowledge of cookery—she would earn the country's gratitude.

[4] No notice of the book appeared in either.

[5] Dealt with in the Preface to *A Summary Account*, p. xviii.

[6] Sir James Phillips Kay-Shuttleworth, MD (1804–77; *DNB*), educational reformer: see Vols. III, p. 557*n* and IV, p. 526*n*; 1st Bart 1849.

[7] For CD's earlier comment to Miss Coutts on Kay-Shuttleworth's "supernatural dreariness" and his comment, a few months after this letter, on "Kayshuttleworthian nonsense", see Vol. VII, p. 56 and *To* Miss Coutts, 9 Dec 56. He clearly included Kay-Shuttleworth among the targets of his satire on Gradgrind's teaching methods in *Hard Times*, Ch. 2: see Vol. VII, p. 354 and *n*.

[8] Nothing on Miss Coutts's "Common Things" appeared in *Punch*.

sour.[1] But, if it will be the slightest satisfaction to you, I will take that vowel up again, and fight for it as long as I live. U and I shall be inseparable, and nothing shall ever part us.

Pray give my kind love to Mrs. Brown, in which Mrs. Dickens and Georgina and all here join. The parcel shall be sent for directly.

I have reserved the subject of Walter to the last, because your kindness touches me so tenderly that I hardly know my dear Miss Coutts how to acknowledge it. I shall have no difficulty, I hope and fully believe, in remitting that sum to India with him; but if, at any time or in any design of my life, I should want such help as your generosity and friendship could give me, I would ask it of no one else in the World and would unfalteringly turn to you.

Having copied all that part of the letter which refers to Walter, I return the original, enclosed.

Ever Dear Miss Coutts | Most Faithfully and affecy. Yours

CD.

To WILKIE COLLINS, 13 JULY 1856†

MS Morgan Library.

Villa des Moulineaux, Boulogne
Sunday July Thirteenth 1856

My Dear Collins.

I answer your letter at once, because we expect Peter and his wife tomorrow; and between them and Little Dorrit, I am not likely to have much time.

We are all sorry that you are not coming until the middle of next month; but we hope that you will then be able to remain so that we may all come back together, about the 10th. of October. I think (recreation allowed &c for), that the Play will take that time to write. The Ladies of the Dram Pers. are frightfully anxious to get it under way, and to see you locked up in the Pavilion.[2] Apropos of which noble edifice, I have omitted to mention that it is made a more secluded retreat than it used to be, and is greatly improved, by the position of the door being changed. It is as snug and pleasant as possible; and the Genius of Order has made a few little improvements about the house (at the rate of about tenpence apiece) which the Genius of Disorder will, it is hoped, appreciate.

I think I must come over for a small Spree, and to fetch you. Suppose I were to come on the 9th. or 10th. of August to stay three or four days in town, would that do for you? Let me know at the end of this month.

I cannot tell you what a high opinion I have of Anne Rodway. I took "Extracts" out of the title, because it conveys to the many-headed, an idea of incompleteness—of something unfinished, and is likely to stall some readers off. I read the first part at the office with strong admiration, and read the second on the Railway coming back here (being in town just after you had started on your cruise.) My behaviour before my fellow passengers was weak in the extreme, for I cried as much as you could possibly desire. Apart from the genuine power and beauty of the little narrative, and

[1] Presumably questioned by Miss Coutts in a recent letter.

[2] One of the cottages in the grounds of the Villa.

the admirable preservation of the girl's identity and point of view, it is done with an amount of honest pains and devotion to the work, which few men have better reason to appreciate than I, and which no man can have a more profound respect for. I think it excellent—feel a personal pride and pleasure in it which is a delightful sensation—and know no one else who could have done it.[1]

Of myself I have only to report that I have been hard at it with Little Dorrit, and am now doing No. X.[2] This last week, I sketched out the notion, characters, and progress, of the Farce, and sent it off to Mark who has been ill of an ague. It ought to be very funny.

The Cat business is too ludicrous to be treated of in so small a sheet of paper, so I must describe it, viva voce, when I come to town. French has become so insufferably conceited since he shot Tigerish Cat No. 1 (intent on the noble Dick, with green eyes three inches in advance of her head), that I am afraid I shall have to part with him. All the boys likewise (in new clothes and ready for Church) are at this instant prone on their stomachs behind bushes, whooshing, and crying, (after Tigerish Cat No. 2) "French! Here she comes! There she goes!" &c. I dare not put my head near my window, for fear of being shot (it is as like a coup d'Etat as possible), and tradesmen coming up the Avenue, cry plaintively "Ne tirez pas, Monsieur Frenche; c'est moi—boulanger—ne tirez pas, mon ami!"

Likewise I shall have to recount to you, the secret history of a Robbery at the Pavilion at Folkestone. Which you will have to write.

Tell Piggot[3] when you see him, that we shall all be much pleased if he will come at his own convenience while you are here, and stay a few days with us.

Forgues ought not to have done that. I shall not buy the translation,[4] lest that passage should put me out of humour with him[5]—though I should much like to see it.

I shall have more than one notion for future work to suggest to you while we are beguiling the dreariness of an Arctic Winter in these parts. May they prosper!

Being on the salt sea, you probably did not see a speech of Samivel Carter Hall's[6] at Mr. Peabody's annual American Dinner.[7] The snivelling insolence of it, the concentrated essence of Snobbery in it, the dirty Pecksniffianity[8] that pervaded it, and the Philoprogullododgeitiveness wherein it was steeped, have so affected me, that I have flown to Cockle[9] for succour. As my eye wandered over the type, I felt my bile begin to shake and swell, like Green's[10] balloon with the gas turned on into it. The Colonel[11] himself is not so bilious as I have been since.

[1] See *To* Macready, 8 July and *fn.*

[2] Chs 33–6 for Sep, published 31 Aug.

[3] Thus in MS for Pigott.

[4] See *To* Collins, 6 June, *fn.*

[5] CD would object to the glance at his private life in the final paragraph and the mention of a relative "qui lui a consacré sa vie (sa belle-soeur, Miss Hogarth").

[6] Samuel Carter Hall (1800–89; *DNB*): see Vol. I, p. 483*n* and later vols.

[7] The annual American Independence Dinner on 4 July given in London by George Peabody (1795–1869; *DAB*), American merchant and philanthropist, to foster Anglo-American friendship; there must have been a report which CD saw and Collins missed; but not found.

[8] For CD's basing Pecksniff on Hall, see Vols I, p. 483*n* and IV, p. 5 and *n.*

[9] Cockle's Anti-Bilious Pills, much advertised: see Vol. VII, p. 43 and *n.*

[10] Charles Green (1785–70; *DNB*), constructor of the Great Nassau balloon 1836: see Vol. VI, p. 508*n.*

[11] Their nickname for Augustus Egg: see Vol. VII, pp. 322, 425 and *nn.*

Kind regard from all to the Dramatic Poet of the Establishment, and to the D.P's mother and brother.

Ever Yours

CD.

If the Flying Dutchman[1] should be done again, pray do go and see it. Webster expressed his opinion to me that it was "a neat piece". I implore you to go and see a neat piece.

To JOHN FORSTER, [13 JULY 1856]

Extract in F, VII, iv, 602. *Date:* 13 July 56, according to Forster.

About four pounds of powder and half a ton of shot have been fired off at the cat (and the public in general) during the week. The finest thing is that immediately after I have heard the noble sportsman blazing away at her in the garden in front, I look out of my room door into the drawing-room, and am pretty sure to see her coming in after the birds, in the calmest manner, by the back window. Intelligence has been brought to me from a source on which I can rely, that French has newly conceived the atrocious project of tempting her into the coach-house by meat and kindness, and there, from an elevated portmanteau, blowing her head off. This I mean sternly to interdict, and to do so to-day as a work of piety.

To W. H. WILLS, 14 JULY 1856*

MS Robert H. Taylor Collection, Princeton University.

Villa des Moulineaux, Boulogne
Monday Fourteenth July, 1856

My Dear Wills.

Peter arrived this morning, and brought the "odds and ends".

I have no No. here—have returned all Nos. in Proof, promptly, by post. I suppose you to have received the last from me since you wrote the note which Peter brought. I have not been able to write anything for H.W.—have thought of two or three things, but matured nothing.

Sala[2] we must not begin to print, at any rate until we shall have received another batch of Copy.

Will you be so kind as to go round to Coutts's, and see our little friend Mr. Esse[3] on the following point.

In my banking-book (received by Cunningham this morning) I find this entry on my Dr. side:

"4th. July—To J. Serle's bill—£24."

I know nothing about any J. Serle, and was at first made uneasy by this, until I

[1] See *To* Webster, 1 July, *fn.*

[2] The first of 22 instalments of "A Journey Due North"; it did not appear until 4 Oct (XIV, 265).

[3] Charles Frederick Esse, of 5 Hartland Terrace, Camden Town: see Vol. VI, p. 601*n*.

supposed it must mean J. *Poole*. I want to know if that be what is really meant? And then on the other hand, I observe that I am not credited with that amount—though I suppose you have paid it in? Will you set this straight?[1]

Ever Faithfully
CD.

P.S. You send me, by Cunningham, a letter from a Madame Persano[2] whom I know at Genoa, proposing to translate from week to week for H.W—D'Azeglio's[3] Records of Italian life.[4] Therein, she says "In a day or two, I will send you the first number, and you will let me know how much you think it worth". Have you received such first No. and is it worth any thing? The letter without that necessary light upon it, is useless. Pray answer at once, as there has already been delay, and I ought to write to her.

To MISS BURDETT COUTTS, 15 JULY 1856†

MS Morgan Library. *Address:* Miss Burdett Coutts | Prospect Hill | Reading.

Boulogne, Tuesday Fifteenth July, 1856

My Dear Miss Coutts.

I am extremely unwilling to return the enclosed; firstly, because it is a son's remembrance of his father; and secondly because it is a tribute to the worth of one for whom I had a sincere admiration and a high regard.[5] But it would distinctly be out of place in Household Words—would not look natural there—and would not have its right effect there. Accustomed to consider all kinds of compositions with this reference, I am quite sure that your misgiving is correct, and that your impression is exactly the impression that its appearance in Household Words would make upon its best readers. Will you be so kind as to let Mr. Julian Young[6] know that if it had contained any facts about his excellent father's life or career, to which I could have given a character like the prevailing tone of Household Words, I *would have* taken any pains to do so; and further, that on the first natural opportunity I have of writing about the dramatic art, I will assuredly make such an allusion to his father's example, as shall present this point in the clearest light?[7] (You suppose yourself to have sent me Mr. Julian Young's letter to you—but you have not.)

[1] In CD's Account-book "J. Serle" has been corrected to "John Poole" (MS Messrs Coutts).

[2] Countess Fanny di Persano, translator of G. M. Ferrero's *Journal d'un Officier de la Brigade de Savoie sur la Compagnie de Lombardie*, Turin, 1848; transl. 1850.

[3] The Marquis Massimo Taparelli d'Azeglio (1798–1866), Italian patriot, painter and writer, Prime Minister of Piedmont-Sardinia 1849.

[4] Clearly an earlier autobiographical record than his *Recollections* (*I mei Ricordi*, 1867), transl. by Count Maffei, 2 vols, 1868; presumably running up to his accompanying King Victor Emmanuel and Cavour to Paris and London in Autumn 55 for the peace negotiations that ended the Crimean War. The Countess Persano's translation did not appear in *HW*. CD rarely in fact accepted translations.

[5] Julian Young's (see below) memoir of his father, the actor Charles Mayne Young (1777–1856; *DNB*: see Vol. I, p. 592*n*), who had died on 28 June; eventually expanded into 2 vols, 1872.

[6] The Rev. Julian Charles Young (1806–73), friend of Miss Coutts, at whose house CD had met him in 1846: see Vol. V, p. 588*n*; now Rector of Southwick, Sussex.

[7] No mention of Young has been found in any subsequent *HW* article.

Yes, I see that Mr. Dunn[1] is at last disposed of. But I could not help saying when I read the case, that it is remarkable how brisk people are to perceive his madness, the moment he begins to trouble the blood royal. As to his being mad, I believe he is as mad as any other obstinate and persistent scoundrel—and no more.[2]

Pray read a story in two parts, in Household Words—next No. and the following one—called Anne Rodway's Diary. It is by Mr. Collins, and I think possesses very remarkable merit—especially the close of it. I forget whether I have already mentioned it in a former note. If I have, forgive the repetition.

Charley is in some apprehension that he will have no holiday, Mr. Bates[3] being reported in the House to have enunciated the dismal sentiment that the Juniors are to have none. I write him, however, that I cannot believe that, in these times, and that we persist in expecting him. I am afraid he really requires a little reviving from the dust and heat of London.

The man on duty in the Man of War, broke down this morning at Inspection-time, and was found guilty of having omitted to open one of the windows. In consideration, however, of previous good character, and of this being the first offence on board he was not superseded.

☛[4] Mr. Forster is going to marry a widow—five or six and thirty, agreeable, and rather pretty—with as many thousand pounds as she is years of age.[5] Thereupon, he will relinquish the editing of the Examiner;[6] which is to be regretted, as he is one of the most responsible and careful of literary men associated with newspapers—though he *does* hustle an unoffending Company, sometimes.

And this is all the secret history I know of this morning.

With love to Mrs. Brown

Ever Dear Miss Coutts | Most Faithfully and affecy. Yours

CD.

To MISS MARY BOYLE, 20 JULY 1856*

MS Morgan Library.

Villa des Moulineaux, Boulogne
Sunday Twentieth July, 1856

Beloved Mary.

This from your own and only Joe. Come by the Tidal train from London Bridge station, which will relieve you of any necessity of looking after, or so much as thinking of, that box, until you arrive here. By which conveyance, my precious gal, you can take a through ticket at one nine six. Mr. and Mrs. Peter Cunningham are

[1] Richard Dunn: see Vols II, p. 207*n* and V, p. 51*nn*.

[2] Dunn had been brought before the Magistrate at Bow St on 10 July to inquire into the state of his mind, after writing love-letters to the Duchess of Cambridge and Princess Mary suggesting they had made advances to him; he had threatened to shoot the first person he found "watching him". The Magistrate ordered him to be put under restraint.

[3] Joshua Bates: see *To* Georgina Hogarth, 8 Feb and *fn*.

[4] CD has drawn a pointing hand.

[5] Colburn left her *c.* £35,000.

[6] For Forster's resignation as editor of the *Examiner* after his appointment in Dec 55 as Secretary to the Lunacy Commission, and his helping with editorial duties until his marriage, see 1 Jan 56, *fn*.

staying here, and he is this day a going to Manchester wherefrom he proposes fur to return a wensday—purr-tidal. Consequence of which if you should change to wensdy your own self my duck, he will take charge on you and if not innocence and wirtue will. O do not be cast down about the passage for at this time of the year it is in general a mere O. O breezes waft[1] (or at least don't waft, but keep yourselves out of the way altogether) my Mary to my arms!

Ever to distraction

Joseph

(In name and natur')

To THOMAS CARLYLE, 20 JULY 1856

MS National Library of Scotland.

Boulogne, | Sunday Twentieth July, 1856

My Dear Carlyle.

This is to present you to my printers and old friends, Messrs. Bradbury and Evans. They desire to have the honor of seeing their imprint attached to the proposed collected Edition of your works.[2] Now, they have not only printed my books from the first page thereof to this hour, but have been closely associated with me in matters of trust and confidence. And I believe that when I assure you they are not only the best and most powerful printers in London, but have in all our transactions won my affectionate esteem and regard, you will believe that you cannot do better than entrust your Edition to them. I am perfectly sure you will never repent it, or have a moment's dissatisfaction with them. I cannot say too much for them, and no man could say anything for them out of a closer knowledge of them than mine is.

Ever My Dear Carlyle | Cordially Yours

CHARLES DICKENS

To W. H. WILLS, 20 JULY 1856†

MS Houghton Library, Harvard.

Boulogne, Sunday Twentieth July, 1856

My Dear Wills.

I hope and trust the eyes are getting better. I have not written since I heard of their being affected, because I deemed it best to leave them and you alone.

No. 333 proof,[3] I have not received; but there is no hurry, and you probably know that it is not sent.

The Post I have enquired into, and think I have discovered the cause of those two delays, and provided against a repetition of such an important mischance. Of course you will let me know of any other failure.

[1] Probably from a song; but not discovered.

[2] The Cheap Edn of Carlyle's works, 16 vols, published by Chapman & Hall and printed by Bradbury & Evans, monthly from Jan 57.

[3] *HW*, 9 Aug, XIV, 73.

You will be amazed to receive (as I have no doubt you have received or will receive) letters from Custom House Agents, informing you of a case of Wine lying for you at that agreeable public establishment, and proposing to clear it. I have bought it for Macready,[1] and it contains 3 dozen of Champagne. Will you authorize the most respectable of these correspondents (in address &c) to clear the same and pay all charges, and forward it to W. C. Macready Esqre. Sherborne House, Sherborne, Dorsetshire. Then if you let Macready know what you have paid for him, he will forthwith remit cheque.

Pray let me know how you are, and whether I am to see you, and whether you can see anything.

Ever Faithfully
CD.

To WILKIE COLLINS, 29 JULY 1856

MS Morgan Library.

Boulogne, | Tuesday Twenty Ninth July 1856

My Dear Collins.

I write you at once, in answer to yours received this morning, because there is a slight change in my London plans—necessitated by Townshend's intention of coming to the Pavilion here on the 5th. or 6th. and hoping to have me pretty much at his disposal for a week or so.

Therefore, if Wills should purpose returning to London, on Friday or on Saturday, I shall come up with him, and return here on the fourth or fifth of August. Will you hold yourself disengaged for next Sunday until you hear from me? I think I am very likely to be on the loose that day.

(Having done this morning, I am only waiting here for Wills—whom I don't like to despoil of his trip by going across now.)

On the fifteenth we shall of course delightedly expect you, and you will find your room in Apple Pie Order. I am charmed to hear you have discovered so good a notion for the play. Immense excitement is always in action here on the subject, and I don't think Mary and Katey will feel quite safe until you are shut up in the Pavilion on pen and ink.

I like that view of the picture controversy (what a World it is!) very much, and shall be glad, and much assisted, if you will tell me, *by return*, when you can have the Copy ready, and about how long it will be. My reason is this:—To facilitate poor Wills's getting a holiday (his stomach has been manufacturing all sorts of unheard-of gases lately, and has been constantly blowing him up, to the great terror of his neighbours who look upon him as a kind of Powder Magazine) we are getting more than usual in advance; and if you can satisfy me on these points while I have Wills beside me, I can keep a No. open, and lead it off with that paper.[2]

[1] See 9 July. [2] See *To* Wills, 12 Aug and *fn*.

The chateau continues to be the best known, and the Cook is really special. All send their kindest regard, and their welcome for the 15th. or beforehand.

Ever Faithfully
CD.

To THE REV. EDWARD GIRDLESTONE,[1] 30 JULY 1856*

MS John F. Fleming, Inc.

Villa des Moulineaux | Boulogne Sur Mer
Thirtieth July, 1856

Dear Sir

Your letter has just now been forwarded to me. I am passing the Summer here, for the more uninterrupted pursuit of my avocations.

The correspondence to which you refer, related to a reading of my Christmas Carol, and not to the delivery of a Lecture—a task I never undertake. I regret to assure you that I am at present too much occupied and shall be for many months to come, to have it reasonably within my power to make any promise to visit my Bristol friends.[2]

Faithfully Yours
CHARLES DICKENS

The Reverend E Girdlestone

To W. H. WILLS, 7 AUGUST 1856

MS Huntington Library.

Boulogne Thursday Seventh August 1856

My Dear Wills

I do not feel disposed to record those two Chancery cases;[3] firstly, because I would rather have no part in engendering in the mind of any human creature, a hopeful confidence in that den of iniquity:

And Secondly, because it seems to me that the real philosophy of the facts is altogether missed in the narrative. The wrong which *chanced* to be set right in these two cases, was done, as all such wrong is, mainly because these wicked Courts of Equity, with all their means of evasion and postponement, give scoundrels confidence in cheating. If justice were cheap, sure, and speedy, few such things would be. It is because it has become (through the vile dealing of these Courts and the vermin they have called into existence) a positive precept of experience that a man had better endure a great wrong than go, or suffer himself to be taken, into Chancery with the dream of setting it right,—it is because of this, that such nefarious speculations are made.

[1] The Rev. Edward Girdlestone (?1805–84; *DNB*), scholar, Balliol College, Oxford; MA 1829; Canon of Bristol 1854; Vicar, St Nicholas with St Leonard, Bristol 1855–8; known as "the Agricultural Labourers' friend" from his work on their behalf; published sermons and pamphlets.

[2] His next visit was in Aug 1858.

[3] Probably cases. Wills thought CD might want to take account of in the *HW* article he was writing, "Nobody, Somebody and Everybody" (30 Aug 56, XIV, 145); but in fact its emphasis is much more on the breakdown of civil law.

Therefore I see nothing at all to the credit of Chancery in these cases, but everything to its discredit. And as to "owing" it to Chancery to bear testimony to its having rendered justice in two such plain matters, I have no debt of the kind upon my conscience.

In haste | Ever Faithfully
CD.

To MRS BROWN, 8 AUGUST 1856*

MS Morgan Library.

Boulogne, Friday Eighth August 1856

My Dear Mrs. Brown.

I have considered your question very carefully, and with that anxious desire to make no mistake, which my interest in the subject naturally awakens.[1]

First, I cannot too strongly agree with you in objecting to leave any discretion to the Committee.[2] Incalculable abuse, perverted intention, and mischief, come of that, nine times out of ten.

Secondly, it would be very objectionable to bind yourself to any division or disposition of the money among the more deserving students. Cases might easily arise in which your help or encouragement might be of little value to any of them. On the other hand, cases might arise in which you would most ardently desire, perhaps to give the whole year's money to one of them. Suppose, for instance, a deserving young man just to fall short (in a year when no one was up to the mark) through having fallen ill for a time in the course of his hard and anxious study; or through having had to tend a sick sister; or to having devoted himself to a dying widowed mother. Such an occurrence is not out of the reach of probability—not to stop short at possibility—and might be very affecting and meritorious.

What I recommend you to do, is, to stipulate without any reserve, that in case there should be no candidate possessing the necessary amount of qualifications, the money shall revert to you.[3] Retain, yourself, the power of rewarding any competitor or competitors as you think best, and I am sure you will never repent it.

I conceive this supposititious failure of all the competitors, to be very unlikely ever to occur. But, it is quite right to provide for it; and, if it should occur, I say let

[1] Mrs Brown had consulted CD about her decision to found an Exhibition for students of St George's Hospital, by examination, "out of respect and affection to the memory" of her husband (Dr William Brown, *d.* 23 Oct 1855: see Vols IV, p. 237*n* and VII, p. 727 and *n*), who had been a pupil at its Medical School. After discussion of the Exhibition's conditions with CD and her solicitors, Farrer, Ouvry, she sent a draft Deed to the Governors of the Hospital on 11 Oct 56. The first award was made in July 57 to one of the "perpetual pupils", i.e. those studying for further qualifications (Minutes, St George's Hospital Board of Governors, 15 Oct 56 and 22 July 57). *HW*, 10 Apr 52 had carried an article, "Saint George and the Dragon" (V, 77), by Andrew Wynter, MD, on the Hospital's devoted voluntary work.

[2] Who were to make the awards.

[3] See *To* Mrs Brown, 10 Aug. This clearly did not become part of the Deed, as, in a letter of 30 Oct to the Governors, Mrs Brown referred to "the present arrangement" as "intended to avoid any confusion or trouble in reference to an unawarded Exhibition—meaning that the next three years' Exhibition should immediately commence for other competitors—thus avoiding any lapse" (Minutes, above, 5 Nov 56).

the money come back to you or your representative. In considering the matter before I thought of this, I felt that I was always wandering about among *some* uneasy chances; but, in this direction, the road seems to me to be clear, safe, and light.

This little place looks very beautiful, but the leaves are beginning to be tinged with yellow, and the berries are turning red, and we have already begun to talk sometimes of our return home early in October. They all send best love to you and to Miss Coutts. Mary is acquiring an immense reputation as an arranger of flowers, and we have some new device on the table at dinner every day. The Cats at the Mill, are still the great topic of the house, and Mr. Plornish mentions them after dark, in a low voice. One of the porters at the Pavilion at Folkestone, trained and sent him over a little goldfinch who draws all the water he drinks, in a thimble. He hangs in my room all the morning, that he may be safe from these ravaging cats. I observe that when he draws the thimble up, he has to put a foot upon the tiny cord, to keep it in its place while he drinks—and that he knows that when he takes his foot away, the thimble will tumble down into the glass with a chink that will frighten him. So sometimes he stands thinking about letting it go, without being able to make up his mind to take his foot off the cord—and the moment he at last does so, he flys away to the remotest end of his perch, that he may hear the chink from a respectful distance. He won't drink when I look at him; but I have beaten him by looking in the glass. Then he exults over me (supposing me to have my eye on the cathedral), and drinks bumpers.[1]

—Which brings me over-leaf to sign myself—which I have no need to do—

Ever Faithfully Yours
CHARLES DICKENS

To W. C. MACREADY, 8 AUGUST 1856†

MS Morgan Library.

Boulogne | Friday August Eighth 1856

My Dearest Macready

I like the second little Poem[2] very much indeed, and think (as you do) that it is a great advance upon the first.[3] Please to note that I make it a rule to pay for everything that is inserted in Household Words—holding it to be a part of my trust, to make my fellow-proprietors understand that they have no right to any unrequited labor. Therefore, when Wills (who has been ill and is gone for a holiday) does his invariable spiriting, gently,—don't make Katey's case different from Adelaide Procter's.[4]

I am afraid there is no possibility of my reading Dorset-shire-wards. I have made many conditional promises thus: "I am very much occupied; but, if I read at all, I will read for your Institution in such an order on my list." Edinburgh which is No. 1,

[1] See *To* Collins, 1 June 57 and *fn.*

[2] Catherine Macready's "The Angel of Love", *HW*, 30 Aug 56, XIV, 156.

[3] "The Shadow of the Hand": see *To* Macready, 8 July and *fn.*

[4] Adelaide Anne Procter (1825–64; *DNB*), one of the most frequent contributors of verse to *HW* since Feb 53: see Vol. VII, p. 26*n*. In fact, Macready had his way and Catherine was not paid (*To* Wills, 12 Aug).

I have been obliged to put so far off as next Christmas twelvemonth. Bristol stands next. The working men at Preston come next. And so, if I were to go out of the record and read for your people, I should bring such a house about my ears as would shake Little Dorrit out of my head.

Being in town last Saturday, I went to see Robson[1] in a burlesque of Medea.[2] It is an odd but perfectly true testimony to the extraordinary power of his performance (which is of a very remarkable kind indeed), that it points the badness of Ristori's[3] acting, in a most singular manner, by bringing out what she might do and does not. The scene with Jason is perfectly terrific; and the manner in which the comic rage and jealousy does not pitch itself over the float at the stalls is in striking contrast to the manner in which the tragic rage and jealousy does. He has a frantic song and dagger-dance, about two minutes long altogether, which has more passion in it than Ristori could express in fifty years.[4]

We all unite in kindest love to Miss Macready, and all your dear ones: not forgetting my Godson, to whom I send his godfather's particular love twice over. The Hammy boy is so brown that you would scarcely know him.

Ever My Dear Macready

Affectionately Yours

CD.

To MRS BROWN, 10 AUGUST 1856*

MS Morgan Library. *Address: Angleterre:* | Mrs. Brown | Miss Burdett Coutts | Prospect Hill | Reading.

Boulogne, Sunday Tenth August 1856

My Dear Mrs. Brown.

I think your letter received here this morning, has crossed my reply to your former letter.

My opinion as to the Sixth clause[5] is quite unaltered, and I repeat my former advice. It seems to be highly objectionable that the sum intended to have been awarded in any year, shall, in case of failure or forfeiture, go in augmentation of the next Exhibition. It might positively lead to the future reward of a Student, for present negligence; or it might lead (I don't say would), under some exceptional

[1] Thomas Frederick Robson (?1822–64; *DNB*), actor: see Vol. VII, p. 179*n*.

[2] A burlesque of Legouvé's *Médée*, by Robert Brough, at the Olympic; the *Athenaeum*, 19 July, highly praised Robson's Medea in terms very like CD's: he is "at bottom a tragedian, and his burlesque efforts result merely in exaggerations of tragic passion. He rises to the sublime before he passes into the ridiculous." It praises his "burst of pathos" at the end as showing "the true and pathetic Medea". The same review dismissed a performance of Lemon's burlesque of *Medea* at the Adelphi as marked by "dullness and tedium".

[3] Name omitted in MDGH and N. She had been performing Italian tragedy at the Lyceum since the beginning of July, playing Silvio Pelico's *Francesca da Rimini* for her benefit on 14 July; her first appearance, in Alfieri's *Rosmunda*, was praised in the *Examiner*, 5 July, but her performance not held as sufficient to "justify great extravagance of admiration."

[4] An exhibition of Ristori's bust on the stage, "encircled with theatrical glories", just before the final curtain, was intended as a compliment to her (she was in the first night audience).

[5] Of the draft Deed containing the rules for the award of Mrs Brown's Exhibition; it has not survived.

circumstances, to a compact among the Students to fail this year, and try for the Exhibition of increased value next year. Besides, I think it essential to the dignity and usefulness of your remembrance of your good husband, that it should be a substantial, unchanging, solid thing—liable to no fluctuations or vacillations arising out of the heedlessness of young men; but fixed and settled as your own mind and heart are on all associated with him.

I can quite understand why the Hospital Authorities may, in perfect honor and good faith, desire to lose none of this money through the negligence of their pupils. But that is not the question. The question is how you can best satisfy your own desire to help young men treading in your husband's footsteps, and also how you can best satisfy the sentiment that belongs to that desire. With these views, I again say—When this money is not won, let it come back to you or your representative. Can you not easily imagine that, in the chances and difficulties of life, it might then even come to be a help of vast importance to some young man who in a former year had carried off the Exhibition triumphantly, and perhaps made it famous for ever?

Again—don't disparage the Exhibition—don't make it a game—so much in the pool this time—so much more or less, next time. It will do nobody good.

With affectionate regard to Miss Coutts | Believe me Ever | Faithfully Yours

CD.[1]

To W. H. WILLS, 10 AUGUST 1856*

MS Free Library of Philadelphia.

Boulogne, Sunday August Tenth 1856

My Dear Wills

I am heartily glad you have let your house, and cordially congratulate you thereupon. It is even worth a slight inroad upon your holiday.

Ansell's[2] bill that you write about, I gave John a cheque to pay, full a week ago. I am vexed that the poor man has had to ask for it. Will you ascertain from John that it is not still unpaid; and tell him whenever he has money to pay, to pay it immediately?

Enclosed is a paper by Townshend[3]—not brilliant, but good enough. As I have rejected innumerable articles of his, I want it to go into the next No. you make up. It will do very well for the last article in the No.[4]

As I am writing, I give you on the other side, an order, *dated next Wednesday*, for

[1] A slip of paper, in CD's hand, may have accompanied this letter; it reads: "It appears from Articles 2nd. and 3rd. at page 3 of the draft deed, that although the Scholarship would be awarded in the presence of several gentlemen, the examination for it might take place in the presence of only one other person besides the competing Pupil, and that person the Examiner himself. Is this according to the usual custom?" (MS Morgan.)

[2] The superintendent of the shared garden at Tavistock House; probably Thomas Ansell, nursery and seedsman, Rochester Rd, Camden Rd Villas. The cheque, for £10.2.6, was cashed on 23 Aug (CD's Account-book, MS Messrs Coutts).

[3] "Fly Leaves", *HW*, 13 Sep 56, XIV, 201, on the nuisance-value of flies and other insects, with related personal recollections.

[4] It appeared as the third article in No. 338.

my book at Coutts's.[1] If John gets it on Wednesday afternoon and takes it on Thursday to Collins (who is coming on Friday), he will bring it, and any thing else you may have to send.

Ever Faithfully
CD.

I have the Pirate-parcel,[2] safe.
In last Wednesday's Times there is a very remarkable letter from the Colliers in the Pit where the last great accident was,[3] stating their case, and making out with every appearance of truth that they "struck", to save their poor lives.[4] Watch the case. If they be not very decidedly disproved in their assertions, then it is a case to go into, and on which to communicate with their attorney and represent their grievance (when the enquiry shall be concluded), in a history of the whole matter.[5] The same paper contains a fearful accident at Sheffield from unfenced machinery.[6]

To JOHN FORSTER, [?8–10 AUGUST 1856]

Extracts in F, VII, iv, 601. *Date:* after CD's return on 5 Aug which was also the day the Fair[7] began; probably the following weekend.

The last of the camp was now at hand. It had only a battalion of men in it, and a few days would see them out. At first there was horrible weather, storms of wind, rushes of rain, heavy squalls, cold airs, sea fogs, banging shutters, flapping doors, and beaten down rose-trees by the hundred; *but then came a delightful week among the corn fields and bean fields and afterwards the end.* It looks very singular and very miserable. The soil being sand, and the grass having been trodden away these two years, the wind from the sea carries the sand into the chinks and ledges of all the doors and

[1] His Account-book.

[2] Possibly connected with the play which Collins had begun.

[3] On 15 July 114 men and boys had been suffocated through lack of adequate ventilation in the Oaks Colliery, nr Barnsley, Yorks, the subject of the colliers' powerfully argued letter to *The Times* of 6 Aug. The letter, written in reply to a letter from the colliery owners attempting to justify their position, was signed "Corresponding Secretary to the Oaks Colliers on Strike", on behalf of the "poor illiterate colliers". The accident was followed by the deaths of 10 men in an English mine on 13 Aug, through an explosion of foul air, and by the deaths of a further 15, through flood, on 1 Oct.

[4] The colliers had struck for the first 16 weeks of 1854, because the manager of the mine had dismissed two firemen whom they trusted and appointed two in their place, whom they did not.

[5] In "Lost in the Pit", *HW*, 1 Nov 56, XIV, 361, Morley gives a damning report on the neglect of safety precautions which had led to the worst of these accidents.

[6] A young woman silver polisher had been killed by her clothes becoming entangled in the shaft of a steam machine on 4 Aug. Both the accident and inquest were reported fully in *The Times*, 5 and 6 Aug; the jury found the shaft not sufficiently protected.

[7] Called la Madeleine, it was held on the Esplanade, near the Ramparts, and lasted 15 days. Temporary wooden stalls and shops were constructed, selling a large variety of objects; there were exhibitions of wild beasts; mountebanks and other curiosities (J. Brunet, *New Guide to Boulogne-sur-mer and its Environs*, 1851). Clearly the Crimean War added new sideshows. Berger recalls CD going to the Fair "with his baby-boy on his shoulders or on his head all the way" (F. G. Kitton, *CD by Pen and Pencil*, Suppl., 1891, p. 18).

windows, and chokes them;—just as if they belonged to Arab huts in the desert. A number of the non-commissioned officers made turf-couches outside their huts, and there were turf orchestras for the bands to play in; all of which are fast getting sanded over in a most Egyptian manner. The Fair is on, under the walls of the haute ville over the way. At one popular show, the Malakhoff[1] is taken every half-hour between 4 and 11. Bouncing explosions announce every triumph of the French arms (the English have nothing to do with it); and in the intervals a man outside blows a railway whistle—straight into the dining-room. Do you know that the French soldiers call the English medal "The Salvage Medal"[2]—meaning that they got it for saving the English army? I don't suppose there are a thousand people in all France who believe that we did anything but get rescued by the French. And I am confident that the no-result of our precious Chelsea enquiry[3] has wonderfully strengthened this conviction. Nobody at home has yet any adequate idea, I am deplorably sure, of what the Barnacles and the Circumlocution Office have done for us.[4] But whenever we get into war again, the people will begin to find out.

To W. H. WILLS, 12 AUGUST 1856*

MS Yale University Library.

Boulogne Tuesday Twelfth August 1856

My Dear Wills.

H.W.[5]

I have gone over the No.[6] and return it herewith.

Collins's paper I have entitled (I repeat the title here as it is not very plain upon the Proof):

To Think, or to be thought for?[7]

[1] See *To* Collins, 19 Jan and *fn.*

[2] The presentation of it to the French soldiers was reported in *The Times*, 25 July.

[3] The Crimean Board of Enquiry, a Board of General Officers, presided over by Gen. Sir Alexander Woodford, to inquire into the severely critical Report of Sir John McNeill and Col. Alexander Tulloch on the Commissariat and general organisation of the troops in the Crimea, 1855; it sat in the Military College, Chelsea, 29 Mar–19 May 56 and presented its report to Parliament. Tulloch was justly dissatisfied with the way it was conducted and composed (no member had ever been to the Crimea); his pamphlet *The Crimean Commission and the Chelsea Board, being a Review of the Proceedings and Report of the Board*, published in Jan 1857 (delayed by his illness), exposed its inconsistencies, omissions, and inaccuracies in convincing detail. CD read this closely and devoted three cols of his article "Stories for the First of April" (*HW*, XV, 217; 7 Mar 57), to a sympathetic and satirical account. He included an attack on Abraham Hayward, who had defended the Board in the *North British Review*.

[4] There could hardly be a better example, Lord Lucan (a member of the Board) being an obvious "Barnacle". CD remembered him in writing Ch. 28 (No. XVIII) of *Little Dorrit* in the following Feb.

[5] Underlined with short double strokes.

[6] *HW* No. 338, 13 Sep, XIV, 193.

[7] Beginning with a recent controversy over the worth of a Bellini, recently bought for the National Gallery, the paper attacks "the Cant of Criticism" (CD's phrase), the imposition of authoritative rules over individual judgment, much as CD had done in *Pictures* in 1846. Collins continued his attack in a Chip, "The National Gallery and the Old Masters", 25 Oct 56, XIV, 347, arising out of another controversy over the restoration of Velasquez's *A Boar Hunt*.

Mr. Speckles on Himself,[1] is so weak, that it would be hardly possible to put King Leopold's Curiosity Shop (which is mere Ditch Water Make Weight) in a worse place. Can't you substitute some better paper for this curiosity Shop?[2] And Miss Macready's poem, the Angel of Love or whatever it's called, is immeasurably better than the poem in the proof.[3]

(*Apropos of Miss Macready, Macready particularly wishes her not*[4] to be paid for her first two poems)

Six Years in a Cell[5] is extremely good. I shall be much interested in seeing the writer[6] when I come home.

Perfectly Contented,[7] I don't adequately understand. The joke is too fine for me.[8] But let it be.

I think Townshend in King Leopold's place would be better and would be about the requisite length, if you have nothing of superior merit.

MISS BESSIE FORSTER[9]

has thrown the Chateau into ecstacies.

Ever Faithfully
CD.

To WILKIE COLLINS, 13 AUGUST 1856

MS Morgan Library.

Villa des Moulineaux | Wednesday Thirteenth August 1856

My Dear Collins

When I saw (on returning here) the unconscionable hour on Friday, I expected to hear from you. But you don't know that on that day there are two boats, the last of which leaves Folkestone for this place at *8 in the Evening*. Now this would be better than next morning, because you could leave town on Friday afternoon at ½ past 4, and even then have an hour at Folkestone, and be here by the usual time of going to

1 A story by Morley, p. 198.

2 This did not appear; Townshend's "Fly Leaves" was substituted.

3 See *To* Macready, 8 Aug and *fn*. No poem appeared in this No.

4 Underlined twice.

5 By Otto von Corvin and Morley, p. 205: von Corvin's second account in *HW* of solitary confinement in a German prison (see also "Beating against the Bars", 30 Aug 56, XIV, 147).

6 Otto Julius Bernhard von Corvin-Wiersbitzki (1812–86), journalist and writer. Born in East Prussia; sentenced to death after prominent part in 1848–9 revolution; sentence commuted to six years' imprisonment; settled in London 56; *Times* correspondent for American Civil War 61; *New York Times* correspondent in Berlin; contributed 8 articles to *HW* 9 Aug 56–7 Nov 57 (in 7 helped by Morley); also to *AYR* and *Temple Bar*. Learnt English in prison by reading 30 vols of Tauchnitz Edn of *HW*. Met and greatly admired CD, to whom he paid tribute in "Charles Dickens", *Europa*, 1870. Published his autobiography, transl. as *A Life of Adventure*, 1871 (favourably noticed in *AYR*, 4 Mar 71), and other books.

7 By Brown and Morley, p. 213 (the last of eight *HW* papers by "Brown", not otherwise identified).

8 The paper consists of complacent recollections (inspired by street cries) by an elderly London bachelor; there is no obvious irony.

9 Underlined with short double strokes. Probably a story with this title which provoked hilarity over Forster and Eliza Colburn.

bed. However, unless I hear from you to the contrary, I shall assume that you come on Saturday morning.[1]

The last atrocity set me up with brilliancy. I shall have to relate to you with minute particulars (the merit of the narrative, its surprising character excepted, lies in them),

THE STORY OF MRS. BELL[2]

—as achieved by an individual whom I will call The Gentle Shepherd, at the appointed hour.

Ever Yours
CD.

I am forgetting the Picture-Paper, which I went over, yesterday, and liked very much. I altered the title, and it stands thus.

TO THINK, OR BE THOUGHT FOR?[3]

I also changed "Criticism" once or twice, to "Cant of Criticism". If you should have time, I wish you would ask Wills to let you see my marked proof.

One[4] or two trifles will probably be sent to you on Thursday to bring over.

To MISS BURDETT COUTTS, 13 AUGUST 1856†

MS Morgan Library.

Villa des Moulineaux | Wednesday Thirteenth August, 1856

My Dear Miss Coutts

I believe there will always be a qualified competitor,[5] unless the terms of the Exhibition should by an unfortunate mistake, give the qualified competitor a reason for stopping short of full success. By dividing it between two, in the event of no marked superiority on the part of one, you might readily (though unintentionally) appeal to a generous mind, to abstain from rising above the level of the next best man, and content himself with half the prize.

Mrs. Brown ought certainly to know with distinctness the nature of the Examination. That clearly laid down, I should not be afraid of the Committee rewarding an incompetent person. The credit of their School of Medicine would be more impaired by their so doing, than by their admitting "We have no student, this year, qualified for the Exhibition, *who has been a Candidate for it.*" They would always have that saving clause.

The deed should by all means be revocable. It is the only efficient protection, I am convinced, against abuse.

Many thanks for the clue to the outfit,[6] which will be of the greatest assistance to me. Charley shall go to the place and make a copy of the whole list.

[1] According to Berger, who was staying in Boulogne, CD and Collins were already at work on the new play for Jan 57 (F. G. Kitton, *CD by Pen and Pencil*, Suppl., p. 18). See *To* Mamie Dickens, 4 Oct.

[2] Doubly underlined. Not discovered; possibly one of the many rejected contributions by Townshend (see *To* Wills, 10 Aug).

[3] Doubly underlined.

[4] Oblique stroke before "One" in MS.

[5] See *To* Mrs Brown, 8 Aug and *fn*.

[6] Presumably for Walter Dickens's journey to join his Regt in India, though he did not sail until 20 July 57.

When I was last at Folkestone, the picture was strongly before me which your note suggests. I have never been there since, without thinking of it, and of you two.[1]

Pray tell Mrs. Brown with my love, that the flowers are beautiful, and that Mary is improving in her powers of floral arrangement every day. In two parts of the garden, we have sweet peas nearly seven feet high, and their blossoms rustle in the sun, like Peacocks' tails. We have a honey-suckle that would be the finest in the world—if that were not at Gad's Hill. The house is invisible at a few yards' distance, hidden in roses and geraniums. The little bird is gradually getting less afraid of his thimble, and draws a world of water this hot weather. He hangs in the drawing-room now, with the two other birds; and a tremendous sensation was created yesterday just before dinner by his being found hanging by the leg, upside down, in the cord from which one of their cages depends—twirling round and round as if he were roasting for a course of poultry. It took about half an hour to untwist him. He was prodigiously ruffled, and staggered about as if he had been to the public house; but soon recovered.

I crossed from Folkestone a week ago, and found Townshend on board, fastened up in his carriage, in a feeble wide-awake hat. It was rather windy, and the sea broke pretty heavily over the deck. With sick women lying among his wheels in various attitudes of despair, he looked like an Ancient Briton of a weak constitution—say Boadicea's father—in his war-chariot on the field of battle. I could not but mount the Royal Car, and I found it to be perforated in every direction with cupboards, containing every description of physic, old brandy, East India Sherry, sandwiches, oranges, cordial waters, newspapers, pocket handkerchiefs, shawls, flannels, telescopes, compasses, repeaters (for ascertaining the hour in the dark), and finger-rings of great value. He was on his way to Lausanne, and he asked me the extraordinary question "how Mrs. Williams,[2] the American Actress, kept her wig on?" I then perceived that mankind was to be in a conspiracy to believe that he wears his own hair.

Some gravel got into my bath the other morning, and cut my left elbow, deep, in so complicated a manner that I was obliged to send into the town for a surgeon to come and strap it up. This reminds me of the political Surgeons, and of the fearful mess they have made of the Peace.[3] But I have never doubted Lord Palmerston[4] to be (considering the age in which he lives) the emptiest impostor and the most dangerous delusion, ever known. Within three months of the peace, here are its main conditions broken and the whole World laughing at us![5] I am as certain that these men will get us conquered at last, as I am that I shall die. We have been feared and hated a long time. To become a jest after that, is a very,

[1] CD is clearly recalling the death of Dr Brown in 1855.

[2] Mrs Barney Williams: see *To* Lemon, 2 July, and *fn.*

[3] The Peace established by the Congress of Paris (25 Feb–30 Mar 56), that ended the Crimean War.

[4] "Palmerstone" in MS.

[5] The main provisions were the neutralization of the Black Sea; the guaranteeing of Turkey against foreign aggression; the cession by Russia to Rumania of the mouths of the Danube and part of Bessarabia; and Russia's surrender of her claim to protect the Christians in Turkey. Russia already had naval ships in the Black Sea and was interfering in Turkish affairs.

very, serious thing. Nobody knows what the English people will be when they wake up at last and find it out. (N.B. This is the gravel that gets into my mind).

Loves from all.

Dear Miss Coutts | Ever Faithfully and AffYrs

CD.

To JOHN FORSTER, [15 AUGUST 1856]

Extract in F, IX, i, 715–16. *Date:* 15 Aug 56, according to Forster.[1]

Writing of the limitations placed upon the artist in England. Similarly I have always a fine feeling of the honest state into which we have got, when some smooth gentleman says to me or to some one else when I am by, how odd it is that the hero of an English book is always uninteresting—too good—too natural, &c. I am continually hearing this of Scott from English people here, who pass their lives with Balzac[2] and Sand. But O my smooth friend, what a shining impostor you must think yourself and what an ass you must think me, when you suppose that by putting a brazen face upon it you can blot out of my knowledge the fact that this same unnatural young gentleman (if to be decent is to be necessarily unnatural), whom you meet in those other books and in mine, *must be* presented to you in that unnatural aspect by reason of your morality, and is not to have, I will not say any of the indecencies you like, but not even any of the experiences, trials, perplexities, and confusions inseparable from the making or unmaking of all men!

To MRS CHARLES DICKENS, 25 AUGUST 1856

MS British Library.

Boulogne, Monday Twenty Fifth August | 1856.

My Dearest Catherine

I write hastily, after having been caught in a very heavy squall—and having got wet through and through—and having changed, and being now in expectation of the Dinner-bell.

Mr. Gibson[3] was here this morning, with the result of his enquiries among the Doctors in the town. It appears on their showing, that the Epidemic[4] has undoubtedly been very bad, and that it was considered at its worst about the end of June, when twenty children died of it in a day. That there are at present no cases, and that there have been none for two or three weeks. That there has never been a single case in the Haute Ville. That Dr. Scott,[5] finally, proves his belief that the

[1] Written from Paris, according to Forster, but mistakenly: see *To* Collins, 13 Aug and F, 1872–4, III, 299.

[2] The first collected edn of Balzac's *La Comédie humaine* had appeared 1842–8; he was much read in England and his *Droll Stories*, 1864, was in the Gad's Hill Library at CD's death.

[3] See *To* Pigott, 17 Jan 56.

[4] Of malignant sore throat, i.e. diphtheria. On 24 Aug CD received a warning from Olliffe (see Wilkie Collins *to* his mother, 1 Sep, MS Morgan, wrongly endorsed 8 Sep); the same day he sent Mrs CD and the younger children back to England.

[5] J. Scott, of rue de l'Écu, 33, one of the English doctors resident in Boulogne.

danger is over, by intending to have his son, who is now in London, brought back to Boulogne for the opening of Mr. Gibson's school.

Under these circumstances Mr. Gibson and Mr. Bewsher consider that there is no reason for postponing the opening of the school on the regular day, and that they incur no unusual risk or responsibility in opening it. I have said that as the boys are in London, I shall prefer to keep them there some fortnight or so after the opening of the School, and that if I should then receive Mr. Gibson's assurance that all continues well and that the disease has made no new head, I shall send them to him.

I have not the least doubt of Mr. Gibson's perfect honor and good faith. The interval I propose will enable us to see (I hope) that there are no dangers behind or facts behind, which are unknown to him.

We are afraid you had a rather rough passage, though a fast one. I hope the Noble Plorn did not suffer from the commotions or fatigues of his journey. Give him all our loves, and tell him that we missed the Hammy boy terribly, at breakfast this morning, when there was no one to bring up the rolls.

All unite too in love to you, and Frank, Alfred, Syddy (Giant I mean) and Harry. And all send kind remembrances to Nurse.

Ever affectionately
CD.

To SIR JOSEPH OLLIFFE, [25 AUGUST 1856]

Envelope only, MS Benoliel Collection. *Address:* Sir Joseph Olliffe | Trouville | Calvados. *Date:* PM 25 Août; year illegible but no doubt 1856: see *To* Mrs CD, 25 Aug.[1]

To JOHN FORSTER, [?30 AUGUST 1856]

Extracts in F, VII, iv, 603. *Date:* first extract almost certainly immediately after A'Beckett's death; second extract probably same letter.

Gilbert A'Beckett,[2] *finding his small son dangerously ill, sank under an illness from which he had been suffering*[3] *and died*[4] *two days after the boy.* He had for three days shown symptoms of rallying and we had some hope of his recovery; but he sank and died, and never even knew that the child had gone before him. A sad, sad story.[5]

[1] No doubt CD wrote to tell Olliffe that he had followed his advice: see *To* Beard, 8 Sep.

[2] Gilbert Abbott A'Beckett (1811–56; *DNB*), playwright, humorous writer and metropolitan police magistrate since 1849; regular contributor to *Punch* and *The Times*: see Vols I, p. 208*n* and VI, p. 135*n*. He and his family had been staying in Boulogne (rue Neuve Chaussée) since 17 July. A'Beckett visited Paris, evidently returning on 26 Aug. For Jerrold's visiting him while he lay ill, see *To* Russell, 10 June 57.

[3] Typhus.

[4] On 30 Aug. Jerrold's notice in *Punch* appeared on 13 Sep 56, a short, black-bordered notice, paying tribute to A'Beckett as both contributor to *Punch* since its first issue, "singularly gifted with the subtlest powers of wit and humour", and as metropolitan magistrate.

[5] See *To* Miss Coutts, 8 Sep, *fn.*

Poor M. Beaucourt was inconsolable when the family left. The desolation of the place is wretched. When Mamey and Katey went,[1] Beaucourt came in and wept. He really is almost broken-hearted about it. He had planted all manner of flowers for next month, and has thrown down the spade and left off weeding the garden, so that it looks something like a dreary bird-cage with all manner of grasses and chickweeds sticking through the bars and lying in the sand. "Such a loss too," he says, "for Monsieur Dickens!" Then he looks in at the kitchen window (which seems to be his only relief), and sighs himself up to the hill home.

To MRS CHARLES DICKENS, 2 SEPTEMBER 1856

MS British Library. *Address:* Angleterre. | Mrs. Charles Dickens | Tavistock House | Tavistock Square | London.

Boulogne, Tuesday Second September 1856

My Dearest Catherine.

We are in all the confusion and bewilderment of moving. I leave tomorrow—Georgy and the Servants, next day. We were all coming away together tomorrow; but there is so much to do, that the new arrangement has sprung up today.

Georgina had already got in the small hatter's bill.[2] I enclose a £5 cheque, in case you want it.

We are all shocked by the idea of another of those poor children being ill; but I hope the removal may bring him round.[3]

With love to all | Ever affecy.

CD.

To JOHN FORSTER, [?7 SEPTEMBER 1856]

Extract from F, VIII, iii, 650. *Date:* "July" 56, according to Forster; but see below.

Returning to England through Kent with Wilkie Collins,[4] *advantages of Gadshill*[5] *occurred to him.* A railroad opened from Rochester to Maidstone, which connects Gadshill at once with the whole sea coast,[6] is certainly an addition to the place, and an enhancement of its value. Bye and bye we shall have the London, Chatham and Dover, too; and that will bring it within an hour of Canterbury and an hour and a

[1] They left a few days after the others, probably 26 or 27 Aug: for Katey, see *To* Miss Coutts, 8 Sep and *To* Mrs Watson, 7 Oct.

[2] CD then wrote, but deleted, "She shall".

[3] If the reference is to another A'Beckett son, Arthur William, born 1844, lived until 1897.

[4] CD left Boulogne with Collins and Pigott on 3 Sep, and they walked part of the way from the Kent coast, evidently reaching London on 6 or 7 Sep (Collins *to* his mother, MS Morgan). From Folkestone to Maidstone is about 40 miles; they may have made use of the railway (opened in June).

[5] The passage is at the beginning of Forster's Gadshill chapter, immediately after a quotation from a letter of 13 Feb and followed by letters of 1855 and details of purchase.

[6] "The Maidstone Railway" from Strood to Maidstone, linking Rochester with Folkestone, Dover, Margate, Ramsgate and Deal, was opened on 20 June 56.

half to Dover.[1] I am glad to hear of your having been in the neighbourhood. There is no healthier (marshes avoided), and none in my eyes more beautiful. One of these days I shall show you some places up the Medway with which you will be charmed.

To CLARKSON STANFIELD, [?7 SEPTEMBER 1856]

Mention in *To* Roberts, 13 Sep 56. *Date:* immediately on CD's return to London.

To THOMAS BEARD, 8 SEPTEMBER 1856

MS Dickens House. *Address:* Thomas Beard Esquire | 42 Portman Place | Edgeware Road.

Tavistock House | Monday Eighth September 1856

My Dear Beard.

We have all come away from Boulogne!—Not deliberately to jockey you out of your share in the Moulineaux, but because I received a warning so pressing from my friend Dr. Olliffe in Paris, of the necessity of removing the children out of the reach of a dangerous Epidemic there, that I had nothing for it but to send them off by the next boat, and follow myself, a fortnight afterwards. Poor A'Beckett's death had saddened the air of the place besides, and my people were all gloomy.

So here we are!—

Can you make a day for a walk in the Gad's Hill neighbourhood, and a dinner of consolation at Gravesend? I am your man for that, or any other similar expedition.

Ever Cordially

CD.

To MISS BURDETT COUTTS, 8 SEPTEMBER 1856

MS Morgan Library. *Address:* Miss Burdett Coutts | Prospect Hill | Reading.

Tavistock House | Monday Eight September 1856.

My Dear Miss Coutts.

We have all come home from Boulogne. A letter of the strongest possible warning, from my friend Dr. Olliffe at Paris, induced me to send the children home a fortnight ago. The rest of us have followed by driblets, and I have brought up the rear. You will have seen in the papers I dare say, that poor Mr. A Beckett died there, unconscious that one of his children lay dead in the next room.[2]

[1] Lines from Chatham to Faversham and from Strood to Chatham were opened in Jan and Mar 1858; and authority was given in 1858 to the new Co., renamed the London, Chatham and Dover Railway in 1859, for an extension to London.

[2] Walter Horace Callander A'Beckett, aged nine, had died on 28 Aug, of "malignant sore throat", i.e. diphtheria, according to the notice in *The Times*, 2 Sep. But according to a letter of 5 Sep from the Maîtres d'Hôtel to the Mayor of Boulogne, he was convalescing from an attack of nephritis; and he died of a fever after dancing "more than his powers allowed him to" at a ball given where he was staying (MS Boulogne Archives). *The Times* notice, 2 Sep, gave his father's cause of death as "congestion of the brain, greatly augmented by anxiety, consequent upon the illness of his son". The Maîtres d'Hôtel, in the same letter as above, denying that he had typhus fever (suggested in *The Times* of 3 Sep), said that he had died of "a

He was a very conscientious man and an admirable magistrate, and is a real loss.

I hope to get out to Shepherd's Bush on Wednesday, and forthwith to re-establish the regular meetings. After a plunge of four and twenty hours duration among the wrecks of my dismantled study, I have happily fished up all the fragments of that noble ship and pieced them together. The neat result is afloat again, and looks none the worse!

I am sorry to say that Katey has come home the worse for her absence, and is very far from well. She has a bad cough, and lost her usual pretty looks with extraordinary suddenness. I was very anxious for her to be seen by Dr. Watson,[1] but we found him out of town and not expected back for a month or six weeks. So I sent her in the meantime to Dr. Hastings,[2] who says she will come right. The noble Baby, after having been the admiration of our gallant neighbours, and the most popular person in Boulogne, has returned to defy competition at home.

We all send kindest regard to Mrs. Brown and I am Ever My Dear Miss Coutts

Affecy. and faithfully Yours

CD.

To [T. J.] MOLYNEUX,[3] 8 SEPTEMBER 1856†

MS Free Library of Philadelphia.

Tavistock House | Tuesday Eighth September 1856

Sir.

I am sorry that in the hurry of being newly returned to town after a long absence, and having a great deal to do, I could not wait for you this morning.

It is unnecessary for me to assure you that I feel a real interest in the project to which your letter invites my attention.[4] I regret to add, however, that I cannot comply with your request. My time is at present so fully occupied that I am obliged to forego all such engagements; and if I were to make an exception in this case, I should immediately be reminded of conditional promises, and overwhelmed by a flood of correspondence, for which I have no leisure.

grave and incurable disease of the brain" contracted a long time since in London. The hotel proprietors were, of course, extremely anxious to dispel tourist alarm about an epidemic. In Oct Mrs A'Beckett was granted a Civil List pension of £100 p.a.

[1] Thomas Watson (1792–1882; *DNB*), MD, FRCP, leading London physician; FRS 1849; 1st Bart 1866.

[2] J. Hastings, MD, of 14 Albemarle St: see Vol. v, p. 355 and *n*.

[3] Secretary, People's Concerts Committee, St Martin's Hall (see envelope, 19 Aug 57); perhaps Thomas John Molyneux, music seller and stationer, 19 Cross St, Newington.

[4] A concert of "cheap and good music" for "the people" with singers, small choir, and organ was held on Monday, 6 Oct "under the patronage of eminent men of letters" among others, at St Martin's Hall (*Athenaeum*, 11 Oct). A notice in *The Times*, 7 Oct 57, stated that 45 "Monday Evening Concerts for the People" had been given the previous season, attended by 50,000: their aim had been "to maintain the influence of music in promoting the moral elevation of the people". The notice appealed for subscriptions to the Guarantee Fund, to liquidate the Committee's debt of £200 and to enable the Concerts to continue. The venture was the forerunner of Chappell's very successful Monday and Saturday Popular Concerts ("Monday Pops"), the former started in Dec 1858.

With this sufficient reason for avoiding public meetings while my own avocations occupy my time and attention, it is scarcely necessary perhaps to hint at any other. But in my desire to be quite frank with you and the friends you represent, I will add that even if I had been more at leisure, I doubt very much whether I should not, on consideration, have requested you to excuse my compliance with your proposal. I am not at all clear in the first place that I have a right to assume such a position in reference to an entertainment over the arrangements of which I have no power, and in the direction of which I assume no responsibility. In the second place I most earnestly desire to see a working man in that position—one of your own body—personally identified with the merit of the scheme and with the working of it out. The recognition of such a President would have a meaning in it, and a becoming expression of self-reliance, which I think would be as agreeable to many thousands as it would to me. I confess to having an uneasy feeling in all such cases, that the term "self-supporting" includes, of right, much more than the mere money question; and I wish your Society would be self supporting in the much higher sense of putting its own men and its own members in its high places. If I were then invited as its guest, to take my place among the general auditory, listen to the music, and bear my testimony to the humanizing and improving influences of such good efforts, through such channels as I have open to me, I should respond with great pleasure.

I am Sir, Faithfully Yours

Mr Molyneux. CHARLES DICKENS

To [MRS BATEMAN],[1] 9 SEPTEMBER 1856*

MS University of Virginia.

Office of Household Words,
Tuesday Ninth September 1856

My Dear Madam.

Your story has been awaiting my return to town.

I regret that I cannot have the pleasure of accepting it. Although it has many points of merit, it is too long in doing what it does, and has too little incident and movement in it, for the purposes of this journal.

Hoping to be a more agreeable correspondent on a future occasion, and begging you to give my kind regard to Mr. Bateman,[2]

I am Dear Madam | Faithfully Yours
CHARLES DICKENS

[1] See *To* Wills, 10 July and *fn.*
[2] John Bateman, of 7 Albion Terrace, Folkestone.

To THE REV. MATTHEW GIBSON, 9 SEPTEMBER 1856*

MS Free Library of Philadelphia.

Tavistock House | Tuesday Ninth September 1856.

My Dear Sir

I thought it right to let you know what Mr. Jerrold[1] had told us; deeming it possible that some person might, in ignorance or interest, have misrepresented the case of the poor little boy to you. Nothing can be more distinct and emphatic than Dr. Cookesley's[2] note—but it is undeniable on the other hand that the family do consider the child to have died of malignant sore throat, and did positively record in the obituary of the newspapers at home here, that he died of that disorder.

The medical testimony to which you refer in the note I had the pleasure of receiving from you yesterday, appeared in yesterday's Times.[3] I fear that the good effect it might otherwise have produced, will be much impaired by its being signed by only one of the resident *English* medical practitioners.[4]

The three boys are all well, and I shall not keep them at home much longer unless you have (as I do not expect you will have) any new reason for recommending caution. We are all sorry to have had our pleasant summer-quarters so suddenly broken up.

With kind regard from my whole house, Believe me My Dear Sir

Ever Faithfully Yours

The Reverend M. Gibson CHARLES DICKENS

To WILKIE COLLINS, 12 SEPTEMBER 1856

MS Morgan Library.

Tavistock House | Twelfth September 1856.

My Dear Collins

[a]*An admirable idea.*[a5] It seems to me to supply and include everything the play wanted. But it is so very strong, that I doubt whether the man[6] can (without an anti climax) be shewn to be rescued and alive, until the last Act. The struggle, the following him away, the great suspicion, and the suspended interest, in the second. The relief and joy of the discovery in the third.

Here again, Mark's part[7] seems to me to be suggested. An honest bluff man previously admiring and liking me[8]—conceiving the terrible suspicion—watching its growth in his own mind—and gradually falling from me in the very generosity and

[1] Douglas Jerrold was a friend of the A'Beckett family.

[2] John Moore Cookesley, Rue des Vieillards, 19, Boulogne.

[3] A letter, signed by four delegates of the Medical Society of Boulogne, attempting to allay panic over recent deaths; they pointed out that there were only 13 more deaths in Boulogne in July–Aug 56 than in the previous year (in fact 12 of them were of children); that only 22 children had died of "malignant sore throat" (diphtheria)—mainly in the poorer quarters; and they denied, on their honour, any other "epidemic malady whatever".

[4] Cookesley.

[aa] Doubly underlined.

[5] The "idea" was presumably Nurse Esther's second sight, used to heighten the tension in Act I: see *To* Collins, 13 Sep and *fn.*

[6] Frank Aldersley.

[7] Lieut. Crayford.

[8] i.e. Richard Wardour, CD's part.

manhood of his nature[1]—would be engaging in itself, would be what he would do remarkably well; would give me capital things to do with him (and you know we go very well together); and would greatly strengthen the suspended interest aforesaid.[2]

I throw this out, with all deference of course to your internal view and preconception of the matter. Turn it how you will, the strength of the situation is [a]*prodigious*[a]—and if we don't bring the house down with it, I'm a—Tory. (an illegible word which I mean for TORY.)[3]

Hoping to see you to night,

Ever Cordially
CD.

P.S.

I may as well mention that I have made out the trip accounts. The total disbursements were, £16..0..6. Being £5..6..10 each.[4]

To W. D. [?BOWATER],[5] 13 SEPTEMBER 1856

MS Mr Marshall R. Anspach. Text from owner's transcript.

Tavistock House | Saturday Thirteenth September | 1856

Sir

In reply to your letter, I beg to express my regret that I cannot comply with the request preferred in it. But my avocations occupy so much of my time and press so constantly on my attention, that I am at present obliged to forego all attendance at public meetings.

I am Sir | Faithfully Yours
CHARLES DICKENS

W. D. Boneter Esquire

To DAVID ROBERTS,[6] 13 SEPTEMBER 1856*

MS Mr Anthony R. Turner. *Address:* David Roberts Esquire. R.A.

Tavistock House | Saturday Thirteenth September | 1856

My Dear Roberts

I answer your letter myself, in order that the arrangements may be quite plain.

We purpose sending the boys back by the General Steam Navigation Co's boat which leaves London Bridge Wharf on Friday Morning at about 3 o'Clock—that is to say, they will go aboard about 9 or 10 on *Thursday night*. You should take your grandson's[7] berth at the office in Regent Circus.

I am heartily obliged to you for the hint you gave Mrs. Dickens about Stanny. It

[1] In Act II.

[2] Collins followed CD's suggestion.

[aa] Doubly underlined.

[3] Written in Roman caps.

[4] In Kent with CD and Pigott. See *To* Forster, 7 Sep and *fn*.

[5] Possibly a relation of Thomas Bowater, 2 Wilmot Place, Camden Town; owner's reading of "Boneter" seems unlikely.

[6] David Roberts (1796–1864; *DNB*), painter: see Vol. v, p. 522*n*, and later vols.

[7] The son of Henry Bicknell and Roberts's daughter, Christine: see Vol. v, p. 596 and *n*.

perfectly amazed me (for I could have no earthly reason to imagine such a thing), but of course I instantly wrote to him and set it all right.[1]

Ever Cordially Yours

David Roberts Esquire. CHARLES DICKENS

To WILKIE COLLINS, 13 SEPTEMBER 1856

MS Morgan Library.

Tavistock House
Saturday Night | Thirteenth September 1856

My Dear Collins

Another idea I have been waiting to impart.—I dare say you have anticipated it. *Now*, Mrs. Wills's second sight is clear as to the illustration of it, and greatly helps that suspended interest. Thus. "You ask *me* what I see of those Lost Voyagers! I see the lamb in the grasp of the Lion—your bonnie bird alone with the hawk—What do I see? I see you and all around you crying Blood! The stain of his Blood is upon you, (C.D.)!"—[2]

—Which would be right to a certain extent, and absolutely wrong as to the Marrow of it.[3]

Ever Yours
CD.

To [?T. R. EELES],[4] 15 SEPTEMBER 1856

Mention in Pickering & Chatto, *The Book Lovers Leaflet*, No. 13 (9 Feb 1888); dated Tavistock House, 15 Sep 56.

Referring to the re-binding of Catlin's Indians.[5]

[1] This incident undiscovered.

[2] This is used to end Act I, where it appears in Scots dialect: "Does the Sight show me Frank? Aye! and anither beside Frank. I see the lamb i' the grasp o' the lion. I see your bonnie bird alone wi' the hawk. I see you and all around you crying bluid! The stain is on *you*! Oh my bairn, my bairn, the stain o' that bluid is on *you*!"

[3] The point of the play is, of course, that Nurse Esther's prophecy is unfulfilled: see *To* Wills, 7 Jan 57, *fn*.

[4] Probably Thomas Robert Eeles of 22 Cursitor St, CD's main bookbinder since at least 1846: see Vol. IV, p. 517*n*.

[5] George Catlin's *Letters and Notes on the Manners, Customs, and Condition of the North American Indians*, 2 vols, 1841; CD possessed the 2nd edn, 1842 (Inventory, May 1844: Vol. IV, p. 722).

To GEORGE AUGUSTUS SALA, 15 SEPTEMBER 1856

MS Rosenbach Foundation.

OFFICE OF HOUSEHOLD WORDS,
Monday Fifteenth September 1856

My Dear Mr. Sala.

In the No. we have made up to day,[1] I have begun your Journey.[2] This No. will be published on Wednesday the 1st. of October.

As I have found it necessary to take a good deal out of the two first papers, I am anxious that you should perfectly understand from myself, my only reason for having done so. It seemed to me to be essential to get the first two papers so compressed together, as that you might be fairly on your way *to Russia itself* in the first periodical portion of your book.[3] Otherwise, you would have staved some readers off, and might have missed the most important stage (the first) at which to attract attention. All the passages taken out, shall be carefully preserved for you;[4] and I have taken pains so to select them for omission as to do no damage to the descriptions that remain.

I like the opening very much, and hope the result of this undertaking will realize the best hopes with which it was begun. I have been concerned to hear from Wills, on more than [one][5] occasion, of your not being well. But I trust you have now health and spirits to carry you pleasantly through the work.

We shall follow the first portion up with the others, in weekly succession.

Believe me | Faithfully Yours

G. A. Sala Esquire CHARLES DICKENS

To MISS BURDETT COUTTS, 16 SEPTEMBER 1856*

MS Morgan Library. *Address:* Miss Burdett Coutts | Prospect Hill | Reading.

Tavistock House | Tuesday Sixteenth September | 1865

My Dear Miss Coutts.

To my shame and mortification Mr. Wills reminded me incidentally yesterday, that I had appointed Saturday Afternoon at 4 for a Meeting of our Guild Committee (which we are obliged by the Act of Parliament[6] to hold formally), and that the Summonses had duly gone out.

If you please, take particular notice that this otherwise disgraceful obliviousness is not to be recorded against my model punctuality. The pocket ledger which defies all competition in its exactness, had not been entered up, in the distractions of moving and settling, and editing and writing. Hence the deplorable result.

May I faintly and afar off, hint at Saturday Week? May I also falteringly send my

[1] *HW*, No. 341, for 4 Oct.

[2] "A Journey Due North": see 19 Sep, *fn.*

[3] The first instalment ends with his leaving Prussia and sailing up the Oder, bound for Russia.

[4] When published by Bentley in Aug 1858, the omitted passages were included.

[5] Omitted in MS.

[6] The Private Act to incorporate the Guild of Literature and Art, passed on 2 June 54: see Vol. VII, p. 330*n*.

penitent regard to Mrs. Brown? They trample on me here as much as they dare—which is not much.

Ever Dear Miss Coutts | Most Faithfully Yours
CD.

To JOHN GIBBON,[1] 16 SEPTEMBER 1856

MS Private (seen before destruction in Prestwick air-crash, Dec 1954).

Tavistock House, London | Sixteenth September 1856.

Sir.

Allow me to acknowledge the receipt of your letter, and to assure you (which I hope is unnecessary), that I shall respect your confidence. You already know through the pages of the work to which you refer, that I am not indifferent to the truths you state, and that I earnestly desire to impress the necessity of a better and juster system on the general mind.

Your faithful Servant

John Gibbon Esquire. CHARLES DICKENS

To W. H. WILLS, 16 SEPTEMBER 1856

MS Huntington Library.

Tavistock House | Tuesday Sixteenth September 1856.

My Dear Wills

I have been thinking a good deal about Collins, and it strikes me that the best thing we can just now do for H.W. is to add him on to Morley, and offer him Five Guineas a week. He is very suggestive, and exceedingly quick to take my notions. Being industrious and reliable besides, I don't think we should be at an additional expence of £20 in the year by the transaction.

I observe that to a man in his position who is fighting to get on, the getting his name before the public is important. Some little compensation for its not being constantly announced, is needed, and that I fancy might be afforded by *a certain engagement*. If you are of my mind, I wish you would go up to him this morning, and tell him this is what we have to propose to him today, and what I wish him, if he can, to consider beforehand. You could explain the nature of such an engagement to him, in half a dozen words, far more easily than we could all open it together. And he would then come prepared.

Of course he should have permission to collect his writings, and would be handsomely and generously considered in all respects. I think it would do him, in the long run, a world of good; and I am certain that by meeting together—dining three instead of two—and sometimes calling in Morley to boot—we should knock out much new fire.

What it is desirable to put before him, is the regular association with the work, and the means he already has of considering whether it would be pleasant and use-

[1] Perhaps John Burdett Gibbon, 7 Downing Terrace, Compton Rd, Islington.

ful to him to work with me, and whether any mere trading engagement would be likely to render him as good service.[1]

Ever Faithfully
CD.

To MRS BROWN, 18 SEPTEMBER 1856

Mention in N, II, 801.

To W. H. WILLS, 18 SEPTEMBER 1856

MS Huntington Library.

Tavistock House | Thursday Eighteenth September | 1856

My Dear Wills.

Don't conclude anything *un*favourable with Collins, without previous reference of the subject, and the matter of your consultation, to me. And again put before him clearly, when he comes to you, that I do not interpose myself in this stage of the business, solely because I think it right that he should consider and decide without any personal influence on my part.

I think him wrong in his objection, and have not the slightest doubt that such a confusion of authorship[2] (which I don't believe to obtain in half a dozen minds out of half a dozen hundred) would be a far greater service than dis-service to him. This I clearly see. But, as far as a long story is concerned, I see not the least objection to our advertising, at once, before it begins, that it is by him. I *do* see an objection to departing from our custom of not putting names to the papers in H.W. itself; but to our advertizing the authorship of a long story, as a Rider to all our advertisements, I see none whatever.[3]

Now, as to a long story itself, I doubt its value to us. And I feel perfectly convinced that it is not one quarter so useful to us as detached papers, or short stories in four parts. But I am quite content to try the experiment.[4] The story should not, however, go beyond six months, and the engagement should be for twelve.

Faithfully Ever
CD

[1] Collins joined the *HW* staff from 4 Oct 56, receiving a regular salary instead of payment for contributions (*CD as Editor*, p. 222*n*).

[2] That contributions by him would be credited to CD.

[3] Collins's first long story, *The Dead Secret*, which ran weekly in *HW* 3 Jan–13 June 57, XV, 12–565, was advertised beforehand (early Dec), with his name; not done before except for CD himself.

[4] CD may have been remembering the trouble over Mrs Gaskell's *North and South*.

To GEORGE AUGUSTUS SALA, 19 SEPTEMBER 1856

MS Free Library of Philadelphia.

Tavistock House, London
Friday, Nineteenth September 1856

Dear Mr Sala.

Nothing can be better than your list of subjects.[1] It promises admirably, and I have no doubt of your performance.

I beg that you will not suppose that you "have long ceased to be interested commercially" in this design. I have no knowledge of that kind. The passage in your note has grated upon me and pained me but would have done so in a much deeper degree if I could have admitted its truth. It is a mistake.

May you be as much mistaken in your despondent view of your health! Encouraged by your being wrong in one case, I hope you may be wrong in the other, and that I may add you, twenty years hence, to the prosperous list I have of men who were going to die between twenty five and thirty five, and are strong and happy, fifteen years afterwards, this day.

I believe (with reason arising out of my own observation) that there is no human malady in which doctors make such extraordinary mistakes as in that attributed to you. I have hardly ever known a recovered patient of a year or two's standing, who had not been at one time declared to have a disease of the heart. Near home here, I can at once lay my hand on two people, man and woman, most notable instances of this truth.

Always Faithfully Yours
CHARLES DICKENS

To DR R. B. CARTER,[2] 20 SEPTEMBER 1856

Mention in *American Book Prices Current*, 1973, p. 1034; *MS* 1 p.; addressed Dr R. B. Carter; dated 20 Sep 56.

Accepting an article on health and education.[3]

[1] Of sub-titles to his serial, "A Journey Due North". By this time, having returned from Russia, Sala was in Brussels writing up his experiences; he had run short of money and had been unable to visit Moscow, but spent much time in or near St Petersburg. In Nov he had a spell of illness which he supposed to be a disease of the heart (*Life and Adventures of G. A. Sala*, Chs 27 and 28; and Ralph Straus, *Sala*, 1942, p. 122): see *To* Wills, 24 Dec and *fnn*.

[2] Robert Brudenell Carter (1828–1918), ophthalmic surgeon; staff surgeon in Turkey during Crimean War; ophthalmic surgeon to St George's and other hospitals; FRCS 1864; wrote for *Lancet* and *The Times*; evidently introduced to CD by Mowbray Morris: see next; published *Students' Manual on Ophthalmology* and other medical works; contributed 8 articles to *HW* 18 Oct 56–1 May 58.

[3] "Health and Education", *HW*, 18 Oct 56, XIV, 313, on neglected health in girls' schools.

To W. H. WILLS, 21 SEPTEMBER 1856*

MS Huntington Library.

Tavistock House | Sunday Twenty First September | 1856.

My Dear Wills

I send you a paper by Mowbray Morris's[1] man, which will suit us very well, and will perfectly answer for the first paper in the next No. you make up.

I hope he may turn out a very useful acquisition to us. He will call upon you soon, no doubt. His name and address are

Mr. R. B. Carter
12 Crawley Terrace
Fulham Road

Ever Faithfully
CD.

To JAMES E. RONEY,[2] 23 SEPTEMBER 1856*

MS Dickens House.

Tavistock House | Tuesday Twenty Third September | 1856.

My Dear Roney.

I am delighted to get your letter, and shall be more than delighted to see you. I am unfortunately obliged to dine out tomorrow, but am quite free, both for Thursday and Friday. Tell me on which day you will dine with me at 6 o'Clock, and I will have nobody else at the family table.

Lord! To think of a Colonial Chief Justice![3] And it was but the day before yesterday that we gave our first dinner at the Mansion of Mrs. Rogers in Buckingham Street, Adelphi. I bought the soup myself (it was hard, and looked like a bit of a mantel-piece), and you provided some inheritance of family tea-spoons for the decoration of the festival.

Ever Cordially Yours
James E Roney Esquire. CHARLES DICKENS

To MRS BROWN, 24 SEPTEMBER 1856*

MS Morgan Library. *Address:* Mrs. Brown | Miss Burdett Coutts | Prospect Hill | Reading.[4]

Tavistock House
Wednesday September Twenty Fourth | 1856.

My Dear Mrs. Brown

I called on Mr. Ouvry very soon after you left me on Monday, but he had gone

[1] Mowbray Morris (1819–75), Manager of *The Times*: see Vol. V, p. 291*n*.

[2] James Edward Roney (*b.*?1812), barrister and journalist; had shared lodgings in Buckingham St, Adelphi, with CD, probably during 1831: see Vol. I, p. 59*n*. This was recalled in *Copperfield* (Mrs Crupp's lodgings).

[3] Roney had emigrated to Demerara, British Guiana, 1838, where, after a successful career as a barrister, he was appointed Chief Justice.

[4] The letter is endorsed, obviously by Mrs Brown: "Abt. Trust Deed for Exhibition".

from his office for the afternoon. Yesterday he came here to me, and we went through the draft with great care, three times. I think he is now in complete possession of your wishes on the subject and fully understands the suggested alterations. He quite agreed with me that it is but reasonable that you yourself should retain, during your lifetime, the power of appointing any new trustees who may be rendered necessary by the death or resignation of any one of those first appointed. As soon as the amended draft shall be prepared, he will forward it to you for your approval.

You will have to reduce the number of your trustees to four, as the Bank of England does not receive more in such a case.[1]

With affectionate regard to Miss Coutts

Believe me ever | Faithfully Yours
CHARLES DICKENS

To MISS BURDETT COUTTS, 26 SEPTEMBER 1856

MS Morgan Library.

Tavistock House | Friday Twenty Sixth September | 1856

My Dear Miss Coutts

I grieve to say that I must deny myself a holiday tomorrow. Destiny seems to be against my coming to Prospect Hill. After having been greatly put-out by the unexpected necessity of chopping and changing at Boulogne, I have come home to such an immense arrear of demands on my attention, that I am falling behind-hand with that reserve of Little Dorrit which has kept me easy during its progress, and to lose which would be a serious thing. All the week I have been hard at it[2] with a view to tomorrow; but I have not been in a quick vein (which is not to be commanded), and have made but tardy way. If I stick to it resolutely now, next week will bring me up. If I let a day go now, there is no saying when I may work round again and come right. You will see what a hard necessity it is that makes me decide so much against my wishes.

With kind regard to Mrs. Brown

Ever Dear Miss Coutts | Affecy. and faithfully Yours
CD.

[1] The others, besides Mrs Brown herself, were W. J. Farrer, Lady Falmouth and no doubt Miss Coutts. CD stood down.

[2] Writing No. XII for Nov, Book II, Chs 5–7, published 31 Oct.

To GEORGE DOLBY,[1] 28 SEPTEMBER 1856

Extract in Samuel T. Freeman & Co catalogue, May 1932; *MS* 1 p.; dated Tavistock House, 28 Sep 56; misread as "Donly" in catalogue.

I don't care much for the weather and am off to the Foundling,[2] and (unless it should rain Tiger cats and Newfoundland dogs), to Hampstead afterwards.

To CLARKSON STANFIELD, 28 SEPTEMBER 1856

MS Private.

Tavistock House | Sunday Twenty Eight September | 1856.

My Dear Stanny.

I write this to leave at your house at Hampstead, in the course of my walk to day. You promised to write to me as soon as you should arrive in Wales. I have been uneasily waiting from day to day in the hope of hearing from you and receiving your assurance that you are getting strong and jolly; and day after [day][3] has passed over, and I have heard nothing! Pray when you get this (God knows when it may reach you) write me a line—only one line—and say how you are, where you are, and when I shall see you. I really have gradually come to that pass, through daily hope deferred, that I have a strong inclination on me to throttle the Postman.

Ever Affectionately Yours

Clarkson Stanfield Esquire CHARLES DICKENS

To W. H. WILLS, 28 SEPTEMBER 1856

MS Huntington Library.

Tavistock House

Sunday Morning Twenty Eight September | 1856

My Dear Wills

I suddenly remember this morning, that in Mr. Carter's article, Health and Education, I left a line which must come out. It is, in effect, that the want of Healthy Training leaves girls in a fit state to be the subjects of Mesmerism.[4] I would not on any consideration hurt Elliotson's feelings (as I should deeply) by leaving that depreciatory kind of reference in any page of H.W. He has suffered quite enough without a stab from a friend.[5] So pray, whatever the inconvenience may be in what

[1] George Dolby (1831–1900), third son of Samuel Dolby, born in London; brother of Charlotte Helen, later Sainton-Dolby (1821–85; *DNB*; see Vol. VI, p. 242*n*), contralto. For his managing of CD's readings 1866–70, see later vols.

[2] The Chapel at the Foundling Hospital, Guilford St, where CD rented a pew.

[3] Omitted in MS.

[4] This probably followed the reference to the susceptibility of girls to "various injurious influences" (unspecified) on p. 316.

[5] For the increasing hostility from the rest of the medical profession Elliotson incurred, after his mesmeric experiments in public 1837–8 and his consequent resignation from his chair at London University, see Vol. I, p. 461*n*.

Bradbury calls "The Friars",[1] take that passage out. By some extraordinary accident, after observing it I forgot to do it.

Ever Faithfully
CD

To W. H. WILLS, 29 SEPTEMBER 1856*

MS Huntington Library.

Tavistock House
Monday Night | Twenty Ninth September 1856

My Dear Wills.

Yes as to Miss Parr's story.[2] A word or two, in the face making and tooth grinding way, wants alteration;[3] but I can easily do that on the Proof.

Monmouth would be well enough, but for its breaking down so direfully at the end. Still I think there is sufficient merit in it to justify its acceptance.[4]

I enclose you the next portion of Sala—that is to say, two portions together, to be made one.

The Two Lions won't do—but I would encourage the author[5] to send something else. He seems to me to have a something stalwart in him.

We had better meet at the office to talk of things in general in going over the next No.[6] We can afterwards dine at the Albion.[7] Will Wednesday at 4 suit you? Send me word in reply.

Ever Faithfully
CD.

Do you think it worth while to see 12 in 10 Queen's Bench?[8] Letter now returned.

[1] Bradbury & Evans's printing office in Whitefriars.

[2] "A Day of Reckoning", *HW*, 1 and 8 Nov, XIV, 366 and 402.

[3] In this melodramatic narrative, in 7 chs, one character in Ch. 1 gnaws his lips with "a darkling look", but nothing worse.

[4] "Monmouth", a poem by George Meredith, 1 Nov, XIV, 372: an account of the Duke of Monmouth's proclamation as King at Taunton on 20 June, 1685 and his defeat two weeks later. The final stanzas do not obviously break down.

[5] Unidentified.

[6] Probably No. 343, for 25 Oct.

[7] The Albion Tavern, Russell St.

[8] Presumably Case No. 12 in the Queen's Bench Court No. 10; unexplained, but possibly connected with "Two Difficult Cases" in *HW* (8 Nov, XIV, 385 by Miss French and "Miss Jewsbury's friend", and 29 Nov, XIV, 473, by Morley).

To CONTRIBUTORS TO HOUSEHOLD WORDS, 30 SEPTEMBER 1856*

MS Huntington Library.

Mem: For Christmas Number.[1]

OFFICE OF HOUSEHOLD WORDS,
30th.[2] September 1856

[a]I beg to convey to you the scheme of our Christmas number for the present year: to which Mr. Dickens would be glad if you would Contribute:—[a] An English Trading-Ship (with passengers aboard), bound for Australia, is supposed to have got foul of an Iceberg, and become a wreck. The Crew and passengers not being very many in Number, and the Captain being a cool man with his Wits about him, one of the boats was hoisted out and some stores were got over the side into her, before the Ship went down. Then all Hands, with a few exceptions, were got into the Boat—an open one—and they got clear of the wreck, and put their trust in God.

The Captain set the course and steered, and the rest rowed by spells, when the sea was smooth enough for the use of the oars. They had a sail besides. At sea in the open boat for many days and nights, with the prospect before them of being swamped by any great wave, or perishing with hunger, the people in the boat began after a while to be horribly dispirited. The Captain remembering that the narration of stories had been attended with great success on former occasions of similar disasters, in preventing the shipwrecked persons' minds from dwelling on the horrors of their condition, proposed that such as could tell anything to the rest, should tell it. So the stories are introduced.

The adventures narrated, need not of necessity have happened in all cases to the people[3] in the boat, themselves. Neither does it matter whether they are told in the first or in the third person. The whole narrative of the Wreck will be given by the Captain to the Reader in introducing the stories. Also, the final deliverance of the people. There are persons of both Sexes on the boat. The writer of any story may suppose any sort of person—or none if that be all—as the Captain will identify him if need be. But, among the Wrecked there might naturally be The Mate, The Cook, the Carpenter, the Armourer (or Worker in Iron), the Boy, the Bride Passenger, the Bridegroom passenger, the sister passenger, the brother passenger, the Mother or father passenger or son or daughter passenger, the child passenger, the Runaway passenger, the old Seaman, the toughest of the Crew, &c &c[4]

[a]It will be necessary that we receive your contribution not later than the 10th. of November.

Believe me | Ev faithfully[a]

[1] "The Wreck of the Golden Mary", the Christmas No. for 1856, published 6 Dec.

[2] In Wills's hand, written above "16th" in CD's hand, cancelled.

[aa] In Wills's hand; the rest in CD's.

[3] "The Wreck" (the Captain's Account) is by CD; "John Steadiman's (the Chief Mate's) Account" and "The Deliverance" by Wilkie Collins.

[4] The stories told in "The Beguilement in the Boats" are "The Armourer's Story", by Percy Fitzgerald; "Poor Dick's Story", by Harriet Parr; "The Supercargo's Story" by Fitzgerald; "The Old Sailor's Story" (in verse), by Adelaide Procter; and "The Scotch Boy's Story", by James White. For suggestions as to CD's authorship of linking passages in the stories, see *Uncollected Writings of CD*, ed. Harry Stone, II, 563–69, who also reproduces the letter as an illustration.

To THOMAS BEARD, 1 OCTOBER 1856

MS Dickens House. *Address:* Thomas Beard Esquire | 42 Portman Place | Edgeware Road.

Tavistock House | First October 1856.

My Dear Beard

How's the foot? How are you getting on? What does the doctor say? What do *you* say? Can you walk? Can you eat and drink? Is there a probability of your being able to toe the scratch[1] on a bright cool October day (a fine month October!), and punish the Consolation-Dinner?

Ever Faithfully
CD.

To CHARLES EDMONDS,[2] 1 OCTOBER 1856*

MS Mr J. Stevens Cox. *Address:* Charles Edmonds | Messrs. Wills and Co. | 136 Strand.

Tavistock House | First October 1856

My Dear Sir

Accept my best thanks for your obliging letter. But I know Eustace[3] well, and formed Byron's opinion of him (as a solemn Humbug)[4] when I was first in Italy.[5] I wanted him,[6] when I sent to you for him, that I might lay my hand upon an instance or two of his worthlessness.[7]

You don't mention in your List, what seems to me to be the honestest and best of all the books, as written by a man who was not afraid to form his own opinions or unable to give good reasons for them—Simond.[8]

Faithfully Yours
CHARLES DICKENS

Charles Edmonds Esquire.

[1] Boxing slang.

[2] Charles Edmonds, bookseller, bibliographer and editor of *Poetry of the Anti-Jacobin*: see Vol. VI, p. 782*n*.

[3] John Chetwode Eustace (?1762–1813; *DNB*), antiquary, author of *A Tour Through Italy*, 1813 (8th edn, 3 vols, 1841, in the Gad's Hill library at CD's death: *Catalogue of the Library of CD*, ed. J. H. Stonehouse). See Vol. IV, pp. x*n* and 323*n*.

[4] Not found, but CD may be recalling the comment by Byron's friend, John Cam Hobhouse (later, Lord Broughton), given in Appx, No. XXXII, Byron's *Poetical Works*, 1850, p. 785: "This author is in fact one of the most inaccurate, unsatisfactory writers that have in our times attained a temporary reputation, and is very seldom to be trusted even when he speaks of objects which he must be presumed to have seen."

[5] CD, with his whole family, had first visited Italy in Summer 1844, reaching Albaro on 16 July: see Vol. IV, p. 156 and *n*.

[6] He was writing *Little Dorrit*, No. XII, Book II, Chs 5 and 7, for Nov, published 31 Oct, which describes the Dorrit family in Venice and Rome.

[7] Eustace is treated with sarcasm in both Chs 5 and 7. In Ch. 5 Mrs General, always conventional, says that she has told Amy "it is better not to wonder" at Venice, when "the celebrated Mr. Eustace, the classical tourist, did not think much of it"; and in Ch. 7 CD himself comments on travellers in Rome: "The whole body of travellers seemed to be a collection of voluntary human sacrifices, bound hand and foot, and delivered over to Mr. Eustace and his attendants". See also Vol. VII, p. 218*n*.

[8] Louis Simond (1767–1830), French emigré, linked by marriage with Lord Jeffrey; CD discovered his *Tour in Italy and Sicily*, 1828 (in the Gad's Hill Library at CD's death) in 1844, took his copy with him to Italy and wrote of it in glowing terms to Forster: see Vol. IV, pp. xi*n*, 164 and *n* and 276. He cites him in other letters and in *Pictures*, 1846. No doubt he also took his copy on his 1853 visit.

To MRS BROWN, 3 OCTOBER 1856

MS Morgan Library. *Address:* Mrs. Brown.

Tavistock House | Third October 1856

My Dear Mrs. Brown

I will write tonight, after having seen Mr. Ouvry. He is coming here presently. Will you tell Miss Coutts that I will answer her kind note at the same time.

I think you have decided right about the Trustees. You can always make me one when you have a vacancy, if I am still forthcoming myself. The enclosed note seems to me to say everything that is necessary. I would use the word "found", in the place where you are uncertain.

Ever Faithfully Yours
CD.[1]

To MRS BROWN, 3 OCTOBER 1856*

MS Morgan Library. *Address:* Mrs. Brown.

Tavistock House | Friday Third October 1856.

My Dear Mrs. Brown

I have gone over the deed again, with Mr. Ouvry, and will tell you the result of our deliberation in no deed-like manner—that is to say, in the fewest and plainest words.

As to that "order" and "direct" point (which after all only refers to the payment of the money) Mr. Ouvry considers that the addition of "with the consent of the Trustees", would place the Trustees in difficulty, would place the Medical Council in difficulty, and might easily place the foundation in Chancery. I am on the whole of his opinion, and would waive that objection.

As to the stipulation you wish inserted in reference to the examination on the case-books, and to examination by written question as well as orally—the necessary words are inserted.

As to the moral conduct, it is expressed in the deed that the Foundation has in view both moral conduct and general fitness for the exercise of the Medical Profession. As to who is to judge of the moral conduct (this is in answer to a question put to me in a note this morning by Miss Coutts), we are both of opinion that that *must be* left to the Medical Committee. They have on the whole the best means of judging: and we think that any sort of body for the revision or reversal of their judgment, would complicate the Foundation beyond all foresight.

As to the lapsing, there will be no lapse to speak of—*can* be none—and therefore it is not necessary to embarrass the Deed with provisions for the addition of unbestowed Interest to the Principal. If the Exhibition became vacant, say in the first year, through death or misconduct, the three years term would not be waited out,

[1] The letter is endorsed: "Concerning Trusteeship-Exhibition Whitehall Gardens | Falmouth | G. Hospital": i.e. the Countess of Falmouth, who lived at 3 Whitehall Gardens, a Trustee of the William Brown Exhibition Fund, St George's Hospital: see *To* Miss Coutts, ?31 Dec 56, *fn*.

but the new Examination for a new award would come on at once.[1] As we have altered the Clause (Clause 6) it stands thus, in effect:

That at the usual time of Examination which shall next follow after a vacancy from any cause shall have occurred in the Exhibition, a new examination and a new award shall take place.

As to those words which last night were in the same clause, about "manner, time, and place" of examination, and which Miss Coutts pointed out to be inconsistent with Clause 3, we have taken them out altogether. The examination must then necessarily be according to Clause 3.

As to your power of revocation, you retain it on 3 years notice.

Lastly, as to the date of the Deed, I have informed Mr. Ouvry, on what day you would like it to be dated, and why.

I hope to be able to send you the new Draft itself with this (leaving my envelope open for that purpose); but, whether or no, these are its provisions. And I think you may now decide to have it submitted to the St. George's Luminaries.[2]

I return your draft letter.

Ever My Dear Mrs. Brown | Faithfully Yours
CHARLES DICKENS[3]

To MISS BURDETT COUTTS, 3 OCTOBER 1856

MS Mr. Roger W. Barrett.

Tavistock House | Third October 1856.

My Dear Miss Coutts.

This is briefly in answer to your kind and considerate note of this morning—briefly, for your sake, not mine.

Your remark upon the Deed, I have replied to, for the sake of clearness and having all the case together, in a note to Mrs. Brown which accompanies this.

I have no doubt that it will be best for Walter to go out at once.[4] I believe it will be far better for his health, and certainly for his spirits, and no less for his duties. The staying with his brothers and sisters with that unsettled purpose on him and cloud of departure hanging over him, would do him no good and would be (I much suspect from what I see of him), a kind of cruelty. Mr. Brackenbury reports that he will be ready for his examination next March, when he will just have turned his Sixteenth year. With a little holiday here, I should like him to be considered ready to go out. His Presidency (if I can choose it?), is of course the Presidency you recommended.[5]

Perhaps you will kindly tell Mr. Lock[6] this, as he knows you, and does me the great service for your sake.

[1] See *To* Mrs Brown, 8 Aug 56, *fn*.

[2] It was submitted to the Governors on 11 Oct: see *To* Mrs Brown, *ibid*.

[3] The letter is endorsed, no doubt by Mrs Brown: "Concerning Trust Deed. Whitehall Gardens [Countess F.'s]."

[4] i.e. after his examination for an East Indian Co. cadetship. After being successful, he went to India in July 57.

[5] Of the three Presidencies of British India, Madras, Bombay and Bengal; Walter went to Bengal.

[6] CD's mistake for John Loch, a Director of the East India Co. At Miss Coutts's request, Loch had given Walter "a direct Cadetship to Bengal", subject to his examination, on 6 Mar 56 (MS India Office).

Immense excitement was occasioned here last night by the arrival of Mr. Collins in a breathless state, with the first two acts of his play in three. Dispatches were sent off to Brighton,[1] to announce the fact. Charley exhibited an insane desire to copy it. There was talk of a Telegraph Message to Mr. Stanfield in Wales. It is called The Frozen Deep, and is extremely clever and interesting—very serious and very curious.

Ever Dear Miss Coutts | Most Faithfully Yours

CD.

To MISS MARY DICKENS, 4 OCTOBER 1856†

MS Miss Gladys Storey.

Tavistock House | Saturday Fourth October 1856

My Dear Mamey.

[a]Before starting off to Birmingham on a little trip with Mr. Lemon, I send you a cheque for the amount of the Riding Bill, thinking it will be less inconvenient to you than a Post Office order. Mr. Evans will kindly get it changed for you, if necessary.[a]

The preparations for the Play are already beginning, and it is christened (this is a great dramatic secret, which I suppose you know already), The Frozen Deep.

Tell Katey with my best love, that if she fail to come back six times as red, hungry, and strong, as she was when she went away,[2] I shall give her part to somebody else.[3]

We shall all be very glad to see you both back again; when I say "we", I include the birds (who send their respectful duty), and the Plorn.

Kind regard to all at Brighton.

Ever My Dear Mamey | Your Affectionate father

Miss Dickens. CHARLES DICKENS

To J. E. MAYALL,[4] 4 OCTOBER 1856*

MS Alderman Library, University of Virginia.

Tavistock House | Saturday Fourth October 1856

Dear Sir

I am much obliged to you for your kind letter. I fear it will not be in my power to sit,—I have so much to do and such a disinclination to multiply my "counterfeit presentments",[5]—but I am not the less sensible of your valuable offer.[6] I shall hope,

[1] For Mamie and Katey.

[aa] Omitted in MDGH and N.

[2] For her poor health in Boulogne, see *To* Miss Coutts, 8 Sep; she had whooping cough (see *To* Mrs Watson, 7 Oct).

[3] Rose Ebsworth.

[4] John Edwin Mayall (1810–91), photographer in London 1847–67; then at Brighton: see Vol. VI, p. 834*n*.

[5] *Hamlet*, III, iv, 54. For CD's photograph by Mayall in 1852, see Vol. VI, pp. 834, 838, 840 and *nn*. An engraving of one of Mayall's photographs of CD was included in the *National Magazine*, 1 Dec, and advertised in *Little Dorrit*.

[6] In July 1856 Mayall announced the opening of a new gallery of pictures for the "Exhibition of Photographic Portraits of Eminent Individuals" with a detailed catalogue; the 1852 photograph of CD would be included, but Mayall naturally wanted a more up-to-date one.

about Christmas time, to shew you some dramatic groups[1] here, which you may perhaps feel an interest in presenting. In which case, I am sure that all concerned (including myself) will be delighted to give you the opportunity.

Faithfully Yours

J. E. Mayall Esquire CHARLES DICKENS

To EDWARD WALFORD,[2] 4 OCTOBER 1856*

MS Free Library of Philadelphia.

Tavistock House | Saturday Fourth October 1856.

Sir.

I regret that my absence from town should have been the occasion of your letter lying for a long time unanswered.

I have two reasons against furnishing information to form the basis of a Biographical Memoir of myself.[3] The first is, that I do not desire to identify myself with such memoirs during my life time; the second is, that I may probably leave my own record of my life for the satisfaction of my children.

But perhaps I shall sufficiently comply with your request by informing you that there was published in a weekly Parisian Journal called L'Ami de la Maison, sometime about last Midsummer, an account of myself (as an introduction to a translation of The Lighthouse by Mr. Wilkie Collins), which I believe is generally quite accurate. I have not got it, nor have I ever read it; but Mr. Collins himself described it to me.

I am Sir | Faithfully Yours

Edward Walford Esquire CHARLES DICKENS

[1] MS reads "groupes".

[2] Edward Walford (1823–97; *DNB*), classical scholar, biographer, antiquary and editor. MA Oxford 1847; ordained 1846 (twice joined and left Roman Catholic Church). Edited the *Court Circular* 1858–9; *Gentleman's Magazine* 1866–8; *Men of the Time*, new edn 1862. Published *Life of Prince Albert*, 1861; edited *County Families of Great Britain*, 1860, and many other similar compilations.

[3] Walford was clearly hoping to include CD in his biographies in *Photographic Portraits of Living Celebrities*, the series of five-shilling monthly nos which ran from May 1856 to Aug 1859, started by Herbert Fry (see *To* Fry, 15 Mar 56) and continued by Walford from Sep 1856, making a total of 40 nos. All comprised two-page "biographical notices" with quarto-size photographs of high quality. Among Walford's were Cruikshank, Stanfield, Buckstone, and (strikingly) Maclise, but few subjects who were primarily authors. The whole series was finally collected in a handsome volume, called "Vol. 1", but with no successor. Its Preface, by Walford, does not announce discontinuance; he thanks his subjects, notes that most had corrected his proof-sheets, and that many had stipulated before sitting that the biography should be confined to "the barest possible narrative of facts" without any comment of his own.

To JOHN THOMPSON, 5 OCTOBER 1856*

MS Fales Collection, New York University Library.

Hen and Chickens Hotel, Birmingham.
Sunday, October 5th., 1856.

I find, John, on measuring here with Mr. Lemon, that the proposed rake of the stage in the schoolroom is too much. Let Rudkin[1] alter the measurements, so as to make it still 7 inches (seven inches) above the floor of the room, at the float;[2] but only one foot four inches above the floor of the room at the back of the bow. It will then slope sufficiently, and not too much.

Tell Mrs. Dickens I shall be home tomorrow (Monday) night.

Yours,
CHARLES DICKENS

To MRS BROWN, 7 OCTOBER 1856*

MS Morgan Library.

Tavistock House | Tuesday Seventh October 1856.

My Dear Mrs. Brown

Since I wrote to you last, I have been obliged to go to Birmingham, whence I returned last night at Midnight. I then found awaiting me, the enclosed draft and letter from Mr. Ouvry. The draft is exactly as I described it to you, but will you look it over before it is sent to the Medical School people, to make sure that you approve.

With kindest and truest regard to Miss Coutts,

Ever Dear Mrs. Brown | Faithfully Yours
CHARLES DICKENS

To THE HON. MRS RICHARD WATSON, 7 OCTOBER 1856

MS Yale University Library.

Tavistock House | Tuesday Seventh October 1856

My Dear Mrs. Watson.

I *did* write it for you;[3] and I hoped, in writing it, that you would think so. All those remembrances were fresh in my mind—as they often are—and gave me an extraordinary interest in recalling the past. I should have been grievously disappointed if you had not been pleased, for I took aim at you with a most determined intention.

Let me congratulate you most heartily on your handsome Eddy[4] having passed his examination[5] with such credit. I am sure there is a spirit shining out of his eyes

[1] Henry Rudkin, carpenter and builder, 8 Paddington St, Marylebone: see Vol. IV, p. 313 and *n*.

[2] The front of the stage.

[3] The account of the Great St Bernard Convent in *Little Dorrit*, Book II, Ch. I (No. XI) for Oct, published on 30 Sep 56. CD was recalling the expedition he and a party, including Georgina, Catherine and the Watsons, had made 1–3 Sep 46 (see Vol. IV, pp. 618–20 and *nn*).

[4] Edward Spencer Watson.

[5] At the Naval School, Southsea, for entry into the Navy: see *To* Mrs Brown, 5 July and *fn*.

which will do well in that manly and generous pursuit. You will naturally feel his departure very much, and so will he, but I have always observed within my experience that the men who have left home young, have [a]many long years afterwards[a] had the tenderest love for it and of all associated with it. That's a pleasant thing to think of, as one of the wise and benevolent adjustments in these lives of ours.

I have been so hard at work (and shall be for the next 8 or 9 months) that sometimes I fancy I have a digestion—or a head—or nerves—or some odd incumbrance of that kind, to which I am altogether unaccustomed, and am obliged to rush at some other object for relief. At present the house is in a state of tremendous excitement on account of Mr. Collins having nearly finished the New Play we are to act at Christmas, which is very interesting and extremely clever. I hope this time you will come and see it. We purpose producing it on Charley's birthday, Twelfth Night, but we shall probably play four nights altogether—the Lighthouse on the last occasion[1]—so that if you would come for the two last nights you would see both the pieces. I am going to try to do better than ever, and already the schoolroom is in the hands of carpenters; men from underground habitations in Theatres, who look as if they lived entirely upon smoke and gas, beset me at unheard of hours—Mr. Stanfield is perpetually measuring the boards with a chalked piece of string and an umbrella, and all the elder children are wildly punctual and businesslike, to attract managerial commendation. If you don't come, I shall do something antagonistic—try to unwrite No. XI I think. I should particularly like you to see a new and serious piece so done. Because I don't think you know, without seeing, how good it is!!!

None of the children suffered, thank God, from the Boulogne risk. The three little boys have gone back to school there, and are all well. Katey came away ill, but it turned out that she had the whooping-cough for the second time. She has been to Brighton, and comes home to day. I hear great accounts of her, and hope to find her quite well when she arrives presently. I am afraid Mary Boyle has been praising her Boulogne life too highly. Not that I deny, however, our having passed some very pleasant days together, and our having had great pleasure in her visit.[2]

You will object to me dreadfully, I know, with a beard (though not a great one), but if you come and see the Play, you will find it necessary there, and will perhaps be more tolerant of the fearful object afterwards. I need not tell you how delighted we should be to see George[3] if you would come together. Pray tell him so with my kind regard. I like the notion of Wentworth[4] and his philosophy, of all things. I remember a philosophical gravity upon him—a state of suspended opinion as to myself, it struck me—when we last met, in which I thought there was a great deal of oddity and character.

[aa] Added over caret.

[1] This was not done.

[2] Though she gives 1853 for her stay in Boulogne, her account in *Mary Boyle: her Book* clearly refers to this visit, its "halcyon days ... suddenly clouded over by the outbreak of ... diphtheria ... at first called the 'Boulogne sore-throat'." She crossed with Peter Cunningham on 23 July; other guests included Wilkie Collins (in Aug) and Douglas Jerrold; she refers to the fair and the camp and to CD's "most extensive walks", often accompanied by Georgina and herself (p. 237).

[3] George Watson (b. 1841), Mrs Watson's eldest son, who inherited Rockingham Castle.

[4] Wentworth Watson (1848–1925), Mrs Watson's third son; educated at Eton and Christ Church, Oxford; BA 1869; ordained 1871. Vicar of Monmouth 1872–92; of St Thomas the Martyr, Oxford, 1892–6; of Abingdon 1896–1900.

Charley is doing very well at Barings, and attracting praise and reward to himself. Within this fortnight there turned up—from the West Indies where he is now a Chief Justice—an old friend of mine,[1] of my own age, who lived with me in Lodgings in the Adelphi, when I was just Charley's present age. He had a great affection for me at that time, and always supposed I was to do some sort of wonders. It was a very pleasant meeting indeed—and he seemed to think it so odd that I shouldn't be Charley!

This is every atom of No-News that will come out of my head, and I firmly believe it is all I have in it—except that a Cobbler at Boulogne who had the nicest of little dogs, that always sat in his sunny window watching him at work, asked me if I would bring the dog home, as he couldn't afford to pay the Tax for him. The Cobbler and the dog being both my particular friends, I complied. The cobbler parted with the dog, heart-broken. When the dog got home here, my man like an Idiot as he is, tied him up, and then untied him. The moment the gate was open, the dog (on the very day after his arrival) ran out. Next day, Georgy and I saw him lying, all covered with mud, dead outside the neighbouring church. How am I ever to tell the cobbler? He is too poor to come to England, so I feel that I must lie to him for life, and say that the dog is fat and happy. (Mr. Plornish, much affected by this Tragedy, said: "I spose Pa I shall meet him [a](the Cobbler's dog) in Heaven."

Georgy and Catherine send their best love and I send mine. Pray write to me again some day, and I can't be too busy to be happy in the sight of your familiar hand—associated in my mind with so much that I love and honor. Ever My Dear Mrs. Watson

Most Faithfully Yours CD[a]

To WILKIE COLLINS, 9 OCTOBER 1856

MS Morgan Library.

Tavistock House | Thursday Ninth October 1856.

My Dear Collins

I should like to shew you some cuts I have made in the second act (subject to Authorial sanction of course). They are mostly verbal, and all bring the Play closer together.[2]

Also I should like to know whether it is likely that you will want to alter anything in these first two acts. If not, here are Charley, Mark, and I, all ready to write, and we may get a fair copy out of hand. From said fair copy, all my people will write out their own parts.

I dine at home to day, but not tomorrow. On Saturday and Sunday likewise, I dine at home. We must perpetually "put ourselves in communication with the view of dealing with it"—as Wills says—the moment you have done. How do you get on? And will you come at 6 to day—or when?

I am more sure than ever of the effect.

Ever Faithfully

CD.

[1] James Roney: see 23 Sep and *fn.*

[aa] Written on p. 1 above address.

[2] The cuts, more extensive than this suggests, were aimed to keep Wardour central to Act II and so to preserve the "suspended interest" (see 13 Sep).

To MR AND MRS COWDEN CLARKE,[1] 10 OCTOBER 1856

MS Brotherton Library, Leeds.

Tavistock House | Tenth October 1856

My Dear Mr. and Mrs. Clarke.

An hour before I received your letter, I had been writing your names. We were beginning a list of friends to be asked here on Twelfth Night to see a new play by the Author of the Lighthouse and a better play than that. I honestly assure you that your letter dashed my spirits, and made a blank in the prospect.

May you be very happy at Nice,[2] and find in the climate and the beautiful country near it, more than compensation for what you leave here. Don't forget among the leaves of the vine and olive, that your two green leaves[3] are always on my table here, and that no weather will shake them off.

I should have brought this myself on the chance of seeing you, if I were not such a coward in the matter of Good Bye, that I never say it, and would resort to almost any subterfuge to avoid it.[4] Mrs. Dickens and Georgina send their kindest regard. Your hearty sympathy will not be lost to me, I hope, at Nice, and I shall never hear of you without true interest and pleasure.

Always Faithfully Your friend
CHARLES DICKENS

To G. F. HUDSON,[5] 10 OCTOBER 1856

Extract in Dobell catalogue No. 281 (1919); *MS* 2 pp.; addressed G. F. Hudson; dated Tavistock House, 10 Oct 56.

Friday, Tenth October, 1856

The post brought me, from Windermere, a few days ago, a letter from the Bridegroom.[6] You will be amazed to hear that he was excessively happy![7] In answering it,

[1] Charles Cowden Clarke (1787–1877; *DNB*): see Vol. V, p. 532*n*, and his wife Mary Victoria (1809–98; *DNB*): see Vol. IV, p. 477*n*.

[2] The Cowden Clarkes and the Novellos moved to Nice that autumn and in 1861 to Genoa.

[3] The green Morocco leather blotting case Mrs Cowden Clarke and her sister, Emma Novello, had given him in Sep 48, after the amateur theatricals: see Vol. V, p. 408 and *n*.

[4] See *To* Mary Boyle, 8 Jan 56 and *fn*.

[5] G. F. Hudson, private printer, of the Heath Press (later called the Burgh Heath Press), Tadworth Heath, Surrey; produced 25 small pamphlets 1862–7, all in the Forster Collection (V & A), some inscribed to Forster. See Will Ransom, *Private Presses and their Books*, New York, 1929, p. 314. His home was presumably Tadworth Court, which belonged to the Hudson family 1776–1862; occupied by the widow of Robert Hudson (probably G. F.'s elder brother or cousin) as Lady of the Manor since 1841.

[6] Forster, who married Eliza Colburn (see *To* Mrs CD, 9 May 56 and *fn*) on 24 Sep 56; Whitwell Elwin came to London to take the service. The Forsters were spending a two months honeymoon in the Lake District.

[7] It was a very happy marriage. In his Preface to *The Forster Collection, South Kensington Museum*, 1888, Elwin wrote of Forster: "Cared for in everything, he was released from the need to look after himself, and enjoyed the luxury he prized most in the world, a companionship which interfused itself through all his labours without interrupting them" (p. xxii). There is a charming crayon sketch of Eliza Forster by Sir William Boxall in Richard Renton, *John Forster and his Friendships*, facing p. 96.

I took care to render justice to your pedestrian performances, and to describe your vigorous style as being without a blemish.

To ALFRED DICKENS,[1] 11 OCTOBER 1856

MS Berg Collection.

Tavistock House, London
Saturday Eleventh October 1856.

My Dear Alfred.

I don't know whether you would care to be in a new play by Collins (which I am going to get up for Twelfth Night) for the mere sake of being in the social amusement of the thing, or whether you are so certain of your movements as to be safely available if you do care.

But it has come into my head in casting about for somebody of your build and look, for a certain Sea-Captain who has some six lines to speak, and a little that is picturesque and requires care, to do in action, that you might like to be in the interest of the getting-up. Therefore I mention it to you first of all. Do exactly as you feel inclined, for I shall have no difficulty in finding this Captain's representative anyhow.[2]

I will tell you all about it whenever you like. The preparations are tremendous, and the arrangements will be of stupefying grandeur.

With love to Helen[3] and all the children,[4] in which all here join,

Ever affectionately
CD.

To MARK LEMON, 11 OCTOBER 1856

Mention in Dickens Exhibition, New Dudley Gallery catalogue, 1909; *MS* 1 p., with envelope; addressed Mark Lemon; dated 11 Oct 56.

Relating to platform and covering.[5]

To THOMAS BEARD, 14 OCTOBER 1856

MS Dickens House. *Address:* Thomas Beard Esquire | 42 Portman Place | Edgeware Road.

Tavistock House | Tuesday Fourteenth October | 1856.

My Dear Beard

I will write to poor old Guy,[6] telling him (Heaven save the mark, it is true!) that I

[1] Alfred Lamert Dickens (1822–60), CD's second surviving brother, railway engineer and, since 1854, Superintendent Inspector, Board of Health: see Vol. I, p. 44*n* and later vols. 13 of his Reports on water supply, sewerage, sanitary conditions and parish boundaries, made under the Public Health Act, were published by the General Board of Health, mostly with plans, 1854–7; towns he reported on included Leamington, Swindon and Tonbridge.

[2] Alfred played Capt. Helding, of *The Wanderer*.

[3] Née Dobson (?1823–1915); they were married on 16 May 46: see Vol. IV, p. 563*n*.

[4] They had five children.

[5] i.e. the stage and its floor.

[6] Joseph Guy the younger (1784–1867), private tutor and schoolmaster; author of numerous school books (21 by 1857); he had suffered from low rewards for his books and the

have no influence with the Barnacles.[1] Between ourselves, I think it hardly a case with a literary claim.

Let me know when you are able to walk.

Kindest regard from all. | Ever Faithfully

CD

To UNKNOWN CORRESPONDENT, 14 OCTOBER 1856

Text in Walter M. Hill catalogue, Dec 1901; *MS* 2 pp.; dated Tavistock House, Tuesday, 14 Oct 56.

Sir

In reply to your letter I beg to inform you that my son resided with Professor Müller[2] in order that his general life might be well looked after, and that that gentleman might superintend the classical part of his studies. German, of course, was the language of the house. For such other branches of knowledge as he devoted himself to in Germany he had masters who read with him at Professor Müller's. I was in all respects well satisfied. The Professor looked sharply after him, wrote to me from time to time, and did his duty conscientiously. My boy considered him "a Dragon in respect of his ardour for work", &c &c

I am Sir, your faithful servant,

CHARLES DICKENS

To HENRY AUSTIN, 15 OCTOBER 1856*

MS Morgan Library.

Tavistock House | Wednesday October Fifteenth | 1856.

My Dear Henry.

If you will like to be in the "Lark", I want to offer you a responsible post (of the most awful importance, or everybody will be fainting away) in the Christmas Theatre. Said Post is to see it thoroughly ventilated, according to the state of the weather &c as the performances go on, each night. Without a judicious and practised head, it can never be done in the winter time. And I should greatly like to shew you the available means for the purpose, now that the Carpenters are at work.

Of course the mysteries of the Coulisses[3] are open to so distinguished an officer—and his wife. We read the New Play (a very fine one, I think) to the Company, next Monday evening at a quarter before 8. Will you come, and bring Letitia? I can warrant your finding it very interesting.

(The sounds in the house are like Chatham Dockyard—or the building of Noah's Ark.)

Ever affectionately

CD.

scarcity of private pupils; his supporters included the publisher George Routledge. Between Dec 50 and Feb 63 the Royal Literary Fund gave him eight grants, totalling £135 (MSS Royal Literary Fund).

[1] The Royal Literary Fund committee.

[2] O. C. Müller of Leipzig: see Vol. VII, p. 34*n*.

[3] The side-scenes or wings between them in a theatre; i.e. behind the scenes.

To WILKIE COLLINS, 15 OCTOBER 1856

MS Morgan Library.

Tavistock House | Fifteenth October 1856

My Dear Collins

Will you read Turning the Tables[1] (in my old Promptbook)[2] enclosed, and let me know whether you care to play Edgar de Courcy.[3] There is very good business in it with Humphreys[4] (Mark). My great difficulty is Patty Larkins.[5]

Send me back the book, when you answer.

Ever Faithfully
CD.

I wish Berger[6] were—a little farther. Hogarth says, that some of the best people out of the Queen's Private Band[7] would have been charmed to play for nothing, and would have esteemed it a privilege to take all manner of pains; but that of course they can't be put under said B.

P.P.S. Here is Animal Magnetism[8] to read too. Will you get another copy for yourself at some theatrical shop? We play it in two Acts.[9]

To ALFRED DICKENS, [15 OCTOBER 1856]

Envelope only, MS Mr B. G. Meakin. *Date:* PM 15 Oct 56. *Address:* Alfred Dickens Esquire | 2 St John's Villas | Hampstead Road.

To FRANK STONE, 15 OCTOBER 1856

MS Benoliel Collection.

Tavistock House | Wednesday Fifteenth October | 1856.

My Dear Stone.

The Play is so difficult and will give us all so much to do (not mentioning the Manager), that Mark and I, on solemn Council holden, resolve to abandon the idea of a New Farce.[10] Therefore, for two nights, do your old friend Knibbs[11] instead!

Ever affecy.
CD.

[1] Poole's one-Act farce played by the Amateurs in July 1847 and by a different group at Knebworth in Nov 1850. For the plot see Vol. V, p. 115*nn*.

[2] CD's own copy is at Dickens House: see Vol. VI, p. 229 and *n*.

[3] Articled clerk to an attorney and the romantic lover of Sally Knibbs.

[4] The chief character, played by Mark Lemon at Knebworth, 1850.

[5] The maid of all work, played at Knebworth by Anne Romer.

[6] Franceso Berger (1834–1933); composer of the overture and incidental music for *The Frozen Deep*: see Vol. VII, p. 502*n*.

[7] The Queen's string band. Marie Mallet, a Maid of Honour, records its playing, on one occasion, selections from *Carmen*, Grieg's *Norwegian Rhapsody*, and "a lovely gavotte by Gillet" in an icy room, where "our teeth chattered audibly" (*Life with Queen Victoria*, ed. Victor Mallet, 1968, Introduction, p. xx).

[8] The popular farce by Mrs Inchbald, adapted from the French; played several times by the Amateurs in 1848 (see Vol. V, *passim*), at Knebworth in 1850 and at Rockingham, Jan 54.

[9] It was written in three.

[10] See *To* Lemon, 8 July 56.

[11] In *Turning the Tables*; Stone's part at Knebworth in 1850: see Vol. VI, p. 193 and *n*.

To W. H. WILLS, 15 OCTOBER 1856

MS Huntington Library.

Tavistock House | Wednesday October Fifteenth | 1856.

My Dear Wills

Will you and Mrs. Wills come to the reading of the Play, next Monday Evening at a quarter before 8. Stanfield has not returned yet; but there is so much to do with it that I think it best not to wait for him, so far as the Dram: Pers: is concerned.

Ever Faithfully

CD.

To THE REV. WHITWELL ELWIN,[1] 17 OCTOBER 1856

Extract in Anderson Galleries catalogue, Apr 1916; *MS* 2 pp.; dated Tavistock House, 17 Oct 56; addressed the Rev. W. Elwin.

You shall have due reminder of Twelfth Night. Already the clink of hammers gives awful note of preparation,[2] and in the evening hours my elder children go through fearful drill under their rugged parent. It not only unites us in a pleasant amusement, but it is a wonderful discipline in punctuality, perseverance and ingenuity. One of these days I may read at Norwich, when there are no Little Dorrits, and no plays holding on round my neck.

To JOHN FORSTER, [18 OCTOBER 1856]

Extract in F, VIII, i, 628. *Date:* 18 Oct 56, according to Forster.

In the difficulty of obtaining more space for audience as well as actors he applied to Mr Cooke[3] *of Astley's.* One of the finest things I have ever seen in my life of that kind was the arrival of my friend Mr. Cooke one morning this week, in an open phaeton drawn by two white ponies with black spots all over them (evidently stencilled), who came in at the gate with a little jolt and a rattle, exactly as they come into the Ring when they draw anything, and went round and round the centre bed of the front court, apparently looking for the clown. A multitude of boys who felt them to be no common ponies rushed up in a breathless state—twined themselves like ivy about the railings—and were only deterred from storming the enclosure by the glare of the Inimitable's eye. Some of these boys had evidently followed from Astley's. I grieve to add that my friend, being taken to the point of difficulty, had no sort of suggestion in him; no gleam of an idea; and might just as well have been the popular minister from the Tabernacle in Tottenham Court Road.[4] All he could say was—answering me, posed in the garden, precisely as if I were the clown asking him a riddle at night—that two of their stable tents would be home in November, and that

[1] The Rev. Whitwell Elwin (1816–1900; *DNB*): see Vol. VII, p. 602*n*.

[2] Cf. *Henry V*, IV, Prologue, l. 14.

[3] William Cooke (*d.* 1886), lessee and manager of Astley's Amphitheatre 1855–60.

[4] Tottenham Court Rd (Methodist) Chapel, No. 79, also known as Whitefield Tabernacle.

they were "20 foot square," and I was heartily welcome to 'em. Also, he said, "You might have half a dozen of my trapezes, or my middle-distance tables,[1] but they're 6 foot and all too low sir." Since then, I have arranged to do it in my own way, and with my own carpenter. You will be surprised by the look of the place. It is no more like the schoolroom than it is like the sign of the Salutation Inn at Ambleside in Westmoreland.[2] The sounds in the house remind me, as to the present time, of Chatham dockyard—as to a remote epoch, of the building of Noah's ark. Joiners are never out of the house, and the carpenter appears to be unsettled (or settled) for life.

To MARK LEMON, 18 OCTOBER 1856*

MS Robert H. Taylor Collection, Princeton University Library.

Tavistock House | Saturday Eighteenth October | 1856.

My Dear Mark

Sorry you can't come tomorrow.

As to asking Telbin[3] to the Reading on Monday, I have a lingering doubt whether Stanny (you know him to be a little touchy where his strong affection is concerned), might not wince at another Painter's knowing the Play before he did!!—Don't you feel this?

What I would say to Telbin therefore, is, "would he and Grieve[4] paint me a little set of a room in a country house with a backing of Landscape outside the window, for the new piece with which we are taking great pains, and in which Stanny is going to do wonders?[5] If yes and they would like to hear the piece read, I will make an appointment when Stanny returns, for that purpose."

We will settle about Cooke[6] on Monday Evening.

Ever affecy.
CD.

[1] Used by acrobats.

[2] Where Forster and his wife were spending their honeymoon. Forster had probably sent CD a picture of the Salutation Inn, the famous inn with Wordsworthian associations; many such views were on sale. He may well have chosen Westmorland because of his interest in Wordsworth (he owned some MSS and several early edns) and may also have just been reading Robert Ferguson's *The Northmen in Cumberland and Westmoreland*, published early 1856 (copy in his library). Also in his library was Harriet Martineau's *Complete Guide to the English Lake District*, published Apr 55.

[3] William Telbin (1813–73), scene-painter; painted the Overland Route panorama with Thomas Grieve for the Gallery of Illustration and the Holy Land panorama for the Haymarket; exhibited one landscape at RA and six at British Institution. He and Grieve had painted some of the scenes for Lytton's *Not so Bad as we Seem* in 1851: see Vol. VI, p. 337 and *n*.

[4] Thomas Grieve (1799–1882; *DNB*), scene-painter: see Vols VI, p. 337 and VII, p. 633*n*.

[5] See *To* Telbin, 2 Dec 56.

[6] His payment.

To ARTHUR RYLAND,[1] 18 OCTOBER 1856*

MS Benoliel Collection.

Tavistock House, London
Saturday Eighteenth October | 1856.

My Dear Sir

This Christmas I can read nowhere—partly, because of the weight of my own avocations while I have Little Dorrit in progress; partly, because we are going to produce a new play here on Twelfth Night, which has already become the occupation of spare time in the evenings, and which would be quite irreconcileable with my absence from home at that time of year. In reference to which Play, Mrs. Dickens begs me to say that if there should be any probability as the time approaches, of your and Mrs. Ryland's being in town on any one of the four nights when we propose to play it, it would afford us cordial pleasure to see you both. In any case she will not fail, she says, to write upon the subject bye and bye.

I hope we may manage a Reading at Birmingham after Little Dorrit's fortunes shall be closed. I will not lose sight of that agreeable expectation, and will beg Mr. Wills to communicate with you when I find myself with some leisure again. Your account of your Institution is particularly interesting to me.[2]

You will be glad to hear that Charley gets on very well indeed, in Baring's House. He has already raised himself, and has been much commended for his business qualities and attention

He, Mrs. Dickens, her sister, and all my house, unite in kindest regard to yourself and your house.

Believe me always | Very faithfully Yours

Arthur Ryland Esquire. CHARLES DICKENS

To MARK LEMON, 19 OCTOBER 1856

MS Benoliel Collection.

Tavistock House | Sunday Nineteenth October | 1856

My Dear Mark

I doubt if there be anything in this book, to make a good little Poem of,[3] unless it depended for its merit, mainly on its manner. It is a common tale of chivalry, with all the usual things in it. Some of the incidents asserted in the Preface to be discernible in Don Quixote, were really taken, I don't doubt, from this Romance; but others were not—The only novelty I see in it, is the people falling foul of any questioner who asks them what in Heaven's name they are howling about, when they fall into those periodical fits of grief. But this is so very poorly accounted for, that I don't think it comes to anything.

Ever affectionately
CD.

[1] Arthur Ryland (1800–77), founder of the Birmingham and Midland Institute 1853: see Vol. IV, p. 29*n*.

[2] For CD's reading for the Institute in Dec 53, see Vol. VII, p. 233 and *n*. He did not read at Birmingham again until 1858.

[3] Presumably as a contribution to *HW*; book untraced.

To MRS HORNE, 20 OCTOBER 1856

MS Berg Collection.

Tavistock House | Twentieth October 1856.

My Dear Mrs. Horne.

I answer your note by return of Post, in order that you may know that the Stereoscopic Nottage[1] has not written to me yet.[2] Of course I will not lose a moment in replying to him when he does address me.

We shall all be greatly pleased to see you again. You have been very, very often in our thoughts and on our lips, during this long interval.

And "*She*" is near you, is she? O I remember her well! And I am still of my old opinion! Passionately devoted to her sex as I am (they are the weakness of my existence), I still consider her a failure. She had some extraordinary Christian Name which I forget. Lashed into verse by my feelings, I am inclined to write—

My heart disowns
Ophelia Jones;

—only I think it was a more sounding name.

Are these the Tones,—
Volumnia Jones?

No, again it seems doubtful.

God bless her bones
Petronia Jones!

I think not.

Carve I on stones,
Olympia Jones?

—can *that* be the name? Fond memory[3] favors it more than any other.[4] My love to her.

Ever My Dear Mrs. Horne | Very faithfully Yours
CHARLES DICKENS

To THE HON. MRS WATSON, 20 OCTOBER 1856*

MS New York Public Library.

Tavistock House | Monday Twentieth October 1856.

My Dear Mrs. Watson

I greatly regret that I am quite unable to make any promise to read for the Northampton people. This Christmas coming, I have excused myself from reading anywhere: having as much to do, as I can reasonably perform. Next Christmas following, if all go well, the task from selecting from conditional promises, will be very difficult, and will leave me still with a long list of claims. Bristol, Birmingham,

[1] George Swan Nottage (1822–85), photographer; founder and owner of the London Stereoscopic and Photographic Co. 1856; Sheriff of London 1877–8; Lord Mayor 1884–5.

[2] Clearly concerning employing Mrs Horne: see 29 May 57 and *fn*.

[3] From "Oft in the Stilly Night" in Thomas Moore's *National Airs*.

[4] The joke, according to MDGH, I, 415, was about the name of a friend of Mrs Horne's, once brought by her to Tavistock House.

and Edinburgh disposed of, I have then the most urgent appeals (now growing old) from various places in Lancashire, in Yorkshire, in Ireland, in Scotland, away in the Eastern Counties, and Heaven knows where not.[1] Things have come to such a pass in this connexion, that I am positively afraid to think of putting down a new name or faintly hinting at a remote period when I may be disengaged.

I write thus shortly, in order that I may write at once, and help you to a complete clearance of your conscience.

Ever My Dear Mrs. Watson | Most Faithfully Yours
CHARLES DICKENS

To W. H. WILLS, 21 OCTOBER 1856*

MS Huntington Library.

Tavistock House | Tuesday Twenty First October | 1856.

My Dear Wills.

Here is this unfortunate French!—come to me this morning, after having been considerably battledored about Whitefriars for a week or two, to say (which he might have known at first) that B and E have nothing for him to do that he is fit for. Will you see Peter[2] in his Newcastle Street Retreat,[3] and ask him whether there is anything in connexion with the Manchester scheme,[4] in which he can get employment? I don't like to trouble Cunningham with a direct letter, as he has recently taken pains in behalf of Johnson.[5] French has a very fair business capacity and a good address, can write and keep plain accounts correctly, and has a fair smattering of French—enough to get on easily, with any one. The immense difficulty in his way, is, his being ruptured and unable to do work in the way of lifting and carrying, and going up and down stairs. Otherwise he would be in no need.

Miss Coutts's letters have arrived this morning. I will bring them with me before dinner-time tomorrow.

Ever Faithfully
CD.

To MISS BURDETT COUTTS, 22 OCTOBER 1856

MS Morgan Library. *Address:* Miss Burdett Coutts | Star Hotel | Oxford.

Tavistock House | Wednesday Twenty Second October | 1856.

My Dear Miss Coutts.

The letters are all in train of enquiry; and your desire to avoid the association of your name with them, will, of course, be strictly observed.

[1] These accumulated requests led to his later decision to undertake paid readings, but he read for charity at Bristol in Jan 58 and at Edinburgh in Apr 58, as well as other places: see *To* Mrs Watson, 7 Dec 57.

[2] Peter Cunningham.

[3] The Branch Audit Office, 21 Newcastle St, Strand. Cunningham was now Senior Examiner, 1st class, in the Audit Office, Somerset House.

[4] The Manchester Art Treasures Exhibition, opened by Prince Albert on 5 May 57: see *To* Macready, 3 Aug 57, and *fnn.*

[5] One of the *HW* Office staff.

I will make an appointment with Mr. Bentley,[1] immediately; and he shall make a Report in writing of what is necessary to be done to Rogers's[2] pictures. Mr. Stanfield has not returned yet; but, it is pretty clear that we don't want him.

Will you read the enclosed from Cooper, and let me know by return whether I shall say Yes. On considering the matter and balancing the reasons for and against, I do not doubt that it is advisable for all parties, that she should be received;[3] but I would like to be fortified by your approval.

With kind regards to Mrs. Brown

Ever Dear Miss Coutts | Most Faithfully Yours

CD.

To L. J. NATHAN,[4] 24 OCTOBER 1856*

MS Ohio Historical and Philosophical Society.

Tavistock House | Friday Twenty Fourth October | 1856

Mr. Charles Dickens begs to let Mr. Nathan know that Mr. Lemon and himself will call upon him tomorrow (Saturday) evening between 7 and 8, to have a word with him about the dresses for the new play.

To FRANK STONE, 24 OCTOBER 1856*

MS Benoliel Collection.

Tavistock House | Twenty Fourth October 1856 | Friday

My Dear Stone

Thanks for your note. I can easily manage it; there being abundance of people. I write shortly, having been writing my head off[5]—or rather, round and round like a Harlequin's—all day.

Ever affecy.

CD.

[1] William Bentley: see 12 May 56 and *fn*.

[2] Samuel Rogers had died on 18 Dec 55. Miss Coutts bought several of his finest paintings at the sale after his death, including Raphael's *The Agony in the Garden*, Rembrandt's *Forest Scene*, two Gainsboroughs and three Joshua Reynolds: see Edna Healey, *Lady Unknown*, 1978, p. 170.

[3] Clearly on a visit, on her return: see 15 Nov 56.

[4] Lewis Jacob Nathan, head of L. & H. Nathan, theatrical costumiers; had supplied costumes for the Amateurs regularly since 1847: see Vol. V, p. 100*n*.

[5] *Little Dorrit*; probably No. XIII for Dec, published 30 Nov, but possibly No. XIV, to get ahead on account of the play.

To WILKIE COLLINS, 26 OCTOBER 1856

MS Morgan Library.

Tavistock House
Sunday Night | Twenty Sixth October 1856.

My Dear Collins. Will you tell Pigott of the Rehearsal Arrangements, when that Ancient Mariner[1] turns up?

Will you dine at our H.W. Audit dinner, on Tuesday the 4th. of November at ½ past 5?[2]

Will you come and see the ladies, in the rough,[3] next Thursday at ½ past 7?—

Though mayhap you may come here before, for you will be glad to know that Stanfield arrived from Holyhead,[4] at Midnight last night, and sent a Dispatch down here the first thing this morning, proposing to fall-to, tomorrow. I have appointed him to be here at from 3 to ½ past, tomorrow (Monday) afternoon to hear the Play—to dine at ½ past 5—and to go into the Theatre after dinner and settle his whole plans for the Carpenters. If you can come at the first of these times, or the second, or the third, it will be well. I have had an interview with the Nathans, and primed them. I begin with the mazy Berger, tomorrow night. I have found a very good farce (with character parts for all) in lieu of Turning the tables.[5] On the whole, have not been idle.

Ever Faithfully
CD.

Took 20 miles to day, and got up all Richard's[6] words—to the great terrors of Finchley, Neasdon, Willesden,[7] and the adjacent country.

To AUGUSTUS TRACEY, 27 OCTOBER 1856*

MS University of Texas.

Tavistock House
Monday Twenty Seventh October | 1856.

My Dear Tracey

I am so exceedingly sorry to have missed you again.

[1] Pigott was a passionate yachtsman and he and Collins made many yachting expeditions together.

[2] Collins had just become a member of the *HW* editorial staff, having received his last payment for a contribution on 25 Oct: Anne Lohrli, *Household Words*, p. 234 (not on 4 Oct, as given in *CD as Editor*, p. 222*n*).

[3] Just as they are, not dressed up. Cf. *Martin Chuzzlewit*, Ch. 28: "You'll have a party? ... No ... he shall take us in the rough."

[4] He had been in Wales and Ireland since Sep, but was in London in early Oct: see *To* Mrs Watson, 7 Oct.

[5] Either *Animal Magnetism*, or *Uncle John*.

[6] Richard Wardour. Rehearsals continued for many weeks. According to Berger "one long scene" was omitted in the early rehearsals. This was Wardour's soliloquy in Act II. He thought this "a most finished and thrilling piece of acting" by CD and recalled that it included "a big D"—in fact "Damn the fellow and his sweetheart too". But this had "seemed so necessary to the passion of the moment that nobody felt shocked" (F. G. Kitton, *CD by Pen and Pencil*, Suppl., p. 18).

[7] Then villages to the north of London.

Is there any chance of your being in town on Tuesday the 4th. November, and able to dine at the Household Words Office at ½ past 5 sharp? It is our half yearly Audit Day, when we close the examination of the accounts with something to eat.

My kind regard to Henry.[1]

To EDWARD CHAPMAN, 28 OCTOBER 1856

Extract in *Autograph Prices Current*, V, 1919–21; *MS* 2 pp.; addressed Edward Chapman; dated Tavistock House, 28 Oct 56.

The Oliver Twist as usual.[2] Bradbury and Evans have nothing to do with the cheap edition of the Christmas Books[3] that I know of.... When I considered the idea of publishing the 8vo books in two volumes each, on a former occasion,[4] I did not think it a desirable one.

To MISS BURDETT COUTTS, 30 OCTOBER 1856†

MS Morgan Library. *Address:* Miss Burdett Coutts | Veale's Royal Hotel | Teignmouth | Devon.

Tavistock House | Thursday Thirtieth October 1856.

My Dear Miss Coutts.

I have seen Mr. Bentley (a very respectable grey-haired, high-dried little man, compounded of a Master of the Ceremonies in former years, a Collector of Assessed Taxes, a highly trustworthy Book-keeper, and a Parish Clerk of five and thirty years standing), and I have this day received from him the enclosed letter.[5]

He cannot say what his doings will cost, but he observes that of course they will be charged as such things are charged to Mr. Baring, the National Gallery, and everybody else. His having the pictures at home, is indispensable. He does not expect the work to be difficult. He can restore all the frames, and re-gild them. There is no doubt at all of his reliability.

I did not mention to him your wish that your bidder should be employed in their removal, because I perceived him to be a man so much trusted and so thoroughly accustomed to do his own work completely, that I thought it desirable to be avoided. I mistrust collision in such case; none the less because Mr. Bentley himself bid for most of these very pictures, having commissions to that effect from Thomas Baring and others.

Everything that needs to be done, can be done and is to be done, before the Manchester Exhibition gets into form. And I now only await your authority to let him

[1] Ending and signature missing.

[2] CD received £163.3.6 from Chapman on 12 Nov (CD's Account-book, MS Messrs Coutts).

[3] They concluded the 1st Series of the Cheap edn in Oct 52: see Vol. VI, p. 758*n*.

[4] All novels in the Cheap edn were in 1 vol, and so, at this date, were first edns.

[5] It enclosed a list of 24 paintings at 1 Stratton St needing cleaning or other attention; they included the Raphael, the Rembrandt, the two Gainsboroughs and two of the three Reynolds Miss Coutts had bought at the Samuel Rogers sale (see 22 Oct). Bentley added: "I have not acknowledged the merits of the Pictures, as they have already been acknowledged as fine specimens of their respective Masters." (MS Morgan Library.)

take the pictures away. Will you write by return? If you still wish your man to be suggested, of course I can do it, and (I hope) with all due discretion. But I myself would leave that alone.

The very curious Old Bailey case to which one of those letters referred, was truly stated.[1] It being ante-dated some time (meaning as to its receipt by me from you), the Sessions coming on, and time pressing, Mr. Wills asked me what I thought he had best do at once? I told him, engage a respectable Counsel to defend the man, and go to legal expences within ten pounds for that purpose. There is no trace of you in the matter.[2]

I found the Home going on very well the other day, and both Mrs. Marchmont and Mrs. Macartney[3] tremendously cast down by your having had occasion for blame. They really seem so sorry and depressed, and it is so necessary that they should have self-reliance and a sustaining pride in what they do, that I comforted them with what majestic consolation I felt it Ministerial to impart. I think if you would deem it right, gradually to soften down the frequency of Mrs. Engelbach's[4] visits, it would set them up and reassure them more than anything else. They have a notion that they have waned in your confidence.

I have been, and am, so busy that my head simmers—occasionally approaches boiling point. Therefore I will only add my love to Mrs. Brown.

One thing I have forgotten. Charley is in great glory, and much surveyed and admired in "the House", by reason of his being on a week's visit to Mr. Bates at Sheen:[5] going down with him every night, and coming up every morning.

I enclose Thomas Baring's letter agreeably to your wish.

Ever Dear Miss Coutts | Most Faithfully Yours

CD.

To JAMES GRESHAM,[6] 31 OCTOBER 1856†

MS Free Library of Philadelphia.

Tavistock House, London | Thirty First October 1856.

Dear Sir

My opinions on the subject of Public Executions were expressed in two letters addressed to the Editor of the Times Newspaper,[7] immediately after the execution of the Mannings, husband and wife.[8] I am far too busy to repeat them here; but it is the less necessary, by reason of their having undergone no kind of modification.

Your faithful Servant

James Gresham Esquire CHARLES DICKENS

[1] Possibly connected with the Crystal Palace fraud, by larceny and forgery of shares; William James Robinson, when detected, fled to the continent; captured 7 Dec; tried at Old Bailey 1 Nov 57 and sentenced to 20 years' transportation.

[2] Miss Coutts may well have had shares in the Crystal Palace.

[3] Assistant Matron at the Home since 1849.

[4] No doubt the wife of either Lewis J. or Charles William Engelbach, both clerks in Coutts & Co., one of whom had acted also as a secretary to Miss Coutts: see Vol. V, p. 435*n*.

[5] In Surrey; Bates's country home.

[6] Unidentified.

[7] Of 13 and 17 Nov 1849 (Vol. V, pp. 644 and 651).

[8] Frederick George Manning and his Swiss wife Maria: see Vol. V, p. 642 and *nn*.

To AUGUSTUS TRACEY, 31 OCTOBER 1856*

MS University of Texas.

H.M.S. Tavistock | Port of London
Thirty First October 1856.

My Dear Commodore

I was out on Sunday, on a twenty mile cruise, getting a dramatic code of Signals up for that ould Salt, Stanfield.

Whenever you come aboard, you shall have the best bottle of wine in the locker, and the best Irish stew in the Caboose.[1]

So no more at present from Yours Ever, in whatsoever waters,

Harry Bluff.[2]

To WILKIE COLLINS, 1 NOVEMBER 1856

MS Morgan Library.

Tavistock House
Saturday Evening First November | 1856.

My Dear Collins

Forster came here yesterday afternoon to ask me if he might read the Play, and I lent it to him. This afternoon I get the enclosed from him

(which please to read at this point.)

You know that I don't agree with him as to the Nurse[3]—[a]and indeed I have no doubt his demur is founded on his seeing that it requires more Stage Go than our dear Janet[4] possesses.[a] But I think his suggestion that the going away of the women might be suggested at the Close of the First Act as a preparation for the last, an excellent one.[5] Will you think of it? By an alteration that we could make in a quarter of an hour it might be done, and moreover—this suggestion upon a suggestion arises in my mind—it might be made the Nurse's position in the Play that her blood-red Second Sight *is the first occasion of their going away at all.*[6] [Forster does not clearly understand the circumstances of their going; but never mind that.]

His notion that Clara tells too much,[7] has been strong in my mind since I first got that Act in Rehearsal. But, doubtful whether it might not unconsciously arise in me from a paternal interest in my own part, I had, as yet, said nothing about it; the rather as I had not yet seen the Second Act on the stage.

Stanfield wants to cancel the chair altogether, and to substitute a piece of rock on the ground, composing with the Cavern. That, I take it, is clearly an improvement.

[1] Merchantmen's kitchen on deck.

[2] The hero of a song in Isaac Pocock's nautical melodrama *For England Ho!*, 1818: see Vol. IV, p. 515 and *n*, where CD signs a letter to Stanfield "Henry Bluff".

[3] Forster probably had doubts about the effectiveness of her "second sight".

[aa] Omitted in *CD to WC* and N.

[4] Mrs Wills.

[5] Not suggested in the Prompt-Book.

[6] At the end of Act I; but not made the occasion of Clara and Lucy going away from their home.

[7] In Act I, Clara tells Lucy the whole story of Richard Wardour's original passion for her and her later engagement to Frank Aldersley.

He has a happy idea of painting the ship which is to take them back, ready for sailing, on the sea.[1]

Nothing would induce Telbin, yesterday, to explain what he was going to do, before Stanfield; and nothing would induce Stanfield to explain what *he* was going to do, before Telbin. But they had every inch and curve and line in that bow, accurately measured by the Carpenters, and each requested to have a drawing of the whole made to scale. Then each said that he would make his model in cardboard, and see what I "thought of it". I have no doubt the thing will be as well done as it can be.

Will you dine with us at 5 on Monday before Rehearsal. We can then talk over Forster's points? If you are disengaged on Wednesday, shall we breathe some fresh air in dilution of Tuesday's "alcohol",[2] and walk through the fallen leaves in Cobham Park? I can then explain how I think you can get your division of the Christmas No. very originally and naturally. It came into my head to day.

Ever Faithfully
CD.

P.S. I re-open this, to say that I find from Wills that next Tuesday being the Audit Day at all, is his mistake. It is Tuesday *Week*. Therefore, if Tuesday is a fine day, shall we go out then?

To PROFESSOR GEORGE WILSON,[3] 4 NOVEMBER 1856*

MS Yale University Library.

Tavistock House, London | Fourth November, 1856.

My Dear Sir

I am truly honored by your kind remembrance in having sent me the Five Gateways of Knowledge,[4] and I beg to assure you that I have read that charming little book with the highest interest and gratification. Wise, elegant, eloquent, and perfectly unaffected, it has delighted me. I should find it very difficult indeed to tell you, to my own satisfaction, how unusually it has pleased me.

Accept my cordial thanks.

Very faithfully Yours
CHARLES DICKENS

Professor George Wilson

[1] The scene for Act III is reproduced from the *Illustrated London News*, 17 Jan 57, in *Catalogue of Exhibition*, 1979, p. 160, showing both the rock in the foreground and the ship in the distance. See Vol. VII, p. 627*n*.

[2] The Audit dinner; but see P.S.

[3] George Wilson (1818–59; *DNB*), chemist and religious writer; MD, Edinburgh, 1839; "extra-mural" lecturer on chemistry at Edinburgh; Director of Scottish Industrial Museum and Regius Professor of Technology, Edinburgh University, 1855; President Royal Scottish Society of Arts. His many books include the *Life of Henry Cavendish*, 1851, and *Researches on Colour-Blindness*, 1855.

[4] Wilson's popular account of the five senses, *Five Gateways of Knowledge*, published Oct 56 (advertised Aug 56; 8th edn 1860); the book fully justifies CD's high opinion of it.

To MRS AUSTIN,[1] 5 NOVEMBER 1856

MS Free Library of Philadelphia.

Tavistock House | Fifth November 1856.

My Dear Mrs Austin

I have not seen anything of your Protegée, and I humbly hope she will not come to me. If she should, I shall entreat her to excuse me from hearing her; firstly, because, from simply hearing her in a room, I could form no opinion worth giving or having, of her powers as an actress; secondly, because I shrink with horror from the idea of sending any one to a Manager, and throwing any fresh ingredient into the sooty soup of theatrical difficulties and jealousies.

I thoroughly agree in all you say of the Drama. It has been my constant effort for years past to shew in many ways that an amusement so wholesome and humanizing is more needed by an over-worked, over-driven, over-repressed, over-lectured, over-bothered People, than all the Blue Book writing and Didactic speechifying whereof my soul is sick, and wherewith my liver (in the Persian idiom) is turned upside down.[2]

I wish you would come, in the holidays of this next Christmas, and see a New Play here. I think it will be very pretty, and I know it will have some specialities which can be seen nowhere else. We will write to Lady Gordon,[3] and give her more than a month's notice of the great event.

My Dear Mrs Austin

Faithfully Yours

CHARLES DICKENS

To HABLOT K. BROWNE, 8 NOVEMBER 1856

MS Widener Collection, Harvard.

Tavistock House | Saturday Eighth November, 1856.

My Dear Browne.

All right. Please keep Clennam, always, as agreeable and well-looking as possible.[4] He is very good in the Flintwinch scene here.[5] Mrs. Clennam's expression, capital.[6]

Letterings below.[7]

Ever Faithfully CD.[8]

[1] Sarah Austin, née Taylor (1802–66; *DNB*): see Vol. VII, p. 200*n*.

[2] Cf. James J. Morier, *Hajji Baba in England*, 1828: see Vols III, p. 196 and *n*, and IV, p. 535 and *n*.

[3] Née Lucie Austin (1821–69; *DNB*): see Vol. V, p. 44*n*.

[4] CD has seen sketches for the two plates in No. XIII for Dec, published 30 Nov, and is cautioning Browne over Clennam's appearance in "Rigour of Mr. F's Aunt".

[5] "Mr Flintwinch receives the embrace of friendship", Book II, Ch. 10 (No. XIII, published 30 Nov 56).

[6] Her expression in the plate is impassive.

[7] Cut off; tops of a few letters showing.

[8] In top left corner of letter the initials "R.Y." are written (not in CD's hand): Robert Young (1816–1907), Browne's assistant, who helped him in biting-in the plates: see Vol. VI, p. 594*n*.

To MRS CHARLES DICKENS, 8 NOVEMBER 1856

MS British Library.

Tavistock House | Saturday Eighth November 1856.

My Dearest Catherine

I must make very short work of this letter, for I have been writing hard all day (being now engaged on the Xmas No. of Household Words) and only leave off as the darkness begins.

The Rehearsal came off last night, and the progress was satisfactory. Especially, considering that Lemon had the Rheumatism in his jaw, and that Berger had such a cold as to be wrapped up like a Stage Coachman, and screened in with the Print-Screen.[1]

The only two bits of news, are, that the Half year's balance of Household Words is very indifferent indeed,[2] and that I don't think the Cook will do. She seems too sulky a woman to tolerate in a house where the other servants deserve anything but mortification of spirit.

Shrieks of amazement and delight today, proclaimed the return of Cobbler, looking wonderfully fat and well. Immediately afterwards, he ran away again—and then it was discovered that it was not Cobbler at all, but a dog very like him, belonging to the Adelphi Theatre, who had come up with a Carpenter.

My best love to dear Macready, and Miss Macready, and Katie, and the dear little girls, and Henry my godson, and Johnny. Tell Macready that if he doesn't come to the Play, I shall join the Tory ranks in Politics immediately afterwards, and become one of whatsoever religious denomination most requires me, in the words of Miggs "to hate and despise my feller creeters, as every practicable Christian should."[3] Tell him I have not yet settled the exact church I shall favor, there being so many of this kind.

All well, and all send loves. I went over Forster's house a day or two ago, which is very pretty indeed, and very excellently done.[4]

Ever affectionately

CD.

To [?B. H.] BECKER,[5] 9 NOVEMBER 1856

Extract in Anderson Galleries catalogue No. 2029 (1926); *MS* (3rd person) 1 p.; dated Tavistock House, 9 Nov 56.

Mr. Charles Dickens ... begs to say that he has referred Mr. Becker's note to the Author of Sister Rose;[6] in doing which his power of interference in the matter to which it refers, ends.

[1] A folding screen decorated with prints.

[2] The total income for the half-year to 30 Sep 56 was £384.12.9 (of which CD's share was £216.7.2), as against £832.1.7 for the previous half-year.

[3] Miggs in fact says: "I hate and despise myself and all my fellow-creatures as every practicable Christian should" (*Barnaby Rudge*, Ch. 13).

[4] 46 Montague Sq.

[5] Probably Bernard Henry Becker (1833–1900), journalist and miscellaneous writer; on staff of *Daily News*; special commissioner in Sheffield and Manchester, 1878–9; in Ireland 1881; his books included *Disturbed Ireland*, 1881.

[6] *HW*, 7–28 Apr 55, XI, 217–93, a story in four instalments by Wilkie Collins.

To WILLIAM TELBIN, 10 NOVEMBER 1856

MS Berg Collection.

Tavistock House
Monday Evening Tenth November | 1856.

My Dear Sir

I am very much indebted to you for your kind letter, and look forward with the greatest interest and pleasure to seeing your scene.

It happens that I was within five minutes of writing to you when your letter came. With the view of securing the large audience we shall have, distributed over the four nights of performance, before out of town Christmas engagements are settled, we are going to give them so much notice that it is necessary to get the bills and invitations &c in hand.

So the questions, are:

First, am I to call the Scenery of the First Act by you *and Grieve*? Or by you, only? I presume the latter.[1]

Secondly, will you let me know (when you have thought of it), the names and addresses of any friends you would wish to have asked to see the play? It will then give Mrs. Dickens the greatest pleasure to send them regular invitations.

Thirdly, what colored drugget would you prefer on the ground in the chamber. Red (which always tells), or green, or brown? The furniture being showy, I think the drugget should have no pattern on it.

The men have begun putting up the outer room, and Stanfield is in ecstacies at its proportions. He swelled just now, with his great intentions.

Very faithfully Yours

William Telbin Esquire CHARLES DICKENS

To MRS BROWN, 11 NOVEMBER 1856

MS Morgan Library. *Address:* Mrs Brown | Royal Hotel | Teignmouth | Devon.

Tavistock House | Eleventh November, 1856. | Tuesday

My Dear Mrs. Brown.

A hurried reply to yours. After considering the point with my utmost care and attention, I do not see anything to object to in it. The case they put,[2] is on the whole a reasonable one, which you yourself would wish to guard against.[3] I have therefore this morning sent your letter on to Mr. Ouvry. His letters to you, I return.

I am hard at the Christmas No. of Household Words—a shipwreck story.

With affectionate regard to Miss Coutts

Ever Faithfully and truly

CD.

[1] The playbill gives only Telbin's name for Act I, "an old Country House in Devonshire".

[2] Either the St George's Hospital authorities or the Trustees of her gift to the Hospital.

[3] Probably the danger of a lapse after an unawarded Exhibition: see *To* Mrs Brown, 8 Aug, fn. On 7 Nov the Medical School Council reported that Ouvry had attended their meeting and the Board had agreed to "the proposed Alterations in the Deed of Foundation", "subject to Mrs Brown's approval" (Minutes, Board of Governors, 12 Nov).

To W. H. WILLS, 13 NOVEMBER 1856

MS Huntington Library.

OFFICE OF HOUSEHOLD WORDS,
Thursday Evg. 13th. Novr. 1856

My Dear Wills.

Yes, to the Christmas Carol.[1]—No, to the Song of the Stars.

I am glad you like the Wreck—though you have not seen all of it, I think. I find the Narrative too strong (speaking as a reader of it; not as its writer) to be broken by the stories. I have therefore devised with Collins for getting the stories in between his Narrative and mine, and breaking neither.[2]

I never wrote anything more easily, or I think with greater interest and stronger belief.

The almanack[3] I returned to the Printer tonight. I chose the longer quotation, because the quotation without the Sun seems to want its source of Life.[4]

Ever Faithfully
CD.

To WILKIE COLLINS, 14 NOVEMBER 1856

MS Morgan Library.

Tavistock House | Friday Fourteenth Novr. | 1856.

My Dear Collins

I could not send you the books[5] before I went out this morning for a 12 miler, the collection being curiously spare in pick-up cases,[6] and it being a work of time to find them.

Will you exchange proofs of the Captain[7] with me. The proofs you have, have markings of mine upon them which will be useful to me in correcting. You can bring me those when you come tonight.

Ever Faithfully
CD.

[1] "A Christmas Carol", a poem, *HW*, 27 Dec 56, XIV, 565, author unknown.

[2] The five stories ("The Beguilement in the Boats": see *To* Contributors to *HW*, 30 Sep 56), come in fact between Collins's "John Steadiman's Account" (following CD's "The Wreck") and his "The Deliverance".

[3] The *HW Almanac* (by Henry Morley) published 20 Nov 56 at 4*d*: see Vol. VII, p. 741*n*. This was the second and last of the Almanacs, the sales of which had evidently proved disappointing. Besides the usual advertisements on 1 Nov, there were two prominent insets in *Little Dorrit* for Dec, reminding purchasers that the *Almanac* was not included with the ordinary weekly issue of *HW*.

[4] At top of title-page is the quotation, "O Ye Nights and Days, Bless Ye The Lord: Praise Him and Magnify Him for Ever", from the *Benedicite*, in both *Almanacs*: CD's suggested change to "O Ye Sun and Moon, Bless Ye The Lord ...", was not implemented, probably to save the expense of re-setting.

[5] Probably to use in his "A Petition to the Novel-Writers", *HW*, 6 Dec 56, XIV, 451.

[6] Examples casually found; CD's library probably contained few of the popular novels Collins needed.

[7] i.e. "The Captain's Account of the Wreck", the opening section.

To DANIEL MACLISE, 14 NOVEMBER 1856*

MS Benoliel Collection.

Tavistock House | Friday Fourteenth November | 1856.

My Dear Mac

Stanny, seeing my big brown Punch Jug t'other night (a genuine old article), said, with his face shining before the Lord, that it was just the thing you wanted to paint.[1] Is my young man right, and shall I send it to you? If you were to see my young man perpetually painting here for the Christmas Play, in the midst of 70 paint pots and a cauldron of boiling size, you would never forget the spectacle.

Faithfully Ever

CD.

To MISS BURDETT COUTTS, 15 NOVEMBER 1856

MS Morgan Library. *Address:* Miss Burdett Coutts | Apsley House Hotel | Torquay | Devon.

Tavistock House | Saturday Fifteenth November | 1856.

My Dear Miss Coutts

I return Derry.[2] I have no doubt it's a capital article, but it's a mortal dull color. Color these people always want, and color (as allied to fancy), I would always give them.[3] In these cast-iron and mechanical days, I think even such a garnish to the dish of their monotonous and hard lives, of unspeakable importance. One color, and that of the earth earthy, is too much with them early and late. Derry might just as well break out into a stripe, or put forth a bud, or even burst into a full blown flower. Who is Derry that he is to make quakers of us all, whether we will or no!

You will immediately hear from Mr. Wills, with all the information you want, drawn fresh from the fountain head.

At Shepherd's Bush on Wednesday, all were in excellent order. Mr. Dyer and I represented the august Committee. It was very pleasant to see Louisa Cooper, nicely dressed and looking very well to do, sitting with Mrs. Macartney in the Long Room. She brought me for a present,[4] the most hideous Ostrich's Egg ever laid—wrought all over with frightful devices, the most tasteful of which represents Queen Victoria (with her crown on) standing on the top of a Church, receiving professions of affection from a British Seaman.

How long are you going to stay in Devonshire? And don't you mean to come to town at Christmas Time? I always want to know, and you never will tell me.

[1] Perhaps used by him as one of the "assemblage of bottles and glasses"—"a quiet allusion to Peter's predilection for the bottle"—in *Peter the Great, Czar of Muscovy, working as a shipwright . . . in the Dockyard at Deptford, during the winter of 1697–8 . . . visited by William the Third*, exhibited RA 1857 (*Art Journal*, 1857).

[2] Drab cotton material which Miss Coutts was proposing for working clothes for girls at the Home. Attached to the letter is a piece of material marked "Derry 3 3/4" and some figures.

[3] Miss Coutts disagreed with CD on this, convinced that an interest in dress was a strong temptation to working-class girls; she included letters from two prison governors, Augustus Tracey (see Vol. II, p. 270*n*) and G. L. Chesterton (see Vol. I, p. 101*n*) in the Preface to her *A Summary Account* Appx, strongly in her support. See *To* Miss Coutts, 5 Mar 56 and 9 Apr 57.

[4] See *ibid.*, 5 July and *fn.*

With kind regard to Mrs. Brown,

Ever Dear Miss Coutts | Most Faithfully Yours
CHARLES DICKENS

I re-open this to say that I have just received the enclosed from Mr. Macready, who is very anxious indeed that you should have it. Would you like Mr. Wills to see the boy,[1] and give him a suit of clothes?

To W. H. WILLS, 19 NOVEMBER 1856

MS Huntington Library.

Tavistock House | Nineteenth November 1856.

My Dear Wills

On the lists being added up, I find that we can still (as I hope), book some more names. I have therefore put down Mr. Payn. And if you have any names to suggest, now is the time.[2]

Of course if you have any at any time, wherein you may be interested or not, you will let me know what they are. But this is the time at which such lines have the best chance of falling into pleasant places.[3]

Ever Faithfully
CD.

To GEORGE BRACE,[4] 20 NOVEMBER 1856*

MS Dickens House.

Tavistock House | Thursday Twentieth November | 1856.

Sir

In reply to your letter of yesterday's date, I beg to assure you that I would immediately appoint a time for receiving a Deputation from your Society,[5] or its President, but that I am convinced I should occasion them useless trouble by doing so. No doubt the visit would refer to some public function the Society does me the honor to wish me to discharge. I am bound therefore to let you know at once, that my own avocations at present demand so much of my time and attention, as to oblige me to forego all public engagements without any exception, until after next Midsummer.

I am Sir | Faithfully Yours
CHARLES DICKENS

George Brace Esquire

[1] See *ibid.*, 8 Apr and *fn*.

[2] On p. 2 of this folded sheet Wills has jotted down a list of 15 names, not all legible, but including Frederick and Nina (Lehmann), Payn and wife, and Novello and wife.

[3] Cf. Psalm XVI: 6 "The lines are fallen unto me in pleasant places" (*Authorized Version*).

[4] Probably George Brace, solicitor, of 24 Surrey St, Strand.

[5] Not discovered.

To FRANK STONE, 20 NOVEMBER 1856*

MS Benoliel Collection.

Tavistock House | Twentieth November, 1856.

My Dear Stone

I hear you were in, this morning. I have been restraining my impatience to ask you to come and see the Theatre, until it should be finished. Now you *have* seen it, I should like to explain to you all that it is going to be. I want to make it something that shall never be seen again.

Will you come in after 8 this evening?

Ever Affecy.
CD.

To FRANK STONE, 21 NOVEMBER 1856*

MS Benoliel Collection.

Tavistock House | Friday Twenty First November 1856.

My Dear Stone

If you are disengaged, come to the Rehearsal tonight. If not disengaged tonight, say Monday.

Ever Affecy.
CD.

To [CHARLES] LEE,[1] 22 NOVEMBER 1856

Extract in N, II, 812.

OFFICE OF HOUSEHOLD WORDS,
22nd November 1856

Mr. Charles Dickens presents his compliments to Mr. Lee and begs to thank him for the ticket for the dinner at the North Surrey Industrial Schools.[2]

Should Mr. Dickens have an opportunity of going over the establishment, he will have the pleasure of accepting Mr. Lee's kind offer to accompany him.

[1] Probably Charles Lee of 5 Bellevue Villas, Putney.

[2] Not traced under this title, but probably connected with the Sir William Perkins Charity, by which 130 boys and 130 girls of Chertsey received a free education.

To [?WILLIAM BRADBURY],[1] 24 NOVEMBER 1856*

MS Houghton Library, Harvard.

Tavistock House | Monday Twenty Fourth November | 1856.

My Dear Sir

I received a note from you yesterday, about the Little Dorrit Proofs.[2]

I have not got them. Mr. Forster tells me he has returned them to Whitefriars; but I have not yet had the Revise. If you will send me the Revise, your messenger may wait to bring it back to you again. I have only two very slight alterations to make in it.

Faithfully Yours
CHARLES DICKENS

To W. H. WILLS, 24 NOVEMBER 1856*

MS Huntington Library.

Tavistock House
Monday Night | Twenty Fourth November | 1856.

My Dear Wills.

I forgot, in the tremendous hurry and storm of to night, to ask you if you can be here for a little while on Wednesday from a quarter before Four.

The Fire Insurance Office are going to send an Inspector that day "between 4 and 5",[3] and it is so much better that he should be attended over the "Works" by some one who is not the Principal. I will tell you beforehand, the points I wish him to understand.

Ever Faithfully
CD.

To FRANK STONE, 26 NOVEMBER 1856*

MS Benoliel Collection.

Tavistock House
Wednesday Twenty Sixth November 1856.

My Dear Stone

I have put you down on the List—*two places on each of the Four Nights*, which I hope will answer your purpose well. There will always be a good lounging-place by the door, besides, with a good view.

[1] Probably Bradbury, but possibly one of his printers.

[2] Of No. XIII for Dec, Book II, Chs 8–11, published 30 Nov.

[3] Because of the additional risk for the theatre and its audience: see *To* Mitton, 3 Dec.

We are getting on. But the amount of Carpenter's Work, through having to make the Scenes in small pieces, is quite extraordinary.

Ever affecy.

CD.

To THE SECRETARY OF THE EAGLE INSURANCE OFFICE, [27 NOVEMBER 1856]

Mention in *To* Mitton, 3 Dec 56. *Date:* no doubt the same day that he received the Secretary's letter, 27 Nov (see *To* Wills, 24 Nov and *To* Mitton, 3 Dec).

To MESSRS WILLIAMS & NORGATE,[1] [27 NOVEMBER 1856]

MS (envelope) Mr John Brancher. *Address:* Messrs. Williams and Norgate | 14 Henrietta Street | Covent Garden. PM 27 Nov 56.

To MESSRS BRADBURY & EVANS, 29 NOVEMBER 1856

MS Free Library of Philadelphia.

Tavistock House
Saturday Twenty Ninth November | 1856

My Dear B and E.

You have made a most fatal mistake, which puts me in greater concern than I can possibly describe. You have omitted a correction of mine in the Revise of No XIII, of the last importance. It is a reference certain to be mischievously perverted, and used against me. I wrote it in the text, more as a joke which Forster shewed me in the Proofs than for any other purpose. I knew he would see that it was unsafe, and he came here directly to ask me to take it out. The moment I saw him, I said "I know what it is; I have already taken it out in my mind". How is it possible for me ever to explain that the grossest carelessness at the Printers', and their placing me in the damned absurd position of making corrections which are pitched into the fire, occasions its going forth? The passage is at page 404, 4 lines from the bottom, where I most carefully took out from the revise a reference to "baptismal water on the brain".[2] If it were not too late, I would suppress the whole issue.[3] I never was so vexed in my life.

Faithfully Ever

CD.

[1] Tauchnitz's London agents: see Vol. IV, p. 384*n* and later vols.

[2] In his description of Casby in Book II, Ch. 9, CD had written "making his polished head and forehead look as christian" (proof, "as largely christian") "in every knob as if he had got baptismal water on the brain". This was a joke to tease Forster, who had warned CD in the past about offending religious susceptibilities (see his revision of christening scene in Ch. 5 of *Dombey and Son*, Clarendon edn, ed. E. A. Horsman, pp. xix, 60 and *To* Forster, Vol. IV, p. 628). It was never intended to get past proof stage (see Clarendon edn, ed. H. P. Sucksmith, Introduction, p. xxxiv).

[3] Despite CD's letter being at the last minute, the No. appeared without the offending phrase (Clarendon edn, p. 524).

To THE DUKE OF DEVONSHIRE, 1 DECEMBER 1856

MS Devonshire Collections, Chatsworth.

Tavistock House | First December, 1856

My Dear Duke of Devonshire

The moment the first bill is printed for the first night of the New Play I told you of,[1] I send it to you, in the hope that you will grace it with your presence. There is not one of the old actors whom you will fail to inspire as no one else can. And I hope you will see a little result of a friendly union of the Arts, that you may think worth seeing, and that you can see nowhere else.

We purpose repeating it on Thursday the 8th. Monday the 12th. and Wednesday the 14th. of January. I do not encumber this note with so many bills, and merely mention those nights in case any one of them should be more convenient to you than the first.

But I shall hope for the first, unless you dash me. (N.B. I put Flora into the current No.[2] on purpose that this might catch you, softened towards me and at a disadvantage.)

If there is hope of your coming, I will have the Play clearly copied, and will send it to you to read beforehand. With the most grateful remembrances and the sincerest good wishes for your health and happiness,[3]

I am Ever | My Dear Duke of Devonshire | Your faithful and obliged

The | Duke of Devonshire CHARLES DICKENS

To WILLIAM TELBIN, 2 DECEMBER 1856

MS Free Library of Philadelphia.

Tavistock House | Tuesday Night | Second December, 1856

My Dear Mr Telbin

I send you our bills for all the nights; and I am sure I need not tell you what pleasure it will give us all to see you, both before and behind the curtain, throughout the prodigiously long season.

Before you receive this, you will probably have received all the remaining pieces of your scene;[4] for at this moment they are all completed and lying on the stage. I had a pair of wings made for the back, outside the windows, and canvassed on both sides, so that they might be used both by you and Stanfield.[5] Now, Stanfield, finding

[1] 6 Jan 57.

[2] Arthur Clennam calls on Flora in Book II, Ch. 9, No. XIII for Dec, published 1 Dec (Monday). She and Mr F.'s Aunt are both at their comic best.

[3] The Duke's state of health evidently precluded him from coming.

[4] For Act I. The *Examiner*, 17 Jan 57, commented: "The Scenery is wonderfully good on its tiny scale." The view from the drawing-room window it described as "thoroughly English.... As the light fades with the advancing evening a grey tone comes over the landscape with the most natural effect."

[5] Stanfield painted the sets for Act II, a hut in the Arctic, and Act III, a cavern on the Newfoundland coast. Of the Act II set, the *Examiner*, above, commented: "We are next shivering in a hut in the Arctic regions, all bare, dreary, and grim. As the door opens ... we see the falling snow and the far-spreading frozen waste." It refers to the "masterly hand of Stanfield" in both scenes. "Who else, indeed, could paint such a sea?"

that they made a disagreeable shadow and did not screen in well after all, has set them flat against the wall and made them out with unframed canvass so as to cover the whole distance within sight. As he has only painted them sky and sea, I hope you will find when you come to look at the stage again that they will screen in—at all events with a little masking—sufficiently for your set.

Very faithfully Yours always

W. Telbin Esquire CHARLES DICKENS

To THE LORD CAMPBELL,[1] 3 DECEMBER 1856*

MS Brigadier Lord Stratheden and Campbell.

Tavistock House | Third December, 1856.

My Dear Lord

I cannot sufficiently thank you for your letter, which has gratified me beyond expression. Mrs. Dickens addresses a note to Lady Stratheden[2] in leaving this: and we shall look for Lady Stratheden, your daughter,[3] and yourself, on the 14th. with the greatest interest and pleasure.

My Dear Lord | Yours faithfully and obliged

The | Lord Campbell. CHARLES DICKENS

To MISS BURDETT COUTTS, 3 DECEMBER 1856*

MS Morgan Library.

Tavistock House | Wednesday Third December 1856.

My Dear Miss Coutts

I received your note this morning, and will go over the little MS[4] tomorrow, and return it by post tomorrow night.

In the meantime I *must* send you the enclosed to read, because I feel sure you will be pleased with it. Will you kindly return it, for the family archives?[5]

With kind love to Mrs. Brown

Ever Dear Miss Coutts | Most Faithfully Yours

CD.

Over

Have you disposed of your votes for the Medical officer of "The St. George's and St. James's Dispensary, King Street, Regent Street"?[6] If not, will you give them to me.

[1] John, 1st Baron Campbell (1779–1861; *DNB*), Chief Justice Queen's Bench, since 1850; known to CD through his judgment over the Booksellers' Association in 1852: see Vol. VI, 671*n*.

[2] Lord Campbell's wife Mary, daughter of Sir James Scarlett, later Baron Abinger; created Baroness Stratheden in her own right 1836.

[3] Perhaps Mary Scarlett, his eldest unmarried daughter.

[4] Of the new edn of her *Summary Account*, published 1857.

[5] Probably a letter from one of the children.

[6] 60 King St; the medical officer by 1860 was J. W. Johnstone.

To THOMAS MITTON,[1] 3 DECEMBER 1856

MS Benoliel Collection.

Tavistock House | Wednesday Third December | 1856.

My Dear Mitton

The Inspector from the Fire Office[2]—Surveyer, by the bye, they called him—duly came. Wills described him as not very pleasant in his manners. I derived the impression that he was so exceedingly dry, that if *he* ever takes fire, he must burn out, and can never otherwise be extinguished.

Next day, I received a letter from the Secretary, to say that the said Surveyer had reported great additional risk from Fire, and that the Dirctors, "at their meeting next Tuesday", would settle the Extra amount of Premium to be paid.

Thereupon, I thought the matter was becoming complicated, and wrote a common-sense note to the Secretary, (which I begged might be read to the Directors), saying that I was quite prepared to pay any extra Premium, but setting forth the plain state of the case. (I did not say that the Lord Chief Justice, the Chief Baron, and half the Bench were coming:[3] though I felt a temptation to make a joke about burning them all).

Finally, this morning comes up the Secretary to me (yesterday having been the great Tuesday), and says that he is requested by the Directors to present their compliments, and to say that they could not think of charging for any additional risk at all: feeling convinced that I would place the gas (which they considered to be the only danger) under the charge of one competent man. I then explained to him how carefully and systematically that was all arranged, and we parted with drums beating and colors flying on both sides.

Ever Faithfully
CD.

To MISS BURDETT COUTTS, 4 DECEMBER 1856

MS Morgan Library. *Address:* Miss Burdett Coutts | Meadfoot House | Hesketh Crescent | Torquay | Devon.

Tavistock House | Thursday Fourth December | 1856.

My Dear Miss Coutts

I have gone over the additional MS, and hope I have made it quite plain. I enclose my draft.[4] You will observe at the bottom of page 2, that I have used this expression:

[1] Thomas Mitton (1812–78), solicitor: see Vol. 1, p. 35*n* and later vols.

[2] The Eagle Insurance Office, to which he had paid his annual premium of £124.11.8 on Tavistock House, valued at £5,000, on 20 Nov (CD's Account-book, MS Messrs Coutts).

[3] See *To* Mrs Brown, 14 Jan 57 and *fnn*.

[4] The passage in the Preface to Miss Coutts's *A Summary Account*, new edn (1857), introduced as "The following quotation, taken from the letter of a much valued friend [*clearly CD*], whose sympathy for the working-classes is very sincere" (p. vii). The passage, within quotation-marks, is as follows: "Not only a man's own happiness, but the happiness of many others, would be much advanced by his reflecting, while yet young, that an income which is quite sufficient, or something more than sufficient for the expenses of one person, can be with difficulty eked out to cover the charges of a family; and by his considering that a few years of saving and forethought at that period of his life would lay the certain foundations of a comfortable home. Nor is it requiring

—"distinctly shewing how much a workman receiving so much pr. week at so many years of age, *could, by properly investing a steady saving from it, accumulate in five years.*"—This I suppose to be the effect of the calculation referred to?[1]

Enclosed, you will also find the Christmas No. I am the Captain of the Golden Mary; Mr. Collins is the Mate. We are out very early,[2] as I want it to get all over England Ireland and Scotland, a good fortnight before Christmas Day.

With love to Mrs. Brown | Ever Dear Miss Coutts | Most Faithfully Yours

CD.

It is freezing, thawing, and snivelling. It is also densely foggy. Nobody can stand in the streets, and nobody can quite fall. Mr. Stanfield, after undergoing unspeakable perils in the passage from Hampstead, is being held on a board fixed between two tall ladders (on account of Rheumatism, held) by two Carpenters. It is exactly like a Coat of Arms.

To JAMES DUNN,[3] 4 DECEMBER 1856

MS Goodspeed's Book Shop.

Tavistock House, London | Fourth December, 1856.

Sir.

I do not like to leave your letter without an answer under my own hand, though I have no satisfactory reply to give at present. The book[4] has been an expensive one to print, and has but very modestly repaid me for the time devoted to its composition. Being stereotyped too, it would involve some sacrifice to alter its form;[5] and it could not be cheaply issued in its present form. These considerations make me doubt the practicability, in any reason, of reducing its price until a time shall have elapsed.[6] But I am exceedingly desirous that it should be as useful as possible, and should be

too much of him to take these things to heart; because it is not to be doubted that he may be by this means enabled to establish himself in life with even less of exertion, postponement, and anxiety, than often has to be endured by his employer before he can attain the same ardently-desired end. It is of unspeakable importance to their own happiness, self-respect, and rational enjoyment of life, that the youth of both sexes among the working-classes should accustom themselves to thus much of preparation and honourable forethought before they take upon themselves the responsible duties of heads of families. Surely this would not be incompatible with that help to morality, domestic virtue, and religious habits, which many whose opinion is entitled to all respect, hold to be furnished by early marriages, notwithstanding the many privations and evils that often follow in their train." (Preface, p. viii.)

[1] After the passage above comes the gist of this sentence (not in quotation-marks), with the addition of "or ten years" followed by a tabular calculation of accumulated savings for both periods (pp. viii–ix).

[2] Apparently on same day, though advts in *HW* are still only announcements saying "Early in December".

[3] Perhaps James Dunn, engraver, 52 Myddelton St, Clerkenwell.

[4] Clearly *A Child's History*.

[5] The original 3 vol. edn, 1852–4, was priced at 10*s* 6*d*; Bradbury & Evans, anxious to improve its sales, were that month unusually advertising separate vols at 3*s* 6*d*; it was not published in one vol. at this time.

[6] The real reason was no doubt the unsold stock of the 3 vol edn which Bradbury & Evans still had on hand.

suggestive to the large class whom you so well represent. I will therefore consult my publishers on the subject, and keep your representation steadily in my mind.

Faithfully Yours

Mr. James Dunn. CHARLES DICKENS

To HERBERT FRY, 4 DECEMBER 1856*

MS National Portrait Gallery.

Tavistock House | Fourth December, 1856.

Dear Sir

I regret that I cannot comply with the request you do me the favor to prefer.[1] My wish is, to avoid sittings at all, for any sort of portrait; but if it should fall out that I cannot have my wish, I am already under conditional promises enough in the Photographic way, to haunt mankind with my countenance.

Faithfully Yours

Herbert Fry Esquire CHARLES DICKENS

To HABLOT K. BROWNE, 6 DECEMBER 1856

MS Widener Collection, Harvard.

Tavistock House | Saturday Sixth December 1856.

My Dear Browne

Don't have Lord Decimus's hand put out, because that looks condescending; and I want him to be upright, stiff, unmixable with mere mortality.[2]

Mrs. Plornish is too old, and Cavalletto a leetle bit too furious and wanting in stealthiness.[3]

Faithfully Always

CD.

[1] See *To* Fry, 15 Mar and *fn.* Those refusing a similar request included John Stuart Mill, Carlyle, Ruskin, Matthew Arnold, Mrs Gaskell and Tennyson; those accepting included Leigh Hunt and Wilkie Collins (MSS National Portrait Gallery).

[2] CD is again commenting on Browne's sketches. The changes he wanted were all made in the plates. In "The Patriotic Conference", Book II, No. XIV, Ch. 12, for Jan 57, published 31 Dec, Lord Decimus sits with Merdle on a sofa, with both hands on his knees. By this time CD had probably seen the premature adaptation of *Little Dorrit* by Frederick Fox Cooper based only on Book I and Cooper's ingenious conjectures (Lord Chamberlain's Collection, MS BL). It had run for nearly three weeks at the Strand Theatre from 10 Nov, with Neville as Mr Dorrit and Emma Wilton as Little Dorrit. For evidence that he knew it, whether from attending a performance or (more probably) hearing or reading a full account, see *To* Macready, 28 Feb 57 and *To* Hudson, 11 Apr 57, *fn.* Cooper (1806–79), manager, journalist, and minor dramatist, was responsible for several other Dickens adaptations; T. J. Taylor's *Dombey and Son* was also produced at the Strand under his management in Aug 1847, when only half the novel had been published. Both were themselves pirated in the drastically abridged *Penny Pictorial Series* (n.d.), intended for provincial actors; Malcolm Morley in *D*, L (June 1954), 136–7, who had not seen MS BL, wrongly says this version was "entirely different".

[3] "Mr. Baptist is supposed to have seen something" in the same No., Ch. 13; Cavaletto, "Mr. Baptist", looks stealthy rather than furious as he enters the Plornishes' cottage, and Mrs Plornish quite young.

To MISS BURDETT COUTTS, 6 DECEMBER 1856*

MS Morgan Library.

Tavistock House | Saturday Sixth December | 1856.

My Dear Miss Coutts.

I return the Scraps.[1] Wherever, in my proposed emendations I have made a cabalistic mark, the Printer will understand it. The last slip I have re-written—all but the last sentence—which I

can not[2]

(Beast that I am!) make out. I therefore send both the original of that slip, and the transcript: that you may supply my shortcoming.

The letter I would print, omitting your name, and also the autograph. He merely means by that odd expression, that the poor man was anxious you should have his grateful testimony *under his own hand*.[3]

I write very hastily at the end of the day, to save the post.

With love to Mrs. Brown | Ever Dear Miss Coutts | Most Faithfully Yours

CD.

To MESSRS JUSTERINI & BROOKS,[4] 8 DECEMBER 1856

MS (in Wills's hand) Professor Harry Stone.

OFFICE OF HOUSEHOLD WORDS,
8 December 1856

Mr. Charles Dickens would feel obliged to Messrs. Justerini and Brooks, if they would send *immediately* to his house, Tavistock House, Tavistock Square One dozen of the best Gin.

The bearer will pay for it.

To MISS BURDETT COUTTS, 9 DECEMBER 1856

MS Morgan Library.

Tavistock House | Tuesday Ninth December, 1856.

My Dear Miss Coutts.

I send you the last Addition enclosed.[5] I omitted to say the other day that I

[1] See *To* Miss Coutts, 9 Dec.

[2] Written very large.

[3] Probably another testimony from a working man who could not write well enough himself, perhaps given to J. Newman, builder (*Summary Account*, pp. 81–2), but which Miss Coutts must have decided to omit. The three reports mentioned contain no "odd expression", and the letter, though it opens "Dear Sir", gives Miss Coutts's name in line 2.

[4] Foreign liqueur, wine and brandy merchants, 2 Colonnade, Pall Mall, and Adelaide St, Strand.

[5] To her *Summary Account*. Perhaps the account in CD's hand (MS Dickens House; published in *D*, XXIII [1927], 106–7 as

thoroughly agree with you on that point of sending girls to school. There is a vast deal of Kayshuttleworthian nonsense[1] written, sung, and said, on that subject; and I turn into a Man-Trap on it very often, and seize unsuspicious holders-forth by the leg, when they supposed themselves to be promenading among flower beds.[2]

Beauty and the Beast are therefore united, amidst the cheers of thousands, as they were in the Story.

I should not like to give you an opinion on the arrangement of the little book, without having it complete before me. But when I have the sheets, I hope I shall put it into the most orderly and convenient form it can be made to take.

Charley will be very proud indeed of a letter from you. I shall not tell him you are going to write, in order that he may have the additional pleasure of a surprise.

You delight me by what you say of the Golden Mary. It strikes me as the prettiest Christmas No. we have had; and I think the way in which John Steadiman[3] (to whom I shall give your message) has got over the great difficulty of falling into my idea, naturally, is very meritorious indeed. Of course he could not begin until I had finished; and when he read the Wreck he was so desperately afraid of the job, that I began to mistrust him. However, we went down to Gad's Hill and walked through Cobham Woods, to talk it over; and he then went at it cheerfully, and came out as you see. I wish you would read a Petition to the Novel Writers (by him) in last week's Household Words.[4] It strikes me as uncommonly droll, and shrewdly true.

And now I come round to his Play—must do it—can't help it. I really cannot bear that it should pass over, without your seeing it.[5] Mr. Stanfield's part in the thing will never be seen again, for I am sorry to say he is getting infirm and ill. Nor do I think (if I may say so) that anything like the thing itself will ever be seen again. I have put up a wooden house at the back of the schoolroom (my own Architect!—) to help the effect, and the Stage is 30 feet long. You would be quite charmed, I think, with the girls; and there is a tenderness pervading the whole design which I believe would thoroughly interest and please you. There are no reminders in the place, for it is utterly changed and different. You would have no idea where you were. Finally, I am quite sure (you may suppose I have watched it a little), that its whole influence is softening and good, and that if Mrs. Brown could be induced to come,[6] she would afterwards be glad of having done so. Now, I don't suggest her coming when the

"Women in the Home", by CD) of education and the influence of women in the home; first shown by K.J. Fielding in *D* (XLVII), 1951, 140–2, to be not CD's original composition, but a re-writing of part of Miss Coutts's Preface (the first two-thirds of it correspond very closely—verbatim in places—to pp. xx–xxii). Fielding, above, lists five further fragments of the Preface, in Miss Coutts's hand, with corrections by CD, including the passage above, before being rewritten by CD (p. 141). A further essay in CD's hand, published by Cumberland Clark in *Dickens and Democracy and Other Studies*, 1930, pp. 42–4, as "The Condition of the Working Classes", corresponds even more closely to the Preface: the first part to pp. vi–vii; the second, which includes the passage given in *To* Miss Coutts, 4 Dec, *fn*, to pp. vii–viii.

[1] i.e. Kay-Shuttleworth's utilitarian views on education: see *To* Miss Coutts, 11 July, *fn*.

[2] Cf. his reference to "flowers on the carpets" to Henry Cole in June 54 and the allusion to *Hard Times*, Ch. 2 (Vol. VII, p. 354 and *n*).

[3] Wilkie Collins, "the Mate" of the story.

[4] "A Petition to the Novel-Writers", *HW*, 6 Dec 56, XIV, 481: a defence of the novel, with some ironical comments on women novelists.

[5] No doubt Miss Coutts was reluctant to attend, because she wished to avoid a public appearance; but see *To* Miss Coutts, 31 Dec.

[6] She did not come, still being affected by her husband's death in Oct 55, and recalling their visit to the Tavistock Theatre in June 55. But see *To* Mrs Brown, 2 Jan 57.

place would be full of people she knows; but on the night before Twelfth Night, Monday the 5th. we do it exactly as it will be done on Twelfth Night, in the minutest respect; and only our tradespeople and the Servants' relations come. Couldn't you two sit beside Mrs. Dickens that night? Do think of it. It made me quite unhappy last night, looking at Mary,[1] to reflect that you would not see something that seems so fresh and wholesome to me.

With kind love

Ever Dear Miss Coutts | Most Faithfully Yours

CD.

To THE REV. CHARLES JOSEPH GOODHART,[2] 10 DECEMBER 1856*

MS Baron Dan de Calinescu.

Tavistock House, London | Tenth December, 1856.

Mr. Charles Dickens presents his compliments to Mr. Goodheart,[3] and begs to say that his engagements prevent his acceptance of the invitation with which he is favored by the Directors of the Annual Soirée.[4]

To CLARKSON STANFIELD, 11 DECEMBER 1856

MS British Library.

Tavistock House

Thursday Night | Eleventh December 1856.

My Dear Stanny

I send an Express up to say that just now (9 o'Clock) Powell gave the alarm, just as he was going away, that the tremendous rain was making its way in on the Snow-cloth.[5] We immediately got it down on the roller, and found it (I grieve to relate) already heavily wetted in two places right down the sky in long streaks. I am taking the best precautions possible for the night, and have lighted all the Gas to dry it. I let you know at once, as I am of course most anxious that you should see it as soon tomorrow as you can.

We had not a drop of wet (as you know) through the heavy thaw; but the torrent to night was in, in one place, right across the stage back, within half an hour.

Ever affectionately

CD.

[1] She played Clara Burnham, the heroine.

[2] The Rev. Charles Joseph Goodhart (?1803–92); MA Trinity College, Cambridge, 1831; Minister, Park Chapel, Chelsea, 1852–68; Secretary, Society for Promoting Christianity among the Jews, 1863–8; published sermons.

[3] Misspelt by CD.

[4] Almost certainly the Royal Female Philanthropic Society, established 1822 for reception of first-time convicted and imprisoned young women, the ignorant and destitute, Manor Hall, West Brompton; Goodhart was Hon. Chaplain and lived near, at 1–2 Hollywood Grove, West Brompton (the Secretary in 1853 was the Rev. William Quekett: see Vol. VI, p. 269*n*). The Society had a shortfall of income in 1853.

[5] A device for producing snow, which falls throughout Act II.

To FREDERICK DICKENS,[1] 12 DECEMBER 1856

MS Huntington Library.

Tavistock House | Friday December Twelfth | 1856.

My Dear Frederick

I am very sorry to receive your letter; not only on account of the position it makes known to me, but because it forces me to write a very plain answer.

I have already done more for you than most dispassionate persons would consider right or reasonable in itself.[2] But, considered with any fair reference to the great expences I have sustained for other relations, it becomes little else than monstrous. The possibility of your having any further assistance from me, is absolutely and finally past.

Affectionately Yours
CHARLES DICKENS

To J. E. RONEY, 12 DECEMBER 1856*

MS Mr R. P. Roney-Dougal. *Address:* James E. Roney Esquire | Parthenon Club[3] | Regent Street.

Tavistock House | Twelfth December, 1856.

My Dear Roney

I was very glad to see your Card yesterday, for rumours have reached me of your having been ill. Pray let me know whether you dine with us on Christmas Day. Also that you are good for Twelfth Night.

Further. Tell me how I am to describe you in the Athenæum book, and whereof? In my uncertainty on these heads, and in my daily expectation of seeing you, I have not been able to put your name down.[4]

Faithfully Yours always
James E. Roney Esquire. CHARLES DICKENS

[1] Frederick William Dickens (1820–68), CD's younger brother: see Vol. I, p. 47*n* and later vols. He had moved from the Treasury to the War Dept Commissariat, as a second class clerk, in 1856. His relations with CD were happy and affectionate until his engagement to Anna Weller.

[2] CD had paid Frederick's debts of over £80 shortly before his marriage on 30 Dec 48 and a bill of £250 on 14 Feb 50, no doubt towards furnishing his home (Vols V, p. 424*n* and VI, p. 256*n*). He refused to guarantee a loan, probably of £600, on 26 Sep 50, but on 25 Oct 50 offered to become security for a loan of the same amount (Vol. VI, pp. 180 and *n*, 198). For Frederick's marital problems see Vol. VII, p. 361 and *n*.

[3] A convivial club at 16, Regent St: see Vol. I, p. 380 and *n*; CD was a member from 1838 to *c*. 1847.

[4] Roney was not elected to the Athenaeum.

To WILKIE COLLINS, 13 DECEMBER 1856*

MS Morgan Library.

Tavistock House
Saturday Night | Thirteenth December 1856.

My Dear Collins

Here is Tauchnitz's answer,[1] which perhaps you will give me back when you have done with it. Observe that in his English, "anything" means "something".

O[2] the ventilation question!!!!![3]

Ever Faithfully
R Wardour

To MISS BURDETT COUTTS, 13 DECEMBER 1856

MS Morgan Library. *Address:* Miss Burdett Coutts | Meadfoot House | Hesketh Crescent | Torquay | Devon.

Tavistock House
Saturday Night | Thirteenth December, 1856.

My Dear Miss Coutts

As we have now both relieved our minds on the subject of the Play, I cheerfully leave the rest to the result that opens out. I could not quite give you up without a struggle; but, having made it, I can be as quiet as a lamb. If you tell me on the morning of the Fifth that you are coming, either alone or with Mrs. Brown, I shall have the happiness of expecting you. If you do not, I shall know that you could not see your way to it—and with a perfect faith in your seeing clearly out of kind eyes, shall want no sort of explanation.

Beauty is mistaken in supposing Beast[4] to have retained any scrap of matter, either printed or in Manuscript. Beast appeals to habits of order and method as yet unchallenged by Beauty—lays his paw upon his heart—and declares upon his honor, to the best of his knowledge information and belief, "*Not Guilty*".

B was at S.B.[5] the other day, and held Committee in due form. All most satisfactory. He begs to send his love to Mrs. B (rown).

Dear Miss Coutts | Ever Yours faithfully & affecly.
CHARLES DICKENS

[1] Almost certainly relating to terms for his publication of *The Dead Secret*, Chs 1–21, as part of *Novels and Tales from HW*, Vol. 4; Chs 22–8 followed later in Vol. 5 (both in 1857). Collins's name was not given.

[2] Not underlined, but written *c.* four times its normal size.

[3] Of the theatre: see *To* Austin, 15 Oct.

[4] Continuing the joke of 6 and 9 Dec.

[5] Shepherd's Bush.

To W. C. MACREADY, 13 DECEMBER 1856†

MS Morgan Library.

Tavistock House
Saturday Evening | Thirteenth December 1856.

My Dearest Macready.

We shall be charmed to squeeze Willie's friend in—and it shall be done, by some undiscovered power of compression, on the Second Night—Thursday the 14th. Will you make our compliments to his Honor the Deputy Fiscal,[1] present him with the enclosed bill, and tell him we shall be cordially glad to see him? I hope to entrust him with a special shake of the hand, to be forwarded to our dear boy (if a hoary Sage like myself may venture on that expression), by the next Mail.

I would have proposed the first night, but that is too full.

You may faintly imagine, my venerable friend, the occupation of these also-grey hairs, between Golden Marys, Little Dorrits, Household Wordses, four stage-carpenters entirely boarding on the premises, a carpenter's shop erected in the back-garden, size always boiling over on all the lower fires, Stanfield perpetually elevated on planks and splashing himself from head to foot, Telbin requiring impossibilities of swart gasmen, and a legion of prowling nondescripts ever slinking in and out. Calm amidst the wrack, your aged friend glides away on the Dorrit stream, forgetting the uproar for a stretch of hours—refreshes himself with a ten or twelve miles walk—pitches himself head-foremost into foaming rehearsals—placidly emerges for Editorial purposes—smokes over buckets of distemper with Mr. Stanfield aforesaid—again calmly floats upon the Dorrit waters.

[a]One piece of News I have, that I think you will be pleased to hear. Lord Gardner[2] has married Miss Fortescue,[3] and they are living quietly and very happily.[a]

With my best love to Miss Macready, and to all the rest,

Ever My Dear Macready | Most affectionately Yours
CHARLES DICKENS

To MARK LEMON, 14 DECEMBER 1856

MS Benoliel Collection.

Tavistock House | Sunday, Fourteenth December | 1856.

My Dear Mark

Stanfield wants an appointment made now, for an evening "within a week or ten days of the Play", when you, he, and I, "and nobody else but the Snow-boys", may meet and give a few hours to the Snow and Ice. It seems to me that Saturday the 27th. would be a very good time. Will that suit you?

Hadn't you better send a Box here for your accumulating dress? A heavy coat of obtrusive appearance, a heavy pair of trousers, and a red shirt, which I find disport-

[1] No doubt Willie's friend's post in Ceylon, where Willie had been since 1854.

[aa] Omitted in MDGH and N.

[2] Alan Legge Gardner, 3rd Baron Gardner (1810–83): see Vol. v, p. 303 and *n*.

[3] Julia Sarah Hayfield Fortescue (1817–99), actress: see Vol. II, p. 331 and *n*; by now she had five children by him.

ing themselves on my study-chairs, will otherwise—I feel persuaded—somehow get upon Little Dorrit, to the astonishment of the Public.

Ever affecy.
CD.

To MESSRS COUTTS & CO., 15 DECEMBER 1856*

MS Fales Collection, New York University Library.

London, Fifteenth December, 1856.

Messrs. Coutts and Co.

Please deliver my banking-book to the Bearer for me.

CHARLES DICKENS

To CHARLES DE LA PRYME,[1] 15 DECEMBER 1856†

MS Free Library of Philadelphia.

Tavistock House | Monday Fifteenth December | 1856.

Dear Sir

In reply to your obliging letter, I beg to assure you that I have not the slightest reason to suppose that Andersen is coming to England at all, otherwise than that I have seen it stated in some newspapers that he is coming on a visit to me.[2] I have not heard from him these six months, and, when he last wrote, he certainly had no more idea of visiting London than of going to the Antipodes.

Faithfully Yours

C. De La Pryme Esquire CHARLES DICKENS

To MISS MARGUERITE POWER, 15 DECEMBER 1856

MS Berg Collection.

Tavistock House | Fifteenth December 1856.

My dear Marguerite

I am not *quite*[3] clear about the story—not because it is otherwise than exceedingly pretty, but because I am in rather a difficult position as to stories just now. Besides beginning a long one by Collins with the new year (which will last five or six months), I have, as I always have at this time, a considerable residue of stories written for the Christmas No.—not suitable to it—and yet available for the general purposes of Household Words. This limits my choice, for the moment, to stories that have some decided speciality (*or a great deal of story*) in them.

[1] Charles De la Pryme (1815–99), of Wistow Lodge, Huntingdon: see Vols V, 484*n* and VII, Addenda, pp. 905–6 and *nn*.

[2] Andersen did not visit CD until June 57.

[3] Doubly underlined.

But I will look over the accumulation before you come, and I hope you will never see your little friend again but in print.[1]

You will find us expecting you on the night of the 24th. and heartily glad to welcome you. The most terrific preparations are in hand for the Play on Twelfth Night. There has been a carpenter's shop in the garden, for six weeks—a painter's shop in the schoolroom—a gas fitter's shop all over the basement—a dressmaker's shop at the top of the house—a tailor's shop in my dressing room. Stanfield has been incessantly on scaffoldings for two months, and your friend has been writing Little Dorrit &c &c in corners, like the Sultan's groom who was turned upside down by the Genie.[2]

Kindest loves from all, and from me

Ever Affectionately

CD.

To WILKIE COLLINS, 16 DECEMBER 1856

MS Morgan Library.

Tavistock House

Tuesday Evening | Sixteenth December, 1856.

My Dear Collins

I send round to ascertain that you are all right. Not that I have any misgiving on the subject, for when I shook hands with you last night, you were as cool and comfortable as an unlucky Dog could be.

All progressing satisfactorily. Telbin painting on the stage. Carpenters knocking down the Drawing Room.

We are obliged to do Animal Magnetism[3] on Thursday evening at 8.[4] If you are strong enough to come, I know you will. If you are not—I know you won't.

Ever Cordially

CD.

To WILLIAM CULLENFORD,[5] 17 DECEMBER 1856*

MS Private.

Tavistock House | Wednesday Seventeenth December | 1856.

My Dear Mr. Cullenford

I am too closely occupied, to make an appointment to go into the City until after Christmas Day. But any appointment for eleven o'Clock in the forenoon that you

[1] "The Painter's Pet" did not appear until 23 May 57 (XV, 484): a sentimental tale of a little ill-treated French gipsy girl whom an eccentric English painter rescues and eventually marries.

[2] CD quotes the same story from *The Arabian Nights* in Vol. VII, p. 616 and *n*.

[3] See *To* Collins, 26 Oct, when this farce was being considered.

[4] i.e. a rehearsal; Collins was to play Gregorio.

[5] William Cullenford (1797–1874), actor and Secretary, General Theatrical Fund, since 1839: see Vol. IV, p. 467*n*.

may make for me with Messrs. Hill[1] after that day, I will attend to, on your letting me know of it.

Faithfully Yours
CHARLES DICKENS

To MESSRS. BRADBURY & EVANS, 18 DECEMBER 1856*

MS Berg Collection.

Tavistock House | Thursday Eighteenth December | 1856.

My Dear B and E.

In asking you again kindly to undertake the commission of sending Wills a big turkey and ham, I am reminded that I don't think you charged the last in our cash account. Will you remember to clear the said ham and turkey score, in the account of this Christmas?

Ever Faithfully Yours
CD.

To W. J. EASTWICK,[2] 21 DECEMBER 1856

MS Boston Public Library. *Address:* William J. Eastwick Esquire | &c &c &c | East India House.

Tavistock House | Twenty First December, 1856.

Dear Sir.

I cannot sufficiently express to you the gratification I have derived from your kindest of letters.[3] Apart from the valuable and welcome nature of its generous offer, the spirit in which that offer is made to me and the terms in which you assure me of the causes of your feeling of interest in my behalf, will always remain deeply impressed on my mind. It has been my good fortune to receive many of the greatest spontaneous rewards that can attend an author's life; but I doubt if I have ever had occasion to feel more sensible of my high privileges than I feel when with all my heart I thank you.

I do not know at what age a youth can become the subject of nomination to a cadetship. I have a boy named Alfred,[4] now educating in France—a boy of a remarkable character as a combination of self-reliance, steadiness, and adventurous spirit—whom I have always purposed to send abroad, and whom I believe to be particularly qualified for this opportunity. I have another, Francis Jeffrey,[5] now thirteen (this Alfred is eleven) for whom I should like a cadetship *next best*, but whose abilities I think more of a character to force some way of their own, peacefully, at

[1] Probably Hill & Sons, bankers and agents, 17 West Smithfield and 2 Bank Buildings, Metropolitan Cattle Market.

[2] William Joseph Eastwick (1808–89), former acting Resident at Hyderabad; Director, East India Co. 1847; Deputy Chairman 1858; member of Council of India 1858–68; author of *Lord Lytton and the Afghan War*, 1879.

[3] Eastwick may have been doing something for Walter, as well as offering to help Alfred and Frank.

[4] Alfred D'Orsay Tennyson Dickens (1845–1912), CD's fourth son.

[5] Francis Jeffrey Dickens (1844–86), CD's third son.

home. I am aware that no boy can go up for examination until he is Sixteen; but if one can be nominated so long beforehand, I should be delighted to accept your offer for one of these, and decidedly for Alfred rather than the other, supposing both to be equally available. I only mention Frank, on the chance of its being possible to nominate a boy of thirteen, and not possible to nominate a boy of eleven.

I shall be happy to call upon you at any time that may best suit your convenience. I cannot feel quite easy until I have thanked you in person. You may be as sure that I cannot forget your esteem and the proof of it (whatever the result), as that any son of mine who may owe his calling in life to you, will be honestly trained to support it with credit, and to feel a double duty in distinguishing himself.

I am My Dear Sir | Yours faithfully and truly obliged

William J Eastwick Esquire CHARLES DICKENS

To THE MARQUIS OF LANSDOWNE,[1] 21 DECEMBER 1856*

MS Private.

Tavistock House | Twenty First December, 1856.

My Dear Lord.

Will you allow me to ask you if you will have any objection to forwarding the enclosed Memorial[2] to the Prime Minister. The names appended to it, are purposely few in number; but I hope they are such as may be considered expressive on such a subject; and I know that the name to which they refer will have its own weight with you.

It is only desired that the Minister should receive the Memorial from fit hands. No acknowledgement, promise, or explanation of any sort, is solicited. His difficulties in the bestowal of literary pensions are perfectly understood; and all that is sought, is, that he should receive an earnest recommendation—but one not made in formâ pauperis—and attach such weight to such a case as his opportunities and sense of its claims on the public respect may seem to him to justify.

I am My Dear Lord | Yours always faithfully and obliged

The | Marquis of Lansdowne CHARLES DICKENS

To JOHN FORSTER, [?20–21 DECEMBER 1856]

Extract in F, VIII, i, 628. *Date:* near Christmas (see below); probably weekend, 20–1 Dec.

As Christmas approached, the house was in a state of siege. All day long, a labourer heats size over the fire in a great crucible. We eat it, drink it, breathe it, and smell it. Seventy paint-pots (which came in a van) adorn the stage; and three Dansons (from the Surrey Zoological Gardens)[3] all painting at once!! Meanwhile, Telbin, in a

[1] Sir Henry Petty-Fitzmaurice, 3rd Marquis of Lansdowne (1780–1863; *DNB*), Whig statesman; member of the Cabinet without office 1852–63.

[2] Possibly on behalf of Marguerite Power: see *To* Milnes, 4 Jan 57.

[3] One was George Danson (1799–1881), scene-painter; eight of his paintings were shown at the Surrey Zoological Gardens 1837–50 (the final one being *Napoleon's Passage of the Alps*); also exhibited four landscapes at RA. The other two were perhaps his sons, not otherwise identified.

secluded bower in Brewer-street, Golden-square,[1] plies *his* part of the little undertaking.

To THOMAS BEARD, 23 DECEMBER 1856

MS Dickens House. *Address:* Thomas Beard Esquire | Morning Herald Office | Shoe Lane | Fleet Street.

Tavistock House | Tuesday Twenty Third December 1856

My Dear Beard

I am vexed to have seen your card twice, and not to have seen you. New servant[2]—unlearned in the privileged faces.

If it should be a fine dry day next Sunday, what do you say to a walk at Gad's Hill?

Ever Faithfully

CD.

To SIR EDWIN LANDSEER, 23 DECEMBER 1856*

MS British Library.

Tavistock House | Tuesday Twenty Third December | 1856.

My Dear Landseer

Mrs. Dickens on coming home from Eastlake's last night, told me you had assured her that Lord Lyndhurst[3] would be pleased to come to the Play. I write to you immediately, as few things could give me greater pleasure than to have the soundest head I ever saw and the finest speaker I ever heard, among the audience.

I will call and leave a card for Lord Lyndhurst to day. But as it is now some years since I met him at Lord Brougham's,[4] and as you know of his desire at first hand, perhaps I had best leave the arrangement of the night with him to you.

We act four nights, and I enclose you the bills. I think the best night for Lord Lyndhurst would be either the first or the last. (The last is of an awfully judicial character, ranging from the Lord Chief Justice to the youngest of the Puisnes).[5] All I want to know, is, which night he selects; and that you must let me know *as soon as you possibly can*, in order that I may arrange accordingly; for the run upon the seats passes belief.

On any of the four nights I will make the best seat his, and shall be heartily

[1] Presumably a studio Telbin rented; he lived at 5 Rosedale Terrace, Notting Hill.

[2] Perhaps Mitchell, mentioned in CD's instructions to John Thompson for an evening party: see *To* Wills, 7 Jan 57, *fn.*

[3] John Singleton Copley, Baron Lyndhurst (1772–1863; *DNB*), Lord Chancellor for the third time 1841–6: see Vol. III, p. 297 and *n.* High Steward of Cambridge University since 1840.

[4] Henry Peter, Baron Brougham and Vaux (1778–1868; *DNB*), Lord Chancellor 1830–4: see Vol. II, p. 373*n.*

[5] Junior Judges; the youngest of the Judges who came on the last night was Sir James Shaw Willes: see *To* Mrs Brown, 14 Jan and *fnn.*

gratified by the presence of so great an intellect and so wonderful a man. Pray say as much, like Osric in Hamlet, "after what flourish your nature will".[1]

Hour, halfpast seven.

Always My Dear Landseer | Cordially Yours

Sir Edwin Landseer. CHARLES DICKENS

To MISS BURDETT COUTTS, 24 DECEMBER 1856*

MS Morgan Library. *Address:* Miss Burdett Coutts.

Tavistock House | Christmas Eve, 1856.

My Dear Miss Coutts

Many, many, many happy Christmases and New Years to both of you.

The letter weights shall have henceforth, the place of honor—and love—on my table. They take their places as Households Gods to night, and shall have but one dethronement. Beautiful in themselves—"tidy"—orderly—congenial in all such respects, they have deeper and invisible value to me, never my dear friends to be stated in words.

I will come round tomorrow about 2. You say "Stratton Street", and to Stratton Street my Compass shall direct me.

Ever Dear Miss Coutts | Most Faithfully and affecly. Yours

CHARLES DICKENS

Kindest love and regard from all here.

To THE REV. R. H. DAVIES,[2] 24 DECEMBER 1856

MS Free Library of Philadelphia. *Address:* The Reverend R. H. Davies.

Tavistock House | Christmas Eve, 1856.

My Dear Sir

I beg to thank you for your very acceptable letter—not the less gratifying to me, because I am myself the writer [a]of "The Wreck" in the Christmas Number[a] to which you refer.[3]

There cannot be many men, I believe, who have a more humble veneration for the New Testament or a more profound conviction of its all-sufficiency than I have. If I am ever (as you tell me I am) mistaken on this subject, it is because I discounten-

[1] *Hamlet*, v, ii, 176.

[2] The Rev. Robert Henry Davies (1821–1908), MA Trinity College Dublin. Incumbent of the Old Church, Chelsea, from 1855 to death.

[aa] Omitted by Forster (F, XI, iii, 820), who implies that Davies had written to CD of the hymn, "Hear my prayer, O! Heavenly Father", sung by poor Dick in "Poor Dick's Story", Harriet Parr's contribution to "The Wreck" (and later published by her in *The Congregational New Hymn Book*, 1859: see *To* Allon, 1857). This resulted in F. G. Kitton's misattribution of the hymn's authorship to CD (*Minor Writings of CD*, 1900, p. 252).

[3] Whether or not Davies had referred to the hymn, he should surely have been struck by the simple piety and God-fearingness of Capt. Ravender in CD's own description of "The Wreck": hence CD's emphatic profession of his own faith in reply.

ance all obtrusive professions of, and tradings in, Religion, as one of the main causes of real Christianity's having been retarded in this world; and because my observation of life induces me to hold in unspeakable dread and horror, those unseemly squabbles about the Letter, which drive the Spirit out of hundreds of thousands.

Faithfully Yours
CHARLES DICKENS

To MISS EMILY JOLLY,[1] 24 DECEMBER 1856

Extract in John Heise catalogue No. 2468 (1935); *MS* 1 p.; dated Tavistock House, Christmas Eve, 1856; addressed Miss Emily Jolly according to N, II, 818 (*aa*)

[a]Constant occupation since the receipt of your book,[2] has prevented my acknowledging it sooner.... I have read it with much pleasure, and find in it all the power that strongly impressed me when I first perused the story to which you refer.[a3] If I still venture to whisper counsel very similar to that which I formerly offered to you, it is because I observe it to be less needed than before, and wish to support you—as far as my poor word may—in the great advance you have made.

To WILLIAM KENT,[4] 24 DECEMBER 1856

MS Dickens House.

Tavistock House | Christmas Eve, 1856.

My Dear Sir

I cannot leave your letter unanswered, because I am really anxious that you should understand why I cannot comply with your request.

Scarcely a week passes, without my receiving requests from various quarters, to sit for likenesses, to be taken by all the processes ever invented. Apart from my having an invincible objection to the multiplication of my countenance in the Shop-Windows, I have not—between my avocations and my needful recreation—the time to comply with these proposals. At this moment there are three cases out of a vast number, in which I have said "If I sit at all it shall be to you first—to you second—and to you third". But I assure you I consider myself almost as unlikely to go through these three conditional achievements, as I am to go to China. Judge when I am likely to get to Mr. Watkins![5]

I highly esteem and thank you for your sympathy with my writings. I doubt if I have a more genial reader in the world.

Very faithfully Yours
CHARLES DICKENS

William Charles Kent Esquire.

[1] Emily Jolly, novelist; contributor to *HW* and *AYR*: see Vol. VII, p. 676*n*.

[2] *Mr. Arle*, her first novel, published 1 Nov 1856 by Hurst & Blackett. For CD's reassurance to her about it, see 10 Apr 57.

[3] No doubt "A Wife's Story", *HW*, 1–22 Sep 66, XII, 97–180: see Vol. VII, pp. 676–7, 681 and *nn*.

[4] No doubt William Charles Kent, photographer, 52 St George's Place.

[5] Herbert Watkins or his brother John, photographers, of 34 Parliament St.

To W. H. WILLS, 24 DECEMBER 1856

MS Huntington Library.

Tavistock House | Twenty Fourth December, 1856.

My Dear Wills.

Will you represent to Mr. Sala the necessity and vital importance—quite as much to himself as to Household Words—of his being punctual and faithful in the performance of the work he has undertaken.[1]

Pray take care that he distinctly understands beyond all possibility of misconception, that he can have money from you while he is at work, as he wants it;[2] and that when we come, on the completion of Due North, to close our accounts I shall arrange all things with him for his advantage, in exactly the same spirit as if he had not given me occasion to decide that Household Words must not do him the injury of accepting any further service at his hands.[3]

Faithfully Always

W. H. Wills Esquire. CHARLES DICKENS

To W. H. WILLS, 25 DECEMBER 1856*

MS Huntington Library.

Tavistock House | Christmas Day, 1856.

My Dear Wills.

All good wishes of the Season and of all good Seasons, to you and yours!

I am delighted to have the Pocket Book from you, and hope to enter much business in it of interest to us both.

Ever Faithfully

W. H. Wills Esquire CHARLES DICKENS

[1] Instalments are regular up to 3 Jan. No instalment appeared on 10 Jan 57: Sala simply sent a short Chip correcting a previous error; those on 17, 24, 31 Jan contained little further travel, and on 7 Feb there was no instalment.

[2] Sala states that he asked Wills for £10, to pay his expenses home (he had been in Brussels for some months), and this Wills sent him (*Life and Adventures of G. A. Sala*, Ch. 28).

[3] The quarrel with CD arose out of Sala's request for his travelling expenses to St Petersburgh to be reimbursed; CD had given him a monthly credit of £40, which, Sala states, left him little over his travel and living expenses; and this was regarded as the fee for his articles. CD then exercised his right of not allowing republication of "A Journey Due North". Sala gives details of the quarrel in *Life and Adventures*, Ch. 28. They were reconciled the following summer; and Sala made over 30 contributions to *AYR*.

To THE REV. WILLIAM J. FOX,[1] 30 DECEMBER 1856

Mention in Parke-Bernet catalogue No. 1190 (Oct 1950); *MS* 2 pp.; dated Tavistock House, 30 Dec 56; addressed William J. Fox.

Discussing literary matters, mentions Household Words *and Horne's*[2] Orion.[3]

To DAVID HASTINGS,[4] 30 DECEMBER 1856

MS Dickens House.

Tavistock House | Tuesday Thirtieth December 1856

Dear Sir

I ought to let you know that I don't wish to coquet about next Tuesday's play, and that if you should think it of any public interest or merit I beg you to use your own free discretion as to noticing it; not being restrained by the supposition that any privacy on that head is implied in the invitation. I have written both to Oxenford and Hogarth (who will also be here on the first night) exactly to this effect, by this same post. The Play will be seen by so many people of various conditions, that I feel it would be an affectation in me to make a mystery of it—while it would be hardly fair moreover, to the other public men who have taken pains with it.[5]

Faithfully Yours

— Hastings Esquire CHARLES DICKENS

To GEORGE HOGARTH, 30 DECEMBER 1856

MS John Rylands Library.

Tavistock House | Tuesday Thirtieth December, 1856.

My Dear Hogarth

I write today both to Oxenford and Hastings, to this effect:

That if they think the Play of any public interest or merit, I beg them to use their own free discretion as to noticing it; not being restrained by the supposition that any privacy on that head is implied in the invitation. That it will be seen, first and last, by representatives of all sorts and conditions of people, and that I feel it would be an affectation in me to make a mystery of it, while it would be hardly fair moreover to the other public men who have taken pains with it.

[1] See *To* Georgina Hogarth, 9 May 56 and *fn*. CD was probably inviting him to the play.

[2] Richard Henry (or Hengist) Horne (1803–84; *DNB*), poet and journalist: see Vol. I, p. 500*n* and later vols. Had been in Australia since June 52 (see Vol. VII, p. 8 and *n*). Now living with Jessie Taylor, by whom he had a son, Percy Hazlitt Horne, on 3 Feb 57 (*d*. 15 Sep 57); she had left him by 1862 (Ann Blainey, *The Farthing Poet*, 1968, p. 224).

[3] His epic poem, published at a farthing in 1843.

[4] Dramatic critic of the *Morning Herald*.

[5] Hastings no doubt wrote the highly appreciative review of *The Frozen Deep*, of over a column, in the *Morning Herald*, 8 Jan 57. It begins "Private theatricals have never been seen in such high and absolute perfection as at Tavistock House, the performances at which [*including* The Lighthouse] have ... created an epoch in the history of amateur efforts." CD gave Wardour "a most powerful and impressive significance", and Mary Dickens acted Clara "with a sweetness and naturalness that won the sympathies of all". Several of the "poetically conceived" effects were also noticed.

As I want you to be on exactly the same footing with them, I send you this summary of my note by the same post.[1]

Ever affecy.
CHARLES DICKENS

To JOHN OXENFORD,[2] [30 DECEMBER 1856]

Mention in *To* Hogarth, 30 Dec 56. *Date:* written same day.

To MISS BURDETT COUTTS, [31 DECEMBER 1856]*

MS Morgan Library. *Date:* clearly the Wed before the dress rehearsal of *The Frozen Deep* on Mon 5 Jan 57, to which both Miss Coutts and Lady Falmouth came; formation of "CD" supports.

Tavistock House | Wednesday Night

My Dear Miss Coutts.

Monday stands fixed. Shall Mrs. Dickens write to Lady Falmouth—or call—or how? I ask, simply because I don't want to make a fuss about it, as if it were a great thing. Will you direct me?

I fear, I cannot make sure of *myself* for Wednesday, until Friday morning. I am already half engaged.

A word as to Lady Falmouth.[3]

Ever Faithfully and affecy.
CD.

To LORD LYNDHURST, 1 JANUARY 1857*

MS W. A. Foyle.

Tavistock House | First January 1857.

My Dear Lord

I exceedingly regret that I am particularly engaged on Saturday, or I should have been most happy to have accepted your invitation.

Believe me | Very faithfully Yours

The | Lord Lyndhurst. CHARLES DICKENS

[1] Although music, not dramatic critic of the *Daily News*, Hogarth no doubt wrote the long and warm notice of *The Frozen Deep* that appeared on 7 Jan 57. He praised CD's performance as "a display of tragic power which has seldom been surpassed"; and, next to CD, he found most striking the acting of Mary Dickens as Clara and Mrs Wills as Nurse Esther.

[2] John Oxenford (1812–77; *DNB*), dramatist, critic and translator; dramatic critic on *The Times* since *c.* 1850; contributed to *HW* (see Vol. VII); wrote over 60 plays 1835–75; made many translations from German, Italian, French and Spanish. In his review in *The Times*, 7 Jan 57, he praised the power of CD's acting. For his second review, on 13 July 57, see *To* Beard, 9 July 57, *fn.* For the long review in the *Leader*, 10 Jan, see *To* Wills, 7 Jan 57, *fn.*

[3] Née Anne Frances Bankes (*d.* 1864); widow of 1st Earl of Falmouth (1787–1841; *DNB*): see Vol. VII, p. 734*n.*

To DANIEL MACLISE, [1 JANUARY 1857]

Mention in *To* Wills, 3 Jan 57.

To CLARKSON STANFIELD, 1 JANUARY 1857*

MS Benoliel Collection.

Tavistock House | Thursday, New Year's Day 1857.

My Dear Stanny

In the excitement of the G Picture[1] yesterday, I forgot that there are all those Icicles to be made.[2] Could you manage to come tomorrow afternoon—direct that operation before dinner—take your mutton with us—and then take the Rehearsal? Do if you can.

Ever Affecy.
CD.

To MRS BROWN, 2 JANUARY 1857

MS Morgan Library.

Tavistock House | Friday Second January 1857

My Dear Mrs. Brown.

Shall we say, One o'Clock tomorrow? I will be ready for you at that hour. The preparations, however, are very difficult to understand in the day; because they have been made by the Painters, for their purposes, extraordinarily ingenious, and require the Carpenters to handle them and put them together.

I should very much like you only to see a Sunset[3]—far better than anything that has ever been done at the Diorama[4] or any such place. There is a Rehearsal to night (no one here but the company), and this Sunset, which begins the play, will be visible at a quarter before 8: lasting ten minutes. If you came, you need speak to nobody but Georgina and me—and nobody need so much as see you to recognize you. But I don't press you, and don't look for any answer.

Tomorrow at One, if I don't see you in the meanwhile. That's all.

Ever Your faithful
CD.

Miss Coutts and Lady Falmouth, Catherine will expect on Monday at ½ past 7. I am delighted to hear of their coming.

[1] The large oil painting, *A Dutch blazer coming out of Monnikendam, Zuyder Zee*, painted for and presented to the Garrick Club in 1856—no doubt with a celebration dinner on 31 Dec.

[2] For Act II.

[3] A series of directions in the prompt-book refers to the sunset effect achieved by gas and red lights after Clara's entrance. During Lucy's long speech, "Lower gas, Setting Sun worked. Red light".

[4] The first Diorama in England was opened 1823 in Regent's Park, but had many lesser imitations, all in decline by the 1850s. CD may be thinking of the one at the Royal Bazaar in Oxford St, opened 1828, to which Stanfield had contributed paintings with changing light effects.

To W. J. EASTWICK, 2 JANUARY 1857

Mention in N, II, 823.

To JOHN LEECH, 2 JANUARY 1857*

MS Johns Hopkins University.

Tavistock | Second January 1857.

My Dear Leech.

Turning over the leaves of your Second Series[1] this morning with infinite pleasure, I am reminded that I have not thanked you for it. Let me do so, cordially. It is full of good things of a most admirable kind. It is not the least of its merits, or of its certain hold on long life, that it comprehends a large variety of classes.[2] Feeling thoroughly sure that nothing, however admirable, will strike root in these days and the days to come, which limits itself to the mere perishing gentilities, it is an unspeakable satisfaction to my mind when I see a man of your genius and rare power doing in this regard what *every one* of the famous lasting English men has done, without a single exception, through the whole circle of the Arts.

Very faithfully Yours always
CHARLES DICKENS

I hope you will see something very pretty and uncommon, in the Play here.

To B. W. PROCTER,[3] 2 JANUARY 1857

Text from MDGH, II, 5.

Tavistock House, January 2nd, 1857

My Dear Procter,

I have to thank you for a delightful book,[4] which has given me unusual pleasure. My delight in it has been a little dashed by certain farewell verses,[5] but I have made up my mind (and you have no idea of the obstinacy of my character) not to believe them.

Perhaps it is not taking a liberty—perhaps it is—to congratulate you on Kenyon's[6] remembrance.[7] Either way I can't help doing it with all my heart, for I

[1] *Pictures of Life and Character, From the Collection of Mr. Punch*, 2nd series of five (1854–69), published by Bradbury & Evans, Dec 56 (1857 on the title-page).

[2] All the drawings are concerned with the working classes ("some from the mining districts"), often in contrast with higher classes.

[3] Bryan Waller Procter (1787–1874; *DNB*), writer (as "Barry Cornwall") and lawyer; Metropolitan Commissioner in Lunacy 1832–61: see Vol. I, p. 314*n* and later vols.

[4] Procter's *Dramatic Scenes. With Other Poems*, published early Dec 56 (1857 on title-page), enlarged edn with illustrations. Copy inscribed by the author "Charles Dickens from his friend and admirer the Author" (Jarndyce catalogue CXIV, Winter 1993–4).

[5] "To the Lamp" and "A Farewell to Verse", the final two poems.

[6] John Kenyon (1784–1856; *DNB*), poet and philanthropist: see Vol. I, p. 554*n*; well-known to CD (see Vol. VI, p. 92). He had died on 3 Dec 56.

[7] A close friend of Procter's, he left him a handsome legacy of £6,500.

know no man in the world (myself excepted) to whom I would rather the money went.

Affectionately yours ever
[CHARLES DICKENS]

To MISS BURDETT COUTTS, 3 JANUARY 1857*

MS Morgan Library.

Tavistock House | Saturday Third January | 1857

My Dear Miss Coutts

Here is the statement. I have made it very plain, and very brief. And it certainly looks very damaging.[1]

Ever Faithfully and affecy. Yours | (With love to Mrs. Brown)
CD.

To W. H. WILLS, 3 JANUARY 1857

MS Huntington Library.

Tavistock House | Saturday Third January | 1857

My Dear Wills

I am sorry that I cannot do what Mr. Payn[2] asks. But the substitution of an uninvited visitor for an invited one, is really put out of the question by the large reserved list of friends whom we have been unable to ask for want of room. No longer ago than Thursday, I could not do exactly the same thing for my old and intimate friend Maclise. His place falling in (through his being unable to move his leg, which is injured), I could not accept his proposed substitute, but gave it to the first on our old neglected list. And I must beg to exercise the same privilege in respect of Mrs. Payn's.[2]

Ever Faithfully
CHARLES DICKENS

To JOHN FORSTER, [?3–4 JANUARY 1857]

Extract in F, VIII, i, 628. *Date:* shortly before the first performance on 6 Jan.

On the pressure for admittance. My audience is now 93, and at least 10 will neither hear nor see.[3]

[1] Presumably his first Memorandum about mismanagement at St George's Hospital, referred to in *To* Miss Coutts, 14 Jan and *fn.*

[2] Name omitted in *CD as Editor* and N. James Payn and his wife, née Louisa Adelaide Edlin; married Feb 54.

[3] It was therefore decided to increase the number of performances.

To FRANCESCO BERGER, 4 JANUARY 1857*

MS Cornell University Library.

Sunday Fourth January | 1857

My Dear Berger

Nothing can possibly be better. I thoroughly agree with you, and am delighted to hear of the Big Bell.[1]

In haste | Ever Faithfully Yours
CHARLES DICKENS

To MISS BURDETT COUTTS, 4 JANUARY 1857*

MS Morgan Library.

Tavistock House | Sunday Fourth January 1857.

My Dear Miss Coutts.

I did not return you this letter yesterday morning, as I meant to have done.

Ever Faithfully Yours
CD.

To RICHARD MONCKTON MILNES, 4 JANUARY 1857*

MS Trinity College, Cambridge.

Tavistock House, London. W.C. | Fourth January 1857

My Dear Mr. Milnes

I have received your kind cheque for Ten Pounds, in favor of Miss Power, safely.

The Emperor[2] has been written to. He did give a Convent-Dowry[3] to Ellen.[4] As I remember its amount, it was five thousand francs.

Faithfully Yours always

R. M. Milnes Esquire. CHARLES DICKENS

To W. H. WILLS, 4 JANUARY 1857

MS Huntington Library.

Tavistock House | Sunday Fourth January 1857

My Dear Wills

I have of course no other reply to your note than that I *cheerfully* acquiesce. I wish however, in thorough good humour, that you did not argue the principle with me, because it does not reasonably admit of any discussion out of myself. The less I

[1] Probably for the chimes at the end of Act I, following Nurse Esther's claim of second sight. The stage-direction (Prompt-book) reads: ... "The Chimes ring in the distance the air of 'Those Evening Bells', the piano in the next room takes up the tune...." (Thomas Moore's well-known song with accompaniment, set by Sir John Stevenson; heard on the piano several times during Act I, but only here is there a reference to chimes).

[2] Napoleon III.

[3] Untraced.

[4] Marguerite Power's younger sister.

know of the people concerned, the more unreasonable such a substitution is in my mind, and the greater the liberty *is* of so misusing an act of attention. (This remark applies solely, I need not add, to Mr. Payn.)[1] It is worth remembering that among nearly four hundred people no such thing has been thought of—except by Maclise, who expressly said in his note that he still did not consider it a kind of thing to be done.

I should like to see you sometime tomorrow morning about the Seats; which will require a little management when you have got the Theatre nearly full, and will need to be perfectly understood beforehand. I am going to Newgate-Market with Mrs. Dickens after breakfast to shew her where to buy fowls; but I shall be back directly. Shall we appoint 12 o'Clock?

I shall then have one or two things to give you for H.W. also, and a question to ask you about Frederick.

Will you impress upon Mrs. Wills from me, this last never-to-be-departed-from rule. Imagine it written in Golden Characters.

WHEN THEY APPLAUD, INVARIABLY STOP, UNTIL THE APPLAUSE IS OVER.

Ever Faithfully
CD.

Yes to the Poems[2]—too golden-haired, and marble, and all that; but meritorious I think.

To RICHARD BENTLEY, 7 JANUARY 1857*

MS Berg Collection.

Tavistock House | Seventh January 1857.

My Dear Sir

I am very much obliged to you for the curious book[3] you have had the kindness to send me. Accept my cordial thanks and all seasonable good wishes.

Faithfully Yours
CHARLES DICKENS

Richard Bentley Esquire.

To W. H. WILLS, 7 JANUARY 1857

MS Huntington Library.

Tavistock House | Wednesday Seventh January | 1857

My Dear Wills

All right. Halfpast one tomorrow!

[1] Name omitted in *CD as Editor* and N.

[2] Probably "A Daisy on a Grave", by Frances Freeling Broderip (1830–78; daughter of the poet Thomas Hood), 17 Jan 57, XV, 60; and "Gone Before", by Edmund Yates, 24 Jan 57, XV, 84: both inspired by the death of children.

[3] The most "curious" book Bentley had just published was *Letters of James Boswell, addressed to the Rev. W. J. Temple*, 18 Dec 56 (title-page 1857), in the Gad's Hill library at CD's death. The letters had been discovered in a Boulogne shop, where they were being used to wrap up parcels.

I am in perfect order. Calm—perfectly happy with the success[1]—about to make more Gin Punch. Draught of that article enormous.

Macready[2] has just been here, perfectly raging because Forster took him away, and positively shouldered him out of the Green Room Supper,[3] on which he had set his heart.

You write Diabolically plain this morning. I can't do *that*.

Ever Faithfully
CD.

To FREDERICK DICKENS, 8 JANUARY 1857

MS Benoliel Collection.

Tavistock House | Thursday January Eighth 1857

My Dear Frederick

Either Alfred[4] has made a mistake in his communication with you (of which I

[1] Of the first performance. In a long review, the *Leader*, 10 Jan, praised the play, the acting and CD as "a genuine manager, 'creating' new pieces as well as reviving old". The play's "atmospheric effects" it found "absolutely superior to those at the public theatres". CD's performance "of [*his*] most touching and beautiful part" wrote the reviewer, "might open a new era for the stage, if the stage had the wisdom to profit by it" . . . he "has all the technical knowledge and resources of a professed actor; but these, the dry bones of acting, are kindled by that soul of vitality which can only be put into them by the man of genius and the interpreter of the affections". The acting of Kate and Mary Dickens was "exquisitely pure"; Mrs Wills's Esther was played with "true feeling and subdued power". *Uncle John*, too (Buckstone's farce, 1833, substituted for *Animal Magnetism* from 8 Jan onwards), was "acted with immense spirit by all"; Lemon and Collins "delightfully aided by the refined vivacity of Miss Hogarth, the dramatic instinct of 'Miss Mary', and the fascinating simplicity of 'Miss Kate'". The review prints CD's Prologue to *The Frozen Deep*, delivered by Forster from behind the scene, in full; in 17 couplets, it begins "One savage foot-print on the lonely shore | Where one man listen'd to the surge's roar" (MS Yale University Library; given in MDGH, I, pp. 461–2). On 10 Jan 57 Sir Charles Eastlake, PRA, wrote to Collins to congratulate him, particularly on the Nurse's unfulfilled prophecy: "You have used the exciting machinery of superstitious prophecy & apparent fatalism and have still quietly exposed their fallacy." Walter Scott, he wrote, could not have thus stigmatized such prophecies. "I am", he ended, "among the warmest admirers of your play & of the accuracy & truth of the representation" (MS Morgan).

[2] He wrote to Lady Pollock, clearly after this performance: "It was remarkably, extraordinarily clever, in all respects; I mean positively so, and rendered so much more effective by the general harmony of the party. I do not wonder at your having recourse to your cambric, the performance excited me very much" (*Macready's Reminiscences*, ed. F. Pollock, 1875, II, 409).

[3] CD gave the following written instructions, no doubt to his servant, John Thompson, on 5 or 6 Jan: "HALL AND STAIRCASE. | The Inner Hall Doors must be closed as soon as the Gas is lighted, and must be kept closed all night. They must never on any account be opened while the street-door is open. The Dancing-Room Curtains are to be drawn, when the gas is lighted. | Everybody who comes, is to be shewn up into the Drawing Room to Mrs. Dickens. Hats and Cloaks are to be given up, on the Study-Landing. | WINE. | With the evening-refreshments before supper, 2 large Decanters of Sherry and 2 small decanters of Barsac may be kept on the Refreshment-table. Put no more wine there. | Mitchell or John to keep Gin Punch in ice under the table all the evening, and to give it only to myself, or Mr. Lemon. | At Supper, let there be a good supply of Champagne all over the table. No Champagne before supper: and as little Wine as possible, of any sort, before supper" (MS Mr David Low).

[4] Alfred Dickens.

know nothing but from yourself), or you have mistaken him. I asked Wills for no advice whatever, but asked him what was the present state of the kind responsibility he incurred for you, against my strong representation that I felt certain it was useless and you would abandon him. He told me how it stood, and I found you to have deserted him and Henry,[1] with a greater coolness than I had been prepared for.

Now, as this is a plain matter of fact which no representation can alter, and as my interference begins and ends with my asking for that information and leaving Wills (as he fully understands) free to do exactly what he thinks necessary, without any sort of check or influence from me, I must decline entering on the subject any further, and therefore make no appointment.

Affectionately always

Frederick Dickens Esquire C.D.

To THE DEAN OF ST. PAUL'S, 9 JANUARY 1857

MS (fragment) Yale University Library; transcribed before partial destruction in Prestwick air-crash, 1954.

Tavistock House | Friday Ninth January 1857

My Dear Dean

I have delayed this reply to your letter, awaiting the chance of some seat reverting to us by an accident, that we might offer to Miss [M'Lennan].[2] I am sorry to let you know however, after all, that I fear it will be impossible to find room for that lady. Although every seat in our little Theatre has its occupant's name upon it beforehand, we are well night distracted by the fearful accumulation of names that some undiscovered principle of compound Interest brings to bear upon the places. We acted last night to exactly the number who are coming on Monday; and the difficulty of seating them (intensified by Crinoline)[3] was so great, that I am afraid to add one more. You will understand the difficulty better, when you see the place; but I am sure I need not ask you to give me credit in the meantime for its being insurmountable.

Very faithfully Yours always

The | Dean of St. Paul's. CHARLES DICKENS

To SIR JAMES EMERSON TENNENT, 9 JANUARY 1857

MS Berg Collection. *Address: Private* | Sir James Emerson Tennent | &c &c &c | Board of Trade | Whitehall.

Tavistock House | Friday Evening | Ninth January 1857.

My Dear Tennent

I must thank you for your earnest and affectionate letter. It has given me the

[1] Henry Austin.

[2] Difficult to read; but possibly a relation of Mrs M'Lennan, of 14 Osnaburgh St, Regent's Park.

[3] The fashion had just appeared, but was not yet so general or excessive as it became.

greatest pleasure, mixing the Play in my mind, confusedly and delightfully, with Pisa—the Valetta—Naples—Herculanaeum[1]—God knows what not.

As to the Play itself; when it is made as good as my care can make it, I derive a strange feeling out of it, like writing a book in company. A satisfaction of a most singular kind, which has no exact parallel in my life. A something that I suppose to belong to the life of a Labourer in Art, alone, and which has to me a conviction of its being actual Truth without its pain, that I never could adequately state if I were to try never so hard.

You touch so kindly and feelingly on the pleasure such little pains give, that I feel quite sorry you have never seen this Drama in progress during the last ten weeks here. Every Monday and Friday evening during that time we have been at work upon it. I assure you it has been a remarkable lesson to my young people in patience, perseverance, punctuality, and order: and, best of all, in that kind of humility which is got from the earned knowledge that whatever the right hand finds to do, must be done with the heart in it, and in a desperate earnest.

When I changed my dress last night (though I did it very quickly), I was vexed to find you gone. I wanted to have secured you for our Green Room Supper, which was very pleasant. If by any accident you should be free next Wednesday night (our last), pray come to that Green Room Supper. It would give us cordial pleasure to have you there.

Ever My Dear Tennent | Very Heartily Yours
CHARLES DICKENS

To WILKIE COLLINS, 10 JANUARY 1857

MS Morgan Library.

Tavistock House | Saturday Tenth January 1857

My Dear Collins.

On second thoughts, I am afraid of wasting the spirits of the Company by calling the Dance[2] at 6 on Monday. Therefore I abandon that intention. I hope we may get it right by speaking to one another in the Dressing Room.

On Play Days (only two more! How they fly!) Mark and I dine at 3, off steak and stout, at the Cock in Fleet Street.[3] If you should be disposed to join us, then and there you'll find us.

Ever Cordially
CD.

[1] For CD, Collins and Augustus Egg travelling with the Tennents on the *Valetta* from Genoa to Naples in Nov 53 and visiting the places named, see Vol. VII, pp. 183–9.

[2] CD's acting copy of *Uncle John* (now in the Beinecke Library, Yale University) with many notes in his own hand and underlining of his own part (the title role), with cues, shows that he composed a new ending in place of the famous speech about its being "a beautiful world". Uncle John says to his friend Thomas (Mark Lemon), "... dance Sir. *Thomas* I can't. *Uncle John* You're always dancing Sir—you're never doing anything else—from morning to night, you're perpetually rolling and pitching yourself about like a Jack in the Green. Dance everybody! The comfortable polka! | *Dance and curtain.*" This may have been confined to the final performance.

[3] 201 Fleet St: see Vol. VI, p. 830*n*.

To LADY EASTLAKE,[1] 10 JANUARY 1857*

MS Öffentliche Bibliothek der Universität Basel.

Tavistock House | Saturday Tenth January | 1857

My Dear Lady Eastlake.

I must acknowledge the receipt of your kind note, because I have derived the greatest pleasure from it. No recognition of the *Art* of the representation, could be more valuable than yours and your good husband's; and you sum up in a single sentence all our aims and hopes as to the influences of that noble amusement which has unhappily been made so mean.

You make me wish now, that you could have seen something of the progress of the Play during the last two months, and of the lesson it has been to all concerned, in patience, perseverance, punctuality, order, and care in little things. I very much doubt whether the younger people concerned in it would in all their lives have been made by any other means as respectful students of Art, or would have gained from any other source so much of that humility which knows that nothing satisfactory can be done by halves or without trying hard to do it.

I hope our green curtain will not close for the last time next Wednesday night. Visions of another Play in another year, already rise before my mind's eye. If I write it myself, I shall desire no higher appreciation and sympathy to address it to, than your's and Sir Charles's—to whom I send my kind regard.

Always My Dear Lady Eastlake | Very faithfully Yours

CHARLES DICKENS

To C. H. HAZLEWOOD,[2] 10 JANUARY 1857*

MS Berg Collection.

Tavistock House, London | Tenth January 1857.

Mr. Charles Dickens presents his Compliments to Mr. Haslewood and begs to say that he cannot positively answer Mr. Haslewood's question, but that he fully believes Mr. Wilkie Collins's Frozen Deep will not be represented in the country.

To DAVID HASTINGS, 10 JANUARY 1857

Mention in N, II, 826.

[1] Née Elizabeth Rigby (1809–93; *DNB*), authoress: see Vol. VII, p. 95*n*.

[2] Misspelt by CD. Colin Henry Hazlewood (1823–75), dramatist and stage-manager: see next vol.

To J. T. LOVEDAY,[1] 10 JANUARY 1857

Extract in Sotheby's catalogue, Oct 1980; *MS* 2 pp.; addressed James Thomas Loveday; dated Tavistock House, 10 Jan 57.

Regretting that his avocations have obliged him to forego all public engagements, but assuring him that his letter needs no shadow of apology. . . . My only refuge against the numerous solicitations I receive, is in an unvarying rule that admits of no exception. Without it, I could not do what I have to do, with the necessary freedom of mind, or with the indispensable aids of rest and recreation.

To CLARKSON STANFIELD, 11 JANUARY 1857*

MS British Library.

Tavistock House | Sunday Eleventh January | 1857.

My Dear Stanny

I forgot;—I am obliged to go to Gad's Hill to day. Therefore I send Catherine up to see after you, and to bring me back the fullest particulars about you she can get together. I trust and hope my dear fellow you are by this time growing so much better, as to see a good chance of being able to come on Wednesday. You shall not go behind, but shall have a snug invalid seat, out of all draughts and difficulties.

Telbin was faithful at his post on Thursday night, and looked after you with the greatest care. Everything went to perfection.

Of course you are not to trouble yourself to write any answer to this, except what Catherine will bring me by word of mouth.

Ever affectionately

CD.

To BENJAMIN WEBSTER, 12 JANUARY 1857*

MS New York University Library.

Tavistock House | Monday Twelfth January | 1857.

My Dear Webster

You were obliged to go away the other night, before I could see you. Wednesday is our last night. Will you come and join the Green Room Supper after the play, and be jovial for an hour or so?

Ever Faithfully

CHARLES DICKENS

Benjamin Webster Esquire.

[1] James Thomas Loveday, undertaker, 9 Cleveland St, Mile End Rd.

To FRANCESCO BERGER, 13 JANUARY 1857

Facsimile in Francesco Berger, *Reminiscences, Impressions and Anecdotes*, 1913, p. 30.

Tavistock House | Tuesday Thirteenth January | 1857.

My Dear Berger.

Will you do me the favor to accept the little memorial[1] I send with this, in remembrance of our pleasant play and the obligations it owes to you. I can never forget the pains you have taken with it, or the spirit and genius with which you have rendered it high service.[2] I hope these slight ornaments may lie lightly on your breast during some part of a brilliant career, and I heartily assure you that your fortunes will always be full of interest to me.

Very faithfully Yours

Francesco Berger Esquire CHARLES DICKENS

To MR. ELLIS,[3] 13 JANUARY 1857*

MS Mitchell Library, Sydney.

Tavistock House | Thirteenth January | 1857.

Mr. Charles Dickens presents his compliments to Mr. Ellis, and begs to acknowledge the receipt of Mr. Ellis's obliging proposal. He cannot entertain it, however, as he has no intention of sitting to any one. If he had, several friends of his, who are artists, would have a prior claim upon him and would naturally have his preference.

To MRS BROWN, 14 JANUARY 1857

MS Morgan Library. *Address:* Mrs. Brown | Meadfoot House | Hesketh Crescent | Torquay | Devon.

Tavistock House | Wednesday Fourteenth January | 1857.

My Dear Mrs. Brown.

The letter printed in the little paragraph[4] I return, is perfectly delightful. The ship is true to her name, and I trust in God will go about the world prosperously, doing good, as long as she floats.[5] It is one of those exquisitely touching and affecting things that make one smile and cry together.

I do not myself doubt the good result of the enquiry at the Hospital; nor do I, I must add, doubt the gentlemen engaged in it. If there be a conscientious and

[1] A set of three shirt-front studs, with diamonds set in blue enamel, each engraved on the back "C.D. to F.B." (Francesco Berger, *Reminiscences, Impressions & Anecdotes*, [1913], p. 31).

[2] Berger's music was highly praised in the *Daily News*, 7 Jan, by George Hogarth (see 30 Dec 56 and *fn*): "There was a beautiful overture, with some effective melodramatic music, by Mr Francesco Berger, a younger composer of much merit, nicely performed by a small chamber orchestra consisting of first-rate players." His incidental music was also praised in the *Leader*, 10 Jan, for its "perfect fidelity of expression".

[3] Possibly "H. Ellis", or "Thomas Ellis", who each exhibited one or two pictures at RA in early 1850s.

[4] Not traced; perhaps connected with Mrs Brown's Exhibition at St George's Hospital.

[5] Probably metaphorical; unlikely to be a real ship.

humane body of men in existence, I am convinced they are to be found among the honorable and upright medical men who have attained eminence in London. Whatsoever I have seen of them has won my utmost respect; and I am all but sure that those of them who are associated with St. George's Hospital can have no desire but to do their duty. Consequently I have a strong trust in their putting this matter right for the future—just as I have in your scholarship helping to raise up worthy successors to them.[1]

I am delighted to hear that Mr. Marjoribanks[2] was so much pleased by the Play. Its effect on the three other audiences we have had, has been the same; and I certainly have never seen people so strongly affected by theatrical means. To night is our closing night. By an absurd coincidence three fourths of the Judges I know, preferred this night to another. Please to imagine the Lord Chief Justice,[3] the Lord Chief Baron,[4] Mr. Baron Bramwell,[5] and Mr. Justice Willes,[6] all sitting on the front row to night, to try the case. Cockburn[7] the new Chief Justice of the Common Pleas, rather spoils the effect of the absurdity by having been here on Monday. He wouldn't go after the Play, but would come and make speeches at the Green Room Supper. I never saw anything better of its kind than the genuine and hearty way in which, without the least affectation, he shewed his pleasure.

Ever Dear Mrs. Brown | Faithfully Yours

CD.[8]

To MISS BURDETT COUTTS, 14 JANUARY 1857†

MS Morgan Library. *Address:* Miss Burdett Coutts | Meadfoot House | Hesketh Crescent | Torquay | Devon.

Tavistock House | Wednesday January Fourteenth | 1857.

My Dear Miss Coutts

I was at the Home yesterday, and found the favorable change in the poor girl still continuing. Her constitution is evidently poor and weak, and I doubt her ever entirely recovering. But there seems to be every hope, now, that she will get the better of this attack. She is almost as weak as she *can* be, but is happy in not suffering, and is very grateful. The impression made by her illness on the rest appears to have been very good, and they have all shewn great sympathy.

You do not send me the note you received from the Hospital.[9] Neither do I send you my second Memorandum of the circumstances, supposing you not to want it,

[1] See *To* Mrs Brown, 8 Aug 56, and *fn.*

[2] Edward Marjoribanks (1776–1868), banker, former senior partner in Coutts's Bank: see Vol. I, p. 527 and *n.* CD probably first met Miss Coutts at his house in 1838 or 1839, but date not known.

[3] Lord Campbell: see 3 Dec 56, *fn.*

[4] Sir J. F. Pollock (1783–1870; *DNB*), Chief Baron of the Exchequer 1844–66: see Vol. VI, p. 393*n.*

[5] Sir George William Wilshere Bramwell (1808–92; *DNB*), Judge of the Exchequer 1856; Lord Justice 1867–81.

[6] Sir James Shaw Willes (1814–72; *DNB*), Judge of Common Pleas 1855.

[7] Sir Alexander James Edmund Cockburn (1802–80; *DNB*), Chief Justice of Common Pleas 1856; Lord Chief Justice 1859.

[8] Letter endorsed: "... Returning paragraph. Concerning the Ship. Angela Burdett Coutts | Meadfoot House."

[9] St George's.

after having spoken with Mr. Barlow.[1] I will keep it by me of course. It is not exactly the same as the first, for I dare say I do not remember the exact form and sequence of the words in which I wrote it; but it is, of course, substantially the same.

You may remember my conveying to you in Whitehall Gardens,[2] my impression of the truth, exactly to the effect of what Mr. Barlow tells you—namely, that there was nothing wrong in the place, and probably nothing wrong in its arrangements, if the officials entrusted with them were properly looked after.

I have received this morning (by the Post which brought me your letter) the enclosed from Clara Novello.[3] Do you happen to have any sort of presentation available, now or presently, that you think would suit such a case?

We are in a mighty bustle for our closing performance tonight. The impression that the Play has made, has been delightfully strong.[4] I certainly have never seen Audiences so affected. Your suggestion to Mrs. Dickens I immediately carried out. Your friend now chops down pieces of wood with the letters carved upon them.[5]

Ever Dear Miss Coutts | Most Faithfully Yours

CD.

To THE COUNTESS GIGLIUCCI, 14 JANUARY 1857*

MS Brotherton Library, Leeds.

Tavistock House | Wednesday Fourteenth January | 1857.

My Dear Genius

I am afraid Miss Coutts has no presentation that will do for the poor boy.[6] I have, however, written to her to day (she is at Torquay) asking her if she can do any thing for the case. You shall know her reply, as soon as I receive it. My impression is, that she has no means of help at hand.

What you say of the humility to be learnt from the over-ready acceptance of mediocrity and incapacity, is as true as—your singing. There are few things more discouraging, in the whole round of the Arts.

[1] Perhaps, as CD's later charge of mismanagement at the hospital (see *To* Miss Coutts, 3 Feb) concerned a death, William John Barlow, Superintendent Registrar of births, deaths and marriages, 40 Holford Sq.

[2] At Lady Falmouth's.

[3] Clara Anastasia Novello, Countess Gigliucci (1818–1908; *DNB*), fourth daughter of Vincent Novello, music publisher, leading oratorio and opera soprano; made her debut at 14; soon, leading soprano at all important English concerts; sang in Germany; first appeared in opera in Italy 1841, with immense success; Nov 43 married Count Gigliucci, Governor of Fermo, near Rome, where she had been detained under arrest owing to her agent's mismanagement. Lived in Italy; then re-appeared in London and Milan 1850–6; sang at reopening of Crystal Palace 1854 and at Handel Festival there 1859; retired 1860.

[4] Writing to a friend on 15 Jan, William Howitt recorded: "I think Dickens as great an actor as a writer. Thackeray, who was there, said—'If that man would go upon the stage he would make his £20,000 a year'" (George Smith's typescript "Recollections", National Library of Scotland).

[5] Near the end of Act II Wardour cuts up Frank's berth for fuel, finds the initials of Clara and Frank and therefore starts questioning Frank. The improvement must be that the letters are actually on the wood and can be seen by the audience.

[6] Probably Richard, Mrs Warner's son; "Poor Richard" in *To* The Countess Gigliucci, 3 Feb: see *To* Miss Coutts, 8 Apr 56 and *fn*.

With my kind regard to Count Gigliucci. Believe me always

Very faithfully Yours
CHARLES DICKENS

Our Audiences have been excellent, with a wonderful power of crying. We finish tonight.

To THE HON. MRS RICHARD WATSON, 16 JANUARY 1857

MS Huntington Library.

Tavistock House | Sixteenth January 1857.

My Dear Mrs. Watson

Though in the depressed agonies of smashing the Theatre, I must in half a dozen words thank you for your kind note of this morning.

I never can tell you how much I regret your absence. I believe that nothing so complete will ever be done again; and I had made up my mind (and had often said so here), to surprise you—you especially.

My only comfort is, that the dear children may be considered well again. But I shall never separate from the Frozen Deep, the drawback of your not having seen it.

Kind love from all, | Ever Faithfully Yours
CHARLES DICKENS

To LOUIS HACHETTE, 17 JANUARY 1857

MS Librairie Hachette.

Tavistock House, London
Saturday Seventeenth January | 1857

My Dear Sir

I have been so much occupied with other matters since the receipt of your letter, that I have not had time to answer it until to day.[1] I do so in few words, wishing to avoid the delay of another Post.

Enclosed is the Address to be prefixed to the Translated series, and which you will of course cause to be translated into French.[2] I hope you will agree with me that it says, briefly, all that is necessary.

Your account of the excellent revision the translations have undergone, gives me great pleasure. I do not doubt that they will be admirably done, after so much care, and under the excellent superintendence of M. Lorain.[3]

[1] See 14 Jan 56.

[2] "L'Auteur Anglais Au Public Français", signed by CD and dated London, 17 Jan 57, appears before the text of *Nicholas Nickleby*, Vol. 1, 1857; it was translated from CD's "Address | of the English Author | *To* The French Public", which immediately follows it. "The present translation", wrote CD, was proposed to him "in a manner equally spirited, liberal and generous. It has been made with the greatest care, and its many difficulties have been combated with unusual skill, intelligence and perseverance." (MS Librarie Hachette.)

[3] Paul Lorain (1799–1861), an old friend of Louis Hachette's; Professor of Latin Rhetoric, l'École normale 1830; Rector, Academy of Lyon; his books include *Mémoire sur l'Université d'Oxford*, Paris, 1850; directed translations

Accept my dear Sir the assurance of my high regard, and Believe me

Always | Yours faithfully

Monsieur L. Hachette. CHARLES DICKENS

To WILKIE COLLINS, 19 JANUARY 1857

MS Morgan Library.

Tavistock House | Monday Nineteenth January | 1857.

My Dear Collins

Will you come and dine here, next Sunday at 5?

There is no one coming but a poor little Scotchman domiciled in America[1]—a musical composer and singer—who brought me a letter yesterday from New York, and quite moved me by his simple tale of loneliness. He is Davy Roberts,[2] softened by trouble—with all the starch out of his collar, and all the money out of his Bank. O reaction, reaction!—

Ever Faithfully

CD.

To THE REV. GEORGE WILKINSON,[3] 19 JANUARY 1857

MS Texas University Library. *Address* (*The A. Edward Newton Collection*, Parke-Bernet Catalogue, 18 Apr 1941)*:* The Reverend George Wilkinson | Rectory | Whicham | Whitehaven.

Tavistock House, London | Nineteenth January 1857.

Dear Sir

I highly esteem your confidence, and wish it were in my power to return any hopeful or useful reply to your enquiry. I cannot, however, offer you any advice on the subject. I hear (as you do) on high and learned authority, that there need no longer be delays in Chancery.[4] Highly gratifying and convincing perhaps; but if that pestilent Court cannot, or do not, make its own agents do their duty, it is, in my poor opinion, body and soul a Humbug. Against such a dragon I know no remedy but a Saint George.

Faithfully Yours

The Reverend George Wilkinson CHARLES DICKENS

of Bulwer Lytton for Hachette as well as CD, and himself translated *Nicholas Nickleby*, which opened the series. CD describes him in his "Address" as "an accomplished gentleman perfectly acquainted with both languages, and able, with a rare felicity, to be perfectly faithful to the English text while rendering it in elegant and expressive French." (MS *ibid.*)

[1] Untraced.

[2] Name omitted in all previous texts; but CD simply means that the man's appearance reminds him of David Roberts, the painter.

[3] The Rev. George Wilkinson (?1782–1865), BD St John's, Cambridge, 1833; Rector of Whicham, Cumberland, 1847–65; antiquary.

[4] CD clearly does not believe it.

To WILLIAM TELBIN, 19 JANUARY 1857

MS Free Library of Philadelphia.

Tavistock House
Monday Evening | Nineteenth January 1857

My Dear Telbin.

It is an odd coincidence that I had actually dipped my pen in the ink to write this note to you, when your note was brought to me. It came quite Providentially, to enable me to give this a new turn. And the turn shall be on the stereoscope glass.

Our servants have been discharged on suspicion of breaking that valuable article, and the Policeman on duty that night has been suspended for the same dread reason. As you appear on your own confession to be the culprit, the sentence of the Court on you is, that you receive from the Court's bookbinder (the Court supposes in about a fortnight) a complete set of the Court's books;[1] and that you read the same as often as your constitution can possibly bear that punishment without fatal consequences.

Plainly, I have asked my binder to put up a set, in a cheerful serviceable dress that I always use myself; in order that I might have the pleasure of asking you to accept them with my kindest regard. Perhaps you will put the accompanying leaf into one of them.

And believe me that if I lose sight of you soon, the fault shall be yours and not mine. Mrs Dickens, her sister, my daughters, son, everybody, send you their cordial remembrance.

Faithfully Yours always
William Telbin Esquire CHARLES DICKENS

To THE REV. CHAUNCY HARE TOWNSHEND, [?19 JANUARY 1857]

Mention in *To* de Cerjat, 19 Jan 57. *Date:* probably written the same day.

To W. W. F. DE CERJAT,[2] [19] JANUARY 1857

MS Berg Collection. *Date:* CD's mistake; Monday was 19 Jan 57. *Address:* A Monsieur W. W. F. de Cerjat | Elysée | Lausanne | Switzerland.

Tavistock House, London
Monday Night | Seventeenth January 1857.

My Dear Cerjat.

So wonderfully do good (epistolary) intentions, become confounded with bad execution, that I assure you I laboured under a perfect and most comfortable conviction that I had answered your Christmas Eve letter of 1855. More than that—in spite of your assertion to the contrary, I still strenuously believe that I did so! I have more than half a mind (Little Dorrit and my other occupations notwithstanding), to

[1] Presumably the Cheap edn, 1st series, 9 vols, 1847–52.

[2] William Woodley Frederick de Cerjat (*d.* 1869), one of the circle of CD's friends in Lausanne in Summer 1846: see Vol. IV, p. 574*n*.

charge you with having forgotten my reply!! I have even a wild idea that Townshend reproached me, when the last old year was New, with writing to you instead of to him!!! Wait till I come back to Elysée,[1] and we will argue it out—as well as we can argue any thing without poor dear Haldimand.[2] In any case, however, don't discontinue your annual letter, because it has become an expected and a delightful part of the season to me.

With one of the prettiest houses in London,[3] and every conceivable (and inconceivable) luxury in it, Townshend is voluntarily undergoing his own sentence of transportation at Nervi—a beastly little place near Genoa where you would as soon find a herd of wild elephants in any Villa, as Comfort. He has a notion that he must be out of England in the winter; but I believe him to be altogether wrong (as I have just told him in a letter), unless he could take his Society with him.

Talking of Society, two things arise in my mind.

Firstly, when you offered your respected Pastor[4] that testimonial, why didn't you make it conditional on his lowering his shirt-collar behind? I don't think a man with that article of dress scraping the hair off the crown of his head ought to have a testimonial.

Secondly, workmen are now battering and smashing down my Theatre here, where we have just been acting a new play of great merit, done in what I may call (modestly speaking of the getting-up, and not of the acting), an unprecedented way. I believe that any thing so complete, has never been seen. We had an act at the North Pole, where the slightest and greatest thing the eye beheld, were equally taken from the books of the Polar Voyagers.[5] Out of 30 people, there were certainly not 2 who might not have gone straight to the North Pole itself, completely furnished for the winter. It has been the talk of all London for these three weeks. And now it is a mere chaos of scaffolding, ladders, beams, canvass, paint pots, sawdust, artificial snow, gas pipes, and ghastliness. I have taken such pains with it for these ten weeks in all my leisure hours, that I feel, now, shipwrecked—as if I had never been without a Play on my hands, before.

A third topic comes up, as this ceases.

Down at Gad's Hill near Rochester in Kent—Shakespeare's Gad's Hill, where Falstaff engaged in the robbery[6]—is a quaint little country house of Queen Anne's time.[7] I happened to be walking past it, a year and a half or so ago, with my Sub Editor of Household Words,[8] when I said to him "You see that house? It has always a curious interest for me, because, when I was a small boy down in these parts, I thought it the most beautiful house (I suppose because of its famous old Cedar

[1] L'Elysée, a large country-house above Lausanne and the lake, rented by the Watsons in Summer 1846: see Vol. IV, p. 560 and *nn*.

[2] William Haldimand (1784–1862) of Lausanne: see Vol. IV, p. 574 and *n*.

[3] 21 Norfolk St, Park Lane.

[4] The Rev. Isaac Cheesbrough, Minister of the English church at Lausanne from 1846; CD had commented on his cravat in Nov 46: see Vol. IV, p. 667 and *n*.

[5] Particularly Sir John Franklin's two *Narratives of his Journeys to Shores of the Polar Sea*, 1823 and 1828; and Sir John Richardson's *Journal*, 1851.

[6] Falstaff and his followers robbed the travellers near Gad's Hill, and in turn ran away from Prince Hal and Poins, in *1 Henry IV*, II, ii.

[7] In fact, George III's; built in 1779/80 by James Stevens, a self-made man and well-known local character, who became Mayor of Rochester.

[8] See Vol. VII, p. 531 and *nn*; though there are differences in the two accounts.

Trees) ever seen. And my poor father used to bring me to look at it, and used to say that if I ever grew up to be a clever man, perhaps I might own that house, or such another house. In remembrance of which, I have always in passing, looked to see if it was to be sold or let; and it has never been to me like any other house, and it has never changed at all." We came back to town, and my friend went out to dinner. Next morning he came to me in great excitement, and said, "It is written that you were to have that house at Gad's Hill. The lady[1] I had allotted to me to take down to dinner yesterday began to speak of that neighbourhood. 'You know it?' I said 'I have been there to day'. 'O yes', said she,'I know it very well; I was a child there, in the house they call Gad's Hill Place. My father was the Rector, and lived there many years.[2] He is just dead, has left it to me, and I want to sell it'. So," says the Sub Editor,"you must buy it. Now or never!"—I did, and hope to pass next Summer there; though I may perhaps let it afterwards, furnished, from time to time.

All about myself, I find, and the little sheet nearly full! But I know, my dear Cerjat, the subject will have its interest for you. So I give it its swing. Mrs. Watson was to have been at the Play, but most unfortunately had three children sick of Gastric Fever, and couldn't leave them. James[3] was here. She was here herself some three weeks before, looking extremely well in the face but rather thin.—I have not heard of your friend Mr. Percival Skelton; but I much misdoubt an Amateur Artist's success in this vast place.[4]—I hope you detected a remembrance of our happy visit to the Great St. Bernard, in a certain No. of Little Dorrit?[5] Tell Mrs. Cerjat[6] with my love, that the opinions I there expressed to her on the subject of Cows, have become matured in my mind by experience and venerable age; and that I denounce the race as Humbugs—who have been getting into Poetry and all sorts of places, without the smallest reason. The best thing they do, is Shoeing-Horns, and those you can make of brass—to say nothing of Gutta Percha.—Haldimand's housekeeper is an awful woman to consider. Pray give him our kindest regard and remembrance, if you ever find him in a mood to take it. "Our" means, Mrs Dickens's, Georgina's, and mine. We often, often, talk of our old days at Lausanne, and send loving regard to Mrs. Cerjat and all your house. We saw Miss Forbes's[7] death in the Paper. She wasn't half [a]old enough, I thought. Adieu my dear fellow. Ever Cordially Yours CD.[a]

[1] Eliza Lynn, later Mrs W. J. Linton.

[2] The Rev. James Lynn (1776–1855) had bought Gad's Hill Place and remained its owner while Rector of Caldbeck, Cumberland, 1813 to his death. Eliza lived there 1833–8. See *ibid.*

[3] A "Mr James" whose brother evidently had a small part in the Rockingham theatricals in Jan 51 (Vol. VI, p. 250 and *n*); but nothing known of him; since Cerjat knows him, he must have visited Lausanne.

[4] Skelton (of Upper Norwood), in fact, had two pictures exhibited at RA 1850: *Gipsy Encampment* and *Market Day*.

[5] See *To* Mrs Watson, 7 Oct 56 and *n*.

[6] Maria, daughter of Peter Holmes of Peterville, co. Tipperary: see Vol. IV, p. 574*n*.

[7] One of the "two old ladies", sisters, living near the church in Lausanne, the subject of CD's amusing "gossip" to Forster in Oct–Nov 46: see Vol. IV, pp. 651 and *n*; CD had joked about the age of those "damask-eyed virgins" (see p. 664).

[aa] Written above address on p. 1 through lack of space.

To JOHN FORSTER, [20 JANUARY 1857]

Extract in F, VIII, i, 628. *Date:* 20 Jan 57, according to Forster.

He described the workmen smashing the last atoms of the theatre.

To THE REV. EDWARD TAGART, 20 JANUARY 1857

MS Berg Collection.

Tavistock House | Tuesday Night | Twentieth January 1857

My Dear Mr. Tagart.

All that is personal to me and mine in your affectionate note, is so delightfully earnest, that I cannot refrain from thanking you for it and telling you that I know it has given me exactly the pleasure you designed it to convey. It gratified me exceedingly to hear from Mrs. Dickens that you were evidently pleased and moved by the Play. I had hoped to shake hands with you when I came upstairs, and that was the best substitute you could have left behind. Of course it (I come to the Play again) was a great trouble, but a labor of love. I very much doubt, apart from its being a lesson in patience, order, punctuality, and perseverance; and being a bond of union among all concerned; whether (so prepared and done) it is not about the best training in Art and respect for Art, that my young people could receive. When we do another ("when will that be, says the bell of Step-ney!")[1] I should like you to see the preliminary process, and judge for yourself.

Now to Mrs. Williams.[2] Let me say to you, in the perfect confidence I may impose upon you, that I am not at all likely, with my own concurrence, to see her. *I do not believe that narrative*. I unhesitatingly say to you that I do not believe it. Even allowing for some large suppression, I still do not believe it. I recommend you to be extremely cautious. I know of three incredible women, either of whom might be this person; one of whom I strongly suspect to be this person. Mind! I never saw any of these particular statements before, and have no direct reason (but their own want of basis and coherence) for discrediting them. It is true that I never heard the faintest reference from Macready to any such lady; but that might be, and her story might still be strictly true. But, in the case of the particular female monstrosity to whom I have specially referred, there were characteristics exactly answering to those which have interested you; and there was a narrative, in its general features sufficiently like this (to one, as I am, in the habit of constructing fictions and curiously watching them), to awaken great suspicion. You have here my whole reasons for recommending you to be very careful. They are twofold. First, as I might mistrust a strong personal likeness to a bad person, I mistrust the strong general resemblance I perceive here to a bad case, in which Forgery was one of the commonest elements. Secondly, if I had met with this lithographed narrative anywhere, I should have said, "On the face of it, highly suspicious and extremely improbable."

This is for your own guidance and self-restraining if you think right,—and it may be all wrong. I would write it to few other people. If with this caution any new

[1] From "Oranges and Lemons", the singing game.

[2] Mrs Williams and her stories have not been traced.

circumstances of doubt should come before you—let me know what it is, and it may piece into my previous knowledge.

Ever Faithfully Yours
CD.

P.S. My eye falls on the Lithograph as I fold this note.

Do you know the "London Bank Threadneedle Street",[1] where "the Memorial with the Government Endorsement" is to be seen? *I* don't.

Do you know of any state of the English law which, proving Bigamy against Mr. Seymour, would have failed to nullify the second marriage?—I don't.

Do you see any sort of allusion to the friends to whom she "fled" in March 1849—or to the place where she lived as Mr. Seymour's wife—or to the place from which she married—or to the situation of her property which he nefariously got hold of—or to the means by which she gained, either her "terrible suspicion" or her "dreadful certainty" within seven days of her marriage—or any tangible reference to "the many eminent persons" in England and France, who know her history? Have you ever been face to face with one such, who can vouch for it?

To MRS MORGAN,[2] 21 JANUARY 1857

MS Charles W. Traylen.

Tavistock House | Twenty First January 1857.

Mr. Charles Dickens presents his compliments to Mrs Charles Morgan, and begs to express his regret that her letter is one of an incredible number, in reference to which he can only assure the writers that he is unable to serve the objects in which they are benevolently interested, and that he will respect their confidence.

To W. J. ADAMS,[3] 28 JANUARY 1857*

Facsimile in B. Altman & Co. catalogue.

Tavistock House | Wednesday Twenty Eighth January | 1857

Dear Sir

Allow me to thank you for your very obliging note which I have received with much pleasure, and for the very useful London Guide and Hand Book accompanying it.[4] Such a volume was much wanted and will, I have no doubt, be extensively purchased.

Faithfully Yours
CHARLES DICKENS

William James Adams Esquire

[1] i.e. the Bank of England.

[2] Possibly the wife of Charles Morgan, Esquire, of East St, Maidstone.

[3] William James Adams (1809–73), publisher; published *Bradshaw's Railway Guide* from 1841, and several guides and handbooks by Edward Litt Leman Blanchard.

[4] Blanchard's *Bradshaw's Guide through London and its Environs*, W. J. Adams, 1857.

To THOMAS BEARD, 28 JANUARY 1857

MS Dickens House. *Address:* Thomas Beard Esquire | 42 Portman Place | Edgeware Road | W.

Tavistock House | Wednesday Twenty Eighth January 1857

My Dear Beard

Will you "make a note,"[1] to the effect that you dine with me on my Birthday, Saturday Week the 7th. of February? I will let you know whether we dine at Gravesend[2] or at home here: which will mainly depend on the weather. In the first-named contingency, how is the foot?

Ever Faithfully
CD.

To SIR EDWARD BULWER LYTTON,[3] 28 JANUARY 1857

MS Lytton Papers.

Tavistock House | Wednesday Twenty Eighth January | 1857.

My Dear Bulwer

Hachettes gave me £350 for my consent to a complete translation of my books to this time.[4] And they are to have the same right in respect of forthcoming books (if they choose to claim it), at the rate of £40 each. They are a very large house, and have a place of business, over the water in old Paris,[5] quite as extensive, I should say, as Longmans.[6]

I thought Wills had told you as to the Guild[7] (for I begged him to), that we can do absolutely nothing until our Charter is 7 years old. It is the stringent and express prohibition of the Act of Parliament[8]—for which things you Members, thank God, are responsible and not I. When I observed this clause (which was just as we were going to grant a pension, if we could agree on a good subject), I caused our counsel's opinion to be taken on it. And there is not a doubt about it. I immediately recommended that there should be no expences—that the interest on the Capital should be all invested as it accrued—that the chambers should be given up and the Clerk discharged—and that the Guild should have the use of the household Words office rent free, and the services of Wills on the same terms. All of which was done.

A letter is now copying, to be sent round to all the Members, explaining, with the New Year, the whole state of the thing. You will receive this. It appears to me that it looks wholesome enough. But if a strong Idiot comes and binds your hands, or mine, or both, for 7 years, what is to be done against him?

As to greater matters than this, however—as to all matters on the face of this teeming earth—it appears to me that the House of Commons and Parliament

[1] Like Capt. Cuttle in *Dombey & Son*.

[2] At Wates's Hotel.

[3] Sir Edward George Earle Lytton Bulwer Lytton, Bart, later 1st Baron Lytton (1803–73; *DNB*): see Vol. I, p. 337*n*.

[4] See *To* Forster, 30 Jan 56; although he there says £440.

[5] At Rue Pierre-Larrazin, 14.

[6] Longmans published from 38–41 Paternoster Row.

[7] The Guild of Literature and Art, set up in 1851 by CD and Bulwer Lytton: see Vol. VI, *passim*.

[8] The private Act incorporating the Guild, of 2 June 54: see Vol. VII, p. 330 and *n*.

altogether, is just the dreariest failure and nuisance that ever bothered this much bothered world.

Ever Yours
CD.

I duly forwarded your letter to the Secretary of the Dramatic Authors.[1]

To W. C. MACREADY, 28 JANUARY 1857

MS Morgan Library.

Tavistock House | Twenty Eighth January 1857

My Dearest Macready

Your friend and servant is as calm as Pecksniff, saving for his knitted brows now turning into cordage over Little Dorrit.[2] The Theatre has disappeared, the house is restored to its usual condition of order, the family are tranquil and domestic, dove-eyed Peace[3] is enthroned in this Study, fire-eyed Radicalism[4] in its master's breast.

Mrs. Meredith's[5] paper[6] I retain for insertion. There is nothing in it very new, but it is very agreeable.

I am glad to hear that our Poetess is at work again; and shall be very much pleased to have some more contributions from her.

Love from all, to your dear sister, and to Katie, and to all the house.

We dined yesterday at Frederick Pollock's.[7] I begged an amazing Photograph of you, and brought it away. It strikes me as one of the most ludicrous things I ever saw in my life. I think of taking a Public-House, and having it copied large, for the Sign. You may remember it? Very square and big—the Saracen's Head with its hair cut—and in modern gear? Staring very much?—As your particular friend I would not part with it on any consideration. I could never get such a wooden head again.

Ever Affectionately
CD

[1] Of 10 Lancaster Place, Strand; Secretary, since 1856, Joseph Stirling Coyne (1803–68; *DNB*), dramatist and member of the Guild of Literature and Art Committee: see later vols.

[2] Probably a reference to the "great pains" he was taking over Ch. 21, Miss Wade's story: see *To* Forster, 9 Feb and *fn.*

[3] Perhaps an allusion to "Innocence, | The dove, and very blessed spirit of peace" (*2 Henry IV*, IV, i, 45), recalling also Milton's "meek-eyed peace" (*Nativity Ode*, st. 3).

[4] Cf. "fire-ey'd fury", *Romeo and Juliet*, III, i, 126 and "fire-ey'd maid of smoky war", *1 Henry IV*, IV, i, 114.

[5] Née Louisa Anne Twamley (1812–95), miscellaneous writer and illustrator; after marriage, settled first in Sydney, then in Tasmania; her books included *The Romance of Nature* (dedicated to Wordsworth), 1836; and *Some of my Bush Friends in Tasmania* (dedicated to the Queen), 1860, which made her a leading authority on Tasmanian life: see Anne Lohrli, *Household Words*, p. 366.

[6] "Shadows of the Golden Image", *HW*, 4 Apr 57, XV, 313: an account of the disruptive effect on Tasmania of the discovery in 1851 of gold in New South Wales.

[7] William Frederick Pollock (1815–88; *DNB*), lawyer and close friend of Macready: see Vol. VI, p. 523*n*.

To MARK LEMON, 29 JANUARY 1857*

MS Fales Collection, New York University Library.

Tavistock House | Thursday Twenty Ninth January | 1857

My Dear Mark

I enclose a cheque (crossed) for Nathan.[1] Will you let him put a receipt stamp to his bill, and then send it to me.

There is a little bill for skins,[2] which you kindly ordered. Will you let me know its amount?

Ever affectionately

CD.

To THE MEMBERS OF THE GUILD OF LITERATURE AND ART, [LATE JANUARY 1857]

Mention in *To* Lytton, 28 Jan 57; the original letter surely written by CD. *Date:* shortly after that letter.

To UNKNOWN CORRESPONDENT, [?1–2 FEBRUARY 1857]

Mention in *To* Tagart, 4 Feb. *Date:* before Tagart's call on 3 Feb.

To MISS BURDETT COUTTS, 3 FEBRUARY 1857

MS Morgan Library. *Address:* Miss Burdett Coutts | Meadfoot House | Hesketh Crescent | Torquay | Devon.

Tavistock House | Tuesday February Third, 1857

My Dear Miss Coutts.

I have no doubt that your excellent interposition will cause the Hospital to manage these sad matters (clearly, I take it, mismanaged before), in a better way.[3] But I am sorry in the letter to you which I now return, to observe, either carelessness or dishonesty. I recollect my written summary distinctly. And I do most positively declare—not only that it did *not* represent Mrs. Bragg[4] to have seen the body in the

[1] CD's Account-book shows a payment to Lemon, 30 Jan 57, of £50 (MS Messrs Coutts).

[2] Animal skins worn in Acts II and III and the facing of the walls of the hut and cavern.

[3] This clearly refers to the misconduct of the St George's Hospital Hall porter and Surgery man in neglecting to inform the Medical Officer that a woman who had taken poison had been brought into the hospital. The woman had subsequently died. The Hall porter, intoxicated while on duty, and the Surgery man, who had left the hospital while on duty, were dismissed by the Hospital Steward (Minutes, St George's Hospital Board of Governors, 14 Jan 57).

[4] Almost certainly Mrs Harriet Bragg, mistress of Miss Coutts's school for girls at St Stephen's, Westminster. Several times mentioned in *The Summary Account* and praised for her "zeal and energy". Her connection with the scandal at the hospital unexplained.

Hospital—which she plainly stated to me she did not—but, in so many clear words, described it to have been seen by the two men, who, after having dressed it as they best could, *took it to her*. In such a case as this, of all others, there is no defence for carelessness, and it is excessively suspicious. If I were conducting the case, I would most decidedly put them in the wrong on their own Resolution and make them acknowledge it. I don't say you should do so—your position being so different—but I would allow no body of men on earth to deal so grossly with me as to make their own misrepresentation and then coolly contradict it as mine. I have never seen a worse thing of this kind in my life. The connexion of the word "exaggerated" with the only hint in its support—that is, that Mrs. Bragg never saw the body—which you never represented that she did—is Old Bailey from the crown of its head to the sole of its foot—or, untidy and slipshod muddling.

I will go to the Bishop of Exeter[1] on Monday Morning; until when, my mornings will be occupied. Publicly, I think he has done about as much harm to real Christian brotherhood and good will, by his uniform conduct since he has been a Bishop,[2] as any mere mortal man could well do in his life time. Privately, I can of course have no other feeling towards him than that you commend him,[3] and that is enough. I will explain everything to him with my utmost pains.[4]

(I find the foregoing two sides and a half, have a savage aspect! I now subside into ethereal mildness.)

The drainage at Shepherd's Bush has got all at once into such a dreadful condition, fraught with so much danger of sickness to the Inmates, that I was obliged on Saturday, after referring the matter to the Builder, to give him directions for going to work to remove the evil, instantly. I was really afraid to wait, to refer the matter to you (the parlor had then become uninhabitable, and the whole house was fast becoming so); and I knew besides, that it must unfortunately be done. I am going out there to day, to see how they are getting on.

I read your letter at breakfast (with great gravity and a general rustic sensation which I associated with the field and a vague idea of a syllabub in the garden), to the effect that "Mr. Tennent[5] will probably speak about a COW."[6] Coming shortly afterwards to an unknown girl in the country (otherwise unintroduced) I found it was Case.[7]

[1] Henry Phillpotts (1778–1869; *DNB*), Bishop of Exeter 1830–69; Fellow of Magdalen College, Oxford, 1795–1804; Prebendary of Durham 1809; Dean of Chester 1828.

[2] As a High Church and polemically Tory Bishop, Phillpotts stood in the opposite camp to CD on almost every issue: before becoming Bishop, he had defended the Poor Law and the "Peterloo massacre" of 1819; as Bishop, he opposed the Reform Bill in the House of Lords (leading to an attack on his palace by the Exeter mob) and Lord Grey on the Tithes Bill; of his many lawsuits against clergymen in his diocese, the most notorious arose out of his refusal to institute the Rev. G. C. Gorham on the grounds of his unorthodoxy on baptism; on appeal to the Privy Council, Gorham was instituted in Mar 50.

[3] Miss Coutts was a close friend of Phillpotts; she owned his portrait by J. S. W. Hodges (1829–1900), exhibited at RA 1866. He was Vice-President of the National Society for Promoting the education of the poor in the principles of the Established Church, which covered Whitelands as a training institution.

[4] Unexplained.

[5] CD's mistake; he was obviously thinking of his friend Sir James Emerson Tennent. The Rev. William Tennant (?1814–79), first Vicar 1847–79 of St Stephen's Rochester Row, Westminster; on the Committee of Miss Coutts's Home: see Vol. v, p. 231 *n*.

[6] Written in large printed letters.

[7] Written in ordinary writing, but twice as large as rest of text.

I don't know who wrote the African articles in the Times;[1] but I will enquire, and tell you. Without at all disparaging Dr. Livingstone[2] or in the least doubting his facts, I think however that his deductions must be received with great caution. The history of all African effort, hitherto, is a history of wasted European life, squandered European money, and blighted European hope—in which the generous English have borne a great share. That it would be a great thing to cultivate that cotton and be independant of America, no one can doubt; but I think that happy end, with all its attendant good results, must be sought in India. There are two tremendous obstacles in Africa; one, the climate; the other, the people.

It rejoices me to hear such good news of Nova Scotia.[3]

With kind regard to Mrs. Brown, Ever Dear Miss Coutts. Most Faithfully Yours CD.

P.S. The wildest legends are circulating about town, to the effect that the Queen proposes to ask to have the Frozen Deep at Windsor.[4] I have heard nothing of it otherwise, but slink about, holding my breath.—Please don't say any thing about fine weather, when you write. It is too much to bear.

To THE COUNTESS GIGLIUCCI, 3 FEBRUARY 1857

MS Brotherton Library, Leeds. Envelope (MS Dickens House) Countess Gigliucci | Great Western Hotel | Paddington. PM Feb 1857

Tavistock House | Tuesday Third February | 1857

My Dear Countess Gigliucci

I ought to have told you that Miss Coutts immediately replied (as indeed I knew beforehand), that she had no vacant presentation of any kind which she could give to "Poor Richard."[5]

May he succeed in his new effort! But there is so much of electioneering, canvassing, and rushing about red hot, in all these things, that I have no faith in their solidity.

With kind regard to Count Gigliucci. Believe me always

Very faithfully Yours
CHARLES DICKENS

[1] Presumably "Exploration of Central Africa", 15 Oct 56, five articles, "The French in Central Africa", 16 Oct–25 Nov 56; and "Peculiarities of Central Africa", 15 Dec 56; author not traced.

[2] David Livingstone (1813–73; *DNB*), FRS, African missionary and explorer; had just completed his great four-year exploring expedition northwards from Cape Town.

[3] i.e. Columbia Square, the four large blocks of flats for *c.* 180 working-class families, built by Miss Coutts in what was formerly Nova Scotia Gardens, a slum district in Bethnal Green. For CD's advice, taken by Miss Coutts, to build flats rather than small houses, see Vol. VI, pp. 644–5 and *n.* Building was delayed until 1859; the "good news" CD refers to was probably that building could begin in two years. See later vols.

[4] See *To* Collins, 5 Feb.

[5] See *To* Macready, 28 Feb and *fn*; also with joking reference to Benjamin Franklin's *Poor Richard's Almanac*.

To THE REV. EDWARD TAGART, 4 FEBRUARY 1857

MS Morgan Library.

Tavistock House | Fourth February 1857

My Dear Mr. Tagart

I was very sorry to miss you yesterday.—Had my Seven league boots on, and was striding over the frosty country.

I had already received and answered a note from this gentleman. I told him that the pressure of my own avocations would not admit of my complying, and, more than that, that I am not going, and have not within these five years had the faintest intention of going, to that dreary old Bath for any purpose under the Sun.[1]

Ever Faithfully Yours

The Rev. Edward Tagart. CHARLES DICKENS

To THOMAS BEARD, 5 FEBRUARY 1857

MS Dickens House. *Address:* Thomas Beard Esquire | 42 Portman Place | Edgeware Road | W.

Tavistock House | Thursday Fifth February 1857

My Dear Beard

The weather being so severe, we will dine *here* on Saturday. Hour, 6. Best wine on the premises (and that "not bad," as Mitton says) to be broached on the occasion.

Ever Faithfully

CD

To MESSRS BRADBURY & EVANS, 5 FEBRUARY 1857

MS Dickens House.

Tavistock House | Thursday February Fifth 1857

Dear B and E.

I find an odd mistake in the last No. which none of us observed, and which nobody seems to have discovered yet.[2]—I shouldn't have done so, I think, but that I have been working today on that part of the story. It is explained on the other side, which we must have printed as a slip for the next No.[3] Will you have the corrections made immediately in the type, if standing? If not, in the stereotype plates?[4]

Ever Faithfully

CD.

[1] Although CD enjoyed his many visits to Landor at Bath, he never liked the city; his dislike is reflected in *Pickwick*, Chs 35–7. When the Amateurs were there in Autumn 1851, he found the audience "horribly dull" (Vol. VI, p. 536). But he gave readings there in 1867 and 1869.

[2] The use of "Rigaud" instead of "Blandois" in Book II, Ch. 17 (No. XV): see below.

[3] The "other side" must have been copy for the slip inserted in No. XVI, beginning "By an oversight of the Author's, which he did not observe until it was too late for the first impression of the Number for last month": see Clarendon Edn, ed. H. P. Sucksmith, pp. xxxv–vi. It is also listed under "Errata" of No. XIX–XX and in the vol. Copies of later issues of No. XV have "Blandois" correctly.

[4] Where it was made: see *To* Cerjat, 16 Feb.

To WILKIE COLLINS, 5 FEBRUARY 1857

MS Morgan Library.

Tavistock House | Thursday Fifth February 1857.

My Dear Collins.

The weather being so severe, we will dine *here* on Saturday. Hour, 6.

I was at the Garrick on Monday. Comes De Bathe[1] and says to me, "So you are going to Windsor!"—"Am I?—I know nothing about it."—"Pardon me! I mean, with the Frozen Deep"—"Well! I tell you I know nothing about it."—"Pardon me again," said he, "I can only say that I have been at the Court, and that I heard it from the Court's own people. Further; the Queen has a strong idea of following it up with some of the Crimean Amateur Performances,[2] by the Divisional Officers who played there"—"I can only assure you," I repeated, "that I know nothing about it."

An idea has come into my head that they may be waiting to close the Professional Windsor Season, and get rid of Kean[3]—that then the Queen may mean to lie by for her confinement[4]—and that then the Amateur Plays may be designed for a season at Easter.

Ever Faithfully

CD.

To FREDERICK DICKENS, 5 FEBRUARY 1857

MS Free Library and Museum, Welshpool.

OFFICE OF HOUSEHOLD WORDS,
Thursday Fifth February 1857.

My Dear Frederick

I am sorry to be obliged to reply to you as before.

I cannot lend you the £30. Firstly because I cannot trust you, and because your bad faith with Wills and Austin makes the word "lend" an absurdity.[5] Secondly because if this were otherwise it would do you no real good and would not in the least save you against creditors who have already power of taking you in execution.

Affectionately

CD.[6]

[1] Lieut.-Col. Sir William Plunkett De Bathe, 3rd Bart (1795–1870), retired Army officer. Member of the Garrick since 1845.

[2] Untraced.

[3] Kean had first taken his company to play at Windsor Castle in Jan 53. The Queen wrote that "Kean acts admirably," after seeing his Lear at the Princess's in Apr 58 (*Dearest Child: Private Correspondence of Queen Victoria and the Crown Princess of Prussia, 1858–61*, ed. Roger Fulford, 1964, p. 95).

[4] Her youngest child, Princess Beatrice, was born on 14 Apr.

[5] See 8 Jan 57.

[6] For Frederick's reply, see *To* Wills, 7 Feb and *fn*.

To MISS BURDETT COUTTS, 6 FEBRUARY 1857

MS Morgan Library. *Address:* Miss Burdett Coutts | Meadfoot House | Hesketh Crescent | Torquay | Devon.

Tavistock House | Friday Sixth February 1857.

My Dear Miss Coutts.

No. I *won't* look upon it in extremis,[1]—but I have an indignant objection to any thing like unfair dealing, which puts my blood up to boiling point. A blow would not incense me more than a shuffle.

I knew of Mrs. Bragg's having offered the money, but wholly separated it from the Hospital treatment of the Dead, because it had nothing to do with it. If *you* had connected the two things, they would instantly have told you that they had no connexion.

The drainage is distinctly our business (I am sorry to say), the main drain being provided. What is being done will cost, according to estimate, from Thirty to Forty Pounds. But I am pretty sure that when you see what it is, you will think the money well spent. We must have had illness without it. It is surprising that some obstinate disorder had not already broken out.

The gas is now at the gate. Would you like it taken into the house? The expense will be the usual fittings and nothing more. If we had it at all, I would recommend a jet in the fanlight, kitchen, wash-house, bathroom, over the chimney piece in each bedroom. Then, no light would ever be carried about the house. Just as we do here.

Between ourselves, I too should feel a little jealous of our own speciality if it should turn out that the Queen resolves to make that request. I *know* now, that she strongly entertains the idea. However, I should of course stipulate for as complete mastery and inaccessibility on the stage, as if we were at home—and should put a cheerful and dutiful face on the matter. Mr. Collins would like it very much, thinking it would express to the Theatres that they are not doing their duty, and that their noble Art is sliding away from them. He is of course a great consideration, and, knowing his feeling, I am ready with my reply if I should have occasion to give one.

With love to Mrs. Brown

Ever Dear Miss Coutts | Most Faithfully Yours

CD.

To MISS MARY BOYLE, 7 FEBRUARY 1857

MS Morgan Library.

Tavistock House | Seventh February 1857

My Dear Mary

Half a dozen words on this my Birthday, to thank you for your kind and welcome remembrance, and to assure you that your Joseph is proud of it.

For about ten minutes after his death—on each occasion of that event occurring—Richard Wardour was in a floored condition. And one night, to the great terror of Devonshire, the Arctic Regions, and Newfoundland, (all of which local-

[1] See *To* Miss Coutts, 3 Feb and *fn.*

ities were afraid to speak to him as his Ghost sat by the kitchen fire in its rags), he very nearly did what he never did—went and fainted off, dead—again. But he always plucked up, on the turn of ten minutes,[1] and became facetious.

Likewise he chipped great pieces out of all his limbs (solely, as I imagine, from moral earnestness and concussion of passions, for I never knew him to hit himself in any way), and terrified Aldersley[2] to that degree by lungeing at him to carry him into the Cave, and the said Aldersley always shook like a mould of jelly, and muttered "By G— this is an awful thing!"

Ever affectionately
CHARLES DICKENS

I shall never cease to regret Mrs. Watson's not having been there.

To W. H. WILLS, 7 FEBRUARY 1857*

MS Huntington Library.

Tavistock House | Seventh February 1857

My Dear Wills.

A touch of simple manly gratitude, fresh from the honest and overcharged heart, is so delightful in this world, that I am sure you will like to see the enclosed.[3]

Pray keep it, and when you see Austin shew it to him. (I need not say that there was nothing in my letter but the plain declaration of the reason for being obliged to repeat my refusal.)

Ever Faithfully
CD.

To MARK LEMON, 8 FEBRUARY 1857

Extract in Dickens Exhibition, New Dudley Gallery catalogue, 1909; *MS* 1 p.; addressed Mark Lemon; dated Tavistock House, 8 Feb 57.

Stanny will order the dinner.... Will you secure a box *for the Adelphi.*[4]

[1] Evidently the actors retired to the kitchen in the half hour's interval before the farce.

[2] Wilkie Collins.

[3] Fred's reply to CD's letter of 5 Feb; it runs: "WAR DEPART. Seventh February 1857 | My dear Charles. | I cannot help saying that the tone of your letter is as cold & unfeeling, as one Man could pen to another—much less—one Brother to another—this too—in the face of all your protestations of affection & regard for me in years gone bye. | With respect to Wills & Austin, I say, most emphatically, that you have misjudged me upon an ex parte statement,—& that if they had carried out their part of the Contract, I should have been enabled to perform mine. | It is very easy to sit in Judgment on others—nothing more so—The World fancy from your writings that you are the most Tolerant of Men—let them individually come under your lash—(if one is to judge from your behaviour to your own flesh & blood) & God help them! | For a quarter of a century you have had the world at your foot—such a blessing ought at any rate to make you charitable in respect to the shortcomings of others—instead of placing yourself upon a Pinnacle, upon the assumption that poor human nature is perfection—(or ought to be so—) & you her Judge when e'er she errs! | Yrs affectionately | FREDERICK DICKENS | Many happy returns of the day" (MS Huntington).

[4] Probably for the following night, Mon.; the programme was *The Customs of the Country*, with Mrs Barney Williams; *A Night at Notting-*

To THE REV. JAMES WHITE, 8 FEBRUARY 1857

Text from MDGH, II, 11–12.

Tavistock House, Sunday, Feb. 8th, 1857.

My dear White,

I send these lines by Mary and Katey, to report my love to all.

Your note about the *Golden Mary* gave me great pleasure; though I don't believe in one part of it; for I honestly believe that your story,[1] as really belonging to the rest of the narrative, had been generally separated from the other stories, and greatly liked. I had not that particular shipwreck that you mention in my mind (indeed I doubt if I know it), and John Steadiman merely came into my head as a staunch sort of name that suited the character.[2] The number has done "Household Words" great service, and has decidedly told upon its circulation.

You should have come to the play. I much doubt if anything so complete will ever be seen again. An incredible amount of pains and ingenuity was expended on it, and the result was most remarkable even to me.

When are you going to send something more to H. W.?[3] Are you lazy?? Low-spirited??? Pining for Paris????

Ever affectionately
[CHARLES DICKENS]

To MRS WILLS, 8 FEBRUARY 1857

MS Huntington Library.

Tavistock House | Eighth February 1857

My Dear Mrs. Wills

Pray accept my cordial thanks for your elegant little present.[4] It has a treble value to me. Firstly as a mark of your remembrance. Secondly, as replacing a loss that I have much regretted. Thirdly, as a gift from Nurse Esther, and an association with the pleasant times in which I made that worthy woman's acquaintance, and conveyed to her previously benighted mind the complete assurance that I am not a Dragon, but a villified Lamb. (Note. An L too many in the last word but one.)

Believe me always | Very faithfully Yours
CHARLES DICKENS

Hill, a sketch by Edmund Yates and H. Harrington; *The Irish Tutor*, with Barney Williams, adapted from the French by the Earl of Glengall; and a pantomime, *Mother Shipton—Her Wager*.

[1] "The Scotch Boy's Story" in the second part of the Christmas No., 1856, pp. 27–9.

[2] Perhaps White thought CD had recalled the 18th-cent. explorer, John Gabriel Stedman.

[3] His next contribution was on 4 Apr.

[4] Not discovered.

To W. H. WILLS, 9 FEBRUARY 1857

MS Huntington Library.

Tavistock House | Monday Night | Ninth February 1857

My Dear Wills.

Will you be so kind as to make an explanation to the India House for me? I get so mobbed if I go to a place of that sort myself, that I ask the favor. I did not know of the necessity when you were here to day.

Walter Landor Dickens, being now of an age[1] to go up to be examined for a Direct Appointment as a Cadet to which he is nominated, (the Director nominating him, being, as I remember, Mr. Lock),[2] the business merely is to ask for his necessary papers. I suppose the Secretary's office to be the right one; but the name Walter sends me this evening as the name of the gentleman to be asked for, is Mr. Hollyer.[3]

It is a mere matter of form. Walter is going up in about a fortnight. He is now with Messrs. Brackenbury and Wynne at Wimbledon[4] (if that be anything to the purpose). The papers are wanted, I believe, directly—or at all events should be applied for directly.

Ever Faithfully

CD.

To JOHN FORSTER, [?9 FEBRUARY 1857]

Extract in F, VIII, i, 626. *Date:* shortly after 5 Feb while working on proof of Ch. 20 (No. XVI), published 28 Feb 57.

I don't see the practicability of making the History of a Self-Tormentor, with which I took great pains, a written narrative. But I do see the possibility of making it a chapter by itself,[5] which might enable me to dispense with the necessity of the turned commas. Do you think that would be better? I have no doubt that a great part of Fielding's reason for the introduced story, and Smollett's also, was, that it is sometimes really impossible to present, in a full book, the idea it contains (which yet it may be on all accounts desirable to present), without supposing the reader to be

[1] He was just 16 (*b.* 8 Feb 41).

[2] Loch: see *To* Miss Coutts, 3 Oct 56, *fn.*

[3] John Hollyer, of the Military Dept, East India House.

[4] The Rev. John Matthew Brackenbury (1816–95), MA St John's College, Cambridge, assistant master at Marlborough 1843–9, and the Rev. Charles James Wynne (*b.* ?1832), MA Jesus College, Oxford, founders and from 1860 joint headmasters of the newly-built Wimbledon School; it trained boys for Indian cadetships and the British Army artillery and engineers: see Vol. VII, p. 508*n*. In 1892 it became the Roman Catholic Wimbledon College. For further details see R.J. Milward, *History of Wimbledon*, priv. printed, Wimbledon, 1969, pp. 154–6. Brackenbury was also chairman of the local Board of Education 1871–6.

[5] Miss Wade's story became both a written narrative and a separate chapter (Ch. 21), added to the No. which previously consisted of Chs 19, 20 and what then became Ch. 22. See Clarendon edn, pp. xxxvi and 641–4; and for the No. plans, p. 822, with reproduction on facing page. *To* Bradbury & Evans, 5 Feb indicates that CD then had first proof of the No. which had also gone to Forster: they had probably met on 7 Feb, CD's birthday, and discussed the question. Forster mistakenly implies a later dating which misled N and others into giving an obviously impossible date at end of Mar.

possessed of almost as much romantic allowance as would put him on a level with the writer.[1] In Miss Wade I had an idea, which I thought a new one, of making the introduced story so fit into surroundings impossible of separation from the main story, as to make the blood of the book circulate through both. But I can only suppose, from what you say, that I have not exactly succeeded in this.[2]

To HABLOT K. BROWNE, 10 FEBRUARY 1857*

MS Berg Collection.

Tavistock House | Tuesday Tenth February 1857

My Dear Browne.

In the dinner scene,[3] it is highly important that Mr. Dorrit should not be too comic. He is too comic now. He is described in the text as "shedding tears", and what he imperatively wants, is an expression doing less violence in the reader's mind to what is going to happen to him, and much more in accordance with that serious end which is so close before him.[4]

Pray do not neglect this change.

Ever Faithfully
CD.

Over

LETTERING FOR THE SUBJECTS.
An unexpected After-Dinner Speech.
The Night.[5]

To J. WESTLAND MARSTON,[6] 11 FEBRUARY 1857*

MS Huntington Library.

Tavistock House | Wednesday Eleventh February | 1857.

My Dear Marston

A thousand thanks for your note. I am unfortunately obliged to dine out on Saturday, or I should have accepted the enclosed[7] with great interest and pleasure. The underlining in the bill had not escaped me, and was not dissociated in my mind from

[1] Examples of such "introduced" stories are "The Man of the Hill" in *Tom Jones* (Book IX) and several in *Peregrine Pickle*. Their practice was in the tradition of "romance" such as *Don Quixote*, but it would not serve CD's purpose for the history of an important character.

[2] CD's first plan of having the equivalent of eight printed pages (Clarendon edn, Ch. 21) spoken by Miss Wade to Clennam is certainly implausible, as can be seen by the footnotes to Ch. 20 (*ibid.*, pp. 641–4).

[3] No. XVI, Book II, Ch. 19, for Mar, published 28 Feb.

[4] CD is again looking at the sketches. The change was made; in the plate, "An Unexpected After-Dinner Speech", William Dorrit looks pathetic and bewildered.

[5] It shows the dying Frederick Dorrit, kneeling by his dead brother's bed.

[6] John Westland Marston (1819–90; *DNB*), poet and dramatist: see Vol. III, p. 370*n*.

[7] Admission to the rehearsal before the first night, Monday, 16 Feb, at the Lyceum, of Marston's new verse play, *A Life's Ransom*, set in the period of the Revolution of 1688.

the old remembrances of the Patrician's Daughter.[1] I still hope, of course, to see the Play; but I am very sorry to miss the first night.

Believe me | Very faithfully Yours

Westland Marston Esquire CHARLES DICKENS

To JOHN FORSTER [?13 FEBRUARY 1857]

Extracts in F, VIII, i, 630*n*; VIII, i, 629 and 629*n*. *Date:* first extract 13 Feb, day of visit to Zoo (see *To* Miss Coutts, 14 Feb); next extracts both same letter in Feb according to Forster, and probably same date, just after Gad's Hill visit on 12 Feb with Wills.[2]

I have been (by mere accident) seeing the serpents fed to-day, with the live birds, rabbits, and guinea pigs—a sight so very horrible that I cannot get rid of the impression, and am, at this present, imagining serpents coming up the legs of the table, with their infernal flat heads, and their tongues like the Devil's tail (evidently taken from that model, in the magic lanterns and other such popular representations), elongated for dinner. I saw one small serpent, whose father was asleep, go up to a guinea pig (white and yellow, and with a gentle eye—every hair upon him erect with horror); corkscrew himself on the tip of his tail; open a mouth which couldn't have swallowed the guinea pig's nose; dilate a throat which wouldn't have made him a stocking; and show him what his father meant to do with him when he came out of that ill-looking Hookah into which he had resolved himself. The guinea pig backed against the side of the cage—said "I know it, I know it!"—and his eye glared and his coat turned wiry, as he made the remark. Five small sparrows crouching together in a little trench at the back of the cage, peeped over the brim of it, all the time; and when they saw the guinea pig give it up, and the young serpent go away looking at him over about two yards and a quarter of shoulder, struggled which should get into the innermost angle and be seized last. Everyone of them then hid his eyes in another's breast, and then they all shook together like dry leaves—as I daresay they may be doing now, for old Hookah was as dull as laudanum.... Please to imagine two small serpents, one beginning on the tail of a white mouse, and one on the head, and each pulling his own way, and the mouse very much alive all the time, with the middle of him madly writhing.

Announcing that he had taken possession of Gad's Hill Place and subscribing himself as the Kentish Freeholder on his native heath, his name Protection.[3]

You remember little Wieland[4] who did grotesque demons so well. Did you ever hear how he died? He lay very still in bed with the life fading out of him—suddenly sprung out of it, threw what is professionally called a flip-flap,[5] and fell dead on the floor.

[1] Marston's first play, produced by Macready at Drury Lane, with a Prologue by CD, Dec 42: see Vol. III, p. 370 and *nn*.

[2] See *To* Austin, 15 Feb.

[3] "My foot is on my native heath, and my name's MacGregor" (Scott, *Rob Roy*, Ch. 34).

[4] George Wieland, actor and dancer, retired 1844: see Vol. IV, p. 14*n*; died 6 Nov 1848, aged 35. He first appeared at Sadler's Wells at age 5; he was regarded as unique for his representation of a stage monkey.

[5] A somersault in which the performer lands on feet and hands alternately.

To WILKIE COLLINS, 14 FEBRUARY 1857

MS Morgan Library.

Tavistock House | Fourteenth February 1857

My Dear Collins

Will you come and dine at the office on Thursday at ½ past 5. We will then discuss the Brighton or other trip-possibilities. I am tugging at *my* Oar too—should like a change—find the Galley a little heavy[1]—must stick to it—am generally in a Collinsian state.[2]

Ever Faithfully

CD.

To MISS BURDETT COUTTS, 14 FEBRUARY 1857

MS Morgan Library.

Tavistock House | Fourteenth February 1857

My Dear Miss Coutts

I have the necessary form of certificates to fill in before Walter goes up for his examination; and it seems to me that you are the proper person to fill up *The First* on the 3rd. page of this form. Will you do so, if you see no objection? I was going to fill it up myself, and had almost written on it, when—reading it again—it appeared to me that I ought to ask you.[3] You will see that the first blank in the certificate is for the Presidency.[4]

Yesterday at the Zoological Gardens I saw (accidentally, for I had no idea of such a thing until I got into the room), the Serpents being fed with live birds, Guinea Pigs, rabbits, &c. A most horrible spectacle, and I have ever since been turning the legs of all the tables and chairs into Serpents and seeing them feed upon all possible and impossible small creatures.

Ever Dear Miss Coutts | Yours faithfully & affecy.

CD.

To ANTHONY PANIZZI, 14 FEBRUARY 1857

Extract in *A Collection of Autograph Letters and Historical Documents formed by Alfred Morrison* (2nd Series, 1882–93), 1896, III, 120; *MS* 2 pp.; addressed Panizzi; dated Tavistock House, 14 Feb 57.

Dear Sir,

Pray excuse the trouble I am going to give you in asking you to read this short note.

[1] He had now begun work on No. XVII (Chs 23–6). The first chapter was to "pave the way" for the catastrophe at Mrs Clennam's; the rest would include Merdle's suicide and its consequences.

[2] i.e. restless and ready for the kind of distraction he associates with Collins.

[3] Miss Coutts signed the first certificate, that she had received Loch's nomination of Walter "gratuitously and expressly"; and CD the Parent's certificate confirming it, on 14 Feb. The other certificates were of his baptism and from his school and a doctor (MSS BL, India Office).

[4] See *To* Miss Coutts, 3 Oct 56 and *fn*.

A young man who has a claim on my recommendation has some special assurance that I don't know how many scores of assistants will be wanted this spring some time at the Museum. He was a servant of mine for some years, but left me in consequence of a surgical disorder, which rendered it dangerous for him to be always skirmishing from the top of the house to the bottom. He is under thirty, sharp, well accustomed to public ways and public men, knows something of French, has seen a good deal of the world with his late master, and I can strongly recommend him.[1]

To HENRY AUSTIN, 15 FEBRUARY 1857*

MS Morgan Library.

Tavistock House | Sunday Fifteenth February | 1857.

My Dear Henry

I take the opportunity of a few spare minutes, to write you a short yarn concerning Gad's Hill Place. Wills and I were down there, this last Thursday.

Mr. Hindle the old Rector says that the builder in the neighbourhood of whom he hears the best account (though he has never had occasion to employ him, himself) is Naylor of Strood.[2] As you spoke of enquiring about the repute of some neighbouring Professor, perhaps you will bear this artist in mind. The advantage of employing a Strood man (all other things being equal) is, that it is the nearest place.

It occurs to me that if we could decide upon our man, it would be a good plan, as tending to fill his mind with a solemn sense of his responsibilities, if you were to write to him, asking him if he would be disposed to attend us at the house on the 26th. of March, with a view to the immediate preparation of an estimate of the probable cost of the necessary repairs, and (that being agreed upon), *the immediate execution of the work*. The Drainage I suppose must have an estimate to itself, as we can not tell what is wanted, until it is all laid open. But the preparations for painting and papering, and the raising of the Roof 6 feet (the roof itself seems to be in want of great repair) could all be going on at the same time as the Drainage. And the great point is, to arrange for everything being done at once, out of hand, and got rid of.

Or, if you should think it better, we might, after you had chosen the builder, make an appointment with Mr. Hindle for going through the house with him and checking off the things to be done, so that (if you approved of his estimate) his man might get to work on the 26th. of March. Perhaps this would be the preferable course. I think if you would make the builder, whoever he shall be, come and see you first, before he goes into the house at all, and distinctly understand that if he is chosen to do the work it is to be *done* without pause or postponement (any taste of Circumlocution being inadmissible), we shall fall-to, at a great advantage. The

[1] Charles French, who had left CD's service because of a rupture. Panizzi replied on 18 Feb, asking CD to send French to the British Museum to collect an application-form, to be submitted to "the Principal Trustees, the Archbishop of Canterbury, the Lord Chancellor and the Speaker who alone appoint". If he could serve him, he would (MS BL). There is no record that he was employed in the Museum and in Jan 60 he became Bulwer Lytton's servant.

[2] Probably CD's mistake for James George Naylar, builder, in fact of Maidstone Road, Rochester, the only builder of similar name listed in the Strood district.

whole business ought to be disposed of in 6 weeks—don't you think so? And it will be an immense thing for the garden and its summer appearance and enjoyment, to get the workmen out before the Spring is far advanced.

I have begun the furnishing, and have already bought a good many things at a very fair advantage, by picking them up wherever I see them—sending John to buy them as if for himself—and permitting him to bring them away ignobly, in Vans, Cabs, barrows, trucks, and costermonger's trays. If you should meet such a thing as a Mahogany dining table or two marble washing-stands, in a donkey cart anywhere, or in a cats'-meat cart or any conveyance of that kind, you may be sure the property is mine. Or any shabby man with a porter's knot and a gigantic Crown of legs of chairs upon it, will be on his way here.

Ever Affectionately
CD.

To W. W. F. DE CERJAT, 16 FEBRUARY 1857

MS Free Library of Philadelphia. *Address:* Affranchie | William. F. De Cerjat Esqre. | Elysée | Lausanne | Switzerland.

Tavistock House, London | Sixteenth February 1857

My Dear Cerjat.

A hasty line after my day's work. You are quite right. Always knowing the man in my own mind by his real name of Rigaud, I made the mistake. I observed it very soon, but not soon enough to correct it in the first large issue for the month, though it was immediately set right in the stereotype plates. Also, a notice has been printed for issue with the next No. explaining the error.[1]

Ah! I wish you *had* seen the Play! Though I say it as shouldn't, I am pretty sure nothing so complete was ever seen before, or will ever be seen again.

I hear very frequently from Townshend. He is pretty well, but evidently lonely out there[2]—and no wonder.

Kindest loves from all mine to all yours.

Ever Heartily Yours | My Dear Cerjat,
CHARLES DICKENS

To THOMAS PHINN,[3] 17 FEBRUARY 1857

MS Gresham's School, Holt.

Tavistock House | Seventeenth February 1857

My Dear Sir

Allow me to thank you for your letter, and to assure you that you did not need any recalling to my remembrance.

[1] See *To* Bradbury & Evans, 5 Feb and *fnn.*

[2] At Nervi.

[3] Thomas Phinn (1814–66), lawyer; educated at Eton and Exeter College, Oxford (scholar); called to Bar 1840; QC and Bencher, Inner Temple, 1854; Recorder of Portsmouth 1848–52; MP Bath 1852–5 (Liberal); Counsel to Admiralty 1854; 2nd Secretary to Admiralty 1855. Friend of Thackeray (often mentioned in his Diary), through whom CD no doubt met him. He might also have met him through Landor; Phinn was the counsel consulted by Landor's solicitors in July 1858 and in the trial that followed after Landor's flight to Italy.

As I had not heard of the application, I made some enquiry about it on receiving your favor. It comes from the second son[1] of the late Magistrate, and I have not the slightest hesitation in thoroughly recommending him. A'Beckett was remarkably careful and conscientious in the training of his boys. They have been exceedingly well educated, and well brought up in all respects.[2] I do not doubt that this young man is much above the average, and would do great credit to the service.

My Dear Sir | Faithfully Yours

Thomas Phinn Esquire. CHARLES DICKENS

To W. M. THACKERAY, 17 FEBRUARY 1857

Mention in Henry Hellssen catalogue, Copenhagen, Jan 1958; *MS* 1 p.; addressed W. M. Thackeray; dated Tavistock House, 17 Feb 57. *Address:* W. M. Thackeray Esquire | Onslow Square | Brompton | S.W. PM Feb 57.

Recommending a former valet.[3]

To FRANK STONE, 18 FEBRUARY 1857*

MS Benoliel Collection.

Tavistock House
Wednesday Night | Eighteenth February 1857.

My Dear Stone

I send you on the other side, the counterpart of a Memorandum of the estate disbursements[4] for this last year, which I am now sending to Mr. Powell.[5]

We never see anything of you. Can you and Mrs. Stone[6] and the namesake of my deceased heroine,[7] come and dine with us on Sunday—alone—at 5? We will have no one here, and will dine off roots and water. Say yes—unless one of your Corner banquets should happen to be coming off on that day, and the Burton air[8] should be intended to be laden with the steams of Epicurean cookery.

Ever affectionately
CHARLES DICKENS

[1] Albert A'Beckett (1840–1904), second son of Gilbert Abbot A'Beckett (see *To* Forster, 30 Aug 56, *fn*); midshipman, Indian Navy, 1856–7; appointed to War Office 1858; Private Secretary to several Ministers of War; Asst Accountant Gen. of Army; knighted 1904.

[2] The eldest son, Gilbert Arthur (1837–91), was at Westminster School, like his father; the third son, Arthur William, was at Felsted and perhaps earlier at Mr Gibson's school in Boulogne.

[3] Possibly Charles French: see *To* Panizzi, 14 Feb.

[4] For the three Tavistock Square houses.

[5] Nathaniel Powell, CD's next-door neighbour since 1854: see Vol. VII, p. 619 and *n*.

[6] Elizabeth Stone: see Vol. VII, p. 69*n*.

[7] Stone's elder daughter Ellen, *b.* ?1836, evidently known as Nell: see *ibid*.

[8] Presumably coming from the nearby Burton Arms: see *To* Yates, 28 Apr 58 and *fn*.

	£	S	D
One third of gardener's contract half yearly charge for front court, extra the purchase of five new lime trees at 7/- each	1.	19.	4
One third of gardener's contract half yearly charge for front enclosure	1.	5.	0
One third of painter's bill for "preparing and painting quadrangle railings, piers, and gates, and re-writing names"	3.	0.	10
	£6.	5.	2

To UNKNOWN CORRESPONDENT, 20 FEBRUARY 1857

Mention in Christie's catalogue, July 1974.

To MISS BURDETT COUTTS, 21 FEBRUARY 1857*

MS Morgan Library. *Address:* Miss Burdett Coutts | Meadfoot House | Hesketh Crescent | Torquay | Devon.

Tavistock House
Twenty First February 1857 | Saturday

My Dear Miss Coutts

A hasty line before the Post goes out. Will you be so kind as to return me Walter's paper,[1] for it is wanted and they press me for it.

Ever Faithfully & affYours
CD.

To THOMAS BEARD, 24 FEBRUARY 1857

MS Dickens House. *Address:* Thomas Beard Esquire | 41 Portman Square | Edgeware Road | W.

Tavistock House
Tuesday Night | Twenty Fourth February 1857.

My Dear Beard

I had heard of the first calamity,[2] but not of the second.[3] Your letter is a painful

[1] See 14 Feb.

[2] The bankruptcy of Edward Baldwin, proprietor of the *Morning Herald*, on which Beard worked, listed in *The Times*, 24 Feb.

[3] Charles Baldwin's (no doubt Edward's father) enforced sale of the *Morning Herald* and *Standard* to James Johnstone (1815–78), accountant, for £16,500.

surprise to me in so far as it concerns your own treatment—if I can say, without making an Ass of myself, that any thing would surprise me in that association.

If Saturday evening will suit you equally well, let me propose that we dine at the Garrick at 6. We will be alone of course. A glass of good wine may take the taste of that Scum out of our mouths—and it must be pretty strong in yours by this time. If this should not suit you, of course I am at your disposal in the morning of the same day; but the evening is better, as being more like one of our old Saturdays. Write me just a word in reply.

I went down yesterday to look at your country quarters.[1] I said when I came home at night, that they would set you up; and now I feel that they are fresh enough—Ah! even to get you in training for another Baldwin—if there should be another in reserve for the sons of men and Holy Church.

Don't be cast down. Cheer up, and you will soon be the better for this. IF I WERE YOU, I WOULD ABOVE ALL THINGS LEAVE A CARD FOR DELANE[2] WITHOUT A DAY'S DELAY.[3] You need do no more,—but do that.

Ever Heartily CD.

To MISS BURDETT COUTTS, 24 FEBRUARY 1857†

MS Morgan Library. *Address:* Miss Burdett Coutts | Meadfoot House | Hesketh Crescent | Torquay | Devon.

Tavistock House
Twenty Fourth February 1857 | Tuesday Night.

My Dear Miss Coutts

When do you want to publish the Summary?[4] I ask, because it requires revision *for the Press* (that is, according to the Printer's habits) entirely through the Preface. You put your corrections in the text, and we always put them in the Margin; besides which, your additions require every one to be introduced in another way, so that the Printer may understand them at a glance. I should like to have a morning at this; but cannot get one just at this moment, as I am obliged to work at Little Dorrit. Can you let me keep it—say, until the 6th. or 7th. of March? I could then return it, so that it would be mere A B C to a printer.

In page 8 as to the Missing Calculation, there is no difficulty. I think. I have taken out all reference to such a Calculation, but have left in, all that refers to the principle.[5] The passage has legs of its own, and is really not much weakened.

I see no objection to the present arrangement of the 3 parts.[6]

[1] Gad's Hill.

[2] John Thadeus Delane (1817–79; *DNB*), editor of *The Times* since 1841: see Vol. VII, p. 145*n*.

[3] Whole sentence doubly underlined.

[4] The new edn of *A Summary Account of Prizes for Common Things*, published early May. Pages 1–120 are completely new.

[5] This clearly refers to p. viii of the Preface, following the passage taken from CD on the advantages of saving (see *To* Miss Coutts, 4 Dec 56 and *fn*). Miss Coutts has restored the reference to the "calculation" of saving at 3%, having obviously found it; and it appears on p. ix.

[6] Part I. New preface, pp. i–xxiv and pp. 1–101. Part II. Reprint of Certain Prizes for Common Things ... awarded ... 1854; Part III. Prizes awarded 1855 and offered 1856; Lessons on Common Things; Appx (reprint of 1st edn).

I would put Mr. Newman's letter[1] exactly in his own words and way.

As to the Record,[2] I cannot too strongly express my sympathy with your opinion. It is a shameful practice that you justly object to, and one which ought to be steadily and inexorably discountenanced. I would by no means send them the book.

I am so addle-headed tonight after a long day's work, that I am not quite sure I see this paper. So I will only add, pray don't let any body alter J. Newman. He is an honest fellow, who expresses himself in a genuine way that is very wholesome and good.

Let me know in a line, how long you can give me. I will turn back to the Summary as soon as my thoughts are clear of the complications they are running upon.

With love to Mrs. Brown | Ever Dear Miss Coutts | Yours faithfully and affy.

CD.

I was obliged to go to Gad's Hill yesterday, and so did not get your book and letter until to day.—Wonderful climate!—People sitting out of doors!—

To WILLIAM HEPWORTH DIXON,[3] 24 FEBRUARY 1857*

MS Rosenbach Museum.

Tavistock House

Tuesday Evening Twenty Fourth February | 1857

My Dear Mr. Dixon

I am unfortunately engaged for Monday night, or I would have come with pleasure, and denied all manner of humbugs[4] from A[5] to Z[5]: including P[5](olitical), the greatest perhaps of all.

Very faithfully Yours

Hepworth Dixon Esquire CHARLES DICKENS

To HENRY MORLEY, 24 FEBRUARY 1857*

MS Dickens House.

Tavistock House

Tuesday Night | Twenty Fourth February 1857

My Dear Morley.

I accept the last (to this time) of the goodly company, with great pleasure, and

[1] Given in Appx to Part I, pp. 81–2; from J. Newman, the builder who obtained the "real expenditures" of various families (pp. 16–33). Written on 19 Nov 56, it gives the enthusiastic response of three of the workmen to whom Miss Coutts had sent the book. Addressed "Dear Sir", it was probably sent to the Chaplain of the Whitelands Institution (the Rev. Harry Baber), who was clearly acting for Miss Coutts. CD wished his letter to be given verbatim, not in extracts or paraphrases.

[2] The Low Church and evangelical newspaper, established 1828; notorious for its attacks on other parties in the Church.

[3] William Hepworth Dixon (1821–79; *DNB*), historian, journalist and traveller: see Vol. v, p. 686*n*. Editor of the *Athenaeum* since 1853.

[4] Probably including the Royal Literary Fund Committee.

[5] All written heavily for emphasis.

with the certainty of a good book to read. The "dead men" are not buried here, believe me.[1]

I reply to your letter without a moment's loss of time, because it would be very painful to me to leave you for one unnecessary hour under the supposition that I could possibly do anything so ungenerous as throw the slightest impediment in the way of your very reasonable wish. I assure you that I have not the faintest "disinclination" to your making such a volume as you describe, from your esteemed contributions to Household Words.[2] Let me go beyond this negative assent, and declare to you that it gives me cordial pleasure to think that they may be profitable and pleasant to you (and many others) in a new form.

I have been writing all day, and my pen blots and erases of its own accord, evidently under the impression that this is going to the Printer's. So I send it to the Post, out of hand.

Always Faithfully Yours

Henry Morley Esquire. CHARLES DICKENS

To FRANK STONE, 26 FEBRUARY 1857*

MS Benoliel Collection.

Tavistock House

Thursday Twenty Sixth February | 1857

My Dear Stone

I have omitted to reply to your question about the Gardener's bills. What you have still to pay, is one item of my memorandum repeated—that is, the £1 odd, half year's share of keeping the front court, here, under the windows in order.[3]

Seriously as to Gad's Hill,—don't make any prospective arrangements for finding a light place to paint in during the winter months, until you shall have become familiar with it. It is highly probable that it would suit me as well as you, that you should have it at your busy time for what you can afford to pay—what it is worth to you in short—and if there is a pretty little place in England, accessible at all times by railway or steamboat, I believe that house to be it.

Ever Affecy.

CD.

[1] Morley's article "Across Country", *HW*, 14 Mar 57, XV, 260, is based on the book describing Col. Frémont's journey to Utah, written and illustrated by S. N. Carvalho, *Incidents of Travel and Adventure . . . across the Rocky Mountains*, 1857 (published Nov 1856): a journey of great hardship and at least one death. CD would also be thinking of Morley's article "Mummy", 28 Feb 57, XV, 196.

[2] Morley reprinted 46 of his contributions (June 1850–Mar 57), together with some poems, as *Gossip . . . Reprinted from "Household Words"*, late May, 1857.

[3] See 18 Feb.

To W. C. MACREADY, 28 FEBRUARY 1857*

MS Morgan Library.

Tavistock House.
Saturday Twenty Eighth February | 1857.

My Dearest Macready

Miss Coutts being still at Torquay, there has been an unavoidable delay in approaching the subject of the poor boy[1]—no avoidable delay, you will readily understand. I took the first occasion of presenting it to her, but with scarcely the least hope of success. For I know that when she resists her own strong impulse to do a kindness, she does so on some principle the necessity of which she has proved to her own satisfaction. And I also perceived the difficulty, that young Warner does not represent an individual in her consideration, but Legion. She writes thus—after having written me several letters, on other matters, always avoiding this.

"I really was foolish, and could not write about Warner. I feel so sorry for him, and so vexed not to do it, in a case which interests you and Mr. Macready. But I feel that every boy I have ever put anywhere, will come upon me, if I break through my rule *only* to provide for the education. Of course it is very uncomfortable personally to me, that a boy who passes more as a protegé of mine than he really is, should be in such a state; but I foresee what would happen if I did otherwise. What is the boy's age? If there are no funds available—and it seems to me something should have been put aside or allowed for such a purpose—would it not be better to withdraw him and try to place him somewhere? This I would assist in."

By "somewhere", no doubt she means in some sort of situation. Now, does it appear to you that anything can be done in that direction? To continue him at school under the circumstances, seems a hopeless kind of thing.

I am transcendently busy, drawing up the arteries of Little Dorrit.[2] Very hard work, but deeply interesting to me. This short letter is all along of her. We are all well, and all send most affectionate loves to all at Sherborne House. Mamey and Katey have been at Bonchurch[3] these three weeks, but come home to day.

Ever My Dearest Macready | Most affectionately Yours
CD.

[1] Richard.

[2] This unusual and expressive phrase suggests that, besides starting work on No. XVIII (Book II, Chs 27–9), he was already thinking ahead to the problems of his conclusion. His notes for Ch. 28 include special emphasis on "Prepare finally for the last scene in the old house." Entitled "An Appearance in the Marshalsea", it describes Clennam's visits from Rigaud, Cavaletto, and Flintwinch, in which CD must be recalling, perhaps unconsciously, similar interviews in the closing scene of Frederick Fox Cooper's play adapted from Book I in Nov 1856 (see *To* Browne, 6 Dec 56). Setting, situation, and characters are identical, though the outcome was of course the disclosure of Mr Dorrit's inheritance. Probably at about the same time CD made elaborate notes headed "Mems for working the Story round—Retrospective" and "Prospective ... To work out in Nos. XIX and XX" (see Clarendon, pp. 824–6), which represent the "arteries" of the plot and include much that he had clearly not planned in advance. See also *To* Hudson, 11 Apr 57 and *fn*.

[3] Staying with the Whites.

To THOMAS BEARD, 1 MARCH 1857

MS Dickens House. *Address:* Thomas Beard Esquire | 42 Portman Square | Edgeware Road | W.

Tavistock House | First March 1857

My Dear Beard

I have been preached against here, for forgetting an engagement—as I always do, unless I consult a neat pocket Ledger, which I invariably carry and—as invariably—never look at. I am bound over to eat a dinner on Wednesday.

Therefore let us postpone our theatrical trip for a little while. I will keep my eye on the bills, and look out for the American actress's[1] most characteristic piece.

I shall be very much interested in knowing what passes between you and the vinous old dotard,[2] next Thursday. Perhaps you will write me the result, on Friday or Saturday, addressed to the Bedford at Brighton.

Ever Cordially

Thomas Beard Esquire. CD

To MISS BURDETT COUTTS, 1 MARCH 1857*

MS Morgan Library.

Tavistock House | Sunday First March 1857.

My Dear Miss Coutts

I do not see any thing to object to, in the accompanying report.[3] You have done great good; an obviously bad thing is set right; and although it would have been much better ingenuously done in the beginning than disingenuously, done it is, and many poor people will be the happier and better for it.

I will not fail to return the pamphlet on Common Things, and the corrections, in the course of the week.

Ever Faithfully & affYours

CHARLES DICKENS

To JOHN MURRAY,[4] 1 MARCH 1857*

MS Miss Barbara Murray.

Tavistock House | First March 1857.

My Dear Murray

I shall have great pleasure in dining with Mrs. Murray[5] and yourself, on Thursday the Twelfth.

Believe me | Faithfully Yours always

John Murray Esquire. CHARLES DICKENS

[1] Mrs Barney Williams.

[2] Edward Baldwin: see 15 Mar 57.

[3] No doubt concerning the treatment of the dead woman at St George's Hospital: see *To* Miss Coutts, 3 Feb and *fn*.

[4] John Murray III (1802–92; *DNB*), publisher: see Vol. II, p. 422*n*; he had met CD at the Booksellers' Association and over copyright questions in 1852.

[5] Marion, daughter of Alexander Smith, banker, of Edinburgh; married 1847.

To SIR JOSEPH PAXTON, 1 MARCH 1857

MS Berg Collection.

Tavistock House | Sunday First March 1857.

My Dear Paxton

A thousand thanks for your kind and prompt note. My idea of the weekly wages was merely a sporting guess, and I am thoroughly sure that whatever you tell me is right in that respect, *is* right.

I have a tenant in the place at this moment (an old clergyman who has lived in it 30 years), but I take possession myself on Lady Day. I don't care, however, how soon I engage the gardener, as I dare say that the summer aspect of the spot will be materially improved by his looking to it soon.

Whenever you are so kind as to send the accredited man here, I will see him; or, if I should happen by any chance to be away, Mrs. Dickens or Miss Hogarth will have full powers from the source of all domestic authority, to conclude treaties. About 10 in the morning is the best time. I shall not think it necessary to make any enquiries about his character, as your recommendation is conclusive on that head and all others.[1]

You must let me remind you of this correspondence when the Midsummer weather comes, and ask you to accompany me one Saturday to the extensive freehold, where Cigars and Lemons grow on all the trees.

☛The House of Commons[2] seems to me to be getting worse every day.[3] I solemnly declare to you that direfully against my will, I have come to the conclusion that representative Government is a miserable failure among us. See what you are all about, down at Westminster at this moment with the wretchedest party squabble, and consider that poor Working Mens' Meeting about Emigration, within a few yards of you all, the other night![4] When your gardener grows me a gooseberry bush with its roots in the air, and Epping sausages for its fruit springing from a fountain of vitriol, I shall believe in the likelihood of a country's long going on, under the auspices of such a Club as the Devil has got together (present Company always excepted) under the big bell which will ring on some strange occasions before it's an old one.

Always Very faithfully Yours
CHARLES DICKENS

Sir Joseph Paxton

[1] See *To* Milner, 1 Apr and *fn*. Charles Barber first appears as head gardener at Gad's Hill on 3 Aug (*To* Paxton, that day).

[2] A hand, pointing to it, is drawn in the margin here. Paxton was Liberal MP for Coventry 1854 to his death.

[3] After stormy debates in both the Lords and Commons on the war in China, the Govt was defeated on 3 Mar and Parliament dissolved on 5 Mar.

[4] A meeting of the British Workman's Association on 24 Feb, held to obtain assistance for emigration; reported sympathetically by *The Times* on 26 Feb.

To C. W. DILKE, 2 MARCH 1857*

MS Professor Helena M. Gamer.

Tavistock House | Monday Evening | Second March 1857

My Dear Mr. Dilke.

Will it be convenient to you if I call upon you at 4 on Wednesday, to confer about the Bloomsbury Humbug?[1] I am going to Brighton on Friday morning, but of course arrange to be back for Wednesday week.[2] I only suggest my hour, in order that you may be spared the trouble of answering this note. In case it should be in the least unsuitable, then (and then only) write to name another, and I will make it answer my purpose. I have really nothing to do on that day.

Very faithfully Yours

C. W. Dilke Esquire CHARLES DICKENS

To JOSEPH ELLIS,[3] 2 MARCH 1857*

MS Bedford Hotel, Brighton. *Address:* Mr. Joseph Ellis | The Bedford Hotel | Brighton.

Tavistock House, London. | Monday Second March 1857

Dear Mr. Ellis.

As I have not been in Brighton for sometime and want a walk on the Downs, I purpose coming to you next Friday, with a literary friend (Mr. Wilkie Collins) for about three days. Will you be so good as let me know whether you have room enough to give us a sitting-room and two bedrooms? If you reply yes, perhaps you will let your people know that we shall come down early in the afternoon, and that we will dine at Six.

Faithfully Yours

Mr. Joseph Ellis CHARLES DICKENS

[1] i.e. the Royal Literary Fund, of 73 Great Russell St, Bloomsbury: see Vols V, p. 62*n* and VII, *passim*.

[2] The Annual General Meeting of the Fund on 11 Mar. CD returned for it. Dilke made a long speech, as an amendment to adopting the annual Report, requesting the General Committee to "pledge themselves to reconsider the whole of the management and Expenses of the Institution", on the grounds that they spent much too much on administration and the annual dinner. The Fund gave away £1500 p.a.; to do this, it appealed to the public for donations, while having £30,000 funded property and landed estate yielding £200 p.a. But "the reformers are conquering their ground", he said. They "rejoice to see that their principles are finding a way into the Society". (MS Royal Literary Fund.) Both CD and Forster spoke for the amendment; Robert Bell, the Bishop of Oxford and Monckton Milnes against it. CD's speech (see *Speeches*, ed. K. J. Fielding, pp. 226–7) was widely reported in the Press. Much of it concerned a disputed "House Fund" of £6,540, which he showed to be merely the original rent since 1821 capitalized; the *Athenaeum*, in a very full report (5 cols) obviously by Dilke, the editor, recorded that the Literary Members "feel, as Mr. Dickens said very forcibly, that the issues lie beyond the indiscretions of the Committee—with that great public which, by means of its reporters, the Literary Members have brought into the management of the Fund. To this public, rather than to the benches of officers, the debate ... was addressed" (14 Mar). The amendment was seconded by Lemon; but defeated by 69 votes to 11 (*ibid.*, 14 Mar). The *Publishers' Circular*, 16 Mar, in a brief, unfavourable comment, hoped that the result would convince the minority of "the uselessness of continuing an opposition evidently repugnant to the general feeling of the subscribers".

[3] Joseph Ellis the younger (1815–91), proprietor of the Bedford Hotel, Brighton, 1845–65: see Vol. III, p. 265*n*.

To THE CHAIRMAN OF THE METROPOLITAN FREE HOSPITAL,[1] 3 MARCH 1857

Extract in Maggs Bros catalogue, No. 258 (1910); *MS* 2 pp.; dated Tavistock House, 3 Mar 57; addressed Chairman of the Metropolitan Free Hospital.

Expressing his respect for the Christian zeal by which their labour is animated and regretting his inability to help in it. In the midst of many pressing demands on my continuous attention, I am so beset by entreaties to preside on public occasions, ... that I am almost every day obliged to decline. ... I consider only my inability to help it, consistent with the punctual and useful discharge of other duties.

To WILKIE COLLINS, 4 MARCH 1857

MS Morgan Library.

Tavistock House | Wednesday Fourth March 1857

My Dear Collins

I *cannot tell you* what pleasure I had in the receipt of your letter yesterday Evening, or how much good it did me in the depression consequent upon an exciting and exhausting day's work. I immediately arose (like the desponding Princes in the Arabian Nights, when the old woman—Procuress evidently, and probably of French extraction—comes to whisper about the Princesses they love),[2] and washed my face, and went out; and my face has been shining ever since.

Ellis responds to my letter that rooms shall be ready. There is a train at 12 which appears to me to be the train for the distinguished Visitors. If you will call for me in a Cab at about 20 minutes past 11, my hand will be on the latch of the door.

I have got a book to take down with me, of which I have not yet read a line, but which I have been saving up, to get a pull at, in the nature of a draught.—The Dead Secret—By a Fellow Student.[3]

Plornish has broken ground with a Joke which I consider equal to Sydney Smith.

Ever Faithfully

CHARLES DICKENS

[1] At 8 Devonshire Sq., Bishopsgate, founded 1836; no Chairman discovered (Treasurer J. G. Hoare and Secretary Charles Nash).

[2] In the tale of "Taj El-Mulook and the Lady Dunya", transl. E. W. Lane, 1839–41, I, 523–603; though it has a single princess and prince (attended by a friend), an old woman is the intermediary in his long courtship.

[3] Collins's *The Dead Secret*, not completed in *HW* until 13 June; probably the manuscript: see *To* Mrs Watson, 8 Mar.

To WILLIAM HOWITT,[1] 4 MARCH 1857

MS Brotherton Library, Leeds.

Tavistock House | Fourth March 1857

My Dear Sir

Many thanks for your kind note. I know all the walks,[2] well. There is not an inch of all that ground which is not familiar with the print of my foot.

I hope to be in town, to call and see Miss Howitt's[3] pictures.[4] But I am very hard at work finishing a long story; and at such times wildnesses come over me, and I go off unexpectedly into strange places and write in inaccessible fastnesses.

Very faithfully Yours

William Howitt Esquire. CHARLES DICKENS

To MISS BURDETT COUTTS, 5 MARCH 1857†

MS Morgan Library. *Address:* Miss Burdett Coutts.

OFFICE OF HOUSEHOLD WORDS,
Thursday Fifth March 1857

My Dear Miss Coutts.

I have gone over your corrections, and return them and the Summary.[5] My fingers have itched to put your various insertions on the Margin, in the proper places of their introduction, where the Printer might have them under his eye without perpetual reference backward and forward. I have, however, of course observed your wish, and have only made such erasures in those parts of the text, as are calculated to prevent a Wilderness of repetitions and confusion. Some of the more obvious printers' mistakes I have also marked, where they have impaired the spirit and plainness of a passage.

Now, you will presently go on to say to Mrs. Brown, "What a queer man he is! What odd ideas he has sometimes!" Nevertheless, I can't help saying that I don't agree with you in your approval of the little essays about Dress.[6] I think them not natural—overdone—full of a conventional sort of surface morality—disagreeably like one another—and, in short, just as affected as they claim to be unaffected. Catherine Stanley[7] (page 36) who finds out that the reason for not liking a little bit of finery—which almost every young person on earth does, remember—human nature is "a common thing", and it is of no use to dream of putting it aside—Catherine, I say, who finds out that the reason for not liking it and putting it on, is,

[1] William Howitt (1792–1876; *DNB*), author: see Vol. IV, p. 501*n.*

[2] Perhaps the places Howitt described later in *The Northern Heights of London: or Historical Associations of Hampstead, Highgate, Muswell Hill, Hornsey and Islington*, 1869.

[3] Anna Maria Howitt (1824–84), writer and artist, the Howitts' elder daughter: see Vol. VI, p. 361*n.*

[4] Presumably drawings she did as a medium after giving up painting in 1856: see *ibid.*

[5] Miss Coutts's *Summary Account of Common Things*, new edn, 1857.

[6] Answers to Miss Coutts's Question II, "How would you teach that the possession or want of self-respect is betokened by dress, and that moral habits are influenced by dress", by seven pupils at Whitelands (pp. 43–9). All took a puritanical attitude towards any finery.

[7] One of those awarded a £1 prize.

that she will be "More really admired", without it, ought to be her successor—Miss Sly. I should call Catherine the only honest person of those Seven.

With these exceptions—respecting which I nail my flag to the Mast with a tenpenny nail at each corner—I have been greatly interested in, and pleased with, the whole book. And I heartily congratulate you upon it.

Wills has just had Mr. Bentley's (the Picture-cleaner's) address from me, and is now gone after him. I have been writing in a shaded room (the Sun shining full on the windows) and did not at first see that the opening part of this paper might have been sent to the same Mr. Bentley to be freed of its discoloration. You will excuse it, I know.

I am going to Brighton tomorrow for a breezy walk on the Downs, and shall be at the Bedford until Monday afternoon. After that, at home again.

With kind regard to Mrs. Brown, and hurling defiance at

Elwig
Morgan
Sproston
Wheeler
Stanley
Sly
and[1]
Higinbotham[2]

Ever dear Miss Coutts Yours most faithfully & affy.

CD.

To HENRY AUSTIN, 6 MARCH 1857*

MS Morgan Library.

Tavistock House | Friday Sixth March 1857

My Dear Henry

Your letter with its dark reference to a "proposition", brings my Gad's Hill fever to a height. I am a mere infant, babbling incessantly "Proposition—proposition".[3]

My work has tired me so, that I arranged a few days ago to go to Brighton this morning until Monday. The dark note reaches me, just on the point of starting.

Can you dine with me at the Garrick on Monday at 6?—Or I could come out to you at Ealing on Tuesday Morning. I want to avoid an hour's unnecessary delay. Will you on receipt of this, write me a line addressed to me at the Bedford Hotel, Brighton, and tell me what our appointment shall be? And do—I implore on my bended knees—hurriedly glance at the nature of the Proposition. Wild to know what it is, I beseech to be informed in a general way.

The Greater part of the furniture is got. The last double-tooth I had out, was the order for the bedsteads, beds, and bedding.

[1] Has flourish round it, like that of his signature.

[2] Five of these had won prizes.

[3] Making a study out of the china cupboard: see *To* Miss Coutts, 9 Apr.

Ha ha ha!—Proposition—Ha ha—(Don't mind this. It is the harmless wandering of my mind).

With love to Laetitia | Ever affectionately
CD.

To H. K. BROWNE, 6 MARCH 1857

MS Comtesse de Suzannet.

Tavistock House | Friday Sixth March 1857

My Dear Browne

Very good subjects, both.[1] The Lettering below.

Faithfully Yours always
CD.

(I can't distinctly make out the detail—but I take Sparkler to be getting the tortoise-shell knife from the box.—am I right?)[2]

Flora's tour of inspection[3]
Mr. Merdle a borrower.[4]

To JOSEPH ELLIS, 6 MARCH 1857*

MS Mrs K. M. Jonas. *Address:* Mr. Joseph Ellis.

Bedford Hotel | Friday Evening | Sixth March 1857

Dear Mr. Ellis

I have been kept out later than I intended, and have only just now (9 o'Clock) returned. I shall hope to have the pleasure of seeing you at any time tomorrow that may best suit your convenience.

Faithfully Yours
CHARLES DICKENS

To HENRY AUSTIN, 8 MARCH 1857*

MS Morgan Library.

Brighton | Sunday Eighth March 1857

My Dear Henry

Noble idea—brilliant conception—enticing in the extreme—the only question will be, *How Much*?[5]

[1] Illustrating No. XVII, Book II, Chs 23 and 24, published 31 Mar for Apr.

[2] CD is correct.

[3] Flora exploring Mrs Clennam's house, escorted by Arthur.

[4] Sparkler getting the knife from the box for Merdle, while Fanny looks on. Merdle's suicide comes in the next chapter, Ch. 25, reflecting the suicide of John Sadleir on 16 Feb 56, which had caused a sensation. For H. P. Sucksmith's suggestion that the imaginative treatment of Merdle derives from Samuel Warren's "The Forger", *Passages from the Diary of a Late Physician*, 1830–7, see *Little Dorrit*, Clarendon Edn, p. xxvii.

[5] See *To* Austin, 6 Mar and *fn*.

On Tuesday morning at Tavistock House at your own hour, I will expect you.

Ever affecy.

CD.

To F. M. EVANS, 8 MARCH 1857

Extract in Phillips catalogue, Nov 1990; *MS* 2 pp.; dated Brighton, 8 Mar 57; addressed F. M. Evans.

Acknowledging receipt of Evans's accounts[1] *and arranging a meeting to discuss a query concerning them.*

I observe the amount to be from three to four hundred pounds *less* than the balance on the last half year.[2] I have of course no means at hand of comparing the items; but you have the matter more readily at your fingers' ends than I have, at all times; and I wish you would tell me how this in the main comes about? Is it that the sale in the gross, is less by about 1500?[3]

To THE HON. MRS RICHARD WATSON, 8 MARCH 1857*

MS Benoliel Collection. *Address:* The Hon. Mrs. Watson | 92 King's Road.

Bedford[4] | Sunday Eighth March 1857

My Dear Mrs. Watson

I have had such a burst on the Downs—have been so rained upon, hailed upon, snowed upon, and blown—that I have been obliged to tumble into a warm bath, and *have not got a hat to come out in, until my own is dried*. I brought it back, if you can believe it, a solid cake of ice, half an inch thick.

If I do not go away too early in the Morning, I will call at your door, on the chance of saying Good bye. If I lose that chance, I will send you down The Frozen Deep on Tuesday. If you have done with The Dead Secret,[5] will you let the Bearer have it, as it is Mr. Collins's copy. If you have not, don't on any account send it. (N.B. Mr.

[1] For the half year ending Christmas 56.

[2] The balance paid to CD was £1,841.13.3, as against £2,250.8.5 paid the previous half year. There was a fall in the amount due for *Little Dorrit* for £3,601.17.7 to £3,252.4, and no payment for *A Child's History*. (Bradbury & Evans's Accounts, MS V & A.)

[3] i.e. copies of total sales, including *HW*.

[4] The Bedford Hotel, Brighton.

[5] The book was published in 2 vols. on 10 June (before the final instalment); Tauchnitz published Chs 1–21 in May and 22–8 later. In March or April CD had drafted the following for Bradbury & Evans to send to Ticknor & Fields: "Mr Wilkie Collins the author of the story called The Dead Secret now publishing in Household Words, and which will probably be completed at about the end of May, has communicated to Mr. Charles Dickens that he has received a proposal from Messrs Harper of New York (through their agent here) 'to be supplied with the last two or three chapters in MS., so that the American Edition may be completed in book-form, about the time it is completed here.' For this accommodation £25 English money is offered to Mr. Collins. | Mr Dickens deems it both courteous and honorable—and we quite agree with him—that you should be asked whether you have any desire to make a similar offer to Mr. Collins. In that case, Mr. Dickens would represent to that gentleman that your regular connection with Household Words gives you a prior title to the concession on the same terms." (N, II, 841 and *n.*)

Collins's head being triangular with a knob in the middle, and small besides, his hat is of no use to anybody but himself).

Ever Most Faithfully Yours | My Dear Mrs. Watson

CD.

To THE HON. MRS RICHARD WATSON, 10 MARCH 1857

MS Huntington Library.

Tavistock House | Tuesday Tenth March 1857

My Dear Mrs. Watson

I left the Bedford, early yesterday morning, leaving the Invalid behind to follow with the baggage. (My face is like a cullender from the hail and ice on Sunday).

Here is the Frozen Deep, accompanied by love and regard from all. I lose no time in sending off the packet.

My Dear Mrs. Watson | Ever Most Faithfully Yours

CHARLES DICKENS

To RICHARD MONCKTON MILNES, 11 MARCH 1857*

MS Trinity College, Cambridge. *Address:* Richard Monckton Milnes Esquire M.P. | Upper Brook Street | Grosvenor Square.

Tavistock House | Wednesday Night | Eleventh March 1857.

My Dear Milnes

As you made a reference to the Guild to day,[1] I wish—merely as between yourself and myself—to make an important little point known to you. Pray understand,—not because I can have the slightest quarrel, either with the matter or the manner of what you said (which were, both, worthy of you, and of all respect), but because it is a plain fact, essential to any such reference.

I do not assert that the principles of the Guild are successful. I could have no warrant for making any such statement to you. But they are placed *altogether in abeyance*, by the Act of Parliament under which the Guild is incorporated.[2] That Act is the least stringent we could obtain, but it disqualifies the Institution from appropriating any of its money to any of its purposes, until it shall have been in existence seven years from the date of the Bill. Consequently, the Society is forced (very much against its will), to remain inactive until the prescribed term is out. In the meanwhile it incurs no expences of management, and re-invests the interest upon its capital as the interest becomes due. You see how clear the case is, that it cannot be regarded as under the test of experience until the period of probation shall have expired.

Very faithfully Yours always

R. M. Milnes Esquire CHARLES DICKENS

[1] In his speech at the Annual meeting of the Royal Literary Fund.

[2] See *To* Lytton, 28 Jan 57 and *fn*.

To [E. F. PIGOTT], 12 MARCH 1857

Extract in Parke Bernet catalogue, Dec 1947; *MS* 1 p.; dated Tavistock House, 12 Mar 57; addressed Mr Bigott according to the catalogue.

My Dear [Pigott]

Will you come and dine with us Monday next at 6 sharp? We have no party. Thackeray's daughters[1] are coming to see the girls that day, but otherwise we are en famille.

To FRANCESCO BERGER, 13 MARCH 1857

MS Ohio Historical and Philosophical Society.

Tavistock House | Thirteenth March 1857 | Friday

My Dear Berger

I am sorry to assure you that my Vote for the Royal Hospital[2] has long been promised in behalf of another distressing case, or you should have had it with the greatest readiness and pleasure.

Faithfully Yours always

Francesco Berger Esquire CHARLES DICKENS

To CHARLES DE LA PRYME, 14 MARCH 1857

MS Brotherton Library, Leeds. *Address:* Private | C. De La Pryme Esquire | &c &c &c | Reform Club | Pall Mall.

Tavistock House | Fourteenth March 1857

My Dear Sir

I feel exceedingly obliged to you for your kind note; but the Lovers[3] cannot be brought together without some prospect of a mutual attachment. Reciprocity of liking, on my side, is wholly out of the question.

I beg to assure you that I thoroughly satisfied myself long ago, that I can be far more useful and far more independent, in my own calling than in the House of Commons; and that I believe no consideration would induce me to become a Member of that amazing Assembly.[4]

Faithfully Yours

C. De la Pryme Esquire CHARLES DICKENS

[1] Anne Isabella, "Annie" (1837–1919; *DNB*), novelist and essayist, and Harriet Marian, "Minnie" (1838–75).

[2] The Royal Hospital for Incurables: see *To* Moore, 14 May 57 and *fn.*

[3] CD and the House of Commons.

[4] For similar replies to other invitations to stand in the coming General Election (which began 26 Mar) from unknown correspondents, this month, see 17 and 14–17 Mar; and, for several earlier rejected proposals, see Vol. VI, p. 692 and *n.* De la Pryme wrote a similar letter asking CD to stand for Lambeth in Jan 65 (see Vol. XI).

To MRS LING,[1] 14 MARCH 1857*

MS Mr J. Wilson.

Tavistock House | Fourteenth March 1857

Mr. Charles Dickens presents his Compliments to Mrs. Ling, and regrets that the case to which the enclosed paper refers, is one of scores upon scores that he is quite unable to assist.

To THOMAS BEARD, 15 MARCH 1857

MS Dickens House. *Address:* Private | Thomas Beard Esquire | Morning Herald Office | Shoe Lane | Fleet Street | E.C.

Tavistock House | Sunday March Fifteenth 1857

My Dear Beard

I had begun to think that the vinous dotard and feeble Bacchus of Bankruptcy,[2] might be playing fast and loose. Consequently your letter was a great relief to me, and I am now confirmed in my hopes, that whatever becomes of the Paper, your position is permanently improved.[3]

As to those two incurable corns in Shoe-Lane, Baldwin and Knox[4]—it is quite clear that eradication is the only possible resource.

Your hard work will only leave you Saturdays for a chance of a Play. Next Saturday I am engaged; but if you will bind yourself over for Saturday week the 28th and will appoint—a day or two before—your own hour for our meeting at the Household Words office, we will go and dine somewhere, and I will be ready with the place of entertainment.

Ever Heartily Yours

CD.

Your summer quarters are progressing favorably. I shall not let you see them, now, until the workmen are out, and they have got their clean shirt on.

To W. C. MACREADY, 15 MARCH 1857*

MS Morgan Library.

Tavistock House | Sunday Fifteenth March 1857

My Dearest Macready.

I have only one vote for the Royal Hospital. It has long been promised in behalf of a very sad case (they are all sad cases), and is already anticipated for next year too, by another afflicted applicant.

Our poor dear boy![5]—We speak of him every day, and look for any scrap of news

[1] Possibly of 39 Albert St, Mornington Crescent.

[2] See 24 Feb and *fn.*

[3] He remained on the *Morning Herald* until the end of 1863, when he was appointed Court Newsman.

[4] Robert Knox (1808–59), editor of the *Morning Herald* 1846–57: see Vol. II, p. 81*n.*

[5] Henry.

of him from Sherborne, with the deepest interest. What an extraordinary assertion of native strength in him breaks through all his illnesses! But we think most, now, of his father and his aunt. We never can get either of you out of our minds.

Please God you will come and look at Gad's Hill this Summer and will like it none the less for the sign of the Sir John Falstaff over the way. I am getting it up, very plainly, but comfortably; and I hope it is the best thing I could do for the boys—particularly Charley, who will now be able to have country air and change all through the fine weather; the railway enabling him to go up for business, and come down for dinner.

The annual fight at the Literary Fund came off last Wednesday.[1] I am resolved to reform it or ruin it—one or the other.

God bless you. Our most affectionate love and sympathy to yourself and your dear sister and all the dear ones in the house.

Ever affectionately and faithfully

CD.

To THE HON. SECRETARY, WALLINGFORD MECHANICS' INSTITUTE, [?15–16 MARCH 1857]

Mention in *To* Gregson, 17 Mar 57. *Date:* clearly written a day or two earlier.

To [?THE SECRETARY],[2] ROYAL LITERARY FUND, 16 MARCH 1857

Mention in Anderson Galleries, Feb 1922; *MS* 1 p.; dated Office of Household Words, 16 Mar 57.

Sending draft of a resolution to appoint a committee to help Mrs Haydn.[3]

To THE REV. JOHN GREGSON,[4] 17 MARCH 1857

Text from N, II, 840.

Tavistock House, London | Seventeenth March 1857

Dear Sir,

I feel much obliged to you for your proffered hospitality, and entreat you to accept my thanks. But I beg to assure you (as I have already assured the honorary

[1] i.e. the Annual General Meeting: see *To* Dilke, 2 Mar and *fn*, and 19 Mar and *fn*.

[2] Octavian Blewitt (1810–84; *DNB*): see Vol. I, p. 602*n* and later vols.

[3] Mrs Haydn was granted £25 by the Fund in Mar 56. CD was no doubt concerned in appointing a committee to raise funds for the election of Mrs Haydn's second son, Thomas, to a place at St Ann's Society School; over £60 was raised and the boy was elected in Mar 57 (MSS Royal Literary Fund). A letter to *The Times* from Mrs Haydn (16 Jan 56), appealing for help, aroused Press controversy over the amount of the grant made by the Royal Literary Fund, the *Morning Chronicle* describing the Fund as lying "rusting in its large and gilded cage in Bloomsbury" (21 Jan 56; Press cuttings, Royal Literary Fund).

[4] The Rev. John Gregson (?1817–59), of Castle Priory, Wallingford; MA Brasenose College, Oxford, 1841; Vicar of the Abbey, Sutton Courtenay, Berks in 1847.

Secretary of your Institution) that my avocations render my compliance with the request that I will read at Wallingford,[1] wholly out of the question. I receive such an incredible number of similar applications, that it is no light task to answer them, however briefly.

Dear Sir | Yours faithfully and obliged
[CHARLES DICKENS]

To UNKNOWN CORRESPONDENT,[2] [14–17 MARCH 1857]

Extract in F, XI, iii, 827. *Date:* "apparently about the same date" as next, according to Forster; not later than 27 Mar; the election began 26 Mar.

I declare that as to all matters on the face of this teeming earth,[3] it appears to me that the House of Commons and parliament altogether is become just the dreariest failure and nuisance that ever bothered this much-bothered world.[4]

To UNKNOWN CORRESPONDENT, 17 MARCH 1857

Extract in Sotheby's catalogue, July 1890; *MS* 1 p.; dated 17 Mar 57.

I have however thoroughly satisfied myself, having often had occasion to consider the question, that I can be far more usefully and independently employed in my chosen sphere of action than I could hope to be in the House of Commons; and I believe that no consideration would induce me to become a member of that extraordinary assembly.

To HENRY AUSTIN, [19 MARCH 1857]

Mention in next. *Date:* posted the same day.

To HENRY AUSTIN, 19 MARCH 1857*

MS Morgan Library.

Tavistock House
Thursday Night | Nineteenth March 1857

My Dear Henry.

A letter I posted to you from the Household Words office this afternoon has crossed a letter from you which I find here on coming home.

I am delighted to find that the Builder got in.[5] Certainly, as to going down as early as will suit you next week. As to tomorrow (Friday) I will remain at home here until

[1] In Berks.

[2] According to Forster, this was in answer to a request from one of the Metropolitan constituencies, i.e. the City, Finsbury, Marylebone, Tower Hamlets, Westminster. After the election there were more "reformers" than before. But see pp. 269–70.

[3] Cf. *1 Henry IV*, III, i, 27: Hotspur mocks Glendower ("diseased nature oftentimes breaks forth in strange eruptions of this teeming earth").

[4] But see *To* Lytton, 28 Jan.

[5] See *To* Miss Coutts, 9 Apr.

4, expecting either to see or hear from you. Any summons from you in the course of the day to come to your office (if that should suit you better), will immediately produce me.

Ever affectionately
CD.

To C. W. DILKE, 19 MARCH 1857*

MS Churchill College, Cambridge.

OFFICE OF HOUSEHOLD WORDS,
Thursday Nineteenth March 1857

My Dear Mr. Dilke

Forster has another notion about the Literary Fund. Will you name a day next week—that day being neither Thursday nor Saturday—when we shall hold solemn council here at ½ past 4.

For myself I beg to report that I have my War Paint on—that I have buried the Pipe of Peace—and am whooping for Committee Scalps.[1]

Ever Faithfully Yours
C. W. Dilke Esquire CHARLES DICKENS

To MARK LEMON, 19 MARCH 1857

MS Brotherton Library, Leeds.

Tavistock House | Thursday Nineteenth March | 1857

My Dear Mark

Stanny is delighted with the prospect of tomorrow, and will meet us at the H.W. Office at a quarter before five.

Ever affecy.
CD.

To SAMUEL PHELPS,[2] 24 MARCH 1857

MS Rosenbach Foundation. *Address:* Samuel Phelps Esquire | 8 Canonbury Square | N.

Tavistock House | Tuesday Twenty Fourth March | 1857

My Dear Mr. Phelps.

Can you come and join our family dinner (we shall be perfectly alone) on Sunday at 5? If this proposal should not be convenient to you, I should be happy to see you on Saturday at halfpast 2. I should prefer the former appointment, as it would enable us to discuss our subject[3] at the fireside after dinner; but I suggest two

[1] See *To* Dilke, 2 Mar, *fn.*

[2] Samuel Phelps (1804–78; *DNB*), actor; joint-manager, Sadler's Wells, since 1844: see Vol. VII, p. 281 and *n.*

[3] The coming Annual Festival of the Royal General Theatrical Fund on 6 Apr. Phelps had been persuaded to be Chairman, for the first time, having overcome his "reluctance to be placed before the public in such a position", and was naturally anxious to seek advice from his

opportunities of meeting, in order that the end may be the more readily brought about.

Write me a word in answer, and I shall expect you according to your reply,

Faithfully Yours

Samuel Phelps Esquire CHARLES DICKENS

To F. FREDERICK BRANDT,[1] 27 MARCH 1857

Extract in Sotheby's catalogue, Mar 1984; *MS* 1 p.; dated Tavistock House, 27 Mar 57. *Address:* F. Frederick Brandt Esquire | Inner Temple.

Sympathising with his love for the fountain[2] *and his* righteous indignation against the insensitive and bibulous old benchers.[3] May the Water-Gods confound them! *But declining to write to* The Times *on the subject* when scores of men who are well able to do so, live within sound of the Fountain and make no sign.

To ROBERT BELL,[4] 30 MARCH 1857

Extract from Christie's catalogue, Mar 1985; *MS* 1 p.; addressed Robert Bell; dated Tavistock House, 30 Mar 57.

He has a pleasant remembrance of his last visit[5] *to Bell and regrets his inability to accept an invitation owing to an engagement to dine at Gravesend on 7 April.* It is, however, an engagement—and a grim business one to boot[6]—and you know the reliability of your old Manager.[7] (I will be as disagreeable at Gravesend as I possibly can).

To MARK LEMON, 30 MARCH 1857

MS Benoliel Collection.

Tavistock House | Monday Thirtieth March 1857

My Dear Mark

Stanny wants to know if you will come and dine at the Jack Straw at Hampstead

friend CD. He made excellent speeches, warmly received, and proposed the usual toasts, including one to CD and his fellow Trustees to which CD replied in a complimentary speech (*Speeches*, ed. K. J. Fielding, pp. 228–32). For a full account of the occasion see W. May Phelps and John Forbes-Robertson, *The Life and Life-Work of Samuel Phelps*, 1886, pp. 244–53.

[1] Francis Frederick Brandt (1819–74; *DNB*), barrister and author; called to Bar 1847.

[2] In the Temple Gardens; where Ruth Pinch and John Westlock met (*Chuzzlewit*, Ch. 53).

[3] In his autobiographical novel, *Frank Marland's Manuscripts*, 1859, Brandt refers to this letter (from "one of the greatest authors of the day") and makes it clear that the Benchers wished to remove the fountain in order to build a library on the site, "the old one being required for their private festivities".

[4] Robert Bell (1800–67; *DNB*), journalist and miscellaneous writer: see Vols I, p. 543*n* and VI, p. 89*n*.

[5] Probably in Apr 1855, when Bell was one of the group requesting a special meeting of the Royal Literary Fund: see Vol. VII, p. 600.

[6] Unspecified business connected with Gad's Hill.

[7] Bell had acted in the amateurs' production of *Not so Bad as we Seem*, 1851: see Vol. VI, p. 385*n*.

next Friday, seeing his Pictures[1] first. Answer me as soon as you can, and, if Yes, meet here at 3.

Ever affecy.
CD.

To GEORGE HODDER,[2] [?MARCH 1857]

Text from George Hodder, *Memories of my Time*, 1870, p. 10. *Date:* soon after receiving Hodder's verses on the death of his wife, Agnes, who died in Mar 57.

I sympathize with you in the feelings which have prompted the verses, and I beg to offer you my condolences on the great loss which they very tenderly and touchingly deplore. But I think they express a private sorrow, and have not that public scope of address which is necessary to the purposes of "Household Words."[3]

To CHARLES MILNER,[4] 1 APRIL 1857*

MS Mr Maurice I. Packington.

Tavistock House | First April, 1857 | Wednesday Evening

Mr. Charles Dickens presents his Compliments to Mr. Milner, and begs to say that he has engaged Charles Barber,[5] and hopes to be well suited with him. He will feel much obliged to Mr. Milner, if he will have the goodness to let Barber have the enclosed note as soon as convenient. He would not trouble Mr. Milner, but for not knowing Barber's address.

To FRANK STONE, [?1 APRIL 1857]*

MS Benoliel Collection. *Date:* shortly before *To* Stone, 6 Apr 57; handwriting supports. 1 Apr was Wednesday in 1857.

Wednesday Morning

My Dear Stone

What are you doing to day? I am off to Gad's Hill. Are you disposed for a country walk?

Ever Affecy.
CD.

[1] Stanfield exhibited four pictures at RA this year: *Fort Socoa, St Jean de Luz*; *Port na Spania, near the Giant's Causeway, Antrim, Coast of Ireland*; *Calais Fishermen taking in their Nets—Squall coming on*; and *Calm—in the Gulf of Salerno*.

[2] George Hodder (1819–70), journalist: see Vol. IV, p. 95 and *n*, 96*n*.

[3] Entitled "A Lament of the Heart", they were published elsewhere, according to Hodder. Introducing CD's letter, Hodder writes of him: "to whose kindness and assistance in the struggle of life I have often been deeply indebted". (*Memories*, p. 10.)

[4] Charles Milner (*b.* ?1802), formerly of Preston Hall, Farlingham, a few miles south of Rochester. Educated at Eton; BA Brasenose College, Oxford, 1824.

[5] As head gardener at Gad's Hill Place. Probably Milner was his present or former employer.

To HANS CHRISTIAN ANDERSEN, 3 APRIL 1857

MS Royal Library, Copenhagen.

Tavistock House, London | Third April, 1857.

My Dear Hans Andersen.

I received your welcome letter, the day before yesterday, and immediately proceed to answer it. I hope my answer will at once decide you to make your summer visit to us.[1]

We shall not be at home here in London itself, after the first week in June, but we shall be at a little country house I have, only twenty seven miles away. It is on a line of Railroad, and within an hour and a half of London, in a very beautiful part of Kent. You shall have a pleasant room there, with a charming view, and shall live as quietly and wholesomely as in Copenhagen itself. If you should want, at any time while you are with us, to pass the night in London, this house, from the roof to the cellar, will be at your disposal. A servant who is our friend also, who lived with us many years and is now married, will be taking care of it; and she will take care of you too, with all her heart.[2]

So pray make up your mind to come to England. We shall be at this place I mention, within an hour and a half's ride, all through the summer, and if you will let me know when we may expect you, we shall look forward to that time with most cordial pleasure.

I am very much interested by what you tell me of your new Novel,[3] and you may be very sure that it will have no more attentive and earnest reader than it will find in me. I am impatient for its publication. Little Dorrit at present engages me closely. I hope to finish her story by about the end of this month, and that you will find me in the summer quite a free man, playing at cricket and all manner of English open-air games.

The two little girls you saw at Broadstairs when you left England, are young women now, and my eldest boy is more than 20 years old. But we have children of all sizes, and they all love you. You will find yourself in a house full of admiring and affectionate friends, varying from three feet high to five feet nine. Mind! you must not think any more of going to Switzerland. You must come to us.

With kind regard from all my family, Believe me

My Dear Andersen | Affectionately | And Cordially Yours

Hans Christian Andersen. CHARLES DICKENS

[1] For Andersen's stay at Gad's Hill 11 June–15 July 57, see *To* Miss Coutts, 10 July and *fnn.*

[2] Anne Cornelius.

[3] *To Be, or Not to Be*, transl. by Mrs Bushby; announced in May and published early June by Bentley.

To P. W. CURRIE,[1] 3 APRIL 1857*

MS New York University Library.

Tavistock House, London | Third April, 1857.

Dear Sir

I beg to acknowledge the receipt of your obliging letter, and to thank you for the trouble its subject has occasioned you.

If you will have the kindness to reply to the gentleman whose letter I return, that you find such photographs as he required are not to be obtained, you will tell him the exact truth. I am so sensible of being a notorious personage, and am always to unwilling to make any unnecessary flourish of myself before the general eye, that I constantly decline to have myself multiplied in the Print Shops. Hence it really is the fact that what the sculptor wants is not in existence.

I am naturally very much flattered by his proposal and the assurance I derive from it that I have interested readers even in Russia: but I may confess to you that I should be greatly embarrassed by his carrying it into execution. For I am sure he would be disappointed by the reception his work would meet with here, simply because I am sure that no likeness sufficiently striking and characteristic to bear comparison with life, could be made out of such materials.

Renewing my thanks to yourself I have the honor to be Dear Sir

Your faithful Servant

Philip W Currie Esquire CHARLES DICKENS

I do not quite understand whether or no N. Borytshevski[2] is aware that you have referred his letter directly to me. If he be, may I beg you to assure him of my most grateful and cordial appreciation of the honor he would confer upon me.

To LOUIS HACHETTE, 3 APRIL 1857

MS Librairie Hachette.

Tavistock House, London | Third April, 1857

Dear Sir.

I have received your two obliging letters, with much interest and satisfaction. The copies of Nickleby[3] which you had the kindness to forward to me, I have also received safely, and have carefully read. Touching them, and the high opinion I have formed of the translation, I enclose a letter to M. Lorain which perhaps you will have the kindness to place in his hands.

Bleak House[4] has not yet reached me.

[1] No doubt Philip Henry Wodehouse Currie, later 1st Baron Currie of Hawley (1834–1906; *DNB*), diplomat; joined Foreign Office 1854; served in St Petersburg and Denmark; permanent Under-Secretary of State for Foreign Affairs, 1889; KGB 1885; Baron 1899. Wrote *Memoir of Richard Cosway, RA*, for *Catalogue Raisonné of his engraved works* (of which he had a major collection), ed. F. B. Daniell, 1890.

[2] Probably Ivan Peter Borichevskii, 97 Fontanki St, St Petersburg, Privy councillor; presumably an amateur sculptor or acting for a friend. Currie would have met him when attached to the British Legation in St Petersburg.

[3] Vols I and II of Hachette's translated edn.

[4] Also published in two vols in Hachette's edn, 1857.

I am charmed to learn that the series is progressing with so much vigour, and I sincerely hope that the result of the undertaking may be in all respect satisfactory to you.[1]

Accept my dear Sir the assurance of my consideration and regard.

Very faithfully Yours

A Monsieur L. Hachette CHARLES DICKENS

To PAUL LORAIN, 3 APRIL 1857

Mention in last. *Date:* written the same day.

To JOHN FORSTER, [?5 APRIL 1857]

Extract in F, VIII, i, 627. *Date:* shortly after 3 Apr 57 (see below).

I was ludicrously foiled here[2] the other night in a resolution I have kept for twenty years not to know of any attack upon myself, by stumbling, before I could pick myself up, on a short extract in the *Globe* from *Blackwood's Magazine*, informing me that *Little Dorrit* is "Twaddle."[3] I was sufficiently put out by it to be angry with myself for being such a fool, and then pleased with myself for having so long been constant to a good resolution.

To FRANK STONE, 6 APRIL 1857*

MS Benoliel Collection.

Tavistock House | Monday Morning Sixth April | 1857

My Dear Stone

Many thanks for your note. I will come in, early tomorrow morning before the Visitors begin.[4] Yesterday I was engaged, and to day I have no end of botherations. I

[1] The *Publisher's Circular*, 2 Mar 57, referred to the edn of the complete works "now in course of publication" and "translated into French under the author's superintendence".

[2] This suggests that CD is writing from one of his clubs—probably the Athenaeum.

[3] The *Globe* of 3 Apr gives extracts from *Blackwood's* of 1 Apr which, though very disparaging, do not include the actual word "twaddle". CD must have turned to *Blackwood's* itself: *To* Forster, mid-Apr shows he was reading the magazine. He would find in the lengthy article, "Remonstrance with Dickens" (pp. 490–503), anonymous, but by (Sir) Edward Bruce Hamley, a regular contributor, a complaint first of his "post-Pickwickian works", and then in great detail an attack on *Little Dorrit.* The writer deplores CD's attempt to write on social questions, also criticising the novel's "cumbrous array of characters" and "aimless" construction. "Old Dorrit", at first a well-drawn character "becomes on his accession to wealth, a prosy old driveller, whose inanities are paraded and circumstantially described in a long succession of twaddle" (p. 497). Mrs General "twaddles ... through a great number of scenes" (p. 500). The word is applied to characters rather than the whole novel; but all the criticism is damaging, and with the closing chapters still to come CD must have found it disturbing. Forster, placing the extract in his general discussion of the novel, notes that it did not add to CD's reputation, though the public showed no falling-off; the letter shows "his anxiety to avoid any set-off from the disquiet that critical discourtesies might give".

[4] For the usual private view in Stone's studio of pictures for the RA.

am of course anxious to see what you have done, before it goes away.[1] I have seen nobody's pictures but Stanfield's; being closely occupied with my book—and Gad's Hill.

Ever Affecy.
CD

To FRANK STONE, 7 APRIL 1857*

MS Benoliel Collection.

OFFICE OF HOUSEHOLD WORDS,
Seventh April 1857

My Dear Stone

I have unfortunately been kept here until the last moment, and have to fly for my Train.[2] Never mind! I will study the Picture on the Academy wall.

In great haste | Every affecy.
CD.

To MISS BURDETT COUTTS, 9 APRIL 1857

MS Morgan Library. *Address:* Miss Burdett Coutts | Meadfoot House | Hesketh Crescent | Torquay | Devon.

Wates's Hotel, Gravesend
Thursday Night | Ninth April, 1857

My Dear Miss Coutts.

I am working here for a few days (that I may have an eye on the little repairs at Gad's Hill), and must thank you for your letter. Not that I thought you "queer" for not writing sooner. You must be very much queerer than that, to be queer in my mind!

My uneasiness on the Dress point, arose, first of all, from the nature of the girls' remarks. I do not feel them to be true, and I have a very great misgiving that they were written against nature, under the impression that they would have a moral aspect. I attach no blame to the young women—have not a doubt that they deceived themselves far more than they will ever deceive any body else—and believe them to have written in a love of commendation; in a rather more disagreeable phase of it than a love of dress would shew.[3]

I have also, long felt the question to be an excessively difficult one. Apart from what you so gently and delightfully write in your letter (you must not mind my praising it, because it really does charm me), of that little womanly vanity and desire to please, which a wisdom in comparison with which the best of our lights are mere ignorance and folly, has implanted in women, as one of their distinguishing marks, for the happiness of mankind; I have to add an observation which I believe to be a

[1] Stone exhibited at RA that year *Margaret. "My peace is gone, my heart is heavy"* and *Bon Jour, Messieurs*, a painting of a French family in a horse and cart. For his collecting material in Boulogne for his new paintings of boatmen, peasants and fish-wives, see Vol. VII, p. 390*n*.

[2] *To* Gravesend: see next.

[3] See *To* Miss Coutts, 5 Mar and *fn*.

true one. I constantly notice a love of color and brightness, to be a portion of a generous and fine nature. I feel sure that it is often an innocent part of a capacity for enjoyment, and appreciation, and general adornment of everything, which makes a buoyant, hopeful, genial character. I say most gravely that I do *not*[1] know what I may take away from the good influences of a poor man's home, if I strike this natural common thing out of the girl's heart who is going to be his wife.

It is like the use of strong drinks or the use of strong any thing. The evil is in the abuse, and not in the use. The distinction between the two, and the perception of the medium in which taste and propriety are to be found, is the result—one of the results—of a generally good, sound, plain education. The natural tendency of the sex through all its grades, is to a little finery—and I would not run counter to that (I make bold to say), agreeable, wholesome, and useful characteristic. The frivolous women of a better degree who disgust you and all sensible people, have really had no education whatever that deserves the name.

You will I know be glad to hear that Walter appeared here yesterday, radiant and gleaming. He passed his examination[2] on Tuesday in a most creditable manner, and was one of a small number of boys out of a large number, who emerged from the Ordeal triumphant. I have now taken order for his learning to swim, to ride, to fence, to become acquainted with the use of gun and pistol, and to "go in" for a trifle of Hindustanee, in the course of the three months he will probably remain at home. I started him up again last night to his brothers and sisters (Mary, Katey, and Charley, are keeping house), laden with his credentials to the different professors of these Arts. He was perfectly happy, and they had received him with torrents of applause, and he was very anxious that I should "tell Miss Coutts that he hadn't been spun"—which means, rejected.[3]

Mr. Wates, who is one of my particular friends (and whom you liked, I remember) is in great force, and his house is as orderly and comfortable as ever. If you don't like Gad's Hill, I shall set it on fire—particularly as it is insured. I have devised an immense number of small inventions, which it will require a Summer's day for you and Mrs. Brown to appreciate. There *is*[4] a little study (I am sorry to say that the merit of hewing it out of a china-closet is Mr. Austin's) which—but you must see it. According to Charley's plans, Walter is to destroy his constitution at Cricket in the field, before starting for India: which will be a great comfort to him. Mrs. Dickens and Georgina and the two little boys are with me, [a]and send best love to you and Mrs. Brown. I add mine, and am Ever dear Miss Coutts Yours most faithfully & affecy.

CD.

P.S. Very much interested in the Geologist.[a5]

[1] Underlined twice.

[2] For his commission in the East India Co. A certificate that he had qualified himself for admission was signed on 7 Apr by the three examining professors, of Mathematics and Classics, Fortification and French (MS BL, India Office).

[3] Slang used in military training establishments.

[4] Underlined twice.

[aa] Written above address on p. 1.

[5] Hugh Miller, who had recently died: see *To Mrs Miller*, 16 Apr and *fn*.

To MISS EMILY JOLLY, 10 APRIL 1857

Text from MDGH, III, 181–3.

Gravesend, Kent, 10th April, 1857.

Dear Madam,

As I am away from London for a few days, your letter has been forwarded to me. I can honestly encourage and assure you that I believe the depression and want of confidence under which you describe yourself as labouring to have no sufficient foundation.

First as to "Mr. Arle."[1] I have constantly heard it spoken of with great approval, and I think it a book of considerable merit. If I were to tell you that I see no evidence of inexperience in it, that would not be true. I think a little more stir and action to be desired also; but I am surprised by your being despondent about it, for I assure you that I had supposed it (always remembering that it is your first novel) to have met with a very good reception.

I can bring to my memory—here, with no means of reference at hand—only two papers of yours that have been unsuccessful at "Household Words." I think the first was called "The Brook." It appeared to me to break down upon a confusion that pervaded it, between a Coroner's Inquest and a Trial. I have a general recollection of the mingling of the two, as to facts and forms that should have been kept apart, in some inextricable manner that was beyond my powers of disentanglement. The second was about a wife's writing a Novel and keeping the secret from her husband until it was done. I did not think the incident of sufficient force to justify the length of the narrative. But there is nothing fatal in either of these mischances.

Mr. Wills told me when I spoke to him of the latter paper that you had it in contemplation to offer a longer story to "Household Words." If you should do so, I assure you I shall be happy to read it myself, and that I shall have a sincere desire to accept it, if possible.[2]

I can give you no better counsel than to look into the life about you, and to strive for what is noblest and true. As to further encouragement, I do not, I can most strongly add, believe that you have any reason to be downhearted.

Very faithfully yours
[CHARLES DICKENS]

To G. F. HUDSON, 11 APRIL 1857

Text from *Daily News*, 9 Oct 1905. *Address:* name of addressee given in shorter extract in Anderson Galleries catalogue, Mar 1917.[3]

Gravesend | 11th April, 1857

My dear Sir,

Your kind note has been forwarded to me here, and I received it with much

[1] See 24 Dec 56, *fn.*

[2] No further contribution by her appeared until "An Experience" in *AYR*, 1869: see later vols.

[3] Catalogue reads "G.B." in error.

pleasure. But I cannot (unfortunately) accept your agreeable invitation,[1] for I am busy here with a race of my own—bringing a pretty large field of characters up to the winning-post,[2] and spurring away with might and main.—

Believe me, very faithfully yours,

CHARLES DICKENS

To WILLIAM J. CLEMENT,[3] [?8–14 APRIL 1857]

Mention in *To* Clement, 10 July 57. *Date:* if, as CD "strongly" believed, written from Gravesend, then probably between 8 and 15 Apr.[4]

To THE EARL OF CARLISLE,[5] 15 APRIL 1857

MS Lord Howard of Henderskelfe.

Gravesend, Kent | Wednesday | Fifteenth April, 1857

My Dear Lord Carlisle.

I am writing by the river-side for a few days, and, at the end of last week, Mrs. Webb[6] appeared here with your note of introduction. I was not in the way; but, as Mrs. Webb[6] had come express from London with it, Mrs. Dickens opened it, and gave her (in the limited sense which was of no use to her), an audience. She did not quite seem to know what she wanted of me. But she said she had understood at Stafford House,[7] that I had a Theatre in which she could read; with a good deal of modesty and diffidence she at last got so far. Now, my little Theatre turns my house out of window—costs fifty pounds to put up—and is only two months taken down. Therefore is quite out of the question. This, Mrs. Dickens explained, and also my profound inability to do anything for Mrs. Webb's[6] readings, which they could not do for themselves. She appeared fully to understand the explanation, and indeed to have anticipated for herself how powerless I must be in such a case.

[1] Since Hudson lived at Tadworth Heath, close to Epsom Downs, clearly to the Derby (27 May). CD did not in fact go to the Derby this year.

[2] During the next four weeks, and especially 20 Apr–9 May (see *To* Paxton, 3 May), CD is strenuously at work on the final double number (Chs 30–4 and Preface). His "Mems to be done" list almost all the characters who then duly appear, with a further note for Ch. 32 "Take up characters to be disposed of". Again, as for No. XVIII (see *To* Macready, 28 Feb, *fn*), he drew on his memories of Fox Cooper's 1856 play. While the use in both of the recovered papers, Flintwinch's box and Affery's dreams might be coincidence, an obvious reminiscence is the passage early in Ch. 31 where Mrs Clennam kneels to ask Little Dorrit's forgiveness. The closing scene of the play also showed her repentant: "I come to beg forgiveness on my knees … *Mr Dorrit endeavours to raise her and Little Dorrit takes her hand and tries to soothe her*" (MS BL). Then she forgives her, in the spirit of the New Testament. CD describes the afterglow of the sunset and its rays as an emblem of divine Grace, recalling a passage in Wordsworth's *The Excursion*, Book IX (the resemblance first pointed out by Alan Hill in *Wordsworth's "Grand Design"*, 1986).

[3] William James Clement (1804–70), FRCS, of Shrewsbury, surgeon: see Vol. VI, p. 484*n*.

[4] About returning a MS written by a boy and sent to him by Clement.

[5] George William Frederick Howard, 7th Earl of Carlisle (1802–64; *DNB*): see Vol. II, p. 447*n*.

[6] Name omitted in MDGH; not further identified.

[7] The London home of the Duchess of Sutherland, who had given a "demonstration" of women there in Nov 52, in support of Mrs Beecher Stowe: see Vol. VI, p. 808*n*.

She described herself as being consumptive, and as being subject to an effusion of blood from the lungs—about the last condition, one would think poor woman, for the exercise of public elocution as an art.

Between ourselves, I think the whole idea a mistake, and have thought so from its first announcement. It has a fatal appearance of trading upon Uncle Tom, and am I not a Man and a Brother—which you may be by all means and still not have the smallest claim to my attention as a public reader. The town is over-read from all the white squares on the draught-boards; it has been considerably harried from all the black squares—now with the aid of Old Banjoes, and now with the aid of Exeter Hall—and I have a very strong impression that it is by no means to be laid hold of from this point of address. I myself for example am the meekest of men, and in abhorrence of Slavery yield to no human creature—and yet I dont admit the sequence that I want Uncle Tom (or Aunt Tomasina)[1] to expound King Lear to me. And I believe my case to be the case of thousands.

I trouble you with this much about it, because I am naturally desirous you should understand that if I could possibly have been of any service or have suggested any thing to this poor lady, I would not have lost the opportunity. But I cannot help her, and I assure you that I cannot honestly encourage her to hope. I fear her enterprise has no hope in it.

In your absence I have always followed you through the papers, and felt a personal interest and pleasure in the public affection in which you are held over there.[2] At the same time I must confess that I should prefer to have you here, where good public men seem to me to be dismally wanted. I have no sympathy with Demagogues, but am a grievous Radical, and think the political signs of the times to be just about as bad as the spirit of the people will admit of their being. In all other respects I am as healthy, sound, and happy, as your kindness can wish. So you will set down my political despondency as my only disease.

On the tip top of Gad's Hill between this and Rochester—on the very spot where Falstaff ran away—I have a pretty little old-fashioned house which I shall live in hope of shewing to you one day. Also I have a little story respecting the manner in which it became mine, which I hope (on the same occasion in the clouds) to tell you.

Until then and always | I am dear Lord Carlisle

Yours very faithfully and obliged

The | Earl of Carlisle CHARLES DICKENS

To J. E. BRADFIELD,[3] 16 APRIL 1857*

MS Private.

Tavistock House | Sixteenth April, 1857

Sir.

I beg to assure you that I think your movement in the matter of Toll Reform, an excellent one; but I cannot accept the honor you propose to me of becoming a

[1] This makes it clear that Mrs Webb was coloured. Carlisle had written a preface to one of the many English edns of *Uncle Tom's Cabin* in 1852.

[2] Carlisle had been Lord Lieut of Ireland since 1855.

[3] John E. Bradfield, Secretary, Toll Reform Office, 19 Strand.

Member of the Committee, simply because I am very closely occupied, and I make it a rule never to connect myself *in name alone*, with anything.

Your faithful Servant

J. E. Bradfield Esquire. CHARLES DICKENS

To MARK LEMON, 16 APRIL 1857

Extract in John Waller catalogue No. 90; *MS* 1 p.; dated 16 Apr 57.

I understand you covered yourself with GLORY on the way home the other night.

To DR HENRY MADGE,[1] 16 APRIL 1857

Extract in N, II, 898; *MS* 1½ pp; dated 1857; addressed Dr. Madge. Mention in *American Book Prices Current*, III, 80; MS 1½ pp; dated 16 Apr 57; addressed Dr Madge, St Pancras Literary Institute.

Before accepting the compliment which you have the kindness to propose to me, I would desire to be better acquainted with some details of the Institution, and the facilities it affords for a fusion of several classes on a good, common, mutual ground. This appears to me to be one of the highest uses of such establishments, and one of their most ordinary failures.

To MRS HUGH MILLER,[2] 16 APRIL 1857

Text from N, II, 845.

Tavistock House, London | Thursday 16th April, 1857

Dear Madam,

Allow me to assure you that I have received the last work[3] of your late much-lamented husband[4] with feelings of mournful respect for his memory and of heart-felt sympathy with you. It touches me very sensibly to know, from the inscription

[1] Henry Madge, MD, MRCS, of 54 Howland St, Fitzroy Sq; Medical Officer under Board of Health 1854; physician to St Pancras Royal General Dispensary, 1855; published a letter, "Sanitary Improvement in St Pancras", *The Times*, 1855; and wrote on Asiatic cholera in the *Lancet*, 1857.

[2] Née Lydia Falconer Fraser (?1811–76; *DNB*), writer, under the pseudonym "Harriet Myrtle", mainly of moral and religious children's stories, including *The Ocean Child*, 1857; married Hugh Miller 1837 and assisted him on the *Free Church Witness* (see below); helped Peter Bayne in preparing Miller's *Life*.

[3] Miller's *Testimony of the Rocks; or Geology in its Bearings on the Two Theologies, Natural and Revealed*, Edinburgh, June 1857; proof corrections completed by Miller on the day he died; Mrs Miller clearly sent CD an early copy.

[4] Hugh Miller (1802–56; *DNB*), geologist and writer; originally a stonemason; accountant in Commercial Bank, Cromarty, 1834; editor, the *Free Church Witness*, Edinburgh, 1840; his books included *Scenes and Legends of the North of Scotland*, 1835; *The Old Red Sandstone*, 1841; *Footprints of the Creator*, 1849 (a reply to Robert Chambers's *Vestiges of the Natural History of Creation*, 1844); and *The Testimony of the Rocks* (above). Took his own life 2 Dec 1856.

appended to the Volume, that he wished it to be given to me.[1] Believe me, it will fill no neglected place on my book-shelves, but will always be precious to me, in remembrance of a delightful writer, an accomplished fellow of science, and an upright and good man.

I hope I may, dear Madam, without obtrusion on your great bereavement, venture to offer you my thanks and condolences, and to add that, before I was brought into this personal association with your late husband's final labour, I was one of the many thousands whose thoughts had been much with you.

Yours faithfully and obliged
[CHARLES DICKENS]

To WILLIAM WILSON,[2] 16 APRIL 1857*

MS Free Library of Philadelphia.

Tavistock House | Sixteenth April, 1857.

Dear Sir

Returning to town last night after a short absence of ten days, I found your note and book[3] awaiting me. I hasten to assure you that I received them with very great pleasure and that I am sincerely sensible of your kind feeling towards me. My knowledge of the book has not, in these few hours, extended beyond the two first pages,[4] but those have touched my heart.

Very faithfully Yours

William Wilson Esquire CHARLES DICKENS

To BENJAMIN WEBSTER, [?16 APRIL] 1857

Mention in Sotheby's catalogue, April 1885; *MS* 1 p.; dated 1857; addressed Benjamin Webster. *Date:* after publication of *Proceedings* (see below) on 11 Apr, and probably on CD's return to London 16 Apr.

Enclosing the Proceedings of the Theatrical Fund Festival.[5]

[1] The presentation copy in the Gad's Hill Library is inscribed "from Mrs. Hugh Miller, by the expressed desire of her late Husband" (*Catalogue of the Library of CD*, ed. J. H. Stonehouse, p. 80).

[2] William Wilson, verse and prose writer, son of the publisher Effingham Wilson; used the pseudonym "Doubleyou"; besides the book below, published *A Little Earnest Book upon a great old Subject*, chapters upon poetry and prose, under his own name, 1851; and *Poems*, 1860. He had earlier sent CD his two pamphlets, *A House for Shakespeare*, dedicated to Bulwer Lytton, 1848 and 1849, advocating a National Theatre (information kindly given by Mr Robin Whitworth).

[3] *Such is Life. Sketches* [and poems] *By "Doubleyou"*, 1857, dedicated to CD. The dedication runs: "By his kind permission | This little book is dedicated to | Charles Dickens, Esq., | as a | very slight token of a very great admiration | for his | rich and original genius | by the | gratified and obliged | Author."

[4] They contain the Dedication and sonnets to CD; the first sonnet ends "Thine is the largest heart-mind ever writ", and the second, explaining how CD "battles for the helpless in the land", ends "Thy bettering perception is so fine, | To read these books is like a draught of wine!" There are also sonnets to Macready (1854) and to Carlyle (1855).

[5] i.e. the Anniversary Dinner of the General Theatrical Fund on 6 Apr (see *To* Phelps, 24 Mar 57 and *fn*); the Proceedings were published as a pamphlet. Webster (as Vice-President) is not recorded as being present.

To JOHN FORSTER, [?MID–APRIL 1857]

Extract in F, IV,i, 292. *Date:* probably after return to London on 15 Apr.

Calling Forster's attention very earnestly to two tales then in course of publication in Blackwood's Magazine.[1] Do read them. They are the best things I have seen since I began my course.

To L. MACKENZIE,[2] 18 APRIL 1857

Extract in Sotheby's catalogue, July 1983; dated Tavistock House, 18 Apr 57. *Address:* L. Mackenzie Esquire | 81 Ebury Street | S.W.

Sir.

Allow me to thank you for your note. *Replying to Mackenzie who has pointed out a resemblance between Miss Wade and a character in one of Mrs. Opie's*[3] *books,*[4] *he informs him that he does not know the story to which his correspondent refers, nor does he have her books in his library, but that he will look into the matter more fully when he has completed the novel.* I have observed Miss Wade in real life (as I dare say Mrs. Opie observed her gentleman), and know the character to be true in every respect. It quite fascinated me in its singular anatomy and I devoted great pains to it in the little narration.

I observe it to be out of the familiar experience of most people and that they regard it with an incredulous kind of astonishment,—though in reality it is often before them.

[1] "Scenes of Clerical Life" by George Eliot (unknown by this name) appeared monthly in *Blackwood's*, Jan–Nov 57; "The Sad Story of the Reverend Amos Barton" was completed in Feb and followed by Part II, "Mr. Gilfil's Love Story", completed in June. CD's "in the course of publication" suggests that the second tale was already appearing; therefore April, at its mid-point, is the likeliest; the final tale, "Janet's Repentance", appeared July–Nov 57. For CD's letter to "George Eliot", identity still unrevealed, see 18 Jan 58.

[2] Unidentified.

[3] Amelia Opie, née Alderson (1769–1853; *DNB*), novelist and poet; wife of the painter, John Opie; best-known for *Father and Daughter*, 1801, and *Adeline Mowbray*, 1804.

[4] Perhaps Madeline, heroine of her *Madeline, A Tale*, 2 vols, 1822, the daughter of a Scottish cottager; the story of her adoption by an upper-class English family, her return to her parents at age 16, and the rivalry for her of two lovers, is told through her strained, introspective Journal; but any resemblance with Miss Wade ends there: she marries a Scottish laird and her story ends happily.

To STEWARDS AND COMMITTEE OF ST. ANN'S SOCIETY,[1] 18 APRIL 1857*

MS Dickens House.

Tavistock House | Saturday Eighteenth April, 1857.

Mr. Charles Dickens presents his compliments to the Stewards and Committee of St. Ann's Society, and begs to say that his engagements do not admit of his accepting the invitation with which they have favored him.[2]

To DR W. C. HOOD,[3] 19 APRIL 1857*

MS Dickens House.

Tavistock House | 19 April, 1857 | Saturday Night.

Dear Sir

I beg to assure you that you require no better introduction to me than your own, and that I shall be happy to receive you here on Tuesday Afternoon at 5 o'Clock.

Faithfully Yours

Dr. Hood. CHARLES DICKENS

To CHARLES COOTE,[4] 22 APRIL 1857*

MS Mr Peter Goodricke. *Address:* Charles Coote Esquire | Devonshire House | Piccadilly.

Tavistock House | Wednesday Twenty Second April | 1857

My Dear Sir

I am sorry that I am not free to support your friend. But I have already pledged myself to vote for two gentlemen recommended by the Founder of the Institution.[5]

Always Faithfully Yours

Charles Coote Esquire CHARLES DICKENS

[1] For St Ann's Society, the educational charity long supported by CD, see Vols. III, p. 485*n* and VII, p. 23 and *n*.

[2] Clearly to attend its Anniversary Festival; he had accepted a similar invitation in May 43, but declined it at the last moment (Vol. III, *ibid.*).

[3] William Charles Hood (1824–70), MD, FRCP, Medical Superintendent of Bethlehem Hospital since 1852 and physician to other asylums; Treasurer, Bridewell and Bethlehem Hospital 1868–70; Lord Chancellor's Visitor in Lunacy (Forster being Secretary to the Commissioners since 1856); knighted 1868. Author of *Statistics of Insanity*, [1856] and *Criminal Lunatics*, 1860. The reforms he made in Bethlehem Hospital benefited the painter, Richard Dadd, especially the conversion in 1857 of a ward for the "better class" of criminal patients (including him). Hood is described by Patricia Allderidge in the *Richard Dadd Catalogue* (*The Late Richard Dadd*, 1974) as "a man of vision and industry, of compassion, culture and commonsense".

[4] Charles Coote (1807–79), musician; the Duke of Devonshire's pianist: see Vol. VI, p. 493*n* and *passim*.

[5] Probably the Royal Society of Musicians.

To THOMAS BEARD, 23 APRIL 1857

MS Dickens House. *Address:* Thomas Beard Esquire | 42 Portman Place | Edgeware Road | W.

Tavistock House | Thursday Twenty Third April | 1857

My Dear Beard

I have engaged Delane to dine here on Saturday the Ninth of May at half past 6, sharp. Will you hold yourself engaged accordingly.

Ever Faithfully
CD.

To HENRY BOWIE, 25 APRIL 1857*

MS Edinburgh Central Library.

Tavistock House, London
Twenty Fifth April, 1857 | Saturday Night

Dear Sir

I beg to reply to your letter that I cannot possibly pledge myself thus long beforehand, to the precise day on which I may be able to redeem my promise to your Society. Nor do I think it reasonably probable that I shall be able to do so, until September at the earliest.[1]

Faithfully Yours

Henry Bowie Esquire. CHARLES DICKENS

To THE REV. ARCHER GURNEY,[2] 25 APRIL 1857*

MS Free Library of Philadelphia.

Tavistock House
Saturday Evening | Twenty Fifth April, 1857.

My Dear Sir

I am no stranger to the worth of your opinions,[3] and the force they derive from your knowledge, feeling, and habits of reflection.

Your letter has afforded me the greatest pleasure. Believe me, whatever gratification I have been so fortunate as to give you, you have most generously and

[1] See *To* Bowie, 3 Oct. CD did not give this reading until 26 Mar 58: see *To* Mrs Forster, 28 Mar and *fn.*

[2] The Rev. Archer Thompson Gurney (1820–87; *DNB*), miscellaneous writer; called to Bar 1846, but ordained 1849; curate, St Mary's, Soho, 1851–4; Buckingham 1854–8; Court Chapel, Paris, 1858–71; transl. *Faust. Part the Second*, 1842; published many vols of verse, 1845–60; and, later, theological articles in periodicals and pamphlets.

[3] CD perhaps refers to Gurney's *A Satire for the Age—"the Transcendentalists"*, 1853, a poem somewhat in the manner of Pope's *Dunciad*; CD would approve of the strictures on "Conventionality", but not of the virulent attack on Tennyson's *Maud*, added to the 2nd edn, 1855. Both edns mention CD and Thackeray favourably.

handsomely repaid. I cannot sufficiently express to you the estimation in which I hold a tribute so spontaneously and affectionately rendered.

It cannot be more agreeable to you to find me writing without satire, than it is to me to find myself in the height of geniality. But, a writer with a great audience, who deeply feels certain salient public vices of his time, must not let them altogether go by him. He has his duty to do, and he must do it—yoking it to his pleasanter fancy as well as he can.

My Dear Sir | Very faithfully Yours

The Reverend Archer Gurney. CHARLES DICKENS

To SIR JOSEPH PAXTON, 3 MAY 1857

MS British Library.

Rochester | Sunday Third May, 1857

My Dear Paxton

Don't be dismayed when I tell you in the outset of this note, that I cannot come to Coventry on Wednesday—but read on.

You know I am an exact man, and that nothing short of necessity would induce me to break such an engagement as I have made with you. But it *is* absolute necessity that urges me to write. I am finishing my book—a task to which it is essential to devote much time and care—I have other and pressing matters requiring my prompt attention; and I really can not make a gap in the march to those two words "The End", which now absorbs me. It is not the actual time that this little journey would cost me, but it is the sense of having to go anywhere and do anything but what I am upon, next week of all the weeks in the fifty two, that would disable me. Therefore I am forced—really forced by the peculiar nature of my work which cannot be left and resumed at pleasure—to stick to my writing and ask your friendship to believe that I am, in my own despite, unavailable for Wednesday.

But, you once asked me to read my Carol for your Coventry people. Now, I will empower you to announce at the Dinner, if you think it worth while, that, as a little mark of my interest in and regard for you, I will do so, please God, on any day that you may appoint within a fortnight before Christmas Day or a fortnight after it. It shall be done for the pleasure—or benefit—or both—of any public Society in Coventry, you choose to name. You shall be at full liberty to pledge me at the Dinner, and to bind me then and there. The only promise I ask from you in return, is, that we go down together on the occasion, go to no man's dwelling-house, but cosily and jollily sup at the Inn, after the reading.

I should be exceedingly—in all truth and sincerity, seriously—pained, if you were to take my defalcation to heart, and let it throw the faintest cloud on your Wednesday's triumph. I do hope, however, that I have struck out a way of putting this right, and that you will feel that you take me down in your pocket with one of my best suits on.

So all Health and Prosperity to you, at Coventry and everywhere else—on Wednesday and on all the days in the year!—And don't suspect me of any thing but the truth: which is, that I am in the full flight and mid career of the close of my book, and must finish it at a heat, and until it is finished am fit for nothing else.

Ever Faithfully Yours

Sir Joseph Paxton. CHARLES DICKENS

To THE REV. ALEXANDER HOWELL,[1] 6 MAY 1857*

MS Professor K. J. Fielding.

Tavistock House, London | Sixth May, 1857.

Mr. Charles Dickens presents his Compliments to Mr. Howell, and begs to reply to Mr. Howell's note, that his avocations do not admit of his undertaking to read at Darlington.

To JOHN FORSTER, [7 MAY 1857]

Extract in F, VIII, i, 626–7. *Date:* CD visited the Borough on 6 May 57.[2]

Went to the Borough yesterday morning before going to Gadshill, to see if I could find any ruins of the Marshalsea. Found a great part of the original building—now "Marshalsea Place." Found the rooms that have been in my mind's eye in the story.[3] Found, nursing a very big boy, a very small boy, who, seeing me standing on the Marshalsea pavement, looking about, told me how it all used to be. God knows how he learned it (for he was a world too young to know anything about it), but he was right enough.[4] ... There is a room there—still standing, to my amazement—that I think of taking! It is the room through which the ever-memorable signers of Captain Porter's petition filed off in my boyhood.[5] The spikes are gone, and the wall is lowered, and anybody can go out now who likes to go, and is not bedridden; and I said to the boy "Who lives there?" and he said, "Jack Pithick." "Who is Jack Pithick?" I asked him. And he said, "Joe Pithick's uncle."[6]

[1] The Rev. Alexander James Howell (*b.* ?1811), BA, Magdalen College, Oxford, Vicar of Darlington 1846–60.

[2] In his Preface to the 1st edn of *Little Dorrit*, CD says that he "went to look" on "the sixth of this present month" (May 1857).

[3] The Preface has a much fuller account of the same visit.

[4] CD describes him in the Preface as "this young Newton".

[5] i.e. in 1824 during John Dickens's imprisonment for debt: see CD's personal recollections in Forster (I, ii, 32–3).

[6] The Preface reads "Tom Pythick" and "Joe Pythick's Uncle" and calls him the tenant of William Dorrit's room.

To EDWARD CHAPMAN, 8 MAY 1857*

MS Free Library of Philadelphia.

Tavistock House | Friday Evening | Eighth May, 1857

Dear Sir

I am very glad to find the state of the accounts so much improved,[1] and thoroughly concur in your hope that we may find the improvement lasting.[2]

Please to pay in the balance as usual, now that I have gone over them.

Faithfully Yours

Edward Chapman Esquire. CHARLES DICKENS

To THE EARL STANHOPE,[3] 11 MAY 1857*

MS Stanhope Papers.

Tavistock House | Eleventh May, 1857

My Dear Lord Stanhope.

It would have given me great pleasure if I could have had the honor of accepting your kind invitation—and Mrs. Dickens also, would have been proud to respond to Lady Stanhope's[4] remembrance of her—but that I am unfortunately engaged for Wednesday the 20th. A promise of long standing, to go out of town that morning, ties me fast.[5]

My Dear Lord | Faithfully Yours

The | Earl Stanhope CHARLES DICKENS

To WILKIE COLLINS, 11 MAY 1857

MS Morgan Library.

Tavistock House | Monday Evening | Eleventh May, 1857

My Dear Collins

I am very sorry that we shall not have you tomorrow. Think you would get on better if you were to come, after all.

Yes Sir. Thank God, I *have* finished! On Saturday last, I wrote the two little words of three letters each.[6]

[1] The half-yearly accounts to Christmas 1856: CD's total balance went up from £416.15.0 to £605.3.8 (including a special account for *Oliver Twist*, not returned till Mar 57): MS V & A.

[2] For the first six months of 1857 total sales were not down, but the account was "not so good as last time", Chapman wrote to CD, "owing to the heavy reprints" (MS V & A).

[3] Philip Henry Stanhope, 5th Earl Stanhope (1805–75; *DNB*), DCL, historian and politician. Had been close friend of Peel. Procured passing of Copyright Bill 1842; President Society of Arts 1846–75; Chairman of Trustees, National Portrait Gallery, 1857. The first of his many historical works was *History of the War of Succession in Spain*, 1832. Deputy Lord Lieut of Kent. Letter makes clear they had met.

[4] Emily Harriet, daughter of General Sir Edward Kerrison, Bart; married 1834.

[5] In fact he was away 17–20 May.

[6] The final double No. for June, Nos XIX and XX, Book II, Chs 30–4, was published 30 May 57.

Any mad proposal you please, will find a wildly insane reponse in.

Yours Ever
CD.

We shall have to arrange about Tuesday at Gad's Hill. You remember the engagement?[1]

To HANS CHRISTIAN ANDERSEN, 12 MAY 1857*

MS Royal Library, Copenhagen.

Tavistock House, London | Twelfth May, 1857.

My Dear Hans Christian Andersen.

I have just now finished Little Dorrit, and devote my first leisure to writing to you, in answer to your welcome and much-valued letter.

My house in the country is *not* upon the straight main railway-line between Dover and London. There is a station upon that line, where you could turn off, and come to me by a Branch Railroad; but it would be rather a complicated business for a stranger. Therefore, if you should be alone, I would recommend you to come to London, and then, *at another part of the Station at which you would arrive*—the London Bridge Terminus—to take the North Kent Railway, to a place called Higham (HIGHAM) which is a mile from my house.

But, when you know exactly when you will come, and how you will come, I will meet you somewhere—either at the station in London, or at some other part of the journey—if you will tell me what your arrangements are.

You write English so extraordinarily well, that I am quite surprised by what you tell me of your speaking it. I feel sure, however, that you will become a perfect Englishman among my family, in a very few days. We all speak French, and some Italian. My eldest boy speaks German too. So I am not in the least afraid of our failing to be talkative.

I may as well mention while I think of it, that I wear a moderate beard. As I wore none when you were last in England, your knowing of the change may enable you to recognize me the sooner, when you see me.

Do not write until you know all about your journey. And then be sure that you will find me somewhere, waiting to receive and welcome you.

With kindest regard from all my house, | Ever Faithfully Yours
CHARLES DICKENS

[1] For 19 May: see *To* Collins, 17 May.

To THOMAS BEARD, 12 MAY 1857

MS Dickens House. *Address:* Thomas Beard Esquire, Morning Herald Office.

OFFICE OF HOUSEHOLD WORDS,
Tuesday Twelfth May 1857

My Dear Beard

I am sorry to find (your card being sent down to me here, with my letters), that you called at home this morning. Could you call at Tavistock House again tomorrow morning at 10?

Are you engaged *this afternoon*? If not, we dine here (B and E, Lemon, and Forster). It is our half yearly Audit Day. Half past five. Can you come? If you can—do.

Ever Faithfully
CD.

To JOHN FORSTER, 13 MAY 1857

MS Churchill College, Cambridge.

Tavistock House | Thirteenth May, 1857.

My Dear Forster.

I have gone over Dilke's memoranda, and I think it quite right and necessary that those points should be stated. Nor do I see the least difficulty in the way of their introduction into the Pamphlet.[1]

But I do not deem it possible to get the Pamphlet written and published before the dinner.[2] I have so many matters pressing on my attention, that I cannot turn to it immediately on my release from my book, just finished. It shall be done and distributed early in next month.

As to anything being lost by its not being in the hands of the people who dine (as you seem to think), I have not the least misgiving on that score. They would say, if it were issued, just what they will say without it. Lord Granville is committed to taking the chair[3] and will make the best speech he can in it. The pious Blewitt[4] will cram him with as many distortions of the truth as his stomach may be crooked enough to receive. Bell,[5] with Bardolphian eloquence, will cool his nose in the modest merits of the Institution. Thackeray[4] will make a neat and appropriate speech on both sides, round the two corners, and over the way.[6] And all this would be done to exactly the

[1] *The Case of the Reformers in the Literary Fund*, 1858, written by CD, with the help of Forster and C. W. Dilke.

[2] On 19 May, in the Freemasons' Tavern. *The Times*, 20 May, gave it a full report.

[3] In fact he was unable to attend and his place was taken by William Cowper, MP (later 1st Baron Mount-Temple). The longest speech was made by a guest, Mr Justice Haliburton, of Canada.

[4] Names omitted in MDGH.

[5] Name omitted in MDGH. Robert Bell, a member of the committee. He read out the list of donations and subscriptions, but did not make a speech.

[6] Thackeray proposed the main toast, "Prosperity to the Royal Literary fund". He could see in the room, he said, nothing "which did not augur well for the prosperity of the fund". There were 151 present and subscriptions amounted to over £1,200.

same purpose and in just the same strain, if twenty thousand copies of the Pamphlet had been circulated.

Ever affecly.
CD

To JOSEPH HOGARTH,[1] 13 MAY 1857

Text in *Outlook*, 18 Oct 1913, checked from MS Sotheby's, Oct 1963.

Tavistock House | Wednesday Thirteenth May 1857

Mr. Charles Dickens presents his compliments to Mr. Hogarth, and begs to say that if the Prints are taken to Gad's Hill Place on *Saturday morning*, he will be there himself to direct the hanging of them. He would prefer red cord.

To THE EARL STANHOPE, 13 MAY 1857*

MS Stanhope Papers.

Tavistock House | Thirteenth May, 1857

My Dear Lord Stanhope

I feel exceedingly obliged to you for your second kind note. We are very unfortunate in not being able to come. But our engagement is just this;—I have a little old-fashioned house in the country, near Rochester, which I have just now been altering and polishing, to live in in the summer-time. The Nineteenth being Mrs. Dickens's birthday,[2] I gave a promise that she should make her first appearance there on that occasion, and asked some of her friends to come down for two or three days. Hence we are engaged on the nineteenth, exactly as on the twentieth.

Faithfully Yours
CHARLES DICKENS

The | Earl Stanhope.

To GEORGE MOORE, 14 MAY 1857*

MS Dickens House.

Tavistock House | Fourteenth May, 1857.

My Dear Sir

I have the pleasure of enclosing you my Royal Hospital[3] proxy, in redemption of my promise.

Faithfully Yours
CHARLES DICKENS

George Moore Esquire

[1] Joseph Hogarth, printseller, 5 Haymarket.

[2] Her 42nd.

[3] The Royal Hospital for Incurables. In his speech at the Hospital's Anniversary dinner a week later, CD said there were 121 candidates for that election, of whom only 10 could be elected: see *To* Lord Raynham, ?19–20 May 57.

To BENJAMIN WEBSTER, 14 MAY 1857

MS Free Library of Philadelphia.

Tavistock House | Fourteenth May, 1857.

My Dear Webster

I have been away, and am only this afternoon in the receipt of your letter.

The Champagne has been steadily rising and becoming more difficult to get. It is now (very good indeed) 54/– per dozen. The Merchant is Mr. Charles Ellis, Richmond, Surrey.[1]

Faithfully Yours always

Benjamin Webster Esquire CHARLES DICKENS

To MR DÜHRSSEN,[2] 16 MAY 1857*

MS Dickens House.

Gad's Hill, Higham by Rochester | Sixteenth May, 1857.

I am happy to acknowledge the interest felt in my books by Mr. Dührssen, my young friend unknown; and I send him my signature with much pleasure. In reference to his enquiry concerning my portrait, I have to inform him that the only portrait for which I have sat to any painter within the last fifteen years or so, is now being engraved in Paris (from a picture by Ary Scheffer) and will probably be published before long. Another, by Maclise, was published about 16 years ago, as I remember, by Chapman and Hall, Piccadilly, London.[3]

CHARLES DICKENS

To THOMAS BEARD, 17 MAY 1857

MS Dickens House. *Address:* Thomas Beard Esquire | Morning Herald Office | Shoe Lane | London | E.C.

Waites's Hotel Gravesend | Sunday Seventeenth May, 1857

My Dear Beard

The train which will bring down the compact body of attackers of cold meat for the first time, "on the premises", will leave London Bridge Station on Tuesday afternoon at 3..40. If you came by that, you would take Return Ticket for Gravesend. But you were saying you would have the whole day in the country. Being still in that mind (and able to walk a mile to my Numble abode), take ticket for Higham, *one* station beyond this. Then, *by return of post*, let me know, *in a note addressed here*,

[1] Charles Ellis (1824–1908), manager of the Star & Garter Hotel, Richmond, and wine merchant, of Hill St, Richmond: see earlier vols.

[2] Unidentified; clearly German, and possibly connected with Dr Jacobus Dührssen of Kiel who published medical works in Latin in the 1850s.

[3] As frontispiece to *Nickleby*, Oct 39: see Vol. 1, p. 558 and *nn*.

by what train you intend to come to Higham, and the Inimitable Kentish Freeholder will be on the spot to receive you.

Ever Heartily

Thomas Beard Esquire CHARLES DICKENS

To WILKIE COLLINS, 17 MAY 1857

Text from N, II, 847.

Waite's Hotel, Gravesend | Sunday Seventeenth May 1857

My Dear Collins,

The train which will bring down the main body of the small and noble army who inaugurate Gad's Hill Place with cold meat next Tuesday, leaves London Bridge Station at 3.40—twenty minutes before 4. Take return for Gravesend. Put yourself under the guidance of the gallant Wills, and he will lead you to Victory.—Have you done????[1]

Ever Faithfully

[CD]

To VISCOUNT RAYNHAM,[2] [?20 MAY 1857]

Summary from Minutes of Board of Management, Royal Hospital for Incurables, 23 May 57. *Date:* just before the Anniversary Dinner on 21 May.

Telling Lord Raynham that he had visited the house[3] *and referring to the want of ventilation and other inconveniences which rendered the place in his view very undesirable for its present purpose.*[4]

To CLARKSON STANFIELD, 20 MAY 1857

MS Comtesse de Suzannet.

Tavistock House

Wednesday Evening | Twentieth May, 1857

My Dear Stanny

Binders of books are rather slow. I know that some weeks may elapse before the copy of Little Dorrit that I have asked my binder to put into a cheerful dress for you, will be ready. And as I hope you may like to know it is coming, and also to know the end of the book before the rest of its readers can, I send you the Proof Sheets of the closing Nos. Of course I don't want them back.

[1] i.e. finished writing *The Dead Secret.*

[2] The Hospital's Treasurer.

[3] In Carshalton, Surrey.

[4] CD referred to these drawbacks at the dinner: see *Speeches*, ed. K. J. Fielding, p. 234. A special meeting of the Board was called for 23 May, to consider CD's letter, read out by Lord Raynham. Dr Andrew Reed (1787–1862; *DNB*), Independent minister of Wycliffe Chapel, London, and philanthropist, founder of the Hospital in 1854, undertook to reply to CD, explaining that they hoped that the house at Carshalton was only temporary and that "the points of his letter were under careful consideration" (Minutes, above).

I say nothing of the pleasure it has been to me to put your name on the opening page, or to leave behind us both (as I hope its being there, may), a little record importing that we loved one another.[1]

Ever My Dear Friend | Affectionately
CHARLES DICKENS

Clarkson Stanfield Esquire

To SIR ALEXANDER DUFF GORDON,[2] 21 MAY 1857*

MS Berg Collection.

Tavistock House | Twenty First May, 1857

My Dear Gordon

Coming to town to day, to preside (for my sins) at a Public Dinner, I find your kind note.

I am amazed to hear that Scheffer is in England, and should greatly like to see him, for I hold him in the highest regard and respect. Unfortunately, however, I am in the burst of engagements consequent on being newly released from a long book, and fear I cannot come to Esher.[3] On Sunday I have promised to go down to Cockburn's,[4] and on Monday I am away into Kent, where I have a little old fashioned house (on the top of Gad's Hill), which I have been putting to rights these two months, and where a number of things have been awaiting my freedom, to be looked to. When you see Scheffer again, will you remember me to him heartily.

You play the very Devil with me on my weakest point, when you mention the dear delightful little German girl.[5] *Her* feelings on the night of the Play, were nothing to mine. I have loved her, ever since, distractedly.

Ever Faithfully Yours
CHARLES DICKENS

Sir Alexander Duff Gordon

To LADY JOHN RUSSELL, [21] MAY 1857

Text from *Lady John Russell*, ed. Desmond MacCarthy and Agatha Russell, 1910, p. 171. *Date:* 21 May, the day after his return to London.

May 22, 1857

Dear Lady John,

Coming to town yesterday morning out of Kent, I found your kind and welcome note referring to the previous day. I need not tell you I hope, that although I have not had the pleasure of seeing you for a long time, I have of late been accompanying Lord John at a distance with great interest and satisfaction. Several times after the City election was over I debated with myself whether I should come to see you, but I

[1] The final No. included the preliminary pages, with the dedication of the volume: "Dedicated | to | Clarkson Stanfield, R.A., | by his Attached Friend".

[2] Sir Alexander Cornewall Duff Gordon (1811–72), 3rd Bart, Commissioner of Inland Revenue since 1856: see Vol. v, p. 44*n*.

[3] Gordon House, Esher, Surrey, the Duff Gordons' country-home.

[4] Sir Alexander Cockburn (see *To* Mrs Brown, 14 Jan 57, *fn*).

[5] No doubt Janet Duff Gordon's friend, Mathilde, of 23 Jan 58.

abstained because I knew you would be overwhelmed with congratulations[1] and I thought it was the more considerate to withhold mine.

I am going out of town on Monday, June 1st, to a little old-fashioned house I have at Gad's Hill, by Rochester, on the identical spot where Falstaff ran away, and as you are so kind as to ask me to propose a day for coming to Richmond, I should very much like to do so either on Saturday the 30th of this month or on Sunday the 31st.

I heard of you at Lausanne from some of my old friends there, and sometimes tracked you in the newspapers afterwards. I beg to send my regard to Lord John and to all your house.

Do you believe me to remain always your very faithfully,

CHARLES DICKENS

To WILLIAM HOWARD RUSSELL,[2] 21 MAY 1857*

MS Dickens House.

Tavistock House | Thursday Twenty First May, 1857

My Dear Sir

I have been out of town, and am only now in the receipt of your note. I will not fail to be at the Gallery of Illustration at 3 tomorrow.[3]

Always Faithfully Yours

W. H. Russell Esquire CHARLES DICKENS

To WILKIE COLLINS, 22 MAY 1857

MS Morgan Library.

Tavistock House

Friday Evening, Twenty Second May, 1857

My Dear Collins

Hooray!!![4]

From our lofty heights, let us look down on the toiling masses with mild complacency—with gentle pity—with dove eyed benignity.

[1] At the recent General Election at end of Mar, Russell had retained his seat for the City of London, as third of four in the poll; his supporters had not expected he would be elected and the Liberal Registration Association had attempted to oust him. The defeated candidate was Raikes Currie: see Vol. VII, p. 696 and *n*.

[2] William Howard Russell (1820–1907; *DNB*), *Times* war-correspondent. Brought up in Dublin; began working for *The Times* in 1841; reported the Schleswig-Holstein campaign against Denmark 1850; reported the Crimean War for *The Times*, his letters about the mismanagement of the Commissariat and Medical Dept leading directly to reforms and playing a substantial part in the fall of the Aberdeen Ministry in Jan 55. For his reporting the Indian mutiny, see 7 July 58 and *fn*; in 1861–2 reported the beginning of the American Civil War. Founded and ed. the *Army and Navy Gazette* from 1860. For his opinion of the *Daily News*, see Vol. IV, p. 478*n*. No doubt long known to CD through the Garrick Club (see Vol. VI, p. 642*n*).

[3] To rehearse Russell's three lectures on the Crimean War, "Mr. W. H. Russell's Personal Narrative", given in Willis's Rooms, 23 and 28 May and 1 June: see *To* Russell, 30 May and *n*; and, for Douglas Jerrold's also being asked to help with the rehearsals, Appx K.

[4] Because he had finished *The Dead Secret*.

Tomorrow, I am bound to Forster—on Sunday, to solemn Chief Justices in remote fastnesses beyond Norwood[1]—on Monday, to Geographical Societies dining to cheer on Lady Franklin's Expedition[2]—on Tuesday, to Procters. On Wednesday Sir—on Wednesday, if the mind can devise any thing sufficiently in the style of Sybarite Rome in the days of its culminating voluptuousness, I am your man.

Shall we appoint to meet at the Household Words office, at 1/2 past 5? I have an appointment with Russell (W.H.) at 3 that afternoon, which *may*, but which I don't think will, detain me a few minutes after my time. In that unlikely case, will you wait for me at the Office?

If you can think of any tremendous way of passing the night, in the meantime—do. I don't care what it is. I give (for that night only) restraint to the Winds!——

I am very much excited by what you tell me of Mr. F's Aunt.[3] I already look upon her as mine. Will you bring her with you.

☛[4] Wills tells me that he thinks the principles of story-writing, are scarcely understood in this age and Empire.

Ever Faithfully
CD.

To MISS BURDETT COUTTS, 22 MAY 1857†

MS Morgan Library. *Address:* Miss Burdett Coutts | The Star Hotel | Oxford.

Tavistock House | Twenty Second May, 1857

My Dear Miss Coutts.

Mr. Bentley[5] has handed to me the enclosed account. I hope you will find it extremely reasonable, considering what he has had to do, and the skill with which he has done it.

Ages seem to have rolled by, since I saw you. I never hear of you, except when I reverentially approach Mr. Wills with humble enquiries as to where you may be and how you may be. What a monstrous state of existence you appear to have fallen into! If you don't return home soon, I shall insert a mysterious and pathetic Advertisement to A.B.C. in the Times.

After the first of June, I shall be inconsolable until I have fairly laid hold of you and Mrs. Brown and taken you in captivity down to Gad's Hill. I want you so much to see it. It is full of the ingenious devices of the inimitable writer, and I really think

[1] Cockburn's country house was Kingswood Lodge, nr Croydon, Surrey, several miles south of Norwood.

[2] The Anniversary Dinner of the Royal Geographical Society at the Freemasons' Tavern, 25 May. Toasts were drunk to "the final projected search for Sir John Franklin", replied to by Capt. McClintock, who, after the Admiralty had given up the 12-year search, fitted out and commanded the *Fox Yacht*, for a final quest; and to "The Healths of the Explorers of Distant Regions", replied to by Dr Livingstone. CD answered on behalf of "Our Periodical Literature and the Press"; but no record of his speech has been found.

[3] See *To* Gale, 11 June and *fn.*

[4] Preceded by a drawing of a pointing hand.

[5] William Bentley, the picture-restorer.

is as comfortable a little place as you will find out of Torquay[1]—which place I consider to be an Impostor, a mockery, a delusion, and a snare.

Ever Dear Miss Coutts | Most Faithfully Yours

Miss Burdett Coutts. CHARLES DICKENS

To [?MR ELLIS], 22 MAY 1857

Extract from P. F. Haag catalogue, 1957; *MS* 1 p.; dated Tavistock House, W.C., 22 May 57.

About sitting for his portrait. Have no doubt that I expressed myself imperfectly in my former note,[2] since it conveyed a wrong impression to you. I meant that I [a]quite firmly say[a] no and I beg to excuse myself from sitting.

To THE REV. JAMES WHITE, 22 MAY 1857

Text from MDGH, II, 15.

Tavistock House, Friday, May 22nd, 1857.

My dear White,

My emancipation having been effected on Saturday, the ninth of this month, I take some shame to myself for not having sooner answered your note. But the host of things to be done as soon as I was free, and the tremendous number of ingenuities to be wrought out at Gad's Hill, have kept me in a whirl of their own ever since.

We purpose going to Gad's Hill for the summer on the 1st of June; as, apart from the master's eye being a necessary ornament to the spot, I clearly see that the workmen yet lingering in the yard must be squeezed out by bodily pressure, or they will never go. How will this suit you and yours? If you will come down, we can take you all in, on your way north; that is to say, we shall have that ample verge and room enough,[3] until about the eighth; when Hans Christian Andersen (who has been "coming" for about three years) will come for a fortnight's stay in England. I shall like you to see the little old-fashioned place. It strikes me as being comfortable.

So let me know your little game. And with love to Mrs. White, Lotty, and Clara,[4]

Believe me, ever affectionately yours

[CHARLES DICKENS]

To MISS BURDETT COUTTS, [24] MAY 1857*

MS Morgan Library. *Date:* CD's mistake; Sunday was 24 May. *Address: Miss* Burdett Coutts | The Star Hotel | Oxford.

Tavistock House | Sunday Twenty Fifth May | 1857

My Dear Miss Coutts

I will look out the street you mention,[5] in the Map of London (for I am quite a

[1] For the next 20 years Miss Coutts and Mrs Brown spent many months of every year in Torquay (Meadfoot House illustrated in Edna Healey, *Lady Unknown*, pp. 142–3).

[2] Probably to Mr Ellis, 13 Jan 57.

[aa] Catalogue reads "quiet say".

[3] Cf. Gray "The Bard", stanza 2.

[4] A younger daughter, *d.* 1864.

[5] Clearly a joke, since she had been away so long.

stranger to it), and will endeavour to present myself there, next Thursday, punctually at 7. You don't mention the number.—I shall begin my enquiries at Number one.

With love to Mrs. Brown

Ever Dear Miss Coutts | Yours most faithfully & affecy.
CHARLES DICKENS

To JOHN THOMPSON, [24] MAY 1857*

MS Fales Collection, New York University Library.

Tavistock House | Sunday Twenty Fifth May 1857

I think, John, on reconsidering the matter, that it will be as well for the Foreman to cut some holes in the top of Mr. Charles's bedroom door, like those that are already cut in the women servants' bedroom.

I shall be down on Thursday, if not before; very likely, before.

CHARLES DICKENS

To THE HON. MISS EMILY EDEN,[1] 25 MAY 1857*

MS Bodleian Library.

Tavistock House. | Twenty Fifth May, 1857.

My Dear Miss Eden.

I have been sensibly touched by your note, and have read it with no common interest. I need scarcely add that I have particular pleasure in taking charge of your handsome subscription, and forwarding it to the Secretary.

No one can know better than you, the quiet fortitude and resignation of which invalids are capable. But if you could have seen these poor sufferers as I saw them the other day—walking in among them perfectly unknown—you would have been scarcely less impressed, I think, by their cheerful submission than I was myself. I merely told the company at the dinner,[2] exactly what I had seen. And they were affected by it in consequence, just as they would have been by the reality.

As to the time when I had the pleasure of talking with you at Broadstairs,[3] you know how certain particular scenes will sometimes fix themselves in the mind. Inseparable from my remembrance of that coast, and I verily believe from my abstract idea of a Lighthouse, is an Autumn afternoon in a little garden full of red geraniums, on the road to the North Foreland—you on your couch—Lord Clarendon[4] on one side of it—myself on the other—a bright sky over the cornfields, and the ships sailing away in the distance. All this has, ever since that hour, been still and unchangeable in my memory;—got itself daguerrotyped there in some indelible

[1] The Hon. Emily Eden (1797–1869; *DNB*), traveller and novelist: see Vol. VI, p. 409*n*.

[2] See *To* Viscount Raynham, 20 May and *fn*.

[3] Miss Eden and CD were both there in Autumn 51; the afternoon CD remembers must have been then: see Vol. VI, p. 499 and *n*.

[4] George William Frederick Villiers, 4th Earl of Clarendon (1800–70; *DNB*), Foreign Minister 1853–8.

way, and has gone up Swiss mountains with me and gone floating about Venice and gone drumming and dancing about France, as distinct as ever, everywhere.

Always Faithfully Yours

The Hon. Miss Eden. CHARLES DICKENS

To J. E. PFEIFFER,[1] 25 MAY 1857*

MS Yale University Library.

Tavistock House. W.C. | Monday Twenty Fifth May, 1857

Dear Sir

I cannot imagine by what accident your most obliging note and its accompanying book,[2] came to be laid aside on my library shelves, unopened and unknown to me, until yesterday. I can only suppose that some unlucky hand must have incautiously put the little packet there, to make room on an adjoining table for some momentary purpose, and must have forgotten it. How long an interval of apparent neglect it might have reproached me for, but for its having been laid on the top of a book I wanted yesterday, I blush to think.[3]

Pray allow me to offer you the assurance of my sincere regret that I should have seemed indifferent to a mark of remembrance so very courteously conveyed to me. In thanking you and its authoress,[4] I can with a clear conscience promise the best acknowledgement and atonement in any reader's power.—I have just packed up the book to take into the country with me, and I purpose reading it under the trees on the next sunny day.

Dear Sir | Yours faithfully and obliged

J. E. Pfeiffer Esquire CHARLES DICKENS

To [ARTHUR SMITH],[5] 26 MAY 1857

MS Yale University Library.

Tavistock House. W.C. | Twenty Sixth May, 1857.

My Dear Sir

I am not going to the Derby this year (being tired of it), but I fancy from your note that you are! Therefore I shall *not* come to the Gallery,[6] unless I hear at the Household Words office between 1 and 2, that you will be there at 3.

I have a promise already given for Sunday; but I will try to get out of it, if it can be

[1] J. E. Pfeiffer (*d.* 1889), German merchant resident in London.

[2] *Valisneria; or a Midsummer Day's Dream: a Tale in Prose*, 1857, by Pfeiffer's wife, Emily Jane.

[3] Published in early Feb and no doubt sent to CD then.

[4] Emily Jane Pfeiffer, née Davis (1827–90; *DNB*), poetess, painter and advocate of women's work; made a substantial bequest to Somerville College, Oxford.

[5] Mention of Albert Smith and "the Gallery" make Arthur Smith virtually certain as addressee: Arthur Smith (1825–61; *DNB*), who managed CD's readings 1858 and 1861 (until his death in Oct): see Vol. VII, p. 475 and *n.*

[6] The Gallery of Illustration, where Arthur Smith managed his brother Albert's entertainments.

handsomely done. I sincerely reciprocate your wish that we may know one another intimately (I hope we are already friends), and I assure you it shall not be my fault if we fail. I must get you, before I leave town on Monday, to fix a Sunday for coming down with Albert, to see me in a little house I have, on the identical spot where Falstaff ran away when they set upon the travellers—most appropriate ground for being jovial on.

Very faithfully Yours
CHARLES DICKENS

To MRS HORNE, 29 MAY 1857*

MS Dickens House.

Tavistock House | Twenty Ninth May, 1857

My Dear Mrs. Horne.

I will not fail to keep my eye upon the subject of your brother's[1] interest, or to read the account of it.

When I was at Bennet's[2] the other day, I did deliberate about coming to see you. But I thought you would be busy and I should be in the way, and—so I didn't.

We are just going out of town for the summer, to a house I have set up near Rochester—only an hour and a half from town—a good little old-fashioned breezy, shady, sunny, leafy place. Catherine is going to write to you in a week or two, when we get settled, to ask you to come and pass a Sunday with us. And when you have once seen the place and know how easily it is got at, I have a strong personal hope (which I hereby confess to you) that you will come very often, through the fine weather, and restore yourself after the fatigues of the week.[3]

My Dear Mrs. Horne | Always Faithfully Yours
CHARLES DICKENS

To LADY JOHN RUSSELL, 29 MAY 1857

MS Myers & Co.

Tavistock House. | Friday Twenty Ninth May, 1857.

Dear Lady John.

I am extremely sorry to let you know that I must make up my mind to be disappointed, and not to come to you tomorrow. I have been for some days a perfect Victim to influenza—or Hay Fever—or whatever it is—and have been a terror to

[1] Probably either James Foggo (1789–1860) or his younger brother, George (1793–1869), both painters trained in Paris and exhibitors to RA; they frequently worked together and were well-known as painters of altar pieces. Horne was negotiating with George Foggo for a divorce under the new Matrimonial Causes Act, 1857, presumably to enable him to marry Jessie Taylor (see *To* Fox, 30 Dec 56); he agreed to pay Kate £100 *p.a.* and sent the papers for her to sign in Sep; but the death of his child that month ended the negotiations (Ann Blainey, *The Farthing Poet*, 1968, pp. 215–16).

[2] Possibly John Bennett (1814–97, watchmaker: see 17 Dec and next vol.).

[3] See *To* Moore, 11 Feb 56. The Ladies' Guild, for whom she had worked, broke up in 1856; she was now working as an assistant to the photographer G. S. Nottage: see 20 Oct 56 and *fn*.

my fellow creatures by incessantly sneezing, coughing, and weeping. Yesterday I distinguished myself in these feats to that wonderful extent, in a railway carriage, that I became an object of hatred to seven other people, who were really resentful of me. To day, after a week of it, I am so much worse and in such a ridiculous state, that I feel that the only thing to be done, is, to go away to Gad's Hill and get rid of the enemy.

(I would enclose a tear if it were worth any thing,—but I am shedding so many while I write, that my feelings have nothing to do with them.)

I have asked my binder to put Little Dorrit into a new frock for your kind reception. When he has done so, I will call with her in Chesham Place[1] one day when I am in town, in the hope that I may have a chance of seeing you. If I should not succeed, then I will leave her, and, on another morning when I am in town, will try again, either there or at Richmond, as I hear of the family movements. I beg to be remembered to Lord John (if he should ever want a Kentish Freeholder's vote, I know of one at his service to the death), and am always with thanks.

Very faithfully Yours

The | Lady John Russell CHARLES DICKENS

To CHARLES EDMONDS, 29 MAY [?1857][2]

Extract in Anderson Galleries catalogue No. 1236 (June 1916); *MS* 1 p.; addressed Charles Edmonds; dated Tavistock House, 29 May 47. *Date:* 1857 since from Tavistock House.

I have mislaid the monthly circular[3] last received; but I observed in it a number of curious little books, following one another in regular succession over some couple of pages, concerning Newgate, its former prisoners and turnkeys, and such subjects.[4] Will you have the kindness to send them all to me? I need not ask you for the list. You will know what I mean.... Faithfully yours, CHARLES DICKENS

To MISS EMILY JOLLY, 30 MAY 1857

Text from MDGH, III, 183–6.

Tavistock House, Saturday Morning, 30th May, 1857.

Dear Madam,

I read your story, with all possible attention, last night. I cannot tell you with what reluctance I write to you respecting it, for my opinion of it is *not* favourable, although I perceive your heart in it, and great strength.

Pray understand that I claim no infallibility. I merely express my own honest opinion, formed against my earnest desire. I do not lay it down as law for others, though, of course, I believe that many others would come to the same conclusion. It appears to me that the story is one that cannot possibly be told within the compass to which you have limited yourself. The three principal people are, every one of them, in the wrong with the reader, and you cannot put any of them right, without

[1] No. 37, the Russells' town-house.

[2] Catalogue gives 29 May 1847, clearly in error.

[3] Edmonds's monthly catalogue.

[4] Not at Gad's Hill on CD's death; but see *To* Georgina Hogarth, 29 July and *fn*.

making the story extend over a longer space of time, and without anatomising the souls of the actors more slowly and carefully. Nothing would justify the departure of Alice, but her having some strong reason to believe that in taking that step, *she saved her lover*. In your intentions as to that lover's transfer of his affections to Eleanor, I descry a striking truth; but I think it confusedly wrought out, and all but certain to fail in expressing itself. Eleanor, I regard as forced and overstrained. The natural result is, that she carries a train of anti-climax after her. I particularly notice this at the point when she thinks she is going to be drowned.

The whole idea of the story is sufficiently difficult to require the most exact truth and the greatest knowledge and skill in the colouring throughout. In this respect I have no doubt of its being extremely defective. The people do not talk as such people would; and the little subtle touches of description which, by making the country house and the general scene real, would give an air of reality to the people (much to be desired) are altogether wanting. The more you set yourself to the illustration of your heroine's passionate nature, the more indispensable this attendant atmosphere of truth becomes. It would, in a manner, oblige the reader to believe in her. Whereas, for ever exploding like a great firework without any background, she glares and wheels and hisses, and goes out, and has lighted nothing.

Lastly, I fear she is too convulsive from beginning to end. Pray reconsider, from this point of view, her brow, and her eyes, and her drawing herself up to her full height, and her being a perfumed presence, and her floating into rooms, also her asking people how they dare, and the like, on small provocation. When she hears her music being played, I think she is particularly objectionable.

I have a strong belief that if you keep this story by you three or four years, you will form an opinion of it not greatly differing from mine. There is so much good in it, so much reflection, so much passion and earnestness, that, if my judgment be right, I feel sure you will come over to it. On the other hand, I do not think that its publication, as it stands, would do you service, or be agreeable to you hereafter.

I have no means of knowing whether you are patient in the pursuit of this art; but I am inclined to think that you are not, and that you do not discipline yourself enough. When one is impelled to write this or that, one has still to consider: "How much of this will tell for what I mean? How much of it is my own wild emotion and superfluous energy—how much remains that is truly belonging to this ideal character and these ideal circumstances?" It is in the laborious struggle to make this distinction, and in the determination to try for it, that the road to the correction of faults lies. [Perhaps I may remark, in support of the sincerity with which I write this, that I am an impatient and impulsive person myself, but that it has been for many years the constant effort of my life to practise at my desk what I preach to you.]

I should not have written so much, or so plainly, but for your last letter to me. It seems to demand that I should be strictly true with you, and I am so in this letter, without any reservation either way.

Very faithfully yours
[CHARLES DICKENS]

To WILLIAM HOWARD RUSSELL, 30 MAY 1857

MS Dickens House.

Tavistock House | Saturday Thirtieth May, 1857

My Dear Sir

As we do not move the Caravan until Monday, I received your note at dinner just now (7 o'Clock).

Mrs. Dickens would be glad to kill the Dragon—as glad, let us say, as Miss Saint George[1]—and would triumph in the act, but that she has unfortunately some sisterly, motherly, paternal, or other family engagement for tomorrow. She is very anxious that I should explain her aright to Mrs. Russell[2] through you—and you see how distinctly I do it!

It is tomorrow, Sunday, at 12.30, that you expect me at the Gallery,[3] is it not? Unless you reply in the negative, I intend to be there. I should have no doubt on the point, but for your having written from the Gallery this afternoon, and not precisely saying in two syllables, Sunday, in your former note.

Very faithfully Yours always

W. H. Russell Esquire CHARLES DICKENS

To UNKNOWN CORRESPONDENT, [?29–30 MAY 1857]*

MS (fragment) Dunedin Public Library. *Date:* probably the Friday or Saturday before going to Gad's Hill.

I[4] go out of town on Monday, but only to the neighbourhood of Rochester, where I purpose remaining during the whole summer and autumn. As there is now a Railroad into those parts, it is as good—though not as bad—as being in London.

Kind regard from Mrs. Dickens and Georgina.

Faithfully Always

CHARLES DICKENS

To RICHARD BENTLEY, 31 MAY 1857*

MS Berg Collection.

Tavistock House, W.C. | Thirty First May, 1857

My Dear Sir

I received Hans Christian Andersen's letter, and answered it; giving him all needful instructions for finding me at Gad's Hill. I hope you will come down one day and meet him there while he is with me.

Faithfully Yours

Richard Bentley Esquire CHARLES DICKENS

[1] Marguerite-Joséphine Weyma George (1787–1867), actress and once Napoleon's mistress: see Vol. IV, p. 239 and *n.*

[2] Née Mary Burrowes (*d.* 1867), great-niece of Peter Burrowes, Irish Judge and politician; married 1846.

[3] To rehearse Russell's final lecture on 1 June.

[4] First part of letter cut away.

To [?C. W. SEPTIMUS PIESSE], 31 MAY 1857

Extract in Maggs Bros catalogue No. 427 (Autumn 1922); *MS* 1 p.; dated Tavistock House, 31 May 57.

I am happy to receive your book[1] with the additions, and wish it and you every possible success.... I think it is scarcely worth while to send another copy to the Household Words office. I will inform the gentleman who wrote the article[2] of your remembrance of him.

To WILKIE COLLINS, 1 JUNE 1857

MS Morgan Library.

OFFICE OF HOUSEHOLD WORDS,
First June (Monday) 1857

My Dear Collins

In consequence of bedevilments at Gad's Hill, arising from the family luggage wandering over the face of the earth, I shall have to pass tomorrow behind a hedge, attired in leaves from my own fig tree. Will you therefore consider our appointment to stand for next day—Wednesday.

When last heard of, the family itself (including the birds,[3] and the Goldfinch on his perch)[4] had been swept away from the stupefied John, by a crowd of Whitsun holiday-makers, and had gone (without tickets) somewhere down into Sussex. A desperate calmness has fallen upon me. I don't care.

Faithfully Ever
CD.

To T. H. HERBERT,[5] 1 JUNE 1857*

MS Morgan Library.

Tavistock House, London | First June, 1857.

Sir

In reply to your letter of enquiry, I have to inform you that I never at any time had in my employment, in any capacity, any one bearing the name of Winthrop Park.[6]

I am Sir | Your faithful Servant

T. H. Herbert Esquire CHARLES DICKENS

[1] This must refer to *The Art of Perfumery* by Charles William Septimus Piesse (1820–82), whose business address was 2 New Bond St.

[2] Eliza Lynn's "Perfumes", *HW*, XV, 236 (7 Mar 57). When writing the article she would naturally use the 1st edn (1855); the 2nd edn was published in Dec 56.

[3] Including Dick, the canary.

[4] Presumably the goldfinch of his *Uncommercial Traveller* paper, "Shy Neighbourhoods", *AYR*, 26 May 60, III, 155, found "drawing his own water" in "a dirty court in Spitalfields" and bought by CD.

[5] Unidentified; perhaps an autograph hunter.

[6] Untraced; perhaps fictitious.

To HENRY MORLEY, 1 JUNE 1857

MS Benoliel Collection.

OFFICE OF HOUSEHOLD WORDS,
Monday First June 1857

My Dear Morley

I send you a Biography of George Stephenson, which perhaps may make an interesting article for us.[1]

Faithfully Yours always

Henry Morley Esquire. CHARLES DICKENS

To FRANK STONE, 1 JUNE 1857

MS Free Library of Philadelphia.

OFFICE OF HOUSEHOLD WORDS,
Monday First June 1857

My Dear Stone.

I know that what I am going to say will not be agreeable; but I rely on the authoress's[2] good sense; and say it, knowing it to be the truth.

These notes are destroyed by too much smartness. It gives the appearance of perpetual effort—stabs to the heart, the nature that is in them—and wearies by the manner, and not by the matter. It is the commonest fault in the world (as I have constant occasion to observe here), but it is a very great one. Just as you couldn't bear to have an épergne or a candlestick on your table, supported by a light figure always on tiptoe and evidently in an impossible attitude for the sustainment of its weight; so all readers would be more or less oppressed and worried by this presentation of everything in one smart point of view, when they know it must have other and weightier and more solid properties. Airiness and good spirits are always delightful, and are inseparable from notes of a cheerful trip; but they should sympathize with many things as well as see them in a lively way. It is but a word or a touch that expresses this humanity, but without that little embellishment of good nature, there is no such thing as humour. In this little MS. everything is too much patronized and condescended to, whereas, the slightest touch of feeling for the rustic who is of the earth earthy, or of sisterhood with the homely servant who had made her face shine in her desire to please, would make a difference that the writer can scarcely imagine without trying it. The only relief in the twenty one slips is the little bit about the Chimes. It *is* a relief, simply because it is an indication of some kind of sentiment. You don't want any sentiment laboriously made out in such a thing—you don't want any maudlin show of it—but you do want a pervading suggestion that it is there. It makes all the difference between being playful and being cruel. Again, I must say, above all things—especially to young people writing—For the love of

[1] For his "Inch by Inch Upward", see *HW*, 18 July (XVI, 49). Probably based on Samuel Smiles's *Life of George Stephenson*, 1857, though this is not named.

[2] See *To* [Ellen Stone], 4 June.

God, don't condescend! Don't assume the attitude of saying "See how clever I am, and what fun everybody else is!" Take any shape but that.[1]

I observe an excellent quality of observation throughout, and think the boy at the shop, and all about him, particularly good. I have no doubt whatever that the rest of the Journal will be much better, if the writer chooses to make it so. If she considers for a moment within herself, she will know that she derived pleasure from everything she saw, because she saw it with immeasurable lights and shades upon it, and bound to humanity by innumerable fine links. She cannot possibly communicate anything of that pleasure to another, by shewing it from one little limited point only—and that point, observe, the one from which it is impossible to detach the exponent as the patroness of a whole universe of inferior souls. This is what everybody would mean in objecting to these notes (supposing them published), that they are too smart and too flippant.

As I understand this matter to be altogether between us three, and as I think your confidence and hers imposes a duty of friendship on me, I discharge it to the best of my ability. Perhaps I make more of it than you may have meant or expected;—if so, it is because I am interested, and wish to express it. If there had been anything in my objection not perfectly easy of removal, I might after all have hesitated to state it; but that is not the case. A very little indeed would make all this gaiety as sound and wholesome and good-natured in the reader's mind as it is in the writer's.

Affectionately always
CHARLES DICKENS

To MISS BURDETT COUTTS, 3 JUNE 1857†

MS Morgan Library.

Gad's Hill Place, Higham | Third June, 1857.

My Dear Miss Coutts.

Would Thursday, Friday, or Saturday, *in next week* suit you for a day here? If neither will do, will you and Mrs. Brown appoint your own day, in the week following. You come from London Bridge Station (North Kent Railway) to Higham—the station next beyond Gravesend. A manly figure will of course be awaiting you on the Platform. The train that I think will be most convenient to you, starts at *12*. Take return tickets, unless you will stay a day or two with us. I have some faint hopes that you might do even that!

Hans Christian Andersen may perhaps be with us, but you won't mind *him*—especially as he speaks no language but his own Danish, and is suspected of not even knowing that.

With love to Mrs. Brown, and looking for your answer,

Ever Dear Miss Coutts | Yours most faithfully & affecy.
CHARLES DICKENS

[1] *Macbeth*, III, iv, 101.

To GEORGE BOUGHEY,[1] 4 JUNE 1857

MS Mr W. A. Foyle. *Address:* George Boughey Esquire | 33 Mecklenburgh Square | London | W.C.

Gad's Hill Place, Higham, Kent. | Fourth June, 1857

Dear Sir

Your obliging note has been forwarded to me in my summer retreat, where I have read it with much pleasure. Allow me to thank you for it sincerely.

Faithfully Yours

George Boughey Esquire CHARLES DICKENS

To [MISS ELLEN STONE], 4 JUNE 1857

Text from MDGH, II, 18.

Gad's Hill Place, Higham, | Thursday, June 4th, 1857.

My dear ——,[2]

Coming home here last night, from a day's business in London, I found your most excellent note awaiting me, in which I have had a pleasure to be derived from none but good and natural things. I can now honestly assure you that I believe you will write *well*, and that I have a lively hope that I may be the means of showing you yourself in print one day. Your powers of graceful and light-hearted observation need nothing but the little touches on which we are both agreed. And I am perfectly sure that they will be as pleasant to you as to anyone, for nobody can see so well as you do, without feeling kindly too.

To confess the truth to you, I was half sorry, yesterday, that I had been so unreserved; but not half as sorry, yesterday, as I am glad to-day. You must not mind my adding that there is a noble candour and modesty in your note, which I shall never be able to separate from you henceforth.

Affectionately yours always

[CHARLES DICKENS]

To GEORGE BEADNELL,[3] 5 JUNE 1857

MS Dickens House.

Gad's Hill | Friday Fifth June 1857.

My Dear Mr. Beadnell

I am exceedingly obliged to you for your great kindness in behalf of my boy, and beg you to accept my heartfelt thanks. He is tempted by your kind invitation, and

[1] N gives "Boughley" in error. George Boughey (1837–1910), second son of 3rd Bart; succeeded 1906; BA Christ Church, Oxford 1860; ordained 1861.

[2] This letter, and *To* Stone, 1 June (especially "between us three") point to Ellen, his daughter, as writer of the story. Later, having clearly profited from CD's advice she contributed "Rather Low Company" to *HW* (19 Feb 59, XIX, 269). It is an attractive sketch of village life as seen by a young schoolmistress, but unrelated to the story rejected here.

[3] George Beadnell (1775–1862), father of Maria; retired banker: see Vols I, p. 2 and *n*, and VI, 659*n*.

has wild ideas of making his way to your part of the country;[1] but, between ourselves, as he is here with us in his spare time—and as he sails next month—and as his outfit is being got ready—and as he is taking lessons in Hindustanee—and as he is "looking at" the Chatham fortifications (without appearing to me to make head or tail of them) out of swimming lessons, fencing lessons, riding lessons, and a general course of cricket—my impression is, that he will find himself at the Himalayas on his way to Carshalton.

I return Mr. Oswald Smith's[2] letter, and beg you to let him know whenever you have the opportunity, that Barkis is very grateful.[3]

Barkis, however, must take the liberty (this with my love to Mrs. Lloyd)[4] of defying Surrey, and writing up "Kent" in his vehicle,[5] as the object of his enthusiastic affections. Surrey is very well in its way, but all the eyes since Falstaff's—he ran away on the very spot where this house stands—never saw in Surrey, such a green landscape as I see from this hill-top, this morning.

With kindest regard | Believe me always
My Dear Mr. Beadnell | Very faithfully Yours

George Beadnell Esquire CHARLES DICKENS

To HENRY AUSTIN, 6 JUNE 1857

MS Morgan Library.

Gad's Hill | Saturday Sixth June, 1857

My Dear Henry

Here is a very serious business on the great estate respecting the water Supply. Last night, they had pumped the well DRY[6]—merely in raising the family supply for the day; and this morning (very little water having been got into the Cisterns), it is DRY[6] again! It is pretty clear to me that we must look the thing in the face, and at once bore, deepen, dig, or do some beastly thing or other, to secure this necessary in abundance. Meanwhile I am in a most plaintive and forlorn condition without your presence and counsel. I raise my voice in the Wilderness and implore the same!!!

Wild legends are in circulation among the Servants, how that Captain Goldsmith[7] on the knoll above—the skipper in that Crow's Nest of a house—has millions of gallons of water always flowing for him. Can he have damaged my Well? Can we imitate him, and have our millions of gallons? Goldsmith or I must fall, as I conceive.

If you get this, send me a telegraph message informing me when I may expect

[1] Surrey, where he was staying with his daughter Margaret.

[2] Oswald Smith, banker, of Smith, Payne & Smith's Bank, 1 Lombard St.

[3] Smith must have quoted "Barkis is willing" from *Copperfield*.

[4] Margaret, Beadnell's eldest daughter, married to David Lloyd (1800–59), tea-merchant: see Vol. VI, p. 660*n*.

[5] Beadnell had evidently wrongly addressed his letter to Higham, Surrey.

[6] Doubly underlined.

[7] Probably George Goldsmith, Capt. RN since Sep 42, though no house in Higham listed as his: see later vols.

comfort. I am held by four of the family while I write this, in case I should do myself a mischief—it certainly won't be taking to *drinking water*.

Ever affectionately | (now despairingly)

CD.

To MISS BURDETT COUTTS, 7 JUNE 1857*

MS Morgan Library. *Address:* Miss Burdett Coutts | 1 Stratton Street | Piccadilly | London | W.

Gad's Hill | Sunday Seventh June 1857.

My Dear Miss Coutts

On Thursday we shall be delighted to see you. We will give you and Mrs. Brown a country room together,[1] and your Maid shall be lodged close to you.

Wednesday is our Committee Day at Shepherd's Bush. I will be there.

The fogs that welcome you to London, have no existence in these parts. An ethereal mist or so is sometimes seen in the distance—nothing grosser.

With love to Mrs. Brown

Ever Dear Miss Coutts | Yours faithfully and affecy.

CD.

To MRS GORE,[2] 7 JUNE 1857*

MS Baron Dan de Calinescu.

Gad's Hill, by Rochester. | Seventh June 1857

My Dear Mrs. Gore

Many thanks. I will get the book,[3] and read it on your advice. But see how Imitations may deceive even the elect! The "New Boy"[4] is none of mine.

Mrs. Dickens and her sister beg to thank you beforehand for your book,[5] and assure you that they are good and confiding readers.

Very faithfully Yours always

Mrs. Gore CHARLES DICKENS

[1] Probably at the Sir John Falstaff or the Darnley Arms, Cobham, since Gad's Hill would obviously not be ready for three overnight guests.

[2] Catherine Grace Frances Gore (1799–1861; *DNB*), née Moody, novelist and dramatist; widowed 1846: see Vols II, p. 200*n* and VII, pp. 17 and *n* and 308.

[3] This sounds like some imitation of CD.

[4] "The New Boy at Styles's", by Henry Spicer, *HW*, 9 May 57, XV, 433 (see Kathleen Tillotson, *D*, LXXXIV [Summer 1988], 67).

[5] *The Two Aristocracies*, 3 vols, published 1 June 57.

To DR F. H. RAMSBOTHAM,[1] 7 JUNE 1857

Extract in Sotheby's catalogue, Mar 1981; *MS* 2 pp.; dated Gad's Hill, 7 June 57. *Address:* Dr. Ramsbotham | 7 Portman Square | London W.

My Dear Sir

I am very heartily obliged *for Dr Ramsbotham's giving an introduction for his son* [Walter] *but as his passage is already taken on the Peninsular & Oriental, he needs no help there.*

According to my annual custom I have left for the country for four or five months ... an old-fashioned house on top of a hill built on the very spot where Falstaff ran away and here I live like a sort of honest Robin Hood among the green trees.

PS *He has the pamphlet about the College*[2] *already.*

To W. S. HOOLE,[3] [?7 JUNE 1857]

MS Dickens House. *Date:* probably within the week of the final No. of *Little Dorrit*, published 30 May 57 (Chs 30–4).

Gad's Hill, Higham, by Rochester

Mr. Charles Dickens presents his compliments to Mr. Hoole, and begs to acknowledge the receipt of his obliging note. As the window in St. George's Church appropriately carried out the pervading spirit of the tale at its conclusion,[4] Mr. Dickens made reference to it. He knew it was not as old as the date of the story,[5] but did not consider that slight anachronism of any importance.

To JOHN FORSTER, [10 JUNE 1857]

Extract in F, VIII, i, 629–30. *Date:* Jerrold died on 8 June; letter written two days later.

On the death of Douglas Jerrold. I chance to know a good deal about the poor fellow's illness, for I was with him on the last day he was out. It was ten days ago, when we dined at a dinner given by Russell at Greenwich. He was complaining much when we met, said he had been sick three days, and attributed it to the inhaling of white paint from his study window. I did not think much of it at the moment, as we were very social; but while we walked through Leicester-square he suddenly fell into a white, hot, sick perspiration, and had to lean against the railings. Then, at my urgent request, he was to let me put him in a cab[6] and send him home; but he

[1] Francis Henry Ramsbotham (1801–68), MD, FRCP, leading obstetric physician; lecturer in Obstetric and Forensic Medicine, London Hospital; President Hunterian Society 1848; Harveian Society 1855; published *Principles of Obstetric Medicine and Surgery*, 1841.

[2] Possibly King's College: see *To* Miss Coutts, 10 July and *fn.*

[3] William Spencer Hoole (1823–78), son of Henry, Vicar of St George's, Southwark; BA Brasenose College, Oxford, 1845, Vicar of Briercliffe, Lancs, 1851–75.

[4] On the last page of the final chapter CD wrote: "they were married, with the sun shining on them through the painted figure of Our Saviour on the window".

[5] The Marshalsea prison was demolished *c.* 1830; the window above the altar, depicting Christ in Majesty, was probably fitted during major alterations to the church in 1855.

[6] See Appx K for CD's much fuller account.

rallied a little after that, and, on our meeting Russell, determined to come with us. We three went down by steamboat that we might see the great ship,[1] and then got an open fly and rode about Blackheath: poor Jerrold mightily enjoying the air, and constantly saying that it set him up. He was rather quiet at dinner—sat next Delane—but was very humorous and good, and in spirits, though he took hardly anything. We parted with references to coming down here and I never saw him again. Next morning he was taken very ill when he tried to get up. On the Wednesday and Thursday he was very bad, but rallied on the Friday, and was quite confident of getting well. On the Sunday he was very ill again, and on the Monday forenoon died; "at peace with all the world" he said, and asking to be remembered to friends. He had become indistinct and insensible, until for but a few minutes at the end. I knew nothing about it, except that he had been ill and was better, until, going up by railway yesterday morning, I heard a man in the carriage, unfolding his newspaper, say to another "Douglas Jerrold is dead." I immediately went up there, and then to Whitefriars.... I propose that there shall be a night at a theatre when the actors (with old Cooke)[2] shall play the *Rent Day* and *Black-ey'd Susan*; another night elsewhere, with a lecture from Thackeray;[3] a day reading by me; a night reading by me; a lecture by Russell;[4] and a subscription performance of the *Frozen Deep*, as at Tavistock House. I don't mean to do it beggingly; but merely to announce the whole series, the day after the funeral, "In memory of the late Mr. Douglas Jerrold," or some such phrase. I have got hold of Arthur Smith as the best man of business I know, and go to work with him to-morrow morning—inquiries being made in the meantime as to the likeliest places to be had for these various purposes. My confident hope is that we shall get close upon two thousand pounds.

To WILLIAM HOWARD RUSSELL, 10 JUNE 1857

MS Berg Collection.

OFFICE OF HOUSEHOLD WORDS,
Wednesday Tenth June 1857

My Dear Russell.

Although I can quite understand that a generous nature is quick to give itself the pain you describe, I am perfectly sure that you have nothing whatever to reproach yourself with in association with the poor dear fellow. I do not doubt that he would have died in the same hour, though he had not dined with us; and that he was happy that day, and recalled the air of our ride, on his bed but a day or two before he passed away, I know from Lemon, to whom he spoke of it with great cheerfulness

[1] I. K. Brunel's *Great Eastern*, then known as the *Leviathan*, being built for the Eastern Steam Navigation Co in Napier's yard on the Thames. With a 692 ft hull and a 82 ft beam, its displacement was six times greater than that of any previous ship; it attracted immense public interest. Finally launched on 31 Jan 1858, after several abortive attempts.

[2] Thomas Potter ("Tippy") Cooke (1786–1864; *DNB*), actor; his most famous part was William in *Black-eyed Susan* (1829) constantly revived: see Vol. III, p. 534*n*. *The Rent Day*, another success, was played and published in 1832.

[3] "Week-day Preachers", given on 22 July: see *To* Dickers, 11 July and *fn*.

[4] He gave his lecture, "Personal Narrative of the Late Crimean War", in St Martin's Hall on 7 July.

and pleasure. He was taken very ill on the next day—the Monday. He tried to get up as usual, rolled over on his bed, and fell into great pain. On the Wednesday and Thursday, they were very much alarmed; but on the Friday he rallied again, and was free from pain, though exceedingly weak. It was then that Lemon saw him for the last time. He had begun to be confident of getting better, and he told Lemon about our riding over Blackheath, and about the air having been so fresh and pleasant to him. On the Saturday he turned worse; on the Sunday, he was in terrible pain, and suffered severely; on the Monday morning, the pain left him, but he was greatly exhausted, and knew himself to be dying. He said that if he had spoken at all hardly of any one or to any one, he had not meant it, and that he died at perfect peace. His son William[1] was holding him in his arms. He went on to mention friends to whom he desired to be remembered, when he became indistinct, and in a few moments died.

I had heard at Gad's Hill, in a note from Evans, that he had been seriously ill; but I supposed him to be recovering, and thought it quite past. I was coming up by the Railway yesterday morning, with my wife, and her sister (of whom he had always been fond) when a gentleman in the carriage looking over his newspaper told another "Douglas Jerrold was dead". You may imagine how shocked we were. I went up there as soon as we reached town, and then went to Whitefriars[2] to urge the immediate necessity of exertion in behalf of the Widow and daughter. I found that Brooks[3] had already acted with a kindness and judiciousness that I can never forget in him, and I suggested a plan for certain benefit nights which I hope to be able to mature this afternoon;—I am only now waiting while Brooks confers with his son. Arthur Smith, invaluable where promptitude and sagacity are wanting, wrote to me this morning, like a good sound fellow, saying his aid is ready. I hope and believe that if nothing arises to prevent our turning to, in earnest, we may easily—and not beggingly—raise £1500 at least. I would have the Actors (and old T. P. Cooke) play The Rent Day and Black eyed Susan, one night. On another night, I would have Thackeray lecture. On another night, I would read, or do any thing. On another night I hope you could lecture to a good, large, liberal comprehensive public audience. All this series I would announce as a tribute of his friends to his memory—or in some such way—so that it should not be a pitiful appeal. You shall hear more, as soon as I know more.

Poor dear fellow. I went up to him before I left Greenwich that Sunday night, and asked him how he was. He said, much better—much the better for coming—had only taken a little weak brandy and water to drink, and had enjoyed it and some curried fish. I said he was all right now, and he said "Oh yes my dear boy, all right now—that paint you know—nothing more", and we shook hands heartily, and parted. I cannot believe it now, or that we three were laughing together in that sunshine and summer wind with schemes and plans before us.

Last Autumn at Boulogne, day after day while poor A Beckett lay ill, he used to come up to me with his report, and would walk about the garden talking about these sudden strikings down of men we loved, in the midst of us. When he sent to Lemon a

[1] William Blanchard Jerrold (1826–84; *DNB*), Douglas Jerrold's eldest son; journalist and writer: see Vol. v, p. 676*n*.

[2] The office of Bradbury & Evans, owners of *Punch*.

[3] Shirley Brooks.

little notice of A Beckett after his death, for Punch,[1] he wrote in the envelope "My dear Mark, who among us will be the next, and who will write a word or two of *him*"—[2]

Again my dear Russell let me impress upon you my perfect conviction that his dining at Greenwich did not by a hair's breadth hasten his death. I am quite convinced it had no sort of bearing on it. As I told you when we walked from the Garrick after him, I had found him at the Gallery of Illustration, very ill—and had been greatly struck by his account of his illness, and by his becoming very weak and white in Leicester Square. I have no doubt that the mortal malady had its hand upon him at that time, and had had it on him during the whole attack. If he could have been got into the country, at rest and away from some family troubles, a month before, I think he might have recovered—if it is not mere idleness to speculate on such a possibility when the Almighty had numbered his days. But that his time was come, when we were with him, I feel assured. When I went home that Sunday night, I could not leave off saying that I was afraid Jerrold was in a bad way, or recalling his condition in Leicester Square. On the Monday night of his death—the night of the day on which he died at noon—I dreamed that he came and shewed me a writing (but not in his hand) which he was pressingly anxious that I should read for my own information, but I could not make out a word of it. I awoke in great perplexity with its strange character quite fresh in my sight.

Ever Faithfully Yours
CD.

To LIEUT. COLONEL THE HON. C. B. PHIPPS,[3] [?10 JUNE 1857]

Mention in *To* Miss Coutts, 20 June 57. *Date:* before talking to Miss Coutts on 11 June: see 20 June.

To WILLIAM GALE, 11 JUNE 1857

Extract in Francis Edwards catalogue No. 971 (1973); *MS* 1 p.; dated Gad's Hill Place, 11 June 57.

Thanking him for his note and picture.[4] . . . I esteem myself very fortunate in the possession of your highly characteristic and humorous picture.

[1] See *To* Forster, 30 Aug 56, *fn.*

[2] *Punch*, 20 June, had a black-bordered, six-stanza poetic tribute to Jerrold, praising his wit in particular; no doubt by Lemon.

[3] Lieut-Col the Hon. Charles Beaumont Phipps (1801–66; *DNB*), equerry to the Queen since Aug 46; KCB 58: see Vol. v, p. 371*n.*

[4] *Mr. F's Aunt*, exhibited RA, May 1857, where Collins evidently saw it (see *To* Collins, 22 May). Bought by CD from Gale for ten guineas (CD's Account-book, MS Messrs Coutts); at Gad's Hill at his death (*Catalogue of the . . . Pictures . . . of CD*, ed. J. H. Stonehouse, p. 126).

To LEIGH HUNT,[1] 11 JUNE 1857

Extract in N, II, 856.

My Dear Hunt.

This summer retreat (on the spot where Falstaff ran away) will be my home until the winter probably; but I shall be often in town and will come to you one day.... Nothing but the death of poor Jerrold prevents my naming the day now;—I hope to do his family some good, and shall be for a few days overwhelmed with that business.

To FRANCESCO BERGER, 12 JUNE 1857

Mention in *Autograph Prices Current*, I, 51 (1914–16); *MS* 1 p.; dated 15 June 57; addressed Francesco Berger.

Respecting other performances.

To WILKIE COLLINS, 12 JUNE 1857*

MS Morgan Library.

Garrick | Twelfth June 1857 | Friday

My Dear Collins

You will readily understand the accompanying Proof.[2] I should like to see you as soon as convenient, about the Frozen Deep. (I am trying for the Queen).[3] Could you run down on Sunday? Perhaps?

Ever Faithfully

Wilkie Collins Esquire CHARLES DICKENS

To T. P. COOKE, 12 JUNE 1857

MS (telegram) Benoliel Collection.

THE ELECTRIC AND INTERNATIONAL TELEGRAPH COMPANY

The following message forwarded from Strand Station. And received at Portsea[4] Station June 12 1857

[1] James Henry Leigh Hunt (1784–1859; *DNB*): see Vol. I, p. 341*n* and Vols. IV–VI *passim*.

[2] A proof of the programme for "the Fund in Remembrance of the late Mr Douglas Jerrold", given to Yates to take round to editors of the principal journals on 15 June: see *To* Yates, 14 June. They included the *Literary Gazette* and *Examiner*. The *Literary Gazette*, 20 June, welcomed the proposal as "most gratifying evidence of the kindliness of spirit and true sympathy which should connect in a common bond of union all literary men". The bill of the programme itself, including a fuller list of names of the Committee, is given in Francesco Berger, *Reminiscences, Impressions and Anecdotes*, pp. 33–4. See also Appx D.

[3] See *To* Forster, 21 June.

[4] Telegrams were received on this side of the Solent.

FROM Charles Dickens Garrick Club
TO T. P. COOKE St. Vincent Villa Ryde[1]
On twenty ninth July will you play William at the Adelphi for its late Author,[2] Every body joins, Reply.

To THE COUNTESS GIGLIUCCI, 12 JUNE 1857*

MS Haverford College.

Garrick Club | Friday Twelfth June 1857

My Dear Countess Gigliucci.

Will you allow me to call your attention to the accompanying Proof. It is the committee's wish that it should be left to speak for itself.

If, on the occasion against which I have set a mark, you could possibly render this endeavour the immense service of singing once,[3] you would—I am sure—gratify your own generous impulses quite as much as my wishes.

Ever Faithfully Yours

The | Countess Gigliucci CHARLES DICKENS

To SIR EDWARD BULWER LYTTON, 12 JUNE 1857

MS Lytton Papers.

Garrick Club | Friday Twelfth June 1857

My Dear Bulwer.

You will understand the enclosed Proof. I believe I need not ask you for leave to use your name. Nothing but our names is sought.

Ever Faithfully

Sir Edward Bulwer Lytton. CHARLES DICKENS

To SIR JOSEPH PAXTON, 12 JUNE 1857*

Text from typescript, Huntington Library.

Garrick Club | Friday Twelfth June 1857.

My Dear Paxton,

You will readily understand the accompanying Proof.

I know I need not ask you for leave to use your name. Nothing but your name is sought here in our poor friend's behalf.

Ever Faithfully

Sir Joseph Paxton. CHARLES DICKENS

[1] Cooke's seaside home on the Isle of Wight.

[2] See *To* Cooke, 30 July and *fn*.

[3] As she did, at the Concert given on 27 June in St Martin's Hall: see 15 June.

To SAMUEL PHELPS, 12 JUNE 1857

MS Rosenbach Foundation. *Address:* Please forward.[1] | Samuel Phelps Esquire | Canonbury Square | Islington.

Garrick Club | Friday Twelfth June 1857

My Dear Phelps.

Let me call your attention to the accompanying proof. It is the wish of the Committee that it should be left to speak for itself.

I am not wrong, I believe, in having taken upon myself to say that I am certain your co-operation may be counted on, on the occasion against which I have set a mark?*[2]

Faithfully Yours always

Samuel Phelps Esquire CHARLES DICKENS

To SIMS REEVES,[3] 12 JUNE 1857*

MS Private.

Garrick Club | Twelfth June 1857

Dear Sir

Will you allow me to call your attention to the accompanying Proof. It is the Committee's wish that it should be left to speak for itself.

If, on the occasion against which I have set a mark, your engagements would admit of your singing one song,[4] your generous aid would be most highly esteemed by all concerned in this endeavour, and by none more highly than

Yours faithfully

Sims Reeves Esquire CHARLES DICKENS

To UNKNOWN CORRESPONDENT, 12 JUNE 1857

Mention in *Autograph Prices Current*, III, 80; *MS* 1 p.; dated Gad's Hill, 12 June 57.

Referring to Gad's Hill and Douglas Jerrold.

[1] The Sadler's Wells season had closed before Easter, and Phelps was not on tour but on holiday: see *To* Mrs Phelps, 20 June.

[2] Against this asterisk the Circular announced that Phelps would appear in *The Housekeeper* (see *To* Georgina Hogarth, 9 May 56 and *fn*) with the Keeleys and Webster; in fact, he also appeared in Jerrold's *The Prisoner of War* at the Haymarket on 15 July, with the Keeleys, Buckstone and Henry Compton.

[3] John Sims Reeves (1818–1900; *DNB*), tenor; sang in Macready's company at Drury Lane 1842–3; made his name in oratorio at the Worcester and Norwich musical festivals 1848; henceforward the leading English tenor; towards end of his life Professor of Singing, Guildhall School of Music.

[4] Sims Reeves was one of the vocalists at the Concert on 27 June.

To EDMUND YATES, [?14 JUNE 1857]

Mention in Yates, *Recollections and Experiences*, I, 293. *Date:* received on the morning of Douglas Jerrold's funeral (15 June).

Asking him to dine at the Garrick to talk on a matter of business. [1]

To WILLIAM CRESWICK,[2] 15 JUNE 1857

MS Dickens House.

Garrick Club | Monday Fifteenth June 1857.

My Dear Sir

Allow me to call your attention to the accompanying Proof. It is the wish of the Committee that it should in all cases be left to speak for itself.

But I may add that if it should suit your convenience and inclinations, and those of Mr. Shepherd[3]—to whom I do not write separately, as I have not the pleasure of personally knowing him—to propose a night in aid of the objects, at the Surrey Theatre,[4] your generous aid would be highly esteemed. I do not hold myself at liberty to say more, or to urge the point upon you.

I will only add that in such a case, I am sure Mr. and Mrs. Keeley[5] would readily strengthen your company for the occasion.

My Dear Sir | Faithfully Yours

W. Creswick Esquire CHARLES DICKENS

I am in town this evening and would drive round to you at the Theatre after half past 9.

To [MISS CHARLOTTE DOLBY],[6] 15 JUNE 1857

Extract in Parke-Bernet catalogue, Nov 1946; *MS* $1\frac{1}{2}$ pp.; dated Garrick Club, 15 June 57.

if, in such an exceptional case and cause, we could have your invaluable aid at the concert, a most important service would be rendered by one of the finest of living artists, to the nearest and dearest relatives of an admirable dramatic writer.

[1] Yates says that he found Albert and Arthur Smith also present.

[2] William Creswick (1813–88; *DNB*), actor; joint-lessee, Surrey Theatre, 1849–62; had previously played many Shakespearean roles under Phelps at Sadler's Wells 1846.

[3] Richard Shepherd (1869–86), actor, especially of sailor parts; joint-lessee, Surrey Theatre, with Creswick, 1850–63.

[4] This did not come off (the Surrey was where *Black-eyed Susan* had originally been played).

[5] Robert Keeley (1793–1869; *DNB*), comic actor: see Vol. III, p. 247*n*; and his wife, née Mary Ann Goward (?1805–99; *DNB*), comic actress; married 1829; they frequently played together.

[6] No doubt Charlotte Dolby. Letters survive to the other major soloists at the Fund's Concert on 27 June; CD certainly admired Miss Dolby and she sang at the Concert.

To T. P. COOKE, 15 JUNE 1857*

MS Benoliel Collection.

Tavistock House, London
Monday Evening | Fifteenth June 1857

My Dear Sir

Coming to town this morning to attend poor Jerrold's funeral,[1] I found your note. It is like yourself, and I don't know that I could easily say any thing higher in its praise.

I beg my compliments to Mrs. and Miss Cooke, and am always

Very faithfully Yours

T. P. Cooke Esquire CHARLES DICKENS

To THE COUNTESS GIGLIUCCI, 15 JUNE 1857

MS Dickens House. *Address:* The Countess Gigliucci | Great Western Royal Hotel | Paddington.

Garrick Club | Monday Evening | Fifteenth June, 1857

My Dear Countess Gigliucci.

Your earnest and generous letter has occasioned me almost as much pleasure in hearing from you, as I have in hearing you.

You will not be inconvenienced, I hope, by our having been obliged to make a change in the arrangements for the concert. It is settled to take place at *St. Martin's Hall* on Saturday the 27th. of June.[2]

With kind regard to Count Gigliucci, Believe me ever

Very faithfully Yours
CHARLES DICKENS

To T. F. ROBSON, 15 JUNE 1857

Mention in Smith catalogue No. 72 (1912–13); *MS* 2 pp.; dated Garrick Club, Monday Evening, June 15, 1857; addressed F. Robson.

On behalf of the committee CD requests the [actor's] *invaluable aid at a concert.*

[1] The funeral was at Norwood Cemetery. CD, with Hepworth Dixon, led the ten pall-bearers who were Bradbury, Forster, Charles Knight, Lemon, Horace Mayhew (Jerrold's son-in-law), Monckton Milnes, Paxton and Thackeray. Besides the family mourners, many literary friends and eminent people, there was a "vast concourse" of 5 or 6 thousand. The burial service was read by the Rev. Thomas Hugo of Bishopsgate. After the interment the Memorial Committee was announced and their printed programme issued (*The Times*, 16 June and *Athenaeum*, 20 June).

[2] Besides Sims Reeves and herself, Charlotte Dolby sang; T. F. Robson (see *To* Macready, 8 Aug 56) sang "The Country Fair"; and the German Reeds gave one of their entertainments. The *Globe*, 29 June, recorded the Concert's "unequalled variety" and announced CD's reading of the *Carol* the following evening.

To EDITORS OF THE PRINCIPAL JOURNALS, [15 JUNE 1857]

Mention in Yates, *Recollections and Experiences*, I, 294.

Enclosing a Memorandum for the Committee.[1]

To JULES BENEDICT,[2] [16 JUNE 1857]

Mention in next. *Date:* written the same day.

To JULES BENEDICT, 16 JUNE 1857

Extract in Sotheby catalogue, Mar 1974; *MS* 1 p.; dated Garrick Club, 16 June 57.

Concerning an invitation to Benedict to perform in a concert, Dickens explains that when he wrote "conduct", in his letter that morning, he meant there will not be an orchestra, and therefore I mean, to direct and accompany—in which latter office Mori[3] will assist; *he adds that an announcement about the concert must be made immediately; he will send a messenger to Benedict the same evening.*

To FRANCESCO BERGER, 16 JUNE 1857

Text from Francesco Berger, *Reminiscences, Impressions and Anecdotes*, p. 31.

Dear Berger,

A thousand thanks for your kind and cordial letter. I am delighted to accept the compliment you offer me,[4] as I am always truly proud to be associated with you. I have ventured to put you down as one of the Conductors at the Concert. It is finally arranged to take place at St. Martin's Hall on Saturday, June 27. It will be very good indeed, and I hope you will like to be associated with it. We are all out of town. Can you dine with me here[5] on Thursday next at half-past-five? or if you can come down to Gad's Hill with Charley on Saturday we shall all be pleased to see you. As to dining with me, send me one line here.

Faithfully yours ever
CHARLES DICKENS

[1] According to Yates (*ibid.*, I, 294–5) he took the Memorandum to the *Morning Post*, *Morning Chronicle*, *Daily Telegraph*, *Advertiser*, and *The Times*.

[2] Julius Benedict (1804–85; *DNB*), composer and conductor, born in Stuttgart: see Vols V, p. 353*n* and VII, p. 372*n*; knighted 1871.

[3] Francis Mori (1820–73), musician; composed many songs and comic operas; Professor of Singing at Crystal Palace, Sydenham.

[4] The dedication of his *Overture* to *The Frozen Deep* (Francesco Berger, *ibid.*).

[5] Berger has added in square brackets: "Garrick Club, King Street, Covent Garden"; CD has probably simply put "Garrick Club" at head of letter, omitted by Berger.

To WILKIE COLLINS, 16 JUNE 1857

MS Morgan Library.

H.W. Office | Sixteenth June 1857

My Dear Collins

What an unlucky fellow you are! What a foot you have for putting into anything! I write this to Harley Place,[1] having been unable to write yesterday. I must be in town on Thursday, and will come up to you. I will try to come at about 12.

Mrs. Wills's lameness, makes a new Esther the first thing wanted. You once said you knew a lady[2] who could and would have done it. Is that lady producible?

Ever Faithfully
CD.

To MISS HELEN HOGARTH, 16 JUNE 1857

MS Mrs J. Felix-Davies.

Tuesday Evening Sixteenth June | 1857

My Dear Helen.

It is all excellent.[3] Pryor's name I will use,[4] and will write to him.[5] Whitworth[6] it will be best to let alone. If you have anything to report tomorrow, will you write to Arthur Smith? I shall be in town on Thursday.

Ever affecy.
CD

To MISS BURDETT COUTTS, 17 JUNE 1857*

Facsimile in F. G. Kitton, *Dickens Ana*, Dickens House.

Gad's Hill | Wednesday Evening | Seventeenth June 1857.

My Dear Miss Coutts

I think I may as well send you the enclosed exactly as I have received it; merely observing that the Institution[7] to which it refers is an admirable project, and that Mr. Ryland, the writer of the note, is one of the most upright and respected men in Birmingham.

Ever Faithfully and affecYours
CHARLES DICKENS

[1] Collins's mother's home since 1856.

[2] Frances Dickinson: see *To* Collins, 26 June and *fn.*

[3] The arrangements for the concert at St Martin's Hall on 27 June, in aid of the Jerrold Fund.

[4] Unexplained. The only Pryor known to be connected with music is Richard Pryor, author of a work on church music, 1874.

[5] If CD wrote, his letter has not survived.

[6] H. Whitworth, baritone: see Vol. V, p. 363 and *n.*

[7] The Birmingham and Midland Institute: see Vol. VII, pp. 4–5 and *nn.* In Feb 1855 CD had promised "to give the institution in all £500" by means of readings: see p. 549. He did not read for them until 1858, and had perhaps suggested an appeal to Miss Coutts.

To WILKIE COLLINS, 19 JUNE 1857*

MS Morgan Library.

Gallery of Illustration | Friday June Nineteenth 1857

Dear Sir

We beg to inform you that we have taken the liberty of adding your name to this Committee, in the full assurance that you would readily extend that sanction and support to the object in view.

We are Dear Sir | Faithfully Yours
CHARLES DICKENS
ARTHUR W. W. SMITH

Wilkie Collins Esquire

To WILLIAM HEPWORTH DIXON, 19 JUNE 1857*

MS Rosenbach Museum.

Gallery of Illustration | Friday June Nineteenth, 1857

Dear Sir

We beg to inform you that we have taken the liberty of adding your name to this Committee, in the full assurance that you would readily extend that sanction and support to the object in view.[1]

We are Dear Sir | Faithfully Yours
CHARLES DICKENS
ARTHUR W. W. SMITH

Hepworth Dixon Esquire

To DANIEL MACLISE, 19 JUNE 1857†

MS Berg Collection.

Gallery of Illustration | Friday June Nineteenth, 1857

Dear Sir

We beg to inform you that we have taken the liberty of adding your name to this Committee, in the full assurance that you would readily extend that sanction and support to the object in view.

We are Dear Sir | Faithfully Yours
CHARLES DICKENS
ARTHUR W. W. SMITH

Daniel Maclise Esquire R.A.

To SAMUEL PHELPS, 19 JUNE 1857

MS Rosenbach Museum.

Gallery of Illustration | Friday June Nineteenth 1857

Dear Sir

We beg to inform you that we have taken the liberty of adding your name to this

[1] Dixon owed much to Jerrold: he first wrote under his own name in Jerrold's *Illuminated Magazine*, Dec 43; moved to London in Summer 46 on Jerrold's strong recommendation.

Committee, in the full assurance that you would readily extend that sanction and support to the object in view.

We are Dear Sir | Faithfully Yours
CHARLES DICKENS
ARTHUR W. W. SMITH

Samuel Phelps Esquire

To UNKNOWN CORRESPONDENT, 19 JUNE 1857

Mention in Puttick & Simpson catalogue, Dec 1877; *MS* 1 p.; dated Gallery of Illustration, 19 June 57.

To MRS PHELPS,[1] 20 JUNE 1857*

MS Rosenbach Museum. *Address:* Mrs Phelps | 8 Canonbury Square | Islington | N.

GARRICK CLUB
Saturday Twentieth June 1857

My Dear Mrs. Phelps

Many thanks for your note. I heard from Mr. Phelps the other day. There is no hurry as to my two later notes. So that he finds them when he comes home, it will be time enough.

Very faithfully Yours
CHARLES DICKENS

To MISS BURDETT COUTTS, 20 JUNE 1857

MS Morgan Library. *Address:* Miss Burdett Coutts | 1 Stratton Street | Piccadilly | London | W.

Gad's Hill | Saturday Night | Twentieth June 1857

My Dear Miss Coutts.

As you and I had a little talk here[2] about the Frozen Deep, in which your kindness and sense were as conspicuous as they always are—and as deeply felt by me as they always are—I am anxious to let you know what has since passed about it with the Queen.

I had written (at the time we spoke together) to Colonel Phipps in the usual way, stating what I was trying, with others, to do "In remembrance of the late Mr. Douglas Jerrold", and adding that I had no poor case to make, or pitiful thing to say—that I had resolved never to travel out of those words. I added that if the Queen would come to see the Frozen Deep, it would be a great honor, &c. To this Phipps replied (as I knew he would), that the Queen could never do anything in that way for the memory of an Individual, as it would involve perpetual engagements or constant grievous offence; but that she very much wanted to see the Play, and could it be done otherwise? Could he and I talk about it? I then went to see him, and he proposed, on the Queen's behalf, its being done at Buckingham Palace. I begged him to

[1] Née Sarah Cooper (*b.* ?1810); married 1826, aged 16.

[2] During her visit: see *To* Miss Coutts, 7 June.

represent to the Queen that I felt difficulties on that score—that I should not feel easy as to the social position of my daughters at the Court under such circumstances—and that I would, with all duty and so forth, suggest that the Queen would relieve us of that difficulty by coming, on a private night of her own, to the Gallery of Illustration, and inviting her own guests to see the Play privately. But I added that she had always been most kind and considerate to me on other occasions, and that if she could not act upon my suggestion, we would, however much I might desire to avoid it, go to the Palace. He received it in the best manner, and *she* received it in the best manner; and the result is, that she has a night of her own at the Gallery, a week in advance of the public, on Saturday the 4th. of July.

I hope you think this right, as to all parties?

In reference to the point you suggested to me, I spoke confidentially to Collins, who immediately felt with me that your having suggested it or thought of it, at once closed and settled the case. I have turned over in my mind a way of changing the action of that scene; and I think (as you did) that it can be made more affecting and natural, with the change,[1] than without it.

This is all. With kind love to Mrs. Brown, Believe me ever

Faithfully and affecy. Yours

CD.

To MEMBERS OF THE CAST OF *THE FROZEN DEEP*, 20 JUNE 1857

MS Benoliel Collection.

IN REMEMBRANCE OF THE LATE MR. DOUGLAS JERROLD.

COMMITTEE'S OFFICE, GALLERY OF ILLUSTRATION, REGENT STREET.

Saturday Twentieth June 1857.

Rehearsals of The Frozen Deep
on the stage, here.

Friday 26th. June, at 3 in the afternoon
Monday 29th. June, at 3 in the afternoon
Thursday 2nd. July, at ¼ past 10 at night.
Friday 3rd. July, at ¼ past 10 at night.

On Saturday July 4th, the piece will be *privately* acted here, to the Queen. And on Saturday July 11th. it will be acted here, agreeably to the printed Programme.

[1] In Act I: see *To* Collins, 26 June; most probably making Nurse Esther's "second sight" more natural (Miss Coutts may even have thought that as originally presented, it might disturb the Queen). The Morgan MS shows that, in revising Collins's original MS for the professional performance in 1866, CD modified the "second sight" throughout; and in that performance Nurse Esther and her "second sight" were removed and a "vision" by Clara substituted.

To JOHN FORSTER, [21 JUNE 1857]

Extract in F, XI, iii, 830. *Date:* 21 June 57 according to Forster.

Saying that the Queen, through Col. Phipps, had requested that he would select a room in the palace, do what he would with it, and let her see The Frozen Deep *there*. I said to Col. Phipps thereupon that the idea was not quite new to me; that I did not feel easy as to the social position of my daughters, etc., at a Court under those circumstances; and that I would beg her Majesty to excuse me, if any other way of her seeing the play could be devised. To this Phipps said he had not thought of the objection, but had not the slightest doubt I was right. I then proposed that the Queen should come to the Gallery of Illustration a week before the subscription night, and should have the room entirely at her own disposal, and should invite her own company. This, with the good sense that seems to accompany her good nature on all occasions, she resolved within a few hours to do.

To JOHN DEANE,[1] 23 JUNE 1857*

MS Free Library of Philadelphia.

Gallery of Illustration | Regent Street
Twenty Third June 1857

My Dear Sir

Your letter has interested me very much, and is another proof (if I needed any) of your promptitude, quick sense, and consideration.

I had not thought of doing the Frozen Deep at Manchester; but I would, if a sum of any importance could be gained by it. The difficulty is this:—it cannot be done in any *very large* place. Firstly, because the scenery is not of sufficient width to display its great delicacy and completeness in a great building. Secondly, because I doubt if my ladies would be as good as they really are—that is, could express themselves for as much—in a wilderness of space. If we could get such high prices as would make a Concert Room or the like, pay, I would not mind the trouble. But it is to be remembered that a Railway Truck would be wanted to carry the rollers and set pieces, and that very expert Carpenters would be necessary, of whom at least two must be London-men to whom the piece is known in the working. Again—the gas fitting for a sunset of Telbin's, and a sea beach by Stanfield, is of a very nice kind; and although it involves no material which is not likely to be in any good Gas Fitter's shop, the gas would have to be brought in from the Main in a considerable quantity, and would require two intelligent men to work it, besides the personal direction of one of those two painters. Again, the stage must be a raised one. Again a little hanging platform is wanted from the roof, to hold two boys to "snow". Again, the stage

[1] John Connellan Deane (1816–87), son of the Irish architect Sir Thomas Deane; General Commissioner of the Manchester Art Treasures Exhibition. Called to the Irish Bar; Poor Law Inspector 1846; associated with Paxton in the Great Exhibition, Crystal Palace, 1851 and with Great Exhibitions at Cork 1852 and Dublin 1853. Wills described him as joint conceiver of the Manchester Exhibition and its general manager, presenting "a rare instance of the union, in one person, of a bold and comprehensive projector with an exact and able executant" ("The Manchester School of Art", *HW*, 10 Oct 57, XVI, 351). A member of the Jerrold Fund Committee.

must be from 30 to 40 feet deep. These are not terrific requirements, but they are indispensable, and are perhaps more than you have thought of. And so much trouble was taken when I got the piece up, to render it curiously complete, that it is impossible to chop any little mechanical nicety out of it without spoiling it all—the whole thing so coheres and goes together.

Lastly, there are 30 people in it; and the moving of such a party for such a distance is expensive.

If any scheme should occur to you for making Manchester cry, through these means—say two nights, I would attentively consider it. But I do not myself know a suitable place, nor do I see any hopeful means of making two or three hundred pounds by it, after deducting all charges.

Faithfully Yours always

John Deane Esquire. CHARLES DICKENS

To DANIEL MACLISE, 24 JUNE 1857

MS Huntington Library.

IN REMEMBRANCE OF THE LATE MR. DOUGLAS JERROLD.

COMMITTEE'S OFFICE, GALLERY OF ILLUSTRATION,
REGENT STREET.
Wednesday Twenty Fourth June 1857.

My Dear Maclise.

Perhaps you know that the Queen has commanded a private performance of our last Tavistock House play, here, on Saturday Week the 4th. of July? As your name is on the Committee and as she knows you very well, will you be one of three or four (not more) to receive her, quietly? If you say yes, I will let you know, as soon as I know myself from Phipps, at what hour she will come. I cannot receive her myself, as I must be half dressed in North Polar costume, and busy.

Write me a word in answer, to this address.

Ever affecy.
CHARLES DICKENS

To SIR JOSEPH PAXTON, 24 JUNE 1857

MS British Library.

IN REMEMBRANCE OF THE LATE MR. DOUGLAS JERROLD.

COMMITTEE'S OFFICE, GALLERY OF ILLUSTRATION,
REGENT STREET.
Wednesday Twenty Fourth June 1857.

My Dear Paxton

The Queen has commanded a private performance of the Frozen Deep, here, on Saturday Week, the fourth of July. As your name is on the Committee and as the Queen knows you well, I have no doubt it would be a very good thing altogether if you could be here to receive her. Will your engagements admit of it? If (as I hope) yes, and you answer me to that effect, I will let you know, as soon as I know myself, at what hour she will arrive.

Ever Faithfully Yours

Sir Joseph Paxton. CHARLES DICKENS

To RICHARD BENTLEY, 25 JUNE 1857*

MS Berg Collection. *Address:* Richard Bentley Esquire | New Burlington Street | London | W.

Gad's Hill, Higham, by Rochester
Twenty Fifth June 1857

My Dear Sir

When I get a day to myself from the business in which poor Jerrold's death has immersed me, I will not fail to read the book of which you give me so interesting an account. In the meantime I will have it read by some one else, on whom, if it be really deserving, it will not be lost.[1]

Will you come down and dine with us on Sunday the 5th.? We shall be quite alone. We have to act to the Queen on the previous night, but shall return here by a train which leaves London Bridge at ten minutes to eleven in the forenoon. If the day will suit you, we might all come down together. And if the country be half as beautiful then as it is now, I think you will be pleased with this neighbourhood.

There are various trains in the evening, for getting back to town.

Believe me | Faithfully Yours

Richard Bentley Esquire. CHARLES DICKENS

To HENRY WASHBOURNE,[2] 25 JUNE 1857*

MS Free Library of Philadelphia. *Address:* Henry Washbourne Esquire | 25 Ivy Lane | Paternoster Row | London | E.C.

Gad's Hill, Higham, by Rochester
Twenty Fifth June 1857

Dear Sir

I am greatly obliged to you for the book[3] you have done me the favor to send me, and for the very pleasant letter accompanying it. It commends the book to me, I assure you, in a most agreeable manner, and I hope to be as good a reader in your case as you have been in mine.

Faithfully Yours

Henry Washbourne Esquire CHARLES DICKENS

[1] Possibly "Berkeley Aikin"(pseudonym of Frances Aikin Kortright), *Anne Sherwood or, the Social Conditions of England*, a 3-vol. novel, published by Bentley, 30 May 57.

[2] Of Henry Washbourne & Co., publishers.

[3] *The Book of Family Crests*, 8th edn, 2 vols, 1856; enlarged by Washbourne from J. P. Elven's *Heraldry* (1815) in 1829 and successive edns. CD's "crest" is in Vol. II, p. 143, heraldically described as "a lion couchant, or, holding up in the dexter paw a cross patonce, sa"; illustrated in Vol. I as No. 19 in plate 7. CD used it as his bookplate: see letter in N, III, 717, saying it was John Dickens's crest (see title-page to this edn).

To WILKIE COLLINS, 26 JUNE 1857

MS Morgan Library.

Tavistock House | Friday Night | Twenty Sixth June, 1857

My Dear Collins

I am so sensible of that First Act's requiring—for the old hands—so much care in a less feverish atmosphere than the Theatre, that I must propose Rehearsals of the Ladies here (our house is stripped, and has plenty of room), on Tuesday, Wednesday, and Thursday.[1] The hour must rest principally with Mrs. Dickenson,[2] but I should like it best in the evening—say at 8. However, my time is the Play's. There is a great deal at stake, and it *must be* well done. Will you see Mrs. Dickenson between this and Monday's Rehearsal, and consult her convenience on the point?

I shall be at the Gallery during the greater part of tomorrow, and shall dine at the Garrick at 6 before going to the Concert.

Ever Faithfully

CD.

[1] Four rehearsals in the Gallery of Illustration had already been arranged between 26 June and 3 July, the last two at 10.15 p.m. ("Rehearsal Call", in CD's hand, 20 June 57, MS FLP).

[2] i.e. Dickinson. Frances Vickriss Dickinson (1820–98), only child and heiress of Charles Dickinson of Farley Hill Court, Berks, and miscellaneous writer, clearly introduced to CD by Wilkie Collins; she played the part of Nurse Esther for the four Gallery of Illustration performances in July. She appears as "Mrs. Francis" ("Giles née Dickenson" against her name in CD's hand) in playbill advertising performance of 18 July (*D*, XXXVI, [1940], 201). Married Nov 1838 John Edward Geils, of Shinfield, Berks and Dumbuck, Dumbartonshire, Lieut. in the 4th Dragoons; they had four daughters. She had inherited a fortune of £3,200 p.a. from her father; Geils had virtually nothing outside his Lieut's pay (and an entailed but heavily encumbered Scottish estate). She left him in Sep 45. In a peculiarly unsavoury divorce case, tried in the Court of Arches July 46–Aug 48 (its lurid details reported at great length in *The Times*), she was granted a judicial separation on grounds of Geils's adultery, the Judge non-suiting her pleas of cruelty and unnatural behaviour; she finally won a full Scottish divorce (made possible since the couple had cohabited in Scotland) on 7 Dec 55 (Scottish Record Office): see Catherine Peters, *The King of Inventors*, pp. 173–4. As Miss Peters shows, Collins's "A New Mind" (*HW*, 1 Jan 59 XIX, 107), bases the reference to Scottish divorce law on her experience. (In all other respects his story is entirely fictitious.) On 23 Jan 48, at the end of the day's proceedings, the Judge, Sir Herbert Jenner Fust, pronounced: "I can hear no more. I am disgusted. It is quite disgraceful to the Court, the public, and the profession. The manner in which this case has been argued is disgraceful" (*The Times*, 24 Jan 48). The case was described in the *Critic*, 7 Jan 60, as "perhaps the worst . . . that ever was reported in the English press". Mrs Geils emerges from the case as wilful and self-centred, but not vicious. In 1863 she married the Rev. Gilbert Elliot, Dean of Bristol (see Vol. VI, p. 538*n*), and for the help CD gave her in her new marital difficulties, see later vols. She was an intimate friend of Hepworth Dixon and godmother of one of his daughters; another daughter, Ella, described her as having "all the poise and authority of a woman of birth", as "vitality itself" even when quite an old woman", and as living "in a social whirlwind". (Ella Dixon, *As I Knew Them*, [1930], pp. 29–39.)

To DANIEL MACLISE, 26 JUNE 1857*

MS Benoliel Collection.

IN REMEMBRANCE OF THE LATE MR. DOUGLAS JERROLD.

COMMITTEE'S OFFICE, GALLERY OF ILLUSTRATION,
REGENT STREET.
Friday Twenty Sixth June 1857.

My Dear Maclise. I am very happy to have your note. The greatest desire I had in asking you to receive H.M. was that you should see the play. We were all much disappointed that you lost it before, because we believed you would appreciate it. You will find plenty of room for yourself and the best situation.

Ever Faithfully
CD.

To C. [M.] SMITH,[1] 27 JUNE 1857

Extract in Carnegie Book Shop catalogue, No. 228; *MS* 1 p.; dated Tavistock House, London, 27 June 57; addressed C. D. Smith.

I . . . shall not fail to send the order you have had the goodness to give me, to the bookseller forthwith.

To JOHN THOMPSON, 28 JUNE 1857

Mention in *American Book Prices Current*, No. 79, 1973; *MS* 1 p.; addressed John; dated 28 June 57.

Enclosing a list of things to be fetched from Mr. Stanfield's.

To J. E. MAYALL, 30 JUNE 1857*

MS Mrs Gladys Wheen Ross. *Address:* J. E. Mayall Esquire | 224 Regent Street | W.

Tavistock House | Tuesday Thirtieth June 1857

My Dear Sir

I thank you heartily for your admirable photograph of poor Jerrold, and I shall carefully preserve it.

Faithfully Yours always
J. E. Mayall Esquire CHARLES DICKENS

[1] Initials probably catalogue's error for "C. M.": Charles Manby Smith, whose *Curiosities of London Life* (1853) was published in a new cheap edn in Mar 1857.

To SIR JOSEPH PAXTON, 30 JUNE 1857*

MS British Library.

IN REMEMBRANCE OF THE LATE MR. DOUGLAS JERROLD.

COMMITTEE'S OFFICE, GALLERY OF ILLUSTRATION, REGENT STREET.
Tuesday Thirtieth June 1857.

My Dear Paxton

It will be necessary to assemble here by half past 8 on Saturday, as the Queen has appointed to be here precisely at 9.

Can you lend us any plants in pots, for the occasion, and give us any cut flowers? All such contributions, Chiswickian, Sydenhamian, or Devonshirian,[1] will be joyfully received.

Faithfully Yours Ever

Sir Joseph Paxton M.P. CHARLES DICKENS

To JOSEPH LANGFORD,[2] 2 JULY 1857

Mention in Royal Commission on Historical Manuscripts (1974); dated 2 July 57; addressed Joseph Langford.

Enclosing invitation cards for "Queen's Night" and reading of Christmas Carol.

To SAMUEL PHELPS, 2 JULY 1857

MS Rosenbach Museum.

IN REMEMBRANCE OF THE LATE MR. DOUGLAS JERROLD.

COMMITTEE'S OFFICE, GALLERY OF ILLUSTRATION, REGENT STREET.
Second July 1857.

My Dear Phelps.

We shall not have above 20 people on the Queen's night, but I have managed to lay violent hands on these two cards for yourself and Mrs. Phelps. Observe the directions as to time.

Faithfully Yours always
CHARLES DICKENS

[1] i.e. from Chiswick House, one of the Duke's houses; the Crystal Palace; or Chatsworth.

[2] Joseph Munt Langford (1809–84), manager of London branch of Blackwood's 1845–81: see Vol. VI, p. 461*n*.

To W. M. THACKERAY, 2 JULY 1857

MS University of Texas.

IN REMEMBRANCE OF THE LATE MR. DOUGLAS JERROLD.

COMMITTEE'S OFFICE, GALLERY OF ILLUSTRATION,
REGENT STREET.
Thursday Second July 1857.

My Dear Thackeray.

I send you two tickets for the Queen's night here. Perhaps you may not care to use them, but I have written them off on the list as yours. There will not be above five and twenty present, over and above the Queen's party.

Faithfully Yours always
W. M. Thackeray Esquire. CHARLES DICKENS

To DR CHARLES MACKAY,[1] 3 JULY 1857*

MS Berg Collection.

Tavistock House | Friday Night | Third July 1857.

My Dear Mackay.

I need not tell you that the labor of making the arrangements to get the money to which Mr. Ashurst's[2] letter refers, is something enormous. It is a kind of work impossible to be discharged by more than two or three men; and upon them it falls, while the arrangements are working themselves out, with a weight which really crushes out all other occupation.

Hence, and because the getting of the money necessarily precedes the discussion of the question How it shall be disposed of, I have not yet called the Committee together. That shall be done, however, as a matter of form, next week:—though I do not think that they can come to any decision even then, pending the raising of the fund. I reserve my own opinion on Mr. Ashurst's view of the case until we come together. I apprehend that there is very little probability of our differing among ourselves, when we can have but one interest and one desire.

Faithfully Yours
Charles Mackay Esquire CHARLES DICKENS

[1] Charles Mackay (1814–89; *DNB*), poet and journalist: see Vol. I, p. 485*n*.

[2] William Henry Ashurst, of Ashurst & Morris, 6 Old Jewry, the solicitor handling Douglas Jerrold's estate.

To WILLIAM IRVINE,[1] 4 JULY 1857*

MS Free Library of Philadelphia.

IN REMEMBRANCE OF THE LATE MR. DOUGLAS JERROLD.

COMMITTEE'S OFFICE, GALLERY OF ILLUSTRATION,
REGENT STREET.
Saturday Fourth July 1857.

Sir

I beg to say in reply to your letter, that I shall be happy to take charge of the subscription to which it refers; but that I can only do so, on behalf of this Committee, by recording it as payment for a ticket or tickets for one or more of the occasions set forth on the other side.[2] In remitting it, you will do me the favor, perhaps, to let me know what tickets shall be sent to you.

As the body whom I represent in this communication never address any solicitation or explanation to any quarter, beyond such as may be supposed to be conveyed in the printed line at the head of this sheet of paper, I can only very slightly follow your reference to the money-affairs of the late Mr. Jerrold's family. It is not true that Mr. Jerrold left no provision whatever; but the other printed paragraph to which you refer (by whom originated I don't know) is as preposterously exaggerated as anything I have ever seen in my life.[3]

I am Sir | Your faithful Servant
CHARLES DICKENS

Mr. William Irvine.

To UNKNOWN CORRESPONDENT, 4 JULY 1857

Extract in Bangs & Co. catalogue Nos 739 & 741 (*c.* 1893); *MS* (3rd person) 2 pp.; dated 4 July 57.

Mr. Dickens receives letters from unknown[4] correspondents by hundreds rather than scores, and he can only respect their confidence and lament his inability to serve them.

[1] Unidentified.

[2] A copy of the printed programme of concerts, plays and readings (headed by the names of the Committee).

[3] The printed paragraph is probably a letter signed "Anti-Humbug", which appeared in *Reynolds' Weekly Newspaper*, 5 July. Sunday papers were published a few days earlier. The letter, alleging "the cruel neglect by Mr. Jerrold of the most sacred duties and ties", stated that Douglas Jerrold had for some years before his death made "at least 2,000l. a year—Yet he never insured his life, and has left his family without a shilling ... he spent all he had in indulgence, and left his family to the charity of the public, or rather to the whim and vanity of a set." Those who went to Jerrold's funeral, to connect themselves with "the set"—"a certain literary and dramatic league" (CD, Thackeray, Carlyle, Tennyson and Paxton are mentioned) were accused of "cliquism", "snobbery" and "flunkeyism".

[4] No doubt named, but unknown to CD.

To JOHN FORSTER, [5 AND 6 JULY 1857]

Extracts in F, XI, iii, 830–1 and VIII, iii, 653. *Date:* 5 and 6 July according to Forster.

My gracious sovereign was so pleased that she sent round begging me to go and see her and accept her thanks.[1] I replied that I was in my Farce dress, and must beg to be excused. Whereupon she sent again, saying that the dress[2] "could not be so ridiculous as that," and repeating the request. I sent my duty in reply, but again hoped her Majesty would have the kindness to excuse my presenting myself in a costume and appearance that were not my own. I was mighty glad to think, when I woke this morning, that I had carried the point.

Difficulties over water supplies for Gad's Hill. We are still boring for water here, at the rate of two pounds per day for wages.[3] The men seem to like it very much, and to be perfectly comfortable.

[1] The Queen recorded in her Journal: "July 4 1857. Buckingham Palace.... At 9 went with dear Uncle [*King Leopold I of the Belgians*], our other guests [*they included his two children, Princess Charlotte and Philip, Count of Flanders; Prince Frederick William of Prussia; Charles Anthony, Prince of Hohenzollern-Sigmaringen*], and 4 eldest children, to the Gallery of Illustration, to see an amateur performance of a Play, a romantic Melodrama in 3 acts, by Wilkie Collins, called 'The Frozen Deep',—a tale of the Northern Arctic Expedition,—most interesting, intensely dramatic, and most touching, and moving, at the end. The Play was admirably acted by Charles Dickens, (whose representation of Richard Wardour was beyond all praise and not to be surpassed) his 3 daughters [*one was in fact Helen Hogarth*] and son,—Mark Lemon, the author, etc.. There was charming scenery and almost constant accompaniment of music, which adds so much to the effect of a melodrama. We were all kept in breathless suspense, and much impressed. The Performance ended with the Farce of 'Two o'clock in the Morning', acted by Charles Dickens and Mark Lemon" (MS Royal Archives). Colonel Phipps wrote to CD on the Queen's behalf the next day: "Buckingham Palace | July 5th. 1857. | My Dear Mr Dickens, | It is no formal compliment to say that the Queen and Prince Consort, and the whole of the Royal party were delighted with the rich dramatic treat of last night. I have hardly ever seen Her Majesty and HRH so much pleased. | I cannot to yourself repeat all that was said of your own acting, but I may say that Mr. Mark Lemon's performance was particularly (and I may add from myself deservedly) admired. | The Ladies represented what Ladies would have done and said under similar circumstances.... | The Queen commanded me particularly to express her admiration of the piece itself—not only on account of its interest, and striking situations, or of the very superior language in which it is written, but on account of the high tone which is preserved in it. There was every temptation to an Author to increase the effect of the play by representing the triumph of the Evil [*prophet*], but it was particularly pleasing to Her Majesty to find a much higher lesson taught in the Victory of the better and nobler feelings—and of the Reward—the only one he could obtain—to Richard, in his self-content before his death. | This is not a small thing—and her Majesty particularly wishes that Her high approval should be conveyed to Mr. Wilkie Collins. | All the arrangements were excellent, and though the hour of the termination was rather late I saw no symptoms of fatigue. | Her Majesty had intended to convey to you personally how much She had been pleased with the performance but the dress in which the farce was concluded was a sufficient reason for your non appearance. | Unofficially I may tell you—everything went off as well as possible. | Sincerely Yours | C. B. PHIPPS (MS Morgan).

[2] As Snobbington in *Two o'Clock in the Morning*, presumably Mrs Gore's version of 1839 (called *Two in the Morning*), in which CD had acted in Montreal in 1842: see Vol. III, p. 237*n*.

[3] CD had paid £12 for "Well Workmen" on 25 June; no doubt eight further payments for "Workmen" July–Sep, totalling £109, were mainly for them (CD's Account-book, MS Messrs Coutts). They may have included Slegg, the plumber (see *To* Austin, 21 July).

To EDWARD EDWARDS,[1] 6 JULY 1857*

MS Miss L. E. Godden.

Gad's Hill Place, Higham, by Rochester
Sixth July 1857

Sir

I beg to acknowledge with many thanks, the receipt of your kind letter and its accompanying curious and interesting book.[2] I accept the work with much pleasure, and am truly gratified by your manner of offering it to me.

Faithfully yours
E. Edwards Esquire CHARLES DICKENS

To RICHARD BENTLEY, 8 JULY 1857*

MS Berg Collection.

Tavistock House | Eighth July, 1857

My Dear Mr. Bentley

The terms of your note make me fear that you over-rate my power of being serviceable to you.[3] Many people do so, in many ways, almost daily. I am always afraid of it.

I shall be here on Saturday morning at half past ten. You may command my attention at that hour, if it should suit your convenience.

Faithfully Yours
Richard Bentley Esquire CHARLES DICKENS

To DANIEL MACLISE, 8 JULY 1857

MS Dickens House.

Tavistock House | Eighth July, 1857

My Dear Maclise

We may cry quits. I cannot possibly have given you more pleasure through Richard Wardour,[4] than you have given me through your appreciation of it. In that perpetual struggle after an expression of the Truth, which is at once the pleasure and the pain of the lives of workers in the Arts, the interest of such a character to me is that it enables me, as it were, *to write a book in company* instead of in my own solitary room, and to feel its effect coming freshly back upon me from the reader. With such a reader as you to send it back, it is a most fascinating exercise. I could blow off my superfluous fierceness, in nothing so curious to me.

[1] Edward Edwards (1812–86; *DNB*), first Librarian of the Manchester Free Library 1850–8 and miscellaneous writer; Sec. of Art Union; his books included *The Fine Arts in England*, 1840 and a biography of Sir Walter Raleigh, 1865.

[2] Perhaps his *Comparative Table of the Principal Schemes . . . for the Classification of Libraries*, Manchester, 1855.

[3] Helping to arrange terms for a new edn of Shirley Brooks's novel, *Aspen Court*: see *To* Bentley, 16 July and *fn*.

[4] Maclise had missed CD's first performance of the part on 6 Jan because of an injured leg.

I shall take you at your word! When we have done, I shall send you the book[1] to annotate.[2]

You should have seen the Company's appreciation of *your* appreciation, when I told them of it. You really would have felt pleased with their thorough knowledge of its worth.

The Queen was undoubtedly wonderfully taken.[3] I had a letter on Sunday, of the most unofficial and uncourtly character. She sent for me after the Play, but I beg[4] to be excused from presenting myself in any dress but my own.

When will you come down to Gad's Hill?[5]

Ever Faithfully
CD.

To MESSRS CHAPMAN & HALL, 8 JULY 1857

MS Mr St John G.A. Sechiari. *Date:* Printed heading gives 185— on date-line; only in 1857 was 8 July a Wednesday; handwriting supports.

OFFICE OF HOUSEHOLD WORDS,
Wednesday Evening Eighth July 185[7]

Messrs. Chapman and Hall

Please deliver to the Bearer, one copy of the American Notes, Cheap Edition,[6] for me.

CHARLES DICKENS

To TOM TAYLOR,[7] 8 JULY 1857

MS Huntington Library.

Household Words Office
Wednesday Night | Eighth July 1857

My Dear Taylor

By all means as to Wigan's[8] committee,[9] and delighted to join it. I should take

[1] The prompt-book, copied by a clerk or professional copyist from CD's MS, with at least one whole page in his hand, and used for the 1857 performances (MS Morgan). For CD's substantial revisions, which continued after rehearsals began, see R. L. Brannan, *Under the Management of Mr CD*, Cornell University Press, 1966. A copy, embodying Collins's changes for the Olympic in 1866, was printed that year for the cast, but not published (copy, with further changes in MS by Collins and CD and a facsimile page of MS by CD, in BL).

[2] Maclise had presumably offered to do some sketches of scenes or characters from *The Frozen Deep*. If he did so, they have not survived. Two drawings in January of CD and Lemon in the Arctic hut, early in Act II, by Nathaniel Powell, CD's next-door neighbour, are reproduced by *D*, LVI (1960), 158. Powell's great-grand-daughter, Miss Audrey Baker, possesses the originals, larger and in colour wash, showing more detail; together with a third drawing showing Wardour feeling for his knife, towards the end of Act II.

[3] Written over "pleased", cancelled.

[4] Thus in MS.

[5] Maclise was beginning to be a recluse and probably never went to Gad's Hill.

[6] Published 1850.

[7] Tom Taylor (1817–80; *DNB*), dramatist and journalist: see Vols V, p. 82*n* and VII, p. 278*n*.

[8] Alfred Sydney Wigan.

[9] To arrange his farewell benefit (on the grounds of illness) on 24 July; it took place at the Olympic Theatre. His wife played the

shame to myself for having forgotten to reply, if I had not been perpetually busy in one way or other with poor Jerrold's matter.

It seems to me that the best thing you can do as to the Prologue[1] is to choose your own speaker.[2] Let me know who it is to be, and I will nail that name on Webster's forehead. Webster or other, man, woman, or child, surely you are the proper man to say "I have such an idea, and I desire it to be done in such a way."

Faithfully Yours Ever

Tom Taylor Esquire. CHARLES DICKENS

To BENJAMIN WEBSTER, [8 JULY 1857]

Envelope only,[3] MS British Library. *Address:* Benjamin Webster Esquire | Theatre Royal | Liverpool. PM 8 July 1857.

To THOMAS BEARD, 9 JULY 1857

MS Dickens House. *Address:* Thomas Beard Esquire | 42 Portman Place | Edgeware Road | W.

Tavistock House | Thursday Evening | Ninth July, 1857.

My Dear Beard

I omitted to ask you yesterday, whether you would like to see the Play from the Proscenium Wing, on Saturday night.[4] If you would, managerial potentiality can

heroine in Taylor's comedy, *A Sheep in Wolf's Clothing*; he gave a Farewell Address, reported in full in the *Morning Chronicle*, 25 July. Lady Glanville and her party occupied the Queen's box; Stanfield, Maclise, Procter and Taylor were reported as present; CD was not mentioned. Wigan, in fact, returned to the stage the following year after several months' convalescing at Scarborough.

[1] To Jerrold's *The Rent Day* and *Black-Eyed Susan*, performed on the Douglas Jerrold Remembrance Night, 29 July, written by Taylor.

[2] See *To* Webster, 24 July and *fn*.

[3] Probably contained a letter about the Haymarket performance of Jerrold's *Housekeeper* and *Prisoner of War* on 15 July, as announced. In the former Webster took the part of Father Oliver, in which he had first made his reputation in 1833. In *The Prisoner of War*, Phelps and the Keeleys played their original parts of 1842; also in the cast were Buckstone, Compton, Webster and Maria Ternan. A Prologue written by Samuel Lucas (1818–68; *DNB*) was spoken by Phelps (printed as a single sheet; copy in BL stamped 1 Aug 57). It opens "Welcome in Jerrold's name! From Jerrold's tomb | This greeting chases half the gathering gloom, | And turns our sorrow for his mortal part | To joy and pride in his immortal art." After referring to the plays' "savour and zest ... surging and sparkling", the conclusion praises the man, as "still more worthy of regard .. he fought a fair, a brave and generous fight, | And struck in honour's name for truth and right, | —*Hopeless of cross or riband*—taking heed | Less for his fortunes than the common need— | So,—for his guerdon and the common cause, | Do you now crown him with your just applause."

[4] 11 July, the first performance of *The Frozen Deep* at the Gallery of Illustration. Oxenford, in *The Times*, 13 July, gave it a long and warm notice; much of CD's "art" he found in his "minutest variations of voice and gesture"; his performance was, "in the truest sense of the word, a creation ... the creation of a literary man. He gave the full casts of both *The Frozen Deep* and *Uncle John*. The *Athenaeum*, 18 July, acclaimed Collins at length as an original and theatrically effective dramatist; called CD "a great actor" who "might teach professionals much that they will never learn"; he "depended on truth of detail, not vehemence of manner—on pathetic inflections, not violent emphases". It also praised Lemon, Egg, Mamie Dickens and Georgina Hogarth.

achieve it. In that case, be in the entrance hall (where we went in yesterday) at $\frac{1}{4}$ before 8, and Walter shall be waiting to bring you round to the stage.

Ever Heartily
CD.

To ARTHUR RYLAND, 9 JULY 1857*

MS Mrs Quinney.

[a]*In Memory of the late Mr. Douglas Jerrold.*

Gallery of Illustration, Regent Street[a]
Thursday Ninth July 1857

My Dear Mr. Ryland

I want to consult you about the hopefulness of doing the Frozen Deep, two nights running, in Birmingham.

I am afraid of the Town Hall.[1] It would be too large for the ladies, and too large for the scenery. Dee's large room[2] (if there should be none larger and better) would be the place, I think, for the purpose. We should have to take off 28 feet deep for the stage—and we should have by the way to contract with a Carpenter to put up the stage. Now, what could we get into that room, each night, in money? What do you think we might charge for such a performance, and how many would the place hold? And could we get the necessary audience at the price necessary to remunerate us, two consecutive nights.

The thing is making such a noise here,[3] that I believe we could fill St. Paul's if we played there. But the difficulty is, that we must not play in too large a space.

Taking it out of London at all, I would rather take it to Birmingham than anywhere. The question is, can it be done? Can you suggest any better place than Dee's Room? Will you counsel me generally?[4]

In great haste | Ever Faithfully Yours
CHARLES DICKENS

Arthur Ryland Esquire.

[aa] In CD's hand.

[1] In Paradise St, begun 1832; its principal architect was J. A. Hansom (1803–82; *DNB*), inventor of the Hansom cab.

[2] In Frederick Dee's Commercial Hotel and Posting House, 26 Temple St.

[3] For the publicity CD had sought for the Tavistock House performance in Jan, and the ensuing reviews, see *To* George Hogarth, *To* Oxenford and *To* Hastings, 30 Dec 1856 and *fnn*, and *To* Wills, 7 Jan 57, *fn*. The performance for the Queen and her party at the Gallery of Illustration on 4 July was fully and warmly reviewed in the *Morning Chronicle*, 6 July. By 4 July all the seats for the first two public performances on 11 and 18 July had been sold (*Athenaeum*, 4 July). Reviews continued to be highly favourable: although "there is much in dramatic art which is of a higher kind" wrote the *Saturday Review*, 1 Aug, "there is nothing to be seen at present on the English stage which equals *The Frozen Deep*". CD's acting it described as "quiet, strong, natural, and effective ... free from exaggeration ... a work of art, but the art is concealed".

[4] On inside blank page of letter Ryland jotted down calculations of the number and price of seats and the cost of renting the hall; but the play was not performed in Birmingham.

To WILLIAM J. CLEMENT, 10 JULY 1857

MS Huntington Library.

Tavistock House | Friday July Tenth 1857.

My Dear Clement

Your note received this morning amazes me. Within two or three days after the receipt of the poor boy's[1] Manuscript,[2] I returned it to you in a letter replying to yours on the subject. I cannot quite accurately recall whether I was here or at Gravesend; but I strongly incline to the belief that I was at the latter place.[3] In that case I posted the letter with my own hand; *but in any case I most positively* KNOW[4] that I dispatched my reply to you, and sent the MS with it.

The exact words of my answer I have necessarily forgotten; having an immense correspondence and a constantly occupied mind. I remember that I had felt in a difficulty what to write, without encouraging hopes that might prove to be fallacious. I believe I told you in effect that there were many little points of merit in the juvenile production, but that I saw no signs in it of the author being able to make an advance on a very general kind of ability, or being able to do more than many young men do—not very successfully. I hinted at the difference between what is clever and meritorious among private friends, and what is addressed to the Public—who have nothing whatever to do with the circumstances under which any work is produced, and can only be expected to accept it for its own sake. I have an impression that I finished by saying that if the young man should ever wish to offer anything to Household Words, I would read it myself if you would send it to me.

Pray understand that I have not the slightest doubt of this letter's having been posted; and that I have a conviction very little short of certainty, that I posted it myself.

I must indeed have changed very much, and cast my nature as a snake does his skin, if I could have neglected you for whom I have a truly affectionate regard, and whom I first knew through our poor dear Talfourd.[5]

Mrs. Dickens unites with me in cordial remembrances to Mrs. Clement, and all your house.

Very faithfully Yours

William J. Clement Esquire

CHARLES DICKENS

[1] Untraced.

[2] Not discovered.

[3] Where he was staying to superintend the improvements at Gad's Hill: see *To* Clement, 8–14 Apr.

[4] Underlined twice.

[5] Sir Thomas Noon Talfourd (1795–1854; *DNB*), barrister and Judge of the Common Pleas since July 1849: see Vols. I, p. 290*n* and VII, p. 89 and *n*. In his last Diary entry of 11 Mar 54, two days before his death, he had written: "I hope I shall encounter no festive temptation till I dine with Clement at Shrewsbury" (Private Personal Memoranda, 1852–4, MS Reading Central Library).

To MISS BURDETT COUTTS, 10 JULY 1857†

MS Morgan Library. *Address:* Miss Burdett Coutts | 1 Stratton Street | Piccadilly | W.

Tavistock House | Friday Tenth July, 1857

My Dear Miss Coutts.

I have been obliged to postpone Walter's photograph visit,[1] because, between the outfitter,[2] and the Hindustanee, and the India House, and the Passage preparations, I thought I descried that he was getting dazed, and had best have a few quiet hours with his brothers, just home from Boulogne after a year's absence.[3] I have sent him down to them again to day; but tomorrow he will go to King's College.[4] I a little doubt there being time left for him to learn the Art to any real purpose—but I have not said this to him; I only say it to you, in order that you may understand that he has not been remiss in his appreciation of your great kindness.

At Shepherd's Bush on Wednesday, all was in excellent order. No complaints or shortcomings of any kind. Alice Matthews however, very poorly again. I went carefully through my proposed alteration; and left instructions with the builder[5] to send me an estimate. When I get it, I will propose an appointment, if you will make one with me, to explain to you exactly what I mean.

I know my plan is a good one,—because it is mine! Seriously, I am certain it has the merit of being simple, easy, cheap, rather ingenious, and easily made with the people in the house. It brings in all the existing materials—would make the long room remarkably airy and healthy—would give us a better bedroom (much better) than we now have over it—and a room for a sick girl besides.

At Gad's Hill, we have left off digging for water, and are now boring. I watch the process with the resignation of despair.

We are suffering a good deal from Andersen.[6] The other day we lost him when we

[1] Miss Coutts had offered to have Walter taught photography before he left for India.

[2] CD made two payments for Walter's outfit: 8 guineas on 28 July and £106.3.9 on 1 Sep (CD's Account-book, MS Messrs Coutts).

[3] Frank, Alfred and Sydney, all at Mr Gibson's school at Boulogne.

[4] Presumably for his lessons in Hindustani. He sailed for India on 20 July.

[5] Edward Bird, of Hammersmith.

[6] Andersen stayed with CD and his family at Gad's Hill 11 June–15 July, after he had originally announced a visit of a week or a fortnight. He clearly outstayed his welcome. The visit is fully documented in Elias Bredsdorff, *Hans Christian Andersen*, 1975, pp. 210–16. Bredsdorff shows, from Andersen's diary and letters, that, although he remained entirely happy with CD himself and with Catherine, he became convinced that Georgina and the children disliked him. The children clearly found him trying. According to Henry, then aged eight, Andersen on his first morning sent to Charley to shave him, "to the intense indignation of the boys" (*Recollections*, 1934, p. 35). Katey, according to Gladys Storey, summed him up as "a bony bore [*who*] stayed on and on"; Miss Storey reports her as saying that CD put up a card in Andersen's room saying "Hans Andersen slept in this room for five weeks—which seemed to the family AGES!" (Gladys Storey, *Dickens and Daughter*, 1939, pp. 21–2). But Andersen's diary shows that CD himself was a perfect host (although he was often away); and on 23 June he wrote of him to his friend Weidemann in Leipzig: "He is a singularly lovable character. Pick out of his writings what is heartiest, absurdest, liveliest. Out of that, fashion to yourself a man, and you have his portrait" (MS Morgan; transl. from Danish). Andersen himself was delighted with his visit and felt it had been a great success. Wilkie Collins caricatured him as an eccentric German visitor, Herr von Muffe, in "The Bachelor Bedroom", *AYR*, 6 Aug 59, I, 355.

came up to London Bridge Terminus,[1] and he took a Cab by himself. The Cabman driving him through the new unfinished street at Clerkenwell,[2] he thought he was driving him into remote fastnesses, to rob and murder him. He consequently arrived here, with all his money, his watch, his pocket book, and documents, *in his boots*—and it was a tremendous business to unpack him and get them off. I have arrived at the conviction that he cannot speak Danish; and the best of it, is, that his Translatress[3] declares he can't—is ready to make oath of it before any magistrate.

With love to Mrs. Brown

Dear Miss Coutts | Ever Affecy. & faithfully Yours

CD.

To F. W. HAMSTEDE,[4] 10 JULY 1857*

MS Mr Nicolas Bentley.

Gallery of Illustration | Friday Tenth July, 1857

My Dear Sir

I did not quite understand the exact purport of your note, until I looked at it again a minute ago, after hearing from Webster.

It is my impression that it would scarcely do to introduce the duet to which you refer, in Black Eyed Susan. The situation is not favorable to it, and it does not belong to the piece—which is well known to the Public. But if you approve of my asking Mr. Allen[5] to sing Black Eyed Susan, I will immediately write to him.[6]

Faithfully Yours

F. W. Hamstede Esquire CHARLES DICKENS

To W. C. MACREADY, 10 JULY 1857*

MS Morgan Library.

Tavistock House | Friday Tenth July 1857

My Dearest Macready

Will you let me know what you did respecting money for Ned when he went out to India? As what you gave him in hand, after paying his passage, and what credit

[1] CD took Andersen on several visits to London; to the Crystal Palace, to several theatres, to the special performance of *The Frozen Deep* given for the Queen, to Parliament, Westminster Abbey, the British Museum and *The Times*; Miss Coutts gave a dinner-party in his honour; and he visited Bentley, his publisher, now living in St John's Wood. He also met CD's circle of close friends: Forster, Lemon, Wilkie Collins, Shirley Brooks (Bredsdorff, above, pp. 210–2).

[2] Clerkenwell Rd, connecting Theobald's Road with Hackney and the City.

[3] No doubt Mary Howitt (1799–1888; *DNB*: see Vol. IV, 501*n*), who had translated Andersen's first two novels and the German edn of his autobiography (*The True Story of My Life*, 1847); but had broken off relations with him on his accepting another translator from Bentley (Bredsdorff, above, p. 190).

[4] Frederick William Hamstede, retired city clerk; Hon. Secretary of Our Club, founded by Douglas Jerrold: see Vol. VII, p. 719 and *n*.

[5] Henry Robinson Allen (1809–76), tenor and ballad composer. Born in Cork; made his London debut as Elvino in *La Sonnambula*. Wrote the popular ballad, "The Maid of Athens".

[6] See *To* Webster, 18 July.

you lodged for him at Calcutta. I am particularly anxious not to do too much in this regard; but at the same time not to do too little, and to do right.

I still hope you may come to Gad's Hill before the summer is out. It is a place to repose in, and admire the beautiful Kentish country from. It goes sorely against the grain with me to come among London streets, heat, gas, and crowds; but I have gone into this Jerrold matter, and won't come out without a round sum.[1] (I wish you could have heard the Carol reading in St. Martin's Hall! I never saw such an audience in my life.)[2]

Catherine and Georgina, Mary, Katey, Charley, and Walter—the rest are at Gad's Hill—send their loves to all Sherborne House. You may be sure I send mine.

Ever and Ever affectionately
CD.

P.S. You will be charmed to hear that Ristori is making a dismal failure here this season, as to drawing.[3]

To FRANK STONE, 10 JULY 1857*

MS Benoliel Collection.

Tavistock House | Tenth July, 1857

My Dear Stone

The half year's account for the Front Court Gardening is £ 2. 5. 6
For the Front Enclosure ———————————— 3.15. 0
Making a Total of £ 6. 0. 6.

Which, divided by three, leaves us £2.0.0 each, to pay.[4]

Affecy. Ever
CD.

[1] Arthur Smith sent a circular letter to Committee members of the Fund, calling a meeting on 13 July, for CD to report on arrangements in progress (given in George Smith's typescript "Recollections", National Library of Scotland).

[2] CD had read the *Carol* for the Jerrold Remembrance Fund on 30 June: his first public reading in London. Yates in the *Daily News*, 1 July (see *To* Yates, 19 July), recorded: "A more appreciative set of people we have never seen." At the end, the packed audience "rose to their feet and cheered and waved their hats and handkerchiefs". He repeated the reading on 24 July.

[3] Newspaper reports hardly support this. She gave six performances as Lady Macbeth, in Italian, at the Lyceum between 3 and 29 July, interspersed with Medea and Camma, as an addition to the Italian Opera season. The *Morning Chronicle* (4 July) reported a "crowded audience" at her first night as Lady Macbeth and recorded "an equally great effort of genius" as Mrs Siddons. The *Leader*, 11 July, pronounced her success as "complete".

[4] Stone paid by cheque the next day (endorsed by him on letter).

To A. DICKERS SENR,[1] 11 JULY 1857*

MS Berg Collection. *Address:* Mr. A. Dickers Senr. | Golder Farm | Tetsworth | Oxon.

[a]*In remembrance of the late Mr. Jerrold.*

Gallery of Illustration | Regent Street London[a]
Eleventh July, 1857.

Sir.

I beg to acknowledge the safe receipt of your cheque for two guineas in aid of this Memorial Fund. Allow me to enclose you four stall tickets; two, admitting to Mr. Thackeray's lecture announced in the accompanying printed paper;[2] two, to my own Reading.

I think it right to inform you that Mr. Jerrold has not left his family in want; but that he was in the course of making a good provision for them, and would have succeeded in doing so, if his life had been spared a little longer.

Your plain and sincere letter *has* interested me very much, I assure you, and has given me great pleasure.

I am Sir | Faithfully Yours

Mr. A Dickers Senr. CHARLES DICKENS

To THOMAS EDELSTON,[3] 11 JULY 1857

MS Mr Lawrence Smith. *Address:* Thomas Edelston Esquire | 13 Lancaster Road, | Preston.

[a]*In remembrance of the late Mr. Douglas Jerrold*

Gallery of Illustration, Regent Street.[a]
Saturday July eleventh, 1857

Dear Sir

We beg to acknowledge, with many thanks the safe receipt of your remittance of £14.4.5, the balance of profit on the[4] performance[5] at the Theatre Royal Preston.[6]

Without in the least recognizing the veracity of any statement you may have seen in print respecting the pecuniary affairs of the late Mr. Jerrold's family (we make no representation whatever on the subject, and so no other form of address to the public, than the line at the top of this sheet of paper), we beg to add that we most cordially approve of your having paid the night's expenses of the Theatre. We

[1] Obviously a relation of James Dickers, farmer, of the same address, 1854.

[aa] In CD's hand.

[2] "Week-day Preachers", given on 22 July in St Martin's Hall; his subjects were Addison, Steele, Goldsmith, Fielding, Sterne, Béranger, Burns, Lamb, Hood, *Punch*, A'Beckett, and Jerrold himself; the lecture included "a very high encomium" of CD (*Morning Chronicle*, 23 July).

[3] Clearly Manager of the Theatre Royal, Preston.

[4] "benefit" deleted by CD.

[5] On 1 July, of *The Rent Day* and *Black-Eyed Susan*, in "memory of one who combined the qualities of author, actor, philosopher, wit, and philanthropist" (*Preston Pilot*, 27 June). Between the plays a verse tribute to Jerrold was delivered by Miss Seaman, no doubt the daughter of one of the two lessees. The main parts were played by H. Vandenhoff and Miss Mostyn. A warm notice in the *Preston Pilot*, 4 July, praised the actors, recorded that the house was "tolerably well filled", and ended "Altogether the entertainment was eminently successful."

[6] In Arcade Buildings, Fishergate.

particularly desire on all occasions that no one should be permitted to make any sacrifice in this cause which cannot be reasonably made and well afforded. And this is our anxious wish, not only because the thing is right in itself, but because we are well acquainted with the late Mr. Jerrold's feeling on such subjects.

Repeating our acknowledgements to yourself, and to all Preston friends, we have the honor to be,

Dear Sir | Your faithful Servants
CHARLES DICKENS
Thomas Edelston Esquire[1] ARTHUR W. W. SMITH

To CHARLES RIEU,[2] [?12 JULY 1857]

Envelope only, MS Dr Andrew Sanders. *Address:* Charles Rieu Esquire | Department of MSS. | British Museum | London, W.C., PM 12 July 57.

To FRANCESCO BERGER, [13 JULY 1857]

Mention in *Autograph Prices Current*, I (1914–16), 51; *MS* 2 pp.; dated 13 July 57; addressed Francesco Berger. *Address* (envelope, Sotheby's catalogue, June 1955): Francesco Berger Esquire | 36 Thurloe Square | Brompton | S.W. PM 13 July 1857.

Referring to the Douglas Jerrold memorial concert.

To W. C. MACREADY, 13 JULY 1857

MS Morgan Library.

Tavistock House | Monday July Thirteenth, 1857.

My Dearest Macready

Many thanks for your Indian information. I shall act upon it in the most exact manner, [a]except that as Walter is not so manly in appearance or manner as Ned was when he went out,[3] I shall strike off £20 from the letter of credit.[a] He sails next Monday.[4] Charley and I go down with him to Southampton, next Sunday.

We are all delighted with the prospect of seeing you at Gadshill. These are my Jerrold-engagements. On Friday the 24th. I have to repeat my reading at St. Martin's Hall.[5] On Saturday the 25th. to repeat The Frozen Deep at the Gallery of Illustration for the last time. On Thursday the 30th. or Friday the 31st. I shall

[1] Written at bottom of first page.

[2] Charles Pierre Henri Rieu (1820–1902; *DNB*), orientalist. Born in Geneva; studied at Geneva and Bonn Universities; settled in London 1847. Assistant, Dept of MSS, British Museum, May 1847, as Arabic and Sanskrit scholar; first Keeper of Dept of Oriental MSS, 1867–91. Compiled catalogues of the Museum's Persian and Turkish MSS. Professor of Arabic and Persian, University College, London, 1857–94; Adams Professor of Arabic, Cambridge, 1894; father of E. V. Rieu, the eminent translator. He was giving Walter lessons in Hindustani.

[aa] Omitted in MDGH and N.

[3] Walter was 16; Edward Macready 18, when he sailed to India.

[4] CD had paid £105 to the P. & O. Co. on 23 May, for Walter's voyage (CD's Account-book, MS Messrs Coutts).

[5] Of the *Carol*.

probably read at Manchester. Deane, the General Manager of the Exhibition is going down tonight, and will arrange all the preliminaries for me. If you and I went down to Manchester together and were there on a Sunday, he would give us the whole Exhibition to ourselves. It is probable I think (as he estimates the receipts of a night at about £700) that we may, in about a fortnight or so after the Reading, play The Frozen Deep in Manchester. But of this contingent engagement I at present know no more than you do.

Now, will you upon this exposition of affairs, choose your own time for coming to us, and, when you have made your choice, write to me at Gad's Hill? I am going down this afternoon for rest (which means violent cricket with the boys), after last Saturday night—which was a teazer, but triumphant. The St. Martin's Hall audience[1] was, I must confess, a very extraordinary thing. The two thousand and odd people were like one, and their enthusiasm was something awful.

—Yet I have seen that, before, too. Your young remembrance cannot recall the man, but he flourished in my day—a great actor Sir—a noble actor—thorough artist! I have seen him do wonders in that way. He retired from the stage early in life (having a monomaniacal delusion that he was old), and is said to be still living in your County.

All join in kindest love to your dear sister and all the rest.

Ever my Dearest Macready | Most affectionately Yours

CHARLES DICKENS

To FRANK STONE, 13 JULY 1857*

MS Benoliel Collection.

Gallery of Illustration | Monday Thirteenth July, 1857.

My Dear Stone.

I have booked you here for 3 Stalls for the 25th. in a capital place. If you will call or send, on or after Thursday, they will be ready for you in an envelope—3 guineas to pay.

Ever Affecy.

CD.

To RICHARD BENTLEY, 16 JULY 1857*

MS Free Library of Philadelphia.

Gad's Hill Place, Higham, by Rochester
Thursday Sixteenth July 1857

My Dear Mr. Bentley.

I have not yet had an opportunity of seeing Mr. Evans;—I mention the circumstance, merely that you may rest assured I have not forgotten our conversation.

Mr. Shirley Brooks, I *have* seen. And I hope I may now be able to arrange that

[1] On 30 June

matter.[1] As I must be in town and in your neighbourhood, on Saturday, I will endeavour to call in New Burlington Street from 12 to 1.

Faithfully Yours

Richard Bentley Esquire. CHARLES DICKENS

To CHARLES DE LA PRYME, 17 JULY 1857†

MS Doheny Memorial Library.

Tavistock House | Seventeenth July 1857

My Dear Sir

Although the poor boy's[2] writing is admirable, considering the circumstances in which he has been placed, I am strongly inclined to think that the less he is encouraged to do in that way for the future, the happier he will be. I would most decidedly gratify his own inclination—which appears to me to be a proof of his good sense—and send him to Australia.[3]

I cannot remember whether I sent you my subscription to the book.[4] In case I did not, will you have the kindness to let me know as much in one line.

My Dear Sir | Faithfully Yours

The Reverend Charles De la Pryme.[5] CHARLES DICKENS

To CHARLES KENT,[6] 18 JULY 1857*

MS Free Library of Philadelphia.

IN REMEMBRANCE OF THE LATE MR. DOUGLAS JERROLD.

COMMITTEE'S OFFICE, GALLERY OF ILLUSTRATION, REGENT STREET.

Saturday Eighteenth July 1857.

Dear Sir

On coming here from the country this morning, I found your note—just brought down to me from Tavistock House. I have to act here tonight, and tomorrow morning early to take my second boy to Southampton where he embarks for India.

Under these circumstances, I think it will be best for you to see Mr. Wills (who is altogether in my confidence), at the Household Words, say at 12 on Monday. My

[1] The publication by Bentley of a revised edn of Brooks's novel *Aspen Court* (3 vols, 1855): see *To* Brooks, 7 Aug, *fn*.

[2] Richard Realf (1834–78; *DAB*), poet, then aged 23, who had left his previous employment and gone to Brighton: see Vol. VII, Addenda, p. 906*n*.

[3] Realf had originally gone to Brighton with the intention of becoming a sailor, but found employment and encouragement with Mrs Parnell Stafford.

[4] *Guesses at the Beautiful. Poems*, 1852, with a 14 pp. Preface by De la Pryme (from 7 Marine Parade, Brighton), and a 6-line verse dedication to Mrs Stafford from "A humble EDITOR and grateful BARD": see Vol. VII, Addenda, p. 906*n*. CD did subscribe; no complete list of subscribers was included, but 23 were thanked by name, though not CD (no doubt omitted because he wished only for his initials).

[5] De la Pryme was not in fact ordained.

[6] William Charles Mark Kent (always known as Charles) (1823–1902; *DNB*), poet and journalist; see Vol. V, p. 280 and *n*.

ability to be of use to you there, necessarily depends on your ability to propose any kind of papers likely to be available for the Journal.[1] But I shall be heartily glad to serve you, if I possibly can. Trust me for that.

In great haste | Faithfully Yours

W. Charles Kent Esquire CHARLES DICKENS

To BENJAMIN WEBSTER, 18 JULY 1857

MS Dickens House. *Address:* Benjamin Webster Esquire | Theatre Royal Adelphi.

IN REMEMBRANCE OF THE LATE MR. DOUGLAS JERROLD.

COMMITTEE'S OFFICE, GALLERY OF ILLUSTRATION, REGENT STREET.
Saturday 18th. July 1857.

My Dear Webster

Allen will sing Black Eye'd Susan on your night.[2]

Faithfully Yours always

Benjamin Webster Esquire. CHARLES DICKENS

To EDMUND YATES, 19 JULY 1857

MS Robert H. Taylor Collection, Princeton University.

Tavistock House | Sunday Nineteenth July, 1857

My Dear Yates.

Although I date this as above, I really write it from Southampton (dont notice this fact in your reply, for I shall be in town on Wednesday). I have come here on an errand which will grow familiar to you before you know that Time has flapped his wings over your head. Like me, you will find those babies grow to be young men, before you are quite sure they are born.[3] Like me, you will have great teeth drawn with a wrench, and will only then know that you ever cut them. I am here to send Walter away over what they call in Green Bush Melodramas[4]

[1] He contributed ten literary and biographical sketches (later reprinted in *Footprints on the Road*, 1864) and two poems to *HW*, most of them in 1857–8. The first sketch, "Béranger", appeared on 22 Aug (XIV, 185).

[2] The "Jerrold Remembrance Night", 29 July, at the Adelphi, when Jerrold's *Black-Eyed Susan*, followed by his *The Rent Day*, were performed. The occasion was fully supported by the acting profession: T. P. Cooke played his original part of William in *Black-Eyed Susan*, 1829, supported by Buckstone as Gnatbrain; in *The Rent Day*, 1832, Henry Wallack played Silver Jack, his original part; Webster played Martin; Mme Celeste, Rachel Heywood; Mrs Keeley, Polly Briggs. Both productions were warmly praised in *The Times*, 30 July.

[3] Yates had three infant sons: Frederick, *b.* 14 Oct 54; Charles (CD's godson: see *To* Yates, 2 Jan 56), and Frank, twins, *b.* 27 Sep 55.

[4] So called after Buckstone's highly popular play, *The Green Bushes*, first performed at the Adelphi 1845 and frequently revived; also known as the "Adelphi drama"; written by Buckstone, Jerrold and Edward Fitzball in particular. Earlier examples were Fitzball's *The Pilot*, 1825, and Buckstone's *The Wreck Ashore*, 1830, and *The Flowers of the Forest*, 1847. Daniel Terry and Yates had managed them; and Mrs Yates (then Elizabeth Brunton) had acted in several.

"the Big Drink"[1] and I dont at all know this day how he comes to be mine, or I, his.

I don't write to say this—or to say how, seeing Charley and he going aboard the Ship before me just now, I suddenly came into possession of a photograph of my own back at 16 and 20, and also into a suspicion that I had doubled the last age. I merely write to mention that Telbin and his wife are going down to Gad's Hill with us, about mid-day next Sunday, and that if you and Mrs. Yates will come too, we shall be delighted to have you.[2] We can give you a bed, and you can be in town (if you have such a savage necessity) by 20 minutes before 10 on Monday morning.

I was very much pleased (as I had reason to be) with your account of the Play in the Daily News.[3] I thank you heartily.

[a]Monday morning.

Faithfully Yours
CHARLES DICKENS

It is now half-past 5 by Greenwich time—whatever that is—I never did know and never shall. Wills, I believe, knows all about it.[a]

To MISS BURDETT COUTTS, 20 JULY 1857

MS Morgan Library. *Address:* Miss Burdett Coutts | 1 Stratton Street | Piccadilly | W.

Radley's Hotel, | Opposite the Terminus & Dock House, Southampton.
Monday Twentieth July 1857.

My Dear Miss Coutts

I hasten to report that I have just now (one o'Clock) come back in the Steam Tender, from putting the poor boy on board. He was cut up for a minute or so when I bade him good bye, and also yesterday morning when he took leave of them in

[1] Used to describe the Atlantic by the Indian woman Mrs Gong in *The Green Bushes*, III, iii; the Mississippi River in US slang of 1840s.

[2] Yates accepted the invitation and later wrote of the visit: "We had a most delightful day, lying out on the grass under a tree. Dickens was greatly amused at a story of Telbin's about a Scotchman at the play, who, in the ecstasy of his delight, thumped the man sitting next him; and he himself told some capital stories of Rogers the poet, of whom he gave a ludicrous imitation" (Yates, *Recollections and Experiences*, II, 95–6).

[3] On 13 July Yates had written glowingly in the *Daily News* of CD's performance in *The Frozen Deep*: "the greatest triumph of dramatic art . . . which . . . we have ever witnessed. On the English stage there is no one who can approach him in his delineation of intense power and feeling, nor was Frederic Lamaître, in his best days, a greater artist." He also praised Lemon as Lieut. Crayford; Egg as the comic ship's cook, John Want; and the scenery and effects by Stanfield and Telbin.

[aa] Rest of letter cut away. It is possible, if CD dispensed with his flourish or signed with initials only, that the missing piece, from bottom of pp. 3 and 4 of a folded sheet, might be the "bit from one of his letters" Yates told Kitton he had stuck under a photograph of CD in an album, "representing a jolly, genial, middle-aged man, with his arm over the back of a chair": CD had written: "It is now half-past 5 by Greenwich time—whatever that is—I never did know and never shall. Wills, I believe, knows all about it" (Yates *to* F. G. Kitton, given in *CD by Pen and Pencil*, p. 169). A clock in a Southampton hotel may well have had "Greenwich Time" written on it.

town, and also on Saturday when he left his little brothers at Gad's Hill; but on all three occasions he recovered directly, and conducted himself like a Man.[1] He leaned over the side looking after Charley and me, quite composed and comfortable. He had already found an old schoolfellow on board, and the Captain came away with me to assure me that he should have every possible protection, assistance, and encouragement. He was anxious that I should send his love to you and Mrs. Brown, and a thousand thanks to you for your kind letters. I add mine for all your kindness, out of a heart almost full.

I have appointed to meet Mr. Bird[2] about my plan, at Shepherds Bush on Wednesday at 12. As I come back from there, I will take the chance of finding you in Stratton Street.

Ever Faithfully and affecy.

Miss Burdett Coutts — CHARLES DICKENS

To HENRY AUSTIN, 21 JULY 1857*

MS Morgan Library.

Gad's Hill Place | Tuesday July Twenty First, 1857

My Dear Henry

I really begin to think we are a little unfortunate here. The whole of that Drain from the wash-house is stopped up through a considerable part of the pipe; and the garden (just beginning to recover from the workmen and look pretty), is dug up again by people whom I have been obliged to have in from Strood;[3] the whole place having been stopped. The chief of those local operatives shews how it is impossible that the present Drain *could* do—how it chokes at the "elbow"[4]—which it certainly does—how a big pipe meets a little pipe "what can't carry on it off"—with various other binding chains of argument. The result is that in perfect despair, infidelity, and misery, I have told him to do what he thinks best. And what he thinks best, is to make two little cesspools, one at the "elber" and one at the "washers"—which works "will receive any sileage as may appear to flow, and leave the water free for to pass, which likeways if anythin should be wrong then, why you only takes up a stone or wotever you thinks most proper, instead of making this here frightful mess." Conscious of nothing but a frightful mess I have feebly acceded. I had some idea of running away from the place altogether, but have acceded instead.

(They are now forcing long sticks through the choked pipes, which I foresee will come out into the eye of a man who is at present lying on his stomach looking in at the other end of the pipe—who will be blinded—and who will have a claim to be supported for life.)

[1] The next day Georgina Hogarth wrote to Mrs Winter: "the dear boy bore it a very great deal better than we could have hoped.... when they left him finally he looked a great deal less sad than they did" (*The Love Romance of Charles Dickens*, ed. Walter Dexter, 1946, pp. 104–5).

[2] The builder: see *To* Miss Coutts, 10 July and *fn*.

[3] The only plumber listed in Strood in 1855 was James Slegg, Cage Lane.

[4] Opening quotation marks omitted in MS.

No change in the Well. "Ned" says, "still flint, but whether a lane of flint or only a Wane[1] is as yet unbeknownst."

Ever affecy.
CD.

To JOHN DEANE, 21 JULY 1857

MS Mr W. A. Foyle.

Gad's Hill, Higham, by Rochester
Tuesday Twenty First July, 1857

My Dear Deane.

I don't like to answer the enclosed letter,[2] without first shewing it to you, and asking you what answer you would recommend me to give.

Many thanks for your two letters in behalf of my boy. I left the poor fellow on board the Indus yesterday, in good spirits—as little cast down as, at 16, one could reasonably hope to be with the world of India before one.

I go to town tomorrow, and purpose remaining there until Sunday

Very faithfully Yours
John Deane Esquire CHARLES DICKENS

To WILLIAM JERDAN,[3] 21 JULY 1857

MS Dickens House.

Gad's Hill, Higham, by Rochester
Tuesday Twenty First July, 1857

My Dear Jerdan

In addition to the whirl and fatigue of the Jerrold Remembrance matter, I have been at Southampton these two days, embarking my second boy for India. The poor fellow steamed away yesterday, and I have a day's rest on the grass here, to think whether the best definition of man may not be, after all, that he is (for his sins) a parting and farewell-taking animal.

I have not the means of reference at hand, but I think I may say I am *sure* that the brief contribution has been published—that both the brief contributions have been published.[4]

Andersen went to Paris, to go thence to Dresden and thence home, last Wednesday morning. I took him over to Maidstone, and booked him for Folkestone.[5] He had been here, five weeks. He had spoken of you with much regard, and, I under-

[1] i.e. vein.

[2] Probably about his reading at Manchester.

[3] William Jerdan (1782–1869; *DNB*), Tory journalist, editor of the *Literary Gazette* 1817–50: see Vols I, p. 207*n* and VI, p. 204*n*.

[4] Jerdan's first two contributions to *HW*: "The Gift of Tongues", 10 Jan 57, XV, 41 (4 cols), and "Old Scraps of Science", 11 Apr 57, XV, 355 (5 cols). He contributed twice more.

[5] Andersen recorded in his diary: "Dickens drove me as far as Maidstone; my heart was so full; I did not speak very much, and at parting I said almost nothing; tears choked my voice" (given in Elias Bredsdorff, *Hans Christian Andersen*, p. 214).

stood or fancied, had seen you.[1] But whenever he got to London, he got into wild entanglements of Cabs and Sherry, and never seemed to get out of them again until he came back here, and cut out paper into all sorts of patterns, and gathered the strangest little nosegays in the woods.[2] His unintelligible vocabulary was marvellous. In French[3] or Italian, he was Peter the Wild Boy[4]—in English, the Deaf and Dumb Asylum.[5] My eldest boy swears that the ear of man cannot recognize his German;[6] and his translatress[7] declares to Bentley that he can't speak Danish!

One day he came home to Tavistock House, apparently suffering from corns that had ripened in two hours. It turned out that a Cab Driver had brought him from the City, by way of the new unfinished thoroughfare through Clerkenwell. Satisfied that the Cabman was bent on robbery and murder, he had put his watch and money into his boots—together with a Bradshaw, a pocket book, a pair of scissors, a penknife, a book or two, a few letters of introduction, and some other miscellaneous property.

These are all the particulars I am in a condition to report. He received a good many letters—lost (I should say) a good many more—and was for the most part utterly conglomerated—with a general impression that everything was going to clear itself up, "tomorrow".

Ever Faithfully
CHARLES DICKENS

[1] Jerdan had become a personal friend of Andersen. For his welcoming him on his first visit to England in 1847 and introducing him to English writers, see Vol. v, pp. 47 and *n*, 130 and *n*; he had particularly wanted him to meet CD (*ibid.*). Andersen had wished to dedicate his *Pictures of Sweden* (of which he sent CD a copy in Spring 1851) to Jerdan; but he took Bentley's advice against doing so, on grounds of "the enmity of the Athenaeum" (Elias Bredsdorff, *Hans Andersen and CD*, 1956, p. 37). But Jerdan was no longer living in London and they did not meet this time.

[2] On one occasion he garlanded Wilkie Collins's hat with daisies, causing great amusement when Collins walked into Higham (Sir Henry Dickens, *Recollections*, p. 34).

[3] Andersen no doubt spoke it badly; but he wrote a letter to Bulwer Lytton from Lisbon in 1866 in perfectly reasonable French (MS Lytton Papers).

[4] A Hanoverian boy, found walking on all fours, climbing trees and unable to articulate more than sounds, whom George I brought to England. Dr Arbuthnot took care of him and christened him "Peter". He eventually lived with a Berkhamsted farmer who gave him a brass collar inscribed "Peter the Wild Boy", with his address.

[5] Andersen had been worried by his poor English when he accepted CD's invitation: "Pray do not lose patience that in English I shall express myself so heavily and awkwardly" (Bredsdorff, *Hans Christian Andersen*, pp. 209–10).

[6] Charley and he clearly did not get on. On 22 June Andersen wrote in his diary: "Charles was far from agreeable, and I returned in very bad humour which I could not conceal. This is the first disagreeable day in England" (Bredsdorff, above, p. 213).

[7] See *To* Miss Coutts, 10 July, *fn*.

To ROBERT PEMBERTON,[1] 21 JULY 1857*

MS Brotherton Library, Leeds. *Address:* Robert Pemberton Esquire | 33 Euston Square | London | N.W.

Gad's Hill, Higham, by Rochester | Twenty First July, 1857

Sir

I beg to thank you for your obliging letter, and your book.[2] I have read the latter with a strong conviction of your earnest sincerity in a great object, and of your true desire to do good. You will excuse my adding that I am not so clear as to your proposed means in their extreme assertion, or as to the machinery through which in "The Infant Drama" you set them forth. I mention this as the truth, without the least intention of arrogantly putting my opinion up, and yours down. But I cannot honestly say that I think "The Philosopher" a happy exponent of his theory: or, that I think the compliments paid by the other characters to that personage, likely to advance it.[3]

Your faithful Servant

Robert Pemberton Esquire. CHARLES DICKENS

To TOM TAYLOR, 22 JULY 1857

Extract in Phillips catalogue, Nov 1993; *MS* 1 p.; addressed Tom Taylor; 22 July 57.

Wednesday Evening Twenty Second July 1857

About the Prologue.[4] When will you send it to me at the Gallery of Illustration, and who is to speak it?[5] You know what our friends of the theatres are.

To HENRY AUSTIN, 23 JULY 1857*

MS Morgan Library.

OFFICE OF HOUSEHOLD WORDS,
Thursday Twenty Third July 1857

My Dear Henry

Your letter and I have been crossing each other in the wildest way. I have only

[1] Robert Pemberton, FRSL, educationalist, follower of Robert Owen and the Christian Owenite philanthropist, John Minter Morgan (1782–1854; *DNB*). Published several books on teaching foreign languages to children, and in Aug 57 inaugurated his "New Philosophical Model Infant School, for teaching Languages, Native and Foreign, on the Natural or Euphonic System", based on his theory of the "science of mind-formation".

[2] *The Infant Drama: a Model of the True Method of Teaching All Languages*, published by himself for the Infant Euphonia Institution, June 1857.

[3] "The Philosopher", in charge of the Infant Prince's upbringing, is Pemberton himself. His main theory is the teaching of language to infants through sounds. He receives, in turn, the allegiance of the Prince's nurse, her sister, and finally the Emperor and Empress.

[4] Some drafted lines are written by Taylor on the verso, wherein he alludes to "kind hands" drying "the widow's and the orphan's tear"; included in the final version: see *To* Webster, 24 July, *fn.*

[5] Albert Smith: see *ibid.*

now got it—5 this afternoon. The mischief is done; the little cesspools (very small) are made; if harm should prove to be done, it must be undone again.

What could I do? Forlornly overflown with black mud and choked with the same—cook in tears—all that trouble and expence of Nye's[1] men, useless—garden chaotically dragged up by the roots—everybody tearing their own hair and mine too—what *could*[2] I do!

Ha ha ha! Yah—Ho ho!

Maniacally
CHARLES DICKENS

To GEORGE BELL,[3] 23 JULY 1857*

MS Messrs G. Bell & Sons.

Tavistock House | Twenty Third July, 1857.

Mr. Charles Dickens presents his Compliments to Mr. Bell, and begs to thank him for his obliging note. Mr. Dickens's absence from town has delayed his receipt of it until this morning.

He will be here at 2 tomorrow. But he may add that international copyright is a question of deferred justice, as to which he has no present faith or hope whatsoever.[4]

To RICHARD BENTLEY, 23 JULY 1857*

MS Berg Collection. *Address:* Private. | Richard Bentley Esquire | New Burlington Street | W.

Tavistock House | Thursday Twenty Third July | 1857

My Dear Mr. Bentley

Coming here yesterday Afternoon, I found your note awaiting me. I write this at once, without having seen Mr. Brooks, because I wish to have one question plainly comprehended between us—I mean, between you and me.

When the publication of the novel in a serial form, was first referred to between you and me at Gad's Hill, I understood such serial form to apply to its publication in monthly portions *in your Miscellany*. Your note dated the 20th. and received by me yesterday evening, mentions "a Monthly Serial". The words may have the same meaning, but I wish to ask you whether they have or no?[5] Because, what I have as

[1] Either George Nye, bricklayer, King Street, Troy Town, Rochester; or John P. Nye, bricklayer and painter, Medway St, Chatham.

[2] Heavily underlined.

[3] George Bell (1814–90), bookseller and publisher, of 186 Fleet St; in partnership with F. R. Daldy 1855–73; founder of George Bell & Sons, York St, 1872. Specialized in school and theological books; first publisher of *Notes and Queries*, 1850; bought J. and J. J. Deighton, of Cambridge, 1856.

[4] For the failure of American attempts to pass an international copyright bill in Feb 1854, see Vol. VII, p. 236 and *n*.

[5] CD makes the necessary distinction between instalments in a monthly periodical and independent monthly parts.

yet said to Mr. Brooks, has been altogether based on the idea that he should supply the story in portions, for monthly publication in "Bentley's Miscellany."[1]

Faithfully Yours always

Richard Bentley Esquire CHARLES DICKENS

To SIR CULLING EARDLEY,[2] 23 JULY 1857*

MS Mr Edward V. E. Fremantle.

Tavistock House, London. | Twenty Third July, 1857.

Mr. Charles Dickens presents his compliments to Sir Culling Eardley, and begs to express his regret that his absence from town has prevented his receiving Sir Culling Eardley's obliging and highly interesting invitation[3] until this morning—when it is his misfortune to have business engagements and appointments for the whole of the day.

To JOEL PINNEY,[4] 23 JULY 1857*

MS Mr Harry E. Gould, Jr.

Private

Tavistock House, London
Thursday Twenty Third July, 1857

Dear Sir

As I reside in Kent during the summer, I have only this morning received your obliging letter and its accompanying book.[5]

The latter I have not yet had time (I need scarcely add) to read. But I have made a general acquaintance with its contents, and I purpose to know them better.

As you refer to my own habits, you may be interested to learn that for the last fifteen or twenty years they have been of the most exact and punctual nature. I portion out my time methodically, take a great deal of exercise and fresh air regularly, am probably as much in all the winds that blow as any country gentleman, bathe in large quantities of cold water all the year round, and can keep a Swiss guide on his mettle during a day's journey. A large part of my life is necessarily passed at my desk, but never to the interruption of these compensatory habits.[6]

Your faithful Servant

J. Pinney Esquire CHARLES DICKENS

[1] See *To* Bentley, 16 July, *fn*.

[2] Sir Culling Eardley, Bart (1805–63; *DNB*), philanthropist; founder of the Evangelical Alliance 1846; supporter of many Protestant and liberal causes.

[3] Eardley lived at Erith in Kent (ten miles west of Gravesend) and had no doubt invited CD to some local event.

[4] Joel Pinney, who published six books on health and disease 1838–60, three of them in 1856.

[5] Probably *The Influence of Occupation on Health and Life*, published Jan 56.

[6] Evidently in the letter; but the books emphasise the drawbacks of long periods of sedentary work.

To GEORGE BELL, 24 JULY 1857*

ME Messrs G. Bell & Sons.

OFFICE OF HOUSEHOLD WORDS,
Friday Twenty Fourth July 1857

Mr. Charles Dickens presents his Compliments to Mr. Bell, and begs to say that he is unfortunately prevented from keeping his appointment to day; but that he will write in a day or two, and make another.

To W. R. SAMS,[1] 24 JULY 1857*

MS Huntington Library.

Gallery of Illustration, Regent Street
Friday Twenty Fourth July, 1857.

Dear Sir

Excuse my observing that I must beg you to bring no one on the stage here, either during or after a performance. It is an infringement of a rule I have always made,[2] and the strict observance of which I feel it necessary to uphold.

Faithfully Yours

W. R. Sams Esquire CHARLES DICKENS

To BENJAMIN WEBSTER, 24 JULY 1857*

MS Free Library of Philadelphia.

Gallery of Illustration | Twenty Fourth July 1857 | Friday

My Dear Webster

Here is the Prologue.[3] Tom Taylor wishes you to speak it. I hope you will like it.[4]

Faithfully Ever

Benjamin Webster Esquire CHARLES DICKENS

To MISS BURDETT COUTTS, 25 JULY 1857*

MS Morgan Library.

Tavistock House | Saturday Twenty Fifth July 1857

My Dear Miss Coutts

I send you this note to say that I received a letter early this morning from Arthur

[1] William Raymond Sams, bookseller and publisher, 1 St James's St; tickets for performances were obtainable from him.

[2] See for example Vol. IV, p. 433 and *n.*

[3] See *To* Taylor, 8 July, and *fn.*

[4] Apparently Webster did not; verses by Tom Taylor were spoken at the Adelphi on 29 July as an "Address" by Albert Smith between the acts of *Black-Eyed Susan* (given in full in *The Times*, 30 July) they ended: "While Dibdin's song on English decks is sung, | While Nelson's name lives on the sailor's tongue, | Still Susan's tenderness and William's faith | Shall weave for Jerrold's tomb a lasting wreath." The theatre had just been re-opened under the new management of Robson and W. S. Emden (see *To* Emden, 31 July, *fn*).

Smith, in which no allusion was made to you in any way, but in which I immediately perceived your ever kind and thoughtful influence. The truth is, we had been suddenly thrown on a decision yesterday,[1] but that I doubted it very much when I was before that vast assembly last night,[2] and resolved that I would to day discuss our engaging actresses. We are committed to nothing, and have resolved not to act there[3] at all, but to play once more (this day fortnight) at the Gallery of Illustration, which is in effect but a great Drawing Room.

We must get £2,000 free of expences, before we leave off. I hope I shall be left free for Gad's Hill by the middle of August. It is rather hard work, after a long book.[4]

With love to Mrs. Brown
Ever Faithfully and affecy.
CD.

To HENRY ATTWELL,[5] 27 JULY 1857*

MS Dickens House. *Address:* Professor Attwell | Romford | Essex.

Gad's Hill Place, Higham, by Rochester
Twenty Seventh July, 1857

Dear Sir

I am exceedingly obliged to you for the interesting and artistic poems[6] you have had the kindness to send me, and for your charming letter. Constant occupation has involved me in a week's arrear of correspondence which I am only mastering this Evening, or I should have written to you sooner.

Between an occasional day's rest at my little place of retirement here, and various public engagements which just now beset me, I find it very difficult to make an appointment in London. But I purpose being there on Thursday next; and if it should not be inconvenient to you to call at the Household Words Office (16 Wellington Street North, Strand) at 5 in the Afternoon, I shall be heartily glad to see you and to thank you in person.

Dear Sir | Yours faithfully and obliged
Professor Attwell.[7] CHARLES DICKENS

[1] There must have been a meeting of the cast and some of the committee to discuss the visit to Manchester.

[2] At his reading at St Martin's Hall.

[3] At Manchester.

[4] *Little Dorrit.*

[5] Henry Attwell (*b.* 1834), privately educated; writer of school books and prolific editor and translator of French and German texts, ranging in date from the 1850s to the 1890s. Founded a school in Barnes, Surrey, 1859, and taught there until 1880.

[6] Either his *Poems*, published in Leiden, or his translation of Hugo's *Les Orientales* as *Phantoms*, both of 1856.

[7] He held a lectorship at the University of Leiden and taught the Prince of Orange.

To JOHN HOLLINGSHEAD,[1] 27 JULY 1857

Extract in Dodd, Mead & Co. catalogue (Nov. 1901); *MS* 1 p.; addressed John Hollingshead; dated Gad's Hill Place, 27 July 57.

I will not say that I think the thing too low and too degrading to literature to be honored with such notice.[2] This was certainly my first impression when I began to read your Proof, but as I proceeded I felt that I need not spoil such tenderness of appreciation as yours, or wish for any reason to lose the utterance of it.[3]

[1] John Hollingshead (1827–1904; *DNB*), son of an Irish barrister; journalist and, later, theatre manager. After working as a clerk and commercial traveller, became a prolific contributor to periodicals; wrote for *Punch*, the *Leader*, *Cornhill*, the *Train* (see below), *HW* and *AYR*, and many others. For a time dramatic critic on *Daily News*. Contributed regularly to *HW* from Oct 57; became a member of the staff 1859, and found CD "an excellent editor to write under.... In business ... sympathetic, though not over liberal." In *My Lifetime* (1894), I, 98–101, he recalled his first dinner with CD at the *HW* Office, the others present being Wilkie Collins, Lemon, Wills and Townshend (whom he wrongly describes as "the Hon."). He greatly admired CD: in *My Lifetime* he includes himself among the "Dickens young men" (I, 96) and refers to CD as "the master" (I, 97); but stresses that he did not imitate CD and that CD very rarely altered his articles (I, 96). Published many collections of his periodical contributions, presenting five of them (*Old Journeys In and Out of London*, 1860, *Rubbing the Gilt Off*, 1860, *Under Bow Bells*, 1860, *Ways of Life*, 1861, and *Underground London*, 1862) to CD, inscribed "from his affectionate friend", or with similar inscriptions (see *Catalogue of the Library of CD*, ed. J. H. Stonehouse, pp. 59–60). Worked for abolition of paper duty and reform of copyright law. Manager of Gaiety Theatre 1868–86; Director of several Music Hall companies.

[2] CD's article in *HW*, "Curious Misprint in the Edinburgh Review" (1 Aug 57, XVI, 97–100), written at high speed on 24 July (see *To* Macready, 3 Aug), is his reply to James Fitzjames Stephen's long unsigned review, "The Licence of Modern Novelists" (*Edinburgh Review*, July 57, CVI, 124–56); Stephen had attacked both *Little Dorrit*—and especially the satire on the Circumlocution Office—and Charles Reade's prison novel, *It is Never Too Late to Mend*, 3 vols, 1856; 1 vol, 1857. One charge, to support his contention that CD selected "one or two of the popular cries of the day" to season each novel, was that "even the catastrophe in *Little Dorrit* is evidently borrowed from the recent fall of houses in Tottenham Court Road". The falsity of this CD proved by date in his reply. Stephen's review continued the onslaught he had already mounted in "Mr Dickens as a Politician" (*Saturday Review*, 3 Jan 57, III, 8), continued in the *Saturday Review*, 4 July 57, IV, 15. For other reviews, see *CD: The Critical Heritage*, ed. Philip Collins, 1971, p. 356. Of CD's *HW* article, Hollingshead wrote: "This was his last answer to his critics or defamers. From that time till his death he read nothing and answered nothing" (letter of Hollingshead given from Cat. source above, in Kitton's "Dickens Ana", IV, 14).

[3] The proof of his forthcoming article in the *Train* (see *To* Yates, 2 Jan 56, *fn*), "Dialogues of the Living. No. IV. Mr Dickens and his Critics" (Aug 57, IV, 76), in which he described the recent onslaughts on *Little Dorrit* as largely politically motivated. A substantial part is reprinted in *CD: The Critical Heritage*, p. 375. Hollingshead had also defended *Little Dorrit* from the "shrivelled souls" of "certain University-bred reviewers", in an unsigned review in the *Leader*, 27 June 1857. CD would have particularly liked Hollingshead's praise of "those delicate and beautiful creations of his fancy, that ideal family, the children of his pen"; and his ending: "And yet this man, great critics, is only a mere buffoon, and nothing more? Truly a fit companion for that low player of olden time, who wrote *King Lear*, and acted at the Globe."

To CHARLES RIEU, 27 JULY 1857*

MS Dr Andrew Sanders. Address: Charles Rieu Esquire | Department of MSS. | British Museum | London | W.C.

Gad's Hill Place, Higham by Rochester
Monday Evening Twenty Seventh July | 1857

Dear Sir

I have the pleasure of enclosing you a cheque for the amount in which I am indebted to you.[1] Allow me to add my best thanks to it.

It was pretty clear to me when Walter began with you that the unsettled state of mind which necessarily preceded his departure, was unfavorable to his making any great advance. But I hoped that your tuition would be of great service to him, in giving him the means of improving himself in India. I have no doubt that it has had that effect, and I was not so ungenerous or unreasonable as to expect more.

Believe me | Faithfully Yours

Charles Rieu Esquire CHARLES DICKENS

To MISS BURDETT COUTTS, 27 JULY 1857*

MS Morgan Library. *Address:* Miss Burdett Coutts | 1 Stratton Street | Piccadilly | W.

Gad's Hill Place
Monday Night Twenty Seventh July | 1857

My Dear Miss Coutts

Enclosed is the builder's estimate. What do you say to it? It is for carrying the long room up to the ceiling of the first floor—cancelling that first floor bedroom—and making one large bedroom and one very good one, over the Laundry and wash-house.[2]

I purpose being in town on Wednesday evening. If you would like me to come to you at any time on Thursday before 5 and will write me a line to Tavistock House making an appointment, I shall be delighted to come to you. I go away on Friday Morning, to read at Manchester.

Dear Miss Coutts | Ever Faithfully and affecy.
CHARLES DICKENS

To RICHARD BENTLEY, 28 JULY 1857*

MS Berg Collection.

Gad's Hill Place | Tuesday Twenty Eighth July, 1857

My Dear Mr. Bentley

I certainly had been aware that you had disposed of the Miscellany to Ainsworth;[3] but I had as entirely forgotten it, until you reminded me of the fact, as if I had never heard of such a thing in my life.

[1] CD paid him £5.15.6 on 15 Aug (CD's Account-book, MS Messrs Coutts).

[2] Bird's estimate was for £195 (MS Morgan).

[3] William Harrison Ainsworth (1805–82; *DNB*): see Vol. 1, p. 115*n*; CD had seen comparatively little of him in recent years.

I shall be in town on Thursday and will then see Mr. Brooks. I have little doubt of being able to write you my proposed way of arranging the details,[1] in the course of that afternoon.

Faithfully Yours always

Richard Bentley Esquire CHARLES DICKENS

To MISS GEORGINA HOGARTH, 29 JULY 1857

MS Dickens House.

OFFICE OF HOUSEHOLD WORDS,
Wednesday Twenty Ninth July 1857

My Dear Georgy.

In the bottom of my bookcase, nearest the window, are three collections of old cuttings, pamphlets, and pictures—one referring to Newgate—one to Bartholomew Fair[2]—one to Ludgate Hill. I want the whole of the Newgate collection (that is to say, all that refers to Newgate in any way) made a parcel of, and sent up by Railway to Wilkie Collins, 2 Harley Place, New Road.[3] Will you do this, and send Mitchell without delay to book the parcel at Higham Station? I write to you (very hurriedly), because you have seen the different packets in my hands, and can no doubt make out the Newgate one, pretty readily. Just look at the other two, to assure yourself that no Newgate scraps have fallen by mistake into either.

Love to Catherine and to all | Ever affectionately

CD.

To HENRY REEVE,[4] 29 JULY 1857

Mention in Catalogue of the Bodley Book Shop, No. 119; *MS* 1 p.; dated Tavistock House, 29 July 57.

Calling his correspondent's attention to the opening paper in Household Words.[5]

To SHIRLEY BROOKS, 30 JULY 1857

MS Brotherton Library, Leeds.

Household Words Office | Thirtieth July 1857

My Dear Brooks.

Unfortunately I shall merely pass through town on Sunday morning, on my way

[1] See *To* Brooks, 7 Aug, *fn*.

[2] See the detailed description in *Catalogue of the Library of CD*, ed. J. H. Stonehouse, p. 10.

[3] As material for Collins's forthcoming article, "The Debtor's Best Friend" (*HW*, 19 Sep 57, XVI, 279); its only source is *An Accurate Description of Newgate* ..., by "B.L.", 1724, which perhaps was included in CD's collection. Newgate had been a continuing interest of CD's since his visit in 1835 (Vol. I, p. 88 and *n*) and the subject of powerful descriptions in *Sketches* ("A Visit to Newgate"), *Barnaby Rudge* and *Oliver Twist*. CD's collection, clearly similar to Bartholomew Fair, is not in Stonehouse, so possibly was retained by Collins.

[4] Henry Reeve (1813–95), editor of the *Edinburgh Review* 1855–95.

[5] See *To* Hollingshead, 27 July, *fn*.

back from Manchester. But I shall leave the station for Gad's Hill on Sunday at 1, and shall be delighted to take you down with me if you can go. If not, I hope to be there until Thursday inclusive, and shall be glad to see you at any time. But I would impress upon you that I think we had best close with Bentley as soon as we can.

I send you the note to which I, having drunk of the waters of Oblivion[1] as to Ainsworth's purchase of the Miscellany, returned the cautious reply I told you of.[2] It now only needs to settle the money-terms;[3] and as to those, I await the confidential knowledge of your wishes.

Believe me always | Faithfully Yours

Shirley Brooks Esquire CHARLES DICKENS

To T. P. COOKE, 30 JULY 1857

MS Benoliel Collection. *Address:* T. P. Cooke Esquire | Woburn Square | W.C.

IN REMEMBRANCE OF THE LATE MR. DOUGLAS JERROLD.

COMMITTEE'S OFFICE, GALLERY OF ILLUSTRATION,
REGENT STREET.
Thursday Thirtieth July 1857.

My Dear Mr. Cooke.

I cannot rest satisfied this morning, without writing to congratulate you on your admirable performance of last night.[4] It was so fresh and vigorous, so manly and gallant, that I felt as if it splashed against my Theatre-heated face, along with the spray of the breezy sea.[5] What I felt, everybody felt. I should feel it quite an impertinence to take myself out of the crowd therefore, if I could by any means help doing so. But I can't—so I hope you will feel that you bring me on yourself, and have only yourself to blame.

Always Faithfully Yours

T. P. Cooke Esquire. CHARLES DICKENS

[1] Cf. John Martin's famous picture, *Sadak in search of the Waters of Oblivion*, 1812, from *Tales of the Genii*.

[2] *To* Bentley, 28 July.

[3] See *To* Brooks, 7 Aug, *fn*.

[4] See *To* Webster, 18 July, *fn*.

[5] Cooke had first played the part in 1829. Now, aged 71, he "exhibited extraordinary energy and acted, sang and danced the sailor's hornpipe, with 'all his original brightness'" (*Leader*, 1 Aug, VIII, 740).

To THOMAS FAIRBAIRN,[1] 30 JULY 1857*

Text from transcript by owner of MS, Mr Ulysses Walsh.

IN REMEMBRANCE OF THE LATE MR. DOUGLAS JERROLD.

COMMITTEE'S OFFICE, GALLERY OF ILLUSTRATION,
REGENT STREET.
Thursday, Thirtieth July 1857.

Dear Sir

I am exceedingly obliged to you for your kind invitation, and cordially assure you that it would give me great pleasure to accept it, if I possibly could. But I am obliged to be at Manchester on Saturday afternoon.[2] These exertions have fatigued me so much, that a rest at my little old house in the country, is indispensable; and I have arranged to return accordingly.

Mrs. Dickens will, I am sure, be very sensible of Mrs. Fairbairn's[3] remembrance and invitation. As I have left her in Kent, I shall send her down your Postscript by this afternoon's post.

Always Dear Sir | Very faithfully Yours
CHARLES DICKENS

Thomas Fairbairn Esquire

To FREDERICK HUDSON,[4] 30 JULY 1857*

MS Free Library of Philadelphia.

IN REMEMBRANCE OF THE LATE MR. DOUGLAS JERROLD.

COMMITTEE'S OFFICE, GALLERY OF ILLUSTRATION,
REGENT STREET.
Thursday Thirtieth July 1857.

Dear Sir

Constant occupation and exertion have disabled me from keeping pace with the correspondence pouring in upon me, for many days past.

In reply to your obliging letter I beg to say that I have at present made no arrangements for the performance of The Frozen Deep, in Manchester, and that I do not know that any representation of that Play will take place there. But I am bound to add, with many thanks, that if such a thing should come to pass, I should seek the local assistance I might require, from the friends I have in the Art Treasures Exhibition: to whose sympathy and aid I am already in other respects much beholden.[5]

Dear Sir | Faithfully Yours
CHARLES DICKENS

Dr. Hudson

[1] Thomas Fairbairn (1823–91), Manchester engineer, son of Sir William Fairbairn, FRS (1789–1874; *DNB*), engineer (see Vol. VII, p. 309*n*.). Chairman of Executive Committee of the Manchester Art Treasures Exhibition and on Jerrold Fund Committee: see Vol. VII, p. 326*n*. Succeeded as 2nd Bart in 1874.

[2] Manchester, where he was to read the *Carol* on 31 July. The *Manchester Guardian*, 1 Aug, reported that the audience "crowded every part of the great room at the Free Trade Hall" and that it was "completely under the sway of the story and its reader".

[3] Née Allison Calloway of Chislehurst.

[4] Presumably Frederick Hudson, surgeon, of 13 Heaton Lane, Heaton Norris, Manchester.

[5] CD had in mind mainly John Deane: see 23 June and *fn*.

To SIR JOSEPH PAXTON, 30 JULY 1857

Mention in unidentified catalogue in *Chadwick Collection of Dickensiana*; *MS* 1 p.; dated 30 July 57; addressed Paxton.

Telling him of the Duke of Devonshire's promise to subscribe £100 to the fund in memory of the late Douglas Jerrold.

To W. S. EMDEN,[1] 31 JULY 1857

Extract in N, II, 865–6; *MS* 2 pp.; dated Tavistock House, 31 July 57; addressed W. S. Emden.

I beg to acknowledge the receipt of your note, and the Proof of your proposed bill.[2] As I made no mention of myself in association with the Prologue, when I produced the Play here,[3] I wish to avoid any mention being made of me now. I shall therefore be obliged by your merely announcing that "The original Prologue will be spoken by Mr. Frederick Vining."[4]

To MRS FRANCES DICKINSON, [?1 AUGUST 1857]

Mention in next. *Date:* written between his promise on 31 July to act *The Frozen Deep* and his telling Collins of it on 2 Aug.

To WILKIE COLLINS, 2 AUGUST 1857

MS Morgan Library.

Tavistock House | Sunday Morning | Second August, 1857

My Dear Collins

I write this, on my way back to Gad's Hill from Manchester.

As our sum is not made up,[5] and as I had urgent Deputation and so forth from Manchester Magnates at the Reading on Friday night, I have arranged to act the Frozen Deep in the Free Trade Hall on Friday and Saturday nights, the 21st. and 22nd.[6] It is *an immense place*, and we shall be obliged to have actresses—though I

[1] William Samuel Emden (?1801–72), theatre manager and playwright. Prompter at Covent Garden under Madame Vestris 1839; subsequently acting manager; was about to succeed Alfred Wigan (retired 27 July) on 10 Aug as lessee and manager of the Olympic, of which he had previously been treasurer. Wrote five plays 1837–59.

[2] For the professional performance of *The Lighthouse* at the Olympic, opening on 10 Aug, as the second item in a triple bill following *The Subterfuge*, an anonymous comedy, and succeeded by Robson's burlesque *Masaniello*. A rhymed Address celebrating the new management, written by Robert Brough, was delivered by Robson.

[3] At Tavistock House, 16 June 1855: see Vol. VII, pp. 650 and *n* and 667 and *n*. CD spoke the Prologue, but did not say he had written it.

[4] Frederick Vining (?1790–1871; *DNB*), comic actor; first appeared in London at Covent Garden 1813.

[5] The £2,000 named in *To* Paxton, 3 Aug.

[6] After the reading, CD told the audience that some of "the leading men in this city" had asked him, in the interval, whether the Amateurs would perform there. The proposal was greeted with "loud applause and cries of Yes,

have written to our prononcée[1] friend, Mrs. Dickinson, to say that I don't fear her, if she likes to play with them.[2] (I am already trying to get the best who *have been* on the stage.)[3]

Whether Charley can play his part or not, I will tell him to let you know directly.[4] I had a letter from the Olympic the other day, begging me to go to a Rehearsal.[5] I have appointed next Friday, if agreeable and convenient.

In haste | Ever Faithfully
CD.

To JOHN DEANE, 2 AUGUST 1857*

MS Private.

Tavistock House | Sunday Morning, Second August | 1857

My Dear Deane.

This scrap on my way to Gad's Hill, to say that I have written to Telbin to come straight to you by Thursday morning's express—and have written to Berger to let you know his Band requirements at once.

I cannot, on consideration, be quite sure whether yesterday's first violin[6] was my Frozen Deep first violin, or whether I was confounding him with Seymour,[7] long of Manchester. It is no matter.

Ever Faithfully Yours
John C Deane Esquire CHARLES DICKENS[8]

To FRANCESCO BERGER, 2 AUGUST 1857

Text from *Royal Leamington Spa Courier*, 24 Mar 1922.

Tavistock House, | Sunday, Second August, 1857.

My Dear Berger,

I write to you very hurriedly on my way back to Gad's Hill from Manchester.

It is arranged that we shall act in the Free Trade Hall[9] at Manchester on Friday and Saturday evenings, 21st. and 22nd. It is an immense hall and my girls will have to be replaced by actresses.[10]

Will you write as soon as you can to J. C. Deane, Esquire, Art Treasures

yes!" He had, he said, no intention "to go any other place out of London", but "too lively a remembrance of the generosity of Manchester in a similar case [*the performance for Leigh Hunt in June 1848: see Vol. V*] not to give the request full consideration" (*Manchester Examiner and Times*, 1 Aug). The decision to act in Manchester was clearly made at once (*Speeches*, ed. K. J. Fielding, pp. 237–8).

[1] Ebullient. Omitted in *CD to WC*.

[2] See *To* Collins, 26 June. She did not play at Manchester.

[3] At this date this would mean Mrs Compton (see *To* her, same day).

[4] He played Lieut. Steventon in *The Frozen Deep*.

[5] Of Collins's *The Lighthouse*, before its professional production on 10 Aug.

[6] See *To* Berger, 2 Aug and *fn*.

[7] Alexander Seymour, "professor of music", 77 Coupland St, Greenheys, Manchester; leader of the Art Treasures Exhibition Orchestra.

[8] Several letters of this date show some shakiness: either because written on the train from London to Gad's Hill or through stress from so much travel.

[9] The New Free Trade Hall in Peter St, opened Oct 56; its main hall, designed for public meetings and concerts, seated 4,000.

[10] See *To* Stone, 17 Aug and *fn*.

Exhibition,[1] Manchester (addressing him as Dear Sir and observing that you write by arrangement with me) telling him what performers you require for the Band? He will then at once engage them from the Exhibition Orchestra (a very good one—I heard them play beautifully yesterday)[2] and all will be ready for you.[3] Exercise your own discretion in augmenting the Band by two or three, if you think it necessary. I would ask Mr. Deane to call them for rehearsal—say at 10 or 11 (as you think best) on the morning of Friday 21st. Do not lose time in this, as there will be an Italian Opera in the town at the same time.[4]

I shall be at [a]Gad's Place,[a] Higham, by Rochester, Kent, until next Friday.

Faithfully yours

Francesco Berger, Esquire. CHARLES DICKENS

To MISS BURDETT COUTTS, 2 AUGUST 1857*

MS Morgan Library.

Gad's Hill Place, Higham, by Rochester
Second August 1857.

My Dear Miss Coutts

I am a little uneasy about you. I wrote to you some days ago,[5] sending you the builders estimate for the proposed alterations at Shepherd's Bush, and asking you to tell me at what time last Thursday, I could see you. Finding no letter from you in town, I thought you might by mistake have written here. Yesterday I come home here from Manchester, and still find no letter. Hereupon I become inconsolable.

I must be in town next Saturday (for the last Frozen Deep),[6] and could come to you at any time between 11 and 2.

With kind regard to Mrs. Brown, Ever Dear Miss Coutts

Yours faithfully and affecy.

Miss Burdett Coutts. CHARLES DICKENS

To WILLIAM TELBIN, [2 AUGUST 1857]

Mention in *To* Deane, 2 Aug 57. *Date:* written the same day.

[1] See *To* Macready, 3 Aug and *fn.*

[2] The orchestra, of over 50 players, formed by Charles Hallé (1819–95; *DNB*), performed daily throughout the Exhibition; on "reserved and half-a-crown days", Hallé himself conducted, as Musical Director; on ordinary days, Mons. Becquier de Peyreville, of the Italian Opera, Paris. On the Opening Day and on the day of the Queen's visit, the orchestra was increased to 82 and a chorus of 560 voices added (*Exhibition of Art Treasures . . . Report of the Executive Committee*, 1859, p. 43 and Appx XVII).

[3] The music—both Berger's *Overture* and his incidental music—was praised by the *Manchester Examiner and Times*, 22 Aug. For Berger's reminiscences of the visit to Manchester—the cast making up conundrums on the delayed train and singing songs far into the night after the first performance (he would never forget CD's look of "amusement and assumed horror combined" when he burst in on them)—see *Reminiscences, Impressions and Anecdotes*, pp. 35–7.

[4] 21 Aug was the last night of Italian plays at the Theatre Royal, with Mme Ristori playing Medea; and 22 Aug the first night of the Royal Italian opera, from the Lyceum (*Fra Diavolo*).

[aa] Thus in text.

[5] On 27 July.

[6] At the Gallery of Illustration.

To W. H. WILLS, 2 AUGUST 1857

MS Huntington Library.

Tavistock House | Sunday Second August 1857

My Dear Wills

I[1]

write hurriedly, on my way back to Gad's Hill.

YOU[1]

I suppose are somewhere in Cheshire or Staffordshire—as you didn't turn up yesterday.[2]

FROZEN DEEP.[1]

Get the Circular[3] out, directly. Nights of acting, Friday 21st. and Saturday 22nd. Company to go down on the afternoon of Thursday 20th. Rehearsal of 3rd. act to be called in town beforehand, on account of Actresses instead of Amateur ladies. Also in the Free Trade Hall on the Friday Morning at 11.

H.W.[1]

Can you come down to Gad's Hill with the next proofs?[4] If yes, when? I purpose not coming up (unless obliged), before Friday.

Ever Faithfully
CD.

To MRS COMPTON,[5] 2 AUGUST 1857

MS Free Library of Philadelphia.

Gad's Hill Place, Higham, by Rochester
Sunday Night Second August 1857.

My Dear Mrs. Compton

We are going to play the Frozen Deep (pursuant to requisition from Town Magnates &c) at Manchester, at the New Free Trade Hall, on the nights of Friday and Saturday, the 21st. and 22nd. August.

The place is out of the question for my girls.[6] Their action could not be seen, and their voices could not be heard. You and I have played, there and elsewhere, so sociably and happily,[7] that I am emboldened to ask you whether you would play my sister in law, Georgina's part[8] (Compton[9] and Babies[10] permitting).

[1] Underlined with short double strokes.

[2] At Manchester.

[3] i.e. to the cast as far as then known.

[4] Of *HW*, No. 387, published 22 Aug.

[5] Mrs Henry Compton, née Emmeline Montague: see Vol. v, p. 319*n*.

[6] See *To* Stone, 17 Aug, *fn*.

[7] They had played together in *The Merry Wives* at Manchester, but not in the New Free Trade Hall, and *Every Man in his Humour* at Birmingham, in 1848, and in *Not so Bad as we Seem* in London and the provinces in Sep 1852. According to T. E. Pemberton, Mrs Compton later described CD as "an actor whose tact, talent, and resource would be equal to any emergency that might arise". Her husband used to declare, she said, "that had CD adopted the stage as a profession, he would have made upon it fame and fortune" (T. E. Pemberton, *CD and the Stage*, 1888, p. 134).

[8] Mrs Compton declined.

[9] Henry Compton (1805–77; *DNB*), actor: see Vol. v, p. 326*n*.

[10] She acted with the Amateurs several times in 1851 and 1852 in spite of children, many of her final family of nine being born in the first ten years of marriage (1848–57).

We shall go down in the old pleasant way, and shall have the Art Treasures Exhibition to ourselves on the Sunday—when even "He" (as Rogers always called every pretty woman's husband),[1] might come and join us.

What do you say? What does He say? And what does Baby say? When I use the term "Baby", I use it in two tenses—Present, and Future.

Answer me at this address, like the Juliet I saw at Drury Lane—when was it?—yesterday.[2] And whatever your answer is, if you will say that you and Compton will meet us at the North Kent Station London Bridge, next Sunday at a quarter before One, and will come down here for a breath of sweet air, and stay all night, you will then give your old friends great pleasure. Not least among them,

Yours faithfully
CHARLES DICKENS

To RICHARD BENTLEY, 3 AUGUST 1857

MS Berg Collection. *Address:* Richard Bentley Esquire | New Burlington Street | London | W.

Gad's Hill Place | Monday August Third, 1857

My Dear Mr. Bentley

I could not see Mr. Brooks on the day in last week when I expected to do so, by reason of his engagements clashing with mine. But I have seen him to day, and beg to send you, now, the result of our conference.

If the new story be written in 12 monthly Nos. of two sheets[3] each (beginning at the date we have already agreed upon), it will contain a much larger quantity of matter than an ordinary novel in 3 Volumes.[4]

And I assume that the Nos. should contain two sheets each, as that is the public experience of that form of publication.

It does not appear to me—and I hope it will not appear to you—that it is at all unreasonable to ask another Hundred Pounds for this additional labor. I may go further, and add that I sincerely regard it as a very modest proposal.

I would therefore suggest that we have a new agreement between you and Mr. Brooks for such a serial, for which you agree to give him in all Four Hundred Pounds. One hundred pounds he has already received, and will, in the agreement, duly acknowledge the receipt of; the remaining £300 you covenant to pay him in ready-money payments of £25 each, on the publication of each of the twelve Nos.

In return for these payments, you will have the copyright of the work for 3 years from the date of its completion; with the restriction that its form in twelve Nos. or one Volume is not to be altered, without Mr. Brooks's consent.

I shall be ready to conclude this agreement on Mr. Brooks's part, and to obtain his signature to it, as soon as you please. On Friday I shall be in town, and at the Household Words office at 4 O'Clock. If you see no objection to the terms I propose, Mr.

[1] Cf. Vols VI, p. 635 and IV, p. 612*n*, where he is quoted as referring to CD as *Him*.

[2] Her London debut in 1839.

[3] i.e. of 16 pp., 32 pp. being the standard length for separate Nos.

[4] Because the type of a monthly No. is always much smaller and the page much larger.

Brooks would very gladly meet you there at that time (supposing it to suit your convenience), and close the arrangement.

Faithfully Yours always

Richard Bentley Esquire. CHARLES DICKENS

To W. C. MACREADY, 3 AUGUST 1857

MS Morgan Library.

Gad's Hill Place, Higham, by Rochester
Monday Third August 1857

My Dearest Macready

I write to you in reference to your last note, as soon as I can positively know our final movements in the Jerrold matter.

We are going to wind up by acting at Manchester (on solemn requisition) on the evenings of Friday and Saturday, the 21st. and 22nd. (Actresses substituted for the girls, of course.) We shall have to leave here on the morning of the 20th. You thought of coming on the 16th. Can't you make it a day or two earlier, so as to be with us a whole week? Decide and pronounce. Again—cannot you bring Katey with you? Decide and pronounce thereupon, also.

I read at Manchester last Friday. As many thousand people were there, as you like to name.[1] The collection of Pictures in the Exhibition is wonderful.[2] And the power with which the modern English School asserts itself, is a very gratifying and delightful thing to behold.[3] The care for the common people, in the provision made for their comfort and refreshment, is also admirable, and worthy of all commendation. But they want more amusement, and particularly (as it strikes me) *something in motion*, though it were only a twisting fountain. The thing is too still, after their lives of machinery, and Art fires over their heads in consequence.[4]

I hope you have seen my tussle with the Edinburgh. I saw the chance last Friday week, as I was going down to read the Carol in St. Martin's Hall. Instantly turned to, then and there, and wrote half the article.[5] Flew out of bed early next morning, and

[1] The reading, in the New Free Trade Hall, was an immense success; receipts were over £300. The audience included the Tennysons, who broke their journey to the Lakes, to see the Manchester Art Treasures Exhibition (*Letters of Alfred, Lord Tennyson*, ed. Cecil Y. Lang and Edgar F. Shannon, Jr, Oxford, II (1987), 183–8).

[2] The Manchester Art Treasures Exhibition, housed in a building specially erected on Old Trafford, the Manchester cricket ground, had been opened on 5 May. One wing of the great collection of paintings on loan was devoted to Old Masters (Raphael, Giorgione, Titian, etc.) and the other to the "modern English school". There were numerous other works of art, including carvings, jewellery and armour, on display. During the six months it was open nearly a million people visited it, at a shilling a head. The idea of the Exhibition was conceived by John Deane (see 23 June, *fn*) early in 1856; Peter Cunningham placed the portraits and wrote the historical part of the catalogue. Building began in Aug 56; it cost £35,000.

[3] It began with Hogarth, Reynolds and Gainsborough; included Etty, Wilkie, Turner and Charles Collins; and was hung by Egg.

[4] The failure of the Exhibition to attract the working classes is a major point made by Wills in "The Manchester School of Art", *HW*, 10 Oct 57, XVI, 349. The chief reason he gives is their "uninstructed eye", faced by various schools of painting; and their being totally uninformed about the technicalities of modern pictures (p. 350).

[5] See *To* Hollingshead, 27 July and *fn*.

finished it by Noon. Went down to Gallery of Illustration (we acted there that night), did the day's business, corrected the proof in Polar costume in dressingroom, broke up two numbers of Household Words to get it out directly,[1] played in Frozen Deep and Uncle John, presided at Supper of company, made no end of speeches, went home and gave in completely for four hours, then got sound asleep, and next day was as fresh as—you used to be in the far off days of your lusty Youth.

All here send kindest love to your dear good sister and all the house. Ever and ever affectionately. CD.

To SIR JOSEPH PAXTON, 3 AUGUST 1857*

MS British Library.

Gad's Hill Place | Monday Third August, 1857

My Dear Paxton

I have safely received the Duke's munificent donation, and beg most earnestly to tender the thanks of the Committee for that princely gift.[2]

As to your own kind promise of assistance to Tom,[3] I should say, Wait a little. *Between ourselves*, I have no faith in the Farm project;[4] because I believe it to be based on the assumption that the Fund we are raising will be placed at the disposal of the whole family—like a sort of pecuniary skittles, to be bowled down by whomsoever may have a fancy to Go in. This idea I, for one, shall very strenuously oppose, when we meet to consider the Trust that shall be established.

It is obvious that the Money must be got, before it can be disposed of. Therefore it is beating the wind to discuss the question at present. I hope we shall finish our exertions, at Manchester on the 22nd. by then turning the round corner of £2,000—the point at which I have always designed to stop.[5] As soon as possible thereafter, I will call the Committee together, at reasonable notice. In the meantime, if I were you, I would do nothing, and would in no wise commit myself to any thing.

Faithfully Yours always

Sir Joseph Paxton M.P. CHARLES DICKENS

P.S. I re-open this letter to say (at the urgent solicitation of the Gardener) that if you can send me any "cuttings", of any kind, out of your great wealth in such things, "here's an empty house and empty grounds"—I quote the gardener—"and nothing from Sir Joseph could possibly come amiss".—That's *his* opinion.

[1] i.e. Nos 384 and 385, published 1 and 8 Aug. He must have removed Eliza Lynn's "Witches of England", which is of equivalent length, from 1 to 8 Aug, and possibly altered the order of other articles.

[2] See *To* Paxton, 30 July.

[3] Thomas Serle Jerrold (1833–1907), Jerrold's youngest son; he had learnt gardening at Chatsworth under Paxton *c.* 1851–5.

[4] Tom had taken up farming in 1855 and spent a year on a farm near Liverpool. He no doubt now wanted to set up on his own. He became a writer on gardening subjects, publishing *Our Kitchen Garden*, 1881, and similar books, and contributing to periodicals. Spent 18 years in Canada.

[5] See *To* the Editor of *The Times*, 1 Sep 57.

To ARTHUR RYLAND, 3 AUGUST 1857*

MS Benoliel Collection.

Gad's Hill Place, Higham, by Rochester
Monday Third August, 1857

My Dear Mr. Ryland

Many thanks for your careful and explicit letter, with all the information I could possibly have required.[1]

In your absence, your partner Mr. Martineau[2] did me the favor to write me a sensible and practical letter, which discouraged me in respect to Birmingham, and which your letter confirms. I did not receive yours until I came home here yesterday from Manchester, but it fully confirmed me in a previous relinquishment of the Birmingham idea.

I read at Manchester last Friday night. Between the parts, some of the foremost people in the place, came to me with a representation that they particularly wished to have the Frozen Deep done in their City, and that they were absolutely certain of the success of two consecutive nights in the Free Trade Hall. They even offered to guarantee a certain profit, but I did not think it right to accept that generous proposal. However, I felt it incumbent on me to take the Play there, if careful calculations should prove the likelihood of a good result.[3] We went into them immediately after the reading—worked them out—and got the advertisement into next day's paper, before going to bed.[4] These two representations will finish the Jerrold business.

The number of people to be moved, the number of skilled workmen to be employed, and the quantity of material to be carried about, make up such a cost, that it would not be worth while to play once only, in any place I know of. But playing twice, the second night becomes sheer profit.

The Free Trade Hall is too large and difficult, and altogether too public for my girls however. So we shall take down Actresses in their stead.

[1] See *To* Miss Coutts, 17 June and *fn*.

[2] Thomas Martineau (1828–93), solicitor, partner since 1852. Mayor of Birmingham 1884–7; established Victoria Law Courts there and knighted 1887.

[3] See *To* Collins, 2 Aug and *fn*.

[4] The advertisement appeared in both the *Manchester Guardian* and the *Manchester Weekly Examiner and Times* on 1 Aug. The copy that CD supplied is as follows: "IN REMEMBRANCE OF THE LATE MR. DOUGLAS JERROLD. | The public are respectfully informed, that | THE ONLY TWO REPRESENTATIONS OUT OF LONDON | of Mr. Wilkie Collins's new romantic Drama, | THE FROZEN DEEP. | with Mr. Buckstone's farce of | UNCLE JOHN | will take place in the large room of | THE FREE TRADE HALL, MANCHESTER, | With the original Scenery by MR. STANFIELD R.A. and MR. TELBIN, | ON FRIDAY AND SATURDAY EVENINGS, THE 21ST. AND 22ND. AUGUST, | UNDER THE MANAGEMENT OF MR. CHARLES DICKENS. | STALLS, cushioned, reserved, and numbered, Ten Shillings each. (DRESS). RESERVED SEATS IN THE GALLERY, five shillings each. (DRESS.) UNRESERVEDSEATS, half a crown each. Every ticket sold, for any part of the Hall, will have a seat belonging to it, and no Standing-Room will be let, on any terms. | Tickets will be on sale on and after Monday August 10th. In the mean time communications may be addressed to J. C. DEANE ESQUIRE, Belgrave House, Old Trafford." A French translation, in another hand, was probably intended for foreign visitors to the Art Treasures Exhibition. According to Deane, the advt was written in the Royal Hotel, Manchester, "on Friday July 31st or rather Saturday Morning the 1st. of August, and taken by me for insertion in the Papers" (MS Houghton Library, Harvard).

All here send kindest regard to Mrs. Ryland and yourself, in which I very heartily join.

Always Most Faithfully Yours

Arthur Ryland Esquire. CHARLES DICKENS

To W. H. WILLS, 3 AUGUST 1857*

MS Berg Collection.

Gad's Hill Place | Monday Night Third August | 1857

My Dear Wills

I omitted in my last, to remind you that the ladies' parts in the 1st. and 3rd. acts Frozen Deep, should be immediately copied, and that we should be armed likewise with 3 new copies of Uncle John.[1]

Ever Faithfully

CD.

To WILLERT BEALE,[2] 4 AUGUST 1857*

MS Mr Cyril Staal.

Gad's Hill Place, Higham, by Rochester
Tuesday Fourth August, 1857

My Dear Sir

I propose being in town on Friday,[3] and will come to the Gallery of Illustration at ¼ before 5 on that day in the hope of seeing you. If this appointment should be inconvenient, I will propose another for Saturday forenoon.

Faithfully Yours

Willert Beale Esquire CHARLES DICKENS

[1] A copy of the printed text with MS annotations is in the Beinecke library at Yale University.

[2] Thomas Willert Beale (1828–94; *DNB*), impresario; as lessee of the Gallery of Illustration, Feb 1856–Dec 1857, he gave the Gallery free to the Jerrold Fund. Managed Italian operas in London 1856 and opera recitals in provinces from Aug 1856. Published songs, piano pieces, two plays, *The Enterprising Impresario*, 1867, and his memoirs, *The Light of Other Days*, 2 vols, 1890. For his long-standing friendship with Douglas Jerrold and admiration of his wit, see *ibid.*, 1, Ch. 6 ("Our Club", of which he and Jerrold were members). They were guests at the dinner given by W. H. Russell at the Trafalgar Hotel, Greenwich, eight days before Jerrold's death: see *To* Forster, 10 June 57. He "looked pale and wan", Beale recorded, "spoke little, and was evidently suffering". "'I am very ill'", he said, "'and am here against the doctor's orders'" (*ibid.*, 1, Ch. 14, 159–60).

[3] For the final London performance the next evening of *The Frozen Deep* and *Uncle John* the playbill twice emphasises "For the Last Time"; for its success see *To* Fairbairn, 13 Aug.

To RICHARD BENTLEY, 6 AUGUST 1857*

MS Berg Collection.

Gad's Hill Place | Thursday August Sixth 1857

My Dear Mr. Bentley.

By all means, as to asking Mr. Evans's[1] opinion. We must wait, I suppose, until he returns; for he has been very unwell, and his holiday will be useless to him unless it is free from business.

His indisposition has been the occasion of my not having seen him since you were here. I have several matters to see him upon—one of them, a rather pressing one—but have forborne, in the hope that he would get well of his liver-disorder.

I cannot leave town on Saturday, for we act that night. If you wish to see me, I shall be at the Gallery of Illustration Regent Street, at one that day.

Faithfully Yours always

Richard Bentley Esquire. CHARLES DICKENS

To SHIRLEY BROOKS, 6 AUGUST 1857

MS Brotherton Library, Leeds.

Gad's Hill Place | Thursday Sixth August, 1857

My Dear Brooks.

In reply to the enclosed from Bentley, I have said that I by all means consent to taking Evans into council, but that I suppose we must wait until his return to town.

If I understand Bentley's position, he *cannot* make the contract we have proposed to him, without the consent of the gentlemen before whom his affairs are "under inspection."[2] Of these, Evans is one.

I have further told him that if he wants to see me, he will find me at the Gallery of Illustration on Saturday at One.

Faithfully Yours always

Shirley Brooks Esquire. CHARLES DICKENS

To MISS GEORGINA HOGARTH, 7 AUGUST 1857

MS Wellcome Historical Medical Library, London.

Tavistock House | Friday Morning Seventh August | 1857

My Dearest Georgy

I have had an excellent night (a little opiate in the medicine), and have had no

[1] F. M. Evans.

[2] Bentley had been in financial difficulties for many years; and on 1 Apr 55 an arrangement had been made for the firm to carry on under "inspectors", including the well-known printers, William Clowes and G. A. Spottiswoode. After two years, debts had been reduced by a third to £6,718 and a £3,000 loan repaid; although the business was declared "perfectly solvent" and "rapidly improving", a four-day sale of Bentley's copyrights by Southgate & Barrett began on 18 June 57. On 31 Mar 58 George Bentley recorded in his diary "The inspection terminated"; but Clowes and Spottiswoode were still exercising some control in 1863 (Royal Gettmann, *A Victorian Publisher: a Study of the Bentley Papers*, Cambridge, 1960, pp. 25–6).

return whatever of the distress of yesterday morning. Come to me at the Garrick, in a Cab, at ½ past 8.

Ever Affectionately

CD.

To SHIRLEY BROOKS, 7 AUGUST 1857

MS Brotherton Library, Leeds.

OFFICE OF HOUSEHOLD WORDS,
Friday Seventh August 1857

My Dear Brooks.

Will you give me the enclosed from Bentley, back again tomorrow night? Will you in the meantime think of the point he puts, and of what you would suggest upon it? I will then give you my own suggestion, and out of the two we will compound a shot.[1]

Faithfully Yours always

Shirley Brooks Esquire CHARLES DICKENS

To MR STEVENS,[2] 8 AUGUST 1857*

Text from transcript by owner of MS, Mrs Joyce Shorter.

IN REMEMBRANCE OF THE LATE MR. DOUGLAS JERROLD.

COMMITTEE'S OFFICE, GALLERY OF ILLUSTRATION,
REGENT STREET.
Saturday August Eighth 1857.

Mr. Charles Dickens presents his compliments to Mr. Stevens and begs with thanks to acknowledge the receipt of Mr. Stevens' obliging communication. It reached Mr. Dickens only yesterday in consequence of his having been out of town.

To FRANK STONE, 9 AUGUST 1857†

MS Benoliel Collection.

Tavistock House | Sunday Afternoon | Ninth August 1857

My Dear Stone

Now, here, without any Preface, is a good, confounding, stunning question for you.

—Would you like to play Uncle John, on the 2 nights at Manchester?

It is not a long part, you could have a full Rehearsal on the Friday, and I could sit in the Wing at night and pull you through all the business. Perhaps you might not object to being in the thing, in your own native place; and the relief to me would be enormous.

This is what has come into my head, lying in bed to day (I have been in bed all day), and this is just my plain reason for writing to you.

[1] See *To* Bentley, 1 Sep, and *fn*.

[2] Unidentified.

It's a capital part, and you are a capital old man. You know the Play as we play it,[1] and the Manchester people don't. Say the word, and I'll send you my own book by return of post.

The agitation and exertion of Richard Wardour are so great to me, that I cannot rally my spirits in the short space of time I get. The strain is so great, to make a show of doing it, that I want to be helped out of Uncle John, if I can.[2] Think of yourself far more than me; but if you half think you are up to the joke,[3] and half doubt your being so—then give me the benefit of the doubt, and play the part.

Answer me at Gad's Hill. The full address is as follows:

Gad's Hill Place
Higham
by
Rochester
Kent.

Kind regard to all with you.
Ever affectionately
CD.

If you play, I shall immediately announce it to all concerned. If you don't, I shall go on[4] as if nothing had happened, and shall say nothing to any one

To WALTER LACY,[5] 10 AUGUST 1857

MS Mr John Williams.

Tavistock House | Monday Tenth August 1857

My Dear Mr. Lacy.

I have read your letter with the sincerest gratification; and I beg most cordially to assure you that in its generous and earnest words, you have amply repaid me any pleasure I have ever been so fortunate as to give you.

Very faithfully Yours
CHARLES DICKENS

Walter Lacy Esquire.

[1] Though not in the cast he would have seen it at Tavistock House on 8 Jan and probably at the Gallery of Illustration. (Marcus Stone was in *The Frozen Deep*.)

[2] Clearly CD was suffering from the strain of the previous night's performance of both parts, added to his other anxieties about the Manchester visit, and probably also fearing an anticlimax in the rapid change from a tragic and emotional plot to a farcical one.

[3] Uncle John, hearty, fit and sanguine at 60, decides to marry the 19-year-old Eliza. His niece, a shameless legacy-hunter, and her husband manipulate a match between her and the young drawing-master, Edward Easel. Uncle John trumps their intrigues to break the marriage off on his wedding-day by marrying Eliza's mother instead.

[4] Stone accepted, but see *To* Stone, 17 Aug, *fn* and 18 Aug.

[5] Walter Lacy, stage name of Walter Williams (1809–98; *DNB*), actor; originally doctor in the penal colony in Van Diemen's Land; narrowly escaped when his ship was seized by convicts; a chief witness when the convicts were tried for piracy. Made his London debut at Haymarket Aug 38 as Charles Surface; played John of Gaunt and Edmund with Charles Kean; sufficiently well-known by 1843 to appear in CD's cast for his joke comedy, "The One Thing Needful" (Vol. III, p. 509); took Forster's part in *Not so Bad as we Seem* at Bristol in 1851 and Liverpool in 1852: see Vol. VI, pp. 537*n* and 606*n*. Well-known figure at the Garrick Club since 1850. (Information about his early career kindly given by his great-grandson, Mr John Williams.)

To FRANCESCO BERGER, 11 AUGUST 1857*

MS Victoria and Albert Museum.

Gallery of Illustration | Tuesday Eleventh August 1857.

My Dear Berger.

I have another suggestion to make. Would it not be much better to hang the Bell[1] behind,—out of sight? You would only have to shew me on Friday morning, exactly when and how it should be struck, and I would take upon myself to do it.

Faithfully Ever
CHARLES DICKENS

To WILLIAM DONNE,[2] 11 AUGUST 1857*

MS Dickens House.

Gallery of Illustration, | Regent Street.
Eleventh August, 1857

My Dear Sir

We are going to close our exertions in behalf of the Jerrold Fund, by acting The Frozen Deep at Manchester. With this view, it is necessary that it should be approved by the Licenser.[3] Will you excuse my begging your kind and early attention to it?

Very faithfully Yours

William Donne Esquire CHARLES DICKENS

To DANIEL MACLISE, 11 AUGUST 1857*

MS Benoliel Collection.

Gallery of Illustration | Tuesday Eleventh August | 1857

My Dear Mac. I should have been delighted to come, if I had known it yesterday. But I am pledged to go down to Gad's Hill, almost directly.

In haste | Faithfully Ever
CD.

[1] This is the Big Bell of *To* Berger, 4 Jan, evidently part of the musical effects.

[2] William Bodham Donne (1807–82; *DNB*), writer and Examiner of Plays in the Lord Chamberlain's Office Mar 1857–Apr 74; previously Librarian of the London Library (1852–7) and Deputy Examiner of Plays; a family tradition claimed direct descent from John Donne. Published *Essays upon the Drama*, 1858. He made a joking reference to "An Official Scarecrow" (*HW*, 24 July 58, XVIII, 143), by John Hollingshead (see 27 July 57, *fn*), a satire on his office (*W. B. Donne and his Friends*, ed. C. B. Johnson, 1905, p. 227).

[3] A licence would certainly be required for a public theatre (see *To* Deane, 12 Aug), and must have been granted. No record survives in the Lord Chamberlain's Collection; Donne would give it by letter, but the official correspondence is incomplete. The performance at the Olympic in 1866 was given a new licence.

To JOHN DEANE, 12 AUGUST 1857*

MS Free Library of Philadelphia.

Gad's Hill Place, Higham, by Rochester.
Wednesday Twelfth August, 1857

My Dear Deane.

I have been making out the List of the Manchester Expedition this morning, with the view of being able, to give you, in the rough, a notion of the Hotel accommodation we shall want at the Royal.[1] It will be

A Sitting room
A Dining room
And *about* 23 Bedrooms.

Detailed particulars will come, in due course from Arthur[2] and Wills, but this is very near the mark. Arthur will write to you soon (probably when you get this, you will have already heard from him), respecting the accommodation for the professional ladies—which is altogether separate, and not included here.

You know, no doubt, that the Solicitors, after all, sent me a form of application for a License, to fill up. It extends only to the two nights, Friday and Saturday. But it has occurred to me that if the Play should be (as I hope it will, and as I mean to do my best to make it) a great go—a very marked impression and success—it would make a wonderful addition to the Profits and a very small addition to the success, if we could play on the Monday at Theatre prices.[3] What do you think of the idea? If we entertain it, we must keep it impenetrably close, of course. But we *might* bring bills down to post on Saturday Evening to that effect. Now, if we could do this, I suppose we must hazard the License for that night?—I mean, hazard the playing without one? *Or*, we could be armed with a Travelling License too, from the Chamberlain? I want particularly, to know your opinion on these points.

Faithfully Yours always

John Deane Esquire. CHARLES DICKENS

P.S. We have made a very advantageous arrangement with the Great Western.

To W. C. MACREADY, 12 AUGUST 1857*

MS Morgan Library.

Gad's Hill Place, Higham, by Rochester
Wednesday Twelfth August | 1857

My Dearest Macready

The time you suggest will be perfectly convenient to us in all respects; and we have booked you and Katie, with joy, accordingly.

Next week we go to Manchester, and I hope the Jerrold task will end.

Faithfully and affecy. Ever
CD.

[1] In Mosley St, close to the Free Trade Hall; the chief Manchester hotel.

[2] Arthur Smith.

[3] As they did, adding unreserved seats at 2*s*. 6*d*. and 1*s*.

To T. GERMAN REED,[1] 12 AUGUST 1857*

MS Dickens House.

Gad's Hill Place, Higham, by Rochester
Wednesday Twelfth August 1857

My Dear Mr. Reed.

Mr. Macready has altered his time for coming to us, from the Sixteenth of this month, to the fifth (or thereabouts) of next month, September. We still hope that Mrs. Reed[2] and you may be able to come and pass a day with us, while he is here. If you are within reach, I shall write and bring our conversation to your remembrance, when I have safely laid hold of him.

With kind regard to Mrs. Reed, | Always Faithfully Yours

T. German Reed Esquire. CHARLES DICKENS

To WILLIAM TELBIN, 12 AUGUST 1857

Text from N, II, 869.

Gad's Hill Place, Higham by Rochester, Kent
Wednesday Twelfth August 1857

My Dear Telbin,

I don't know where to address Mr. Cuthbert.[3] Will you kindly tell him from me that I count on the pleasure of his joining our party to Manchester; and that I have put him down among the rest of us, both in our Railway and Hotel accommodation. We shall make a family party of it, just as though we were staying in a country house.

Full particulars as to starting-time and so forth, to be had of Arthur Smith.

Always cordially yours
[CHARLES DICKENS]

[1] Thomas German Reed (1817–88; *DNB*), musician; first appeared at Bath concerts as pianist and singer, aged 10; musical director of Haymarket 1838. Scored and adapted many new operas. With his wife (see below) began "Miss P. Horton's Illustrative Gatherings", mainly adaptations of musical dramas, at St Martin's Hall in Mar 1855; these became widely known as "Mr and Mrs German Reed's Entertainment", performed at the Gallery of Illustration since 1856 and until 1871. They had given a selection from their "Entertainment" at the Concert in memory of Jerrold at St Martin's Hall, 27 June.

[2] Née Priscilla Horton (1818–95; *DNB*), actress and singer; made her debut at the Surrey Theatre aged 10; played the Fool in *King Lear* in Macready's restoration of the part at Covent Garden Jan 1838, Ariel in his revival of *The Tempest* in Oct, and Ophelia at the Haymarket with Macready and Phelps 1840. Married T. G. Reed 1844. Played Hecate on Macready's last appearance 26 Feb 1851. Of her contralto voice, she told of Macready's inviting friends to hear "a new young man with a wonderful voice", while she sang behind a curtain (*The German Reeds and Corney Grain*, ed. D. Williamson, 1895, p. 12).

[3] Presumably John Spreckley Cuthbert, who exhibited at RA 1852–65 (mainly portraits).

To FRANCESCO BERGER, 13 AUGUST 1857

Mention in *Autograph Prices Current*, I, 51 (1914–16); *MS* 2 pp.; addressed Francesco Berger; dated 13 Aug 57.

Referring to performances at Manchester.

To THOMAS FAIRBAIRN, 13 AUGUST 1857*

MS Bodleian Library, Oxford.

Gad's Hill Place, Higham, by Rochester
Thursday Thirteenth August, 1857

My Dear Mr. Fairbairn

A thousand thanks for your kind letter. But I am sorry to reply that the business of the thing crushes the pleasure, and that the unfortunate Manager must stay in London until Thursday afternoon, and then come down with the main body, and keep with them.

When I hoped to be able to come to your house,[1] I had quite forgotten the professional ladies. They have to be rehearsed, however, and drilled into situations that are quite new to them. Hence, both on the Tuesday and on the Wednesday I have made engagements to go through the two pieces with them at the Gallery of Illustration. On the Thursday I must keep the Company together; and on the Friday morning at Manchester the aforesaid ladies will look to me to put them through all they have to do, with everybody concerned, scenery, band, and what not, for the first and only time. I have not a chance of a spare halfhour.

I hope to bring Mrs. Dickens but she is at present extremely unwell. My daughters and sister in law plead hard to come too, in order that they may see their substitutes. I suppose I must yield.

We had a wonderful account from our representative,[2] of the onslaught made upon him on the opening day. It is very cheering, and I should like him to be yet torn to pieces. We left off in London last Saturday with a greater house than ever, and I believe we might have played the piece for twelve months to come.

Believe me ever | Very faithfully Yours

Thomas Fairbairn Esquire CHARLES DICKENS

To JOHN THOMPSON, 13 AUGUST 1857

MS Berg Collection. *Address* (envelope, MS Walter T. Spencer): Mr. John Thompson | Household Words Office | 10 Wellington Street North | Strand | London | W.C. PM 13 Aug 57.

Gad's Hill Place | Thursday Thirteenth August | 1857.

John.

Mr. Berger wishes you to take the Bell that is struck in the Frozen Deep, to Manchester, among the properties. (It was left in the Orchestra). My little handbell[3] must

[1] Northwood, Prestwich, four miles north-west of Manchester.

[2] Arthur Smith.

[3] Used to call the maid in Act I.

be strongly mended, or a new one bought. The clapper always comes out of it, when I want it most.

See that the Snow[1] you take to Manchester, is better made than the last. It was very badly cut, and much too large.

CD.

To W. H. WILLS, 13 AUGUST 1857

MS Huntington Library.

Gad's Hill Place | Thursday Thirteenth August 1857

My Dear Wills

I send this up to town to be posted by our Doctor[2]—come down to Mrs. Dickens—still very poorly.[3]

I have altered the names thus:

A Journey in Search of Nothing
The Self-made Potter.
Burning, and Burying.
The Leaf
Sepoy Symbols of Mutiny.
Eleanor Clare's Journal[4]
On Her Majesty's Service[5]

—But I have a misgiving that we have used the last title before.[6] If we have not, retain it. If we have, call the article either

PUBLIC BUSINESS.[7]

or

HOW THE WRITER WAS DISPATCH-BOXED.[7]

Perhaps the latter is the better title of the Two. On Her Majesty's Service is the best title of the three, if we have not anticipated it.

I will try to knock out a subject or two.[8] In the event of my Sleepy Head engendering any thing, the great suggestion shall come to you by Post.[9]

Ever Faithfully
CD.

[1] See *To* Stanfield, 11 Dec 56 and *fn*. An important feature of the dramatic effects in Act II, especially near the end of the Act when Wardour and Frank are seen leaving together over the snow.

[2] Thomas Watson.

[3] She recovered in time to go to Manchester.

[4] All articles in *HW*, 5 Sep 57, XVI, 217–40; respectively by Wilkie Collins, John Robertson, Henry Morley, Owen O'Ryan (a poem), John Robertson, Harriet Parr (Ch. 2).

[5] Changed to "How the Writer was Despatch-Boxed" (on Govt red tape), by Dr R. B. Carter (see 20 Sep 56).

[6] Used for an article on the diplomatic corps by CD and Grenville Murray (7 Jan 54, VIII, 433).

[7] Underlined with short double strokes.

[8] He may have considered writing on the Manchester Arts Exhibition.

[9] No article by CD appeared in Aug (after "Curious Misprint" on 1 Aug), or Sep.

To HENRY AUSTIN, 15 AUGUST 1857

MS Morgan Library.

Gad's Hill Place, | Saturday Fifteenth August, 1857

My Dear Henry

At last, I am happy to inform you, we have got at a famous spring!! It rushed in this morning 10 foot deep—And our friends talk of its supplying "a ton a minute for yourself and your family, Sir, for hevermore".

They ask leave to bore ten feet lower, to prevent the possibility of what they call "a choking with sullage". Likewise, they are going to insert "a rose-headed pipe"; at the mention of which implement, I am (secretly) wellnigh distracted: having no idea what it means. But I have said "Yes", besides instantly standing a Bottle of Gin. Are you come back, and can you get down on Monday Morning, to advise, and endeavour to decide on the mechanical forces we shall use for raising the Water?[1] I would return with you, as I shall have to be in town until Thursday,[2] and then to go to Manchester until the following Tuesday.

I send this by hand to John, to bring to you.

Ever affectionately
CD.

To JOHN DEANE, 15 AUGUST 1857*

MS Houghton Library, Harvard.

Gad's Hill Place | Saturday Fifteenth August, 1857

My Dear Deane

I merely write to say that I received your letter this morning with great pleasure.

Also, as to the Orchestra, that I think the two Rehearsals had best come off, as Berger proposes. I have lately had occasion to find fault in that Department, and he is very anxious to put it right.

Faithfully Yours Ever

John C Deane Esquire CHARLES DICKENS

To H. G. ADAMS,[3] 17 AUGUST 1857

MS Huntington Library. *Address* (MS Yale University Library): H. G. Adams Esquire | Rochester. PM 17 Aug 57.

Gad's Hill Place | Monday August Seventeenth 1857

Dear Sir

Your letter finds me leaving this, for London and Manchester, to bring to a close

[1] On a visit to Gad's Hill in Aug 1888, W. R. Hughes and F. G. Kitton were told that the well, in a pumping-room, was 217 ft deep, and that there was never less than 20 ft of water in it. The water was drawn by a horse-driven pump (W. R. Hughes, *A Week's Tramp in Dickens-Land*, p. 181).

[2] 19 Aug, for the three days of rehearsals.

[3] Henry Gardiner Adams (?1811–81), Secretary of the Mechanics' Institute, Chatham and Rochester: see Vol. II, p. 11*n*.

the exertions that have been for some weeks in progress, in remembrance of the late Mr. Jerrold. I cannot therefore have the pleasure of making an appointment at present to receive the Deputation from the Chatham and Rochester Mechanics Institution. On my return however, which I hope will be within a fortnight, I will write to you again, proposing a time for that purpose.

But I think it well to assure you beforehand, that if the gentlemen who purpose coming to me have it in contemplation to ask me to make any public appearance, of any kind, in aid of their Institution, I shall be obliged to decline. I have lately devoted to the cause referred to in the beginning of this note, as much time and personal exertion as I can possibly give away; and nothing new must stand between me and my own pursuits and recreations.

I am Dear Sir | Faithfully Yours

H. G. Adams Esquire CHARLES DICKENS

To FRANK STONE, 17 AUGUST 1857

MS Yale University Library.

Gad's Hill Place | Monday Seventeenth August, 1857

My Dear Stone

I received your kind note this morning, and write this reply here to take to London with me and post in town—being bound for that village, and three days drill of the professional ladies[1] who are to succeed our Tavistock girls.

My book, I enclose. There is a slight alteration[2] (which does not affect you) at the end of the First Act, in order that the piece may be played through, without having the Drop Curtain down. You will not find the situations or business difficult, with me on the spot to put you right.

Now, as to the Dress. You will want a pair of pumps, and a pair of white silk socks. Those you can get at Manchester. Two extravagantly and anciently-frilled shirts that I have had got up for the part, I will bring you down. Large white waistcoat, I will bring you down. Large white hat, I will bring you down. Dressing gown, I will bring you down. White gloves and ditto choker, you can get at Manchester. There then remain, only a pair of common nankeen tights to button below the calf, and blue wedding coat. The nankeen tights you had best get made at once; my Uncle John coat, I will send you down in a parcel by tomorrow's train, to have altered in Manchester to your shape and figure. You will then be quite independent of Chris-

[1] In *The Frozen Deep*, these were Mrs George Vining who played Mrs Steventon (previously Helen Hogarth's part), Ellen Sabine for Rose Ebsworth (Kate Dickens's part), Maria Ternan for the heroine, Clara Burnham (Mamie Dickens's part), Ellen Ternan for Lucy Crayford (Georgina's part), and Mrs Ternan for Nurse Esther (Mrs Wills's part at Tavistock House and Mrs Frances Dickinson's at the Gallery of Illustration). In *Uncle John*, Maria Ternan played Mrs Hawk (Georgina's part), Ellen Ternan Eliza (Kate's part) and Mrs Ternan Mrs Comfort (Mamie's part). The female parts in both plays that required the greatest acting ability were taken by Maria Ternan; but in both pieces all are important and would require considerable rehearsal—presumably at least partly with the male parts, though this is not stated. For the Ternan family, see *To* Miss Coutts, 5 Sep and *fnn*.

[2] Presumably to avoid the characters' exit at the end of Act I.

tian chance, and Jewish Nathan: which latter Potentate is now at Canterbury with the Cricket Amateurs,[1] and might fail.[2]

A Thursday's Rehearsal is (unfortunately) now impracticable; the passes for the Railway being all made out, and the Company's sailing orders issued. But, as I have already suggested, with a careful Rehearsal on Friday morning, and with me at the Wing at night to put you right, you will find yourself sliding through it easily. There is nothing in the least complicated in the business. As to the Dance, you have only to knock yourself up[3]for a twelvemonth, and it will go nobly.

After all too, if you *should*, through any unlucky break-down, come to be afraid of it, I am no worse off than I was before, if I have to do it at last. Keep your Pecker[4] up with that.

I am heartily obliged to you my dear old boy for your affectionate and considerate note. And I wouldn't have you do it— really and sincerely, immense as the relief will be to me—unless you are quite comfortable in it, and able to enjoy it.

Kind love from mine to yours.

In haste | Ever affecy.
CD.

To WILKIE COLLINS, 17 AUGUST 1857

MS Morgan Library.

GARRICK CLUB
Monday Evening Seventeenth August | 1857

My Dear Collins

Fred Evans's[5] grandmother[6] being evidently on the point of Death, no Evans[7] is available (as I learn on coming to town tonight), for Manchester. This leaves to be supplied, Easel,[8] and Bateson.[9] I immediately think of your brother Charles,[10] and Luard.[11] If it had been a purely managerial and not personal case, I should have proposed to Luard to do one of the parts, and to your brother to do the other. But I think it right that Charles Collins should first select for himself.[12] Now, will you,

[1] i.e. the amateurs who performed in the Canterbury Theatre during the "Grand Cricket Week", 17–21 Aug.

[2] He went to Manchester and had a walk-on part in Act II of *The Frozen Deep*.

[3] Perhaps in joking sense of "knock out" in boxing.

[4] Spirit, courage (slang, 1848).

[5] F. M. Evans's son: see Vol. VII, p. 144*n*.

[6] If this is Mrs Mary Evans, of Bath, she lingered until June 58 and died aged 96.

[7] The cast had also included Tom and George Evans in non-speaking parts.

[8] Edward Easel, the young drawing-master in *Uncle John*, eventually paired off with Eliza; he has very few speeches.

[9] One of the *Sea-Mew*'s crew.

[10] Charles Collins played Darker, the other member of the *Sea-Mew*'s crew.

[11] John Dalbiac Luard (1830–60; *DNB*), painter. Had walk-on part of a sailor in *The Frozen Deep* at Manchester and played Easel in *Uncle John*. Son of Lieut.-Colonel John Luard; served in 82nd Foot Regt 1848–53; then studied painting; friend of Millais, with whom he shared chambers, and Charles Collins; appears in sketches by Millais (J. G. Millais, *Life and Letters of J. E. Millais*, 1899, I, 243–4); first exhibited in RA 55; visited his brother serving in the Crimea Winter 55–6 and exhibited four paintings in RA 55–8, three based on scenes in the Crimea and on journey home (*The Welcome Arrival*, 1857, officers opening a hamper, became famous); his health failed 1859.

[12] As the playwright's brother.

before you come to the Rehearsal tomorrow, arrange with him whether he will play one—which one—or both; and if he leaves one, will you call on Luard as you come down, and offer that one to him?

I write at Express pace, but you will understand all I mean.

Ever Faithfully
CD.

To FRANK STONE, [17 AUGUST 1857]

Telegram, mentioned in *To* Stone, 18 Aug. *Date:* night before that letter.

To FRANK STONE, 18 AUGUST 1857†

MS Benoliel Collection.

OFFICE OF HOUSEHOLD WORDS,
Tuesday Eighteenth August 1857

My Dear Stone. I sent you a telegraph message last night, in total contradiction of the letter you received from me this morning.

The reason was simply this:—Arthur Smith, and our other business men, both in Manchester and here, urged upon me in the strongest manner that they were afraid of the change—that it was well known in Manchester that I had done the part in London—that there was a danger of its being considered disrespectful in me to give it up—also, that there was a danger that it might be thought that I did so at the last minute, after an immense Let, whereas I might have done it at first &c. &c. &c. Having no desire but for the success of our object, and a becoming recognition on my part of the kind Manchester public's cordiality, I gave way and thought it best to go on.[1]

I do so against the grain, and against every inclination,[2] and against the strongest feeling of gratitude to you. My people at home will be miserable, too, when they hear I am going to do it.[3] If I could have heard from you sooner and got the bill out sooner, I should have been firmer in considering my own necessity of relief. As it is—I knock under. And I hope you will feel the reasons, and approve?

[1] CD's Uncle John was praised for its "lively sparkle" in the *Manchester Weekly Examiner and Times*, 22 Aug. Berger in 1891 wrote that he had never seen anything funnier than CD's Uncle John in the final scene, especially the last speech where he is struggling to get his arms into a tight-fitting wedding coat and says (elaborating Buckstone's text), "there are just a few devilish disagreeable people, ... but it's a beautiful world" (F. G. Kitton, *CD by Pen and Pencil*, Suppl., p. 18). The *Manchester Guardian*, 24 Aug, recorded that the play was performed "with a gusto and comic breadth very rarely equalled"; it also commented on Charley Dickens's "gentlemanly demeanour" as Andrew the footman (the *Manchester Weekly Examiner*, 22 Aug, praised him for his "smart bit of character").

[2] Perhaps CD was reluctant to act an old man, but the chief reason was clearly the physical and nervous strain of this part following that of Wardour: see *To* Stone, 9 Aug and *fn*.

[3] They would be anxious about his health; he had been "in bed all day" after the last performance instead of returning to Gad's Hill with Georgina and his daughters.

[a]I have been rehearsing the ladies for hours, and have just time to get this into the post.[a]

Ever affectionately
CD.

To RICHARD BENTLEY, 19 AUGUST 1857*

MS Berg Collection.

OFFICE OF HOUSEHOLD WORDS,
Wednesday Nineteenth August 1857

My Dear Mr. Bentley

Passing through town on my way to Manchester (whence I purpose returning within a week), I write this line or two to let you know that I have not troubled you on Mr. Shirley Brooks's matter, pending Mr. Evans's return to business; but that I shall be quite ready to close it when you please. I think, in reference to the Cheap Edition, that he should have some little interest in it. Probably we should find it easy enough to agree on that point.

Faithfully Yours
Richard Bentley Esquire. CHARLES DICKENS

To TIMOTHY YEATS BROWN,[1] 19 AUGUST 1857*

MS Mrs R. E. Yeats-Brown.

OFFICE OF HOUSEHOLD WORDS,
Wednesday Nineteenth August 1857

My Dear Browne.[2]

All the world knows Mr. Albert Smith. Innumerable people who know nothing of Mont Blanc itself, perhaps know more about it of him than they have ever known of their own fathers and mothers.

He is an intimate friend of mine, for whom I have a great regard, and in whose prosperity in all ways, I am much interested. In passing through Genoa, it is not unlikely that he may desire to have a good letter of introduction. I give him this, and earnestly commend him to you, nothing doubting that you, and Mrs. Browne,[3] and yours, will be good to him—first for my sake, and then for his own.

With kind regard and remembrance

Ever My Dear Browne[2] | Yours Very faithfully
T. Yeats Browne[2] Esquire. CHARLES DICKENS

[aa] Omitted in MDGH.

[1] Timothy Yeats Brown (1789–1858), British Consul at Genoa, whom CD had met in Nov 1844: see Vol. IV, p. 222*n*; and for CD's revisiting him, see Vol. VII, p. 177 and *n*.

[2] CD's error for Brown.

[3] Stuarta (1810–93), daughter of the 2nd Lord Erskine.

To EMILE DE LA RUE,[1] 19 AUGUST 1857*

MS Berg Collection.

Tavistock House, London | Nineteenth August, 1857

My Dear De la Rue.

If you knew what a constant correspondent I am (in the spirit); how often I think of you, and Madame De la Rue,[2] and our old times; how true my memory is, under all changes of time and distance, and how firmly what has once got into my heart, rests rooted there; you would never be angry with me—if you ever are—for writing so rarely.

I do not write, even now, to say this (though I say it), but to ask your kind offices in behalf of my friend Mr. Albert Smith. You will be familiar with his reputation, and will know him well beforehand, and will be pre-interested in so distinguished a man. But I have told him that I give him this letter of introduction, in order that he may go straight to the wisest and kindest of people in Genoa, for any information or help he may want there. I have assured him that if he wants to know anything about the Genoese tongue—which one would think nobody did—our dear Madame De la Rue has an unfathomable knowledge of it and speaks it to frightful perfection. That if he wants to know anything about Genoa, you are Genoa compressed. And that if he wants to see the most beautiful apartment in the world, he has only to make an ascent a trifle shorter than his ascent of Mont Blanc, and look at the beloved old rooms at the top of the Brignole Rosso.[3]

With affectionate love to Madame

Ever Your faithful friend

Emile De la Rue. CHARLES DICKENS

To W. J. EASTWICK, 19 AUGUST 1857*

MS Mr Cyril D. B. Hawksley. *Address:* William J. Eastwick Esquire | 12 Leinster Terrace.

Tavistock House | Nineteenth August, 1857

My Dear Sir

Coming to town on my way to Manchester, I find your interesting letter, and its accompanying volume. I will read the book attentively, and bearing in my mind what you say of it. Perhaps I may see my way to the preparation of an account of it for Household Words, which may help to make it better known.[4]

Allow me to thank you for your kind remembrance of my second boy. I have just

[1] Emile de la Rue (*d.* 1870), banker, whom CD had met in Genoa in Nov 44: see Vols IV, p. 223*n* and VII, p. 177 and *n*.

[2] Née Augusta Granet (*d.* 1887): see Vols IV, *ibid.* and VI, p. 364; and, for CD's mesmerizing her in Italy, Vol. IV, p. 243 and *n*.

[3] See Vol. IV, p. 294.

[4] *The Autobiography of Lutfullah Khan*, ed. by Edward Eastwick (William's brother and Professor of Urdu at Haileybury College), published late July 57. Article on it by E. Townsend, who had written other articles on India, in *HW*, 21 Nov, XVI, 490, warmly praises the book and says it is "admirably edited".

heard from him (from Gibraltar[1] on his way out), and he seems to have become habituated to his new life, with wonderful ease.

Always My Dear Sir | Yours faithfully and obliged

William J. Eastwick Esquire. CHARLES DICKENS

To DR W. C. HOOD, 19 AUGUST 1857

Text from N, II, 872.

OFFICE OF HOUSEHOLD WORDS,
19th August 1857

The reference to yourself in Mr. Morley's article is his own honest tribute to your merit.[2] . . . It will give me real pleasure to improve the interesting beginning of our personal knowledge of one another when the approach of winter shall bring me back to London.[3]

To WILLIAM JERDAN, 19 AUGUST 1857*

MS Benoliel Collection.

OFFICE OF HOUSEHOLD WORDS,
Wednesday Nineteenth August 1857

My Dear Jerdan.

I am sorry that I cannot use the Paper on the Highlands. There is curious matter in it; but it comes too barely and dryly, for this purpose.

Old Hawtrey[4] I am very glad to retain. Wills has "estimated" the old man's size (in Household Words feet), and I enclose said Wills's official cheque.[5] If he should have made a mistake in the way of under-measurement, I will take care that it is set right.

Faithfully Yours

W. Jerdan Esquire. CHARLES DICKENS

To T. J. MOLYNEUX, [19 AUGUST 1857]

MS (envelope only) Walter T. Spencer. *Address:* Mr. J. Molyneux | People's Concerts Committee | St. Martin's Hall | Long Acre | W.C. PM 19 Aug 57.

[1] "Gibralter" in MS.

[2] In "The Star of Bethlehem" (*HW*, 15 Aug 57, XVI, 145), Morley, describing the many changes in Bethlehem Hospital effected by Hood, had mentioned, as an instance of his humanity, two or three of Hood's own children playing with the insane patients and his "noble little boy" standing upon the staircase of one of the men's wards (p. 147). Hood's book *Statistics of Insanity* is cited as showing how constantly insanity is related to "a depressing influence".

[3] They may have met through Forster: see *To* Hood, 19 Apr 57, *fn.*

[4] *HW*, 26 Sep 57 (XVI, 308). It describes the narrator's meeting an old countryman of 84 near Windsor and his early memories. Jerdan himself was 73.

[5] Obviously paid on acceptance; amount not stated in Office Book, but probably £2.2.0, as for his two earlier contributions.

To MISS BURDETT COUTTS, 20 AUGUST 1857†

MS Morgan Library. *Address:* Miss Burdett Coutts | 1 Stratton Street | Piccadilly.

Tavistock House
Thursday Morning | Twentieth August, 1857

My Dear Miss Coutts.

I have been asked by a very old friend indeed, of my school days,[1] to lay the enclosed letter before you. He is well acquainted with the writer, and has a high esteem and respect for him. I do not under the circumstances feel it is quite kind to be as firm on the subject of such entreaties as I usually am, and I have therefore consented. But, strictly on the understanding that with the delivery of the letter my function ends, and that I encourage no hope or further prospect of any kind.

I am away to Manchester this morning, to finish the Jerrold matter (N.B. Professional ladies.)[2]

With kind regard to Mrs. Brown,

Ever Dear Miss Coutts | Yours faithfully and affecy.
CHARLES DICKENS

To W. S. EMDEN, 20 AUGUST 1857

Text from N, II, 873.

Tavistock House | Twentieth August 1857

Dear Sir,

I am exceedingly obliged to you for your polite attention and kind note of last evening. Pray accept in return my heartiest good wishes.

I was astonished by the great improvement in The Lighthouse[3] since the first night; it appeared to me to be admirably done in all respects and its effect upon the audience was not to be mistaken. A veteran dramatic writer of high reputation[4] (who wishes in his retirement to be known in no new effort) has given me the enclosed farce[5] with an earnest request that I will do what I can for him in the way of disposing of it outright. His expectations of it are very reasonable. I have had it

[1] Possibly John Bowden, who had been in touch with CD in Dec 47 (see Vol. V, p. 204 and *n*).

[2] Emphasised to allay her anxiety about public performances by Georgina and his daughters.

[3] See Vol. VII, p. 650 and *n*. The first professional performance, at the Olympic on 10 Aug, under Frederick Robson and Emden; given a warm review on 11 Aug by *The Times*, which acclaimed it as a "great event:" "a very charming story, very effectively acted"; but despite its merits, "rather a dramatic anecdote than an actual drama", missing the "compactness" of Tavistock House. Robson played CD's part of Aaron Gurnock. It ran until 17 Oct.

[4] John Poole.

[5] It must have been John Poole's one-act farce, "A Pair of Razors", of 39 pp. (Forster Collection, MS V & A), presumably an early work, never performed or published. Its two characters, Biddy Sharp and Bob Sharper, disguise themselves to outdo each other as their employers, Lady O'Ranter and Admiral Broadsides, and as another servant, Nick Dumps, a "Somersetshire lout". Biddy as Lady O'Ranter has a terrible Irish temper; Bob as the Admiral has suitably ferocious nautical language. They end up with hopes of being "comfortably married". It is quite funny enough to be performed, but was declined: see *To* Webster, 9 Nov and 8 Dec.

fairly copied,[1] have read it myself and have until now shown it to no one. I think I should have known the hand if I had come upon it by chance, but that is not to the purpose. Will you ask Mr. Robson in my name to look at it, and will you tell me if there is any likelihood of its suiting your company? Pray expressly understand that I expect you to give it no weight or favour because I forward it, beyond a decision at your first convenience.

Faithfully Yours
[CHARLES DICKENS]

To RICHARD BENTLEY, 26 AUGUST 1857*

MS Berg Collection.

Tavistock House | Wednesday Twenty Sixth August, 1857.

My Dear Mr. Bentley.

My reply to your letter (I found it here this morning, having come from Manchester late last night), is the result of daily experience, and enforced consideration a thousand times reiterated.

The best thing Miss Pardoe[2] can do for herself, or that any friend of hers can do for her, with the view of attracting Miss Coutts's attention to her case,[3] is to address Miss Coutts, describing the case plainly and correctly. If Miss Coutts should feel it to be one in which she can render assistance, she will very probably refer it to me. *Then*, I shall deem it my duty, and make it my business, to supply the strong confirmation I have derived from you.

But, I know the task of refusal to be an unwelcome one that is forced upon Miss Coutts an absolutely incredible number of times, every week. And I have long been compelled to establish it as a rule, that I have no right to add to the pain and irksomeness of that so-often unavoidable necessity, the weight of a personal explanation to myself.

In haste | Faithfully Yours

Richard Bentley Esquire CHARLES DICKENS

[1] A fair "Prompter's Copy" is in the Forster Collection. Forster also possessed an incomplete, untitled farce by Poole and numerous letters from other people to him, so obviously acquired many of his manuscripts.

[2] Julia Pardoe (1806–62; *DNB*), travel-writer, popular historian and novelist: see Vol. III, p. 274*n*.

[3] She had been given three grants by the Royal Literary Fund since Dec 44, totalling £165; the most recent in June 57 (£65), the grounds including death in her family and "severe physical suffering"; she was given a further grant in Apr 59 (£60) (MSS Royal Literary Fund). She was still writing, but no doubt had difficulty in finding publishers to succeed Bentley, formerly the main one; her only work this year, *Pilgrimages in Paris*, was not published till Dec, by William Lay, who also published an *Arabian Nights Selection for the Young, a Thousand and One Days*, with a Preface by her. Bentley had sold his copyrights of her historical works and they were not reprinted. She was granted a Civil List pension of £100 p.a. in 1860, "in consideration of 30 years' toil in the field of literature".

To W. C. MACREADY, 26 AUGUST 1857*

MS Morgan Library.

Tavistock House | Wednesday Twenty Sixth August, 1857

My Dearest Macready

I came home from Manchester late last night, and, on going out this morning, was shocked by the announcement in the Times.[1] Though we have long entertained the sad probability of the poor dear boy's blessed relief, the tidings came so suddenly at last, that—for the moment—they seemed like the heralding of an unexpected calamity.

So, I greatly fear, this new bereavement may at first come upon you. But, apart from the confidence I have (God knows, with reason!) in your fortitude under all afflictions, I hope and believe that you will soon be reconciled to this one, and that the thought of the dear over-burdened child, released from his long endurance and gone to his mother in the great land, the shadow of which is for ever on this earth while its radiant light is shed another way, will have great comfort in it and but little pain. Every year that under a less merciful wisdom had dawned upon his heavy head, must have brought greater trial upon it and upon all of you; and I have a great faith, even on an hour's reflection, in no man's power of knowing it more religiously and thankfully, than in my dear, beloved friend's.

Forgive me for these few words. I had a mind, but a few minutes ago, not to write until tomorrow. But as I could not, if I had been near you and your true sister, have refrained from coming and pressing your hands, so I *cannot* go away to Gad's Hill without writing this note.

Catherine and Georgina and the two girls are here; and what they say, and what loving words they send, you know.

Ever my Dearest Macready | Most affectionately Yours
CHARLES DICKENS

To HENRY AUSTIN, 26 AUGUST 1857*

MS Morgan Library.

Gad's Hill | Wednesday Evening | Twenty Sixth August, 1857

My Dear Henry. I got back from Manchester to Tavistock House, late last night. There, I found the enclosed for you.[2] I went down to your office about noon to day, but you were gone. I came back here at 6, and found your note to Catherine unopened—she too, as you now know, having been in Manchester. I write in great haste, to save the Messenger going over to Rochester to fetch Charley, who will post this.

Ever affecy.
CD.

[1] Of the death of his third son, Henry Frederick Bulwer, aged 18, on 22 Aug; the first of his children to be stricken with tuberculosis, when aged two.

[2] Presumably a letter from one of the two Nyes whom CD was employing at Gad's Hill (see 23 July and *fn*): he paid him £300 on 24 Aug and a further £300 on 24 Sep (CD's Account-book, MS Messrs Coutts).

To HENRY AUSTIN, 28 AUGUST 1857*

MS Morgan Library.

Gad's Hill | Friday Twenty Eighth August, 1857

My Dear Henry

This is the enclosure that I thought I had sent you. It is from the Chief Conspirator.[1]

I hope the Pump will not be long a-making. The aggravation of knowing that the water is at the bottom of the well—and of paying for that accursed water-cart that comes jogging backwards and forwards—and of looking at the dry bath, morning after morning—is gradually changing the undersigned honey-pot, into a Mad Bull.

Ever Affecy.

CD.

To W. H. WILLS, [?27–8 AUGUST 1857]

Mention in next. *Date:* probably written the same day.

To MRS BROWN, 28 AUGUST 1857

MS Morgan Library. *Address:* Mrs. Brown | Holly Lodge | Highgate.

Gad's Hill | Friday, Twenty Eighth August, 1857

My Dear Mrs. Brown.

The address of that letter to Miss Coutts, which you enclosed me, is about as bad as bad can be. There are not many worse places. However, there may be something in the case for all that; and I have written to Mr. Wills upon it (the street is very near the Household Words office),[2] and have told him what I think about it, and have begged him to try to see the writer, straightway.

In Mr. Ford's[3] matter, I have caused "A Lady"[4] to be put down for a subscription of Five Pounds.

I have just come back from Manchester, where I have been tearing myself to pieces, to the wonderful satisfaction of thousands of people,[5] with Neuralgia—or something like it—in my face half the time. That work is now over, and more than two thousand Guineas are in store for the widow and daughter.

[1] See 26 Aug 57 and *fn.*

[2] Perhaps Holywell St, off the Strand.

[3] Probably the Rev. Richard Robert Ford: see *To* Wills, 26 Sep 57 and *fn.*

[4] i.e. Miss Coutts.

[5] For CD's short speech from the stage, after the first performance on 21 Aug, thanking the audience for their reception, see *Speeches*, ed. K. J. Fielding, p. 238. The *Manchester Guardian*, 22 Aug, gave it a long and warm review, particularly praising CD's Wardour and Lemon's Crayford and the acting of CD, Lemon and Collins in *Uncle John*; it also commented on "the clever acting of the professional ladies". Of the second performance on 22 Aug, before an audience of 3,000, Collins wrote much later: "This was, I think, the finest of all the representations of 'The Frozen Deep'. The extraordinary intelligence and enthusiasm of the great audience stimulated us all to do our best, Dickens surpassed himself. The trite phrase is the true phrase to describe that magnificent piece of acting. He literally electrified the audience" (*The Frozen Deep and Other Stories*, 1874, Introductory Lines, pp. 4–5).

Last Saturday week, the well-workmen here burst at last upon a beautiful spring of bright clear water which is reported to be exhaustless. I am now having a pump made to pump it up. When the first glassful is drunk at the surface, it will have cost £200. But of course there was no going on without it, and I comfort myself (as well as I can) with the reflection that the spring might have lain much deeper, or might not have been at all.

The restlessness which is the penalty of an imaginative life and constitution—we all hold whatever we possess, on the strict tenure that it must and shall be used—so besets me just now, that I feel as if the scaling of all the Mountains in Switzerland, or the doing of any wild thing until I dropped, would be but a slight relief.[1] The vague unhappiness which tracks a life of constant aim and ever impels to some new aim in which it may be lost, is so curious to consider, that I observe it in myself sometimes, with as much curiosity as if I were another man. Wonderful to think how wise the ordering of it is, and how it works to the doing of what is to be done!

Walter has written from Gibraltar and Malta. Quite well, and wonderfully settled to his new life. He does not seem, as yet, to have a backward glance or regret. Will you kindly ask Miss Coutts from me whether the enclosed refers to *that* helmet? I am quite at a loss to understand it, and only get the idea into my head as I write, that it may possibly be so.

All here unite in kind love and regard.

Ever Dear Mrs. Brown | Affectionately Yours
CHARLES DICKENS

To THE REV. S. HADDEN PARKES,[2] 28 AUGUST 1857*

MS Mr John Schroder.

Gad's Hill Place, Higham, by Rochester
Friday, Twenty Eighth August, 1857.

Sir.

My absence at Manchester has occasioned a delay (which I beg you on that account to excuse), in my receiving and replying to your letter.

I was perfectly satisfied with Charles French when he was in my employment, and always found him a very good and zealous servant. I can recommend him with confidence. Indeed I have already recommended him to Mr. Panizzi, in association with his desire to obtain employment at the Museum.

I am Sir | Very faithfully Yours
The Rev. Shadden[3] Parkes. CHARLES DICKENS

[1] See *To* Collins, 29 Aug and *fn*.

[2] The Rev. Samuel Hadden Parkes (?1831–1906), newly appointed Curate of St George's, Bloomsbury; BA, Jesus College, Cambridge, 1854; Curate of St George's, Wolverhampton, 1855–7; Rector of Wittersham, Kent, 1872–1906.

[3] CD's error for S. Hadden.

To WILKIE COLLINS, 29 AUGUST 1857

MS Morgan Library.

Tavistock House | Saturday Twenty Ninth August | 1857

My Dear Collins.

Partly in the grim despair and restlessness of this subsidence from excitement, and partly for the sake of Household Words,[1] I want to cast about whether you and I can go anywhere—take any tour—see any thing—whereon we could write something together. Have you any idea, tending to any place in the world? Will you rattle your head and see if there is any pebble in it which we could wander away and play at Marbles[2] with? We want something for Household Words, and I want to escape from myself. For, when I *do* start up and stare myself seedily in the face, as happens to be my case at present, my blankness is inconceivable—indescribable—my misery, amazing.[3]

I shall be in town on Monday. Shall we talk then? Shall we talk at Gad's hill? *What* shall we do? As I close this, I am on my way back by train.

Ever Faithfully

CD.

To THE EDITOR OF *THE TIMES*, [?31 AUGUST–1 SEPTEMBER 1857]

Text from *The Times*, 2 Sep 57. *Date:* final draft as agreed at meeting of Fund Committee (see below).

IN REMEMBRANCE OF THE LATE MR. DOUGLAS JERROLD.

Sir,

The work we have carried on being now brought to a close, we beg leave, through your columns, briefly to make its result known to the public.

We have first to observe that the committee whom we represent decided in the outset to state no case and to make no appeal or representation beyond the line which forms the heading of the present letter. They considered that in taking this course they had a due regard both to the independence of literature and to the personal character of their deceased friend; and therefore they have never for a moment deviated from it, nor do they now depart from it.

They have considered their personal responsibility a sufficient refutation of any untrue and preposterous statements that have obtained circulation as to property asserted to have been left by Mr. Jerrold,[4] and they now merely add that, unless they

[1] CD had contributed nothing since 1 Aug, and only one article since June, which evidently caused a drop in circulation. Collins had three historical articles in July and Aug and must have already supplied the three published on 5, 19 and 26 Sep. Those of 5 and 26 Sep seem to be related to personal experience.

[2] Possibly in the low slang sense.

[3] Perhaps the first sign of his infatuation with Ellen and Maria Ternan: see *To* Miss Coutts, 5 Sep.

[4] Letters of Administration were granted on 31 July to his widow Mary Anne (née Swann), then living at Greville Place, Kilburn Priory: his "Goods, Chattels and Credits" were valued at £3,500 (Public Record Office); but, of course, there were debts to be met. On 13 Sep Blanchard Jerrold published a statement in *Lloyd's*

had thoroughly known, and beyond all doubt assured themselves that their exertions were needed by the dearest objects of Mr. Jerrold's love, those exertions would never have been heard of.

The audited accounts show that the various performances, readings, and lectures have realized, after the payment of all expenses, a clear profit of 2,000*l.* This sum is to be expended in the purchase (through trustees) of a Government annuity for Mrs. Jerrold and her unmarried daughter, with the remainder to the survivor.[1]

We are happy to add, in conclusion, that, although we have been most generously assisted on many hands, and especially by members of the musical profession, we have never consciously accepted a sacrifice that could not be afforded, and have furnished good employment and just remuneration to many deserving persons.

We are, Sir, your faithful servants,

CHARLES DICKENS, Chairman.
ARTHUR W. W. SMITH, Hon. Secretary.[2]

To RICHARD BENTLEY, 1 SEPTEMBER 1857*

MS Berg Collection.

Gad's Hill Place | Tuesday Evening | First September 1857

My Dear Mr. Bentley

I had so much to do before leaving town this afternoon, that I omitted to answer your letter. If it will suit you to come to the Household Words office on Friday at 2

Weekly London Newspaper, which he edited; it had obviously circulated earlier. In it he referred to "fifty rumours, one and all erroneous", which had "cast false light" on his father's character, and denied that his family needed charity. His father, he wrote, had left £3,000, together with £100 p.a. from the copyright of his plays. His father's family, moreover, would have helped his mother and sister, had it been necessary. With reference to the "Remembrance" performances, he had "declined emphatically to receive anything that should wear the appearance of a charity—such charity being needless". He had been distinctly assured that they would be in honour of his father's name, and be "offered as an addition to his estate". He thanked his "earnest friends" for their "zeal and kind intentions"; but made it clear to the public that there was no "need to pass the hat round—however gracefully—in the name of Douglas Jerrold". The *Era*, 20 Sep, commented unfavourably on the "tardiness" of this statement, made after the Remembrance performances; and characterised his acceptance of the Fund not as charity, but as an "addition to his father's estate", as a "jargon of words", "juggling with the facts". Of CD's efforts, it wrote that his "conduct stands as a monument to his friendship and perseverance".

[1] Jerrold's widow, Mary Ann, died on 6 May 59, at Fairfield Farm, near Broadstairs; her estate was under £1,000 and Letters of Administration were granted to her son (MS Central Registry of Wills, Somerset House). Her unmarried daughter, also Mary Ann, who died on 30 Mar 1910, left the capital of the Fund to Christ Church, Oxford, to found a "Douglas Jerrold Scholarship in English Literature".

[2] Although signed by them both, the letter was written by CD, as the minutes of a meeting of the Jerrold Fund committee held to approve it (clearly in late Aug) make clear (Minutes in CD's hand, MS Private). CD's draft was agreed to, after "some discussion and a few minor alterations". It was also decided that a copy of the letter should be sent to Mrs Jerrold. Besides *The Times*, the *Morning Chronicle*, *Morning Herald* and *Daily News* (and no doubt other newspapers) published it on 2 Sep. In addition to CD and Arthur Smith, the other committee members present were Lemon, Shirley Brooks, Edward Lloyd (1815–90; *DNB*; founder of *Lloyd's Weekly London Newspaper*, ed. Douglas Jerrold 1852–7), Wilkie Collins, Forster, Wills and Maclise.

(as I shall assume it will, unless I hear from you to the contrary), Mr. Shirley Brooks will meet you there; and we will endeavour to conclude the business[1] there and then, fairly to all.

Faithfully Yours

Richard Bentley Esquire. CHARLES DICKENS

To JOHN FORSTER, [?1 SEPTEMBER 1857]

Extract in F, VIII, i, 630. *Date:* soon after meeting Collins (see *To* Collins, 29 Aug).

I have arranged with Collins that he and I will start next Monday on a ten or twelve days' expedition to out-of-the-way places, to do (in inns and coast-corners) a little tour in search of an article and in avoidance of railroads.[2] I must get a good name for it, and I propose it in five articles, one for the beginning of every number in the October part.[3]

To HANS CHRISTIAN ANDERSEN, 2 SEPTEMBER 1857

MS Royal Library, Copenhagen.

Gad's Hill Place, Higham, by Rochester
Wednesday Second September 1857

My Dear Andersen.

I have been away from here—at Manchester—which is the cause of this slow and late reply to your two welcome letters.[4]

You are in your own home again by this time; happy to see its familiar face, I do not doubt; and happy in being received with open arms by all good Danish men, women, and children.

Everything here, goes on as usual. Baby (too large for his name, this long while!) calls "Aunty" all over the house, and the dogs come dancing about us and go running down the green lanes before us, as they used to do when you were here. But the days are shorter, and the evenings darker, and when we go up to the Monument to see the Sunset, we are obliged to go directly after dinner, and it gets dark while we are up there, and as we pass the grim dog who rattles his chain, we can hardly see his dim old eyes as we feed him with biscuit. The workmen who have been digging in that well in the Stable Yard so long, have found a great spring of clear bright water,

[1] For the Agreement of 4 Sep (signed by Brooks and Bentley, witnessed by CD), see Appx E. Bentley had previously published *Aspen Court* with etchings by Leech in *Bentley's Miscellany*, 1853–5, and in 3 vols in June 1855. The cheap edn was published Oct 57; 4,720 copies were sold by Apr 1858, when Brooks received a cheque for £39.6.8.

[2] As in Collins's *Rambles beyond Railways* (in Cornwall), 1851.

[3] i.e. the monthly part of *HW*, combining the five weekly parts of 3 to 31 Oct.

[4] On 1 Aug Andersen had written a long letter of thanks for his visit: "My visit to England, my sojourn with you, is a highlight in my life. . . . I realized every minute that you were good to me, that you were pleased to see me and were my friend"; ending "Forget in friendship the dark side which proximity may have shown you in me. I would so much like to live in good remembrance by one whom I love as a friend and brother" (given in Elias Bredsdorff, *Hans Christian Andersen*, pp. 216–17). His second letter has not apparently survived.

and they got rather drunk when they found it (not with the water, but with some Gin I gave them), and then they packed up their tools and went away, and now the big dog and the Raven have all that place to themselves. The corn-fields that were golden when you were here, are ploughed up brown; the hops are being picked; the leaves on the trees are just beginning to turn; and the rain is falling as I write—very sadly—very steadily.

We have just closed our labors in remembrance of poor Jerrold, and have raised for his widow and daughter, Two Thousand Pounds. On Monday I am going away (with Collins) for a fortnight or so, into odd corners of England, to write some descriptions for Household Words. When I come back, I shall find them dining here by lamplight. And when I come back, I will write to you again.[1]

I never meet any of the friends whom you saw here, but they always say "How's Andersen—Where's Andersen"—and I draw imaginary pictures of where you are, and declare that you desired to be heartily remembered to them. They are always pleased to be told this. I told old Jerdan so,.the other day, when he wrote to me asking when he was to come and see you!—

All the house send you their kind regard. Baby says you shall not be put out of window when you come back. I have read To Be or Not To Be, and think it a very fine book—full of a good purpose admirably wrought out—a book in every way worthy of its great author.[2]

Ever My Dear Andersen | Affectionately Your friend

Hans Christian Andersen CHARLES DICKENS

[1] Andersen replied immediately to this letter with the same gratitude and cordiality as before (see Bredsdorff, above, p. 217); but CD did not answer it, nor several letters that Andersen subsequently wrote, including letters of introduction for two of his Danish friends. In the extended edn of his autobiography, *Mit Livs Eventyr* (written 1868–9), Andersen wrote of his relationship with CD: "Later, letters came more seldom, in the last few years none at all. 'Done with! Done with!' and that's what happens to all stories!" (Bredsdorff, *ibid.*). They did not meet again. Bredsdorff's explanation for CD's silence may well be right. In Aug 60, *Bentley's Miscellany* (XVIII, 181) reviewed a sketch by Andersen, "A Visit to Charles Dickens in the Summer of 1857", from his collection in German, *Aus Herz und Welt*. The review contained many quotations about CD's happy family life and gave unstinted praise to Catherine (Andersen knew nothing of the real state of affairs in 1857); and Andersen was criticized for "the way in which he had betrayed private confidence" (p. 185). If CD, as is probable, saw this review, it would certainly have made him angry with Andersen. See Bredsdorff, above, p. 218.

[2] *To Be or Not to Be*, a mixture of novel and religious tract, transl. by Mrs Bushby, May 1857 and dedicated to CD "by his sincere friend Hans Christian Andersen". An unfavourable review of its religious direction—"In one word, the book is dangerous", despite being "charmingly written"—in the *Athenaeum* (27 June 57) had greatly upset Andersen—it "lay upon my heart like a nightmare", he recorded in his diary—and only CD had been able to cheer him up: "I told him of it, and he took me in his arms, pressed a kiss upon my cheek and spoke most kindly, bade me feel how immensely much God had given me, how great was my vocation—these are his words, which I repeat; he bade me, like himself, never read newspaper notices; 'they are forgotten in a week, but your book will live!' We walked up Gad's Hill, he scratched with his foot in the sand. 'That is criticism,' he said, and stroked over it with his foot: 'Gone!—But that which God has given you, that will remain!'" (Andersen *to* Henriette Wulff, given in Bredsdorff, above, p. 213).

To HENRY AUSTIN, 2 SEPTEMBER 1857†

MS Morgan Library.

Gad's Hill Place | Wednesday Second September 1857

My Dear Henry.

[a]Thanks for your note of yesterday. Nye understands, I suppose, that the new Water Closet is to be made?[a]

The Second Conspirator has been here this morning, to ask whether you wish the Windlass to be left in the Yard, and whether you will want him and his Mate any more, and if so when? Of course he says (rolling something in the form of a pellet, in at one broken tooth all the while, and rolling it out at another), that they could wish fur to have the Windlass if it wasn't any ways a hill conwenience fur to fetch her away. I have told him that if he will come back on Friday, he shall have your reply. Will you therefore send it me by return of Post? He says he'll "look up" (as if he was an Astronomer) a' Friday arterdinner.

On Monday I am going away with Collins for ten days or a fortnight, on a "Tour in Search of an Article" for Household Words. We have not the least idea where we are going, but *he* says "let's look at the Norfolk Coast", and *I* say, "let's look at the back of the Atlantic". I don't quite know what I mean by that; but I have a general impression that I mean something knowing.[1]

I am horribly used up after the Jerrold business. Low spirits, low pulse, low voice, intense reaction. If I were not, like Mr. Micawber, "falling back for a spring"[2] on Monday, I think I should slink into a corner and cry.

Ever affectionately

CD.

To COLIN RAE BROWN,[3] 2 SEPTEMBER 1857

MS Burns Memorial Museum and Library, Kilmarnock.

Tavistock House, London
Wednesday Second September 1857

Dear Sir

I am favored with your letter, dated on the 31st. of August.

There must necessarily be a limit to such great personal exertion and fatigue, as I and my associate friends have lately undergone in the cause which enlists your generous sympathy. The bound I appointed in the beginning, was the realization of two thousand pounds profit. That point having happily been reached, we have

[aa] Omitted in MDGH, II, 28 and N.

[1] See *To* Forster, same day.

[2] "You find me, fallen back, for a spring" (*Copperfield*, Ch. 27).

[3] Colin Rae Brown (1821–97), born in Greenock; journalist and poet; ed. the *Scottish Annual*, Glasgow, 1859; manager of the *Glasgow Daily Bulletin*, the first daily penny newspaper in Britain, 1855–61. Played leading part in raising monuments to Sir William Wallace, Burns, Scott, etc. Founded Burns Club 1868. Published *Lyrics of Sea and Shore*, 1848, dedicated to De Quincey, *Lays and Lyrics*, 1859, and other poems; *Ethel Dewar; or Glimpses of Scottish Life and Manners in the Nineteenth Century*, 3 vols, 1875.

audited the accounts, formally closed the business, and—as to this effort—parted company.

Dear Sir | Your faithful Servant

C. R. Brown Esquire CHARLES DICKENS

To JOHN FORSTER, [?2 SEPTEMBER 1857]

Extract in F, VIII, i, 631. *Date:* "next day" after *To* Forster, 1 Sep, according to Forster.

Our decision is for a foray upon the fells of Cumberland; I having discovered in the books[1] some promising moors and bleak places thereabouts.

To MRS OWEN,[2] 2 SEPTEMBER 1857

MS Benoliel Collection.

Gad's Hill Place, Higham, by Rochester
Wednesday Second September 1857

My Dear Mrs. Owen

Your pleasantest of letters finds me here, stopping to breathe after the fatigues of the last two months: which have been on the whole as great as I have ever undergone, and which have left me, for the moment, just a little dashed. However, we have happily gained the limit I prescribed to myself in setting out—we have raised Two Thousand Pounds—and our success has been enormous.

On Monday I am going away for a run to certain out of the way places in opposite corners of the Map of England, with an eye to Household Words. It is probable that I shall not be back here, until September is far advanced. I shall then have to give myself up for a week or two to some friends who are coming, and then the dreary leaves will begin to fall and my wintry plans will gather about me.

So I am afraid I shall not see the old house[3] *this* summer. But you describe it so wonderfully well, that I seem to have seen it already, and to be perfectly acquainted with it. That—and your, and Owen's remembrance of me—are my consolation.

With kindest regard to him and to your son,[4] in which all here join, Believe me

Always Most Faithfully Yours

Mrs. Owen. CHARLES DICKENS

[1] *Beauties of England and Wales*, according to Forster (F, VIII, i, 631); by John Britton, E. W. Brayley and others (26 vols, 1801–15). CD had bought the set on 30 Dec 39 (Vol. I, p. 621*n*). Cumberland is in Vol. III.

[2] Née Caroline Amelia Clift (*d.* 1873), daughter of the naturalist, William Clift (1775–1849; *DNB*); married Richard Owen 1835.

[3] According to the Rev. Richard Owen, *Life of Richard Owen*, 1894, II, 65*n*, "An old house in Mortlake which CD had said he would like to see." Glossed as "Cromwell House" on MS in unknown hand: a manor-house belonging to Thomas Cromwell, Earl of Essex (?1485–1540), later demolished, according to Maxwell Fraser, *Surrey*, 1975, p. 32 (also claimed as once the residence of Oliver Cromwell).

[4] William Owen (1837–86); educated at Westminster; studied in Germany; 1869 clerk in Foreign Office. Contributed "A German Table d'Hote" to *HW*, 15 Dec 55 (XII, 478); according to Kitton, CD requested it after reading it at Owen's father's and presented him with a complete set of *HW* up to then (F. G. Kitton, *CD by Pen and Pencil*, Suppl., p. 37). Drowned at Kingston, Surrey.

To THE MASTER OF THE ANGEL HOTEL, DONCASTER,[1] 3 SEPTEMBER 1857*

MS Dickens House. *Address:* To | The Master of | The Angel Hotel | Doncaster | Yorkshire.

Tavistock House, London | Thursday Third September | 1857.

Mr. Charles Dickens sends his compliments to the Master of the Angel Hotel at Doncaster, and begs to say that he purposes coming to Doncaster with a friend (Mr. Wilkie Collins) on Sunday the Thirteenth, and that he wishes to engage at the Angel on that day, a sitting room and two bedrooms.

Mr. Dickens is not certain that he may remain all through the race week; but if he can have these apartments, he is quite willing to engage them for the whole time, whether he leaves before the end of the week or no.

As Mr. Dickens leaves London for some other places on Monday Morning next, he begs to receive a line in reply to this, by return of post.[2]

To PETER CUNNINGHAM, 3 SEPTEMBER 1857*

MS Yale University Library.

Gad's Hill Place | Thursday Third September 1857

My Dear Cunningham

I have thought over that riddle, and I fancy I have got it.

It is quite clear that no bargain can be fairly sold, without *a Selling*
That is the first thing:

The Second is, *a Band*
The Third is, Box

And this gives you for the answer

A Sell in a Bandbox.[3]

Ever Faithfully
CD.

To JOHN FORSTER, [?3 SEPTEMBER 1857]

Extract in F, VIII, ii, 640. *Date: To* Forster, 5 Sep, answers Forster's reply to this; therefore about two days before it.

Your letter of yesterday[4] was so kind and hearty, and sounded so gently the many chords we have touched together, that I cannot leave it unanswered, though I have not much (to any purpose) to say. My reference to "confidences" was merely to the

[1] Thomas Pye, Manager of the Angel Inn and Posting House, 3 Frenchgate, Doncaster.

[2] The first evidence that the Doncaster visit was planned early, probably as soon as he knew the Ternans were engaged there. In Ch. 9 of the "Lazy Tour" he pretends that the visit only occurred to himself and Collins on 9 Sep.

[3] Perhaps in the low slang phrase, "my arse to a bandbox", meaning "that won't do" because too small for a seat.

[4] Answering, says Forster, a "previous expression of his wish for some confidences as in the old time". "I give only", he adds, "what is strictly necessary to account for what followed, and even this with deep reluctance" (F, VIII, ii, 640).

relief of saying a word of what has long been pent up in my mind. Poor Catherine and I are not made for each other, and there is no help for it. It is not only that she makes me uneasy and unhappy, but that I make her so too—and much more so. She is exactly what you know, in the way of being amiable and complying; but we are strangely ill-assorted for the bond there is between us. God knows she would have been a thousand times happier if she had married another kind of man, and that her avoidance of this destiny would have been at least equally good for us both. I am often cut to the heart by thinking what a pity it is, for her own sake, that I ever fell in her way; and if I were sick or disabled to-morrow, I know how sorry she would be, and how deeply grieved myself, to think how we had lost each other. But exactly the same incompatibility would arise, the moment I was well again; and nothing on earth could make her understand me, or suit us to each other. Her temperament will not go with mine. It mattered not so much when we had only ourselves to consider, but reasons have been growing since which make it all but hopeless that we should even try to struggle on. What is now befalling me I have seen steadily coming, ever since the days you remember when Mary was born;[1] and I know too well that you cannot, and no one can, help me. Why I have even written I hardly know; but it is a miserable sort of comfort that you should be clearly aware how matters stand. The mere mention of the fact, without any complaint or blame of any sort, is a relief to my present state of spirits—and I can get this only from you, because I can speak of it to no one else.

To MRS BROWN, 4 SEPTEMBER 1857

MS Morgan Library. *Address:* Favored by W. H. Wills Esquire. | Mrs. Brown.

OFFICE OF HOUSEHOLD WORDS,
Friday Fourth September 1857

My Dear Mrs. Brown.

The Postman put your letter, so full of warm heart and interest, in my hands this morning, as I was driving from Gad's Hill to the Railway Station, to come up to town. A thousand thanks for it.

Yes. When I wrote to you, I certainly was exactly in the state you describe. It belongs to such a life as mine, and is its penalty. Thank God while I have health and activity, it does not last long: so after a miserable day or two, I have come out of the dark corner into the Sun again.

Mr. Wills reporting a stimulus to be necessary to Household Words (and the Pump being fitted at this moment in the stable yard, where the newly-driven-out workmen have re-appeared like Mice), I am off, on a wild tour with Wilkie Collins, to write a gossiping description of all that we see and all that we don't see, under the title of The Tour of the Two Idle Apprentices. We start on Sunday night or Monday Morning, and have not the least idea where we are going to. I have a vague notion of the Cumberland Fells, and the Irish look-out on the Atlantic with the winter driving

[1] Mary (Mamey) Dickens was born on 6 Mar 38; there is no sign whatever of their incompatibility at that date, or for long after. Vol. III gives new evidence of their happy relationship in the early 1840s: see Preface, pp. xi–xii.

up—but it's of the most shadowy kind—and we may be at the top of Snowdon instead, in no time.

So according to your account of your movements, I shall not see either of you for another while. I shall not think the less of both.

O the good dog! And what a good thing of the Almighty to shew us our best qualities, moving our own affections and winning our own regard, in these little shapes about us that love and honor us so much!

With most affectionate remembrance to Miss Coutts,

Ever Dear Mrs. Brown | Your faithful friend
CHARLES DICKENS[1]

To MRS CORNELIUS, 4 SEPTEMBER 1857

Text from N, II, 876.

OFFICE OF HOUSEHOLD WORDS,
Friday, Fourth September 1857

My Dear Anne,

Enclosed is a letter from Miss Hogarth about something she wants. Will you send it back by the Bearer, and also my strong lace-up half boots, which I think are on the boot-shelf in the front pantry.

Faithfully Yours
[CHARLES DICKENS]

To DR J. SHERIDAN MUSPRATT,[2] 4 SEPTEMBER 1857*

MS Judd School, Kent.

OFFICE OF HOUSEHOLD WORDS,
Friday Fourth September 1857

My Dear Dr. Muspratt.

There is no copy to be had, of the Frozen Deep. It is not printed, and nothing of it is in existence but the Draft Book.[3]

I am sorry that at this time I know no one in Calcutta. My second boy was there the other day—or is there now—but whither he will be sent, in these distracted Indian times,[4] it is impossible to calculate.

I write in the most hasty way, as I am leaving town directly.

Faithfully Yours
CHARLES DICKENS

With kind regard to Mrs. Muspratt, and all the house.

[1] Letter endorsed in another hand: "Sepr 4th. 57 With Little Dorrit".

[2] Dr James Sheridan Muspratt (1821–71; *DNB*), of Liverpool, industrial chemist; secretary of the local committee which arranged CD's Amateurs' Liverpool performances in July 47: see Vol. V, p. 126*n*.

[3] See *To* Maclise, 8 July 57, *fn*.

[4] The massacre at Cawnpore had taken place on 27 June; Lucknow was still under siege. Walter was to fight at both places: see *To* Spencer Boyle, 5 Feb 58, *fn*.

To MISS BURDETT COUTTS, 5 SEPTEMBER 1857

MS Morgan Library.

Gad's Hill Place | Saturday Fifth September 1857

My Dear Miss Coutts

I think I would head the paper

An independent and useful career for young women of the Middle Classes.[1]

—such a heading as that, something to that effect, arrests the attention directly. So much Boredom, and Red Tape, and what I may call Kayshuttleworry,[2] are associated with the word "Education", that I fear it might repel readers.

The paper itself is very good indeed. Very plain, very easily remembered, very direct to the purpose.

Apprehensive, like Mrs. Brown, of the moist valleys, I have decided on a foray into the bleak fells of Cumberland. So the idle apprentices go to Carlisle on Monday.

Sometimes of late, when I have been very much excited by the crying of two thousand people over the grave of Richard Wardour, new ideas for a story have come into my head as I lay on the ground,[3] with surprising force and brilliancy. Last night, being quiet here, I noted them down in a little book I keep.[4] When I went into the dining room and mentioned what I had been doing, they all called out "*Friday*!" I was born on a Friday, and it is a most astonishing coincidence that I have never in my life, whatever projects I may have determined on, otherwise—never begun a book, or begun any thing of interest to me, or done any thing of importance to me, but it was on a Friday. I am certain to be brought round to Friday. It *must* have been on a Friday that I first dined with you at Mr. Marjoribanks's!

Mentioning Richard Wardour,—perhaps Mr. Wills has not told you how much impressed I was at Manchester by the womanly tenderness of a very gentle and good little girl who acted Mary's part.[5] She came to see the Play beforehand at the Gallery of Illustration, and when we rehearsed it, she said "I am afraid, Mr. Dickens, I shall never be able to bear it; it affected me so much when I saw it, that I hope you will excuse my trembling this morning, for I am afraid of myself." At night when she came out of the cave and Wardour recognized her, I never saw any thing like the distress and agitation of her face—a very good little pale face, with large black eyes;—it had a natural emotion in it (though it was turned away from the audience) which was quite a study of expression. But when she had to kneel over Wardour dying, and be taken leave of, the tears streamed out of her eyes into his

[1] Title underlined with short double strokes. Miss Coutts's paper has not been discovered; no doubt it was related to her *Summary Account of Prizes for Common Things*, 1856, of which a new edn had recently been published, emphasising the importance of trained teachers of domestic subjects.

[2] See *To* Miss Coutts, 11 July and 9 Dec 56.

[3] Cf. the Preface to *A Tale of Two Cities*, 1859.

[4] Presumably his *Book of Memoranda*, for possible use in later novels, begun in Jan 55: see F, IX, vii, 747, and edn by Fred Kaplan, NYPL, 1981. There are in fact no entries that connect specifically with Wardour or the themes of *The Frozen Deep*; but Kaplan may be right in thinking that entry No. 67, p. 14, "Representing London—or Paris, or any other great city—in the new light of being utterly unknown to all the people in the story", was an idea that occurred to him at this time.

[5] Clara Burnham, the heroine, the part taken over by Maria Ternan from Mamie Dickens.

mouth, down his beard, all over his rags—down his arms as he held her by the hair.[1] At the same time she sobbed as if she were breaking her heart, and was quite convulsed with grief. It was of no use for the compassionate Wardour to whisper "My dear child, it will be over in two minutes—there is nothing the matter—don't be so distressed!" She could only sob out, "O! It's so sad, O it's so sad!' and set Mr. Lemon (the softest hearted of men) crying too. By the time the Curtain fell, we were all crying together, and then her mother[2] and sister[3] used to come and put her in a chair and comfort her, before taking her away to be dressed for the Farce. I told her on the last night that I was sure she had one of the most genuine and feeling hearts in the world; and I don't think I ever saw any thing more prettily simple and unaffected. Yet I remember her on the stage, a little child, and I dare say she was born in a country theatre.[4]

[1] The *Leader* (10 Jan 57) had described CD's first public performance as Wardour as "fearfully fine", especially "the appalling misery and supreme emotion of the dying Scene". Berger, in 1891, thought it surpassed anything he had seen on the professional stage.

[2] Frances Eleanor Ternan (1803–73; *DNB*), actress, eldest daughter of John Jarman, prompter at Theatre Royal, York, and his second wife, Martha Maria Mottershed, actress. Born at Hull; played juvenile roles from May 1815; London debut in Covent Garden, Feb 1827, as Juliet to Charles Kemble's Romeo. Alternated between London and provinces in over 20 leading roles for next four years. Acted with T. L. Ternan in Edinburgh 1831 and married him 21 Sep 1834. Thomas Lawless Ternan (?1799–1846), was eldest son of Michael Ternan, grocer and wine-merchant, of Dublin, and Susanna Lawless, daughter of a well-known brewer, also of Dublin; had some success as an actor in Dublin, Edinburgh and the English provinces; began successfully as a lessee-manager in Newcastle, Doncaster and Sheffield, 1839–44; but finally lost money; made his last stage appearance in Newcastle Dec 1844. Taken to the Insane Asylum at Bethnal Green in 1845 and treated for general paralysis of the insane (i.e. syphilis); he died on 17 Oct 46 (but did not commit suicide, as stated by Malcolm Morley in "The Theatrical Ternans", *D*, LIV [1958], 103). The Ternans left for America 22 Sep 34, played together for $2\frac{1}{2}$ years, followed by a tour in Canada. Returned to England early 1837 for birth of second daughter, Maria. Frances played many Shakespearean roles in Drury Lane and provinces, under Macready, Phelps and Kean 1846–56. After acting at Manchester in 1857 virtually retired from stage, to look after her daughters in London. Portraits of Thomas Lawless and Frances Eleanor Ternan, *c.* 1840, are given in Katharine M. Longley, "The Real Ellen Ternan", *D*, LXXXI (1985), 28 and 29. See later vols.

[3] Ellen Lawless Ternan (1839–1914), known almost always as Nelly, later Mrs George Wharton Robinson; youngest daughter of Thomas and Frances Eleanor Ternan; actress; born at Rochester 3 Mar 39 at home of her uncle, William Ternan, prosperous barge-owner. First appeared on stage aged three in Kotzebue's *The Stranger* at Sheffield, 15 Nov 42; then with her sister Maria as the little princes in *Richard III*; for her career as a child-actress in London and the provinces 1843–55, see Malcolm Morley, "The Theatrical Ternans, Part II", *D*, LIV (1958), 100–4. In Spring 55 settled in Park Cottage, Northampton Park, Islington, with her mother and two sisters; her first adult role was the young man Hippomenes in Francis Talfourd's burlesque, *Atalanta*, Apr–July 57, at the Haymarket. Met CD in July 57 when invited, through Alfred Wigan, Manager of the Olympic, to play Lucy Crayford in *The Frozen Deep* and Eliza in *Uncle John*, at Manchester. See also Claire Tomalin, *The Invisible Woman*, 1990.

[4] Maria Ternan had played her first juvenile role, at the age of three, in the Theatre Royal, Newcastle, on 25 Mar 1840, as the child of Cora in Sheridan's *Pizarro*; continued to play juvenile roles in the provinces, with her mother and elder sister Fanny, showing a comic talent (e.g., as Tom Thumb in Kane O'Hara's burlesque). CD may have seen her last appearance as a child as Little Pickle in Mrs Jordan's *The Spoiled Child*, at Drury Lane on 8 Feb 1850, when she was 12.

Very pleasant to know, I submit to you and Mrs. Brown? And if you ever see, at Kean's[1] or elsewhere, Miss Maria Ternan,[2] that is the young lady.

Dear Miss Coutts | Ever most Faithfully & affecy. Yours

Miss Burdett Coutts. CHARLES DICKENS

To ROBERT DUDLEY,[3] 5 SEPTEMBER 1857

Extract in Myers & Co. catalogue, 1952; dated 5 Sep 57.

Thanking him for a photograph of the spirited and accurate sketch.[4]

To JOHN FORSTER, [5 SEPTEMBER 1857]

Extracts in F, VIII, ii, 640–1; iii, 653 and ii, 641. *Date:* all three 5 Sep, according to Forster.

To the most part of what you say[5]—Amen! You are not so tolerant as perhaps you might be of the wayward and unsettled feeling which is part (I suppose) of the tenure on which one holds an imaginative life, and which I have, as you ought to know well, often only kept down by riding over it like a dragoon—but let that go by. I make no maudlin complaint. I agree with you as to the very possible incidents, even not less bearable than mine, that might and must often occur to the married condition when it is entered into very young. I am always deeply sensible of the wonderful exercise I have of life and its highest sensations, and have said to myself for years, and have honestly and truly felt, This is the drawback to such a career, and is not to be complained of. I say it and feel it now as strongly as ever I did; and, as I told you in my last, I do not with that view put all this forward. But the years have not made it easier to bear for either of us; and, for her sake as well as mine, the wish will force itself upon me that something might be done. I know too well it is impossible. There is the fact, and that is all one can say. Nor are you to suppose that I disguise from myself what might be urged on the other side. I claim no immunity from blame. There is plenty of fault on my side, I dare say, in the way of a thousand uncertainties, caprices, and difficulties of disposition; but only one thing will alter all that, and that is, the end which alters everything.

[1] Both Maria and Ellen Ternan had been members of Kean's company since 1854.

[2] Maria Susanna Ternan (1837–1904), second daughter of Thomas Lawless and Frances Eleanor Ternan; actress, later, artist, traveller and journalist; known all her life in the family as "Mia". After her career as a child-actress 1840–50, played Jessica in *The Merchant of Venice* (Jan 1855) at the Princess's Theatre, under Kean and many comedies, including Charles Dance's *A Wonderful Woman*. For her parts in Doncaster that Sep, see *To* Georgina Hogarth, 15 Sep, *fn*. For her many operatic appearances as a contralto in the provinces, with her sister Fanny, see next vol.; and, for her marriage and later career as a journalist, principally in Rome, see later vols. Portrait-photograph on stage given in *D*, LV (Winter 1949), 41.

[3] Robert Dudley (*d.* 1893), illustrator and lithographer from 1858 (contributed that year to *Illustrated London News*); illustrated, with frontispiece and vignette, *Such is Life*, dedicated to CD by "Doubleyou", i.e. William Wilson. Later, painter, mainly of genre pictures and landscapes, exhibiting at RA 1866–89.

[4] No doubt of one of the scenes in *The Frozen Deep* or *Uncle John* at Manchester, possibly for a Manchester newspaper.

[5] Forster introduces this extract with the words "his rejoinder to my reply".

Hop-picking is going on, and people sleep in the garden, and breathe in at the keyhole of the house door. I have been amazed, before this year, by the number of miserable lean wretches, hardly able to crawl, who go hop-picking. I find it is a superstition that the dust of the newly picked hop, falling freshly into the throat, is a cure for consumption. So the poor creatures drag themselves along the roads, and sleep under wet hedges, and get cured soon and finally.

What do you think of my paying for this place, by reviving that old idea of some Readings from my books. I am very strongly tempted. Think of it.[1]

To W. J. SORRELL,[2] 5 SEPTEMBER 1857*

MS Free Library of Philadelphia.

Gad's Hill Place | Saturday Fifth September 1857

My Dear Mr. Sorrell

Many thanks for your note and the photograph. I write by this same post to the Artist,[3] thanking him for his gift.

I am happy to report my face quite well for the time being, and myself in a less despairing condition than at the close of our labors.

Faithfully Yours always

W. J. Sorrell Esquire CHARLES DICKENS

To J. B. BUCKSTONE, [6 SEPTEMBER 1857]

Mention in *To* Wills, 6 Sep.

Sending him the MS of Douglas Jerrold's play, "The Spendthrift".[4]

[1] Both now and in 1858 Forster strongly opposed the proposal. "It was a substitution of lower for higher aims; a change to commonplace from more elevated pursuits; and it had so much of the character of a public exhibition for money as to raise, in the question of respect for his calling as a writer, a question also of respect for himself as a gentleman" (F, VIII, ii, 641).

[2] Clearly a personal friend and almost certainly William J. Sorrell, dramatist and miscellaneous writer. Wrote eight plays, two in collaboration; also, under the pseudonym "Christian Le Ros", a Christmas book for 1853, illustrated by Phiz, its dedication dated from Gray's Inn; and "Drawing Room Theatricals" [1866]. Contributed "A Discursive Mind" to *HW* (14 Nov 57, XVI, 477); its use of Lamb and Hazlitt would appeal to CD.

[3] See *To* Dudley, same day.

[4] A romantic comedy written 1838–9 for Macready, but not performed until 1850 (at the Olympic 3 May) and not published. Walter Jerrold gives the opening comic scene; the serious scenes were in blank verse (*Douglas Jerrold: Dramatist and Wit*, 1918, I, 311–12).

To F. M. EVANS, 6 SEPTEMBER 1857*

MS Free Library of Philadelphia.

Gad's Hill Place | Sunday Sixth September 1857

My Dear Evans

I am very glad to get the accounts, and I think they come out very well indeed.[1]

The payment of £1000 on the 16th., and of the remaining £1,317.11.1 on the 16th. of next month, will suit me quite well.[2]

You do not mention whether you have yet done any thing with Collins as to the Dead Secret,[3] and the £200 bill. I want to set the latter against Walter's outfit: to say nothing of the improvements of this place, and the Well—into which last-mentioned gulf, a good deal of ready money has fallen.

It is clear that we ought to republish the Child's History.[4] In estimating and considering about that, during the next ten days or a fortnight while I am away, I wish you would also give your thoughts for a little while, to the following kindred subject.

Forster has a strong impression that my copyrights are not turned to anything like the account that the time demands; and he sets particular store by the fact that there is no good edition of them for the better class of readers who would buy them for well-furnished bookshelves. I did not at first take his view of the matter when he propounded it to me, but I have gradually come to the conclusion that he is right; and not only that there is money to be made, but that good is to be done, to the place and station (so to speak) of my writings. The question is, in what form, and at what price, and how as to periods and regular intervals, such an Edition could be best devised. It might comprise a selection from the original Illustrations (a few of the best of them), or it might have none. It should be handsome to look at, and easy to read.[5]

If you could make a good project on paper, I have no doubt Chapman would be very glad to jump at any reasonable proposal I might make to him. The result might be very beneficial to all of us, and the course of such an issue of my books, would keep me well before the public, without wasting me—which is a consideration, with an eye to the future.[6]

Now, supposing you able to knock out a scheme which we could settle in a careful interview when I come back, I would not let the grass grow under the plan, but would work Chapman directly, so that we might begin before Christmas.

But this will not interfere with our republication of the Child's History, which, as a Child's book, is still to be considered by itself.

[1] Bradbury & Evans's half-yearly accounts to 30 June 57 showed £3,817.11.1 owed to CD (including £3,612.9.3 for *Little Dorrit*. (MS V & A.)

[2] After payment of £250 a month for six months, CD was owed £2,317.11.1. The payments were made as specified (CD's Account-book, MS Messrs Coutts).

[3] See *To* Mrs Watson, 8 Mar 57 and *fn*.

[4] See *To* Evans, 15 Sep and *fn*. Nothing came of this plan.

[5] The upshot was the Library edition, in 22 vols, 1858–9, eventually 30 vols 1858–70, published under the imprint of both Chapman & Hall and Bradbury & Evans; earlier vols had a vignette title-page unsigned (by H. K. Browne).

[6] The Library edition was not, in fact, a financial success. By June 58, after publication of the first seven vols and sales of 11,300, it showed a deficit of £305. This rose during the next two years and was not worked off until Oct 61, when, after sales that half-year of 6,250, CD received £113 (MS V & A).

I shall be glad to hear what you think of this notion, and will beg Wills to let you know (when I know, myself), where you can write to me at the end of the week.

Faithfully Yours always

F. M. Evans Esquire CHARLES DICKENS

To W. H. WILLS, 6 SEPTEMBER 1857

MS Huntington Library.

Gad's Hill Place | Sunday Sixth September 1857

My Dear Wills

MRS. WILLS[1]

I hope is better. I have filled them with sympathy here, by my vivid descriptions of *your* descriptions. They all send loves and messages. Don't forget to let me know how she goes on, when you write.

H.W.

I find in my official drawer, the card of the Writer of some foreign paper I left for you on your table.[2] In case his address should not be attached to the paper, I send the card to you.

JERROLD REMEMBRANCE[1]

In the left hand drawer of my table at the office, is a Roll of the usual Theatrical MS—the Spendthrift,[3] by poor Jerrold. Will you have it put up in a parcel for Buckstone with the enclosed note, and left at the Haymarket Theatre?

THE IDLE APPRENTICES[1]

Go straight to Carlisle, by 9 AM North Western Train on Monday Morning. After casting about a good deal, the Cumberland Fells look promising to them. I will write you one line from Carlisle on Tuesday, giving you any new address we may fix on. Until you have a new address from me, write (if you have occasion to write), to me at the Post Office there—that is to say, at Carlisle.

I[1]

think I am becoming rather inventive again.[4]

Ever Faithfully

CD.

[1] Underlined with short double strokes.

[2] Probably "Indian Irregulars", *HW*, 12 Sep, XVI, 244, the only foreign paper by a writer whose address would not be already known. The unidentified E. Townsend's address would be needed for paying him.

[3] Never performed.

[4] i.e. the writing of what became "The Lazy Tour of Two Idle Apprentices"; possibly also the Christmas No., "The Perils of Certain English Prisoners".

To MISS GEORGINA HOGARTH, 7 SEPTEMBER 1857*

MS Miss Mary Elspeth Milford. *Address:* Miss Hogarth | Gad's Hill Place | Higham | by | Rochester | Kent.

Carlisle. | Monday Night, Seventh September | 1857.

My Dearest Georgy.

On receipt of this, let me know, addressing me "Post Office Maryport,[1] Cumberland", how dear Mamey is, and how you all are; and give me any little scraps of any home news that your genius, and charming room, may inspire. Where we shall be after Friday, I have no idea. But, up to Friday, Maryport will remain our best address. On Sunday night, we purpose arriving at Doncaster, Yorkshire. After that time, the Post Office at that place will be our safe address always.

Collins is anxious that I should report his brown suit,[2] a noble success.+ We are off tomorrow, to the Fells. As yet we have seen nothing whatever, and consider Carlisle a humbug. Kiss everybody and everything for me. I send all sorts of remembrances to both. My love to the Noble Plorn.

There is just time to save the Post coming through from Scotland. We had a delightful journey, and arrived here to the moment.[3]

I have a bedroom here, not quite so large, and not half so airy, as Turk's Kennel.[4] My portmanteau squeezed up against the bed, represents the Raven in it.

Ever Affectionately

Miss Hogarth. CHARLES DICKENS

+But I don't think so.

To W. H. WILLS, 7 SEPTEMBER 1857

MS Huntington Library.

Carlisle. Monday Night, | Seventh September 1857

My Dear Wills.

Conglomeration prevailing in the Maps—and our minds—to an alarming extent, I have the faintest idea of our trip. But I think I am perfectly right in this direction:— You Writing[5] to me from London not later than Wednesday night, address me at the Post office, Maryport, Cumberland. After that, address me at the Post office, Doncaster. I think we shall leave the Maryport (that is to say, the Coast) regions, about Friday or so. We shall not arrive at Doncaster until Sunday night. It is quite uncertain what we may be about, in the interval. Once at Doncaster, the address is always Doncaster until you hear to the contrary.

Of course you will expect Copy (as we agreed) on Saturday Morning.[6]

[1] On the coast, 28 miles south-east of Carlisle terminus of the branch line. Described in *Beauties of England and Wales*, p. 206, as "extremely pleasant"; in the "Lazy Tour", Ch. 2.

[2] Mentioned in the "Lazy Tour", Ch. 1, p. 316 as a "bran new shooting-jacket" which cost him two guineas.

[3] Vividly described in the "Lazy Tour", after a fanciful opening pretending that they set out on foot.

[4] CD's bloodhound.

[5] Capital "W" in MS, obviously to start the sentence; "You" then squeezed in at margin.

[6] Ch. 1 of the "Lazy Tour".

You will be charmed to hear that 2 bed rooms and a sitting room are not to be got at Doncaster for the race week, at less than the moderate charge of

TWELVE GUINEAS![1]

But we have a grotesque idea of describing the town under those circumstances,[2] which I hope may be worth (if anything can be worth), the money.

Will you let Evans know the directions I give you, as he will probably wish to write to me while we are out.

Collins's kind regard

Ever Faithfully
CHARLES DICKENS

To JOHN STADFIELD, J. JACKSON MITCHELL, JAMES McKEEVER, THOMAS McMECHAN, ROBERT STAMPER,[3] 8 SEPTEMBER 1857*

MS British Library.

Wigton,[4] Tuesday Night | Eighth September 1857.

Gentlemen.

On behalf of my friend Mr. Collins, and myself, allow me to thank you for your very obliging attention. As Mr. Collins however, is worried by an accident, of no importance in itself but which requires repose; and as we leave here, early in the forenoon of tomorrow; perhaps you will excuse our expressing our acknowledgments through this note.

We thank you very sincerely. And I have the honor to remain,

Faithfully Yours
CHARLES DICKENS

John Stadfield
J Jackson Mitchell
James Mc Keever } Esquires
Thomas Mc Mechan
Robert Stamper

To JOHN FORSTER, [9 SEPTEMBER 1857]

Extracts in F, VIII, i, 631 and 632. *Date:* first extract from Wigton dated 9 Sep 57, according to Forster; second extract, same letter, from Allonby (see next).

Looking over the Beauties of England and Wales *before he left London, his ambition was fired by mention of Carrick Fell,*[5] a gloomy old mountain 1500 feet high, *which*

[1] Underlined with short double strokes.

[2] As they did: see *To* Georgina Hogarth, 15 Sep and *fn.*

[3] Only Thomas McMechan, bookseller and printer, of King Street, Wigton, and James McKeever, solicitor, appear in local Directories; the others were presumably not householders.

[4] A market-town in flat country, $11\frac{3}{4}$ miles south-west of Carlisle; featured in *Beauties of England and Wales*, pp. 195–9, for its antiquarian interest.

[5] Carrick or Carrock Fell (both spellings are found) north of Skiddaw, 2174 ft; CD's "1500 ft" approximates to *Beauties of England and Wales*, p. 172 ("520 yds above the surrounding meadows", as distinct from height above sea-level).

he secretly resolved to go up. We came straight to it yesterday. Nobody goes up. Guides have forgotten it. Master of a little inn,[1] excellent north-countryman, volunteered. Went up, in a tremendous rain.[2] C.D. beat Mr. Porter[3] (name of landlord) in half a mile. Mr. P. done up in no time. Three nevertheless went on. Mr. P. again leading; C.D. and C. following. Rain terrific, black mists, darkness of night. Mr. P. agitated. C.D. confident. C. (a long way down in perspective) submissive. All wet through. No poles. Not so much as a walking-stick in the party. Reach the summit, at about one in the day.[4] Dead darkness as of night. Mr. P. (excellent fellow to the last) uneasy. C.D. produces compass from pocket. Mr. P. reassured. Farm-house where dog-cart was left, N.N.W. Mr. P. complimentary. Descent commenced. C.D. with compass triumphant, until compass, with the heat and wet of C.D.'s pocket, breaks. Mr. P. (who never had a compass), inconsolable, confesses he has not been on Carrick Fell for twenty years, and he don't know the way down. Darker and darker. Nobody discernible, two yards off, by the other two. Mr. P. makes suggestions, but no way. It becomes clear to C.D. and to C. that Mr. P. is going round and round the mountain, and never coming down. Mr. P. sits on angular granite,[5] and says he is "just fairly doon." C.D. revives Mr. P. with laughter, the only restorative in the company. Mr. P. again complimentary. Descent tried once more. Mr. P. worse and worse. Council of war. Proposals from C.D. to go "slap down." Seconded by C. Mr. P. objects, on account of precipice called The Black Arches,[6] and terror of the country-side. More wandering. Mr. P. terror-stricken, but game. Watercourse, thundering and roaring, reached. C.D. suggests that it must run to the river, and had best be followed, subject to all gymnastic hazards. Mr. P. opposes, but gives in. Water course followed accordingly. Leaps, splashes, and tumbles, for two hours. C. lost. C.D. whoops. Cries for assistance from behind. C.D. returns. C. with horribly sprained ankle, lying in rivulet! *Great had been the trouble in binding up Collins's ankle and getting him painfully on, shoving, shouldering, carrying him alternately, till* terra firma *was reached.* We got down at last in the wildest place, preposterously out of the course; and, propping up C. against stones, sent Mr. P. to the other side of Cumberland for dog-cart, so got back to his inn, and changed. Shoe or stocking on the bad foot, out of the question. Foot tumbled up in a flannel waistcoat. C.D. carrying C. melo-dramatically (Wardour to the life!)[7] everywhere; into and out of carriages; up and down stairs; to bed; every step.[8] And so to Wigton,[9] got doctor, and here we are! A pretty business, we flatter ourselves! *The next night they were at the Ship Hotel, Allonby.*[10]

[1] The Queen's Head, Hesket New-Market, nine miles south-east of Wigton; 4 miles from Carrick Fell.

[2] The inn, the landlord and their ascent of Carrick Fell are all described in detail in the "Lazy Tour", Ch. I (3 Oct 57, XVI, 315–17).

[3] Joseph Porter.

[4] The summit (not described) is the mountain's most notable feature: an oval of stones, 252 by 122 yards, man-made, perhaps a fort.

[5] Another feature of the mountain, covering its eastern end (*Beauties of England and Wales*, III, 172).

[6] The "Black Crag".

[7] i.e. the scene in Act III of *The Frozen Deep* where Wardour has to carry Frank Aldersley.

[8] The incident is written up in much greater detail in the "Lazy Tour", Ch. I.

[9] See *To* Georgina Hogarth, 9 Sep and *fnn.*

[10] A Posting House, landlord Benjamin Partridge.

Describing Allonby as a small untidy outlandish place: rough stone houses in half mourning, a few coarse yellow-stone lodging houses with black roofs (bills in all the windows), five bathing-machines, five girls in straw hats, five men in straw hats[1] *(wishing they had not come); very much what Broadstairs would have been if it had been born Irish, and had not inherited a cliff.*

But this is a capital little homely inn, looking out upon the sea; with the coast of Scotland, mountainous and romantic, over against the windows;[2] and though I can just stand upright in my bedroom, we are really well lodged. It is a clean nice place in a rough wild country, and we have a very obliging and comfortable landlady.[3]

To MISS GEORGINA HOGARTH, 9 SEPTEMBER 1857

MS Comtesse de Suzannet. *Address* (envelope, MS Professor Harry Stone): Miss Hogarth | Charles Dickens Esquire | Gad's Hill Place | Higham | by Rochester | Kent. PM 11 Sep 57 Allonby.

Allonby,[4] Cumberland
Wednesday Night, Ninth September | 1857

My Dear Georgy.

I walked over to Maryport to day, to see what letters there were, and to ask the Postmaster to send any more he might have, over here. I found none from you; but hardly supposed I should, so soon.

Think of Collins's usual luck with me!!! We went up a Cumberland mountain yesterday—a huge black hill, 1,500 feet high. We took for a Guide, a capital Innkeeper hard by. It rained in torrents—as it only does rain in a hill country—the whole time. At the top, there were black mists and the darkness of night. It then came out that the Innkeeper had not been up for 20 years—and he lost his head and himself altogether, and we couldn't get down again! What wonders the Inimitable performed with his compass until it broke with the heat and wet of his pocket, no matter. It did break, and then we wandered about, until it was clear to the Inimitable that the night must be passed there, and the enterprising travellers probably die of cold. We took our own way about coming down—struck—and declared that the Guide might wander where he would, but we would follow a water-course we lighted upon, and which must come at last to the River. This necessitated amazing gymnastics. In the course of which performances, Collins fell into the said watercourse with his ankle sprained, and the great ligament of the foot and leg swollen I don't know how big.

How I enacted Wardour over again in carrying him down, and what a business it was to get him down, I may say in Gibbs's[5] words, "Vi lascio a giudicare!"[6] But he

[1] In the "Lazy Tour", Ch. 3, *ibid.*, p. 361, "five gentlemen in straw hats ... four ladies in straw hats".

[2] In the "Lazy Tour", *ibid.*, p. 362, CD describes the "fine sunsets at Allonby ... and fine views—on fine days—of the Scottish coast".

[3] Compare Thomas Idle's tribute, despite his anxiety to leave, in the "Lazy Tour", p. 365; see also p. 362.

[4] A small resort on the Solway, 22 miles from Carlisle.

[5] Charles Gibbs, banker, resident of Albaro, near Genoa: CD and Georgina had met him there in Summer 1844: see Vols IV, p. 179*n* and VII, p. 177*n*.

[6] "I leave you to judge!"

was got down somehow—and we got off the mountain somehow—and now I carry him to bed, and into and out of carriages, exactly like Wardour in private life. I don't believe he will stand for a month to come!

He has had a Doctor, and can wear neither shoe nor stocking, and has his foot wrapped up in a flannel waistcoat (dirty), and has a breakfast-saucer of liniment and a horrible dabbing of lotion incessantly in progress. We laugh at it all—but I doubt very much whether he can go on to Doncaster. It will be a miserable blow to our H.W. schemes, and I say nothing about it as yet; but he is really so crippled, that I doubt the getting him there. We have resolved to fall to work tomorrow morning and begin our writing; and there, for the present, that point rests.

This is a little place with 50 houses, 5 bathing-machines, [a]5 girls in straw hats, 5 men in straw hats, and no other company. The little houses are all in half mourning—yellow stone or white stone, and black[a]—and it reminds me of what Broadstairs might have been, if it had not inherited a cliff, and had been born an Irishman. But this is a capital little homely Inn, looking out upon the sea; and we are really very comfortably lodged. I can just stand upright in my bedroom. Otherwise, it is a good deal like one of Ballard's[1] top rooms. We have a very obliging and comfortable landlady; and it is a clean nice place in a rough wild country. We came here, hap-hazard, but could not have done better.

We lay last night at a place called Wigton, also in half mourning[2]—with the wonderful peculiarity that it had no population, no business, no streets to speak of, but 5 linen-drapers within range of our small window, 1 Linen Draper's next door, and 5 more linen drapers round the corner.[3] I ordered a night-light in my bedroom. A queer little old woman brought me one of the common Child's night lights, and, seeming to think that I looked at it with interest, said: "It's joost a vara keeyourious thing Sir, and joost new coom oop. It'll burn awt hoors a 'end, and no gootther, nor no waste, nor ony sike a thing, if you can creedit what I say, seein' the airticle."

Of course I shall go to Doncaster, whether or no (please God), and my postage directions to you remain unchanged. Love to Mamey, Katey, Charley, Harry, and the darling Plorn.[4]

Ever affectionately
Miss Hogarth. CHARLES DICKENS

[aa] The first sentence is almost the same as published in F, VIII, i, 632; the incident of the night light, in the next paragraph, he gives verbatim. MDGH, II, 5 ("1857 Narrative") states that parts of letters in their volume during the expedition with Wilkie Collins had been published "in Mr. Forster's book". They add that this is also the case "with many letters to his eldest daughter and sister-in-law".

[1] James Ballard (?1806–74), landlord of the Albion Hotel, Broadstairs: see Vol. I, p. 303*n*.

[2] Wigton is described by Francis Goodchild (CD) in the "Lazy Tour", Ch. 2, as "what I hope and believe is one of the most dismal places ever seen by eyes"; and its houses as "looking as if they were all in mourning" (*HW*, 10 Oct, XVI, 337).

[3] They are similarly enumerated in the "Lazy Tour", Ch. 2, *HW*, XVI, 338.

[4] The first letter to Georgina in which he does not name Catherine, along with the children, when sending love.

To JOHN FORSTER, [?11 SEPTEMBER 1857]

Extract from F, VIII, ii, 632. *Date:* after *To* Miss Hogarth, 9 Sep 57; probably 11 Sep.

Describing Wigton as a place of little houses all in half-mourning, yellow stone or white stone and black, with the wonderful peculiarity that though it had no population, no business, and no streets to speak of it had five linendrapers within range of their single window, one linendraper next door, and five more linendrapers round the corner.

The day after Carrick there was a mess about our letters, through our not going to a place called Maryport.[1] So, while the landlord was planning how to get them (they were only twelve miles off), I walked off, to his great astonishment, and brought them over.

To JOSEPH SLY,[2] 11 SEPTEMBER 1857

MS Public Library & Museum, Lancaster.

County Hotel, Carlisle | Friday Evening | Eleventh September 1857

Mr. Charles Dickens sends his compliments to the Master of The King's Arms at Lancaster,[3] and begs to say that he wishes to bespeak for *tomorrow* (*Saturday*) afternoon and night, a private sitting-room and two bedrooms; also a comfortable dinner for two persons at half past 5. Mr. Dickens will be accompanied by his friend Mr. Wilkie Collins; and as Mr. Collins has unfortunately sprained his leg, it will be a great convenience to him to have his bedroom as near the sitting-room as possible. For the same reason, Mr. Dickens will be glad to find a fly awaiting them at the station. They purpose leaving here, by the mid-day Train at 12..38.[4]

To MISS GEORGINA HOGARTH, 12 SEPTEMBER 1857

Text from MDGH, II, 31. *Address* (envelope only MS Yale University Library)*:* Miss Hogarth | Gad's Hill Place | Higham | by Rochester | Kent.[5] PM Lancaster Sep 13 1857.

Lancaster, Saturday Night, Sept. 12th, 1857.

My dear Georgy,

I received your letter at Allonby yesterday, and was delighted to get it. We came back to Carlisle last night (to a capital inn, kept by Breach's brother),[6] and came on

[1] Forster reads "Mayport", in error.

[2] Joseph Sly (1814–95), proprietor (1856–77) of the King's Arms (built 1625), which he filled with antique furniture, tapestries and ancient bedsteads. Visitors during his time included several members of the English and Continental Royal families; Ruskin, who frequently stayed there on his way to the Lake District; and Miss Coutts (bedrooms were named after both her and CD). See later vols; and, for further details of Sly and the King's Arms, David Steel, "CD, Lancaster and the Old King's Arms Royal Hotel, Lancaster", *Comment* (Lancaster University Independent Magazine), Nos 87 and 88, 13 Oct 1978, p. 3 and 16 Nov 1978, p. 10.

[3] In Market Street, described in the "Lazy Tour", Ch. 3.

[4] See *To* Wills, 26 Sep and *fn.*

[5] Envelope endorsed at top in Georgina Hogarth's hand, when collecting letters for MDGH: "Tour in the North with Wilkie *1857*".

[6] The County Hotel, Court Square, kept by Benjamin Bodman Breach, no doubt the brother of James G. Breach, proprietor of the Pavilion Hotel, Folkestone (see Vol. VII, p. 697 and *nn*).

here to-day. We are on our way to Doncaster; but Sabbath observance throws all the trains out; and although it is not a hundred miles from here, we shall have, as well as I can make out the complicated lists of trains, to sleep at Leeds—which I particularly detest as an odious place[1]—to-morrow night.

Accustomed as you are to the homage which men delight to render to the Inimitable, you would be scarcely prepared for the proportions it assumes in this northern country. Station-masters assist him to alight from carriages, deputations await him in hotel entries, innkeepers bow down before him and put him into regal rooms, the town goes down to the platform to see him off, and Collins's ankle goes into the newspapers!!![2]

It is a great deal better than it was, and he can get into new hotels and up the stairs with two thick sticks, like an admiral in a farce. His spirits have improved in a corresponding degree, and he contemplates cheerfully the keeping house at Doncaster. I thought (as I told you) he would never have gone there, but he seems quite up to the mark now. Of course he can never walk out, or see anything of any place. We have done our first paper for H. W., and sent it up to the printer's.

The landlady of the little inn at Allonby lived at Greta Bridge, in Yorkshire, when I went down there before "Nickleby,"[3] and was smuggled into the room to see me, when I was secretly found out. She is an immensely fat woman now. "But I could tuck my arm round her waist then, Mr. Dickens," the landlord said when she told me the story as I was going to bed the night before last. "And can't you do it now," I said, "you insensible dog? Look at me! Here's a picture!" Accordingly, I got round as much of her as I could; and this gallant action was the most successful I have ever performed, on the whole.[4] I think it was the dullest little place I ever entered; and what with the monotony of an idle sea, and what with the monotony of another sea in the room (occasioned by Collins's perpetually holding his ankle over a pail of salt water, and laving it with a milk jug), I struck yesterday, and came away.

We are in a very remarkable old house here, with genuine old rooms and an uncommonly quaint staircase.[5] I have a state bedroom, with two enormous red four-posters in it, each as big as Charley's room at Gad's Hill. Bellew[6] is to preach here

[1] He was there on 1 Dec 47, as chairman of the Mechanics' Institute Soirée; but did not complain of it then.

[2] That morning the *Carlisle Examiner and North Western Advertiser* reported their arrival the previous day.

[3] He had stayed there 31 Jan–1 Feb 1838, to see the Yorkshire boarding-schools: see Vol. 1, pp. 365–6.

[4] This appears verbatim in Forster, VIII, ii, 632–3.

[5] Described in the "Lazy Tour", Ch. 4, as having "a certain grave mystery lurking in the depth of the old mahogany panels"; and the scene of the story told them by the old man, the ghost of the murderer hanged at Lancaster Castle a hundred years before, which turns out to be a dream brought on by eating Bride-cake (*HW*, 24 Oct 57, XVI, 385–93).

[6] The Rev. John Chippendall Montesquieu Bellew (1823–74; *DNB*), born in Lancaster and educated at Lancaster Royal Grammar School; son of Capt. Robert Higgin and grandson of John Higgin (for many years Governor of Lancaster Castle), had assumed his mother's name; Curate of St Philip's, Regent St, 1855–7; Permanent Curate of St Mark's, St John's Wood, 1858–62. Became a Roman Catholic 1869. Popular London preacher and, later, public reader of Shakespeare in England and America. Besides several collections of sermons, published a history of Shakespeare's home, a novel, *Blount Tempest*, 1863, and *Poets' Corner*, a poetry manual, 1868. For his later close friendship with Yates and the actor Charles Fechter, see later vols.

to-morrow.[1] "And we know he is a friend of yours, sir,"[2] said the landlord, when he presided over the serving of the dinner (two little salmon trout; a sirloin steak; a brace of partridges; seven dishes of sweets; five dishes of dessert, led off by a bowl of peaches; and in the centre an enormous bride-cake)—"We always have it here, sir," said the landlord, "custom of the house." (Collins turned pale, and estimated the dinner at half a guinea each.)

This is the stupidest of letters, but all description is gone, or going, into "The Lazy Tour of Two Idle Apprentices."[3]

Kiss the darling Plorn, who is often in my thoughts. Best love to Charley, Mamey, and Katie. I will write to you again from Doncaster, where I shall be rejoiced to find another letter from you.

Ever affectionately, my dearest Georgy
[CHARLES DICKENS]

To [F. M. EVANS],[4] 15 SEPTEMBER 1857

Text from transcript, Huntington Library.

Angel Hotel, Doncaster
Tuesday Fifteenth September | 1857.

My Dear [Evans]

I like your notion of the Edition,[5] and, as soon after next Monday (when I return), as you please, let us have a quiet day at Gad's Hill and go into the "facts and figures". In the meantime I have begged Forster to see Chapman, and so to pave the way as that you and Chapman shall have the road open for making all arrangements. I have told Forster that Bradbury and Evans's name must be on all the series as well as Chapman's,[6] and that I must have B and E in all the accounts and all the business, and must have (and will have) no Chapman delays and shortcomings from first to last, but must wholly extinguish the same.

The Child's History looks clearly and plainly readable, and I think the proposed price sufficiently cheap.[7]

I am much interested in knowing what your H.W. notion is.[8] That too must be propounded at Gad's Hill.

Ever Faithfully yours
CHARLES DICKENS

[F. M. Evans] Esquire.

[1] The previous night he had given a public lecture on Palestine in the Assembly Room. CD did not hear him preach.

[2] It is not known when he and CD met; but in Dec 1859 Bellew proposed CD's health at the annual dinner of the Commercial Travellers' Schools Society (*Speeches*, ed. K. J. Fielding, p. 293).

[3] See Ch. 4.

[4] No name given in typescript for salutation or ending; but Evans is obvious addressee: see *To* Evans, 6 Sep.

[5] The Library edition.

[6] This was done: but see next vol.

[7] Not republished until 1864 by Chapman & Hall, no doubt because Bradbury & Evans's next half-yearly accounts showed a small loss on it (MS V & A).

[8] Not discovered.

To JOHN FORSTER, [?15 SEPTEMBER 1857]

Extracts in F, VIII, i, 634*n* and 633. *Date:* written from Doncaster, no doubt same day as last.

At the theatre there had been a performance of Money.[1] I have rarely seen anything finer than Lord Glossmore,[2] a chorus-singer in bluchers,[3] drab trowsers, and a brown sack; and Dudley Smooth,[4] in somebody else's wig, hindside before. Stout[5] also, in anything he could lay hold of. The waiter at the club had an immense moustache, white trowsers, and a striped jacket; and he brought everybody who came in, a vinegar-cruet.[6] The man who read the will began thus: "I so-and-so, being of unsound mind but firm in body . . ."[7] In spite of all this, however, the real character, humour, wit, and good writing of the comedy, made themselves apparent; and the applause was loud and repeated, and really seemed genuine. Its capital things were not lost altogether.[8] It was succeeded by a Jockey Dance by five ladies, who put their whips in their mouths and worked imaginary winners up to the float—an immense success.[9]

Collins had by now so far recovered as to be able, doubled-up, to walk with a thick stick; in which condition, being exactly like the gouty admiral in a comedy, I have given him that name. *The impressions received from the race-week were far from favourable. It was noise and turmoil all day long, and a gathering of vagabonds from all parts of the racing earth. Every bad face that had ever caught wickedness from an innocent horse had its representative in the streets;*[10] *and as he, like Gulliver looking down upon his fellow-men after coming from the horse-country, looked down into Doncaster High-street from his inn-window*, everywhere I see the late Mr. Palmer[11] with his betting-book in his hands. Mr. Palmer sits next me at the theatre; Mr. Palmer goes before me down the street; Mr. Palmer follows me into the chemist's shop where I go to buy rose water after breakfast, and says to the chemist "Give us soom

[1] Lytton's comedy, first performed with great success at the Haymarket in Dec 40, with Macready as Evelyn and the costumes designed by Count D'Orsay: see Vol. IV, p. 406 and *n.* It opened at the Theatre Royal, Doncaster, on 14 Sep.

[2] One of the "chorus" of cousins with thwarted expectations, a die-hard Tory.

[3] Old-fashioned low boots.

[4] The professional card-player, who enters into a plot with the hero, Alfred Evelyn, pretending that he has ruined him.

[5] Another of the cousins: a political economist and follower of Malthus.

[6] In the play it is a snuff-box.

[7] Sharp, the lawyer, begins, of course, correctly: "being . . . of sound mind, though infirm body".

[8] It was warmly reviewed in the *Doncaster, Nottinghamshire and Lincoln Gazette*, 18 Sep: H. Mellon's Graves was "admirably performed" and J. F. Cathcart's Evelyn "very ably" played.

[9] "Loudly encored", according to the *Doncaster Gazette*, above. The programme ended with *The Corsican Brothers*.

[10] In the "Lazy Tour" CD pictured himself as being in a lunatic asylum, and the race-goers as "all mad people under the charge of a body of designing Keepers!" (*HW*, XVI, 410).

[11] William Palmer (1824–56; *DNB*), MRCS, "the Rugeley poisoner", convicted on 27 May 1856 at the Old Bailey, after a 12 days' trial, of murder, almost certainly by strychnine, of his friend John Parsons, a betting man; publicly hanged outside Stafford Gaol on 14 June. The case excited intense interest: see CD's article "The Demeanour of Murderers", *HW*, 14 June 56, XIII, 505–7. A previous inquest had found that he had similarly poisoned his wife and brother.

sal volatile or soom damned thing o' that soort, in wather—my head's bad!"[1] And I look at the back of his bad head[2] repeated in long, long lines on the race course, and in the betting stand and outside the betting rooms in the town, and I vow to God that I can see nothing in it but cruelty, covetousness, calculation, insensibility, and low wickedness.[3]

To MISS GEORGINA HOGARTH, 15 SEPTEMBER 1857

Text from MDGH, II, 33.

Angel Hotel, Doncaster, Tuesday, Sept. 15th, 1857.

My dear Georgy,

I found your letter here on my arrival yesterday. I had hoped that the well[4] would have been almost finished by this time, and the additions to the house almost finished too—but patience, patience!

We have very good, clean, and quiet apartments here, on the second floor, looking down into the main street, which is full of horse jockeys, bettors, drunkards, and other blackguards, from morning to night—and all night. The races begin to-day and last till Friday, which is the Cup Day. I am not going to the course this morning, but have engaged a carriage (open, and pair) for to-morrow[5] and Friday.[6]

"The Frozen Deep's" author gets on as well as could be expected. He can hobble up and down stairs when absolutely necessary, and limps to his bedroom on the same floor. He talks of going to the theatre to-night in a cab,[7] which will be the first

[1] Repeated in the "Lazy Tour", as spoken by "one red-eyed Lunatic" (*HW*, XVI, 412).

[2] A portrait-photograph in G. Fletcher, *Life and Career of Dr William Palmer of Rugeley*, 1925, facing p. 196, shows a thick-set head and a sullen face.

[3] Given, in virtually the same words, as "the uniform Keeper characteristics", in the "Lazy Tour" (*HW*, XVI, 410).

[4] MDGH reads "wall" in error.

[5] The day of the St Leger, described in the "Lazy Tour", Ch. 5. Mr Goodchild's fantasy in the "Lazy Tour" concerning "a pair of lilac gloves and a little bonnet that he saw there" (pp. 411–12) suggests that Maria and Ellen (with their mother), accompanied CD in the carriage.

[6] Both CD and Collins appear in the "List of Company" at the Race Meeting, published in the *Doncaster, Nottinghamshire and Lincoln Gazette*, 18 Sep.

[7] The notice in the *Doncaster, Nottinghamshire and Lincoln Gazette*, 18 Sep reported their attendance at the Theatre Royal on Monday night, an error for Tuesday (CD must have gone alone on Monday to see *Money*: see *To* de la Rue, 23 Oct). It described CD, accompanied by Collins, entering the boxes: "both gentlemen (especially the former) at once became the objects of the most marked attention and conversation. In fact, the distinguished author of the 'Pickwick Papers' ... was evidently the lion of the evening." CD's motive in going to Doncaster was to see Maria and Ellen Ternan act; both were mentioned in the *Doncaster ... Gazette*, 18 Sep, as "in former years ... distinguished as juvenile actresses". (Their father had been lessee of the theatre.) They performed as members of Charles Kean's Princess's Theatre Co. for the first time that evening. Maria Ternan played Mrs Major Mortar, accompanying herself on the guitar, in Mark Lemon's *The Ladies' Club*, in which Ellen had a smaller part; Ellen also had a small part in *The Convent; or The Pet of the Petticoats*, a comic opera with music by J. Barnett. Neither of them seems to have appeared in *The Stranger*, the best known in the week's programme, performed on 19 Sep (see Vol. VII, p. 310 and *n*). On 28 Sep Maria was Jessica in *The Merchant of Venice*. The Ternans' Benefit Night was 30 Sep. The programme began with Tom Taylor's *Victims* and included J. R. Planché's vaudeville, *The Loan of a Lover*, and *A Game of Romps*, a farce by J. M. Morton, first performed at the Princess's on 9 Apr 55, Maria appearing in her

occasion of his going out, except to travel, since the accident. He sends his kind regard and thanks for enquiries and condolence. I am perpetually tidying the rooms after him, and carrying all sorts of untidy things which belong to him into his bed-room, which is a picture of disorder. You will please to imagine mine, airy and clean, little dressing-room attached, eight water-jugs (I never saw such a supply), capital sponge-bath, perfect arrangement, and exquisite neatness. We breakfast at half-past eight, and fall to work for H. W. afterwards. Then I go out, and—hem! look for subjects.

The mayor called this morning to do the honours of the town, whom it pleased the Inimitable to receive with great courtesy and affability. He propounded invitation to public *déjeûner*, which it did *not* please the Inimitable to receive, and which he graciously rejected.

That's all the news. Everything I can describe by hook or by crook, I describe for H. W.[1] So there is nothing of that sort left for letters.

Best love to dear Mamey and Katey, and to Charley, and to Harry. Any number of kisses to the noble Plorn.

Ever affectionately
[CHARLES DICKENS]

To W. H. WILLS, 17 SEPTEMBER 1857

MS Huntington Library.

Angel Hotel, Doncaster
Thursday Seventeenth September, | 1857

My Dear Wills.

The day post has brought me your note, and I write you by return a few words in reply.

The other halves of the notes[2] I believe are all safe. One in Arthur Smith's hands; one in mine. I cannot remember the correspondent's name, or any thing about him, except that he dated from Exchange Buildings, Liverpool.[3]

All of my part—three pages and a half—of the second portion of the Lazy Tour is already here, and in corrected type. Collins is sticking a little with his story, but I hope will come through it tomorrow. He is much obliged by your enquiries and sympathy, and sends his kind regard. He can't walk out, but can limp about the room, and has had two Doncaster rides in a carriage. Is to be treated to another tomorrow, if he has done.

Happy to hear so good an account of Mrs. Wills.

original part of Violet (see Malcolm Morley, "The Theatrical Ternans", Pt IV, *D*, LV [1959], 37).

[1] CD's description of their week in Doncaster fills Ch. 5, of the "Lazy Tour" (*HW*, 31 October 51, XVI, 409–16). In the Appx to F, 1872–4, III, 511, "The Writings of Charles Dickens" (1857), Forster distinguishes the authors of Chs 1–4, and says "the rest" was by Collins; deliberately averting attention from the revealing passages in Ch. 5 (F, 1872–4, III, Appx, 511).

[2] Banknotes sent through the post in two halves, as a precaution against theft; a practice long-continued.

[3] Payments connected with the Jerrold Fund.

[a]Young Jerrold, just contemptible. Poor Jerrold in his grave must not be confounded with him; and in this thought I tore the paper up after I had read the letter, and would not allow myself to be passionate about it.[1] I wish I was as good a boy in all things as I hope I have been, and mean to be, in this.

But Lord bless you, the strongest parts of your present correspondent's heart are made up of weaknesses. And he just come to be here at all (if you knew it) along of his Richard Wardour![2] Guess *that* riddle, Mr. Wills!—[a]

Ever Faithfully
CD

To HENRY AUSTIN, 19 SEPTEMBER 1857

MS Morgan Library.

Doncaster | Saturday September Nineteenth | 1857

My Dear Henry.

Your letter has been forwarded to me here from Gad's Hill, and I enclose you a cheque (payable to "Order") in Nye's favor, for Three Hundred Pounds.[3] Will you address acknowledgment of its safe receipt, to me at Gad's Hill. I expect to return there, on Tuesday or Wednesday.

Pumps deferred make the Heart sick,[4]—but the complaint is not of your engendering, I know very well.

Ever affectionately
[CD.][5]

Over

I reopen this, to say that I am very much disposed, so soon as we go to town at the end of October, to make that Conservatory[6] suggested by Barber,[7] which would relieve the house of the little Drawing Room. I think it would make such a great difference in its value, if I wanted to sell it, to have a conservatory with two openings from the Drawing Room: one on each side of the Fire. Let us carefully devise it while the men are about, and have a careful estimate made of its exact cost.

[aa] Omitted by *CD as Editor* and N.

[1] For Blanchard Jerrold's letter, objecting to his mother being the object of charity, see *To The Times*, 1 Sep, *fn*. On 19 July Hans Andersen, during his stay at Gad's Hill, had written to his sister: "Dickens told me how glad he was that a large sum had been collected for Jerrold's widow. His eyes sparkled. A moment later I read in one of the many papers which were lying about that Dickens had done it all from vanity—he desired to make himself popular. Horrible. It brought tears to my eyes" (given in *D*, XXVII (1931), 272).

[2] This may point to Maria Ternan (see *To* Miss Coutts, 5 Sep) rather than Ellen, but probably both.

[3] The cheque went through Nye's bank account on 24 Sep (CD's Account-book, MS Messrs Coutts).

[4] Cf. Proverbs, XIII: 12, "Hope deferred maketh the heart sick."

[5] The signature has been cut away.

[6] Not built at this time.

[7] The head-gardener at Gad's Hill.

To JOHN FORSTER, [?19 SEPTEMBER 1857]

Extracts and summaries in F, VIII, i, 633–4. *Date:* from Doncaster, where they had arrived on 14 Sep, the day before the St Leger; probably written on 19 Sep, the day after the Cup day (18 Sep).

On the St Leger Day a wonderful, paralysing, coincidence *befell him. He bought a race-card; facetiously wrote down three names for the winners of the three chief races (never in his life having heard or thought of any of the horses, except that the winner of the Derby, who proved to be nowhere, had been mentioned to him); and,* if you can believe it without your hair standing on end, those three races were won, one after another, by those three horses!!![1] *He also thought it noticeable that, though the losses were enormous, nobody had won, for there was nothing but grinding of teeth and blaspheming of ill-luck. On the night of the Cup Day* a groaning phantom *lay in the doorway of his bedroom and howled all night. The landlord came up in the morning to apologise,* and said it was a gentleman who had lost £1500 or £2000; and he had drunk a deal afterwards; and then they put him to bed, and then he—took the 'orrors, and got up, and yelled till morning.

Saying if a boy with any good in him, but with a dawning propensity to sporting and betting, were but brought to the Doncaster races soon enough, it would cure him.

To W. H. WILLS, 20 SEPTEMBER 1857

MS Huntington Library.

Angel, Doncaster | Sunday Twentieth September 1857

My Dear Wills.

[a]I am going [b]to take the little—riddle[b2]—into the country this morning;[3] and I answer your letter briefly, before starting.[a]

I see no other objection to the Manchester article[4] than that [it][5] is commonplace.

The Bristol Prayer Monger[6] I have never had sent me, and therefore can do nothing to. But the name suggests care and caution.

You will see that the second part of the Lazy Tour is very long.[7] The third will be much shorter—not more than half this quantity, if so much.[8]

My next address will be, Gad's Hill. I *think* I shall leave here on Tuesday, but I cannot positively say. Collins and I part company tomorrow. (He can walk now—

[1] The St Leger itself was won by Imperieuse; the Municipal Stakes by Blanche of Middlebie; and the Portland Plate by Meta.

[aa] Enclosed in square brackets, presumably by Lehmann, with the intention of omitting all of it. In fact, he omitted only [bb], here and below.

[2] See *To* Wills, 17 Sep and *fn.*

[3] *To* Roche Abbey, 10 miles south of Doncaster. The *Doncaster Gazette*, 25 Sep, stated that "on Sunday, he viewed the ruins of Roche Abbey and enjoyed a walk in its beautiful grounds". Mrs Ternan would certainly have come as well.

[4] Not Wills's own article on "The Manchester School of Art", published 10 Oct (XVI, 349–52), as no other Manchester article published in Oct–Dec, this must have been something declined and therefore unidentifiable.

[5] Omitted by CD.

[6] Morley's "Brother Muller and his Orphan-Work", *HW*, 7 Nov, XVI, 433.

[7] $12\frac{1}{2}$ pp. as against the average 8 pp., lengthened by the Doctor's story (XVI, 337–49).

[8] In fact, 7 pp. (XVI, 361–7).

walked a mile yesterday, with a stick.) I did intend to return home tomorrow, but have no idea now of doing that.[1] Whatever I do, I shall of course come up to the scratch with the third part. Indeed I have half done it. [b]So let the riddle and the riddler go their own wild way, and no harm come of it![b]

I am very sorry to hear of Mrs. Wills, to whom my kind regard again. But you know how constantly it happens that the first effect of the sea[2] is to exaggerate and stimulate an illness.

Ever Faithfully
CHARLES DICKENS

Collins sends kind regard.

To J. L. BOLTON,[3] 23 SEPTEMBER 1857

Text from transcript of MS in Doncaster Municipal Museum.

Gad's Hill Place, Higham by Rochester, Kent
Twenty Third September 1857

Sir,

I regret I did not receive your obliging letter until yesterday, when I found it on my return home from Doncaster. If it had come to hand sooner I should have had the pleasure of thanking you in person, instead of through the medium of this note.

Faithfully Yours
CHARLES DICKENS

J. L. Bolton Esq.

To SHIRLEY BROOKS, 24 SEPTEMBER 1857*

MS New York Public Library.

Gad's Hill Place, Higham.
Thursday Twenty Fourth September 1857

My Dear Brooks.

No letters have been forwarded to me in my absence, and I have only just got yours.

The absurdity of the thing made me break out into a fit of laughter. I cannot but think that it is the Printer's folly, and that you have already found it to be so. I will

[1] He changed his mind and left for London on the Monday; perhaps discouraged by the Ternans from staying longer; their Doncaster engagement continued until 30 Sep, when they had a benefit.

[2] Perhaps Wills had sent her to Bonchurch, Isle of Wight; he had jotted down in pencil on CD's letter to him of 7 Sep: "Two addresses: Mr. I. [ ] {13 White Rock Place | Mrs. Walter | 17 [Undercliff]." CD had spent Aug and Sep 1849 at Bonchurch, but left disillusioned by the Undercliff and the doctors who praised its health-giving properties: see Vol. V, p. 605 and *n.*

[3] Unidentified.

not say that I doubt [B . . . y's][1] being able to play the knave, but I really don't think he would play the Fool to such extraordinary perfection.[2]

Faithfully Yours always

Shirley Brooks Esquire CHARLES DICKENS

To JOHN FORSTER, [24 SEPTEMBER 1857]

Extracts in F, I, i, 2n and VIII, iii, 653. *Date:* all 24 Sep 57, according to Forster.

Being here[3] again, or as much here as anywhere in particular.

I shall cut this letter short, for they are playing Masaniello[4] in the drawing-room, and I feel very much as I used to do when I was a small child a few miles off, and Somebody[5] (who I wonder, and which way did *She* go, when she died) hummed the evening hymn[6] to me, and I cried on the pillow—either with the remorseful consciousness of having kicked Somebody else, or because still Somebody else had hurt my feelings in the course of the day.

Here are six men perpetually going up and down the well (I know that somebody will be killed), in the course of fitting a pump; which is quite a railway terminus—it is so iron, and so big.[7] The process is much like putting Oxford-Street endwise, and laying gas along it, than anything else. By the time it is finished, the cost of this water will be something absolutely frightful. But of course it proportionately increases the value of the property, and that's my only comfort. . . . The horse has gone lame from a sprain, the big dog has run a tenpenny nail into one of his hind feet, the bolts have all flown out of the basket-carriage, and the gardener says all the fruit trees want replacing with new ones.

[1] Obviously, Bentley's. A square has been cut out from page, with a capital "B" written on blank page below; a clear "s" is visible and the tail of probably "y" preceding it.

[2] Probably the advertisement of *Aspen Court* on 15 Sep in the *Publishers' Circular* (and no doubt elsewhere) for publication on 20 Sep "in Mr. Bentley's new popular series for September". The book was not published until 1 Oct. Brooks is also described as the author of "Miss Violet and Her Offers" which as far as is known was not then published as a book.

[3] At Gad's Hill.

[4] Probably extracts from James Kenney's adaptation of Auber's opera, first performed at Drury Lane 4 May 1829, with Braham in the title role: see Vol. IV, p. 174*n*.

[5] Not Mary Weller (?1804–88, later Mrs Gibson), as given by Robert Langton (*Childhood and Youth of CD*, 1892 edn, pp. 26–9), who elicited, by questioning, her having sung the evening hymn. It must be someone who died in CD's childhood, and the obvious claimant is his maternal aunt, Mary Allen, who died in Sep 1822, having lived with the Dickenses until Sep 1821. (The "death" referred to in F, VIII, v, 674, would be hers.)

[6] Bishop Ken's "Glory to Thee, my God, this night". Mrs Atherfield sings this hymn to the shipwrecked sailors in CD's section of "The Wreck of the Golden Mary" (*HW*, Christmas No., 1856, p. 8).

[7] Forster's reference to sinking of the well as if it were in 1859 (F, VIII, iii, 653) is clearly mistaken.

To CAPTAIN E. E. MORGAN,[1] 24 SEPTEMBER 1857

MS Mrs Richard Armstrong.

Gad's Hill, Higham, by Rochester
Twenty Fourth September 1857

My Dear Morgan.

Another box of Cigars, just now received at this little old-fashioned country-house of mine, perched on the very hill-top where Falstaff ran away! You don't know, my dear fellow, how often you are with me. Two or three times every week, as I light my Cigar after dinner, and sit down in my study or go out walking (according to the season), to muse, I say "I wonder whether Morgan will ever bring one of those big ships back, and beam upon me with the light of his bright face, and hear *me* tell *him* the story of the Wet Lovers and the dry one!" (You must know that I have appropriated that story, and acquired immense reputation by it.)[2]

God bless you and yours! I heartily tell you that every short letter from you, comes to me like a wholesome breeze from the other side of the Atlantic, giving me assurance that fine natures and sound hearts will never die out of any land, so long as the Rainbow shines.

I will inaugurate the first chapter of the next book (whenever it comes into life; it is in the land of shadows now, unknown to me, and waiting to be born) by fumigating it in MS with a Cigar reserved from this very box.

Faithfully Your friend
CHARLES DICKENS

To DAVID [?PERKINS],[3] 24 SEPTEMBER 1857

Extract in Ernest Dressel North catalogue, 1926; dated Gad's Hill Place, 24 Sep 57.

Sir. Your letter has just now been forwarded to me here at my house in the country. I comply with your request with much pleasure, and send this brief autograph accordingly.

Faithfully Yours
CHARLES DICKENS

David L. [P]erkins, Esquire

To PAUL WEINLING,[4] 24 SEPTEMBER 1857

Mention in J. A. Stargardt, Marburg catalogue 1958; addressed Paul Weinling; dated 24 Sep 57.

[1] Capt. Elisha Ely Morgan (?1805–64), of the American merchant service: see Vol. VII, p. 571 and *n.*

[2] For his telling it at the General Theatrical Fund Dinner, 25 Mar 50, see Vol. VI, p. 66 and *n.* He would tell it again at the Railway Benevolent Society Dinner, 5 June 67 (*Speeches*, ed. K. J. Fielding, pp. 364–5).

[3] Catalogue gives Derkins, probably a misreading of CD's initial "P". Unidentified in either case.

[4] Unidentified.

To WILLIAM BANTING,[1] 26 SEPTEMBER 1857*

MS Fales Collection, New York University Library.

Gad's Hill Place, Higham, by Rochester
Saturday Twenty Sixth September | 1857.

Dear Mr. Banting.

Your letter has given me very great pleasure. I saw Mrs. Thompson[2] before she went, and told her that I trusted her with great confidence. I will write to her at once, and encourage her in her excellent course.

Faithfully Yours
CHARLES DICKENS

To CAROLINE THOMPSON, [?26 SEPTEMBER 1857]

Mention in last. *Date:* He probably wrote the same day.

To W. H. WILLS, 26 SEPTEMBER 1857

MS Huntington Library.

OFFICE OF HOUSEHOLD WORDS,
Saturday Twenty Sixth September 1857

My Dear Wills. I write you a line, with such slight official intelligence as I have.

Part 3 of The Lazy Tour, I have corrected, and introduced Collins's copy[3] (received this morning) in to. I have instructed B and E to send him down Proof to Scarborough tonight, and have instructed *him* to send back proof to B and E tomorrow night. There are some descriptions of mine in it (particularly one, of a Railway Station), that I think very good indeed.[4]

Part 4, I am at work on.

Oxenford has sent a paper "Touching the Lord Hamlet",[5] giving a very good account of the old Saxo Grammaticus history.[6] I have sent it to the Printer, with instructions to send proof to him.

I have, at Gad's Hill, a pretty little paper of a good deal of merit,[7] by one Mr. Hollingshead, who addressed me as having tried his hand in the Train.[8] This, too, I will send to the Printer's. (I ought to have brought it from Gad's Hill this morning, but forgot it.) I am inclined to hope that the writer may be very serviceable to us.

Collins I have made the new proposal to, as we agreed.

[1] William Banting (1797–1878; *DNB*), cabinet maker and undertaker: see Vol. VII, p. 730*n*.

[2] No doubt Caroline Thompson, who had presumably carried out her plan to emigrate to Canada: see *To* Miss Coutts, 20 May 56.

[3] Thomas Idle's reflections on the three "disasters" of his past life (*HW*, 17 Oct 57, XVI, 363–5).

[4] The long and imaginative description of the "Junction-Station" (Carlisle, where they spent the night of 10 Sep), XVI, 366–7—of which CD was justifiably proud.

[5] 17 Oct, XVI, 372.

[6] The earliest known version of the story of *Hamlet*.

[7] "Poor Tom.—A City Weed" (the life-story of a poor clerk), 17 Oct 57, XVI, 381.

[8] See *To* Hollingshead, 27 July and *fn*.

Evans has been with me this morning, to ask me, Would I have a Posting-Bill of the Lazy Tour? I replied, most decidedly Yes.[1] I think it will give us a good push into the public mind, at a very dull time—will probably do us good at Christmas.

I spent while I was away, £75. I shall make a very handsome deduction indeed, if I take off £15 for any personal peculiarities in the order of march. That I will do, however; and therefore H.W. has to pay £10 to my account at Coutts's.

Which reminds me:—Will you make a memorandum that whenever you settle accounts with Miss Coutts, I have to receive £5 for her subscription to the Reverend Mr. Ford,[2] which I have paid.

Trusting that Mrs. Wills continues to improve,

Ever Faithfully
CD.

To JOHN FORSTER, [?27–28 SEPTEMBER 1857]

Extract in F, VIII, iii, 653. *Date:* "came in three days" after 24 Sep, according to Forster.

I have discovered that the seven miles between Maidstone and Rochester is one of the most beautiful walks in England. Five men have been looking attentively at the pump for a week, and (I should hope) may begin to fit it in the course of October.

To JOHN THOMPSON, 28 SEPTEMBER 1857*

MS Free Library of Philadelphia. *Address* (Envelope, MS Walter T. Spencer): Household Words Office | 16 Wellington Street North | Strand | London | W.C. PM Rochester 28 Sep 57.

Gad's Hill Place | Twenty Eighth September 1857.

I have always forgotten to ask you, John, whether the Scenery and fittings are all right, and have been all properly put away at Tavistock House. I hope so.

Will you go up there, and look in the Wardrobe in my dressing-room, and see what black ankle-boots are there, with stout soles for walking. And if they require heeling, or any other repairing, please get them done at once.

CHARLES DICKENS

To W. H. WILLS, 28 SEPTEMBER 1857*

MS Huntington Library.

Gad's Hill | Monday Twenty Eighth September 1857

My Dear Wills.

A considerable alteration must be made in this No.[3]

[1] A poster advertising the "Lazy Tour", in addition to the newspaper advts.

[2] Most likely the Rev. Richard Robert Ford (?1821–83), curate of St James's, Clerkenwell 1852–7; the subscription being towards charities in his poor parish.

[3] *HW*, 31 Oct 57, XVI, 409–32.

The Murder of the Agah Abdullah[1] must be shortened and made plainer. I don't understand it as I read it. It does not cohere. I can make nothing of it.

The Two Janes[2] are as bad as need be; but may remain.[3]

Adolphe Adam—positively NO.[4]

If you want papers of merit, there is Oxenford's at the Printers;[5] and I send you, enclosed, the other that I wrote to you of.[6] But the Number must be altered, and will not do.

Ever Faithfully CD.

Over

Will you send Miss Coutts the enclosed letter—she will remember the writer[7] well—and ask her from me what answer I am to return?

To SIR ALEXANDER DUFF GORDON, SEPTEMBER 1857

Mention in S. J. Davey's catalogue No. 42; *MS* 1 p.; dated Gad's Hill, 9 Sep 57, according to catalogue; but clearly in error, as CD was in Cumberland then.

Mentions Household Words.[8]

To MRS MASON,[9] [LATE] SEPTEMBER 1857

Mention in Meridian Bookshop catalogue, No. 48; *MS* 4 pp.; addressed Mrs Mason; dated 18 Sep 57, but must be after return from Doncaster.[10]

To MESSRS BRADBURY & EVANS, [1 OCTOBER 1857]

Mention in *To* Wills, 2 Oct.

To MESSRS BRADBURY & EVANS, [2 OCTOBER 1857]

Mention in *To* Wills, 2 Oct.

1 "Captain Doineau", by John Robertson, 31 Oct 57, XVI, 423: an account of the murder of the Agar Abdullah in Algeria, in 1856. The narrative is clear, but still long (13 cols).

2 By James Payn, 7 Nov 57, XVI, 442 (Lady Jane Grey and Jane Shore); Payn writes as a "Coketown" millhand with literary and antiquarian interests.

3 It was published on 7 Nov.

4 Written large and dark for emphasis.

5 See *To* Wills, 26 Sep and *fn*.

6 By Hollingshead: see 26 Sep and *fn*.

7 Perhaps Mrs Matthews: see *To* Miss Coutts, 4 Oct.

8 Nothing by Duff Gordon appeared in *HW*. His wife, Lucie, who had contributed an article in 1851, had written to CD in Oct 55 to enquire about submitting a translation (Vol. VII, p. 716).

9 Unidentified. But probably same person as in *To* Mrs Mason, 17 Dec 57 (about a case for the Home), since both letters mentioned in same catalogue.

10 18 Sep must be catalogue error; during his fortnight's absence CD had no letters forwarded (except Henry Austin's, a special case).

To JOHN THOMPSON, [2 OCTOBER 1857]

Mention in next. *Date:* clearly written the same day.

To W. H. WILLS, 2 OCTOBER 1857

MS Huntington Library.

Gad's Hill Place | Friday Second October 1857

My Dear Wills

I have yours of yesterday, this morning.

Know, that I yesterday sent to B and E, the greater part of the Lazy Tour Part IV; and that by this post I send the rest—having stuck to it, and finished it this morning. A very odd story, with a wild, picturesque fancy in it.[1]

I write to John, to tell him not to come, *if* he has only to come for copy.

Monday, so far as I know at this moment, will suit me very well. In case I should have occasion to go to town that day (possible, but not probable), I will write to you again in the meantime.

I don't remember whether I have told you that I have made the arrangement [a]with Collins[a]—that he is extremely sensible of the extra Fifty,[2] and was rather unwilling to take it—and that I have no doubt of his being devoted to H.W. and doing great service.

Ever Faithfully
CD.

To HENRY BOWIE, 3 OCTOBER 1857*

MS Deighton Bell & Co.

Gad's Hill Place, Higham, by Rochester
Third October 1857

Dear Sir

I cannot, I regret to inform you, supply the date for which you have left a blank in your Prospectus; nor can I even positively say that I shall be able to read in Edinburgh, at any time during the coming winter. My exertions in that way during the past summer, "In Remembrance of the late Mr. Jerrold" have been so great, and have so much interfered with my fulfilment of other conditional promises to read elsewhere, that I am placed in quite a new condition as to such engagements. To say that I could not foresee it, would be simply to say that I could not foresee the date of a friend's death.

Dear Sir | Your faithful Servant
Henry Bowie Esquire CHARLES DICKENS

[1] The old man's story in the "Lazy Tour", Ch. 4 (see *To* Georgina Hogarth, 12 Sep, *fn*): the whole chapter was written by CD.

[aa] Added over caret.

[2] An increase, after a year, on the five guineas a week he had received since Oct 1856 as a member of the *HW* staff.

To ARTHUR RYLAND, 3 OCTOBER 1857

MS Benoliel Collection.

Gad's Hill Place, Higham, by Rochester
Saturday Evening, Third October 1857

My Dear Sir.

I have had the honor and pleasure of receiving your letter of the Twenty Eighth of last month, informing me of the distinction that has been conferred upon me by the Council of the Birmingham and Midland Institute.

Allow me to assure you with much sincerity that I am highly gratified by having been elected one of the first Honorary Members of that establishment.[1] Nothing could have enhanced my interest in so important an undertaking;[2] but the compliment is all the more welcome to me on that account.

I accept it with a due sense of its worth, with many acknowledgments, and with all good wishes.

I am Ever My Dear Sir | Very faithfully Yours
CHARLES DICKENS

Arthur Ryland Esquire

To MISS BURDETT COUTTS, 4 OCTOBER 1857

MS Morgan Library. *Address:* Miss Burdett Coutts | Queen's Hotel | Alderley | near | Manchester.

Gad's Hill Place. | Sunday Fourth October 1857

My Dear Miss Coutts.

I sent Mrs. Matthews, £20, on receipt of your letter.

Mr. Collins (who never goes out with me on any expedition, without receiving some damage or other), sprained his leg on our second day out; and I had to carry him, à la Richard Wardour, in and out of all the Inns, Railway Carriages &c, during the rest of the Expedition. You will see Our "Lazy Tour" now going on in Household Words. It contains some descriptions (hem!) remarkable for their fanciful fidelity, and two grim stories—the first, of next Wednesday, by the cripple;[3] the second, of next Wednesday fortnight, that is to say in the Fourth Part, by your present correspondent—a Ghost Story—a bit of Diablerie.[4]

When I am clear of this Tour, I shall have to go to the Christmas Number of Household Words;[5] and I fear (as I want to do a great deal to it) that I shall not be in a condition to come, either "here", or there, while you are "here", or "there". But I have put the travelling-scheme in my desk, and shall try.

We have not yet heard from Walter at Calcutta—could not do so, until the next

[1] At a special meeting of the Council on 28 Sep (MS Birmingham and Midland Institute minute-book).

[2] See Vol. VII, p. 233 and *n*.

[3] Collins's story, told by the doctor at Wigton, of the apparently dead medical student he had brought back to life: *HW*, 10 Oct, XVI, 340–9. Collected in Collins's *The Queen of Hearts*, 3 vols, 1859 (published Dec 58), as "Brother Morgan's Story of the Dead Hand" (Vol. II, 173), without acknowledgment to *HW*, and adapted to a fictitious narrator. The volumes were dedicated to Forgues, as translator of *The Dead Secret* and *The Lighthouse*.

[4] There are no devils in the story; CD presumably refers to his own "devilment" or "impishness" in making it a dream.

[5] See *To* Morley, 18 Oct and *fn*.

Mail—but we have had three letters from him: the last, from Suez. He seems to be perfectly happy, in great enjoyment of the novelties surrounding him, and with no more thoughts of home—as yet, at all events—than if he had never had one.

When you next come to see this place, you won't know it. I have made all manner of changes. *The* glass of water has not been drunk yet, and the process of fitting the Pump (which is proceeding as slowly, and in every respect as *un*satisfactorily as possible) is like putting Oxford Street on end, and laying gas up it.

I observed an extraordinary deterioration in Layard,[1] the last time I saw him. I ventured to hint to him[2] that I thought it came of his not leaving the noble game of Politics to the Knaves and Fools and Pococurante,[3] until they had ruined us.[4]

When I see people writing letters in the Times day after day, about this class and that class not joining the Army and having no interest in arms—and when I think how we all know that we have suffered a system to go on, which has blighted generous ambition, and put reward out of the common man's reach—and how our gentry have disarmed our Peasantry—I become Demoniacal.[5]

And I wish I were Commander in Chief in India.[6] The first thing I would do to strike that Oriental race with amazement (not in the least regarding them as if they lived in the Strand, London, or at Camden Town), should be to proclaim to them, in their language, that I considered my holding that appointment by the leave of God, to mean that I should do my utmost to exterminate the Race upon whom the stain of the late cruelties rested;[7] and that I begged them to do me the favor to observe that I was there for that purpose and no other, and was now proceeding, with all convenient dispatch and merciful swiftness of execution, to blot it out of mankind and raze it off the face of the Earth.[8]

[1] Austen Henry Layard (1817–94; *DNB*), archaeologist and radical politician: see Vols VI, p. 555*n* and VII, *passim*.

[2] Layard had suffered periodic bouts of malaria since returning from his excavations.

[3] Taken from Voltaire's Senator Pococurante, a Venetian, the prototype of the man who cares for nothing (*Candide*, Ch. 25).

[4] Layard saw himself as in perpetual war with the Govt. "The country is heartily with me", he had written to his cousin the Marchioness of Huntly in 1855, "and such being the case I have no fear. If only I keep my health I shall be able to carry on the war" (Gordon Waterfield, *Layard of Nineveh*, 1963, p. 217). Politics remained his chief activity for many years. Meanwhile, he left for a six-month tour of India, to assess the causes and effects of the Mutiny.

[5] Many letters to *The Times* in late Aug and Sep criticized the slowness of reinforcements to India. "Why is not the whole of the Militia . . . at once embodied?", demanded a letter of 8 Sep; other letters advocated Negroes and West Indians as the best recruits to replace the sepoys. Most condemned, as CD did, the system of purchasing commissions, which made it virtually impossible for the sons of the middle class to serve. *The Times* criticized it in a leader of 22 Sep.

[6] The Indian Mutiny had broken out at Meerut in the Punjab on 10 May, and was followed by the massacre of Europeans in Delhi the next day. Two Commanders in Chief, Gen. Anson and Lt.-Gen. Barnard, died of cholera before assaulting Delhi; their successor, Lt.-Gen. Sir Archdale Wilson, planned the successful assault on 14 Sep; Brig. John Nicholson commanded the main assault group and was in charge of all four groups during the attack (see Christopher Hibbert, *The Great Mutiny: India 1857*, 1978, pp. 301*ff*).

[7] The massacre in the Ganges at Cawnpore on 27 June, followed by the imprisonment and murder of the surviving women and children in Bibighar, "the House of the Ladies", were the worst atrocities of the Mutiny and provoked the most fury in England. The rebels' siege of the Residency at Lucknow, with all its attendant horrors, had begun on 30 June and was not to be lifted until Mar 58.

[8] CD's imaginary threats of revenge were less horrific than those expressed by many British commanders in the field as well as by

My love to Mrs. Brown, with these sentiments.

Ever Dear Miss Coutts | Most Faithfully & affecy. Yours
CHARLES DICKENS

To F. W. HAMSTEDE, 4 OCTOBER 1857*

MS Free Library of Philadelphia.

Gad's Hill Place, Higham, by Rochester
Sunday Fourth October 1857

My Dear Sir

I received your letter, in Yorkshire. I received Mr. Blanchard Jerrold's published letter[1] at about the same time. I need hardly tell you that it made me sick at heart of the subject, and that I could take charge of no more money, so generously given, and so thanklessly pocketed.

I therefore determined to leave the matter at rest, until I should one day see you at the Garrick.

Equally I had determined to let the whole matter rest until the Resurrection-Day, and never to notice Mr. Blanchard Jerrold's letter. But I find, in other Members of the Committee, an indignant and decided determination that this must not be.

Let me ask you, therefore, if I have your permission to make that public reference to Mr. Ashurst's letter to you, of which I send you a draft enclosed.[2]

My Dear Sir | Faithfully Yours

F. W. Hamstede Esquire CHARLES DICKENS

To JOHN HOLLINGSHEAD, 4 OCTOBER 1857

Extract in *American Book Prices Current*, 1934; *MS* 1 p.; addressed John Hollingshead; dated Gad's Hill Place, 4 Oct 57.

I don't think there is enough in this paper to separate it from some other similar narratives (more or less) that have appeared in Household Words.[3]

sectors of the press in both India and England. The fiercest voice was probably that of Brig. John Nicholson (see above), who wrote in a letter, soon after the Mutiny broke out: "Let us propose a Bill for the flaying alive, impalement, or burning of the murderers of the women and children at Delhi. The idea of simply hanging the perpetrators of such atrocities is maddening. I wish that I were in that part of the world, [*he was then in the Punjab*] that if necessary I might take the law into my own hands" (given by Christopher Hibbert, *ibid.*, p. 193). See *To* de la Rue, 23 Oct and *fn.*

[1] See *To* the Editor of *The Times*, 1 Sep and *fn.*

[2] See *ibid.*, 6 Oct.

[3] Hollingshead's published contributions to *HW* are very numerous from October on.

To MRS CARMICHAEL-SMYTH,[1] [5] OCTOBER 1857*

MS University of California, Los Angeles. *Date:* misdated by CD; Monday was 5 Oct 57.

Gad's Hill | Monday Fourth October 1857.

My Dear Mrs. Smyth.

I very much regret to inform you that I cannot make your friend's story available for Household Words. I observe many good things in it, and much in the descriptions it contains that is felt in a picturesque and striking way; but it is too diffuse; too deficient in character, and too slow in its movement with a reference to its length, to have the requisite address in it to a large Audience.

It would be useless for me to trouble the Authoress with a request to send me the remainder. Howsoever the story ends, I could not overcome the difficulties in its Household-Words-way.

Will you thank the lady from me for her offer? And will you tell her from me, as you most conscientiously may, that I think the idea of the title, and the manner in which an interest in it is derived from the Pedigree, very novel and ingenious?

I beg to send my kind regard to Major Smyth,[2] and am Ever

Very faithfully Yours
CHARLES DICKENS

Mrs. Carmichael Smyth.

To E. W. LANE,[3] 5 OCTOBER 1857*

MS Free Library of Philadelphia.

Gad's Hill Place, Higham, by Rochester
Fifth October 1857

Dear Sir

Coming to my little country-house, after an absence of a few weeks in other parts of England, I find your obliging note. Pray accept my assurance that I accept your little book[4] (still lying at my house in town), with many thanks; and that I should not have been so (apparently) remiss in acknowledging its receipt, but for the reason which I have troubled you by explaining.

Dear Sir | Faithfully Yours
CHARLES DICKENS

Edward W Lane Esquire

[1] Née Anne Becher (1792–1864), Thackeray's mother. Daughter of John Harman Becher, Writer in the East India Co.; married Richmond Thackeray, Secretary of Board of Revenue, Calcutta, 1810; and, 18 months after his death in 1815, Capt. Henry Carmichael-Smyth, whom she had fallen in love with as a girl of 15. They lived in Paris 1838–61: for an account of their life there by Thackeray's daughter, later Lady Ritchie, see *Letters and Private Papers of W. M. Thackeray*, ed. Gordon N. Ray, 1955, I, cxv; Thackeray's letters show his devotion to her, but he is not uncritical in taking her as the model for Helen Pendennis. CD had presumably met her with Thackeray, but not known when.

[2] Her husband, Henry Carmichael-Smyth (1780–1861), retired Major, Bengal Engineers; educated, like Thackeray, at Charterhouse; then at the East India Company's military academy, Addiscombe; for his distinguished active service in India, see H. M. Vibart, *Addiscombe: its Heroes and Men of Note*, 1894, p. 60. Major 1821; Resident Superintendent of Addiscombe 1822–4.

[3] Edward Wickstead Lane, MD: see Vol. VI, p. 783 and *nn*.

[4] *Hydropathy, or the Natural System of Medical Treatment*, published July 1857.

To RICHARD BENTLEY, 5 OCTOBER 1857*

MS Berg Collection.

Gad's Hill Place | Monday Night | Fifth October 1857

My Dear Mr. Bentley

I was in Yorkshire when you addressed your letter of the Seventeenth of last month, to me. I have not been long at home, but have had time to consider and reconsider it.

I cannot overcome my objection to that kind of use of my name with the public;—simply because I cannot overcome the conviction that it would be an abuse of it. For this reason, and no other, I must beg you to excuse me from entertaining your proposal.[1]

But I shall be heartily glad to shew, in the frankest manner on all becoming occasions, that the old wound between us has quite healed up and left no mark.[2] And I hope I may be able to do that, in many little social ways, which will be quite as significant—at least—as if I took money from you.

Faithfully Yours

Richard Bentley Esquire CHARLES DICKENS

To JOHN FORSTER, [?19 SEPTEMBER–6 OCTOBER 1857]

Extract in F, IX, i, 726. *Date:* between 19 Sep and 6 Oct (see below).[3]

Saying that he and Collins had written together the second part of the "Lazy Tour"; in which I think you would find it very difficult to say where I leave off and he comes in;[4] *of the descriptions in the first part he had said* Some of my own tickle me very much;[5] but that may be in great part because I know the originals, and delight in their fantastic fidelity.

To JOHN THOMPSON, 6 OCTOBER 1857

Text from Sawyer's catalogue No. 103 (1931); addressed John Thompson; dated Gad's Hill, 6 Oct 57.

John. These letters are important. Leave them at the different Newspaper Offices[6] to which they are addressed, *as soon as they are delivered into your hands.* Do not delay.—CHARLES DICKENS

[1] Bentley had probably wanted to quote Brooks's dedication to CD of the 1st edn of his *Aspen Court* (see *To* Brooks, 14 Oct and *fn*) in his advt of the cheap edn, published 1 Oct.

[2] Their disputes of 1837–9; see Vol. I, *passim.*

[3] Ch. 2 had been completed on 19 Sep (see *To* Wills, 17 and 20 Sep) and was published in *HW*, 10 Oct (appearing 7 Oct).

[4] In fact CD wrote everything up to the white line on p. 340 (F, 1872–4, III, Appx, p. 511), which shows that the Doctor's story is very skilfully led up to by the introduction of the Doctor himself.

[5] Ch. 1 includes descriptions of the innkeeper near Carrick Fell, and of Thomas Idle himself. Forster uses the quotation as an instance of CD's enjoyment of his own humour.

[6] See *To* the Editor of *The Times*, 1 Sep, *fn.*

To THE EDITOR OF *THE TIMES*, 6 OCTOBER 1857

Text from *The Times*, 7 Oct 57.

October 6, 1857

Sir,

You were so kind as to give publicity to a letter we addressed to you on the termination of our labours "In remembrance of the late Mr. Jerrold," making known their result.[1]

Mr. Jerrold's eldest son thereupon gave to a letter of his own what publicity he could obtain for it, making his own representation of his late father's affairs.[2]

We knew our forbearing and delicate reference to them (forced upon us by exaggerations with which we had been repeatedly met, and which the son had never contradicted) to be perfectly accurate, and we knew his account of them to be highly incorrect. We are extremely sorry to be obliged to produce the proof of this; but it is necessary to the clearance of our own good faith, and that of the gentlemen associated with us.

We have before us, under date the 2d of this present month, a letter *from the solicitor to the late Mr. Jerrold's estate*[3] (a gentleman well known in his profession, Mr. Ashurst, of the Old Jewry), in which, after mentioning that there is a life assurance of 1,000*l.*, which is Mrs. Jerrold's absolutely, and which the estate cannot claim, he informs the correspondent to whom his communication is addressed "that he cannot understand Mr. Blanchard Jerrold's reason for writing this unfortunate letter;" that he thinks "he and his family ought to be set right on the matter;" and that, if a certain claim be urged of which he has received the particulars, "the facts and figures show that the estate will be absolutely insolvent."

We quote this letter with its writer's permission, and we have now done with this subject for ever.[4]

Your faithful servants,
CHARLES DICKENS
ARTHUR W. W. SMITH

[1] *To* the Editor of *The Times*, 1 Sep.

[2] See *To* the Editor of *The Times*, 1 Sep, *fn.* According to Jerrold's grandson, Jerrold "did not leave his family pennyless, as was unwarrantably stated at the time". Besides a life policy, to pay off a debt incurred on the failure of Douglas Jerrold's *Weekly Newspaper* in 1849, and the life policy for his widow, there were rights in some plays, etc. (Walter Jerrold, *Douglas Jerrold, Wit and Dramatist*, II, 657).

[3] Addressed to Hamstede: see *To* him, 4 Oct.

[4] Jerrold's own bitterness at CD's letter to *The Times* of 1 Sep is shown in what he wrote to Hepworth Dixon on 19 Sep. He regarded the letter as an "intentional slight to myself particularly & to the family generally": "you will see how deeply pained we have all been". Despite severe judgement by some, he had "equally strong proofs that the public is with *me*". He felt keenly "the insult" to his father, "in the shape of studied disregard for me as his representative"; he had "reaped a crop of enemies", because "I have not been a very Tame wearer of leading-strings" (MS Private).

To JAMES DAVIS,[1] 7 OCTOBER 1857

MS University of Kentucky.

Gad's Hill Place. | Seventh October 1857

Dear Sir

In acknowledging the receipt of your interesting letter, and in thanking you for it, I have to express my regret that I cannot comply with your request. But, I receive similar requests by hundreds; and I have already promised that whenever I read in this neighbourhood, I will do so for the local[2] Mechanics' Institution.

Dear Sir | Your faithful Servant

James Davis Esquire CHARLES DICKENS

To JOHN HOLLINGSHEAD, 7 OCTOBER 1857

Extract in Dodd Mead Company catalogue No. 69; *MS* 2 pp.; dated Gad's Hill Place, 7 Oct 57.

I am proceeding on a new plan with the Christmas Number this year,[3] and it may be considered as already done.

To JOHN THOMPSON, 7 OCTOBER 1857*

MS Walter T. Spencer.

Tavistock House | Wednesday, Seventh October 1857.

I shall be in town tomorrow (Thursday) afternoon, and shall be glad to have the Dressing-Room comfortable, as I shall want to change at the office. I shall also be glad to have a little bit of fish and a mutton chop for dinner at the office at half past 4.

CHARLES DICKENS

To JOHN FORSTER, [?EARLY OCTOBER 1857]

Extract from F, VIII, ii, 638. *Date:* "early autumn", according to Forster; and after Forster had read the account of CD's "rush up Carrick Fell", published 3 Oct.

Too late to say, put the curb on, and don't rush at hills—the wrong man to say it to. I have now no relief but in action. I am become incapable of rest. I am quite confident I should rust, break, and die, if I spared myself. Much better to die, doing. What I am in that way, nature made me first, and my way of life has of late, alas! confirmed. I must accept the drawback—since it is one—with the powers I have; and I must hold upon the tenure prescribed to me.[4]

[1] Obviously a local man, but not identified.

[2] i.e. Rochester and Chatham.

[3] See *To* Morley, 18 Oct and *fn*.

[4] Marginal note in F, 1872–4, III, 158, has "Reply to a remonstrance".

To MRS CORNELIUS, 11 OCTOBER 1857

Text from N, II, 890.

Gad's Hill Place | Sunday Eleventh October 1857

My Dear Anne

I want some little changes made in the arrangement of my dressing-room and the Bathroom. And as I would rather not have them talked about by comparative strangers, I shall be much obliged to you, my old friend, if you will see them completed before you leave Tavistock House.

I wish to make the Bathroom my washing-room also. It will be therefore necessary to carry into the Bathroom, to remain there, the two washing-stands from my Dressing-Room. Then, to get rid altogether, of the chest of drawers in the Dressing-Room I want the recess of the doorway between the Dressing-Room and Mrs. Dickens's room, fitted with plain white deal shelves, and closed in with a plain light deal door, painted white. Rudkin can do this—or Lillie,[1] being in the house, can do it if he likes.[2] The sooner it is done, the better.

My wardrobe will then stand where the chest of Drawers stands now, and a small iron bedstead will go behind the door, with its side against the wall, as you enter the Dressing-Room; its head towards the stairs, and its foot towards the window. I have ordered the bedstead and bedding, and they will be sent to Tavistock House to you. The chest of drawers shall come down here, when the van comes down to bring our luggage home at the end of the month.

They all send their love.

Ever Faithfully Yours
[CHARLES DICKENS]

To J. B. BUCKSTONE, 13 OCTOBER 1857*

MS Free Library of Philadelphia.

OFFICE OF HOUSEHOLD WORDS,
Tuesday Thirteenth October 1857.

My Dear Buckstone.

No. I do not believe that you have "made out of the matter a mere managerial bargain", and I do not believe that you have done any thing in it but oblige me very readily.[3] For which accept my cordial thanks.

I need hardly tell you that my interest in the young lady does not cease with the effecting of this arrangement, and that I shall always regard your taking care of her

[1] Benjamin Lillie, plumber and painter, 70 High St, Marylebone, who had worked for CD at Devonshire Terrace; at Tavistock House he fitted up the library and the imitation book-backs and moved the furniture to Gad's Hill (W. R. Hughes, *A Week's Tramp in Dickens-Land*, p. 42). See later vols.

[2] CD's Account-book (MS Messrs Coutts) shows four payments to "Workmen" Sep–Nov 57, totalling £52.15.

[3] Buckstone had engaged Ellen Ternan to appear at the Haymarket as Louisa in Augustus Harris's one-Act farce, *My Son, Diana*; her part is a contrast with that of the strong-minded heroine who appears for most of the play in shooting jacket, breeches and boots. Though in the repertory 17–21 Oct, it was not played every night and was still in on 7 Nov, when Ellen appeared.

and remembering her, as an act of personal friendship to me.[1] On the termination of her present engagement, I hope you will tell me, before you tell her, what you see for her, "looming in the future."[2]

I enclose a cheque (which I have not crossed) for Fifty Pounds.[3]

As you are so far as Shooter's Hill[4] on the way to Gad's Hill; I wish you would come from your hill to my hill, and have Sunday dinner. I would meet you at Dartford, and bring you on in a basket-carriage; and I would keep you (with your leave) all night, and send you anywhere in the morning. Could it be done,—on Sunday Week for instance?

Faithfully Yours always
CHARLES DICKENS

J. B. Buckstone Esquire.

To SHIRLEY BROOKS, 14 OCTOBER 1857

MS Brotherton Library, Leeds.

Gad's Hill Place | Fourteenth October 1857

My Dear Shirley Brooks.

As I would on no account notice William Jerrold's[5] letter,[6] myself, so I would on no account have you notice it either. The thing is at an end. I have turned that little entry in the book of my life, and can quite composedly pass to a new page.

In the far different and far more cheering matter of your dedication[7] and the affectionate part of your note referring to it, let me assure you that the new line[8] gives me hearty pleasure, and that you shall never find the sincere friendship fail on my side. Of the old part, which pleased me so much when it was new and which has not faded at all, I will only say again that if I have an object in life, it is to leave my calling (as I do believe I shall), much better than I found it; and that in the unpretending sincerity and constant remembrance of this desire, I am worthy that grasp of your workman's hand.

Ever Faithfully Yours
CHARLES DICKENS[9]

Shirley Brooks Esquire.

[1] Buckstone gave Ellen three further engagements: Fanny Melrose, a small part, but on stage throughout (in "spotted muslin") in John Maddison Morton's new one-Act farce, *Take Care of Dowb*, which ran between 23 Nov and 23 Dec; and in Thomas Morton's two old comedies, well-known to CD, *Speed the Plough*, 1–9 Jan 58, as Susan and *A Cure for the Heartache*, as Jessy Oatland, 12–27 Jan 58. From 17 Mar she played at the Lyceum, under Charles Dillon, in *She Stoops to Conquer*.

[2] Disraeli's phrase in a speech to his electors on 2 June 52, constantly mocked in *Punch*: see Vol. VI, p. 721 and *n*.

[3] Perhaps a present, in return for Buckstone's help; or to pay for Ellen's engagement.

[4] In the parish of Eltham, 8 miles south-east of London, on the Dover road.

[5] N reads "Turrold's". William Blanchard Jerrold.

[6] See *To* the Editor of *The Times*, 6 Oct and *fn*.

[7] The first edn of *Aspen Court*, 3 vols, 1855, had been dedicated to CD "In Earnest Acknowledgment of the Constant | Energetic, and Invaluable Service | Rendered by Him | In Promoting the Recognition and Elevation | Of the Profession Adorned by His Genius."

[8] Brooks's new dedication began: "Not less in Testimony of Sincere Friendship, Than | . . .".

[9] Back at his office that night, or possibly the next night, CD decided to walk out to Gad's Hill. In "Shy Neighbourhoods" (*AYR*, 26 May 60, III, 155) he wrote: "My last special feat was turning out of bed at two, after a hard day pedestrian and otherwise, and walking thirty

To CHARLES COLLINS, 16 OCTOBER 1857*

MS Mr H. E. Quick.

OFFICE OF HOUSEHOLD WORDS,
Friday Sixteenth October 1857

My Dear Charles Collins

I have left a letter of Wilkie's behind me at Gad's Hill, and cannot remember his present address.[1] If you know it (as I dare say you do) will you send on the enclosed[2] to him without loss of time?

Very faithfully Yours

Charles Collins Esquire. CHARLES DICKENS

To MISS GEORGINA HOGARTH, 16 OCTOBER 1857*

MS Fales Collection, New York University Library.

OFFICE OF HOUSEHOLD WORDS,
Sixteenth October 1857

Dearest Georgy

I shall not be able to get home tonight as I had expected, and shall therefore come by the Train on Sunday by which I came last Sunday. Knowing that Charley is not with you and that you have some letters, I send John down for them.

Ever and ever Affectionately[3]

To CLARKSON STANFIELD, 16 OCTOBER 1857

MS Berg Collection.

OFFICE OF HOUSEHOLD WORDS,
Friday Sixteenth October 1857

My Dear Stanny

I am extremely sorry to hear that you have been ill and confined to the house. I have been far away, and very busy, and much distressed by some anxieties, or I should have heard of you sooner.

Tomorrow forenoon I hope to be able to come out to Hampstead and shake you

miles into the country to breakfast" (quoted in F, VIII, v, 675). Forster also recollected his saying that he had "seldom seen anything so striking as the way in which the wonders of an equinoctial dawn ... presented themselves during that walk. He had never before happened to see night so completely at odds with morning, 'which was which' [Macbeth, *III, iv, 127*]." It is just possible that Forster was recording a letter to himself on 15 or 16 Oct. The incident is recalled in *Great Expectations*, Ch. 44, where Pip, distressed and restless after learning of Estella's coming marriage and Miss Havisham's remorse, walks through the night from Rochester to London.

[1] Both Wilkie and Charles Collins lived occasionally with their mother at 2 Harley Place during 1857, but also had lodgings elsewhere. Wilkie took rooms in Howland St temporarily and moved into 124 Albany St with Caroline Graves in Feb 58. (William Clarke, *The Secret Life of Wilkie Collins*, pp. 93–4.)

[2] Untraced.

[3] Signature cut away.

by the hand. In the meantime here is an old little friend in a new frock, who has been long due,[1] and who begs to be tenderly taken in.[2]

Ever affectionately

Clarkson Stanfield Esquire. CHARLES DICKENS

To LORD BROUGHAM, 18 OCTOBER 1857*

MS Brotherton Library, Leeds.

Gad's Hill Place, Higham | by Rochester, Kent
Eighteenth October 1857

My Dear Lord Brougham

I venture to send you the enclosed note from Miss Power, because I believe I know the urgency of her case better than any one else, and because I am sure I have seen her hard struggle to become quietly independent, with great sympathy and admiration. She is no fine lady in these changed times; but a thoroughly hard-working, self reliant, striving woman.[3] Whatever she could get to do, she would do conscientiously and well. I am as certain of it, as I could possibly be if I spoke for myself. If one or two of the most powerful of those who remember that dead and gone house[4] and the attractions of poor D'Orsay,[5] would try to do this little thing for her, they would do a real and a most gracious kindness, and she would always deserve it.[6]

My Dear Lord Brougham | Very faithfully Yours

The | Lord Brougham. CHARLES DICKENS

To HENRY MORLEY, 18 OCTOBER 1857

MS Comtesse de Suzannet.

Gad's Hill Place. | Higham, by Rochester, Kent
Sunday Eighteenth October | 1857

My Dear Morley.

I particularly want a little piece of information, with a view to the construction of something for Household Words.[7] I have not the means of reference here, and I dare

[1] The delay of several months since publication may be explained by the absence from London of both CD and Stanfield besides the time taken for the special binding.

[2] A specially bound copy of *Little Dorrit*, 1857, inscribed "Clarkson Stanfield | With affectionate regard, from | Charles Dickens October 1857" (Berg Collection).

[3] Marguerite Power was now trying to earn her living by writing; she published five novels between 1856 and 1861 (*The Foresters*, 2 vols, 1857, dedicated to CD "as a humble tribute of profound admiration and most sincere regard") and a *Memoir of Lady Blessington*, 1850. Edited the *Keepsake* 1851–7; her periodical contributions included four prose-pieces and a poem for *HW* 1856–8.

[4] Gore House, Kensington, where she had lived with her aunt and Count D'Orsay Sep 1839–May 1849. See Vols. II, p. 58*n* and V, p. 530*n*.

[5] Alfred, Count D'Orsay (1801–52; *DNB*): see Vols. II, p. 219*n* and IV and V, *passim*.

[6] See *To* Thackeray, 4 Dec 57 and *To* Friends of Lady Blessington, 24 Dec 57.

[7] For the Christmas No., "The Perils of Certain English Prisoners, and Their Treasure in Women, Children, Silver, and Jewels", by CD and Collins, 7 Dec 57. CD wrote two of the three chapters: Ch. I, "The Island of Silver-

say you can supply them out of your own reading. It will oblige me very much, if you will consider and reply to the following question.

Whether, at any time within a hundred years or so, we were in such amicable relations with South America as would have rendered it reasonably *possible* for us to have made, either a public treaty, or a private bargain, with a South American Government, empowering a little English Colony, established on the spot for the purpose, to work a Silver-Mine (on purchase of the right). And whether, in that suppositious case, it is reasonably *possible* that our English Government at home would have sent out a small force, of a few Marines or so, for that little Colony's protection; or (which is the same thing), would have drafted them off from the nearest English Military Station.[1]

Or, can you suggest, from your remembrance, any more probable set of circumstances, in which a few English people—gentlemen, ladies, and children—and a few English soldiers, would find themselves alone in a strange wild place and liable to hostile attack?

I wish to avoid India[2] itself; but I want to shadow out in what I do, the bravery of our ladies in India.

Very faithfully Yours

Henry Morley Esquire CHARLES DICKENS

To F.M. EVANS, 20 OCTOBER 1857

Text from N, II, 892.

Ship Hotel, Dover[3] | Tuesday Twentieth October 1857

My Dear Evans,

We decide upon No. 1., at six shillings.[4] I know you will be glad to hear this, and I therefore send you the intelligence.

Mr. Forster will see you as soon as he comes to town—probably on Saturday. He will then see Chapman and arrange other matters with him. This done, I will

Store", and Ch. 3, "The Rafts on the River". Collins contributed Ch. 2, "The Prison in the Woods".

[1] All the factors are present in Ch. 1: the story's teller is one of a detachment of 24 Marines, drafted from Jamaica to Belize, British Honduras, in pursuit of pirates; as a result, they find themselves protecting the small English colony on the island who owned and worked a silver-mine inland. See *To* Collins, 22 Oct and *fnn*.

[2] The story particularly stresses the heroism of the ladies. There had been many reports of atrocities committed on the wives of British officers, who insisted on staying with their husbands, during the Indian Mutiny that summer. (For one particularly horrific one, see Christopher Hibbert, *The Great Mutiny: India 1857*, p. 195; also *To* Miss Coutts, 4 Oct and *fnn*). CD would also have read the previous day of the capture of a boat-full of British men and their wives during the siege of Lucknow: the men were killed first and their wives asked that they should die with them (*The Times*, 17 Oct).

[3] Probably editor's confusion over the owner's address; CD had no reason to be at Dover, *c.* 50 miles from Gad's Hill.

[4] *Pickwick Papers*, Vol. 1, the first vol. of the Library edn, published at 6/–.

appoint with you for our meeting at Household Words to settle the draft of the Prospectus.[1]

Faithfully Yours always
[CHARLES DICKENS]

To WILKIE COLLINS, 22 OCTOBER 1857

MS Morgan Library.

[OFFICE OF HOUSEHOLD WORDS][2]
Thursday Twenty Second October 1857

My Dear Wilkie

The accompanying letter from Morley (as usually happens in these cases) conglomerates and complicates the business, I think.

You will see nothing appropriate about Silver Mines in the book,[3] except at the following references. All in Vol I.

Page 169 to 172[4]
" 224 to 226[5]
" 285 to 290.[6]

Look it over, and let us then come to some conclusion, right or wrong, and follow it out.

Shall we meet here tomorrow between 3 and 5, or shall I come to you between those hours? Let me know, according to your health.

Ever Faithfully
CD.

[1] For the Library edn, 22 vols, 1858–9, issued in monthly vols, advertised as "a far more convenient form, at once for present perusal, and for preservation" than any previous format. See *To* Evans, 6 and 15 Sep and *fnn*.

[2] Part of address torn away but clearly headed office notepaper.

[3] Carl Scherzer, *Travels in the Free States of Central America; Nicaragua, Honduras, and San Salvador*, Longmans, 2 vols, July 1857.

[4] Part of Ch. 10, about Nicaragua and the working of gold and silver mines at Matagalpa.

[5] Ch. 12, "Dipilto and its Silver Mines", still in Nicaragua; describing Scherzer's visits to the mine of St Rafael; the use of Red Indian labour; and how the silver was taken to the "eastern seaboard of Honduras and exchanged for English cotton goods ... and other European productions."

[6] Ch. 14, about Honduras; describing visits to three silver mines: one taken over by a company; one owned by an Irishman; and the third owned by a man from Alsace. This silver is mostly carried to Tegucigalpa (capital of Granada). The proprietors are "far from prosperous". Vol. II has more about robbery and hostility to foreigners, perhaps reflected in Collins's "The Prison in the Woods".

To WILLIAM CRESWICK, 22 OCTOBER 1857

MS Dickens House.

OFFICE OF HOUSEHOLD WORDS,
Thursday Twenty Second October 1857

Dear Sir

I want to see your Drama now in course of representation,[1] of which I think I know something in another form.[2] I shall be in town tomorrow (Friday) evening, and shall be very glad to occupy a Private Box if you can conveniently place one at my disposal.

Faithfully Yours
William Creswick Esquire CHARLES DICKENS

To EMILE DE LA RUE, 23 OCTOBER 1857*

MS Berg Collection.

OFFICE OF HOUSEHOLD WORDS,
Friday Twenty Third October 1857

My Dear De la Rue.

I cannot tell you how delighted I have been to receive your budget of news, or with what interest I have read, and re-read, your letter. I hope you really will produce yourself at Tavistock House before the year is out, and that my dear old patient will appear there before the next year is out. Both of you shall have the heartiest welcome that the Inimitable's house and its inmates can give. Believe that, and take it from my heart to both of yours!—

Between ourselves (I beckon Madame De la Rue nearer with my fore-finger, and whisper this with a serio-comic smile), I don't get on better in these later times with a certain poor lady you know of, than I did in the earlier Peschiere[3] days. Much worse. Much worse![4] Neither do the children, elder or

[1] *Ambition; or The Throne and The Tomb*, by F. L. Phillips (*d.* 1879), playing at the Surrey since 28 Sep; originally licensed (on 18 Sep) as *Catherine Howard*. An exciting melodrama, it featured Henry VIII, Cranmer and Catherine Howard, with Ethelwold, "Earl of Derby", acted by Creswick, as the principal character. Unpublished; but MS BL (Lord Chamberlain's copy). A great success ("filling the house floor to ceiling": *Theatrical Journal*, 7 Oct), it ran until 6 Nov.

[2] The play was adapted from Dumas's *Catherine Howard*, 1835, which CD would certainly have read and probably seen.

[3] See Vols IV, p. 167 and *n* and VII, pp. 884–5 and *n*.

[4] An exaggerated and patently inaccurate report by Harriet Martineau, three years later, claimed that F. M. Evans told her that he and Wills "had for 2 years declined their annual visit to the Ds' country house, because they 'could not stand his cruelty to his wife.' I asked what 'cruelty' meant; and he said 'swearing at her, in the presence of guests, children and servants;'—swearing often and fiercely. He is downright 'ferocious' now, and has quarreled with almost every friend he had. Next to him, Forster behaved worst,—aggravating his discontents with his wife, who 'is not the sort of woman they say', Mr E declares. Dickens had terrified and depressed her into a dull condition; and she never was very clever" (*Harriet Martineau's Letters to Fanny Wedgwood*, ed. Elisabeth Arbuckle, Stanford, 1983, p. 196; letter of 20 Oct 1860). This is the more unlikely because CD abhorred bad language (see his paper, "The Ruffian", *AYR*, 10 Oct 68, XX, 421). But there may be some basis for the report of CD's treatment of Catherine; Katey Dickens told Gladys Storey, probably referring to early

younger.[1] Neither can she get on with herself, or be any thing but unhappy.[2] (She has been excruciatingly jealous of, and has obtained positive proofs of my being on the most confidential terms with, at least Fifteen Thousand Women of various conditions in life, every condition in life, since we left Genoa. Please to respect me for this vast experience.)[3] What we should do, or what the Girls would be, without Georgy, I cannot imagine. She is the active spirit of the house, and the children dote upon her. Enough of this. We put the Skeleton away in the cupboard, and very few people, comparatively, know of its existence.

—Not Albert Smith, for one, I dare say! I thought you would be pleased with him, and rather chuckled when I sent him to you.[4] He is a very good, kind fellow, under certain oddities of manner, and has a most hearty recollection of his intercourse with you. Only yesterday (he being now at home again), he wrote me a letter, asking me when we should go to some place about Town and dine, and then stroll to the Theatre "and talk about the De la Rues and Genoa"? I appointed tomorrow night, so we shall overhaul you at a great rate.

My visual ray[5] has been lately dwelling on the wilds of Cumberland and Yorkshire, where whole towns have turned out (as in duty bound) to greet the Inimitable and offer him homage. One night at Doncaster I was at the Theatre,[6] where I had been behaving excessively ill in the way of gaping and rubbing my head wearily, from 7 to 11, without the slightest idea that anybody knew me; and I was slouching out at the fall of the Curtain, with my hands in my pockets and a general expression upon me of total want of dignity, when the Pit suddenly got up without the slightest warning, and cried out "Three cheers for Charles Dickens Esquire!" Thereupon all the house took it up, the actors came back and joined in the demonstration, and I was obliged instantaneously to convert myself into a most affable, interesting, and beaming personage. [a][I was a little troubled in my mind by not having that other waistcoat on, but made a very splendid appearance, all things considered.][a]

Why did they know nothing of the Hindoo character? Why? Do you ask why? Because it was the system to know nothing of anything; and to believe that England, while doing nothing, was doing everything. There are Thousands of Asses now—and Asses in power: which is the worst of it—who will hold this faith—if one could dignify such idiotcy by the name—until they have done for all of us. It is not three years since there were Indian Princes here; and in the rush after *them*, that baser side of the genteel character which would go Tuft-Hunting after the Devil was exhibited in a most astounding degree. Again and again, I have said to Ladies, spirited enough and handsome enough and clever enough to have known better (*not* of the 15,000, please to observe!), "what on earth do you see in those men to go mad

in 1858, that her father had behaved "like a madman" (Gladys Storey, *Dickens and Daughter*, pp. 94); and Mrs Hogarth reported Catherine telling her of "her trials".

[1] For the untruth of this charge, see *To* Miss Coutts, 9 May 58, *fn*.

[2] They had almost certainly quarrelled about Ellen Ternan by now.

[3] There is no evidence of Catherine's having shown jealousy of any woman apart from Mme de la Rue and Ellen. CD had, of course, flirted with several of the women he was attracted by: in 1841 with Emma Picken (who became Mrs Eleanor Christian; see Vol. III, p. 328 and *nn*), Christiana Weller (see Vol. IV) and Mary Boyle (see Vols VI and VII).

[4] See *To* de la Rue, 19 Aug 57.

[5] An old joke between them, quoting Milton: see Vol. VII, p. 208*n*.

[6] On Mon, 14 Sep, to see *Money*.

[aa] CD's square brackets.

about? You know faces, when they are not brown; you know common expressions when they are not under turbans; Look at the dogs—low, treacherous, murderous, tigerous villains who despise you while you pay court to them, and who would rend you to pieces at half an hour's notice." I suppose a greater mistake was never committed in the world, than this wretched Lord Canning's[1] maudlin proclamation about mercy.[2] It would have been bad enough, if the Hindoos lived in the Strand here, and had the ideas of London vagabonds; but, addressed to the Oriental character, it is hideously absurd and dangerous. I wish I were Commander in Chief over there! I would address that Oriental character which must be powerfully spoken to, in something like the following placard, which should be vigorously translated into all native dialects, "I, The Inimitable, holding this office of mine, and firmly believing that I hold it by the permission of Heaven and not by the appointment of Satan, have the honor to inform you Hindoo gentry that it is my intention, with all possible avoidance of unnecessary cruelty and with all merciful swiftness of execution, to exterminate the Race from the face of the earth,[3] which disfigured the earth with the late abominable atrocities."

Poor Charley Gibbs, poor dear Gibbs.[4] Give him my Love, and tell him everything that is cheery and friendly from me. And poor Browne[5]—the man cast in the same mould as myself—the man formed (as he said) to be my twin brother! Broken his rib! Why the wrong rib? Why not break Mrs. Browne! I have hope of his recovery, poor fellow, if he can only be got to take it into his head that somebody wants him to die. His constitutional obstinacy will then most certainly prevent his doing it.[6]

Perhaps I may see you in Genoa, before I won't say you—but at all events before

[1] Charles John Canning, 1st Earl Canning (1812–62; *DNB*), Governor-General of India since Feb 56.

[2] Not a public proclamation, but a Resolution by the Council of India, of 31 July, circulated to civilian officers. It discriminated between sepoys of Regts which had mutinied and committed bloodshed and sepoys of other units not actively involved in the Mutiny. It soon appeared in Calcutta papers and was published by *The Times* on 17 Oct. *The Times* leader that day sarcastically pilloried it as the "Clemency of CANNING" and on 21 Oct attacked it again as "a silly proclamation". A *Punch* cartoon of 24 Oct, "The Clemency of Canning", showed Canning caressing with his hand the turbaned head of a sepoy, armed with sword and knife. It was savagely attacked by the press in both England and India. But Lord Granville, leader of the House of Lords, strongly supported the document and the Queen wrote to Canning: "how entirely the Queen shares *his* feelings of sorrow and indignation at the unchristian spirit shown—alas! also to a great extent here—by the public towards Indians in general & towards *Sepoys without discrimination*!" (Michael Maclagan, *"Clemency" Canning*, 1962, p. 141.) Prince Albert, too, made it clear to the Cabinet that he entirely supported Canning. Commissioner Pordage's words to Capt. Carton, in command of the English boats at Silver Store Island ("The Perils of Certain English Prisoners", Christmas No., 7 Dec 57, Ch. 1) are obviously a gibe at Canning: "Government requires you to treat the enemy [*the pirates*] with great delicacy, consideration, clemency, and forbearance" (p. 8). The same line is taken in several of the very numerous articles on India published in *HW* between July 57 and Mar 58; e.g. a series of twelve, "Wanderings in India" by John Lang, and "Blown away!" on the execution of sepoys by George Craig, 27 Mar 58 (XVII, 348).

[3] Capt. Carton uses almost the same words about the pirates to Commissioner Pordage in "The Perils of Certain English Prisoners" (above).

[4] De la Rue may have told CD of Gibbs's having been passed over by his firm, Gibbs & Co., Bankers, as agent in Genoa, or he may have been ill.

[5] Timothy Yeats Brown (again misspelt by CD).

[6] He died the following year.

Madame De la Rue—shall come to London. There are times when I think—really think—of coming, en garçon, and staying Weeks in the dear old City. It *may* be a castle in the air—a house in Spain—it *may* turn out to be an idea with a solid foundation.

I met Thompson[1] one day, about two months ago. He told me they were living in the country, about 30 or 40 miles from London.[2] We have been at a house I have in Kent, all the summer, and I have heard no more of them—except that I believe he has been much troubled by his two sisters at Jersey,[3] who get into all manner of Debt, and look to him to be got out.[4]

Wilkie Collins has just come in, and begs me to send his kindest regard to you and Madame. All at home would send their loves, if they knew me to be writing.

Adieu! | Ever and Ever Affectionately
CHARLES DICKENS

To WILLIAM CRESWICK, 24 OCTOBER 1857

MS Dickens House.

OFFICE OF HOUSEHOLD WORDS,
Saturday Twenty Fourth October 1857

My Dear Sir

Many thanks. I thought the Piece (which I know very well) extremely good of its kind, and your own part, if you will excuse my saying so, admirably played.[5]

Faithfully Yours

William Creswick Esquire. CHARLES DICKENS

To PETER CUNNINGHAM, 26 OCTOBER 1857[6]

Extracts in Anderson Galleries catalogue No. 4240 (1936), and Sotheby's catalogue, Dec 1877; *MS* 1 p.; dated Gad's Hill Place, 26 Oct 57; addressed Peter Cunningham.

Can you write me (either at the Household Words Office, or Tavistock House) whether there is a housekeeper to every Public office, or for example to all in Somerset House.[7] . . . I ask with a view to a lady, and not with any private object.[8]

[1] Thomas James Thompson (1812–81): see Vol. I, p. 416*n* and subsequent vols.

[2] Probably at Dorking, where his wife Christiana (see Vol. III, p. 446*n*) gave a piano recital, with her sister Anna Dickens, on 29 Oct (Christiana's Diary, MS Mrs Sowerby).

[3] Presumably Amelia Thompson (*b.* ?1809) and Elizabeth Dorothy Smithson (?1811–60): see Vol. III, p. 5*nn*. Not known whether Thompson had other sisters.

[4] Thompson himself had been particularly worried about money since 1856 (Thompson *to* Christiana, 26 July 56, MS Mrs Sowerby). For CD's loan of £1000 to him in Dec 47 (apparently never repaid), see Vol. V, 122*n*.

[5] See 22 Oct, *fn*.

[6] Some catalogues give the date as 29 Oct.

[7] Where Cunningham worked as a clerk in the Audit Office.

[8] Unexplained. Perhaps CD was writing on behalf of a lady looking for a post as housekeeper.

To WILKIE COLLINS, 1 NOVEMBER 1857*

MS Morgan Library.

Tavistock House | Sunday First November 1857

My Dear Wilkie

I hope I am now ready to start you. I think the best way will be, to send you a Proof of the little I have done, *tomorrow night*. If you will come and dine at the Office on Tuesday at ½ past 5, and will have read it in the meantime, I will explain what more you ought to know beforehand.

Just a word in answer, here.

Ever Faithfully
CD.

Hope you are all right at last?

To SAMUEL SMILES,[1] 2 NOVEMBER 1857*

MS Mr R. Slifer.

Tavistock House | Second November, 1857

Dear Sir

The enclosed passes having expired, allow me with many thanks to return them to you.

Faithfully Yours

S. Smiles Esquire. CHARLES DICKENS

To JOSEPH LANGFORD, 3 NOVEMBER 1857

Mention in Royal Commission on Historical Manuscripts report (1974); dated 3 Nov 57; addressed Joseph Langford.

Sending remainder of Manzanilla—a wine of good repute.

To UNKNOWN CORRESPONDENT, 3 NOVEMBER 1857

Mention in Sotheby's catalogue, Dec 1888; *MS* 1 p.; dated 3 Nov 57.

[1] Samuel Smiles (1812–1904; *DNB*), writer and reformer; Secretary, South-Eastern Railway 1854–66: see Vol. VII, p. 774 and *n*.

To HERBERT WATKINS, 4 NOVEMBER 1857

Extract in American Art Association and Anderson catalogue, May 1934; *MS* 1 p.; addressed Herbert Watkins; dated Gad's Hill Place,[1] 4 Nov 57.

I send you a thousand thanks for the remarkable, interesting, and admirable collection of Photographs you have sent to me.[2] I shall always prize them highly[3] and shall never tire of them. They are not the less agreeable to me for including two capital heads of yourself.

The Library Edition in its Holiday Dress shall not fail to appear, as soon as it is out of the tailor's (or binder's) hands.[4]

To [WILLIAM] OSTELL,[5] 5 NOVEMBER 1857*

MS Mrs Manzie.

Tavistock House | Fifth November, 1857

Sir.

I am happy, in remembrance of the Morning Chronicle time to which you refer, to have it in my power to send you the accompanying Proxy.[6]

Faithfully Yours

Mr. Ostell CHARLES DICKENS

To H. G. ADAMS, 7 NOVEMBER 1857†

MS Mr Alfred C. Berol.

Tavistock House, London. W.C.
Saturday Night, Seventh November | 1857

My Dear Sir

Although the Deputation you did me the honor to present to me at Gad's Hill, did not appear to have a very lively faith in their President,[7] their President thought it right to hold out no hopes that might be fallacious, and to reserve to himself his secret justification of a better faith.

Accordingly I have since tried, with some steadiness, so to disentangle myself from other promises, by a new arrangement of them, as to be able to read my Carol for my Rochester and Chatham Institution. And I am now able to tell you that I will do so for you, please God, on any evening in the week before this next Christmas Day, or in the week after it, that may suit you best.[8]

[1] May be catalogue error; all other Nov letters are from London address.

[2] Almost certainly the Oct and Nov issues of the *National Gallery of Photographic Portraits*, Watkins's series of portraits (starting with Lord Palmerston), with biographical notices by Herbert Fry.

[3] Catalogue reads "high".

[4] Vol. I of *Pickwick*, published in Dec for 1 Jan 58: see *To* Evans, 20 Oct and *fn*.

[5] Perhaps William Ostell, printer (since 1836) and stationer, 24 Hart Street, Bloomsbury; but connection with the *Morning Chronicle* not found.

[6] Probably for the Printers' Pension Fund Society of which CD was a member: he had taken the chair at their Anniversary Dinner in 1843: see Vol. III, pp. 452–3 and *n*.

[7] Of the Rochester and Chatham Mechanics' Institute.

[8] He read it on 22 Dec: see *To* Paxton, 23 Dec, *fn*.

As soon as you can determine, please to do so. Mr. W. H. Wills at the Household Words office, will (whenever you may communicate with him as the time approaches), let you know what my wishes always are as to announcements and room-arrangements.

Faithfully Yours

H. G. Adams Esquire. CHARLES DICKENS

To ROBERT CROZIER,[1] 8 NOVEMBER 1857

MS Messrs Hudson Rogue Co. *Address:* Robert Crozier Esquire | 45 Sidney Street | Manchester.

Tavistock House, W.C.
Sunday Night | Eighth November, 1857.

Sir.

My absence from town has delayed this reply to your letter. Pray excuse the circumstances.

I am sorry that I must beg to decline the honor you propose to me. But in the constant and almost incredible accumulation of such claims, which is a part of my life, I have long observed the rule of never associating myself, in name alone, with any effort, however good.

Faithfully Yours

Robert Crozier Esquire CHARLES DICKENS

To JOHN DILLON,[2] 8 NOVEMBER 1857*

MS University of Texas. *Address* (envelope, MS Yale University Library): John Dillon Esquire | 104 Fore Street | City | E.C. PM London WC 9 Nov 57.

Tavistock House | Sunday Night | Eighth November, 1857

My Dear Sir

Let me thank you for your note, and assure you, both that I am very much obliged by your kind remembrance, and that I greatly regretted your absence from the dinner.[3]

Faithfully Yours

John Dillon Esquire. CHARLES DICKENS

[1] Robert Crozier (?1818–91), one of founders of Manchester Academy of Fine Arts, 1857; Literary Secretary to 1868; President 1878. Painter, mostly of portraits; exhibited five pictures at RA 1854–82. Collector of Old Master prints.

[2] John Dillon, of Morrison, Dillon & Co., merchants, 104–7 Fore St, Cripplegate; philanthropist: see Vol. IV, p. 39*n*.

[3] The Anniversary Dinner of the Warehousemen and Clerks' Schools, held at the London Tavern on 5 Nov, with CD in the Chair: see *Speeches*, ed. K. J. Fielding, pp. 239–44.

To WILLIAM ALLINGHAM,[1] 9 NOVEMBER 1857

MS University of Kentucky.

Tavistock House | Monday Ninth November, 1857

My Dear Sir

I am happy to retain the Poem,[2] which is mournfully true, and has moved me very much. You shall have a Proof without fail.

Faithfully Yours
CHARLES DICKENS

W. Allingham Esquire

To MRS BROWN, 9 NOVEMBER 1857*

MS Morgan Library. *Address:* Mrs. Brown | Miss Burdett Coutts | 1 Stratton Street | Piccadilly | W.

Tavistock House | Monday Ninth November, 1857

My Dear Mrs. Brown.

A very curious letter, and (in its way) both a very sad, and a very pleasant one.[3] Good Heaven, to think of that Doctor!—[4]

This is only to welcome you home, and to say how glad I shall be to see you again. I cannot trust myself to refer to your remembrance of the little—the nothing—I could ever do for you in your grief.[5] You make so much of it, and I such a nothing, that you quite overpower me.

Ever Your affectionate friend
CHARLES DICKENS

To MISS BURDETT COUTTS, 9 NOVEMBER 1857*

MS Morgan Library. *Address:* Miss Burdett Coutts.

Tavistock House | Monday Ninth November, 1857

My Dear Miss Coutts.

This is merely a word to welcome you home again.[6] I should have written to you at Rugby, but that your allusion—of a triumphant sort—to Coventry, was too much for me. For have I not promised to read the Carol at Coventry next Christmas, and am I not gloomily repentant of my sweet nature![7]

[1] William Allingham (1824–89; *DNB*), poet: see Vol. VI, p. 124*n*.

[2] "George Levison; or, The Schoolfellows", *HW*, 12 Dec 57, XVI, 562. It describes a visit from the author's schoolboy hero, now drunken and destitute.

[3] CD's letter is endorsed "Rec. Novr. 10th. | 57 at Peterboro—Returns Letter from [?Mr.] Cooper—to Miss C—concerning [*word illegible*]": probably connected with a case at the Home.

[4] Unidentified.

[5] On the death of her husband on 23 Oct 55: see Vol. VII, p. 732–5 and *nn*; the funeral was on 7 Nov 55.

[6] From her tour of the Midlands.

[7] See *To* Paxton, 23 Dec 57 and *fn*.

I always *knew*[1] Torquay to be a Humbug, and am delighted to find that the Truth is great and will prevail.[2]

Ever Faithfully and affecy. Yours
CHARLES DICKENS

To BENJAMIN WEBSTER, 9 NOVEMBER 1857*

MS Free Library of Philadelphia. *Date:* Lord Mayor's Day was 9 Nov in 1857.

Tavistock House | Lord Mayor's Day, 1857

My Dear Webster

The accompanying Farce–don't be alarmed–it is very short and very stagey–is by an old hand who has entrusted it to me, whose expectations are moderate, and who wants "to sell it".[3] Is it worth any thing to you?

Ever Faithfully
CHARLES DICKENS

Benjamin Webster Esquire.

To MISS HORNER,[4] 16 NOVEMBER 1857

Extracts in Sotheby's catalogue, July 1982 and Dobell catalogue No. 52 (1939); *MS* 2 pp.; dated Tavistock House, Monday Evening, 16 Nov 57; addressed Miss Horner.

Having been away, had a little delayed his answer. The circumstances of the article being a translated pamphlet,[5] already known in its general purport to the English public, is conclusive against its acceptance for Household Words ... *if it were an account, a dissertation and description it would have been different, but as it is he must decline it* very much against my will.

To EDMUND YATES, 16 NOVEMBER 1857

MS Robert H. Taylor Collection, Princeton University.

Tavistock House
Monday Night | Sixteenth November, 1857.

My Dear Yates.

I retain the story[6] with pleasure; and I need not tell you that you are not mistaken in the last line of your note.[7]

[1] Underlined four times.

[2] Cf. 1 Esdras (Apocrypha) IV, 41: "Great is truth, and it prevails."

[3] See *To* Webster, 8 Dec and *fn.*

[4] Ann Susan Horner (?1816–90), translator and miscellaneous writer, daughter of Leonard Horner, geologist and commissioner on Children's Employment (known to CD: see Vol. II, p. 165*n*). She translated Pietro Colletta's *History of the Kingdom of Naples*, 1734–1825, 2 vols, Edinburgh, Dec 1858, and wrote a supplementary chapter on 1825–56; published *A Century of Despotism in Naples and Sicily*, Edinburgh, 1860, and other books.

[5] Probably one of her many Italian sources for the added chapter (see her 2nd vol., p. 473*n*), but not traced.

[6] "Two in a Legion", *HW*, 19 Dec 57, XVII, 20.

[7] Yates may have said he hoped his story was good enough for *HW*; he had thought his early writing clearly "not up to the Household Words standard" (*Edmund Yates: his Recollections and Experiences*, 4th edn, p. 174).

Excuse me—on that ground—if I say a word or two, as to what I think (I mention it with a view to the future),[1] might be better in the paper. The opening is excellent. But it passes too completely into the Irishman's narrative—does not light it up with the life about it, or the circumstances under which it is delivered—and does not carry through it, as I think it should with a certain undefinable subtlety, the thread with which you begin your weaving.[2] I will tell Wills to send me the Proof, and will try to shew you what I mean when I shall have gone over it carefully.

Faithfully Yours always

Edmund Yates Esquire. CHARLES DICKENS

To THOMAS BEARD, 19 NOVEMBER 1857

MS Dickens House. *Address:* Thomas Beard Esquire | 42 Portman Place | Edgeware Road | W.

Tavistock House | Thursday Nineteenth November | 1857

My Dear Beard

I want very much to see you—and to know what you are about—and to be told where you have been hiding all the summer.

Can you come and dine with us next Sunday at half past Five?

Ever Faithfully

Thomas Beard Esquire CHARLES DICKENS

To B. W. PROCTER, 19 NOVEMBER 1857

MS Yale University Library.

Tavistock House | Thursday Nineteenth November | 1857

My Dear Procter

You may be very sure that nothing but a special, made, engagement[3]—not to be broken—prevents my accepting your most interesting and welcome invitation. But, unfortunately I *have* such an engagement, and I cannot come. I could not easily tell you how much I feel your association of me with the day,[4] or with what affectionate thoughts I shall remember it, though absent.

Ever Faithfully Yours

B. W. Procter Esquire CHARLES DICKENS

[1] This was in fact the last of Yates's four contributions to *HW*.

[2] The opening—the author escaping from a boring visit to his uncle and then stranded for two hours at the local railway station—is only a pretext for the Irishman's story of the Spanish Legion that follows. Yates may have added the final paragraph—in which the author dreams of the story's hero as his uncle—to meet CD's criticism.

[3] Untraced.

[4] Procter's 70th birthday, on 21 Nov.

To A. C. KRUSEMAN,[1] 23 NOVEMBER 1857

Facsimile in J. W. Enschedé, *Bijdrage tot de Geschiedenis van de Nederlandse Boekhandel*, 1899, p. 263.

Tavistock House, London.
Monday Twenty Third November, 1857

Dear Sir

I beg to acknowledge, with many thanks, the safe receipt of the translations of my books[2] into the Dutch language, which you have had the kindness to send me. Allow me to thank you heartily, both for that acceptable present, and for the account you give me of the esteem in which I am held in Holland. It causes me great pride and gratification.

Accept the assurance of my high regard Dear Sir, and believe me always
Your faithful Servant
CHARLES DICKENS

To J. A. LANGFORD,[3] 23 NOVEMBER 1857

Extract in City Book Auction catalogue No. 309 (May 1945); *MS* 1 p.; dated Tavistock House, Monday, 23 Nov 57; addressed John Alfred Langford.

Regretting that he is unable to read manuscripts submitted to him for criticism and advice ... and I assure you I have already made as many conditional promises to read, as I can hope to redeem within a long time.

Your faithful Servant
CHARLES DICKENS

To BENJAMIN WEBSTER, 24 NOVEMBER 1857†

MS Free Library of Philadelphia.

OFFICE OF HOUSEHOLD WORDS,
Tuesday Twenty Fourth November 1857

My Dear Webster

My razors, my razors! Don't forget my pair of razors!![4]

I have something to say to you. There is a Christmas No. coming out here—the

[1] Arie Cornelis Kruseman (1818–94), of Haarlem, Holland, bookseller since 1840; publisher 1854–78; the translations of CD he published, at a low price, 1854–62, ended with *Chuzzlewit*; his lack of success probably due to small format and poor typography.

[2] *Nelly* (2 vols in one) 1855 and *Dombey en Zoon* (3 vols), Vol. I, 1856, Vols II and III, 1857. Both were translated by C. M. Mensing and published at Haarlem by Kruseman. In CD's library at his death (*Catalogue of the Library of CD*, ed. J. H. Stonehouse, p. 37).

[3] John Alfred Langford (1823–1903; *DNB*), LLD; Birmingham antiquary and radical journalist; apprenticed to his father's chair-making business at 13; contributed to periodicals, including *Howitt's Journal*, from 1846; on staff of *Birmingham Daily Gazette* 1862–8; taught English Literature in Birmingham and Midland Institute 1868–74; his books included *Religion and Education in Relation to the People*, 1852; *English Democracy*, 1853; *Modern Birmingham and its Institutions*, 2 vols, 1873–7; and other Birmingham histories.

[4] John Poole's farce: see *To* Emden, 20 Aug and *fn*.

whole No. one story, of which I have done the greater part: Wilkie Collins having written one chapter—which I clearly foresee will be dramatized everywhere.[1] [a]I think it will make a prodigious noise, and I am sure it will be laid hold of by all sorts and conditions of Theatres. Now, I don't want it done upon the Stage at all: because I never do want to see any composition there, which is not intended for it.[a] Nevertheless, I can't help its being done; and, done at all, I should like it done well. It would be a three act piece, requiring three very curious scenes. It lights up all the fire that is in the public mind at this time, and you might make your Theatre blaze with it. If you would like to try to do it *thoroughly well*, supposing it to answer this description, you shall have it in Proof some week or ten days before the Public, so as to get a good start in the adapting of it and preparing for it.[2] I make this offer as a friend, and not with any idea of accepting any money.

Your arrangements *may* be such, and you *may* be so much behind with your Pantomime[3] (for even *YOU*,[4] I believe, are occasionally procrastinative in the slightest degree), as to be in no position to contemplate the possibility of getting out such a thing. This is the reason why I write to you at all. In that case, I would not send it to you to read. But if it be on the cards that you could, if you saw reason, undertake such a dash, I know I can trust you to read it, and you should have it at the end of this week. An hour and a half of next Sunday, would carry you through it.

Don't leave this note lying about. I may possibly be able to get down to you tonight. If I can—I will.

Faithfully Yours always
CHARLES DICKENS

To MISS BURDETT COUTTS, 25 NOVEMBER 1857

MS Morgan Library. *Address:* Miss Burdett Coutts | Stratton Street.

OFFICE OF HOUSEHOLD WORDS,
Wednesday Twenty Fifth Novr. 1857

My Dear Miss Coutts.

Would you and Mrs. Brown like to come and dine with us at Tavistock House, either on Monday, Tuesday, or Wednesday at 6, to hear the Christmas No. of Household Words. It is all one story this time, of which I have written the greater part (Mr. Collins has written one chapter), and which I have planned with great care in the hope of commemorating, without any vulgar catchpenny connexion or application, some of the best qualities of the English character that have been shewn

[1] Three dramatizations are recorded: *Perils of Certain English Prisoners* at the Britannia, 15 Jan 58, probably by one of the theatre's regular writers; *Silver Store Island, or the British Flag of the South American Pirate*, at the Strand, 13 Feb, by the notorious Frederick Fox Cooper, who had adapted 11 of CD's novels and stories, beginning with *Master Humphrey's Clock* (1840); and *Silver Store island, or, Pedro Mendez the South American Pirate* (also listed as *Perils*, etc.), at the Victoria, 17 Feb, by H. Young.

[aa] The forgery, *To* Collins, 21 Nov 57 (see Preface), incorporates these two sentences; the forger had probably seen the catalogue extract given in N, II, 894.

[2] It was not dramatized for the Adelphi.

[3] *Harlequin and the Loves of Cupid and Psyche*, "the grand new union Christmas comic pantomime"; first performance Boxing Night.

[4] Written very large and underlined five times.

in India.[1] I hope it is very good, and I think it will make a noise. Naturally therefore, I want you to know what it is, before any body else does.

If you say "Yes", say too what day you choose. And say further, whether there is any one you would like me to ask.

Ever Dear Miss Coutts | Yours faithfully and affecy.
CHARLES DICKENS

To MRS JERROLD, 30 NOVEMBER 1857*

MS Mr J. R. Chamberlain.

Tavistock House | Thirtieth November, 1857

Dear Mrs. Jerrold

Before we can complete the purchase of the Annuity,[2] it is necessary that the Certificates referred to in the accompanying printed Form, should be got, and that the Form should be duly filled up. May I recommend you to employ some Solicitor for the purpose? His charge, if he will have the goodness to send it to me when the business is completed, I will defray out of the Fund.

I beg my kind regard to Miss Jerrold,[3] and am always

Faithfully Yours

Mrs. Jerrold. CHARLES DICKENS

To LADY OLLIFFE, 30 NOVEMBER 1857

MS Comtesse de Suzannet.

Tavistock House | Monday Thirtieth November | 1857

My Dear Lady Olliffe

I have just time to send you this, a week in advance of the Public,[4] and to express my hope that you and Olliffe (to whom my love), will be pleased with it. Chapter 2 is by Wilkie Collins; all the rest by me.

Ever Your faithful
CHARLES DICKENS

To FRANK STONE, 30 NOVEMBER 1857*

MS Benoliel Collection. *Address:* Frank Stone Esquire | Russell House.

H W Office | Thirtieth November 1857

My Dear Stone

Here you are—a week ahead of the Public. Second chapter by Collins; all the rest by me.

With kind regard | Ever affecy. CD.[5]

[1] See *To* Morley, 18 Oct, *fn*.
[2] See *To* the Editor of *The Times*, 1 Sep 1857.
[3] Mary Ann Jerrold.
[4] The *HW* advt of 28 Nov gives "Early in Dec" as the publication date for the Christmas No.; 5 Dec gives no date, but implies it is about to go on sale; 12 Dec says "now ready".
[5] Note written on flap of large envelope.

To W. C. MACREADY, 1 DECEMBER 1857

MS Walter T. Spencer.

Tavistock House | Tuesday Night, First December 1857

My Dearest Macready.

I send you (very hurriedly) an early proof of The Christmas Story. The Second Chapter is by Wilkie Collins; all the rest is by me. I hope you may like it.

Kindest love to all.

Ever Most affectionately CD.

To MISS MARGUERITE POWER, [?1–2 DECEMBER 1857]

Mention in *To* Thackeray, 4 Dec 57. *Date:* probably written two or three days before that letter.

To SIR JOSEPH PAXTON, 2 DECEMBER 1857

Extracts in unidentified catalogue in *Chadwick Collection of Dickensiana* and Sotheby's catalogue, Jan 1883; *MS* $1\frac{1}{2}$ pp.; dated 2 Dec 57; addressed Sir Joseph Paxton.

Making an appointment about a reading in Coventry,[1] *adding that he never accepts invitations* on such occasions, when it is necessary to be composed and unbothered—let us stick to the best Hotel. *He also invites Paxton to visit him at Rochester.*

To ARTHUR RYLAND, 2 DECEMBER 1857*

MS Benoliel Collection. *Address:* Arthur Ryland Esquire | Birmingham.

Tavistock House, London. W.C.
Wednesday Second December 1857

My Dear Mr. Ryland.

I am afraid I cannot possibly read at Birmingham this Christmas. The plain truth is, I have nothing to read. My work in the summer for the Jerrold Fund—and very hard work indeed, it was—completely deprived me of the opportunity I had *expected* to have, of getting some new Reading together. I have now made four promises to read the Carol; I have not a chance of getting to the work of condensing any of my larger books; and when I look at your letter again, I drift away bodily, out to sea.

You know I don't want the will. But what am I to do without the power!

Faithfully Yours always

Arthur Ryland Esquire CHARLES DICKENS

[1] On 15 Dec. See *To* Paxton, 5 and 11 Dec.

To MRS LOCKWOOD,[1] 3 DECEMBER 1857*

MS (in Wills's hand) Dickens House.

OFFICE OF HOUSEHOLD WORDS,
3 December 1857

Mr. Charles Dickens presents his compliments to Mrs. Lockwood, and begs to thank her for her obliging communication of Saturday last, and for the newspaper which accompanied it.[2]

Mrs. Charles Day Lockwood

To JOSEPH SLY, 3 DECEMBER 1857

MS Public Library and Museum, Lancaster. *Address:* Mr. Sly | King's Arms Hotel | Lancaster.

Tavistock House, London. W.C. | Third December, 1857

Sir.

I am sorry that I have, until now, accidentally omitted to answer your letter.

I assure you that I received it with much pleasure. It was very agreeable to me to know that you were gratified by my having associated a little fancy with your excellent house;[3] and I was particularly interested by your account of your honorable career in life.

I wish you every prosperity, and am | Faithfully Yours

Mr. Sly. CHARLES DICKENS

To MISS BURDETT COUTTS, 4 DECEMBER 1857*

MS Morgan Library. *Address:* Miss Burdett Coutts | Stratton Street | Piccadilly | W.

Tavistock House | Fourth December, 1857

My Dear Miss Coutts

On Monday,[4] with pleasure.

Ever Faithfully & affecy.
CD.

To W. M. THACKERAY, 4 DECEMBER 1857

MS Widener Collection, Harvard.

Tavistock House | Friday December Fourth, 1857.

My Dear Thackeray

Your second note stopped me from coming to you, to talk over the subject of your

[1] Mrs Charles Day Lockwood of South Parade, Doncaster; a schoolfellow of Marian Evans's at Miss Franklin's School, Coventry. Her husband owned a stone quarrying business at Levitt Hagg nearby.

[2] No mention of CD found in any Doncaster newspapers now available.

[3] See *To* Miss Hogarth, 12 Sep, *fn*.

[4] Evidently accepting an invitation to Stratton Street.

first—which reached me within an hour before the receipt of a similar proposal from Forster.[1]

In the interval which has followed through your absence from town,[2] I have communicated with Marguerite Power, and have asked her, plainly, whether such a subscription would be acceptable and accepted? She replies, most gratefully and without hesitation, "Yes". It seems to me that the best thing we can do, is, to take out 20 names of old visitors at Gore House[3] and make a subscription of £10 each. This will give us a purse of £200 to present to her.

I will come to you at Brompton, or meet you any where, any day you can name, between 10 and 5. Let us do it as soon as we can, and get it done.

Ever Faithfully

W. M. Thackeray Esquire CHARLES DICKENS

To SIR JOSEPH PAXTON, 5 DECEMBER 1857*

MS Mr Lloyd E. Roscoe.

Tavistock House | Fifth December, 1857

My Dear Paxton.

I am very sorry that I was not at home last evening, and have been too unwell with influenza this morning to get up at my usual hour; thus doubly delaying my reply to your note.

Shall we say next Thursday morning? To meet at the booking Office of the North Kent Railway, London Bridge at 5 minutes past 10. The train starts at a quarter past 10.

Ever Faithfully Yours

Sir Joseph Paxton. CHARLES DICKENS

To MISS BURDETT COUTTS, 6 DECEMBER 1857*

MS Morgan Library. *Address:* Miss Burdett Coutts | Stratton Street.

Tavistock House | Sunday Sixth December 1857

My Dear Miss Coutts

I must ask you to excuse my absence for one hour tomorrow evening—from half past 8 to half past 9. I will go and return so deftly, that no one shall miss me.

My movements are wildly deranged at all hours just now, by my having a very delicate matter to adjust for a very dear friend[4]—with an immense responsibility resting upon me, which I don't see my way out of.

[1] That the three of them should write a joint letter, asking for subscriptions for a present to Marguerite Power: see *To* Unknown Correspondent, 24 Dec.

[2] In Brighton (*Letters and Private Papers*, ed. Gordon N. Ray, IV, 58).

[3] See *To* Friends of Lady Blessington, 24 Dec, *fn*.

[4] Clearly Marguerite Power: CD has told Thackeray he would meet him about her case at any time.

—In addition to which, I now write under the oppression of a most ferocious Influenza.

Ever Faithfully and affy. Yours
CD.

To F. M. EVANS, 6 DECEMBER 1857

MS Free Library of Philadelphia.

Tavistock House | Sunday Night Sixth December 1857

My Dear Evans.

Your printing from the Cheap Edition,[1] had best go on without waiting for me. If I see anything wrong in the sheets you send me, I will let you know of it promptly.

I wish you would get the accompanying Dedication[2] set up as prettily as you possibly can, and then send it at once to Forster, with a note saying that I had begged you to ask him whether it was right.—I want to surprise him. All the old dedications will be cancelled in this Edition, you understand.

Faithfully Ever
CD.

To THE HON. MRS RICHARD WATSON, 7 DECEMBER 1857*

MS Huntington Library.

Tavistock House, London. W.C. | Seventh December, 1857

My Dear Mrs. Watson. I cannot tell you how interested and pleased I have been by the receipt of your letter, or how delightful it is to me to picture you among those beautiful objects, enjoying the life, change, and movement, you must have so drearily wanted at Rockingham. I had been speaking about you to Georgina, over and over again. She had just been telling me that Mary Boyle had spoken of you as being abroad—I had been saying what a good thing that was—and we had set in for a long train of remembrance,[3] in my room one night, while your letter was making its way to me.

You want an egotistical reply from me, and you shall have it. I have been very busy with the Xmas Number of Household Words, in which I have endeavoured to commemorate the foremost of the great English qualities shewn in India, without laying the scene there, or making any vulgar association with real events or calamities. I believe it is rather a remarkable production, and will make a great noise. I should send it with this, but for the uncertainty of its ever getting to you. It is published to day. It is all one story. The Second Chapter by Wilkie Collins; all the rest of it by me.

[1] The Library edn was set up from the Cheap edn.

[2] "This | best edition of my books | is, of right, inscribed to my dear friend | John Forster | Biographer of Oliver Goldsmith. | In grateful remembrance of the | many patient hours he has devoted to the correction | of proof-sheets of the original editions: | and in affectionate acknowledgement | of his | counsel, sympathy, and faithful friendship, | during | my whole literary life" (printed in caps of various sizes).

[3] Of Switzerland: see Vol. IV, *passim*.

It leaves me—as my Art always finds me and always leaves me—the most restless of created Beings. I am the modern embodiment of the old Enchanters, whose Familiars tore them to pieces. I weary of rest, and have no satisfaction but in fatigue. Realities and idealities are always comparing themselves together before me, and I don't like the Realities except when they are unattainable—*then*, I like them of all things. I wish I had been born in the days of Ogres and Dragon-guarded Castles. I wish an Ogre with seven heads (and no particular evidence of brains in the whole lot of them) had taken the Princess whom I adore—you have no idea how intensely I love her!—to his stronghold on the top of a high series of Mountains, and there tied her up by the hair. Nothing would suit me half so well this day, as climbing after her, sword in hand, and either winning her or being killed.—*There's* a state of mind for you, in 1857.

All last summer I had a transitory satisfaction in rending the very heart out of my body by doing that Richard Wardour part. It was a good thing to have a couple of thousand people all rigid and frozen together, in the palm of one's hand—as at Manchester—and to see the hardened Carpenters at the sides crying and trembling at it night after night. Which reminds me of a pretty little story about it. We engaged for Manchester, a young lady from Kean's Theatre—Miss Maria Ternan—born on the stage, and inured to it from the days when she was the little child in Pizarro. She had been brought to the Gallery of Illustration in town, to see the Play; and when she came on to me in the Morning at Manchester, I said, "Why my dear, how cold your hand is, and what a tremble you are in! This won't do at night."—"Oh Mr. Dickens", she said, "I am so afraid I can't bear it, that I hope you'll be very gentle with me this morning. I cried so much when I saw it, that I have a dread of it, and I don't know what to do." She had to take my head up as I was dying, and to put it in her lap, and give me her face to hold between my two hands. All of which I shewed her elaborately (as Mary had done it before), that morning. When we came to that point at night, her tears fell down my face, down my beard (excuse my mentioning that hateful appendage), down my ragged dress—poured all over me like Rain, so that it was as much as I could do to speak for them. I whispered to her, "My dear child, it will be over in two minutes. Pray compose yourself."—"It's no comfort to me that it will be soon over", she answered. "Oh it is so sad, it is so dreadfully sad. Oh don't die! Give me time, give me a little time! Don't take leave of me in this terrible way—pray, pray, pray!!" Whereupon Lemon, the softest-hearted of men, began to cry too, and then they all went at it together. I think I never saw such a pretty little genuine emotion in my life. And if you had seen the poor little thing, when the Curtain fell, put in a chair behind it—with her mother and sister taking care of her—and your humble servant drying her eyes and administering Sherry (in Rags so horrible that they would scarcely hold together), and the people in front all blowing their noses, and our own people behind standing about in corners and getting themselves right again, you would have remembered it for a long, long time.[1]

Our Indian boy was at Dum-Dum (which means a school of musketry, some 6 miles from Calcutta)[2] when last heard of, but expected to be sent up the country in a

[1] See *To* Miss Coutts, 5 Sep and *fn*: CD gives Mrs Watson an even fuller description of *The Frozen Deep* and Maria Ternan.

[2] The Bengal Artillery HQ, claimed as witnessing the immediate cause of the Mutiny, when a low-caste labourer told a sepoy, who had refused him a drink of water from his cup: "You will soon lose your caste altogether. For

few days. Where or why, I don't know; for he belongs to the Bengal Army, which is virtually extinct. He likes the country and the life, of all things, and is quite happy. My usual fortune of falling in with strange people, attended me, by the bye, when I took him down to Southampton. A very strange fellow got into our Railway Carriage, and took such an immense fancy to me, that I couldn't shake him off. He went out in the same ship—died of delirium tremens, within three days of their leaving Southampton—and had no luggage whatever, with him, but 3 shirts and 240 Sovereigns.

I am going to read, twice this month. On the 15th. at Coventry, and on the 22nd. at Rochester. On the 19th. of January I am going to read at Bristol, and, in April, at Edinburgh. After that, if I bind myself to any more promises, I'll—but I won't forswear myself; I *shall* bind myself, I know, in weakly amiable moments.

I hope the badly-stuffed Horse continues to conduct himself as if he were better stuffed? I have taken to Dogs lately,[1] and, when I am at Gad's Hill, go out attended by tall Prowlers that are the terror of the neighbourhood.[2] Six or eight weeks ago, I performed my celebrated feat of getting out of bed at 2 in the morning, and walking down there from Tavistock House—over 30 miles—through the dead night.[3] I had been very much put-out;[4] and I thought, "After all, it would be better to be up and doing something, than lying here." So I got up, and did that.

Poor Stafford![5] I had seen him pretty often, and had made an engagement with him to go down to Chatham, and talk with some of the poor wounded men from the Crimea, to whom he had been very kind. I believe that he was really beloved among them and had been exceedingly good to them. Inquests may come to contrary conclusions five hundred times over, but I make bold to give *my* verdict—"Murdered by the Doctor."

There is a Legend current here, that to pay the Postage of this letter would be to insure its non-delivery, so I have told my servant *not* to pay it. Is it egotistical enough? If not, what DO[6] you want? Kindest loves and remembrances from all. And from no one in the world can they come to you more fervently, my dear Mrs Watson, than from your Ever affectionate friend

CHARLES DICKENS

I am afraid Spencer Lyttelton[7] is not mending his ways.

the Europeans are going to make you bite cartridges soaked in cow and pork fat" (Christopher Hibbert, *The Great Mutiny: India 1857*, p. 63).

[1] Turk, a bloodhound, CD's favourite, and Linda, a St Bernard (daughter of one brought by Albert Smith from the Alps); see F, VII, iii, 657.

[2] Dogs were a necessity at Gad's Hill, Forster says, because of the "tramps and wayfarers of a singularly undesirable description" on the highroad (F, *ibid.*).

[3] See *To* Brooks, 14 Oct, *fn* (describing the same walk).

[4] Cf. the opening of "Night Walks" in *The Uncommercial Traveller* (*AYR*, 21 July 60, III, 348).

[5] Augustus Stafford O'Brien Stafford (1812–57), MP: see Vol. VI, p. 225*n*. He had died in Dublin on 15 Nov.

[6] Underlined twice.

[7] The Hon. Spencer Lyttelton (1818–81), Mrs Watson's cousin: see Vols V, p. 206*n* and VII, p. 738 and *n*.

To BENJAMIN WEBSTER, 8 DECEMBER 1857*

MS Benoliel Collection.

Tavistock House | Tuesday Night | Eighth December, 1857

My Dear Webster.

An excellent idea of yours!—If you will submit it to Mr. and Mrs. Barney Williams[1] as it stands, and tell them the truth—that it is the production of an excellent old dramatic Writer[2] for whom I do what I can, in the dregs and decline of his life, and who wants to sell it for whatever can be got for it—you may add from me, that I will (sub rosâ) re-arrange it for them as they may think best, if they will purchase it; and will make it as ship-shape for them (knowing their acting very well), as I possibly can.

But what I must stipulate for, is *a quick reply*. Young Toole[3] is good at personation, and I think Mr. Dillon[4] might purchase the Farce, if I paid him the small compliment of addressing him myself on the subject. That, of course, should be before he opens.

Ever Faithfully
CHARLES DICKENS

To JOHN DEANE, 9 DECEMBER 1857*

MS Brotherton Library, Leeds.

OFFICE OF HOUSEHOLD WORDS,
Wednesday Ninth December 1857

My Dear Deane.

I had already given Paxton to know that you are going with us[5]—at which he is delighted. Tuesday is the day. I don't know the hour yet, but will inform you of it—in Gordon Square,[6] I suppose?—on Monday afternoon or evening.

In great haste | Ever Faithfully
CHARLES DICKENS

[1] For Mrs Barney Williams, see *To* Lemon, 2 July 56, *fn*. Barney Williams made his English debut at the Adelphi in *Rory O'More*, June 55. Managed the Broadway Theatre, New York, 1867–9; then toured again with his wife. Left a large fortune.

[2] Poole: for his farce see *To* Emden, 20 Aug 57 and *fn*.

[3] John Lawrence ("Johnny") Toole (1830–1906; *DNB*), comic actor and manager: see Vol. VI, p. 607*n*.

[4] Charles Dillon (1819–81), actor and theatre manager. Stage manager and leading actor of Marylebone Theatre 1842; lessee of Lyceum Sep 1856–Apr 1857, and 20 Jan–22 Mar 1858; toured America and Australia 1861–8. Wrote several melodramas.

[5] To Coventry, for CD's reading on the 15th.

[6] Where Deane no doubt was staying.

To THOMSON HANKEY,[1] 11 DECEMBER 1857*

MS University of Kentucky Library.

Tavistock House. W.C. | Eleventh December, 1857

Dear Sir

Will you excuse my taking the liberty of asking you whether you can render me any help towards nominating a young man of great respectability and undoubted business qualifications, for employment in the Bank of England?

The person in whom I am thus interested, is a brother of my wife's,[2] now in a Business-House at Sheffield which has lately failed, and is reducing its establishment.[3] He is twenty five, was thoroughly well educated in Germany, brings from the Sheffield House the highest character and recommendation, and has a thoroughly good acquaintance with business. I know him, of my own knowledge, to be very diligent, steady, and striving; and I should be heartily glad if I could assist him to attain this desire.

Pray forgive my intrusion on your time.

Dear Sir | Faithfully Yours

T. Hankey Esquire M.P. CHARLES DICKENS

To SIR JOSEPH PAXTON, 11 DECEMBER 1857*

MS British Library.

OFFICE OF HOUSEHOLD WORDS,
Friday Eleventh December 1857

My Dear Paxton

I was obliged to go to Birmingham[4] on Wednesday, and was there when you called on me yesterday Morning.

While I am most heartily obliged to your kind and hospitable friend[5] for his invitation—and I beg you earnestly to thank him in my name—I am still in my old mind as to going to the Hotel; the rather as we are sure to have Deane and Wills with us; which circumstance disposes me still more (if anything *can* dispose me still more), to stick to my invariable rule. But I think *you* ought to dine with your friend. And therefore I would propose that you do so, and come to us afterwards.

The conclusion at which I thus arrive, is subject to only one condition of change. If it would really and truly be of the least service to you in Coventry, that I should go to this gentleman's house, and dine with his company, *then*—I *will do it*. Otherwise not. Decide accordingly.

Do we go to Gad's Hill, at 5 minutes past 10 tomorrow morning?

In the matter of Mark Lemon, he has so completely and unreservedly sold his

[1] Thomson Hankey, Jnr (1805–93; *DNB*), banker and Liberal MP: see Vol. VI, p. 104*n*.

[2] Edward Hogarth (1833–?79), Catherine's youngest brother and Helen Hogarth's twin: see Vol. I, p. 690 and *n*.

[3] See *To* Miss Coutts, 2 Feb 58 and *fn*.

[4] Reason unknown, possibly connected with Ryland.

[5] Not traced.

soul to the —— Ingram,[1] that I should say he is not to be got by any other speculator, even on hire for an afternoon.

Ever Faithfully Yours

Sir Joseph Paxton CHARLES DICKENS

To JOHN HOLLINGSHEAD, 12 DECEMBER 1857

Text from N, II, 896.

Tavistock House,
Saturday Night, Twelfth December, 1857[2]

My Dear Sir

Although there is a very droll (and an original) idea in the farce,[3] I doubt if it would do on the stage.[4] I don't think it ends as well as it opens, and I don't see enough for an actor to "make" in it. By far the best part is Mr. Maresnest's,[5] but you could not hold the stage with the piece unless Cranky were done by a good actor; and, as the piece stands, a good Farce-actor would not play the said Cranky, because the character is really not strong enough to win the presence and eye of an audience all that time. I am not giving you this opinion as a writer, but as an actor.

What the farce wants, for the stage, is the throwing of a great deal more into Cranky's hands through some addition to the plot which would place him in a more ludicrous position, by involving him in some new complication of his own respecting it. As, for instance, if he had some tremendous grudge against some common-place man of whom he only knew that his name began with a P—or if he had had a rival of the name of Podgers, before he married Mrs. Cranky—or if a defaulting Podgers had disappeared with Mrs. Cranky's marriage portion—or if the Bank of Dodgers and Dodgers had failed and damaged him—and the thing, whatever it might be, were set right at last by the appearance (to make restitution) of that Podgers, who really was born there, but should explain that it had not been his intention to be born there, but that his mother had been frightened by a Poet in the neighbourhood

[1] Lemon had just accepted the editorship of the weekly *London Journal*, bought by Herbert Ingram in Oct 1857. His reissue of the Waverley novels in it, beginning with *Kenilworth*, was, he announced, "crowned with the most signal success"; *The Fortunes of Nigel* followed, but after declining circulation in 1859, *Ivanhoe* was abandoned and Lemon resigned. See A. A. Adrian, *Mark Lemon: First Editor of* Punch, 1966, pp. 94–5.

[2] According to Forster *to* Maclise, 11 Dec CD had "promised to come" to meet Maclise, who nevertheless did not come.

[3] Hollingshead's *The Birthplace of Podgers*, "an Original Domestic Sketch in One Act", based on W. Moy Thomas's investigations into the poet Chatterton's place of death, which were published in the *Athenaeum*, 5 Dec 57. Hollingshead describes how he wrote the farce "in a few days", after visiting the house in Brook St, Holborn, in which Chatterton had died. After receiving CD's letter, he met J. L. Toole, whom he knew, by chance, and persuaded him to put it on for his benefit, 10 Mar, and to act Cranky ("a Working Man") in it. The *Morning Chronicle*, 11 Mar, praised his acting, but of the farce itself commented: "the less that is said the better". Cranky became, in fact, one of Toole's most successful roles, played for 36 years. CD, Hollingshead says, "handsomely atoned for his original coldness about the farce by paying to go into the pit on the first night" (John Hollingshead, *My Lifetime*, I, 112–14).

[4] It ran at the Lyceum 10–23 Mar 58, and was published in the summer.

[5] Erasmus Maresnest, "a Literary Enthusiast", who invades Cranky's lodgings in Lambeth, convinced that "the immortal poet Podgers" had died there; certainly not the best part.

of Bedlam, and had fled to that apartment (or relations) for refuge in a hackney carriage—then I think you might get Mr. Buckstone to the rescue. The solicitous gentlemen and ladies should then rush off to the neighbourhood of Bedlam in search of the immortal Podgers, and the mortal Podgers should throw the end of the piece into Mr. Cranky's mouth.[1] With some ingenuity and invention in such a direction, I believe the Farce might succeed greatly. Otherwise, no.

Faithfully Yours
[CHARLES DICKENS]

To JOHN BENNETT,[2] 17 DECEMBER 1857*

Text from transcript, Huntington Library.

Tavistock House | Thursday Seventeenth December | 1857.

Dear Sir,

I have the pleasure to enclose you a cheque (payable to Order) for £21.

The clock goes reasonably well, but always loses something.

Faithfully yours

Mr John Bennett. CHARLES DICKENS

To MISS MARY GIBSON,[3] 17 DECEMBER 1857

Text from N, II, 896.

Tavistock House, Tavistock Square, W.C.
Seventeenth December 1857, Thursday

My Dear Madam,

I am bound to assure you that you are altogether mistaken in supposing that any "touch" of my pen, or any introduction from me, would do anything for your writings which they cannot do for themselves. It would be considered as a mere form, by any Editorial or publishing recipient of it, and would be quite unserviceable.

[1] CD's suggestions were not taken and would have overweighted the farce; the revision with the help of Toole must have developed Cranky's part. Hollingshead gave him the credit of "seeing its value as a sketch from life" (*ibid.*, I, 113). Constantly repeating "I'm a working man" and "Is this my house, or is it not?", he is baffled by talk of the "Immortal Podgers" and resents the succession of intruders: Alonso Lexicon ("Editor of the Rosewater Annual") and his sister Penelope ("Authoress of Despair and other Poems") and finally, Erasmus Maresnest; the only Podgers he knows is "the old fool we took this house of", a hopeless drunk who appears at the end, just before Cranky's final words to the audience.

[2] John Bennett (1814–97; *DNB*), elder brother of the poet W. C. Bennett (see Vol. v, p. 43*n*); watchmaker, of 65 Cheapside; lectured on the watch in London and provinces, Nov 58. Common councillor for ward of Cheap 1862–89; member of London School Board 1872–9 and 1885–9; Sheriff of London and Middlesex 1872; knighted 1872. Regularly repaired CD's clocks.

[3] Given wrongly in N as "Giison"; Sotheby's catalogue, 1938, gives the name correctly, as "Miss Mary W. A. Gibson". The *HW* Office Book gives her address as 6 Cottage Place, Brompton.

It is the plainest honesty to tell you this, because I know it to be the truth. If you should desire to offer anything to Household Words, I will promptly read it myself. There is always room there for good and suitable contributions, and it is always a pleasure to me to find them.[1]

As to seeing you, I will do so with the greatest readiness. If you can call here tomorrow (Friday) morning at 11, you will find me at home. If that should be inconvenient, you will find me at home on Monday morning at the same hour.

Faithfully yours
[CHARLES DICKENS]

To JAMES HULKES,[2] 17 DECEMBER 1857*

MS Private.

Tavistock House, London. W.C.
Thursday Seventeenth December | 1857

My Dear Sir

I should have answered your kind note yesterday but that I have been (for my sins) reading at Coventry, and am but now at home again.

I cannot have the pleasure of accepting either of your kind offers, as I shall be accompanied by the gentleman who acts as my Secretary and by another friend, if not by two others. But I am truly obliged to you for your welcome and neighbourly remembrance.

Mrs. Dickens is better, and unites with her sister and myself in compliments to Mrs. Hulkes.

My Dear Sir | Very faithfully Yours
James Hulkes Esquire CHARLES DICKENS

To MRS MASON, [17 DECEMBER 1857]

Mention in Meridian Bookshop catalogue No. 48; *MS* 1 p.; addressed Mrs Mason; dated 17 Dec 57.

Concerning a girl on her way to the Home in Shepherd's Bush.

[1] Miss Gibson contributed two stories, "A Tale of an Old Man's Youth", and "Lost Alice" to *HW* (10 and 24 Apr 58) and four poems (27 Feb and 5 June 58, 19 Mar and 9 Apr 59).

[2] James Hulkes (*b.* ?1827), JP, of the Little Hermitage, Frindsbury, near Higham; gentleman farmer; educated at Eton and Corpus Christi College, Oxford. For his and his wife's reminiscences of CD, see W. R. Hughes, *A Week's Tramp in Dickens-Land*, pp. 196, 204–5. Tennyson knew the family well and on 5 Dec 50 wrote to Hulkes's mother, thanking her for congratulations on the Laureateship, saying he would like to pay a visit and recalling "pleasant little parties in your room at Umberslade", the water-cure centre near Birmingham where Tennyson went in 1847 (*Letters of Alfred, Lord Tennyson*, ed. Cecil Y. Lang and Edgar P. Shannon, I, 345 and *n*).

To UNKNOWN CORRESPONDENT, 17 DECEMBER 1857

Mention in *Autograph Prices Current*, IV, 1918–19; *MS* 1 p.; dated Tavistock House, 17 Dec 57.

To SAMUEL CARTWRIGHT JNR,[1] [?17 DECEMBER 1857]

Summary from Dinner Committee Minutes, Great Ormond St Children's Hospital, given in Jules Klosky, *Mutual Friends*, 1989, p. 188. *Date:* sent by Cartwright to the Committee on 18 Dec; no doubt written shortly before that.

Desiring to be excused from writing any note for issue in lithographed form.[2]

To MESSRS BRADBURY & EVANS, 18 DECEMBER 1857

Extract in N, II, 897.

Tavistock House | Friday Eighteen December 1857

Dear Sirs,

The Solicitor wants, for the purpose of the agreement defining our copyrights, transcripts of the existing entries of Registrations of those copyrights of books by me in which you are interested.[3] Will you cause them to be got, and send them straight to Frederic Ouvry Esquire, Mess^s. Farrer, Ouvry and Farrer, 66 Lincolns Inn Fields.[4]

To JOHN HOLLINGSHEAD, 19 DECEMBER 1857*

MS Mr John J. Curran.

Tavistock House. W.C.
Saturday Nineteenth December 1857

Dear Mr. Hollingshead.

I wish you would put the Farce[5] by, for a little while, and not try Buckstone now. I know his hands are full,[6] and—though they were not—I am almost sure he would not accept it as it stands.

[1] Samuel Cartwright Jr (1815–65; *DNB*), dental surgeon: see Vol. VII, p. 27*n*.

[2] The Dinner Committee had asked Cartwright, as a member, "to request the favour of a short letter from [*CD*], to be lithographed for issue" (Committee Minutes, above). For CD's chairing of the Dinner on 9 Feb, see *To* Miss Coutts, 11 Feb 58 and *fn*.

[3] Under the Copyright Amendment Act of 1842, compulsory registration of all books at Stationers' Hall had been replaced by compulsory delivery by the publishers of every new book seeking copyright protection to the British Museum: this served as registration of the copyright.

[4] Text cut off.

[5] See 12 Dec 57.

[6] CD knew that Buckstone's Haymarket season was already planned: see *To* Buckstone, 13 Oct and *fnn*. The farce was readily accepted by Charles Dillon (see *To* Webster, 8 Dec and *fn*), in whose season at the Lyceum the performances changed nightly; no doubt the March run would have continued but for Dillon's bankruptcy in Apr. The part of Amelia Maresnest, "a pleasing young lady", was played by Maria Ternan.

I very much doubt his approving of that Stomach-ache, and I doubt still more the Audience's approval of it.[1] It seems to me to be by no means an improvement.

He would say to me, I believe, if I wrote him a note for you to send with the MS, "What do you say to the Piece? Honestly tell me that I ought to play it, against my apprehension that I can't make much of it—and I will". Now, I could *not* honestly tell him so, and therefore I would rather not address him about it as it stands.

Faithfully Yours always

John Hollingshead Esquire CHARLES DICKENS

To SIR JOSEPH PAXTON, 23 DECEMBER 1857

MS Free Library of Philadelphia.

Tavistock House

Wednesday Twenty Third December | 1857

My Dear Paxton.

I have just come back (2 P.M.) from reading at Rochester, and I wish you had been there. It was a tremendous success, and quite a wonderful demonstration.[2]

With me at this door, by the best of coincidences, arrives your Hamper. A thousand thanks for it—not less for the seasonable spirit of hearty friendship in which I *know* you send it to me, than for its own jolly sake.

I am quite affected by the generosity of my friends at Coventry. But they shall not spoil me, if I can help it; and I will try to "go" as truly and staunchly as the Repeater itself.[3]

All here unite with me in all good wishes, seasonable and unseasonable, to you and all your house. And I am always, with great regard,

My Dear Paxton | Faithfully Yours

Sir Joseph Paxton. CHARLES DICKENS[4]

P.S. You say "4 Hares and 4 Pheasants". But there are 8 of each, in the miraculous hamper!

[1] No reference to this in the printed play; but it must be Cranky's, caused by the "literary intruders" interrupting his dinner of boiled fowl and "inguns" (i.e. onions).

[2] CD had read the *Carol* in the new Lecture Hall, Chatham, on 22 Dec, in aid of the Chatham and Rochester Mechanics' Institute. A very warm notice in the *Maidstone, Rochester, Chatham and Canterbury Journal*, 26 Dec, reported that "the most crowded assembly" yet gathered in the Hall "was kept spell-bound and delighted for two hours by [*CD's*] magic voice and manner".

[3] After CD's reading at Coventry on 15 Dec, a subscription was opened in order to present him with a locally-made gold watch. £30 was promised in the first week. See *To* Paxton, 6 Dec 58 and *fn*.

[4] Drawn on by the "South Coast Forger": see Preface.

To W. H. WILLS, 24 DECEMBER 1857*

MS Berg Collection.

Tavistock House
Thursday Morning Twenty Fourth December | 1857

My Dear Wills

Perhaps you may know what the enclosed rigmarole[1] means—*I* don't.

Ever Faithfully
CD.

To FRIENDS OF LADY BLESSINGTON, 24 DECEMBER 1857

MS (in unknown hand, except for "24th." in date, salutation, ending and signature) Widener Collection, Harvard.

Confidential

24th. December, 1857

Dear Sir

We have ascertained from Miss Power that a present of £200, would be of very great service to her at this time, and would be gratefully accepted by her, if it were the result of a private subscription among old and confidential visitors at Gore House. We have made a private list of twenty old friends of Lady Blessington and Count D'Orsay, who may make up the required sum among themselves by a contribution of Ten Pounds each.[2]

Such private list contains your name. If you should desire to contribute your Ten Pounds, any one of us will be happy to receive your donation, and the names of the subscribers shall be forwarded to you in the close of the subscription.

Faithfully Yours
W. M. THACKERAY 36 Onslow Sqre. Brompton.
CHARLES DICKENS Tavistock House
JOHN FORSTER 46 Montagu Square

To JOHN P. PARKER,[3] 24 DECEMBER 1857

MS Private. *Address:* Mr. John P Parker | 4 Mercer Street | Long Acre | W.C.

Tavistock House. W.C. | Twenty Fourth December, 1857

Dear Sir

I have received your letter with very great pleasure and interest. Your story,[4] too,

[1] No enclosure with letter now.

[2] It would almost certainly have included Lytton, Landor, Macready, Disraeli, Milnes, Fonblanque, Henry Bulwer, the painter John Varley, perhaps Albert Smith (see *Letters and Private Papers of W. M. Thackeray*, ed. Gordon N. Ray, IV, 59).

[3] Writer of temperance tracts (see below); the owner of 4 Mercer St was William Stocker, silversmith.

[4] Parker's penny *Catechism for Bands of Hope*, published in early Nov, advertises as "just published" a story entitled *Job Brown's Two Glasses*. Probably he also contributed to the *Weekly Record of the Temperance Movement* which included a serial "of thrilling interest".

I think highly meritorious and commendable; and I am heartily proud and glad to receive your assurance that I hold a favored place in your good home.

We can agree to differ on the Total Abstinence question. I have my convictions on that subject, and they are not yours. But you cannot detest drunkenness more than I do, or hold in greater horror the evils that follow in its train. If the two words, Use and Abuse, have very different significations in my mind, so have the two words, Right and Wrong. And I know as well as all the Bands of Hope and anti-alcoholic leagues between this and the Moon, that drunken habits are tremendously wrong, and that nothing can make them out to be right.

I wish you and yours, a Merry Christmas and a happy New Year; and I rest faithfully your friend and well-wisher in all things.

Mr. John P Parker. CHARLES DICKENS

To MRS BALL WILSON,[1] 24 DECEMBER 1857*

MS Yale University Library.

Tavistock House | Thursday Twenty Fourth December | 1857

My Dear Rebecca.

I send you the autographs, with all good wishes, seasonable and unseasonable.

Affectionately Yours

CD.

To [THE SECRETARY], CHATHAM & ROCHESTER MECHANICS INSTITUTE,[2] 28 DECEMBER 1857

MS Dickens House.

Tavistock House W.C. | Twenty Eighth December, 1857

Dear Sir

I am sorry you should have given another thought to so slight a matter as the carriage-hire of Tuesday night. Your note and its enclosure reached me safely this morning.[3]

Faithfully Yours

CHARLES DICKENS

To B. W. PROCTER, [28 DECEMBER 1857]

Envelope only, MS Private. *Address:* B. W. Procter Esquire | 32 Weymouth Street | Portland Place | W. PM London 28 Dec 57.

[1] Née Rebecca Mary Barrow (1817–77), CD's first cousin; widow of Alexander Ball Wilson: see Vol. IV, p. 456*n*.

[2] Clearly an official.

[3] No doubt he was reimbursing CD for the cost of the carriage to Gad's Hill, after his reading on 22 Dec.

To AUGUSTUS TRACEY, 28 DECEMBER 1857*

MS University of Texas.

Tavistock House | Twenty Eighth December, 1857

My Dear Tracey.

On Friday I can dine with you at the Wellington[1] with great pleasure, if it will suit you to dine as early as half past 5, as I shall have to leave you at a little after 8.

Ever Faithfully | (and now hastily)
CHARLES DICKENS

To UNKNOWN CORRESPONDENT, 28 DECEMBER 1857

Mention in C. F. Libbie catalogue, Dec 1895; *MS* 1 p.; dated Tavistock House, 28 Dec 57.

Referring to literary matters; mentioning Oliver Twist.[2]

To FRANK STONE, 30 DECEMBER 1857

MS Benoliel Collection.

Tavistock House | Wednesday Thirtieth[3] December 1857

My Dear Stone

I find on enquiry, that the General Theatrical Fund *has* relieved non-members, in one or two instances; but that it is exceedingly unwilling to do so, and would certainly not do so again, saving on some very strong and exceptional case.[4] As its Trustee,[5] I could not represent to it that I think it ought to sail into those open waters, for I very much doubt the justice of such cruising, with a reference to the interests of the patient people who support it out of their small earnings.

Affecy. Ever
CD.

[1] Probably the Wellington Hotel, 351 Strand.

[2] Probably connected with the Library edn, just started; *Oliver Twist* was published on 1 Dec 58. The correspondent might be F. M. Evans or Edward Chapman (see *To* Evans, 20 Oct 57).

[3] Misdated 13 Dec in MDGH, II, 35.

[4] For the pamphlet laying down the Fund's provisions for relief, see Vol. III, p. 467*n*.

[5] CD had been a Trustee since at least 1843 (*ibid.*).

To THE REV. DR HENRY ALLON,[1] [?1856–57]

Mention in *D*, July 1916, XII, 193. *Date: The New Congregational Hymn Book* (see below) was being prepared in 1856–7, according to *D*.

Referring Allon to Harriet Parr, authoress of the hymn, "Hear my prayer, O! Heavenly Father", in "The Wreck of the Golden Mary",[2] *for her consent*[3] *to publish it in* The New Congregational Hymn Book.

To JAMES DICKENS[4] SENR, 1857

Extract in Charles De F. Burns catalogue (*c.* 1897), *MS* 1 p.; addressed James Dickens Senr; dated 1857.

I call you a thorough good Englishman.

To J. H. FRISWELL,[5] [1857]

Mention in John Anderson Jr catalogue No. 74 (1901); *MS* (3rd person) 1 p.; dated 1857.

To UNKNOWN CORRESPONDENT, [1857]

MS Fales Collection, New York University Library. *Date:* handwriting suggests end of 1857.

Accept my cordial thanks for the elegant umbrella.[6] It will be my frequent companion, and I shall take such care of it—for your sake[7]—that I expect in due course of time to shew it you grown grey under my arm.

Believe me always | Faithfully Yours
CHARLES DICKENS

[1] The Rev. Henry Allon (181–92; *DNB*), Congregational minister; pastor, Union Chapel, Islington, 1852 to his death; joint-editor of the *New Congregational Hymn Book*, revised edn 1859; Chairman, Congregational Union, 1864 and 1881; published memoirs, sermons and musical works. *The Congregational Psalmist* was announced in Mar 58 as "a companion to the *New Congregational Hymn Book*".

[2] The Christmas No., published Dec 56.

[3] Harriet Parr gave her consent and the hymn appeared in this standard collection, approved by the Congregational Union (John Julian, *Dictionary of Hymnology*, 1892, II, 882).

[4] Sadly unidentified; perhaps an Anglophil American.

[5] James Hain Friswell (1825–78; *DNB*), writer: see Vol. III, p. 485*n*. Bentley published his *Ghost Stories and Phantom Fancies* in Dec 1857.

[6] No doubt a Christmas present. Umbrellas, usually of silk, had become elegant and fashionable appurtenances for men as well as ladies. See also "Please to leave your umbrella" (*HW*, 1 May 58, XVII, 457), written in the 1st person.

[7] This suggests a present from a lady—possibly Mrs Brown, or even Mrs Ternan.

To UNKNOWN CORRESPONDENT,[1] [1857]

Extract in Goodspeed's Book Shop catalogue No. 540; dated 1857.

I give my free consent ... to the admission into this country of one copy of a Leipzig reprint of David Copperfield, and one copy of a Leipzig reprint of Pickwick Papers[2] (I being the author of both books).[3]

To H. G. ADAMS, 4 JANUARY 1858

Text from the *South Eastern Gazette*, 12 Jan 58.

Tavistock House, | 4th January, 1858

[My][4] Dear Sir,

I am very happy to receive the handsome acknowledgement of the committee of the Chatham and Rochester Mechanics Institute, and to assure them that they cannot have had more pleasure in accepting the little service I have been able to render them than I have had in giving it.[5] I can never be indifferent to the prosperity of the institution, or otherwise disposed than to help it my any means in my power.

Faithfully yours always

[H.][6] G. Adams, Esq. CHARLES DICKENS

To THOMAS DUFFUS HARDY,[7] 4 JANUARY 1858*

MS Free Library of Philadelphia.

Tavistock House. W.C. | Fourth January 1858

Mr. Charles Dickens presents his Compliments to Mr. Hardy, and begs to say that he will have great pleasure in appending his name to any acknowledgement of the great service Mr. Panizzi has rendered to students who desire to profit by the Library of the British Museum.[2]

[1] Clearly an officer of the Customs and Excise; CD is applying to receive copies for his own use.

[2] Tauchnitz's edns in his *Collection of British Authors: Pickwick Papers*, 3 vols, 1842 (Vols. 2 and 3); *Copperfield*, 3 vols, 1849 (Vols 175–7).

[3] Tauchnitz was licensed to reprint English copyright works for sale in Europe, under the Copyright Acts, 1842 and 1851: see William B. Todd and Ann Bowden, *Tauchnitz Editions in English 1841–1955, a Bibliographical History*.

[4] Omitted in printed text.

[5] See *To* Paxton, 23 Dec 57 and *fn*.

[6] Omitted in printed text.

[7] Thomas Duffus Hardy (1804–78; *DNB*), clerk in Public Records Office 1819–40; Assistant Keeper 1840–61; Deputy Keeper 1861–76; member of Historical MSS Commission 1869 and knighted; published *Memoirs of Lord Langdale* (a friend of Panizzi's), 1852.

[8] Panizzi had been Keeper of Printed Books from 1837 to 1856 and was appointed Principal Librarian on 6 Mar 56. Both appointments had been criticised at the time (because he was a foreigner and former revolutionary), e.g. by Madden within the Museum and in part of the Press; but any opposition to the 1856 appointment had died down, and was in any case futile. In the session of 1856–7 both Houses of Parliament paid tribute to his outstanding merits, and the great new Reading Room, started in 1852, ceremonially opened and available for readers in May 57, had been universally acclaimed. There seems no special reason for formal "acknowledgment" at this late date; as no record has been found, either it was not followed up, or was not public and took the form of a personal letter. Duffus Hardy, as an archivist, may have been interested in the great new Catalogue of Printed Books, started by Panizzi when Keeper and progressing according to his plans.

To W. C. MACREADY, 6 JANUARY 1858*

MS Morgan Library.

Tavistock House, London W.C. | Sixth January 1858

My Dearest Macready.

First, let me reciprocate, you know with how much earnestness and heartiness of affection, all your seasonable good wishes.

Secondly, let me assure you that I perfectly understood your difficulty, and that I do not the less sympathize with it because I have previous experience of the fact that[1] magnates [a]of that Board[a2] are Red Tape made manifest in the flesh. But my dear fellow, for *me* to go to Lord Granville[3] and represent a case of Circumlocution, would be the strangest thing! Apart from its being opposed to the rule I enforced upon myself when I made that burst,[4] to wit that I would have nothing to do with the system or the men, it would put the whole Office into a condition of white-heat, in the noble ardor of its Barnacles, great and small, to prove that what *I* represent, is a thing by no manner of means and in no conceivable condition of circumstances, to be done.[5] Rely upon it, I should be the very worst delegate you could have—that I should flutter all the doves in the cot[6]—that they would erect themselves into very Ravens against me—and that I should "plainly by Lord Granville's looks perceive"[7] that it was all U.P. with your hopes.

Though I think as ill of such bodies and of most things that they do, as it is reasonably possible for man to think, I am not (on the other hand) at all clear but that a temperate representation from yourself might carry the point. I think it tolerably probable that it might. And I recommend you to address Lord Granville straight, upon it.

I quite agree with you in your opinion of the Poem,[8] but its subject places me in the difficulty that I do not see the opportunity for publishing it in Household Words, sooner than next Christmas. We are but now out of a forest of references to Christmas,[9] taking our course through the open country again. Now, shall I keep it so long? I am sensible that it looks like burying it,—and yet, I descry no other way.[10]

[1] CD wrote "fat" before "magnates", but crossed it out.

[aa] Written over caret.

[2] Perhaps the Board of Control, responsible for the Army in India and therefore for Macready's son Edward, who had served in India since 1854 (see 10 Apr 57); its President, Robert Vernon Smith (1800–73; *DNB*), created Baron Lyveden 1859, was very unpopular.

[3] As leader of the House of Lords whenever the Liberals were in office.

[4] Created the Circumlocution Office.

[5] Cf. "Whatever was required to be done, the Circumlocution Office was beforehand with all the public departments in the art of perceiving—HOW NOT TO DO IT" (*Little Dorrit*, Ch. 10).

[6] Cf. *Coriolanus*, V, vi, 115–6.

[7] Cf. *All's Well*, IV, iii, 224.

[8] By his daughter Catherine; not published in *HW*.

[9] There were two long poems referring to Christmas in *HW*, 26 Dec, XVII: "A Christmas Phantasy" (p. 35) and Mrs Macintosh's "An Elfin Charm" (p. 40), as well as two stories.

[10] Lower half of page cut away; impossible to say how much of text missing.

To MISS CATHERINE MACREADY, 8 JANUARY 1858

Extract in Hodson's catalogue, May 1934; dated 8 Jan 58.

Referring to a poem of hers, and concluding With a whole Leviathan-freight of loves and remembrances.

To JOHN DEANE, 10 JANUARY 1858

Extract in N, III, 3 (from catalogue source); dated Tavistock House, 10 Jan 58.

Singularly characteristic and expressive, I think on the part of our Manchester proprietors![1]

There you are, evidently. Printed at Manchester in fast colors, until the expiration of your term. And you may depend upon it that your iron slipper will not fall off, until the clock shall have struck the last stroke of the appointed hour.[2]

What do you think of getting up a little Exhibition of the dry commercial spirit of all nations? And which nation, and which place in which nation, does your experienced commissionership hold likely to carry off the first medal?

To FRANK STONE, 10 JANUARY 1858*

MS Benoliel Collection.

Tavistock House | Sunday Tenth January 1858

My Dear Stone

Why shouldn't such stuff be brought forward, do you ask?[3] Because with all our brag, we are the most humbugged country that the Sun shines (or doesn't shine) on. I know on the best and most direct authority, that the Court influence was most unsparingly used against the Dead Havelock[4]—that its influence is enormous,

[1] See 23 June 57, *fn*. An item in *Punch*, 9 Jan, shows that the lack of recognition of Deane's work for the Art Treasures Exhibition (the original conception, arrangement and catalogue) had drawn comment. *Punch*, supplying the facts, pretends that acknowledgement of Deane's work (and that of Egg, Cunningham and others) had been accidentally omitted from the Report.

[2] An indirect reference both to Cinderella and the iron fetters or instruments of torture. Although the Exhibition had officially closed in Oct 57, after six months, Deane's services had no doubt been retained to organize its dismantling.

[3] Stone had probably commented on Morley's "A Lesson Lost Upon Us", *HW*, 9 Jan 58, XVII, 73. He mainly attacked the appalling sanitary conditions of both the English and French armies in the Crimea, commenting on the vast improvements to the English army brought about by the Sanitary Commission of 1855. But the title made his real point: that soldiers' living conditions were still deplorable both in India and in England itself.

[4] Major-Gen. Sir Henry Havelock (1795–1857; *DNB*), popular English hero of the Indian Mutiny. After recapturing Cawnpore on 17 July 57, reinforcing the Lucknow garrison in Sep and eventually helping Sir Colin Campbell to relieve it on 16 Nov, he had died of dysentery on 24 Nov. His death, reported in England on 7 Jan, caused universal mourning. Promoted to Major-Gen., July 57; made KCB in Sep; and on 26 Nov, before his death was known, created Bart and given £1,000 p.a. pension; a statue of him erected in Trafalgar Square by public subscription. The Duke of Cambridge told Havelock that the Queen herself had suggested his promotion to Major-Gen. (J. C. Pollock, *Way to Glory: The Life of Havelock of Lucknow*, 1957, p. 248).

because Prince Albert is the real Commander in chief,[1] and the Duke of Cambridge his mask[2]—and that Havelock was within a hair's breadth of not being appointed to his command in India by reason of the unblushing obstinacy with which the Court championed Airey[3]—the man of all others who failed in the Crimea, and is in the highest degree responsible for the most frightful of its calamities![4]

Macaulay comes home quite soon enough.[5]

Ever Affecy.
CD.

To FRANK STONE, 13 JANUARY 1858*

MS Benoliel Collection.

Tavistock House | Wednesday Thirteenth January | 1857

My Dear Stone

He is such an Ass,[6] that I really *can't* go. Say you sent me in the Card, and heard I was in the East Indies.

Ever Affectionately
CD.

[1] CD had charged Prince Albert with "interposing in Foreign affairs" in Aug 53; and the Prince had been widely held responsible for using Court influence against Palmerston, until vindicated by Lord John Russell in the Commons in Jan 54; see Vol. VII, p. 127 and *n*. But no evidence has been found for Court influence being used against Havelock or on behalf of Airey.

[2] George William Frederick Charles, 2nd Duke of Cambridge (1819–1904), the Queen's cousin, had succeeded Viscount Hardinge as Commander-in-Chief, British Forces, in July 56. He had served in the Crimea.

[3] Major-Gen. Sir Richard Airey (1803–81; *DNB*), Quarter-master-Gen., British Forces in the Crimea, Sep 54–Nov 55; promoted to Major-Gen. and made KCB Dec 54; Quarter-master-Gen. to the Army Nov 55–65. For attacks on him as responsible for the condition of troops before Sebastopol, and his exoneration, see below. Gen. 1871. Created Lord Airey 1876.

[4] This widely-held view of his blame for the breakdown of the Crimean commissariat and transport led Airey to demand a military enquiry on his return to England in 1855. A Board of Generals, meeting at Chelsea Hospital in 1856, found the commissariat officers themselves responsible and totally exonerated Airey; but CD's view of him as finally responsible persisted among critics of the Govt's conduct of the War.

[5] Stone no doubt recalls Macaulay's widely-reported attack on patronage in the second reading of the India Bill, 23 June 53; he had probably hoped for another speech about India from him in the Lords, when Parliament was recalled in Dec 57 as an emergency; CD thinks that Feb 58, when Parliament reassembles, will be soon enough.

[6] Not traced.

To W. M. THACKERAY, 14 JANUARY 1858*

MS Yale University Library.

Tavistock House | Fourteenth January 1858

My Dear Thackeray

Will you send me as soon as you can, whatsoever you have for Marguerite Power,[1] "in possession, reversion, remainder, or expectancy"[2]—

Ever Faithfully

CD.

To WILKIE COLLINS, 17 JANUARY 1858

Text from MDGH, II, 40.

Tavistock House, Sunday, Jan. 17th, 1858.

My dear Wilkie,

I am very sorry to receive so bad an account of the foot.[3] But I hope it is all in the past tense now.

I met with an incident the other day, which I think is a good deal in your way, for introduction either into a long or short story. Dr. Sutherland[4] and Dr. Monro[5] went over St. Luke's with me (only last Friday), to show me some distinctly and remarkably developed types of insanity. Among other patients, we passed a deaf and dumb man, now afflicted with incurable madness too, of whom they said that it was only when his madness began to develop itself in strongly-marked mad actions, that it began to be suspected. "Though it had been there, no doubt, some time." This led me to consider, suspiciously, what employment he had been in, and so to ask the question. "Aye," says Dr. Sutherland, "that is the most remarkable thing of all, Mr. Dickens. He was employed in the transmission of electric-telegraph messages; and it is impossible to conceive what delirious despatches that man may have been sending about all over the world!"

Rejoiced to hear such good report of the play.[6]

Ever Faithfully

[CD.]

[1] See *To* Thackeray, 4 Dec 57 and *fn.*

[2] Common legal formula; quoted, as a joke, in the opening sentence of *Nicholas Nickleby*, Ch. 22.

[3] Probably his "rheumatic gout", rather than the sprained ankle of Sep 57.

[4] Alexander John Sutherland, FRS (1811–67), physician to St Luke's Hospital for the Insane 1842–67. BA Christ Church, Oxford, 1833; MD 1838; FRCP 1840. Author of *Medical Treatment of Insanity*, 1847, and other books and papers on insanity.

[5] Henry Monro (1817–91; *DNB*), physician to St Luke's Hospital 1855–82, BA Oriel College, Oxford, 1839, MD 1863. Founded House of Charity in Soho 1846. Physician to Bethlehem Hospital 1848. Author of *Remarks on Insanity*, 1850. Published articles calling for reform in private lunatic asylums, 1852.

[6] Collins's new play, *The Red Vial*: see *To* Wills, 22 Feb and *fn.*

To GEORGE ELIOT,[1] 18 JANUARY 1858

MS British Library.

Tavistock House, London. W.C.
Monday Eighteenth January 1858

My Dear Sir

I have been so strongly affected by the two first tales in the book you have had the kindness to send me through Messrs. Blackwood,[2] that I hope you will excuse my writing to you to express my admiration of their extraordinary merit. The exquisite truth and delicacy, both of the humour and the pathos of those stories, I have never seen the like of; and they have impressed me in a manner that I should find it very difficult to describe to you, if I had the impertinence to try.

In addressing these few words of thankfulness, to the creator of the sad fortunes of Mr. Amos Barton, and the sad love-story of Mr. Gilfil, I am (I presume) bound to adopt the name that it pleases that excellent writer to assume. I can suggest no better one; but I should have been strongly disposed, if I had been left to my own devices, to address the said writer as a woman. I have observed what seem to me to be such womanly touches, in those moving fictions, that the assurance on the title-page is insufficient to satisfy me, even now. If they originated with no woman, I believe that no man ever before had the art of making himself, mentally, so like a woman, since the world began.

You will not suppose that I have any vulgar wish to fathom your secret. I mention the point as one of great interest to me—not of mere curiosity. If it should ever suit your convenience and inclination, to shew me the face of the man or woman who has written so charmingly, it will be a very memorable occasion to me. If otherwise, I shall always hold that impalpable personage in loving attachment and respect, and shall yield myself up to all future utterances from the same source, with a perfect confidence in their making me wiser and better.

Your obliged and faithful Servant, | and admirer

George Eliot Esquire CHARLES DICKENS[3]

[1] Marian Evans, "George Eliot" (1819–80; *DNB*). After rejecting her family's Evangelicalism, had completed Miss Brabant's translation of Strauss's *Life of Jesus* 1846; assisted John Chapman with the editing of the *Westminster Review*, 1851–4, through which she met G. H. Lewes; for their decision to live together and departure for Germany in 1854, see Vol. VII, p. 399 and *n*. Her literary gifts were already evident in many critical articles (all anonymous), which appeared in the *Westminster Review*. Lewes persuaded her to try her hand at fiction. See Vol. VI, p. 667*n*; and for CD's admiration of her novels, see later vols.

[2] *Scenes of Clerical Life*, 2 vols, Edinburgh, 1858 (published 5 Jan); for their publication in *Blackwood's Magazine*, see *To* Forster, Mid-Apr 57 and *fnn*. George Eliot had asked Blackwood to send CD a copy, as also to Froude, Thackeray, Tennyson, Ruskin, Faraday, Albert Smith, Mrs Carlyle and Arthur Helps (*The George Eliot Letters*, ed. Gordon S. Haight, II, 418).

[3] On 21 Jan George Eliot sent CD's letter to John Blackwood, asking him to keep its contents confidential to himself and Major Blackwood. "There can be no harm, of course", she wrote, "in every one's knowing Dickens admires the 'Scenes', but I should not like any more specific allusion made to the words of a private letter. | There can hardly be any climax of approbation for me after this, and I am so deeply moved by the finely-felt and finely-expressed sympathy of the letter, that the iron mask of my incognito seems quite painful in forbidding me to tell Dickens how thoroughly his generous impulse has been appreciated. If you should have an opportunity of conveying this feeling of mine to him in any way, you would oblige me by doing so." On 21 Jan also,

To JOSEPH LANGFORD, 18 JANUARY 1858

MS Mrs Dorothy Hicks.

Tavistock House. W.C. | Eighteenth January 1858

My Dear Langford

Will you—by such roundabout ways and methods as may present themselves—convey this note of thanks to the author of Scenes of Clerical life: whose two first stories I can never say enough of, I think them so truly admirable. But, if those two Volumes, or a part of them, were not written by a Woman,—then should I begin to believe that I am a woman myself.

Faithfully Yours always

Joseph Langford Esquire. CHARLES DICKENS

To M. LITTIGNOL,[1] 21 JANUARY 1858*

MS Mr John W. Bridge.

Tavistock House | Twenty First January 1858

Mr. Charles Dickens presents his compliments to M. Littignol, and begs to express his regret that his avocations do not leave him at leisure to accept the responsibility which that gentleman asks him to undertake. He begs to assure M. Littignol, that he is sensible of the confidence reposed in him.

To LADY DUFF GORDON, 23 JANUARY 1858*

MS Free Library of Philadelphia. *Address:* Lady Duff Gordon | Esher.

Tavistock House | Twenty Third January 1858.

My Dear Lady Gordon

Your letter charms me[2]—and emboldens me to make a confession of weakness. Freely confiding it to you and my two other sympathizing correspondents,[3] I hereby assure the blessed triumvirate that I affected myself so strongly by Gill Davis's misplaced love, as to be for days and days, really unable to approach the Proofs. As often as I tried to correct them, I turned them over, looked at the last page, and was so completely overcome, that I couldn't bear to dwell upon it.[4] It was only when the

Jane Carlyle sent George Eliot her warm thanks for *Scenes of Clerical Life*. The first vol. had helped her "during one of the most (physically) wretched nights" of her life. It was, she wrote, "a *human* book—written out of the heart of a live man, not merely out of the brain of an author". The writer she thought of as "a man of middle age, with a wife from whom she had got those beautiful *feminine* touches in his book, a good many children, and a dog ... for the rest, not just a clergyman, but Brother or first cousin to a clergyman.—How ridiculous all this may read, beside the reality!" (*The George Eliot Letters*, ed. Gordon S. Haight, II, 424–6).

[1] Unidentified. Possibly a teacher connected with Lord Kingsdown's schools at Teston, nr Maidstone, where family of owner lived.

[2] Praising "The Perils of Certain English Prisoners".

[3] Her daughter Janet and her German friend, Mathilde: see below and *To* Alexander Duff Gordon, 21 May 57.

[4] The humble private who has rescued the prisoners and guarded "Miss Maryon" is called out of the ranks by Capt. Carton, publicly thanked and offered a purse of money. This he declines, saying it would break his heart; but "ignorant and common" though he is, he begs

Steam Engine roared for the sheets, that I could find it in my heart to look at them with a pen in my hand dipped in any thing but tears!

The Second chapter[1] was done, on the perusal of my first and third,[2] by Wilkie Collins. We planned it out, and it seems to me a very notable and happy piece of execution.

I should have been very happy to have immediately acted on your suggestion concerning M. De Wailly,[3] but that I have "conceded" (which is polite for sold), to a Publishing House in Paris, the right of translating any thing and everything I may write, if the said house choose to claim the right within twelve months of the original publishing in English.[4]

What am I doing? Tearing myself—My usual occupation, at most times. Wild and misty ideas of a story are floating about somewhere (I don't know where), and I am looking after them. One of the most restless of men at all times, I am at such a crisis worse than ever. Nothing would satisfy me at this present writing, but the having to go up a tremendous mountain, magic spell in one hand and sword in the other, to find the girl of my heart (whom I never did find), surrounded by fifty Dragons—kill them all—and bear her off, triumphant.[5] I might finish the story in the usual way, by settling down and living happy ever afterwards—Perhaps; I am not sure even of that.

Forget her?—I mean Mathilde, but my previous antecedent would do—have I ever forgotten her? Sits she not always on my left hand, at the supper-table of The Frozen Deep?[6]

The two old pictures look very bright, and seem so quiet and composed when I sit in my chair and watch them for half an hour.

Dear Lady Gordon | Ever Yours | (and Their—viz: | Janet's[7] and Mathilde's)

Faithful

CD.

for some personal trifle that she has worn. She gives him a ring from her finger as "a gallant and generous man". There follows his "confession" to the reader—that despite the social distance between them, "immense and hopeless", "she as high above him as the sky", he loved her and suffered long agony, "as great as if I had been a gentleman". Years pass, while he continues dutifully in the service far away, not promoted owing to his "utter want of learning". Finally he is brought from a distant hospital to be cared for in the home of Admiral Carton and Lady Carton, where "my Lady", once Miss Maryon, now grey-haired, is supposed to be writing down the entire narrative at his dictation. CD had been correcting these proofs in late Nov 57: see *To* Lady Olliffe, 30 Nov.

1 "The Prison in the Woods".

2 "The Island of Silver-Store" and "The Rafts on the River".

3 Armand François Leon De Wailly. Books he translated include *Tristram Shandy*, *A Sentimental Journey*, *Uncle Tom's Cabin*, *Barry Lyndon*, *Henry Esmond*, and writings by Swift. Lady Duff Gordon's *Stella and Vanessa: a Romance*, from the French, 1850, was a translation from De Wailly.

4 For CD's selling the rights to Hachette, see *To* Forster, 6 Jan 56 and *fn*.

5 Cf. a similar description of his restlessness in *To* Mrs Watson, 7 Dec 57.

6 On 6 Jan 57, after the first performance.

7 Janet Duff Gordon (1842–1927); she married Henry Ross, manager of Briggs's Bank in Alexandria and friend of Layard, on 5 Dec 60; on the bank's collapse in 1866, settled in Florence, where she became a leading member of the English literary colony (see John Pemble, *The Mediterranean Passion*, Oxford, 1987, p. 79). George Meredith ("My Poet", Janet called him) had earlier fallen in love with her.

To WILLIAM KELLY,[1] 23 JANUARY 1858*

MS Free Library of Philadelphia.

Tavistock House, London. W.C.
Twenty Third January 1858.

Sir.

The service you ask of me, is one I cannot possibly render you. So many similar letters are constantly addressed to me, that unless I invariably made a rule of reading no MSS for the purpose of giving abstract opinions on their merits, I could discharge no other avocation in life. I must limit myself to the expression of my regret that your verses are not suitable to Household Words—the only miscellaneous publication over which I have controul.

Your faithful Servant

William Kelly Esquire CHARLES DICKENS

To JOHN STEDMAN[2] AND OTHERS, 25 JANUARY 1858

MS Mr J. C. Taylor. *Address:* John Stedman Esquire | Northfleet | Kent.

Tavistock House, London. W.C.
Twenty Fifth January 1858

Gentlemen.

I beg to express my regret that I cannot possibly comply with your request. You will the better understand my inability to do so, when I assure you that I receive similar requests incessantly, in numbers so incredible, that even to acknowledge their receipt however briefly, is often a serious encroachment on my occupied time and attention.

I am Gentlemen | Your faithful Servant

John Stedman Esquire And Others CHARLES DICKENS

To LADY DUFF GORDON, [26 JANUARY 1858]

Mention in next. *Date:* written the same day.

To MARK LEMON, 26 JANUARY 1858

MS Benoliel Collection.

Tavistock House
Tuesday Morning. Twenty Sixth Jany. | 1858

My Dear Mark

I have been prevented from meeting you this morning, by an unusually violent rush of letters, imposing all sorts of other peoples' botherations on me.

[1] The only William Kelly who wrote verse is the Rev. William Kelly SJ, who seems unlikely. But just possibly the Irish emigrant who wrote on his travels to California and Victoria and whose travel books of 1851–2 show considerable literary capacity.

[2] Builder, of 5 Tabor Place, Northfleet.

Among them, came the enclosed from Lady Gordon. As you know her to be a literary woman of real ability, I send you her note and the pamphlet to which it refers. In telling her I have done so, I have added that my impression of the case is the same as my friend Mr Punch's,[1] but that I will read the Pamphlet (which she sends me in duplicate), with judicial care and attention.

Ever affectionately
CD.

To FRANK STONE, 26 JANUARY 1858*

MS Benoliel Collection.

Tavistock House | Twenty Sixth January 1858

My Dear Stone.

Your one third share of Ansell's charge for Front Court and Front Enclosure, from Midsummer last to the time of the engagement of the new man (in all, £8.11.6), is £2.17.2. I have settled with Ansell, and this latter sum is what you have to pay me.[2]

Ever affecy.
CD.

To JOHN FORSTER, [?27 JANUARY 1858]

Extracts in F, IX, ii, 729 and VIII, iii, 651. *Date:* First extract 27 Jan, according to Forster; second extract from same letter: see *ibid.*, p. 729.

Growing inclinations of a fitful and undefined sort are upon me sometimes to fall to work on a new book.[3] Then I think I had better not worry my worried mind yet awhile. Then I think it would be of no use if I did, for I couldn't settle to one occupation.—And that's all!

You will hardly know Gadshill again, I am improving it so much[4]—yet I have no interest in the place.[5]

[1] No reference to the pamphlet or "case" to which it refers found in *Punch*; "Mr Punch" may simply stand for Lemon.

[2] See *To* Stone, 10 July 57 and *fn.*

[3] The first notion occurred to him while acting in *The Frozen Deep* (as CD himself stated in his Preface to the novel, Nov 59). "But it was only a vague fancy, and the sadness and trouble of the winter of that year (1857–8) were not favourable to it." On 27 Jan "it was again in his thoughts" (F, IX, ii, 729).

[4] For the additions and alterations CD made, see later vols. CD's Account-book (MS Messrs Coutts) shows eight payments to James Shoolbred & Co., linen and woollen drapers and carpet warehousemen, 152–56 Tottenham Court Road (see Vol. VI, p. 487*n*), 28 Oct 56–18 June 58, totalling over £465.

[5] At this time CD regarded the house mainly as an investment and a summer residence (F, VIII, iii, 651).

To W. S. LANDOR, 28 JANUARY [1858]

Mention in Pickering & Chatto, *The Book Lovers Leaflet*, No. 13 (Feb 1888); *MS* 4 pp.; addressed W. S. Landor; dated 28 Jan [58] (see below).[1]

To JOHN FORSTER, [?30 JANUARY 1858]

Extract in F, IX ii, 729. *Date:* Three days after letter of 27 Jan, according to Forster.

If I can discipline my thoughts into the channel of a story, I have made up my mind to get to work on one: always supposing that I find myself, on the trial, able to do well. Nothing whatever will do me the least "good" in the way of shaking the one strong passion of change[2] impending over us that every day makes stronger; but if I could work on with some approach to steadiness, through the summer, the anxious toil of a new book would have its neck well broken before beginning to publish, next October or November.[3] Sometimes, I think I may continue to work; sometimes I think not. What do you say to the title, ONE OF THESE DAYS?[4]

To J. WESTLAND MARSTON,[5] 31 JANUARY 1858*

MS Library of Congress.

Tavistock House | Sunday Thirty First January | 1858.

My Dear Marston

I am unfortunately engaged to dine out tomorrow, as a preliminary to supporting a philosopher[6] in a ballot where the "bishops, priests, and deacons"[7] are expected to be arrayed against him.[8]

But I will come to see the piece[9] on its second night, and I need not tell you that I shall come with interest and pleasure. For this use, I retain the card for which I am indebted to your welcome remembrance and Mr. Dillon's politeness.

I will give you the ten minutes—and as many more as you like—most readily. Will you say next Friday at any time between 10 and 1? If that day should not suit you, say next Saturday between the same hours.

Faithfully Yours always

Westland Marston Esquire. CHARLES DICKENS

[1] The catalogue dates the letter Bath, 1888 and adds "(*Very interesting*)". 1888 must have been wrongly transcribed from the date of the catalogue, and Bath from the address to Landor on the envelope. Probably CD wrote for Landor's birthday on 30 Jan, and may have described his own unhappiness, as in *To* Forster, 30 Jan. CD is not known to have visited Landor in Bath after 1851 and Landor left in July 1858.

[2] His growing insistence on a separation.

[3] He changed his mind, and did not begin writing until Feb 1859.

[4] As Forster says, that title "held its ground very briefly" (F, IX, ii, 729).

[5] John Westland Marston (1819–90; *DNB*), poet and dramatist: see Vol. III, p. 370*n*.

[6] See *To* Miss Coutts, 11 Feb and *fn*. Elliot Grasett, of 6 Chesham St; BA, Emmanuel College, Cambridge, 1842; called to Bar by Inner Temple 1847.

[7] From the Book of Common Prayer.

[8] For his election to the Athenaeum. CD was presumably expected to meet Grasett at dinner.

[9] Marston's *A Hard Struggle* at the Lyceum: see *To* Forster, 3 Feb and *fn*.

To MISS BURDETT COUTTS, 2 FEBRUARY 1858

MS Morgan Library. *Address:* Miss Burdett Coutts | 1 Stratton Street | Piccadilly. W.

Tavistock House | Second February 1858

My Dear Miss Coutts

I am inexpressibly vexed to find that Mrs. Dickens, in my absence[1] and without my knowledge, wrote to you yesterday about her brother.[2] I had not told her of the contents of your last kind note to me, concerning him. That is her only excuse;[3] and I hope you will forgive her more freely and more readily than *I* do.

Ever Faithfully and affecy. Yours
CHARLES DICKENS

To [?T. R. EELES],[4] 2 FEBRUARY 1858

Mention in Pickering & Chatto, *The Book Lovers Leaflet*, No. 13 (Feb 1888); dated Tavistock House, 2 Feb 58.

Relating to the binding of an original MS.[5]

To W. M. THACKERAY, 2 FEBRUARY 1858

MS Comtesse de Suzannet.

Tavistock House | Tuesday Second February 1858

My Dear Thackeray

The wisdom of Parliament, in that expensive Act of its greatness which constistutes the Guild, prohibits that corporation *from doing any thing* until it shall have existed in a perfectly useless condition for Seven Years. This clause (introduced by some Private-Bill magnate of official might) seemed so ridiculous, that nobody could believe it to have this meaning; but as I felt clear about it when we were on the

[1] At the Athenaeum.

[2] Catherine had written: "In case I am not fortunate enough to find you—and dear Mrs Brown—at home when I call at Stratton Street today, I write to tell you what I would have said to you. | You may remember that Charles wrote to you now some weeks ago about my youngest Brother Edward who owing to one of the great failures in Sheffield lost an excellent position there, and had the world to begin again. | Soon after Charles wrote to you about him, he was offered and accepted a situation in the City as Cashier in a large Wholesale Furniture Silk Warehouse, but for reasons with which I need not trouble you, he finds it impossible to continue in it. I ought however to add that it is from no fault of his that he leaves. I venture therefore dear Miss Coutts to ask you if you should hear of any situation likely to suit him, if you would do me the great kindness to bear him in mind, as I need not tell you I am deeply interested in his procuring employment, more particularly as my Father is not able to do much for him, and it is a serious and anxious thing for him, that my Brother should be unemployed. | I know that with your usual friendship and kindness you will pardon my thus troubling you on my brother's behalf, and with best love, Believe me always" (MS Morgan; given in *Letters from CD to Angela Burdett Coutts*, ed. Edgar Johnson, 1953, p. 352).

[3] Surely a sufficient reason; CD clearly should have told her.

[4] "Unknown Correspondent" in catalogue; almost certainly Thomas Robert Eeles.

[5] See *To* Collins, 6 Feb.

very verge of granting an excellent literary annuity, I referred the point to Counsel, and my construction was confirmed without a doubt.[1]

It is therefore needless to enquire whether an association in the nature of a Provident Society could address itself to such a case as you confide to me. The prohibition has still two or three years of life in it.

But, assuming the gentleman's[2] title to be considered an "Author", as established, there is no question that it comes within the scope of the Literary Fund. They would habitually "lend" money if they did what I consider to be their duty. As it is, they only give money, but they give it in such instances.

(I have forwarded the envelope to the Society of Arts,[3] with a request that they will present it to Prince Albert: approaching H.R.H. in the Siamese manner.)[4]

Ever Faithfully
CD.

To EDMUND YATES, 2 FEBRUARY 1858

MS Robert H. Taylor Collection, Princeton University.

Tavistock House | Tuesday Second February 1858

My Dear Yates

Your quotation is—as I supposed—all wrong. The text is NOT[5] "which his owls was organs."[6] When Mr. Harris went into "a empty dog-kennel", to spare his sensitive nature the anguish of overhearing Mrs Harris's exclamations on the occasion of the birth of her first child (the Princess Royal of the Harris family), "he never took his hands away from his ears, or came out once, till he was shewed the baby." On encountering that spectacle he was (being of a weakly constitution), "took with fits." For this distressing complaint he was medically treated; the doctor "collared him and laid him on his back upon the airy stones"—please to observe what follows—"*and she was told, to ease her mind, his owls was organs*."

That is to say: Mrs. Harris, lying exhausted on her bed, in the first sweet relief of freedom from pain, merely covered with the counterpane and not yet "put comfortable", hears a noise, apparently proceeding from the backyard, and says, in a flushed and hysterical manner, "what owls are those! Who is a owling! Not my ugebond!" Upon which, the Doctor, looking round on one of the bottom posts of the bed, and taking Mrs. Harris's pulse in a re-assuring manner, says, with admirable presence of mind, "Howls my dear Madame? No, no, no. What are we thinking of. Howls, my dear Mrs. Harris? Ha ha ha! Organs Ma am, organs. Organs in the streets Mrs. Harris. No howls"— Ever Faithfully CD.

[1] This clause does not appear in the Private Act incorporating the Guild of Literature and Art on 2 June 54 (Statutes, 17 & 18 Vic, Cap 54 and see Vol. VII, p. 330 and *n*); if CD's interpretation is correct, it must have been introduced later.

[2] Unidentified.

[3] The Society for the Encouragement of Arts, Manufactures and Commerce, founded 1754.

[4] i.e. prostration, as to the Siamese King.

[5] Underlined twice.

[6] *Martin Chuzzlewit*, Ch. 49. Cf. Vol. IV, pp. 142–3. Yates says that this was one of the occasions on which he had, in conversation, purposely misquoted CD, in order to receive a letter setting him right (*Recollections and Experiences*, II, 106).

To J. WESTLAND MARSTON, 3 FEBRUARY 1858

Text from MDGH, II, 43.

Tavistock House, Wednesday, Feb. 3rd, 1858.

My dear Marston,

I most heartily and honestly congratulate you on your charming little piece. It moved me more than I could easily tell you, if I were to try. Except "La Joie fait Peur," I have seen nothing nearly so good, and there is a subtlety in the comfortable presentation of the child who is to become a devoted woman for Reuben's sake,[1] which goes a long way beyond Madame de Girardin. I am at a loss to let you know how much I admired it last night, or how heartily I cried over it. A touching idea, most delicately conceived and wrought out by a true artist and poet, in a spirit of noble, manly generosity, that no one should be able to study without great emotion.[2]

It is extremely well acted by all concerned; but Mr. Dillon's performance is really admirable, and deserving of the highest commendation.[3] It is good in these days to see an actor taking such pains, and expressing such natural and vigorous sentiment. There is only one thing I should have liked him to change. I am much mistaken if any man—least of all any such man—would crush a letter written by the hand of the woman he loved.[4] Hold it to his heart unconsciously and look about for it the while, he might; or he might do any other thing with it that expressed a habit of tenderness and affection in association with the idea of her; but he would never crush it under any circumstances. He would as soon crush her heart.

You will see how closely I went with him, by my minding so slight an incident in so fine a performance. There is no one who could approach him in it; and I am bound to add that he surprised me as much as he pleased me.

I think it might be worth while to try the people at the Français[5] with the piece. They are very good in one-act plays; such plays take well there, and this seems to me well suited to them. If you would like Samson[6] or Regnier to read the play (in English), I know them well, and would be very glad indeed to tell them that I sent it with your sanction because I had been so much struck by it.

Faithfully yours always

[CHARLES DICKENS]

[1] Lilian Trevor, betrothed as a girl to her childhood friend Reuben Holt, falls in love with Fergus Graham, who has saved her life on a voyage to Madeira. Reuben discovers this and, after a violent quarrel with Fergus through a misunderstanding, releases Lilian from her engagement, so that she may marry Fergus.

[2] "We have rarely seen so much pathos and real feeling developed in so small a space as it is in this admirable little domestic tragedy" (*Morning Chronicle*, 2 Feb).

[3] Dillon played Reuben; his wife, Lilian. "We never saw Mr. Dillon ... to more advantage"; he displayed "a passion and energy which calls for the highest praise" (*ibid.*).

[4] Lilian's letter to Reuben, in which she hides her love for Fergus. He does not "crush" it in the published text.

[5] The Comédie Français.

[6] Joseph-Isidore Samson (1793–1872), French actor and playwright. Played 250 parts at the Comédie Français from 1826; taught at the Conservatoire from 1829.

To UNKNOWN CORRESPONDENT, 3 FEBRUARY 1858

Mention in American Art Association and Anderson catalogue, Jan 1939; dated Tavistock House, 3 Feb 58.

Thanking his correspondent for a song he has sent him.

To JOHN FORSTER, 3 FEBRUARY 1858

Text from MDGH, II, 42–3.

Tavistock House, | Wednesday Night, Feb. 3rd, 1858.

My dear Forster,

I beg to report two phenomena:

1. An excellent little play in one act, by Marston, at the Lyceum; title, "A Hard Struggle;" as good as "La Joie fait Peur,"[1] though not at all like it.

2. Capital acting in the same play, by Mr. Dillon. Real good acting, in imitation of nobody, and honestly made out by himself!!

I went (at Marston's request) last night, and cried till I sobbed again. I have not seen a word about it from Oxenford.[2] But it is as wholesome and manly a thing altogether as I have seen for many a day. (I would have given a hundred pounds to have played Mr. Dillon's part).[3]

Love to Mrs. Forster.

Ever affectionately
[CD.]

To CAVENDISH SPENCER BOYLE, 5 FEBRUARY 1858*

MS Roger W. Barrett.

Tavistock House | Friday Fifth February 1858.

My Dear Boyle.

Many thanks. I am happy to find that Flora is going to dash into commerce, to distract her own mind and everybody else's at the same time. I heard from Pan, a few weeks since.[4] I also had a charming letter, on New Year's Day, from your sister Mary. Which I have not yet answered—which would be like a Beast, if it were not more like a man who can seldom write any letters that he likes to write, by reason of his writing fifty a day that he doesn't like to write. Love from all out of prison to all

[1] By Mme de Girardin (wife of Emile de Girardin), first performed at the Théâtre Français, 25 Feb 54: see Vol. VII, p. 540 and *n*. The best known of the four plays she wrote 1840–54.

[2] As dramatic critic of *The Times*; it was not noticed there.

[3] The hero nobly renounces the girl he loves, like Wardour in *The Frozen Deep*.

[4] Pan is obviously a member of the Rockingham circle, perhaps Spencer Lyttelton. Flora is probably Eleanor Vere Boyle, Mary's cousin by marriage, known to CD since 1852 (see Vol. VI, p. 835 and *n*). Her first work, *Child's Play*, by E. V. B., 17 drawings, illustrating nursery rhymes, beautifully printed by Addey & Co. of Bond St in 1852, was republished in smaller format with coloured plates at the end of 1858 by a commercial publisher, Sampson Low (Addey had gone out of business in 1857). Perhaps she was also thought to be like Flora Finching.

in prison.[1] (I find that sentence to have an apostolic appearance).[2] I thought of you when I saw Lord Spencer's[3] death[4] in the papers, but I hope the son will follow [*you*][5] in the father's footsteps.[6] My second boy is attached to the 42nd. Highlanders, and in the thick of the Indian tussle.[7] And so no more at present from

Yours Ever

[CHARLES DICKENS]

To WILKIE COLLINS, 5 FEBRUARY 1858

MS Morgan Library.

My Dear Wilkie

Will you come and dine with me at Wates's at Gravesend, next Sunday—my Birthday? Only Forster, besides. We will go from London Bridge Station by the Train which leaves at 3.

I have to report two phenomena[8] at the Lyceum.

1. A very pretty original piece in one Act by Marston. As good as La joie fait peur, and not at all like it.

2. Excellent acting in it by Mr. Dillon. Imitated from no one—honestly and vigorously made out for himself.

!

Ever Faithfully

CD.

To J. W. KNIGHT,[9] 5 FEBRUARY 1858*

Text from transcript, Huntington Library.

Tavistock House, | Fifth February 1858.

Sir,

I would most willingly receive the Deputation from the Master Boot and Shoe Makers' Benevolent Institution,[10] if I could possibly accede to the request they contemplate doing me the honor to proffer to me. But as I can make no new public engagements of that nature for the present season, and as I consequently know that

[1] Boyle had been Governor of the Military Prison, Weedon, Northants, since 1853.

[2] Like St Paul.

[3] Frederick, 4th Earl Spencer, CB (1798–1857): see Vol. VI, p. 266*n*. Lord Steward of the Royal Household 1854–7; Vice-Admiral 1857.

[4] On 27 Dec 57.

[5] CD's square brackets.

[6] Weedon was six miles from Althorp, his cousin Lord Spencer's seat; and, according to Mary Boyle, he had become a "frequent and confidential companion" of Lord Spencer (*Mary Boyle her Book*, ed. Sir Courtenay Boyle, p. 256).

[7] The 42nd Highlanders had fought in the Battle of Cawnpore on 6 Dec 57 and on 9 Mar took part in the relief of Lucknow. "The Black Watch" (originally formed by 1725) was officially added to their title in July 61.

[8] "phenomona" in MS.

[9] Secretary, Master Boot and Shoe Makers' Benevolent Institution.

[10] Founded 1836; gave pensions of £15–£20 *p.a.*; possessed alms-houses at Mortlake for 20 inmates.

their coming to me would be a waste of their time, I deem it right to inform you at once that I cannot have the satisfaction of presiding at the proposed dinner.

I am Sir, | Your faithful Servant,

Mr John W. Knight. CHARLES DICKENS

To WILKIE COLLINS, 6 FEBRUARY 1858

MS Yale University Library.

Tavistock House | Saturday Sixth February 1858

My Dear Wilkie

Thinking it may one day be interesting to you—say, when you are weak in both feet, and when I and Doncaster are quiet and the great race is over[1]—to possess this little memorial of our joint Christmas Work, I have had it put together for you, and now send it on its coming home from the binder.

Faithfully Ever

Wilkie Collins Esquire. CHARLES DICKENS

To SIR CHARLES LOCOCK,[2] 10 FEBRUARY 1858*

MS Free Library of Philadelphia. *Address:* Sir Charles Locock | Hertford Street | May Fair | W.

Tavistock House | Tenth February 1858

My Dear Sir Charles

The undersigned Charmer was extremely sorry to lose you last night.[3] He handed your generous donation to the Secretary, by whom it was duly announced. You will be glad to hear that the Dinner was very successful, and that the subscriptions amounted to the—as far as I know—unprecedented sum of £3,000.[4]

Faithfully Yours ever

Sir Charles Locock. CHARLES DICKENS

[1] i.e. when Collins is permanently crippled and CD himself is dead.

[2] Sir Charles Locock (1799–1875; *DNB*), MD, obstetric physician to the Queen: see Vol. V, p. 58*n*. Bart 1857.

[3] At the first Anniversary Dinner on behalf of the Hospital for Sick Children, Great Ormond St, at the Freemasons' Hall, with CD in the Chair: see *To* Miss Coutts, 11 Feb and *fn*; and, for the opening of the Hospital, see Vol. VI, p. 579*n*.

[4] No doubt including donations; the sum raised at the Dinner was in fact £2,850 (Jules Klosky, *Mutual Friends* [1989], p. 203), an impressive sum, since the Dinner was (like most Hospital dinners), not very well attended. With the contributions, the Hospital opened endowment and building funds. (*Speeches*, ed. K. J. Fielding, p. 246). T. A. Reed (see 12 June 58 and *fn*) later told Kitton that publication of CD's address had "brought many handsome contributions to the hospital exchequer" (F. G. Kitton, *CD by Pen and Pencil*, Suppl., p. 46).

To BENJAMIN WEBSTER, 10 FEBRUARY 1858

MS Dickens House.

Tavistock House, W.C. | Wednesday Tenth February 1858.[1]

My Dear Webster

I am sorry to reply to your note, that I already stand pledged to an engagement for Ash-wednesday,[2] which leaves me no property in myself for that day.

(I wonder, by the bye, how many Orreries[3] you have in the vaults at the Adelphi—about 20, I suppose.)

Faithfully Yours always
CHARLES DICKENS

To MISS BURDETT COUTTS, 11 FEBRUARY 1858*

MS Morgan Library. *Address:* Miss Burdett Coutts | 1 Stratton Street | Piccadilly.

Tavistock House | Thursday Eleventh February | 1858.

My Dear Miss Coutts

I was out of town yesterday and did not receive your note until I came home at night. This morning I have been down to the Athenaeum and have had the pleasure of attaching my name to Mr. Grasett's balloting paper.[4] He may depend upon my going down on Monday night too, and voting for him.[5]

I think this poor girl's letter,[6] a very pathetic and genuine one. It says what we must all think (I mean all we who have any part under you in administering it) of the Home; and says it with great feeling and simplicity.

Ever Dear Miss Coutts | Yours faithfully and affecy.
CHARLES DICKENS

I wish you had been at the first dinner of the Hospital for Sick Children, last Tuesday. I really thought that the Chairman warmed with the subject and turned it well!—[7]

[1] Misdated 8 Feb 58 in N.

[2] 24 Feb.

[3] Perhaps the vaults were explored because of the planned demolition of the old theatre in early June. Orreries were clockwork models, invented in 1715, to show the motions of the planets around the sun, used in Planetaria; named after the 4th Earl of Orrery; clearly still popular: Charles H. Adams, author of *The Explanatory Letter-press to Accompany the Plate of The Solar system*, 1822, used them in lectures on astronomy he gave at the Haymarket Theatre on 10 and 17 Apr 58. CD later recalled the boredom he suffered as a boy at Chatham when he and a childhood sweetheart were taken to see "a slow torture called an Orrery" as a birthday treat: "The terrible instrument was set up in the local Theatre.... It was a venerable and shabby Orrery, at least one thousand stars and twenty-five comets behind the age." It ended their love: "the man with the wand was too much for the boy with the bow" ("The Uncommercial Traveller", *AYR*, 6 June 63, IX, 349; reprinted as "Birthday Celebrations" in *The Uncommercial Traveller*).

[4] The ballot paper, dated 13 Feb, describing Grasett as a Private Gentleman, shows that his proposer was the Rt. Rev Bishop Hinds (Bishop of Norwich), seconded by the late Lieut Gen. Sir W. L. Herries and the Rt. Hon. Edmund Cardwell, M.P. There are three cols of names of supporters.

[5] Grasett was one of the seven who were declared elected on 15 Feb.

[6] No doubt from one of the Home's emigrants to Australia or South Africa; but not discovered.

[7] For a full account of the Dinner, see Jules Klosky, *Mutual Friends*, pp. 183–97; and for CD's speech as Chairman, see *Speeches*, ed. K. J.

To J. WESTLAND MARSTON, 11 FEBRUARY 1858*

MS Free Library of Philadelphia.

Tavistock House | Thursday Eleventh February | 1858.

My Dear Marston

I have sent off the Proof[1] to Regnier; and have told him what I think of the play and of its acting capacities, just as I have already told my opinion to you.

Faithfully Always
CHARLES DICKENS

To FRANÇOIS RÉGNIER, 11 FEBRUARY 1858†

MS Comédie Français.

Tavistock House, London. W.C.
Thursday Eleventh February 1858

My Dear Regnier.

I want you to read the enclosed little play. You will see that it is in one Act—about the length of La joie fait peur. It is now acting at the Lyceum Theatre here, with very great success. The author is Mr. Westland Marston; a dramatic writer of some reputation, who wrote a very well known tragedy called "The Patrician's Daughter", in which Macready and Miss Faucit[2] acted (under Macready's management at Drury Lane), some years ago.[3]

This little piece is so very powerful on the stage, its interest is so simple and natural, and the part of Reuben is such a very fine one, that I cannot help thinking you might make un grand coup with it, if, with your skilful hand, you arranged it for the Français. I have communicated this idea of mine to the author, et la dessus je vous ecris. I am anxious to know your opinion, and shall expect with much interest to receive a little letter from you at your convenience.

Mrs. Dickens, Miss Hogarth, and all the house, send a thousand kind loves and regard to Madame Regnier and the dear little boys.[4] You will bring them all to London when you come, with all the force of the Français—will you not?

Ever My Dear Regnier | Faithfully Your friend
CHARLES DICKENS

Fielding, pp. 248–53. Forster, giving two long passages from it, considered it "the best of the kind spoken by him". "There was a simple pathos ... quite startling in its effect ... and he probably never moved any audience so much as by the strong personal feeling with which he referred to the sacrifices made for the Hospital by the very poor themselves" (F, VIII, ii, 643). T. A. Reed, who reported the speech, wrote to Kitton much later: "I never heard him, or reported him, with so much pleasure.... His speech was magnificent, thoroughly characteristic, and extremely telling" (F. G. Kitton, *CD by Pen and Pencil*, Supplement, p. 46). Soon after the Hospital's opening in 1852, CD and Morley had collaborated in an article upon it in *HW*, "Drooping Buds", 3 Apr 52, V, 45 (*Uncollected Writings*, ed. Harry Stone, II, 401).

[1] Of *A Hard Struggle*, which it must have been intended to publish at once; it was not in fact published until 1861 (T. H. Lacy's *Acting Edn*, Vol. 48).

[2] Helen (later Helena) Saville Faucit (1817–98; *DNB*): see Vol. III, p. 597*n*. She had married Sir Theodore Martin in 1851.

[3] Marston's first play, in verse, for which CD wrote the Prologue; first performed on 10 Dec 42: see Vol. III, p. 370*nn*. Helen Faucit played Lady Mabel.

[4] Born since July 1849, when his 14-year-old daughter, then his only child, had died: see Vol. V, p. 587 and *n*.

To MARK LEMON, 12 FEBRUARY 1858

MS Brotherton Library, Leeds.

Tavistock House W.C. | Twelfth February 1858

My Dear Mark

Many hearty thanks for your remembrance of my Birthday.

Affectionately Ever

Mark Lemon Esquire CHARLES DICKENS

To J. WESTLAND MARSTON, 16 FEBRUARY 1858*

MS Library of Congress. *Address:* Westland Marston Esquire | 1 Camden Park Villas | N.W.

Tavistock House W.C. | Sixteenth February 1858

My Dear Marston

I have received the enclosed from Regnier, this morning. Consider it at your leisure, and tell me what reply I shall send him.[1]

Ever Faithfully

Westland Marston Esquire CHARLES DICKENS

To H. A. BATHURST,[2] 17 FEBRUARY 1858*

MS Hospital for Sick Children.

Tavistock House

Wednesday Evening | Seventeenth February 1858

Dear Sir

I beg to acknowledge the receipt of your obliging letter, and to assure the Committee, through you, of the gratification I derive from their generous recognition of my most willingly rendered services.[3] It will give me great pleasure to become one of the Honorary Governors of the Hospital.

In the matter of my public reading for its benefit, I will presently consult the friend who was Honorary Secretary to the Jerrold Remembrance Fund[4] (for which I read in London last year), and who has a better practical experience of the management of such things than perhaps any one in London. When I shall have taken counsel with him as to time, place, and prices, I will communicate with you again.[5]

[1] Régnier had obviously written that he needed more time to study *A Hard Struggle*. In his reply to CD on 17 Feb, Marston said that he would "most cheerfully" wait until Régnier had decided whether he could interpret the play as he wished; he valued Régnier's good opinion and agreed that, where the central incident had been previously used in other forms, the handling of the material was "even more important than the material itself". He told CD how much he owed to Régnier's "cheering sympathy" (MS Yale).

[2] Henry Allen Bathurst (*b.* 1819), son of Lieut. Gen. Sir James Bathurst, Assistant Adjutant Gen. to Wellington's Peninsular campaign; BA Merton College, Oxford, 1839; one of original founders of Hospital for Sick Children 1850 and Hon. Secretary for 10 years; on Committee of Management until 1884; Registrar of Admiralty Court 1879–90. See Jules Klosky, *Mutual Friends*, pp. 121, 126.

[3] See *To* Miss Coutts, 11 Feb and *fn.*

[4] Arthur Smith.

[5] See *To* Beard, 5 Apr and *fn.*

You will of course understand in the meanwhile, that I only desire to redeem my pledge in the most advantageous and most profitable manner.

Dear Sir | Faithfully Yours

H. A. Bathurst Esquire CHARLES DICKENS

To MISS BURDETT COUTTS, 17 FEBRUARY 1858*

MS Morgan Library. *Address:* Miss Burdett Coutts | 1 Stratton Street | Piccadilly | W.

Tavistock House
Wednesday Evening Seventeenth Feby. | 1858.

My Dear Miss Coutts.

I attended the Committee to day, and thoroughly agreed with Mr. Dyer in the precautionary measure he proposed as to the admission of cases. It is quite understood among us that it shall be always adopted henceforth.

As you had expressed a wish that we would not call in the newer girls to day, we saw but four or five of the Inmates. The two who are going into service, expressed their gratitude with much propriety and modesty, and steered quite clear of Desdemona's fault of protesting too much.[1]

I send you a letter addressed to Mr. Charles Knight, and another from him to me. They relate to the De Foe family,[2] and explain themselves.

With love to Mrs. Brown

Ever Dear Miss Coutts | Yours faithfully and affecy.
CHARLES DICKENS

To LADY HARDING,[3] 19 FEBRUARY 1858

MS Mr A. G. Schaw Miller. *Address:* Lady Harding | 30 St. James's Place | S.W.

Tavistock House. W.C. | Nineteenth February 1858

Mr. Charles Dickens presents his compliments to Lady Harding, and begs to acknowledge the receipt of Lady Harding's interesting note and printed enclosure.[4]

To FRANÇOIS RÉGNIER, 20 FEBRUARY 1858†

MS Comédie Français.

Tavistock House, London.
Saturday Twentieth February | 1858.

My Dear Regnier.

First, let me tell you how extremely sorry we all are to hear of Madame Regnier's illness, and with how much true sympathy and concern we have spoken of it. We

[1] Not Desdemona, but the Player Queen (*Hamlet*, III, ii, 225).

[2] A descendant of Daniel Defoe, whom Knight had found living in poverty; he and CD, with the assistance of Miss Coutts, were helping him: see Vol. VII, p. 273.

[3] Wife of Sir John Dorney Harding (1809–68), Advocate-General 1852–62.

[4] Not discovered.

hope, from the latter part of your account, that she is gradually recovering and will soon be very much better. Pray assure her that we all send her our love and most cordial good wishes, and that none of her friends can be more interested in her, or solicitous for her, than we are.

Next, let me thank you with all my heart, for your most patient and kind letter. I made its contents known to Mr. Marston, and I enclose you his reply.[1] You will see that he cheerfully leaves the matter in your hands, and abides by your opinion and discretion.

You need not return his letter, my friend.

There is great excitement here this morning, in consequence of the failure of the Ministry last night, to carry the Bill they brought in, to please your Emperor and his troops.[2] I, for one, am extremely glad of their defeat.[3]

"Le vieux Poole"[4] I have no doubt will go staggering down the Rue de la Paix today, with his stick in his hand and his hat on one side, predicating the Downfall of everything, in consequence of this event. His hand-writing shakes more and more every quarter, and I think he mixes a great deal of Cognac with his ink. He always gives me some astonishing piece of news (which is never true), or some sagacious public prophecy (which is never verified). And he always tells me he is dying (which he never is).[5]

Adieu my dear Regnier. Accept a thousand thanks from me, and believe me, now and always,

Your affectionate and faithful friend
CHARLES DICKENS

To H. A. BATHURST, 21 FEBRUARY 1858

Facsimile in *Fac-Simile Reporting Notes*, I, 11, Jan 88.

Tavistock House | Monday Twenty First February 1858

My Dear Sir

I send you the speech, with a few slight corrections. It is extremely well done, and with great fidelity.[6] If you should have an opportunity of making my approval of it, known to the gentleman who took it down, I would beg you to do so.

Tomorrow or next day, I do not doubt to be able to write to you in detail, on the subject of the reading.

My Dear Sir | Faithfully Yours
CHARLES DICKENS

H. A. Bathurst Esquire.

1 See *To* Marston, 16 Feb, *fn*.

2 The Conspiracy to Murder Bill, put forward in response to French complaints that most of the conspirators in Orsini's attempt to assassinate Napoleon III in Paris on 14 Jan had been resident in London. See *To* Delane, 28 Feb and *fn*.

3 Palmerston resigned as Prime Minister as a result.

4 "P——" in MDGH, but name given in N, III, 9.

5 Poole did not die until 1872, aged 85.

6 Bathurst wanted the speech for the Hospital's publication of it as a pamphlet. After comparing W. J. Carlton's transcription of T. A. Reed's original shorthand notes (printed in the *Phonographic Reporter*, ed. T. A. Reed, 1858, pp. 38–46), with the speech as published, K. J. Fielding confirms the slightness of CD's corrections: "chiefly . . . the addition or omission of single words", to improve the style (*Speeches*, p. 435): see *To* Reed, 12 June and *fn*.

To CHARLES KNIGHT, 22 FEBRUARY 1858

Extract in Sotheby's catalogue, July 1983; *MS* 1 p.; dated Tavistock House, 22 Feb 58; addressed Charles Knight.

Writing on behalf of Miss Coutts, who is engaged with a sick sister,[1] *he remits £10 from her for* the De Foe survivors *and thanks Knight for his interest. He will not forget the 15th March.*[2]

To W. H. WILLS, 22 FEBRUARY 1858

MS Huntington Library.

Tavistock House
Monday Night Twenty Second February 1858

My Dear Wills.

Letter No. 1, enclosed, is the Stereoscope people's[3] favor that I spoke to you of this morning. Will you kindly write them an obliging reply, to the effect we mentioned?

Letter No. 2, is the usual thing. I know no more about it.

Collins wishes to read his new play[4] to me, next Thursday. I mean to propose to him that you be of the party, and I have no doubt the idea will give him much pleasure. If all things else should be "in a concatenation accordingly",[5] what do you say to our dining at Gad's Hill (under John's[6] convoy), reading there after dinner, sleeping there, and coming up next morning? I have broached this notion to our respected contributor.

I will be in Wellington Street on Wednesday in good time, and we can arrange details then.

Ever Faithfully
CD.

To H. A. BATHURST, [?22–25 FEBRUARY 1858]

Summary in Minute Book, Committee of Management, Great Ormond St Hospital for Sick Children. *Date:* between 22 Feb (see *To* Bathurst, 21 Feb) and 26 Feb, when letter read out to Committee.

Proposing to fulfil his promise to read for the benefit of the Hospital on Thurs 15 Apr, at St Martin's Hall, and recommending that the arrangements be superintended by Mr. [*Arthur*][7] *Smith.*

[1] Probably Clara (wife of the Rev. James Money), of whom she was particularly fond.

[2] Knight's 67th birthday.

[3] No doubt either the London Stereoscopic Co., 54 Cheapside and 313 Oxford St, or the Stereoscopic Views Warehouse, 73 Newgate St, the most likely "Stereoscope Makers" listed. The instrument in its lenticular form (invented by Sir David Brewster), became popular in the 1850s and is often advertised. The firm may have been offering one to CD.

[4] *The Red Vial*, a melodrama set in Frankfort; it ran at the Olympic 11 Oct–13 Nov 58, with Robson and Mrs Stirling in the two main roles. There was a long, respectful review in the *Morning Chronicle*, 12 Oct; but the play was a failure: see *To* Collins, 9 Nov, *fn.*

[5] One of CD's favourite quotations: see earlier vols.

[6] MS reads "John".

[7] The minutes read "Alfred" in error.

To JOHN DELANE, 25 FEBRUARY 1858

MS *The Times* Newspapers Ltd.

Tavistock House, W.C.
Thursday Twenty Fifth February 1858

My Dear Delane[1]

Miss Coutts (no doubt with a kind object) has asked me to try to find out for her, who wrote the one more unfortunate letter in the Times of yesterday.[2] Of course she proceeds on the assumption that it is really written, or prompted, by such a person as it purports to originate with.[3]

Do you feel yourself at liberty to enlighten me on the point, with the view of doing good to some one?

Ever Faithfully
John Delane Esquire CHARLES DICKENS

To [MISS BURDETT COUTTS], 26 FEBRUARY 1858*

MS Father Daniel M. Venglarik.

Tavistock House | Friday Twenty Sixth February 1858.

My Dear [Miss Coutts][4]

I wrote (privately) to the active Editor of the Times, asking him if he could give me the name of that writer, to communicate to you. I send you his reply.[5]

Ever Faithfully and affecy.
CHARLES DICKENS

[1] They had met earlier this month at a dinner given by Lord Alfred Paget (1816–88; *DNB*; equerry and clerk-marshal to the Royal household; MP for Lichfield), along with Lords Stafford, Dufferin and Canterbury (Delane's diary, 16 Feb, quoted by A. I. Dasent, *John Thadeus Delane | His Life and Correspondence*, 1908, Vol. I, p. 296).

[2] In fact, of 11 Feb, the second of two letters from a prostitute (headed "The Delicate Question"), written by "One More Unfortunate", an educated woman, previously a governess. She thanks "Amicus" who had offered her help after her first letter, commenting "and now the thought that I am addressing those who can think of us without levity or loathing is overpowering!" Both Delane's reply, referring to "nearly two columns", and *To* Delane, 28 Feb, saying that the "latter part of it" would have shocked Miss Coutts, make it clear that it was her second letter that Miss Coutts had read; the first was printed on 4 Feb. A letter printed on 24 Feb was from "Another Unfortunate", a "career prostitute" since the age of 14, whose tone of self-justification would have shocked Miss Coutts throughout. She distinguished herself totally from "One More Unfortunate": "I am a stranger to all the fine sentiments which still linger in the bosom of your correspondent" (*The Times*, 24 Feb).

[3] All three letters were contributions to a series of *Times* reports on "The Great Social Evil", recording meetings of the Society for the Suppression of Vice, held 31 Dec 57–28 Jan 58, chiefly attended by the clergy and vestrymen of central London parishes. They all called on the Govt to put down prostitution in the metropolis.

[4] Name erased in MS; but clearly Miss Coutts (see last).

[5] Delane replied the same day: "I am bound under the most solemn adjurations not to reveal the name of the 'Unfortunate' but I will call on her in the course of a day or two and ask if she is willing to be revealed to (Miss Coutts) [*name deleted leaving a gap of* c. *12 letters*]. | What an admirable letter it was! | Except Currer Bell or Mrs Gaskell, I know of no *woman* who could have sustained such a tone through nearly two columns" (MS Yale).

To MISS BURDETT COUTTS, 27 FEBRUARY 1858*

MS Morgan Library. *Address:* Miss Burdett Coutts.

OFFICE OF HOUSEHOLD WORDS,
Saturday Twenty Seventh Feby. 1858

My Dear Miss Coutts

I will come to you at about half past 3 to day. In case that time should not suit you and you should have had occasion to go out, will you leave a note for me, appointing your own hour on Monday.

Ever Faithfully and affecy.
CD.

To JOHN DELANE, 28 FEBRUARY 1858*

MS *The Times* Newspapers Ltd.

Tavistock House | Sunday, Twenty Eighth February | 1858.

My Dear Delane.

It seems that when Miss Coutts spoke to me about that "One more unfortunate" letter, it had just attracted her notice and she had not read it through. It further appears that she is immensely staggered and disconcerted by the latter part of it (so very difficult of presentation to, and comprehension by, a woman), and is even troubled by its being seen by the people in her household.[1] Therefore I think the writer had best remain unknown to her.

Many thanks for your kind note. I was at Gad's Hill on Thursday and the greater part of Friday, and saw Miss Coutts again only yesterday afternoon.

Ever Faithfully Yours
CHARLES DICKENS

I think the attitude of that miserable man Orsini, on his trial, as sad a picture, almost, as this world has to shew at the present time.[2] "Sir", said a noble gentleman

[1] The second half of the letter deals first with the better-known haunts of London prostitutes, and then with "kept ladies".

[2] Felice Orsini (1819–58), Italian patriot, and four others, had attempted to assassinate Napoleon III on 14 Jan, while he and the Empress were arriving at the Paris Opera. The three bombs thrown killed eight people and injured over 100; Napoleon and the Empress narrowly escaped injury. The two-day trial, on 25 and 26 Feb, disclosed that the conspirators had persuaded Thomas Allsop (1795–1880; *DNB*), London stockbroker and friend of Coleridge, Lamb, Hazlitt and Landor, to obtain the bombs; but Orsini stated that Allsop was "entirely ignorant" of the bombs' use (*Morning Chronicle*, 27 Feb). The *Morning Chronicle* referred to Orsini's "sang-froid" throughout the trial; he showed little remorse for the eight deaths he had caused. Landor, known to have entertained Orsini in Bath two years before, was attacked in the press as sympathetic to the attempted assassination. But, the day after the attempt, he wrote to Forster: "Miserable Orsini! he sat with me two years ago at the table on which I am now writing. Dreadful work! horrible crime! To inflict death on a hundred for the sin of one! Such a blow can serve only to awaken tyranny, reverberating on the brass helmets of her satellites" (John Forster, *W. S. Landor. A Biography*, II, 468). Orsini and the eldest of the others, Joseph Pierri, were executed on 13 Mar.

to me when I was last in Italy: "in this country of mine, the greatest social misery is to have a son."

To STEPHEN MASSETT,[1] 1 MARCH 1858*

MS Free Library of Philadelphia.

Tavistock House. W.C. | Monday First March 1858.

Mr. Charles Dickens presents his Compliments to Mr. Massett, and begs to acknowledge the receipt of Mr. Massett's obliging note. His absence from town for a day or two, has delayed his reply.

He begs to add, that Mr. Massett is at perfect liberty to read, at any of the proposed entertainments, the passage from Bleak House descriptive of Jo's death.[2] He merely begs the favor (to save himself from an interminable correspondence with English readers and lecturers), that Mr. Massett will make no special mention of him in the Programmes.

To UNKNOWN CORRESPONDENT, 2 MARCH 1858

Text from N, III, 9–10.

Tavistock House, Londres | Mardi, 2 mars, 1858

Cher Monsieur,

J'ai reçu votre si intéressante et si généreuse lettre avec les plus vives émotions de la sympathie et de l'admiration vers M. de Lamartine, cet homme illustre qui a ennobli à la fois la littérature imaginative et l'histoire politique et sociale du siècle qu'il adorne.

J'ai soigneusement considéré la question sur laquelle vous m'avez fait l'honneur de me consulter; et je suis bien fâché de vous répondre que j'ai grand peur que votre projet ne réussirait pas.[3] Quand j'étais à Paris il y a deux ans, je causai avec M. de Lamartine au sujet de la dernière grande édition de ses Œuvres en quatorze tomes.[4] Il me dit, et je n'ai pu cacher mon étonnement, qu'il n'avait que trois souscripteurs, ou abonnements à cette entreprise, en Angleterre! Je moi-même en avait l'honneur d'être un; et je me souviens que cette édition était annoncée en avance, pas seulement à tous nos hommes de lettres, mais à presque tout le monde enseigné, chez nous.

[1] Stephen Massett, American singer, composer, mimic and elocutionist.

[2] Massett gave an "entertainment" on 8 Mar in the Hanover Square Rooms—his first London appearance. It combined song, anecdote and recitation (including Tennyson's "Charge of the Light Brigade")—but no reading from CD was mentioned (*Morning Chronicle*, 9 Mar). Apparently the first of a series. Meeting him at the American Legation on 5 Mar, Benjamin Moran (see *To* Brooks, 11 Mar and *fn*) describes him as "a dapper good-looking young fellow" and predicts that "he'll not succeed. He talks too fast" (*The Journal of Benjamin Moran, 1857–65*, ed. S. A. Wallace and F. E. Gillespie, Chicago, 1948, I, 259). On 9 Mar, after his reading, he comments: "The London papers of to-day fairly laugh at him. He tried California & Australia clap-trap, but it wouldn't do. The *Times* is very funny about his mode of rendering Tennyson's line 'Rrrrrrode the six hundred'" (I, 262).

[3] See below.

[4] *Oeuvres de A. de Lamartine*, 14 vols, Paris, 1849. See Vol. VII, p. 70 and *n*.

Croyez moi, cher Monsieur, je serais vraiment enchanté d'avoir la grande distinction et la grande félicité de rendre aucun service, quelque petit qu'il soit, à M. de Lamartine qui j'aime et qui j'honore. Mais il faut considérer, d'abord et surtout, M. de Lamartine lui-même; et je vous avoue que je ne voulais pas l'exposer aux chances de notre manquer notre coup. . . .[1]

Agréez cher monsieur l'assurance de ma consideration la plus distinguée et de mes sentiments les plus sincères de l'amitié et de l'estime.

Votre fidèle
[CHARLES DICKENS]

To MISS BURDETT COUTTS, 4 MARCH 1858†

MS Morgan Library.

OFFICE OF HOUSEHOLD WORDS,
Thursday Fourth March 1858

My Dear Miss Coutts

Most unfortunately,—I am engaged to dinner to day, to hear Wilkie Collins read a new play[2] (in the construction of which I have held no end of Councils with him), which he designs for Mr. Robson. I fear I shall not be able to get away in time for the Face.[3] Cannot the Face be reproduced? Whose face is it? What is the hope or danger of the face? I am distracted by doubts and speculations, and must come and ask tomorrow.

Ever Faithfully and affecy.
CD.

To THE REV. WILLIAM HARNESS,[4] 4 MARCH 1858*

MS New York University Library.

Tavistock House W.C. | Thursday Fourth March 1858

My Dear Harness.

It is always such a great pleasure to me to have a talk with you, that you may be sure nothing vanquishable in the way of difficulty would prevent my accepting your kind invitation. Most unfortunately however, the fifteenth is Charles Knight's birthday, and on that anniversary we always dine with him.[5] It is a strange thing that he could not have been born on any other day, when there was a choice of three hundred and sixty five; but as he was not consulted, and as his mother has long been

[1] The next collected edn of Lamartine was *Oeuvres complètes de Lamartine publiés et inedites*, 41 vols, Paris, 1860–6, published "Chez l'auteur" and ed. by him, with new and interesting prefaces.

[2] *The Red Vial*: see *To* Wills, 22 Feb and *fn*.

[3] Another of CD's digs at Miss Coutts's difficult handwriting.

[4] The Rev. William Harness (1790–1869; *DNB*): see Vols I, p. 639*n* and V, p. 228*n*.

[5] See *To* Knight, 22 Feb.

dead, I have not even the consolation of blaming any one for this act of perverseness.

Believe me always | Very faithfully Yours

The Rev. William Harness. CHARLES DICKENS

To RICHARD BENTLEY, 8 MARCH 1858

MS Berg Collection.

Tavistock House | Monday Eighth March 1858.

My Dear Mr. Bentley

Pray do not ask me to see that lady. Believe me, it would only distress and disappoint her. In the present state of the stage, I have no earthly power of helping her, and I wish to spare myself and her the pain of a more detailed assurance to that effect. I do not return this answer to your note, on any vague and indistinct grounds. My experience of such cases has been a large one, and I believe that nothing would now induce me to mediate with a Manager on behalf of any new lady-aspirant whomsoever. Apart from this, if I had any really serviceable influence in such wise, there are claims upon it which would go before all others and exclude all others.

Faithfully Yours

Richard Bentley Esquire. CHARLES DICKENS

To MARK LEMON, 8 MARCH 1858

MS Comtesse de Suzannet.

Tavistock House | Monday Night | Eighth March 1858

My Dear Mark

I trust you are better? You were sadly missed, yesterday and the night before.

Enclosed No. of popular periodical has been shewn to me. If the article I have marked be not yet paid for, please pay *me* for it—I wrote it, and it is taken from Master Humphrey's Clock.[1]

Ever affectionately

CD.

To B. W. PROCTER, 8 MARCH 1858

Text from N, III, 10.

Tavistock House | Monday Eighth March 1858

My dear Procter,

I am afraid my facetious account of my restless energies may have given you a wrong impression of my "case." I habitually keep myself in the condition of a fight-

[1] "A Confession" (a child-murderer on his last night alive), purporting to be "found in the Papers of a deceased Prussian Judge", in the *London Journal* (No. 681), for the current week. It clearly resembles "A Confession found in a prison in the time of Charles the Second" in *Master Humphrey's Clock*, No. 3, 8 Apr 40, collected in Vol. I, pp. 32–6.

ing man in training—And as to sponging, scrubbing, brushing and all manner of such arts, I am the latest addition to the wonders of the world.

Ever affectionately
[CHARLES DICKENS]

To THOMAS TROUGHTON,[1] 8 MARCH 1858

Text from Minute Book of Gravesend and Milton Library and Reading Room.

Tavistock House London | Monday Eighth March 1858

Mr. Charles Dickens presents his compliments to the Mayor of Gravesend and regrets his inability to comply with the request which the Mayor has done him the honor to forward.[2] His inability will be the better understood perhaps when he assures the Mayor of Gravesend that he declines such applications by hundreds and that it is sometimes quite impossible for him even to acknowledge their receipt however briefly.

To SHIRLEY BROOKS, 11 MARCH 1858

MS Brotherton Library, Leeds.

Tavistock House | Thursday Eleventh March 1858

My Dear Brooks.

Many thanks for your note. Forster had seen the article.[3] It *was* Moran[4] who did that disgraceful deed; and I shall take an opportunity of mentioning that interesting circumstance to O'Dowd.[5]

We had a great scene with the Committee yesterday.[6] They did a frightfully injudicious thing on a sudden, in rejecting a motion made by a very moderate outsider[7] for a Sub Committee of Enquiry into the expences.[8] I could have desired or expected nothing half so good. The outsider stood aghast with amazement (for they

[1] Thomas Troughton, JP, 5 Park Place, Gravesend, Mayor of Gravesend.

[2] That CD should give a reading in the Harmer Assembly Room, Gravesend, in aid of the Gravesend and Milton Library and Reading Room, Edwin St. (Minute Book, Gravesend and Milton Library).

[3] Not traced; probably not by Moran himself as no "article" by him is known, but may be connected with something communicated to his intimate companion Thornton Hunt, now editor of the *Leader*.

[4] Benjamin Moran (1820–86; *DAB*), Assistant Secretary of Legation, American Embassy in London, since 1857 (Secretary 1864–74). He never actually met CD, but took a dislike to him before he even saw him, no doubt because of what he heard from Thornton Hunt in Jan 58 about how CD "libelled" Leigh Hunt, but disclaimed it (*The Journal of Benjamin Moran, 1857–1865*, ed. S. A. Wallace and F. E. Gillespie, I, 216). "He is a compound of genius, humanity and a want of principle. One of those men who never adhere long to a friend or have friends long adhere to them. You would distrust him, and my feeling against him is of contempt" (*ibid.*, p. 292).

[5] James Cornelius O'Dowd (1829–1903), Irish barrister and journalist; on Committee of Garrick Club; member since 1854. Part-proprietor and joint editor with W. H. Russell, *Army and Navy Gazette* (1st issue, 7 Jan 60). See *To* Yates, 6 July, *fn.*

[6] At the Annual General Meeting of the Royal Literary Fund: see *Speeches*, ed. K. J. Fielding, pp. 253–8.

[7] Purton Cooper; seconded by John Murray, the publisher.

[8] The motion was lost 66–18.

had been professing all manner of desires to co-operate with those distinguished &c. whose general objections &c.),[1] and came over to me afterwards and said that now he thought they *had* done for themselves and made out the Reform case.[2]

Ah! You should see the virtuous grey hairs of Bentley,[3] in the foreground of a group of two score parson-schoolmasters, he voting on their conservative side, and going direct to Heaven in their company. It's like the apotheosis of an evangelical (and drunken) butler.

Ever Faithfully
CHARLES DICKENS

To JOHN HOLLINGSHEAD, [11 MARCH 1858]

Mention in Hollingshead, *My Lifetime*, 1895, I, 114. *Date:* after first night of *The Birthplace of Podgers*, 10 Mar 58.

Congratulations on the success[4] *of Hollingshead and Toole.*

To DESMOND FITZGERALD,[5] 15 MARCH 1858

Extract in Sotheby's catalogue, Dec 1980; *MS* 2 pp.; addressed Desmond FitzGerald; dated Tavistock House, 15 Mar 58.

Saying that he should be happy to accept FitzGerald's verses, entitled 'Poetry and Philosophy'[6] *if he would* make the last stanza but one plainer to my comprehension. I cannot make out that crown of bay which Science gives as incense to its God.[7]

The Lone Heart's Recollections are not suited to the magazine.

The Ghost Story is an extremely old one. It is usually told of a gentleman who went down into one of the Vaults in Westminster Abbey on a similar expedition. It is very well told in your little paper, but its antiquity is a fatal objection.

[1] CD himself had moved an amendment on the accounts: "That the accounts ... showing a systematic Expenditure of from £40 to £45 in the giving away of every £100 in grants, are not quite satisfactory. That such an appropriation of money subscribed with a clearly defined charitable object is not quite right. That its continuance as a distinctive feature of the Literary Fund is not so consistent with the professions of the Literary Fund as to uphold that Institution in the general confidence. That such continuance, therefore, ought not to be sanctioned from year to year, and is now protested against." This was seconded by Forster and lost 70–14. (MSS Royal Literary Fund.)

[2] See *To* Grattan, 24 Apr 58 and *fnn*, and next vol.

[3] Richard Bentley.

[4] See *To* Hollingshead, 12 Dec 57 and *fn*.

[5] Desmond G. Fitzgerald, analytical chemist; contributed "Natural Science.—Its Adaptation to the Youthful Mind" to *The School and the Teacher*, 1 June 58 (describing his own teaching of chemistry at a Middlesex school); his lecture, *Education*, published as a pamphlet, 1858.

[6] In six stanzas, advocating reconciliation between the two: *HW*, 17 Apr 58, XVII, 420; his only contribution to *HW*.

[7] The fifth stanza reads: "And genius that would scorn the lowly way | Which leads to truth, although by millions trod, | Might humble violets twine with haughty bay, | And learn from children how to soar to God."

To JOHN FORSTER, [15 MARCH 1858]

Extract in F, IX, ii, 729. *Date:* "six weeks" after 27 Jan, according to Forster.

What do you think of this name for my story—*Buried Alive*? Does it seem too grim? Or, *The Thread of Gold*?[1] Or, *The Doctor of Beauvais*?

To W. C. MACREADY, 15 MARCH 1858†

MS Morgan Library.

Tavistock House. W.C. | Fifteenth March 1858.

My Dearest Macready

I have safely received your cheque this morning, and will hand it over forthwith to the Honorary Secretary of the Hospital. I hope you have read the little speech, in the Hospital's publication of it.[2] They had it taken by their own Short Hand Writer, and it is done verbatim.

You may be sure that it is a good and kind Charity. It is amazing to me that it is not at this day ten times as large and rich as it is.[3] But I hope and trust that I have happily been able to give it a good thrust onward into a great course.

We all send our most affectionate love to all the house. I am devising all sorts of things in my mind, and am in a state of energetic restlessness incomprehensible by the calm philosophers of Dorsetshire. What a Dream it is, this work and strife, and how little we do in the Dream after all! Only last night, in my sleep, I was bent upon getting over a perspective of barriers, with my hands and feet bound. Pretty much what we are all about, waking, I think?

But, Lord! (as I said before) you smile—pityingly: not bitterly—at this hubbub, and moralize upon it, in the calm evenings when there is no School at Sherborne.[4]

And *you*[5] are not asked (and what is more, are not obliged to go) to hear MARSTON[6] read a very bad play,[7] at the Beethoven Rooms in Harley Street on a

[1] The idea of the book was obviously already taking shape in his mind; "The Golden Thread" is the title of Bk II.

[2] See *To* Bathurst, 21 Feb and *fn*.

[3] Out of 50,000 annual deaths in London, 21,000 were of children under ten years old. Yet by 1858 there were still only 31 beds in the Hospital (*Speeches*, ed. K. J. Fielding, p. 246).

[4] The "Evening School for the Industrious Classes", founded by Macready and supported by the Sherborne community; held in the parish rooms of the Wesleyan Methodist Chapel. Fifty boys and young men, aged 10 to 20, studied three nights a week for at least five months, paying 1*d.* a week. The master appointed was assisted by members of the Committee and by Macready himself. The State Inspector of Schools found it the best evening school he had visited; he was particularly impressed by Macready's devoting himself to teaching the English language to "the children of a few Dorsetshire labourers" (A. S. Downer, *The Eminent Tragedian*, Cambridge, Mass, 1966, pp. 345–6).

[5] Heavily underlined.

[6] Doubly underlined, with short double strokes.

[7] His five-Act blank verse drama of modern life, *Anne Blake*, had been successfully performed at the Princess's Theatre under Charles Kean's management 28 Oct–26 Nov 1852, with Kean and his wife in the main parts. The published text is dedicated gratefully to them and has a preface of fulsome praise of the cast. The *Morning Chronicle* had praised it as "notably the best" of his plays; but this must have been thanks to the acting. As a private reading it must have been tedious, with a conventional plot, interested parties fomenting misunderstandings between hero, heroine and rival lover—all cleared up at the end, as could have long been foreseen.

Saturday Night:[1] to the intent that you may give your honest opinion on the probabilities of his coining money by reading in public. *You*[2] don't sit in an arm-chair of judgment, in the full glare of the operator's eye; and *you*,[2] in the hour of that Forcible-Feeble[3] triumph, don't feel yourself (with a start of shame and horror) falling asleep, and don't alternate that condition with a state of such appalling sense of the ludicrousness of the situation, that grins carve themselves into your face—tattoo themselves all over your countenance—when you ought to be in floods of tears.

Yet this was *my*[2] condition, only the night before last. And I declare to you that, bringing Wilkie Collins home to refresh himself with a Cigar, I fell into my chair with such a sudden relief from the oppression of bottling off a cask of absurdity through three long hours, that I laughed myself into hysterics.

Ever affectionately and truly
CHARLES DICKENS

To WILLIAM TELBIN, 15 MARCH 1858

MS Mrs J. A. Martin.

Tavistock House. W.C. | Monday Fifteenth March 1858

My Dear Telbin

I should have been extremely glad and ready to have sat to any one in whom you have an interest, but that I am under positive refusals and conditional promises, which altogether exclude my visage from Photography! It is a melancholy fact, but I don't see the remotest chance of my interesting countenance being ever photographed, of my own knowledge and consent, again.[4] If I were to begin, I could never leave off.

Faithfully Yours Ever

William Telbin Esquire CHARLES DICKENS

To F. M. EVANS, 16 MARCH 1858

MS Free Library of Philadelphia.

TAVISTOCK HOUSE, | TAVISTOCK SQUARE, LONDON. W.C.
Tuesday March Sixteenth 1858

My Dear Evans.

I want you to consider this letter as being strictly private and confidential between you and me. I am anxious to have your soundest opinion on the point it refers to you, and I shall give it great weight—though I do not, of course, pledge myself to be bound by it.

The Reading idea that I had, some time ago, sticks to me. Let me read where I

[1] 13 Mar.

[2] Heavily underlined.

[3] Falstaff praising the courage of the woman's tailor when he is pricked for service (*2 Henry IV*, III, ii, 164).

[4] For his sitting in fact twice during the next twelve months, see *To* Watkins, 31 May and *fn* and *To* Thompson, 11 July; by that time photographs would be required because of the public readings.

will, an effect is produced which seems to belong to nothing else; and the number of people who want to come, cannot by any means be got in. I have in my mind this project:—

After reading in London on the 15th. of next month for the Benefit of the childrens' Hospital, to announce by advertisement (what is quite true), that I cannot answer the applications that are made to me, so numerous are they, and that compliance with ever so few of them is in any reason impossible.[1] That therefore I have resolved upon a course of Readings[2] both in town and country,[3] and that those in London will take place at St. Martins Hall on certain evenings—four or six Thursdays—through May, and just into June.

Then, in August, September, and October, in the Eastern Counties, the West of England, Lancashire, Yorkshire, and Scotland, I should read from 35 to 40 times. At each place where there was a great success, I should myself announce that I should come back, on the turn of Christmas, to read a new Christmas Story written for the purpose (and which I should first read in London). Unless I am gigantically mistaken,—by March or April *a very large sum of money* would be cleared—and Ireland would be still untouched; not to speak of America, where I believe I could make (if I could resolve to go there) ten thousand pounds.

Now, the question I want your opinion on, is this:—Assuming these hopes to be well-grounded, would such an use of the personal (I may almost say affectionate) relations which subsist between me and the public, and make my standing with them very peculiar, at all affect my position with them as a writer? Would it be likely to have any influence on my next book? If it had any influence at all, would it be likely to be of a weakening or a strengthening kind?[4]

(It is not to the purpose of this point, to remark that I should confide the whole of the Business arrangements to Arthur Smith. I merely mention it, that you may have the whole case).

Ever Faithfully
CHARLES DICKENS

To T. W. BEALE, [19 MARCH 1858]

Mention in *To* Forster, 20 Mar 58. *Date:* the day before that letter.

Agreeing to see Beale the next day.

[1] He made these points in his short speech before his first paid reading on 29 Apr: see *Speeches*, ed. K. J. Fielding, p. 264.

[2] Curious circular pen-marks top left and bottom right of "Readings", apparently in CD's hand.

[3] i.e. readings for his own profit as distinct from charitable purposes.

[4] Evans probably sent a favourable reply. Soon after, Bradbury & Evans launched the Second Series of the Cheap edn, advertising *Dombey & Son* "in a few days" on 15 Apr, with the promise of *Copperfield* and *Bleak House* "at intervals of about two months". An advt on 1 Sep shows *Copperfield* and *Dombey* were only just ready then and *Bleak House* "in the Press". By 1 June (when they might already have cause for alarm about relations with CD) they were prominently advertising separate Christmas books at 1*s.*, clearly because of the current readings in London. In late June, no doubt in some haste, they brought out *Little Dombey*, and in late July *The Poor Traveller*, *Boots* and *Mrs Gamp*, after the break was complete.

To T. R. EELES, 20 MARCH 1858

MS Free Library of Philadelphia.

TAVISTOCK HOUSE, | TAVISTOCK SQUARE, LONDON. W.C.
Saturday Twentieth March 1858

Dear Mr. Eeles.

Will you be so good as to bind me for my readings:

The Chimes
and
The Haunted Man[1]

Each separately, and both like the Cricket[2]—which I send with this, as a specimen. You will want two copies of each book, for which I send you an order on the other side.

Faithfully Yours
CD

To JOHN FORSTER, [19–20 MARCH 1858]

Extracts in F, VIII, ii, 645–6 and VIII, ii, 642*n*. *Date:* first extract "nearly a month" before 15 Apr; second extract 20 Mar, according to Forster.

Your view of the reading matter I still think is unconsciously taken from your own particular point.[3] You don't seem to me to get out of yourself in considering it. A word more upon it. You are not to think I have made up my mind. If I had, why should I not say so? I find very great difficulty in doing so because of what you urge, because I know the question to be a balance of doubts, and because I most honestly feel in my innermost heart, in this matter (as in all others for years and years), the honour of the calling by which I have always stood most conscientiously. But do you quite consider that the public exhibition of oneself takes place equally, whosoever may get the money? And have you any idea that at this moment—this very time—half the public at least supposes me to be paid? My dear F, out of the twenty or five-and-twenty letters a week that I get about Readings, twenty will ask at what price, or on what terms, it can be done. The only exceptions, in truth, are when the correspondent is a clergyman, or a banker, or the member for the place in question. Why, at this very time half Scotland believes that I am paid for going to Edinburgh!—Here is Greenock writes to me, and asks could it be done for a hundred pounds? There is Aberdeen writes, and states the capacity of its hall, and says, though far less profitable than the very large hall in Edinburgh, is it not enough to come on for? W.[4] answers such letters continually. (—At this place, enter Beale. He

[1] On 30 Mar (see *To* Forster that day) he intended his first readings for profit to be confined to the *Carol*. Eventually, he gave successive readings of *The Cricket*, *The Chimes* and the *Carol*; *The Haunted Man* was prepared, but never given. At this stage he gave almost the entire text, taking between two and three hours.

[2] To give himself more marginal space for interpolations and revisions, he had foolscap octavo pages of an ordinary copy of the story (here, the 7th edition, 1846) inlaid into a larger octavo page; this was then bound by Eeles: the pattern for all the Christmas Books.

[3] CD was replying to Forster's "renewed efforts at remonstrance" over the plan for paid readings.

[4] Wills.

called here yesterday morning, and then wrote to ask if I would see him to-day. I replied "Yes," so here he came in. With long preface called to know whether it was possible to arrange anything in the way of Readings for this autumn—say, six months. Large capital at command. Could produce partners, in such an enterprise, also with large capital. Represented such. Returns would be enormous. Would I name a sum? a minimum sum that I required to have, in any case? Would I look at it as a Fortune, and in no other point of view? I shook my head, and said, my tongue was tied on the subject for the present; I might be more communicative at another time. Exit Beale in confusion and disappointment.)—You will be happy to hear that at one on Friday, the Lord Provost, Dean of Guild, Magistrates, and Council of the ancient city of Edinburgh will wait (in procession) on their brother freeman, at the Music Hall, to give him hospitable welcome. Their brother freeman[1] has been cursing their stars and his own, ever since the receipt of solemn notification to this effect.

He had referred the question to two distinguished ladies of his acquaintance. You may as well know that I went on and propounded the matter to A,[2] without any preparation. Result.—"I am surprised, and I should have been surprised if I had seen it in the newspaper without previous confidence from you. But nothing more. N—no. Certainly not. Nothing more. I don't see that there is anything derogatory in it, even now when you ask me that question. I think upon the whole that most people would be glad you should have the money, rather than other people. It might be misunderstood here and there, at first; but I think the thing would very soon express itself, and that your own power of making it express itself would be very great." As she wished me to ask B,[3] who was in another room, I did so. She was for a moment tremendously disconcerted, "*under the impression that it was to lead to the stage*"!! Then, without knowing anything of A's opinion, closely followed it. That absurd association had never entered my head or yours; but it might enter some other heads for all that. Take these two opinions for whatever they are worth. A (being very much interested and very anxious to help to a right conclusion) proposed to ask a few people of various degrees who know what the Readings are, what *they* think—not compromising me, but suggesting the project afar-off, as an idea in somebody else's mind. I thanked her, and said, "Yes," of course.

To WILKIE COLLINS, 21 MARCH 1858

MS Morgan Library.

TAVISTOCK HOUSE, | TAVISTOCK SQUARE, LONDON. W.C.
Sunday Twenty First March 1858

My Dear Wilkie

I too had intended to come to the enclosed subject,[4]—and I too forgot it.

You (or somebody else) will find the cheque crossed to Coutts's!

All day yesterday I was pursuing the Reading idea. Forster seems to me to be extraordinarily irrational about it. (I have a misgiving sometimes, that his money

[1] See Vol. II, p. 313.

[2] Miss Coutts.

[3] Mrs Brown.

[4] Perhaps connected with *HW*.

must have got into his head.)[1] I propounded it to Miss Coutts, who might have been expected to be dismayed, but *was not*, in the least.[2] I am no further on my road to a decision, than that I resolve I will decide within 7 days from this date. Could you possibly believe that Forster asked me what I thought of consulting (on the Literary-position question)

F.L.A.D.G.A T E[3]

!

The Doncaster unhappiness remains so strong upon me that I can't write, and (waking) can't rest, one minute. I have never known a moment's peace or content, since the last night of the Frozen Deep. I do suppose that there never was a Man so seized and rended by one Spirit. In this condition, though nothing can alter or soften it, I have a turning notion[4] that the mere physical effort and change of the Readings would be good, as another means of bearing it.

—I suppose it is the penalty I pay for having written all these red-backed books[5] upon my shelves—?

Ever Faithfully
CD.

To W. J. CULLENFORD, 23 MARCH 1858*

MS Fales Collection, New York University Library.

TAVISTOCK HOUSE, | TAVISTOCK SQUARE, LONDON. W.C.
Tuesday Twenty Third March 1858

Dear Mr. Cullenford

As I am going to Edinburgh on Thursday morning, to read there next night, I shall not be here in case you wish to say any thing to me about your Dinner.[6] I therefore write, to beg you to reserve a place for me, and another (next to me) for Mr. Chauncy Hare Townshend. I shall return on Saturday night.

Faithfully Yours
CHARLES DICKENS

[1] See *To* Miss Coutts, 15 July 56 and *fn*.

[2] CD began sentence with "So", but cancelled it.

[3] Probably Frank Fladgate (1799–1892), barrister, of Lincoln's Inn, a close friend of Thackeray, or his younger brother William Mark (1806–88) solicitor (see Vol. v, p. 485*n*). Both were active members of the Garrick Club; Frank was on the Garrick Club Committee with CD in 1855, and lived to be its oldest member: "one of the most polished gentlemen and good-natured persons I ever met", recorded R. H. Barham (*The Garrick Club*, New York, 1896), p. 30).

[4] Probably related to "turning-point", which was first recorded in 1856 (OED).

[5] CD's own copies of his first edns were specially bound in half-crimson morocco.

[6] The annual dinner of the Royal General Theatrical Fund, held on 29 Mar, with Thackeray in the chair. For CD's speech, proposing Thackeray's health, see *Speeches*, ed. K. J. Fielding, pp. 261–3. Thackeray appeared so overcome with CD's praise of his writing and avowal of their friendship that he could only say a sentence or two in reply (*Speeches*, above, p. 264).

To W. C. MACREADY, 24 MARCH 1858*

MS Morgan Library.

TAVISTOCK HOUSE,|TAVISTOCK SQUARE, LONDON. W.C.
Wednesday Twenty Fourth March 1858.

My Dearest Macready

As the Children's Hospital Secretary sends me the enclosed, I suppose I had best send it on to you in business-like course. I am slowly recovering from Marston—have weak fits of grinning, occasionally, but am on the whole better.

Kindest love from all. | Ever affectionately
CD.

To MISS ELLEN STONE, [24] MARCH 1858

MS Benoliel Collection. *Date:* misdated by CD; Wednesday was 24 Mar 58.

TAVISTOCK HOUSE,|TAVISTOCK SQUARE, LONDON. W.C.
Wednesday Evening Twenty Sixth March 1858

My Dear Miss Stone

I shall have great pleasure in dining at Russell House next Tuesday.

Your kind note comes to me opportunely, for I am away to Edinburgh tomorrow morning, to read there on Friday night.

With kindest regard | Believe me | Ever Faithfully Yours
CHARLES DICKENS

To M. BAMPS,[1] 25 MARCH 1858

Mention in N, III, 14; *MS* (in French) 1 p.; dated Tavistock House, 25 Mar 58; addressed Monsieur Bamps (of Brussels).

Disclaiming all knowledge of a M. Louis Dickens.[2]

To JOHN FORSTER, [?27 MARCH 1858]

Extract in F, VIII, ii, 646. *Date:* "on his return" from Edinburgh, according to Forster.

I had no opportunity of asking any one's advice in Edinburgh. The crowd was too enormous, and the excitement in it much too great. But my determination is all but taken. I must do *something*, or I shall wear my heart away. I can see no better thing to do that is half so hopeful in itself, or half so well suited to my restless state.[3]

[1] Perhaps Anatole Bamps, "docteur en droit, Bruxelles"; contributed the *Compte rendu* of the Third Session of the International Congress of Americanists at Brussels in 1878; its Proceedings were published in 2 vols, Brussels, 1879.

[2] Perhaps of Brussels also; not further identified.

[3] Forster comments: "What is pointed at in those last words had been taken as a ground of objection, and thus he turned it into an argument the other way. During all these months many sorrowful misunderstandings had continued in his home, and the relief sought from the misery had but the effect of making desperate any hope of a better understanding" (F, VII, ii, 646): see *To* Forster, 30 Mar.

To MRS FORSTER, 28 MARCH 1858*

MS Birthplace Museum, Portsmouth. *Address:* Mrs. Forster.

TAVISTOCK HOUSE, | TAVISTOCK SQUARE, LONDON. W.C.
Sunday Twenty Eighth March 1858.

My Dear Mrs. Forster

I went to Marshall's[1] on the North Bridge (the best place for the purpose), with your drawing.[2] He perfectly understood what was wanted, and shewed me, in fact, the lower portion of it, and the chain. But the heads, he said, it is not usual to keep in stock, and he did not think one could be found in Edinburgh in a completed state. Now, as Wills was to remain behind me for a week's pleasure, I thought it best to ask him (Marshall) under these circumstances, by what day the thing could be got ready? Whereunto he replied, By Tuesday. So I ordered it to be made, and Wills will bring it to London. Mr. Marshall's estimate of the cost is "jast aboot three punds".

The Reading was a tremendous success.[3] Some two thousand people were crammed into the place; and nobody *I* know in Edinburgh, could get admission on any terms.[4] They gave me a gorgeous cup[5] (tell Forster), and I made them a neat and appropriate.[6]

All of which (please also to tell Forster), I saw very faithfully and well described in The Scotsman yesterday morning.[7] But of course I haven't got the Scotsman, or I would forward him to Montagu Square.

My dear Mrs. Forster | Ever affectionately Yours
CHARLES DICKENS

[1] William Marshall & Co., gold and silver-smiths, 62 North Bridge, Edinburgh.

[2] She had evidently asked CD to order her present for Forster's birthday (2 Apr), possibly a watch chain and guard. The birthday was celebrated by the Forsters at the Queen's Hotel, Upper Norwood. Forster's letter to an unknown correspondent, 30 Mar, says that Dickens will be the only other guest, "there will be no-one else—none of his woman kind—in fact, only him & our two selves. I hope you will come. Indeed I count upon your not letting any engagement come in the way of this ..." (MS Sotheby's catalogue, Dec 1964). Perhaps the friend was Procter. On 27 Mar Wills wrote to his wife from 1 Doune Terrace: "Dickens and I began work yesterday morning with Marshall's shop (Scotch jewellery) and at Littlejohns (confectioner), he spending some six or eight pounds in sweeties, cairngorms, shortbread, and Finnan haddys for presents to the girls, &c. Then four times round the Calton Hill: full of admiration.... Then to the Rooms" (Lady Priestley, *The Story of a Lifetime*, 1904, pp. 176–7).

[3] CD read the *Carol* on 26 Mar in the Music Hall, Edinburgh, on behalf of the Edinburgh Philosophical Institution. Wills, who accompanied him, wrote to his wife the following day: "The Reading went off admirably. Capital audience. Wonderful unanimity. Wonderful happiness. Cheers and guffaws and pocket-handkerchiefs all in their right places" (Lady Priestley, above, p. 177).

[4] In the same letter, Wills told his wife that the Secretary of the Philosophical Institution had written to him that "he had neither ate nor drank nor slept for days, he has been so bullied for tickets. None but members could have them ... so many made themselves members to come" (Lady Priestley, *ibid.*).

[5] Described in the *Scotsman*, 27 Mar, as 'a massive silver Christmas or wassail cup', elaborately decorated with animals and birds in a rural scene, specially made for CD; presented to him by the Lord Provost after the reading. Left to Charley Dickens in CD's Will.

[6] For CD's short but delighted speech of gratitude after the presentation, see *Speeches*, ed. K. J. Fielding, pp. 259–60.

[7] The *Scotsman*, 27 Mar, in its full report, warmly praised CD as "a thoroughly practised and finished histrionic artist"; he read with "a singularly clear voice, which though not very powerful, yet made itself well heard through all that large and densely crowded hall, and with precise, steady, well-considered elocution".

To JOHN FORSTER, [30 MARCH 1858]

Extracts in F, VIII, ii, 646–7 and n, and XI, iii, 831. *Date:* first extract "end of March", second extract 30 Mar, according to Forster; no doubt same letter.

It becomes necessary, with a view to the arrangements that would have to be begun next month if I decided on the Readings, to consider and settle the question of the Plunge.[1] Quite dismiss from your mind any reference whatever to present circumstances at home. Nothing can put *them* right, until we are all dead and buried and risen. It is not, with me, a matter of will, or trial, or sufferance, or good humour, or making the best of it, or making the worst of it, any longer. It is all despairingly over. Have no lingering hope of, or for, me in this association. A dismal failure has to be borne, and there an end. Will you then try to think of this reading project (as I do) apart from all personal likings and dislikings, and solely with a view to its effect on that peculiar relation (personally affectionate, and like no other man's) which subsists between me and the public? I want your most careful consideration. If you would like, when you have gone over it in your mind, to discuss the matter with me and Arthur Smith (who would manage the whole of the Business, which I should never touch); we will make an appointment. But I ought to add that Arthur Smith plainly says, "Of the immense return in money, I have no doubt. Of the Dash into the new position, however, I am not so good a judge."[2] I enclose you a rough note of my project, as it stands in my mind.[3]

Here is the rough note. I propose to announce in a short and plain advertisement (what is quite true) that I cannot so much as answer the numerous applications that are made to me to read, and that compliance with ever so few of them is, in any reason, impossible. That I have therefore resolved upon a course of readings of the *Christmas Carol* both in town and country, and that those in London will take place at St. Martin's Hall on certain evenings. Those evenings will be either four or six Thursdays, in May and the beginning of June.[4] ... I propose an Autumn Tour, for the country, extending through August, September, and October. It would comprise the Eastern Counties, the West, Lancashire, Yorkshire, and Scotland. I should read from 35 to 40 times in this tour, at the least. At each place where there was a great success, I would myself announce that I should come back, on the turn of Christmas, to read a new Christmas story written for that purpose. This story I should first read a certain number of times in London. I have the strongest belief that by April in next year, a very large sum of money indeed would be gained by these means. Ireland would be still untouched, and I conceive America alone (if I could resolve to go there) to be worth Ten Thousand Pounds. In all these proceedings, the Business

[1] His announcement of the public readings.

[2] "Mr Arthur Smith", wrote Forster, "a man possessed of many qualities that justified the confidence Dickens placed in him, might not have been a good judge of the 'Dash' into the new position, but no man knew better every disadvantage incident to it, or was less likely to be disconcerted by any. His exact fitness to manage the scheme successfully, made him an unsafe counsellor respecting it" (F, VIII, ii, 647).

[3] Forster notes the original limits CD had set himself: "The first Readings were to comprise only the *Carol*, and for others a new story was to be written. He had not yet the full confidence in his power or versatility as an actor which subsequent experience gave him" (F, VIII, ii, 646–7*n*).

[4] For the actual programme which began on 29 Apr, see *To* Beard, 17 Apr and *fn*.

would be wholly detached from me, and I should never appear in it. I would have an office belonging to the Readings and to nothing else, opened in London; I would have the advertisements emanating from it, and also signed by some one belonging to it; and they should always mention me as a third person—just as the Child's Hospital, for instance, in addressing the public, mentions me.

I was put into a state of much perplexity on Sunday. I don't know who had spoken to my informant, but it seems that the Queen is bent upon hearing the *Carol* read, and has expressed her desire to bring it about without offence; hesitating about the manner of it, in consequence of my having begged to be excused from going to her when she sent for me after the *Frozen Deep*. I parried the thing as well as I could; but being asked to be prepared with a considerate and obliging answer, as it was known the request would be preferred, I said, "Well! I supposed Col. Phipps would speak to me about it, and if it were he who did so, I should assure him of my desire to meet any wish of her Majesty's, and should express my hope that she would indulge me by making one of some audience or other—for I thought an audience necessary to the effect." Thus it stands; but it bothers me.

To ARTHUR SMITH, [?1 APRIL 1858]

Mention in *To* Wills, 3 Apr. *Date:* CD had probably received Wills's letter by 1 Apr; he had written to Smith "immediately".

To UNKNOWN CORRESPONDENT, [2 APRIL 1858]

Mention implied by testimonial dated 2 Apr 58.

Sending a testimonial[1] *for Benjamin Cooper.*

[1] "Tavistock House, Tavistock Square, London, WC., | Friday Second April, 1858 | Benjamin Cooper [*see Vol.* VII, *p.* 109 *and* n], lived in my service as Coachman and Groom, for three years and a half. I parted with him, solely because it became more convenient to me to job my Brougham than to keep it myself. Cooper is married—he is a most respectable and deserving man in all respects—perfectly well acquainted with his business—and an excellent servant. Honest, sober, industrious, and obliging. I never had the slightest fault to find with him, and I shall be glad and ready to give him my personal recommendation in addition to this testimony, whenever he requires it. | CHARLES DICKENS" (MS University of Texas).

To W. H. WILLS, 3 APRIL 1858

MS Huntington Library.

TAVISTOCK HOUSE, | TAVISTOCK SQUARE, LONDON. W.C.
Saturday Third April, 1858

My Dear Wills

I have been so hustled by a crowd of cares since I came home,[1] that I have not written to you—the rather because, until I received yours from Edinburgh, I had nothing to say.

Yours arrived very opportunely. On the previous night, I had been going through Arthur Smith's suggested list of readings, and had demurred to his idea of returning to several large places. His reason for this, was exactly yours. I felt bound to send him your unconscious confirmation of his opinion, immediately. And he was extremely glad to receive it.

It is an unspeakable satisfaction to me, to have left such an impression in Edinburgh. I felt that night, that it was a very great success; but your account of it, even exceeds my hopes.

Arthur Smith told me on my return, that he had written to you in Edinburgh. I suppose you received his letter? I believe he had nothing important to say, in consequence of the Glasgow man,[2] the brother of the Edinburgh Music Seller,[3] having communicated with him direct.

The Queen wants to hear the Carol. I have represented my dutiful hope that she will form one of an Audience, as I consider an Audience necessary.

I have not a scrap of news. The usual papers come tumbling into the Office in the usual way, and John cleans the windows all day in a kind of melancholy stagnation of mind. Holdsworth[4] smiles on me with a limp and sickly benevolence.

All the chance men who have been got in to help the Gardener at Gad's Hill ply the Pump, have run away, one after another (I am serious) and been heard of no more in that country. The last man became so desperate as to work hours, and fly without his money. The machinery must be altered, and I must establish a revolving poney.[5]

All the rest of my world turns as it did,[6] and that's not saying much for it.

With kind regard to Mrs. Wills and all about you,

Ever Faithfully
CD.

[1] They would have included decisions about readings, the Queen's wish to hear the *Carol*, the General Theatrical Fund's Anniversary Dinner on 29 Mar, at which he spoke (Thackeray in the chair), besides continuing anxiety about the separation.

[2] John Muir Wood, of J. M. Wood & Co., pianoforte and music sellers, 42 Buchanan St, Glasgow.

[3] Wood & Co., London pianoforte and Music saloons, 14, 16 and 18 Waterloo Place, Edinburgh.

[4] George Holdsworth of the *HW* Office staff. Sometimes written Holsworth as in *To* Holsworth, 10 Sep 58.

[5] Presumably a real one, rather than a machine: it took 20 minutes to draw sufficient water for a day (Alan Watts, *Dickens at Gad's Hill*, 1989, p. 25).

[6] Perhaps a conflation of Lucio in *Measure for Measure*, "Is the world as it was, man?" (III, i, 317), with the proverb of the world running on wheels.

To THOMAS BEARD, 5 APRIL 1858

MS Dickens House. *Address:* Thomas Beard Esquire | 42 Portman Place | Edgeware Road | W.

TAVISTOCK HOUSE, | TAVISTOCK SQUARE, LONDON. W.C.
Monday Fifth April 1858

My Dear Beard

The Hospital sending me four tickets, I send you one;[1] thinking you may like to use it, either in person or by proxy.

It has become so impossible to comply with these reading Petitions, and the readings attract such very large audiences, that I have all but decided (between ourselves) to read on for my own profit. In that case, I shall read The Cricket, The Chimes, and The Haunted Man, at this same place, in May; and you will have, you may be sure, timely notice of being free of the Temple.[2]

It was a wonderful go, in Edinburgh. Certainly the most intelligent audience (2000 strong) I have ever had to do with; and showing a capacity of being affected by the pathetic parts, such as I never saw before.

Ever Faithfully

Thomas Beard Esquire CHARLES DICKENS

To JOHN FORSTER, [9 APRIL 1858]

Extract in F, VIII, ii, 647. *Date:* 9 Apr 58, according to Forster.

They have let five hundred stalls for the Hospital night;[3] and as people come every day for more, and it is out of the question to make more, they cannot be restrained at St. Martin's Hall from taking down names for other Readings.[4]

[1] For his reading of the *Carol* at St Martin's Hall on 15 Apr for the Hospital.

[2] i.e., a guest at the readings.

[3] *The Times*, 16 Apr, reported that "such was the assembled multitude that the sum produced must have been sufficient to physic all the sick children in the United Kingdom." The reading raised £165.8*s*.

[4] "This closed the attempt at further objection", wrote Forster (F, VIII, ii, 647). *The Times*, 16 Apr, welcomed the announcement that the "benevolent 'reader' is at last about to employ his elocutionary talents for his own advantage".

To W. HOLMAN HUNT,[1] 13 APRIL 1858

MS Mrs Elizabeth Burt.

TAVISTOCK HOUSE, | TAVISTOCK SQUARE, LONDON. W.C.
Tuesday Night, Thirteenth April, 1858

My Dear Sir.

I am pained and shocked by the receipt of your letter,[2] referring to a story called "Calmuck" lately published in Household Words,[3] and which has been a very long time in type there, unused.

When you use the words, "the extremely objectionable nature" of that article, I am quite sure that you use them in reference to your own knowledge of some allusions in it, and not to mine. If I could have had any reason for deeming it objectionable, I need not say (I hope) that you would never have found it in print under my auspices.[4]

I have too great an interest in, and too high a respect for, your calling and yourself, to be otherwise than anxious to understand your cause of complaint, and to remove it, if I can, in the frankest and fullest manner. If it should suit your convenience to call upon me here on Friday at half past twelve, I have not the least fear of

[1] William Holman Hunt (1827–1910; *DNB*), painter; moving spirit in foundation of Pre-Raphaelite Brotherhood with J. E. Millais and D. G. Rossetti, 1848; helped to found their short-lived journal, *The Germ*, Jan 50. One of his first exhibited paintings was *Little Nell and her Grandfather*, British Institution, 1847. His *Christians escaping from Druid Persecution* and Millais's *Christ in the House of His Parents*, both RA 1850, were ridiculed by the press; for CD's attack in *HW*, see below. *Valentine rescuing Sylvia from Perseus*, RA 1851, was again attacked by *The Times*, but defended by Ruskin, henceforth Hunt's public champion and close friend. By now, *The Light of the World*, RA 1854, and *The Scapegoat*, 1856, had made him famous. Had recently done six drawings for Moxon's illustrated *Poems by Tennyson*, 1857. Rejected as Associate RA 1856; and, although later invited, never became RA; OM 1905.

[2] Hunt had written to CD the day before: "May I venture to call your attention to the extremely objectionable nature of an article called 'Calmuck' which recently appeared in Household Words and to beg the favor of an interview with you to consult as to the best means of averting the injurious suspicions that an artist introduced therein is a true portrait of myself ..." (MS [heavily revised draft] Yale). According to Hunt's second wife, Edith, his sister Emily had written him "a furious letter saying 'Everyone knows your character now. Uncle Holman has read in *Household Words*, the DISGRACEFUL story about you and your model.'" According to Edith Hunt, Wilkie Collins also wrote, "describing the article as 'an abominable libel', urging Holman to write at once to Dickens" (Diana Holman-Hunt, *My Grandfather, his Wives and Loves*, 1969, p. 190)—but this seems very improbable.

[3] On 3 Apr 58 (XVII, 361). "Calmuck" by Robert Brough (see 10 June, *fn*) was a thinly-disguised account of Hunt (in the story, "Mildmay Strong") and his association with Emma Watkins (here, an ugly peasant girl nicknamed "Calmuck") who had been his model for the shepherdess in the famous *The Hireling Shepherd*, 1852. Brough's emphasis is on Strong's unworldly devotion to art, regardless of conventions or indeed other people's feelings; Calmuck's husband becomes jealous and Strong is then terrified of being attacked. Hunt had met Emma, a "fieldgirl", when staying with Millais, on a farm at Ewell, Surrey; she lived for a time in his Chelsea lodgings; and was nicknamed by Hunt's friends "The Coptic" (Diana Holman-Hunt, above, p. 81).

[4] Hunt could hardly have forgotten or forgiven CD's attack on the Pre-Raphaelite Brotherhood in "Old Lamps for New Ones", *HW*, 15 June 50, I, 265: see Vols VI, pp. 106–7 and VII, p. 517 and *n*. CD's links with Wilkie and Charles Collins affected his attitude to the PRB, as well as their changes in reputation and, to some extent, style.

our going wrong, because I have a perfect faith in our both equally desiring to do right.[1]

My Dear Sir | Faithfully Yours
CHARLES DICKENS

To A. U. THISELTON,[2] 13 APRIL 1858*

Text from copy, Minute Book, Artists' Benevolent Fund.

TAVISTOCK HOUSE,|TAVISTOCK SQUARE, LONDON. W.C.
Tuesday Night. Thirteenth April 1858

Sir,

Although I have been compelled, by want of leisure, to decline a host of proposals, to preside at public dinners, of late, I cannot for a moment resist the claims of my brother Artists. I beg you to assure your Committee that they are most heartily welcome to my poor services, and that I place myself at their disposal with all possible cheerfulness and good will.[3]

Your faithful Servant
CHARLES DICKENS

To MISS BURDETT COUTTS, 14 APRIL 1858*

MS Morgan Library. *Address:* Miss Burdett Coutts | 1 Stratton Street | Piccadily | W.

TAVISTOCK HOUSE,|TAVISTOCK SQUARE, LONDON. W.C.
Wednesday Fourteenth April, 1858

My Dear Miss Coutts.

It was Committee Day to day at Shepherd's Bush. Mr. Dyer, Mr. Tennant,[4] and I, attended.

We had a disagreeable circumstance to investigate, which was made known to me yesterday. Yesterday morning at between 4 and 5 (to make the matter very short), the Police Constable *employed to watch the place* was found in the parlor with Sarah Hyam, by Mary Lugg, whose suspicions had been excited by the early rising of Hyam. As soon as the thing was told to me yesterday, I sent to the Acting Inspector of the District, desiring him to attend at Urania Cottage to day, when we should have a very serious charge to investigate, against one of his men. He came, with the

[1] Hunt, according to Edith, was "by no means satisfied" with this interview. He was "bombarded with abusive letters from disillusioned admirers" (Diana Holman-Hunt, above, p. 192).

[2] Augustus Union Thiselton, printer, of 26 College Place, Camden Town; Secretary of the Artists' Benevolent Fund since Mar 1855.

[3] Viscount Goderich having declined, CD took the Chair at the Fund's 48th Anniversary Dinner, held at the Freemasons' Tavern on 8 May. In his speech, he praised not only the Artists' Benevolent Fund for its grants of annuities to the widows and children of deceased artists; but also the Artists' Annuity Fund, a mutual Assurance Co. (founded on similar principles to the Guild of Literature and Art: see Vol. VI, *passim*); and a third fund, the Artists' General Benevolent Fund, which gave money to relieve artists. It "makes no pretensions to gentility, squanders no treasure in keeping up appearances" (an obvious allusion to the Royal Literary Fund): see *Speeches*, ed. K. J. Fielding, pp. 266–69, and *To* Thiselton, 12 June.

[4] Misspelt "Tennent" by CD.

man implicated, and another officer. I examined into the case with great minuteness and care (Mr. Dyer and Mr. Tennant[1] assisting), in the presence of the three men. Not a doubt was left on our minds as to its nature, and I formally required the Inspector, in writing, to report it to Sir Richard Mayne.[2] The girl (who in other respects had conducted herself well in the Home), we discharged. She behaved quietly and respectfully—told no lies, and made no defence. A few household precautions which seemed desirable to us, we directed to be taken.

I don't think the management was to blame, or could help it. Mrs. Marchmont has been in great distress, and if you will rest satisfied, in so difficult a matter, with what we have done, I believe it to be impossible to do more.

I saw the girl in Vincent Square,[3] in due course (you remember giving me the letter about her?), and directed the Matron to bring her for approval to day. We thought it a good case, and agreed to take it.

I have omitted to say that the neighbouring clergyman interested in Hyam's case, came, with his son. He was extremely sensible and kind, and seemed really impressed with the pains we bestowed upon it.

With love to Mrs. Brown | Ever Dear Miss Coutts
Yours faithfully and affecy.
CHARLES DICKENS

To THE ACTING INSPECTOR, HAMMERSMITH & WANDSWORTH POLICE OFFICE,[4] [14 APRIL 1858]

Mention in *To* Miss Coutts, 14 Apr 58. *Date:* written same day.

To MRS HOGGE,[5] 14 APRIL 1858†

MS Walter T. Spencer.

TAVISTOCK HOUSE, | TAVISTOCK SQUARE, LONDON. W.C.
Wednesday Fourteenth April, 1858

My Dear Mrs Hogge.

My enforced disposals of myself have been so numerous and so uncertain since I had the happiness of seeing you,[6] that I have been afraid to write to you. I DID[7] "mean it", and have often thought of it; and it is you who commit the direst cruelty in doubting (as I clearly see you do) the faithful and devoted wretch who pens these lines.

Mrs Dickens very rarely dines out, and I had best not include her in my answer to

[1] Misspelt "Tennent" by CD.

[2] Sir Richard Mayne, KCB (1796–1868; *DNB*), Chief Metropolitan Police Commissioner.

[3] A different girl, from the Westminster Police Court.

[4] The Superintendent was Septimus Finn.

[5] Mary (or Polly) Hogge, daughter of Capt. Richard Harness, RN; the Rev. William Harness's "lovely" niece (Caroline M. Duncan-Jones, *Miss Mitford and Mr Harness*, 1955, p. 41; and see Vol. II, p. 178); wife of George Hogge. Thackeray recorded her kindness to his daughters in Baden in July 53 (*Letters and Private Papers*, ed. Gordon Ray, III, 288).

[6] The last time they are known to have met was in May 54; see Vol. VII, p. 334.

[7] Underlined three times.

your heart-breaking note. I myself am as free as I ever can be (being your slave)[1] for Monday or Wednesday in next week, or for any day in the following week, except Thursday the 29th.

[a]I grieve to hear that you have been ill, but I hope that the Spring—when it comes—will find you blooming with the rest of the flowers.[a]

Very Faithfully Yours
CHARLES DICKENS

Mrs Hogge.

To CHARLES ELLIS, 16 APRIL 1858

MS Chas Ellis & Co.

TAVISTOCK HOUSE, | TAVISTOCK SQUARE, LONDON. W.C.
Friday Sixteenth April, 1858

Dear Mr. Ellis

I send you a cheque (crossed) for my account.[2] Before I go out of town for the summer, I will look over my wine and see what I want. Having done so, I will write you a note and ask you to call on me.

Faithfully Yours
CHARLES DICKENS

To THOMAS BEARD, 17 APRIL 1858

MS Dickens House. *Address:* Thomas Beard Esquire | 42 Portman Place | Edgeware Road. W.

TAVISTOCK HOUSE, | TAVISTOCK SQUARE, LONDON. W.C.
Saturday Morning Seventeenth April | 1858

My Dear Beard

I have begged Arthur Smith (who directs all the business) to send you 2 stalls for each of my readings,[3] and I hope I shall never miss my old friend's face. If you will follow into my little room when I go out for the free five minutes, you will always find Sherry and Ice there.

Ever Faithfully
CD.

[1] Perhaps a Shakespearian echo (the opening words of Sonnet 57).

[aa] Given in MDGH, 1880, II, 46 and N, III, 17 with paragraphs from 28 May 58 and 5 Mar 59; rest of letter unpublished.

[2] Of £29.1; it went through Ellis's bank account on 20 Apr (CD's Account-book, MS Messrs Coutts).

[3] The first three readings, for Thurs, 29 Apr, 6 and 24 May, of the *Cricket*, *Chimes*, and *Carol* respectively, had now been advertised: "Mr. Charles Dickens | will read at St. Martin's Hall . . .". The time was "Eight exactly" and each was to last two hours; the prices were quite high—"Stalls (numbered and reserved), Five Shillings; Area and Galleries, Half-a-crown; Unreserved seats, One Shilling" and tickets obtainable from Chapman & Hall's office and at St Martin's Hall.

To WILKIE COLLINS, 17 APRIL 1858*

MS Morgan Library.

TAVISTOCK HOUSE, | TAVISTOCK SQUARE, LONDON. W.C.
Saturday Morning Seventeenth April | 1858

My Dear Wilkie

I have begged Arthur Smith to send you 2 Stalls for each of my readings, and I hope you'll come to them.—You will find some Sherry and Iced-Water in my little room when I go there.

Ever Faithfully
CD.

To CHARLES DANCE,[1] 19 APRIL 1858*

MS Private.

TAVISTOCK HOUSE, | TAVISTOCK SQUARE, LONDON. W.C.
Monday Evening | Nineteenth April, 1858

My Dear Dance

I am sorry to say in reply to your note just received, that I am to be relied upon for nothing on Friday. I put down my name for the Dinner,[2] as a mark of respect to Mr. Kean—and I intend being at the dinner—but an older engagement will oblige me to leave directly after it. I shall be obliged to go, at a quarter before Nine.

Otherwise, wouldn't I have brought you up with a neat and appropriate!—[3]

Faithfully Yours always
Charles Dance Esquire. CHARLES DICKENS

To MRS FRANCES DICKINSON, 19 APRIL 1858

MS Free Library of Philadelphia.

TAVISTOCK HOUSE, | TAVISTOCK SQUARE, LONDON. W.C.
Monday Nineteenth April, 1858

My Dear Mrs Dickinson

If I burn your letter, may I be D—— I mean B—u-r-n-t myself! It is much too earnest and cordial for any such fate. I shall put it by, until I get another as good; and then I must get you to write me a better.

[1] Charles Dance (1794–1863; *DNB*), dramatist: see Vol. v, p. 485*n*; member of the Garrick Club since 1836. Yates remembered him as friend and often collaborator of Planché and says his "bright intellignce would never have been suspected from his heavy appearance" (*Recollections and Experiences*, II, 6). *The Stock Exchange*, the latest of his numerous farces, had been running at the Princess's Theatre since 5 Apr.

[2] The Shakespeare Birthday Dinner at the Garrick Club, 23 Apr.

[3] In fact, CD was called on to make a speech: see *To* Thackeray, 28 Apr. No record has been found of it.

I am charmed by your having been so pleased.[1] If you don't come again, I shall have the Drapery dyed black.

O yes (as to your party) O[2] yes! It is all very well to break your Manager's[3] heart by not asking him, and then when you know he is going somewhere else, to shew him (as if he were Scrooge), the shadows of the things that might have been![4] But he feels it, and encloses a tear

This is

His Tear.

Believe me always | Very faithfully Yours
CHARLES DICKENS

To W. HOLMAN HUNT, 20 APRIL 1858

MS Mrs Elizabeth Burt.

TAVISTOCK HOUSE, | TAVISTOCK SQUARE, LONDON. W.C.
Tuesday Twentieth April, 1858

My Dear Sir

I feel it to be useless to express my astonishment that you and your friends can possibly conceive the Bishop of Jerusalem[5] to be, by any remote contingency, between the centre of the earth and the centre of the Sun, in any danger of associating you as a responsible and individual gentleman, with the hero of this story.[6] I believe with much confidence, however, that he would never have come to *be* the Bishop of Jerusalem, if he were in the least hazard of so committing himself.

My judgment is unchanged. It is altogether against the insertion of a contradiction. I have not a doubt that it would suggest to the public what they have not the faintest idea of, and that its effect would be exactly the reverse of your desire.

But as it is quite out of the question that the text of the article can be altered in future copies (for it is printed and stereotyped and done with), I must ask you to

[1] By his reading in aid of the Children's Hospital on 15 Apr. It was highly praised by *The Times*, 16 Apr: "A 'reading' by Mr. Charles Dickens is something altogether *sui generis*, a happy blending of the narrative and dramatic style, by which the author ... astonishes the auditor by revelations of meaning that had escaped the solitary student." Benjamin Moran (see *To* Brooks, 11 Mar 58, *fn*) admitted that, after the reading, he was "not so much inclined to kick him as before (because of his 'evident insincerity of character')". But he was still patronizing: "As a performance however his reading was still defective ... [*he*] reads tolerably and that is all" (*Journal of Benjamin Moran, 1857–65*, ed. S. A. Wallace and F. E. Gillespie, I, 292).

[2] Doubly underlined.

[3] i.e. himself, in the 1857 theatricals.

[4] See Stave Four of the *Carol*: "Shadows of the things that may be".

[5] The Rt Rev. Samuel Gobat (1799–1879), resident Bishop since 1846; a naturalised Swiss, had earlier been a missionary in Abyssinia.

[6] See *To* Hunt, 13 Apr and *fnn*. Hunt had had a theological feud with Gobat during his stay in Jerusalem in 1854; he apparently feared that, if the Bishop identified him with the painter, Strong, of Brough's story, he would use this as a weapon to prevent his return to the Holy Land. (Diana Holman-Hunt, *My Grandfather, his Wives and Loves*, p. 192).

decide whether there shall be a contradiction or no. If yes, I will take care to make it emphatic and plain.

My Dear Sir | Very faithfully Yours

W. Holman Hunt Esquire CHARLES DICKENS

To W. H. WILLS, 21 APRIL 1858*

MS Berg Collection.

TAVISTOCK HOUSE, | TAVISTOCK SQUARE, LONDON. W.C.
Wednesday Twenty First April 1858

My Dear Wills.

Will you write a line round to Arthur Smith, telling him about Brooks,[1] and how to address him, and who he is.

I will come to the office to do the No.[2] tomorrow at 2.

Faithfully Ever
CD.

To [OCTAVIAN BLEWITT],[3] 24 APRIL 1858

MS Churchill College, Cambridge

OFFICE OF HOUSEHOLD WORDS,
Saturday Twenty Fourth April 1858

My Dear Sir

I want any annual Report of the Literary Fund, which has their stock-extract from the Quarterly, appended to it.[4] Can you lend me one? And in case this

[1] S. L. Brooks, Station-Master of Euston: see Vol. v, p. 112*n*. No doubt arrangements for the provincial tour were already under consideration.

[2] Probably to settle the contents of No. 424, 8 May; of the seven articles two were by Hollingshead and two by Morley.

[3] The obvious addressee, as Secretary of the Fund.

[4] Each Annual Report included the following extract from the *Quarterly Review* inside its back cover: "The General Committee take this opportunity of returning their best acknowledgements to the Editor and Proprietor of the Quarterly Review, for the following notice of the Royal Literary Fund given in the pages of that Journal. | *Extract* | We hope to be pardoned for taking this opportunity of bearing witness to the wise and generous method in which the Managers of the Literary Fund conduct that admirable Charity. It may not be known in many parts of the Empire that such an Institution exists at all, and even this casual notice may be serviceable to its revenues. We have had occasion to observe the equal promptitude and delicacy with which its Committee is ever ready to administer to the necessities of the unfortunate scholar, who can satisfy them that his misery is not the just punishment of immoral habits. Some of the brightest names in contemporary Literature have been beholden to the bounty of this Institution, and in numerous instances its interference has shielded friendless merit from utter ruin." (In *Annual Report* from 1858 onwards, the date and author were added—Jan 1831, late John Gibson Lockhart.) CD referred to this in *The Case of the Reformers in the Literary Fund; stated by Charles W. Dilke, Charles Dickens, and John Forster* (Mar 58) as a "stock quotation" and suggested substituting a condemnatory passage also from the *Quarterly Review* proposing "the propriety of substituting it" (pp. 15–16) as follows: "The Literary Fund provides no present employment for the hungry and willing labourer, and holds out no hope for the future.... There is neither the grace nor the virtue of charity, in distributions of this kind; and were the money, which is thus

Messenger should miss you, can you send me such Report *to Tavistock House*, any time tomorrow?[1]

To T. C. GRATTAN, 24 APRIL 1858

MS Huntington Library.

TAVISTOCK HOUSE, | TAVISTOCK SQUARE, LONDON. W.C.
Saturday Twenty Fourth April, 1858

My Dear Grattan

An answer to the last pamphlet[2] to which your note refers, is already advertized in the Athenaeum and Times, as about to appear within a few days.[3]

The facts (unobscured by clouds of words), are perfectly clear. I desire nothing so much as that the Members of the Society—and above all, Literary men—should understand them. Nor will I ever leave off—being alive—until they do.

In the Days of our Play, The Frozen Deep, you were looked for here. But you were "there", instead. In the Ages that have elapsed since then, I have often wondered in what blessed foreign haven you were basking.[4]

Faithfully Yours always

T. C. Grattan Esquire. CHARLES DICKENS

To [?F. M. EVANS],[5] 26 APRIL 1858

MS Fales Collection, New York University Library.

TAVISTOCK HOUSE, | TAVISTOCK SQUARE, LONDON. W.C.
Monday Twenty Sixth April, 1858

My Dear [?Evans]

Collins has communicated to me (only tonight) a secret project of my good friend

annually expended, disbursed in well-directed alms, a far greater sum of good would be obtained.... But, in this Joint-Stock Patronage Company, a donation is paid and received like a poor-rate—save only that there is rather more humiliation on the part of the receiver, who, in this case, solicits as a charity what, in the other, he would have claimed as a right." Robert Bell's speech at the Annual General Meeting revealed that the condemnatory passage occurred in the *Quarterly* for Sep 1812, too long ago to be relevant to the argument. This was greeted with cheers and laughter at CD's expense. See also *Summary of Facts*, p. 17. But CD retaliated: see *To* Yates, 15 June, *fn.*

[1] Bottom of page cut off, probably removing ending, signature and addressee.

[2] *Summary of Facts, ... Issued in Answer to Allegations Contained in a Pamphlet Entitled 'The Case of the Reformers of The Literary Fund'*; published by the Fund's General Committee, it incorporated the whole of Robert Bell's official reply, as the Committee's representative, to CD, at the Annual General Meeting of 10 Mar. The subsequent debate, including CD's long speech, is also given. Grattan was a member of the Royal Literary Fund, and a donor; his address was the Athenaeum Club.

[3] The *Athenaeum* of 24 Apr advertised the publication "in a few days" of Royal Literary Fund, *The Answer to the Committee's 'Summary of Facts'*; although given as by Dilke, CD and Forster, it was certainly written by CD himself: see *To* Collins, 29 Apr and *fn.*

[4] Grattan never returned to America after his Consulship ended in 1846, nor did he reside in Europe in the 1850s, but no doubt went there for holidays.

[5] Name blotted out in MS; a publisher, therefore F. M. Evans; length of blot and parts of letters appearing above and below confirm.

Townshend's, concerning a pamphlet of championship of me,[1] which I have no doubt originates in the best and most affectionate intentions, but which I certainly would not have published for a Thousand Pounds. In returning your answer concerning said projected pamphlet, to Collins, pray say that you would on no account publish, or print, anything concerning me, without my previous knowledge and concurrence.

Ever Yours
CHARLES DICKENS

To MISS BURDETT COUTTS, 28 APRIL 1858*

MS Morgan Library.

TAVISTOCK HOUSE,|TAVISTOCK SQUARE, LONDON. W.C.
Wednesday Twenty Eighth April, 1858

My Dear Miss Coutts

I think it worth doing.[2] If you wish me to do it—of course I will, with the greatest pleasure.[3]

As I have heard no more from you about Friday, I conclude that I am not engaged to you.

I know you will be glad to hear that whereas they usually make some 250 stalls at St. Martin's Hall, Arthur Smith has made 560, and they are all gone. They will be in great demand to day and tomorrow, but all stall applicants will have to go over to another night.

Ever Faithfully
CD.

To W. M. THACKERAY, 28 APRIL 1858*

MS Carl H. Pforzheimer Library.

TAVISTOCK HOUSE,|TAVISTOCK SQUARE, LONDON. W.C.
Wednesday Twenty Eighth April, 1858

My Dear Thackeray

Charles Dance made a Beast of himself in the matter of that Toasting. I wrote to tell him—two days before, when he sent me the list of toasts—that I could only dine, and that he must not look to me to say any thing whatever, as I should be gone.

Sunday the 9th. of May, with pleasure.[4] I am uncertain whether the other man

[1] No doubt supporting his attempts to reform the Royal Literary Fund: see last and *fn.*

[2] The Secretary of the Reformatory and Refuge Union, 118 Pall Mall, had asked Miss Coutts to send them an account of the Home for Homeless Women, for insertion in a pamphlet "containing a short account of the various Penitentiaries and Homes for females" (MS Morgan).

[3] CD no doubt wrote the entry for the Home in *A Hand-Book of Penitentiaries and Homes for Females, in Great Britain and Ireland*, published by the Union (4th edn, 1860; only known copy, in BL, destroyed in Second World War).

[4] Thackeray's dinner party included Maclise, Landseer, Lord Stanley and Turgenev (Thackeray's Diary, *Letters and Private Papers of W. M. Thackeray*, ed. Gordon N. Ray, IV, 392, Appx XX).

who "didn't answer" on Monday, came, and was a failure; or didn't answer and didn't come?[1]

I met a stately lady[2] yesterday, in whom I recognized the lineaments of that distinguished Novelist Who.

Ever Faithfully
CD.

To MISS BURDETT COUTTS, 28 APRIL 1858*

MS Morgan Library.

At Townshend's[3]
Wednesday Evening | Twenty Eighth April, 1858

My Dear Miss Coutts

I am dining here, before going down to see Mr. Arthur Smith. Rely upon it—but of course you do—that I will manage to get the Bishop of Cape Town[4] in, *somehow*. I hope to be able to contrive a Chair near you,—but I cannot speak with confidence, because I trust all these things to my trusty man of business, and I suppose him to have been beset all day. I will write to you again, after seeing him, between 8 and 9 tonight.

Ever Faithfully and affy
CD.

To MISS BURDETT COUTTS, 28 APRIL 1858*

MS Morgan Library.

MR.
CHARLES DICKENS'S
READING[5]

Wednesday Evening Twenty Eighth April | 1858.

My Dear Miss Coutts

Mr. Arthur Smith has achieved the thing, and sends the enclosed "Chair" by you, for the Bishop of Cape Town.

Ever Faithfully and affecy.
CD.

[1] Perhaps to the Garrick Club dinner on 23 Apr.

[2] Thackeray's mother, Mrs Carmichael-Smyth: see 5 Oct 57, *fn*.

[3] 21 Norfolk St, Park Lane.

[4] The Rt. Rev. Robert Gray (1809–72; *DNB*): see Vol. v, p. 591*n*.

[5] Heading embossed on writing paper and also on the envelope. CD is presumably writing from St Martin's Hall.

To EDMUND YATES, 28 APRIL 1858

MS Robert H. Taylor Collection, Princeton University.

TAVISTOCK HOUSE, | TAVISTOCK SQUARE, LONDON. W.C.
Wednesday Twenty Eighth April, 1858

My Dear Yates

I send you an Orthopaedic shield, to defend your manly bosom from the pens of the enemy.[1]

For a good many years, I have suffered a great deal from Charities, but never anything like what I suffer now. The amount of correspondence they inflict upon me, is really incredible. But this is nothing. Benevolent men get behind the piers of the gates, lying in wait for my going out; and when I peep shrinkingly from my study-windows, I see their pot-bellied shadows projected on the gravel. Benevolent bullies drive up in Hansom Cabs (with engraved portraits of their benevolent Institutions hanging over the aprons, like banners on their outward walls),[2] and stay so long at the door, that their horses deposit beehives of excellent manure all over the front court. Benevolent Area-Sneaks[3] get lost in the kitchens, and are found to impede the circulation of the knife-cleaning Machine. My man has been heard to say (at the Burton Arms)[4] "that if it was a wicious place, well and good—*that* an't door-work; but that wen all the Christian wirtues is always a shoulderin and a helberin on you in the All, a tryin to git past you and cut upstairs into Master's room, wy no wages as you couldn't name, wouldn't make it up to you."

Persecuted Ever

Edmund Yates Esquire CD.

To WILKIE COLLINS, 29 APRIL 1858

MS Morgan Library.

TAVISTOCK HOUSE, | TAVISTOCK SQUARE, LONDON. W.C.
Thursday Twenty Ninth April, 1858

My Dear Wilkie

I send you a proof of what will begin, tomorrow, to be abundantly circulated,

[1] At a friend's request, Yates had asked CD to take the chair at a dinner in support of the Orthopaedic Hospital (*Recollections and Experiences*, II, 108). He did not do so.

[2] Cf. *Macbeth*, V. v. I.

[3] Flash slang for thieves who get into a house through the basement area.

[4] Not listed under that name; clearly near Tavistock House (see *To* Stone, 18 Feb 57), and perhaps in Burton Rd, Place or Crescent, under another name.

besides being printed at length in the Athenaeum of next Saturday.[1] It is a facetious facer—which I have given to those solemn impostors, con amore.[2]

Ever Faithfully

CD.

To W. HOLMAN HUNT, 30 APRIL 1858

MS Mrs Elizabeth Burt.

TAVISTOCK HOUSE, | TAVISTOCK SQUARE, LONDON. W.C.

Friday Thirtieth April, 1858

My Dear Sir

With the sincerest desire to do what is right, and what is best calculated to remove any disagreeable association that anybody may have made between you and that preposterous story of Calmuck, I have considered and reconsidered the question of inserting an explanation in Household Words, to the effect that you have no more to do with it than I have.[3] But I am quite sure and certain that such a proceeding (however carefully your name might be detached from it), would defeat its own object, and would instantly set all sorts and conditions of people speculating on "who the artist may be who is not to be connected with it". And thus the very association, however ridiculous and baseless, which we wish to avoid, would be got into numbers of heads which are innocent of it, as my own was, when you first wrote to me.[4]

As I have already told you—I never liked the story, and it has been lying at the office, unused, a long time. I am sorry now, that I did not strike out of it the pretence that it is true.[5] But that is so common a pretence in fiction, that it really did not attract my attention or make any impression on me. I assure you that I had no idea there was such a statement *in* the paper, until I looked for it expressly.

It seems such a superfluous proceeding to tell you, "I know it is *not* true", that I really hesitate to write what I should suppose all reasonable human creatures must be already convinced of. But I do it, nevertheless. Rest satisfied, I beg, that I accepted the story, with much doubt, as a very weak fiction—that it *is* a very weak

[1] The *Answer to the Committee's 'Summary of Facts'* (see *To* Grattan, 24 Apr, *fnn*). It was printed complete in the *Athenaeum*, 1 May, extending to almost 10 columns.

[2] The "Answer" is hard-hitting, sarcastic, contemptuous of the arguments put forward by the Fund's Committee to justify their expenses. The only facetiousness is in the beginning where CD draws an analogy between the Committee and "Mr. Rarey, the horse-tamer"; and in col. 3, where the Committee is compared with Swift's Laputans, employing "Flappers". The *Athenaeum*'s "Our Weekly Gossip" returned to the attack on 8 May, fuelled by the President's claim at the annual Dinner that the Fund lacked adequate funds: "Why, the society is obese, lazy, and plethoric with too much prosperity. It has too much money." Its "extravagance and useless expenditure" are again pilloried. "To the share of Literature", it ends, "in whose name [*public donations are*] given, there falls absolutely nothing but the shame."

[3] According to Edith Hunt, Hunt had asked CD to write another letter "which he could show to his family, repeating his, Dickens', dismay even more *forcibly* to reassure them that the article was fiction" (Diana Holman-Hunt, *My Grandfather, his Wives and Loves*, p. 193).

[4] No contradiction appeared in *HW*. It seems extraordinary that Brough reprinted the piece in his *Heads and Tales: A Medley*, 1859.

[5] The story ends: "There is not much matter in it; but it is entitled to the apology claimed by Ben Jonson for his imperfect rhymes—it is thoroughly true."

fiction, and nothing else—that if I could have contemplated the possibility that anybody (not to say you, but anybody) could be absurdly and wrongfully associated with it in the least particular, nothing would have induced me to print it—and that I am heartily sorry I ever did print it, seeing that it is an arrow, with anything but a sharp point, shot vaguely over a house-top, and glancing off, in a manner wholly unaccountable to and unforeseen by me, against a brother-artist.[1]

Dear Sir | Faithfully Yours always

W. Holman Hunt Esquire CHARLES DICKENS

To EDMUND YATES, 30 APRIL 1858

MS Robert H. Taylor Collection, Princeton University.

TAVISTOCK HOUSE, | TAVISTOCK SQUARE, LONDON. W.C.

Friday Thirtieth April, 1858

My Dear Yates

I have derived great gratification of heart from what I have read of yours to day,[2] and I cordially thank you;—not alone because you have written it, but because I am sure you have earnestly felt it.

Ever Faithfully

CHARLES DICKENS

To THOMAS BEARD, 1 MAY 1858

MS Dickens House.

TAVISTOCK HOUSE, | TAVISTOCK SQUARE, LONDON. W.C.

Saturday First May 1858

My Dear Beard

I was heartily sorry to learn (before I received your kind note last night), that that abominable foot of yours, wouldn't come to the Hall last Thursday.[3] If it should keep away next Thursday, I should begin to think, from its beastly persistence in Unreason, that it must be Somebody else's foot, which you have laid [hold][4] of by mistake.

They crammed 70 more people into the place, the other night, than were ever got

[1] Cf. *Hamlet*, v. ii. 235–6.

[2] Yates's glowing notice in the *Daily News*, 30 Apr, of CD's reading of the *Cricket* in St Martin's Hall the previous night, his first paid reading. After giving his short prefatory speech in full (see *Speeches*, ed. K. J. Fielding, p. 264), Yates gives the reading itself his highest praise: "this great and God-gifted genius holds the hearts of his audience in his hand"; in the women's speeches "the artist's true genius shines most brightly"; it was "no public entertainment, but a very large family party, gathered round the kindest, the dearest, the best of their friends." In *Recollections and Experiences*, II, 98–9 (in a passage wrongly implied as of June 58) Yates describes CD stepping on to the platform, "walking rather stiffly, right shoulder well forward, as usual, bud in button-hole, and gloves in hand.... He was received with a roar of cheering which might have been heard at Charing Cross, and which was again and again renewed." *The Times*, 3 May, gave the reading a very warm notice: CD infused into it "a life that was perfectly marvellous". "Hundreds" had to be turned away.

[3] See last.

[4] Omitted in error.

into it before—though we were quite clear, on the Children's Hospital Night, that one more could by no means by crammed in. I think some people are a little afraid of the Chimes.[1] To tell you the truth, I am—as yet—a little so myself, for I CAN[2] NOT[3] yet (and I have been at it all the morning) command sufficient composure at some of the more affecting parts, to project them with the necessary force, the requisite distance.[4]

I must harden my heart, like Lady Macbeth.[5]

Wills will write to you about coming down to Gad's Hill next Tuesday Week (Household Words Audit Day), and staying all night.[6]

Ever Faithfully

Thomas Beard Esquire. CHARLES DICKENS

To JOHN B. MORGAN,[7] 1 MAY 1858

Extract in Henry Bristow of Ringwood catalogue No. 291 (1987); *MS* (3rd person) 1 p.; addressed John B. Morgan; dated Tavistock House, Saturday, 1st May 1858.

Mr. Charles Dickens presents his compliments to Mr. Morgan, and begs to say that it has become quite impossible for him to read in aid of any Institution whatever.

To [?R. P.] TEBB,[8] 1 MAY 1858*

MS Mr Alan G. Thomas.

TAVISTOCK HOUSE, | TAVISTOCK SQUARE, LONDON. W.C.

Saturday First May, 1858

Mr. Charles Dickens presents his Compliments to Mr. Tebb, and regrets that he cannot have the honor of accepting the office of a Vice President of the Crosby Hall Cricket club.[9] But his public engagements and positions are at present so numerous, that he has been obliged to resolve to make no additions to them, even though they should be merely nominal.

[1] See *To* Beard, 7 May and *fn*.

[2] Doubly underlined.

[3] Trebly underlined.

[4] His only previous readings of *The Chimes* had been to friends at Forster's on 3 and 5 Dec 1844; after the first of which Maclise had written: "there was not a dry eye in the house" (see Vol. IV, p. 234 and *n*). Forster saw them as the germ of his public readings (F, IV, vi, 363).

[5] Recalling her soliloquy in I, v.

[6] Beard could not come, as 7 May makes clear.

[7] Unidentified.

[8] Perhaps Robert Palmer Tebb, auctioneer and estate agent, of 3 Adelaide Place, E.C.; presumably on the Committee of Crosby Hall (see below).

[9] Of Crosby Hall, Bishopsgate, which provided evening classes for young men, a library and reading room. It began as a Literary and Scientific Institution 1842; then became "Metropolitan Evening Classes for Young Men", 1848; by 1860, on re-purchase by the freeholder, the classes moved to Sussex Hall, Leadenhall St, and developed into the City of London College. Crosby Hall itself became a "Public Dining Establishment". Tebb had probably deduced CD's interest in cricket from the match between All-Muggleton and Dingley Dell in *Pickwick*, Ch. 7.

To W. S. TROOD,[1] 5 MAY 1858

Text from N, III, 20.

TAVISTOCK HOUSE, | TAVISTOCK SQUARE, LONDON. W.C.
Fifth May 1858

Mr. Charles Dickens begs Mr. Strood[2] to be so good as to give directions that no rubbish or refuse from the Falstaff be thrown into the shrubbery of Gad's Hill Place. Mr. Dickens also hopes that Mr. Strood will advise his customers not to trespass on that ground in going from the Falstaff to the village.

He wishes very earnestly to live on good terms with his neighbours; and he hopes that they know it, and will not feel disinclined to respect his property. He is sure that Mr. Strood can have no desire not to do what is obliging and right, and he therefore addresses this note to Mr. Strood in good will and good humour.[3]

To THE REV. C. T. [WEATHERLEY],[4] 5 MAY 1858

Mention in Retz & Storm catalogue, *c.* May 1940; *MS* (3rd Person) 1 p.; dated London, 5 May 58.

Saying that he is unable to comply with his correspondent's wishes.

To THOMAS BEARD, 7 MAY 1858

MS Dickens House. *Address:* Thomas Beard Esquire | 42 Portman Place | Maida Hill | W.

TAVISTOCK HOUSE, | TAVISTOCK SQUARE, LONDON. W.C.
Friday Evening Seventh May, 1858

My Dear Beard

Shall I come and see you? If you would like to behold the countenance of the Inimitable—say so by Post, and I'll come on Sunday.

Gad's Hill shall not yet be given up. It shall *not* be given up, by——said my Uncle Toby.[5]

Some of the people about me, were also doubtful of The Chimes. *I* was rather so myself, but, having written it, thoroughly resolved to read it, whether or no.[6] As

[1] William Stocker Trood, landlord 1849–72 of the Sir John Falstaff Inn, Gad's Hill, on the north side of the Dover Rd, a little below Gad's Hill Place. In later recollections, he recalled CD and Catherine staying at the Falstaff before Gad's Hill Place was ready, and visitors—including Forster, Collins and Stone—staying there when the house was full (W. R. Hughes, *A Week's Tramp in Dickens-Land*, p. 207; Trood's further reminiscences of CD, showing that they were on very good terms, are on pp. 208–9).

[2] CD's error; he no doubt confused the name with the nearby town.

[3] This letter implies that he has been at Gad's Hill 2–4 May.

[4] The Rev. Charles Thomas Weatherley (catalogue reads "Weatherby" in error), Curate of Harmondsworth, Middlesex, 1857; chaplain of Morecroft Asylum 1858.

[5] Cf. Sterne, *Tristram Shandy*, Bk VI, ch. 8: "He shall not die, by G—, cried my uncle Toby." For the whole passage quoted, see Vol. VI, p. 711 and *n*.

[6] See *To* Beard, 1 May. A further doubt, shared by others, no doubt concerned the relevance then of the social protest, particularly as embodied in Will Fern.

soon as I began to lay hold of it, I told Arthur Smith that I believed it would be a tremendous success—and I think there is no doubt that it topped the others by a great height last night. I have heard in all directions to day that the effect was amazingly strong.[1]

Ever Faithfully
CD.

To MISS BURDETT COUTTS, 9 MAY 1858

MS (copy in the hand of C. C. Osborne)[2] British Library.

Sunday Ninth May, 1858

My Dear Miss Coutts,

You have been too near and dear a friend to me for many years, and I am bound to you by too many ties of grateful and affectionate regard, to admit of my any longer keeping silence to you on a sad domestic topic. I believe you are not quite unprepared for what I am going to say, and will, in the main, have anticipated it.

I believe my marriage has been for years and years as miserable a one as ever was made. I believe that no two people were ever created, with such an impossibility of interest, sympathy, confidence, sentiment, tender union of any kind between them, as there is between my wife and me. It is an immense misfortune to her—it is an immense misfortune to me—but Nature has put an insurmountable barrier between us, which never in this world can be thrown down.

You know me too well to suppose that I have the faintest thought of influencing you on either side. I merely mention a fact which may induce you to pity us both, when I tell you that she is the only person I have ever known with whom I could not get on somehow or other, and in communicating with whom I could not find some way to some kind of interest. You know that I have the many impulsive faults which often belong to my impulsive way of life and exercise of fancy; but I am very patient and considerate at heart, and would have beaten out a path to a better journey's end than we have come to, if I could.

We have been virtually separated for a long time.[3] We must put a wider space between us now,[4] than can be found in one house.

[1] The "more affecting parts"—Lilian's "fall" in the third Quarter and Meg's would-be suicide in the fourth, in Trotty's dream—were particularly praised by the critics. Hollingshead, in a long and appreciative article in the *Critic*, claimed that Trotty Veck "produced more tears and laughter combined than anything within the whole range of the acted drama" (4 Sep 1858).

[2] Miss Coutts's private secretary 1882–98; his "Material collected for the biography of the Baroness Burdett-Coutts by C. C. Osborne" is in the BL; this letter, which is a transcript by Osborne, is prefaced by a note saying that it is not proposed to use it. Our text has replaced "&" by "and" according to CD's own usage.

[3] There were no births after Plorn's in 1852; Catherine was still under 40.

[4] According to Catherine's aunt, Helen Thomson, CD had made various "absurd" or "insulting" proposals to her to keep up appearances, including Catherine's "going abroad to live alone, or keeping to her own apartment in his house in daily life, at the same time to appear at his parties still as mistress of the house, to do the honors". Helen Thomson claimed that Catherine "had no desire to leave her home or children so long as that home was endurable to her" (see Helen Thomson *to* Mrs Stark, [30] Aug 58: Appx F). This is a very different view from CD's statement in the "Violated Letter" that "for some years past Mrs.

If the children loved her, or ever had loved her, this severance would have been a far easier thing than it is. But she has never attached one of them to herself, never played with them in their infancy, never attracted their confidence as they have grown older, never presented herself before them in the aspect of a mother.[1] I have seen them fall off from her in a natural—not *un*natural—progress of estrangement, and at this moment I believe that Mary and Katey (whose dispositions are of the gentlest and most affectionate conceivable) harden into stone figures of girls when they can be got to go near her, and have their hearts shut up in her presence as if they closed by some horrid spring.

No one can understand this, but Georgina who has seen it grow from year to year,[2] and who is the best, the most unselfish, and the most devoted of human

Dickens has been in the habit of representing to me that it would be better for her to go away and live apart" (see Appx F). It is impossible to determine the truth of either statement now; but, to keep up appearances on the verge of his public readings, CD may have suggested some such arrangement as Miss Thomson claimed.

[1] There is virtually no foundation for this charge, repeated more vehemently to Miss Coutts on 23 Aug and, publicly, in the "Violated Letter" (see Appx F). Catherine may have been less outgoing to her children than was CD (especially when the children were very young); but CD himself admitted that he was "chary of showing my affections, even to my children" (see *To* Maria Winter, 22 Feb 55). But there is a great deal of evidence to show that she and the children were devoted to each other. From the 1840s on, CD's letters to her, when they are apart, always end with expressions of the children's love; in a letter of 11 Aug 1870, to G. W. Rusden, Alfred Dickens (aged 13 in 1858), said of his parents: "we their children always loved them both equally having free intercourse with both as of old" (given in Mary Lazarus, *A Tale of Two Brothers*, Sydney, 1973, p. 2); Henry Dickens recorded that, after the separation, "I used regularly to visit my dear mother ... we lived on terms of mutual affection until her death" (*Recollections*, p. 19). Catherine showed her feelings for her youngest boys in a letter to her aunt Helen Thomson, after a visit from them very shortly after the separation: "I need hardly tell you, dearest Aunt, how very happy I have been with my dear boys, although they were not allowed to remain with me so long as I wished.... I cannot tell you how good and affectionate they were to me ..." (quoted in Helen Thomson *to* Mrs Stark, 20 Aug 58: Appx F.) Bequests of small personal belongings in her will, often given to her by the children, again show her fondness for them. On the other side are two of Georgina Hogarth's remarks: the first in a letter to Mrs Winter of 31 May 58, during the separation arrangements themselves: "Unhappily ... by some constitutional misfortune & incapacity, my sister always from their infancy, threw her children upon other people, consequently as they grew up, there was not the usual strong tie between them and her"—"in short, for many years, although we have put a good face upon it, we have been very miserable at home" (given in *The Love Romance of CD*, ed. Walter Dexter, 1936, pp. 290–1); the second, much later, to Annie Fields on Catherine's response to Sydney Dickens's death at sea in 1872: that she had felt it "as much as she can feel anything, but she is a very curious person—unlike anyone else in the world" (Georgina Hogarth *to* Mrs Fields, 5 Aug 1872; given in Arthur Adrian, *Georgina Hogarth and the Dickens Circle*, 1957, p. 172; but this surely says more of Catherine's reticence towards Georgina than of her feelings for Sydney). Michael Slater, in *Dickens and Women*, 1983, makes the convincing psychological point that, rather than the gratuitous cruelty it seems, this charge against Catherine was something CD "had to get himself to believe so that he could the more freely pity himself in the image of his own children"; and he links this with CD's own acute feelings of rejection by his mother during his sojourn in the blacking-factory 34 years earlier (pp. 146–7).

[2] Georgina Hogarth had lived with CD and Catherine since their return from America in June 1842, when she was only 15; there is, however, no evidence that she had taken over any housekeeping duties until CD's letter to her from Paris of 14 Mar 56. All the children were devoted to her. But, against what CD said in the "Violated Letter": "I do not know—I cannot by any stretch of fancy imagine—what would have become of them but for this aunt..." (see Appx F), may be set Katey's comment: "She was useful to my mother, of course, but that was all. My

Creatures. Her sister Mary,[1] who died suddenly and who lived with us before her, understood it as well though in the first months of our marriage.[2] It is her misery to live in some fatal atmosphere which slays every one to whom she should be dearest. It is my misery that no one can ever understand the truth in its full force, or know what a blighted and wasted life my married life has been.

Forster is trying what he can, to arrange matters with her mother. But I know that the mother herself could not live with her. I am perfectly sure that her younger sister and her brother could not live with her.[3] An old servant of ours[4] is the only hope I see, as she took care of her, like a poor child, for sixteen years. But she is married now, and I doubt her being afraid that the companionship would wear her to death. Macready used to get on better with her than anyone else,[5] and sometimes I have a fancy that she may think of him and his sister. To suggest them to her would be to inspire her with an instant determination never to go near them.

In the mean time I have come for a time to the office, to leave her Mother free to do what she can at home, towards the getting of her away to some happier mode of existence if possible. They all know that I will do anything for her comfort, and spend anything upon her.

It is a relief to me to have written this to you. Don't think the worse of me; don't think the worse of her. I am firmly persuaded that it is not within the compass of her character and faculties, to be other than she is. If she had married another sort of man, she might however have done better. I think she has always felt herself at the disadvantage of groping blindly about me and never touching me, and so has fallen into the most miserable weaknesses and jealousies. Her mind has, at times, been certainly confused besides.[6]

All this is for Mrs. Brown no less than for you. Put a kind construction on it, and hold me in the old place in your regard.

Ever Dear Miss Coutts | Yours faithfully and affectionately
(signed) CHARLES DICKENS

poor, poor mother" (Gladys Storey, *Dickens and Daughter*, p. 24); and—allowing for obvious prejudice against both CD and Georgina—Helen Thomson's indignant defence of Catherine's role, as against Georgina's: with her ten children, "reducing her bodily strength", "was it not natural that she should lean upon the assistance of a sister in the care of her children.... All that Georgina did was to teach the little boys to read and write until they went to school at the age of seven in turn; at that age the girls always had a daily governess ..." (Helen Thomson *to* Mrs Stark, 20 Aug 58: Appx F).

[1] Mary Scott Hogarth (1819–37), who died, aged 17, on 7 May 1837: see Vol. I, p. 65*n*.

[2] Her letter of 15 May 36 to her cousin, Mary Hogarth, certainly does not confirm this (Vol. I, Appx E, p. 689).

[3] Helen and her twin, Edward Hogarth, Catherine's youngest brother.

[4] Anne Cornelius.

[5] See Vol. III, p. 159.

[6] Catherine had suffered a nervous disorder in Mar 51, some months after the birth of her ninth child, sufficiently serious for her to take the water-cure at Malvern: see Vol. VI, p. 309 and *n*. Her illness at Gad's Hill in Summer 1857 may well have been nervous too.

To WILLIAM BOXALL,[1] 10 MAY 1858*

MS Private.

Tavistock House, Monday Tenth May, 1858

My Dear Boxall.

I think that Monday or Tuesday in next week would best suit me, if convenient to you.[2]

Faithfully Yours always
CHARLES DICKENS

To MISS GEORGINA HOGARTH, 10 MAY 1858

MS Dickens House.

Monday Tenth May, 1858[3]

My Dearest Georgy.

Mitchell[4] shall not go down tomorrow. Do you arrange with John to take with you, such plate as you and he may agree to be necessary.

He has brought me the wrong flesh-brush. Will you exchange it for mine—which is much harder.

Have you sent that letter to Forster? If not, send it by John to me.[5]

Best love to the dear girls and to Plornish. | Ever affectionately
CD.

To FRANK STONE, 10 MAY 1858*

MS Benoliel Collection.

OFFICE OF HOUSEHOLD WORDS,
Monday Night Tenth May 1858

My Dear Stone

I am very sorry to say that in the many, many, perplexities of thought that I have been involved in during the last few days, I utterly forgot my engagement to you. I know you will forgive me. I should have forgotten it at no other time than the present.

Ever affectionately
CHARLES DICKENS

[1] William Boxall (1800–79; *DNB*), portrait-painter: see Vols. V, p. 662*n* and VI, p. 249 and *n*.

[2] For the dinner with artist friends mentioned in *To* Morgan, 19–22 May.

[3] CD is at *HW* Office, sending directions to Georgina, who is at Tavistock House and about to leave for Gad's Hill.

[4] The servant mentioned in *To* Wills, 7 Jan 57, *fn*.

[5] This letter does not survive.

To FREDERIC OUVRY, [?10 MAY 1858]

Mention in Ouvry *to* CD, 12 May 58 (MS Messrs Farrer & Co.). *Date:* 10 May, from reference in that letter.

Proposing that Ouvry should seek an amendment of the Act of Parliament incorporating the Guild of Literature and Art to enable the Guild to accept a gift of land from Patrick Allan-Fraser[1] *of Arbroath, Forfarshire.*[2]

To ROBERT CHAMBERS,[3] 11 MAY 1858

Mention in catalogue of Autograph Collection of Ferdinand Julius Dreer, Philadelphia, 1890.

To LADY EASTLAKE, 11 MAY 1858*

MS Private (destroyed in Prestwick air-crash, Dec 1954).

TAVISTOCK HOUSE, | TAVISTOCK SQUARE, LONDON. W.C.
Tuesday Eleventh May 1858

My Dear Lady Eastlake.

I send you a Report of a little speech of mine[4]—in trust for Sir Charles, who asked me for it.

It would give me great pleasure if you could come and hear my "Chimes" on Thursday the 27th. I have an idea it might interest you. I have therefore begged Mr. Arthur Smith, my business-Director, to send you 2 stalls for that night, which I hope you will use.

With kind regard, | Believe me always | Very faithfully Yours

Lady Eastlake. CHARLES DICKENS

[1] Patrick Allan-Fraser (1813–90), born Patrick Allan, son of an Arbroath stocking weaver; successively, house painter and artist; assumed additional name of Fraser 1851, after marrying in 1843 heiress of nearby estate of Hospitalfield. Devoted himself to managing his wife's estate and collecting works of art. Under his Will formed a Trust (1) to maintain Hospitalfield as an Art College for young students, and (2) to assist aged and infirm professional men, including specifically "painters, sculptors or literary men". Only the first provision was carried out. (Information kindly given by Angus District Council).

[2] This would have been contrary to the Act of George II (Geo II 9, Cap. 36), making such gifts of land void, except under stringent conditions. On 23 Apr Ouvry had told CD that there was "no mode of carrying out the effect except by an alteration in the Act of Parliament. It is too late now to apply to Parliament during this Session." He added: "Possibly Mr. Fraser might be induced to modify his liberal offer and give say 40 acres of land, with an endowment of £10,000 cash, as we [*i.e. the Guild*] can take any amount of personal property that may be offered" (MS Messrs Farrer & Co.). On 12 May Ouvry told CD that neither he nor the Town Clerk of Forfar "can stir a finger in the business till next November" (MS *ibid.*). Nothing came of the intended gift.

[3] Robert Chambers (1802–71; *DNB*), publisher, of Edinburgh: see Vol. VII, p. 306 and *n*.

[4] At the Artists' Benevolent Fund on 8 May: see *To* Thiselton, 13 Apr and *fn*.

To P. S. FRASER,[1] 12 MAY 1858

MS National Library of Scotland.

TAVISTOCK HOUSE, | TAVISTOCK SQUARE, LONDON. W.C.
Wednesday Twelfth May, 1858

My Dear Sir

A thousand thanks for the Glorious Whiskey. It arrived in safety. It is housed in a rare cellar, deep in the Kentish Chalk. I have called it Mary Morrison.[2]

Ever Faithfully Yours

P. S. Fraser Esquire CHARLES DICKENS

To FRANK STONE, 12 MAY 1858*

MS Benoliel Collection.

Household Words | Twelfth May 1858 | Wednesday

My Dear Stone

Not having been at home[3] for some days, I did not know that you had written to me there, at the time when I received your very kind note here, this afternoon. I shall be here to night from 8 to ½ past 9. Or tomorrow morning from 10 to 11.

Ever affectionately

CD.

To EDWARD CHAPMAN, 15 MAY 1858

Extract in Samuel T. Freeman & Co. catalogue, Nov 1924; dated Tavistock House, 15 May 58; addressed Edward Chapman.

Pray do not suppose that in speaking of Mr. Arthur Smith on the subject of your kind sale of tickets for my readings, I expressed the least irritation, or the least doubt of your readiness to assist me. Not giving Mitchell[4] credit for the extraordinary power of lying that he seems to possess I asked Mr. Smith to see you, in the course of his transaction of the business of management to ask you if you really did find it inconvenient.

[1] Peter S. Fraser, publisher, bookseller (of Fraser & Co.) and agent for the UK Life Assurance Co., of 45 North Hanover St, Edinburgh; later of 15 Queen St. Wrongly identified as Patrick Fraser, Vol. VI, p. 665 and *n*; though the reference to Forster's naming him as one Edinburgh friend of CD's is correct (*ibid.*).

[2] For "Morison", named after the girl addressed in Burns's poem, "Mary Morison" (1786), with the last four lines of the second stanza in his mind: "Though this was fair, and that was braw, | And yon the toast of a' the town, | I sigh'd, and said amang them a'; | 'Ye are na Mary Morison'."

[3] i.e. Tavistock House.

[4] John Mitchell (1806–74; *DNB*), bookseller, theatrical manager and agent, of 33 Old Bond St: see Vol. IV, p. 344 and *n*, and Vol. VII.

To B. HOMER DIXON,[1] 15 MAY 1858*

MS Dickens House.

TAVISTOCK HOUSE, | TAVISTOCK SQUARE, LONDON. W.C.
Saturday Evening Fifteenth May 1858

Dear Sir

Pray allow me to thank you for your obliging note, and its accompanying book.[2] I am honored by your kind remembrance, and have always a true gratification in being kindly thought of by a traveller from your side of the Atlantic.

Faithfully Yours

B Homer Dixon Esquire CHARLES DICKENS

To CARL WERNER,[3] 15 MAY 1858

MS Private.

TAVISTOCK HOUSE, | TAVISTOCK SQUARE, LONDON. W.C.
Saturday Evening Fifteenth May, 1858

Dear Sir

I beg to acknowledge the receipt of your obliging communication, and to thank you for your courtesy. I hope to have the honor of visiting your atelier and thanking you in person, when I am next in town for a few days together.

Dear Sir | Allow me to remain | with much consideration
Your faithful Servant

Carl Werner Esquire. CHARLES DICKENS

To MRS YATES, 15 MAY 1858

MS Robert H. Taylor Collection, Princeton University.

TAVISTOCK HOUSE, | TAVISTOCK SQUARE, LONDON. W.C.
Saturday Evening Fifteenth May 1858

My Dear Mrs Yates

Pray believe that I was sorry with all my heart to miss you last Thursday,[4] and to learn the occasion of your absence.[5] Also, that whenever you *can* come, your presence will give me a new interest in that evening. No one alive can have more delightful associations with the lightest sound of your voice than I have; and to give

[1] Benjamin Homer Dixon (1819–99), American miscellaneous writer. Published a tract on the Bible, *Golden Moments*, Toronto, 1865; a comedy, *Behind a Mask*, performed 1871; and several family histories, including *The Scotch Border Clan Dickens*, priv. printed, Toronto, 1884.

[2] Perhaps *Surnames*, priv. printed, Boston, 1855, which included material on the Dickens name.

[3] Carl Friedrick Heinrich Werner (1808–94), of Leipzig, landscape and architectural painter and lithographer; exhibited at New Water Colour Society after 1851; travelled and painted throughout Europe; spent Summer 1856 in England. He had perhaps approached CD through Tauchnitz and Charley Dickens's Leipzig teacher.

[4] At his reading of the *Carol*.

[5] Her bad health. For her death, after a long illness, in Sep 1860, see next vol.

you a minute's interest and pleasure, in acknowledgement of the uncountable hours of happiness you gave me when you were a Mysterious Angel to me, would honestly gratify my heart.[1]

Very faithfully | (and gratefully) | Yours

Mrs Yates. CHARLES DICKENS

To MISS BURDETT COUTTS, 19 MAY 1858

MS Dickens House.

Household Words Office | Nineteenth May 1858

My Dear Miss Coutts.

I think I know what you want me for.[2] How I value your friendship, and how I love and honor you, you know in part, though you never can fully know. But nothing on earth—no, not even you—no consideration, human or Divine, can move me from the resolution I have taken.

And one other thing I must ask you to forgive me. If you have seen Mrs. Dickens in company with her wicked mother, I can not enter—no, not even with you—upon any question that was discussed in that woman's presence.[3]

I will come round, almost as soon as your messenger; but I foresee that there is nothing left to us to say.

My Dear Miss Coutts | Ever affectionately | And Faithfully Yours

C D.

To MISS BURDETT COUTTS, 19 MAY 1858*

MS Morgan Library.

OFFICE OF HOUSEHOLD WORDS,
Wednesday Nineteenth May 1858

My Dear Miss Coutts.

It is very, very, kind of you to send the letters, and I return you a thousand thanks. I hope you will think it right to hint to Charley when you see him, that perhaps he might have let the Race[4] pass him at such a time.

Ever Faithfully and affecy.

Miss Burdett Coutts. CHARLES DICKENS

[1] CD had seen her act many times at the Adelphi, managed by her husband 1825–42; she played Nancy in his adaptation of *Oliver Twist*, Feb 1839, and Dolly Varden in his *Barnaby Rudge*, Dec 1841; left the stage 1849, after a final season at the Lyceum.

[2] Catherine had clearly asked Miss Coutts to intervene on her behalf. Miss Coutts must have told her the same day that her attempt had been fruitless, since Catherine wrote to her at once, also on 19 May: "Many many thanks for your true kindness in doing what I asked. | I have now—God help me—only one course to pursue. | One day though not now I may be able to tell you how hardly I have been used. | With sincere love to yourself and dear Mrs Brown" (MS Morgan). Miss Coutts, according to Helen Thomson, even invited Catherine to share her home, "before matters were settled" (Helen Thomson *to* Mrs Stark, 20 Aug 58: Appx F).

[3] CD's fury here shows that the damaging rumours about both Ellen and Georgina, which he attributed to Mrs Hogarth and her daughter Helen, had already begun to circulate: see *To* Thackeray, 22–9 May, *fn*.

[4] The Derby, run that day.

To CAPTAIN E. E. MORGAN, [?20–22 MAY 1858]

Extract in "A Yankee Tar and his Friends", *Scribner's Monthly*, XIV, No. 6, Oct 77, p. 772. *Date:* 1858, according to article; a few days after the dinner on 18 May (see below).

I really cannot tell you how highly and heartily I esteem your friendship. What if I were to come to America and try to tell you myself? More unlikely things have happened since the world began. I have been making an extraordinary sensation in divers places by reading my Christmas books[1] to immense audiences, and sometimes I have thought, dreaming with my eyes open, "Lord! I should not wonder if they would be very glad to hear me in America, after all!" I saw Leslie not long ago looking very well, but, on the whole, exceedingly like Don Quixote, with a grizzled beard. All your other artist friends are flourishing. I dined with a dozen of them last Tuesday,[2] and they all smelt horribly of oil and varnish....

We have as much public humbug here as usual, and I should very much like (in imitation of your Washington legislature).to dodge it with a stoneware spittoon, and dash its brains out.

To C. C. FELTON,[3] 22 MAY 1858

MS Dickens House.

TAVISTOCK HOUSE, | TAVISTOCK SQUARE, LONDON. W.C.
Saturday Twenty Second May, 1858

My Dear Felton.

You may be very sure—and are, I know—that no slight occasion would have prevented my seeing you, during your present short stay in London.[4]

I have been much beset and distressed for some weeks past, by domestic matters. Although they are not finally arranged, they were last night (through Forster's kindness) as good as settled;[5] the end being, that Mrs. Dickens and I have agreed to live apart henceforth.

When you come back to London, you will find Georgina, and my girls, and me, (I hope) quite happy and at home. Not one among us will ever forgive you, if you don't come to us then.

We shall be at my little place in Kent (on the top of Falstaff's Gad's Hill—only an hour and a half from London), and you cannot have a better few days' preparation for the Voyage home, than in that still and beautiful country.

[1] i.e. the *Carol* outside London and other Christmas Books at St Martin's Hall.

[2] The dinner arranged by Boxall: see *To* Boxall, 10 May.

[3] Cornelius Conway Felton (1807–62; *DAB*): see Vol. III, p. 28*n*; and, for his last visit, Vol. VII, p. 77 and *n*.

[4] Felton was visiting Europe for his health and to further his research in Greece.

[5] On 21 May Lemon, acting for Catherine, told Forster, acting for CD, that "Mrs. Dickens thankfully accepts the proposal—as made by you on May 7th." (*The Love Romance of CD*, ed. Walter Dexter, p. 277.) CD's terms then included a maintenance allowance of £400 *p.a.* and a brougham (see *To* Mrs CD, 4 June). Forster clearly felt agreement had been reached and wrote at once to Ouvry: "It is highly necessary that no time whatever should be lost in proceeding to completion." (MS Messrs Farrer & Co.) At this stage no Deed of Separation had been mentioned; and CD refused any further negotiations until Mrs Hogarth and her daughter, Helen, formally repudiated the rumours he attributed to them (*To* Miss Coutts, 19 May and *To* Ouvry, 26 May).

Mind! I count upon your giving notice of your coming, either to Georgina or to me.

I have been shocked and surprised by Forster's telling me that you were one of the sufferers by that unfortunate poisonous accident which attracted much attention here.[1] I heartily hope that you are taking the best conceivable remedy, in change and travel, and that you will go back to your class, a young man—and the old one too, for you will never beat *him*.[2]

Don't be disturbed by the news I give you. It is all for the best. We have tried all other things, and they have all broken down under us.[3]

Ever affectionately

Professor Felton. CHARLES DICKENS

To FRANK STONE, 22 MAY 1858*

MS Benoliel Collection.

TAVISTOCK HOUSE,|TAVISTOCK SQUARE, LONDON. W.C.
Saturday Twenty Second May 1858

My Dear Stone

I am back here again—just come. Can you use the enclosed box for the Covent Garden Opera tonight.[4]

Ever Affectionately
CD.

To WILKIE COLLINS, 25 MAY 1858

MS Morgan Library.

TAVISTOCK HOUSE,|TAVISTOCK SQUARE, LONDON. W.C.
Tuesday Night, Twenty Fifth May 1858

My Dear Wilkie

A thousand thanks for your kind letter: I always feel your friendship very much, and prize it in proportion to the true affection I have for you.

Your letter comes to me only tonight. Can you come round to me in the morning (Wednesday) before 12. I can then tell you all in lieu of writing. It is rather a long story—over, I hope, now.

Ever affectionately
CD.[5]

[1] Felton had suffered severe effects from bad drinking-water at a hotel. Both CD and Forster attributed his death in Feb 1862, aged 54, to them (*To* Forster, 8 Apr 62; N, III, 292).

[2] Heavily underlined.

[3] See *To* Miss Coutts, 9 May and *fn*.

[4] The first night of Meyerbeer's *Les Huguenots*, performed by the Royal Italian Opera, with Mario and Grisi. Covent Garden had just re-opened after the fire of 1856.

[5] A badly ink-spotted, messy letter, showing the strain CD was going through.

To ARTHUR SMITH, 25 MAY 1858

Text from *Mr. & Mrs. CD*, ed. Walter Dexter, 1935, p. 276.

TAVISTOCK HOUSE, | TAVISTOCK SQUARE, LONDON. W.C.
Tuesday, May 25th, 1858.

My Dear Arthur,

You have not only my full permission to show this, but I beg you to show, to any one who wishes to do me right, or to any one who may have been misled into doing me wrong.[1]

Faithfully Yours

Arthur Smith, Esqre. CHARLES DICKENS

To FREDERIC OUVRY, 26 MAY 1858*

MS Messrs Farrer & Co. *Address: Private*: | Frederic Ouvry Esquire | 66 Lincolns Inn Fields.

TAVISTOCK HOUSE, | TAVISTOCK SQUARE, LONDON. W.C.
Wednesday Evening | Twenty Sixth May 1858

My Dear Ouvry

I saw Forster this afternoon, and he told me what you had arranged. In which I fully concur.[2]

It is right—as we agreed—that I should tell you that I received today, at first hand, from a very honorable and intelligent gentleman,[3] information of Mrs. Hogarth's having repeated these smashing slanders to him in a concert Room, *since our negotiations have been pending*.[4] I do not tell you this in any

[1] This note to Smith enclosed what, after its publication in Aug, CD always referred to as the "Violated Letter" (given in Appx F). According to Forster, it was intended "as an authority for correction of false rumours and scandals" and Smith gave "a copy of it, with like intention, to the [*New York*] *Tribune* correspondent in London". For its publication in the *Tribune* "without his sanction" (F, VIII, ii, 648) on 16 Aug 58, as being "in circulation among friends of Mr. and Mrs. Dickens", see *To* Ouvry, 5 Sep and *fnn*. Widely reprinted in both English and American newspapers.

[2] Ouvry and George Frederick Smith (of Smith & Shepherd, 15 Golden Sq, Parliamentary Agents, Catherine's solicitor) had agreed that Catherine's annuity should be £600 p.a. Smith had then drawn up a Deed of Separation and sent it to George Jessel (later, Master of the Rolls), to settle (MS Messrs Farrer & Co., given in Katharine Longley, unpublished transcript).

[3] Arthur Smith, K. J. Fielding suggests in "Dickens and the Hogarth Scandal" (*Nineteenth-Century Fiction*, June 1955, X, 67*n*); likely to have met Mrs Hogarth at a concert (see below), through his working for Chappells. Also possible is Mrs Yates: see *To* Yates, 31 May.

[4] On a demand by Ouvry, G. F. Smith at once obtained from George Hogarth a denial that the Hogarth family had "at any time stated or insinuated that any impropriety of conduct had taken place" between CD and Georgina. "It is of course a matter of grief to us", Hogarth added, that Georgina should remain with his family, "but while we regret what we regard as a mistaken sense of duty we have never for one instant imputed to her any improper motive for so doing" (copy, Messrs Farrer & Co.; given in K. J. Fielding, "Dickens and the Hogarth Scandal", *ibid.*, X, 68). Ouvry replied immediately that he was not satisfied with this: "The slanders in circulation go beyond the specific charge which Mr. Hogarth repudiates, and with reference to the disgusting and horrible nature of that charge, I cannot think it desirable that it should be distinctly written down even for the purpose of denial." He then stated: "Mr Dickens will not sign any deed with these charges hanging over him, and supposed to be sanctioned by some members of his wife's family"

anger, but simply that you may know the stern necessity of being relentless with her.

Pray do me the kindness, expressly to detach Mrs. Dickens from these wrong-doings, *now*. I do not in the least suspect her of them, and I should wish her to know it. She has a great tenderness for me, and I sincerely believe would be glad to shew it. I would not therefore add to her pain by a hair's breadth. It would be a pleasure to her (I think) to know that I had begun to trust her so far; and I believe that it would do her lasting good if you could convey that assurance to her.[1]

Ever Faithfully Yours
Frederic Ouvry Esquire. CHARLES DICKENS

To MRS HOGGE, 28 MAY 1858

MS Walter T. Spencer. *Address:* Mrs Hogge | 16 Hyde Park Gate South | Kensington Gore | W.

TAVISTOCK HOUSE, | TAVISTOCK SQUARE, LONDON. W.C.
Friday Twenty Eighth May, 1858

My Dear Mrs Hogge.

After the profoundest cogitation, I come reluctantly to the conclusion that I do not know that Orphan.[2] If you were the lady in want of him, I should certainly offer myself.[3] But as you are not, I will not hear of the situation.

It is wonderful to think how many charming little people there must be, to whom this proposal would be like a revelation from heaven. Why don't I know one, and come to Kensington, boy in hand, as if I had walked (I wish to God I had) out of a Fairy Tale! But no. I do *not* know that Orphan. He is crying somewhere, by himself, at this moment—I can't dry his eyes. He is being neglected by some Ogress of a nurse—I can't rescue him.

Ever Faithfully Yours
CHARLES DICKENS[4]

(MS *ibid.*). With his letter Ouvry enclosed a statement for Mrs Hogarth and Helen Hogarth to sign, totally clearing CD from the imputations: see *To* Yates, 31 May and *fn*.

[1] Ouvry added to his letter: "You will not understand me as in any way referring to Mrs. Dickens. She does not believe the charges made against her Husband, and has indignantly expressed her disbelief of them" (copy, *ibid.*, given in K. J. Fielding, above, p. 69).

[2] Unexplained, but possibly connected with CD's Life Governorship of the Orphan Working School: see Vol. III, p. 497 and *n*.

[3] Italicised in MDGH, II, 46, followed by N.

[4] For MDGH and N giving text of this letter as first two paragraphs of *To* Mrs Hogge, 14 Apr 58, see 14 Apr, *fn*.

To W. C. MACREADY, 28 MAY 1858*

MS Morgan Library.

TAVISTOCK HOUSE, | TAVISTOCK SQUARE, LONDON. W.C.
Friday Twenty Eighth May, 1858

My Dearest Macready

I am deeply sensible of your affection, and have been strongly moved by your letter.

It is perfectly clear to me that the change had become indispensable and unavoidable, and that we must all be the happier and better for it. I have not the faintest lingering doubt upon the subject.

If I were to write more, I could not help straying into some reference to what is past and gone.[1] And I steadily desire to dismiss it.

With love to your dear sister and all the house,

Ever my Dearest Macready | Your attached and affectionate

W. C. Macready Esquire. CHARLES DICKENS

To MADAME CELESTE, 29 MAY 1858

MS Cornell University Library.

TAVISTOCK HOUSE, | TAVISTOCK SQUARE, LONDON. W.C.
Saturday Twenty Ninth May, 1858.

My Dear Madame Celeste

With the greatest pleasure. If you will have the kindness to send the book[2] here, I will write in it immediately.

Faithfully Yours always
CHARLES DICKENS

To W. P. FRITH, 29 MAY 1858

Text from N, III, 24.

TAVISTOCK HOUSE, | TAVISTOCK SQUARE, LONDON. W.C.
Saturday Twenty-Ninth May 1858

My dear Frith,

Plain Charles Dickens by all means.[3] I shrink with horror from the notion of Esquire. A thousand thanks for your note.

Ever faithfully yours
[CHARLES DICKENS]

[1] Macready had probably recalled 1842, when he and his wife looked after the Dickens children, and his and his family's affection for Catherine.

[2] No doubt her copy of a Christmas Book which she would like inscribed.

[3] Presumably refers to the engraving of one of the pictures that Frith painted for Dickens, probably *Kate Nickleby*. This had been engraved in 1848; but what must have been a similar picture, exhibited RA 1857, was perhaps the one now being engraved.

To RICHARD NELSON LEE,[1] 29 MAY 1858

MS Berg Collection.

TAVISTOCK HOUSE,|TAVISTOCK SQUARE, LONDON. W.C.
Saturday Twenty Ninth May, 1858.

Dear Sir

An unusual addition to the general demands upon my time and attention, has prevented my looking over the Manuscript of your life, until within the last two or three days.

I cannot too highly extol the modesty of its tone, or a certain unobtrusive and becoming manliness which everywhere pervades it. It strongly corroborates all that I ever heard to your advantage, and presents you in a very natural and agreeable aspect.

But I am sorry to add that I do not think its interest is by any means of a character to awaken a response in the general public. It seems to me, to lie purely within the circle of the Theatrical profession, and not even to comprehend the whole of that. I greatly doubt, for this reason, whether any publisher would undertake the risk of it; I should think any publisher mistaken who did; and I am very much mistaken myself, it if would return its expences.[2]

Fiction has done a good deal with wandering lives of all sorts, and with the showman's life among others. Fact has done much too, in the same directions. I fail to see, in your experiences, that variety and oddity of adventure which people attracted by the nature of the subject, would expect to find there. And as to all the Minor-Theatre management, benefit, and play-bill part of the book, I am quite sure that its interest does not pass beyond a mere handful[3] of persons. I remember many instances in which the question has been tried, and I do not know of ONE[4] in which my position has been disproved.

The life of any persevering, industrious, and honorable man, is a lesson. But it is a lesson to be acted—not written. I do not see in your biography sufficient reason for your writing it, except as a subject of just pride and interest to your own family, and perhaps to a portion of your own profession. It is in confounding either or both with the great body of the Public, that I think the root of the mistake of publishing it, would strike.

Faithfully Yours
CHARLES DICKENS

Nelson Lee Esquire

[1] Richard Nelson Lee (1806–72; *DNB*), actor-manager and pantomime-writer; acted at Surrey from 1827; wrote over 200 pantomimes and plays, many for Surrey, then for Frederick Yates and Mathews at the Adelphi, acting in many himself. Joint owner of "Richardson's Show" 1836–53; joint proprietor and manager of Marylebone, Pavilion and other City theatres until 1867. Member of several theatrical benevolent committees supported by CD.

[2] Although referred to several times, Lee's autobiography was never published. A notice in *The Players*, 26 Apr 60, I, 138, states that it would contain "a sketch of his entire life, the ups and downs of forty years, with the whimsicalities of a strolling life"; also mentioned in his obituary in the *Era* (7 Jan 72). But the whereabouts of the MS is unknown. (Information kindly given by Lee's great-grandson, Mr Alan Ruston.)

[3] "handfull" in MS.

[4] Written large.

To FREDERIC OUVRY, 29 MAY 1858*

MS Messrs Farrer & Co.

TAVISTOCK HOUSE, | TAVISTOCK SQUARE, LONDON. W.C.
Saturday Evening Twenty Ninth May 1858

My Dear Ouvry

I cannot possibly assent to Mr. Smith's[1] terms.[2] His proposal to hand you that paper "in exchange for the Deed when completed", has far too much the air of a bargain, and is not the way in which to do a simple act of justice that can be, at the best, but a most imperfect reparation of the great wrong and injury these two people have done.

I must have that paper at once.[3] I must have it in the course of Monday, or not at all. This is my conclusion, and Forster strongly agrees.[4]

Faithfully Yours always
Frederic Ouvry Esquire CHARLES DICKENS

To MISS MARY BOYLE, 29 MAY 1858*

MS Morgan Library.

TAVISTOCK HOUSE, | TAVISTOCK SQUARE, LONDON. W.C.
Saturday Night Twenty Ninth May 1858

My Dear Mary

I myself answer your letter to Georgy, in order that I may have an opportunity of assuring you how deeply sensible I am of the affectionate remembrance in which you always hold me.

My only surprise in the matter of your note, is, that you have heard nothing worse!!! I have been the hero of such bewildering and astonishing Lies during this last week,[5] that this merely Infernal one seems quite a favor.

It is the penalty I pay for my conspicuous position. It is a very heavy one; but it is what I owe to the knaves and the fools, and I must take their receipt for it.

You have seen something of the great misfortune of my life, and you know the

[1] See *To* Ouvry, 26 May, *fn*.

[2] Smith had written to Ouvry that day: "I shall be prepared to hand to you the Papers which you forwarded yesterday—signed by Mrs. Hogarth and her Daughter, in exchange for the Deed when completed" (copy, Messrs Farrer & Co.; given in K. J. Fielding, "Dickens and the Hogarth Scandal", p. 69).

[3] The paper had in fact been signed the day before, though "after considerable discussion" (copy, Messrs Farrer & Co., given in Katharine Longley, unpublished typescript). This makes clear that Mrs Hogarth and her daughter could not have "stood out against" signing it "during a fortnight, costing them many tears and sleepless nights", as stated by Miss Thomson *to* Mrs Stark, [30] Aug 58 (Appx F).

[4] Smith handed over the signed statement to Ouvry at once, "upon his assurance that there was no objection to the Deed as drawn" (Smith and Shepherd's itemized bill, copy, Messrs Farrer & Co.: see K. J. Fielding, above, pp. 66 and 70).

[5] They had clearly crossed the Atlantic: on 3 June 58 Longfellow wrote to Charles Sumner: "What a sad affair is this of Dickens. Immensely exag. no doubt; but sad enough at least. How discouraging it is, and disgusting, to see how eagerly and recklessly a fair reputation is dragged thro' the mire of the streets." (*Letters of H. W. Longfellow*, ed. Andrew Hilen, Harvard, IV [1972], 82.)

truth. Mrs. Dickens and I have agreed to live apart, and we have arranged that Charley shall take care of her, and that Mary shall keep my house; and between me and the children there is in all things absolute accord and confidence; and Mrs. Dickens (really, generously indignant at the baseless scandals she hears, whatever her weakness may once have done circuitously, towards originating them)[1] has hastened to declare in writing that there is no other cause for our separation than our having lived unhappily together for some time, and having agreed to live asunder. Lastly, the friend who represents her,[2] writes for her that she "thankfully and gratefully accepts" the terms of our separation.[3]

Nothing can be done that I know of, but to circulate the Truth. And if you will do that, so far as you can, you will gratify your own earnest and generous nature in serving the friend who loves you.

Ever truly and affectionately
CHARLES DICKENS

To W. M. THACKERAY, [?22–29 MAY 1858]

Mention in Thackeray to James Wilson,[4] ?May 58 (*Letters and Private Papers of W. M. Thackeray*, ed. Gordon N. Ray, IV, 83–4). *Date:* CD's reference to "Lies during this last week" in *To* Miss Boyle, 29 May, must refer to Wilson's letter to Thackeray; CD would have answered Thackeray at once.

Authorizing Thackeray to contradict a rumour[5] on his own solemn word and his wife's authority.

To MRS GORE, 31 MAY 1858*

MS Berg Collection.

TAVISTOCK HOUSE, | TAVISTOCK SQUARE, LONDON. W.C.
Monday Thirty First May 1858

My Dear Mrs. Gore.

Do not for an instant suppose that I could take your kind letter otherwise than cordially and gratefully; or that I could possibly reconcile it to my heart, to leave it unanswered.

I have heard such thronging multitudes of wonderful and inexplicable lies about

[1] Presumably her seeking sympathy from her mother.

[2] Mark Lemon.

[3] For the terms of the Deed of Separation, see *To* Mrs CD, 4 June, *fn* (the day on which she signed it).

[4] Thackeray's neighbour at 19 Onslow Sq.

[5] A "common report derogatory to the honor of a young lady whose name has been mentioned in connection with his" (Thackeray *to* Wilson, above). In a letter to his mother Thackeray wrote: "Last week going into the Garrick I heard that D is separated from his wife on account of an intrigue with his sister in law. No says I no such thing—its with an actress—and the other story has not got to Dickens's ears but this has—and he fancies that I am going about abusing him. We shall never be allowed to be friends that's clear" (*Letters and Private Papers of W. M. Thackeray*, ed. G. N. Ray, IV, 86; dated late May by Ray; but since Thackeray must refer to CD's "Personal" statement, first published in *The Times*, 7 June, early June seems certain).

myself during the last week, that it almost bewilders me to find you in possession of the truth.

—Except that you are not to suppose that the children are to be "divided". Charley takes care of his mother at my express request, and all the rest remain with me: my eldest daughter keeping my house. Charley undertakes his part of the arrangement as an act of duty, and on the express stipulation that there is to be nothing in the nature of a parting between him and us.[1]

Believe me, I had already so strongly felt what you say as to long absences and so forth, that I had myself most strenuously proposed it and stood out upon it. That I did so, unsuccessfully, I really believe to be in the nature of the case itself, and not the fault of Mrs. Dickens.

Our separation is the natural end of a course of years. I have felt the force of our example, and have, for a long time urged it and sacrificed to it. But it would be a poor example to be driven mad myself, or to drive Mrs. Dickens mad; and one or both of the two results must have happened, if we had gone on living together.

There is no anger or ill-will between us. I believe, not the slightest. Our elder children are at least as sensible that the thing *must be*, as we are. Between them and myself, there is a confidence as absolute and perfect as if we were of one age. Mrs. Dickens's sister (who has devoted her whole youth to them, and brought them up from their cradles), and an attached woman-servant, always in Mrs. Dickens's confidence, who has also lived with us for sixteen years, both know perfectly well that they have long exerted themselves to prevent our going apart, but that it has become inevitable.

I do not doubt that we shall all be much the better for it. I only want to impress upon you that it is calmly and moderately done; that whatever doubt or passion there has ever been on either side, has already died out; that I am sure we only want to forgive and forget, and live at peace; that it was an unhappy day for both, when two such strongly contrasted people came together, but that we quietly accept all that, and do not blame the day, and only seek to make the best of it.

What I tell you, is quite at your disposal to tell again, when and where you will.

Ever My Dear Mrs. Gore | Your faithful

CHARLES DICKENS

To JOHN LEECH, 31 MAY 1858

MS Benoliel Collection.

TAVISTOCK HOUSE, | TAVISTOCK SQUARE, LONDON. W.C.
Monday Thirty First May 1858

My Dear Leech.

In making the domestic change which we all here know (I believe, equally) to have become unavoidable, and to be for the good of all, and which is made without anger or ill will, I expect, of course, the misconstruction of the knaves and fools. I should be but a poor writer, if I did not know the penalty I owe to *them*, and for which I must take their receipt.

[1] See next and *fn*.

But you have been my friend, and know my nature. And when you misrepresent me, however unconsciously—as when you tell Luard it is a point in the case, that Charley sides with his mother—you strike me in a tender place, and wound me deeply.

Between the children and me, there is absolute confidence and accord throughout. Charley's living with his mother to take care of her, is *my* idea—not his. I beg you to read the copy of a note from him which I send you on the other side,[1] and to do me justice.

He wrote it soon after he had seen me at the office one morning; where I had asked him if he thought he could decide to live with his mother. That is what he refers to, when he says, "What you told me this morning."

Faithfully Yours

CD

To J. PALGRAVE SIMPSON,[2] 31 MAY 1858*

MS Dickens House.

TAVISTOCK HOUSE, | TAVISTOCK SQUARE, LONDON. W.C.

Monday Thirty First May 1858

My Dear Simpson.

To my horror, I discover this morning by chance, that I have omitted to return you the enclosed wonderful document.[3] This sheet of paper will arrive red;—it was blue when I began to blush upon it.[4]

Ever Yours

J. Palgrave Simpson Esquire. CHARLES DICKENS

[1] Charley's note, prefaced by *Copy* (doubly underlined) in CD's hand, reads: "City May 10, 1858 | My Dear Father | What you told me this morning so completely took me by surprise, that I am afraid I did not completely make myself understood to you, and I think I can write you better what I mean than say it to you | Don't suppose that in making my choice I was actuated by any feeling of preference for my mother to you. God knows I love you dearly, and it will be a hard day for me when I have to part from you and the girls. | But in doing as I have done, I hope I am doing my duty, and that you will understand it so. | I remain my dear father | Ever Your affectionate Son" (MS FLP). This makes it clear that, despite CD's letter, it was Charley's own decision to live with his mother.

[2] John Palgrave Simpson (1807–87; *DNB*), dramatist and novelist. After Cambridge (MA, Corpus Christi College, 1832), travelled in Europe. In Paris during the 1848 Revolution; collected his reports of it as *Pictures from Revolutionary Paris*, 2 vols, 1849. Settled in London 1850. Published four novels and had *c.* 60 plays performed, many very popular. Like CD, a member of both the Garrick Club (since 1851), and the Athenaeum.

[3] Perhaps connected with an Athenaeum election.

[4] An old joke of CD's.

To HERBERT WATKINS, 31 MAY 1858*

MS Free Library of Philadelphia. *Address:* Herbert Watkins Esquire | Photographer | 179[1] Regent Street | W.

TAVISTOCK HOUSE, | TAVISTOCK SQUARE, LONDON. W.C.
Monday Thirty First May, 1858

Dear Sir

I wish, without any regard to cost, to get the best photograph of myself that can be produced, to send to a friend in Italy.[2] As I wish it to be tolerably easy to carry about in some elegant little case, I presume it should be a head merely.[3]

If you will have the kindness to undertake this little commission, I shall have perfect confidence in the result.

May I ask you to be so good as to favor me with an appointment, either for Wednesday Afternoon after 2, or for any time next Saturday or the following Monday, after 10 in the morning.

Dear Sir | Your faithful Servant

Herbert Watkins Esquire CHARLES DICKENS

To EDMUND YATES, 31 MAY 1858

MS Robert H. Taylor Collection, Princeton University.

TAVISTOCK HOUSE, | TAVISTOCK SQUARE, LONDON. W.C.
Monday Evening Thirty First May, 1858

My Dear Edmund

You will readily believe that I shall never make an ungenerous use of the paper of which I send you a copy on the other side,[4] though I believe that nothing will ever reconcile me to the two who have signed it. But, as I know Mrs Yates's ears to have been abused, I think it simply just that she should see it. If you think so too (but not otherwise), shew it to her with my kind regard.

Ever Faithfully

Edmund Yates Esquire. CHARLES DICKENS

[1] "179" crossed through, "215" written beside it in unknown hand.

[2] Emile de la Rue.

[3] See *To* Watkins, 17 July, *fn*; published in the *Critic*, 4 Sep 58, facing Hollingshead's article on the readings (see *To* Hollingshead, 6 Sep 58, *fn*) and described there as "exquisite . . . one of the happiest specimens of even that excellent photographer". It became one of CD's best-known photographs, later a *carte*. On 31 Dec 58 the *Publishers' Circular* reported that it had been mistaken by the Paris police for a caricature of Napoleon III and removed by them from the shop where it was exhibited; the *Critic*, 24 Dec, commented on the original report: "A caricature of the Emperor! What nauseous flattery! What similitude can be said to exist between that cold, sinister face, so deeply seamed with care and crime, and a face that never beamed with anything but genius and good to mankind?" Their beards were no doubt the supposed likeness.

[4] See Appx F for the statement signed by Mrs Hogarth and her daughter Helen on 29 May.

To JOHN HOLLINGSHEAD, 2 JUNE 1858

Extract in James Cummins catalogue No. 32 (1991), *MS* 1 p.; dated Tavistock House, London, 2 June 58; addressed John Hollingshead.

I want to speak to you, if you will give me the opportunity, on two little matters of business which I hope may prove both agreeable and useful to you.[1] Could you call on me tomorrow morning? I shall certainly be at home here from 10 to 11.

To FREDERIC OUVRY, 2 JUNE 1858*

MS Huntington Library.

TAVISTOCK HOUSE,|TAVISTOCK SQUARE, LONDON. W.C.
Wednesday Second June 1858

My Dear Ouvry

I have arranged to see Forster in Whitehall Place,[2] this afternoon at 4. It is perfectly clear to me that his American idea[3] is altogether untenable. Surely on your knowledge of human nature (to say nothing of the peculiarity of the American character, though that is highly important to consider too), you cannot think it feasible that I should write to any distinguished man in America, asking him to do for me, *what I have not done for myself here*! It is absurd. And it is just because no public step can possibly be taken for my good, anywhere, until I have taken one here, that I feel I *must* move—somehow.[4]

Faithfully Always
CD.

Frederic Ouvry Esquire

To FREDERIC OUVRY, 3 JUNE 1858*

MS Huntington Library.

TAVISTOCK HOUSE,|TAVISTOCK SQUARE, LONDON. W.C.
Thursday Third June 1858

My Dear Ouvry

Forster writes me this morning, that our meeting at Whitehall Place is to be at 2—*not* 4—as he had forgotten an engagement.

Faithfully Yours
CHARLES DICKENS

Frederic Ouvry Esquire

[1] No doubt to discuss the scale of payment and permission to collect his contributions. Before 2 June Hollingshead had already had 26 articles published in *HW*; 23 more appeared by the end of the year.

[2] No. 19, the office of the Commissioners in Lunacy, of which Forster was Secretary.

[3] Perhaps to ask some prominent American to deny on his behalf any rumours that had reached the US.

[4] To justify the separation, as he attempted to do in the "Personal" statement (*The Times*, 7 June, followed by other newspapers; *HW*, on 12 June, i.e. 9 June, given in Appx F). Besides being designed to scotch the widespread rumours, involving both Georgina and Ellen, it was clearly intended to protect CD's new career as a public reader. Both Ouvry and Forster had advised strongly against its publication (originally by his solicitors: MS Messrs Farrer & Co., given in Katharine Longley, unpublished typescript); but for CD's following his friend Delane's advice to publish, see *To* Macready, 7 June.

To MISS BURDETT COUTTS, 4 JUNE 1858*

MS Morgan Library.

TAVISTOCK HOUSE,|TAVISTOCK SQUARE, LONDON. W.C.
Friday Fourth June 1858.

My Dear Miss Coutts.

Rather a ridiculous thing has occurred, in reference to the enclosed letter of introduction.[1] The lady—distinguished, in her way—has three times sent it to you, and three times had it returned. At last, in terror, affliction, and despair, she has brought it here.[2]

I sincerely hope Mrs. Brown is better. I send her my love, and hope to be able to come and enquire for her tomorrow.

Ever affecy. and faithfully
CD.

To MRS CHARLES DICKENS, 4 JUNE 1858

MS British Library.

TAVISTOCK HOUSE,|TAVISTOCK SQUARE, LONDON. W.C.
Friday Fourth June 1858

Dear Catherine.

I will not write a word as to any *causes* that have made it necessary for me to publish the enclosed in Household Words.[3] Whoever there may be among the living, whom I will never forgive alive or dead, I earnestly hope that all unkindness is over between you and me.[4]

[1] Hans Andersen's letter to Miss Coutts, of 21 Apr 58, introducing the well-known Danish painter, Elizabeth Jerichau-Baumann. He had written to her: "Much honoured Miss Coutts. ... How often do I think with gratitude on these beauteous hours I had the happiness to spend at Your house in London. | The bearer of this letter, Mrs. Jerichau-Baumann, is a distinguished painter, of great talent ... a lady of great mind and pious heart! It was her wish to get a few words from me to You; she is particularly recommended to Her Majesty Queen Victoria by the danish Queen dowager ..." (MS Morgan).

[2] Andersen had sent a letter of introduction to CD too. On 12 June 62 he wrote to Mrs Jerichau, about to travel to London again: "You were the first and only person with a letter from me who was received warmly by the [*Dickens*] family. None to whom I later gave a letter has spoken to him, and therefore I shall not do it any more" (given in Elias Bredsdorff, *Hans Andersen and Charles Dickens*, p. 129). See *To* Andersen, 2 Sep 57, *fn*.

[3] It appeared on 12 June (9 June), XVII, 601: see Appx F.

[4] The terms of the Deed of Separation had now been agreed. Catherine was to receive the generous allowance of £600 *p.a.* and moved to 70 Gloucester Terrace, Regent's Park, where she lived until her death in 1879; Charley (by his own choice: see *To* Leech, 31 May, *fn*) was to live with her; the other children, still at home, with CD; Catherine was to have free access to them: see *To* Charley Dickens, 10–12 July. Catherine signed the Deed at Brighton, where her mother had taken her, on 4 June; CD, after an unexplained delay, on 10 June; and Catherine's two Trustees, Lemon and F. M. Evans, on 12 June. For Catherine's belief that CD had "expressed a wish that we should meet in society, and be at least on friendly terms", see Helen Thomson to Mrs Stark (Appx F).

But as you are referred to in the article, I think you ought to see it. You have only to say to Wills (who kindly brings it to you),[1] that you do not object to the allusion.[2]

CHARLES DICKENS

To RICHARD NELSON LEE, 4 JUNE 1858

MS University of Texas.

TAVISTOCK HOUSE, | TAVISTOCK SQUARE, LONDON. W.C.
Friday Fourth June 1858.

Dear Sir

In case I should not be at home when you call for your Manuscript,[3] I write these few words to be left out with it.

Pray do not suppose that I arrogate any thing like infallibility in behalf of my opinion. It is merely a sincere one. It may be wrong.

Faithfully Yours

Nelson Lee Esquire CHARLES DICKENS

To W. C. MACREADY, 7 JUNE 1858*

MS Morgan Library.

TAVISTOCK HOUSE, | TAVISTOCK SQUARE, LONDON. W.C.
Monday Morning Seventh June 1858

My Dearest Macready.

You will see that some printed words of mine were laid on the breakfast-table this morning in the Times,[4] along with the affectionate words of your kindest of notes.

The question was not I myself; but others. Foremost among them—of all people in the world—Georgina! Mrs. Dickens's weakness, and her mother's and her youngest sister's wickedness, drifted to that, without seeing what they would strike against—though I warned them in the strongest manner.[5]

Forster advised with Delane for an hour and a half on Saturday. And Delane on

[1] Wills must have gone to Brighton and back that day, since the decision to publish the "Personal" statement was made the next day, Sat 5 June.

[2] Catherine, in Brighton, raised no objection; but, after giving Wills, who had brought the statement, her consent, sent it to her solicitor, G. F. Smith. He attempted, on 6 June, to have its publication postponed, obviously since neither CD nor Catherine's Trustees had yet signed the Deed of Separation; but unsuccessfully, since it appeared in *The Times* the following morning (MS Messrs Farrer & Co. given in Katharine Longley, unpublished typescript).

[3] See *To* Lee, 29 May.

[4] CD's "Personal" statement: see Appx F.

[5] According to Helen Thomson, the Deed of Separation was finally agreed upon as "a compromise, to avoid a public court" (see Helen Thomson *to* Mrs Stark, [30] Aug 58: Appx F). By threatening an action in the new Matrimonial Court for Judicial Separation, set up under the Matrimonial Causes Act, 1857, the Hogarths had been in danger of unwittingly implicating Georgina, whose name rumours had already coupled with CD's.

the whole decided *in favor of the publication.*[1] This turned the balance,—as we had settled that it should, either way.[2]

In great haste (for I am going to Gad's Hill with Mary, on household matters), and with love to all,

Ever affectionately
CD.

To F. M. EVANS, 8 JUNE 1858

MS Free Library of Philadelphia.

TAVISTOCK HOUSE, | TAVISTOCK SQUARE, LONDON. W.C.
Tuesday Morning Eighth June 1858

My Dear Evans.

Since you forwarded to me the enclosed letter from Mr Joyce,[3] I have investigated its subject[4] thoroughly—have recurred to it at intervals, again and again—and have taken time and pains to arrive at the truth.

My information in the first instance was positive, direct and plain. It was given me, with a full knowledge that I should consider it necessary to act upon it.

But I am bound to say that it does *not* retain its direct and positive character, on being examined and re-examined. And setting (as I feel bound to do), Mr Joyce's direct denial against it, and giving that denial the full weight that it is incumbent on me to attach to the word of a man whose truthfulness I have no right or reason to doubt, I must not hesitate to acquit Mr Joyce of the offence I imputed to him. I

[1] Forster recorded: "All he would concede to my strenuous resistance against such a publication was an offer to suppress it, if, upon reference to the opinion of a certain distinguished man (still living) [*i.e. Delane*], that opinion should prove to be in agreement with mine" (F, VIII, ii, 647–8). In the 1st edn Forster has a marginal note, "Unwise printed statement" (F, 1872–4, III, vii, 175).

[2] Most of the literary world was shocked by the "Personal" statement. In an undated letter to his mother, (also quoted in *To* Thackeray, 22–29 May, *fn*), Thackeray wrote: "Well what to say? Here is sad news in the literary world—no less than a separation between Mr & Mrs Dickens—with all sorts of horrible stories buzzing about.... There is some row about an actress in the case, and he denies with the utmost infuriation any charge against her or himself—but says that it has been known to any one intimate with his family that his and his wife's tempers were horribly incompatible.... To think of the poor matron after 22 years of marriage going away out of the house! O dear me its a fatal story for our trade." On 12 June the *Illustrated London News* recorded: "A great author has this week thought it necessary to appeal in print to his fellow-authors against certain scandals—stupid, foul, and lying enough—which nobody of name believed for a single moment. An appeal from such a quarter should not be made in vain; we therefore (unnecessarily) acknowledge this appeal, and, knowing his noble nature—knowing the facts (better still)—appeal to him in print to forget the follies of malice and envy, and rely as before on the well-assured affection of his many friends, who know how incapable his nature is of aught that is mean—of aught that is contrary to truth and to his own writings. And the public (the world) is of our opinion" (probably written by the editor, Herbert Ingram). G. H. Lewes, in Munich with "George Eliot" and the eminent German chemist, Baron Liebig (see Vol. VI, p. 471 and *n*), "spoke sorrowfully of Dickens's public separation from his wife, which is making a scandal here as well as in England" (Lewes's Journal, MS Yale, 14 June 58; given in Rosemary Ashton, *G. H. Lewes: A Life*, Oxford, 1991, p. 191).

[3] Felix Joyce (*d.* 1865), Bradbury & Evans's accountant: see Vols IV, p. 506 and *n*, and VI, pp. 740–1 and *n*.

[4] Untraced.

therefore do so, freely, and I must beg to express my regret to him, through you, for having, most unintentionally and innocently, done him wrong.

Faithfully Yours Ever

F. M. Evans Esquire. CHARLES DICKENS

To MR AND MRS G. B. GREGORY,[1] 8 JUNE 1858*

MS (in Mrs CD's hand)[2] Thomas Coram Foundation for Children.

Tavistock House | June 8th. | 58.

Mr. and Mrs. Charles Dickens regret extremely that, as they will be out of town on Sunday the 13th. next, they cannot have the pleasure of accepting Mr. and Mrs. Gregory's kind invitation to Luncheon on that morning.

To W. BLANCHARD JERROLD, [8 JUNE 1858]

Mention in *To* Knight, 11 June. *Date:* CD would have answered Jerrold's letter to him of 7 June at once.

To EDMUND YATES, 8 JUNE 1858

MS Robert H. Taylor Collection, Princeton University.

TAVISTOCK HOUSE, | TAVISTOCK SQUARE, LONDON. W.C.
Tuesday Eighth June 1858

My Dear Edmund

Of course I can have nothing to say to this,[3] but that I deeply feel it. If you could know how much I have felt within this last month, and what a sense of Wrong has been upon me, and what a strain and struggle I have lived under, you would see that my heart is so jagged and rent and out of shape, that it does not this day leave me hand enough to shape these words.[4]

Ever Faithfully
CD.

To [?FREDERIC OUVRY],[5] [?9 JUNE 1858]

Mention in MS Farrer & Co. Papers. *Date:* probably about a week before 16 June, when John Burrell stated that he had settled the draft of CD's Will.

Asking Farrer, Ouvry to revise and condense the draft Will[6] they had drawn up for him.

[1] George Burrow Gregory, Treasurer of the Foundling Hospital, Guilford St, and his wife.

[2] The reply was Catherine's responsibility and should have been sent earlier.

[3] Presumably a letter sympathizing with CD, perhaps from Yates's friend, Robert Brough (see 10 June and *fn*).

[4] In the penultimate line of letter he first wrote "too", then substituted "so". The writing of his initials shows signs of stress.

[5] Almost certainly to Ouvry, who dealt with most of CD's personal affairs.

[6] This was drawn up from CD's own "Memoranda for the Draft" (Appx G), instructing Farrer, Ouvry to make Georgina Hogarth, Forster and Wills Trustees and

To ROBERT BROUGH,[1] 10 JUNE 1858*

MS Mitchell Library, Sydney.

TAVISTOCK HOUSE,|TAVISTOCK SQUARE, LONDON. W.C.
Thursday Tenth June 1858.

My Dear Sir

I assure you I have been deeply affected by your letter. Few things could have been more welcome to me, and I thank you for it heartily.

As to the policy of *my* publishing the poem at present, after having spoken for myself, I have a great doubt. With your leave I will think of it. But in any case I will retain it for its own sake, with great pleasure, and will gladly avail myself of it as a literary composition of unusual merit, when the immediate occasion of it shall be less apparent.[2]

Again I thank you, out of the depths of my heart.

Very faithfully Yours
CHARLES DICKENS

Robert B Brough Esquire

To LEIGH HUNT, 11 JUNE 1858

MS Iowa University Library.

TAVISTOCK HOUSE,|TAVISTOCK SQUARE, LONDON. W.C.
Friday Eleventh June 1858.

My Dear Hunt

Your letter has moved me very much. I heartily thank you for it. It is worth suffering something, to be so remembered.

God bless you.

Ever affectionately Yours
CD.

Executors. The draft Will expanded CD's "Memoranda" from two quarto pages to 17 pages of foolscap; at CD's request, this was drastically shortened by Burrell and a fair copy made on 19 June (MSS Messrs Farrer & Co.). See next vol.

[1] Robert Barnabas Brough (1828–60; *DNB*), miscellaneous writer: see Vol. VII, p. 680*n*. Was still contributing to many periodicals and helped to launch the *Train* (1856–8): see *To* Yates, 2 Jan 56, *fn*. His novel, *Marston Lynch*, serialized there, was published as a "yellowback" after his early death, with a sympathetic memoir by Sala, who knew him well; sub-titled "a personal biography", it records much of his own life and those of his Bohemian associates.

[2] Brough's poem, "The Last Devil's Walk" (based on Coleridge's "The Devil's Thoughts"), was published in *HW* on 17 July (XVIII, 109); the last of his eight contributions. The last four lines identify this Devil as "Calumny".

To CHARLES KNIGHT, 11 JUNE 1858

Extract in Sotheby's catalogue, July 1983; *MS* 1 p.; dated Tavistock House, 11 June 58; addressed Charles Knight.

He is touched by Knight's letter. On the anniversary of Jerrold's death he had an excellent letter from his eldest son. I immediately replied to it, and gave him my hand across his father's grave.

To SIR EDWARD BULWER LYTTON, 11 JUNE 1858

Extract in Sotheby's catalogue, Feb 1973; *MS* (3rd person) ½ p.; dated Tavistock House, 11 June 58.

Regretting that his absence from town[1] *on 26 June will prevent him from having the honour of dining with Sir Edward Bulwer Lytton.*[2]

To J. E. McINTYRE,[3] 11 JUNE 1858

Mention in N, III, 27.

To T. J. THOMPSON, 11 JUNE 1858

MS Mrs Sowerby.

TAVISTOCK HOUSE,|TAVISTOCK SQUARE, LONDON. W.C.
Friday Eleventh June 1858

My Dear Thompson

I cannot leave your letter unanswered. For I know it comes out of your heart, as I know it has gone straight to mine.

Upon my soul I don't know—and I never have known—what has been amiss between us![4] But I shall be heartily glad to be on the old cordial terms, if you and Christiana[5] will give us the opportunity.[6]

On the first of August I am going away on a long series of Readings. But we shall be at Gad's Hill (I have a house there, two miles and a half this side of Rochester) all through July; and if you would both come and see us for a day or two, you would find that a certain sugar-basin[7] has never been off the table.

I don't know where to address you, so I sent this to Mitton to direct and post.

[1] i.e. at Gad's Hill.

[2] It seems impossible that CD should address an old friend so formally.

[3] Possibly James McIntyre, of Simms & McIntyre, booksellers and publishers of Belfast and also 13 Paternoster Row.

[4] See below.

[5] Née Christiana Jane Weller (1825–1910): see Vol. III, p. 446*n*; married 1845. For CD's criticism of her in Aug 46, see Vol. IV, pp. 604 and 615. He had not seen the Thompsons since visiting them in Italy in Oct 53 (Vol. VII, p. 178).

[6] Clearly as the result of this letter, Thompson and Christiana spent 29–31 July at Gad's Hill.

[7] Obviously a gift from the Thompsons.

It has grieved me to hear of your domestic distress.[1] In the hope that it is mended or has passed, and that our inexplicability has passed too, I am ever

Very faithfully Yours

T. J. Thompson Esquire. CHARLES DICKENS

To [?DANIEL MACLISE],[2] [?11 JUNE 1858]

MS (fragment) Berg Collection. *Date:* 11 June, the day after the reading.

We had an amazing scene of weeping and cheering, at St. Martin's Hall, last night. I read the Life and Death of Little Dombey; and certainly I never saw a crowd so resolved into one creature before, or so stirred by any thing.[3]

I tell you this, my dear fellow, because I know you will read it with interest. Mary (now my housekeeper) Katie, and Georgina, send their kindest and best love. I cordially embrace you. You may be sure that I shall always deserve your steady confidence, and always be your affectionate and attached friend.

CHARLES DICKENS

To THE SECRETARY OF THE PLAYGROUND SOCIETY,[4] [?11 JUNE 1858]

Mention in *To* Reed, 12 June 58. *Date:* probably written the day before that letter.

Returning the shorthand transcription of his speech at the Society's dinner on 1 June.[5]

To HENRY AUSTIN, 12 JUNE 1858*

MS Morgan Library.

TAVISTOCK HOUSE, | TAVISTOCK SQUARE, LONDON. W.C.
Saturday Twelfth June 1858

My Dear Henry

All right. We don't go down[6] till Friday.

[1] His son Mel's mental illness had reached a crisis. On 9 June Christiana recorded in her diary: "Poor dear Tom returned about 10—in a heart broken state about poor Mel who is out of his mind and worse has happened—alas! a fearful thing—staid awake with Tom all night poor creature." On 14 June: "Tom off to London & saw C. Dickens about Mel he returned at Eve." On 15 June Thompson made arrangements for Mel to go into a private asylum at Alton, Hampshire; but on the 18th: "Bad news of poor Mel who has been removed to Southampton" (MS Mrs Sowerby).

[2] Substance and tone of letter make him a probable recipient.

[3] The first *Dombey* reading and not part of the original plan (see *To* Forster, 30 Mar and *n*). The *Globe*, 11 June, recorded: "the interest of the story was immensely increased by the admirable reading of Mr. Dickens".

[4] Edward West (office at 17 Bull and Mouth St, St Martin's le Grand). Its object was "to provide playgrounds for poor children in populous places": see Morley's "A Plea for Playgrounds" (*HW*, 30 Jan 58, XVII, 160).

[5] *Speeches*, ed. K. J. Fielding, pp. 270–5.

[6] To Gad's Hill.

It certainly was a prodigious success. It frightened Arthur Smith. The people cried so, going out, that he thought "it wouldn't do" to put it up again![1]

Love to Lætitia. | Ever Affectionately

CD.

To G. L. CHESTERTON,[2] 12 JUNE 1858*

MS Somerville College, Oxford.

TAVISTOCK HOUSE, | TAVISTOCK SQUARE, LONDON. W.C.

Saturday Twelfth June 1858.

My Dear Chesterton.

An unusual combination of occupations, has prevented my writing you an earlier acknowledgement of the receipt of Miss Edwards's[3] book.[4]

Pray thank that lady in my name, and tell her that Hand and Glove and I are presently going down together into Kent, there to become closely acquainted under the shadow of a great Oak Tree.

Faithfully Yours always

G. L. Chesterton Esquire. CHARLES DICKENS

To C. W. CROCKER,[5] 12 JUNE 1858*

MS Private.

TAVISTOCK HOUSE, | TAVISTOCK SQUARE, LONDON. W.C.

Saturday Twelfth June 1858

Sir.

Allow me to assure you that I have read the article[6] you have had the kindness to send me, with very great pleasure; and that I have deeply felt its earnestness and sincerity of purpose.

Faithfully Yours

C. W. Crocker Esquire CHARLES DICKENS

[1] *Little Dombey*: see *To* Maclise, 11 June and *fn*.

[2] George Laval Chesterton (*d*. 1868), former Governor of the Middlesex House of Correction; a Governor of the Home: see Vol. I, p. 101*n* and later vols.

[3] Amelia Ann Blandford Edwards (1831–92; *DNB*), novelist, miscellaneous writer and Egyptologist. Contributed to periodicals, including one story to *HW* ("The Patagonian Brothers", 23 Jan 58, XVII, 126) and to the *AYR* 1861 and 1866 Christmas Nos. Published eight novels, children's books, travel books and verse. Her novel *Half a Million of Money* was serialized in *AYR*, 1865. From 1874 devoted her life largely to Egyptology.

[4] Her most recent novel, *Hand and Glove*, published in one vol., early May 58.

[5] Charles Crocker (1797–1861), of Chichester, shoemaker (1809–39) and poet; employed by W. H. Mason, Chichester publishers, 1839–45; sexton, Chichester Cathedral 1845–61; author of *The Vale of Obscurity . . . and Other Poems*, priv. printed, 1830; his *Poetical Works* published, Chichester 1860; also published *A Visit to Chichester*, 1860.

[6] Untraced.

To THOMAS A. REED,[1] 12 JUNE 1858

Facsimile in *Fac-Simile Reporting Notes*, I, 11 (Jan 88).

TAVISTOCK HOUSE, | TAVISTOCK SQUARE, LONDON. W.C.
Saturday Twelfth June 1858.

Sir.

Many occupations have combined to prevent my looking over your notes of my observations at the dinner of the Playground Society[2] until to day. I have now returned them to the Secretary, with an expression of my high satisfaction with their great and rare accuracy.[3] Allow me to convey the same assurance to yourself.

Faithfully Yours

Thomas A Reed Esquire CHARLES DICKENS

To DAVID ROBERTS, 12 JUNE 1858*

MS Dr L. Warnock. *Address:* David Roberts Esquire R.A. | 7 Fitzroy Street | Fitzroy Square | W.

TAVISTOCK HOUSE, | TAVISTOCK SQUARE, LONDON. W.C.
Saturday Twelfth June 1858

My Dear David Roberts.

I cordially thank you for your friendly and loving words. I did not need them, to assure me of your worth—for I have known *that*, a long long time. But they are most heartily welcome to me, and they touch me home.

Believe me, I shall never regard our friendship as a common one, and that I shall ever be while I live,

Yours affectionately and truly

David Roberts Esquire CHARLES DICKENS

To A. U. THISELTON, 12 JUNE 1858

Text from copy in Minute Book, Artists' Benevolent Fund.

TAVISTOCK HOUSE, | TAVISTOCK SQUARE, LONDON. W.C.
Saturday Twelfth June 1858

Sir,

I beg to acknowledge the receipt of the flattering resolution of which the Committee of the Artists' Benevolent Fund have made me the Subject, and to assure

[1] Thomas Allen Reed (1826–99), shorthand-writer and teacher of shorthand, of Reed, Robeson & Woodward, of 6 Southampton Buildings, Chancery Lane and 41 Chancery Lane. Founded the Metropolitan Reporting Agency 1849; edited the *Phonographic Reporter* 1848–80. Author of *The Reporters' Reading Book*, 1851, and other books on shorthand.

[2] See 11 June.

[3] CD had earlier praised Reed—probably without knowing his identity—for his reporting of his speech at the Dinner for the Hospital for Sick Children: see *To* Bathurst, 21 Feb and *fn*.

those gentlemen, that I am heartily and unaffectedly glad to have rendered them the least Service.[1]

Your faithful Servant
CHARLES DICKENS

To THE REV. EDWARD TAGART, 14 JUNE 1858

MS Dickens House.

TAVISTOCK HOUSE, | TAVISTOCK SQUARE, LONDON. W.C.
Monday Fourteenth June 1858

My Dear Mr. Tagart.

I have had the greatest pleasure in the receipt of your kind and affectionate note. The only drawback is, that I was at home when you brought it, and should have been delighted to have seen you.

Though I have unquestionably suffered deeply from being lied about with a most wonderful recklessness, I am not so weak or so wrong-headed as to be in the least changed by it. I know the world to have just as much good in it as it had before; and no one has better reason to thank God for the friendship it contains, than I have.

So I hope to regain my composure in a steady manner, and to live to be good and true to any innocent people who have been traduced along with me. For the rest, I am already thoroughly sure that the change which has been made at home, is a beneficial one for us all.

With kindest regard from all here to yourself, Mrs. Tagart, and all your house,

Believe me ever | Affectionately Yours
The Rev. Edward Tagart. CHARLES DICKENS

To THOMAS MITTON, 15 JUNE 1858

MS Huntington Library.

TAVISTOCK HOUSE, | TAVISTOCK SQUARE, LONDON. W.C.
Tuesday Fifteenth June 1858

My Dear Mitton

I cannot answer for my being free, next Saturday. I have so much to attend to just now, and am so liable to be troubled by some untoward thing or other, that I am afraid to make so early an engagement with you.

But we can still avoid the Fruit-time.[2] I shall be often back, from Saturday to Monday, in August and September, and we will try then.

Faithfully Ever
CD.

[1] The resolution had thanked CD for presiding at the Anniversary Dinner on 8 May and for "the effective and eloquent manner in which he advocated the cause of the institution" (Minute Book, Artists' Benevolent Fund). For his speech, see *Speeches*, ed. K. J. Fielding, pp. 266–9. He also subscribed 10 guineas.

[2] Mitton had lived at Lampton, near Hounslow, Middlesex, since 1845; occupying two houses there, North Lodge and South Lodge; besides his practice as a solicitor, he had taken up market-gardening (W. J. Carlton, "The Strange Story of Thomas Mitton", *D*, LVI [1960], 144–5). He may have worked with C. T. Hennell, the one market gardener listed in Lampton.

To EDMUND YATES, 15 JUNE 1858

MS Robert H. Taylor Collection, Princeton University.

TAVISTOCK HOUSE, | TAVISTOCK SQUARE, LONDON. W.C.
Tuesday Fifteenth June 1858

My Dear Yates

Come!—We dine at Dilkes,[1] but don't go out until past 6. I needn't tell you that you may in all things count upon

Yours Ever
CD[2]

To THE MARQUIS OF LANSDOWNE, 15 JUNE 1858*

MS The Bowood Collection.

TAVISTOCK HOUSE, | TAVISTOCK SQUARE, LONDON. W.C.
Tuesday Evening Fifteenth June 1858.

My Dear Lord.

I take the liberty of returning an informal answer to your kind card, in order that I may express my regret that I came home just as you were driving away, and so lost the great pleasure and gratification I should have felt in seeing you.

Unfortunately I am going into Kent on Friday morning (I live on the top of Falstaff's Gad's Hill when I am there), for a little country peace, of which I stand much in need. Unfortunately, I have given my daughters free permission to dispose of me in the mean time. Unfortunately, they have availed themselves of this concession for tomorrow and thus I come to the crowning misfortune that I cannot have the honor of dining with you.

[1] i.e. himself and Forster; they would by now be completing the *Answer to the Committee's Summary of Facts* for the Royal Literary Fund, published later as a 6*d.* pamphlet. Though all three names are on the title-page, most of it is clearly the work of CD, and had been begun soon after 14 Apr. Forster was concerned with the controversial question of admitting reporters to meetings, and Dilke with his own reports in the *Athenaeum*.

[2] Yates had asked CD if he could consult him about what became known as "the Garrick Club Affair". In a new periodical, *Town Talk*, 12 June, Yates had, in "Literary Talk", written a sketch of Thackeray, a fellow-member of the Club. Thackeray's "style of conversation" he characterized as "either openly cynical or affectedly good-natured and benevolent"; of his lectures he wrote: "No one succeeds better than Mr. Thackeray in cutting his coat according to his cloth": in "the English Humourists of the Eighteenth Century" he had adulated the aristocracy; in America "George Washington became the idol of his worship, the 'Four Georges' objects of his bitterest attacks." (Article given in full in *Letters and Private Papers of W. M. Thackeray*, ed. Gordon N. Ray, IV, 90, and in Edmund Yates, *Recollections and Experiences*, II, 21–3). In a furious letter, two days later, Thackeray accused Yates of imputing insincerity to him in private talk, assigning "dishonourable motives" to him in public statements, and of basing his sketch on private conversation at the Garrick. He described the article as "not offensive & unfriendly merely, but slanderous and untrue" (letter given in *Letters and Private Papers*, ed. G. N. Ray, IV, 89–90). CD found Yates's first intended reply to this "too flippant and too violent"; and, following their meeting, a much shorter and curter letter was sent, saying that Yates did not accept Thackeray's "understanding" of the phrases complained of, in the least: "I altogether reject it." On 19 June Thackeray placed his complaints against Yates before the Committee of the Garrick: for the outcome, see *To* Yates, 6 July and *fn.*

Allow me to assure you of my grateful respect and esteem, and of my ever being

My Dear Lord | Most Faithfully Yours

The | Marquess of Lansdowne. CHARLES DICKENS

To T. J. THOMPSON, 17 JUNE 1858

Mention in list of letters from CD to Thompson made by his son-in-law Wilfrid Meynell; *MS* 1 p.; dated Tavistock House, 17 June 58.

To JAMES T. FIELDS,[1] 19 JUNE 1858

MS Houghton Library, Harvard.

GAD'S HILL PLACE, | HIGHAM BY ROCHESTER, KENT.
Saturday Nineteenth June 1858.[2]

My Dear Sir

I write to you from my little Kentish Country-house, on the very spot where Falstaff ran away.

I cannot tell you how very much obliged to you I feel for your kind suggestion,[3] and for the perfectly frank and unaffected manner in which it is conveyed to me.

It touches, I will admit to you frankly, a chord that has several times sounded in my breast, since I began my Readings. I should very much like to read in America. But the idea is a mere Dream as yet. Several strong reasons would make the journey difficult to me, and—even were they overcome—I would never make it, unless I had great general reason to believe that the American people really wanted to hear me.[4]

Through the whole of this Autumn I shall be reading in various parts of England, Ireland, and Scotland.[5] I mention this, in reference to the closing paragraph of your esteemed favor.

Allow me once again to thank you most heartily, and to remain

Gratefully | And Faithfully Yours
CHARLES DICKENS

[1] James Thomas Fields (1817–81; *DAB*), publisher and writer; partner in Ticknor, Reed & Fields of Boston, later CD's main American publishers. See Vol. III, p. 49*n* and later vols.

[2] Fields wrongly dates this as 1859 in *Yesterdays with Authors*, Boston, 1872, p. 154; followed by N, who misdates it Circa June 1859 (N, III, 108).

[3] In *Yesterdays with Authors*, *ibid.*, Fields wrote: "As long ago as the spring of 1858 I began to press [*CD*] very hard to come to America and give us a course of readings from his works." See later vols.

[4] "I thought him over-sensitive with regard to his reception here," wrote Fields. He tried to remove, he says, any obstructions in CD's mind against a second visit (*Yesterdays with Authors*, *ibid.*).

[5] Already planned: see *To* Cerjat, 7 July and *fn.*

To G. M. TOWLE,[1] 19 JUNE 1858*

MS Yale University Library. *Address:* George Makepeace Towle Esquire | Yale College | New Haven | Conn. | U.S. of America.

GAD'S HILL PLACE, | HIGHAM BY ROCHESTER, KENT.
Nineteenth June 1858.

Dear Sir

I am very happy to send you the autograph which you desire to add to your collection.

Allow me to thank you for the pleasant and obliging terms in which your letter is couched.

I am Dear Sir | Faithfully Yours
CHARLES DICKENS

George Makepeace Towle Esquire

To HENRY AUSTIN, [19–20 JUNE 1858]

Mention in next. *Date:* written same day or day before that letter.

To HENRY AUSTIN, 20 JUNE 1858*

MS Morgan Library.

GAD'S HILL PLACE, | HIGHAM BY ROCHESTER, KENT.
Sunday Twentieth June 1858

My Dear Henry

You will receive—probably with this—a former note of mine, posted to you from Rochester today. Since that letter was posted, *the Pump has broken down again—the same rod.* And the Rochester man says "he'd rather have nothink to do with that 'ere infernal ma-sheen."

Pray help me! Pray, pray, save me from bankruptcy and Despair!!

Affecy Ever
CD.

To HENRY BICKNELL, 24 JUNE 1858*

MS Dickens Fellowship, Boston, Mass.

TAVISTOCK HOUSE, | TAVISTOCK SQUARE, LONDON. W.C.
Thursday Twenty Fourth June 1858.

My Dear Bicknell.

I am exceedingly unwilling to say No to the proposal with which the Directors of

[1] George Makepeace Towle (1841–93; *DAB*), at school in Massachusetts; BA Yale 1861; LLB 1863; later, journalist and writer.

the Crystal Palace Company honor me;[1]—and yet I fear I must. The truth is, that I abstain, on principle, from associating myself *in name alone* with any project; I know I have not leisure to bestow on any new occupation at present; and I feel it right, not only towards myself, but also towards the projectors of this scheme, to give these plain reasons for declining, though very unwillingly.

Faithfully Yours always

Henry Bicknell Esquire CHARLES DICKENS

To DR F. H. RAMSBOTHAM, 24 JUNE 1858

Summary from Sotheby's catalogue Mar 1981; *MS* (copy in unknown hand) 1 p.; addressed Dr Ramsbotham; dated Tavistock House, 24 June 58.

Saying he cannot accept invitation as he is in town only for a day and a half to read,[2] *and has friends staying in Kent, so must return.*

To W. M. THACKERAY, [?24–27 JUNE 1858]*

MS (fragment) Yale University Library. *Date:* near the date of the Special meeting of the Garrick Club Committee on 26 June; handwriting supports.

of any other person, in it or out of it?[3]

Faithfully Yours

W. M. Thackeray Esquire CHARLES DICKENS

To WILLIAM MOY THOMAS, 28 JUNE 1858

MS Walter T. Spencer.

OFFICE OF HOUSEHOLD WORDS,
Monday Twenty Eighth June 1858

My Dear Sir

I shall be at Gad's Hill again tomorrow evening, but not in time to communicate with you before it will be necessary for you to send to Edinburgh. I will write to you after reading your article.[4]

[1] To join the Council of the Crystal Palace Art-Union (endorsement, presumably by Bicknell, on letter), formed to promote art and "art-industry", chiefly through commissioning works for distribution to its subscribers. Established 1859 and warmly welcomed by the *Art Journal* (articles in 1858 and 1859); its first Committee headed by the Earl of Carlisle.

[2] *Little Dombey* on Wed afternoon, 23 June, and the *Carol* on Thurs evening.

[3] i.e., the matter lies between Thackeray and Yates; is it really the business of the Committee or "of any other person . . .?"

[4] "The Literary Fund", *North British Review*, Aug 58, XXIX, 244. A note by Thomas, accompanying the letter, states that the proprietor, W. P. Kennedy, had asked CD to name a writer to contribute such an article; CD and Dilke had recommended Thomas. No further letter to him survives, but an editorial note (obviously Dilke's) in the *Athenaeum*, 7 Aug, praised this "calm and sagacious paper" and quoted its closing paragraphs.

I am sure it will be manly and right, and I have not the least uneasiness about it; my confidence being—believe me—Thorough.[1]

Faithfully Yours always

William Moy Thomas Esquire CHARLES DICKENS

To G. A. SALA, [?29–30 JUNE 1858]*

MS (fragment)[2] British Library. Date: "1858" pencilled at top of page; June likely, as a month before publication of *A Journey Due North* as a separate book, and probably written from Gad's Hill.[3]

glad to see it there. If no such reason should arise I am content to let my wound heal quietly.

The "Journey Due North" is henceforth at your own disposal. I hereby declare you to be the owner of the copyright of that work, collected and republished as a separate book;[4] and I hope it may be a pleasant and profitable possession.

Faithfully Yours

George A Sala Esquire CHARLES DICKENS

[1] CD must have given Thomas a copy of his *Answer to the Committee's Summary of "Facts"* (see *To* Yates, 15 June, *fn*), listed among other pamphlets at the head of the article, along with *Annual Reports* and the founder's *Claims of Literature* (1802). After an introduction on charitable societies and the dangers of "waste and mismanagement", Thomas effectively restates and defends the reformers' case against the present constitution and the cost of administration. He makes it clear that the Special Committee appointed to look into this included members who afterwards opposed the reformers (e.g. Robert Bell), and that "the tide of reform suddenly turned" in 1858. The reformers wanted only "men of letters" on the governing committee, and not those who were merely "great names". The *Answer* made the reformers' condition clearer (some of the aristocratic members were men of letters). Thomas does not cite CD's triumphant rebuttal over the *Quarterly Review* quotation, in which he showed the "stock quotation" in the Fund's *Reports* was also undated: see *To* Blewitt, 24 Apr. Nor, perhaps wisely, does he refer to CD's sarcastic invectives against the *Summary*'s "haystack of words" and disregard of the "sharp needle of facts". But he concludes by quoting CD's comment on the Committee as "a remarkable instance of the condition into which good-enough men will often lapse when they get behind a large table". The *Answer* had continued "with a fatal clean sheet of foolscap and ... two fatal clean pens".

[2] First part of letter torn away.

[3] On pale blue paper, usually used at Gad's Hill.

[4] *A Journey Due North* was eventually published by Bentley on 30 July. According to Sala's recollections (*Life and Adventures*, Ch. 2, p. 387), CD "took the embargo off" republication from *HW* in the summer (for their earlier quarrel, see *To* Wills, 24 Dec 56 *fn*). Advertised first as *Russian Notes* and later under the present title. See *To* Sala, 19 Sep 56 and *fn*.

To FRANCIS WAUGH,[1] 30 JUNE 1858*

MS Free Library of Philadelphia. *Address:* Master Francis G. Waugh | 6 Mecklenburgh Street | London | W.C.

GAD'S HILL PLACE, | HIGHAM BY ROCHESTER, KENT.
Wednesday Thirtieth June 1858.

My Dear Young friend

I am quite ashamed to find that your letter was written to me so long ago as on the eighteenth of this month. For I am (as you have been truly told) very fond of children, and I should be pained by your supposing that I could neglect you.

The truth is, I have been very busy. Otherwise I should have sent you this present autograph, on the very next day after I received your letter. "Better late than Never", however, and here it is.

I don't write as plainly as you do. But printers can read anything, and they have made me lazy about the shapes of my letters, and the clearness of my loops, and the roundness of my O's (there's a round one though), and all that. But I am not lazy in anything else, so I hope to retain your good opinion on the whole.

Affectionately Yours
CHARLES DICKENS

Perhaps you'll wonder why I make that flourish. I don't know. I have not the least idea.

Master Francis G Waugh

To CHARLES KEAN, [1 JULY 1858]

Extract in N, III, 28 (from catalogue source); *MS* 1 p.; dated Tavistock House, 1 July 58.

I have received your letter on my arrival in town this morning, and I shall have great pleasure in meeting you at the Athenaeum at half past one to-morrow, if that time will suit your convenience.[2]

[1] Perhaps a relation of Lieut-Col. W. P. Waugh, of Campden House, Kensington: see *To* Waugh, 9 May 56, *fn.* Francis Waugh's mother, a widow since 1846, lived at 6 Mecklenburgh St.

[2] Kean had been manager of the Princess's Theatre since 1850. He was no doubt consulting CD about the proposed "Dramatic College": see *To* Kean, 23 July and *fnn.*

To HENRY BRADBURY,[1] 3 JULY 1858*

MS Professor K. J. Fielding.

GAD'S HILL PLACE, | HIGHAM BY ROCHESTER, KENT.
Saturday Third July, 1858

My Dear Sir

I send you enclosed, a List of "Reprinted Pieces". They are all in Household Words, and I have appended to each, the No. of the Vol. in which each is to be found. I wish them to be printed in the Library Edition, in the order in which I send them.[2] If there be too many, I will strike some out. If there be not enough, I will add some more. It will be best to let me have the Proof Sheets of this part of the Volume, *all together*, so that we may know exactly what we are about as to quantity.

Faithfully Yours
CD.

Henry Bradbury Esquire

To MISS HARNESS,[3] [?5 JULY 1858]

Mention in next. *Date:* probably written the same day.

To HENRY CHORLEY,[4] 5 JULY 1858

Text from N, III, 28.

TAVISTOCK HOUSE, | TAVISTOCK SQUARE, LONDON. W.C.
Monday Fifth July 1858

Dear Chorley,

The enclosed is from Miss Harness, asking you to dine there with me.

I have replied for myself, that I have left off dining out, until my reading Tour[5] shall be over. I have added for you, that I *think* you are engaged out of town, but that you will answer for yourself. They are very agreeable and excellent people, you know.

Ever affectionately
[CHARLES DICKENS]

[1] Henry Riley Bradbury ("'Arry") (1831–60; *DNB*), writer on printing, eldest son of William Bradbury, of Bradbury & Evans (see Vol. V, p. 691); pupil at Imperial Printing Office, Vienna, 1850; became an expert on "nature-printing", about which he wrote and lectured; produced folio plates for *Ferns of Great Britain and Ireland*, 1855, and *British Sea Weeds*, 4 vols, octavo, 1858. His lecture, *Printing: its Dawn, Day, and Destiny*, was delivered at the Royal Institution on 14 May 58 and privately printed later that month. Founded Henry Bradbury & Co., banknote engravers, 12 and 13 Fetter Lane.

[2] The Library edn (published by Chapman & Hall, printed by Bradbury & Evans) had been appearing monthly as planned, and Vol. VIII, containing *Reprinted Pieces* was due on 1 Aug. 31 articles were published in this and the Illustrated Library edn, taken from Vols I–XI of *HW*, beginning with "The Long Voyage" and ending with "A Christmas Tree" (later moved to *Christmas Stories*). Four illustrations were later supplied by Frederick Walker (1840–75; *DNB*), ARA 1870, then a student at RA.

[3] Mary Harness (*b.* 1801), the Rev. William Harness's only sister, who kept house for him: see Vol. III, p. 364*n*.

[4] Henry Fothergill Chorley (1808–72; *DNB*), music critic and miscellaneous writer: see Vol. V, p. 360*n*.

[5] See *To* Cerjat, 7 July, *fn*.

To THOMAS BEARD, 6 JULY 1858

MS Dickens House. *Address:* Thomas Beard Esquire | 42 Portman Place | Edgeware Road | W.

GAD'S HILL PLACE, | HIGHAM BY ROCHESTER, KENT.
Tuesday Evening Sixth July 1858

My Dear Beard

I am anxious that you should come (if you can and will), and have a little country idleness here, this month. I say this month, because on the 2nd. of August I go away on a long Reading Tour, which, with occasional Saturday rushes to London, will hold me engaged until November. Now, see how I stand. On Wednesday and Thursday the 14th. and 15th. I read.[1] On Friday the 16th. I return here. Can't you come too? The Forsters may be with us for a day or two, but you know we are elastic in our accommodations, and more than elastic in our welcome to you. Can you manage to come then, and stay until I roam away into the wide world of Readings?

Write me a word in answer here, or see me in my room at St. Martin's Hall between the parts next Thursday night.[2] There is always Sherry and Ice for you, and you never come to take it.

Ever Affectionately

Thomas Beard Esquire CHARLES DICKENS

To EDMUND YATES, 6 JULY 1858

MS Robert H. Taylor Collection, Princeton University.

GAD'S HILL PLACE, | HIGHAM BY ROCHESTER, KENT.
Tuesday Sixth July, 1858

My Dear Edmund

I have been thinking about the General Meeting.[3] My considerations and reconsiderations thereupon, induce me to recommend you *not* to attend it in person.

Firstly, I think it pretty certain that Thackeray will stay away.[4] If he should do so, it would be regarded as an act of delicacy in him; and your doing the reverse, would be regarded as an act of *in*delicacy in you.

Secondly, though he should come; still, your staying away, would shew well by the side of his presence.

Thirdly, it is very difficult indeed for anyone, even though practised in public

[1] He read the *Carol* for the last time on Wednesday afternoon; on Thursday evening, also for the last time, *The Poor Traveller*, *Boots*, and *Mrs Gamp*.

[2] i.e. 8 July, when he read *The Chimes*.

[3] Of the Garrick Club, called for 10 July: for the events leading up to it, see *To* Yates, 15 June, *fn*.

[4] Neither Yates nor Thackeray attended the meeting. For a letter, justifying his action, which Thackeray addressed to the Chairman of the General Meeting, but did not send, see *Letters and Private Papers of W. M. Thackeray*, ed. Gordon N. Ray, IV, 101–2. He referred in it to "the doubt, distrust, recrimination, & heart burning, wh. conduct like that of wh. I complain, must bring upon our or any Society!" His drawing of Yates and himself in the Garrick, Yates with large ears, smiling, with a knife behind his back, as he shakes hands, is given, *ibid.*, facing p. 102.

meetings and appearances, to keep quiet at such a discussion: the said "anyone" being a principal therein.

Fourthly, you could do nothing, if you were there, but deny that you ever intended to abide by the Committee's decision. That, I will say for you, if necessary.

In case you should be staggered by this advice of mine, ask one or two men of experience and good judgement, whom you can trust, what *they* say. I am pretty sure that on careful consideration they will agree with me.[1]

I suppose the Meeting is not to take place so soon as next Saturday, seeing that I have not yet received any Circular.[2]

Ever Faithfully
CHARLES DICKENS

Edmund Yates Esquire

To W. W. F. DE CERJAT, 7 JULY 1858

MS Yale University Library. *Address:* Affranchie | A Monsieur | William. W. F. De Cerjat | Campagne Elysée | Lausanne | La Suisse.

GAD'S HILL PLACE, | HIGHAM BY ROCHESTER, KENT.
Wednesday Seventh July, 1858.

My Dear Cerjat.

I should vainly try to tell you—so I *won't* try—how affected I have been by your warm-hearted letter, or how thoroughly well convinced I always am of the truth and earnestness of your friendship. I thank you, my dear fellow, with my whole soul. I fervently return that friendship, and I highly cherish it.

[a]Ah! If Prudence only knew how far out she was when she plucked you by the sleeve, she would marry Generous Impulse without delay and have a charming family. What good the children of that match would do on earth!

Dear Cerjat, I know very well that a man who has won a very conspicuous position, has incurred in the winning of it, a heavy debt to the Knaves and Fools, which he must be content to pay, over and over again, all through his life. Further, I know equally well that I can never hope that any one out of my house can ever compre-

[1] On 23 June Yates sent a letter, to be read out, apologizing for his article to the Club—but not to Thackeray. He maintained that, despite its being, as he admitted, "in exceedingly bad taste", it had made no reference to the Club and therefore was no business of the Committee (*Recollections and Experiences*, II, 31); this was unanimously rejected at a Special Meeting on 26 June, which resolved that Thackeray's complaints were well founded and that Yates must either "make an ample apology" to Thackeray or resign from the Club. Yates, advised by Forster, Wills, Albert and Arthur Smith, as well as by CD, then appealed to a General Meeting of the Club (*ibid.*, II, 34–5). Six resolutions, confirming those previously passed by the Committee in Thackeray's favour, were proposed by J. C. O'Dowd and passed by 70 to 26 votes. The fifth called on Yates again to apologize to Thackeray, to spare the Meeting "a most disagreeable duty" (i.e., requesting Yates's expulsion from the Club). All the Committee, except CD, voted for their previous resolutions. Besides CD, Wilkie Collins, Robert Bell, Lover and Palgrave Simpson spoke in Yates's favour, according to Yates. On 20 July his name was erased from the list of members. (Edmund Yates, privately printed pamphlet, *Mr Thackeray, Mr Yates and the Garrick Club*, 1859, p. 10; *Recollections and Experiences*, II, 25–8).

[2] No doubt CD's notice of the meeting on 10 July had gone to Tavistock House.

[aa] Omitted in MDGH, II, 48–51.

hend my domestic story.[1] I will not complain. I have been heavily wounded, but I have covered the wound up, and left it to heal.[2] Some of my children or some of my friends will do me right if I ever need it in the time to come. And I hope that my Books will speak for themselves and me, when I and my faults and virtues, my fortunes and misfortunes, are all forgotten.[a]

You want to know all about me? I am still reading in London every Thursday, and the Audiences are very great, and the success immense. On the 2nd. day of August I am going away, on a tour of some four months, in England, Ireland, and Scotland. I shall read, during that time, not fewer than four or five times a week.[3] It will be sharp work; but probably a certain musical chinking will come of it, which will mitigate the hardship.

At this present moment I am on my little Kentish freehold (*not* in top boots, and not particularly prejudiced that I know of), looking on as pretty an English view out of my study window, as you would find in a long day's English ride. My little place is a grave red brick house (Time of George the First, I suppose)[4] which I have added to, and stuck bits upon, in all manner of ways: so that it is as pleasantly irregular, and as violently opposed to all architectural ideas, as the most hopeful man could possibly desire. It is on the summit of Gad's Hill. The Robbery was committed

[1] On 11 July Elizabeth Barrett Browning wrote to a friend: "What is this sad story about Dickens and his wife? Incompatibility of temper after twenty-three years of married life? What a plea!—Worse than irregularity of the passions it seems to me. Thinking of my own peace & selfish pleasure, too, I would rather be beaten by my husband once a day than lose my child out of the house—yes, indeed. And the Dickens's have children younger than Penini! [*only Plorn*]—Poor woman! She must suffer bitterly—that is sure" (Browning Collection, University of Texas Library).

[2] Two London newspapers in particular had repeated scurrilous rumours in comments on CD's "Personal" statement: the *Court Circular* (despite its name, an entirely unofficial weekly paper) and *Reynolds's Weekly Newspaper*. The *Court Circular* in its editorial, 12 June, attributed CD's separation, according to one "story in circulation", to "that talented gentleman's preference of his wife's sister to herself, a preference which has assumed a very definite and tangible shape". It ended: "if half of what we have heard about his temper in his own domestic circle be correct, Mr. Dickens is in a fair way to figure in the new Matrimonial Court, and in a mode which will add little to his laurels." In *Reynolds's Weekly Newspaper*, 13 June, G. W. M. Reynolds commented: "The names of a female relative, and of a professional young lady, have both been, of late, so freely and intimately associated with that of Mr. Dickens, as to excite suspicion and surprise in the minds of those who had hitherto looked upon the popular novelist as a very Joseph in all that regards morality, chastity, and decorum. ... Let Mr. Dickens remember that the odious—and we might almost add unnatural—profligacy of which he has been accused, would brand him with life-long infamy." "Can such an accusation, then, be satisfactorily dismissed with the scratch of a pen, or a few well-rounded sonorous phrases?" Reynolds returned to the attack in the next issue, 20 June: "The Charles Dickens scandalum magnatum rolls along the highways and byways of public conversation, and gathers as it rolls.... The rumours that are now afloat about this unhappy affair are innumerable." On 14 June Wills consulted Ouvry and Forster about the expediency of bringing an action for criminal libel against the *Court Circular* (considering Reynolds "too small to be thought about"); but no prosecution was brought (MS Farrer & Co.; given in K. J. Fielding, "Dickens and the Hogarth Scandal", p. 71).

[3] On 24 July the *HW* advt announced: "Mr Dickens will also read at CLIFTON, on the 2nd of August; at EXETER on the 3rd; at PLYMOUTH on the 4th and 5th; at CLIFTON on the 6th; at WORCESTER on the 10th; at WOLVERHAMPTON on the 11th; at SHREWSBURY on the 12th; and at CHESTER on the 13th of August." The advt, 14 Aug, adds Liverpool (4 readings), Dublin (4), Cork (2) and Belfast (2).

[4] See *To* Cerjat, 19 Jan and *fn*.

before the door, on the men with the Treasure, and Falstaff ran away from the identical spot of ground now covered by the room in which I write. A little rustic alehouse, called The Sir John Falstaff, is over the way—has been over the way, ever since, in honor of the event. Cobham Woods and Park are behind the house; the distant Thames in front; the Medway, with Rochester and its old Castle and Cathedral, on one side. The whole stupendous property is on the old Dover Road: so, when you come, come by the North Kent Railway (not the South Eastern) from Canterbury to Strood or Higham, and I'll drive over to fetch you.

The blessed woods and fields have done me a world of good, and I am quite myself again. The children are all as happy as children can be; [a]and the girls are happier than they ever were.[a] My eldest daughter, Mary, keeps house—with a state and gravity becoming that high position. Wherein she is assisted by her sister Katie, and by her Aunt Georgina, who is, and always has been, like another sister. Two big dogs—a bloodhound, and a St. Bernard, direct from a convent of that name[1] where I think you once were—are their principal attendants in the green lanes. These latter, instantly untie the neck-kerchiefs of all Tramps and Prowlers who approach the Presence,[2] so they wander about with any escort, and drive big horses in basket phaetons through murderous bye-ways, and never come to grief. They are very curious about your daughters, and send all kinds of loves to them and to Mrs. Cerjat. In which I heartily join.

You will have read in the papers that the Thames at London is most horrible. I have to cross Waterloo or London Bridge to get to the Railroad when I come down there, and I can certify that the offensive smells, even in that short whiff, have been of a most head-and-stomach distracting nature. Nobody knows what is to be done; at least, everybody knows a plan, and everybody else knows it won't do; in the meantime cart-loads of chloride of Lime are shot into the filthy stream, and do something—I hope.[3] You will know before you get this, that the American Telegraph Wire has parted again; at which most men are sorry, but very few surprised.[4] This is all the news, except that there is an Italian Opera at Drury Lane[5]—price eighteen pence to the Pit—where Viardot, by far the greatest artist of them all, sings, and which is full, when the dear Operas can't let a box;[6] and except that the weather has been excessively hot, but is now quite cool. On the top of this hill, it has been even cold—actually cold—at night, for more than a week past.

I am going over to Rochester to post this letter, and must write another to Townshend before I go. My dear Cerjat I have written lightly enough, because I want you

[aa] Omitted in MDGH, II, 48–51.

[1] Turk and Linda respectively: see *To* Mrs Watson, 7 Dec 57, *fn.*

[2] "their presence" in MDGH, in error.

[3] *The Times*, 17 June, carried an article on the Thames: "the grandsire of English streams basks, and welters, and wallows in his mud.... No metropolis but London could make such a dirt, and foul so large a wash-pot.... We believe this to be the uncleanest, foulest river in the known world."

[4] The British and American Govts had in June jointly commissioned HMS *Agamemnon* and the American frigate *Niagara* to lay the first electric telegraph cable between Europe and America; but this project was abandoned after the number of fractures to the first 140 miles. The cable was successfully laid by 5 Aug.

[5] In June and July several operas were performed there, including *Don Giovanni*, with Mme Viardot as Donna Anna, and Bellini's *La Sonnambula*.

[6] There were seasons of Italian Opera at Covent Garden, Her Majesty's and St James's. Prices at all of them were considerably higher than at Drury Lane.

to know that I am becoming cheerful and hearty. [a]I have been sadly put out, and sorely unlike myself; but it is past, I hope, and a brighter [b]sky is shining.[a] God bless you. I love you, and I know that you love me. Ever your attached and affectionate CD[b]

To THE REV. CHAUNCY HARE TOWNSHEND, [?7 JULY 1858]

Mention in last. *Date:* probably written the same day.

To W. H. RUSSELL, 7 JULY 1858†

MS Morgan Library.

GAD'S HILL PLACE,|HIGHAM BY ROCHESTER, KENT.
Wednesday Evening, Seventh July, 1858.

My Dear Russell.

I cannot let another Mail go from Marseilles,[1] without sending you my hearty and cordial word of thanks, for your great kindness about my boy, and without saying to you (which is most superfluous) with what unspeakable pleasure I shall see you at home again.[2] I write from the top of that hill where I did hope to have seen you long ago, and where I have a prophetic assurance and fore-knowledge that I shall see you and Mrs. Russell many a time. Divers wonderful drinks are in the capital cellar in the chalk below, which I reserve for these occasions. And then I shall tell you all that I leave out of this letter—so prepare and resign yourself. There being nothing *in* this letter, Heavens! how long-winded I shall have to be!

No doubt, by some wonderful means or other, you get all the news from Printing House Square,[3] at about the same time as I get it here. How the Atlantic Telegraph Wire broke again, the day before yesterday or so, you know, of course. Also, how your friend reads his shorter books in public (Arthur Smith, Manager) with a success which his modesty forbids him to expatiate upon. Also how he has asked Mrs. Russell as a Guest to such intellectual banquet—who came, he hopes. Also, how Albert Smith starts for Hong Kong, viâ Marseilles, tomorrow night,[4] a hot and a weary journey for the man of his figure; as an improvement upon which I have recommended Sheridan's advice as to saying he saw it, and not putting himself out of the way to go to see it.[5] But you don't know—no, not even from Printing H.S.—

[aa] Omitted in MDGH, II, 48–51.

[bb] Written very small transversely across p. 1 above the address.

[1] Russell had been in India, inquiring into reports of the Mutineers' atrocities for both *The Times* and the Govt, since Jan 58. He spent most of the summer in Simla. *My Diary in India in the Years 1858–59*, 2 Vols, 1860, runs from his journey out, at the end of 1857, to 2 Mar 59.

[2] He returned in Spring 1859.

[3] The offices of *The Times*.

[4] Smith was away for five months, reaching Hong Kong on 21 Aug. He spent 9–20 Sep in Canton. On 25 Sep he gave an "entertainment" on the "Travelling English", at the Hong Kong Club, raising £200 for local charities. "His success was unprecedently brilliant in the annals of China", reported the *Hong Kong Daily Press* (details from his *To China and Back* [1859]), but his health never recovered.

[5] "Who has not laughed", says Forster in *The Life and Times of Oliver Goldsmith*, "at Sheridan's remark to his son, on the latter proposing to descend a coal-pit for the pleasure of saying he had done so?" (2nd edn, 1854, II, 341*n*).

that on the anniversary of poor dear Jerrold's death,[1] I had a very good and tender letter from his eldest son, expressing his regret that he had ever been so ill-advised as to be less grateful to certain of his father's friends than he might have been.[2] In reply to which, I stretched out my willing hand to him over his father's grave, and made an end of that incongruity at least, I hope for ever.[3]

Everybody talks about your letters, and everybody praises them.[4] No one says, or can say, more of them than they deserve. I have been deeply impressed by your suggestion, in your note to me, of the miseries and horrors by which you are surrounded; and I can well understand what a trial the whole frightful, revengeful, morally and physically burning, business must be to an affectionate and earnest man. Are there good chances of its being so far ended, as to enable you to come home? That is the turning-point in the War, that I (and Mrs. Russell) think most about.

The gentleman to whom you gave a letter of introduction, called on me one afternoon last month, and left word that he was going away directly.[5] I called on him next day. He was out, as I had been, but I saw a very good serving-man who told me how he was "joost awa' into Scotland yon, airly the morrow mornin'". So I left him my card, with an intimation that I hoped to know him better on his return.

The Garrick is in convulsions. The attack is consequent on Thackeray's having complained to the Committee (with an amazing want of discretion, as I think), of an article about him by Edmund Yates, in a thing called Town Talk.[6] The article is in bad taste, no doubt, and would have been infinitely better left alone. But I conceive that the Committee have nothing earthly, celestial, or infernal, to do with it.[7] Committee thinks otherwise, and calls on E.Y. to apologize or retire. E.Y. can't apologize (Thackeray having written him a letter that really renders it impossible),[8] and

[1] 8 June 57.

[2] See *To* the Editor of *The Times*, 1 Sep 57 and *fn*.

[3] On 14 June Blanchard Jerrold wrote to Hepworth Dixon: "By the way you will be glad to learn that Dickens & I are friends—firm friends:—& that he has asked me to go & see him" (MS Private). In his *Life and Remains of Douglas Jerrold*, 1859, he wrote: "I accept the 'Remembrance' efforts of Mr Dickens and others—all angry words forgotten—on behalf of my father's family, without a touch of rancour or a qualifying word. Hands have long since been heartily shaken all round" (p. 346).

[4] Russell's letters on the ending of the Mutiny, the Mutineers' atrocities and the British Govt's reprisals, had been appearing in *The Times* since late Feb 58. In *My Diary in India*, above, I, 170, Russell stressed that the Commander-in-Chief, Sir Colin Campbell, whom he had met in Cawnpore in early Feb, had imposed no censorship on them. On 8 May, after Russell's account of the British capture of Lucknow, Delane, the Editor, had written to him: "I have nothing but to congratulate you on the perfect success with which you have sustained your fame. . . . I . . . hear everybody saying, that we are at last beginning to learn something about India, which was always before a mystery" (J. B. Atkins, *The Life of W. H. Russell*, 1911, I, 311). On 18 Sep the *Saturday Review*, usually severely critical of *The Times*, wrote: "Mr Russell's Indian letters display the vivid genius of Froissart"; and on 9 Oct, praising the part the letters had played in leading opinion away from indiscriminate reprisals, "They have been the means of preserving English public opinion from dangerous and disgraceful error" (*The History of The Times*, 1938, II, 318). Delane supported Russell throughout and on 8 July wrote to him: "You will have seen, I hope, how I have backed every one of your suggestions by leading articles" (J. B. Atkins, above, I, 335).

[5] Unidentified.

[6] See *To* Yates, 15 June and *fn*.

[7] See *To* Yates, 6 July, *fn*.

[8] In his privately-printed pamphlet, *Mr. Thackeray, Mr. Yates, and the Garrick Club*, Yates took it as clear that Thackeray's letter was "intentionally arrogant and offensive" (p. 5). Much later the architect Edward

won't retire. Committee thereupon call General Meeting, yet pending. Thackeray *thereupon*, by way of shewing what an ill thing it is for writers to attack one another in print, denounces E.Y. (in Virginians) as "Young Grub Street".[1] Frightful mess, muddle, complication, and botheration, ensue. Which Witch's broth is now in full boil.

Why, you are better with a Turban round your hat, over there,—than here, with all this nonsense going on! As to me, I have come to the blessed woods and fields to forget several things (you are not among them my dear Russell), and to calm down before I go a-reading God knows where—including Dublin, Cork, Belfast, and Limerick: I never having set foot in Ireland before.

Behold all my news, and the end of my paper! I send you a cordial and vigorous shake of my hand with my heart in it—which was the way in which Rogers's Ginevra (or some one else) gave hers to her lover[2]—and a very pretty and loving way too. Where is your old Map this night, I wonder, and the Wand you used to point with![3] Lord Lord! and Joe Robins[4] playing (with indifferent success, I am afraid) far [a]North!! And Delane looking as if he lived on morning dew and horseback!!!

God bless you, and send you back to us, ruddy and bould. Believe me Ever Heartily and affectionately Yours

CHARLES DICKENS[a]

To EDMUND YATES, 7 JULY 1858

MS Robert H. Taylor Collection, Princeton University.

GAD'S HILL PLACE, | HIGHAM BY ROCHESTER, KENT.
Wednesday Seventh July, 1858

My Dear Edmund

Yes. I will dine at the Albion[5] tomorrow, at 4.

Pray don't think—or pretend to think—for a moment that I can fail to be interested in your letters, be they ever so numerous.[6]

Faithfully Yours always
CD.

Solomons said that Thackeray had told him that, although convinced his course of action was justified, he was sorry he had written this letter (MS Garrick Club).

[1] "Young Grubstreet, who corresponds with three penny papers and describes the persons and conversations of gentlemen whom he meets at his 'clubs'" (*The Virginians*, No. IX, Ch. 35, published 1 July).

[2] "And in the lustre of her youth, she gave | Her hand, her heart in it, to Francesco" (Samuel Rogers, "Ginevra", in *Italy*, 1830).

[3] In his lectures on the Crimean War: see *To* Russell, 21and 30 May 57 and *fnn.*

[4] Joseph Henry (or Hulme) Robins (1827–78), mainly comic actor; nephew of the auctioneer G.H. Robins, former owner of Tavistock House (Vol. VI, p. 357*n*). After a medical education, travelled to the East with his close friend Albert Smith 1849; played the Cardinal in Bulwer Lytton's *Richelieu*, Drury Lane, 1852; the clown in the Fielding Club's amateur pantomime, *Harlequin Guy Fawkes*, Olympic, Mar 55; and parts in other pantomimes. Played in his own comic entertainments. See Edmund Yates, *Recollections and Experiences*, I, 215–17, 253.

[aa] Written very small across top of p. 1.

[5] The Albion Tavern, Great Russell St.

[6] His correspondence with the Garrick Club since 26 June which CD would not have seen, owing to his being at Gad's Hill; he needed to see it before attending the General Meeting on 10 July, as he clearly did.

To LORD ROBERT GROSVENOR,[1] 9 JULY 1858

Mention in Charles J. Sawyer catalogue (undated); *MS* (3rd person) 1 p.; dated 9 July 58; addressed Lord Robert Grosvenor.

To JOHN THOMPSON, 11 JULY 1858

Extract in N, III, 32 (from catalogue source); dated Gad's Hill Place, 11 July 58.

John, Please take a cab to Mr. Watkins's Photographic Gallery Regent St. . . . and take away to Tavistock House my writing table and brown cloak.[2] Also, please call at Hall's,[3] my bootmakers, and order me another pair of shepherd's plaid, ankle, spring boots,[4] like the two last pairs.

To CHARLES DICKENS JNR, [?10–12 JULY 1858]

Extracts in Charley Dickens *to* Mrs CD, 13 July 58, MS Huntington Library.[5] *Date:* CD probably wrote to Charley 2–3 days before Charley found his letter.

[a]I myself took out of our Deed of separation the usual formal clause inserted by her own solicitors; that she should have access to the children except at Tavistock House.[6] That exception seemed to me to convey an unnecessary slight upon her, and I said that she should see them there or anywhere. . . .[a]

[b]I positively forbid the children ever to utter one word [c]to their grandmother or to Helen Hogarth.[c] If they are ever brought into the presence of either of these two, I charge them immediately to leave your mother's house and come back to me. . . .[b]

[1] Lord Robert Grosvenor (1801–93; *DNB*), politician: see Vol. VII, p. 659 and *n*. CD clearly did not know he had been created Baron Ebury in 1857.

[2] Used by Watkins in taking CD's photograph on 17 June: see 31 May.

[3] Matthew Hall & Co., 88 Leadenhall St.

[4] Boots fitted with springs; new in 1766.

[5] Charley wrote to his mother: "Although I much regret being the medium of the communication I have to make to you, still, as I know it is part of the duty I have set before myself, I accept it without hesitation. | It is this. | On arriving this morning from Henley I found awaiting me a letter from my father referring to your letter to Frank [*home for the holidays from the school at Boulogne*]. | He says [[aa], *quoted above*] | You see therefore that you have a distinct right to see the children when where or how you please, but he places these restrictions on their visits, which I am particularly desirous to impress upon you (*from myself*, and not from him) he has the most perfect right and power to do. [[bb], *quoted above*]—and further in reference to Mr. Lemon [*name omitted in* Mr. & Mrs. CD, *see below;* [dd] *quoted above*] You will see that as far as you are concerned he has no desire, and, in fact no power, if he had the wish to keep them from you, but he has, as their father, an absolute right to prevent their going into any society which may be distasteful to him, as long as they remain under age. I think it necessary to point this out to you *strongly*, in order that there may be no unnecessary and useless talk on this matter. And here, I trust, the subject will rest between us. | I shall sleep at Queen's Road tonight as I have a good deal to pack up there. I will be home to dinner tomorrow at six & will then permanently take up my quarters with you. Till then I remain, ever your most affectionate son | CHARLEY" (MS Huntington).

[6] The formal clause in such a Deed usually excluded the separated spouse from visiting the marital residence.

[cc] Omitted in *Mr & Mrs CD his Letters to her*, ed. Walter Dexter, 1935, pp. 280–1.

[d]I positively forbid the children ever to see or to speak to him,[1] and for the same reason I absolutely prohibit [e]their ever being[e] taken to Mr. Evans's house.[d]

To THE COMMITTEE OF THE GARRICK CLUB, 12 JULY 1858

MS The Garrick Club.

GAD'S HILL PLACE, | HIGHAM BY ROCHESTER, KENT.
Monday Twelfth July, 1858.

Gentlemen

As I had the misfortune to differ from you on the whole principle of last Saturday's discussion, and as I cannot take upon myself the very difficult and unsatisfactory functions which you understand to attach to your Body, but which I believe that Body has no right to assume, I beg your permission to resign my seat at your Board.

I am Gentlemen | With much regard | Faithfully Yours
The Committee | of | The Garrick Club CHARLES DICKENS

To OCTAVE LACROIX,[2] 12 JULY 1858

Facsimile in *Catalogue de Mme G. Whitney Hoff*, Paris, 1934.

GAD'S HILL PLACE, | HIGHAM BY ROCHESTER, KENT.
Monday Twelfth July, 1858

Dear Sir

I feel exceedingly obliged to you for your flattering and interesting letter. I have a great ambition to be extensively read and well understood, in France; and you give me the liveliest and most cordial pleasure when you predict that I shall become widely known among the great French people.[3]

I owe you many apologies for not having answered your letter sooner. But I have been constantly occupied, and it was unfortunately mislaid, and has but this day been recovered.

It would gratify me very much if I could give you any details that would be useful to you, or interesting to your readers. But all that I could say *of* my books I have said *in* them. They originate in my own reflections and fancies, and in my observation of the world around me. Little Dorrit is my last published work. It was published monthly (de mois en mois) and completed in 20 parts (livraisons). Hard Times was

[1] Lemon. A few days after this letter, Lemon wrote to Paxton: "I know you will excuse the freedom I am taking in asking if the Dickens [*thus*] are coming to your fete on Wednesday as just at present I do not wish my young people to meet them" (MS BL). CD did not apparently meet or speak to Lemon again until 18 May 1867, when, he told Lemon's son Harry, sending him condolences for his father's death in 1870, they "embraced affectionately" at Stanfield's grave; in the same letter (25 May 1870; N, III, 780–1) he disclaimed "any serious estrangement" between them.

[ee] *Mr & Mrs CD* reads "them ever to be".

[2] Octave Lacroix (*b.* 1827), French journalist and miscellaneous writer. Secretary to Sainte-Beuve 1851. His books include *Chanson d'Avril*, 1851 and *Du culte de la Vierge au point de la Poétique Religieuse*, 1858. His comedy, *L'Amour et son Train*, was performed in 1855. Secretary to the Senate 1876.

[3] See *To* Forster, 30 Jan 56 and *fn*.

originally published from week to week (de semaine en semaine), in my own literary Journal, Household Words. I have no dates, here, in the country, to refer to; but I think Hard Times was completed about 4 years ago.[1] Little Dorrit was completed and published entire, in May 1857.

Accept the assurance of my great regard and esteem and Believe me always, My Dear Sir

Yours faithfully

Monsieur Octave Lacroix. CHARLES DICKENS

To JOHN HILLS,[2] 13 JULY 1858

Mention in N, III, 32.

To DR W. C. HOOD, [?15 JULY 1858]

Envelope only, MS Brown University Library. *Address:* Dr. Hood | Bethelehem Hospital | S. PM 15 July 58 London.

To ALFRED NOVELLO,[3] 15 JULY 1858

Mention in N, III, 33; *MS* 1 p.; dated Tavistock House, 15 July 58.

Asking for the address of Countess Gigliucci, the singer.

To RICHARD SPOFFORD,[4] 15 JULY 1858*

MS Morgan Library.

TAVISTOCK HOUSE, | TAVISTOCK SQUARE, LONDON. W.C.
Thursday Fifteenth July, 1858

My Dear Sir

I have a hope that it will not be displeasing to you, to receive a letter under my hand. I have an absolute certainty that it is a great pleasure and relief to me to write it.

[1] In Aug 54.

[2] No doubt the John Hills who acted as intermediary for Richard Oliver's articles in *HW* on "The Treatment of the Insane": see Vols VI, pp. 454 and *n*, 610 and VII, p. 347*n*.

[3] Joseph Alfred Novello (1810–96), Countess Gigliucci's brother; eldest son of Vincent Novello (1781–1861; *DNB*), music publisher; succeeded his father as head of Novello & Co.; published the *Musical Times* from 1844; introduced Mendelssohn's works to England. Bass singer; sang in oratorios and concerts. Treasurer, Association for Promoting Repeal of Taxes on Knowledge, 1852–70.

[4] Richard Smith Spofford, Jnr (1833–88), lawyer and politician; son of Dr Richard Smith Spofford, of Newburyport, Mass; descended from an old New England family. Studied law in office of Caleb Cushing (Attorney-Gen. 1853–7) and acted as his private secretary. Practised in US Circuit Court, Washington, 1856; and in Essex and Suffolk Counties, Mass, from 1857. Senator for Massachusetts. Married Dec 65 the poet and essayist Harriet ("Hally") Elizabeth Prescott (1835–1921; *DAB*), close friend of Annie Fields.

Your Cousin[1] Fanny[2] has shewn me a letter of yours in which reference is made to me. I would not for the world do her or you the wrong of giving you any assurance upon a subject on which your own generous nature is perfectly clear. But what I wish to do, is to thank you most heartily for the comfort and strength I have derived from the contemplation of your character as it is expressed in that letter beyond the possibility of mistake, and to convey to you, in a manner as plain and unaffected as your own, my admiration of the noble instinct with which the upright know the upright, all the broad world over. Your Cousin well deserves to be its subject.

From the first month, I think, of my knowing your Cousin Fanny, I have confided in her, have taken great interest in her, and have highly respected her. You may be sure (as I know her mother and sisters are, and as I know my own two daughters are), that there could not live upon this earth a man more blamelessly and openly her friend than I am, or to whom her honor could be dearer than it is to me.

I desire to avoid troubling you with my personal feelings under such wild misrepresentation and amazing falsehood.[3] I will only say on that head that while I know this kind of evil to be a dark place in the social life of many countries, and especially of America, I know well—as no one can have better reason—the chivalry and integrity of the general American character, and I trust myself to it with implicit confidence.

My dear Sir, my wish is gratified. I have stretched out my hand across the Ocean to grasp yours, and I can bear even the misfortune of most innocently causing your Cousin one painful moment, the better for it.

Believe me | With much regard | Faithfully Yours

Richard S Spofford Esquire CHARLES DICKENS

[1] Spofford's mother, née Frances Maria Mills, was a grand-daughter of Mrs Ternan's uncle; therefore a second cousin, once removed, of Fanny, Maria and Ellen Ternan. Fanny knew him as "Cousin Richard".

[2] Frances Eleanor Ternan (1835–1913), eldest daughter of Thomas Lawless Ternan and Frances Eleanor Ternan; born in Aug 35 on a paddle steamer in Delaware Bay, while her parents were acting in America. As actress, opera singer and, later, novelist, the most widely gifted of the three Ternan sisters; she "did everything with panache" and was "brimming over with vitality" (Helen Wickham, daughter of Ellen Ternan's intimate friend, Rosalind Wickham, quoted by Katharine M. Longley in "The Real Ellen Ternan", *D*, LXXXI [1985], 33). Particularly devoted to Ellen. Played juvenile roles in London and the provinces 1840–6, including Mamillius in *The Winter's Tale*, the young Duke of York in *Richard III*, Arthur in *King John*, and Young Norval in John Home's *Douglas*. The three sisters probably then went to school in Birmingham (perhaps at the Misses Adelaide and Thérèse Duchemin's "Ladies' School", 34 Albion St), living with their uncle Henry Rolfe, a civil engineer; Fanny was given singing lessons by Louis Michel Duchemin, "Professor of Languages", later organist at Birmingham Oratory, of the same address, probably father of Adelaide and Thérèse (Katharine Longley, above, p. 38). In London with her mother and two sisters from 1850. Made her début as an adult singer at Exeter Hall concert, 2 Nov 53; other concerts and singing roles followed; sang in opera from 1858. For her spending the next two years studying singing in Florence, see next vol. Other details of her acting and singing career are given in Claire Tomalin, *The Invisible Woman*, 1990, *passim*. A photograph of the three sisters is given in *D*, LIII (1957), 43.

[3] Rumours in America had clearly coupled CD's name with Fanny's.

To THE COUNTESS GIGLIUCCI, 16 JULY 1858*

MS Brotherton Library, Leeds.

TAVISTOCK HOUSE, | TAVISTOCK SQUARE, LONDON. W.C.
Friday Sixteenth July, 1858.

My Dear Countess Gigliucci

I want to ask your kind advice, and I know you will give it me.

A young lady for whom I have a great friendship and in whom I am much interested, is going to study in Italy, the better to qualify herself as a professional singer. She has already been pretty well trained and taught here, but wishes to complete her musical Education and make it a sound one, under good Italian instruction.[1]

She has asked me to what part of Italy I could recommend her going, and under what kind of master I could recommend her placing herself. I have not the least idea! But it suddenly comes into my head that nobody can enlighten me so well as you.

Will you write to me a word or two of enlightenment: understanding that it is not an Amateur affair, but a thorough working one.

I beg to send my kind regards to Count Gigliucci, and Am Ever

Faithfully your friend | And admirer
CHARLES DICKENS

To THOMAS HEADLAND,[2] 16 JULY 1858

Text from Brentano's catalogue, No. 124.

St Martin's Hall | 16 July 1858

To Mr. Headland

This set of my Books, with thanks

CHARLES DICKENS

To ROBERT ORRIDGE,[3] 17 JULY 1858

MS Mr Alex Robertson. *Address:* Robert Orridge Esquire | 3 Paper Buildings | Temple | London | E.C.

GAD'S HILL PLACE, | HIGHAM BY ROCHESTER, KENT.
Saturday Seventeenth July 1858

My Dear Sir

I am sorry that my being here, except when business takes me to London for a

[1] Fanny studied, presumably in Florence, under the distinguished singing-teacher, Pietro Romani, and learnt Italian.

[2] Thomas Hughes Headland (?1806–88); silversmith in Clerkenwell 1842–59; assistant to Arthur Smith in CD's first series of public readings 1858; kept Sussex Hotel, Eastbourne, 1869–72. For his taking over as manager of CD's reading tours on Arthur Smith's death in Oct 61, see next vol.

[3] Robert Orridge (*d.* 1866), barrister, son of Charles Orridge of Regent St, Cambridge; called to Bar by Middle Temple Jan 53; married eldest daughter of F. M. Evans, 1860.

few hours at a time, has deprived me of the pleasure of seeing you in reference to the very kind note of Mr. Macrory.[1]

May I ask you to be so good as to assure that gentleman that I am exceedingly sensible of his father's[2] hospitable offer,[3] and that I thank him very heartily for his great courtesy. But I have been obliged to resolve that I will deny myself all such pleasures during my tour. It will be so very fatiguing, that I am quite sure I can intermingle no social enjoyments with its occupations. I have therefore (putting a virtuous constraint upon myself with a very bad grace), doggedly made up my mind to confine myself to Inns. Even when I shall be in Scotland among many old friends, I shall stick to this heroic resolution.

I am not the less indebted to Mr. Macrory, and I cannot too warmly acknowledge or respond to his invitation.

My Dear Sir | Faithfully Yours
CHARLES DICKENS

To HERBERT WATKINS, 17 JULY 1858*

MS Free Library of Philadelphia. *Address:* Herbert Watkins Esquire | 215 Regent Street | London | W.

GAD'S HILL PLACE, | HIGHAM BY ROCHESTER, KENT.
Saturday Seventeenth July, 1858

My Dear Mr. Watkins

I owe you many thanks for your most obliging note. I am glad to hear so good an account of the Portraits,[4] and I do not doubt that they will be admirable.

It would give me great pleasure to have some five and twenty impressions for private friends, if those should not be too many.

I hope the colored Portrait will be ready in the last week of this month.[5] I go away on a tour, on the 1st. of August, and particularly wish to send that packet to its destination (I have already forsworn myself for a long time), before I leave.

Faithfully Yours
Herbert Watkins Esquire CHARLES DICKENS

[1] Edmund Macrory, barrister. Educated at Trinity College, Dublin; called to Bar by Middle Temple Jan 53; Bencher 1878; QC 1890; Treasurer 1897.

[2] Adam John Macrory (1799–1881), Belfast solicitor; Director of Great Northern Railway (Ireland); Governor of Belfast Lunatic Asylum for *c.* 50 years. (Information kindly given by his grandson, Mr Alex Robertson.)

[3] Clearly to stay with him, when giving his readings in Belfast that Aug.

[4] When posing on 17 June, CD was asked by Watkins to write the following words on a sheet which he was holding "I want you to write very strong, and as large as you can: so that the light may catch it—which done, believe me to remain | Always very faithfully Yours | CHARLES DICKENS | Thursday | June Seventeenth, 1858." CD went on to add in French "Je vous avoue que je suis fache de tout cela, mon cher", and to make a rough sketch of a head with what may be a photographer's hood. At the top of the sheet, presumably in Watkins's hand, is "Written for me when posing" (MS Free Library of Philadelphia).

[5] For the *Critic*'s use of it as an illustration in its series of celebrities (4 Sep 58), see *To* Watkins, 31 May 58, *fn.*

To F. M. EVANS, 22 JULY 1858

Text from N, III, 33.

GAD'S HILL PLACE, | HIGHAM BY ROCHESTER, KENT.[1]
Thursday July Twenty-Second 1858[2]

Dear Sir,

I have had stern occasion to impress upon my children that their father's name is their best possession and that it would indeed[3] be trifled with and wasted by him, if, either through himself or through them, he held any terms with those who have been false to it, in the only great[4] need and under the only great wrong it has ever known. You know very well, why (with hard distress of mind and bitter disappointment), I have been forced to include you in this class. I have no more to say.[5]

[CHARLES DICKENS]

P.S.—Your letter reached me, only yesterday.

To S. L. BROOKS, 23 JULY 1858*

MS Mr Frank North.

TAVISTOCK HOUSE, | TAVISTOCK SQUARE, LONDON. W.C.
Friday Twenty Third July, 1858.

Dear Sir

I write this letter to be presented to you by my friend Mr. Arthur Smith, who is the business-manager of my Public Readings.

Those readings will take me nearly all over England Ireland and Scotland, during the months of August, September, October, and November. My present object is, to ascertain whether the liberality of your Company towards a public man, will concede me, during that time, any advantages on your line.

It will be necessary for me to travel—two first class, and three second or third;

[1] Although on headed paper, almost certainly from London where he was at the Princess's, 21 July (see *To* Kean, 23 July), and gave his final reading of *Little Dombey*, on 22 July.

[2] Date not given in *CD and Maria Beadnell. Private Correspondence*, ed. G. P. Baker, priv. printed, Bibliophile Society of Boston, Mass, 1908, p. 145.

[3] Omitted in Bibliophile Society of Boston text, above.

[4] Bibliophile Society of Boston reads "greatest".

[5] Bradbury & Evans had not printed CD's "Personal" statement of 7 June in *Punch*, despite his appeal to his fellow-journalists "to lend their aid to the dissemination of my present words". In their statement in June 59, *Mr. Charles Dickens and His Late Publishers* (included with No. XX of Thackeray's *The Virginians*), they maintained that for this reason alone CD decided to end his "business transactions" with them. But the quarrel with Evans, as with Lemon (see *To* Charley Dickens, 10–12 July 58 and *fn*), may well have been more personal. Evans was Catherine's co-trustee, with Lemon, under the Deed of Separation; Catherine's solicitors, Smith & Shepherd, were also Bradbury & Evans's; CD may well have felt that Evans had too openly, at some stage, espoused Catherine's cause against his own. CD may also have believed that Evans had re-told or at any rate believed in the scandal about Georgina and himself. This would explain Georgina's continuing animosity against the Evans family. He never met Evans socially again.

and my luggage may probably somewhat (but not greatly) exceed in weight what would be ordinarily allowed to such passengers.

If, on conferring with Mr. Arthur Smith, you should think it not inconsistent with the usual consideration of your Company, to afford me any facilities, I should feel very truly obliged.[1]

I am Dear Sir | Your faithful Servant

S. L. Brooks Esquire CHARLES DICKENS

To EDWARD CHAPMAN, 23 JULY 1858*

MS Benoliel Collection.

TAVISTOCK HOUSE, | TAVISTOCK SQUARE, LONDON. W.C.
Friday Twenty Third July, 1858

My Dear Sir

I quite agree with you as to the proposal you communicate.[2] It is altogether out of the question, and is, in the pecuniary part of it, ridiculous.

Will you tell me, for the information of an accursed correspondent,[3] when the Pickwick Papers were first published.

Faithfully Yours always

Edward Chapman Esquire CHARLES DICKENS

To MISS MARY BOYLE, 23 JULY 1858

Extract in *American Book Prices Current*, 1923; dated 23 July 58; mention in Walter M. Hill catalogue No. 77 (Nov 1918); *MS* 1 p.; addressed Miss Mary Boyle.

1st no. of Pickwick appeared (April 1st:) 1836 last do of do do ed (1st: Novr:) 1837.

So certified, on the authority of His Publisher's Books,

CHARLES DICKENS

To CHARLES KEAN, 23 JULY 1858*

MS Mr Edwin A. Elsbach.

TAVISTOCK HOUSE, | TAVISTOCK SQUARE, LONDON. W.C.
Friday Twenty Third July, 1858

My Dear Mr. Kean.

Let me assure you most unaffectedly and earnestly, in acknowledgement of your kind note, that I was heartily glad to be present last Wednesday;[4] and that my

[1] Letter endorsed at bottom of second page: "I am quite unable to see what special privileges can be granted, except not being too particular with the luggage. Mark Huish" (Capt. Mark Huish, Manager, London Office, London & North Western Railway, Euston).

[2] Probably connected with Bradbury & Evans, printers of the Library edn, and their joint arrangement.

[3] Mary Boyle! (see next).

[4] At a public meeting held at the Princess's Theatre to discuss the foundation of a proposed "Dramatic College": the result of a gift to the Royal General Theatrical Fund of five acres of

reference to yourself, faithfully expressed the admiration with which I listened to what you said, and with which I contemplated your highly becoming share in the proceedings.[1]

Nothing could have been better commenced than this business.[2] I shall be more interested in it than ever,[3] if it should prove (as I trust it may) the beginning of a better acquaintance between us.

With regard and good wishes, believe me to remain

Very faithfully Yours

Charles Kean Esquire. CHARLES DICKENS

To C. A. SAUNDERS,[4] 23 JULY 1858*

MS Dickens House.

TAVISTOCK HOUSE, | TAVISTOCK SQUARE, LONDON. W.C.
Friday Twenty Third July, 1858

Dear Sir

I write this letter to be presented to you by Mr. Arthur Smith, who is the business-manager of my public readings.

Those readings will take me nearly all over England Ireland and Scotland, during the months of August, September, October, and November. My present object is, to ascertain whether the liberality of your company towards a public man, will concede me, during that time, any advantages on your line.

It will be necessary for me to travel—two first class, and three second or third; and my luggage may probably somewhat (but not greatly) exceed in weight, what would be ordinarily allowed to such passengers.

If, on conferring with Mr. Arthur Smith, you should think it not inconsistent with the usual consideration of your company to afford me any facilities, I shall feel very truly obliged.

I am Dear Sir | Your faithful Servant

C. A. Saunders Esquire. CHARLES DICKENS

land in Bucks, together with 100 guineas, by a wealthy brickmaker and dust contractor, Henry Dodd. Kean was in the Chair; CD, as a Trustee of the Theatrical Fund, proposed that the gift and its proposed use be "joyfully" accepted. For his speech, see *Speeches*, ed. K. J. Fielding, pp. 275–77; originally published in the official report of the meeting, entitled *Royal Dramatic College, For Aged and Infirm Actors and Actresses, and for the Maintenance and Education of the Children of Actors* (see *Speeches*, above, p. 437). There were speeches and proposals also by Cullenford, Creswick, T. P. Cooke, Harley, Robert Bell and Webster. Subscriptions from the public and theatres had produced £4,230 by 22 Aug; CD subscribed ten guineas on 5 Aug (CD's Account-book, MS Messrs Coutts).

[1] CD referred to Kean's "manly advocacy" of the proposed scheme and described it as blending "the large spirit of an artist, the feeling of a man, and the grace of a gentleman" (*Speeches*, above, pp. 275–6).

[2] CD's resolution was carried unanimously, T. P. Cooke calling on his "old friend—I mean my young friend—Mr. Harley" to second it; CD, Kean, Webster and Thackeray were elected Trustees and Webster Chairman. But, for the breakdown of the original scheme, see next vol.

[3] A similar scheme for a dramatic college had originally been devised in March and reported in theatrical papers (including the *Theatrical Journal*, 21 Mar), and subscriptions collected.

[4] Charles Alexander Saunders (1797–1864), Secretary and General Superintendent of Great Western Railway since 1833.

To J. PALGRAVE SIMPSON, 23 JULY 1858

MS Dickens House.

TAVISTOCK HOUSE, | TAVISTOCK SQUARE, LONDON. W.C.
Friday Twenty Third July 1858

My Dear Simpson

The Committee seem to me to have gone perfectly mad. I really never met with such ridiculous assumption and preposterous imbecility, in my life before.[1]

Like you, I should "boil with indignation", if I had not a vent. But I have. Upon my soul, when I picture them to myself in that backyard, conceiving that they shake the earth, I fall into fits of laughter which make my daughters laugh—away at Gad's Hill—until the tears run down their cheeks.

—But this is not to the purpose, concerning Edmund Yates. Before I received your note last night, I had recommended him to ascertain, from good sound legal authority, the exact state of the legality of the question. This he is now doing.[2] If he can fix them on that, it will be far better than any protest. If he can not, *then* let us take counsel as to that step. Meanwhile, wait.

I cannot too warmly assure you of my hearty admiration of your generous feeling in this matter,[3] or of my desire to render steady, unflinching, and enduring support. It is amazing to me that so many men can be the tools of such a wonderful small Inquisition. But I conceive that every day's notoriety makes the whole thing, and the whole club, more absurd; and I believe that with a fine retributive justice, there are the seeds of certain decay and destruction in this rottenness.

Very Cordially Yours
CHARLES DICKENS

J. Palgrave Simpson Esquire.

To AUGUSTUS TRACEY, 24 JULY 1858*

MS University of Texas. *Address:* Lieutenant Tracey R.N. | 5 Windsor Terrace | Plymouth.

GAD'S HILL PLACE, | HIGHAM BY ROCHESTER, KENT.
Saturday Twenty Fourth July, 1858

My Dear Commodore.

I have not answered your kind note sooner, for the best of all possible reasons, my brave old Salt—because I have only just received it, along with a hold-full of correspondence from Tavistock House.

You know that if it were possible for me to come aboard o' the Windsor Terrace, I should answer your signal, joyfully, out of hand. But I *must* be at an Inn, and by myself, and *must* avoid engagements, under these circumstances. As to Arthur Smith, he will live, in a high fever, for the next four months, and will (I know beforehand) always dine standing. But I tell you what. If you will give us a glass of pale ale

[1] Yates was expelled from the Garrick Club on 20 July, after the Secretary's giving him three days further grace to apologize to Thackeray had met with no response (see *Letters and Private Papers of W. M. Thackeray*, ed. Gordon N. Ray, IV, pp. 105–6).

[2] In compliance with his counsel's advice, he had had himself forcibly removed from the Club on his second attempt (*ibid.* p. 106). See *To* Thackeray, 24 Nov 58, *fn.*

[3] Simpson had spoken in support of Yates at the Special General Meeting of 10 July.

and grog, on the Wednesday or Thursday night, after the reading,[1] we will come to you with delight. Being positively our first, last, and only appearance off the Inn Boards during the whole Tour.

I send something as near my love as I may, to Mrs. Tracey. Forster is staying here, and adds his particular regard.[2]

To EDWARD WALFORD, 24 JULY 1858*

MS Chas. J. Sawyer Ltd.

GAD'S HILL PLACE, | HIGHAM BY ROCHESTER, KENT.
Saturday Twenty Fourth July, 1858.

Sir

Your obliging note is not dated, but I fear it may possibly be some days old, as it reaches me this morning along with a great arrear of correspondence.

I always have it in my mind to leave my own auto-biography for my childrens' information. Although I have seen various lives of myself surprisingly new to me in all their details, I have never, therefore, taken their correction upon myself.[3] If there should be any dates that you desire to know and will tell me what they are, I will supply them, if I can.[4]

Your faithful Servant
CHARLES DICKENS

E. Walford Esquire
&c &c &c

To H. G. ADAMS, 24 JULY 1858

Text from N, III, 34.

GAD'S HILL PLACE, | HIGHAM BY ROCHESTER, KENT.
Saturday Night Twenty Fourth July 1858

Dear Sir,

Mr. Arthur Smith (to be addressed at my house in London) is the business-manager of my Readings, and conducts all the correspondence arising out of them. But as he has a perfect understanding beforehand with me that they are always my own enterprise, and that I am never to be engaged by any Institution or by any person, I let you know as much, to save you the trouble of writing to him.

I shall be here at intervals during the summer (for a day or two at a time) and shall be happy to make an appointment with you, if you should desire to see me. But there is not the slightest chance of my being able to read for your Institution.[5]

Faithfully yours always
[CHARLES DICKENS]

[1] He read at Stonehouse and Plymouth on 4 and 5 Aug: see *To* Miss Georgina Hogarth, 5 Aug and *fnn.*

[2] Ending and signature cut away.

[3] But in fact he had done so in *To* The Editor of the *Durham Advertiser*, 3 Feb 38: Vol. I, p. 367 and *nn.*

[4] See *To* Walford, 28 July and *fn.*

[5] The Chatham Mechanics' Institution. He did however read there on 29 Dec: see *To* Adams, 30 Nov.

To WILLIAM J. CLEMENT, 25 JULY 1858*

MS Morgan Library.

GAD'S HILL PLACE, | HIGHAM BY ROCHESTER, KENT.
Sunday Twenty Fifth July, 1858.

My Dear Clement.

I have received your letter with much pleasure, and count upon shaking hands with you at Shrewsbury.[1] But I am sorry to say that I *must*[2] deny myself, all through my tour, the pleasure of visiting my friends. Its fatigues will be very great indeed, and I know I can only hope to triumph over them, by observing a rigid system in this regard.

You can scarcely think what a noble spectacle of virtue I feel myself to be, when I announce this resolution. It is so excessively disagreeable to me that I become, in my own eyes, almost sublime.

With kind regard at home
Ever Very faithfully Yours
CHARLES DICKENS

William Clement Esquire

To MRS CORNELIUS, 27 JULY 1858

Text from N, III, 34.

OFFICE OF HOUSEHOLD WORDS,
Tuesday Twenty Seventh July 1858

My Dear Anne,

Will you please call me in the morning at a quarter before 8, and let me have breakfast at a quarter before 9. I am going back by an early Train.[3]

Faithfully yours
[CHARLES DICKENS]

To T. J. THOMPSON, 27 JULY 1858

Mention in list of letters from CD to Thompson made by his son-in-law Wilfrid Meynell; *MS* 1 p.; dated Gad's Hill, 27 July 58.[4]

To HENRY MORLEY, 27 JULY 1858*

MS Mr Douglas C. Ewing.

TAVISTOCK HOUSE, | TAVISTOCK SQUARE, LONDON. W.C.
Tuesday Night | Twenty Seventh July 1858

My Dear Morley

Coming to town for the evening, I find the accompanying packet at Tavistock House here. I send it to you. Will you kindly write an acknowledgement, of its

[1] Where he read on 12 Aug.
[2] Doubly underlined.
[3] i.e. to Gad's Hill; his overnight visit to London was presumably for the regular *HW* meeting.
[4] Before leaving for London: see next.

receipt from the office, to the effect that the Writer of the article in H.W.[1] begs to say that it has been laid before him by Mr. C.D.

In haste | Faithfully Yours always
CHARLES DICKENS

To EDWARD WALFORD, 28 JULY 1858†

MS University of Texas. *Address:* E. Walford Esquire. M.A. &c &c &c | Hampstead | near London | N.W.

GAD'S HILL PLACE, | HIGHAM BY ROCHESTER, KENT.[2]
Wednesday Twenty Eighth July, 1858

Dear Sir

I beg to return you the accompanying Proof.[3]

In adherence to the rule I always observe, I have not touched it.

[a]But I would suggest to you that it is hardly well to rest any thing connected with the origin of the Pickwick Papers, on a vague "it is said";[4] when their origin has been for some years, exactly described by my own hand, and before the Public, in the Preface to the "Cheap Edition" of that work.[a5]

With thanks to you for your courtesy, I beg to remain

Faithfully Yours
CHARLES DICKENS

E. Walford Esquire
&c &c &c

[1] Perhaps "Sarawak", 24 July 58, XVIII, 130, which has a Chip as its "Postscript" on 31 July, Morley's most recent *HW* article; but he had many other articles in *HW* this month.

[2] CD was at Gad's Hill from Wed 28 July to Sun 1 Aug, clearly for the Thompsons' visit, with his London readings over and his provincial tour not starting until the following week. On 29 July Christiana recorded in her diary: "This was the day. Fine & lovely.... Saw Dickens sitting in chaise awaiting us. He very cordial & hearty.... At Dickens Mr. & Mrs. Austin, Mr. Beard, Miss Power ... a wonderful decolté old maid—Nice dinner. I next D.—Passed off very well." And on the 31st: "had lunch & came away.... Got over it pretty well. D. is brilliant as ever & looks well—& dresses do. His face is most intense & has the nota[bi]lity of no ordinary man" (MS Mrs Sowerby).

[3] Probably Walford was already at work (in alphabetical order) on his rewriting of notices for his *Men of the Time*, published early 1862. But it is also possible that he had renewed hopes of including CD in his monthly series of *Photographic Portraits of Living Celebrities* (see 4 Oct 56); the most recent was No. 27 for July, of Maclise, and Stanfield was to be No. 30, for October. Although these are much fuller than the 1862 notices, the substance and tone are similar and many sentences identically worded. The series continued until Aug 59.

[aa] Given in N at end of June 56, although dated [1858]; remainder not published.

[4] The biographical notice merely says that, after seeing the *Sketches*, Chapman & Hall requested a serial in monthly parts. If the proof said more, it must have been further revised.

[5] Published 1847: for Edward Chapman's confirmation of its strict correctness, see Vol. V, p. 575*n*.

To EDWARD CHAPMAN, 30 JULY 1858

MS Berg Collection.

GAD'S HILL PLACE, | HIGHAM BY ROCHESTER, KENT.
Friday Thirtieth July, 1858

My Dear Sir

This will present to you, my friend Mr. Edmund Yates, whose literary career I wish to assist and advance, if I can.

He has asked my opinion on a question he had an idea of propounding to you.[1] As I cannot form an opinion on the subject (not knowing what your engagements may be), I give him this letter that he may state it for himself. I am quite sure you will answer it frankly.

Faithfully Yours always

Edward Chapman Esquire CHARLES DICKENS

To CHARLES FAIDER,[2] 31 JULY 1858*

MS Berg Collection. *Address:* À Monsieur Ch: Faider | &c | &c &c | Bruxelles.

GAD'S HILL PLACE, | HIGHAM BY ROCHESTER, KENT.
Samedi Juillet 31, 1858

Monsieur.

J'ai l'honneur distinguée de reçevoir votre letter.

Je regrette extremement que ma presence au Congres a Bruxelles[3] est absolument impossible; mais permettez-moi de vous assurer, Monsieur, que je sens vivement l'importance de l'idee, et que je vous envois mon adhesion avec le plus grand interet et plaisir.

Agreez Monsieur l'assurance de ma consideration tres distinguée.

Monsieur Ch: Faider. CHARLES DICKENS

[1] Probably about publishing a collection of his contributions to *HW* and other periodicals; but Chapman never published Yates, whose next such volume did not appear till early 1861: *After Office Hours*, published by W. Kent & Co., and in 1862 by Maxwell as a yellowback, containing four *HW* pieces.

[2] Charles Jean Baptiste Florian Faider (1811–88), Belgian lawyer and statesman. Minister of Justice 1852–55; Advocate-General in Court of "Cassation" 1855–70; Procureur-General 1870–86. Wrote several studies of the Belgian Constitution.

[3] A Congress on "Literary and Artistic Property" held 27–30 Sep 58, with Faider in the chair; proceedings published by Edouard Romberg, Brussels, Paris and London, 2 vols, 1859. There was some disappointment over the lack of any official deputation from the UK; but Robert Bell was present.

To THOMAS BEARD, 1 AUGUST 1858

MS Dickens House. *Address:* Thomas Beard Esquire | 42 Portman Place | Edgeware Road | London | N.W.

GAD'S HILL PLACE, | HIGHAM BY ROCHESTER, KENT.
Sunday First August, 1858.

My Dear Beard

I bring with me to Tavistock House, "to be left till called for", a little writing-case in a cover, which I think belongs to you.

Ever affecy
CD.

To WILKIE COLLINS, 1 AUGUST 1858

MS Morgan Library.

GAD'S HILL PLACE, | HIGHAM BY ROCHESTER, KENT.
Sunday First August 1858.

My Dear Wilkie

I am off from here to-day, and enclose you (hastily) my Tour,[1] and my address at each place. I hope you are enjoying yourself at Broadstairs—holding on by your great advance in health—and getting into the condition, physically, of Ben Caunt[2]—morally, of William Shakespeare.

Charley's paper[3] has a great deal in it that is very droll and good. I have sent it to the Printer.

With kind regard | Ever affecy.
CHARLES DICKENS

To PERCY FITZGERALD,[4] 2 AUGUST 1858

Mention in N, III, 35.

[1] Given in *CD as Editor*, p. 239: see Appx H.

[2] Benjamin Caunt (1815–61; *DNB*), pugilist; "Champion of England" 1840; proprietor of *Coach and Horses*, St Martin's Lane, 1843. His last big fight was in 1857.

[3] Charles Collins's "Her Face", *HW*, 28 Aug 58, XVIII, 258 the story of the pursuit of a girl whose photograph has entranced the teller, finally successful and leading to marriage.

[4] Percy Hetherington Fitzgerald (1831–1925), son of Thomas Fitzgerald, MP, of Fane Valley, Dundalk, Ireland; novelist and miscellaneous writer. BA Trinity College, Dublin, 1855; called to Irish Bar; Crown prosecutor; married 1869 the Hon. Dorcas Louisa Skeffington, daughter of 10th Viscount Massareene. Early turned to writing and established himself in a variety of periodicals. Prolific contributor to *HW* since July 56; his first story, "At the Sign of the Silver Horn", 26 July 56, XIV, 41, was, according to him, accepted with Forster's help, and "considered a striking success" (*Memories of CD*, 1913, p. 4); contributed two stories to the 1856 Christmas No., "Wreck of the Golden Mary", and by Aug 58 had contributed over 30 stories and articles. His claims of a "close and familiar" friendship with CD, a relationship of "precious intimacy" (*Memories*, above, p. 5), were exaggerated; but CD was fond of him, encouraged him and admired some of his writing. First President of the Dickens Fellowship.

To EDMUND YATES, 4 AUGUST [1858]

Extract in *Edmund Yates: His Recollections and Experiences*, I, 303; dated Plymouth,[1] 4 August. *Date:* see next.

We had a most noble night at Exeter last night,[2] and turned numbers away. Arthur is something between a Home Secretary and a furniture-dealer in Rathbone Place.[3] He is either always corresponding in the genteelest manner, or dragging rout-seats[4] about without his coat.

To MISS GEORGINA HOGARTH, 5 AUGUST 1858†

MS Huntington Library. *Address* (Envelope, MS Mr W. Miller)*:* Miss Hogarth, | Gad's Hill Place | Higham | by Rochester | Kent.

West Hoe, Plymouth | Thursday Fifth August 1858

My dearest Georgy

I received your letter this morning with the greatest pleasure, and read it with the utmost interest in all its domestic details. [a]On the Beard[5]—or Thompson[6] question, I am quite clear, without the shadow of a doubt. Decidedly, take Thompson! There is no comparison between them. He is not wearisome—really has tact—and is far more formable and mouldable altogether.[a][7]

We had a most wonderful night at Exeter. [a]Only two things are[a] to be regretted [a]in reference to it. Firstly, that even Arthur could not squeeze more than £75 into the room. Secondly,[a] that we cannot take the place again on our way back. It was a prodigious cram, and we turned away no end of people. But not only that. I think they were the finest Audience I have ever read to; I don't think I ever read, in some respects so well; and I never beheld anything like the personal affection which they poured out upon me at the end.[8] It was really a very remarkable sight, and I shall always look back upon it with pleasure.[9]

Last night here, was not so bright.[10] There are quarrels of the strangest kind,

[1] He read at Stonehouse (near Plymouth), once on 4 Aug, and twice on 5 Aug.

[2] CD read the *Carol* in the Royal Public Rooms on 3 Aug. The warm notice in *Chambers's Exeter Journal*, 7 Aug, reported "the most rapturous applause" at the end; he "must be heard to be appreciated. A higher literary treat can scarcely be imagined."

[3] Off Oxford St; No. 11 was William Hope's rout furniture warehouse.

[4] Chairs for hire (*OED*, which refers to this letter).

[aa] Omitted in MDGH and N.

[5] Thomas Beard.

[6] T. J. Thompson; referring to a visit to Gad's Hill, probably for the weekend of 14–16 Aug, on CD's return.

[7] Perhaps because Thompson would fit in better with the children, at home for their holidays.

[8] The writer of the notice in *Chambers's Exeter Journal*, 7 Aug, may well have been voicing the audience's feelings when he went on to write: "We regret to hear that the vile poisonous calumny is continued to be whispered in reference to his domestic affairs, notwithstanding his own manly explanation ... the reptiles who bite at his heel he can well despise. That he is the greatest author of modern time, all must admit. His teachings work wonders in his own day, and his name will go down to posterity with Shakespeare and Scott."

[9] Except for omitting "It was really ... remarkable sight", the passage from "I think ..." appears verbatim in F, VIII, iv, 661–2.

[10] He read the *Carol* in St George's Hall, Stonehouse.

between the Plymouth people and the Stonehouse people. The room is at Stonehouse (Tracey says, the wrong room: there being a Plymouth room in this Hotel, and he being a Plymouth-ite).[1] We had a fair house, but not at all a great one. All the Notabilities come this morning to Little Dombey, for which we have let 130 Stalls—which local admiration of local greatness considers very large. For Mrs. Gamp and the Boots, at night, we have also a very promising Let. But the races are on,[2] and there are two public balls tonight,[3] and the Yacht Squadron are all at Cherbourg[4] to boot. Arthur is of opinion that "Two Sixties" will do very well for us. I doubt the "Two Sixties"[5] myself. Mais, nous verrons.[6]

The room is a very handsome one, but it is on the top of a windy and muddy hill leading (literally) to nowhere; and it looks (except that it is new and *mortary*) as if the subsidence of the waters after the Deluge might have left it where it is. I have to go right through the Company to get to the Platform. Big doors slam and resound when anybody comes in; and all the company seem afraid of one another. Nevertheless they were a sensible audience last night, and much impressed and pleased.

Tracey is in the room (wandering about, and never finishing a sentence), and sends all manner of Sea-Loves to you and the dear girls. I send all manner of Land-Loves to you from myself out of my heart of hearts, and also to my dear Plorn and the boys.

[a]The letter *was* from Mrs. Dickinson, and conveys a hospitable invitation for tomorrow night.[7] Of course I am not going to her.[a]

Arthur sends his kindest love. He knows only two characters. He is either always corresponding, like a Secretary of State: or he is transformed into a Rout-Furniture-Dealer of Rathbone Place, and drags forms about with the greatest violence without his coat.

I have no time to add another word.

Ever Dearest Georgy | Your most affectionate

CD.

[1] The notice in the *Plymouth Mail* (see below) complained of its distance from Plymouth.

[2] The Plymouth, Devonport, and Cornwall Races took place in Plymouth on 5 and 6 Aug.

[3] Notice of only the Race Ball has been discovered, "very thinly attended" (*Plymouth, Devonport and Stonehouse Herald*, 7 Aug).

[4] To take part in the fêtes to celebrate the visit of the Queen and Prince Albert to the Emperor and Empress of France. The Queen had arrived at Cherbourg, attended by a British flotilla, on 4 Aug.

[5] i.e. takings of £60 a night.

[6] The notice in the *Plymouth Mail*, 11 Aug, was unusually sharp. Of the third reading CD gave on the evening of 5 Aug, it found *The Poor Traveller* "terribly tedious; it unsuccessfully attempts pathos"; and *Mrs Gamp* "vulgar and revolting, as well as untrue to nature"; only *Boots* gave the reviewer "unmixed pleasure". CD himself it found, "as a reader of narrative ... below the average; as a reader of farcical conversation, rather above". It was also critical about paid readings: "What a pity Sir Walter Scott, in his days of difficulty, did not think of so easy a way of collecting coppers. But would the proud spirit of the great Magician have stooped thereto?"

[aa] Omitted in MDGH and N.

[7] At the Manor House, Queen Charlton, a family home, between Bristol and Bath.

To MISS MARY DICKENS, 7 AUGUST 1858

Text from MDGH, II, 52–3.

London, Saturday, Aug. 7th, 1858.

My dearest Mamey,

The closing night at Plymouth was a very great scene, and the morning there was exceedingly good too. You will be glad to hear that at Clifton last night,[1] a torrent of five hundred shillings bore Arthur away, pounded him against the wall, flowed on to the seats over his body, scratched him, and damaged his best dress suit. All to his unspeakable joy.

This is a very short letter, but I am going to the Burlington Arcade, desperately resolved to have all those wonderful instruments put into operation on my head, with a view to refreshing it.[2]

Kindest love to Georgy and to all.

Ever your affectionate
[CD]

To PERCY FITZGERALD, 9 AUGUST 1858

MS University of California, Los Angeles.

GAD'S HILL PLACE, | HIGHAM BY ROCHESTER, KENT.
Monday Ninth August, 1858.

My Dear Sir

I am exceedingly obliged to you for your kind note; and I cordially assure you that I have received it with much pleasure and interest, as coming from a fellow-labourer whose writings I highly esteem.

I am not the less sensible of your proffered hospitality, because I cannot accept it. But my tour is of such a very fatiguing nature that I know it to be impossible to unite any social enjoyments with its business. I have therefore forsworn all pleasure engagements whatsoever, during its progress. I accept no invitations, see no one, and am perfectly heroic against my nature and my will.

Believe me | My Dear Sir | Faithfully Yours
Percy Fitzgerald Esquire CHARLES DICKENS

[1] He read twice at Clifton, in the large Victoria Room: *The Chimes* on 2 Aug, the *Carol* on the 6th. A short but enthusiastic notice in the *Bristol Mercury*, 7 Aug, particularly praised *The Chimes*: its "more sombre and tragic scenes were depicted with a power which excited to the utmost the sensibilities of the company".

[2] i.e. to Henry Paul Truefitt, hairdresser and perfumer, 20 and 21 Burlington Arcade.

To UNKNOWN CORRESPONDENT, 9 AUGUST 1858*

MS University of Kentucky.

GAD'S HILL PLACE, | HIGHAM BY ROCHESTER, KENT.
Monday Ninth August 1858

Dear Sir

I have been travelling about, followed by your letter, until it has at length reached me during a day's holiday at my own little country-house.

My engagements, I beg to assure you, render my compliance with the request you do me the honor to prefer to me, absolutely impossible[1]

To CHARLES WATKINS, 9 AUGUST 1858*

MS Yale University Library.

GAD'S HILL PLACE, | HIGHAM BY ROCHESTER, KENT.
Monday Ninth August 1858

Dear Sir

I received your packet[2] safely at Exeter, and am much obliged to you for your courteous attention.

Will you have the kindness to ask your brother[3] to let me know the amount in which I am indebted to him.

Faithfully Yours
CHARLES DICKENS

Charles Watkins Esquire.

To W. H. WILLS, 9 AUGUST 1858

MS Huntington Library.

GAD'S HILL PLACE, | HIGHAM BY ROCHESTER, KENT.
Monday Ninth August 1858.

My Dear Wills

H.W.[4]

I was at the office on Saturday at Noon, but did not expect to find you there.

Send me a Proof of the next No. you make up.[5] I must put a new name to Charles Collins's story.[6]

I hope Mrs. Gaskell will not stop, for more than a week at all events.[7]

[1] Ending and signature cut off.

[2] The coloured portrait-photograph of himself he had asked Herbert Watkins to send him, on 17 July.

[3] Herbert Watkins.

[4] Underlined with short double strokes.

[5] No. 440, published 28 Aug 58.

[6] See *To* Collins, 1 Aug and *fn.*

[7] Instalments of "My Lady Ludlow" stopped for one week, 21 Aug.

I am very glad to hear from Wilkie that he is at work again.[1]

I[2]

Have done exceedingly well, I think, so far. It is out of the season at Clifton, and half the houses are shut up. The Yacht Squadron too, was gone from Plymouth to Cherbourg, and there were races at Plymouth, and public balls.[3] Nevertheless we took nearly £400 last week. Exeter was tremendous. You never saw such a reception, and we might have stayed there a week. The first night at Plymouth (very wet) not good. The next morning (great talk about it spreading in the town) admirable. That night (greater talk about it spreading in the town), enormous. Similarly at Clifton. There was a very great increase of Numbers on the second night, and the local magnate said "Now they know what it is, Mr. Dickens might stay a month and always have a cram." Contrary to my impression of those Western people, I have never seen a finer or more subtly apprehensive Audience than at Exeter. Nor did I ever know the minutest touches in Little Dombey, go better in London than at Plymouth. As to the Boots at Plymouth, the people gave themselves up altogether (Generals, Mayors, and Shillings, equally) to a perfect transport of enjoyment of him and the two children.[4]

Arthur shall have the packet tomorrow morning (when we start for Worcester), that I received from you this morning.

I have no printed lists of my tour here, but will send Miss Coutts one straight.[5]

I think that's all at present,

Ever Faithfully
CD.

To MISS BURDETT COUTTS, 9 AUGUST 1858

MS Morgan Library.

OFFICE OF HOUSEHOLD WORDS,
Monday Evening Ninth August 1858

My Dear Miss Coutts

Passing through town to resume my country Readings after two days peace and quiet at Gad's Hill, I write this short note to you. Wills tells me that you want my various addresses, and I am delighted to send them,[6] and have so good an excuse for writing to you.

You will observe that a few of the addresses are at Booksellers' and the like.[7] This is to ensure my getting letters at towns where Mr. Arthur Smith does not know—or did not know, when he made out the list—the best Hotels.

Our first week was an immense success. I miss the quiet of my own desk, but I look forward to resuming it—and it is a great sensation to have a large Audience in one's hand.

[1] Probably on his serial, "The Poisoned Meal", published in Sep and Oct. He had contributed nothing from May to July, apparently owing to illness.

[2] Underlined with short double strokes.

[3] See *To* Miss Hogarth, 5 Aug and *fn*.

[4] See *ibid*.

[5] See next.

[6] See Appx H.

[7] Booksellers are named, e.g., at Worcester, Shrewsbury and York.

Charley was with us yesterday at Gad's Hill, and talked of passing his fortnight's holiday in Ireland with me. I encouraged him in the idea, as I thought it would do him more good than any other Holiday he is likely to take.[1]

It would be too happy a chance to find you any where in the Tour, but I shall hope to hear from you somewhere.

With kindest love and regard to Mrs. Brown,

Ever Dear Miss Coutts | Most affecty and faithfully Yours

CHARLES DICKENS

To WILLIAM GILES,[2] 10 AUGUST 1858

MS New York University Library.

Worcester[3] | Tuesday Tenth August 1858.

My Dear Sir

I am exceedingly obliged to you for your letter, and scarcely need assure you that your late good father[4] lives in my respect and remembrance.

My present tour is of so rapid and fatiguing a nature, that all social pleasures are incompatible with it, and I forego all invitations and engagements of whatsoever kind, and see no one. But I am not the less glad to hear from your father's son, or the less indebted for the hospitality that I cannot accept.

Faithfully Yours

W. T. Giles Esquire CHARLES DICKENS

To EDMUND YATES, 11 AUGUST 1858

MS Robert H. Taylor Collection, Princeton University Library.

Swan Hotel, Worcester | Wednesday Eleventh August 1858

My Dear Edmund

We have been immensely amused by the enclosed cutting. It must be Cole![5] Nobody else, I think, could have struck out that gentle and playful epithet, "an emasculated Caliban."

Arthur sends his kindest regard. To night's room has to be transformed (after 4 o'Clock, if you please), from a Corn Exchange into a St. Martin's Hall. He has consequently, in some strange way, covered himself with dust and ashes, as a preparation for work. In which costume he is going to dine with me at 3, to the end that he may drag the forms about without a moments loss of time.

[1] Charley did not in fact accompany CD.

[2] No doubt William Giles, factor, of 37 Sandwell St, Walsall, Staffs.

[3] In his Tour (Appx H) he gives as his address, i.e., for receiving letters, Mr Stratford's Music Warehouse, the Cross, Worcester, and stayed at the Swan. He read the *Carol* at the Music Hall that night. His reception was "hearty, even enthusiastic. Never was the Music Hall better attended." (*Worcestershire Chronicle*, 11 Aug.)

[4] The Rev. William Giles (1798–1856), CD's first schoolmaster: see Vol. I, p. 429*n*.

[5] No doubt Henry Cole, caricatured in *Hard Times* (see Vols V, p. 40 and *n* and VII, p. 354 and *n*) and well-known to CD; he had probably been criticizing CD's readings, the "enclosed cutting" being one that had amused CD and Arthur Smith, the latter being the "emasculated Caliban".

I do not see my way to making a safe appointment for Saturday. But I am going to dine with Wills at the Reform Club, on Tuesday at 1/2 past 5. And I will expect you at the H.W. office, at, or after, 4.

What a little [serpent],[1] that daughter of poor honest good [Hogarth]![1]

Ever Faithfully

CD.

To WILKIE COLLINS, 11 AUGUST 1858

MS Morgan Library.

Swan Hotel, Worcester[2]

Wednesday Evening | Eleventh August | 1858

My Dear Wilkie

I have just now toned down the capital Unknown Public article,[3] a little, here and there. Not because I dispute its positions, but because there are some things (true enough), that it would not be generous in me, as a novelist and a periodical editor, to put too prominently forward.[4] You will not find it essentially changed, anywhere.

Your letter gave me great pleasure, as all letters that you write me are sure to do. But the mysterious addresses, O misconstructive one, merely refer to places where Arthur Smith did not know aforehand the names of the best Hotels. As to that furtive and Don Giovanni purpose at which you hint—that may be all very well for *your* violent vigor, or that of the companions with whom you may have travelled continentally, or the Caliphs Haroon Alraschid with whom you have unbent metropolitanly;[5] but Anchorites who read themselves red hot every night are chaste as Diana (I suppose *she* was by the bye, but I find I don't quite believe it when I write her name).

We have done exceedingly well since we have been out—with this remarkable (and pleasant) incident; that wherever I read twice, the turn-away is invariably on the second occasion. They don't quite understand beforehand what it is, I think, and expect a man to be sitting down in some corner, droning away like a mild bagpipe. In that large room at Clifton, for instance, the people were perfectly taken off their legs by the Chimes—started—looked at each other—started again—looked at me—and then burst into a storm of applause. I think the best audiences I have yet had, were at Exeter and Plymouth. At Exeter, the best I have ever seen. At Plymouth, I read three times. Twice in one day. A better morning audience for Little Dombey, could not be. And the Boots at night, was a shout all through.

I cannot deny that I shall be heartily glad when it is all over, and that I miss the thoughtfulness of my quiet room and desk. But perhaps it is best for me not to have

[1] Both words erased and virtually illegible; but both are of *c.* 7 letters and the "s" and "t" of the first seem clear. They certainly fit CD's view of Helen Hogarth and of George.

[2] The Swan, High St.

[3] See *To* Wills, 9 Aug, *fn.*

[4] No doubt Collins's strictures on the bad writing and "extraordinary sameness" of the stories in five journals he had read. Comments such as "the same dead level of the smoothest and flattest conventionality" (p. 221) may have been even stronger before CD's "toning down".

[5] In the "Adventure of Haroon Al Rusheed", *The Arabian Nights' Entertainments*, transl. Jonathan Scott, VI, 343, the Caliph Haroon and his Grand Vizier travel round his capital disguised as foreign merchants.

it just now, and to wear and toss my Storm away—or as much of it as will ever calm down while the water rolls—in this restless manner.

Arthur Smith knows I am writing to you, and sends his kindest regard. He is all usefulness and service. I never could have done it without him.—Should have left the unredeemed Bills on the walls, and taken flight.

This is a stupid letter, but I write it before dressing to read; and you know what a brute I am at such times.

Ever Affectionately
CD.

P.S. I miss Richard Wardour's dress, and always want to put it on. I would rather, by a great deal, act. Apropos of which, I think I have a very fine notion of a part.[1] It shall be yours.

To JOHN T. LAWRENCE,[2] 11 AUGUST 1858*

MS Dickens House.

Wolverhampton | Wednesday Eleventh August 1858

My Dear Mr. Lawrence.

I have received your kind letter, with the pleasure I always feel in hearing from or seeing you.

I am greatly obliged to your hospitable friends Mr. and Mrs. Charles Potts,[3] for their hospitable invitation, and beg you to thank them cordially in my name. But I cannot have the satisfaction of accepting it. My tour is so rapid and fatiguing that I am obliged, while it is in progress, to deny myself all social pleasures, and to forego all invitations and engagements. Apart from that heroic resolution, I could not under any circumstances dine out on a day on which I read. And I have promised my daughters and the rest of my children that I will rejoin them for three days at my little country house in Kent, next Saturday. In redemption of which pledge, I shall leave Chester at the earliest possible moment after my reading is done.

Allow me to send my kindest regard and remembrance to your daughters, and to remain as ever

Very faithfully Yours
John T Lawrence Esquire CHARLES DICKENS

[1] Perhaps CD was thinking ahead to a dramatic version of what became *A Tale of Two Cities*, which has some likenesses to *The Frozen Deep*.

[2] Of Balsall Heath, Birmingham: see Vol. v, p. 319*n*.

[3] Charles Potts, JP, Northgate St, Chester, and his wife.

To MISS MARY DICKENS, 12 AUGUST 1858

Extract in MDGH, II, 53.

Shrewsbury, Thursday, Aug. 12th, 1858.

A wonderful audience last night at Wolverhampton.[1] If such a thing can be, they were even quicker and more intelligent than the audience I had in Edinburgh.[2] They were so wonderfully good and were so much on the alert this morning by nine o'clock for another reading, that we are going back there at about our Bradford time.[3] I never saw such people. And the local agent would take no money, and charge no expenses of his own.

This place looks what Plorn would call "ortily" dull. Local agent predicts, however, "great satisfaction to Mr. Dickens, and excellent attendance." I have just been to look at the hall, where everything was wrong, and where I have left Arthur making a platform for me out of dining-tables.[4]

If he comes back in time, I am not quite sure but that he is himself going to write to Gad's Hill. We talk of coming up from Chester *in the night to-morrow, after the reading*; and of showing our precious selves at an apparently impossibly early hour in the Gad's Hill breakfast-room on Saturday morning.

I have not felt the fatigue to any extent worth mentioning; though I get, every night, into the most violent heats. We are going to dine at three o'clock (it wants a quarter now) and have not been here two hours, so I have seen nothing of Clement.

Tell Georgy with my love, that I read in the same room in which we acted,[5] but at the end opposite to that where our stage was. We are not at the inn where the amateur company put up,[6] but at The Lion,[7] where the fair Miss Mitchell[8] was lodged alone. We have the strangest little rooms (sitting-room and two bed-rooms all together), the ceilings of which I can touch with my hand. The windows bulge out over the street, as if they were little stern-windows in a ship. And a door opens out of the sitting-room on to a little open gallery with plants in it, where one leans over a queer old rail, and looks all downhill and slantwise at the crookedest black and yellow old houses, all manner of shapes except straight shapes. To get into this room we come through a china closet; and the man in laying the cloth has actually knocked down, in that repository, two geraniums and Napoleon Bonaparte.

I think that's all I have to say, except that at the Wolverhampton theatre they played "Oliver Twist" last night (Mr. Toole the Artful Dodger),[9] "in consequence

[1] Where he had read the *Carol* in the Corn Exchange. The notice in the *Wolverhampton Chronicle*, 18 Aug, was one of the warmest he had. It referred to his "masterly delivery" and to the crowded audience's "tumultuous enthusiasm".

[2] i.e., his last reading for charity on 26 Mar: see *To* Beard, 5 Apr.

[3] CD, according to the *Wolverhampton Chronicle* notice, said that the audience was "the quickest and most sympathetic before which he had read". As promised, he gave another reading there, on 3 Nov.

[4] The *Shrewsbury Chronicle*, 13 Aug, described the Music Hall, where he read the *Carol*, as a "wretched place to speak in". Despite that, the numerous audience was "delighted".

[5] On 10 May 52, for the Guild of Literature and Art: see Vol. VI, p. 657.

[6] Not discovered.

[7] The Lion Hotel, Wyle Cop, Shrewsbury.

[8] One of the professional actresses: see Vol. VI, p. 596 and *n*.

[9] At the Theatre Royal, since 9 Aug (the *Era*, 15 Aug, which added: "a part ... he has made entirely his own").

of the illustrious author honouring the town with his presence." We heard that the device succeeded very well, and that they got a good many people.

John's spirits have been equable and good since we rejoined him. Berry[1] has always got something the matter with his digestion—seems to me the male gender of Maria Jolly,[2] and ought to take nothing but Revalenta Arabica.[3] Bottled ale is not to be got in these parts, and Arthur is thrown upon draught.

My dearest love to Georgy and to Katey, also to Marguerite. Also to all the boys and the noble Plorn.

Ever your affectionate father

[CD]

To JOHN GRIFFITH,[4] [12 AUGUST 1858]

Envelope only, MS Houghton Library, Harvard. *Address:* John Griffith Esquire | Mill Fields | Bilston, Staffordshire PM Shrewsbury, 12 Aug 1858.

To WILLIAM PARKE,[5] 12 AUGUST [1858]

Extract in *Autograph Prices Current*, II; addressed W. Parke; dated Shrewsbury, Thursday Twelfth August. *Date:* CD was in Shrewsbury on this day in 1858.

Thanking him for his disinterested and generous assistance at Wolverhampton last night.

To JOHN FORSTER, [15 AUGUST 1858]

Extract and summary in F, VIII, iv, 661. *Date:* 15 Aug, according to Forster.

On Friday we came from Shrewsbury to Chester; saw all right for the evening; and then went to Liverpool.[6] Came back from Liverpool and read at Chester.[7] Left Chester at 11 at night, after the reading, and went to London. Got to Tavistock House at 5 A.M. on Saturday, left it at quarter past 10 that morning, and came down here.[8]

[1] Francis Berry, one of the reading staff.

[2] Probably a fictional character.

[3] A preparation of lentil and barley flour, then a popular invalid's food.

[4] Not further identified.

[5] William Parke, of Horse Fair, Wolverhampton; Forster describes him as "a wealthy old gentleman in a very large way . . . who did all the business for love, and would not take a farthing" (see *To* Forster, 3–4 Nov). He also told CD that the readings increased the sale of the reading copies (F, 1874, III, ix, 205*n*).

[6] To prepare for his first reading there on 18 Aug.

[7] He read the *Carol* in the Music Hall on 13 Aug. The notice in the *Chester Chronicle*, 21 Aug (repeating a paragraph from the *Liverpool Daily Post*, 17 Aug: see *To* Miss Hogarth, 20 Aug, *fn*) discussed the *pros* and *cons* of writers reading their own books. It also thought CD gave his short introductory speech "in rather a condescending way", to "the provincials"; and that he read "slightly too fast to be followed by the bulk of the audience". None the less, the reading gave "intense enjoyment"; it was "a miracle of dramatic art"; and in his facial expression and voice inflections, it found CD reminiscent of "the elder Mathews at home".

[8] Gad's Hill. Forster gives this letter as typical of "one day's work" to show "something of the fatigue . . . involved even at [*the*] outset".

To MRS WINTER, 16 AUGUST 1858

MS Huntington Library.

GAD'S HILL PLACE, | HIGHAM BY ROCHESTER, KENT.
Monday Sixteenth August, 1858.

My Dear Mrs. Winter

I have read poor dear Anne's[1] prayer, with great sorrow, and with many emotions of sadly affectionate remembrance. It was written, no doubt, under a presentiment of Death; but it must always be remembered that such a presentiment often exists when it fails to be fulfilled; and it is very commonly engendered in the state of mind belonging to the condition in which she composed the prayer.

It would give me great pleasure to see you at Liverpool,[2] if I had the least confidence in my own freedom for a moment under the circumstances which will take me there. But I have so much business to transact at times, and have to keep myself so quiet at other times, and have so many people to give directions to, and make arrangements with (four travel with me), that I see no one while I am on this Tour, and have to be always grimly self-denying and heroic. So I shall hope to see you in London, at some time when I am in a less virtuous, and less hurried and worried, condition.

With my love to Ella, and kindest regard to Mr. Winter,

Ever Affectionately Yours

Mrs. Winter CHARLES DICKENS

To MRS CORNELIUS, 17 AUGUST 1858

Text from N, III, 40.

OFFICE OF HOUSEHOLD WORDS,
Tuesday Seventeenth August 1858

My Dear Anne,

I enclose you a letter from Miss Hogarth. I have taken an exceedingly bad cold at Gad's Hill. In case I should not be at Tavistock House tonight before you go to bed, will you leave me two mustard poultices—one for my throat, and one for my chest.

Tomorrow morning, call me at 7 please, and let me have breakfast at 8.

Always affecly. yours

[CHARLES DICKENS]

[1] Mrs Winter's elder sister, Anne Beadnell, who had married CD's friend Henry Kolle in 1833 and died in May 1836 (Vol. I, p. 5*n*).

[2] Mrs Winter was temporarily in Liverpool, because of her husband's business; according to Dexter, they had asked CD to stay with them during his readings there (*The Love Romance of Charles Dickens*, ed. Walter Dexter, p. 110).

To MISS GEORGINA HOGARTH, 18 AUGUST 1858

MS Dickens House.

TAVISTOCK HOUSE, | TAVISTOCK SQUARE, LONDON. W.C.
Wednesday Morning Eighteenth August 1858

My Dearest Georgy

I write this hurried line before starting, to report that my cold is decidedly better, thank God (though still bad), and that I hope to be able to stagger through, tonight.[1] After dinner yesterday, I began to recover my voice, and I think I sang half the Irish Melodies[2] to myself as I walked about, to test it.[3] I got home at ½ past 10, and mustard-poulticed and barley-watered myself, tremendously.

Love to the dear girls and to all.

Ever Affectionately
CD.

To JOHN SMITH,[4] 19 AUGUST 1858

Extract in John Wilson catalogue No. 40 (1979); *MS* 2 pp.; dated Adelphi Hotel, Liverpool, 19 Aug 58;[5] addressed John Smith Esquire | 11 Lord Street Liverpool.

Declining an invitation having many demands on my time and attention while I am away from Household Words *and because* I am at present obliged to nurse a very severe cold, which I took last Sunday, when I was playing among my children at my little country place in Kent.... I had a very good audience last night, and a very apprehensive one.[6] I don't know what is to be done tonight.[7] But I hear there is to be a great press tomorrow.[8]

To JOHN FORSTER, [20 AUGUST 1858]

Extracts in F, VIII, iv, 662 and F, 1872–4, III, ix, 198*n*. *Date:* both extracts dated 20 Aug 58, according to Forster.

An audience of two thousand three hundred people (the largest he had had) greeted him at Liverpool and, besides the tickets sold, more than two hundred pounds in money was taken at the doors. They turned away hundreds, sold all the books, rolled on the ground of my room knee-deep in checks, and made a perfect pantomime of the whole thing.[9]

[1] At Liverpool: see next.

[2] For CD's frequent allusions to Moore's *Irish Melodies*, see Vol. V, p. 496*n*.

[3] From "I think ..." is given by Forster (VIII, iv, 662) as an instance of his "having still to acquire the art of husbanding his voice".

[4] Not further identified.

[5] Misdated "29" in catalogue: CD was not then in Liverpool.

[6] At his first reading of the *Carol*, in the Philharmonic Hall. According to the *Liverpool Daily Post*, 19 Aug, the audience was "fashionable, though not full"; the "galleries were the greatest success". CD was "well received".

[7] He read *Little Dombey*; the *Liverpool Daily Post*, 20 Aug, commented: "up to this time the gifted author ... may not dread a tarnishing of his well-won laurels by his platform appearance".

[8] When he read *The Poor Traveller*, *Boots*, and *Mrs Gamp*.

[9] He wrote in the same words to Georgina (see next).

We are reduced sometimes to a ludicrous state of distress by the quantity of silver we have to carry about. Arthur Smith is always accompanied by an immense black leather-bag full.

To MISS GEORGINA HOGARTH, 20 AUGUST 1858

MS Dickens House. *Address* (MS Heritage Book Shop Inc): Miss Hogarth | Gad's Hill Place | Higham by Rochester | Kent. PM Liverpool 20 Aug 58.

Adelphi Hotel, Liverpool
Friday Night, Twentieth August | 1858

My Dearest Georgy

I received your welcome and interesting letter today, and I write you a very hurried and bad reply. But it is after the reading, and you will take the will for the deed under those trying circumstances, I know.

We have had a tremendous night. The largest house I have ever had since I first began. 2,300 people. [a]Over £200 in money. Last night, and the night before, we had over £100 each night.[a] Tomorrow afternoon at 3, I read again.[1]

My cold has been oppressive, and is not yet gone. I have been very hard to sleep too, and last night I was all but sleepless. This morning I was very dull and seedy. But I got a good walk, and picked up again. It has been blowing all day, and I fear we shall have a sick passage over to Dublin tomorrow night.

Tell Mamie (with my dear love to her and Katie), that I will write to her from Dublin: probably on Sunday. Tell her too, that the stories she told me in her letter were not only capital stories in themselves but *excellently told* too.

[a]You may say the same to yourself (if you like) of your description of Sydney.[a2]

What Arthur's state has been tonight—he, John, Berry, and Boycett,[3] all taking money and going mad together—you cannot imagine. They turned away hundreds, sold all the books, rolled on the ground of my room knee deep in checks, and made a perfect Pantomime of the whole thing. He has kept quite well, I am happy to say, and sends a hundred loves.

[a]So do I—to the darling Plorn—and to all the boys—and most of all to you. Wills had best be written to, to write to Chambers for the exact longer address. I have not the least remembrance of it. Frank's note to Miss Coutts, also, had best go to him.[a]

In great haste and fatigue, | Ever affecy.

CD.

[aa] Omitted in MDGH. ○

[1] The *Liverpool Daily Post*, 17 Aug, prefaced its notice of the four readings to come with a two-column article on CD himself as writer and reader. It acclaimed him as a Radical, particularly since *Little Dorrit*; but had a quite sharp discussion of his readings "experiment": "It is a speculation—a business." Nevertheless, the audience's pleasure was the answer: "The reading is, indeed, a miracle of dramatic art."

[2] Sydney Dickens.

[3] A member of the reading staff, in charge of the gas.

To PATRICK ALLAN-FRASER, 21 AUGUST 1858†

MS Private.

Adelphi Hotel, Liverpool.
Saturday Twenty First August 1858

My Dear Sir

I have received your letter here this morning with great pleasure—though that feeling is dashed by two circumstances. I cannot come to Arbroath,[1] and I cannot come to see you. Simply, because my Tour is now made up and completed, and every moment of my time is parcelled out and allotted.[2] I must therefore hope to receive a visit from you in Dundee.

What a dreadfully Southern fellow Egg is! What an awful enquiry that of his, respecting Arbroath! If *I* had asked a question of you concerning that town (in which I most devoutly believe), it would have been, whether there was a public room in it, small enough for my modest purpose. I tremble when I think of its Provost.[3] Richard Whittington was never thrice Provost of Arbroath. If he had been, what a story his Life would have made!

I am heartily sorry not to be able to accept either of your kind invitations; but it is a consequence of the work in which I am now engaged, that it obliges me to forego all social pleasures for the time.

My Dear Sir | Very cordially Yours
Patrick Allan Fraser Esquire CHARLES DICKENS

To W. H. WILLS, 21 AUGUST 1858

MS Huntington Library.

Adelphi Hotel, Liverpool.
Saturday Twenty First August |1858

My Dear Wills

I send this to Sheffield at a flying venture.

The Liverpool Audience has been altogether different from our Theatrical experience of it.[4] Quite as good as St. Martin's Hall. A great call, every night. Every point taken. The nicest and finest bits in Little Dombey, hitting like chain-shot. Last night, we had the greatest house, both in numbers and money, we have ever had: London included. There were 2,300 people and 200 guineas. The turn-away from the Shilling part, was very large. On each of the two previous nights we had 100 guineas, and (if the day should keep moderately fine) we expect a very good afternoon to day at 3.

The crossing to Ireland tonight is not likely to be very agreeable, for it has been exceedingly squally these last two days.

I observe in H.W. that "Running the Gauntlet"[5] (an article with good stuff in it)

[1] An ancient port in Forfarshire (now Angus), 17 miles north-east of Dundee.

[2] "Alloted" in MS.

[3] John Lumgair, Provost 1855–8.

[4] On 13–14 Feb and 3 Sep 52, for the Guild of Literature and Art: see Vol. VI, p. 600 and *n.*

[5] "The Last Victim of the Gauntlet", by Von Goetznitz, *HW*, 21 Aug 58, XVIII, 222; a description of the last infliction of this savage punishment in the Austrian Army in 1851.

has been very badly looked over. "That" is constantly put for "Who", which is a great vulgarity.[1] Such an expression too, as "vowed him revenge"[2] is extremely bad.

Wilkie's paper,[3] very funny. Just what we want.

With kind regard to Mrs. Wills, and all kinds of remembrances from Arthur,

Ever Faithfully

CD.

P.S. As new places are constantly proposing themselves to be brought into the Tour, I have arranged with Arthur that it shall now be wound up, so that I may be able to get to work in London, *on the 15th. of Novr.*—with a view to the Xmas No. I will talk over my idea with Wilkie, and ascertain if he feels up to it.[4] If he should not, when I expound it to him,—then perhaps it might be best to have a round of Stories. But nous verrons.

To EDMUND YATES, 21 AUGUST 1858

MS Robert H. Taylor Collection, Princeton University.

Adelphi Hotel, Liverpool
Saturday Twenty First August | 1858.

My Dear Edmund

I return you Ouvry's letter. It is all right. I think he should *not* proceed to issuing of a Writ, however, until we have thoroughly ascertained that the Action is to go on. Ascertained (I mean), that you are properly supported in it, and are not to be left to bear too much of the expence. Nothing is lost, during the Long Vacation, by this pause.[5]

The Portrait-Circular[6] has amused us immensely.

A wonderful house here last night. The largest in numbers, and the largest in money we have ever had, including St. Martin's Hall. There were 2,300 people, and 200 guineas. The very books were all sold out, early in the evening, and Arthur bathed in checks—took headers into tickets—floated on billows of passes—dived under weirs of shillings—staggered home, faint with gold and silver.

He sends his kindest regard.

Ever Faithfully

CD.

I re-open this, to tell you that I encountered Thackeray and Fladgate[7] on the steps of the Reform Club. We spoke as if nothing had happened—except that Fladgate's eyebrows went up into the crown of his hat, and he twisted himself into extraordinary forms.

[1] Examples are "those that shed their blood" (p. 223) and "some that had even married afterwards" (p. 224).

[2] On p. 223.

[3] "Sea-Breezes with the London Smack", 4 Sep 58, XVIII, 274.

[4] See *To* Collins, 6 Sep and *fnn*.

[5] Yates did not serve his writ until 5 Dec (see *To* Thackeray, 24 Nov 58, *fn*), and he abandoned the action by Feb 59: see next vol.

[6] See *To* Yates, 11 Aug and *fn*.

[7] Frank Fladgate: a special friend of Thackeray's.

To MISS BURDETT COUTTS, 23 AUGUST 1858

MS Berg Collection. *Address:* Miss Burdett Coutts | Care of W. H. Wills Esquire | 16 Wellington Street North | Strand | London | W.C.

Morrison's Hotel,[1] Dublin
Monday Twenty Third August. 1858.

My Dear Miss Coutts.

I shall address this to Mr. Wills, as I am not certain where you may be. I passed through Bangor last Saturday night at midnight, and wondered whether you were there.

My dear friend, I quite understand and appreciate your feeling that there must be no reservation between us, and that we must not have a skeleton in a closet, and make belief it is not there. But I must not enter on the wretched subject, upon false pretences. I must not do what would make my dear girls out to be a sort of phænomona, and what would make my own relations with Mrs. Dickens, incomprehensible. Since we spoke of her before, she has caused me unspeakable agony of mind; and I must plainly put before you what I know to be true, and what nothing shall induce me to affect to doubt. She does not—and she never did—care for the children; and the children do not—and they never did—care for her. The little play that is acted in your Drawing-room is not the truth, and the less the children play it, the better for themselves, because they know it is not the truth.[2] (If I stood before you at this moment and told you what difficulty we have to get Frank, for instance, to go near his mother, or keep near his mother, you would stand amazed.) As to Mrs. Dickens's "simplicity" in speaking of me and my doings, O my dear Miss Coutts do I not know that the weak hand that never could help or serve my name in the least, has struck at it—in conjunction with the wickedest people, whom I have loaded with benefits![3] I want to communicate with her no more. I want to forgive her and forget her.

I could not begin a course of references to her, without recording, as between you and me, what I know to be true. It would be monstrous to myself, and to the children also. From Walter away in India, to Little Plornish at Gad's Hill there is a grim knowledge among them, as familiar to them as their knowledge of Day light that what I now write, is the plain bare fact. She has always disconcerted them; they have always disconcerted her; and she is glad to be rid of them, and they are glad to be rid of her.[4] No more of it here.

The country expedition has been doing extremely well. The expenses are large (including Mr. Smith's share, about 50 per cent), but the returns come out handsomely. At Liverpool last week, I read 4 times. The audiences amounted to about 6,300 people. My clear profit, after all deductions, was £260.9.0. What we are going to do here, I don't know. The Dublin audience are accustomed to do nothing in the way of taking places, until the last moment, or until they actually "take them" by

[1] Robert Morrison's Hotel, 1 Dawson St.

[2] For the substantial evidence against this, see *To* Miss Coutts, 9 May 58, *fn*.

[3] Whatever Catherine had said or done since CD's letter to her of 4 June was clearly connected with her mother and Helen Hogarth. She may have repeated the earlier rumours about Ellen; for gossip about her discovering the bracelet intended by CD as a present to Ellen, at a dinner-party given by Thackeray in 1860, when she was present, see Michael Slater, *Dickens and Women*, p. 152.

[4] See *To* Miss Coutts, 9 May 58, *fn*.

walking in at the Doors. We are therefore quite in the Dark. I read the Carol here tonight[1]—the Chimes tomorrow—Little Dombey on Wednesday morning—and the Poor Traveller &c on Thursday evening. We had a five hours passage from Holyhead in the night of Saturday, and it was very, very, nasty.

I am greatly surprised by this place. It is very much larger than I had supposed, and very much more populous and busy. Upon the whole it is no shabbier than London is, and the people seem to enjoy themselves more than the London people do. The old town of Edinburgh is a thousand times more squalid than the bye places I have seen in Dublin; and I have wandered about it for 6 or 8 hours in all directions. It may be presumed that it has greatly improved of late years. There are far fewer spirit shops than I have been used to see in great cities. And even Donnybrook Fair[2] (which is on now, though sought to be abolished)[3] is less disagreeable than Chalk Farm;[4] and I have seen numbers of common people buying the most innocent and *un*life-like of Dolls there, for their little children.

Among my English audiences, I have had more clergymen than I ever saw in my life before. It is very curious to see how many people in black come to Little Dombey. And when it is over they almost uniformly go away as if the child were really Dead—with a hush upon them. They certainly laugh more at the Boots' story of the Little Elopement,[5] than at anything else; and I notice that they sit with their heads on one side, and an expression of playful pity on their faces—as if they saw the tiny boy and girl.[6] Which is tender and pleasant, I think? The Chimes is always a surprise. They fall into it with a start, and look at me in the strangest way before they begin to applaud. The Cratchit family in the Carol are always a delight. And they always visibly lie in wait for Tiny Tim. The little books sell extraordinarily[7] well. Besides being in every bookshop window in every place, my men alone will sell from 6 to 12 dozen in a night. I think I have now told you every bit of egotism I can screw out of myself. But I know that you and Mrs. Brown (to whom I send my love) will be interested in these scraps.

I shall hope to find another letter from you, somewhere, soon, telling me how you

[1] The *Dublin Evening Post*, 24 Aug, gave him a very warm notice on his reading of the *Carol* on 23 Aug and reported his short introductory speech: "Let the first public words I have spoken on Irish ground be words of thankfulness to you for your cordial and generous welcome. You cannot, believe me, be more glad to see me than I am to see you."

[2] A notorious fair held on the edge of Dublin, near the river Dodder.

[3] Officially abolished in 1855.

[4] Then a public-house and tea-garden in Hampstead.

[5] In "The Boots at the Holly-Tree Inn", Cobbs, the Boots, tells the traveller the story of the little boy and girl, aged eight and seven, who "elope" with the intention of marrying at Gretna Green.

[6] After his reading of *Boots* on 26 Aug, the *Dublin Evening Mail*, 27 Aug, commented: "The way in which Mr. Dickens read this piece is inimitable, and kept his audience convulsed with merriment." It noted his "chuckling tone and merry twinkle of the eye" as he read. It remained one of his most popular readings.

[7] Copies of the first series of his reading texts, green-covered paperbacks, published by Bradbury & Evans, at 1/–. The three Christmas Books were in fact simply reprints of the original texts; but *The Story of Little Dombey* and the triple reading, *The Poor Traveller*, *Boots*, and *Mrs. Gamp* were reprints of his privately printed versions. The sales were not, in fact, particularly large: 7,500 copies of *Little Dombey* and 8,000 of *The Poor Traveller* (etc.) were printed; unsold copies of both were handed over to Chapman & Hall on 31 May 1861 (Bradbury & Evans's Accounts, MS V & A). For detailed figures of the sales, see Robert L. Patten, *CD and his Publishers*, pp. 258 and 411.

both are, and whether you have found any place to breathe in. Then I will report further of my proceedings. Ever Dear Miss Coutts, Yours affecy. & faithfully

CD.

To MISS KATE DICKENS, [?23 AUGUST 1858]

Mention in *To* Georgina Hogarth, 25 Aug. *Date:* presumably written the day before the proposed visit.

Telling her of his plan to visit Queenstown[1] *on 24 Aug.*

To MISS MARY DICKENS, 23 AUGUST 1858

Extract in MDGH, II, 56.

Morrison's Hotel, Dublin, Monday, Aug. 23rd, 1858.

We had a nasty crossing here. We left Holyhead at one in the morning, and got here at six. Arthur was incessantly sick the whole way. I was not sick at all, but was in as healthy a condition otherwise as humanity need be. We are in a beautiful hotel. Our sitting-room is exactly like the drawing-room at the Peschiere in all its dimensions.[2] I never saw two rooms so exactly resembling one another in their proportions. Our bedrooms too are excellent, and there are baths and all sorts of comforts.

The Lord Lieutenant[3] is away, and the place looks to me as if its professional life were away too. Nevertheless, there are numbers of people in the streets. Somehow, I hardly seem to think we are going to do enormously here; but I have scarcely any reason for supposing so (except that a good many houses are shut up); and I *know* nothing about it, for Arthur is now gone to the agent and to the room. The men came by boat direct from Liverpool. They had a rough passage, were all ill, and did not get here till noon yesterday. Donnybrook Fair, or what remains of it, is going on, within two or three miles of Dublin. They went out there yesterday in a jaunting-car, and John described it to us at dinner-time (with his eyebrows lifted up, and his legs well asunder), as "Johnny Brooks's Fair;" at which Arthur, who was drinking bitter ale, nearly laughed himself to death. Berry is always unfortunate, and when I asked what had happened to Berry on board the steamboat, it appeared that "an Irish gentleman which was drunk, and fancied himself the captain, wanted to knock Berry down."

I am surprised by finding this place very much larger than I had supposed it to be. Its bye-parts are bad enough, but cleaner, too, than I had supposed them to be, and certainly very much cleaner than the old town of Edinburgh. The man who drove our jaunting-car yesterday hadn't a piece in his coat as big as a penny roll, and had had his hat on (apparently without brushing it) ever since he was grown up. But he

[1] CD must have confused it with Kingstown (Dun Laoghaire), a watering-place six miles south-east of Dublin; he could not conceivably have travelled to Queenstown, 177 miles from Dublin, and back in a day. He was due to read in Dublin again on the 25th.

[2] See Vol. IV, pp. 167 and *n* and 177.

[3] The 13th Earl of Eglinton (1812–61; *DNB*); holder of the "Eglinton Tournament" in 1839.

was remarkably intelligent and agreeable, with something to say about everything. For instance, when I asked him what a certain building was, he didn't say "courts of law" and nothing else, but: "Av you plase, sir, it's the foor coorts o' looyers, where Misther O'Connell[1] stood his trial[2] wunst, ye'll remimber, sir, afore I tell ye of it." When we got into the Phœnix Park,[3] he looked round him as if it were his own, and said: "THAT's a park, sir, av yer plase." I complimented it, and he said: "Gintlemen tills me as they'r bin, sir, over Europe, and never see a park aqualling ov it. 'Tis eight mile roond, sir, ten mile and a half long, and in the month of May the hawthorn trees are as beautiful as brides with their white jewels on. Yonder's the vice-regal lodge, sir; in them two corners lives the two sicretirries, wishin I was them, sir. There's air here, sir, av yer plase! There's scenery here, sir! There's mountains—thim, sir! Yer coonsider it a park, sir? It is that, sir!"

You should have heard John in my bedroom this morning endeavouring to imitate a bath-man, who had resented his interference, and had said as to the shower-bath: "Yer'll not be touching *that*, young man. Divil a touch yer'll touch o' that insthrument, young man!" It was more ridiculously unlike the reality than I can express to you, yet he was so delighted with his powers that he went off in the absurdest little gingerbeery giggle, backing into my portmanteau all the time.

My dear love to Katie and to Georgy, also to the noble Plorn and all the boys. I shall write to Katie next, and then to Aunty. My cold, I am happy to report, is very much better. I lay in the wet all night on deck, on board the boat, but am not as yet any the worse for it. Arthur was quite insensible when we got to Dublin, and stared at our luggage without in the least offering to claim it. He left his kindest love for all before he went out. I will keep the envelope open until he comes in.

Ever, my dearest Mamie, | Your most affectionate Father

[CD]

To JOHN FORSTER, [?23 AUGUST 1858]

Extracts in F, VIII, iv, 662. *Date:* probably the same day as *To* Mamie Dickens, 23 Aug.

He had found Dublin to have altogether an unexpectedly thriving look, being almost as big, he first thought, as Paris; of which some places in it, such as the quays on the river, reminded him. Half the first day he was in Dublin [Sunday, 22 Aug] *he had spent exploring, walking till tired, and then taking a car.* Power,[4] dressed for the character of Teddy the Tiler, drove me: in a suit of patches, and with his hat unbrushed for twenty years. Wonderfully pleasant, light, intelligent, and careless.

The number of common people he saw in his drive, also riding about in cars as hard as they could split, *reminded him, but for the dresses, of the Toledo at Naples.*[5]

[1] Daniel O'Connell (1775–1847; *DNB*), "the Liberator".

[2] In 1844, on a charge of creating discontent and disaffection; his sentence of a fine of £2000 and a year's imprisonment reversed on appeal.

[3] In West Dublin, 1735 acres in extent, containing the Viceroy's Lodge, the Chief Secretary's house, and the People's Gardens.

[4] i.e. an Irishman who looked like the Irish comedian Tyrone Power (1797–1841; *DNB*: see Vol. II, p. 104*n*). Acted the leading part in *Teddy the Tiler*, a farce adapted from the French by G. H. Rodwell, first performed at Covent Garden, Feb 1830.

[5] Now the Via Roma.

To PERCY FITZGERALD, 24 AUGUST 1858

MS Mr G. V. Roberts.

Morrison's Hotel
Tuesday Evening Twenty Fourth August | 1858

My Dear Sir

A thousand thanks for your letter.[1] But my availing myself of your kindness is quite impossible. I read tomorrow afternoon at 3—and you may faintly imagine (but not sufficiently), what my correspondence is with London, when I get a few hours to devote to it.

I shall hope to see you before I leave this—that is to say, sometime on Thursday Morning, when I shall do myself the pleasure of calling on you.[2] It will give me great pleasure to assure you personally, of the interest and satisfaction I shall have, in seeing you in London when you come there.

Pray believe that I shall be delighted to know you better, and that my present determination is a "hard" one to myself, and is not in the least meritorious.

Faithfully Yours always
Percy Fitz Gerald Esquire CHARLES DICKENS

To EDWARD DOUDNEY, [25 AUGUST 1858]

Mention in next.

To MISS GEORGINA HOGARTH, 25 AUGUST 1858

Extract in MDGH, II, 58–63.

Morrison's Hotel, Dublin, Wednesday, Aug. 25th, 1858.

I begin my letter to you to-day, though I don't know when I may send it off. We had a very good house last night, after all, that is to say, a great rush of shillings and good half-crowns, though the stalls were comparatively few. For "Little Dombey,"

[1] Written the same day as Fitzgerald's first Diary entry, recording CD's reading the previous night: "Tuesday. | One of those red-letter nights in my life was last night, when I heard Dickens's charming and artistic and refined performance—perhaps enjoyed it more than anything for some years. Those exquisite bits of humour of his own seem to me as if incapable of being pointed by anyone else.... Everybody was delighted, enchanted—convulsions of the most genuine laughter and keenest enjoyment I have ever witnessed" (*Memories of CD*, p. 7). Two days later he recorded: "This has been a gala week with me by reason of this great man. Saw him in street on Tuesday, and spent a feverish day tracking him about the town. Then wrote and received back such a note! Good nature and geniality in every line—announcing too that he would call on me this day" (*ibid.*).

[2] "Dickens came not after all", Fitzgerald recorded, "but good-naturedly sent his card by post" (*ibid.*). But the following Monday, the day of CD's departure, he resolved to "waylay him at South-Western Railway", and described the meeting in his Diary. CD "was in a check suit: he looked a fine, bold, well-made, sturdy, striding Englishman, with the redness (not of paint, as we fancied) but of glowing health on his face". They talked mainly of Landor (see *To* Georgina Hogarth, 29 Aug, and *fn*). "It would be impossible", wrote Fitzgerald, "to give an idea of his cordial heartiness ... and the perfect genuineness of his welcome" (*ibid.*, pp. 7–9).

this morning, we have an immense stall let—already more than two hundred—and people are now fighting in the agent's shop to take more. Through some mistake of our printer's, the evening reading for this present Wednesday was dropped, in a great part of the announcements, and the agent opened no plan for it. I have therefore resolved not to have it at all. Arthur Smith has waylaid me in all manner of ways, but I remain obdurate. I am frightfully tired, and really relieved by the prospect of an evening—overjoyed.

They were a highly excitable audience last night, but they certainly did not comprehend—internally and intellectually comprehend—"The Chimes" as a London audience do.[1] I am quite sure of it. I very much doubt the Irish capacity of receiving the pathetic; but of their quickness as to the humorous there can be no doubt. I shall see how they go along with Little Paul, in his death, presently.

While I was at breakfast this morning, a general officer was announced with great state—having a staff at the door—and came in, booted and plumed, and covered with Crimean decorations. It was Cunninghame,[2] whom we knew in Genoa—then a captain. He was very hearty indeed, and came to ask me to dinner. Of course I couldn't go. Olliffe has a brother at Cork,[3] who had just now (noon) written to me, proposing dinners and excursions in that neighbourhood which would fill about a week; I being there a day and a half, and reading three times. The work will be very severe here, and I begin to feel depressed by it. (By "here," I mean Ireland generally, please to observe.)

We meant, as I said in a letter to Katie, to go to Queenstown yesterday and bask on the seashore. But there is always so much to do that we couldn't manage it after all. We expect a tremendous house to-morrow night as well as to-day; and Arthur is at the present instant up to his eyes in business (and seats), and, between his regret at losing to-night, and his desire to make the room hold twice as many as it *will* hold, is half distracted. I have become a wonderful Irishman—must play an Irish part some day—and his only relaxation is when I enact "John and the Boots," which I consequently do enact all day long. The papers are full of remarks upon my white tie, and describe it as being of enormous size, which is a wonderful delusion, because, as you very well know, it is a small tie. Generally, I am happy to report, the Emerald press is in favour of my appearance, and likes my eyes.[4] But one gentleman comes out with a letter at Cork, wherein he says that although only forty-six I look like an old man. *He* is a rum customer, I think.

The Rutherfords[5] are living here, and wanted me to dine with them, which, I

[1] *The Chimes* was perhaps too local in its references for a non-English audience. The notice in the *Dublin Evening Post*, 25 Aug, mostly praised CD as a writer, laying particular stress, as a Roman Catholic newspaper naturally would, on his "manly exposure" of the Protestant-inspired Gordon Riots in *Barnaby Rudge*. His welcome, it said, was "flattering in the extreme"; and the entertainment "fully appreciated by the crowded audience".

[2] Misspelt by CD. Sir Arthur Augustus Thurlow Cunynghame (1812–84; *DNB*): see Vol. IV, p. 360*n*. As Quartermaster-Gen. 1854, fought at Inkermann and held fortress of Kertch in Crimean War; Major-Gen. 1855; knighted 1869. Published travel-books and recollections. Besides being a CB and Officer of the Legion of Honour, he held the English and Turkish Crimean War medals.

[3] Henry B. Olliffe, JP, Secretary to Cork, Blackrock & Passage Railway Co., of Mount Verdon House, 66 Summer Hill.

[4] The *Cork Herald*, 4 Sep, commented that he had "a bright blue eye".

[5] Misspelt by CD. Major James Hunter Rutherfurd, Royal Engineers, brother of Andrew, Lord Rutherfurd, late Lord Advocate, whom CD had met in Edinburgh in June 41 (see

needn't say, could not be done; all manner of people have called, but I have seen only two. John has given it up altogether as to rivalry with the Boots, and did not come into my room this morning at all. Boots appeared triumphant and alone. He was waiting for me at the hotel-door last night. "Whaa't sart of a hoose, sur?" he asked me. "Capital." "The Lard be praised fur the 'onor o' Dooblin!"

Arthur buys bad apples in the streets and brings them home and doesn't eat them, and then I am obliged to put them in the balcony because they make the room smell faint. Also he meets countrymen with honeycomb on their heads, and leads them (by the buttonhole when they have one) to this gorgeous establishment and requests the bar to buy honeycomb for his breakfast; then it stands upon the sideboard uncovered and the flies fall into it. He buys owls, too, and castles, and other horrible objects, made in bog-oak (that material which is not appreciated at Gad's Hill); and he is perpetually snipping pieces out of newspapers and sending them all over the world. While I am reading he conducts the correspondence, and his great delight is to show me seventeen or eighteen letters when I come, exhausted, into the retiring-place. Berry has not got into any particular trouble for forty-eight hours, except that he is all over boils. I have prescribed the yeast, but ineffectually. It is indeed a sight to see him and John sitting in pay-boxes, and surveying Ireland out of pigeon-holes.

Same Evening before Bed-time.

Everybody was at "Little Dombey" to-day, and although I had some little difficulty to work them up in consequence of the excessive crowding of the place, and the difficulty of shaking the people into their seats, the effect was unmistakable and profound. The crying was universal, and they were extraordinarily affected. There is no doubt we could stay here a week with that one reading, and fill the place every night. Hundreds of people have been there to-night, under the impression that it would come off again. It was a most decided and complete success.[1]

Arthur has been imploring me to stop here on the Friday after Limerick, and read "Little Dombey" again. But I have positively said "No." The work is too hard. It is not like doing it in one easy room, and always the same room. With a different place every night, and a different audience with its own peculiarity every night, it is a tremendous strain. I was sick of it to-day before I began, then got myself into wonderful train.

Here follows a dialogue (but it requires imitation), which I had yesterday morning with a little boy of the house—landlord's son, I suppose—about Plorn's age. I am sitting on the sofa writing, and find him sitting beside me.

INIMITABLE.[2] Holloa, old chap.

YOUNG IRELAND. Hal-loo!

INIMITABLE (*in his delightful way*). What a nice old fellow you are. I am very fond of little boys.

YOUNG IRELAND. Air yer? Ye'r right.

INIMITABLE. What do you learn, old fellow?

Vol. II, p. 315*n*); and his wife, née Elizabeth Young, daughter of Alexander Young of Harburn, Edinburgh lawyer.

[1] The *Dublin Evening Post*, 26 Aug, highly praised it: "we consider it impossible now for anyone who had heard him once not to wish to hear him again and again".

[2] Forster gives "Old England", which is probably what CD wrote.

YOUNG IRELAND (*very intent on Inimitable, and always childish, except in his brogue*). I lairn wureds of three sillibils, and wureds of two sillibils, and wureds of one sillibil.

INIMITABLE (*gaily*). Get out, you humbug! You learn only words of one syllable.

YOUNG IRELAND (*laughs heartily*). You may say that it is mostly wureds of one sillibil.

INIMITABLE. Can you write?

YOUNG IRELAND. Not yet. Things comes by deegrays.

INIMITABLE. Can you cipher?

YOUNG IRELAND (*very quickly*). Wha'at's that?

INIMITABLE. Can you make figures?

YOUNG IRELAND. I can make a nought, which is not asy, being roond.

INIMITABLE. I say, old boy, wasn't it you I saw on Sunday morning in the hall, in a soldier's cap? You know—in a soldier's cap?

YOUNG IRELAND (*cogitating deeply*). Was it a very good cap?

INIMITABLE. Yes.

YOUNG IRELAND. Did it fit unkommon?

INIMITABLE. Yes.

YOUNG IRELAND. Dat was me!

There are two stupid old louts at the room, to show people into their places, whom John calls "them two old Paddies," and of whom he says, that he "never see nothing like them (snigger) hold idiots" (snigger). They bow and walk backwards before the grandees, and our men hustle them while they are doing it.

We walked out last night, with the intention of going to the theatre; but the Piccolomini establishment[1] (they were doing the "Lucia")[2] looked so horribly like a very bad jail, and the Queen's[3] looked so blackguardly, that we came back again, and went to bed. I seem to be always either in a railway carriage, or reading, or going to bed. I get so knocked up, whenever I have a minute to remember it, that then I go to bed as a matter of course.

I send my love to the noble Plorn, and to all the boys. To dear Mamie and Katie, and to yourself of course, in the first degree. I am looking forward to the last Irish reading on Thursday, with great impatience. But when we shall have turned this week, once knocked off Belfast, I shall see land, and shall (like poor Timber[4] in the days of old) "keep up a good heart." I get so wonderfully hot every night in my dress clothes, that they positively won't dry in the short interval they get, and I have been obliged to write to Doudney's[5] to make me another suit, that I may have a constant change.

Ever, my dearest Georgy, most affectionately

[CD]

[1] The Italian Opera were performing at the Theatre Royal, with Mlle Marietta Piccolomini (1834–99) as the leading soprano. The performances were enthusiastically reviewed in the *Dublin Evening Post*.

[2] They performed Donizetti's *Lucia di Lammermoor* on 21 and 26 Aug.

[3] The Queen's Theatre, Great Brunswick St, South: a small theatre, "well adapted for the production of melodramas, farces, &." (*Dublin: What's to be Seen*, 1872).

[4] His white terrier, given to him in New York, who had died of old age in Boulogne on 5 Oct 55 (F, VII, v, 616*n*).

[5] Edward Doudney: see Vol. VII, p. 773*n*.

To MRS RUTHERFURD, 25 AUGUST 1858*

MS National Library of Scotland.

Morrison's Hotel, Dublin
Wednesday Twenty Fifth August | 1858.

My Dear Mrs. Rutherford

I owe you many thanks for your kind note, and I much regret that the constant occupation of my time during my hurried visit here disables me from making any engagements or calls whatever. I am a perfect galley-slave at this time. Nor have I any of my family with me; for, though it would have been delightful to me to bring my girls, my movements are so rapid and comfortless, that I denied myself that pleasure too.

I am sorry to receive so Nelsonic an account of Major Rutherford's right hand. But I am sure he knows that he cannot have a better one than he finds in you.

With kind regard to him and all your house, I am ever

Dear Mrs. Rutherford | Faithfully Yours

Mrs. Rutherford CHARLES DICKENS

To P. MEADOWS TAYLOR,[1] 26 AUGUST 1858

MS Fales Collection, New York University Library.

Morrison's Hotel. | Thursday, Twenty Sixth August 1858

My Dear Sir

I thank you heartily for your token of remembrance.[2] It will have a great interest for me as long as it lasts—and much longer. I shall not easily dissociate Dublin from the remembrance of your cordial and cheery visit.

With hearty good wishes | My Dear Sir | Very faithfully Yours

P. Meadows Taylor Esquire CHARLES DICKENS

To MISS MARY DICKENS, 28 AUGUST 1858

Extract in MDGH, II, 63–5.

Belfast, Saturday, Aug. 28th, 1858.

When I went down to the Rotunda at Dublin on Thursday night, I said to Arthur, who came rushing at me: "You needn't tell me. I know all about it." The moment I had come out of the door of the hotel (a mile off), I had come against the stream of people turned away. I had struggled against it to the room. There, the crowd in all the lobbies and passages was so great, that I had a difficulty in getting in. They had broken all the glass in the pay-boxes. They had offered frantic prices for stalls.[3]

[1] Philip Meadows Taylor (1808–76; *DNB*), Indian Army officer and novelist: see Vol. VI, p. 92*n*. His family home was Old Court, Harold's Cross, Dublin. A new edn of his *Confessions of a Thug*, 1839, his best known novel, came out in 1858.

[2] Perhaps Irish whiskey.

[3] Quoting from this letter, F reads: "[*they*] were offering £5 freely for a stall" (MDGH characteristically omits precise sums); and continues "Half of my platform had to be taken down, and people heaped in among the ruins" (F, VIII, iv, 663).

Eleven bank-notes were thrust into that pay-box (Arthur saw them) at one time, for eleven stalls. Our men were flattened against walls, and squeezed against beams. Ladies stood all night with their chins against my platform. Other ladies sat all night upon my steps. You never saw such a sight. And the reading went tremendously! It is much to be regretted that we troubled ourselves to go anywhere else in Ireland. We turned away people enough to make immense houses for a week.[1]

We arrived here yesterday at two. The room will not hold more than from eighty to ninety pounds.[2] The same scene was repeated with the additional feature, that the people are much rougher here than in Dublin, and that there was a very great uproar at the opening of the doors, which, the police in attendance being quite inefficient and only looking on, it was impossible to check. Arthur was in the deepest misery because shillings got into stalls, and half-crowns got into shillings, and stalls got nowhere, and there was immense confusion.[3] It ceased, however, the moment I showed myself; and all went most brilliantly, in spite of a great piece of the cornice of the ceiling falling with a great crash within four or five inches of the head of a young lady on my platform (I was obliged to have people there), and in spite of my gas suddenly going out at the time of the game of forfeits at Scrooge's nephew's, through some Belfastian gentleman accidentally treading on the flexible pipe, and needing to be relighted.[4]

We shall not get to Cork before mid-day on Monday; it being difficult to get from here on a Sunday. We hope to be able to start away to-morrow morning to see the Giant's Causeway[5] (some sixteen miles off), and in that case we shall sleep at Dublin to-morrow night, leaving here by the train at half-past three in the afternoon. Dublin, you must understand, is on the way to Cork. This is a fine place, surrounded by lofty hills. The streets are very wide, and the place is very prosperous.[6] The whole ride from Dublin here is through a very picturesque and various country; and the amazing thing is, that it is all particularly neat and orderly, and that the houses (outside at all events) are all brightly whitewashed and remarkably clean. I want to climb one of the neighbouring hills before this morning's "Dombey." I am now waiting for Arthur, who has gone to the bank to remit his last accumulation of treasure to London.

Our men are rather indignant with the Irish crowds, because in the struggle they don't sell books, and because, in the pressure, they can't force a way into the room

[1] The *Dublin Evening Mail*, 27 Aug, reported "an overflowing audience"; "the crush at the entrance doors was immense; and his reception even more marked and enthusiastic" than at his first reading on the 23rd.

[2] He gave three readings in the Victoria Hall, Belfast: the *Carol* on Fri 27 Aug, *Little Dombey* at 3 p.m. on Saturday and *The Poor Traveller*, *Boots* and *Mrs Gamp* on Saturday evening.

[3] The *Belfast News-Letter*, 28 Aug, reported that the gallery was over-full and, as a result, there were "frequent and most unpleasant interruptions" during the first half-hour of the reading. There were complaints in the Press and criticism of the manager and of "the person in charge of the seats" (Arthur Smith).

[4] The *Belfast News-Letter*, 28 Aug, gave the reading a very warm notice; it also reported both of what it called these "singular occurrences".

[5] Impossible, since 60 miles north west of Belfast; possibly the Giant's Cradle, a rocking-stone in Brown's Bay, near Larne, *c.* 20 miles away.

[6] According to Percy Fitzgerald, who met him in Dublin three days later, CD thus described Belfast: "Tremendous houses, curious people, they seem all Scotch, but quite in a state of transition." CD also told him that he "walked a long way by sea to Carrickfergus" (in Co. Antrim, 9½ miles north of Belfast): *Memories of CD*, pp. 7–8.

afterwards to sell them. They are deeply interested in the success, however, and are as zealous and ardent as possible. I shall write to Katie next. Give her my best love, and kiss the darling Plorn for me, and give my love to all the boys.

Ever, my dearest Mamie, | Your most affectionate Father

[CD]

To JOHN FORSTER, [?29 AUGUST 1858]

Extracts in F, VIII, iv, 664, 1872–4, III, ix, 198*n* and VIII, iv, 661. *Date:* first two extracts same day as *To* Georgina Hogarth, 29 Aug; third extract undated but possibly from same letter.

Answering Forster's letter on a personal matter,[1] *and inviting him and Mrs Forster to Gad's Hill. Belfast he liked quite as much as Dublin in another way.* A fine place with a rough people; everything looking prosperous; the railway ride from Dublin quite amazing in the order, neatness, and cleanness of all you see; every cottage looking as if it had been whitewashed the day before; and many with charming gardens, prettily kept with bright flowers.

Mr. Smith had an illness a couple of days later,[2] *and CD describes his rapid recovery on discovering the state of their balances.* He is now sitting opposite to me on a bag of £40 of silver. It must be dreadfully hard.

The greatest personal affection and respect *had greeted him everywhere. Nothing could have been more* strongly marked or warmly expressed; *and the readings had* gone *quite wonderfully.*

To MISS GEORGINA HOGARTH, 29 AUGUST 1858

MS Dickens House.

Morrison's Hotel, Dublin
Sunday Night Twenty Ninth August 1858

My Dearest Georgy

I am so delighted to find your letter here tonight (11 o'Clock), and am so afraid that in the wear and tear of this strange life I have written to Gad's Hill in the wrong order and have not written to you as I should—that I resolve to write this before going to bed. You will find it a wretchedly stupid letter, but you may imagine my dearest girl that I am tired.

[a]For novelty's sake, I will give you some statistics. To understand which, you must be informed that Arthur charges every place with its proportion of the next prospective expenses. For instance, before my profit is declared here, it is debited with the journey to Belfast; and before my profit is declared at Belfast, it is debited in its turn with *its* share of our expenses home to London. After all these deductions,

[1] See *To* Miss Hogarth, 29 Aug.

[2] Forster mistakenly dates this two days later than 20 Aug.

[aa] Omitted in MDGH.

and after paying Arthur's share, I made here £210, and at Belfast (in two days) £130. With a good return at Cork,[1] and nothing very great at Limerick[2] from which we don't expect much (except pretty women, for which it is famous), I shall have made a handsome Thousand Pounds since I left Gad's Hill on our country Tour! That is, no doubt, immense; our expenses being necessarily large, and the travelling party being always five.[a]

The success at Belfast has been equal to the success here. Enormous![3] I think them a better audience on the whole than Dublin;[4] and the personal affection there, was something overwhelming. I wish you and the dear girls could have seen the people look at me in the street—or heard them ask me, as I hurried to the hotel after reading last night to "do me the honor to shake hands Misther Dickens and God bless you Sir; not ounly for the light you have been to me this night; but for the light you've been in mee house Sir (and God love your face!) this many a year." Every night, by the bye, since I have been in Ireland, the ladies have beguiled John out of the bouquet from my coat. And yesterday morning, as I had showered the leaves from my geranium in reading Little Dombey, they mounted the platform after I was gone, and picked them all up, as keepsakes.

I have never seen *men* go in to cry so undisguisedly as they did at that reading yesterday afternoon. They made no attempt whatever to hide it, and certainly cried more than the women. As to the Boots at night—and Mrs. Gamp too—it was just one roar with me and them.[5] For they made me laugh so, that sometimes I *could not* compose my face to go on.

You must not let the new idea of poor dear Landor, efface the former image of the fine old man.[6] I wouldn't blot him out, in his tender gallantry, as he

[1] Where he read, at the Athenaeum, the *Carol* on 30 Aug, *Little Dombey* on the afternoon of 31 Aug, and that evening *The Poor Traveller*, *Boots* and *Mrs Gamp*.

[2] He read, in the Theatre Royal, the *Carol* on 1 Sep, and *The Poor Traveller*, *Boots* and *Mrs Gamp* on the 2nd. The *Limerick Reporter*, 3 Sep, devoted most of its long and appreciative review, with some criticism of his "curious peculiarities of pronunciation", to the *Carol*; *Boots* was praised; but not *Mrs Gamp* ("in a great measure coldly received"). Though the theatre was not "so crowded as it might have been", CD was warmly applauded at the end.

[3] Quoting this letter, F reads: "Enormous audiences. We turn away half the town" (VIII, iv, 664). MDGH also inserts: "We turned away half the town" (II, 65).

[4] At his third reading, on Saturday evening, CD told the audience, "crowded in every part", that he had never had one "more competent to appreciate the points of his narrative" (*Belfast News-Letter*, 30 Aug).

[5] The *Belfast News-Letter*, 30 Aug, particularly praised *Mrs Gamp* and referred to the audience's "irrepressible laughter".

[6] The 83 year-old Landor had been widely abused in the Press after being successfully sued for libel by Mrs Yescombe in the Bristol Assizes on 23 Aug. Mrs Yescombe, married to the Rev. Morris Yescombe, and settled in Bath, had been an intimate friend of Landor's; after a long drawn-out quarrel the previous year, in which he had accused her in two pamphlets of theft and perjury, she had begun a libel action against him, only halted after a signed retraction drawn up by Forster and an undertaking not to repeat the charges. The new action was based on three abusive poems in his *Dry Sticks, Fagoted*, Edinburgh, 1858, supported by scurrilous anonymous letters and poems he was alleged to have sent her, and breach of the 1857 undertaking. Mrs Yescombe was awarded £750 for the three libels, £250 for the breach of the undertaking, and costs. For a history of the whole affair, see R. H. Super, *W. S. Landor: a biography*, pp. 454–60. Landor's political enemies in the Press made the most of the scandal. *The Times* carried a two-column report on 24 Aug, followed by a long and hostile leader the next day. The *Saturday Review*, 28 Aug, was the most abusive ("Filth and obscenity are never so unnaturally nauseous as from the chattering lips of age"); and even the *Daily News*,

sat upon that bed at Forster's that night, for a million of wild mistakes at 80 years of age.[1]

[a]I received at Belfast this morning, a very watchful and true and excellent letter from Forster, on a personal matter.[2] I answered it immediately. I asked him if he and Mrs. Forster could come to Gad's Hill next Sunday, and stay Monday. If they could, I begged them to write to dear Mamie.[a]

I hope to be at Tavistock House before 5 o'Clock next Saturday morning, and to lie in bed half the day, and to come home by the 10.50 on Sunday.

Tell the girls that Arthur and I have each ordered at Belfast a trim, sparkling, slap-up *Irish jaunting car*!!![3] I flatter myself we shall astonish the Kentish people. It is the oddest carriage in the world, and you are always falling off. But it is gay and bright in the highest degree. Wonderfully Neapolitan.

What with a sixteen mile ride before we left Belfast, and a sea Beach walk, and a two o'Clock dinner, and a seven hours' railway ride since, I am—as we say here—"a thrifle weary". But I really am in wonderful force, considering the work. For which I am, as I ought to be, very thankful.

Arthur was exceedingly unwell last night—could not cheer up at all. He was so very unwell that he left the Hall (!) and became invisible after my five minutes' rest. I found him at the Hotel in a jacket and slippers, and with a hot bath just ready. He was in the last stage of prostration. The local agent was with me, and proposed that he (the wretched Arthur) should go to his office and balance the accounts then and there. He went, in the jacket and slippers, and came back, in 20 minutes, *perfectly well*, in consequence of the admirable balance. (He is now sitting opposite to me, ON THE BAG OF SILVER[4] (£40; it must be dreadfully hard), writing to Boulogne.[5]

I suppose it is clear that the next letter I write, is Katie's. Either from Cork, or from Limerick, it shall report further. At Limerick I read in the Theatre: there being no other place.

[a] Fancy FREDERICK[6] presenting himself here, in this house, to me, last Thursday a few minutes before Dinner. I was dreadfully hard with him at first; but relented.[a7]

normally sympathetic to Landor, described the libels as "the most atrocious . . . which have ever been read in a court of justice", and charged him with having "disgraced the literature of his country" (*Leader*, 25 Aug). Only Shirley Brooks supported Landor in a signed article in the *Literary Gazette*, 28 Aug, proposing that his damages and costs be defrayed by public subscription.

[1] At his solicitor's insistence, Landor had been persuaded to sell his personal effects and leave England before the trial. His niece Kitty had brought him to the Forsters, in 46 Montagu Square, on 12 July. CD, who was dining there, had visited him in his room: far from finding him wretched, as he expected, he reported that he was "very jovial, and that his whole conversation was upon the character of Catullus, Tibullus, and other Latin poets" (Forster, *W. S. Landor. A Biography*, II, 556). But, as R. H. Super comments on CD's claim for Landor of "tender gallantry": "It was not courage . . . it was oblivion" (Super, above, p. 456). Landor sailed for Boulogne on 16 July; and thence to Fiesole.

[aa] Omitted in MDGH.

[2] Forster had probably heard the rumour about the "violated letter", published in the *New York Tribune*, 10 Aug, and had reason to fear English papers republishing it.

[3] See *To* Finlay, 2 Sep and *fn.*

[4] Underlined twice.

[5] CD forgot to close the second bracket.

[6] His brother; underlined twice.

[7] See *To* Thompson, 22 Nov 58 and *fn.*

Best love to Mamie and Katie, and dear Plorn, and all the boys left when this comes to Gad's Hill; also to my dear good Anne,[1] and—her little woman.

Ever affectionately
CD.

To MRS MADDEN,[2] 31 AUGUST 1858*

MS Fales Collection, New York University Library.

Imperial Hotel, Cork. | Tuesday Thirty First August, 1858.

Mr. Charles Dickens presents his compliments to Mrs. Madden, and, in reply to Mrs. Madden's obliging note, begs to express his great regret that his arrangements do not admit of his reading again in Dublin. It would have given him the greatest pleasure to do so, had such a thing been possible.

To MRS CORNELIUS, 2 SEPTEMBER 1858

Text from N, III, 49.

Limerick | Thursday Second September 1858

Dear Anne,

The trains and boats are so arranged that I doubt if I can get home before about eleven in the forenoon of Saturday. Will you keep breakfast laid up for two, *in case* Mr. Arthur should come home with me to have some.

Affectionately yours always
[CHARLES DICKENS]

To F. D. FINLAY,[3] 2 SEPTEMBER 1858

MS Free Library of Philadelphia.

TAVISTOCK HOUSE, | TAVISTOCK SQUARE, LONDON. W.C.
(which means, Limerick)
Thursday Second September 1858.

My Dear Mr. Finlay

We are not deterred from the achievement of our desperate purpose, by the

[1] Mrs Cornelius.

[2] Née Harriet Elmslie, born in Jamaica; married 1828 Richard Robert Madden (see Vol. VII, p. 38*n*), Secretary to the Loan Fund Board, Dublin Castle, since 1850 and friend of Lady Blessington.

[3] Francis Dalziel Finlay (1832–1917), owner and editor 1857–74 of the strongly Unionist *Northern Whig*, Belfast, founded 1824 by his father, also Francis Dalziel Finlay (1793–1857). Sold the paper in mid-70s and settled in London. Married 1865 Janet Russel, daughter of Alexander Russel, editor of the *Scotsman*. Asked at various times to stand for Parliament; for some years Secretary to political committee of Reform Club; contributed to periodicals on theatre and travel. Knew several of CD's friends, including Frith, Marcus Stone, Luke Fildes and Yates (see Suzannet in *D*, XXX [Autumn 1934], 273).

additional cost. Therefore, if you will have the kindness to order the Cars,[1] we will astonish the counties of Kent and Sussex.[2]

Cork was an immense success. We found upwards of a thousand Stalls let, for the three readings.[3] A great many people were turned away too, on the last night. I did not think them, when I read the Carol, nearly as good an audience as Dublin or Belfast, in respect of demonstrative satisfaction. But they were excellent as to Dombey and the Boots too. Perhaps, on the occasion of the first reading, the fault was in myself. For I was not in very good spirits that evening.

There is not much to be done here, but it is a charming little Theatre[4] for seeing and hearing (I read in the Theatre), and they were a highly sensitive, quick, and agreeable audience last night.

Tomorrow morning we turn our faces towards London. I shall carry there with me (and keep there with me) the remembrance of your most friendly aid, and the hope of seeing you in my own house.[5]

P.S. Mr. Arthur Smith sends his kindest regard, and says (mysteriously) "he will write, about the color of his crest".[6]

To LORD WILLIAM PITT LENNOX,[7] 2 SEPTEMBER 1858

Text from Lord William Pitt Lennox, *My Recollections from 1806 to 1873*, 1874, II, 212.

Royal Hotel, Limerick, | Thursday, 2nd Sept., 1858.

Dear Lord William,

I have just received the extract[8] you kindly sent me, and I cannot refrain from

[1] Irish jaunting-cars, which Finlay sent to both CD and Arthur Smith. CD used his frequently to convey guests from Higham Station to Gad's Hill.

[2] Arthur Smith's home was Bailsborough, Henfield (where Albert also lived), a village 11 m. north of Brighton.

[3] In the Athenaeum: the *Carol* on 30 Aug, *Little Dombey* on 31 Aug (afternoon), *The Poor Traveller*, *Boots* and *Mrs Gamp* that evening. The *Constitution; or, Cork Advertiser*, 2 Sep, gave him a very warm notice. The *Cork Herald*, 4 Sep, devoted half a column of its "Gossip Club" to the readings. It contained more criticism than praise: CD "read many passages too rapidly and in a sing-song tone, ascending from a low to a high key"; the readings "seem to indicate an exhausted intellect"—like *Little Dorrit* which it described as "sheer trash". It ended with gossip about the separation ("an intrigue ... with a pretty actress" has been "scandalously" attributed to him). While at Cork CD sat for a pencil sketch portrait by Edward Sheil, RHA (*d.* 1869); the drawing, autographed by CD, "Friday Night, Thirty First August", was sold at Sotheby's on 4 June 1929.

[4] The Theatre Royal.

[5] "Signature [*on p. 3 of letter*] begged by an Autograph-hunter", Finlay noted. PS written in five short lines on p. 2.

[6] Referring, Finlay noted, to the crest which Smith wanted on his jaunting-car.

[7] Lord William Pitt Lennox (1799–1881; *DNB*), son of 4th Duke of Richmond, miscellaneous writer; Capt. in Army 1822 and ADC to Duke of Wellington; MP for King's Lynn 1852–4. Published five novels, reminiscences of Wellington and books on sport; owner and editor of the *Review* (2 Jan 58–31 Dec 59); had often been attacked in *Punch*, especially by Jerrold.

[8] From his long and extremely appreciative notice in the *Liverpool Mail* of CD's three readings in the Philharmonic Hall, Liverpool, on 17, 19 and 20 Aug. It stressed the audience's delight and applause and encouraged others to hear "the greatest litterateur of the age embodying with wonderful success, the most brilliant emanations of his matchless genius". In *My*

writing to thank you for the interest you feel in its concluding subject,[1] and for the graceful manner in which that interest is expressed. I am sure you will be glad to know that you have given me a very great pleasure, and that I feel heartily obliged to you.

Faithfully yours always,
CHARLES DICKENS.

To W. H. WILLS, 2 SEPTEMBER 1858

MS Huntington Library.

Royal Hotel, Limerick | Thursday Second September 1858

My Dear Wills. I purpose being at the office *next Tuesday afternoon*, before starting again.[2] I hope to be at Tavistock House at noon on Saturday, and to start for Gad's Hill on Sunday forenoon.

Belfast and Cork, as great successes as Dublin. Fancy, at Cork (by no means a large place) more than 1000 stalls being engaged for the three readings. I made last week, clear profit, £340; and have made, in the month of August, a profit of One Thousand Guineas! This, after paying our expences back to London, and halfway to Huddersfield. Pretty well, I think?

This is the oddest place—of which nobody in any other part of Ireland seems to know anything.[3] Nobody could answer a single question we asked about it. There is no large room, and I read in the Theatre—a charming Theatre. The best I ever saw, to see and hear in. Arthur says that when he opened the doors last night, there was a rush of—three Ducks! We expect a Pig to-night. We had only £40; but they seemed to think *that*, amazing! If the two nights bring £100, it will be as much as we expected. I am bound to say that they are an admirable audience. As hearty and demonstrative as it is possible to be. It is a very odd place in its lower-order aspects, and I am very glad we came—though we could have made heaps of money by going to Dublin instead.[4]

[a]Frederick appeared in my room in Dublin! I was very hard with him at first, but relented.[a]

Arthur sends you his kindest regard. He has been nearly torn to pieces in the

Recollections from 1806 to 1873, Lennox wrote of the reading: "Anything more perfect I never heard, and yet I have listened to Charles Kemble, to Fanny Kemble, to Mr. and Mrs. Bartley, and other elocutionists, none of whom were to my mind so forcible, yet so true to nature, as Dickens" (II, 211).

[1] The final paragraph praised "the unexceptionable arrangements for the comfort of the audience", giving the credit to the Secretary of the Philharmonic Society and to Arthur Smith.

[2] For an unbroken series of 11 Yorkshire readings, 8–17 Sep.

[3] Surprising, since Limerick is an ancient and historic city, also a thriving port on the Shannon estuary, 130 m. south west of Dublin. But it was CD's furthest point west and probably those he talked to in Dublin resented his going there.

[4] Instead of returning to Dublin, he gave two readings in Limerick: the *Carol* on 1 Sep and *The Poor Traveller*, *Boots* and *Mrs Gamp* on 2 Sep. The *Limerick Chronicle*, 4 Sep, referred to the crowded audiences for both; it applauded CD as a writer, but "as a general reader we cannot give him unqualified praise"; several descriptive passages he read "in a sing-song, schoolboy style that was below par". It praised *Mrs Gamp* as "the strong point of the evening".

[aa] Omitted in *CD as Editor* and N.

shilling rushes, and has been so flattened against walls that he is only now beginning to "come round" again. My kindest remembrance to Mrs. Wills.

Ever Cordially

CD.

To FREDERIC OUVRY, 5 SEPTEMBER 1858

MS (copy in Mrs Dickens's hand) British Library.

Copy.

Gad's Hill Place | Kent. | Sunday Fifth Septr. 1858

My dear Sir

On coming home here to day from Ireland, for a rest of eight and forty hours, I am exceedingly pained to find that a letter written to me as a private and personal communication,[1] has found its way into some of the London papers, extracted from an American paper.[2] The letter was painfully necessary at the time when it was forced from me, as a private repudiation of monstrous scandals, but that it was never meant to appear in print, I suppose to be quite manifest from its own nature and terms.

I wish you would do me the favor to lose no time in informing Mr. Smith[3] who acted for Mrs. Dickens in our separation, that I am no consenting party to this publication; that it cannot possibly be more offensive to any one in the world than it is to me; and that it has shocked and distressed me very much.[4]

[1] For the "Violated letter", see *To* Arthur Smith, 25 May and *fn*, and Appx F. The *New York Tribune*, in publishing the letter, strongly criticized CD for writing it. "That lying rumor should be busy" with the separation "was inevitable", it wrote. "Every libertine in Anglo-Saxondom, male or female, is sure of course that there is another lady in the case, if not several ladies." CD should have stopped after his "solemn, emphatic denial" in *HW* and remained silent. In such a case the public instinctively sympathized with "the weaker party", the wife "—unless she persists in proving herself a vulgar shrew and virago like Lady Bulwer; but where the wife maintains perfect silence and the husband issues bulletin after bulletin, he is sure to lose ground with each succeeding hour. One more uncalled-for letter from Mr. D. will finish him." In fact Katharine Longley has shown (in *D*, LXXXV, 1989, 178) that the *Tribune*'s comment on the "letter" in the same issue is incompatible with its having been first published there. At the end of the letter, after the signatures of Mrs Hogarth and her daughter Helen, appear the initials "D.J.A", probably a Journalist's Association or Agency, which had supplied the letter; and possibly, she suggests, of Delaware, in retaliation for the satire on its Brandywine Emett Repeal Association as the Watertoast Association, in *Chuzzlewit*, Ch. 21 (see Vol. III, p. 540*n*). The absence of any known quarrel with Smith, the manager of his readings, over its publication, supports this.

[2] The *New York Tribune*, 16 Aug, under the heading "The Dickens Domestic Affair". It was reprinted in both the *Morning Chronicle* and *Morning Herald* on 31 Aug, headed "Mr. Charles Dickens and his Wife", together with CD's letter to Arthur Smith of 25 May and the statement signed by Mrs Hogarth and her daughter Helen. Not reprinted in *The Times*. The *Daily Telegraph*, 2 Sep, regretted its publication, commenting: "First to give [*the letter*] publicity and then to accuse Mr Dickens for circulating certain charges it contains, seems to us a peculiarly base and malignant proceeding."

[3] Ouvry commented in his letter to CD on 6 Sep: "It is very unfortunate that your Letter should have got into print." On 9 Sep he sent CD a letter he had received from G. E. Smith, and on 11 Sep wrote to him: "Smith shall know your feeling" (MSS Messrs Farrer & Co.).

[4] The feeling of shock was widespread. On 5 Oct Elizabeth Barrett Browning wrote from Paris to a friend: "What a dreadful letter that

In short if you will send Mr. Smith this note when you have read it, you will express my present object in the briefest and plainest manner.

Faithfully Yours

Frederick Ouvry Esq. CHARLES DICKENS

To WILKIE COLLINS, 6 SEPTEMBER 1858

Text in MDGH, II, 67–9, checked from MS Sotheby's, Apr 1968.

GAD'S HILL PLACE,| HIGHAM BY ROCHESTER, KENT.
Monday Sixth September 1858

My Dear Wilkie.

First, let me report myself here, for something less than eight and forty hours. I come last (and direct—a pretty hard journey) from Limerick. The success in Ireland has been immense, and, entre nous, I made by the Readings *in this last month of August*, clear profit, over and above all expences and Arthur Smith's share, One Thousand Guineas!

The work is very hard—sometimes, almost overpowering. But I am none the worse for it, and arrived here quite fresh.

Secondly, will you let me recommend the enclosed letter from Wigan,[1] as the groundwork of a capital article, in your way, for H.W. There is not the least objection to a plain reference to him. Or to Phelps; to whom the same thing happened, a year or two ago, near Islington, in the case of a clever and capital little daughter of his. I think it a capital opportunity for a discourse on gentility, with a glance at those other schools which advertize that the "sons of gentlemen only" are admitted—and a just recognition of the greater liberality of our public schools. There are tradesmens' sons at Eton, and Charles Kean was at Eton, and Macready (also an actor's son) was at Rugby.[2] Some such title as Scholastic Flunkeydom—or anything infinitely contemptuous—would help out the meaning.[3] Surely such a schoolmaster must swallow all the silver forks that the Pupils are expected to take away with them when they go. And of course he could not exist, unless he had Flunkey customers by the dozen.[4]

Secondly—no, this is thirdly now—about the Xmas No. I have arranged so to stop

last was! And what a crime, for a man to use his genius as a cudgel against his near kin, even against the woman he promised to protect tenderly with life and heart—taking advantage of his hold with the public to turn public opinion against her. I call it dreadful." (Extract in Maggs Bros catalogue, Summer 1922.)

[1] Alfred Wigan, the actor: see *To* Miss Hogarth, 14 Mar 56, *fn.* He and his wife had recently returned from Scarborough after his two-month absence from the stage through ill-health; his recovery was confirmed by residence in Brighton; he acted again, in Brighton, in Nov. His letter clearly protested against his son's exclusion from a private school, on the grounds of his father's profession; other papers, including the *Brighton Herald*, also protested; the *Theatrical Journal* had a series of three articles, 6, 13 and 20 Oct, entitled "The Climax of Cant", giving the headmaster's name as "Mr. Wigsby".

[2] The article mentions both Kean and Macready to support "the wholesome contrast" of the public schools.

[3] Collins's "Highly Proper!", appeared on 2 Oct 58 (XVIII, 361): see *To* Wills, 24 Sep and *fn.*

[4] The article condemns the parents for the pressure they exerted on the proprietors of such schools.

my Readings, as to be available for it on the [a]*15th. of November*,[a] which will leave me time to write a good article, if I clear my way to one. Do you see your way to our making a Xmas No. of this idea that I am going very briefly to hint? Some disappointed person, man or woman, prematurely disgusted with the world for some reason or no reason, [b](the person should be young, I think)[b] retires to an old lonely house, or an old lonely mill, or any thing you like, with one attendant: resolved to shut out the world and hold no communion with it. The one attendant sees the absurdity of the idea—pretends to humour it—but really tries to slaughter it. Everything that happens—everybody that comes near—every breath of human interest that floats into the old place from the village, or the heath, or the four cross roads near which it stands, and from which belated travellers stray into it—shews beyond mistake that you can't shut out the world—that you are in it to be of it—that you get into a false position the moment you try to sever yourself from it—and that you must mingle with it, and make the best of it, and make the best of yourself into the bargain.[1]

If we could plot out a way of doing this together, I would not be afraid to take my part.[2] If we could not, could we plot out a way of doing it, and taking in stories by other hands? If we could not do either (but I think we could) should we fall back upon a Round of Stories again? That, I would rather not do, if possible. Will you think about it?

And can you come and dine at Tavistock House, on *Monday the 20th. Septr. at ½ past 5*? I purpose being at home there with the girls, that day.

Answer this, according to my printed list for the week. I am off to Huddersfield on Wednesday morning.

[c]I have been greatly vexed by the wantonness of some of our English papers in printing what is evidently on the face of it a private document of mine, violated in America and sent home here. But it is one of the penalties and drawbacks of my position. Any man who wants to sell his paper, has but to lay hold of me for a fillip. And if such men could only make a guess at the pain they give me—well, in that case, I suppose they would only do it the more!—

You know how often I have told you that granting the circulation of the Penny Periodicals[3] (which is greatly exaggerated), I know they cannot pay.[4] Forster tells

[aa] Doubly underlined.

[bb] Added over caret.

[1] A theme CD returned to with Miss Havisham, and much more strongly in "Tom Tiddler's Ground", the Christmas Number for 1861.

[2] The Christmas Number, "A House to Let", published 7 Dec, abandoned the main theme CD outlines; but it kept the "old lonely house" (though now in London, across the road from the house rented by the story's main character, an old lady).

[cc] Omitted in MDGH and N.

[3] By 1850 the number of cheap periodicals in London, offering either fiction or instruction, had reached *c.* 100, with many more in the 1860s after repeal of the paper duty. CD had no doubt chiefly in mind the *London Journal* (see below); G. W. M. Reynolds's periodicals, especially his *Penny Post* (1851–96), *Miscellany of Romance* and *Mysteries of London*; and similar cheap magazines published by William Strange (see Vol. IV, p. 75*n*), John Cleave and G. Purkess. For a full account of such publications up to 1850, see Louis James, *Fiction for the Working Man 1830–1850*, 1963, pp. 28–44.

[4] In fact, the circulation of the *London Journal* reached 500,000 in the 1850s, with exceptional profits of between £10,000 and £12,000; the total circulation of cheap periodicals throughout England had reached 2,900,000 by 1850. Several of the publishers made fortunes. (Louis James, above, p. 44.)

me that he hears on good authority that Mr. Ingram is going about like a Madman as to that London Journal[1]—declaring that he can get nothing out of it[2]—that it is the paper maker's profit (which I know very well)—and that he, Ingram, will never be safe from ruin, until he has got rid "of all his bloodsuckers—with—

Mark Lemon

at their head"!!![3]

With this improving anecdote[c] I think I will leave off: merely adding that I have got a splendid brogue (it really is exactly like the people), and that I think of coming out as the only legitimate successor of poor Power.

Ever My Dear Wilkie | Affectionately Yours

CD

I direct this to Broadstairs.—I hope you are there.[4]

To J. T. GORDON, 6 SEPTEMBER 1858*

MS Free Library of Philadelphia.

GAD'S HILL PLACE, | HIGHAM BY ROCHESTER, KENT.

Monday Sixth September 1858.

My Dear Gordon.

I most heartily congratulate you on being once more at home; and I am touched and gratified by your so soon thinking of me under your own roof, and feeling assured of my cordial sympathy with you and interest in you, there and everywhere.

My life when I am reading, is of that arduous and hurried kind that I never stir out of Hotel quarters, or have the pleasure of visiting any friend while I am so engaged. Moreover, Arthur Smith is always with me, and I mean to bring Mamie and Katie to Edinburgh to shew them something of Scotland. But of course we shall meet, please God.

To my knowledge, I have no acquaintance whatever with the gentleman about whom you enquire. Some indistinct idea floats about in my head that I have been asked the like question concerning him, by some one else. I cannot get it into any tangible shape. Perhaps I may have met him somewhere. I certainly don't know him.

I am only just now at home for eight and forty hours, direct from Ireland. My success has been something wonderful.

With kind regard and remembrance | Ever Faithfully

John T.[5] Gordon Esquire CHARLES DICKENS

[1] The *London Journal*, an illustrated weekly serializing stories and novels, founded by George Stiff 1845; bought by Ingram Oct 57. Its first editor was G. W. M. Reynolds.

[2] Ingram sold it back to Stiff within a year of buying it; it continued until Jan 1912.

[3] See *To* Paxton, 11 Dec 57, *fn.*

[4] Collins had gone to Broadstairs to recuperate early in Aug and no doubt stayed into Sep. References to "my wife" in his "Sea-breezes with the London Smack" (*HW*, 4 Sep 58, XVIII, 274), almost certainly based on this visit, make it virtually certain that he took Caroline Graves, who had been living with him since Jan 1856. His brother Charles also joined him; Charles's two *HW* articles, "The Small-port Monte-Cristo" (16 Oct, XVIII, 423) and "The Great Dunkerque Failure" (30 Oct, XVIII, 476), clearly give further details of their stay.

[5] CD wrote "D" in error.

To JOHN HOLLINGSHEAD, 6 SEPTEMBER 1858

Extract in Dodd Mead catalogue No. 83; *MS* 2 pp.; dated Gad's Hill Place, 6 Sep 58; addressed Hollingshead.

I need not tell you that I have read your article[1] with very great gratification,[2] and that I heartily thank you for it. I know it expresses your honest opinions, manfully and well. The pride I have in it, is therefore an unalloyed one; and the welcome it gives me on coming home to rest for eight and forty hours, is therefore a delightful one....

I am very curious and anxious to know how you got on in the Barges.... I have never seen a Barge these four weeks past—and I have seen many—but I have looked for you, smoking a pipe at the rudder.[3]

To MISS BURDETT COUTTS, 6 SEPTEMBER 1858

MS Morgan Library.

GAD'S HILL PLACE, | HIGHAM BY ROCHESTER, KENT.
Monday Evening | Sixth September 1858

My Dear Miss Coutts

I am at home here tonight, after great fatigue (and great success, thank God!) in Ireland,—for no longer than eight and forty hours. Charley has come down to see me,[4] and he tells me that he thinks the present is a time, in which a word of reminder at Baring Brothers, from a good source, might lead to his removal before long into one of their business opportunities out of London,[5] no matter where, which would present a better opening than London does, to a young man of such capacity, education, and energy, as he possesses.

If you could find an occasion of mentioning this to Mr. Bates, would you object to do so? I know, and I always tell him—I mean Charley—that his rise must in the main depend upon himself. But I hope and believe he deserves well, and of course I know that any sign of *your* interest in him could not fail to serve him.

I would have gone to Mr. Bates myself in the course of tomorrow, but that I have the greatest delicacy in obtruding myself, either on his kindness, or on that of any other partner in the house. What a private gentleman need not scruple to do, my

[1] "Mr. Charles Dickens as a Reader", in the *Critic*, 4 Sep 58 (reprinted in *Hollingshead's Miscellanies*, 1874, II, 275–83). Describing CD as "an elocutionary illustrator", Hollingshead applauded his individual readings, defending them as an additional art to the novel and drama, against the opposition of "the Harold Skimpoles of our literature".

[2] CD would have particularly appreciated Hollingshead's claim for the educational possibilities of the readings: "Mr. Dickens scarcely knows the force of the engine which he holds in his hands—has scarcely mastered the scope and destination of his great design."

[3] The first instalment of Hollingshead's "On the Canal", describing a recent journey by fly-boat (a swift barge) on the Grand Junction Canal, from London to Birmingham, appeared in *HW* on 11 Sep (XVIII, 289); two further instalments followed, on 18 and 25 Sep. Hollingshead was accompanied by Moy Thomas, called "Cuddy" in the article (Hollingshead, *My Lifetime*, 104).

[4] The reading version of *The Chimes* was inscribed to him "From his affectionate father Charles Dickens Seventh September 1858." (Copy in A. Edward Newton Collection, Parke-Bernet catalogue, Apr 1941.)

[5] See next vol.

consciousness of my own notoriety shrinks from. I have a dread of seeming to force it on attention, when I desire nothing more than to be as quiet and modest under it as possible. Hence it is that I trouble you!

I beg to report myself as strong and well as if I had been doing nothing. With love to Mrs. Brown, Believe me ever

Yours faithfully and affecy.

Miss Burdett Coutts. CHARLES DICKENS

To [?PERCY FITZGERALD],[1] [?6 SEPTEMBER 1858]

Fragment from Walter Spencer catalogue No. 196(b). *Date:* shortly after CD's return to England from his reading tour of Ireland 23 Aug–3 Sep 58.

I certainly have no thought of coming to Ireland again, but I hope you will let me see you in England whenever you come here.

Believe me | Very faithfully Yours

CHARLES DICKENS

To MESSRS BRADBURY & EVANS, 7 SEPTEMBER 1858*

MS Dickens House.

OFFICE OF HOUSEHOLD WORDS,
Tuesday Seventh September 1858

Messrs. Bradbury and Evans.

Please to deliver to the Bearer for me

1 Copy Carol
1 Do. Chimes
1 Do. Dombey
1 Do. Poor Traveller &c

—all, of the Reading Edition.

CHARLES DICKENS

To MISS GEORGINA HOGARTH, 7 SEPTEMBER 1858

MS Dickens House. *Address:* Miss Hogarth | Gad's Hill Place | Higham | by Rochester | Kent.

OFFICE OF HOUSEHOLD WORDS,
Tuesday Seventh September 1858

My Dearest Georgy.

I have forgotten to pay Gibson and Bewsher's bill, and I cannot remember how much it is—a hundred and forty odd, I think.[2]

Enclosed is the key of my Writing Table. Sit down at it. The second drawer from the bottom, on your right, will then contain the said bill, with a summary on it, in

[1] Almost certainly to Fitzgerald, and included by Spencer in a lot with other letters addressed to him.

[2] He paid "Gibson & Co" £143.12.9 on 22 Sep (CD's Account-book, MS Messrs Coutts).

my writing, of the gross amount for the four boys. Write and tell me what that amount is, and also who are Gibson's bankers. You will see that, stated in print, on the top of one of the sheets of paper whereon the bills are made out.

I am not at all disposed to go away again.—Don't take to the idea at present, in the least. However, the time will go by, pretty quickly, please God.

With my dear love to the darling girls and to the solitary Plorn.

Ever your most affectionate[1]

To MRS GORE, 7 SEPTEMBER 1858*

MS Berg Collection.

TAVISTOCK HOUSE, | TAVISTOCK SQUARE, LONDON. W.C.
Tuesday Seventh September 1858

My Dear Mrs. Gore.

Being in town this morning for a few hours, in an interval in my series of Readings—which bind me hand and foot until November—I find your note. Believe me (but I know you will), I find it with the truest sorrow and the deepest sympathy. I am touched to the heart by your affectionate remembrance of me at such a time. Depend upon my having nothing to say to the sordid speculation in question—the nature of which, I perfectly understand.

Be of good heart about your brave boy.[2] *My* boy was invalided long ago, and carried in a litter God knows how far and how long. But he began to get well, the moment he arrived at a Hill-Station, and his only care now, in the letters he writes home, is to get away from that easy life and be on service again.[3] He had sun-stroke, a passing attack of small pox, and smart Fever.[4] But he rallied, gaily—and so will your boy, please Heaven, before you can believe in his having had time to think of it.

If I do not hear of you in the meantime, I must write again to ask how your health[5] and spirits are, when I next come to town for a few hours—about the middle of October. Until then and always, believe in the faithful, grateful, and affectionate regard of yours with all his heart

Mrs. Gore. CHARLES DICKENS

To GABRIEL LEGOUVÉ, 7 SEPTEMBER 1858*

MS M. Jean Paladilhe.

GAD'S HILL PLACE, | HIGHAM BY ROCHESTER, KENT.
Tuesday Seventh September 1858.

My Dear Legouvé.

I cannot tell you how much pleasure I have had in the receipt of your letter, or what delight it gives me to be so remembered and honored by you.

[1] Bottom of letter cut away.

[2] Probably Capt. Augustus Wentworth Gore, her only surviving son at her death in 1861.

[3] Walter had been in India since Aug 57, at first in the 26th Native Infantry Regt, then in the 42nd Highlanders: see *To* Cavendish Boyle, 5 Feb 58.

[4] Severe, but of short duration.

[5] She was losing her sight.

Yet I am made more impatient than I can express either, by an omission you have accidentally made. The poem[1] is *not* enclosed in your letter! Pray, pray, send it to me.

I write to you from my little country house, about 30 miles from London. As I shall be absent from here, and from London too, until the middle of November, I fervently hope that you will not make your projected visit to London before that time. I shall be charmed to take you by the hand again, and to renew and increase a friendship, the memory of which is one of my happiest souvenirs of Paris.

Believe me always | With very great regard | Your faithful friend

A Monsieur Legouvé CHARLES DICKENS

To THOMAS BODDINGTON,[2] 10 SEPTEMBER 1858*

MS Free Library of Philadelphia.

Station Hotel York | Friday Tenth September 1858.

Dear Sir

I have received here to day, a note from our friend Miss Mary Boyle, explaining to me the nature of the honor you courteously propose to do me on the 29th. of this month.[3]

Allow me to express my regret that I cannot have the gratification of accepting your kind invitation. I have arranged to be in Edinburgh on that day, and my engagement is a public one.

Dear Sir | Yours faithfully and obliged

Thomas Boddington Esquire CHARLES DICKENS

To MISS MARY BOYLE, 10 SEPTEMBER 1858†

MS Morgan Library.

Station Hotel, York | Friday Tenth September 1858

Dearest Meery.

First let me tell you that all the Magicians and spirits in your employ have fulfilled the instructions of their wondrous Mistress, to admiration. Flowers have fallen in my path wheresoever I have trod; and when they have rained upon me at Cork I was more amazed than you ever saw me.[4]

Secondly, receive my hearty and loving thanks for that same.—(Excuse a little Irish in the turning of that sentence, but I can't help it).

Thirdly, I have written direct to Mr. Boddington, explaining that I am bound to be in Edinburgh on the day when he courteously proposes to do me honor.

[1] His *Un Souvenir de Manin*, Paris, 1858, tribute to Daniele Manin, Italian patriot, now living in exile in Paris: see Vol. VII, p. 732 and *n*.

[2] Perhaps father or brother of the two Boddington girls Mary Boyle had met in Lucca in 1833, the elder of whom became a great friend (*Mary Boyle her Book*, ed. Sir Courtenay Boyle, p. 117); possibly of the same family as Boddington & Co., West India merchants, 9 St Helen's Place, Bishopsgate.

[3] Occasion not discovered.

[4] Mary Boyle, as descendant of Sir Richard Boyle, 1st Earl of Cork 1620, the "Great Earl", no doubt had a special feeling for CD's being there.

[a]Finally, touching that other matter on which you write so tenderly and with a delicacy of regard and interest that I deeply feel. I hope I may report that I am calming down again. I have been exquisitely distressed. It is no comfort to me to know that any man who wants to sell any thing in print, has but to anatomize my finest nerves, and he is sure to do it—It is no comfort to me to know (as of course these dissectors do), that when I spoke in my own person[1] it was not for myself but for the innocent and good, on whom I had unwittingly brought the foulest lies—Sometimes I *cannot* bear it. I had one of these fits yesterday, and was utterly desolate and lost. But it is gone, thank God, and the sky has brightened before me once more.

Ever, with great regard and affection | Yours dearest Meery

CHARLES DICKENS[a]

To GEORGE HOLSWORTH, 10 SEPTEMBER 1858

MS Dickens House.

Station Hotel York | Friday Tenth September 1858

Dear Mr. Holsworth

Will you be so good as to cut out and put together for me, the Lazy Tour of the Two Idle Apprentices, complete.[2] Send it, by return of post, addressed to me, "Assembly Rooms,[3]

To JOHN FORSTER, [11 SEPTEMBER 1858]

Extracts in F, VIII, iv, 665. *Date:* since from York, clearly 11 Sep; for Forster's misdating first extract as Oct, see below.[4]

I was brought very near to what I sometimes dream may be my Fame, when a lady whose face I had never seen stopped me yesterday in the street, and said to me, *Mr. Dickens, will you let me touch the hand that has filled my house with many friends.*

At York I had a most magnificent audience,[5] and might have filled the place for a week.... I think the audience possessed of a better knowledge of character than any I have seen. But I recollect Doctor Belcombe[6] to have told me long ago that they

[aa] Omitted in MDGH and N. In its place MDGH, followed by N, inserts two paragraphs and the ending belonging to *To* Mary Boyle, 8 Dec 59.

[1] In the "Violated letter": see Appx F.

[2] CD was perhaps considering making "The Lazy Tour" into a separate publication; but, if so, this was not done; or he may have wanted a copy for a Yorkshireman, because of the local interest.

[3] Bottom of letter cut off: first missing word was clearly "Scarborough" (see *To* Miss Hogarth, 12 Sep and *fn*).

[4] Although CD's only reading at York was on 10 Sep, up to 22 Oct he intended to read there again on 25 Oct: see *To* Mamie Dickens, 22 Oct. Forster either forgot or did not know of the change of plan and referred to the printed list.

[5] For the *Carol* in the Festival Concert Room. The *York Herald*, 11 Sep, recorded that the large audience listened "with unflagging attention and uninterrupted delight"; his "style of reading is, perhaps, as near perfection as it is possible to conceive".

[6] Henry Stephens Belcombe, MD (1790–1856), late Senior Physician to the York County Hospital: see Vol. I, pp. 368–9 and *n*.

first found out Charles Mathews's[1] father,[2] and to the last understood him (he used to say) better than any other people.... The let is enormous for next Saturday at Manchester, stalls alone four hundred! I shall soon be able to send you the list of places to the 15th of November, the end. I shall be, O most heartily glad, when that time comes! But I must say that the intelligence and warmth of the audiences are an immense sustainment, and one that always sets me up. Sometimes before I go down to read (especially when it is in the day), I am so oppressed by having to do it that I feel perfectly unequal to the task. But the people lift me out of this directly; and I find that I have quite forgotten everything but them and the book, in a quarter of an hour.

To MISS GEORGINA HOGARTH, [12] SEPTEMBER 1858

MS Dickens House. *Address:* Miss Hogarth | Gad's Hill Place | Higham | by Rochester | Kent. *Date:* misdated by CD; Sunday was 12 Sep 58.

Royal Hotel, Scarborough.[3] | Sunday Eleventh September 1858.

My Dearest Georgy. .[a]You will be surprised when I begin my letter by telling you that I have had an excellent opportunity of setting Katey quite right in that matter of Andrew.[4] Coming home to the hotel at York from reading in that city on Friday night, who should I find, established in our room, but—Gordon! He had seen in Household Words where I was, and had come for a holiday, he said, intending to keep company with us as far as Hull, and thence go back by Steamer. Arthur not having yet come up from the room, Gordon and I were alone; and he very soon took the opportunity of saying, with a kind of confidentially smirking satisfaction, that Andrew was uncommonly sweet indeed, upon a certain young lady at Gad's Hill. I immediately turned very grave, and said I had been quite uneasy about it, and had not known what to do. Gordon instantly changed, and asked "Why?"—"O! my good fellow", I said, "Why? Only because the difference is so obvious between a boy of eighteen, and a young woman of 19 or 20—and I like Andrew so very much, and should be so heartily grieved if he were to make himself unhappy." It was clear that this dashed Gordon exceedingly. You know how self-possessed he can be, but he couldn't carry it off at all. His countenance fell, and he walked up and down the room musing about it, and rubbing his chin with his pocket handkerchief. Then he stopped short, and said: "You see it would be such a difficult thing to speak to Andrew about it."—"Exactly so," I said; "I feel that, or I might have done it myself." Having got it to this point, I felt that all I had to do was to leave it alone, so I said this in an offhand easy way, and said no more.[a]

We had a very fine house indeed at York.[5] All kinds of applications have been

[1] Charles James Mathews (1803–78; *DNB*), actor: see Vol. II, p. 385*n*.

[2] Charles Mathews (1776–1835; *DNB*), popular comedian: see Vol. I, p. 3 and *n*; had made his reputation in York, in 1797, and performed his first "At Home", "The Mail Coach, or Rambles in Yorkshire", at Hull, 30 miles away, in Apr 1808.

[3] Where he read *Little Dombey* on the afternoon of 13 Sep and the *Carol* in the evening, in the Assembly Rooms. The *Scarborough Mercury*, 18 Sep, reported "the most fashionable audiences" of the season; though confessed it preferred CD as an author than as "a descriptive reader".

[aa] Omitted in MDGH.

[4] Andrew Rutherford Gordon.

[5] See *To* Forster, 11 Sep and *fn*.

made for another reading there, and no doubt it would be exceedingly productive; but it cannot be done. At Harrogate yesterday,—the queerest place, with the strangest people in it, leading the oddest lives of dancing, newspaper reading, and tables d'hôte—I made a clean profit of £50.[1] The piety of York obliging us to leave that place for this at 6 this morning, and there being no night-train from Harrogate, we had to engage a Special Engine. We got to bed at one, and were up again before five; which after yesterday's fatigues, leaves me a little worn at this present.

I have no accounts of this place as yet, nor have I received any letter here. But the Post of this morning is not yet delivered, I believe. We have a charming room, overlooking the sea. [a]Upon the whole I could easily dispense with Gordon, but I don't care much about it.[a] Leech is here (living within a few doors), with the partner of his bosom, and his young family. I write at ten in the morning, having been here two hours; and you will readily suppose that I have not seen him.

Of news, I have not the faintest breath. I seem to have been doing nothing all my life, but riding in railway carriages and reading. The railway of the morning brought us through Castle Howard[2] and under the woods of Easthorpe,[3] and then just below Malton Abbey where I went to poor Smithson's funeral.[4] It was a most lovely morning, and tired as I was, I couldn't sleep for looking out of the window.

[a]I don't know whether I told Mamey or Katey—but I think not—that Mr. Smith, your sister's legal representative, wrote Ouvry a very good note about that published letter: saying that he was much obliged by the assurance that I had not sanctioned its publication, but that it was quite unnecessary to him, as he had been quite certain of that, from the moment when he saw it. I had a letter from "Meery",[5] at York, which I answered. Very affectionate!—but really sincere and earnest.[a] Yesterday, at Harrogate, two circumstances occurred which gave Arthur great delight. Firstly, he chafed his leg sore, with his black bag of silver. Secondly, the landlord asked him as a favor, "if he could oblige him with a little silver". He obliged him, directly, with some forty pounds worth; and I suspect the landlord to have repented of having approached the subject. After the reading last night, we walked over the moor to the railway—3 miles—leaving our men to follow with the luggage in a light cart. They passed us, just short of the railway, and John was making the night hideous and terrifying the sleeping country, by *playing the horn* in prodigiously horrible and unmusical blasts.

[a]Gordon is sitting in the sunshine at the bow window, surveying the sea through an opera glass. He is too big for the room, and his collars are too big for him. Arthur, after touzling his head in the most frightful manner in the railway carriage, by sleeping with it rolled up in the window curtain, has gone to shave, and freshen himself up a little. This really is the very last and latest scrap of intelligence I have.

[1] He had given two readings, of *Little Dombey* and the *Carol*, in the Cheltenham Room. The *Harrogate Herald*, 15 Sep, praised him as "a good reader, without any extravagances of voice or gesture, and perfectly free from trickery and clap-trap".

[aa] Omitted in MDGH.

[2] Five miles south-west of Malton; the seat, then, of the Earl of Carlisle.

[3] Easthorpe Park, near Malton, former home of CD's late solicitor Charles Smithson (?1804–44: see Vol. I, p. 427*n*); for CD's and Catherine's visit there in July 43, see Vol. III, p. 519 and *n*.

[4] In Apr 1844 (Vol. IV, p. 96). The Smithsons had moved to Malton Abbey in Autumn 1843.

[5] Mary Boyle.

It is to be regretted, of course, that that little accident happened at Cobham;[1] but nothing could be more discreet than the course taken to set it right, and nothing could be better than Lord Darnley's quick response. I *think* I will still write him a note.—I am not sure, but it is no matter.[a]

My dearest love, of course, to the dear girls, and to the noble Plorn. Apropos of children, there was one gentleman at the Little Dombey yesterday morning, who exhibited—or rather concealed—the profoundest grief. After crying a good deal without hiding it, he covered his face with both his hands, and laid it down on the back of the seat before him, and really shook with emotion. He was not in mourning, but I supposed him to have lost some child in old time.[2] There was a remarkably good fellow of 30 or so, too, who found something so very ludicrous in Toots that he *could not* compose himself at all, but laughed until he sat wiping his eyes with his handkerchief. And whenever he felt Toots coming again, he began to laugh and wipe his eyes afresh; and when he came he gave a kind of cry, as if it were too much for him. It was uncommonly droll, and made me laugh heartily.

[a]I received the key all right. It had escaped my memory that I had changed the place where I keep the bills. I will leave this open for an hour or two, to acknowledge the receipt of any letter if I get one from Gads Hill this morning.[a]

Ever dearest Georgy | Your most affectionate

CD.

To MISS MARY DICKENS, 15 SEPTEMBER 1858

MS Robert H. Taylor Collection, Princeton University.

Scarborough Arms, Leeds.
Wednesday Fifteenth September 1858.

My Dearest Mamie.

[a]Although I received the bills from Georgy this morning, I write to you, because it is your turn. Tell her so with my dearest love.

I quite agree with her as to the amounts. The objectionable week is certainly large, but it is scarcely reasonable to hope that the servants will all be methodically saving and economical at once. It is only by looking closely and systematically, into any excess, of any kind, and letting them see that it [b]*will not do*,[b] that we can hope to come to a perfectly satisfactory result. I think the other bills quite fair and very promising. I have no doubt, please God, that we shall get the machine into perfect order. And I know thoroughly well, that you are all three most anxious to bring it into that condition.[a]

I have added a pound to the cheque. I would recommend your seeing the poor Railwayman again, and giving him ten shillings, and telling him to let you see him again in about a week. If he be then still unable to lift weights and handle heavy things, I would then give him another Ten Shillings, and so on.

[1] Cobham Park, Lord Darnley's seat, close to Gad's Hill Place. The "accident" has not been discovered.

[2] He was the Rev. Thomas Sheepshanks (1819–1912), Perpetual Curate of Bilton.

[aa] Omitted in MDGH and N.

[bb] Each word separately underlined.

[a]In the matter of Frank, let me say at once, while I remember it, that I think Dr. Crüger[1] perfectly right in wishing him to have no more pocket-money than the rest of the boys. Will you write to Mrs. Crüger, and say that I wish the Dr. to do exactly what he feels to be right and best in this matter.[a2]

Since I wrote to Georgy from Scarborough we have had, thank God, nothing but success. [a]I made £50 profit there, and made more than £50 profit at Hull last night.[a3] The Hull people (not generally considered excitable, even on their own showing), were so enthusiastic that we were obliged to promise to go back there for Two Readings![4] I have positively resolved not to lengthen out the time of my tour, so we are now arranging to drop some small places, and substitute Hull again and York again.[5] But you will perhaps have heard this in the main, from Arthur. I know he wrote to you after the Reading last night. This place I have always doubted, knowing that we should come here when it was recovering from the double excitement of the Festival and the Queen.[6] But there is a very large Stall Let indeed, and the prospect of to-night consequently looks bright. [a](It is not a large room. I doubt if Arthur can squeeze more than £70 into it.)[a]

Arthur told you, I suppose, that he had his shirt front and waistcoat torn off, last night. He was perfectly enraptured in consequence. Our men got so knocked about, that he gave them five shillings apiece on the spot. John passed several minutes upside down against a wall, with his head amongst the peoples' boots. He came out of the difficulty in an exceedingly touzled condition, and with his face much flushed. For all this, and their being packed as you may conceive they would be packed, they settled down the instant I went in, and never wavered in the closest attention for an instant. It was a very high room, and required a great effort.

Oddly enough, I slept in this house three days ago last year,[7] with Wilkie. Arthur has the bedroom I occupied then, and I have one two doors from it, and Gordon has the one between. Not only is he still with us, but he *has* talked of going on to Manchester, going on to London, and coming back with us to Darlington next Tuesday!!! [a]I hope however, that I observe him to be gradually getting disgusted with the smoke and ashes of these manufacturing towns.[a]

[b]These streets look like a Great Circus with the season just finished. All sorts of garish Triumphal arches were put up for the Queen, and they have got smoky, and have been looked out of countenance by the sun, and are blistered, and patchy, and

[aa] Omitted in MDGH and N.

[1] Carl Crüger, D. Phil, St Georg, Langereihe 15–16, headmaster of Frank's new school in Hamburg.

[2] He paid Crüger's bill of £39.3.2 on 21 Dec (CD's Account-book, MS Messrs Coutts); it would have included Frank's pocket money.

[3] When he read the *Carol* in the Music Hall, gaining "eager, unflagging attention from first to last".... "Such a numerous and fashionable audience as we have seldom witnessed." Many were excluded, "the pushing and murmuring" showing "how keenly they felt their disappointment" (*Hull News*, 18 Sep).

[4] As he did on 26 and 27 Oct: see *To* Forster, 18 Oct.

[5] He did not in fact read at York again: see *To* Mary Dickens, 22 Oct and *fn*.

[6] The Queen and Prince Albert had visited Leeds on 6 Sep, on their way to Scotland. They stayed the night with the Mayor, the Queen receiving the Corporation in the Town Hall the following day. The crowded and successful Music Festival, in aid of the Leeds General Infirmary, followed, 8–10 Sep. It included performances of Mendelssohn's *Elijah* and Handel's *Messiah* and *Israel in Egypt*.

[7] On 13 Sep, between Lancaster and Doncaster: see *To* Georgina Hogarth, 12 Sep 57.

[bb] For the use he and Collins made of this in *HW*, see *To* Wills, 24 Sep and *fn*.

half up and half down, and are hideous to behold.[b] Spiritless men (evidently drunk for some time in the Royal honor) are slowly removing them, and on the whole it is more like the clearing away of the Frozen Deep at Tavistock House, than any thing within your knowledge—with the exception that we are not in the least sorry, as we were then. Vague ideas are in Arthur's head that when we come back to Hull, we are to come here, and are to have the Town Hall (a beautiful building) and read to the Million. I can't say, yet. That depends.[1] I remember that when I was here before (I came from Rockingham, to make a speech),[2] I thought them a dull and slow audience.[3] I hope I may have been mistaken. I never saw better audiences than the Yorkshire audiences generally.

I am so perpetually at work, or asleep, that I have not a scrap of news. I saw the Leech family at Scarboro', both in my own house (that is to say, Hotel), and in theirs. They were not at either reading. Scarboro' is gay and pretty, and I think Gordon had an idea that we were always at some such place. [a]I have a strong hope that he has had a new light or two on that subject,[4] since we got among the tall chimnies.[a5]

Kiss the darling Plorn for me, and give him my love—dear Katey too, giving her the same. I feel sorry that I cannot get down to Gad's Hill this next time, but I shall look forward to our being there with Georgy, after Scotland. Tell the servants that I remember them, and hope they will live with us many years. Ever My Dearest Mamie Your most affectionate father CD.

[b]P.S. Arthur sends his love. Gordon too.[b]

To ALBERT SMITH, 16 SEPTEMBER 1858

MS Morgan Library.

Halifax, Yorkshire. | Thursday Sixteenth September 1858.

My Dear Albert. As Arthur is always writing to you on every railway in England, and has, up to this day, overset his inkstand in 374 first class carriages (I keep a reckoning of that casualty, in an account book), he has left me very little to tell you. But I have two whimsical anecdotes to relate, which you won't find in the Newspapers.

I[6]

When I was last in town, eight or nine years ago (I mean, days; but you know what enormous intervals seem to elapse under these circumstances), Forster told me that Frederic Chapman of Piccadilly had just told him that Ingram was going about town declaring like a madman as to his wildness and ferocity, that there was not a

[1] He gave another reading of *The Poor Traveller*, *Boots* and *Mrs Gamp*, at Leeds on 28 Oct; but again in the Music Hall. The *Leeds Mercury*, 30 Oct, praised it even more highly than the first one, and defended CD from the criticism of being "theatrical".

[2] On 1 Dec 47, as chairman, of a meeting of the Leeds Mechanics' Institute: see Vol. v, p. 204 and *n*.

[3] CD in fact described the occasion to Forster as a "most brilliant demonstration"; and the *Leeds Times* recorded that his speech was received with "reiterated cheering" (*ibid.*).

[aa] Omitted in MDGH and N.

[4] The smokiness of Leeds and Hull.

[5] Thus in MS.

[bb] Written above the address on p. 1.

[6] Underlined with short double strokes.

penny to be got out of the London Journal by anybody but the Paper-Maker, and that he (Ingram) would never be safe from ruin; until he had got rid of "the whole gang of bluid-soockers, beginning with"——O! whom do you think?—"Mark Lemon"!!![1]

2[2]

My little boy Frank, was dispatched the other day, per steamer, to a new School at Hamburg. I knew the Captain, and gave the child a letter to him, knowing that he would be taken excellent care of. Mary wrote to the lady of the school, the wife of one Doctor Crüger, saying when Frank would arrive, and begging that he might be met by some trustworthy person at the Boat's wharf on the Boat's arrival. Gad's Hill was paralysed in the due course by the receipt of a letter from Frank, dated "Aboard the John Bull"—with this astonishing postscript. "The passengers have all been gone, some hours. Nobody has come for me, and nobody knows anything of the name of KRUGGENS.[3] I am dining with the Captain and Mate. The dinner is beefsteak and onions. It is very good, and there is lots of it. The Captain having just regretted and apologized for being unable to offer me a dessert, I have been to my box, and brought out a quantity of the Gad's Hill apples and nuts. The Captain has produced a bottle of wine, and we are very jolly." Since then, he has never been heard of. My own impression is, that he will sail backwards and forwards in the John Bull, like a Young Flying Dutchman, for many years, and will vainly try, until he arrives at a green old age, to get to School. Either this will happen, or a fraudulent and ill-conducted school will kidnap him on false pretences, or he will work out the usual story-book career by entering Hamburg without any boots, selling matches in the streets, gradually realizing an enormous fortune, and finally laying it out in endowing an establishment for 80 one-eyed old men with wooden legs, who will never get anything that he bequeaths to them, but will be pillaged by fifteen trustees in the Banking and Legal lines of life who will live and die in great esteem on the plunder.

Do you understand the following Chinese sentence yet?

[a] [a]

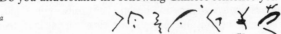

It is a poetical idea, I think, and very expressive of the general virtues of the Tea Plant. Is it really in the works of their great poet[4] [a] [a]

When this reaches you, you will be running home as hopefully and happily as possible.[5] Aden will seem like Fleet Street, Cairo like the Strand, camels like cabs—all so near home and so familiarly. God speed you. We will talk Chinese (I have a smattering of that tongue) always.

Ever Cordially
CHARLES DICKENS

[1] See *To* Collins, 6 Sep and *fn.*
[2] Underlined with short double strokes.
[3] Large ornamental caps.
[aa] Joke Chinese characters.
[4] Perhaps the "Chinese Shakespeare" described in detail in "The Hero of a Hundred Plays" by Fox Bourne and Morley, *HW*, 18 Sep 58, XVIII, 324.
[5] Smith left Hong Kong on 28 Sep.

To UNKNOWN MUSICIAN, 16 SEPTEMBER 1858

Text from *Musical Age*, 1 Jan 1891.

Halifax, Thursday, Sixteenth September, 1858.

Sir,

My time, at all times very much occupied, is so completely absorbed just now, that I have not had leisure to answer your letter until to-day.

If you should ever desire to offer anything for insertion in *Household Words*, it shall be honestly read. You have but to address it to me at the office of that journal. But I cannot undertake to read compositions generally designed for publication, and write opinions upon them;[1] simply because I am so constantly asked to do it, that unless I had a rule from which I never departed, in this respect, I could do nothing else in life.

You repose a confidence in me very honestly and unaffectedly. I should not deserve it if I were otherwise than plain with you.

The course on which you seek to enter is a very difficult one, and I have a very strong doubt, (suggested to me by your letter itself) of your being qualified for it. I know more than you can easily imagine of the wretchedness of failure in it. Do not neglect your respectable and useful certainty for a desperate chance.

Faithfully yours

Mr. —— CHARLES DICKENS

To RICHARD BENTLEY, 17 SEPTEMBER 1858*

MS Berg Collection. *Address:* Richard Bentley Esquire | New Burlington Street | London | W.

Sheffield. | Friday Seventeenth September | 1858.

My Dear Mr. Bentley

Your letter of the Thirteenth has just found me here. I regret to learn from it that my mediation has not been attended with more satisfactory results.[2]

Under the circumstances, I can now do no more than make Mr. Shirley Brooks acquainted with the contents of your communication. That I will take care to do by the present post.

Faithfully Yours

Richard Bentley Esquire CHARLES DICKENS

To SHIRLEY BROOKS, [17 SEPTEMBER 1858]

Mention in last. *Date:* written the same day.

[1] The *Musical Age*, in a preface to CD's letter, describes his correspondent as "a well-known musician in the North of England", who had requested his opinion "as to whether he should embrace literature as a profession".

[2] Clearly over Brooks's novel, *The Gordian Knot*, published by Bentley in monthly parts from 1 Jan 58; its part publication never completed; not published as a vol. until 1860, though announced for "ensuing season" in Nov 58. See next vol.

To MISS GEORGINA HOGARTH, 17 SEPTEMBER 1858

MS Dickens House.

King's Head, Sheffield
Friday, Seventeenth September 1858.

My Dearest Georgy.

I write you a few lines to Tavistock House, thinking you may not be sorry to find a note from me there, on your arrival from Gad's Hill.

Halifax was too small for us. I never saw such an audience though.[1] They were really worth reading to for nothing—though I didn't do exactly that. It is as horrible a place as I ever saw,[2] I think. [a]Of course the local agent (a Music Seller)[3] used to play duetts with your father,[4] and told me a lot about him, after the reading—in which I was deeply interested.[a]

The run upon the Tickets here is so immense, that Arthur is obliged to get great bills out, signifying that no more can be sold.[5] It will be by no means easy to get into the place the numbers who have already paid. It is the Hall we acted in,[6] crammed to the roof and the passages. We must come back here towards the end of October, and are again altering the List, and striking out small places. [a]I suppose I shall get from £60 to £70 profit tonight.[a]

The trains are so strange and unintelligible in this part of the country that we were obliged to leave Halifax at 8 this morning, and breakfast on the road—at Huddersfield again, where we had an hour's wait. Wills was in attendance on the Platform, and took me (here at Sheffield I mean) out to "Frederick's"[7] house, to see Mrs. Wills. She looked pretty much the same as ever, I thought, and was taking care of a very pretty little boy.[8] The house and grounds are as nice as anything *can* be, in this smoke.

[1] He read the *Carol* in the Odd Fellows' Hall, on 16 Sep. A warm notice in the *Halifax Guardian*, 18 Sep, reported a "large and enthusiastic audience", whose interest "never for one moment flagged".

[2] It was a horrible place then, dominated by ironworks; cf. the old saying "From Hell, Hull, and Halifax | The Lord deliver us!"

[aa] Omitted in MDGH.

[3] Probably William Bentham, teacher of music and instruments and music seller, 23 and 24 Southgate.

[4] During 1831–4, when Hogarth and his family were living in Halifax; he was first editor of the *Halifax Guardian* from 1 Dec 32 and a founder of the Halifax Orchestral Society. There were many musical evenings at his house (A. A. Adrian, *Georgina Hogarth and the Dickens Circle*, pp. 3–4).

[5] He read *The Poor Traveller*, *Boots* and *Mrs Gamp* in the Music Hall, Sheffield, that night. The *Sheffield and Rotherham Independent*, 18 Sep, reported a "crowded and delighted audience" and a "most enthusiastic" reception. It praised the "marvellous versatility of [CD's] genius" and his "masterly skill". Most of its long and appreciative notice repeated Hollingshead's "Mr. Charles Dickens as a Reader" in the *Critic*, 4 Sep: see *To* Hollingshead, 6 Sep and *fn*.

[6] The Music Hall, Surrey St; presumably the Free Trade Hall of 1854 re-named, where they had acted in Aug 52: see Vol. VI, p. 751.

[7] Augustus Frederick Lehmann (1826–91), youngest son of Leo Lehmann, portrait-painter, of Hamburg. Came to England to make a career in commerce and by 1851 was living in Leith, near Edinburgh, where he met and married Jane (Nina) Chambers in Nov 52: see Vol. VII, p. 36*n*. Through his brother-in-law, Ernst Benzon, joined engineering firm of Naylor Vickers, working first in Liverpool, then Sheffield. Settled in London 1859, becoming senior partner in Naylor, Benzon & Co., merchants, of 20 Abchurch Lane. Left over £540,000. An excellent violinist, he gathered many musicians around him; also formed a fine collection of paintings. Became a close friend of CD, Browning, Wilkie Collins and James Payn.

[8] Rudolf Chambers Lehmann, *b.* 3 Jan 56; (father of Beatrix, Rosamond and John).

[a]Gordon is still with us and shows no signal of departure. His luggage has been left behind at Halifax, and he is sitting disconsolate.[a] A heavy thunderstorm is passing over the town, and it is raining hard too.

[a]If you should have time to go (*with the girls or one of them*) to Mr. Hill's[1] at Bell's, will you ask him if he will send me in the course of Monday to Tavistock House, a fresh supply of "Voice Jujubes," and also of the "Astringent Lozenges." I have found them both, admirable.

I hope to be at home by 5 on Sunday morning. Will you leave the spirit-stand and a rusk or two, in the Hall? The door to be left on the latch, of course.[a]

This is a stupid letter my dearest Georgy, but I write in a hurry, and in the thunder and lightning, and with the crowd of tonight before me. My best love to dearest Mamie and Katie, and to the Darling Plorn.

Ever Most affectionately.
CD.

To HENRY BURNETT, 18 SEPTEMBER 1858

MS Copy in Dickens House.[2]

Royal Hotel Manchester
Saturday Eighteen September | 1858

My dear Burnett

I have not a moment in which to answer your Letter before going down to the Hall—Believe me I have never had an unkind thought of you—I was very glad to hear of your marrying again—thought it most natural & right—Have always had the best feeling towards yourself and your second Wife[3]—Have always been glad to hear of you. I should have liked to have heard of your marriage from yourself—may (perhaps) have said so—certainly have never said so with the least unkindness or ill will.... God knows it is not in me—We must all go poor Fanny's way, and we shall all want sorely the gentle construction that we cannot do better than give.... Dismiss all uneasiness as to me from your mind. I have always thought of you and do think of you affectionately.

Faithfully Yours
CHARLES DICKENS

[aa] Omitted in MDGH.

[1] Thomas Hyde Hills, pharmaceutical chemist; partner in John Bell & Co., of 338 Oxford St and 2, 4 and 6 Hills Place, Regent Circus. Fellow of Linnaean Society.

[2] This is one of a group of transcripts in a notebook given to Dickens House through descent from Henry Burnett's second wife. The copyist is unidentified. He or she has sometimes misread CD's hand and clearly not troubled about punctuation. We have added only obvious full stops, corrected wrong names and, where possible, suggested omitted words. Elision dots are those of the copyist and seem to affect passages concerning money. For some of the letters given in the notebook and others not included we have the original MSS. (See Vol. VII, p. 838 *n*).

[3] Née Sarah Hargreaves (?1825–89), of Heirs House, Colne, Lancs, daughter of Reginald Hargreaves. They were married at Rusholme Road Independent Chapel, Chorlton, on 29 June 57. Burnett was then living at 55 Shakespeare St, Chorlton.

To THE MARCHIONESS OF NORMANBY,[1] 20 SEPTEMBER 1858

Summary from The Marquis of Normanby.

TAVISTOCK HOUSE, | TAVISTOCK SQUARE, LONDON. W.C.
Twentieth September 1858

A letter of recommendation to the Marchioness of Normanby, for Miss Fanny Ternan to take with her to Florence,[2] *where she is going with her mother, to complete a professional musical education.*[3]

To ARTHUR RYLAND, 20 SEPTEMBER 1858*

MS Mr L. E. S. Gutteridge.

TAVISTOCK HOUSE, | TAVISTOCK SQUARE, LONDON. W.C.
Monday Twentieth September 1858

My Dear Mr. Ryland

A thousand thanks for your kind note. I do not know that I need trouble you before I come to Birmingham, but if I *should* see occasion to do so, I will not scruple to tax the friendship to which I have already been often indebted.

I am at home for only a day. My success is very great indeed—quite indescribable in some cases—as at Manchester last Saturday night.[4]

Charley begs to send you his kindest regard. He wishes me to report that he passed his short holiday from Barings, in rowing and playing cricket-matches. His sisters have just given astonishing evidence of bad taste. I asked them to choose whether they would go with me to Birmingham, or to Scotland. And they said—— Scotland!

Always Very faithfully Yours
Arthur Ryland Esquire. CHARLES DICKENS

I heard of you at Sheffield on Friday, from Mr. Fisher.[5]

[1] Née the Hon. Maria Liddell (1798–1882), wife of the 1st Marquis; see Vol. V, p. 109 and *n.*

[2] Where the Marquis was English Minister 1854–8.

[3] See *To* the Countess Gigliucci, 16 July 58, *fn.*

[4] He had read *The Poor Traveller, Boots* and *Mrs Gamp* in the Free Trade Hall. The *Manchester Guardian*, 20 Sep, found *The Poor Traveller* "somewhat uninteresting", but the other two "quite unapproachable". CD was "exceedingly well received on entering the hall, and was also loudly cheered as he left it". His reading of the characters in *Boots*, above all, showed that he would have been "a consummate actor". He announced two further readings: *Little Dombey* on 16 Oct and the *Carol* on 23 Oct.

[5] William Fisher, Jnr (*d.* 1880), former Mayor of Sheffield: see Vol. VII, p. 482 and *n*; probably of William Fisher & Sons, dealers in ivory, etc., 27 Orchard Place, Orchard St.

To MRS TROLLOPE,[1] 20 SEPTEMBER 1858*

MS University of Texas.

TAVISTOCK HOUSE, | TAVISTOCK SQUARE, LONDON. W.C.
Monday Twentieth September 1858.

My Dear Mrs. Trollope.

If you should be still in Florence when the bearer of this letter comes to that old City, let me beg you to shew her any aid or attention in your power: assuring you that if you bestowed it on one of my daughters, it could not be more welcome to me.

Miss Fanny Ternan (I mean that strange-looking word for T e r n a n) is a professional young lady of great accomplishments and the highest character, who purposes establishing herself in some very respectable family in Florence, probably for a year, that she may complete her musical education under some eminent master there. She travels to Florence accompanied by her Mama; but Mrs. Ternan will return to England when she has settled her daughter to their mutual satisfaction, and will leave her to pursue her studies alone.

In this young lady and in her family, I have the warmest interest. I have given her such letters as I think most likely to serve her, and I cannot resist the temptation I feel to add this to the List, because I know that she must naturally have a great desire to see you, and because I am not less sure that you will appreciate her.

My Dear Mrs. Trollope | Very faithfully Yours

Mrs. Trollope CHARLES DICKENS

To MONTAGU YEATS BROWN,[2] [?20 SEPTEMBER 1858]

Mention in next. *Date:* no doubt written the same day.

To EMILE DE LA RUE, [?20 SEPTEMBER 1858]

MS (fragment) Berg Collection. *Date:* 20 Sep according to endorsement.[3]

serve her,[4] on to the Poste Restante at Florence. I have given her a letter to Monty Brown too, but I am particularly anxious that she should have the advantage of your personal introduction.

Affectionately Yours
CHARLES DICKENS

[1] Frances Trollope (1780–1863; *DNB*), novelist: see Vols I, p. 499*n* and VII, pp. 205, 651, 657 and *nn*; had settled in Florence in 1855, living at her son Thomas Adolphus's house, the Villa Trollopino, in the Piazza Maria Antonia (now Piazza dell' Indipendenza) until her death.

[2] Montagu Yeats Brown (1834–1921), son of Timothy Yeats Brown (see Vol. IV, p. 222*n*), British Consul in Genoa, whom CD had seen frequently 1844–5. Montagu was Vice-Consul in Genoa 1856; succeeded his father as Consul 1859; Consul-General in Boston, Mass., 1893.

[3] Endorsed by de la Rue "20.7.1858", following his usual practice of adhering to the Roman calendar, where Sep is the seventh month; for another instance see Vol. VII, p. 220 and *n*.

[4] Fanny Ternan: see *To* the Marchioness of Normanby.

To JOHN FORSTER, [?20–21 SEPTEMBER 1858]

Extract in F, VIII, iv, 665. *Date:* soon after his Manchester reading of 18 Sep.

When I came to Manchester on Saturday I found seven hundred stalls taken! When I went into the room at night 2500 people had paid, and more were being turned away from every door. The welcome they gave me was astounding in its affectionate recognition of the late trouble,[1] and fairly for once unmanned me. I never saw such a sight or heard such a sound. When they had thoroughly done it, they settled down to enjoy themselves; and certainly did enjoy themselves most heartily to the last minute.[2]

To W. H. WILLS, 24 SEPTEMBER 1858

MS Huntington Library.

Station Hotel, Newcastle
Friday afternoon, Twenty Fourth Sept. | 1858.

My Dear Wills.

I return the cheque, duly signed.

I have just now walked over here from Sunderland[3] (1 o'Clock), and have barely had time to look at the Room.[4] It is new since we acted here—large—and capable of holding a good deal of money. I hope it will have a good deal to hold, tonight and tomorrow. The Let is a very good one, and we expect a large Take in payment at the doors.

You will be amazed to hear that we reaped very little profit at Sunderland last night! I read in a very beautiful new Theatre,[5] and it *looked* a fine house. But it was not fine enough to pay well.[6] Half a million of money, *belonging to Sunderland alone*, was lost in the last Bank-Smash there;[7] and the town has never held up its head since, they say.

I suppose the people who were there, had either not lost any money, or had found it again. I never beheld such a rapturous audience. And they—and the stage together: which I never can resist—made me do such a vast number of new things in

[1] "The reception that awaited him at Manchester had very special warmth in it", wrote Forster, "occasioned by an adverse tone taken in the comment of one of the Manchester daily papers, on the letter which by a breach of confidence had been then recently printed".

[2] The immense audience gave him the warmest reception. The *Manchester Daily Examiner*, 20 Sep, praised the reading as both dramatic and "a gentleman reading to his friends".

[3] 12 miles.

[4] The new Town Hall, where he read the *Carol* that night, to "a large and brilliant company" (*Newcastle Guardian*, 25 Sep), and *The Poor Traveller*, *Boots* and *Mrs Gamp* on 25 Sep.

[5] The Theatre Royal.

[6] "The theatre was not so well filled as it would have been had the public conceived the nature of the treat in store for them"; they would not then "have thought for a moment of the price of the tickets" (*Northern Daily Express*, 25 Sep).

[7] The Northumberland & Durham District Bank, of Newcastle, with a branch in Sunderland, had stopped payments on 27 Nov 57. *The Times* reported that the stoppage was "likely to prove the worst calamity that has been known in this district" (27 Nov).

the Carol,[1] that Arthur and our men stood in amazement at the Wing, and roared and stamped as if it were an entirely new book, topping all the others.[2] You must come to some good place and hear the Carol. I think you will hardly know it again.

Little Darlington—in a mouldy old assembly Room without a Lamp abutting on the Street,[3] so that I passed it a dozen times and looked for it, when I went down to read—covered itself with Glory. All sorts of people came in from outlying places, and the town was drunk with the Carol far into the night.[4] At Durham we had a capital audience too—led by Dean and chapter, and humbly followed up by Mayor and local Bores—but the Hall not large enough, and the City not large enough, for such a purpose as your friend's.[5]

So, we are working our way further North. I walked from Durham to Sunderland,[6] and made a little fanciful photograph in my mind of Pit-Country, which will come well into H.W. one day.[7] I couldn't help looking upon my mind as I was doing it, as a sort of capitally prepared and highly sensitive plate. And I said, without the least conceit (as Watkins might have said of a plate of his) "it really is a pleasure to work with you, you receive the impression so nicely."

I mark this note "Immediate", because I forgot to mention that I particularly wish you to look well to Wilkie's article about the Wigan schoolmaster,[8] and not to leave anything in it that may be sweepingly and unnecessarily offensive to the middle class.[9] He has always a tendency to overdo that—and such a subject gives him a fresh temptation. Don't be afraid of the Truth, in the least; but don't be unjust.

[a]I enclose a few hasty notes about the Queen idea.[a10] Arthur sends kindest regard. Give my love to Mrs. Wills. I hope my wholesome influence lasts?

Ever Faithfully

W. H. Wills Esquire CHARLES DICKENS

[1] The particular improvements he made during this reading are not discoverable; but his text varied considerably from reading to reading. The only surviving prompt-copy (MS Berg) has many amendments made at different times. See Philip Collins, *CD: The Public Readings*, p. 2.

[2] CD "vitalized and embodied [the *Carol*] so perfectly" (*Northern Daily Express*, 25 Sep).

[3] The Central Hall, where he read on 21 Sep.

[4] His powers were warmly praised in the *Darlington and Stockton Times*, 25 Sep; and the audience described as "highly gratified". The receipts exceeded £60.

[5] He read the *Carol* in the New Town Hall on 22 Sep. The *Durham County Advertiser*, 24 Sep, reported a large audience, despite the bad weather. It praised the "moral effect" of these "secular sermons": "surely never preacher sought to inculcate a more obvious or apter moral". CD "might have been the greatest actor of his age".

[6] 13 miles.

[7] Possibly more was included in the notes for the 9 Oct article than was published; it has a brief description of a manufacturing town.

[8] See *To* Collins, 6 Sep and *fn*.

[9] The article remains a stinging condemnation of the social prejudices of the middle-class parents of many private school boys and girls. They are described as "led by those three rampant commanders, General Ignorance, General Prejudice, and General Folly" (p. 361); and their prejudice against the stage, exerted on the headmaster, labelled as a "gross abuse" (p. 363).

[aa] Omitted in *CD as Editor* and N.

[10] Embodied in "A Clause for the New Reform Bill", by Collins and himself, *HW*, 9 Oct 58, XVIII, 385 (*Uncollected Writings*, ed. H. Stone, II, 587); a plea for cities visited by the Queen to remain themselves, rather than indulge in all the theatrical paraphernalia he had just ridiculed in Leeds: see *To* Mary Dickens, 15 Sep and *fn*.

To D. O. HILL,[1] 25 SEPTEMBER 1858

MS The Royal Scottish Academy.

Newcastle on Tyne
Saturday Twenty Fifth September 1858.

My Dear Sir

I am cordially obliged to you for your kind note, and have little need to assure you that it would have given me the greatest pleasure to have dined with the Academy:—particularly on the occasion of their receiving my two old friends, Stanfield and Roberts.[2] But unfortunately, while I am heartily gratified in being so remembered and honored, I cannot possibly accept the invitation. I read twice in Edinburgh on Wednesday—in the afternoon, and in the evening—and I grieve to say that I can no more go to the Academy than the Academy can come to me.

By this post, I return a formal reply to the invitation. If you will do me the favor to say for me in a less constrained manner, to the President,[3] that I am unfeignedly and exceedingly sorry that I cannot profit by this mark of the Academy's courtesy, you will very much oblige me.

Believe me My Dear Sir | Very faithfully Yours

D. O. Hill Esquire CHARLES DICKENS[4]

To THE PRESIDENT OF THE ROYAL SCOTTISH ACADEMY, [25 SEPTEMBER 1858]

Mention in last.

To JAMES B. MANSON,[5] 25 SEPTEMBER 1858

MS Private.

Newcastle on Tyne
Saturday Twenty Fifth September 1858.

My Dear Sir

Your note has touched me[6] to the heart. I deeply feel, and shall always remember, its sincerity, modesty, and manliness. It makes what you have written of me, of new worth to me; and I can truly say, in thanking you, that I am proud of it.

[1] David Octavius Hill (1802–70; *DNB*), landscape and portrait painter and photographer; Secretary, Royal Scottish Academy 1838–70. Pioneer in use of calotypes for portraiture, of which he and Robert Adamson of St Andrews made an important collection.

[2] The Dinner was given on 29 Sep in the Academy's Rooms on the Mound; other guests were the Lord Provost and Adam Black, MP for the City (*The Scotsman*, 2 Oct).

[3] Sir John Watson Gordon (1788–1864; *DNB*), portrait-painter; exhibited at Scottish Academy 1836–64; President 1850. RA 1851; knighted 1850.

[4] CD's letter was read out by Hill after dinner (*ibid.*).

[5] James Bolivar Manson (1823–68), journalist and art critic; BA Aberdeen; schoolmaster at Bannockburn; editor successively of *Stirling Observer* and *Northern Daily Express*, Newcastle-upon-Tyne. Principal leader writer on *Edinburgh Daily Review* 1862–8. Published *The Bible in School*, 1852, on Scottish education.

[6] A long article, "Literature and Charles Dickens", in the *Northern Daily Express*, 25 Sep, welcoming CD to Newcastle.

The view you take of the literary character in the abstract, or of what it might and ought to be, expresses what I have striven for, all through my literary life.[1] I have never allowed it to be patronized, or tolerated, or treated like a good child or like a bad child. In simply doing my plain duty by it, I am always animated by the hope of leaving it, a little better understood by the thoughtless than I found it.[2]

You will forgive me if I cannot conclude this hasty note without a word of reference to three Sonnets I have read in your paper to-day, and of which I suppose you to be the writer.[3] They would have attracted my attention under any circumstances, by their unusual merit. The second, particularly, has a very profound thought in it most happily turned.[4]

My Dear Sir | Faithfully Yours

James B Manson Esquire. CHARLES DICKENS

To MISS GEORGINA HOGARTH, 26 SEPTEMBER 1858

Extract in MDGH, II, 75–6.

Station Hotel, Newcastle-on-Tyne, | Sunday, Sept. 26th, 1858.

The girls (as I have no doubt they have already told you for themselves) arrived here in good time yesterday, and in very fresh condition. They persisted in going to the room[5] last night, though I had arranged for their remaining quiet.

We have done a vast deal here. I suppose you know that we are going to Berwick, and that we mean to sleep there[6] and go on to Edinburgh on Monday morning, arriving there before noon? If it be as fine to-morrow as it is to-day, the girls will see the coast piece of railway between Berwick and Edinburgh to great advantage. I was anxious that they should, because that kind of pleasure is really almost the only one they are likely to have in their present trip.

Stanfield and Roberts are in Edinburgh, and the Scottish Royal Academy give[7] them a dinner on Wednesday, to which I was very pressingly invited. But, of course, my going was impossible. I read twice that day.

Remembering what you do of Sunderland, you will be surprised that our profit there was very considerable.[8] I read in a beautiful new theatre, and (I thought to myself) quite wonderfully. Such an audience I never beheld for rapidity and enthusiasm. The room in which we acted (converted into a theatre afterwards) was

[1] The article's main theme is the writer's "intimate relations with the age"; his possession of "the practical spirit that the business of the time or the problems of the day requires". Of this CD is seen as a major representative. Few "have striven more earnestly and more successfully", the article ends, to bring about the ultimate ending of social problems,—including "the final reconciliation of class with class, and man with man"—than CD in his novels.

[2] Most of this paragraph is quoted by Forster (XI, iii, 819*n*), who was sent the letter sometime before 1874.

[3] The same issue of the *Northern Daily Express* contains three sonnets by the Editor: I. "Harvest". II. "Past and Present". III. "Bound in Affliction and Iron". All are on religious subjects.

[4] The "Past" is the alchemist seeking gold; the "Present" our new awareness that "though no stone has yet turned aught to gold, | There is a gold that turneth all to stone."

[5] See *To* Wills, 24 Sep, *fn*.

[6] At the King's Arms, Berwick-on-Tweed.

[7] MDGH reads "gave" in error. The dinner was on Wed. 29 Sep.

[8] But see *To* Wills, 24 Sep.

burnt to the ground a year or two ago.[1] We found the hotel, so bad in our time, really good.[2] I walked from Durham to Sunderland, and from Sunderland to Newcastle.

Don't you think, as we shall be at home at eleven in the forenoon this day fortnight, that it will be best for you and Plornish to come to Tavistock House for that Sunday, and for us all to go down to Gad's Hill next day? My best love to the noble Plornish. If he is quite reconciled to the postponement of his trousers, I should like to behold his first appearance in them. But, if not, as he is such a good fellow, I think it would be a pity to disappoint and try him.

And now, my dearest Georgy, I think I have said all I have to say before I go out for a little air. I had a very hard day yesterday, and am tired.

Ever your most affectionate

[CD]

To JAMES PAYN, 29 SEPTEMBER 1858*

MS Boston Public Library.

Waterloo Hotel, Edinburgh.

Wednesday Twenty Ninth September 1858.[3]

My Dear Mr. Payn.

All to-day I am, as you may suppose, pretty closely occupied. Tomorrow morning I am going to take my girls out to Hawthornden. But I will arrange to be back here by 3 o'Clock, if it should suit your convenience to have some talk with me then.

The hours and days run away while I am thus occupied, so imperceptibly, that I do nothing that I propose to myself to do. I thought we should have walked twenty miles together, by this time.

On second thoughts, it occurs to me to ask if you could spare time to go with us on our tomorrow morning's expedition?[4] We will leave here at 11. Perhaps you will tell me, or Mr. Arthur Smith, tonight.

Always Very faithfully Yours

J. Payn Esquire CHARLES DICKENS

To JOHN FORSTER, [?1 OCTOBER 1858]

Extracts in F, VIII, iv, 666. *Date:* written on his arrival in Dundee, on 1 Oct; first extract clearly before dinner, second perhaps after it.

At first the look of Edinburgh was not promising. We began with, for us, a poor room.[5] ... But the effect of that reading (it was the *Chimes*), was immense; and on the next

[1] The newly-completed Lyceum, in 1852 rumoured to be structurally unsafe: see Vol. VI, pp. 748–9.

[2] The Bridge Hotel.

[3] Misdated 19 Sep 58 in N.

[4] Payn went with them and describes the expedition in *Some Literary Recollections*, 1884, p. 187. Hawthornden was not open to the public that day, and they had difficulty in seeing the glen. Payn went to the house to expostulate with the servants, who did not know CD's name, and protested "for a long time and without success". They were eventually successful. CD drew a fanciful picture of Payn's "detention in that feudal abode, and of the mediaeval tortures which had probably been inflicted" upon him.

[5] See next.

night, for *Little Dombey*, we had a full room. It is our greatest triumph everywhere. Next night (*Poor Traveller*, *Boots* and *Gamp*) we turned away hundreds upon hundreds of people; and last night, for the *Carol*, in spite of advertisements in the morning that the tickets were gone, the people had to be got in through such a crowd as rendered it a work of the utmost difficulty to keep an alley into the room. They were seated about me on the platform, put into the doorway of the waiting-room, squeezed into every conceivable place, and a multitude turned away once more. I think I am better pleased with what was done in Edinburgh than with what has been done anywhere,[1] almost. It was so completely taken by storm, and carried in spite of itself. Mary and Katey have been infinitely pleased and interested with Edinburgh. We are just going to sit down to dinner and therefore I cut my missive short. Travelling, dinner, reading, and everything else, come crowding together into this strange life.

He thought Dundee an odd place, like Wapping with high rugged hills behind it. We had the strangest journey here—bits of sea, and bits of railroad, alternately;[2] which carried my mind back to travelling in America. The room[3] is an immense new one, belonging to Lord Kinnaird,[4] and Lord Panmure,[5] and some others of that sort. It looks like something between the Crystal Palace and Westminster-hall (I can't imagine who wants it in this place), and has never been tried yet for speaking in. Quite disinterestedly of course, I hope it will succeed.[6]

To W. H. WILLS, 2 OCTOBER 1858

MS Comtesse de Suzannet.

TAVISTOCK HOUSE, | TAVISTOCK SQUARE, LONDON. W.C.
That is to say: | Dundee. Saturday Second October 1858.

My Dear Wills. Pray, *pray*, dont have Poems unless they are good. We are immeasurably better without them. "Beyond",[7] is really Beyond anything I ever saw, in utter badness.

You instructed Payn and White, that no story-Teller must have been a Lodger in the House. I don't understand that, at all. A Lodger may give variety to the thing, and cannot possibly (that I see) weaken the carrying out of the Idea.[8]

To Wilkie's queries I reply:

1. I *think* I had best write the framework in the first person—*unless* I should think

[1] See next and *fn.*

[2] i.e., crossing the estuaries of the Forth and Tay.

[3] Kinnaird Hall, "just ... splendidly decorated and painted" (*Dundee Courier*, 6 Oct).

[4] Arthur FitzGerald Kinnaird, 10th Baron Kinnaird (1814–87; *DNB*), philanthropist; Liberal MP for Perth 1837–9 and 1852–78.

[5] Fox Maule, 2nd Baron Panmure (1801–74; *DNB*), Liberal MP for Perth 1841–52.

[6] A letter to the *Dundee Courier*, 6 Oct, from one of the audience, complained of the Hall's acoustics and said that over 200 in the back seats had left in the interval, unable to hear.

[7] Nine pious stanzas on the inadequacy of human love, by Adelaide Procter (*HW*, 2 Oct, XVIII, 372).

[8] In the Christmas No, "A House to Let": see *To* Wills, 20 Nov. Neither Payn nor White eventually contributed to it. None of the story-tellers were in fact lodgers in the house.

of any new and odd way of doing it. I will certainly avoid the plain third person in which the stories will be narrated.[1]

2. I am not clear about following up the old Materials, and making them doomed and destructive. I think it would end the thing with unseasonable grimness. If I could build them into a good school, or infirmary, or child's hospital, or something of that sort, it might be a more pleasant end, and a working round of the thing to something brighter.[1]

3. If I were Wilkie, unless I got an idea which would not admit of it, I would certainly make the story of some people who kept the house, *the* story.[1] Indeed, I supposed that to have been understood.

There was certainly in Edinburgh, a coldness, beforehand, about the Readings. I mention it, to let you know that I consider the triumph there, by far the greatest I have made. The City was taken by storm, and carried. The Chimes shook it; Little Dombey blew it up. On the two last nights, the crowd was immense, and the turnaway enormous.[2] Everywhere, nothing was to be heard but praises—nowhere more than at Blackwood's shop,[3] where there certainly was no predisposition to praise.[4] It was a brilliant victory, and could have been represented in no mere money whatever.

My profit there was £200. My profit at Newcastle, £170 (the room in the latter place, very large). My profit in September is £900. No doubt in reason this sum will have passed £1,000 before I begin the next Thousand in Glasgow.

The Carol will be read one night at Birmingham, and at Nottingham. Those are the places nearest to your hand I think.[5]

My love to Mrs. Wills in which the girls unite. They were delighted with Edinburgh, and saw it, and all about it, on beautiful days. Payn went with us to Hawthornden, and we laughed all day.[6] Conceive his telling me that Miss Martineau once told him and a certain Lake Doctor, face to face, that the reason why the Times succeeded with their Foreign correspondence, was because ————[7] they kept a clairvoyante to do it!!![8] "You may observe", says she, "that the Daily News

[1] See *ibid.*

[2] CD gave five readings in the Queen St Hall: *The Chimes* on 27 Sep, *Little Dombey* on the 28th, *The Cricket on the Hearth*, *The Poor Traveller*, *Boots* and *Mrs Gamp* on the 29th, and the *Carol* on the 30th. The *Scotsman* had only a short notice on the 29th, reporting that, although the first reading "was not crowded", CD was repeatedly applauded; its notice for the three final readings (on 2 Oct) was much longer and very appreciative: on the 29th "every corner of the Hall" was "filled to overflowing"; the *Carol*, read to a "crowded and delighted audience", was "perhaps [*his*] greatest triumph".

[3] *Blackwood's* head office, 45 George St, Edinburgh, for many years a centre of Edinburgh literary society.

[4] Reviews in the Tory *Blackwood's Magazine* had been consistently critical of CD. Samuel Warren had patronized *American Notes* in Dec 42 (see Vol. III, pp. 412–13 and *n*); Mrs Oliphant had been unsympathetic to *Hard Times* in Apr 55 and E. B. Hamley to *Bleak House* and *Little Dorrit* in Apr 57 (see *To* Hollingshead, 27 July 57 and *fn*). Selections from these reviews are given in *CD: The Critical Heritage*, ed. Philip Collins, pp. 120, 327, and 358.

[5] Wills was still at Sheffield.

[6] See *To* Payn, 29 Sep, *fn*.

[7] Dash thus long in MS.

[8] Miss Martineau had found clairvoyant powers in Jane Arrowsmith, the 19 year-old niece of her landlady; in 1855 Jane had used them to predict the rescue of the crew of a wrecked ship (R. K. Webb, *Harriet Martineau, A Radical Victorian*, 1960, p. 229). Payn had visited her many times at "The Knoll", her home near Ambleside; for his recollections of her, see his *Some Literary Rcollections*, pp. 100–36.

is rapidly improving in that particular. Why? Because they have lately engaged a clairvoyante too!"

With which large button of arrogant conceit from the head and front of a strait waistcoat,[1] I beg to subscribe myself

Ever Anti Politico-Economically[2] | [a]Anti De Morganically,[3], | and the like,[a]

CD

To WILLIAM LOGAN,[4] 8 OCTOBER 1858*

MS Joseph M. Maddalena. *Address* (Phillips catalogue, June 1983): William Logan Esq | 21 Maxwell Street (not through post; clearly belongs to this letter).

Royal Hotel, Glasgow[5] | Friday Eighth October 1858.

Dear Sir

I am greatly obliged to you for your kind note received this morning, and for its accompanying Volumes.[6] Accept my cordial thanks.

As the Christmas Carol is a favorite of yours, may I hope that you will do me the favor to come and hear it tonight, if you are not otherwise engaged.

Faithfully Yours

William Logan Esquire CHARLES DICKENS

[1] For CD's earlier exasperation with her, see *To* Wills, 3 Jan 56.

[2] Another hit at Harriet Martineau.

[aa] Added as an afterthought, squeezed in between "Ever ... Economically" and "CD".

[3] Wills may have made a joke about the mathematical references in Payn's story in *HW*, 2 Oct (XVIII, 337), "Segment's Shadow" (a Cambridge reading party in Wales, conducted by a mathematics tutor) and the mass of figures in "A Very Old Gentleman" (same issue, p. 369). CD himself was on good terms with Augustus De Morgan (1806–71; *DNB*), first Professor of Mathematics, University College, London: see Vol. II, p. 51*n*. Their meeting in Sep 1851 at Broadstairs, according to Mrs De Morgan, "gave pleasure to both". Mrs De Morgan contributed a Chip, "A Plea for Playgrounds", to *HW* with Morley (30 Jan 58, XVII, 160); De Morgan contributed a Chip, "Edmund Waller", to *HW* on 24 Oct 57 (XVI, 402).

[4] William Logan (1813–79), b. in Lanarkshire; originally a loom weaver; then district missionary in London, Leeds, Rochdale and Glasgow; author of *An Exposure of Female Prostitution*, 1843; *Moral Statistics of Glasgow*, 1849; *Words of Comfort for Parents Bereaved of Little Children*, 1861 (8th edn, 1874); and other books. His "Dining and Coffee rooms ... conducted on strictly Temperance Principles" were at 21 Maxwell St in the centre of Glasgow.

[5] Where he read *The Chimes* on 6 Oct, *The Poor Traveller*, *Boots* and *Mrs Gamp*, on 7 Oct, the *Carol* on 8 Oct, and *Little Dombey* on the 9th. The *Glasgow Herald*, 8 Oct, reporting "a crowded and very brilliant audience", commented, on the first two readings: "they afford one of the most refined, intellectual and delightful entertainments that it is possible to conceive". The notice was repeated on 11 Oct. Freedom of the City had clearly been proposed for him, since a letter in the *Glasgow Herald*, 8 Oct, answering objections to it "in present circumstances" (i.e., his separation), hoped it would be conferred on literature's "greatest chief since the days of Scott"; but no further mention of it discovered.

[6] No doubt *An Exposure* and *Moral Statistics*, above.

To THE SUPERINTENDENT, GLASGOW STATION,[1] 9 OCTOBER 1858

MS Brotherton Library, Leeds. *Address:* To The Superintendent | at the Station.

Royal Hotel | Saturday Ninth October 1858.

Mr. Charles Dickens presents his compliments to the Superintendent of the Station, and begs the favor of having a first-class compartment reserved for his party of four, by the 8.17 Train South, tonight, which they can retain all the way to London.

Mr. Dickens's men will have with them, a quantity of luggage which is to be left at Bradford tomorrow.[2] It would be a great additional convenience to Mr. Dickens if the Superintendent's kindness could possibly arrange for its not being shifted at Lancaster, but going the whole way through to Bradford, in the Van in which it will leave Glasgow.

To JOHN FORSTER, 10 OCTOBER 1858

Composite text from MDGH, II, 76–8 and F, VIII, iv, 666–7; first two paragraphs in MDGH only; third paragraph all in Forster (MDGH with omissions *aa*); final paragraph in MDGH only.

TAVISTOCK HOUSE, | TAVISTOCK SQUARE, LONDON. W.C.
Sunday, Oct. 10th, 1858.

My dear Forster,

As to the truth of the readings, I cannot tell you what the demonstrations of personal regard and respect are. How the densest and most uncomfortably-packed crowd will be hushed in an instant when I show my face. How the youth of colleges, and the old men of business in the town, seem equally unable to get near enough to me when they cheer me away at night. How common people and gentlefolks will stop me in the streets and say: "Mr. Dickens, will you let me touch the hand that has filled my home with so many friends?"[3] And if you saw the mothers, and fathers, and sisters, and brothers in mourning, who invariably come to "Little Dombey," and if you studied the wonderful expression of comfort and reliance with which they hang about me, as if I had been with them, all kindness and delicacy, at their own little death-bed, you would think it one of the strangest things in the world.

As to the mere effect, of course I don't go on doing the thing so often without carefully observing myself and the people too in every little thing, and without (in consequence) greatly improving in it.

The people (of Dundee) he thought, in respect of taste and intelligence, below any other of his Scotch audiences; but they woke up surprisingly, and the rest of his Caledonian tour was a succession of triumphs. At Aberdeen we were crammed to the street, twice in one day.[4] At Perth (where I thought when I arrived, there literally could be

[1] Henry Ward, Superintendent, Central Station, Caledonian Railway.

[2] To await his reading there on 14 Oct.

[3] The remark quoted is almost identical with F, VIII, iv, 665, where it is attributed to a lady in York.

[4] He read the *Carol* in the morning and *Little Dombey* in the evening of 4 Oct. The *Aberdeen Journal*, 6 Oct, warmly reviewed both.

nobody to come) the gentlefolk[1] came posting in from thirty miles round, and the whole town came besides, and filled an immense hall.[2] [a]They were as full of perception, fire, and enthusiasm as any people I have seen. At Glasgow, where I read three evenings and one morning, we took the prodigiously large sum of six hundred pounds! And this at the Manchester prices, which are lower than St. Martin's Hall.[a] As to the effect—I wish you could have seen them after Lilian died in the *Chimes*,[3] or when Scrooge woke [a]in the *Carol*[a] and talked to the boy outside the window.[4] And at the end of *Dombey* yesterday afternoon,[5] in the cold light of day, they all got up, after a short pause, gentle and simple, and thundered and waved their hats with such astonishing heartiness and fondness that, for the first time in all my public career, they took me completely off my legs, and I saw the whole eighteen hundred of them reel to one side as if a shock from without had shaken the hall. [a]Notwithstanding which, I must confess to you, I am very anxious to get to the end of my Readings, and to be at home again, and able to sit down and think in my own study. There has been only one thing quite without alloy.[a] The dear girls have enjoyed themselves immensely, and their trip with me has been a great success. I hope I told you (but I forget whether I did or no)[6] how splendidly Newcastle[7] came out. I am reminded of Newcastle at the moment because they joined me there.

I am anxious to get to the end of my readings, and to be at home again, and able to sit down and think in my own study. But the fatigue, though sometimes very great indeed, hardly tells upon me at all. And although all our people, from Smith downwards, have given in, more or less, at times, I have never been in the least unequal to the work, though sometimes sufficiently disinclined for it. My kindest and best love to Mrs. Forster.

Ever affectionately
[CHARLES DICKENS]

To JAMES LAWSON,[8] 11 OCTOBER 1858

Mention in *Autograph Prices Current*, III, 18; *MS* 1 p.; dated Tavistock House, 11 Oct 58; addressed James Lawson.

Assuring him of his sympathy with the People's Concerts.[9]

[1] MDGH reads "nobility".

[2] He read the *Carol* in the City Hall on 5 Oct. The *Perthshire Journal and Constitutional*, 7 Oct, reported "a very large and fashionable audience", whose interest was "intensely excited".

[3] At the end of the Second Part, in the reading text.

[4] In Stave Four (Stave Five in the original). Three of the boy's replies are capitalized in the reading text: "EH?", "CHRISTMAS DAY", and "Walk-ER!", on being told to buy the turkey: here, "Dickens, as the boy, put his thumb to his nose, and spread out his fingers, with a jeer", recalled by Rowland Hill, a Bedford journalist, in his "Notes on Charles Dickens' Christmas Carol", 1930 (given in *The Public Readings*, ed. Philip Collins, p. 31; see also his Introduction, p. xli). Every word of the dialogue was "watched for and listened to by audiences like celebrated passages from a great standard play" (Hollingshead in the *Critic*, 4 Sep 1858).

[5] When he read *Little Dombey* at Glasgow.

[6] He had not yet told Forster of his two readings at Newcastle. See *To* Wills, 24 Sep and *fn*.

[7] Forster's birthplace and home until he was 16.

[8] Perhaps of Steel & Lawson, wholesale hardwaremen, 22 Houndsditch and 22 Duke St, Aldgate; presumably a member of the People's Concerts Committee.

[9] At St Martin's Hall: see *To* Molyneux, 8 Sep 56, *fnn*.

To GEORGE STRUTT,[1] 11 OCTOBER 1858*

MS New York Public Library.

TAVISTOCK HOUSE, | TAVISTOCK SQUARE, LONDON. W.C.
Monday Eleventh October 1858.

My Dear Sir

I am heartily obliged to you for your kind note, and should have been most happy to accept your kind invitation,[2] had it been possible. But the fatigues of my trip are so great, that I find all social pleasures to be incompatible with it, and never go to any place but an Hotel, and never visit any friend. There is not the least virtue in this self-denial; it is forced upon me; and I observe it with the worst grace in the world.

Pray accept my cordial thanks, and present my regard to Mrs. Strutt.[3]

My Dear Sir | Very faithfully Yours

George H Strutt Esquire CHARLES DICKENS

To H. B. DOWNING,[4] 12 OCTOBER 1858*

MS Harrogate College. *Address:* H. B. Downing Esquire | 48 Guilford Street.

GAD'S HILL PLACE, | HIGHAM BY ROCHESTER, KENT.
Twelfth October 1858

Mr. Charles Dickens presents his compliments to Mr. Downing, and begs to acknowledge the receipt of that gentleman's letter of yesterday. Mr. Dickens is obliged by Mr. Downing's confidence and by the terms in which Mr. Downing's proposal is communicated, but he cannot entertain it.[5]

To MRS CORNELIUS, 13 OCTOBER 1858

Text from N, III, 62.

OFFICE OF HOUSEHOLD WORDS,
Wednesday Thirteenth October 1858

My Dear Anne,

Please call me at 7 in the morning. Breakfast at 8.

Yours always
[CHARLES DICKENS]

[1] George Henry Strutt, of William, George & Joseph Strutt, cotton-spinners, of Derby and Belper, Derbyshire: see Vol. VI, p. 757*n*; but known to CD since 1847: see Vol. VII, p. 880 and *n*.

[2] Evidently to stay with him when he was at Derby on 22 Oct.

[3] Née Agnes Ann, daughter of Edward Ashton, of West End, Prescot, Lancs; married 1847.

[4] Henry Bourne Downing, general merchant.

[5] Proposal not discovered.

To THOMAS BEARD, 14 OCTOBER 1858

MS Dickens House. *Address:* Thomas Beard Esquire | 42 Portman Place | Edgeware Road | N.W.

TAVISTOCK HOUSE, | TAVISTOCK SQUARE, LONDON. W.C.
Thursday Fourteenth October 1858

My Dear Beard

I write to you in the greatest haste—just home from Glasgow—before starting again, this morning, for Bradford.[1]

Edmund Yates has brought me the enclosed advertisement,[2] and has asked me whether I thought it likely to have attracted your notice? He tells me that he has reason for confidently believing that there *is* decidedly capital.[3]

The Inimitable's success, enormous. Between ourselves, the clear profits of the readings, after payment of all the charges, which are necessarily heavy—one thousand pounds per month!

Ever affectionately
CD.

To H. B. MACPHAIL,[4] 16 OCTOBER 1858

Extract in N, III, 63 (no authority); dated Royal Hotel, Manchester, 16 Oct 58.

Dear Sir,

Your amazing letter which I have received here to-day, places me in a very distressing position.[5] For Mr. [Colin][6] Rae Brown's[7] lie is too monstrous and intolerable to be borne. And I fear it is impossible that I can, in any decent spirit of respect for myself or any other human being, accept your communication as confidential. A slander so infamous and so wanton and inconceivably baseless, must positively be stopped short and published. I now dispatch a special messenger to London, who is a trustworthy friend,[8] to communicate with my solicitors instantly on the subject.[9]

I thank you very much for making this thing known to me. If I fear that I cannot possibly receive it in confidence, it is because I can get no prospect of redress for so

[1] Where he read *The Poor Traveller*, *Boots* and *Mrs Gamp*: the *Bradford Advertiser*, 16 Oct, reported an audience which listened "with rapt attention" and gave frequent "bursts of delighted applause".

[2] The National Newspaper League Co. Ltd., of 35 New Bridge St., Blackfriars, had advertised on 7 Oct for a General Manager, to establish a proposed newspaper, *The Dial*. "None but gentlemen of position and influence need apply, as the appointment is a highly responsible one, and the remuneration will be liberal", the advt added (copy in Dickens House). The National League's 13 Directors included five clergymen. Intended as a London daily paper, *The Dial* eventually ran as a weekly 7 Jan 60–4 June 64; established, according to its first issue, to exercise "a just and vigilant censorship in the interest of the country" and to instruct "the great body of the people" morally and intellectually. *To* Beard, 20 Oct, makes it clear that he was not engaged.

[3] £120,000 had already been subscribed; shares of £10 each were being offered to the public.

[4] H. Buchanan MacPhail, Assistant-Inspector of the Poor, Barony Parish, Glasgow. He lived at 41 Commercial Rd.

[5] For MacPhail's letter, see Appx I.

[6] N reads "John" in error; CD knew Brown's correct name (see Appx I).

[7] See 2 Sep 57, *fn*.

[8] Obviously Arthur Smith.

[9] For a draft letter to Brown threatening legal action, taken to CD's solicitors, see Appx I.

unspeakable a wrong, but through bringing this Mr. [Colin][1] Rae Brown to answer in a Court of Justice for his abominable words.[2]

To MISS GEORGINA HOGARTH, 18 OCTOBER 1857*

MS Free Library of Philadlephia

Hen and Chickens, Birmingham
Monday Night, Eighteenth October 1858.

My Dearest Georgy

Only a line to say we arrived here prosperously, and that I found the letters waiting me, and that I will write to dear Mamie next.

We had not a *great*[3] house tonight—between seventy and eighty pounds—but I never saw people more honestly and completely delighted, and it was (and is) as wet a night as wet can be.[4]

Best love to Mamie and Katie, and my dear old Plorn.—Arthur joins. Also engages himself for Katie's birthday.[5]

Ever Affectionately
CD.

To W. H. WILLS, [18 OCTOBER 1858]

Mention in next.

To W. H. WILLS, 18 OCTOBER 1858

MS Huntington Library.

Hen and Chickens Hotel, Birmingham.
Monday Night | Eighteenth October 1858.

My Dear Wills.

I forgot three things in my hurried note of to day from London.[6]

[1] See p. 679, n. 6.

[2] For Brown's immediate letter to CD, his solicitors' reply to Farrer, Ouvry and the final paragraph of a letter from Farrer, Ouvry asking Counsel's opinion, following an outline of the facts, see Appx I. On 21 Oct Ouvry wrote to CD, telling him that, unless he could serve a writ for slander on Brown in England, "a Writ in the English Courts would not be of any avail"; the only alternative was to sue him in Scotland; he also warned him that the trial might be reduced to a question of credibility between McPhail and Brown. CD was still anxious to sue and Ouvry went ahead with finding the best counsel to undertake the case in Glasgow. But clearly Ouvry was reluctant; and by 15 Nov CD had decided to proceed no further. (MS Messrs Farrer & Co., given in Katharine Longley, unpublished typescript.) Six weeks later CD answered politely a letter from Brown on another subject: see *To* Brown, 6 Dec 58.

[3] Underlined twice.

[4] *Aris's Birmingham Gazette*, 25 Oct, reported that the Music Hall was "only moderately filled" on 18 and 19 Oct, because of bad weather; but there was "scarcely a vacant seat" on the 20th. "The audience on each occasion were evidently much delighted." He read *The Poor Traveller*, *Boots* and *Mrs Gamp*, on 18 and 20 Oct; *Little Dombey* and *The Trial Scene from Pickwick* on the 19th.

[5] On 29 Oct, her 19th.

[6] Evidence of his dash to see his solicitors.

1.—After the Smallport Monte Christo (which is very whimsical and good), I think the Great Dunkerque Failure may go in.[1] It should be in the next No. you make up. (Let me see the Proof of any other printed paper by him. A very little erasure here and there, makes a considerable difference in his case.)

2.—When you come to advertize in H.W. my readings for November, put, and keep as long as the advertisement stands, this line after Brighton 13 Novr.—*in small caps—in a line by itself—*

WHICH WILL TERMINATE THE SERIES OF READINGS.[2]

3.—The Carol is not read here. It is read at Nottingham on Thursday, and at Manchester on Saturday.[3]

A very, very, wet night.

Ever Faithfully

W. H. Wills Esquire CD.

To H. G. ADAMS, [?19 OCTOBER 1858]

Mention in H. G. Adams *to Rochester, Chatham and Strood Gazette*, 20 Oct 58 (printed 26 Oct). *Date:* very shortly before Adams's letter of 20 Oct.

Assuring Adams that there was no foundation for the report that he would be reading at Rochester on 26 or 27 Oct. I know nothing whatever of your "best authority", except that he is, as he always is, preposterously wild and monstrously wrong.[4]

To FREDERICK DICKENS, 19 OCTOBER 1858

MS Benoliel Collection.

Hen and Chickens, Birmingham
Tuesday Nineteenth October 1858.

Dear Frederick

I found your letter here yesterday. I shall be at Gad's Hill next Sunday Week, the 31st. but I am not to be depended on for any appointment before then.

Affectionately

C.D.

[1] For Charles Collins's two stories, *HW*, 16 Oct 58, XVIII, 423 and 30 Oct, XVIII, 476, see *To* Collins, 6 Sep, *fn*; the second, also set in Smallport, is a kind of sequel to the first.

[2] Underlined with short double strokes. Added to the advertisements of 30 Oct and 6 Nov.

[3] He read both the *Carol* and *The Trial* at Manchester on 23 Oct. The *Manchester Guardian*, 25 Oct, reported that "Call Samuel Weller!" was "greeted with a loud burst of applause"; and that CD was recalled to the platform at the end "by the acclamations of the audience". The previous Sat, 16 Oct, he had read *Little Dombey* and, by request, *Boots*; though the audience was smaller, he had been "repeatedly applauded during his reading" (*Manchester Guardian*, 18 Oct).

[4] Adams had written to the *Gazette*: "A while since the public were informed by a contemporary journal, and that on 'the best authority'," that CD would give a reading in Rochester. The dates given were impossible, since CD was reading in Hull on both those nights. After repeating CD's denial of the report, Adams assured the paper that CD would read at Chatham, probably on 29 Dec (as he did). The "contemporary journal's" report has not been discovered.

To THOMAS BEARD, 20 OCTOBER 1858

MS Dickens House. *Address:* Thomas Beard Esquire | 42 Portman Place | Maida Hill | London | W.

Hen and Chickens, Birmingham
Wednesday Twentieth October 1858

My Dear Beard

I don't think I ever was more impressed by an absurdity, than by the wonderful project you describe. It is amazing.[1]

Have you made any applications to these men who are now in power,[2] for any sort of public employment? I really think that you might stand a reasonably fair chance of getting something, on a statement of your history, and on a reference to the Inimitable as an old fellow 'Prentice, and a comrade of some quarter of a century and more.[3] *Do think of this*. Forster was speaking to me with all his best earnestness, about it, the other day.

I took it into my head last night, to read the Trial from Pickwick here.[4] It was a great go. And when Mr. Sergeant Buzfuz said "Call Samuel Weller!", they gave a great thunder of applause, as if he were really coming in.

Kindest regard to all at home.

Ever affectionately
CHARLES DICKENS

Thomas Beard Esquire

To GEORGE FLETCHER,[5] 20 OCTOBER 1858

MS University of Texas.

Hen and Chickens, Birmingham.
Wednesday Twentieth October 1858.

Sir

I beg to acknowledge with thanks, the receipt of your little book[6] and its accompanying letter. It is very pleasant to me to hear of you again, and to hope that you are doing well.

Faithfully Yours
CHARLES DICKENS

Mr. George Fletcher.

[1] See *To* Beard, 14 Oct, *fn*.

[2] Lord Derby, with Disraeli's support, had taken office on 21 Feb 58, on the defeat of Palmerston's Conspiracy to Murder Bill. His Administration lasted only until Apr 59.

[3] Beard had become a free-lance journalist not long after his employer Edward Baldwin's bankruptcy in early 1857.

[4] Only *Little Dombey* had been advertised. The *Birmingham Daily Post*, 20 Oct, reported that, during *The Trial*, the audience were "in an almost unbroken roar of laughter".

[5] George Fletcher, of Birmingham, miscellaneous writer: see Vols II, p. 416 and *n* and III, p. 500 and *n*.

[6] *The Provincialist: a Series of Tales, Essays, and Stanzas*, Birmingham, 1857.

To MISS MARY GIBSON,[1] 20 OCTOBER 1858

MS Brotherton Library, Leeds.

Birmingham | Wednesday Twentieth October | 1858

My Dear Miss Gibson.

Your warm-hearted and earnest letter has truly affected me. I cordially thank you for it.

Don't change the picture in your mind;[2]—I hope there is no cause for your doing so. The energies with which God has blessed me, are not the spasms of an hour. Their vitality and mine will end, I think, together.

Few homes can have more wholesome and loving young faces in it than mine has. Wherever I go, I find myself affectionately cherished in the homes of honest men and women, and associated, as their friend, with their domestic joys and troubles. If I owe a heavy penalty to the knaves and fools, so do all notorious people who are neither. I hope I can pay it, and go my way.

Believe me | Very faithfully Yours
CHARLES DICKENS

To ABRAHAM HOLROYD,[3] 20 OCTOBER 1858*

MS Yale University Library.

Birmingham | Wednesday Twentieth October | 1858.

Dear Sir

I beg to acknowledge with many thanks, the receipt of the two little books[4] you had the kindness to send me at Bradford. I have been much interested by them, and shall have great pleasure in receiving the remainder of the series, if—as I hope—it should proceed to a tolerably prosperous issue.

Dear Sir | Faithfully Yours
Abraham Holroyd Esquire CHARLES DICKENS

[1] Probably the Mary Gibson to whom CD had written on 17 Dec 57.

[2] No doubt she had written suggesting that his home was not happy since his separation.

[3] Abraham Holroyd (1815–88), of 15 Westgate, Bradford; bookseller, publisher, miscellaneous writer and local historian. Originally a handloom weaver; then served in the Army in Canada and was a bookseller in New Orleans. Published books on Bradford; the Rev. Patrick Brontë's *The Cottage in the Wood*, 1859; also *A Life of Sir Titus Salt*, Saltaire, 1871. His *Collection of Yorkshire Ballads* was ed. by Charles F. Forshaw, Secretary to a Memorial Fund (stone unveiled in Clayton churchyard, 1893), 1892.

[4] The first two of his six penny pamphlets, each of 16 pp., of "Selections from the Poets of Yorkshire" (*Spice Islands passed in the Sea of Reading*); the series was collected in a vol. in 1859; among them are poems by the Brontës, Monckton Milnes, the Earl of Carlisle, as well as minor local poets, including Holroyd himself. Milnes's "London Churches", attacking snobbery, concludes No. 2.

To DR F. H. RAMSBOTHAM, 20 OCTOBER 1858*

MS Free Library of Philadelphia.

Birmingham | Wednesday Twentieth October | 1858.

My Dear Dr. Ramsbotham.

Your note and its enclosure have been forwarded to me here. I am still reading in the country, and shall be until the middle of next month.

I have read your Cherbourg Stanzas with much interest and pleasure, and am truly obliged to you for the offer of them to Household Words. But the subject,[1] as to the public, is too decidedly gone by, and they have been too much bothered about it, to admit of my having the gratification of publishing the verses.

My boy received every attention that your kind introduction could possibly procure for him. He was soon, and still is, attached to the 42nd. Highlanders.[2] He went through the last campaign[3] until he was invalided (from fever), and sent up to the hills. When he wrote by the last mail, he was coming down again, quite strong and well, and was about to rejoin the regiment.

Very faithfully Yours

Dr. Ramsbotham CHARLES DICKENS

To MISS MARY DICKENS, 22 OCTOBER 1858

Text from MDGH, II, 78.

Royal Hotel, Derby, Friday, Oct. 22nd, 1858.

My dearest Mamie,

I am writing in a very poor condition; I have a bad cold all over me, pains in my back and limbs, and a very sensitive and uncomfortable throat.[4] There was a great draught up some stone steps near me last night, and I daresay that caused it.

The weather on my first two nights at Birmingham was so intolerably bad—it blew hard, and never left off raining for one single moment—that the houses were not what they otherwise would have been. On the last night the weather cleared, and we had a grand house.

Last night at Nottingham was almost, if not quite, the most amazing we have had. It is not a very large place, and the room is by no means a very large one, but three hundred and twenty stalls were let, and all the other tickets were sold.[5]

Here we have two hundred and twenty stalls let for to-night, and the other tickets are gone in proportion.[6] It is a pretty room, but not large.

[1] Clearly the meeting of the Queen and Prince Albert with Napoleon III and the French Empress on 4 Aug: see *To* Miss Hogarth, 5 Aug and *fn.*

[2] See *To* Cavendish Boyle, 5 Feb 58 and *fn.* The 26th Native Regt in which Walter had been originally gazetted had been disbanded at the start of the Mutiny.

[3] See *ibid.*

[4] The *Derby and Chesterfield Reporter*, in its notice of his reading, recorded that his "face [*was*] somewhat furrowed by the effects of long and hard mental toil—it might be also of care".

[5] He read the *Carol* in the Mechanics' Hall. The *Nottinghamshire Guardian*, 28 Oct, gave him a very warm notice and reported a large and welcoming audience. It also published an enthusiastic letter from one of them.

[6] He read that night in the Lecture Hall, Derby, "filled to overflowing by a distinguished and fashionable audience" (*Derby Mercury*, 27 Oct). The *Mercury* attacked him for "stooping

I have just been saying to Arthur that if there is not a large let for York, I would rather give it up, and get Monday at Gad's Hill. We have telegraphed to know. If the answer comes (as I suppose it will) before post time, I will tell you in a postscript what we decide to do.[1] Coming to London in the night of to-morrow (Saturday), and having to see Mr. Ouvry on Sunday,[2] and having to start for York early on Monday, I fear I should not be able to get to Gad's Hill at all. You won't expect me till you see me.

Arthur and I have considered Plornish's joke in all the immense number of aspects in which it presents itself to reflective minds. We have come to the conclusion that it is the best joke ever made. Give the dear boy my love, and the same to Georgy, and the same to Katey, and take the same yourself. Arthur (excessively low and inarticulate) mutters that he "unites."

[a][We knocked up Boycett, Berry, and John so frightfully yesterday, by tearing the room to pieces and altogether reversing it, as late as four o'clock, that we gave them a supper last night. They shine all over to-day, as if it had been entirely composed of grease.][a]

Ever, my dearest Mamie, | Your most affectionate Father

[CD]

To W. C. MACREADY, 22 OCTOBER 1858*

MS Morgan Library.

Royal Hotel, Derby | Friday Twenty Second October 1858

My Dearest Macready

I received your letter here, to day; found it awaiting me when I came from Nottingham.

Wills wrote to me by the same post, touching Mrs. Meredith's paper.[3] I have begged him to shew it, and her, all possible attention, and to communicate with you about the payment for it; so that you may have the thing in writing to refer to her.

Over and over and over again, my dear dear friend, since I have been away, have I been thinking and talking of you. I have never once been home for a few stray hours, but the girls and Georgy and I have gone in our talk to Sherborne. Your dear good sister has never been held higher in any love and respect than in ours. God knows I *have* "always entertained a sincere and cordial affection" for her, and that when I last took leave of her in your hall, I loved and honored her with all my heart.[4]

Dear Macready, I think you *must* come to London and bring the children with

to exhibit himself ... he has done what in him lay to lower the position of literary men in the social scale", and damaged the future of his own reputation and influence. It also attacked him for substituting the three readings for the previously advertised *Carol*, "in compliance with what he believed to be a general wish"; castigating "the repulsive coarseness of Mesdames Gamp, Harris, and Betsey Prig" (*ibid.*).

[1] No postscript given but he did not give a second reading at York.

[2] Concerning his proposed action for slander against C. R. Brown: see *To* McPhail, 16 Oct and *fn*.

[aa] Probably CD's square brackets (not given in N, III,65).

[3] See next and *fn*.

[4] Macready's sister, Letitia Margaret (1794–1858), who lived with him, died at Sherborne House on 8 Nov.

you. I have said this so often to Forster, that I cannot help saying it now to you. You ought to be near to us, and more of us, and among us. For your own sake, because our affectionate companionship might lighten your load; for ours, because it is so sad to us to think of you away down there.

God bless you, and all yours, and comfort you!

My Dearest Macready | Ever Your most affectionate | and attached friend

CHARLES DICKENS

To W. H. WILLS, 22 OCTOBER 1858

MS Huntington Library.

Royal Hotel, Derby | Friday Twenty Second October 1858.

My Dear Wills.

If you look at the passage in Macready's letter, which refers to Mrs. Meredith, you will see what I mean when I ask you if you will write to him, and enquire whether he will receive the money for the paper,[1] or what is to be done with it: telling him at the same time how much the sum is.[2]

Was she paid for her former paper or papers?[3] That passage in her note looks to me as if she never had been paid.

Immense at Nottingham last night. Immense final night at Birmingham. Let, very good here.

I have a bad cold all over me.

Ever Faithfully

CD.

To W. H. WILLS, 25 OCTOBER 1858

MS Huntington Library.

TAVISTOCK HOUSE, | TAVISTOCK SQUARE, LONDON. W.C.

Monday Night Twenty Fifth October | 1858

My Dear Wills

Since I left you tonight, I have heard of a case of such extraordinary, and (apparently) dangerous and unwarrantable conduct in a Policeman, that I shall take it as a great kindness if you will go to Yardley[4] in Scotland Yard when you know the facts for yourself, and ask him to enquire what it means.

I am quite sure that if the circumstances as they stand were stated in the Times, there would be a most prodigious public uproar.

Before you wait upon Yardley, saying that you know the young ladies and can answer for them and for their being in all things most irreproachable in themselves and most respectably connected in all ways, and that you want to know what the Devil the mystery means—see the young ladies and get the particulars from them.

[1] "Little Bell" (verse), *HW*, 11 Dec 58, XIX, 35. Mrs Meredith, in Tasmania, had obviously suggested this.

[2] Three guineas.

[3] See *To* Macready, 28 Jan 57 and *fn*; she was paid £5.

[4] Charles Yardley, Chief Clerk, Metropolitan Police Office: see Vol. VI, p. 345*n*.

No. 31 Berners Street Oxford Street,[1] is the address of the young ladies, and the young ladies are Miss Maria and Miss Ellen Ternan, both of whom you know. You are to understand, between you and me, that I have sent the eldest sister to Italy, to complete a musical education[2]—that Mrs. Ternan is gone with her, to see her comfortably established in Florence; and that our two little friends are left together, in the meanwhile, in the family lodgings.[3] Observe that they don't live about in furnished lodgings, but have their own furniture. They have not been many weeks in their present address, and I strongly advised Mrs. Ternan to move from their last one,[4] [a]which I thought unwholesome.[a]

Can you call and see them between 3 and 5 tomorrow (Tuesday)? They will expect you, unless you write to the contrary. If you can't go, will you write and make another appointment.

(N.B. Maria is a good deal looked after.[5] And my suspicion is, that the Policeman in question has been suborned to find out all about their domesticity by some "Swell". If so, there can be no doubt that the man ought to be dismissed.)

They will tell you his No. They don't seem so clear about his letter, but that is no matter. The division on duty in Berners Street, is of course ascertainable by Scotland Yard authorities.

Ever Faithfully
CD.

To FRANK COOPER,[6] 26 OCTOBER 1858*

MS Mr Lewis P. Kinsey, Jr.

Hull,[7] Tuesday Twenty Sixth October | 1858

Dear Sir

In answer to your most obliging letter, for which I cordially thank you, I beg to assure you that it would have been quite conclusive with me, even if this day's post had brought me no other to the same effect. The days on which I hope to read in Oxford[8] shall be changed, and I trust they will be so re-arranged as to meet the general convenience and ensure me the pleasure of your attendance.

Dear Sir | Yours faithfully and obliged,
F. Cooper Esquire CHARLES DICKENS

[1] The owner of the house was Mme Zélie Dewailly, milliner.

[2] See *To* the Marchioness of Normanby, 20 Sep, *fn*. Although there is no evidence from his accounts that CD paid for Fanny, the wording suggests that he did. Her niece, Mrs Reece, stated that he had been "*influential* in getting Fanny to Italy to study singing and also in getting her the position as companion-governess" to Thomas Trollope's daughter (given in Katharine Longley, unpublished typescript).

[3] They were both acting: Maria at the Strand, Ellen in walk-on parts at the Haymarket, for Buckstone.

[4] Park Cottage, Northampton Park, Canonbury.

[aa] Apparently added as an afterthought.

[5] i.e. run after.

[6] Perhaps Frank Cooper, grocer, High Street, who created the firm of Frank Cooper, marmalade manufacturers, in 1874.

[7] He gave two readings in the Music Hall, Hull: *The Poor Traveller*, *Boots* and *Mrs Gamp*, that night; and *Little Dombey* and *The Trial*, on the 27th.

[8] The planned dates were 5 and 6 Nov. His readings there were cancelled and did not take place until Oct 59.

To THE ROYAL HUMANE SOCIETY,[1] 26 OCTOBER 1858*

MS Myers & Co.

Tavistock House, London | Twenty Sixth October 1858.

Understanding Mr. George Hodder to be a candidate for the office of Secretary to the Royal Humane Society,[2] I readily certify to my knowledge of that gentleman's qualifications. He is very persevering, active, zealous, and obliging. He has a good knowledge of business, and is highly trustworthy. He once fulfilled the duties of an Honorary Secretary, under my chairmanship;[3] and I had constant occasion to observe his possession of these qualities, and to esteem myself fortunate in his co-operation.

CHARLES DICKENS

To MRS BROWN, 27 OCTOBER 1858*

MS Morgan Library. *Address:* Mrs. Brown.

Hull | Wednesday Twenty Seventh October | 1858.

My Dear Mrs. Brown.

If I could be made uncomfortable by any expression of your affectionate friendship and interest, I should be rendered as nearly so as possible, by your attaching so much importance to a very little service. But I set myself up again with the reflection that you treasure up the remembrance of the sympathy and the tender and helpful spirit that really animated me in that sad time,[4] and that really would have done a great deal for you, if any way had been open to it.

I have been telling Miss Coutts, in a note I send with this, that I hope to be able to call and see you both, next Monday. I shall be so happy to see your faces again. I seem to have been wandering about, so long!

Ever Believe me | Your faithful and affectionate
CHARLES DICKENS

To MISS BURDETT COUTTS, 27 OCTOBER 1858

MS Morgan Library. *Address:* Miss Burdett Coutts | Great Western Hotel | London | W.

Hull, Wednesday Twenty Seventh October | 1858.

My Dear Miss Coutts.

I was very glad indeed to receive your kind note when I went to London for a few hours last Sunday morning. This shall be but a very short reply to it, as this is mainly to say that I hope to be able to call upon you *next Monday*, during another short rest.

My tour is now drawing to a close, and I am heartily glad to think that it is nearly

[1] Founded in London 1774, "for the recovery of persons apparently drowned".

[2] Hodder was not appointed. The previous year he had acted as manager for a series of Thackeray's lectures, *The Four Georges*, given in the provinces.

[3] In fact twice: to the Committee of the Elton Fund, 1843 (Vol. III, p. 527*n*) and for Miss Kelly's benefit, 1853 (Vol. VII, p. 81 and *n*).

[4] Recalling the week of Dr Brown's death in 1855.

over, and that I shall soon be at home in my own room again. It has been wonderfully successful. My clear profit—my own, after all deductions and expences—has been more than a Thousand Guineas a month. But the manner in which the people have everywhere delighted to express that they have a personal affection for me and the interest of tender friends in me, is (especially at this time) high and far above all other considerations. I consider it a remarkable instance of good fortune that it should have fallen out that I should, in this Autumn of all others, have come face to face with so many multitudes.

Mr. Arthur Smith is everything I could desire, and has made the way as smooth as possible. His extraordinary practical knowledge, and his great zeal, and his gentle way of dealing with crowds and putting people at their ease, have been of the greatest service and comfort to me.

Many thanks for so kindly writing to Mr. Bates[1] about Charley. Charley wrote to me at the time, expressing himself about it, most sensitively and properly.

Mrs. Matthews is by far the most perplexing female I have ever encountered in that way.[2] I thought you ought to see the letter,[3] and yet I feel with you that hers is a most unsatisfactory and difficult case. She has certainly become hardened in begging—gradually and surely, since she first began, as I remember, a dozen years ago, or more—in a very remarkable manner. I suppose her statements are correct. Indeed, I recollect that you once made some enquiries respecting her husband.[4] And yet, granting them all, it seems possible to do her but very little good, and this last remonstrance[5] (for it is quite that), has a dogged perseverance in it that is far from impressing one favorably. When I got the letter, I was so bothered and bewildered by it, that I felt strongly disposed to quarrel with the Postman for not having lost it.

My Dear Miss Coutts | Ever Faithfully and affecy. Yours

CHARLES DICKENS

To R. H. HORNE, 27 OCTOBER 1858

MS Brotherton Library, Leeds. *Address:* Australia | R. H. Horne Esquire | Care of | Charles Panwell Esquire | Town Hall | Melbourne.

Hull | Wednesday Twenty Seventh October 1858

My Dear Horne.

I am busily travelling about, and I have been since the beginning of August, and I shall be until the middle of November.

Your letter has been forwarded to me from London, but not your Tragedy. It has arrived safely, however, and lies in my desk awaiting my return. You will therefore

[1] Joshua Bates: see *To* Miss Coutts, 6 Sep 58.

[2] See Vol. VII, p. 12*n*.

[3] Mrs Matthews had written to CD on 14 Oct, saying that she had that day received £5 from Wills (clearly much less than she had expected). "It is nearly 2 months since I addressed you Sir, and ever since I may safely say, I have not had one peaceful moment. I owe £17 to the flour man and £24 to the butcher, and these two are my torments...." Two of her children, she wrote, were in urgent need of nourishment. (MS Morgan.)

[4] On 16 Jan 53 (see Vol. VII, p. 12*n*).

[5] "On your Friends help I had *rested* so nobly had it been given;—last year £20—the year before £40—then what was my distress at the receipt of the note today! ... Oh Sir, I beseech your Friend as you so well know how to do—to further assist us."

at once perceive that what I am now going to write, must be wholly irrespective of the Tragedy's merits, which I do not doubt.[1]

I cannot discharge the trust you propose to me;—simply because I thoroughly know its satisfactory discharge to be impossible. Here is the state of the Theatres. Buckstone has a Comedy and Farce Company which fills his Theatre[2] with any stock piece he chooses to play. It is rarely worth his while to produce a new Farce; a tragedy (as I know from himself) is wholly out of the question with him. The English Opera House is open for what they call Comedy, and for Burlesque.[3] Drury Lane opens at Christmas for Pantomime, and any cheap thing that can be crammed into the same bill.[4] Charles Kean is open for his "Farewell Season",[5] and has announced his intention of going through his series of revivals and successful plays, and of doing nothing else.[6] There remains but Phelps. I never had more than one negociation with him respecting a Play and its Writer. That transaction began so hopefully, progressed so wretchedly, and terminated so fatally and dismally,[7] that I then resolved that nothing should induce me ever to enter upon such relations with him again. And, if I know myself, nothing ever will.

In this condition of things, I am quite unable to help. You know I would, if I could. I cannot, and I am heartily sorry for it.

Faithfully Yours

R. H. Horne Esquire. CHARLES DICKENS

To T. J. THOMPSON, 27 OCTOBER 1858*

MS Morgan Library.

Hull | Twenty Seventh October, 1858.

My Dear Thompson.

I don't know whether you are aware that for some time past I have known nothing of Frederick. I had my reasons for declining to see him, and no one in the world was stranger to me than he, until, towards the end of last August, he amazed me by presenting himself in my room at Morrison's Hotel in Dublin.

Thus severed from him, I would on no consideration have discussed his affairs. And they have been so entirely unknown to me that I do not now know what you mean when you mention "that astonishing Dorking business."[8]

[1] Horne's pencil note on the envelope reads "London Theatres | 9—d—a M.S. tragedy". Evidently a new work, and untraced.

[2] The Haymarket, where he had engaged Charles Mathews and his wife. On 27 Oct they played Boucicault's comedy, *London Assurance*, followed by two farces, *He Would be an Actor*, by Mathews, and J. H. Stocqueler's *Any Port in a Storm*; and a popular ballet, *Jack's Return from Canton*.

[3] It opened for its First English Opera Season, under Louisa Pyne and W. Harrison, with Balfe's *Satanella*, on 20 Dec; but no advts have been found before that.

[4] It opened on Boxing Day with a lavish pantomime, *Robin Hood*, and Mr and Mrs Barney Williams in J. S. Coyne's farce, *The Latest from New York*.

[5] As manager of the Princess's Theatre.

[6] On 27 Oct he played *King John* (with J. M. Morton's farce, *Away with Melancholy*); in Nov, *The Merchant of Venice* and *Much Ado about Nothing*.

[7] His failed negotiations to put on Saunders's *Love's Martyrdom* in Dec 54: see Vol. VII, pp. 445 and 586.

[8] Anna Dickens's allegation, in the case she was about to bring for judicial separation, that in Apr 57 Frederick "at Dorking . . . committed Adultery with a woman whose name is to your

Ignorant of the details of the relations between him and his wife, I can, of course, form no judgement upon them. But quite apart from their complications and merits, I cannot doubt that your proposals to him to mediate between the two, was a kind one, and a considerate one, and a most discreet one. I have not the least doubt upon that head, and, begging you to understand so, I can say no more.

My tour is drawing to a close: and although it has been *amazingly successful*, I am glad to think of its fatigues as being nearly over, and of my own quieter pursuits as being again before me. I have been wandering about so long, that my writing desk has become permeated with the grease of the United Kingdom, and the state of this paper is a dismal evidence of its condition.

Pray give my love to Christiana, and believe that it will always be a real pleasure to me, and to all of us at home, to see you both. On looking back to what I have written, I find that I have not actually said that I wish to Heaven that Frederick had accepted your offer. I don't wish to leave this, merely implied.

Faithfully Yours always

T. J. Thompson Esquire CHARLES DICKENS

To MISS ALICE TAYLOR,[1] 28 OCTOBER 1858

Extract in T. F. Madigan catalogue, Dec 1935.

At Leeds, Thursday Night Twenty Eighth October 1858.[2]

'And so, as Tiny Tim observed, God bless us everyone!'[3]

In which he expressed himself, less theologically but perhaps on the whole more acceptably to Heaven, than Miggs (Miss Miggs, of Mr. Varden's household) when she hoped 'she hated and despised herself and all her feller creeturs, as every practicable Christian should'.[4]

For Miss Alice Taylor.

To JOHN FORSTER, [?28 OCTOBER 1858]

Extracts in F, VIII, iv, 665–6 and F, 1872–4, III, ix, 205*n*. *Date:* just after his second readings at Hull.

Saying that at Hull the vast concourse had to be addressed by Arthur Smith on the gallery stairs of the Music Hall and additional readings had to be given day and night, for the people out of town and for the people in town.

petitioner wholly unknown" (Principal Probate Registry: Divorce Files). See *To* Thompson, 22 Nov, *fn.*

[1] Daughter of Bridges Taylor, British Consul in Copenhagen.

[2] Where he read *The Poor Traveller*, *Boots* and *Mrs Gamp*, that night, in Leeds Music Hall. The *Leeds Express*, 30 Oct, recorded that the readings were "the very best we have ever heard".

[3] CD also gave this quotation to an unknown correspondent on 4 Oct 58 at Aberdeen, where he had read the *Carol* the same day (Sotheby's catalogue, 4 Mar 1980).

[4] "I hope I know my own unworthiness, and that I hate and despise myself and all my fellow-creatures as every practicable Christian should" (*Barnaby Rudge*, Ch. 13).

The net profit to himself, thus far, had been upwards of three hundred pounds a week. That is no doubt immense, our expenses being necessarily large, and the travelling party being always five. *Another source of profit was the sale of the copies of the several Readings prepared by himself.* Our people alone sell eight, ten, and twelve dozen a night.

To MRS WHITFORD,[1] 29 OCTOBER 1858

Extract in Sotheby's catalogue, July 1972; *MS* 2 pp.; dated Sheffield, 29 Oct 58; addressed Mrs. Thomas Whitford, Belgrave,[2] near Leicester.[3]

Declining her invitation received at Leeds that morning, on the grounds that he never accepted invitations while on tour. The "very grand folks" and the very plain folks everywhere have been equally shut out from me.

Says that his mother will be greatly interested to know that Mrs. Whitford had written to him. Laetitia and her husband he often sees.[4]

I beg to send my regards to your liege Lord, and to that most wonderful of all the prodigies I have ever heard of—the only child—who is not a prodigy.

To FREDERICK DICKENS, [?31 OCTOBER 1858]

Mention in *To* Thompson, 8 Nov 58. *Date:* immediately after Thompson's "second letter" (his reply to CD's of 27 Oct).

To JOHN FORSTER, [?1 NOVEMBER 1858]

Extract from F (1872–4), III, ix, 205*n*. *Date:* "A later letter" than *To* Forster, ?28 Oct, according to Forster; probably early Nov, a week or so after his second reading in Manchester on 23 Oct.

The men with the reading books were sold out, for about the twentieth time, at Manchester. Eleven dozen of the *Poor Traveller*, *Boots* and *Mrs Gamp* being sold in about ten minutes, they had no more left; and Manchester became green with the little tracts, in every bookshop, outside every omnibus, and passing along every street. The sale of them, apart from us, must be very great.[5]

[1] Mrs Thomas Whitford; clearly an early friend of the Dickens family who had written to CD after seeing an announcement of his 4 Nov reading at Leicester.

[2] A large village about 2 miles north-east of Leicester. Thomas Whitford is listed among "Gentry".

[3] Where he read the *Carol* in the New Music Hall on 4 Nov; the *Leicester Chronicle*, 6 Nov, reported that "every part of the room was crowded" ... he "entirely absorbed" the audience's attention.

[4] This suggests a particular friendship with Laetitia (who married Henry Austin in 1837). As "Laetitia" is mentioned in CD's letter of Oct 33 to an unidentified "Miss Urquhart", who had acted with his family and friends in *Clari* on 27 Apr (as Pelgrino's wife) and was then invited by CD and Henry Austin to act in another unnamed play, this might be the same person: see Vol. I, p. 31 and *nn*.

[5] But see *To* Miss Coutts, 23 Aug 58, *fn*.

To MISS BURDETT COUTTS, 3 NOVEMBER 1858†

MS Morgan Library. *Address:* Miss Burdett Coutts | Great Western Hotel | London | W.

Wolverhampton | Wednesday Third November, 1858.

My Dear Miss Coutts

I was very sorry—especially as I *could* have seen you, for the Fog cleared on purpose!

My Tour will end, please God, at Brighton, next Saturday week, the 13th. It will seem so strange and quiet and pleasant to me, to sit down at my desk again.

With love to Mrs. Brown

Ever faithfully and affecy. Yours

Miss Burdett Coutts. CHARLES DICKENS

To MISS GEORGINA HOGARTH, 3 NOVEMBER 1858

MS Dickens House.

Wolverhampton | Wednesday Third November 1858.

My Dearest Georgy.

[a]This is a very short note, merely to report myself "all right", and to add that I purpose being down on Saturday morning by the Chandelier-man Train.[1] I shall have (I am sorry to add) to leave Gad's Hill on Sunday, for I *must* dine with Forster that day. We have to confer about Whitefriars, and he has been so injured by my never accepting any of his many invitations, that I have atoned by proposing this appointment.[a]

Little Leamington came out in the most amazing manner yesterday. We took £130, and turned away hundreds upon hundreds of people. They are represented as the dullest and worst of audiences. I found them very good indeed—even in the morning.[2]

There awaited me at the hotel, a letter from the Reverend Mr. Young,[3] Wentworth Watson's tutor, saying that Mrs. Watson wished her boy to shake hands with me, and that he would bring him in the evening. I expected him at the Hotel, before the reading. But he did not come. He spoke to John about it in the room at night. The crowd and confusion, however, were very great, and I saw nothing of him. In his letter he said that Mrs. Watson was at Paris on her way home, and would be at Brighton at the end of this week. I suppose I shall see her there, at the end of next week.

[aa] Omitted in MDGH.

[1] Perhaps the train taken by the chandler (or "chandleer") man who travelled to Kent to sell candles.

[2] He read twice in the Music Hall, Leamington, on 2 Nov: the *Carol* at 3 p.m.; and *The Poor Traveller*, *Boots* and *Mrs Gamp*, at 8 p.m. He stayed that night in the Regent Hotel. The *Leamington Advertiser*, 4 Nov, contained a long and warm notice of both readings: on Tues there was "a large assembly"; on Wed the Hall was "crowded by the elite of Leamington and Warwick", and CD "possessed the sympathies of his audience" from beginning to end. Welcoming him as the inventor of "The Circumlocution Office", the *Royal Leamington Spa Courier*, 30 Oct, used it to attack the Local Board for its vacillation over adopting both a new drainage system and a site for the National Schools (given in Bryan Homer, *CD and Leamington Spa*, Coventry, 1991, pp. 32–4).

[3] The Rev. Julian Charles Young (1806–73): see Vol. V, p. 588*n*; just appointed Rector of Ilmington, Warwickshire.

We find a Let of 200 stalls here, which is very large for this place. The evening being fine too, and Blue being to be seen in the sky beyond the smoke, we expect to have a very full hall.[1] Tell Mamey and Katey that if they had been with us on the railway today between Leamington and this place, they would have seen (though it is only an hour and ten minutes by the Express), Fires and Smoke indeed. We came through a part of the Black Country that you know, and it looked at its Blackest. All the furnaces seemed in full blast, and all the CoalPits to be working.

It is Market Day here, and the Iron Masters are standing out in the street (where they always hold High Change),[2] making such an iron hum and buzz, that they confuse me horribly. In addition there is a Bellman announcing something—not the reading, I beg to say—and there is an excavation being made in the centre of the open-place, for a statue, or a pump, or a Lamp Post, or something or other, round which all the Wolverhampton boys are yelling and struggling.

And here is Arthur, begging to have dinner at half past 3 instead of 4, because he foresees "a wiry evening"[3] in store for him. Under which complication of distractions, to which a waitress with a tray at this moment adds herself, I sink, and leave off.

My best love to the dear girls, and to the noble Plorn, and to you, Marguerite and Ellen Stone not forgotten. All yesterday and to-day I have been doing everything to the tune of—

—"And the day is dark and dreary"[4]

Ever Dearest Georgy | Your most affectionate and faithful

CHARLES DICKENS

I hope the Brazier is intolerably hot, and half stifles all the family. Then, and not otherwise, I shall think it in satisfactory work.

To W. H. WILLS, 3 NOVEMBER 1858

MS Huntington Library.

Wolverhampton | Wednesday Third November, 1858.

My Dear Wills.

H.W.

You remember that at one of our Audit Meetings—I think, the last[5]—I suggested to Mr. Evans that we ought to have the vouchers for the payments made, and charged as being made, by their Firm, on account of H.W. It arose out of our speaking of paying for the paper in ready money.

[1] He read *The Poor Traveller*, *Boots* and *Mrs Gamp* in the Corn Exchange, that night. The *Wolverhampton Chronicle*, 10 Nov, reported that "the large room was filled in every part", and CD "heartily applauded from every part of the room"—though the pathetic (in *The Poor Traveller*) was by no means his forte. "His voice, when first heard, was not pleasing."

[2] No record of this found; but presumably their settling of accounts, following the Bank of England's six-monthly accounting date on 1 Nov.

[3] i.e. a tough one.

[4] From the setting in 1851 by John Lodge Ellerton (later, Lodge) of Longfellow's "The Rainy Day", St. 3: "Into each life some rain must fall | Some days must be dark and dreary."

[5] In May.

Mr. Evans replied to that, that we, the other proprietors in H.W.[1] were not responsible for the paper. He said so, with confidence; and I did not urge the point, though I had great doubts of his being legally right.

I have now ascertained that we *are* legally responsible. Will you therefore let Mr. Evans know that at the Audit of next week,[2] we wish to have produced to us, the Vouchers for their payments on account of Household Words. There can be no Audit, I am assured, without such Vouchers, except in the mere name.

Pray do not fail to see to this.

Ever Faithfully

W. H. Wills Esquire CHARLES DICKENS

To MESSRS BRADBURY & EVANS, [3 NOVEMBER 1858]

Mention in next.

To W. H. WILLS, 3 NOVEMBER 1858

MS Huntington Library.

Swan, Wolverhampton | Wednesday Third November 1858.

My Dear Wills.

I enclose you the note that I think best calculated to be shewn or sent by you to B and E on the voucher question.

In reference to my own copyrights, you seem to have omitted by accident, the most important question of all. It is, *whether I, being the largest proprietor in the books,*[3] *can change the printer and publisher of them if I choose*? On this, the whole question of the extent of our power and the manner of its exercise, depends. There is no sub-agreement whatever, as to printing and publishing.

Now, will you again see Ouvry on this vital question—which absolutely governs our proceeding as to Household Words—and communicate his opinion on that point, to Forster, along with his opinion on the other points? I cannot consult with Forster[4] to any purpose, until we know exactly how we stand on this head.

As to Wilkie's paper.[5]—I see no necessity whatever, for altering Fauntleroy's name.[6] But I wouldn't use it in the title. I would call it A Paradoxical Experience—or A Curiosity of Life—or something like that.

I purpose being at the office, at 1 on Friday.

Little Leamington came out amazingly yesterday. We took £130, and turned

[1] CD and Wills. Under the original articles of agreement, CD held a half share, Bradbury & Evans a quarter, and Forster and Wills an eighth share each. Forster's eighth share, which he relinquished in Feb 1856, was divided equally between CD and Wills.

[2] On 9 Nov. CD could not attend himself, as he was at Southampton.

[3] i.e., the vols of *HW*.

[4] To whom CD was about to give a power of attorney to act for him, in matters relating to *HW*: see *To* Wills, 10 Nov.

[5] "A Paradoxical Experience", *HW*, 13 Nov 58, XVIII, 518.

[6] Collins's story was based on the execution for forgery of the banker Henry Fauntleroy (1785–1824; *DNB*). His name remains in the story; the "paradox" was his kindness to a young man and secret warning to him just before the Bank stops payment.

away many hundreds of people. We have 200 stalls let here for to night; which, considering the size of the town, is unusually large.

And I think that's all I have to say, at present.

Ever Faithfully
CD.

To JOHN FORSTER, [?3–4 NOVEMBER 1858]

Extract in F, 1872–4, III, ix, 205*n*. *Date:* "another letter", according to Forster; perhaps a few days later.

Did I tell you that the agents for our tickets who are also book-sellers, say very generally that the readings decidedly increase the sale of the books they are taken from? We were first told of this by a Mr. Parke,[1] a wealthy old gentleman in a very large way at Wolverhampton, who did all the business for love, and would not take a farthing. Since then, we have constantly come upon it; and M'Glashin and Gill[2] at Dublin were very strong about it indeed.

To J. COUCHMAN,[3] [4] NOVEMBER 1858

Text in W. R. Hughes, *A Week's Tramp in Dickens-Land*, p. 224. *Date:* Thursday was the 4th in 1858.

GAD'S HILL PLACE,|HIGHAM BY ROCHESTER, KENT.
Thursday, 5th Nov., 1858

Mr. Couchman,

Please to ease the coach-house doors, and to put up some pegs, agreeably to George Belcher's[4] directions.

To VINCENT WANOSTROCHT,[5] 5 NOVEMBER 1858*

MS Yale University Library.

OFFICE OF HOUSEHOLD WORDS,
Friday Fifth November 1858

Dear Sir

I am much obliged to you for your kind letter, and beg you to accept my cordial thanks. I cannot, however, prolong my series of Readings at this time.

Being in town for a few hours only, I answer your favor very hastily.

Faithfully Yours

V. Wanoshocht[6] Esquire — CHARLES DICKENS

[1] William Parke.

[2] McGlashan & Gill, publishers, 50 Upper Sackville St, Dublin, established 1856.

[3] John Couchman, carpenter and undertaker, 1 High St, Strood. He worked for CD from Whit Monday 1856, the day he took possession of Gad's Hill, until his death; for his high opinion of CD as an employer, see Hughes above, p. 221. The first work he did for him was to make a dog-kennel.

[4] CD's coachman.

[5] Vincent Wanostrocht, merchant, of 31 St Swithin's Lane; probably son of Nicholas Wanostrocht, French scholar.

[6] Misspelt by CD.

To THE REV. JAMES WHITE, 5 NOVEMBER 1858

Text from MDGH, II, 81.

TAVISTOCK HOUSE, | TAVISTOCK SQUARE, LONDON. W.C.
Friday, Nov. 5th, 1858.

My dear White,

May I entreat you to thank Mr. Carter[1] very earnestly and kindly in my name, for his proffered hospitality; and, further, to explain to him that since my readings began, I have known them to be incompatible with all social enjoyments, and have neither set foot in a friend's house nor sat down to a friend's table in any one of all the many places I have been to, but have rigidly kept myself to my hotels. To this resolution I must hold until the last. There is not the least virtue in it. It is a matter of stern necessity, and I submit with the worst grace possible.

Will you let me know, either at Southampton or Portsmouth, whether any of you, and how many of you, if any, are coming over, so that Arthur Smith may reserve good seats?[2] Tell Lotty I hope she does not contemplate coming to the morning reading; I always hate it so myself.

Mary and Katey are down at Gad's Hill with Georgy and Plornish, and they have Marguerite Power and Ellen Stone staying there. I am sorry to say that even my benevolence descries no prospect of their being able to come to my native place.[3]

On Saturday week, the 13th, my tour, please God, ends.

My best love to Mrs. White, and to Lotty, and to Clara.

Ever, my dear White, affectionately yours
[CHARLES DICKENS]

To THE REV. MATTHEW GIBSON, 6 NOVEMBER 1858

MS Robert H. Taylor Collection, Princeton University.

GAD'S HILL PLACE, | HIGHAM BY ROCHESTER, KENT.
Saturday Sixth November, 1858.

My Dear Sir

Will you and Mr. Bewsher tell me whether you think the gigantic Sydney[4] really has any sort of Call to the Sea Service? He has often talked of it at home here, and has lately written an odd characteristic letter to one of his sisters, entreating her to ask me to make the Navy his profession, as he is devoted to it "without any sham", and longs to follow it.[5]

[1] Perhaps W. Carter of 1 Onslow Place, New Town, Southampton, the only likely host of that name in Southampton or Portsmouth.

[2] He gave three readings in the Royal Victoria Rooms, Southampton; *The Poor Traveller*, *Boots* and *Mrs Gamp*, on the evening of 9 Nov and at 3 p.m. on the 10th; the *Carol* on the evening of the 10th. The *Hampshire Advertiser*, 13 Nov, reported that the large room was crowded on each occasion, and *c.* 200 were unable to get in.

[3] Portsea. CD was born at Mile End Terrace. He gave two readings at Portsea, in St George's Hall, on 11 Nov: the *Carol* at 3 p.m. and *The Poor Traveller*, *Boots* and *Mrs Gamp* at 8 p.m. The *Hampshire Telegraph*, 13 Nov, reported that both were crowded and "afforded the utmost delight".

[4] Sydney Smith Haldimand Dickens (1847–72), CD's seventh child and fifth son.

[5] Sydney joined the Navy; for his training, see next vol.

I cannot make out in my own mind, how much of this ardour is in-bred in the boy, and how much of it is referable to the frequent appearances here, in the last holidays, of a young Midshipman, the son of an Edinburgh friend of mine,[1] in glorious buttons and with a real steel weapon in his belt. As you have so many more opportunities of observing Sydney than I have, I should be very glad of your opinion: though of course I am not so unreasonable as to expect you to pronounce oracularly on so difficult a question.

But he is a boy of such remarkable energy and purpose, considering his years and inches, that if I supposed him to be quite in earnest and to have made up his small mind, I would give him his way, because I really believe he would then follow it out with spirit.

My daughters and Miss Hogarth unite in kind regard to yourself and Mr. Bewsher; and I am always

My Dear Sir | Very faithfully Yours

The Rev. M. Gibson CHARLES DICKENS

To MISS GEORGINA HOGARTH, 8 NOVEMBER 1858

MS Dickens House.

TAVISTOCK HOUSE, | TAVISTOCK SQUARE, LONDON. W.C.
Monday Eighth November, 1858.

My Dearest Georgy

Knowing that the enclosed from Mrs. Watson would refer to me, I opened it, to see if there were anything that I could answer. Discovering nothing of that kind, I send it on to you to answer for yourself.

I have added Davies & Son[2] to the House cheque: making the total £33..11..5. Enclosed is a cheque for £33..11..6.

Enclosed also is a cheque in the Blacksmith's[3] favor, for £5..18..7—the amount of his bill.

I am in no humour for going away again this morning, and should be in the worst of humours but for seeing Land so close before me.

Best love to dearest Mamey and Katey, and the good and gallant Plorn,[4]

[1] Andrew, son of J. T. Gordon.

[2] Probably James Davies & Son, boot, shoe and leather warehouse, 9 Gracechurch St and 1 and 2 Corbet Court.

[3] George Rayfield, blacksmith and wheelwright, Higham.

[4] Ending and signature cut off.

To T. J. THOMPSON, 8 NOVEMBER 1858*

MS Morgan Library.

TAVISTOCK HOUSE, | TAVISTOCK SQUARE, LONDON. W.C.
Monday Eighth November, 1858.

My Dear Thompson

On the receipt of your second letter,[1] I wrote to Frederick. He has been here by appointment this morning, and I have spoken to him on the wretched subject.

I told him that the Dorking matter[2] had been made known to me, but I did not say by whom. He asked me by whom, but I declined to tell him. I said that it seemed to me that you were the natural person whom he should have asked to negociate. He did not reply that you had offered to do so; but Alfred (to whom I spoke, similarly, on the matter last Thursday) bore testimony to that circumstance, with all becoming earnestness.

I particularly mentioned to Frederick that I desired to know nothing of the differences between him and his wife and his wife's family,[3] and that in point of fact I *would* know nothing about them, and would not enter upon their discussion. I limited myself, I told him, to the one Dorking circumstance, and the accompanying circumstance that he refused to make his wife any allowance. Upon that state of things only, discarding everything about it and around it, I expressed my opinion to him in the strongest manner and advised him with the greatest emphasis. My belief is, that I made no impression upon him whatever. He left me, declaring that I had made none; and I have not the faintest reason to suppose that he attached a feather's weight to any thing I said.

Ever Faithfully Yours
T. J. Thompson Esquire. CHARLES DICKENS

To W. H. WILLS, 8 NOVEMBER 1858*

MS Huntington Library.

TAVISTOCK HOUSE, | TAVISTOCK SQUARE, LONDON. W.C.
Monday Eighth November, 1858.

My Dear Wills

I enclose you the notice[4] to be delivered to B and E with awful gravity and portentous demeanour.[5]

Did you think of Beard, in connexion with the Daily News Wants?[6]

[1] Clearly written after receiving CD's letter of 27 Oct.

[2] See *To* Thompson, 27 Oct, *fn*.

[3] The Wellers: see Vol. III, p. 446*n*.

[4] See next.

[5] CD exaggerates the formality, because he had quarrelled irrevocably with Bradbury & Evans; on the grounds, according to their statement in May 59, of their failure to publish his "Personal" statement in *Punch*. But in reply to this, Forster wrote to them: "Your statement does not set forth truly the communication I made to you. Both in what it asserts and in what it suppresses, it is incorrect" (C. J. S[awyer] and F. J. H. D[arton], *Dickens v. Barabbas, Forster intervening*, 1930, p. 66). See next vol.

[6] The *Daily News* must have advertised a vacancy; but not discovered.

You will write to me by tomorrow night's post, of course.
I can make no impression on Frederick.

Ever Faithfully
CD.

To MESSRS BRADBURY & EVANS, 9 NOVEMBER 1858*

MS Berg Collection.

TAVISTOCK HOUSE, | TAVISTOCK SQUARE, LONDON. W.C.
Tuesday Ninth November, 1858.

Gentlemen

I request you, in compliance with the provisions of the deed of partnership in Household Words, to be so good as to convene a special meeting of the partners, to be held within seven days from this date,[1] for the consideration of a Resolution I shall have to propose.[2]

Messrs. Bradbury and Evans. CHARLES DICKENS

To WILKIE COLLINS, 9 NOVEMBER 1858

MS Morgan Library.

Royal Hotel, Southampton
Tuesday Evening Ninth November | 1858.

My Dear Wilkie

I was under the impression that I was to finish at Brighton on the *afternoon* of Saturday. I find however, that I read, both in the afternoon and in the evening. I would propose to you to come and celebrate the end of the Tour, by dining with us that day at the Bedford;[3] but, between two readings, I am afraid it would rather bore than gratify your digestive functions?

Assuming it not to be worth your while to take a Saturday "Return" to Brighton,

[1] It was held on the 15th. Wills and Forster attended, Forster acting for CD.

[2] "That the present partnership in Household Words be dissolved by the cessation and discontinuance of that publication on the Completion of the Nineteenth Volume" ("Extract from Household Words Minute-book", entered by Wills; copy in CD's hand: MS Messrs Farrer & Co., given in K. J. Fielding, "Bradbury v. Dickens", *D*, L [1954], 76). The resolution was proposed by Forster, seconded by Wills; they voted in its favour; Bradbury and Evans declined to vote, not accepting Forster's right to represent CD at the meeting through his power of attorney. In a separate statement they recorded: "Believing the resolution to be contrary to the conditions of the deed of partnership and therefore illegal—we decline to vote" (MS *ibid.*).

[3] No doubt partly to cheer him up after the failure of his play, *The Red Vial*, at the Olympic, 11 Oct. The *Athenaeum*, 16 Oct, recorded that it seemed to have been written "for the purpose of introducing the Dead House at Frankfurt, to which every corpse is brought before burial". The more macabre scenes "did not prove effective" . . . and were "displeasing to the audience". On 23 Oct the *Athenaeum* reported that Collins "had removed some of the objectionable incidents"; but it had "little faith in changes in a piece once condemned". Collins was "deeply humiliated" by the failure and refused to allow the play to be published or ever performed again: Catherine Peters, *The King of Inventors*, p. 183.

then, will you arrange to go down to Gads Hill on Sunday in good time for dinner? I will go down, by some train or other, in good time for dinner too. How do you feel about having the big bedroom, and writing there through the week? I would go to work too, and we might do Heaven knows how much[1]—with an escapade to town for a night, if we felt in the humour.

I pause for a reply.[2]—Let me find it at the Bedford at Brighton, when I get there on Friday forenoon.

Wills arranged with me that you were presently to receive sacks of Christmas "matter;"—not much "mind" with it,[3] I am afraid.[4]

You have furnished Costello's[5] wing with a feather, for an eagle flight into the Pension List.[6]

Ever affectionately

Wilkie Collins Esquire CHARLES DICKENS

To W. H. WILLS, 10 NOVEMBER 1858

MS Huntington Library.

Royal Hotel, Southampton | Wednesday Tenth November 1858

My Dear Wills.

The Audit Meeting appears to have gone off, pretty much as I expected it would. I felt sure of their producing the documents—I meant to have written, Vouchers.[7]

In the Forster Matter I do not agree with you. For this reason. It is clear to my mind that no discussion *can* take place between me and Bradbury and Evans. My being there would shut up any approach to it,—simply because I have steadily refused to enter on any approach to it, however distant, and have left Evans's advances disregarded. Now, with Forster they are under no such restraint. And even in the event of no discussion taking place with him at the Meeting[8] (which is the most probable aspect of Monday), they still have him legitimately in the business, and can at any time go to him or write to him. They could not do so with me, because they have already proved it to be unavailing.

As to his management of the interview, I have not a doubt of his arranging it as I shall entreat him to do. And I can write to him from Brighton, expressly laying down the course that I want him to take. That course shall be, accommodation if it be possible. It is not possible with me, in a matter in which I have so deep a personal feeling.[9]

[1] See *To* Wills, 20 Nov and *fn.*

[2] *Julius Caesar*, III, ii, 33.

[3] No doubt drawing on jokes against the philosopher Berkeley and J. S. Mill; see also *Don Juan*, Canto XI, st. i.

[4] For the Christmas No.; but Mrs Gaskell and Adelaide Procter were eventually the only contributors besides CD and Collins.

[5] Dudley Costello (1803–65; *DNB*), journalist and author: see Vol. I, p. 552*n* and later vols. He contributed over 40 papers to *HW*.

[6] He was granted a Civil List pension of £75 *p.a.* in Apr 61.

[7] See *To* Wills, 3 Nov.

[8] Of 15 Nov.

[9] Forster refers to "painful personal disputes" with Bradbury & Evans arising out of CD's separation. "The disputes turned upon matters of feeling exclusively" (F, VIII, v, 670). Besides their refusal to reprint his "Personal" statement in *Punch*, there were other, more personal causes which involved both Evans and Lemon as Catherine's advisers: see *To* Evans, 22 July.

It never can come about, unless they have a third person before them, without seeking such person.

For these reasons, I would get the Power of Attorney—a Power to Forster to act for me, in matters relating to H.W. I must execute it. Could you not come down to Brighton with it? We shall be there by mid-day on Friday. I would write my letter to Forster then and there, and you should see it, and see that it is to your satisfaction. I feel convinced that he would not depart from a course agreed upon.[1] You know how emphatically he feels that the first thing above all others, is, not to injure the property.

In order to avoid unnecessary conglomeration of our accounts, let me give you a cheque[2] for your part of the Audit Day balance. [a]It is enclosed.[a]

Don't go to press with Wilkie's paper about Sydney Herbert, Guizot, the heir of Redcliffe, and Dr. Dulcamara, without my seeing it.[3]

Ever Faithfully
CD.

To THE INDEPENDENT STUDENTS,[4] GLASGOW UNIVERSITY, [?10 or 11 NOVEMBER 1858]

Mention in *To* McTear, 22 Nov 58.

Objecting to being nominated for the Rectorship.[5]

[1] For the letters Forster, acting on his power of attorney, exchanged with Bradbury & Evans, see Appx J.

[2] "when I see you" cancelled.

[aa] Written in, after cancellation, at end of paragraph.

[3] "Doctor Dulcamara, M.P.", *HW*, 18 Dec 58, XIX, 49. CD had evidently seen it already, or at least knew its substance and drift. He may have wished to tone down the attacks on Guizot and especially Herbert, for whom in 1850–2 he had shown considerable respect (see Vol. VI, p. 535 and *passim*). Collins takes him as a type of Dulcamara (recalling the travelling quack and charlatan in Donizetti's *L'Elisir d'Amore*, 1832) for his address at the opening of the Warminster Athenaeum on 28 Oct ("On Newspaper Literature and Politics": *The Times*, 29 Oct). He is offended by a politician's presumption in treating novels as "nostrums, in a tone of indulgence", while citing Guizot's authority for praising English "domestic novels" with *The Heir of Redclyffe* as his example. Four cols are then given to mocking summary and quotation, probably as counterblast to the remarkable popularity of Charlotte Yonge's novel (published 1853, anonymously, it had an immediate and long-continued success; 17 edns by 1868). It is here treated merely as a "Pusey-novel", improbable and trivial. In two of the quoted passages Collins jeers at the young hero's passionate enthusiasms for Charles I and for Malory's *Morte d'Arthur*. CD might agree, but should have known that neither Herbert nor (obviously) Guizot was sympathetic to "Pusey-ism". The article was probably planned to open Vol. XIX on 4 Dec, and its postponement suggests some revision; but it is in no sense a collaboration.

[4] A "group of independent medical students", bringing CD forward "as the nominee of the Independent interest", according to the *Glasgow Morning Journal*, 10 Nov.

[5] The *Publishers' Circular* for 1 Dec has the following editorial item: "The *Glasgow Morning Journal* states 'we have seen a letter from Mr. Dickens, in which he strongly repudiates his being put into nomination for the Lord Rectorship, and says, that the movement was not only without his sanction, but expressly opposed by him.'"

To MISS GEORGINA HOGARTH, 11 NOVEMBER 1858

Mention in N, III, 71.

To WILKIE COLLINS, 13 NOVEMBER 1858

MS Morgan Library.

Bedford Hotel | Saturday Thirteenth November | 1858.

My Dear Wilkie

I am reading, this afternoon. Dinner is ordered at 5 punctually. They will shew you up into the sitting-room when you have read this, and will also shew you your bedroom, which I have duly commanded.—Think of our finding ready-taken here, *One Thousand Stalls*![1]

Ever affectionately
CD.

To THE HON. MRS RICHARD WATSON, 13 NOVEMBER 1858

MS Huntington Library.

Bedford | Saturday Evg. 13th. Novr. 1858.

My Dear Mrs. Watson

The Audience are always "dense" in the morning. There is hardly an exception to the rule. Sometimes, in London—not often.

Pray ask for Arthur Smith again, and he will do his best.[2] For he knows how much I love you, and how many old dear remembrances surround you in my mind.

Ever Yours
CD.

To H. L. WINTER, 13 NOVEMBER 1858

MS Huntington Library. *Address:* — Winter Esquire.

Brighton | Saturday Thirteenth November 1858

My Dear Mr. Winter

In the hope that a friendly word of remembrance in season, may not be unacceptable to you, I write to assure you of my sympathy with you in your trouble.[3] Pray do not let it cast you down too much. What has happened to you, has happened to

[1] He gave three readings in the Town Hall, Brighton: the *Carol* on Friday evening, 12 Nov; *Little Dombey* at 3 p.m., Saturday; and on Saturday evening, *The Poor Traveller*, *Boots* and *Mrs Gamp*. The *Brighton Examiner*, 17 Nov, reported that his reception was "warm and friendly"; but the impulse to hear him perhaps "a little heightened by the notoriety of his transpiring domestic relations". It criticized his reading of *Little Dombey*: "The great novelist is, we think *not* a great elocutionist . . . his voice, distinct and audible enough, is not of the kind that makes its way directly to the heart."

[2] To find her a place for the evening reading.

[3] Winter, described in *The Times*, 3 Nov, as of New North St, Finsbury, millowner, had been declared bankrupt on 3 Nov; his Court hearing was on 12 Nov. For his subsequent career as a clergyman see next vol.

many thousands of good and honorable men, and will happen again in like manner, to the end of all things. If you should feel the bitterness of losing belief in any nature you had previously trusted in, consider that the truth is always better than a falsehood, even though the truth involves the detection of such skin-deep friendship as that which can cool towards a man in temporary misfortune. It is better lost than kept, as all things worthless are.

Be strong of heart for yourself, and look forward to a better time.

You will not think, I know, that I obtrude myself upon you in asking to be borne in mind among the friends who feel truly towards you.—

Faithfully Yours always
CHARLES DICKENS

To MRS WINTER, 13 NOVEMBER 1858

MS Huntington Library.

Brighton, Saturday Thirteenth November | 1858

My Dear Mrs. Winter.

I have been so constantly and rapidly changing from place to place during the past week, that I am only just now in receipt of the intelligence of your misfortune. With the utmost sincerity and earnestness of which my heart is capable, I condole with you upon it, and assure you of my true sympathy and friendship. It has distressed me greatly. Not because I am so worldly or so unjust as to couple the least reproach or blame with a reverse that I do not doubt to have been unavoidable, and that I know to be always easily possible of occurrence to the best and most fortunate of men, but because I know you feel it heavily.

I wish to Heaven it were in my power to help Mr. Winter to any new opening in life. But you can hardly imagine how powerless I am in any such case. My own work in life being of that kind that I must always do it with my own unassisted hand and head, I have such rare opportunities of placing any one, that for years and years I have been seeking in vain to help in this way a friend of the old days[1] when the old house stood unchanged in Lombard Street.[2] To this hour, I have not succeeded, though I have strenuously tried my hardest, both abroad and home. Commercial opportunities, above all, are so far removed from me, that I dare not encourage a hope of my power to serve Mr. Winter with my good word, ever coming within a year's journey of my will and wish to do it.

But I really think that your father,[3] who could do much in such a case without drawing at all heavily upon his purse, might be induced to do, what—I may say to you, Maria—it is no great stretch of sentiment to call his duty. Has not Margaret[4] great influence with him? Have not you *some*? And don't you think that if you were to set yourself steadily to exert whatever influence you can bring to bear upon him, you would do the best within your reach for your husband, your child, and yourself? Is it not all important that you should try your utmost with him, at this time?[5]

[1] Just possibly Thomas Beard.

[2] The office of Smith, Payne & Smith's Bank, where her father had worked.

[3] George Beadnell.

[4] His daughter, Margaret Lloyd.

[5] Maria's parents had opposed her marriage, so he was doubtless not prepared to help financially, though he could well afford to (he died in Nov 1862, leaving £40,000).

Forgive my recommending this, if you have so anticipated the recommendation as to have done all that possibly can be done to move him. But what you tell me about George[1] seems so strange, so hard, and so ill-balanced, that I cannot avoid the subject.

I write in the greatest haste, being overwhelmed by business here. On Monday I hope to be at Gad's Hill, and to remain either there or at Tavistock House for months to come. I enclose a few lines to Mr. Winter, and am ever

Your faithful friend
CHARLES DICKENS

To MISS DOLBY, 16 NOVEMBER 1858†

MS Brotherton Library, Leeds.

GAD'S HILL PLACE,| HIGHAM BY ROCHESTER, KENT.
Tuesday Sixteenth November, 1858.

My Dear Miss Dolby.

I received your letter here, this morning. Pray do not suppose for a moment, that the least explanation or apology was a necessary part of it. My reply is rendered short, by the one circumstance, solely, that it originates in a mistake. I have not, I assure you, the remotest idea of severing myself from Arthur Smith.[2] If I were to enter upon any other series of readings, I should consider him an essential part of them. No other end has come to our relations with one another, than the end of my Tour. I have every conceivable reason to regard him as one of my most trusty friends, nor can I easily imagine myself treading the same road again without him.

Believe me always | Very faithfully Yours
Miss Dolby. CHARLES DICKENS

To W. H. WILLS, 20 NOVEMBER 1858

MS Huntington Library.

OFFICE OF HOUSEHOLD WORDS,
Saturday Twentieth Novr. 1858

My Dear Wills.

As I find you are not coming here to day, I post this to let you know that we have returned to Tavistock House.

Also, that Wilkie and I have arranged to pass the whole day here, on *Monday Week, the 29th.* to connect the various portions of the Xmas No. and get it finally together.[3] If you arrange to have them ready at the Printers, for such cuts, and such

[1] Maria's younger brother: see *Catalogue of Suzannet CD Collection*, 1975, pp. 136 and 148; died *c.* 1864.

[2] Charlotte Dolby had perhaps heard gossip about the "Violated letter", suggesting, wrongly, that CD had quarrelled with Smith. She had evidently proposed that her brother George (see 28 Sep 56, *fn*) might replace him.

[3] The six parts of "A House to Let" were "Over the Way", by Collins, "The Manchester Marriage" by Mrs Gaskell, "Going into Society" by CD, "Three Evenings in the House", poem by Adelaide Procter, "Trottle's Report" by Collins, "Let at Last" by CD and Collins. The second, third and fourth purported to be papers read by Trottles and Jarber,

short bits of copy as we shall send them from time to time in the course of that day, we can finally correct it before we leave here that night, and you can send your last revise for Press next day.

This will enable you, now to settle on what day the Xmas No. shall be published, and to announce the said day in our No. sent to Press next week.[1]

Ever Faithfully

CD.

To T. J. THOMPSON, 22 NOVEMBER 1858*

MS Morgan Library.

TAVISTOCK HOUSE, | TAVISTOCK SQUARE, LONDON. W.C.

Monday Twenty Second November 1858.

My Dear Thompson

Frederick has been again to me, and has said that after weighing and considering what I said to him, he will make any reasonable terms with his wife. Still entirely with-holding from him that I had heard from you on the subject, I said I would communicate with you, if he chose to authorize me, but that I would communicate with no one else. Then he *did* authorize me, and this note follows thereupon.

It was only last night that I saw him here.

The first thing to be done by your influence is (I take it) to stay the legal proceedings.[2] The next question is, what does his wife think he ought to allow her, and what is it, with his burdened means, in his power to allow her? If you and I can strike this medium—and surely you and I who have no interest but in doing right, *can* strike it, if we try—this wretched business may be brought to a quiet end.[3]

Kind love from all. | Ever Faithfully

T. J. Thompson Esquire CHARLES DICKENS

I was in your old Pall Mall rooms[4] yesterday, seeing Edwin James.[5]

characters in the frame-story, about previous tenants; the fifth leads up to the explanation of why the house had not been let. Most of these linking sections are included, with the first and last sections, by Harry Stone in his *Uncollected Writings of CD*, II, 595–617, and the attributions suggested; but the frame-story was evidently done in close collaboration.

[1] The Christmas No. was published on 7 Dec; the title, with "Early in December", had been announced in the Nos for 6, 13 and 20 Nov; the exact date was announced in the No. for 4 Dec, XIX, 240.

[2] Anna Dickens had petitioned for judicial separation in the new Matrimonial Court of Probate and Divorce, alleging adultery, on 30 Oct 58 (Principal Probate Registry: Divorce Files). Frederick denied adultery or, alternatively, claimed that, "if any, [*it*] was condoned" (*ibid.*, 6 Dec 58), since, after their first separation in June 1854, Anna had returned to live with him in Jan 1855 (in a succession of 10 different addresses, mainly in London and Surrey). For the Judge's Decree for judicial separation, see next vol.

[3] CD was clearly hoping for a Deed of "voluntary separation" without publicity.

[4] No. 63.

[5] Edwin John James, QC: see *To* Thackeray, 24 Nov and *fn*.

To ROBERT McTEAR,[1] 22 NOVEMBER 1858*

MS Glasgow University Library. *Address:* Robert McTear[2] Esquire | 21 Gordon Street | Glasgow.

TAVISTOCK HOUSE, | TAVISTOCK SQUARE, LONDON. W.C.
Monday Evening, Twenty Second November 1858

Dear Sir

I am truly obliged to you for your kind letter, and am truly touched by the affectionate and earnest remembrance of my esteemed friend, Sheridan Knowles.[3] But here my interest in the subject ends. To my great surprise and indignation I was put up as a "Candidate" (God save me!) for the Lord Rectorship of the College, without my own knowledge or consent.[4] As soon as the independent students (*very* independent, as it appeared to me), thought fit to notify that circumstance to me, I replied that if I were elected, I should decline the office,[5] and that I had a constitutional objection to being so coolly handled.

Dear Sir | Faithfully Yours

Robert McTear[2] Esquire CHARLES DICKENS

To W. M. THACKERAY, 24 NOVEMBER 1858

Text from Edmund Yates, *Mr. Thackeray, Mr. Yates, and the Garrick Club*, p. 13.

TAVISTOCK HOUSE, | TAVISTOCK SQUARE, LONDON. W.C.
Wednesday, 24th November, 1858.

My dear Thackeray,

Without a word of prelude, I wish this note to revert to a subject on which I said six words to you at the Athenaeum when I last saw you.[6]

Coming home from my country work, I find Mr. Edwin James's[7] opinion taken on

[1] Robert McTear, of Robert McTear & Kempt, Glasgow auctioneers, of 33 St Mary's Hall and 37 Renfield St.

[2] CD wrote "McGear" by mistake here and at the end of the letter.

[3] James Sheridan ("Paddy") Knowles (1784–1862; *DNB*), dramatist: see Vols. II, p. 71*n* and V, p. 222*n*. To support CD, Knowles had evidently written a letter to a Glasgow paper (but publication not found), recording CD's obtaining of help from the Royal Literary Fund for Joseph Haydn (see Vol. V, p. 685 and *n*). In their final broadside of 15 Nov, the Glasgow Independent students referred to this letter to win CD further support: see Ada Nisbet, "Dickens Loses an Election", *Princeton University Library Chronicle*, Summer 1950, XI, 157 (facsimile of broadside, facing p. 164).

[4] The Independent students had announced their nomination of CD on 10 Nov, on the withdrawal of their first candidate, Lord Glencorse, Lord Advocate of Scotland. The Conservatives' candidate was Bulwer Lytton and the Liberals', Lord Shaftesbury. The results of the election, held on 15 Nov, were: Bulwer Lytton 217 votes, Shaftesbury 204, and CD 69. For fuller account, see *ibid.*, pp. 157–76.

[5] No mention of this was made in any of the four broadsides put out in CD's support by the Independents.

[6] See *To* Yates, 15 June and *fn*.

[7] Edwin John James, QC (1812–82; *DNB*), very successful and highly-paid barrister; Recorder of Brighton 1855–61; MP for Marylebone 1858–61. Had in Apr 1858 successfully defended Dr Simon Bernard, charged with conspiring with Orsini to kill Napoleon III (see *To* Delane, 28 Feb 58, *fn*). The model for Stryver in *A Tale of Two Cities*—based on CD's one visit to his chambers (according to Edmund Yates, *Recollections and Experiences*, II, 30–1). Bankrupt and disbarred for unprofessional conduct 1861; practised in New York and later played on New York stage.

this painful question of the Garrick and Mr. Edmund Yates.[1] I find it strong on the illegality of the Garrick proceeding. Not to complicate this note or give it a formal appearance, I forbear from copying the opinion; but I have asked to see it, and I have it, and I want to make no secret from you of a word of it.

I find Mr. Edwin James retained on the one side; I hear and read of the Attorney-General[2] being retained on the other. Let me, in this state of things, ask you a plain question.

Can any conference be held between me, as representing Mr. Yates, and an appointed friend of yours, as representing you, with the hope and purpose of some quiet accommodation of this deplorable matter, which will satisfy the feelings of all concerned?

It is right that, in putting this to you, I should tell you that Mr. Yates, when you first wrote to him, brought your letter to me. He had recently done me a manly service I can never forget, in some private distress of mine (generally within your knowledge),[3] and he naturally thought of me as his friend in an emergency. I told him that his article was not to be defended; but I confirmed him in his opinion, that it was not reasonably possible for him to set right what was amiss, on the receipt of a letter couched in the very strong terms you had employed. When you appealed to the Garrick Committee and they called their General Meeting, I said at that meeting that you and I had been on good terms for many years, and that I was very sorry to find myself opposed to you; but that I was clear that the Committee had nothing on earth to do with it, and that in the strength of my conviction I should go against them.[4]

If this mediation that I have suggested can take place, I shall be heartily glad to do my best in it—and God knows in no hostile spirit towards any one, least of all to you. If it cannot take place, the thing is at least no worse than it was; and you will burn this letter and I will burn your answer.

Yours faithfully,

W. M. Thackeray, Esq. CHARLES DICKENS[5]

[1] After deliberately seeking physical ejection from the Club, Yates brought an action against the Secretary, but found that he had to sue the Trustees through Chancery; this he abandoned because of the probable cost: see Edmund Yates, *Mr Thackeray, Mr Yates and the Garrick Club*, pp. 11–12 and *Recollections and Experiences*, II, 29–31.

[2] Sir Fitzroy Kelly: see *To* Forster, 29–30 Mar 56, .

[3] In a note in *Town Talk*, 19 June, headed "CHARLES DICKENS", Yates had written: "The higher the pedestal to which a man, by the exercise of honour, talent, and industry, has raised himself, the more numerous are his detractors, the more bitter his opponents.... A domestic matter, with which the general public cannot have the slightest concern, and into which it is clearly not our province to enter, has given occasion for the fabrication of certain lies, so preposterous in their malice, as almost to defeat the design of their concocters; but the very nature of which, involving as it did the name of most innocent and worthy persons, demanded instant denial. This denial Mr. Dickens has made in a most solemn and earnest public statement, a statement breathing truth in every line ..." (whole passage reprinted in *D*, XXXV [1939], 91).

[4] He had resigned from the Committee after the meeting: see *To* the Committee of the Garrick Club, 12 July 1858.

[5] Thackeray replied on 26 Nov: "Dear Dickens,—I grieve to gather from your letter that you were Mr. Yates's adviser in the dispute between me and him. His letter was the cause of my appeal to the Garrick Club for protection from insults against which I had no other remedy. | I placed my grievance before the Committee of the Club as the only place where I have been accustomed to meet Mr. Yates. They gave me their opinion of his conduct and of the

To DR JOHN ELLIOTSON, 25 NOVEMBER 1858

Extract in Anderson Galleries catalogue, Apr 1916; *MS* 1 p.; addressed Dr Elliotson.

Tavistock House | November Twenty-Fifth 1858

The husband of that lady whom I mesmerised in [Genoa][1] long ago, and whose case is so very remarkable, is in town for a few days.[2] ... Can you dine with us?

To W. H. WILLS, 25 NOVEMBER 1858

MS Huntington Library.

OFFICE OF HOUSEHOLD WORDS,
Thursday Twenty Fifth Novr. 1858

My Dear Wills.

I want to prepare you for an H.W. disappointment, in case it should come off. My introduced paper for the Xmas No.[3] involves such an odd idea—which appears to me so humourous, and so available at greater length—that I am debating whether

reparation which lay in his power. Not satisfied with their sentence, Mr. Yates called for a General Meeting; and, the meeting which he had called having declared against him, he declines the jurisdiction which he had asked for, and says he will have recourse to lawyers. | You say that Mr. Edwin James is strongly of opinion that the conduct of the Club is illegal. On this point I can give no sort of judgment: nor can I conceive that the Club will be frightened, by the opinion of any lawyer, out of their own sense of the justice and honour which ought to obtain among gentlemen. | Ever since I submitted my case to the Club, I have had, and can have, no part in the dispute. It is for them to judge if any reconcilement is possible with your friend. I subjoin the copy of a letter which I wrote to the Committee, and refer you to them for the issue. | Yours, &c., | W. M. Thackeray." (Edmund Yates, *Mr Thackeray, Mr Yates and the Garrick Club*, p. 14.) On 28 Nov Thackeray passed on to the Committee CD's proposal for a conference, ending his letter: "If you can devise any peaceful means for ending [*the dispute*], No one will be better pleased" than he would be (*ibid.*). On 2 Dec Thackeray wrote to John Blackwood: "But the Beauty of Beauties now comes out that *Dickens advised Yates throughout*. Edwin James says he wrote every word of Yates's letters. | Isn't it a noble creature?" And, sending him a copy of CD's letter some days later, he wrote: "You may see by the enclosed whether Dickens had a share in the business or not. Edwin James told him he should put him in the box and make him confess whether or no—and upon this the godlike man writes me word of his counseling Yates. O for shame, for shame! But what pent up animosities and long cherished hatred doesn't one see in the business! 'There's my rival, stab him now, Yates—' and the poor young man thrusts out his unlucky paw.... | Send me back the letter of the Great Moralist. Do you read of him prating at Coventry about his [']heart of hearts' and at Manchester talking of [']Domini Nostri'? O me O me!" (given in Gordon N. Ray, *Thackeray: the Age of Wisdom*, 1958, pp. 285–6).

[1] Catalogue wrongly gives "Geneva". For CD's mesmerizing Mme de la Rue in 1844–5, mainly in Genoa, see Vol. IV, p. 243*n* and *passim*.

[2] For Elliotson's interest in the case, see Vol. VII, p. 288 and *n*.

[3] "Going into Society", the story of Mr Chops, the dwarf, told by the showman, Mr Magsman.

or no I shall cancel the paper (it has gone to the Printer's to day),[1] and make it the Pivot round which my next book shall revolve.[2]

Ever Faithfully
CD.

To W. BLANCHARD JERROLD, 26 NOVEMBER 1858

MS Mr Douglas Jerrold. *Address:* Blanchard Jerrold Esquire | Fairfield Farm | near | Broadstairs | Kent.

TAVISTOCK HOUSE, | TAVISTOCK SQUARE, LONDON. W.C.
Friday Twenty Sixth November 1858

My Dear William Jerrold

I enclose you the few lines I have written.[3] Do what you like with them, and consider them yours, not mine. [a]It has been a gloomy task, and has made my heart heavy.

Faithfully Yours
CHARLES DICKENS[a]

To MESSRS SMITH ELDER & CO.,[4] 26 NOVEMBER 1858

MS Messrs John Murray (Publishers) Ltd.

TAVISTOCK HOUSE, | TAVISTOCK SQUARE, LONDON. W.C.
Friday Twenty Sixth November 1858

Gentlemen

I beg to acknowledge the receipt of your letter of yesterday's date. I had previously written to Mr. Horne, expressing my regret that I could not undertake to negociate with any Manager respecting any Tragedy; and that I could, consequently, take no charge of this Tragedy.[5]

Faithfully Yours

Messrs. Smith Elder[6] and Co. CHARLES DICKENS

[1] Comma in MS; bracket not closed.

[2] The "next book" can hardly be what became *A Tale of Two Cities*; its "Pivot" was already foreseen (see *To* Forster, 27 Jan) and is not "humourous". CD's imagination is running ahead, and the phrasing curiously resembles what Forster quotes as "the germ of Pip and Magwitch" (F, IX, iii, 733) in 1860. Dr Margaret Cardwell, in her Introduction to the Clarendon *Great Expectations*, 1993, argues that certain resemblances of detail show that "the story used in the event for the 1858 Christmas number ... had its influence in the later novel" and that "threads might gradually, even subconsciously, have been coming together in Dickens's mind for some time before the writing began in 1860" (pp. xiv–xv).

[3] For the enclosure, see Appx K. Blanchard Jerrold's *Life* of his father was announced as "Now Ready" on 15 Dec. CD read it on Christmas Day; for his appreciative letter about it to Jerrold on 11 Jan 59, see next vol.

[aa] MDGH 1882, 1893 and N give the last sentence only, preceded by dots, and followed immediately by the enclosure, as if it were part of the letter itself; neither letter nor enclosure given in MDGH 1880.

[4] Publishers and booksellers, of 65 Cornhill and 4 White Lion Court, Cornhill.

[5] See *To* Horne, 27 Oct 58 and *fn.* Horne must at the same time have written to Smith Elder offering the manuscript for publication.

[6] CD in haste (and perhaps exasperation) wrote "Eder".

To JOHN FORSTER for MESSRS BRADBURY & EVANS, 27 NOVEMBER 1858

MS Messrs Farrer & Co.

Acting under the Power of Attorney which I hold from Mr. Dickens, I address this letter to you on the subject of Household Words.

The publication being discontinued Six months hence, under the letter of the Resolution passed at the Special Meeting, such discontinuance will involve Mr. Dickens in some new business arrangements for which he must provide beforehand, and which he must set about soon. It is therefore essential that I should know from you, within a given short time, whether you are disposed to treat with Mr. Dickens for the sale to him of your interest in the work.

Should you inform me within fourteen days from this date that you are disposed to sell that interest to Mr. Dickens, I shall be prepared to offer you a price for it. Should you make no communication to me to that effect within that time, please to understand that Mr. Dickens can no longer entertain the idea of the purchase, and will finally abandon it.

To EDMUND YATES, [?28 NOVEMBER 1858]

Extract in Edmund Yates, *Mr. Thackeray, Mr. Yates, and the Garrick Club*, p. 13. *Date:* on or very soon after 28 Nov 58.

As the receiver of my letter did not respect the confidence in which it addressed him, there can be none left for you to violate. I send you what I wrote to Thackeray, and what he wrote to me,[1] and you are at perfect liberty to print the two.[2] I am, of course, your authority for doing so.

To H. G. ADAMS, 30 NOVEMBER 1858*

MS Morgan Library.

TAVISTOCK HOUSE, | TAVISTOCK SQUARE, LONDON. W.C.
Tuesday Thirtieth November, 1858.

My Dear Sir

Mr. Arthur Smith is in Paris for a few days, and I therefore answer your letter[3] without waiting for him.

[1] i.e. on 26 Nov. Thackeray also enclosed a copy of his letter to the Committee, dated 28 Nov.

[2] See *To* Thackeray, 24 Nov and *fn.*

[3] Inviting him to give a paid reading to the Chatham and Rochester Mechanics' Institute.

FIRST, AS TO THE SUBJECT. YOU CAN HAVE[1]

The Poor Traveller Boots at the Holly Tree Inn and Mrs. Gamp:[2]	all one reading, observe

or:

Little Dombey and The Trial from Pickwick	Again, one reading, observe.

Pray make your own choice.[3] There is no difference in respect of the time occupied. Each reading is well within two hours—ten minutes to spare, probably.

I do not consider that I have any right to object to your filling any places you *can* fill.[4]

Will you send me (to Gad's Hill, as the time comes on) 4 Gallery Seats, and 2 Below, Reserved.[5] But I must beg to have it distinctly understood that I pay for these.

I think our former light[6] will do very well. But if Mr. Arthur Smith should wish to substitute our own[7] (on just the same plan), he will let you know.

You know, I assume, that Little Dombey ends with the child's Death? It is always a very great impression, and a very sad one. But the Trial is very merry.

In the other reading, the opening scene of the Poor Traveller belongs to Chatham. Moreover, that Reading is by far the merrier of the two. It has less story, however.

This, to assist your decision. I will do my best with either.

Or, there is the Chimes—*very*[8] dramatic, but very melancholy on the whole.

Faithfully Yours

CD.

[1] Underlined with short double strokes.

[2] Two short strokes to divide the suggested programmes.

[3] *Little Dombey* and *The Trial* were chosen. The reading was given in the Lecture Hall, Chatham, on 29 Dec. Booking was opened "on or after Monday 20th instant" (Bill, reproduced in *CD, 1812–70*, Berg Collection, 1970, p. 120). The *Rochester, Chatham and Strood Gazette*, 4 Jan 59, reported that, from the applause, it was "a perfect success"; and, of *Little Dombey*, "so completely was it realized, that the effect was perfectly electrical".

[4] Although CD received a fee, the sale of seats left "a large balance" to the Institute; and CD, its President, added £5 himself (*Rochester, Chatham and Strood Gazette*, 4 Jan 59).

[5] For Georgina, Mamie, Henry, "Plorn", Wilkie Collins and J. T. Gordon.

[6] i.e. that used at his previous reading on 22 Dec 57.

[7] The special gas battens taken to each reading.

[8] Heavily underlined.

To ALBERT SMITH,[1] 1 DECEMBER 1858

Text from MDGH, III, 186.

TAVISTOCK HOUSE,|TAVISTOCK SQUARE, LONDON. W.C.
Wednesday Night, 1st December, 1858

My dear Albert,

I cannot tell you how grieved I am for poor dear Arthur (even you can hardly love him better than I do), or with what anxiety I shall wait for further news of him.[2]

Pray let me know how he is to-morrow. Tell them at home that Olliffe is the kindest and gentlest of men—a man of rare experience and opportunity—perfect master of his profession, and to be confidently and implicitly relied upon. There is no man alive, in whose hands I would more thankfully trust myself.

I will write a cheery word to the dear fellow in the morning.

Ever faithfully,
[CHARLES DICKENS]

To ARTHUR SMITH, 2 DECEMBER 1858

Text from MDGH, III, 187.

TAVISTOCK HOUSE,|TAVISTOCK SQUARE, LONDON. W.C.
Thursday, 2nd December, 1858.

My dear Arthur,

I cannot tell you how surprised and grieved I was last night to hear from Albert of your severe illness. It is not my present intention to give you the trouble of reading anything like a letter, but I MUST send you my loving word, and tell you how we all think of you.

And here am I going off to-morrow to that meeting at Manchester without *you!*[3] the wildest and most impossible of moves as it seems to me. And to think of my coming back by Coventry, on Saturday, to receive the chronometer—also without you![4]

If you don't get perfectly well soon, my dear old fellow, I shall come over to Paris to look after you, and to tell Olliffe (give him my love, and the same for Lady Olliffe) what a Blessing he is.

With kindest regards to Mrs. Arthur[5] and her sister,[6]

Ever heartily and affectionately yours
[CHARLES DICKENS]

[1] Smith had returned from China, via Marseilles and Paris, arriving on 14 Nov. On 22 Dec he began a new and very popular entertainment, "China", at the Egyptian Hall. On 1 Aug 59 he married Mary Lucy Keeley (*d.* 19 Mar 70), actress, daughter of the actor Robert Keeley.

[2] See *To* Miss Coutts, 13 Dec.

[3] CD was Chairman at the Prize-giving of the Institutional Association of Lancashire and Cheshire, held on 3 Dec. For his speech, in which he strongly approved of the prize-winners being working-men, see *Speeches*, ed. K. J. Fielding, pp. 278–85.

[4] See *To* Paxton, 6 Dec and *fn.*

[5] Not further identified.

[6] Unidentified.

To COLIN RAE BROWN, 6 DECEMBER 1858

MS Mitchell Library, Glasgow.

TAVISTOCK HOUSE, | TAVISTOCK SQUARE, LONDON. W.C.
Monday Sixth December, 1858.

Mr. Charles Dickens presents his compliments to Mr. Brown, and regrets that his engagements do not admit of his accepting the invitation with which he is honored, to the Glasgow Burns Festival[1] under the distinguished presidency of Sir Archibald Alison.[2]

To FREDERIC CHAPMAN,[3] 6 DECEMBER 1858*

MS Benoliel Collection. *Address:* Fred. Chapman Esquire | 193 Piccadilly | W.

TAVISTOCK HOUSE, | TAVISTOCK SQUARE, LONDON. W.C.
Monday Sixth December, 1858.

Dear Sir

I am exceedingly glad to hear from yourself of the advancement in your prospects. Let me cordially congratulate you upon it. I am quite sure that Mr. Chapman has exercised a sound as well as a kind discretion in his choice of a business-partner,[4] and I beg you to accept my best wishes for your joint success.

Dear Sir | Faithfully Yours

Frederic Chapman Esquire CHARLES DICKENS

To SIR JOSEPH PAXTON, 6 DECEMBER 1858

MS Dr M. G. J. Beets.

TAVISTOCK HOUSE, | TAVISTOCK SQUARE, LONDON. W.C.
Monday Sixth December 1858.

My Dear Paxton

I received your letter on Friday morning as I was starting for Manchester: where I had to preside at a Meeting, before going to Coventry. I cannot tell you how it surprised and vexed me. For some days I had been expecting to hear from you; and your letter was so different from anything I *had* expected, that it surprised me as much as it annoyed me—which is saying a great deal.

[1] Brown was Hon. Secretary of the Committee which organized the Glasgow Burns Centenary Celebration; there was a Festival in Glasgow on 25 Jan 59 and a Centenary Dinner in the City Hall that night. CD must by now have accepted Brown's denial that he had spread false rumours; he had decided not to bring an action for slander against him: see *To* McPhail, 16 Oct and *fnn*.

[2] Sir Archibald Alison, Bart (1792–1867; *DNB*), lawyer and historian, whom CD had met in Glasgow in Dec 47: see Vol. V, p. 193*n*.

[3] Frederic Chapman (1823–95), Edward Chapman's cousin; joined Chapman & Hall 1841; chief proprietor 1864; managing director 1880–95. See later vols.

[4] Edward Chapman had clearly promoted him, in anticipation of his own planned retirement six years later. On 14 June 1865, Carlyle described him to R. W. Emerson as "my Publisher (a new Chapman, very unlike the old)" (*The Correspondence of Emerson and Carlyle*, ed. Joseph Slater, 1964, p. 543).

Of course you know the local lights and shadows of Coventry, better than I do; but I am strongly of opinion that Mr. Whitten's[1] discretion is not remarkable, and that in this matter he made a mistake. I shewed him plainly that I thought so, and he told me of the additional correspondence he had had with you. It appeared to me, at the little dinner,[2] quite clear that there was no suspicion of the real state of the case, and that if you had been there you would have been heartily received.[3] The members were toasted;[4] and Mr. Whitten, in returning thanks for you, said you were "prevented from coming, by an important engagement".[5] He did not make the faintest reference to his having done any thing to keep you away.

I talked of you to all of them, and I considered with some anxiety whether I should refer to your absence, in speaking. After a careful study of our Blunderheaded Whitten, I came to the conclusion that I had better not. For I saw that (being uneasy), if he could only find a hole big enough to put his foot in, he would unquestionably do it, and that what I had to do, was, to fill up all the holes in his way. I therefore did my very best to hold them all together, in the brightest condition of general good humour. My hope and belief are that I succeeded, and that my inevitable association with you in their minds, is established as a pleasant (and possibly, at some time, not an unserviceable) one.

The whole thing passed brilliantly,[6] and Wren Hoskyns[7] in the chair was exceedingly hearty and manly about you.[8] If there were really any sore place before, I think the Dinner had a very wholesome effect upon it. But that Mr. Whitten's tactics were timid and wrong, I feel quite convinced.

Many thanks for the Game, which arrived in admirable condition. I am glad to

[1] Misspelt by CD. James Sibley Whittem, of Coundon, near Coventry.

[2] Given to CD at the Castle Hotel, Coventry, on 4 Dec; he was presented with a gold watch subscribed for after his reading for the Coventry Institute the previous Dec: see *To* Paxton, 23 Dec 57. The *Coventry Herald*, 10 Dec, devoted $3\frac{1}{2}$ columns to the occasion. For CD's speech of thanks, see *Speeches*, ed. K. J. Fielding, p. 286. The inscription on the watch, a repeater, made in Coventry, bore tribute to his "eminent services in the interests of humanity", as well as to his kindness to "his friends in Coventry". In his Will CD left the watch to his "dear and trusty friend John Forster", who bequeathed it to Carlyle. Wills was present at the Dinner and toasted as sub-editor of *HW*.

[3] Whittem had evidently advised Paxton not to attend the Dinner, perhaps because the other member for the City, Edward Ellice, could not be present. Paxton may have originally been invited to take the chair, since both Hoskyns, as Chairman, and Whittem, as seconder of the presentation to CD, began their speeches by saying that they "unexpectedly" found themselves in those positions.

[4] Hoskyns, proposing the toast, praised Paxton as the only member he knew personally. Whittem, responding, pointed out "the vast claims" of Ellice.

[5] Whittem said that Paxton's absence was "unavoidable": Paxton had written to him to say that only "business of the utmost importance" in London had kept him away.

[6] For CD's enjoyment of the occasion, see *To* Miss Coutts, 13 Dec. He would have been particularly pleased with Hoskyns's saying that he had "done more than any other man living to help to close the gulf" between rich and poor; and with Whittem's comment that in all CD's writings there was not "a single word that tended to irritate one class of society against another" (*Coventry Herald*, 14 Dec).

[7] Chandos Wren Hoskyns (1812–76; *DNB*), of Wroxall Abbey, Warwickshire, second son of Sir Hungerford Hoskyns, Bart; MP for Hereford 1869–70: see *To* Hoskyns, 15 Dec and *fnn*, and later vols.

[8] Paying tribute to the Crystal Palace, Hoskyns also mentioned Paxton's proposal that Shakespeare's house at Stratford be preserved "by a coating of glass". He compared Paxton with CD in aiming at "the improvement of the moral and social condition of the people", through "mechanical art" (*Coventry Herald*, 10 Dec).

find you writing hopefully of your past trouble, and am glad I can write hopefully of mine. Can't you propose a day for coming to dine with me (without company), and smoking a cigar?

Faithfully Always

Sir Joseph Paxton. CHARLES DICKENS

To JAMES PAYN, 6 DECEMBER 1858

MS University of California, Los Angeles.

TAVISTOCK HOUSE, | TAVISTOCK SQUARE, LONDON. W.C.
Monday Sixth December, 1858.

My Dear Mr. Payn

I have received your letter with mingled regret and pleasure. I am heartily sorry to lose you as a fellow-workman,[1] but heartily glad to have gained you as a friend.

In that relation, you must remember that you incur the penalty of not coming to London without coming to see us here. My daughters will be delighted to revert to the day when you were in danger of perpetual imprisonment at Hawthornden.[2] They have often spoken of it since, and always with a great regard for you.

As they have carried off the Forster Brothers[3] (I see I have written it "Forster", because I am always writing to my friend of that name),[4] I am not yet in a condition to say I have made their acquaintance. But you may be sure that I shall not fail to read that book with true interest.

Believe me | Very faithfully Yours

J. Payn Esquire CHARLES DICKENS

To UNKNOWN CORRESPONDENT, 6 DECEMBER 1858

Mention in Sotheby's catalogue, Dec 1963; *MS* 1 p.; dated 6 Dec 58.

Regretting his inability to comply with a request made by his correspondent.

To HENRY BICKNELL,[5] 9 DECEMBER 1858

Mention in J. W. Jarvis "Dickens catalogue", 1884; *MS* 2 pp.; dated Tavistock House, 9 Dec 58; addressed Henry Bicknell Esquire, Crystal Palace.

[1] Payn had continued to contribute to *HW* after his appointment as co-editor of *Chambers's Journal*; his last contribution, "Her First Appearance", appeared on 11 Dec (XIX, 29).

[2] See *To* Payn, 29 Sep 58, *fn*.

[3] *The Foster Brothers*, 1859, but just published, anonymously; Payn's first novel, "being the History of the School and College Life of Two Young Men".

[4] Payn records in *Some Literary Recollections*, p. 266, that he sent CD's letter to Forster after the first vol of *Life of CD* appeared, i.e. in 1872.

[5] About his visit to the Crystal Palace on 11 Dec, with de la Rue; see *To* Miss Coutts, 13 Dec.

To MISS MARY BOYLE, 9 DECEMBER 1858*

MS Morgan Library.

TAVISTOCK HOUSE, | TAVISTOCK SQUARE, LONDON. W.C.
Thursday Ninth December 1858.

My Dear Mary.

I am under no apprehension that you will think me unmindful of your affectionate and true friendship, because I have so long detained the enclosed letter.[1] I have a perfect conviction that you know my heart better.

It reached me in Edinburgh, when my sense of cruel wrong was strongest within me. I had then newly resolved to put the subject away from me, and to know no more of it. I made up my mind, therefore, that I would not read even this letter. And to this minute I never have read one word of it.

Constituted to do the work that is in me, I am a man full of passion and energy, and my own wild way that I must go, is often—at the best—wild enough. But vengeance and hatred have never had a place in my breast. Some little while ago, I felt that they were only to be kept out by this course. So I took it, and hold to it.

Receive my fervent thanks, and ever believe me

Your affectionate | And grateful friend

Miss Mary Boyle. CHARLES DICKENS

To EMILE DE LA RUE, 10 DECEMBER 1858*

MS Berg Collection.

TAVISTOCK HOUSE, | TAVISTOCK SQUARE, LONDON. W.C.
Friday Tenth December 1858.

My Dear De la Rue

I regret to say that Albert Smith's good brother has had a relapse, and that Albert has been hurriedly summoned to Paris, to see him.[2] We will therefore meet tomorrow, *at the Household Words office at One precisely*.

Ever Faithfully
CHARLES DICKENS

To MISS BURDETT COUTTS, 13 DECEMBER 1858

MS Morgan Library.

TAVISTOCK HOUSE, | TAVISTOCK SQUARE, LONDON. W.C.
Monday Thirteenth December, 1858.

My Dear Miss Coutts.

Wills sent Mrs. Brown *her* paper from Manchester, and I sent *you* another paper at the same time.[3]

[1] Clearly a letter in reply to his of 10 Sep, received by CD at Edinburgh, 28–30 Sep.

[2] See 19 Aug 57.

[3] Assuming these were separate copies of the same paper, almost certainly the *Manchester Guardian*, 4 Dec; for his speech, reported there, see *To* Arthur Smith, 2 Dec and *fn*.

Mrs. Matthews's case is clearly hopeless. I have had another letter from her this morning, which I have put in the fire. Her former letter, and the Bishop's,[1] I enclose.

You will be sorry to hear that Mr. Arthur Smith, going over to Paris at the close of our labors, was taken ill there with diptheria[2] and Scarlet fever, and has been in an alarming state. He is now recovering, though very weak and much reduced. The Work of our tour was a little too hard for him, I fear. I thank God that I have been, and am, wonderfully well, and that I have never felt the fatigue; though it came upon me under no commonly harassing circumstances, when I would sometimes as soon have laid myself down and given up all, as I would have gone into a bright crowd and read.

It is to be hoped you have brighter weather on the Devonshire Coast[3] than we have here. London, I really think, was never so dark for so many days together as it has been in this present month. It is like living in a large dirty slate. On Saturday I took a foreign friend from Genoa, down to the Crystal Palace. I asked him to try to imagine the Sun shining down through the glass, and making broad lights and shadows. He said he tried very hard, but he couldn't imagine the sun shining within fifty miles of London under any circumstances.[4]

The Coventry people have given me a seventy five Guinea Watch, which is chronometer, Repeater, and every other terrible Machine that a watch *can* be. It was very feelingly and pleasantly given, and I prize it highly.

This is all the news I have—except that I send my love to Mrs. Brown—which is no news—and that I am ever—which is no news either—

My Dear Miss Coutts | Most Faithfully and affecy. Yours

CHARLES DICKENS

To FRANK STONE, 13 DECEMBER 1858

Text from MDGH, II, 82.

TAVISTOCK HOUSE, | TAVISTOCK SQUARE, LONDON. W.C.

Monday, Dec. 13th, 1858.

My dear Stone,

Many thanks for these discourses.[5] They are very good, I think, as expressing what many men have felt and thought; otherwise not specially remarkable. They have one fatal mistake, which is a canker at the foot of their ever being widely useful. Half the misery and hypocrisy of the Christian world arises (as I take it) from a stubborn determination to refuse the New Testament as a sufficient guide in itself, and to force the Old Testament into alliance with it—whereof comes all manner of

[1] The Bishop of Ripon, Robert Bickersteth (1816–84; *DNB*), had written, in answer to Miss Coutts's enquiry, that Mrs Matthews had applied widely for help; he had relieved her "to some small extent". "Your generosity to her has been far beyond what one [*Diocesan*] Society could afford to any one case." He could not strongly recommend her appeal. (MS Morgan.)

[2] Thus in MS. The new name for what was known, by the English, as "Boulogne sore throat".

[3] At Torquay.

[4] Fog and cloud were continuous from 5 to 18 Dec.

[5] Not discovered; perhaps submitted for *HW* by a friend of Stone's.

camel-swallowing and of gnat-straining.[1] But so to resent this miserable error, or to (by any implication) depreciate the divine goodness and beauty of the New Testament, is to commit even a worse error. And to class Jesus Christ with Mahomet is simply audacity and folly. I might as well hoist myself on to a high platform, to inform my disciples that the lives of King George the Fourth and of King Alfred the Great belonged to one and the same category.

Ever affectionately
[CHARLES DICKENS]

To MESSRS BRADBURY & EVANS, 14 DECEMBER 1858*

MS (draft in CD's hand with Forster's amendments, see below) Messrs Farrer & Co.

TAVISTOCK HOUSE, | TAVISTOCK SQUARE, LONDON. W.C.[2]
Tuesday 14th. December 1858

Dear Sirs

Will you please to understand that in making the present communication to you,[3] I do not waive or suspend a word of the Resolution passed at the last Meeting of the proprietors of Household Words.

[a]On the part of Mr Dickens[a] I beg finally to inform you, that [a]Mr. Dickens[a] ⟨is willing to pay⟩[4] offers[5] the sum of One Thousand ⟨Eighteen Hundred⟩[4] Pounds for your share in the copyright of Household Words, and[6] ⟨will⟩[4] [a]further is willing to[a] purchase your ⟨share⟩[4] interest in the Stock &c at a valuation;—the whole to be paid in ready money.[7]

[1] Cf. "Ye blind guides, which strain at a gnat and swallow a camel", Matthew 23: 24.

[2] Crossed out; "W | 46 Montagu Square" in Forster's hand written above.

[3] Forster has inserted: "under the Power of Attorney I hold from Mr. Dickens,"

[aa] Deleted by Forster.

[4] Deleted by CD.

[5] Amended by Forster to "I offer you".

[6] Forster inserts "I also offer to".

[7] Forster ends with "Y.v.t. | J.F. | Messrs B & E".

To DR CHARLES WEST,[1] 15 DECEMBER 1858†

MS Arnold U. Zeigler.

TAVISTOCK HOUSE,|TAVISTOCK SQUARE, LONDON. W.C.
Wednesday Fifteenth December, 1858.

My Dear Sir

I am sorry that as I read on Christmas Eve,[2] I cannot come to see the interesting sight to which you invite me.[3]

But as you may perhaps be free to come to see (and hear) me instead, I will beg Mr. Arthur Smith to send you two stalls.

Faithfully Yours
CHARLES DICKENS

Dr. West

To MISS ELLA MARIA WINTER, 15 DECEMBER 1858

MS Dickens House.

TAVISTOCK HOUSE,|TAVISTOCK SQUARE, LONDON. W.C.
Fifteenth December, 1858

My Dear little friend.

I have received your pretty book-marker with the greatest pleasure, and you may be sure that it will always lie snugly in some book or other, on some table or other, here in my own study. It will always be valuable to me for your sake, and will often and often carry my mind back to the days when your Mamma was a girl, and I was a boy, and very few people knew the name of

Your affectionate
CHARLES DICKENS

Miss Winter.

[1] Charles West (1816–98; *DNB*), MB, FRCP, physician to the Hospital for Sick Children, Great Ormond St, since 1852 and its virtual founder (see Jules Klosky, *Mutual Friends*, *passim*). Previously physician, Infirmary for Children; lecturer in midwifery, St Bartholomew's Hospital, 1848–60; Harveian Orator 1874; published *Diseases of Infancy and Childhood*, 1848, *Diseases of Women*, 1856, and medical papers.

[2] The first of three Christmas readings given on 24 and 27 Dec and 6 Jan 59. At each he read the *Carol* and *The Trial* in St Martin's Hall, to a packed audience; the Christmas Eve audience included Lord Chief Justice Campbell, whom the *Morning Chronicle*, 25 Dec, reported as greatly enjoying *The Trial*. "Without exaggeration, [CD] is hardly less perfect as an actor than a writer."

[3] No doubt an entertainment at the Hospital for Sick Children.

To CHANDOS WREN HOSKYNS,[1] 15 DECEMBER 1858

MS Brotherton Library, Leeds.

TAVISTOCK HOUSE, | TAVISTOCK SQUARE, LONDON. W.C.
Wednesday Evening Fifteenth December | 1858.

My Dear Sir.

I cannot tell you with what cordial pleasure I have received your letter and re-read your excellent book.[2] Nor, what uncommon gratification I had in meeting you at Coventry and finding you exactly what I had wished you to be. This is not company-speech, I know, but it is simply hearty and true. Your share in that evening has left an impression on my mind which it will always be delightful to me to renew. And I do really hope that it may be reserved for us—in a very different spirit from the usual pulpit-use of the phrase—to "improve the occasion".

Your touching remembrance of our dear Talfourd has struck home to my heart.[3]

Be assured that I shall never come into your neighbourhood, without presenting my own personal clay on the stiff Warwickshire soil you have made so famous. I hope and believe that you will not come to London without doing as much for me. And between our joint endeavours, it will be hard indeed if we do not now and then meet, to become more intimate.

I think I told you that I live, in the summer, on the top of the veritable Gad's Hill where Falstaff committed that little indiscretion. It was done, just outside my house. Our highwaymen in that country have degenerated into tramps, and our Carriers are Pickford and Co. But Rochester is still a queer old place with a savage old castle in it—worth your seeing—and though I have no Farm and no soil but chalk, I have a prospect, and a Mulberry Tree, and a Welcome.[4]

In the earnest hope that we shall refer many a pleasant hour in the future, back to the good offices of our good friends at Coventry, believe me

Very faithfully Yours

Chandos Wren Hoskyns Esquire CHARLES DICKENS

[1] Author of influential articles and books on agriculture and land tenure; evidently a friend of Paxton, through whom CD would know of him and his work. Regular contributor to the *Agricultural Gazette* from 1844, including "Tales of a Landlord"; gave a popular course on the history of agriculture to the Manchester Athenaeum in 1849. See later vols.

[2] *Talpa* [Latin for "mole"]; *or, The Chronicles of a Clay Farm*, 1852; Hoskyns had clearly given him the 4th edn, 1857. There were six edns by 1865. The 1st edn, by "C.W.H.", embodied Hoskyns's contributions to the *Agricultural Gazette* and was illustrated with 24 vignettes by Cruikshank; a lively, personal and humorous account of the author's farming experience, with many literary allusions, it had much to appeal to CD: e.g., Hoskyns's writing at length on the "hateful chasm that lies too broad and forbidding between employer and employed" (Ch. 12).

[3] The 3rd edn of *Talpa*, 1854, records in a footnote to Ch. 12 (pp. 94–5), and gives in the main text of the 4th edn, the death of Talfourd ("the distinguished man and deeply-regretted friend"), on 13 Mar 54, as "an event of almost national grief". Hoskyns's text had received his "earnest acquiescence"; and Hoskyns quotes his last words in court: "And if I were to be asked what is the great want of English Society—to mingle class with class—I would say in one word the want is the want of sympathy." He then quotes the rest of the obituary in the *Examiner*, 18 Mar 54, including the words "The latest breath of one whose whole life was kindness, was thus spent in a solemn enforcement of the duty of kindness to others."

[4] CD entertained Hoskyns in May 1859, but declined several later invitations from him.

To JOHN FORSTER, [17 DECEMBER 1858]

Text in F, 1872–4, III, ix, 209.[1] *Date:* 17 Dec, according to Forster.

After describing an early dinner with Chauncy Townshend, he adds I escaped at half-past seven, and went to the Strand Theatre: having taken a stall beforehand, for it is always crammed. I really wish you would go, between this and next Thursday, to see the *Maid and the Magpie*[2] burlesque there.[3] There is the strangest thing in it that ever I have seen on the stage. The boy, Pippo, by Miss Wilton.[4] While it is astonishingly impudent (must be, or it couldn't be done at all), it is so stupendously like a boy, and unlike a woman, that it is perfectly free from offence. I never have seen such a thing. Priscilla Horton,[5] as a boy, not to be thought of beside it. She does an imitation of the dancing of the Christy Minstrels[6]—wonderfully clever—which, in the audacity of its thorough-going, is surprising.[7] A thing that you *can not* imagine a woman's doing at all; and yet the manner, the appearance, the levity, impulse, and spirits of it, are so exactly like a boy that you cannot think of anything like her sex in association with it. It begins at 8, and is over by a quarter-past 9. I never have seen such a curious thing, and the girl's talent is unchallengeable. I call her the cleverest girl I have ever seen on the stage in my time, and the most singularly original.[8]

[1] F, VIII, iv, 668 gives a slightly abbreviated version.

[2] *The Maid and the Magpie, or The Fatal Spoon*, a "burlesque burletta" by H. J. Byron; opened 11 Oct and widely praised. "Founded on the opera of *La Gazza Ladra*", 1817, by Rossini (with libretto by Gherardini), now *The Thieving Magpie*. The costumes were described as "exaggerated copies of its dresses". It also looked back to the earlier melodrama by Isaac Pocock (1815, but still often revived) and had many topical references, theatrical and social, to the 1850s. Pippo, the smart servant, has theatrical ambitions.

[3] Besides the attraction of Marie Wilton, another motive for CD's going to the burlesque was no doubt the appearance in it of Maria Ternan as Giannetto, described in the playbill as "a Pattern Soldier of a Fast Colour" (with moustache and eyeglass). She had been at the Strand since June and praised for her singing and acting; she had already appeared with Marie Wilton in *Carlo the Devil and his Sister* in Aug; also in Sep–Oct, in two of Charles Selby's comedies, as "Mrs Swellington, a Primrose" (i.e. very prim, but transformed in second act) in *The Last of the Pigtails* and as Kitty Crinoline, a clever servant-girl, in *My Aunt's Husband*.

[4] Marie Effie Wilton, later Lady Bancroft (1839–1921; *DNB*). Gained notice of Macready and Kemble as a child actress in the provinces; acted Henri in Charles Webb's *Belphégor*, Lyceum, 1856. Did not want to play Pippo, but continued to be cast as a boy: e.g., Albert in Leicester Buckingham's burlesque, *William Tell*, Strand, Apr 57; and the young Raleigh in *Kenilworth*, A. Halliday and F. Lawrence's extravaganza, Strand, Dec 58. Had great success in the 1860s in T. W. Robertson's plays. In 1865 re-opened the Queen's Theatre, Tottenham Street, with H. J. Byron, having re-named it the Prince of Wales. Married 1867 Squire Bancroft (1841–1926; *DNB*), actor and theatre manager, knighted 1897. Retired 1885 and wrote a novel and three plays.

[5] See *To* Reed, 12 Aug 57 and *fn.*

[6] Minstrels imitating negroes (after George Christy of New York).

[7] In Scene ii, the "characteristic dance" which follows a song by Isaac the comic Jew and Pippo, to the tune of "When I my banjo play".

[8] Extract given by Forster as an instance of CD's "quick and sure eye for any bit of acting out of the common" and as justified by Marie Wilton's later success (i.e. by 1874).

To B. W. PROCTER, [19] DECEMBER 1858

Text from MDGH, II, 82. *Date:* misdated by CD; Sunday was 19 Dec 58.

Tavistock House, | Sunday, 18th December 1858

My dear Procter,

A thousand thanks for the little song. I am charmed with it, and shall be delighted to brighten "Household Words" with such a wise and genial light.[1] I no more believe that your poetical faculty has gone by, than I believe that you have yourself passed to the better land. You and it will travel thither in company, rely upon it. So I still hope to hear more of the trade-songs, and to learn that the blacksmith has hammered out no end of iron into good fashion of verse, like a cunning workman, as I know him of old to be.[2]

Very faithfully yours, my dear Procter

[CHARLES DICKENS]

To W. H. WILLS, 20 DECEMBER 1858

MS Huntington Library.

TAVISTOCK HOUSE, | TAVISTOCK SQUARE, LONDON. W.C.

Monday Twentieth December 1858

My Dear Wills

You will see from the enclosed, that we are quite right.[3]

Will you go round to Ouvry's, and ask them to write the notice they recommend, for me to sign. *If they approve*, I should wish it to be served on B and E from their office, and it certainly had best be served at once—to day.[4] A duplicate of it should be served upon you. I am finishing my little paper for the New Year,[5] and will wait at home until you bring or send me the legally-copied notices for my signature.

Ever Faithfully

CD.

[1] Almost certainly "Hidden Chords", 8 Jan 59, XIX, 132; although given in the Office Book as by Adelaide Procter, it did not appear among her other *HW* poems reprinted in *Legends and Lyrics*, 1861 (Anne Lohrli, *Household Words*, p. 407).

[2] For Procter's series of 17 "Trade Songs", which appeared in Nos 1–9 of *AYR*, see next vol. The reference here is clearly to "The Blacksmith", *AYR*, 30 Apr 59, I, 20.

[3] CD had presumably sent Wills a copy of Bradbury & Evans's rejection of his offer to buy their share in *HW* for £1,000, made to them by Forster on CD's behalf on 14 Dec. It confirmed his opinion that they had no intention of negotiating a price for *HW*, unless it were sold as a going concern, but would take the case to court, as they did.

[4] Ouvry served notice on Bradbury & Evans on 22 Dec that the *HW* partnership would be dissolved after the final No. on 28 May 1859 and its affairs wound up (MS Messrs Farrer & Co., given by K. J. Fielding in *D*, L [1954], 79). For the subsequent Chancery case brought against CD by Bradbury & Evans, see next vol.

[5] "New Year's Day", *HW*, 1 Jan 59, XIX, 97: an outstanding piece in CD's happiest vein of reminiscence of childhood and youth, also of Italy in 1845 and Paris in 1856; the No. (458) was advertised in the three preceding Nos as "A New Year's Number".

To JAMES BALLANTINE, 22 DECEMBER 1858

Extract in *American Art Association* catalogue, Nov 1923; *MS* 1 p.; addressed James Ballantine; dated Tavistock House, Wed 22 Dec 58.

I beg to express my regret that my engagements render it impossible for me to have the pleasure of accepting the invitation with which you honoured me on behalf of the committee of the Edinburgh Burns Centenary Festival.[1]

To T. J. SERLE,[2] [?22 DECEMBER 1858]

Mention in Forster *to* Serle, 23 Dec 58 (Sotheby's catalogue, Oct 1973). *Address:* see below.[3] *Date:* shortly before letter was received by Forster.

Concerning the Elton Fund[4] *accounts, the manner in which they had been kept, and Serle's true and noble service to the children of his old friend; also making some suggestion about the boy.*[5]

To ARTHUR [SMITH],[6] 23 DECEMBER 1858

Extract in Parke-Bernet catalogue, n.d.; *MS* 1 p.; dated London, 23 Dec 58.

Sending a list of the tickets I want *for Boxing Night.*[7]

To T. J. THOMPSON, 27 DECEMBER 1858*

MS Morgan Library.

TAVISTOCK HOUSE,|TAVISTOCK SQUARE, LONDON. W.C.
Monday Twenty Seventh December 1858.

My Dear Thompson

I don't know that your suspicion of me is unnatural, but I do know that it is unjust. For I should not have dreamed of abandoning the subject,[8] and our joint hope and purpose, without communicating with you.

The plain truth is—if you can believe it—that I have been waiting from day to

[1] The main celebratory dinner was held on 25 Jan 59 in the Music Hall, Lord Ardmillan in the Chair. Copies of a long letter from Lord Brougham, unable to be there, were given to all present (*Caledonian Mercury*, 26 Jan 59). Another dinner took place in the Corn Exchange; Duncan Maclaren, ex-Provost of Edinburgh, presided and there were many speeches; *c.* 3,000 were present.

[2] Thomas James Serle (1798–1889), actor and dramatist: see Vols. I, p. 355*n* and II, p. 151*n*.

[3] Forster's letter begins: "Here is a letter from Dickens", according to catalogue; presumably the letter was addressed to Serle not Forster, but sent to Forster for him to see first and then forward. "In all [*CD*] says," wrote Forster to Serle (above), "I say with all my heart Amen."

[4] See Vols III, p. 527*n*, IV, p. 8*n* and VII, p. 415*n*.

[5] Edward S. Elton, the only son, who became an actor. For the formal letter of thanks addressed to the Trustees by all seven Elton children on 6 Apr 59, see next vol.

[6] Addressed "Dear Arthur", according to catalogue; must be Smith. He had evidently recovered and returned from Paris.

[7] For the second of his Christmas readings.

[8] See *To* Thompson, 27 Oct and 8 Nov.

day, to see Frederick, *who has not once been near me*![1] This morning only, I found on the breakfast-table, side by side with your letter, the enclosed from him.[2] Judge what it is possible to do, under such circumstances!

All here unite in kind love and all good wishes, seasonable and unseasonable.

Believe me | Always Faithfully Yours

T. J. Thompson Esquire CHARLES DICKENS

To ALBERT HARDY,[3] [1858]

Mention in Pickering & Chatto catalogue (undated); *MS* 2 pp.; addressed Albert Hardy; dated Tavistock House, 1858.

Dealing with literary matters.[4]

To J. CORDY JEAFFRESON,[5] 1858

Mention in J. Cordy Jeaffreson, *A Book of Recollections* (2 vols), 1894, I, 272.[6] *Date:* 1858, according to Jeaffreson.

A general invitation to visit him at Gad's Hill.

To MISS SARAH RICHARDSON,[7] 1858

Envelope only, MS Private. *Address:* Miss Sarah Richardson | Summer Hill | Clones | Co. Monaghan | Ireland. PM [?] 5 58.[8]

[1] Each word separately underlined for emphasis.

[2] Evidently refusing any mediation; the case came up for the first of five hearings on 13 Jan 59 (*The Times*, 14 Jan).

[3] Perhaps A. Hardy, Grove St, Lewisham.

[4] Possibly a rejected contributor to *HW*.

[5] John Cordy Jeaffreson (1831–1901; *DNB*), novelist, popular biographer, journalist and archivist; BA Pembroke College, Oxford, 1852; published his first novels in 1854 and 1855; contributed to the *Athenaeum* 1858 to his death; published *Novels and Novelists, from Elizabeth to Victoria*, 2 vols, July 1858. Inspector of documents for the Historical MSS Commission 1874–88. His book on novels includes in Vol. II, pp. 303–4, a portrait of CD and a long section on him as "in every sense the *best* living writer of prose fiction". Perhaps he had sent CD a copy of this book.

[6] "Though I never had any personal intercourse with CD (albeit he wrote me two or three letters in 1858, ...".

[7] One of the four daughters of Sarah Richardson (*d.* ?1823), a relation of Isaac Watts; wife of Joseph Richardson, MP for Newport, Cornwall and author of *Original Poems, Intended for the Use of Young Persons*, 1808, and two tragedies. Her daughter, Sarah, ran a school at Clones; Bulwer Lytton sent her 10/– for it; and Viscountess Combermere wrote to her: "It is quite wonderful, that you have done so much for your school" (undated letters, MSS Private). She was also a graphologist (letter from Lytton, 21 Sep 55, referring to her "remarkable judgments" of handwriting he had sent her, MS Private).

[8] No doubt answering her appeal for funds for her school.

To THE SECRETARY[1] OF THE SHEFFIELD LITERARY AND PHILOSOPHICAL SOCIETY, [1858]

Mention in William Smith Porter, *Sheffield Literary and Philosophical Society. A Centenary Retrospect, Sheffield, 1822–1922*, 1922, p. 60. *Date:* 1858, according to Porter.

Declining an invitation to lecture, CD replied that he never read papers before Societies.[2]

To UNKNOWN CORRESPONDENT, [?LATE 1858]*

MS (fragment) Private. *Date:* Signature suggests late 1858.

Chorley (chronically indistinct) dines at *1/2 past* 7.[3] I will not detain your messenger by writing more now.

Ever Faithfully Yours
CHARLES DICKENS

To UNKNOWN CORRESPONDENT, 1858

Text from Anderson Galleries catalogue, No. 530; dated London, 1858.

Mr. Charles Dickens presents his compliments to Mr. —— and begs to thank that gentleman for his letter of the 23rd ult. and for the enclosure that it contained.

[1] There were two secretaries in 1858, Joseph Kirk and William Baker, FCS.

[2] Porter's reference continues "except on his own account", which is probably a misunderstanding. Thackeray had given the Society "The Four Georges", four lectures, in 1857, for £100.

[3] Emphasized, because unusually late. No doubt a dinner at Chorley's house.

APPENDIXES

A. THOMAS CARLYLE, CHARLES DICKENS and JOHN FORSTER *to* THE EDITOR OF *THE TIMES*, 8 FEBRUARY 1856

Text from *The Times*, 11 Feb 56.

Athenæum Club, Pall-mall, Feb. 8.

Sir,—On behalf of such of your readers as took interest in the subscription for Samuel Johnson's goddaughter, the aged Miss Lowe, and her sister, which was set on foot in November last,[1] will you permit us to announce that the same is about to close?

The sum raised is still but a little over 250*l*.; but, on the other hand, the price of such a life annuity as was proposed proves cheaper than we anticipated; and in addition to this there has been a lucky chance come to help us somewhat. Mauritius Lowe,[2] Miss Lowe's father, is now discovered to have been the benevolent painter by whom Turner, at that time a barber's boy, was first recognized, befriended, and saved to art, in return for which fine action an ardent and renowned admirer of Turner (whose name we need not indicate further)[3] desires to gratify himself by bestowing henceforth 5*l*. annually on the Misses Lowe, and permits us to publish his resolution, if that can make it more binding. So that, on the whole, there is now as good as an "additional annuity of 30*l*.," which was our *minimum* limit, secured for these aged ladies; and thus, by one means and another, our small problem can be considered as done.

One fact must not be omitted. There has been no soliciting, nor shadow of such, anywhere used in this matter. The sum gathered has altogether fallen voluntarily. Very sincerely we beg to thank our fellow-contributors, and dismiss the little transient assemblage with a kindly farewell.

The subscription-books at Messrs. Coutts's, Strand, and at Messrs. Grote and Prescott's, 62, Threadneedle-street, City, will continue open until Wednesday, the 12th of March. After Wednesday, the 12th of March, they will be closed, and the net amount will then promptly be invested in the form of life annuity for the Misses Lowe,—we expect, in the Mitre Insurance-office, 23, Pall-mall,—and, so soon as that operation is complete, the list of subscribers will be published in *The Times*.

We have the honour to be, Sir,
Your obliged and faithful servants,
T. CARLYLE.
CHARLES DICKENS.
JOHN FORSTER.

[1] See Vol. VII, pp. 614–21 and *nn* and 921–25 and *nn*.

[2] Mauritius Lowe (1746–93; *DNB*) painter and friend of Dr Johnson: see Vol. VII, p. 921 and *n*.

[3] Obviously John Ruskin.

B. DRAFT RESOLUTION CONCERNING *HOUSEHOLD WORDS*, FEBRUARY 1856

MS Huntington Library.

Resolved.

That the one eighth share in the property of Household Words relinquished on the 23rd. day of February in the present year by Mr. John Forster, has become the property of Mr. Charles Dickens, and is hereby declared to belong to him during his life.

That one half of that one eighth share, is, on the proposal of Mr. Charles Dickens, now by him conferred upon and made over to, Mr. William Henry Wills (in addition to the share Mr. W. H. Wills already holds), to remain his property so long as he shall continue to be Sub Editor of Household Words, or so long as he and Mr. Charles Dickens shall both live.

That in the event of the death of Mr. W. H. Wills, or of his ceasing to be Sub Editor of Household Words, this said one half of the one eighth share now allotted to him by Mr. Charles Dickens, shall revert to Mr. Charles Dickens; who will then exercise his own discretion as to retaining it, or bestowing it, or any part of it, upon any future Sub-Editor; as he may think most advantageous to the interests of Household Words, and the efficiency of his own connexion with it.

That in the event of the death of Mr. Charles Dickens, the whole one eighth share referred to in the first paragraph of this Memorandum, shall become the property of his successors in his half proprietorship of Household Words under the deed of partnership, and of the other surviving partners, jointly; in trust honorably to employ it according to their discretion in rewarding future Editors, or Sub Editors, or both, with an interest, beyond and over and above a salary, in the character and success of Household Words.

C. MISS COUTTS'S PRIZES FOR COMMON THINGS

(1) DICKENS'S AMENDED DRAFT OF MISS COUTTS'S LETTER *to* THE REV. HARRY BABER, 30 MARCH 1856, GIVEN IN HER *SUMMARY ACCOUNT OF COMMON THINGS*.

MS Morgan Library.

Dear Sir

I have at length visited all the schools where the Schoolmistresses and Pupil Teachers have competed for the Prizes on Common Things; and I have read all the papers proceeding from them, together with those of the Whitelands students. The course I adopted in making these visits, was, to ask the Managers of the schools a few days beforehand if I might come there at an appointed time, accompanied by some friends to whom I am indebted for kind assistance in taking notes of the lessons. The selection of subjects, I usually left to the givers of the lessons. In cases where I was offered a list of subjects to select from, I chose one myself.

The Five Pound Prizes, I think it best not to give. Besides that I cannot find among the competitors for those Prizes, any decided superiority one over another, the subject for which they were offered does not seem to have yet attracted so much consideration as its importance requires. This is probably owing in a great degree to its not being among the subjects brought forward by the Council of Education. So far as it has been attended to, the schoolmistresses merit great praise and have exerted themselves conscientiously. But I hope to see it, before long, more systematically pursued, and with a plainer practical reference to the requirements of schools.

The Four Pound Prizes I would give to Mrs. Cox of Christ Church Schools Albany Street St. Pancras, Mrs B[ragg][1] of St. Stephen's Schools Westminster, and Mrs. Mc Intyre of St. John's Schools Horseferry Road. These schoolmistresses appear to me to evince the best practical knowledge, and to have imparted to their Pupils also, clear views as to a sound manner of teaching, and as to the great utility of industrial training. I cannot judge so well of the results of the Teachers' endeavours in any other schools, as in those of St. Stephen's Westminster, with which I am peculiarly connected. Of the indefatigable zeal and energy of Mrs. B[ragg][1] I can speak from experience, and to the beneficial results of her endeavours I can testify from my own observation. But I have had great pleasure in observing the good management of the Christchurch Schools, just mentioned, and the pains taken there; reflecting the highest credit on its managers and on its mistress. At St. John's Schools too, Mrs. Mc Intyre appeared to be carrying out a very useful work, under great encouragement from the Managers. The children under her care are more particularly the children of the poor than in the other establishments I have named; and the information she communicated to them, struck me as being particularly adapted to their need.

[1] "Mrs. B" in MS.

The Three Pound Prizes I would give to Miss White of St. Peter's Schools Stepney, Miss Wilby of Christ Church Schools Chelsea, and Mrs. Cheadle of [ ][1] Miss White and Miss Wilby gave and wrote very superior lessons and papers; but I had not the means I should have been interested in having, of forming an opinion as to their practical knowledge, on account of their being the Mistresses of Infant Schools only. Mrs. Cheadle shewed much aptitude for teaching, and was particularly active and intelligent in the introduction into her school of industrial training. She had not, however, so much experience as the others.

In making this selection I have been especially guided, firstly by the answers made by the children to the questions of the mistresses; and secondly, by the attention bestowed upon Needlework in the school, in all the branches necessary to the cutting out and making of clothes. In these Schools I found the children accustomed to answer questions with a ready interest and intelligence, and found the great domestic importance of a knowledge of needlework to be appreciated.

The ten shilling prizes to Pupil Teachers, I would give to the eight Pupil Teachers following [ ][1] They are the eight Pupil Teachers who appeared upon the whole, to have best considered the subjects in question, and to have bestowed the greatest amount of thought and method upon the lessons they gave, or the papers they wrote. The Whitelands Students selected for the One Pound Prizes were chosen from their papers only. I gave the preference to those papers which I considered to evince the best information or observation: or which, on any one subject, were the most simply and clearly expressed. I was not influenced by any reference to the hand-writing, composition, &c; but, with very few exceptions, all the papers were more or less defective on these points. I most earnestly wish that a better style of handwriting could be introduced into our female schools; that which at present prevails is so extremely bad, as to become confused and almost illegible after the first few lines. In setting aside the papers that I thought the most clearly expressed, I have always preferred those which were written in plain easy language. It is too much the custom to use hard words which are quite unnecessary, instead of easy words that are equally forcible and expressive. The absurd result, is, that valuable time is lost while a lesson should be in progress, in explaining the meaning or derivation of some word thus used, instead of impressing upon the children the use and history of the thing that it often most imperfectly expresses to them.

Thinking it would be agreeable to the Managers of the Schools and to the Competitors for the Prizes, to see some of the results of the competition now brought to a close, I have made a selection from them. The competitors one and all, have afforded me the highest gratification by shewing an amount of interest in the work, extending far beyond the mere temporary interest in the matter of the prizes, and by so carrying to my mind the conviction that they will always strive to advance it. Having become personally acquainted with them in the progress of this scheme, I cannot cease to feel an interest in their endeavours to do so, and I should be glad that through the possession of this little record they should preserve a remembrance

[1] Blank in MS.

of the help they rendered to an attempt to foster Industrial Teaching; a help that can never be regarded with indifference by those who love children, or who think with me that, next to direct Scriptural instruction, no other teaching renders such valuable aid in the formation of christian character and habits.

The selection I have made, with this object, comprizes a number of selected answers to questions, a description of the plans adopted in different schools, and a portion of each Essay. As the Essays necessarily involved a frequent repetition of one thought, I have taken that portion which appeared to contain any useful remark or suggestion. In my selection of answers, I have taken such as seemed to present the best sample of general information; and to each, I have added such remarks as have suggested themselves to the friends who have assisted me, or to myself. I have also remarked upon the least satisfactory answers, and have tried to point out why I think they come under that denomination. The answers to questions Nos. 13, 14, and 15, contained so much useful simple knowledge, and so many errors very easily and naturally made, that I felt a wish to put all the information together and point out all the mistakes. This, with the help of a medical friend, I have done. And I would recommend that no lessons should be given by Pupil Teachers on the subjects comprehended in these questions, without being first reduced to writing, and approved by the schoolmistress; slight mistakes on such points being peculiarly liable to dangerous or even fatal consequences. This class of answers, I should observe, have been selected from the papers of the Schoolmistresses, and of the Whitelands students, only; the Pupil Teachers, from their youth and consequent inexperience, not being reasonably able to compete with them in this respect. From the answers to question No. 5, however, containing accounts of supposititious Expenditure, I have selected a few of those returned by the Pupil Teachers also; and I have added a few real accounts of similar domestic Expenditure, which I have been enabled to obtain without any intrusion on the private affairs of the persons to whom I am obliged for them: who most willingly furnished this aid when they knew for what object it was required. A comparison of the two may suggest some useful considerations in the management of wages, and in the manner of varying the food and other household articles purchased. Lastly, as to question No. 9. The paper given, is a fair sample of the whole, and is very good for plain, straight-forward, unvarying cookery. But, as the answers to this question shewed no ingenuity in varying the preparation of food and making cheap things pleasant and agreeable, and as I think that the better knowledge young women gain of this necessary art when they are learning how to discharge the duties of later life, the greater power they will have of diffusing around them those fireside enjoyments and comforts which are happily within the reach of the poor unless their condition should be very hard indeed, I have presented some hints in plain and cheap cookery which have been given to me, and have appended some recipes which can be easily understood and followed. These latter have been prepared for me by a very dear friend,[1] who has helped me through the whole of this plan, and to whom I am indebted, not only for whatever information I possess, but for my first interest in these subjects, and the first direction of my mind to the humble admiration of the multitude of objects of usefulness and beauty with which a Merciful Father has surrounded us, and a

[1] Mrs Brown.

humble sympathy with the work He has entrusted to the heads and hearts of all His children; without such feelings, I first learned from her that happiness can be a part of no condition; with such feelings that it is attainable by most people, proceeding out of Common Things and simple pleasures which know no distinctions of fortune, and are, like the great christian religion, free to all.

This reference to my dear friend, brings me to an explanation of the long delay that has arisen in the settlement of these Prizes. Last summer, I was prevented from proceeding with the plan, by the breaking up of many of the schools. Last Autumn the death of Mrs Brown's husband, suddenly, when we were travelling abroad, involved us in great affliction. The resumption of this pursuit, it rendered very painful, and for some time impossible. You who knew him and who will remember the interest with which he helped us on a former occasion, will imagine how much I have missed, in this work, the ever ready and kind help, the ever encouraging and cheering presence, of a dear true friend. You will feel how happy it would have made him to have assisted with his experience and sound sense in making the medical suggestions to which I have referred more useful, and how happy it would have made me to have had his support. But it has pleased God to withdraw him from my daily life, and to leave me with the object of his nearest affections, whose loss is greater than mine.

(2) DICKENS'S AMENDED DRAFT OF MISS COUTTS'S SECOND LETTER *to* THE REV. HARRY BABER, 7 APRIL 1856

MS Morgan Library.

[a]I return the papers written at the examination (with a short remark upon each), in order that they may be restored to the Competitors when you inform them of the Prizes having been awarded. Thinking it would be agreeable both to them and to the Managers of Schools to see some of the results of the competition, I have made a selection from the essays, and the answers to the printed questions, and a list of the subjects of the lessons; to which are appended such remarks as the papers and lessons have suggested, and such additional matter as I have thought likely to make this little record more useful.[a]

The competitors, one and all, shewed an interest in the work which this design was intended to further, extending far beyond the mere temporary interest in the matter of the Prizes, and so carrying to my mind the conviction that they will always strive to advance it. Having become personally acquainted with them in the progress of this scheme, I cannot cease to feel much interested in their endeavours to do so, and I shall always remember with gratification the help they rendered to an attempt to foster industrial teaching;—a subject which must ever excite the deepest interest in those who love children, and who think with me that, next to direct Scriptural instruction, no other teaching renders such valuable aid in the formation of Christian character and habits.

[aa] Moved to end in printed text of Miss Coutts's *Summary Account of Common Things*.

A long delay has arisen in the settlement of these Prizes, which I would thank you to cause to be explained. Last summer I was prevented from proceeding with the plan, by the breaking-up of many of the schools for the holidays. In the Autumn, the sudden death of a dear friend, Mr. Brown, while we were travelling abroad, involved me in great affliction. You, who knew him, and who will remember the interest with which he helped us on a former occasion, will imagine how I have missed in this Work his ever ready and kind aid. You will feel how happy it would have made him to have assisted with his experience and sound sense, in making the medical suggestions contained in this record, plain and useful. But it has pleased God to withdraw from my daily life the encouraging and cheering influence and presence of a dear true friend, and to leave with me the object of his dearest affection, whose loss is far greater than my own. This bereavement rendered the resumption of the scheme now brought to a close, for a time impossible; and, even when that period had passed, made it a very painful duty both to myself and to his widow, the dear friend who has helped me throughout this plan, and to whom I am indebted, not only for whatever information I may possess, but for my first interest in these subjects and for the first direction of my mind to the observation of the multitude of objects of usefulness and beauty with which a Merciful Father has surrounded us. From her I first learnt that happiness and comfort are the exclusive possession of no condition in life, but are attainable by most people; proceeding out of common things and simple pleasures, and seldom indeed, if ever, to be wholly missed by those who walk carefully and reverently in the footsteps of our great example, and who cherish a humble sympathy with all the work He has entrusted to the heads and hearts of His children.

D. PROGRAMME OF EVENTS IN REMEMBRANCE OF DOUGLAS JERROLD, JUNE–JULY 1857

Copy, Free Library of Philadelphia.

In Remembrance

OF THE

LATE MR. DOUGLAS JERROLD.

COMMITTEE.

JOHN BLACKWOOD, Esq.
SHIRLEY BROOKS, Esq.
JOHN B. BUCKSTONE, Esq.
PETER CUNNINGHAM, Esq.
CHARLES DICKENS, Esq.
JOHN FORSTER, Esq.
CHARLES KNIGHT, Esq.
JOHN LEECH, Esq.
MARK LEMON, Esq.
SIR EDWARD BULWER LYTTON, Bart., M.P.
WILLIAM C. MACREADY, Esq.
SIR JOSEPH PAXTON, M.P.
WILLIAM H. RUSSELL, Esq.
ALBERT SMITH, Esq.
CLARKSON STANFIELD, Esq., R.A.
WILLIAM M. THACKERAY, Esq.
BENJAMIN WEBSTER, Esq.
W. HENRY WILLS, Esq.[1]

Honorary Secretary—ARTHUR SMITH, Esq.

OFFICE AT THE GALLERY OF ILLUSTRATION, REGENT STREET,

WATERLOO PLACE.

The Committee, in remembrance of their deceased friend, beg to announce the following occasions:—

On Saturday Evening, June 27th, a Concert will take place in St. Martin's Hall, at which Madame Novello, Mr. and Mrs. T. German Reed, Miss Louisa Vinning, Herr Ernst, Mr. Albert Smith, Mr. and Mrs. Weiss, Mr. F. Robson, Signor Bottesini, Mr. Osborne, Miss Mary Keeley, Miss Dolby, and Mr. Sims Reeves, will assist. Conductors, M. Benedict, Mr. Frank Mori, and Mr. Francesco Berger.

To commence at 8 precisely. Prices of Admission : Stalls, Five Shillings.
Body of the Hall, Centre Gallery, and Orchestra, each Two Shillings.
Back Seats and Side Galleries, each One Shilling.

On Tuesday Evening, June 30th, Mr. Charles Dickens will read his Christmas Carol in St. Martin's Hall.

The reading will commence at 8 precisely, and will last two hours. Prices of Admission : Stalls, Five Shillings.

Body of the Hall and the Centre Gallery, each Two Shillings.
Back Seats and Side Galleries, each One Shilling.

---

[1] Six more names were added later, including Maclise; for the full list see Francesco Berger, *Reminiscences*, pp. 33–4.

On Tuesday Evening, July 7th, Mr. W. H. Russell will deliver his Personal Narrative of the late Crimean War, in St. Martin's Hall.

To commence at 8 precisely, and last two hours. Prices of Admission : Stalls, Five Shillings.

Body of the Hall and the Centre Gallery, each Two Shillings.

Back Seats and Side Galleries, each One Shilling.

On Saturday Evening, July 11th, will be represented at The Gallery of Illustration, Regent Street, Mr. Wilkie Collins's new romantic Drama in three acts, The Frozen Deep, performed by the Amateur Company of Ladies and Gentlemen who originally represented it in private. With the original Scenery, by Mr. Stanfield, R.A., and Mr. Telbin, and the original Music, under the direction of Mr. Francesco Berger. The whole under the management of Mr. Charles Dickens. To conclude with a Farce.

Prices of Admission : Stalls, One Guinea. Area, Ten Shillings. Amphitheatre, Five Shillings.

On Wednesday Evening, July 15th, will be represented, at the Theatre Royal, Haymarket, the late Mr Douglas Jerrold's Comedy, in three acts, The Housekeeper. To conclude with the late Mr. Douglas Jerrold's Drama, The Prisoner of War. Represented by Miss Reynolds, Mr. Buckstone, Mr. Phelps, Mr. Howe, Mr. Chippendale, Mr. and Mrs. Keeley, Mr. W. Farren, Mr. Rogers, Miss M. Ternan, Mr. Compton, Miss M. Oliver, Mr. Benjamin Webster, and the Company of the Theatre.

Prices of Admission : Stalls, Ten Shillings and Sixpence. The rest of the house as usual, except the Private Boxes, which may be had at the Committee's Office, or at Mr. Sams's Library, St. James's Street.

On Wednesday Evening, July 22nd, Mr. W. M. Thackeray will deliver a Lecture on "Week-day Preachers," in St. Martin's Hall.

To commence at 8 precisely, and last one hour and a half. Prices of Admission : Stalls, Five Shillings.

Body of the Hall, and the Centre Gallery, each Two Shillings.

Back Seats and Side Galleries, each One Shilling.

On Wednesday Evening, July 29th, will be represented at the Theatre Royal, Adelphi, the late Mr. Douglas Jerrold's Drama, in three acts, The Rent Day. To conclude with the late Mr. Douglas Jerrold's Drama, Black-Eyed Susan. Represented by Mr. T. P. Cooke (who returns to the stage for one night, for the purpose), Madame Celeste, Mr. Benjamin Webster, Miss Wyndham, Mr. Wright, Miss Mary Keeley, Mr. Buckstone, Miss M. Oliver, Mr. Paul Bedford, Mrs. Chatterley, Mr. Billington, Miss Arden, and the Company of the Theatre.

Prices of Admission: Stalls, Ten Shillings and Sixpence. The rest of the house as usual, except the Private Boxes, which may be had at the Committee's Office, or at Mr. Sams's Library, St. James's Street.

☛ On and after Tuesday, June 23rd, Tickets for any or all of these occasions will be on sale at the Committee's Office, at the Gallery of Illustration, Regent Street, every day between the hours of 12 and 4.

E. AGREEMENT BETWEEN SHIRLEY BROOKS AND RICHARD BENTLEY, 4 SEPTEMBER 1857

MS (2 copies, one in Brooks's hand, one in Dickens's) British Library.

Agreement entered into this 4th. day of September 1857 between Shirley Brooks of 18 Tavistock Street Bedford Square of the one part and Richard Bentley of 8 New Burlington Street of the other part.

The said Shirley Brooks hereby agrees for the consideration hereinafter mentioned that the said Richard Bentley shall be at liberty to publish a novel by the said Shirley Brooks entitled "Aspen Court" in a cheap form. Namely in one volume at the price of Two Shillings. On condition of the said Richard Bentley paying to the said Shirley Brooks the sum of Two Pence upon every copy of such Cheap Edition that shall be sold. Accounts are to be rendered and payments made by the said Richard Bentley in respect of such Cheap Editions quarterly.

The above agreement is to be in force for 5 years from the date hereof and then the copyright in "Aspen Court" is to revert to the said Shirley Brooks as it shall also be provided the said Richard Bentley shall not avail himself of his right above mentioned within two years from the date hereof.

Witness the hands of the parties on the date above

Witness CHARLES DICKENS

SHIRLEY BROOKS
RICHARD BENTLEY

F. THE SEPARATION

(1) JOHN FORSTER *to* FREDERIC OUVRY, 21 MAY 1858

MS Messrs Farrer & Co. (given in K. J. Fielding, *Nineteenth-Century Fiction*, x [1956], 64).

19 Whitehall Place | Friday Morning | 21st May 1858

My Dear Sir

Your letter is very important—so much so, that I shall strenuously urge upon Dickens the propriety of acting upon it.

The Decision must be taken by 3 o'clock today.

As I inferred from what passed between us yesterday that you have not yourself had any cases of this exact kind, and were as yet necessarily imperfectly acquainted with the operation & requirements of the New Act[1]—I venture to ask whether you could, between this and 3 o'clock, *assure yourself with certainty upon the matters stated in your letter of this morning*? I feel perfectly certain already that you are right. But so much depends on this step now taken, that I am perhaps over-anxious, and at any rate, for others' sake more than my own, would ask this great favour from you.

Unfortunately I cannot leave Whitehall until late in the afternoon—and I will therefore beg you to have the kindness to *call here* before 3. We will then make an appointment to meet again at your chambers between ½ p. 4 & 5—*with Dickens*.

Very truly yrs.

JOHN FORSTER

P.S. If not able to come here at 3, *pray write*—and the other Engaget. will stand for D[?] at L. I. Fields at 5.

(2) JOHN FORSTER *to* FREDERIC OUVRY, 22 MAY 1858

MS Messrs Farrer & Co.

Private 46 Montagu Square W. | 22d. May 1858.

My dear Sir

Lemon has written to me this Evening that "Mrs. Dickens thankfully accepts the proposal" as I named it to you—and that she "has named Messrs. Smith Wright and Shepherd as her lawyers."—He adds that he (Lemon) will keep any appointment you may make—and it seems to me advisable that you should, in the first instance, get the details of what she expects or understands on this arrangement *from Lemon & herself*.—I will then confirm it, or point out whether, in any details, it differs from D's proposal. Substantially, as I told you, that was "400£ a year and a brougham."

[1] The Matrimonial Causes Act, 1857: see *To* Macready, 7 June, *fn*.

It is highly necessary that *no time whatever* should be lost in proceeding to completion.

Yours my dear sir | Always truly
JOHN FORSTER

Lemon is at 198 Strand in early part of day—and at 140 Strand after ½ p. 1 or 2.

(3) THE "VIOLATED" LETTER, 25 MAY 1858

Text from *Mr. and Mrs. Charles Dickens*, ed. Walter Dexter, 1935, pp. 273–5.

Tavistock House, Tavistock Square, | London, W.C.
Tuesday, May 25th, 1858.

[a]Mrs. Dickens and I have lived unhappily together for many years. Hardly any one who has known us intimately can fail to have known that we are, in all respects of character and temperament, wonderfully unsuited to each other. I suppose that no two people, not vicious in themselves, ever were joined together, who had a greater difficulty in understanding one another, or who had less in common. An attached woman servant (more friend to both of us than a servant), who lived with us sixteen years, and is now married, and who was, and still is, in Mrs. Dickens's confidence and in mine, who had the closest familiar experience of this unhappiness, in London, in the country, in France, in Italy, wherever we have been, year after year, month after month, week after week, day after day, will bear testimony to this.[a]

Nothing has, on many occasions, stood between us and a separation but Mrs. Dickens's sister, Georgina Hogarth. From the age of fifteen, she has devoted herself to our home and our children. She has been their playmate, nurse, instructress, friend, protectress, adviser and companion. In the manly consideration toward Mrs. Dickens which I owe to my wife, I will merely remark of her that the peculiarity of her character has thrown all the children on someone else. I do not know—I cannot by any stretch of fancy imagine—what would have become of them but for this aunt, who has grown up with them, to whom they are devoted, and who has sacrificed the best part of her youth and life to them.

She has remonstrated, reasoned, suffered and toiled, again and again to prevent a separation between Mrs. Dickens and me. Mrs. Dickens has often expressed to her her sense of her affectionate care and devotion in her home—never more strongly than within the last twelve months.

For some years past Mrs. Dickens has been in the habit of representing to me that it would be better for her to go away and live apart; that her always increasing estrangement made a mental disorder under which she sometimes labours—more, that she felt herself unfit for the life she had to lead as my wife and that she would be better far away. I have uniformly replied that we must bear our misfortune, and fight the fight out to the end; that the children were the first consideration, and that I feared they must bind us together "in appearance."

[aa] CD copied these paragraphs for Anne Cornelius (MS Dickens House); but presumably from another draft, as there are several differences in the text.

At length, within these three weeks, it was suggested to me by Forster that even for their sakes, it would surely be better to reconstruct and rearrange their unhappy home. I empowered him to treat with Mrs. Dickens, as the friend of both of us for one and twenty years. Mrs. Dickens wished to add on her part, Mark Lemon, and did so.[1] On Saturday last Lemon wrote to Forster that Mrs. Dickens "gratefully and thankfully accepted" the terms I proposed to her.

Of the pecuniary part of them, I will only say that I believe they are as generous as if Mrs. Dickens were a lady of distinction, and I a man of fortune. The remaining parts of them are easily described—my eldest boy to live with Mrs. Dickens and take care of her; my eldest girl to keep my house; both my girls and all my children but the eldest one, to live with me, in the continued companionship of their aunt Georgina, for whom they have all the tenderest affection that I have ever seen among young people, and who has a higher claim (as I have often declared for many years) upon my affection, respect and gratitude than anybody in the world.

I hope that no one who may become acquainted with what I write here, can possibly be so cruel and unjust, as to put any misconstruction on our separation, so far. My elder children all understand it perfectly, and all accept it as inevitable. There is not a shadow of doubt or concealment among us—my eldest son and I are one, as to it all.

Two wicked persons who should have spoken very differently of me, in consideration of earned respect and gratitude, have (as I am told, and indeed to my personal knowledge) coupled with this separation the name of a young lady for whom I have a great attachment and regard. I will not repeat her name—I honour it too much. Upon my soul and honour, there is not on this earth a more virtuous and spotless creature than this young lady. I know her to be innocent and pure, and as good as my own dear daughters. Further, I am sure quite that Mrs. Dickens, having received this assurance from me, must now believe it, in the respect I know her to have for me, and in the perfect confidence I know her, in her better moments to repose in my truthfulness.[2]

On this head, again, there is not a shadow of doubt or concealment between my children and me. All is open and plain among us, as though we were brothers and sisters. They are perfectly certain that I would not deceive them, and the confidence among us is without a fear.

C.D.

[1] CD's breach with Lemon no doubt partly stemmed from Lemon's acting for Catherine in the separation negotiations and becoming, with Evans, one of her Trustees. But Lemon's response to a letter of Catherine's of 19 May suggests less than enthusiasm for his role. On its receipt he immediately sent it to Forster, saying "This morning I received the enclosed (the second to the same purpose) and shall decline to forward it to Dickens unless you think he ought to have it at once. Of course I shall never refuse to see Mrs Dickens, but whatever she may do for the future must be without my interference" (*Mr. & Mrs. CD*, ed. Walter Dexter, p. 278). Lemon clearly blamed Forster for the breach, for in 1868, after reconciliation with CD, he showed CD's friendly letter to him of 6 Oct 68 (N, III, 670), to a friend, saying "[This is] more like himself than when his actions are controlled by others" (given in A. A. Adrian, *Mark Lemon*, p. 136).

[2] For Catherine's disbelief in the rumours, see *To* Ouvry, 26 May and *fn*.

STATEMENT SIGNED BY MRS HOGARTH AND HER DAUGHTER HELEN, DATED 29 MAY, ATTACHED TO "VIOLATED" LETTER, according to Dexter.

Copy (in CD's hand) from Facsimile, N, III, facing p. 26.

It having been stated to us that in reference to the differences which have resulted in the separation of Mr. and Mrs. Charles Dickens, certain statements have been circulated that such differences are occasioned by circumstances deeply affecting the moral character of Mr. Dickens and compromising the reputation and good name of others,[1] we solemnly declare that we now disbelieve such statements. We know that they are not believed by Mrs. Dickens, and we pledge ourselves on all occasions to contradict them, as entirely destitute of foundation.

Signed by Mrs Hogarth and her daughter Helen 29th. May, 1858.

(4) FREDERIC OUVRY *to* GEORGE F. SMITH, 28 MAY 1858

MS Messrs Farrer & Co.

66, Lincoln's Inn Fields, | London, W.C.
28 May 1858

Dear Sir,

I have received your Letter of the 27th. with its enclosure. I am sorry that I cannot consider the latter satisfactory.

The slanders in circulation go beyond the specific charge which Mr. Hogarth repudiates, and with reference to the disgusting and horrible nature of that charge I cannot think it desirable that it should be distinctly written down even for the purpose of denial.

I think also that if anything be signed, it should be signed by Mrs. Hogarth & her youngest daughter. Mr. Hogarth's signature there is no necessity to ask for.

The matter is so serious—of such vital importance not only to Mr. Dickens, but to his wife, his children, nay even to the Hogarth family that nothing short of a full & explicit statement clearing Mr. Dickens from the imputations cast upon him, can meet his acceptance.

I have drawn out and send you such a statement, and trust that its signature may have the effect of counteracting the false and scandalous charges which ignorance or malice has invented.

I am sincerely anxious for the sake of all parties that this unhappy business

[1] K. J. Fielding in "Dickens and the Hogarth Scandal", *Nineteenth-Century Fiction*, x (1956), 64–74, based on MSS Messrs Farrer & Co., shows that CD forced Mrs Hogarth and her daughter to sign this statement because he believed they were spreading rumours that Georgina Hogarth was his mistress and even with child by him. This accounts for the vehemence of his behaviour.

should be settled but Mr. Dickens will not sign any deed with these charges hanging over him, and supposed to be sanctioned by some members of his wife's family.

You will not understand me as in any way referring to Mrs. Dickens. She does not believe the charges made against her Husband, and has indignantly expressed her disbelief of them. So far as she is concerned the proposed arrangement will be carried out, though without any legal obligation.

I am dear Sir
[?]
Frederic Ouvry

George F. Smith Esq.
15 Golden Sq.
W.

(5) DICKENS'S "PERSONAL" STATEMENT

Text from *HW*, 12 June 58, XVII, 601.[1]

"Familiar in their Mouths as HOUSEHOLD WORDS."—SHAKESPEARE.

HOUSEHOLD WORDS.

A WEEKLY JOURNAL.

CONDUCTED BY CHARLES DICKENS.

No. 429.] SATURDAY, JUNE 12, 1858. {PRICE 2*d.* STAMPED 3*d.*

PERSONAL.

THREE-AND-TWENTY years have passed since I entered on my present relations with the Public. They began when I was so young, that I find them to have existed for nearly a quarter of a century.

Through all that time I have tried to be as faithful to the Public, as they have been to me. It was my duty never to trifle with them, or deceive them, or presume upon their favor, or do any thing with it but work hard to justify it. I have always endeavoured to discharge that duty.

My conspicuous position has often made me the subject of fabulous stories and unaccountable statements. Occasionally, such things have chafed me, or even wounded me; but, I have always accepted them as the shadows inseparable from the light of my notoriety and success. I have never obtruded any such personal uneasiness of mine, upon the generous aggregate of my audience.

For the first time in my life, and I believe for the last, I now deviate from the principle I have so long observed, by presenting myself in my own Journal in my own private character, and entreating all my brethren (as they deem that they have reason to think well of me, and to know that I am a man who has ever been unaffectedly true to our common calling), to lend their aid to the dissemination of my present words.

Some domestic trouble of mine, of long-standing, on which I will make no further remark than that it claims to be respected, as being of a sacredly private nature, has lately been brought to an arrangement, which involves no anger or ill-will of any kind, and the whole origin, progress, and surrounding circumstances of which have been, throughout, within the knowledge of my children. It is amicably composed, and its details have now but to be forgotten by those concerned in it.

By some means, arising out of wickedness, or out of folly, or out of inconceivable wild chance, or out of all three, this trouble has been made the occasion of misrepresentations, most grossly false, most monstrous, and most cruel—involving, not only me, but innocent persons dear to my heart, and innocent persons of whom I have no knowledge, if, indeed, they have any existence—and so widely spread, that I doubt if one reader in a thousand will peruse these lines, by whom some touch of the breath of these slanders will not have passed, like an unwholesome air.

Those who know me and my nature, need no assurance under my hand that such calumnies are as irreconcileable with me, as they are, in their frantic incoherence, with one another. But, there is a great multitude who know me through my writings, and who do not know me otherwise; and I cannot bear that one of them should be left in doubt, or hazard of doubt, through my poorly shrinking from taking the unusual means to which I now resort, of circulating the Truth.

I most solemnly declare, then—and this I do, both in my own name and in my wife's name—that all the lately whispered rumours touching the trouble at which I have glanced, are abominably false. And that whosoever repeats one of them after this denial, will lie as wilfully and as foully as it is possible for any false witness to lie, before Heaven and earth.

CHARLES DICKENS.

[1] The Statement was published in *The Times*, 7 June 58 under the following heading: "Mr Charles Dickens. | We are requested to anticipate the publication of the following article:— | (From *Household Words* of Wednesday, June 9)."

The most scurrilous of the rumours were those published in the *Court Circular* and *Reynolds's Weekly News*. The *Court Circular* gave as "the worst form" of the rumour the story that CD had preferred "his wife's sister to herself, a preference which has assumed a very definite and tangible shape" (12 June; given in K. J. Fielding, "Dickens and the Hogarth Scandal", *Nineteenth-Century Fiction*, X [1956], 71). G. W. M. Reynolds, editor of *Reynolds's Weekly News*, wrote that the rumours had been "generally credited in literary and artistic circles.... The names of a female relative, and of a professional young lady, have both been, of late, so freely and intimately associated with that of Mr. Dickens, as to excite suspicion and surprise in the minds of those who had hitherto looked upon the popular novelist as a very Joseph in all that regards morality, chastity, and decorum" (13 June). On 20 June he referred to CD's "personal statement" as "one of the most ill-advised things that we have ever known ... a palpable and, perhaps, irremedial blunder." Other rumours were simply ludicrous: a *New York Times* correspondent, e.g., wrote from London on 8 June of the "legends concerning Dickens and an actress, with whom it was at last affirmed that the author of *David Copperfield* had eloped to Boulogne.... There is a story that Mr. Dickens means to go on the stage" (*New York Times*, 21 June; given in Katharine Longley, unpublished typescript). The *Scotsman*, which published the "Personal" statement on 12 June, rallied to CD's defence, saying that "the name of a young lady on the stage has been mixed up with the matter—most cruelly and untruly is the opinion, we hear, of those having the best means of observing and judging" (challenged the next week by Reynolds, who reverted to the "female relative" story). In no account was Ellen mentioned by name.

(6) MISS HELEN THOMSON[1] *to* MRS STARK,[2] [30] AUGUST 1858

Text (copy) given in K. J. Fielding, "CD and his Wife", *Études Anglais*, III, 1955, 213–18.

[30th][3] August, 1858

My dear Mrs. Stark,

My past experience has given me too many strong proofs of the kind interest you take in our family concerns, to doubt your sympathy in the late cruel trial of my poor sister, Mrs. Hogarth has been called upon to endure by the separation of her dear eldest daughter Catherine[4] from her husband after 23 years of married life! And the extraordinary publicity given to it by the mystified and incomprehensible statement Dickens thought fit to insert in his "Household Words," and by his request transmitted to the newspapers.

I cannot pretend on paper to give you a detailed account of this most distressing event, and indeed after frequently having taken up my pen to write to you on the subject, have laid it aside, feeling it difficult to make you understand the painful mention of the case, without entering at more length than could be agreeable to you, but from a recent insertion of a letter which Dickens had written to a friend in America now going the round of the press, in which he talks of his wife occasionally labouring under *mental disorder*, I think it only right to contradict that statement, to such a friend as you; he did indeed endeavour to get the physician who attended her in illness, to sanction such a report, when he sternly refused, saying he considered Mrs. Dickens perfectly sound in mind, consequently he dared not in England assert anything of the kind. That her spirits were low was not surprising, considering the manner in which she had been treated; but I assure you, my dear Mrs. Stark, she had no desire to leave her home or children so long as that home was endurable to her, and long had she borne her trials, even unknown to her Mother, and not till matters had come to extremity did her father think it right to interfere, and then the affair was brought to a compromise, to avoid a public court, that she should agree to a separate maintenance, after various absurd proposals he made, of her going abroad to live alone, or keeping her to her own apartment in his house in daily life, at the same time to appear at his parties still as mistress of the house, to do the honors, and to visit their friends in turn with him, and at another time proposing that when he and his family lived in the town house, she should occupy with a servant the country house or vice versa.

When all such insulting proposals were rejected, he refused to make any settlement upon her at all, merely to depend on his bounty as he chose to give it, unless her parents and sister Helen consented to sign their names to a paper he drew up of

[1] Catherine Dickens's aunt, Mrs George Hogarth's youngest sister.

[2] A relation by marriage of Helen Thomson and Mrs Hogarth, whose eldest sister Catherine had married the Edinburgh architect, William Stark (W. J. Carlton, *Notes & Queries*, Apr 1960, XXV, 145).

[3] "20th" in copy; presumably misread by copier. The "Violated letter" referred to in second paragraph of letter was first published in the *New York Tribune*, 16 Aug; but did not reach the English press until 30 Aug (*Morning Star*), repeated the next day in the *Liverpool Mercury*.

[4] "Catharine" in text.

acquitting him of anything immoral, or that any woman had anything to do with his separation from his wife. This my sister and her daughter stood out against during a fortnight, costing them many tears and sleepless nights, but at length they were over-ruled by the casuistry of the lawyer and the entreaties of Mr. Mark Lemon who acted for Catherine,[1] and knowing the stubborn and unyielding temper of her husband, lost all hopes of bringing things to a proper issue, unless concessions were made. Her eldest son, on his knees, entreated his Mother, Grandmother and Aunts to comply, in order that his poor mother might be released from all the anxious agitation of further delay, and against their better judgment they yielded, and he has artfully availed himself of this in writing to his friend, and thus my poor sister's name and her youngest daughter's is also dragged into public notice.

I deeply regret that they did not abide by their own convictions. One cannot consent to do evil and expect good to come of it, but their feelings were worked up to fever heat by witnessing the distress and agitation of poor Catherine.[1] Mrs. Hogarth took her down to Brighton for a fortnight during the time the deed of separation was being drawn up, and remained with her till it was brought down by the lawyer for signature. Mr. Lemon then invited her to pay his wife and him a visit at Crawley. Leaving her under their kind care and protection, my sister returned to London, where she thought she would be wanted at her home; but alas, her pent up feelings and exposure to cold air sitting out late in the evening air, which poor Kate felt soothing, had so fevered her blood that she was seized with a dangerous illness from which she is now only very slowly recovering.—A deep seated carbuncle on the back of the head or nape of the neck, confined her to bed for some weeks, the lancet leaving a very deep wound. As soon as she could be moved, the Medical Attendant ordered her to Margate, the sea-side being her only chance of recovery. The wound is now healing, but leaving erysipelas around it, and she has every morning, and sometimes every two hours, an attack of neuralgia in the head. A sick-nurse has been with her night and day. I had for the first time since June, a few lines yesterday written in her own handwriting, to say she felt a little better. This trial is an aggravated one to her by the strange conduct of her daughter Georgina, who blinded by the sophistry of her brother-in-law takes his part, and by remaining against the wishes of her parents with him and his daughters, weakens the defence of her sister. His exaggerated praises of her to the depreciation of his wife, is most heart-cruel and unjust.

While during the 22 or 23 years of her married life, Catherine[1] was having her family fast, ten children,—the youngest being now about 4 or 5 years old, and frequently made slow and tedious recoveries, reducing her bodily strength, was it not natural that she should lean upon the assistance of a sister in the care of her children; nor was she at all insensible to her services. But again, ought it not to be felt a natural duty for that sister living under her roof, sharing all the indulgences which she herself had, all her wants liberally supplied &c., to give in her turn her time and attention to lighten her sister's domestic duties when she herself was laid aside and unable to attend to them. All that Georgina did was to teach the little boys to read and write until they went to school at the age of seven in turn; at that age the girls always had a daily governess. Catherine,[1] when well, had no light task to

[1] "Catharine" in text.

manage the household affairs of an establishment where constant company was kept, to receive the many guests that her husband's popularity brought to the house, to travel and visit about with him. Georgina made herself occasionally useful, I believe, as a sort of amanuensis to Dickens, and this was all very right and creditable (within proper bounds) but in no way ought to have eclipsed the more sacred claims of a wife in her husband's esteem and affection; but he has proved a spoiled child of fortune, dazzled by his popularity, and given up to selfish egotism. Georgina is an enthusiast, and worships him as a man of genius, and has quarrelled with all her relatives because they dare to find fault with him, saying "a man of genius ought not to be judged with the common herd of men." She must bitterly repent, when she recovers from her delusion, her folly; her vanity is no doubt flattered by his praise, but she has disappointed us all, as we thought her affectionate and disinterested.

His eldest daughter is 19, the youngest 17; they, poor girls, have also been flattered as being taken notice of as the daughters of a popular author. He, too, is a caressing father and indulgent in trifles, and they in their ignorance of the world, look no further nor are aware of the injury he does them. His love for the stage and theatrical society makes him give up all his time and thoughts to it. I am told he is a great actor, and it is thought he may yet make the stage his profession. I wish he were not so good an actor in private life, appearing in his writings as a philanthropist, the protector of the injured, &c., &c., and yet can forget the vow he took at God's altar, to cherish in sickness and in health, for better, for worse, for richer for poorer, the woman who committed her destiny and put all her earthly trust in him till death should part them. Mrs. Dickens is at present with her mother at Margate; they will remain until the 1st October.

All this distress came upon us like a thunder clap, just after his reading in Edinburgh last April when we had been so gratified by hearing him. Little did we know then!

It is a living death indeed that has parted them, but not the death that will justify his broken faith. As to the platonic attachment he has the bad taste and boldness to profess to a young actress, and which he wrote to his elder children their mother had not character to appreciate, and which he has intruded upon the notice of the public in his foolish and egoistical statement, I can only compare it to "the wicked fleeing where no man pursueth." What has the public to do with what ought to be his private affairs? Conscience makes cowards of men. But I must check my pen. His poor, dear wife is silent and forbearing, and I must try to imitate her. I have had several letters from her, she has borne her heavy trial with dignified and gentle forbearance, and a true Christian patience.

God grant that in permitting this page in her life's history to be turned, it may be for good. Separated from a life of fictitious gaiety on the surface, and beneath carrying about chilled affections and a wounded heart, she may now have time for tranquil reflection, and look for help and consolation from her God and Saviour, who has invited all who labour and are heavy laden to trust in Him, who is the same yesterday, to-day and for ever.

She has been much cheered and soothed by all the friends she most esteemed immediately coming to visit her, and amongst her kindest and warmest friends has been Miss Burdett Coutts, indeed she had invited her before matters were settled, to make her home with her. She had a visit of a few days from her youngest boys during their holidays; she thus writes of it.—"I need hardly tell you, dearest Aunt, how very happy I have been with my dear boys, although they were not allowed to remain with me so long as I wished, yet I think we all thoroughly enjoyed being together. Of course it was not all pleasure, as their presence at times brought bitter recollections and feelings to my mind; for indeed, dear friend, you will understand and feel for me when I tell you that I still love and think of their father too much for my peace of mind. I have been told that he has expressed a wish that we should meet in society, and be at least on friendly terms. Surely he cannot mean it, as I feel that if I were ever to see him by chance it would almost kill me; but to return to my boys. I cannot tell you how good and affectionate they were to me. One of them, little Sydney,[1] was full of solicitude and anxiety about me, always asking what I should do when they were gone, and if I would not be very dull and lonely without them; he should so like to stay. Upon the whole their visit has done me much good, and dear Charlie is so kind and gentle, and tried to cheer me. I trust by God's assistance to be able to resign myself to His will, and to lead a contented if not a happy life, but my position is a sad one, and time only may be able to blunt the keen pain that will throb at my heart, but I will indeed try to struggle hard against it."

Now my dear Mrs. Stark I have troubled you with a very long letter, but I will not apologise, for I feel sure your heart has bled for both mother and daughter. It is well for the pecuniary interests of the Dickens family that he in a manner keeps up his popularity by these readings, the sale of his "Household Words," and other writings. The public have made an idol of him, and even the worshippers of a false deity are slow and unwilling to break their idol, but his sentimentality and professed benevolence are more resembling fairy tales than the philanthropy founded on a religious basis. He is the third Dickens brother who has deserted his wife, and I understand a fourth Dickens is about to be separated from his wife by the desire of her parents.[2]

I trust you have been enjoying good health, as well as your sisters and Mr. Bennatyne[3] and family, that you have good accounts of your friends in India.

With my sisters and my united kind regards to yourself and sisters, believe me with much esteem,

Yours faithfully

HELEN THOMSON

Georgina's youngest daughter, Helen,[4] has been since the beginning of last winter teaching singing successfully, and has many pupils in prospect for this season.

Please remember me to Dr. and Mrs. Anderson[5] when you see them.

Mrs. Stark, 1, Vanbrugh Place, Links Leith, Glasgow,[6] Scotland.

[1] "Sidney" in text.

[2] He was in fact the second. Augustus had left his wife the previous year and Frederick was about to be separated.

[3] Unidentified.

[4] For Helen Hogarth see *To* Wills, 3–4 Jan 56, *fn.*

[5] Unidentified.

[6] W. J. Carlton (above) shows that this address was correct for Edinburgh: presumably another mistake by the copier. George Thomson had lived there during his retirement 1848–51 and other members of his family subsequently. Such mistakes led Walter Dexter (in *D*, XXIII [1936] 61) and Edgar Johnson (*CD: His Tragedy and Triumph*, II, lxxvi) to brand the letter as a forgery; but both K.J. Fielding and W.J. Carlton (above) give convincing evidence for its authenticity.

G. DICKENS'S MEMORANDA FOR HIS DRAFT WILL, 1858

MS Messrs Farrer & Co.

MEMORANDA FOR THE DRAFT.

Georgina Hogarth of Tavistock House
John Forster of 46 Montagu Square
and
William Henry Wills of 22 Regent's Park Terrace
to be Trustees and Executors of my Will.

To whom I leave all my real and personal estate, copyrights, interests in copyrights, money derivable from Policy or Policies of Assurance—everything whatever—in trust for the following purposes.

Firstly, to pay a[1] Legacy,[2] which I wish to bequeath in due form.

Secondly, to manage my real and personal estate, to call it in and sell it, or hold it, or have full power to do what they please with it or with any part of it, for the maintenance and support of Georgina Hogarth, and any unmarried daughters or daughter of mine, and for the maintenance, support, education and establishment in life of such of my children as may be under age at the time of my death. Trustees and executors having full power to advance such sums as they may think proper, for the last mentioned purposes, at their own discretion, and according to their opinion of the exigency and promise of the individual case, and with no strict reference to the children all benefitting alike. Regard to be always had to the genteel and comfortable support of Georgina Hogarth and any unmarried daughters or daughter of mine.

Also in trust to pay a certain sum per annum to Mrs. Dickens until the youngest child shall come of age.

Georgina Hogarth and my eldest daughter Mary (if unmarried) to be joint and sole guardians of my children. If my eldest daughter Mary should be married, then my second daughter Kate (if unmarried), to be joint Guardian with Georgina Hogarth. If Kate should be married too, then Georgina Hogarth, whether married or no, to be sole Guardian.

When the youngest of my children shall come of age, the balance remaining in the hands of my Trustees and Executors, to be divided between Georgina Hogarth, and any unmarried or widowed daughters or daughter of mine, and Mrs. Dickens, share and share alike. If there should be no unmarried or widowed daughters, or daughter, then Georgina Hogarth to receive one half[1.] of the whole balance, and Mrs. Dickens one half[2.] If Mrs. Dickens should be the sole survivor, then Mrs. Dickens to have one

[1] "Money" inserted here over caret, probably by Ouvry. Besides a few additions and deletions, no doubt by Ouvry also, CD himself made three changes in the penultimate paragraph: 1. Miss Hogarth's "one half" was originally "two thirds". 2. Mrs Dickens's "one half" was originally "one third" in both places. 3. "moiety" is written over "two thirds" cancelled. A pencilled cross against the original "two thirds" for Georgina suggests that the change may have been proposed by Ouvry.

[2] Probably to Ellen Ternan, who received £1,000 in his final Will of 2 June 1870.

half,[2] and the remaining moiety[3] to be divided among all my surviving children, share and share alike. If Georgina Hogarth should be the sole survivor, then Georgina Hogarth to take the whole absolutely.

If Georgina Hogarth should die at any time during the minority of any of my children, then my eldest surviving daughter whether married or no, to be joint guardian with my surviving trustees or Executors. [a]And in that case, when the youngest child comes of age, the balance to be divided in this proportion.[a]

[aa] Heavily crossed out by CD, but quite legible. On the back of p. 1 of the expanded draft drawn up from these memoranda, CD inserted two paragraphs, both in 1858, following a new sentence, "And I bequeath unto my eldest son Charles Dickens and my son Henry Fielding Dickens . . ."; these two replacing the names of Georgina Hogarth, Forster and Wills. The first new paragraph, in ink, runs: "the sum of £—— upon trust and to invest the same and from time to time to vary the investments thereof and to pay the sum of the income thereof to my Wife during her life and after her decease the said sum of £——, and the investments thereof shall be in trust for my children [*inserted in pencil*: "other than my daughter Mary Dickens"] who being a Son or Sons shall have attained or shall attain the age of 21 years or being Daughter or Daughters shall have attained or shall attain that age, or marry or be previously married in equal shares if more than one. And I devise and bequeath all my real and personal estate (except such as are vested in me as a Trustee or Mortgagee) unto the said —— Dickens and Henry Fielding Dickens" [*last few words illegible*]. The second, in pencil: "Unto the sd. Charles Dickens & Henry Fielding Dickens the sum of £—— upon trust to invest the same & from time to time to vary the investments thereof and to pay the income thereof to my Daughter Mary Dickens during her life and after her decease the sd. sum of £—— and the investments thereof shall be in trust for my children in the same way as hereinbefore declared concerning the sum of £—— the income whereof is given to my wife for her life. Unto the sd. Charles Dickens and Henry Fielding Dickens the sum of £—— upon trust to invest the sum and from time to time to vary the investments thereof and to pay the annual income thereof to my sister in law Georgina Hogarth for her life and after her decease the sd. sum of £—— and the investments thereof shall be in trust for my children in the same way as hereinbefore declared concerning the sum of £—— the income whereof is given to my wife for her life."

H. THE READINGS, AUGUST–NOVEMBER 1858

MR. CHARLES DICKENS'S TOUR, / DURING THE AUTUMN OF 1858

Text from *CD as Editor*, p. 239.

Place	Day	Month	Date	Hour		Venue
CLIFTON	Monday,	Aug.	2.	.8	o'clock	Bath Hotel.
EXETER	Tuesday,	"	3.	.8	"	London Hotel.
PLYMOUTH	Wednesday,	"	4.	.8	"	Elliot's Royal Hotel.
"	Thursday,	"	5.	.3&8	"	
CLIFTON	Friday,	"	6.	.8	"	Bath Hotel
WORCESTER	Tuesday,	"	10.	.8	"	Mr. Stratford's Music Warehouse, The Cross, Worcester.
WOLVERHAMPTON	Wednesday,	"	11.	.8	"	Swan Hotel.
SHREWSBURY	Thursday,	"	12.	.8	"	Mr. Leake, Bookseller.
CHESTER	Friday,	"	13.	.8	"	Royal Hotel.
LIVERPOOL	Wednesday,	"	18	8	"	Radley's Adelphi Hotel.
"	Thursday,	"	19.	.8	"	
"	Friday,	"	20.	.8	"	
"	Saturday,	"	21.	.3	"	
DUBLIN	Monday,	"	23.	.8	"	Morrison's Hotel
"	Tuesday,	"	24.	.8	"	
"	Wednesday,	"	25.	.3&8	"	
"	Thursday,	"	26.	.8	"	
BELFAST	Friday,	"	27.	.8	"	Imperial Hotel.
"	Saturday,	"	28.	.3&8	"	
CORK	Monday,	"	30.	.8	"	Imperial Hotel.
"	Tuesday,	"	31.	.1½&8	"	
LIMERICK	Wednesday,	Sept.	1.	.8	"	Cruise's Hotel.
"	Thursday,	"	2.	.8	"	
HUDDERSFIELD	Wednesday,	"	8.	.8	"	George Hotel.
WAKEFIELD	Thursday,	"	9.	.8	"	Stafford Arms.
YORK	Friday,	"	10.	.8	"	Mr. Henry Banks, Music Warehouse, Stonegate.
HARROGATE	Saturday,	"	11.	.3&8	"	Mr. W. Dawson, Cheltenham Pump Room.
SCARBOROUGH	Monday,	"	13.	.3&8	"	Assembly Rooms.
HULL	Tuesday,	"	14.	.8	"	Mr. R. Bowser, Music Hall.
LEEDS	Wednesday	"	15.	.8	"	Scarboro' Arms Hotel.
HALIFAX	Thursday	"	16.	.8	"	White Swan Hotel.
SHEFFIELD	Friday	"	17.	.8	"	King's Head Hotel.
MANCHESTER	Saturday,	"	18.	.8	"	Royal Hotel.
DARLINGTON	Tuesday,	"	21.	.8	"	Mr. Robert Swale, Bookseller.
DURHAM	Wednesday,	"	22.	.8	"	Mr. Procter, Bookseller, Market Place.
SUNDERLAND	Thursday,	"	23.	.8	"	Bridge House Hotel.
NEWCASTLE	Friday,	"	24.	.8	"	Mr. T. Horn, Music Warehouse, Grey-street.
"	Saturday,	"	25.	.3&8	"	
EDINBURGH	Monday,	"	27.	.8	"	Waterloo Hotel.
"	Tuesday,	"	28.	.8	"	
"	Wednesday,	"	29.	.3&8	"	
"	Thursday,	"	30.	.8	"	
DUNDEE	Friday,	Oct.	1.	.8	"	Mr. Chalmers, Bookseller.
"	Saturday,	"	2.	.8	"	
ABERDEEN	Monday,	"	4.	.3&8	"	Mr. John Marr, Music Saloon.
PERTH	Tuesday,	"	5.	.8	"	Mr. Drummond, Bookseller.

GLASGOW	Wednesday,	"	6. .8	"	Mr. John Muir Wood, Music Warehouse
"	Thursday,	"	7. .8	"	
"	Friday,	"	8. .8	"	
"	Saturday	"	9. .3	"	
BRADFORD	Thursday,	"	14. .8	"	Mr. C. Ollivier, St. George's Hall.
LIVERPOOL . . .	Friday,	"	15. .3&8	"	Radley's Adelphi Hotel.
MANCHESTER . .	Saturday,	"	16. .8	"	Royal Hotel.
BIRMINGHAM . .	Monday,	"	18. .8	"	Hen and Chickens Hotel.
" . .	Tuesday,	"	19. .8	"	
"	Wednesday,	"	20. .8	"	
NOTTINGHAM . .	Thursday,	"	21. .8	"	Mr. T. Forman, Guardian Office.
DERBY	Friday,	"	22. .8	"	Royal Hotel.
MANCHESTER . .	Saturday,	"	23. .8	"	Royal Hotel, Manchester.
YORK	Monday,	"	25. .8	"	Royal Station Hotel.
HULL	Tuesday,	"	26. .8	"	Royal Station Hotel.
"	Wednesday,	"	27. .3	"	
LEEDS	Thursday,	"	28. .8	"	White Horse Hotel.
SHEFFIELD	Friday,	"	29. .8	"	King's Head Hotel.
LEAMINGTON . .	Tuesday,	Nov.	2. .3&8	"	Assembly Rooms, Leamington.
WOLVERHAMPTON	Wednesday,	"	3. .8	"	Swan Hotel.
LEICESTER	Thursday,	"	4. .8	"	Bell Hotel.
OXFORD	Friday,	"	5. .8	"	Star Hotel, Oxford.
"	Saturday,	"	6. .3	"	
SOUTHAMPTON . .	Tuesday,	"	9. .8	"	Mr. Sharland, Bookseller, High Street.
" . .	Wednesday,	"	10. .3	"	
PORTSMOUTH . .	Thursday,	"	11. .3&8	"	Mr. Atkins, Music Warehouse, Portsea.
BRIGHTON	Friday,	"	12. .8	"	Bedford Hotel.
"	Saturday	"	13. .3&8	"	

1. PROPOSED ACTION FOR SLANDER AGAINST COLIN RAE BROWN

(1) H. B. MACPHAIL *to* CHARLES DICKENS, 14 OCTOBER 1858

MS Messrs Farrer & Co. (given in K. J. Fielding, "CD and Colin Rae Brown", *Nineteenth-Century Fiction*, VII [1952], 103).

41 Commercial Road | Glasgow 14th Oct 1858

Dear Sir,

I know not whether I should write to you regarding a matter which is most unpleasant to me to broach, and must be painful to you to read. It respects your personal character. That no doubt must be dear to you and your children. I myself feel feelingly interested in the matter from the affability and kindness which I experienced in the interview I had with you here, and report from yourself—from my admiration of your high literary name, which I would not like to see by Malignments in this City the least impaired in the circulation of falsehood, even in private life.

How I come to write you thus is simply this, and if I can serve you in the matter in this quarter I will be right glad to do it.

Yesterday one of the acting Directorate of the "Bulletin" Newspaper Co. (and I give you his name meantime confidentially Mr. Colin Rae Brown) accosted me in the street with "he was astonished that I would have written as I did of Dickens in *his* paper,—had he been at *home* no notice would have been taken of him—that he was the outcry of London, and enquired if I knew that Mr. Dickens's sister in law had had three children by him." My answer was short, that I knew no such thing, that what had I to do with his private life in writing as I did?—I wrote not of the *man domestic*, but of the *author* and his writings.

Anything but this I would have liked to have written in my first communication to you on your return to London, and pardon me in saying that a purely friendly feeling for the absent has prompted me in doing so. What hurt this man from his position, may do to you in your personal reputation in Glasgow, by repeating what I have expressed I know not.

I may state that I have no disagreeable feeling with Brown, but I was really struck at the manner, in the presence of another gentleman of the Press, in which he expressed himself (not as to my letter respecting you, for I could have got it inserted in half a dozen papers in Glasgow, but the "Bulletin" is the greatest daily circulation). Not the expressions but the spirit was malignant in which he uttered himself and not what I [would] really have expected of him in speaking of any living author of celebrity.

I have no doubt you will view this communication in the proper light and my services here as I have said are at your command in crushing or strangling falsehood. Brown I may state said he was newly down from London and heard all there, precious creature of hearsay.

Believe me to be | Dear Sir
Most respectfully | Faithfully Yours
H. BUCHANAN MACPHAIL

(2) DRAFT LETTER, ALMOST CERTAINLY DICTATED BY DICKENS TO ARTHUR SMITH ON 16 OCTOBER 1858, FOR MESSRS FARRER, OUVRY & FARRER TO SEND TO C. R. BROWN

MS Messrs Farrer & Co. (given in K. J. Fielding, *ibid.*).

TAVISTOCK HOUSE, | TAVISTOCK SQUARE, LONDON. W.C.

Colin Rae Brown Esq.
Bulletin Newspaper Company,
Glasgow

Sir

On the 13th. Oct instant you thought fit to utter a gross scandalous slander affecting the character of Mr. Charles Dickens. A slander—which if it had the slightest foundation—in fact would render Mr. Dickens an outcast from Society.

Mr. Dickens will give further opportunity of maintaining what you have presumed to say & we have to request that you will by return of post send us the name of your Solicitor to whom we may send the process we are instructed to open against you.

(3) EXTRACT FROM COPY OR DRAFT OF LETTER FROM MESSRS FARRER, OUVRY & FARRER, ASKING COUNSEL'S OPINION [LATE OCTOBER] 1858

MS Messrs Farrer & Co.

Under these circumstances Mr. Dickens feels he must either compel Brown to make the most humble & unqualified admission of his misconduct & the acknowledgment that the slander he uttered is groundless, or an action must be commenced. The latter is a painful alternative but Mr. Dickens feels that much as he should suffer from bringing such a statement before the public, the pain would be infinitely less than he now endures in the thought that Brown or any one else may be whispering about this monstrous charge with impunity.

(4) EXTRACT FROM LETTER FROM H. B. MACPHAIL *to* CHARLES DICKENS, 18 OCTOBER 1858

MS (extract) Messrs Farrer & Co.

41 Commercial Road | Glasgow 18th. Oct 1858.

Dear Sir,

I have your favor of the 16th. inst. As my former letter to you respecting the name of Mr. Colin Rae Brown was confidential, I hasten to say that I give you full liberty to do in the matter in vindication of yourself as may appear to you best.

I sincerely sympathise with you in the diabolical report.

I admire your spirit of determination to put, so far as human means can do it, an end to the dastardly malignity of any one here, in circulating such infamous expressions and charges against you.

You can have no idea of the pain it gave me, the conflicting feeling of what I thought my duty to you and the delicacy of the subject, in writing you formerly. Here believe me you may always rely on one Scotchman that will not stand to see in his absence an Englishman unjustly spoken of or maligned, whatever the personal sacrifice may be that may follow his disclosure to the punishment of the assassin of reputation.

(5) C. R. BROWN *to* CHARLES DICKENS, 19 OCTOBER 1858

MS Farrer & Co. (given in K. J. Fielding, *ibid.*).

Glasgow 19 October 1858

Sir

To the deep feelings of sorrow under which I at present labor, in consequence of the rapidly declining state of my dear wife's health I have this morning had the addition to my troubles of a letter from your solicitors. To say that nothing ever more pained or surprised me, than the communication referred to, would but faintly express the emotions it awakened. That I, above all other men—who have, for a life time almost, been your warm, devoted, admirer,—should have such a charge laid to me, is indeed a grief which it is ill to bear. To your Solicitors, I have at once Caused my agent to write, from his communication you will see that my proceedings are exactly the *Converse* of what has been stated. Finding the Slander without foundation I have dismissed even the faintest remembrance of it from my mind; and as lawyers are tedious sometimes, I could not let a post pass over without communicating directly—without intervention. To sleep a night under such a thought as that any man (especially you) should consider me guilty of traducing his name, is a thing so foreign to my nature, that the bare idea quite upsets me. I heard a very malicious report in London, questioned the truth of it from my informant—made strict enquiry regarding it—and am delighted to say that I found it unsupported. I apprehend that some one, of whom I made such an enquiry, has *misunderstood* or *misrepresented* me grossly: while the pain he (or they) has inflicted is beyond description!

Yours very sincerely
C. R. BROWN

(6) QUINTIN DICK *to* MESSRS FARRER, OUVRY, FARRER, 21 OCTOBER 1858

MS Messrs Farrer & Co. (given in K. J. Fielding, *ibid.*).

48 Buchanan Street | Glasgow 21st October 1858

Gentlemen,

My Client Mr. C. R. Brown of this City has placed into my hands your note of the 10th. current with instructions to answer. Mr. Brown is exceedingly pained and surprized at the contents of that letter, in so far as it accuses him of uttering a slander affecting the character of Mr. Dickens, the more especially as Mr. Dickens must know from the spirit of frequent communications addressed to him by my client, that his opinion of that Gentleman is far otherwise than depreciatory.—Mr. Brown cannot charge himself with and he most emphatically denies either having uttered or given the slightest countenance to any slander affecting the character of Mr. Dickens. It is the case that Mr. Brown when in London a few days ago, heard a report of a somewhat malicious nature which, while he gave no credence to it, he made enquiries concerning in order that when he should next meet it he could be able to give it a decided negative. Mr. Brown so far from slandering Mr. Dickens has always professed an unusual amount of respect & veneration for him and the suspicion of such a charge against him is thereby made doubly painful.

If Mr. Dickens is still advised after this explanation to bring the matter before a Court Mr. Brown will just require to meet the action.

I am Sirs | Your mo. obed. Servt.

QUINTIN DICK[1]

Messrs. Farrer Ouvry Farrer
66 Lincolns Inn Fields
London WC

verified.

[1] Quintin Dick, of Dick & Roberts, Writers to the Signet, 104 West Regent St.

J. LETTERS EXCHANGED BETWEEN JOHN FORSTER, ACTING UNDER A POWER OF ATTORNEY FROM DICKENS, AND BRADBURY & EVANS, TO DISSOLVE THE PARTNERSHIP IN *HOUSEHOLD WORDS*, AND OTHER RELEVANT DOCUMENTS.

(1) EXTRACT FROM *HOUSEHOLD WORDS* MINUTE-BOOK (IN WILLS'S HAND), 15 NOVEMBER 1858

MS Messrs Farrer & Co. (given in K. J. Fielding, "Bradbury *v.* Dickens", *D*, L [1954], 73).

Special meeting held on this 15th. day of November 1858.

Present John Forster (as attorney for Charles Dickens) W. Bradbury, F. M. Evans & W. H. Wills.

The minutes of the former meeting having been confirmed the power of attorney empowering Mr. John Forster to act for Mr. Dickens was read. It was then

Proposed by Mr. John Forster & seconded by Mr. W. H. Wills

That the present partnership in Household Words be dissolved by the Cessation and discontinuance of that publication on the Completion of the Nineteenth Volume.

Mr. Forster & Mr. Wills voted in favour of the resolution,—but Messrs Bradbury and Evans declined to vote.

Memo. Mr. John Forster ceased to be a partner in the concern on the 2nd February 1856.

The 19 Volume of Household Words will be completed at the end of May 1859.

Documents wanting. Copy of Forster's letter of the 27 [?]

CD | [?] | copy and requisition to B & E to call the meeting.

[*With this is a note, written by either Bradbury or Evans*]

Believing the resolution to be contrary to the condition of partnership and therefore illegal—We decline to vote. see under.

(2) BRADBURY & EVANS *to* JOHN FORSTER, 9 DECEMBER 1858

MS Messrs Farrer & Co. (given in K. J. Fielding, *ibid.*).

Whitefriars, London, | December 9th. 1858

Dear Sir

It was needless of you to refer to the attempted Resolution which, as we stated at the Meeting, was, and is, wholly inoperative—But after the communication which you were directed by Mr. Dickens to make relative to ourselves, we can have no wish to protract our connection with him.

We shall, therefore, be quite prepared to entertain a proposal for the purchase of our share and all Works in which we are jointly interested with Mr. Dickens including among them Household Words.

Believe us | Dear Sir | Very truly yours

John Forster Esq. BRADBURY & EVANS

(3) JOHN FORSTER *to* BRADBURY & EVANS, 10 DECEMBER 1858

MS (copy in Dickens's hand) Morgan Library (given in K.J. Fielding, *ibid.*).

46 Montagu Square | Tenth December 1858

Dear Sirs

Acting under the Power of Attorney which I hold from Mr. Dickens to represent his proprietorship of Household Words, I addressed a letter to you on the 27th. November, informing you that if a reply to that letter were not sent to me in a fortnight from its date, proceedings would be taken, in accordance with the Resolution passed at the last Meeting of the Household Words proprietors.

You have addressed to me a letter dated the 9th. December, which reached me this morning. In this letter, you refer to the terms, by which I represented Mr. Dickens's proprietorship at the recent meeting, as a communication I was "directed" by Mr. Dickens to make; you describe the Resolution duly passed on that occasion as an "attempted Resolution"; and you introduce subjects to which, as you well know, my authority under the Power of Attorney in question does not extend.

In so addressing me, in such circumstances, you commit what I might with propriety characterize by a harsh epithet. But I content myself with saying, that I altogether decline to receive this letter dated 9th. December as in any respect whatever a reply to mine of the 27th. November, and I accordingly herewith return it to you, enclosed in the same envelope which contains what I am now writing.

Not having been favored with any reply, therefore, to my letter of the 27th. November, I now inform you, that if I do not receive one before the expiration of tomorrow (Saturday the 11th. December), the proceeding to which I referred in that letter, will be taken in due course.

And I have further to request that in case you send me a reply in the course of today or tomorrow, you will limit it, expressly and solely, to the matter which I have been alone empowered to bring under your notice. Upon any other subject affecting Mr. Dickens, you will be good enough to write to himself. I do not act under his directions. I act, upon the specific business of Household Words, with and by the simple powers which I hold from him under the Law; and in that character only, I communicate with you respecting it.

Nor does Mr. Dickens even know of the present letter, or of the very improper communication you have been pleased to address to me under date of the 9th December, and which is now sent back to you.

(4) BRADBURY & EVANS *to* JOHN FORSTER, 10 DECEMBER 1858

MS Messrs Farrer & Co. (given in K. J. Fielding, *ibid.*).

Whitefriars, London, | December 10, 1858

Dear Sir.

In reply to your communication of the 10th. inst. We beg again to protest against the legality of the attempted Resolution referred to in your letter—it was, and still is, wholly inoperative.

At the same time, and for the reason given to you in our letter of the 9th inst. as the inducement to us to part with our interest in all Mr. Dickens's works we are willing to entertain a proposal from Mr. Dickens for the sale of our interest in "Household Words."—

As we cannot withdraw our letter of the 9th. instant to which you object, we beg to return it to you—

Believe us | Dear Sir | Yours very truly

J. Forster Esq. BRADBURY & EVANS

(5) JOHN FORSTER *to* CHARLES DICKENS, 11 DECEMBER 1858

MS Messrs Farrer & Co. (given in K. J. Fielding, *ibid.*).

W | 46 Montagu Square | Decembr. 11, 1858

My dear Dickens

This letter and enclosure,[1] as you see, arrived last night.

My first impulse was to return it as it stands—without a word. My second, to tear it up and return the fragments. My third, to fling it into the fire, and write them one line saying I had done so. My fourth, and last, to retain it, forward it to you, and utter not another word to them.

[1] Bradbury & Evans's letters to him of 9 and 10 Dec.

It shows not only (as I think) extraordinary weakness but extraordinary eagerness as to parting with "all the works"—which you see they manage to Edge in again, and for submission of which desire to you they alone, as it seems to me, send back the original & rejected letter.

Now—what do you say? Give me one word. Of course this letter, with its "protest", is no more an answer than the last, nor can be received as such. But silently to say no more, & proceed to carry out the Resolution, will be, I fancy, the best answer. I will do, however, as you think best.

Ever affecy. yours
JOHN FORSTER

P.S. Will you kindly give the enclosed draft of first letter to Wills? I sent all else to him last night.—A nice man Mr. Ingram![1]

(6) BRADBURY & EVANS *to* JOHN FORSTER, 14 DECEMBER 1858

MS Messrs Farrer & Co. (given in K. J. Fielding, *ibid.*).

Whitefriars, London | Decr. 14, 1858

Dear Sir.

In reply to your letter of this day's date we beg to decline the offer contained in it, for the purchase of our interest in "Household Words".—

Very truly yours

John Forster Esq. BRADBURY & EVANS

[1] Sarcastic of course: Ingram was involved with Bradbury & Evans financially, and a close friend of Lemon.

K. DICKENS'S REMINISCENCES OF DOUGLAS JERROLD, SENT TO HIS SON BLANCHARD JERROLD ON 26 NOVEMBER 1858

MS Mr Douglas Jerrold.

It is not likely that I can furnish you with any new particulars of interest concerning your lamented father. Such details of his life and early struggles as I have often heard from himself, are better known to you than to me; and my praises of him can make no new sound in your ears.

But, as you wish me to note down for you, my last remembrance and experience of him, I proceed to do so. It is natural that my thoughts should first rush back (as they instantly do) to the days when he began to be known to me, and to the many happy hours I afterwards passed in his society.

Few of his friends, I think, can have had more favorable opportunities of knowing him, in his gentlest and most affectionate aspect, than I have had. He was one of the gentlest and most affectionate of men. I remember very well that when I first saw him, in or about the year 1835—when I went into his sick room in St. Michael's Grove Brompton,[1] and found him propped up in a great chair, bright-eyed, and eager and quick in spirit, but very lame in body—he gave me an impression of tenderness. It never became dissociated from him. There was nothing cynical or sour in his heart, as I knew it. In the company of children and young people, he was particularly happy, and shewed to extraordinary advantage. He never was so gay, so sweet-tempered, so pleasing, and so pleased as there. Among my own children, I have observed this many and many a time. When they and I came home from Italy in 1845, your father went to Brussels to meet us—in company with our friends, *Mr. Forster*[2] and *Mr. Maclise.*[2] We all travelled together, about Belgium[3] for a little while, and all came home together.[4] He was the delight of the children all the time, and they were his delight. He was in his most brilliant spirits, and I doubt if he were ever more humorous in his life. But the most enduring impression that he left upon us who were grown up—and we have, all, often spoken of it since—was, that *Jerrold*,[2] in his amiable capacity of being easily pleased, in his freshness, in his good-nature, in his cordiality, and in the unrestrained openness of his heart, had quite captivated us.

Of his generosity I had a proof, within these two or three years, which it saddens me to think of now. There had been an estrangement between us—not on any personal subject, and not involving an angry word—and a good many months had passed without my once seeing him in the street, when it fell out that we dined, each with his own separate party, in the strangers' room of a club. Our chairs were almost

[1] CD first met Jerrold in Nov 1836 at his home, Thistle Lodge, Chelsea. He does not record, before this, meeting him in Brompton.

[2] Underlined by short double strokes.

[3] "Bâle" written, and not cancelled, before "Belgium". The enclosure, as Blanchard Jerrold said, is "blurred and corrected and re-written—so unlike Dickens" (*The Best of All Good Company: A Day with CD*, 1871, p. 33). CD, he also says, "had seen into the heart of his friend" (*ibid.*, p. 5).

[4] For the week they spent together in Belgium, see Vol. IV, p. 324.

back to back, and I took mine after he was seated and at dinner. I said not a word (I am sorry to remember) and did not look that way. Before we had sat so, long, he openly wheeled his chair round, stretched out both his hands in a most engaging manner, and said aloud, with a bright and loving face that I can see as I write to you—"For God's sake, let us be friends again! Life's not long enough for this!"[1]

On Sunday, May 31st, 1857, I had made an appointment to meet him at the Gallery of Illustration, in Regent Street. We had been advising our friend, Mr. Russell, in the condensation of his lectures on the war in the Crimea,[2] and we had engaged with him to go over the last of the series there at one o'clock that day. Arriving some minutes before the time, I found your father sitting alone in the hall. "There must be some mistake," he said: no one else was there; the place was locked up; he had tried all the doors; and he had been waiting there a quarter of an hour by himself. I sat down by him in a niche in the staircase, and he told me that he had been very unwell for three or four days. A window in his study had been newly painted, and the smell of the paint (he thought it must be that) had filled him with nausea and turned him sick, and he felt quite weak and giddy through not having been able to retain any food. He was a little subdued at first and out of spirits; but we sat there half-an-hour, talking, and when we came out together he was quite himself.

In the shadow I had not observed him closely; but when we got into the sunshine of the streets, I saw that he looked ill. We were both engaged to dine with Mr. Russell at Greenwich, and I thought him so ill then that I advised him not to go, but to let me take him, or send him, home in a cab. He complained, however, of having turned so weak—we had now strolled as far as Leicester Square—that he was fearful he might faint in the Cab, unless I could get him some restorative, and unless he could "keep it down". I deliberated for a moment whether to turn back to the Athenaeum where I could have got a little brandy for him, or to take him on into Covent Garden for the purpose; meanwhile, he stood leaning against the rails of the enclosure, looking, for the moment, very ill indeed. Finally, we walked on to Covent Garden, and before we had gone fifty yards, he was very much better. On our way, Mr. Russell joined us. He was then better still, and walked between us, unassisted. I got him a hard biscuit and a little weak cold brandy and water, and begged him by all means to try to eat. He broke up and ate the greater part of the biscuit, and then was much refreshed and comforted by the brandy; he said that he felt the sickness was overcome at last, and that he was quite a new man; it would do him good to have a few quiet hours in the air, and he would go with us to Greenwich. I still tried to dissuade him, but he was by this time bent upon it, and his natural color had returned, and he was very hopeful and confident.

We strolled through the Temple on our way to a boat and I have a lively recollection of him stamping about Elm Tree Court, with his hat in one hand and the other pushing his hair back, laughing in his heartiest manner at a ridiculous remembrance

[1] For Walter Jerrold's suggestion—surely correct—that this arose in Nov 1849 from the controversy over the abolition of capital punishment, after the public hanging of the Mannings, see Vol. v, p. 615*n*: his grandfather desired to abolish all hanging, public and private, while CD advocated only the abolition of public executions (*Douglas Jerrold, Dramatist and Wit*, [1914], II, 517–18). See Vol. v, p. 650 and *n*.

[2] For Russell's lectures on the Crimean War, see Appx D, and *To* Irvine, 7 July 57, *fn*.

we had in common, which I had presented in some exaggerated light, to divert him. We found our boat, and went down the river, and looked at the Leviathan which was building, and talked all the way. It was a bright day, and as soon as we reached Greenwich we got an open carriage and went out for a drive about Shooter's Hill. In the carriage, Mr. Russell read us his Lecture, and we discussed it with great interest; we planned out the ground of Inkermann, on the heath, and your father was very earnest indeed. The subject held us so, that we were graver than usual; but he broke out at intervals in the same hilarious way as in the Temple; and he over and over again said to me with great satisfaction, how happy he was, that he had "quite got over that Paint".

The dinner-party was a large one, and I did not sit near him at table. But he and I arranged before we went in to dinner that he was only to eat of some simple dish that we agreed upon, and was only to drink sherry and water. We broke up very early, and before I went away with *Mr. Leech*,[1] who was to take me to London, I went round to Jerrold, for whom some one else had a seat in a carriage and put my hand upon his shoulder, asking him how he was? He turned round to shew me the glass beside him, with a little wine and water in it: "I have kept to the prescription; it has answered as well as this morning's, my dear old boy; I have quite got over the paint, and I am perfectly well." He was really elated by the relief of having recovered, and was as quietly happy as I ever saw him. We exchanged "God bless you!" and shook hands.

I went down to Gad's Hill next morning, where he was to write to me after a little while, appointing his own time for coming to see me there. A week afterwards, another passenger in the Railway carriage in which I was on my way to London Bridge, opened his morning-paper, and said "Douglas Jerrold is dead!"

[1] Underlined by short double strokes.

CORRIGENDA

5 *fn* 5 *substitute* Not Charley, who was still in France, but the Yates godson.

384 17 *substitute* MS Mr Joseph R. Sakmyster.
21 *insert new line* My Dear Taylor
22 *after* speak it? *insert* Don't delay.
23 *add two lines* Faithfully Yours Ever
Tom Taylor Esquire CHARLES DICKENS

694 last line of text *after* money *add cue* [6]
after fn 5 *add*

[6] The paper is the actual material, the vouchers being the receipts for this, which CD and the other proprietors will require for the next *HW* audit: see below and p. 701, *To* Wills, 10 Nov.

INDEX OF CORRESPONDENTS

Adams, Henry Gardiner 411, 476, 501, 612, 681, 711
Adams, William James 268
Alberti, Frau Sophie ('Sophie Verena') 40, 104
Aldridge, T. L. 112
Allan-Fraser, Patrick 630
Allingham, William 478
Allon, Rev. Henry 500
Andersen, Hans Christian 144, 307, 323, 425
Angel Hotel, Doncaster, Master of 429
Attwell, Henry 388
Austin, Henry 90, 134, 206, 283, 296, 297, 303, 342, 381, 384, 411, 420, 421, 427, 449, 584, 590
Austin, Mrs Sarah 219

Ballantine, James 38, 724
Bamps, (?Anatole) 537
Banting, William 454
Bateman, Mrs John 183
Bathurst, Henry Allen 520, 522, 523
Beadnell, George 341
Beale, Thomas Willert 402, 533
Beard, Thomas 137, 141, 181, 196, 205, 243, 269, 274, 286, 291, 301, 319, 324, 326, 369, 480, 542, 546, 555, 557, 595, 616, 679, 682
Beaucourt-Mutuel, Ferdinand Henri Joseph Alexandre 11, 64
Becker, (?Bernard Henry) 220
Bell, George 385, 387
Bell, Robert 305
Benedict, (Sir) Julius (Jules) 353
Bennett, John 493
Bentley, Richard 253, 337, 360, 367, 377, 385, 390, 398, 403, 415, 419, 424, 462, 528, 663
Berger, Francesco 252, 259, 300, 348, 353, 376, 395, 406, 409
Bicknell, Henry 129, 590, 716
Blessington, Marguerite, Countess of *see* Friends of Lady Blessington
Blewitt, Octavian 549
Boddington, Thomas 655
Bolton, J. L. 451
Boughey, George 341
(Bowater), W. D. 185
Bowie, Henry 319, 457
Boxall, William 561
Boyle, Captain Cavendish Spencer 515
Boyle, Mary Louisa 14, 71, 165, 276, 572, 609, 655, 717
Brace, George 224
Bradbury & Evans, Messrs 31, 61, 66, 80, 107, 227, 241, 274, 456, 495, 653, 695, 700, 719
Bradbury, Henry Riley 594
Bradbury, William 226
Bradfield, John E. 314
Brandt, Francis Frederick 305
Brooks, (Charles William) Shirley 391, 403, 404, 451, 466, 529, 663
Brooks, S. L. 608
Brough, Robert Barnabas 582
Brougham and Vaux, Henry Peter, Baron 4
Brown, Colin Rae 427, 714
Brown, Montagu Yeats 667
Brown, Timothy Yeats 415
Brown, Mrs William 145, 169, 171, 189, 191, 197, 201, 221, 249, 259, 421, 430, 478, 688
Browne, Hablot Knight ('Phiz') 141, 219, 232, 280, 297
Browning, Robert 86
Buckstone, John Baldwin 435, 465
Burnett, Henry 73, 665

Campbell, John, 1st Baron 229
Carlisle, George William Frederick Howard, 7th Earl of 313
Carlyle, Thomas 166
Carmichael-Smyth, Mrs Henry 461
Carroll, Ellen 102
Carter, Dr Robert Brudenell 190
Cartwright, Samuel, Jr. 495
Celeste, Madame (Celeste Elliott) 570
Cerjat, William Woodley Frederick de 264, 284, 596
Chambers, Mrs 44
Chambers, Robert 562
Chapman & Hall, Messrs 368
Chapman, Edward 215, 322, 563, 609, 615
Chapman, Frederic 714
Chatham and Rochester Mechanics' Institute, The Secretary of 498
Chesterton, George Laval 585
Chorley, Henry Fothergill 594
Clarke, Mr & Mrs Charles Cowden 204
Clement, William James 313, 371, 613
Collins, Charles Allston 467
Collins, William Wilkie 28, 39, 53, 62, 67, 86, 95, 105, 130, 161, 167, 175, 184, 186, 203, 207, 214, 217, 222, 237, 240, 256, 263, 275, 282, 294, 322, 327, 329, 338, 348, 354, 355, 361, 394, 413, 423, 470, 475, 505, 516, 517, 535, 547, 553, 567, 616, 623, 649, 700, 703
Compton, Mrs Henry 397

Cooke, Thomas Potter 348, 352, 392
Cooper, Frank 687
Coote, Charles 318
Copley, John Singleton *see* Lyndhurst, Baron
Cornelius, Mrs Edward (Anne) 431, 465, 613, 627, 645, 678
Couchman, John 696
Coutts & Co., Messrs 107, 239
Coutts, Angela Georgina Burdett 16, 41, 50, 53, 60, 79, 84, 117, 118, 119, 122, 123, 124, 127, 146, 160, 164, 176, 181, 187, 192, 198, 212, 215, 223, 229, 230, 233, 237, 244, 248, 251, 252, 260, 271, 276, 282, 286, 287, 291, 295, 310, 330, 331, 340, 343, 354, 356, 372, 380, 387, 390, 396, 418, 432, 458, 478, 482, 485, 486, 512, 518, 521, 524, 525, 527, 544, 551, 552, 558, 565, 578, 621, 632, 652, 688, 693, 717
Creswick, William 351, 471, 474
Crocker, Charles W. 585
Crozier, Robert 477
Cullenford, William J. 240, 536
Cunningham, Peter 42, 132, 429, 474
Currie, Philip Henry Wodehouse 308

Dance, Charles 547
Davies, Rev. Robert Henry 244
Davis, James 464
Dawkins, Henry 62
Deane, John Connellan 358, 382, 395, 407, 411, 490, 503
de Cerjat, William Woodley Frederick *see* Cerjat, William Woodley Frederick de
Delane, John Thadeus (Editor, *The Times*) 423, 463, 524, 525, 729
De la Pryme, Charles 239, 300, 378
De la Rue, Emile 416, 471, 667, 717
Devonshire, William George Spencer Cavendish, 6th Duke of 128, 149, 228
Dickens, Alfred Lamert 205, 207
Dickens, Catherine Macready (Kate) 634
Dickens, Mrs Charles 42, 47, 108, 113, 142, 178, 180, 220, 578
Dickens, Charles, Jr. 602
Dickens, Frederick William 236, 254, 275, 681, 692
Dickens, James, Sr. 500
Dickens, Mary (Mamie) 199, 619, 625, 634, 640, 659, 684
Dickers, A., Sr. 375
Dickinson, Mrs Frances 394, 547
Dilke, Charles Wentworth 44, 293, 304
Dillon, John 477
Dixon, Benjamin Homer 564
Dixon, William Hepworth 288, 355
Dolby, Charlotte 351, 705
Dolby, George 193
Donne, William Bodham 406
Doudney, Edward 636
Downing, Henry Bourne 678
Dudley, Robert 434
Dührssen, Mr 326
Dunn, James 231
Dyer, William George Thistleton 129

Eagle Insurance Office, The Secretary 227
Eardley, Sir Culling 386
Eastlake, Elizabeth, Lady 257, 562
Eastwick, William Joseph 241, 250, 416
Ebury, Baron *see* Grosvenor, Lord Robert
Edelston, Thomas 375
Eden, Hon. Emily 332
Edinburgh Philosophical Institution, The Secretary (Henry Bowie) 103
Editors of the Principal Journals 353
Edmonds, Charles 196, 335
Edwards, Edward 367
Eeles, Thomas Robert 196, 512, 534
Eliot, George *see* Evans, Marian
Elliotson, Dr John 709
Elliott, Celeste *see* Celeste, Madame
Ellis, Charles 546
Ellis, Joseph, the younger 293, 297
Ellis, Mr (H.? or Thomas?) 259, 331
Elwin, Rev. Whitwell 208
Emden, William Samuel 394, 418
Epps, Dr John 44
Evans, Frederick Mullett 54, 126, 298, 436, 445, 469, 487, 532, 550, 580, 608
Evans, Marian (George Eliot) 506

Faider, Charles Jean Baptiste Florian 615
Fairbairn, Thomas 393, 409
Felton, Cornelius Conway 566
Field, Joshua 122
Fields, James Thomas 589
Finlay, Francis Dalziel 645
Fitzgerald, Desmond G. 530
Fitzgerald, Percy Hetherington 616, 619, 636, 653
Fletcher, George 682
Forster, John 1, 8, 33, 37, 39, 51, 57, 62, 65, 76, 78, 82, 89, 91, 94, 101, 135, 136, 139, 153, 163, 173, 178, 179, 180, 208, 242, 251, 267, 279, 281, 309, 317, 321, 324, 344, 358, 366, 425, 428, 429, 434, 439, 443, 446, 450, 452, 455, 462, 464, 510, 511, 515, 531, 534, 537, 539, 542, 626, 628, 635, 642, 656, 668, 672, 676, 691, 692, 696, 711, 722
Forster, Mrs John 538
Fowler, John 3
Fox, Rev. William Johnson 247
Fraser, Peter S. 563
Fraser, Thomas 85
Friend, Richard 112
Friends of Lady Blessington 497

Friswell, James Hain 500
Frith, William Powell 570
Frozen Deep, The, Members of the Cast of 357
Fry, Herbert 72, 232

Gale, William 347
Galimard, Nicolas Auguste 25
Garrick Club, Committee of 603
Gaskell, Elizabeth Cleghorn 3
Gibbon, John Burdett 188
Gibson, Mary W. A. 493, 683
Gibson, Rev. Matthew 184, 697
Gigliucci, Clara Anastasia, Countess 261, 273, 349, 352, 606
Giles, William 622
Girdlestone, Rev. Edward 168
Glasgow Station, The Superintendent 676
Glasgow University, The Independent Students 702
Goodhart, Rev. Charles Joseph 235
Gordon, Sir Alexander Cornewall Duff 328, 456
Gordon, Lady Duff 507, 509
Gordon, John Thomson 106, 651
Gore, Mrs Catherine Grace Frances 343, 573, 654
Gotschalk, Emmely *see* Hansen, Mrs Emmely
Granville, Granville George Leveson-Gower, 2nd Earl 55
Grattan, Thomas Colley 550
Gregory, Mr & Mrs George Burrow 581
Gregson, Rev. John 302
Gresham, James 216
Griffith, John 626
Grosvenor, Lord Robert (Baron Ebury) 602
Guild of Literature and Art, Members of the 271
Gurney, Rev. Archer Thompson 319
Gye, Frederick 143

Hachette, Alfred 133
Hachette et Cie, Messrs 4, 36
Hachette, Louis Christophe François 22, 262, 308
Hammersmith & Wandsworth Police Office, Acting Inspector 545
Hamstede, Frederick William 373, 460
(?Hancock, Harriet) 144
Hankey, Thomson, Jr. 491
Hansen, Mrs Emmely (*née* Gotschalk) 103
Harding, Lady 521
Hardy, Albert 725
Hardy, Thomas Duffus 501
Harness, Mary 594
Harness, Rev. William 527
Hastings, David 245, 257
Hazlewood, Colin Henry 257
Headland, Thomas Hughes 265, 606
Herbert, T. H. 338
Hill, David Octavius 670
Hills, John 604
Hindle, Rev. Joseph 74
Hodder, George 306
Hogarth, George 26, 247
Hogarth, Georgina 48, 70, 109, 114, 391, 403, 438, 441, 443, 447, 467, 561, 617, 628, 629, 636, 642, 653, 657, 664, 671, 680, 693, 698, 703
Hogarth, Helen 354
Hogarth, Joseph 325
Hogge, Mrs George (Mary, or Polly) 545, 569
Holdsworth (or Holsworth), George 656
Hollingshead, John 389, 460, 464, 492, 495, 530, 577, 652
Holroyd, Abraham 683
Hood, Dr William Charles 318, 417, 604
Hoole, William Spencer 344
Horne, Richard Henry ('Hengist') 689
Horne, Mrs Richard Henry 211, 334
Horner, Ann Susan 479
Hoskyns, Chandos Wren 721
Household Words, Contributors to 195
Howell, Rev. Alexander James 321
Howes, Rev. Charles 74
Howitt, William 295
Hudson, Frederick 393
Hudson, G. F. 204, 312
Hulkes, James 494
Hunt, (James Henry) Leigh 348, 582
Hunt, William Holman 543, 548, 554

Irvine, William 365
Irving, Washington 150

Jackson, Thomas 119
Jameson, Mrs Anna Brownell 117
Jaquet, Madame 55
Jeaffreson, John Cordy 725
Jerdan, William 382, 417
Jerrold, Douglas William 44
Jerrold, Mrs Douglas William 483
Jerrold, William Blanchard 710
Jolly, Emily 245, 312, 335
Justerini & Brooks, Messrs 233

Kean, Charles John 593, 609
Kelly, William 509
Kenny, John 121, 123
Kent, William Charles 245
Kent, William Charles Mark 378
Knight, Charles 68, 523, 583
Knight, J. W. 516
Kruseman, Arie Cornelis 481

Lacroix, Octave 603
Lacy, Walter (Walter Williams) 405
Landor, Walter Savage 152, 511
Landseer, Sir Edwin 18, 24, 73, 243
Lane, Edward Wickstead 461
Langford, John Alfred 481
Langford, Joseph Munt 363, 475, 507
Lansdowne, Henry Petty-Fitzmaurice, 3rd Marquis of 242, 588
Lawrence, John T. 624
Lawson, James 677
Lee, (?Charles) 225
Lee, Richard Nelson 571, 579
Leech, John 51, 250, 574
Legouvé, Gabriel Jean Baptiste Ernest Wilfrid 61, 85, 654
Lemon, Mark 11, 100, 107, 124, 126, 130, 135, 142, 155, 205, 209, 210, 238, 271, 277, 304, 305, 315, 509, 520, 528
Lennox, Lord William Pitt 646
Ling, Mrs 301
Littignol, M. 507
Lockwood, Mrs Charles Day 485
Locock, Sir Charles 517
Logan, William 675
Lorain, Paul 309
Loveday, James Thomas 258
Lowne, (?George Gill) 112
Lyndhurst, John Singleton Copley, Baron 248
Lyttelton, George William, 4th Baron 134
Lytton, Sir Edward Lytton Bulwer- (*later* 1st Baron) 269, 303, 349, 583

McIntyre, James E. 583
Mackay, Dr Charles 364
McKeever, James *see* Stadfield, John
Mackenzie, L. 317
Maclise, Daniel 45, 120, 130, 223, 249, 355, 359, 362, 367, 406, 584
McMechan, Thomas *see* Stadfield, John
MacPhail, H. Buchanan 679
Macready, Catherine 503
Macready, William Charles 74, 77, 156, 157, 170, 238, 270, 290, 301, 373, 376, 399, 407, 420, 484, 502, 531, 537, 570, 579, 685
McTear, Robert 707
Madden, Mrs Richard Robert 645
Madge, Dr Henry 315
Manson, James Bolivar 670
Marston, John Westland 280, 511, 514, 519, 520
Mason, Mrs 456, 494
Massett, Stephen 526
Mayall, John Edwin 199, 362
Metropolitan Free Hospital, Chairman of 294
Miller, Mrs Hugh 315
Milman, Rev. Henry Hart *see* St Paul's Cathedral, Dean of
Milner, Charles 306
Milnes, Richard Monckton (*later* 1st Baron Houghton) 126, 132, 252, 299
Mitchell, J. Jackson *see* Stadfield, John
Mitton, Thomas 230, 587
Molyneux, Thomas John 182, 417
Moore, George 52, 325
Morgan, Mrs 268
Morgan, Captain Elisha Ely 453, 566
Morgan, John B. 556
Morley, Henry 288, 339, 468, 613
Murray, John III 291
Muspratt, Dr James Sheridan 431

Nathan, Lewis Jacob 213
Normanby, Maria, Marchioness of 666
Novello, Joseph Alfred 604

Olliffe, Sir Joseph Francis 35, 179
Olliffe, Laura, Lady 483
Orridge, Robert 606
Ostell, William 476
Ouvry, Frederic 562, 568, 572, 577, 648
Owen, Mrs Richard 428
Oxenford, John 248

Palfrey, John Gorham 127
Panizzi, (Sir) Anthony 282
Parke, William 626
Parker, John P. 497
Parkes, Rev. Samuel Hadden 422
Paxton, Sir Joseph 292, 320, 349, 359, 363, 394, 400, 484, 486, 491, 496, 714
Payn, James 672, 716
Pemberton, Robert 384
(?Perkins), David L. 453
Pfeiffer, J. E. 333
Phelps, Samuel 304, 350, 355, 363
Phelps, Mrs Samuel 356
Phinn, Thomas 284
Phipps, Lieutenant-Colonel the Hon. Charles Beaumont 347
Piesse, Charles William Septimus 338
Pigott, Edward Frederick Smyth 26, 300
Pinney, Joel 384
Playground Society, The Secretary of the 584
Powell, Nathaniel 157
Power, Marguerite 84, 239, 484
Procter, Bryan Waller 250, 480, 498, 528, 723

Quin, Dr Frederic Hervey Foster 129

Ramsbotham, Dr Francis Henry 344, 591, 684
Raynham, John Villiers Stuart Townshend, Viscount (*later* 5th Marquis Townshend) 106, 120, 327

Reed, Thomas Allen 586
Reed, Thomas German 408
Reeve, Henry 391
Reeves, John Sims 350
Régnier, François Joseph Philoclès 83, 519, 521
Richardson, Sarah 725
Rieu, Charles Pierre Henry 376, 390
Roberts, David 185, 586
Robertson, John 98
Robson, Thomas Frederick 352
Rochester and Chatham Mechanics' Institute *see* Chatham and Rochester Mechanics' Institute
Roney, James Edward 191, 236
Ross, Thomas and John Kenny 121
Royal Academy, The Secretary 93
Royal Humane Society 688
Royal Literary Fund, The Secretary 302
Royal Scottish Academy, The President 670
Russell, Lady John 137, 328, 334
Russell, William Howard 329, 337, 345, 599
Rutherfurd, Mrs James Hunter 640
Ryland, Arthur 210, 370, 401, 458, 484, 666

St Ann's Society, Stewards and Committee of 318
St Paul's Cathedral, Dean of (Rev. Henry Hart Milman) 125, 126, 255
Sala, George Augustus 8, 28, 81, 187, 190, 592
Sams, William Raymond 387
Saunders, Charles Alexander 610
Serle, Thomas James 724
Sheffield Literary and Philosophical Society, The Secretary 726
Simpson, John Palgrave 575, 611
Sly, Joseph 443, 485
Smiles, Samuel 475
Smith, Albert Richard 661, 713
Smith, Arthur 333, 540, 568, 713, 724
Smith, Charles Manby 362
Smith, Charles Roach 121
Smith, John 628
Smith, Elder & Co., Messrs 710
Sorrell, William J. 435
Spofford, Richard Smith, Jr. 604
Stadfield, John; J. Jackson Mitchell; James McKeever; Thomas McMechan; Robert Stamper 439
Stamper, Robert *see* Stadfield, John
Stanfield, Clarkson 67, 68, 113, 119, 140, 181, 193, 235, 249, 258, 327, 467
Stanhope, Philip Henry Stanhope, 5th Earl of 322, 325
Stedman, John, and others 509
Stevens, Mr 404
Stone, Ellen 341, 537
Stone, Frank 36, 76, 130, 158, 207, 213, 225, 226, 285, 289, 306, 309, 310, 339, 374, 377, 404, 412, 414, 483, 499, 503, 504, 510, 561, 563, 567, 718
Stracey, Charlotte, Lady 5
Strutt, George Henry 678

Tagart, Rev. Edward 46, 267, 274, 587
Tauchnitz, Bernard 85, 93
Taylor, Alice 691
Taylor, Philip Meadows 640
Taylor, Tom 368, 384
Tebb, Robert Palmer 556
Telbin, William 221, 228, 264, 396, 408, 532
Tennent, Sir James Emerson 255
Thackeray, William Makepeace 285, 364, 485, 505, 512, 551, 573, 591, 707
Thiselton, Augustus Union 544, 586
Thomas, William Moy 591
Thompson, Caroline 454
Thompson, John 201, 332, 362, 409, 455, 457, 462, 464, 602
Thompson, Thomas James 583, 589, 613, 690, 699, 706, 724
Times, The, Editor of *see* Delane, John Thadeus
Towle, George Makepeace 590
Townshend, Rev. Chauncy Hare 264, 599
Tracey, Lieut. Augustus Frederick 100, 214, 217, 499, 611
Trollope, Mrs Frances 667
Trood, William Stocker 557
Troughton, Thomas 529

Unidentified Correspondents 206, 271, 286, 303, 337, 350, 356, 365, 495, 499, 500, 501, 515, 526, 540, 620, 663, 716, 726
Unidentified Staff Surgeon 124

Viardot, Mme Louis 13

Walford, Edward 200, 612, 614
Wallingford Mechanics' Institute, The Hon. Secretary 302
Wanostrocht, Vincent 696
Ward, Edward Matthew 124
Washbourne, Henry 360
Watkins, Charles 620
Watkins, Herbert 476, 576, 607
Watson, Hon. Mrs Richard 201, 211, 262, 298, 299, 487, 703
Waugh, Francis 593
Waugh, Lieutenant-Colonel William Petrie 115
Weatherley, Rev. Charles Thomas 557
Webster, Benjamin Nottingham 46, 77, 111, 113, 116, 134, 136, 140, 141, 155, 258, 316, 326, 369, 379, 387, 479, 481, 490, 518
Weinling, Paul 453

Werner, Carl Friedrich Heinrich 564
West, Dr Charles 720
White, Rev. James 97, 278, 331, 697
Whitford, Mrs Thomas 692
Wilkinson, Rev. George 263
Williams & Clapham, Messrs 43
Williams & Norgate, Messrs 227
Willmore, Mrs Graham 92
Wills, William Henry 2, 6, 9, 16, 19, 24, 26, 32, 38, 49, 56, 57, 58, 59, 63, 64, 69, 80, 81, 83, 88, 90, 93, 94, 97, 99, 139, 158, 163, 166, 168, 172, 174, 188, 189, 191, 193, 194, 208, 212, 222, 224, 226, 246, 251, 252, 253, 277, 279, 397, 402, 410, 421, 437, 438, 448, 450, 454, 455, 457, 497, 523, 541, 549, 620, 630, 647, 668, 673, 680, 686, 694, 695, 699, 701, 705, 709, 723
Wills, Mrs William Henry 49, 278
Wilson, Mrs Alexander Ball 498
Wilson, Professor George 218
Wilson, William 316
Winter, Ella Maria 720
Winter, Henry Louis 703
Winter, Mrs Henry Louis (Maria Sarah Beadnell) 43, 627, 704

Yates, Edmund Hodgson 5, 50, 351, 379, 479, 513, 553, 555, 576, 588, 595, 601, 617, 622, 631, 711
Yates, Mrs Edmund Hodgson 564

INDEX OF NAMES AND PLACES

Buildings, streets, districts, etc are indexed under the town or city to which they belong, e.g. Hampstead under LONDON. If a separate entry is desirable a cross-reference is given from the town to the separate entry, e.g. LONDON: Highgate to HIGHGATE.

Married women are generally indexed under their married names, with cross-references when useful.

Books and writings are indexed alphabetically under the name of the author. Writings of unknown authorship, and periodicals, are indexed under title. References to characters in Dickens's novels are listed as a subsection under the title of the novel within the entry DICKENS, Charles: *Works*.

Abbreviations and symbols

The letter D stands for the name Dickens, CD for Charles Dickens. Works are abbreviated as follows: *LD* for *Little Dorrit*, *HW* for *Household Words*.

Those footnotes which contain substantial particulars about a person are distinguished by an asterisk, e.g. 123n*

The sign ~ is used to show that the reference which follows is linked with the reference which precedes.

The names of Dickens's correspondents are printed in capitals. The Preface is not indexed.

D. M.

Abdullah, Agar 456

A'Beckett, Albert 285 & n*

A'Beckett, Arthur William 180n, 285n

A'Beckett, Gilbert Abbott: death 179 & n*, 181, 347; sons 285 & n; in Boulogne 346

A'Beckett, Mrs Gilbert Abbott 182n

A'Beckett, Gilbert Arthur 285n

A'Beckett, Walter Horace Callander: death 181n, 184

Aberdeen: CD reads at 676, 691n

Aberdeen Journal 676n

Abinger, Sir James Scarlett, 1st Baron 229n

Abrahams, Henry 26n

Adams, Charles H. 518n

ADAMS, H. G. 681n, 711

ADAMS, William James 268n*

Adamson, Robert 670n

Addey & Co., printers 515n

Addison, Robert & Co., music publishers 26 & n

Adrian, Arthur A.: *Georgina Hogarth and the Dickens Circle* 559n, 664n; *Mark Lemon, First Editor of* Punch 492n, 741n

Advertiser (newspaper) 353n

Agamemnon, HMS 598n

Agricultural Gazette 721n

Ainsworth, William Harrison: buys *Bentley's Miscellany* 133, 390, 392

Airey, Major-General Sir Richard (*later* Baron) 504 & n*

Albert, Prince Consort: opens Manchester Arts Treasures Exhibition 212n; attends performance of *Frozen Deep* 366n; supports Canning in Indian policy 473n; and Havelock 504; and Society of Arts and Guild restrictions 513; on state visit to France 618n, 684n; visits Leeds 660n

ALBERTI, Frau (Sophie Mödinger; 'Sophia Verena') 40n*; *Else* 40n, 104

ALDRIDGE, T. L.: *Fear-Nac-Flu* (with G. Curtis) 112n*

Alfieri, Marquis Vittorio: *Rosmunda* 171n

Alison, Sir Archibald 714

ALLAN-FRASER, Patrick 562 & n*, 630

Allderidge, Patricia: *Richard Dadd Catalogue* (*The Late Richard Dadd*) 318n

Allen, Henry Robinson 373 & n, 379

Allen, Mary (CD's aunt) 452n

Alletz, Pierre-Edouard 55n

Alleyn, Edward 74n

ALLINGHAM, William: "George Levison; or, The Schoolfellows" (poem) 478n

ALLON, Rev. Henry 500n*

Allonby, Cumberland 440–1, 443–4

Allsop, Thomas 525n

Amateurs, theatre company 1n, 3n, 207n, 431n

Ami de la Maison, L', journal 131n, 132n, 200

Amiens, France 77

ANDERSEN, Hans Christian: visits CD in England 239 & n, 307, 323, 331, 337, 340, 372–3, 382–3; linguistic incomprehensibility 373, 383; returns to Denmark 382, 425; rift with CD 426n; on CD's conduct of Jerrold fund 449n; letters introducing Elizabeth Jerichau-Baumann 578n; *Mitt Livs Eventyr* 426n; *Pictures of Sweden* 383n; *To Be, or Not to Be*

Andersen, Hans Christian (*cont.*): 307n, 426 & n; "Tommelise" 145 & n; "The Ugly Duckling" 145 & n; "A Visit to CD in the Summer of 1857" 426n
Anderson, John Henry 68n
Ansell, Thomas 172 & n, 510
Anson, General George 459n
Arabian Nights, The 63n, 117n, 240n, 294, 623n
Arago, Etienne and Paul Vermond: *Les Mémoires du Diable* 149 & n, 154
Arbroath, Scotland 630
Arbuthnot, Dr John 383n
Ardmillon, James Crawfurd, Lord 724n
Argyll (Argyle), George Douglas Campbell, 8th Duke of 21 & n
Aris's Birmingham Gazette 680n
Army and Navy Gazette 529n
Arrowsmith, Jane 674n
Art Journal 68n, 108n, 111n, 591n
Artists' Annuity Fund 544n
Artists' Benevolent Fund 544n, 562n, 586n
Artists' General Benevolent Fund 544n
Ashburton, William Bingham Baring, 2nd Baron 160n
Ashton, Edward 678n
Ashton, Rosemary: *G. H. Lewes. A Life* 580n
Ashurst, William Henry 364 & n, 460, 463
Athenaeum (journal): and dispute over Royal Literary Fund reform 293n, 550n, 554n, 588n, 591n; on Jerrold's funeral 352n; praises *Frozen Deep* 369n, 370n; reviews Andersen's *To Be or Not to Be* 426n; and death of Chatterton 492n; criticises Collins's *Red Vial* 700n
Atkins, J. B.: *The Life of W. H. Russell* 600n
Atlas (journal) 152n
ATTWELL, Henry 388n*; *Poems* 388
Auber, Daniel François Esprit 58 & n*; *Manon Lescaut* (with Scribe) 63 & n, 65–6; *Masaniello* 452n
AUSTIN, Henry: surveys Gad's Hill 51; CD invites to Boulogne 91; CD asks to help with *Frozen Deep* 206; and Frederick Dickens 255, 275, 277; and repairs and improvements to Gad's Hill 283, 296, 303, 311, 381, 420, 427, 449; CD invites to Garrick 296; and Gad's Hill water supply 342–3, 411, 421, 449, 590; visits Gad's Hill 584, 614n; marriage 692n
Austin, Mrs Henry (Laetitia, or Letitia Mary Dickens) 91 & n, 206, 614n, 692 & n
AUSTIN, Sarah (*née* Taylor) 219
Azeglio, Marquis Massimo Taparelli d' 164 & n

Baber, Rev. Harry 79n, 288n, 731, 734
Baker, Audrey 368n
Baker, G. P.: (ed.) *CD and Maria Beadnell. Private Correspondence* 608n
Baker, William 726n
Baldwin, Charles 286n
Baldwin, Edward 137n, 286n, 291n, 301
Balfe, Michael William: *Satanella* 690n
BALLANTINE, James 38n*, 724; *Poems* 38n
Ballard, James 442
Balzac, Honoré de 178
BAMPS, (?Anatole) 537n
Bancroft, (Sir) Squire 722n
Barber, Charles 292n, 306, 400, 449, 452
Barham, R. H.: *The Garrick Club* 536n
Baring Brothers, financial house: Charley works at 5n, 41–2, 47, 146, 203, 210, 216; Charley seeks transfer in 562, 689
Baring, Thomas 48 & n, 68n, 118, 215n, 216
Barlow, William John 261
Barnard, Lieut.-General Sir Henry William 459n
Barnett, J.: *The Covenant* 447n
Barrow, Emily Elizabeth *see* Lawrence, Mrs George Frederick
Barrow, John Henry 131n
Barrow, John Wylie 151 & n
Barrow, Thomas Culliford 151n
Bartrip, P. W. J.: "*HW* and the Factory Accident Controversy" 6n
BATEMAN, Mrs John (Jane Carr): "Eric Walderthorn" 139 & n, 159, 183
Bates, Joshua 48 & n, 216, 652, 689
Bath 274n
BATHURST, Henry Allen 520n*, 522n
Bathurst, Lieut.-General James 520n
Baumann, Antoine 101n
BEADNELL, George 341–2, 704 & n
Beadnell, George, Jr. 705
Beadnell, Maria *see* Winter, Mrs Henry Louis
BEALE, Thomas Willert 402n*, 534–5
BEARD, Thomas: CD invites to dine 141, 269, 274, 301, 324, 480; invitations and visits to Gad's Hill 243, 326, 556, 595, 614n, 617; on *Morning Herald* 286, 301n; invited to see *Frozen Deep* 369; invited to CD reading 546, 555; interest in *The Dial* 679n; becomes freelance journalist 682n; and *Daily News* vacancy 699; CD seeks to help 704n
Beatrice, Princess 275n
BEAUCOURT-MUTUEL, Ferdinand Henri Joseph Alexandre: CD rents Boulogne house from 12; CD buys pipe for 31; gardening 135, 137, 180; and Cattermoles 138–9; sorrow at D family departure 180
Beaver, inmate of Home 120
Becher, John Harman 461n
BECKER, (?Bernard Henry) 220n
Bee (magazine) 153n
Belcher, George 696

Belcombe, Dr Henry Stephens 656
Belfast: CD reads at 597n, 601, 639–44, 647
Belfast News-Letter 641n, 643n
BELL, George 385n*
Bell, Jacob 18 & n
BELL, Robert, journalist 305n; opposes Royal Literary Fund reforms 293n, 324, 550n, 592n; and "Garrick Club Affair" 596n; speech at General Theatrical Fund 610n; at Brussels Congress 615n
Bellew, Rev. John Chippendall Montesquieu 444 & n*, 445n
Bellini, Giovanni 174n
BENEDICT, (Sir) Jules 353
BENNETT, John 334n, 493n*
Bennett, William Cox 493n
Bentham, William 664n
Bentley, George 403n
BENTLEY, Richard: and French edition of CD's works 31; publishes Sala's *Journey Due North* 187n; sends book to CD 253; publishes Andersen's *To Be, or Not to Be* 307n; invited to Gad's Hill 337, 360; negotiates agreement for Brooks's *Aspen Court* 367n, 378n, 385, 391, 398–9, 403–4, 415, 424–5, 451–2, 738; Andersen visits 373n; and Andersen's Danish 383; financial problems 403n; and Julia Pardoe 419; disputes with CD 462 & n; at Royal Literary Fund 1858 AGM 530; and publication of Brooks's *Gordian Knot* 663n
Bentley, William 118 & n, 213, 215, 296, 330
Bentley's Miscellany 385–6; Ainsworth buys 390, 392
Benzon, Ernst 664n
BERGER, Francesco: and CD's life in Boulogne 173n, 176n; composes music for *Frozen Deep* 207 & n, 214, 220, 252, 259n, 353n; CD gives present to 259; and Manchester performance of *Frozen Deep* 395, 396n; and CD's acting 433n; *Reminiscences, Impressions and Anecdotes* 259n, 348n, 396n
Berkeley, George, Bishop of Cloyne 701n
Bernard, Dr Simon 707n
Berry, Francis 626, 629, 634, 638, 685
Berton, Pierre: *The National Dream* 122n
Berwick-on-Tweed 671
Bewsher, Rev. James 27 & n, 179, 652n
Bible: allusions to 224, 516, 719
Bickersteth, Robert, Bishop of Ripon 718n
BICKNELL, Henry 185n, 592n
Bicknell, Mrs Henry (Christine Roberts) 185n
Bignon, Eugène 91 & n
Bille, Carl Steen Andersen 144 & n*
Bird, Edward, Hammersmith builder 372n, 381, 390n
Birmingham: CD visits 201, 210n, 211, 491; CD enquires about performing *Frozen Deep* in 370, 401; CD declines invitation to read in 484; CD reads in 666, 674, 680–4
Birmingham and Midland Institute 210n, 354n; CD made Honorary Member 458
Birmingham Daily Post 682n
Birmingham, John 110
Birmingham, Mrs John 110 & n
Black, Adam 670n
Blackmore, Edward 131n
Blackwood, John 506n, 709n
Blackwood's Magazine 309, 317 & n, 506n, 674n
Blainey, Ann: *The Farthing Poet* 247n, 334n
Blanchard, Edward Litt Leman 268n
Blessington, Marguerite, Countess of 497
BLEWITT, Octavian 302n, 324
Board of Control (India) 502n
BODDINGTON, Thomas 655
Bonchurch, Isle of Wight 290, 451n
Boner, Charles 145n
Bonnemet, Monsieur 36n
Book of Common Prayer 511n
Booth, Bradford: "Trollope and Little Dorrit" 40n
Borichevskii, Ivan Peter 308 & n
Boswell, James: *Letters . . . to the Rev. W. J. Temple* 253n
Boucicault, Dion: *The Corsican Brothers* 5n; *London Assurance* 690n; *Used Up* 15n
Boulogne: English school in 27; CD stays in 133–8, 142, 144, 165–7, 170; la Madeleine (fair) 173 & n, 174; diphtheria epidemic in 178 & n, 181, 184n, 202
Bourgeois, Anicet and Philippe Adolphus Dennery: *Le Médécin des Enfants* 91 & n
Bourgois, F. 138
Bourgon, Madame de 70
Bourne, Henry Richard Fox: "The Hero of a Hundred Days" (with Morley) 662n
Bowater, Thomas 185n
Bowden, John 418n
BOWIE, Henry 103n
BOXALL, Sir William 204n, 561, 566n
Boycett, member of CD's reading staff 629, 685
Boyle, Mrs 147
BOYLE, Captain Cavendish Spencer ('Benjamin'; 'Bedgy') 15 & n, 72 & n, 516n
Boyle, Mrs Cavendish Spencer (Rose Alexander) 15n
Boyle, Sir Courtenay 15n
Boyle, Eleanor Vere 515n
BOYLE, Mary: handwriting 15; visits CD in Boulogne 152, 165–6, 202; CD flirts with 472n; on Mrs Watson's absence abroad 487; writes to CD 515; and CD's marriage breakdown 572; and CD's 'violated letter' 656; *Mary Boyle her Book* 15n, 202n, 516n, 655n

Brabant, Elizabeth Rebecca ('Rufa') 506n
Brackenbury, Rev. John Matthew 198, 279
Bradbury, Henry & Co., banknote engravers 594n
BRADBURY, Henry Riley 594n*
BRADBURY, William 352n, 758
BRADBURY & EVANS: Account Book 8n, 54n, 298n; and French translation of CD's works 31, 65; enquire about collection of criticisms 32; payments to CD 54 & n, 61; serialise *LD* 67; payment from Tauchnitz 80; publish *Field* 155n; print Carlyle's works 166; Whitefriars office 194n; and Cheap Edition of CD's works 215; publish CD's *Child's History* 231n; proofs and corrections to *LD* 274, 279n; send accounts to CD 298, 436n; publish CD's Library Edition 436n, 445, 594n, 609n; launch second series of Cheap Edition 533n; CD ends business relations with for not printing 'Personal' statement 608n, 699n, 701n; print texts of CD's readings 633n, 653; accounting vouchers for *HW* 695; and CD's copyrights 695; CD convenes partners' meeting 700–1; resist Resolution to dissolve *HW* partnership 700n, 711, 719, 758–61; reject CD's offer to buy *HW* shares 723n; correspondence with Forster on dissolution proposals 758
Bradford: CD reads at 679
Bradford Advertiser 679n
Bragg, Mrs Harriett 80n, 271–2, 276, 731
Braham, John 136n
Bramwell, Sir George William Wilshere, Baron 260 & n
BRANDT, Francis Frederick: *Frank Marland's Manuscripts* 305n
Brannan, R. L.: *Under the Management of Mr CD* 368n
Breach, Benjamin Bodman 443
Breach, James G. 147, 443n
Bredsdorff, Elias: *Hans Andersen and CD* 383n, 578n; *Hans Christian Andersen* 372n, 373n, 382n, 383n, 425n, 426n
Brewster, Sir David 523n
Brighton 291, 293–4, 296; CD reads in 681, 693, 700–1, 703
Brighton Examiner 703n
Brighton Herald 649n
Bristol 171, 211, 212n, 489
Bristol Mercury 619n
British Museum, London 495n; Reading Room 109n
British Workman's Association 292 & n
Britton, John, E. W. Bailey and others: *Beauties of England and Wales* 428n, 438n, 439n
Broadstairs, Kent 332, 442, 651 & n
Broderip, Frances Freeling (*née* Hood): "A Daisy on a Grave" 253n
Brontë, Rev. Patrick: *The Cottage in the Wood* 683n
BROOKS, (Charles William) Shirley: dines with CD 48; and Jerrold's death 346; Andersen meets 373n; on Jerrold fund committee 424n; supports Landor in libel case 644n; text of agreement with Bentley 738; *Aspen Court* 367n, 378n, 385–6, 391–2, 398–9, 403–4, 415, 425, 451–2, 462n, 466; *The Gordian Knot* 662 & n
BROOKS, S. L. 549 & n, 608
BROUGH, Robert Barnabas 5n, 171n, 394n, 581n, 582 & n*; "Calmuck" 543n, 548, 554; *Heads and Tales: a Medley* 554n; "The Last Devil's Walk" 582n; *Marston Lynch* 582n
Brough, William 5n
BROUGHAM AND VAUX, Henry Peter Brougham, Baron 243 & n, 468, 724n
Broughton de Gyfford, John Cam Hobhouse, Baron 196n
Brown, and Henry Morley: "Perfectly Contented" 175n
Brown, Anne *see* Cornelius, Mrs Edward
BROWN, Colin Rae 427n*; supposed slander against CD 679–80, 685n, 714n, 754–7; CD declines invitation from 714
BROWN, Montagu Yeats 667n*
BROWN, Timothy Yeats 415, 473 & n, 667n
Brown, Mrs Timothy Yeats (Stuarta Erskine) 415 & n
Brown, Dr William: death 17n, 80n, 84n, 177n, 478n, 688n, 733, 735; memorial scholarship (William Brown Exhibition Fund) 169n, 197n
BROWN, Mrs William (Hannah Meredith; 'O'): Catherine writes to 16n; and husband's death 17n, 84, 478, 733; funds memorial medical scholarship (Exhibition) for husband 54 & n, 169n, 171–2, 176, 191–2, 197–8, 201, 221, 259n; character and behaviour 65 & n; on French 109–10; and Charley's birthday play 118; invited to see *Frozen Deep* 234–5, 237, 249; CD invites to Gad's Hill 330; in Torquay 331n; visits Gad's Hill with Miss Coutts 343; CD invites to dine 482; as possible donor of umbrella 500n; CD consults over proposed readings 515; unwell 578; Wills sends newspaper accounts of CD's Manchester speech to 717
BROWNE, Hablot Knight ('Phiz'): illustrates *LD* 141 & n, 219, 232, 280, 297; vignette title-pages for CD Library Edition 436n
Browning, Elizabeth Barrett 86n, 597n, 648n
BROWNING, Robert 86n, 664n
Brunel, Isambard Kingdom 345n
Brunet, J.: *New Guide to Boulogne-sur-mer and its Environs* 173n

Brunnov, Baron Ernst Philip Ivanovich 110 & n
Brussels: Congress on Literary and Artistic Property (Sept. 1858) 615n
Buckingham, Leicester: *William Tell* 722n
Buckland, Francis Trevelyan: "Zoological Auction" 3 & n
BUCKSTONE, John Baldwin: as Treasurer of Royal General Theatrical Fund 32 & n, 45, 140; and Macready's asthma 44–5; photograph of 200n; performs for Jerrold memorial fund 350n, 379n; plays in Jerrold's *Prisoner of War* 369n; CD sends Jerrold's *Spendthrift* to 435, 437; invited to Gad's Hill 466; and Hollingshead's *Birthplace of Podgers* 495 & n; engages Ellen Ternan 564–6 & n; manages Haymarket 690; *The Flowers of the Forest* 379n; *The Green Bushes* 379n; *Uncle John* 214n, 254n, 256n, 369n, 400, 401n, 402, 405, 412n, 413n, 414n, 421n, 434n; *The Wreck Ashore* 379n
Bulwer, Henry 497n
Burnett, Charles Dickens Kneller (Henry's son) 73 & n
BURNETT, Henry 73, 665
Burnett, Mrs Henry (Frances Elizabeth Dickens; Fanny): death 72 & n, 665
Burnett, Mrs Henry (Sarah Hargreaves; H's second wife) 665n
Burns, Dr Richard: *The Justice of the Peace and Parish Officer* 7n
Burns, Robert: centenary celebrations 714 & n, 724 & n; "Mary Morison" 563n
Burrell, John 582n
Bushby, Mrs (Andersen's translator) 307n, 426n
Byron, George Gordon Noel Byron, 6th Baron 196 & n; *Cain* 78
Byron, Henry James: *The Maid and the Magpie* 722 & n

Cabu, Georges (known as Cabel) 66n
Cabu (Cabel), Mme Georges (Marie Josephe Freulette) 66 & n*
Cambridge, George William Frederick Charles, 2nd Duke of 503n, 504
Campbell, Lieut.-General Sir Colin (*later* Field Marshal Baron Clyde) 600n
CAMPBELL, John, 1st Baron (Lord Chief Justice) 21 & n, 229n, 260n, 720n
Candia, Giovanni Matteo di *see* Mario
Canning, Charles John, 1st Earl 473 & n
Canterbury: Grand Cricket Week 413n
Canterbury, Archbishop of *see* Sumner, John Bird
Cardale, John Bate 42n, 94 & n, 130n
Cardwell, Edmund 518n
Cardwell, Margaret 710n
Carlisle 432, 437–8, 443
Carlisle Examiner and North Western Advertiser 444n
CARLISLE, George William Frederick Howard, 7th Earl of 313–14, 591n
Carlton, W. J. 522n, 746n, 749n; "An Echo of Copperfield Days" 131n; "The Strange Story of Thomas Mitton" 587n
CARLYLE, Thomas 60; Cheap Edition of Works 166; William Wilson's sonnets to 316n; and Jerrold's death 365n; on Frederic Chapman 714n; Forster bequeaths CD's watch to 715n; co-signs letter to *Times* on appeal for Lowe sisters 729
Carlyle, Mrs Thomas (Jane Baillie Welsh) 114n, 151 & n, 506n, 507n
Carmichael-Smyth, Captain Henry 461n*
CARMICHAEL-SMYTH, Mrs Henry (Anne Becher) 461n*, 552n
Carrick (or Carrock) Fell, Cumberland 439–40, 443, 462n
Carrickfergus, Co. Antrim 641n
Carshalton, Surrey 327n
CARTER, Dr Robert Brudenell 190n*, 191; "Health and Education" 190n, 193; "How the Writer was Despatch-Boxed" 410 & n
Carter, W. 697 & n
Carvalho, S. N.: *Incidents of Travel and Adventure . . . across the Rocky Mountains* 289n
Catechism for Bands of Hope (Parker) 497n
Cathcart, J. F. 446n
Catlin, George: *Letters and Notes on the Manners, Customs, and Condition of the North American Indians* 186n
Cattermole, Rev. Richard 138 & n*
Cattermole, Vincent 138 & n
Caunt, Benjamin 618
Cavour, Camillo Benso, Count 164n
Cawnpore, India 431n, 459n, 516n, 600n
CELESTE, Madame (Celeste Elliott) 11n, 111, 112n, 141n, 379n, 570
CERJAT, William Woodley Frederick de 284, 596–8
Cerjat, Mrs William Woodley Frederick de (Maria Holmes) 266 & n
Cervantes Saavedra, Miguel: *Don Quixote* 153, 280n
Chalk, inmate of Home 120
Chambers's Exeter Journal 617n
Chambers's Journal 716n
CHAPMAN & HALL, publishers: publish Carlyle's collected works 166n; publish CD's Library Edition of works 436n, 445; sell tickets for CD's readings 563; and publication of *Pickwick* 614n; and printed texts of CD's readings 633n
CHAPMAN, Edward: and French translation of CD's works 31 & n; and accounts 322; CD

Chapman, Edward (*cont.*):
proposes new edition of works to 436; and printing of Cheap Edition of CD works 487; and *Pickwick* 614n; CD recommends Yates to 615; promotes cousin Frederic 714 & n
CHAPMAN, Frederic 661, 714 & n
Chapman, John 505n
Chappell & Co.: "Monday Pops" 182n
Chatelain, Clara de 145n
Chatham: CD reads at 681n
Chatham and Rochester Mechanics' Institute *see* Rochester and Chatham Mechanics' Institute
Chatterton, Thomas 111 & n, 492n
Cheadle, Mrs, of Bayswater Schools, Paddington 80, 732
Cheesbrough, Rev. Isaac 265n
Chester: CD reads at 597n, 624–6
Chester Chronicle 626n
CHESTERTON, George Laval 223n, 585n
Cheveux de ma Femme, Les (play) 57
Chopin, Frédéric 29n
CHORLEY, Henry Fothergill 594, 726
Christian, Mrs Eleanor (Emma Picken) 472
"Christmas Fantasy, A" (poem, *HW*) 502n
Christy, George 722n
Clairville (Louis François Nicolaie, the younger) and Montaugry: *Town and Country Mouse* 37 & n
Clarendon, George William Frederick Villiers, 4th Earl of 57n, 332
Clark, Cumberland: *Dickens and Democracy and Other Studies* 234n
CLARKE, Charles Cowden 204
CLARKE, Mrs Charles Cowden (Mary Victoria Novello) 204
Clarke, William M.: *The Secret Life of Wilkie Collins* 105n, 467n
Cleave, John 650n
CLEMENT, William James 625
Clifton: CD reads at 597n, 619 & n, 621, 623
Clowes, William 403n
Cobbett, William: *Rural Rides* 63n
Cobham Park, Kent 659
Cockburn, Sir Alexander James Edmund 260 & n, 328, 330n
Cockle's Anti-Bilious Pills 162n
Colburn, Henry 165n
Colburn, Mrs Henry (Eliza Crosbie) *see* Forster, Mrs John
Cole, Henry 611 & n
Coleridge, Samuel Taylor: "The Devil's Thoughts" 582n
Colletta, Pietro: *History of the Kingdom of Naples* 479n
COLLINS, Charles Allston: contributes to *HW* 31n; acts in Manchester performance of *Frozen Deep* 413; lives with mother 467n; attitude to Pre-Raphaelite Brotherhood 543n; at Broadstairs 651n; "Her Face" 616n, 620; "The Great Dunkerque Failure" 651n, 681; "The Smallport Monte-Cristo" 651n, 681
Collins, Philip (ed.): *CD: the Critical Heritage* 389n, 674n; *CD: the Public Readings* 15n, 669n, 677n
Collins, William (Wilkie's father) 31n
Collins, Mrs William (Wilkie's mother) 31n*
COLLINS, William Wilkie: visits CD in Paris 20, 24, 27–8, 46n, 47–8, 53; sails with Pigott 27n, 95n, 214n; CD proposes collaborative writing with 37n, 423, 425–6; and Caroline Graves 53n, 105n, 467n, 651n; illnesses 53n, 62, 95 & n, 621n; Forster praises 70; in Paris 77–8; receives payment 81n; collaborates with CD in *HW* 159; visit to CD in Boulogne 161, 167, 175, 202n; leaves Boulogne with CD 180 & n; joins *HW* staff 188–9, 214n, 389n; travels in Italy with CD 256n; visits Brighton with CD 293–4, 703; visits Gad's Hill 327, 701; and Jerrold's memorial fund 348n, 355, 424n; caricatures Andersen 372n; Andersen meets 373n, 383n; acts in *Uncle John* 421n; on CD's acting 421n; CD travels with to Cumberland and the North (as 'Two Idle Apprentices') 425–30, 438–47, 450, 454, 458, 660; salary increase at *HW* 457; homes 467n; contributes to *HW* 1857 Christmas number 482 & n, 483–4, 487, 508; CD gives presentation copy of Christmas *HW* to 517; friendship with CD 532; and Pre-Raphaelites 543n; attends CD readings 547, 712n; and reform of Royal Literary Fund 550–1; stays at Sir John Falstaff Inn 556n; supports Yates in Garrick Club affair 596n; and CD's reading tour 616, 649; contributes to *HW* 1858 Christmas number 649–50, 673–4, 701, 705 & n; invited to dine at Tavistock House 650; at Broadstairs 651n; friendship with A. F. Lehmann 664n
Works:
After Dark 28n, 39n
"The Bachelor's Bedroom" 372n
"Brother Morgan's Story of the Dead Hand" 458n
"The Cruise of the Tomtit" 27n
The Dead Secret 189n, 237n, 294 & n, 298 & n, 329n, 436
"The Debtor's Best Friend" 391n
"The Deliverance" 195n, 222n
"The Diary of Anne Rodway" 156 & n, 159, 161, 165
"Doctor Dulcamara" 702n
The Frozen Deep (with CD): writing 81n, 118, 161, 176n, 184–6, 199, 202–5, 210; scenery and sets 202, 208–9, 213–14, 217–

18, 221, 223, 227–30, 234, 238, 240–2, 249, 258, 358, 380n, 401n; invited guests 205, 219, 226, 228, 234–5, 238, 243, 247, 251; read to company 206, 208–9, 214.; music 207 & n, 214, 220, 252, 259n, 353n; costumes 213; rehearsals and preparations 214, 217, 220, 225; Forster's doubts on 217; playbills 228; Tavistock House performances and reception 247n, 254n, 255–7, 260–2, 267, 276–7, 380n, 394, 396–7; CD's Prologue 254n; Collins plays in 254n, 276 & n; first performance 254 & n; ends 265; Queen Victoria wishes to see 273, 275–6; sent to Mrs Watson 298–9; performed for Queen Victoria 348, 356–64, 366, 368; performed at Gallery of Illustration 356–8, 361n, 366n, 369n, 370n, 376, 380n, 388, 396n, 400; remembrance performance for Jerrold 356–7; revisions 356n, 368n; Manchester performance 358, 377, 393–9, 401, 404–9, 411–12, 414, 418, 421, 432, 434n, 488; proposed Birmingham performance 370, 401; licensed for public performance 406 & n, 407; Ternans in 412n, 432n

The Frozen Deep and Other Stories 421n

"Highly Proper" 649n, 669

"John Steadiman's (Chief Mate's) Account" 195n, 222n, 234, 278

"A Journey in Search of Nothing" 410

"Laid Up in Two Lodgings: My Paris Lodgings" 48n, 53n, 95n

"The Lazy Tour of Two Idle Apprentices" *see under* Dickens, Charles: *Works*

The Lighthouse 65, 130n, 149, 200, 202, 394n, 395n, 418

"My London Lodgings" 132n

"The Monkstones of Wincot Abbey" 80n

"The National Gallery and the Old Masters" 174n

"A New Mind" 361n

"Over the Way" 705n

"A Paradoxical Experience" 695 & n

"A Petition to the Novel-Writers" 222n, 234

"The Poisoned Meal" 621n, 623

"The Prison in the Woods" 469n, 470n

The Queen of Hearts 458n

Rambles Beyond Railways 425n

The Red Vial 505n, 523 & n, 527, 700n

"A Rogue's Life" 58, 59n, 80n

"Sea-Breezes with the London Smack" 631n, 651n

"Sister Rose" 220 & n

"To Think, or to be thought for?" 174, 176

"Trottle's Report" 705n

Combermere, Caroline, Countess 725n

Comic Times (periodical) 5n

Commercial Travellers' Schools 52n

Commercial Travellers' Schools Society 445n

Compton, Henry 350n, 369n, 397n, 398

COMPTON, Mrs Henry (Emmeline Montague) 395n, 397n

Conspiracy to Murder Bill (1858) 522n, 682n

Constitution, or, Cork Advertiser 646n

COOKE, Thomas Potter ('Tippy') 345 & n, 346, 352, 379n, 392, 610n

Cooke, William 208–9

Cookesley, Dr John Moore 184

Cooper, Benjamin 540 & n

COOPER, Frank 687n

Cooper, Frederick Fox: dramatises *LD* 232n, 290n, 313n; dramatises *Silver Store Island* (i.e. *Perils of Certain English Prisoners*) 482n

Cooper, Louise 147, 213, 223

Cooper, Purton 529n

Copley, John Singleton *see* Lyndhurst, Baron

Copyright Amendment Act (1842) 495n

Cork, Ireland: CD reads at 597n, 601, 637, 641, 643–7

Cork Herald 637n, 646n

Cork, Richard Boyle, 1st Earl of 655n

Cornelius, Edward 42n

CORNELIUS, Mrs Edward (Anne Brown) 42 & n, 307n, 560n, 627, 645, 740n; daughter Catherine born 48 & n

Corvin-Wiersbitzki, Otto Julius Bernhard von 175n*; "Beating against the Bars" 175n; "Charles Dickens" 175n; *A Life of Adventure* 175n; "Six Years in a Cell" (with Morley) 175 & n

Costello, Dudley 701 & n

COUCHMAN, John 696n*

Court Circular (newspaper) 597n, 745n

COUTTS & Co., bankers: advise CD on Gad's Hill Place 1; CD's account with 7n, 24, 25, 73n, 163, 164n, 172n, 173, 215n, 230n, 271n, 347n, 366n, 372n, 376n, 390n, 420n, 436n, 449n, 465n, 510n, 546n, 610n, 653n, 660n; help Walter with cadetship 60n; and Lowe sisters' appeal 729

COUTTS, Angela Georgina Burdett, later Baroness Burdett-Coutts: Twelfth Night cake 7n, 16; Wills's employment with 16 & n, 17, 19, 41, 49–50; payments to CD 25 & n; and Home for Homeless Women 36; stays in Torquay 50n, 331n, 479, 718n; financial help for Haydns 139; awards prizes at Whitelands 146 & n, 160n, 731–4; as trustee of Mrs Brown's Exhibition 192n, 197–8; buys paintings from Rogers's collection 213n, 215n; views on dress for working girls 223 & n, 295, 310; invited to *Frozen Deep* 234–5, 237, 249; CD visits 244; and St George's Hospital scandal 271–2, 276, 291n;

Coutts, Angela Georgina Burdett (*cont.*): friendship with Bishop Phillpotts 272n; housing improvements 273n; signs Walter's cadetship certificate 282, 286; and Richard Warner 290; invited to and visit to Gad's Hill 330, 340, 343; offers to have Walter taught photography 372n; and repairs to Home for Homeless Women 372, 390, 396; entertains Andersen 373n; CD describes Maria Ternan in *The Frozen Deep* to 432–3; paper on teacher training 432; stays at King's Arms, Lancaster 443n; donation to Rev. R. R. Ford 455; helps Mrs Matthews 456n, 458, 689, 718; CD invites to dine 482; Catherine seeks help from for brother Edward 512 & n; and prostitutes' letters in *Times* 524–5; handwriting 527n; CD consults over proposed readings 535–6; CD confides in over marriage breakdown 558, 632, 748; ~ Catherine appeals to for help over 565n; Andersen recommends Elizabeth Jerichau-Baumann to 578n; and CD's reading tour 621, 688; CD seeks help over Charley's transfer at Baring's 652, 689; *Summary Account of Common Things* 79n, 146n, 160n, 223n, 229n, 230n, 233, 234n, 271n, 287 & n, 291, 295n, 432n, 731–5

Coventry: CD postpones visit to 320; CD's readings in 478, 484, 489, 490n, 491, 494; Miss Franklin's School 485n; CD visits to receive presentation watch 496 & n, 713–15 & n, 718

Coventry Herald 715n

Cowley, Henry Richard Charles Wellesley, 1st Earl 110 & n

Cowper, William, later 1st Baron Mount-Temple 324n

Cox, Mrs, of Christ Church Schools 731

Coyne, Joseph Stirling 270n; *The Latest from New York* 690n; *Urgent Private Affairs* 112n

Craig, George: "Blown Away" 473n

CRESWICK, William 351, 471n, 474, 610n

Crimean War: French troops return from 1–2, 11; storming of Malakoff tower 28 & n; armistice 31 & n; peace treaty 76n, 177n; celebrations for end of 125n; official enquiries into 174n, 504n; Russell lectures on 345n, 763–4; Luard paintings from 413n; sanitary conditions 503n

Critic, The (journal) 361n, 558n, 576n, 607n, 664n, 677n

CROCKER, Charles W. 585n*

Crosbie, Eliza *see* Forster, Mrs John

CROZIER, Robert 477n*

Crüger, Carl 660, 662

Cruikshank, George 200n

Crystal Palace Art-Union 591n

Crystal Palace Company 591

Crystal Palace fraud 216n

Cubitt, Sir William 35n

CULLENFORD, William J. 610n

Cumberland 428, 430, 432, 438–42

Cumming, John 30 & n*

Cunningham, Allan: "A Wet Sheet and a Flowing Sea" 130n

CUNNINGHAM, Peter: dines with CD 42, 48; edits Walpole letters 132n; visits CD in Boulogne 142, 156, 161, 163, 165–6, 202n; works in Audit Office 212 & n, 474n; and Manchester Art Treasures Exhibition 399n, 503n; *Hand Book of London* 18n

Cunningham, Mrs Peter (Zenobia Martin) 142 & n, 156, 161, 165

Cunynghame, General Sir Arthur Augustus 637 & n*

CURRIE, Philip Henry Wodehouse, 1st Baron Currie of Hawley 308n*

Currie, Raikes 329n

Curtis, G. 112n

Customs of the Country, The (anon. farce) 277n

Cuthbert, John Spreckley 408

Dadd, Richard 318n

Dafforne, James 68n

Daily News: reviews *Jack and the Beanstalk* 11n; W. H. Russell on 329n; praises CD in *Frozen Deep* 380; prints CD's letter on Jerrold fund 424n; on Landor libel case 643n; Harriet Martineau claims employs clairvoyant 674; Beard suggested for vacancy at 699

Daily Telegraph 353n, 648n

Daldy, F. R. 385n

Daley, inmate of Home 120

DANCE, Charles 546n*, 551; *The Stock Exchange* 547n; *A Wonderful Woman* 116n, 434n

Daniell, Dr John Bampfylde 129 & n

Danson, George 242n

Darlington: CD reads at 660, 669

Darlington and Stockton Times 669n

Darnley, John Stuart Bligh, 6th Earl of 51 & n, 659

Dasent, A. I.: *John Thadeus Delane* 524n

Daumier, Honoré 29n

Davies, James & Son 698 & n

Davies, James A.: *John Forster: a Literary Life* 114n

Davies, Richard, Dean of Hereford 160n

DAVIES, Rev. Robert Henry 244n*

Dawkins, Thomas 62n

DEANE, John Connellan: manages Manchester Art Treasures Exhibition 358n*, 377, 393n, 399n, 503 & n; and Manchester performance of *Frozen Deep* 395–6, 401n; accompanies CD to Coventry reading 490–1

De Bathe, Lieut.-Colonel Sir William Plunkett 275 & n
Deburau, Jean 30n
Dee, Frederick 370 & n
Defoe, Daniel 521n; *Robinson Crusoe* 153
Defoe family: descendant 521 & n, 523
DELANE, John Thadeus: Beard and 287 & n, 319; and Jerrold's final illness 345; and Miss Coutts's interest in *Times* prostitutes' letters 524n; and CD's 'Personal' statement 577n, 579, 580n; congratulates W. H. Russell in India 600n
DE LA PRYME, Charles 300, 378n
DE LA RUE, Emile 416, 471–2, 576n, 667, 709, 717
De la Rue, Madame Emile (Augusta Granet) 416, 471, 709n
Delaware: Brandywine Emett Repeal Assocation 648n
Delhi 459n, 460n
De Morgan, Augustus 675n
De Morgan, Mrs Augustus: "A Plea for Playgrounds" (with Morley) 584n, 675n
Derby: CD reads in 684–6
Derby and Chesterfield Reporter 684n
Derby Mercury 684n
Derby, Edward George Geoffrey Smith Stanley, 14th Earl of 682n
DEVONSHIRE, William George Spencer Cavendish, 6th Duke of: Jerrold proposes health 45n; on *LD* 129n; suffers stroke 129n, 149; invited to *Frozen Deep* 228; subscribes to Jerrold fund 394, 400
Dewailly, Mme Zélie 687n
Dexter, Walter 748n; *The Love Romance of CD* 381n, 559n, 566n, 627n; (ed.) *Mr and Mrs CD his Letters to her* 602n, 603n, 740, 741n
Dial, The (weekly newspaper) 679n
Dick, Quintin (of Dick & Roberts) 757 & n
Dickens, Alfred D'Orsay Tennyson ('Ally'; CD's son) 26n, 241–2, 372n, 559n
DICKENS, Alfred Lamert (CD's brother) 205 & n*, 254, 699
Dickens, Mrs Alfred Lamert (Helen Dobson) 205
Dickens, Augustus Newnham (CD's youngest brother) 59, 65 & n, 749n
Dickens, Mrs Augustus Newnham (Harriet Lovell) 65n
DICKENS, Catherine Macready, later Mrs Charles Collins; then Mrs C. E. Perugini (CD's daughter; Kate; Katy): in Paris 96; leaves Boulogne 180; illness 182, 199 & n, 202; plays in *Frozen Deep* 199, 254n, 412n; at Bonchurch 290; on Andersen 372n; on father's behaviour to wife 471n; on Georgina 559n; relations with mother 559; helps keep house for father 598, 697; joins father on reading tour 671, 673–4, 677; in father's will 750
DICKENS, Charles Culliford Boz ('Charley'; CD's eldest son): works at Baring Brothers 41–2, 47, 146, 203, 210, 216; dines with CD 67, 69, 109, 115, 142; at Gad's Hill 69, 302, 622, 652; at theatre 71; 20th birthday 118, 202; hopes for holiday 165; and *Frozen Deep* 199, 203, 395; stays with Müller in Leipzig 206; Miss Coutts writes to 234; Andersen requests to be shaved by 372n; sees Walter off to India 376, 380; disagreements with Andersen 383n; plays in *Uncle John* 414n; inherits CD's Edinburgh cup 538n; and the Derby 565; lives with mother after separation 573–5, 578n, 741; and mother's access to children 602 & n; CD proposes visiting Ireland with 622; CD inscribes reading version of *Chimes* to 652n; seeks transfer in Barings 652, 689; holiday from Barings 666; in CD's will 751n
Dickens, Charles John Huffam
Addresses from which letters written:
Allonby (Cumberland) 441; Belfast 640; Birmingham 201, 680–4; Boulogne 133–7, 140, 143–6, 149–50, 152–8, 160–1, 162–72, 174–6, 178, 180; Brighton 297–8, 703–4; Carlisle 38, 443; Cork 645; Derby 684–6; Doncaster 445–50; Dover 104–6, 469; Dublin 632, 634, 636, 640, 642; Dundee 672–3; Edinburgh 672; Gad's Hill Place (Higham, Kent) 326, 340–4, 347, 350, 354, 356, 360, 367, 377, 381–2, 384, 388–90, 396–403, 407–12, 420–2, 424–5, 427–9, 432, 435–7, 451–8, 460–2, 464–6, 468, 476, 589–90, 592–6, 599, 601–3, 606–8, 611–16, 619–20, 627, 648–9, 651–2, 654, 678, 696–7, 705; Glasgow 675–6; Gravesend 310, 312–13, 326–7; Halifax 661, 663; Hull 687–91; Lancaster 443; Leeds 659, 691; Limerick 645–7; Liverpool 628–31; Manchester 665, 679; Newcastle-on-Tyne 668, 670–1; Paris 2–9, 11, 13–14, 16, 18–19, 22, 24–5, 28, 31, 35–41, 43, 52–64, 66–9, 74, 76–7, 79–81, 83–6, 88, 90, 92–3, 95, 97–100, 102–3; Plymouth 617; Rochester 320; Scarborough 657; Sheffield 663–4, 692; Shrewsbury 625–6; Southampton 380, 700–1; Wigton 439; Wolverhampton 624, 693–5; Worcester 622–3; York 655–6
London 619; Athenaeum 729; Gallery of Illustration 355, 357–9, 362–5, 370, 373, 375, 377–9, 387, 392–3, 404, 406; Garrick Club 348–53, 356, 413; Home for Homeless Women 119, 129; *Household Words* office 41–51, 70–1, 73, 107, 113–14, 117, 132, 141–2, 183, 187, 195, 222, 225, 233, 275, 295, 304, 310, 324, 338–9, 345, 354, 368,

Dickens, Charles John Huffam (*cont.*): 384, 387, 391, 404, 414–15, 417, 430–1, 454, 465, 467, 470–1, 474, 481–3, 485, 490–1, 525, 527, 549, 561, 563, 565, 591, 613, 621, 627, 653, 678, 696, 705, 709; Norfolk Street, Park Lane (Townshend's) 551; St Martin's Hall 606; Tavistock House 50, 72–4, 107–9, 111–13, 115–19, 121–8, 130, 132, 150, 181–94, 196–201, 203–64, 267–71, 273–80, 282–97, 299–309, 314–35, 337–8, 352, 361–2, 364, 367, 369, 371–4, 376, 378–9, 385–7, 394–5, 397, 403–5, 416, 418–20, 423, 427, 464, 475–81, 483–7, 490–9, 501–7, 509–32, 534–8, 541–51, 553–7, 561–4, 566–91, 593–4, 604, 606, 609–11, 613, 628, 654, 666–7, 676–9, 686, 688, 697–700, 706–7, 709–11, 713–14, 716–21, 723–5, 740, 755

Works:

American Notes 39, 133n, 150n, 368, 674n

"Auteur Anglais au Public Français, L'" 262n

Barnaby Rudge: French translation 36 & n; on Newgate 391n; stage adaptation 565n; Gordon riots in 637n

— *Character*: Miggs, Miss 220, 691

"Birthday Celebrations" *see* "The Uncommercial Traveller"

Bleak House 8n, 106n, 526, 533n, 674n

— *Character*: Mrs Jellyby 6n

Book of Memoranda 432n

The Boots 533n; readings 618, 621, 623, 628n, 633, 641n, 643, 646, 647n, 661n, 664n, 666n, 668n, 673, 674n, 675n, 679n, 680n, 681n, 687n, 691n, 693n, 694n, 697n, 703n, 712; printed text 692

The Case of the Reformers of the Literary Fund (with Dilke and Forster) 324n

A Child's History 231n, 298n, 436, 445

The Chimes: readings 534 & n, 542, 546n, 556–7, 619n, 623, 633, 637, 652n, 672, 674, 677, 712; ascribed to Charley 652n; printed text 652

A Christmas Carol 2n; CD reads 14n, 352n, 374 & n, 376, 393n, 399, 478, 484, 496n, 534n, 538n, 539–41, 546n, 564n, 566n, 591n, 617n, 619n, 625n, 626n, 628n, 633, 641n, 643n, 646, 657n, 658n, 660n, 664n, 666n, 669, 673, 674n, 675, 676n, 677, 681, 684n, 685n, 691n, 693n, 697n, 703n, 720n; reading version published 652

Christmas Stories (*Contes de Noel*) 22, 23n, 39, 594n

"A Christmas Tree" 594n

"A Clause for the New Reform Bill" 669n

"The Condition of the Working Classes" 234n

"A Confession found in a Prison in the time of Charles the Second" 528n

Contes de Noel see *Christmas Stories*

The Cricket on the Hearth 534n, 542, 546n, 555n, 674n

"Curious Misprint in the Edinburgh Review" 389n, 399, 410n

David Copperfield 40n; sales 106n; books in 153n; and J. E. Roney 191n; Cheap Edition 533n

— *Character*: Dartle, Rosa 65n

"The Demeanour of Murderers" 128, 446n

"A Dinner at Poplar Walk" 13n

Dombey and Son 227n; stage adaptation 232n; Dutch translation 481n; Cheap Edition 533n

— *Character*: Cuttle, Captain 269n; *see also* "Little Dombey" below

"Drooping Buds" (with Morley) 519n

"A Few Conventionalities" 59

"Foreigners' Portraits of Englishmen" 139n

"The Friend of the Lions" 18n, 24 & n

"Going into Society" 705n, 709n

Great Expectations 467n, 710n; planned 510–11, 531

— *Characters*: Havisham, Miss 650n; Pip 467n, 710n

Hard Times 6n; French translation 22, 23n; Kay-Shuttleworth satirised in 160n; publication 603–4; Mrs Oliphant criticises 674n

— *Character*: Bounderby 159

The Haunted Man and the Ghost's Bargain 534, 542

"The Holly Tree Inn" *see Household Words* Christmas Numbers

"Insularities" 1n, 6n, 10

"The Island of Silver Store" 468n, 473n, 508n

"The Lazy Tour of Two Idle Apprentices" (with Collins) 429n, 436n, 438n, 440n, 441n, 442n, 443n, 444n, 445, 446n, 447n, 448, 450, 454–5, 457–8, 462; CD has copy made 656

"Let at Last" 705n

Little Dombey (reading extract) 584, 585n, 591n, 608n, 618, 621, 623, 628n, 630, 633, 636, 638, 641, 643, 646, 657n, 658n, 659, 666n, 673–4, 675n, 676–7, 680n, 681n, 682n, 687n, 703n, 712; printed text 652

Little Dorrit: on snobs 3n; sales and success 8, 36, 49, 54n, 61n, 106n, 298n; Tauchnitz edition 8n; writing and serialisation 12, 17, 28, 36, 60, 64, 69, 75, 77, 79, 82, 96, 104, 108, 116, 135, 137, 145, 156, 162, 192, 196n, 210, 213n, 238, 240, 264, 270, 279–

80, 282n, 287, 290, 307, 313, 319; Circumlocution Office in 18n, 40, 79, 389n, 502n, 693n; Hachette publish French version 22n, 23n; as song title 26; publication 31, 67, 603–4; St Bernard Pass episode 33, 201n, 266; Trollope criticises 40n; reception 63n, 309, 674n; on Patent Law reform 123n; Duke of Devonshire on 129n; illustrations 141n, 219, 232, 280, 297; proofs and corrections 226–7, 274n, 279n, 284; stage adaptation 232n, 290n, 313n; and 'introduced story' 279–80; completed 322–3, 388n, 604; presentation copies 327, 335, 468 & n; dedicated to Stanfield 328 & n; Stephen attacks 389n

— *Characters*: Amy (Little Dorrit) 67n, 313n; Casby, 227n; Cavaletto, John Baptist 232, 290n; Clennam, Arthur 67n, 82n, 129n, 219, 228n, 280n, 290n, 297n; Clennam, Mrs 282n, 297n, 313n; Decimus, Lord 232; Dorrit, Frederick 280n; Dorrit, William 141n, 280, 290n; F, Mr, aunt 75, 228n; Fanny 297n; Finching, Flora 82, 129n, 149–50, 228, 297, 515 & n; Gowan, Mr 79; Flintwich 219, 290n, 313n; Merdle, Mr 79, 232n, 282n, 297; Plornish, Mrs 232; Rigaud 290n; Sparkler 297; Wade, Miss 270n, 279n, 280

"The Long Voyage" 594n

Martin Chuzzlewit 150n, 214n, 305n, 513n; Dutch translation 481n; Watertoast Association in 648n

— *Characters*: Pecksniff, Seth 162n, 270; Pinch, Ruth 305n; Westlock, John 305n

Master Humphrey's Clock 36, 528

"Memoranda for the Draft [Will]" 581n

Mr Nightingale's Diary (with Lemon) 64n, 155n

Mrs Gamp (reading extract) 533n, 618, 628n, 641n, 643, 646n, 647n, 661n, 664n, 666n, 668n, 673, 674n, 675n, 679n, 680n, 687n, 691n, 693n, 694n, 697n, 703n, 712; printed text 633n, 692

Nelly (Dutch translation of *The Old Curiosity Shop*) 481n

"New Year's Day" 723n

Nicholas Nickleby: frontispiece portrait of CD 104n, 326n; French translation 208, 262n, 263n; and CD's visit to Yorkshire 444; opening 505n

"A Nightly Scene in London" 16n

"Nobody, Somebody and Everybody" 168n

The Old Curiosity Shop 22n, 36 & n

"Old Lamps for New Ones" 543n

Oliver Twist 31, 322n, 391n, 499n, 565n, 625

"On Her Majesty's Service" (with Grenville Murray) 411n

"Our Almanac" 59n

"Out of the Season" 110n

"The Perils of Certain English Prisoners" *see Household Words* Christmas Numbers

'Personal' statement (on marriage separation from Catherine) 573n, 577n, 579–80, 597n, 699n, 701n; text 744

Pickwick Papers: French translation 23n; published 131 & n, 609, 614; Library Edition 469n, 476n; *see also The Trial Scene* below

Pictures from Italy 2n, 39, 174n, 196n

"Please to leave your umbrella" 500n

The Poor Traveller 533n; readings 618n, 628n, 633, 641n, 643n, 646n, 647n, 661n, 664n, 666n, 668n, 673, 674n, 675n, 679n, 680n, 687n, 691n, 693n, 694n, 697n, 703n, 712

"A Preliminary Word" (to *HW*) 59n

"Proposals for a National Jest-Book" 30n, 88n, 93n, 96, 97n

"The Rafts on the River" 469n, 508n

"Railway Dreaming" 98n, 108n

Reprinted Pieces (from *HW*) 594 & n

"The Ruffian" 471n

"Shy Neighbourhoods" 466n

Sketches by Boz 23, 39, 131, 391n

Speeches (ed. K. J. Fielding) 45n, 52n, 60n, 74n, 106n, 293n, 305n, 327n, 395n, 421n, 445n, 453n, 517n, 518n, 522n, 529n, 531n, 536n, 538n, 544n, 555n, 584n, 587n, 610n, 713n, 715n

"Stories for the First of April" 174n

Sunday Under Three Heads 121n

A Tale of Two Cities 432n, 624n, 707n, 710n

"The Toady Tree" 105n

The Trial Scene (reading extract from *Pickwick Papers*) 680n, 681n, 682, 687n, 712, 720n

Uncollected Writings (ed. Harry Stone) 9n, 139n, 195n, 519n, 706n

The Uncommercial Traveller (book) 338n, 489n, 518n

"The Uncommercial Traveller" (reprinted as "Birthday Celebrations") 518n

'Violated letter' 568n, 644n, 648n, 656n, 705n, 746n; text 740–1

"A Visit to Newgate" 391n

"Why?" 15n, 30n, 57n, 59

Will (draft) 750–1

"Women in the Home" 234n

Works: Cheap Edition 264n, 487; French translation 309; Library Edition 436n, 445, 470n, 476, 487n, 594n; Illustrated Library Edition 594n

"The Wreck" 195n, 222n, 244

"The Wreck of the Golden Mary" (with Collins) *see Household Words* Christmas Numbers

DICKENS, Mrs Charles John Huffam (Catherine Thomson Hogarth): takes water-cure 64n; celebrates Charles Knight's birthday 68n; in Paris 95; visits Great St Bernard Convent 201n; visits Macready 220; and appointment of Gad's Hill gardener 292; interviews Mrs Webb 313; 42nd birthday 325; and Mrs Horne 334; at Manchester production of *Frozen Deep* 409–10, 420; ill-health 409–10, 560 & n; Andersen praises 426n; marriage breakdown 430, 434, 442n, 471–2, 539, 558–60, 570, 574, 597n, 739–46; seeks help for brother Edward from Miss Coutts 512 & n; and CD's 'violated letter' 558n, 559n, 568n, 644n, 648n, 740–1; relations with children 558–60, 632, 748; Miss Coutts offers help in marriage breakdown 565n; lives apart from CD 566 & n, 573; separation agreement and deed 566n, 568n, 573n, 578n, 602, 739; and Hogarth family's alleged slanders 569, 573; and CD's 'Personal' statement 573n, 577n, 579n, 597n, 744–5; lives with son Charley 573–5, 578n, 741; access to children 602 & n; disbelieves rumours of CD's extra-marital relations 741n, 742–3; aunt Helen's letter on separation 746–9; in CD's will 750

Dickens, Edward Bulwer Lytton ('Plorn'; 'Mr Plornish'; CD's son): in France 27, 105, 135, 155, 170; on Scheffer portrait of CD 28; black eye 49; as 'The Hammy Boy' 156; on death of dog 203; makes joke 294; first trousers 672; at CD's Chatham reading 712n

Dickens, Francis Jeffrey (CD's son): in Boulogne 26n, 372n; CD recommends for cadetship 241–2; and parents' separation 602n; relations with mother 632; at school in Hamburg 660 & n, 662

DICKENS, Frederick William (CD's brother): CD declines to help 236, 254–5, 275, 277; marriage 236n; calls on CD in Dublin 644, 647; wife sues for judicial separation on grounds of adultery 690–1, 706 & n, 725, 749n; CD remonstrates with 699–700

Dickens, Mrs Frederick William (Anna Delancey Weller): sues Frederick for judicial separation 236n, 690n, 706n; gives piano recital with sister Christiana 474n

Dickens, (Sir) Henry Fielding (CD's son): in France 1n, 27n; on Andersen's visit 372n, 383n; relations with mother 559n; in CD's will 751n; *Recollections of Sir Henry Fielding Dickens, K.C.* 383n, 559n

Dickens, John (CD's father) 321n, 360n

Dickens, Louis 537

DICKENS, Mary ('Mamie'; 'Mamey'; CD's daughter); singing 26 & n; in Paris 95; pet canary 154n; flower arranging 170, 177; leaves Boulogne 180; plays in *Frozen Deep* 235, 247n, 248n, 254n, 369n, 412n, 432, 488; at Bonchurch 290; birth 430 & n; relations with mother 559; keeps house for CD 584, 598, 659, 697; joins CD on reading tour 671, 673–4, 677; at CD's Chatham reading 712n; in CD's will 750, 751n; *My Father as I Recall Him* 7n, 14n

Dickens, Sydney Smith Haldimand (CD's son): in Boulogne 26n, 372n; reproached (as 'man on duty') 165; Georgina on 629; intention to join Navy 697–8; relations with mother 749

Dickens, Walter Landor (CD's son): deafness 17, 152; schooling in Paris 17; birth 60; East India Company cadetship 60n, 152, 176n, 198, 279; returns home 65; takes CD's work to Bradbury & Evans 67; at Wimbledon School 127n, 279; in Boulogne 136, 145; and W. S. Landor 152n; Miss Coutts helps 161, 176n; Eastwick offers help to 241n; takes and passes East India Company exam 282, 286, 311; George Beadnell invites to stay 341–2; sails for India 344, 372n, 376, 379–82, 416–17, 422; at Gallery of Illustration 370; Miss Coutts offers to have photography taught to 372n; prepares for departure 372; learns Hindustani 376n, 390; letters home 416–17, 422, 459; in Indian Mutiny 431n, 516; dress 436; in Calcutta 458–9; at Dum-Dum 488; regimental service 516, 654n, 684; contracts fever in India 654, 684

Dickers, James 375n

Dickinson, Charles 361n

DICKINSON, 'Mrs' Frances Vickriss, formerly Mrs John Edward Geils; then Mrs Gilbert Elliot 354n, 361 & n*, 395, 412n, 547–8, 618

DILKE, Charles Wentworth: and reform of Royal Literary Fund 44 & n, 60n, 293n, 304, 324, 549n, 550n, 588 & n, 591n

Dillon, Charles 466n, 490 & n*, 495n, 514–16

Disraeli, Benjamin (*later* Earl of Beaconsfield) 466n, 497n, 682n

Dixon and Ross, printers 121n

DIXON, Benjamin Homer 564n*

Dixon, Edmund Saul 16, 21; "Attraction and Repulsion" 98n

Dixon, Ella: *As I Knew Them* 361n

DIXON, William Hepworth: complains of inappropriate welfare help 25 & n; and Trollope's criticism of *LD* 40n; and Royal Literary Fund reforms 60n; at Jerrold's funeral 352n; and Jerrold memorial fund 355 & n; friendship with Frances Dickinson 361n; Blanchard Jerrold complains of CD to 463n; ~ and Blanchard Jerrold's reconciliation with CD 600n

Dodd, Henry 610n

DOLBY, Charlotte Helen 193n, 351, 705n
DOLBY, George 193n*, 705n
Dolby, Samuel 193n
Doncaster 429, 438–9, 442, 444–50, 536; Theatre Royal 446n, 447n, 472
Doncaster, Nottinghamshire and Lincoln Gazette 446n, 447n
Donizetti, Gaetano: *L'Elisir d'Amore* 702n; *Lucia di Lammermoor* 639n
DONNE, William Bodham 406n*
Donnybrook Fair, Dublin 633–4
Dorking, Surrey 690, 699
D'Orsay, Alfred, Count 446n, 468n
DOUDNEY, Edward 639
Dover 110
Downer, A. S.: *The Eminent Tragedian* 531n
DOWNING, Henry Bourne 678n
Dublin: CD reads at 597n, 601, 629, 632–40, 642–3; Queen's Theatre 639 & n; Theatre Royal 639n; *see also* Donnybrook Fair
Dublin Evening Mail 633n, 641n
Dublin Evening Post 633n, 637n, 638n
Dublin: What's to be Seen? 639n
Duchemin, Adelaide 605n
Duchemin, Louis Michel 605n
Duchemin, Thérèse: 'Ladies' School', Birmingham 605n
Dudevant-Sand, Maurice (George Sand's son) 34n
DUDLEY, Robert 434n*
Duff, David: *Eugénie and Napoleon* 57n
Duff Gordon *see* Gordon
Dührssen, Dr Jacobus 326n
Dulwich College *see* London: Schools
Dumas, Alexandre, père: *Catherine Howard* 471n; *Crimes Célèbres* 93 & n; *L'Oresteia* 29 & n, 33
Dum-Dum, India 488
Duncan-Jones, Caroline M.: *Miss Mitford and Mr Harness* 545n
Dundee 630; CD reads at 673, 676
Dundee Courier 673n
Dunn, Richard 165 & n
Durham: CD reads at 669, 672
Durham Advertiser 132n, 612n
Durham County Advertiser 669n
Duthie, William: "More Sundays Abroad" 99 & n, 121n; "Some German Sundays" 121n
DYER, William George Thistleton 129n*, 223, 521, 544–5

EAGLE INSURANCE OFFICE 230n
EARDLEY, Sir Culling 386n*
Eastern Steam Navigation Co. 47n
Easthope, Sir John 131
Easthorpe Park, near Malton, Yorkshire 658
Eastlake, Sir Charles Lock 108 & n, 254n, 257, 562
EASTLAKE, Elizabeth, Lady (*née* Rigby) 257n
Eastwick, Edward: (ed.) *The Autobiography of Lutfullah Khan* 416n
EASTWICK, William Joseph 241n*, 416 & n
Ebury, Baron *see* Grosvenor, Lord Robert
EDEN, Hon. Emily 332
Edinburgh 212, 489; CD reads in 536–8, 541–2, 625, 651, 655, 670–4, 748; Burns Centenary Festival 724
EDINBURGH PHILOSOPHICAL INSTITUTION 103, 106, 538n
Edinburgh Review 1n, 160, 389n, 399
Edwards, Amelia Ann Blandford 585 & n*; *Hand and Glove* 585
EDWARDS, Edward 367n
EELES, Thomas Robert 512, 517, 534 & n
Egg, Augustus Leopold: 'Plorn' on 28; buys Henry Wallis painting 111; nicknamed 'The Colonel' 162 & n; travels in Italy with CD 256n; praised for performance in *Frozen Deep* 369n, 380n; and Manchester Art Treasures Exhibition 399n, 503n; on Arbroath 630
Eglinton, Archibald Montgomerie, 13th Earl of 634n
Eliot, George *see* Evans, Marian
Elizabeth Fry Refuge, Hackney *see* London: Buildings, &c
Ellerton, John Lodge 694n
Ellice, Edward 715n
Elliot, Very Rev. Gilbert, Dean of Bristol 361n
ELLIOTSON, Dr John 128 & n, 193 & n, 709
Elliott, Celeste *see* Celeste, Madame
ELLIS, Charles, winemerchant 326 & n, 546
ELLIS, (H. or Thomas): CD declines to be photographed by 259, 331
ELLIS, Joseph, the younger 294
Elton, Edward S. 724n
Elton Fund 688n, 724
Elven, J. P.: *Heraldry* 360n
ELWIN, Rev. Whitwell 60n, 204n, 208
EMDEN, William Samuel 387n, 394n*, 418n
Emerson, Ralph Waldo 714n
Emery, Samuel Anderson 71 & n*
Emmerson, George S.: *John Scott Russell* 47n
Engelbach, Charles William 216n
Engelbach, Lewis J. 216n
Engelbach, Mrs 216 & n
Era (journal) 414n, 571n
Essarts, Alfred des 36n
Esse, Charles Frederick 163 & n
Eugène Louis Jean Joseph Napoléon, Prince Imperial of France 87n, 135 & n
Eugénie (de Montejo), Empress of France 525n, 684n
Eustace, John Chetwode 196 & n
Evans, Frederick Moule 413

EVANS, Frederick Mullet: CD mocks Cockneyisms 48n; crosses to France with CD 53n, 54; sends accounts to CD 298, 436; and Jerrold's illness 346; advises Bentley 403; and dying mother 413 & n; publishes Library Edition of CD's works 445, 469; and posting bill for "A Lazy Tour" 455; on CD's treatment of Catherine 471n; CD consults over effect of proposed readings on book sales 533; as Catherine's Trustee after separation 578n, 608n, 701n; CD's children forbidden to visit 603; CD's rift with 608 & n; and accounting for *HW* 694–5; and *HW* dissolution proposal 748
Evans, George 413n
EVANS, Marian (George Eliot) 506n*; attacks Cumming 30n; praises Meredith's *Shaving of Shagpat* 117n; schooling in Coventry 485n; CD identifies as woman 506–7; in Munich with G. H. Lewes 580n; *Letters* (ed. Gordon S. Haight) 506n, 507n; *Scenes of Clerical Life* 317n, 506–7 & n
Evans, Mrs Mary 413n
Evans, Tom 413n
Evening Chronicle 131n
Examiner, The: Forster resigns from 1n, 165 & n; reviews Collins's *After Dark* 39n; on end of Crimean War celebrations 128n; Landor contributes to 152 & n; praises Ristori 171n; praises *Frozen Deep* scenery 228n; and Jerrold memorial fund 348n; obituary of Talfourd 721n
Exeter: CD reads at 597n, 617, 621, 623

FAIDER, Charles Jean Baptiste Florian 615n*
FAIRBAIRN, Thomas 393n*
Fairbairn, Mrs Thomas (Allison Calloway) 393
Fairbairn, Sir William 393n
Falmouth, Anne Frances, Countess of (*née* Bankes) 192n, 197n, 248–9, 261n
Faraday, Michael 506n
Farrer, Ouvry & Farrer, solicitors (*formerly* Farrer, Parkinson & Co.) 169n, 495, 581, 680n, 755–6
Farrer, W. J. 192n
Faucit, Helen (*later* Helena) Saville (*later* Lady Martin) 519
Fauntleroy, Henry 695n
Fechter, Charles 76n, 444n
FELTON, Cornelius Conway 566 & n, 567n
Ferguson, Robert: *The Northmen in Cumberland and Westmorland* 209n
Fergusson, Dr William (*later* Baronet) 57n, 129 & n*
Ferrero, G. M.: *Journal d'un Officier*... 164n
Ferrère Laffitte, Paris bankers 7 & n
FIELD, Joshua 122n*
Field (weekly journal) 155n
Fielding Club 109n
Fielding, Henry 279; *Tom Jones* 280n
Fielding, K. J. 234n; "Bradbury *v.* Dickens" 700n, 758–61; "CD and Colin Rae Brown" 754; "CD and his Wife" 746, 749n; "Dickens and the Hogarth Scandal" 568n, 569n, 572n, 597n, 742n, 745; *see also* Dickens: *Works*, *Speeches* (ed. K. J. Fielding)
FIELDS, James Thomas: *Yesterdays with Authors* 589n
Fields, Mrs James Thomas (Annie) 559n
Fillonneau, André Guillaume 10 & n
Fillonneau, Mrs André Guillaume (Amelia Austin) 10 & n
FINLAY, Francis Dalziel, Jr. 645n*, 646n
Finlay, Mrs Francis Dalziel (Janet Russel) 645n
Finn, Septimus 545n
Fisher, William, Jr. 666
Fitzball, Edward: and "Green Bush Melodramas" 379n; *The Flying Dutchman* 141n, 163; *The Pilot* 379n
FITZGERALD, Desmond G.: "Poetry and Philosophy" 530 & n
FITZGERALD, Percy Hetherington 616n*, 619, 636n, 641n; "The Armourer's Story" 195n; *Memories of CD* 616n, 636n; "The Supercargo's Story" 195n
Fitzgerald, Hon. Mrs Percy Hetherington (Dorcas Louisa Skeffington) 616n
Fitzgerald, Thomas 616n
FitzLyon, April: *The Price of Genius* 34n
Fladgate, Frank 536 & n*
Fladgate, William Mark 536n, 631
Flaherty, Bernard *see* Williams, Barney
Fletcher, Angus 66n
FLETCHER, George: *Life and Career of Dr William Palmer of Rugeley* 447n; *The Provincialist* 682n
Florence, Italy 606n, 666–7
Florence, William Jermyn 115n
Florence, Mrs William Jermyn (Malvina Pray) 115 & n*, 142 & n
Foggo, George 334n
Foggo, James 334n
Folkestone: theft in 143, 140–8, 162
Fonblanque, Albany W. 497n
Foosters, Henri 96 & n
Forbes, Miss, of Lausanne 266
Forbes, Sir John 140 & n; *Sight Seeing in Germany and the Tyrol* 139n
Ford, Rev. Richard Robert 421, 455
Forgues, Paul Emile Durand 29n*, 65n, 87, 130n, 458n; "Biographies Contemporaines: XXVI. Charles Dickens" 130n, 131n, 132n, 162, 200

Forsham, Charles F. 683n
FORSTER, John 1n*; appointed Secretary to Lunacy Commission 1n, 165n, 577n; resigns editorship of *Examiner* 1n, 165 & n; praises *Train* 5n; on anonymous poems for *HW* 20; on CD and George Sand 33n; dines with CD 48, 67, 69, 115; relinquishes share in *HW* 56 & n, 730; supports reform of Royal Literary Fund 60n, 293n, 304, 325n, 549n, 550n, 588n; visits Gad's Hill 69, 595, 612, 642, 644; marriage 70, 114n, 119n, 165, 175n, 204n, 209n; reads proofs of *LD* 82n, 226–7; owns Wallis's *In Shakespeare's House* 111n; doubts on *Frozen Deep* 217; Montague Square house 220; delivers Prologue to *Frozen Deep* 254n; and writing of *LD* 279 & n; and requests for CD to stand for Parliament 303n; and *Blackwood*'s criticism of *LD* 309n; at Jerrold's funeral 352n; Andersen meets 373n; serves on Jerrold memorial fund committee 424n; and CD's marriage breakdown 429–30, 434, 471n, 537n, 539, 566, 739; and copyright on CD's books 436; and Library Edition of CD's works 445; and CD's "Lazy Tour" 462; CD justifies restlessness to 464; supports appeal for Marguerite Power 486, 497; CD dedicates Library Edition of works to 487n; and CD's proposed new novel (*Great Expectations*) 510–11, 531, 710n; praises CD's speech at Hospital for Sick Children dinner 519n; reservations about CD's public readings 534 & n, 535–7, 539; 46th birthday 538; CD outlines programme for readings to 539–41; and CD's reading for Hospital for Sick Children 542; on CD's reading of *The Chimes* 556n; stays at Sir John Falstaff Inn 557n; and Felton's illness and death 567 & n; and Hogarth family slander 572, 577n; and CD's 'Personal' statement on separation 577n, 580n; named as Trustee and Executor for CD's will 581n, 750; and press criticisms of CD's behaviour 597n; helps P. H. Fitzgerald 616n; and CD's reading tours 628, 642, 656, 668, 672, 676, 691, 696; and Landor libel case 643n, 644n; and CD's 'violated letter' 644, 741; on Chapman's account of Ingram 661; CD gives power of attorney to in respect of *HW* 695n, 702; negotiates with Bradbury & Evans over *HW* 699n, 700n, 701 & n, 711, 719n, 723n, 758–61; CD bequeaths watch to 715n; Payn sends CD letter to 716n; on CD's appreciation of uncommon acting 722n; co-signs letter to *Times* on Lowe sisters appeal 729; Lemon blames for breach with CD 741n; in CD's will 751n; in Belgium with CD and Jerrold 762; *The Life and Times of Oliver Goldsmith* 599n; *Walter Savage Landor* 153n, 525n, 644n; "The Writings of Charles Dickens" 448n
FORSTER, Mrs John (*née* Eliza Crosbie; *then* Mrs Henry Colburn): marriage to Forster 114 & n*, 165, 175n, 204 & n; portrait 204n; CD seeks present for husband 538 & n; visits Gad's Hill with husband 595, 642, 644
Fortescue, Julia Sarah Hayfield (Lady Gardner) 238 & n
FOX, Rev. William Johnson ('Publicola') 115 & n*
Franconi's circus, Paris 37 & n, 96 & n
Franklin, Benjamin: *Poor Richard's Almanack* 273n
Franklin, Sir John 66n, 330n; *Narrative of his Journeys* 265n
Franklin, Lady (Jane Griffin) 66 & n, 330
Fraser, Maxwell: *Surrey* 428n
FRASER, Peter S. 563n*
FRASER, Thomas 85 & n
Fraser's Magazine 80n
Frémont, Colonel John Charles 289
French, Miss: "Billeted at Boulogne" 99 & n; "Two Difficult Cases" 194n
French, Charles, servant 47 & n, 154–5, 162–3, 212, 283n, 285n, 422
FRIEND, Richard 112n*
FRISWELL, James Hain: *Ghost Stories and Phantom Fancies* 500n
FRITH, William Powell 9n; *Kate Nickleby* (painting) 570n; *Many Happy Returns of the Day* (painting) 108 & n; *My Autobiography and Reminiscences* 9n
Froude, James Anthony 506n
FRY, Herbert 72n*, 200n, 476n
Fullerton, Lady Georgiana (*née* Leveson-Gower) 133 & n*
Fust, Sir Herbert Jenner 361n

Gad's Hill: Sir John Falstaff Inn 557n
Gad's Hill Place, Kent: CD purchases 1, 20, 38, 54n, 65, 71, 74, 91, 265–6; CD visits with Wills 48, 50; CD's plans for 50–1; CD describes 51, 597; wine cellar 138; in *1 Henry IV* 265 & n, 589, 597–8; CD occupies 281, 292, 330; repairs and improvements 283, 296, 302–3, 310–11, 330, 332, 371n, 381, 420n, 427, 449, 510, 597; furnishing 284, 296; Beard and 287n; gardener (Charles Barber) 292, 306, 400; CD entertains at 326–7; water supply and well 342–3, 366, 372, 382, 411, 421–2, 425, 436, 447, 449, 452, 455, 459, 541; drainage problems 381–2, 384–5; CD walks to from London 466n, 489; dogs at 489 & n
GALE, William: *Mr. F's Aunt* (painting) 330, 347n

Galignani's Messenger (journal) 11, 20, 28, 29n, 33n, 37n, 57n, 76n, 82n, 89n, 91n, 135n
GALIMARD, Nicolas Auguste 25n*
Gardeners' Benevolent Fund 45n
Gardner, Allan Legge Gardner, 3rd Baron 238 & n
GASKELL, Elizabeth Cleghorn 4n, 117n, 701n, 705n; *Cranford* 4n; *Letters* (ed. J. A. V. Chapple and A. Pollard) 4n; "The Manchester Marriage" 705n; "My Lady Ludlow" 620; *North and South* 117n, 136n, 189n; "The Poor Clare" 4n; *Ruth* 4n
Gaskell, Rev. William 4 & n
Gaumont-Laforce, Countess 101n
Gautier, Théophile 37n
Geils, John Edward 361n
Genoa 415–16, 709
George I, King 383n
George, Marguerite-Josephine Weyma 337n
Geradin, Alfred 22n
Gettmann, Royal: *A Victorian Publisher: a study of the Bentley Papers* 403n
Giant's Cradle, Brown's Bay, near Larne, Northern Ireland 641n
Gibbs, Charles 441, 473
GIBSON, Mary W. A. 683; "Lost Alice" 494n; "A Tale of an Old Man's Youth" 494n
GIBSON, Rev. Matthew 26, 27 & n, 178–9, 285n, 372n, 653–4, 697–8
GIGLIUCCI, Clara Anastasia, Countess (*née* Novello) 261 & n*, 349, 352, 604, 606
Gigliucci, Count 261n
Giles, Rev. William 131n, 622n
Girardin, Emile de 34 & n*, 76, 87, 91, 95, 97
Girardin, Madame Emile de: *La Joie fait Peur* 514–16
GIRDLESTONE, Rev. Edward 168n*
Glanville, Lady 369n
Glasgow: CD reads in 674–5, 677; CD objects to nomination to Rectorship of University 702, 707; Burns Centenary Festival 714 & n
Glasgow Daily Bulletin 427n, 754
Glasgow Herald 675n
Glasgow Morning Journal 702n
Glencorse, John Inglis, Lord 707n
Glengall, Richard Butler, 1st Earl of 278n
Globe newspaper 11n, 309, 352n, 584n
Gobat, Rev. Samuel, Bishop of Jerusalem 548 & n
Goderich, George Frederick Samuel Robinson, Viscount (*later* 2nd Earl of Ripon) 544n
Goetznitz, von: "The Last Victims of the Gauntlet" 630 & n
Goldsmith, Captain George 342
Goldsmith, Oliver 153 & n; *She Stoops to Conquer* 466n
GOODHART, Rev. Charles Joseph 235n*
GORDON, Sir Alexander Cornewall Duff 456n
Gordon, Lieut. Andrew 107 & n
Gordon, Andrew Rutherford 657–8, 660–1, 665, 698n
Gordon, Janet Duff (*later* Mrs Henry Ross) 328n, 507n, 508 & n*
GORDON, John Thomson 106, 651, 712n
Gordon, Mrs John Thomson (Mary Wilson) 107 & n
GORDON, Lady Duff (Lucie Austin) 219, 456n, 510; *Stella and Vanessa* 508n
Gordon, Sir John Watson 670n
Gore, Captain Augustus Wentworth 654 & n
GORE, Mrs Catherine Grace Frances (*née* Moody) 573–4, 654n; *The Two Aristocracies* 343n; *Two in the Morning* 366n
Gorham, Rev. G. C. 272n
Gotschalk, Emmely *see* Hansen, Mrs Emmely
Goy, André de and Mlle de Saint-Romain: translate CD's *Contes de Noel* 23n
Grand Junction Canal 652n
Grange, Eugène and Zavier de Montepin: *Les frères corses* 5n
GRANVILLE, Granville George Leveson-Gower, 2nd Earl 134, 324n, 473n, 502
Grasett, Elliot 511n, 518
GRATTAN, Thomas Colley 127 & n*, 550n
Graves, Caroline 53n, 105n, 467n, 651n
Graves, Elizabeth Harriet (*later* Bartley) 105n
Gravesend 269, 529n; Wates's hotel 516
Gravesend and Milton Library and Reading Room 529n
Gray, Rt Rev. Robert, Bishop of Cape Town 552 & n
Great Eastern (ship; formerly *Leviathan*) 345n
Great St Bernard Convent 201n
Great St Bernard Pass 33
Green family 110
Green, Charles 162 & n
GREGSON, Rev. John 302n*
Greta Bridge, Yorkshire 444
Grieve, Thomas 209 & n, 221
Grinot, Eugène *see* Vermond, Paul
Grisi, Giulia 567n
GROSVENOR, Lord Robert (Baron Ebury) 121n, 601n
Grote and Prescott's, Messrs 729
Groucock, Copestake, Moore & Co., lace manufacturers 52n
GUILD OF LITERATURE AND ART: legal constraints on 187 & n, 269, 299, 512, 513n, 562.; Amateurs acting tour for 625n, 630n
Guizot, François 1n, 702 & n; "The Civil Wars and Oliver Cromwell" 1n
Gully, Dr James Manby 64n

GURNEY, Rev. Arthur Thompson 319n*
Guy, Joseph, the younger 205 & n*
GYE, Frederick, the younger 75 & n, 109 & n, 156

HACHETTE, Alfred 133n*
HACHETTE, Louis Christophe François 22
HACHETTE & CIE, Messrs: CD visits 4; publish Mrs Gaskell 4n; agree terms with CD for French translation of works 8n, 22–3, 31, 36, 39–40, 58, 62n, 262, 269, 308n, 508n; CD dines with translators at 91, 96
Haldimand, William 265
Haliburton, Thomas Chandler (Mr Justice) 324n
Halifax: CD reads at 661, 664
Halifax Guardian 664n
Hall, Matthew & Co., bootmakers 602 & n
Hall, Richard, bootmaker 69 & n
Hall, Samuel Carter 162
Hallé, (Sir) Charles 396n
Halliday, A. and F. Lawrence: *Kenilworth* 722n
Hamburg: Frank D at school in 660, 662
Hamilton, Edward: *Memoir of Frederic Hervey Foster Quin* 129n
Hamilton, Captain William 115n
Hamley, Sir Edward Bruce 309n, 674n
Hampshire Advertiser 697n
Hampshire Telegraph 697n
HANCOCK, Harriet 144 & n
Hand-Book of Penitentiaries and Homes for Females 551n
HANKEY, Thomson 491
HANSEN, Mrs Emmely (*née* Gotschalk) 103n
Hansom, Joseph Aloysius 370n
Harding, Sir Joseph Horney 521n
HARDY, Albert 725n
HARDY, Thomas Duffus 501n*
Hargreaves, Reginald 665n
Harlequin and the Loves of Cupid and Psyche (Webster's pantomime) 482n
Harley, John Pritt 610n
HARNESS, Mary 594 & n
Harness, Captain Richard 545n
HARNESS, Rev. William 527, 545n, 594n
Harper Brothers, US publishers 298n
Harrington, H.: *A Night at Nottingham* (with E. Yates) 278n
Harris, Augustus: *My Son, Diana* (farce) 465n
Harrison, William 690n
Harrogate 658
Harrogate Herald 658n
Hart, J., sculptor 90n
Harvey, William 129 & n
Hastie, manager of Pavilion, Folkestone 143n, 147–8
HASTINGS, David 247
Hastings, Dr J. 182
Havelock, Major-General Sir Henry 503 & n*, 504
Hawthornden 672 & n, 674, 716
Haydn, Joseph Timothy 139 & n, 707n
Haydn, Mrs Joseph Timothy (Mary) 139 & n, 302 & n
Haydn, Thomas 302n
Hayward, Abraham 174n
HEADLAND, Thomas Hughes 606n*
Healey, Edna: *Lady Unknown* 213n, 331n
Helps, Arthur 506n
Henfield, Sussex 646n
Hennell, C. T. 587n
Herbert, George 20n
Herbert, Sydney 702 & n
Herries, Lieut.-General Sir W. L. 518n
Hervé, Florimond Ronger 30n
Hesket New-Market, Cumberland 440n
Hesse, Auguste 25n
Heywood, Sir Benjamin, Bart & Co. 73n
Hibbert, Christopher: *The Great Mutiny* 459n, 460n, 469n, 489n
Higgin, John 444n
Higgin, Captain Robert 444n
Hill & Sons, bankers and agents 241 & n
Hill, Alan: *Wordsworth's 'Grand Design'* 313n
HILL, David Octavius 670n*
Hill, Rowland: "Notes of Charles Dickens' Christmas Carol" 677n
HILLS, John 604n
Hills, Thomas Hyde 665 & n
Hindle, John 53n
HINDLE, Rev. Joseph 20, 50, 53n*, 57, 74, 283
Hinds, Rt Rev. Samuel, Bishop of Norwich 518n
Hoare, J. G. 294n
Hobhouse, John Cam *see* Broughton de Gyfford, Baron
HODDER, George 688; "A Lament of the Heart" 306n
Hodges, E. 155n
Hodges, J. S. W. 272n
Hogarth family: at Tavistock House 7n, 99–100
Hogarth, Edward 491n, 512n, 560n
HOGARTH, George 131n; and *Frozen Deep* 207, 247, 248n; denies scandal-mongering at CD–Catherine separation 568n, 742; CD's view of 623; musical interests in Halifax 664 & n; and CD's marriage breakdown 746
Hogarth, Mrs George (Georgina Thomson): illness 20; and CD's marriage difficulties 472n, 560, 565, 632n, 746–7; CD demands retrac-

Hogarth, Mrs George (*cont.*): tion of slander 566n, 568n, 569n, 572n, 579; ~ signed statement 576n, 742; CD forbids children to see 602; and 'violated letter' 648n

HOGARTH, Georgina: in Paris 15, 95; makes arrangements for Collins's visit to Paris 28n, 47–8; performs in play 82; walks with CD 132n, 202n; Forgues on 162n; leaves Boulogne 180; at Great St Bernard Convent 201n; performs in *Frozen Deep* 254n, 369n, 412n, 418n; and appointment of Gad's Hill gardener 292; and Andersen 372n; on Walter's departure for India 381n; and CD's travels in North 441–3, 447; CD praises 472; and CD's marriage breakdown 559–60, 574, 747–8; role and duties in D household 559n, 560n, 598, 698, 747–8; rumours of relations with CD 565n, 573n, 577n, 579 & n, 597n, 608n, 742n, 745, 754; named as Trustee and Executor for CD's will 581n, 750; animosity to Evans family 608n; at CD's Chatham reading 712n; in CD's 'violated letter' 740; benefits under CD's will 750–1 & n

HOGARTH, Helen Isabella (Catherine's sister) 7n*; and concert 354.; plays in *Frozen Deep* 366n, 412n; supposed slanders of CD 566n, 569n, 572n; gives signed statement of disavowal 576n; CD forbids children to see 602; CD dislikes 623n; Catherine relates rumours about CD and Ellen to 632n; and CD's 'violated letter' 648n

HOGARTH, Joseph 325

Hogarth, Mary Scott (Catherine's cousin) 560n

Hogarth, Mary Scott (Catherine's sister): death 560 & n

HOGGE, Mrs George (Mary, or Polly Harness) 545n*, 569

HOLDSWORTH (Holsworth), George 541

Holland, Elizabeth, Lady 151n

Holland, Henry Edward Fox, 4th Baron 151n

HOLLINGSHEAD, John 389n*; contributes to *HW* 460n, 549n, 577n; on CD's public readings 558n, 576n, 677n; *The Birthplace of Podgers* 492–3, 495 & n; "Mr Charles Dickens as a Reader" 652n, 664n; *My Lifetime* 492n, 652n; "An Official Scarecrow" 406n; "On the Canal" 652n; "Poor Tom—a City Weed" 454n

Hollingshead's Miscellanies 652n

Hollyer, John 279

Holman Hunt, William *see* Hunt, William Holman

Holman-Hunt, Diana: *My Grandfather, his Wives and Loves* 543n, 544n, 548n, 554n

Holmes, Peter 266n

HOLROYD, Abraham 683n*

Home for Homeless Women, Urania Cottage, Shepherd's Bush: medical attendant 36; applicants for admission 44, 521; inmates emigrate from 118n, 119–20; scabies at 146; CD attends Committee 237, 343, 521; drainage problems 272, 276; gas supply 276; building improvements 372, 390, 396; policeman scandal at 544–5; included in *Hand-Book of Penitentiaries and Homes for Females* 551n

Homer, Bryan: *CD and Leamington Spa* 693n

Honduras 470n

Hong Kong Daily Press 599n

HOOD, (Sir) William Charles 318n*, 417

HOOLE, William Spencer 344n*

Horne, Percy Hazlitt 247n

HORNE, Richard Henry ('Hengist') 334n, 689–90, 710; *Orion* 247 & n

HORNE, Mrs Richard Henry (Catherine Clare St George Foggo) 52 & n, 334n

HORNER, Ann Susan 479n

Horton, Priscilla *see* Reed, Mrs Thomas German

HOSKYNS, Chandos Wren 715 & n, 721n*; *Talpa* 721n

Hoskyns, Sir Hungerford 715n

House of Commons: CD declines to stand for 300, 303

Household Words: CD on contributions to 2–3, 16, 32, 38, 63, 81, 83, 88, 93, 98–100, 139, 158–9, 163, 174–5, 193–4, 253, 410, 437, 450, 454–6, 620, 630, 673, 681; and translated articles 4 & n; and factory legislation controversy 6n; Forster relinquishes share 56, 730; CD's contributions sent to Hachette 58; Tauchnitz reprints 81n, 237n; Collins joins staff 188–9, 214n; Audit days and dinners 214–15, 218, 324, 556, 695; accounts and accounting 220 & n, 694–5; Collins's salary increased 457; prints CD's 'Personal' statement on marriage separation 577n, 578, 579n; Reprinted Pieces from 594 & n; advertises CD's readings 681; Forster granted power of attorney for 695n, 702; resolution to dissolve partnership 700 & n, 711, 719, 758–61; Bradbury and Evans reject CD's offer to buy shares 723n; winding up 723n

Household Words Almanac 59n, 222n

Household Words Christmas Numbers: "The Holly Tree Inn" (1855) 2 & n, 36n; "The Wreck of the Golden Mary" (1856) 195 & n, 220–2, 231, 234, 244, 278, 452n, 500, 616n;. "The Perils of Certain English Prisoners" (1857) 437n, 458, 464, 468 & n, 473n, 481–4, 487, 507–8; "A House to Let" (1858) 631, 649–50, 673n, 701 & n, 705–6, 709; "Tom Tiddler's Ground" (1861) 650n

HOWES, Rev. Charles 74n*

Howitt, Anna Maria 295
HOWITT, William 261n; "The Land Shark" 3 & n; *The Northern Heights of London* 295n; *Tallengetta, the Squatter's Home* 3n
Howitt, Mrs William (Mary Botham) 373n, 383
Huddersfield 650
HUDSON, Frederick 393 & n
HUDSON, G. F. 204n*, 313n
Hudson, Mrs Robert 204n
Hudson's Bay Company 122n
Hughes, William L. 23n
Hughes, William R.: at Gad's Hill 411n; *A Week's Tramp in Dickens-Land* 121n, 411n, 465n, 494n, 556n, 696 & n
Hugo, Rev. Thomas 352n
Hugo, Victor: *Les Orientales* (translated as *Phantoms*) 388n
Huish, Captain Mark 609n
HULKES, James 494n*
Hull: CD reads at 660–1, 681n, 687–9, 691
Hull News 660n
Hunt, Emily 543n
HUNT, Leigh 529n, 582
Hunt, Thornton Leigh 529n
HUNT, William Holman: protests at Brough's "Calmuck" 543 & n*, 544n, 548, 554; *Pre-Raphaelitism and the Pre-Raphaelite Brotherhood* 31n
Hunt, Mrs William Holman (Edith) 543n, 544n, 554n
Huntly, Mary, Marchioness of (Maria Pegus) 459n
Huzar, Eugène: *La Fin du Monde par la Science* 88n
Hyam, Sarah 544–5

Illingworth, Rev. Edward Arthur 125
Illuminated Magazine 355n
Illustrated London News 218n, 580n
Inchbald, Elizabeth: *Animal Magnetism* 207 & n, 240, 254n
Incledon, Charles 136 & n*
India Bill (1853) 504n
Indian Mutiny (1857–8) 431n, 459, 469n, 472, 503n, 516n; Russell reports on 599n, 600
Ingram, Herbert 5n, 69 & n, 492, 580n, 651, 661–2, 761
Ingres, Jean Auguste Dominique 25n
Institutional Association of Lancashire and Cheshire 713n
Ireland: CD's reading tour in 597n, 601, 622, 630, 632–49
IRVING, Washington 150n; "The Voyage" 68n, 108n
Italian Opera: performs in Dublin 639n
Italy 196 & n, 256 & n; *see also* Florence; Genoa

Jack's Return from Canton (ballet) 690n
JACKSON, Thomas 119
Jaffray, E. S. & Co., New York 151n
James, Edwin John 706, 707 & n*, 708, 709n
James, Louis: *Fiction for the Working Man* 650n
JAMESON, Mrs Anna Brownell (*née* Murphy) 117 & n*
Jarman, John 433n
Jarman, Mrs John (Martha Maria Mottershed) 433n
JEAFFRESON, John Cordy 725n*
JERDAN, William: friendship with Andersen 383n, 426; "The Gift of Tongues" 382n; "Old Hawtrey" 417; "Old Scraps of Science" 382n
Jerichau-Baumann, Elizabeth 578n
Jerrold, Blanchard *see* Jerrold, William Blanchard
JERROLD, Douglas William: CD requests to chair Royal General Theatrical Fund 45 & n; radicalism 45n; and deaths of A'Beckett and son 179n, 184; visits CD in Boulogne 202n; and W. H. Russell's lectures 329n; illness and death 344–8, 583, 600; memorial fund and concerts for 348n, 349–60, 364 & n, 365, 369n, 374–9, 387–8, 392, 394, 400, 401n, 408n, 418, 448; funeral 352; accused of improvidence 365n; and 'Green Bush Melodramas' 379n; CD announces result of fund 423–4, 463; estate 423 & n, 463; Christ Church (Oxford) Scholarship 424n; attacks Lord William Pitt Lennox 646n; CD's appreciation and reminiscences of 710, 762–4; memorial programme 736–7; opposes capital punishment 763n; *Black-Eyed Susan* 369n, 373, 379n, 387n; *The Housekeeper* 369n; *The Prisoner of War* 350n, 369n; *The Rent Day* 369n, 379n; *The Spendthrift* 435, 437
JERROLD, Mrs Douglas William (Mary Anne Swann) 423n, 424 & n, 449n, 463, 483
Jerrold, Mary Ann (Douglas's daughter) 414 & n, 483
Jerrold, Thomas Serle 400 & n*
Jerrold, Walter: *Douglas Jerrold: Dramatist and Wit* 435n, 463n, 762
JERROLD, William Blanchard: with dying father 346n; letter objecting to fund-raising for father 423n, 449 & n, 460, 463, 466; CD's reconciliation with 583, 600; CD sends appreciation of father to 710; ~ text 762–4; *The Best of All Good Company: a Day with CD* 762n; *Life and Remains of Douglas Jerrold* 600n, 710n
Jerusalem, Bishop of *see* Gobat, Rev. Samuel
Jessel, (Sir) George 568n
Jewsbury, Geraldine Endsor 133 & n, 194n

Johnson, of *HW* staff 65
Johnson, C. B.: (ed.) *W. B. Donne and his Friends* 406n
Johnson, Edgar: *CD: His Tragedy and Triumph* 749n
Johnson, Samuel: and Lowe sisters appeal 729; *The Vanity of Human Wishes* 39n
Johnstone, James 286n
Johnstone, J. W. 229n
JOLLY, Emily: CD declines story from 335–6; "The Brook" 312; *Mr Arle* 245n, 312; "A Wife's Story" 245n
Jones, inmate of Home 120
Jonson, Ben: *Every Man in his Humour* 1n, 397n
Jordan, Dorothea: *The Spoiled Child* 433n
Joyce, Felix 580
Julian, John: *Dictionary of Hymnology* 500n
Jullien, Louis 3n

Kaplan, Fred 432n
Kavanagh, Julia 133 & n*
Kay-Shuttleworth, Sir James Phillips 160 & n, 234 & n
KEAN, Charles John: presents *The Corsican Brothers* 5 & n; at Windsor 275 & n; Lacy acts with 405n; and Ternans 433n, 434, 447n; in Marston's *Anne Blake* 531n; and proposed 'Dramatic College' 593n, 609n, 610n; at Eton 649; farewell season 690
Kean, Mrs Charles 531n
Keeley, Robert 71n, 350n, 351, 369n
Keeley, Mrs Robert (Mary Anne Goward) 71n, 350n, 351, 369n, 379n
Kelly, Sir Fitzroy 79n, 708n
Kelly, Frances Maria (Fanny) 688n
Kelm, Joseph 30 & n
Kemble, Adelaide *see* Sartoris, Mrs Edward John
Kemble, Charles 722n
Ken, Rt Rev. Thomas, Bishop of Bath and Wells: "Glory to Thee, my God, this night" (hymn) 452n
Kennedy, W. P. 591n
Kenney, A. P. 54 & n
Kenney, James 452n
Kent, William Charles 245n
KENT, William Charles Mark (known as Charles) 378–9; "Béranger" 379n
Kent-Peron, English resident of Boulogne 135n
Kenyon, John 250 & n
King's College, London 344n, 372
Kingsley, Charles 117n
Kingstown (Dun Laoghaire), Ireland 634n, 637
Kinnaird, Arthur FitzGerald Kinnaird, 10th Baron 673 & n
Kirk, Joseph 726n
Kitton, F. G.: *CD by Pen and Pencil* 173n, 176n, 214n, 380n, 414n, 428n, 517n, 519n; "Dickens Ana" 389n; *John Leech, Artist and Humorist* 52n; *Minor Writings of CD* 244n
Klosky, Jules: *Mutual Friends* 495, 517n, 518n, 720n
Knebworth, Hertfordshire 207n
KNIGHT, Charles 68n, 131n, 352n, 521, 527, 583
Knight, John Prescott 93n*
Knowles, James Sheridan ('Paddy') 707 & n
Knox, Robert 301
Kolle, Henry 627n
Kolle, Mrs Henry (Anne Beadnell) 627 & n
Kortright, Frances Aikin ('Berkeley Aikin'): *Ann Sherwood* 360n
Kossuth, Lajos 152n
KRUSEMAN, Arie Cornelis 481n*
Kuenzel, Dr J. H. 132n
Kurtz, Harolde: *The Empress Eugénie* 57n

LACROIX, Octave 603n*
Lacy, Thomas Hailes 519n
LACY, Walter (Walter Williams) 405n*
Ladies' Guild, Russell Square, London 52n, 334n
Lamartine, Alphonse Marie Prat de 63; *Oeuvres* 526; *Oeuvres Complètes* 527n
Lambert, Daniel 150 & n
Lampton, near Hounslow, Middlesex 587n
Lancashire and Cheshire Institutional Association *see* Institutional Association of Lancashire and Cheshire
Lancaster 443
Landor, Catherine (Kitty; Walter's niece) 644n
LANDOR, Walter Savage: CD visits in Bath 274n; and Phinn 286n; helps Marguerite Power 497n; and Orsini 525n; CD and Fitzgerald discuss 636n; sued for libel by Mrs Yescombe 643 & n, 644n; leaves England 644n; *Dry Sticks, Fagoted* 643n
LANDSEER, Sir Edwin 18 & n, 24
LANE, Edward Wickstead 294n; *Hydropathy* 461n
Lang, John: "Wanderings in India" 473n
LANGFORD, John Alfred 481n*
LANGFORD, Joseph Munt 363n; *Like and Unlike* (with W. J. Sorrell) 112n
Langton, Robert: *Childhood and Youth of CD* 452n
LANSDOWNE, Henry Petty-Fitzmaurice, 3rd Marquis of 242, 588
La Touche, Willy 127 & n
Law, John 94 & n*
Lawrence, George Frederick 47n

Lawrence, Mrs George Frederick (Emily Elizabeth Barrow) 47 & n
Lay, William 419n
Layard, (Sir) Austen Henry 459 & n
Lazarus, Mary: *A Tale of Two Brothers* 559n
Leader (magazine) 20 & n, 27, 248n, 254n, 259n, 374n, 389n, 392n, 433n, 644n
Leamington: CD reads at 693–4
Leamington Advertiser 693n
LEE, Richard Nelson 571n*, 579
Leech, Ada Rose 52n
LEECH, John: family 52n; illustrates Brooks's *Aspen Court* 425n; and CD's marriage breakdown 574; in Scarborough 658, 661; and CD's account of Jerrold's decline 764; *Pictures of Life and Character*, 2nd series 250 & n
Leech, Mrs John (Ann Eaton) 52n
Leech, John Charles Waddington 52n
Leeds 444; CD reads in 659–61, 691; Queen Victoria visits 660n, 669n
Leeds Express 691n
Leeds Mercury 661n
Leeds Times 661n
LEGOUVÉ, Gabriel Jean Baptiste Ernest Wilfrid 61n*; *Médée* 61 & n, 85n, 89n, 156n, 171n; *Un Souvenir du Manin* 655n
Legrand, Jean 30 & n
Lehmann, Augustus Frederick 224n, 664 & n*
Lehmann, Mrs Augustus Frederick (Jane Chambers; 'Nina') 214n, 664n
Lehmann, Beatrix, Rosamond, and John 664n
Lehmann, Leo 664n
Lehmann, Rudolf Chambers 450n, 664n; (ed.) *CD as Editor* 6n, 49n, 56n, 66n, 189n, 616n, 647n
Leicester: CD reads at 692
Leicester Chronicle 692n
Lemaître, Frederic 380n
Lemon, Alice (Lally) 85–7
Lemon, Betty 85–7
Lemon, Harry 603n
Lemon, Kate 12n
LEMON, Mark: invited to Boulogne 12, 135, 140; visits theatre with CD 46, 70; and Mrs Horne 52 & n; supports Royal Literary Fund reforms 60n, 293n; dines with CD 67, 256; canvasses for Ingram 69n; Fraser escorts daughters 85; at *HW* party 108; at St Paul's 126; illness 140n, 142, 162; edits *Field* 155n; burlesque of *Medea* 171n; and Tavistock House theatre 201; in *Frozen Deep* 203, 213, 220, 238, 254n, 366n, 368n, 369n, 380n, 421n, 433, 488; plays in *Turning the Tables* 207n; rheumatism of jaw 220; plays in *Uncle John* 256n; Stanfield invites to dine 305; and Jerrold's death and funeral 345–7, 352n; Andersen meets 373n; Hollingshead meets at *HW* office 389n; serves on Jerrold fund committee 424n; and editorship of *London Journal* 491, 492n, 651, 662; and plagiarised CD story in *London Journal* 528; represents Catherine on separation 566n, 573n, 578n, 602n, 701n, 739, 741, 747; estrangement and reconciliation with CD 603n, 608n, 741n; *Jack and the Beanstalk* (pantomime) 11 & n, 28; *The Ladies' Club* 447n; *Mr Nightingale's Diary* (with CD) 155n
Lemon, Mrs Mark (Nelly Romer) 12n, 13
LENNOX, Lord William Pitt 646n*; *My Recollections from 1806 to 1873* 647n
Le Sage, Alain René: *Gil Blas de Santillane* 153
Leslie, Charles 153n
Leslie, Charles Robert 151, 566
Lewes, Mrs C. L.: *Dr Southwood Smith: A Retrospect* 90n
Lewes, George Henry 27n, 506n, 580n
Liebig, Justus, Baron von 580n
Lillie, Benjamin 465 & n
Limerick: CD reads at 601, 638, 643–7, 649
Limerick Chronicle 647n
Limerick Reporter 643n
Linton, Mrs W. J. *see* Lynn, Eliza
Literary Gazette 348n, 644n
Liverpool 431n; CD reads at 597n, 626–30, 632, 646n
Liverpool Daily Post 626n, 628n, 629n
Liverpool Mail 646n
Liverpool Mercury 746n
Livingstone, Dr David 273 & n, 330n
Lloyd, David 342n
Lloyd, Mrs David (Margaret Beadnell) 342 & n, 704n
Lloyd, Edward 424n
Lloyd's Weekly London Newspaper 423–4 & n
Loch, John 198 & n, 279 & n, 282n
Lockhart, John Gibson 131 & n, 549n
LOCKWOOD, Mrs Charles Day 485n*
LOCOCK, Sir Charles 517
LOGAN, William 675n*
Lohrli, Anne: *Household Words* 214n, 270n, 723n
London
Buildings, districts, streets, etc., including places now regarded as in Greater London (banks, businesses, societies and institutions are indexed under their own names): Argyll Rooms 96; Borough 321; Burlington Arcade 619; Chalk Farm 633; Columbian Square (*formerly* Nova Scotia Gardens), Bethnal Green 273 & n; Cremorne Gardens 130 & n; Crosby Hall 556n; Crystal Palace 30n, 716n,

London (*cont.*):
718; Egyptian Hall, Piccadilly 118, 713n; Elizabeth Fry Refuge, Hackney 129; Freemasons' Hall 517n; Gallery of Illustration 333n, 356–8, 361n, 366n, 369n, 370n, 376, 388, 396n, 400, 403, 408n; Gore House, Kensington 468n, 486n, 497; Holland House 151 & n; Marshalsea Prison 321, 344n; Newgate 391; Regent's Park Diorama 249n; Royal Bazaar, Oxford Street 249n; St Martin's Hall 182n, 345n, 349n, 352–4, 374, 375n, 376–7, 388n, 399, 533, 539, 542n, 546n, 551, 555, 566n, 584, 595, 677n, 720n; St Paul's Cathedral 125, 128; Stafford House 313; Stationers' Hall 495n; Tavistock House (Theatre) 143 & n, 201–2, 206, 225, 226 & n, 230 & n, 234, 235, 237n, 265, 267; Temple Gardens 305n; Willis's Rooms 329n

Churches: St George's, Southwark 344; Tottenham Court Road (Methodist) Chapel (Whitfield Tabernacle) 208 & n; Union Chapel, Islington 500n

Clubs: Athenaeum 236, 309n, 511n, 512n, 518, 575n; Garrick 156, 275, 287, 296, 329n, 351, 404, 536n, 547n, 588n, 591n, 595n, 596n, 600, 601n, 603, 611n, 708 & n, 709n, 711n; Parthenon 236; Reform 623

Hospitals: Bethlehem 417n; Foundling Hospital, Guilford Street 193 & n; Hospital for Sick Children, Great Ormond Street 495, 517n, 518n, 520, 531 & n, 533, 542n, 548n, 556, 586n, 720n; Orthopaedic 553n; Royal Hospital for Incurables 106 & n; St George's 106n, 169n, 197n, 198, 251n, 260 & n

Hotels, Taverns, Restaurants, etc.: Albion Tavern 194, 601; Blue Posts Tavern 18 & n; Burton Arms 285n; Cock Tavern, Fleet Street 256; Freemasons' Tavern 324n, 330n, 544n; London Tavern 132; Trafalgar Hotel, Greenwich 402n; Wellington Hotel, Strand 499

Schools: Bayswater Schools, Paddington 80n; Christ Church, Chelsea 732; Christchurch, St Pancras 731; Dulwich College 71n, 74, 134 & n, 136; Orphan Working School, Hampstead 569n; St John's, Horseferry Road 731; St Peter's, Stepney 732; St Stephen's, Westminster 271n, 731

Theatres: Adelphi 11n, 32, 71 & n, 74n, 77n, 109, 112n, 115, 136n, 277, 379n, 387n, 518 & n, 565n, 571n; Astley's Amphitheatre 208n; Britannia 482n; Covent Garden 68 & n, 69, 75, 567, 598n; Drury Lane 140n, 143n, 452n, 598, 690; English Opera House 690; Gaiety 389n; Haymarket 369n, 446n, 465n, 495n, 518n, 690n; Her Majesty's 598n; Lyceum 73n, 280n, 396n, 466n, 490n, 492n, 495n, 516, 519, 565n; Marylebone 490n; Olympic 70, 368, 395, 406n, 418n, 523n; Princess's 547n, 593n, 608n, 690n; Queen's (*later* Prince of Wales) 722n; St James's 598n; Strand 232n, 722; Surrey 351n, 571n; Victoria 482n

London, Chatham and Dover Railway 180, 181n

London Journal: Lemon edits 492n, 528, 651; plagiarises CD story 528n; circulation 650n, 651 & n; Ingram on unpopularity of 662

London Stereoscopic Co. 523n

Longfellow, Henry Wadsworth: *Letters* (ed. Andrew Hilen) 572n; 'The Rainy Day' 694n

Longley, Katharine 568n, 572n, 577n, 579n, 648n, 680n, 745; "Letters to the Editor" 47n; "The Real Ellen Ternan" 433n, 605n

Longman's, publishers 269 & n

LORAIN, Paul 96n, 262 & n*, 308

Louis Philippe, King of France 58

LOVEDAY, James Thomas 258n

Lover, Samuel 596n

Lowe, Ann Elizabeth and Frances Melina Lucia 729

Lowe, Mauritius 729 & n

LOWNE, (?George Gill) 112n*

Luard, Lieut.-Colonel John 413n

Luard, John Dalbiac 413 & n*, 414, 575; *The Welcome Arrival* (painting) 413n

Lucan, Field Marshal George Charles Bingham, 3rd Earl of 174n

Lucas, Samuel 369n

Lucknow, India 431n, 459n, 469n, 503n, 516n, 600n

Lucullus, Lucius Licinius 91 & n

Lugg, Mary 544

Lumgair, John 629n

Lunacy Commission: Forster appointed Secretary of 1n, 165n, 577n

LYNDHURST, John Singleton Copley, Baron 243 & n

Lynn, Eliza (Mrs Lynn Linton) 16n, 266n; "Epidemics" 99 & n; "Perfumes" 338n; "Witches of England" 400n

Lynn, Rev. James 266n

LYTTELTON, George William, 4th Baron 134n*

Lyttelton, Hon. Spencer 489, 515n

LYTTON, Sir Edward Lytton Bulwer- (*later* 1st Baron): French translation of 262n; employs Charles French 283n; letter from Andersen 383n; helps Marguerite Power 497n; CD declines dinner invitation from 583; elected Rector at Glasgow University 707n; sends donation to Sarah Richardson's school 725n; *The Lady of Lyons* 75n; *Money* 446, 447n; *Not So Bad as we Seem* 3n, 36n, 209n, 305n; *Richelieu* 601n

Lytton, Edward Robert (*later* 1st Earl of Lytton; 'Owen Meredith') 35n*
Lyveden, Robert Vernon Smith, Baron 502n

Macartney, Mrs 216, 223
Macaulay, Thomas Babington, 1st Baron 72n, 133, 143, 504n
McClintock, Captain 330n
McGlashan & Gill, Dublin publishers 696
MacIlraith, John: *Life of Richardson* 66n
Macintosh, Mrs: "An Elfin Charm" (poem) 502n
McIntyre, Mrs, of St John's Schools 731
MACKAY, Charles 364
MCKEEVER, James 439n
Mackenzie, Shelton 132n
Maclagan, Michael: *'Clemency' Canning* 473n
Maclaren, Duncan 724n
M'Lennan, Miss 255
MACLISE, Daniel: 'Nickleby' portrait of CD 104n, 326; on Eliza Colburn (Forster) 114; dines with CD 115; photograph of 200n; unable to attend *Frozen Deep* 251, 253, 367n; and Jerrold memorial fund 355, 424n; meets Queen at *Frozen Deep* performance 359, 362, 367–8; invited to Gad's Hill 368 & n; reclusiveness 368n; at Wigan's farewell benefit 369n; at Thackeray dinner-party 551n; on CD's reading of *The Chimes* 556n; Walford writes on 614n; in Belgium with CD and Jerrold 762; *Peter the Great, Czar of Muscovy* (painting) 223n
MCMECHAN, Thomas 439n
McNeill, Sir John 174n
MACPHAIL, H. Buchanan 679n, 754–5
MACREADY, Catherine Frances Birch 75 & n, 399, 502n, 503; "The Angel of Love" (poem) 170n, 175; "The Shadow of the Hand" (poem) 156n, 170n
Macready, Cecilia Benvenuta 75 & n
Macready, Edward Nevil Bourne 75 & n*, 373, 376, 502n
Macready, Henry Frederick Bulwer 75 & n, 301–2; death 420
Macready, Jonathan Forster Christian 75 & n
Macready, Letitia Margaret 75n, 685n
Macready, Lydia Jane 75 & n
MACREADY, William Charles: asthma 45; visit to CD in Paris 74, 77, 83–4, 86; pays school fees for Mary Warner's son 84 & n; and Lally Lemon 86; Poole complains of CD to 87; attends *Médée* 89; in Sherborne 89; expenses in Paris 94 & n; visits CD in London 115; friendship with Anna Brownell Jameson 117n; CD gives wine to 157, 167; Catherine Dickens visits 220; invited to *Frozen Deep* 220; and Miss Coutts 224; praises *Frozen Deep* 254 & n; and Mrs Williams 267; photograph of 270; produces and plays in Marston's *Patrician's Daughter* 281n, 519; and Richard Warner 290; invited to Gad's Hill 302, 374, 376; William Wilson's sonnets to 316n; provides for son Ned in India 373, 376; and Mrs German Reed's singing 408n; and death of son Henry 420; in Lytton's *Money* 446n; CD sends 1857 *HW* Christmas number to 484; helps Marguerite Power 497n; founds Sherborne evening school 531n; makes donation to Hospital for Sick Children 531; relations with Catherine Dickens 560n, 570n; and CD's marriage breakdown 570; at Rugby 649; CD invites to London 685–6; and Marie Wilton 722n; *Reminiscences* (ed. Sir F. Pollock) 254n
Macready, William Charles, junior ('Willie') 75 & n, 238
Macrory, Adam John 607n
Macrory, Edmund 607 & n
MCTEAR, Robert 707n
Madden, Sir Frederic 501n
Madden, Richard Robert 645n
MADDEN, Mrs Richard Robert (Harriet Elmslie) 645n
MADGE, Dr Henry 315n*
Maffei, A., Count 164n
Maidstone, Rochester, Chatham and Canterbury Herald 496n
Malleson, J. N. 53n
Mallet, Marie: *Life with Queen Victoria* 207n
Malton Abbey, Yorkshire 658
Manchester: *Frozen Deep* performance in 358–9, 377, 393–5, 397–9, 401, 404–9, 411–12, 414, 418, 421, 434n, 488; CD reads in 377, 382n, 390, 393–4, 399, 401, 660, 666, 668, 681; CD's book sales in 692; CD presides at Institutional Association of Lancashire and Cheshire meeting in 713–14; New Free Trade Hall 394–5, 397, 399n, 401; Theatre Royal 396n
Manchester Art Treasures Exhibition (1857) 212n, 215, 358n, 377, 393, 398–9, 503n; orchestra 396 & n
Manchester Daily Examiner 668n
Manchester Examiner and Times 395n, 396n, 401n, 414n
Manchester Guardian 393n, 401n, 414n, 421n, 666n, 681n, 717n
Manin, Daniele 655n
Manning, Frederick George 216
Manning, Mrs Frederick George 216
MANSON, James Bolivar 670n*, 671 & n
Marchmont, Mrs, matron of Home 119, 128, 147, 216, 545
Mario (singer; i.e. Giovanni Matteo di Candia) 567n

Marjoribanks, Edward 260 & n
Marshall, William & Co., Edinburgh 538 & n
MARSTON, John Westland: *Anne Blake* 531n, 537; *A Hard Struggle* 511n, 514–16, 519n, 520, 522; *A Life's Ransom* 280n; *The Patrician's Daughter* 281, 519
Martell, E. 24–5
Martin, John: *Sadak in search of the Waters of Oblivion* (painting) 392n
Martineau, Harriet: in factory accident dispute 6 & n, 9; on not interfering with trade 22; on CD's treatment of wife 471n; on clairvoyants' employment by press 674; CD criticises 675n; *Complete Guide to the English Lake District* 209n; *The Factory Controversy* 6 & n; *Letters to Fanny Wedgwood* (ed. Elizabeth Sanders Arbuckle) 10n, 471n
Martineau, Sir Thomas 401
Maryport, Cumberland 438, 441, 443
Mason, W. H., Chichester publishers 585n
MASSETT, Stephen 526n
Master Boot and Shoe Makers' Benevolent Institution 516
Masterman, Peters & Co. 73n
Mathews, Charles 626n, 657n
Mathews, Charles James (son of above) 571n, 657, 690n; *He Would be an Actor* 690n
Mathews, Mrs Charles James *see* Vestris, Madame Elizabeth Lucia
Mathilde (Janet Duff Gordon's friend) 328n, 507n, 508
Matthews, Alice 372
Matthews, Mrs William (Antonina) 123, 127, 456n, 458, 689 & n, 718
Maule, Fox *see* Panmure, 2nd Baron
Maull & Polyblank, photographers 72n
MAYALL, John Edwin 199n
Mayhew, Horace 352n
Maynard, Frederick 119n
Mayne, Sir Richard 545
Meason, M. R. L.: "French and English Staff Officers" 21n; "Nob and Snob" 2 & n, 3n
Menière, Prosper 17n, 152n
Mensing, C. M. 481n
Meredith, George 111n, 508n; "Monmouth" (poem) 194n; *The Shaving of Shagpat* 117n
Meredith, Mrs George 111n
Meredith, Mrs (Louisa Anne Twamley): "Little Bell" 685–6; "Shadow of the Golden Image" 270 & n*
'Meredith, Owen' *see* Lytton, Edward Robert
Merwe, Pieter van der and Roger Took: *Clarkson Stanfield* 68n
Metropolitan Reporting Agency 586n
Meyerbeer, Giacomo: *Les Huguenots* 567n
Meynell, Wilfrid 589, 613
Mill, John Stuart 601n
Millais, J. G.: *Life and Letters of Sir John Everett Millais* 413n
Millais, (Sir) John Everett 31n, 413n, 543n
Miller, Hugh 311n, 315n*; *Testimony of the Rocks* 315n
MILLER, Mrs Hugh (Lydia Falconer Fraser; 'Harriet Myrtle') 315n*
MILMAN, Very Rev. Henry Hart, Dean of St Paul's 125n
MILNER, Charles 306n*
MILNES, Richard Monckton (*later* 1st Baron Houghton): and Palfrey 126–7, 132; opposes reform of Royal Literary Fund 293n; ~ speech at 299n; and Guild 299; at Jerrold's funeral 352n; helps Marguerite Power 497n; "London Churches" 683n
Milton, John: *Nativity Ode* 270n; *Paradise Lost* 76, 78
Milward, R. J.: *History of Wimbledon* 279n
Mirror of Parliament, The 131
Miscellany of Romance (journal) 650n
Mistler, Jean: *La Librairie Hachette* 22n, 23n
Mitchell, CD's servant 243n, 254n, 561
Mitchell, Miss, actress 625
Mitchell, John 563 & n
Mitre Insurance Office, Pall Mall 60 & n
MITTON, Thomas 274, 583, 587n
Mohl, Julius 4n
Mohl, Mme Julius (Mary Elizabeth Clarke) 4 & n
Molloy, Charles 131n
MOLYNEUX, Thomas John 182n*
Monro, Dr Henry 505 & n*
Monthly Magazine 131
Moore, F.: *That Blessed Baby* 71n
MOORE, George 52n*
Moore, Thomas: *Irish Melodies* 628n; *National Airs* 211n; "Those Evening Bells" 252n
Moran, Benjamin 529 & n*; *Journal* (ed. S. E. Wallace and F. E. Gillespie) 526n, 529n, 548n
Morgan, Augustus de *see* De Morgan, Augustus
Morgan, Charles, Esq. 268n
Morgan, Charles, surgeon 20
MORGAN, Captain Elisha Ely 453, 566
Morgan, John Minter 384n
Mori, Francis 353 & n
MORLEY, Henry: produces *HW* Almanacs 59n; work at *HW* 188; CD seeks information on South America from 468, 470; contributions to *HW* 549n, 614n; "Across Country" 289n; "Brother Muller and his Orphan-Work" 450n; "Burning and Burying" 410; "A Criminal Trial" 89n; "Drooping Buds" (with CD) 519n; "Far East" 59; "Flowers of British Legislation" 88n; *Gossip . . . Reprinted from 'Household Words'* 289n; "The Hero of a Hundred Days" (with Fox

Bourne) 662n; "Inch by Inch Upward" 339n; "Law and Order" 21n; "A Lesson Lost Upon Us" 503n; "Looking out of Windows" 59; "Lost in the Pit" 173n; "The Manchester Strike" 10n; "More Grist to the Mill" 9n; "Mr Speckles on Himself" 175; "Mummy" 289n; "Not Very Common Things" (with Wills) 146n; "One Cure More" 64; "Our Wicked Mis-Statements" 6n, 9; "Perfectly Contented" (with Brown) 175 & n; "A Plea for Playgrounds" (with Mrs de Morgan) 584n, 675n; "Poison" 22 & n; "The Royal Literary Fund" 60n; "Sarawak" 614n; "School Keeping" 160n; "Six Years in a Cell" (with von Corvin) 175 & n; "The Star of Bethlehem" 417 & n; "Time's Sponge" 88n, 89n

Morley, Malcolm 232n; "The Theatrical Ternans" 433n, 448n

Morning Advertiser see *Advertiser*

Morning Chronicle: CD works for 131; on Royal Literary Fund 302n; receives CD memorandum on Jerrold concert 353n; reports Wigan's Farewell Address 369n; reports performance of *Frozen Deep* for Queen 370n; praises Ristori 374n; on Thackeray's address 375n; publishes letter on result of Jerrold appeal 424n; on Hollingshead's *Birthplace of Podgers* 492n; on Marston's *Hard Struggle* 514n; on Collins's *Red Vial* 523n; on Orsini 525n; on Massett's reading 526n; praises Marston's *Anne Blake* 531n; reprints CD's 'violated letter' 648n; on CD's reading 720n

Morning Herald 286n, 301n, 424n; reprints CD's 'violated letter' 648n

Morning Post 353n

Morning Star 746n

Morris, Mowbray 191

Mortlake: almshouses 516n

Mortlock, Mrs, sender of begging letter 25

Morton, John Maddison: *Away with Melancholy* 690n; *Betsy Baker* 71n; *A Game of Romps* 447n; *Take Care of Dowb* 466n

Morton, Thomas: *A Cure for the Heart-ache* 466n; *Speed the Plough* 466n

Mostyn, Miss, actress 375n

Mother Shipton—Her Wager (pantomime) 278n

Mount-Temple, 1st Baron *see* Cowper, William

Moxon, Edward 543n

Müller, Professor O. C. 206

Muret, M. T.: *Michel Cervantes* 82 & n

Murray, Eustace Clare Grenville: "Messina" 63n; "On Her Majesty's Service" (with CD) 411n; "The Show Officer" 16n; "The Sulina Mouth of the Danube" 38n, 63n

MURRAY, John III 60n, 291n, 529n

Murray, Mrs John (Marion Smith) 291 & n

Musical Age (journal) 662n

MUSPRATT, Dr James Sheridan 431n*

'Myrtle, Harriet' *see* Miller, Mrs Hugh

Mysteries of London (journal) 650n

Napoleon I (Bonaparte), Emperor of France: statue 135n

Napoleon III, Emperor of the French (*formerly* Prince Louis Napoleon) 34n; health 57 & n; gives Convent-dowry to Ellen Power 252; assassination attempt on 522 & n, 525 & n, 707n; CD's photograph mistaken for 576n; Queen Victoria visits 684n

Nash, Charles 294n

NATHAN, Lewis Jacob 213–14, 271, 413 & n

National Association of Factory Occupiers 9n

National Gallery, London 174n

National Gallery of Photographic Portraits, The 72n, 476n

National Magazine 199n

National Newspaper League Co. Ltd. 679n

Naylar, James George 283 & n

Naylor, Benzon & Co. 664n

Naylor Vickers, company 664n

Neville, actor 232n

Newcastle Guardian 668n

Newcastle on Tyne: CD reads at 668, 670–2, 674, 677

New Congregational Hymn Book 500 & n

Newman, J. 233n, 288

New York Times 745

New York Tribune: prints 'violated letter 568n, 644n, 648n, 746n

Niagara, US frigate 498n

Niboyet, Eugénie: translates *Pickwick* into French 23n

Nicaragua 470n

Nice 204

Nicholson, Brigadier John 459n, 460n

Nisbet, Ada: "Dickens loses an election" 707n

Normanby, Constantine Henry Phipps, 1st Marquis of 666n

NORMANBY, Maria, Marchioness of (*née* Liddell) 666

North British Review 591n

Northern Daily Express 668n, 669n, 670n, 671n

North Surrey Industrial Schools 225

Northumberland & Durham District Bank: fails 668n

Northumberland, Algernon Percy, 4th Duke of 21 & n

Notes and Queries 385n

Notes of New Truth (*A Monthly Journal of Homoeopathy*) 44n

Nottage, George Swan 211 & n*, 334n

Nottingham: CD reads at 674, 681, 684, 686

Nottinghamshire Guardian 684n
Novello family 204n
Novello, Clara *see* Gigliucci, Clara Anastasia, Countess
Novello, Emma 204n
NOVELLO, Joseph Alfred 224n, 604n*
Novello, Vincent 261n
Nye, George (or John P.), builder 385n, 420n, 427, 449

Oaks Colliery, near Barnsley, Yorkshire 173n
O'Connell, Daniel 635
O'Connor, Mr 119n
O'Dowd, James Cornelius 529 & n*, 596n
Offenbach, Jacques 30n
O'Hara, Kane 433n
Oliphant, Margaret (Mrs Francis Wilson Oliphant) 674n
Oliver, Richard: "The Treatment of the Insane" 604n
Ollier, Edmund: "A Vision of Old Babylon" 59n
Olliffe, Henry B. 637 & n
OLLIFFE, Sir Joseph 35, 120, 178n, 181, 713
OLLIFFE, Laura, Lady 35n, 120, 483, 713
Opie, John 317n
Opie, Mrs John (Amelia Alderson): *Madeline. A Tale* 317 & n
Orrery, Charles Boyle, 4th Earl of 518n
ORRIDGE, Robert 606n*
Orsini, Felice 522n, 525 & n, 707n
O'Ryan, Owen: "The Leaf" (poem) 410
Osborne, Charles C. 558 & n
OUVRY, Frederic: and CD's purchase of Gad's Hill 38; and Mrs Brown's memorial scholarship (Exhibition) 191, 197–8, 201, 221; and CD's copyright 495; and Allan-Fraser's gift to Guild 562 & n; and CD's marriage breakdown and agreement 566n, 568 & n, 739; and Hogarth family slanders 568n, 569n, 572, 742; advises against CD's 'Personal' statement 577n; ~ and newspaper criticisms of 'Personal' statement 597n; and Yates's writ 631; and CD's 'violated letter' 648, 658; and Colin Rae Brown slander 680n, 685; and *HW*s accounting procedures with Bradbury & Evans 695; ~ and CD's negotiations over *HW* 723; and CD's will 750n
Owen, Richard 72n, 428
OWEN, Mrs Richard (Caroline Amelia Clift) 428n
Owen, Rev. Richard (son of above): *Life of Richard Owen* 428n
Owen, Robert 384n
Owen, William 428n*
OXENFORD, John 247, 248n*, 369n, 515; "Touching the Lord Hamlet" 454, 456
Oxford: CD reads at 687
Oxford, Christ Church; Douglas Jerrold Scholarship 424n

Paget, Lord Alfred 523n
PALFREY, John Gorham 126, 127n*, 132
Palmer, Dr William ('the Rugeley poisoner') 128 & n, 446 & n*
Palmerston, Henry John Temple, 3rd Viscount: and Factory Act 6n; CD's hostility to 90, 177; subscribes to Southwood Smith bust 90 & n; and Sunday music 121n, 123; Prince Albert uses influence against 504n; resigns 522n, 682n
PANIZZI, (Sir) Anthony 109 & n, 283n, 422, 501 & n*
Panmure, Fox Maule, 2nd Baron (*later* 11th Earl of Dalhousie) 673 & n
Paradis Perdu (dramatised version of Milton's *Paradise Lost*) 76, 78
Pardoe, Julia 419 & n; *Pilgrimages in Paris* 419n
Paris: CD stays in 1–31, 35–43, 52–69, 74–103; Crimean military parade in 1–2; 1855 Exhibition 12n, 18n; Georgina in 15, 95; Collins visits 20, 24, 27–8, 46n, 47–8, 53; Macready visits 74, 77, 83–4, 86
Buildings, etc.: Bourse 94; Catacombs 30; English Free School 17n; Jardin d'Hiver 30; Trois frères restaurant 28, 95
Theatres: Ambigu-Comique 11 & n, 76; Cirque Olympique 96n; Folies Nouvelles 30; Gaîté 91n; Odéon 78, 82; Opéra-Comique 63, 66; Porte St Martin 29, 33, 76, 91n; Théâtre Français 37, 95; Théâtre Italien 89n; Théâtre Lyrique 66n, Variétés 57n; Vaudeville 37
Paris, Treaty (and Congress) of (1856) 31n, 76n, 177n
Park, Winthrop 338
PARKE, William 626n*, 696
PARKER, John P.: *Job Brown's Two Glasses* 497n
PARKES, Rev. Samuel Hadden 422n*
Parr, Harriet: "A Day of Reckoning" 194n; "Eleanor Clare's Journal" 410; "Hear my prayer, O! Heavenly Father" 244n, 500; "Madame Freschon's" 98n; "Milverston Worthies" 158n, 159n; "Poor Dick's Story" 195n, 244n
Parsons, John 446n
Partridge, Benjamin 440n
Patten, Robert L.: *CD and his Publishers* 8n, 633n
PAXTON, Sir Joseph: CD entertains 73; puts on weight 150 & n; in Parliament 292n; recommends gardener for Gad's Hill 292; at Jerrold's funeral 352n, 365n; meets Queen Victoria at *Frozen Deep* performance 359,

363; and CD's Coventry reading 484, 490–1; visits Gad's Hill 486; and Lemon's estrangement from CD 603n; absence from CD's Coventry presentation 714–15; friendship with Hoskyns 721n
PAYN, James: contributes to *HW* 22 & n; invited to *Frozen Deep* 224; ~ requests substitution for non-attendance at 251 & n, 253; friendship with A. F. Lehmann 664n; accompanies CD to Hawthornden 672 & n, 674, 716; and 1858 *HW* Christmas number 673 & n; visits Harriet Martineau 674n; appointed co-editor of *Chambers's Journal* 716n; *The Foster Brothers* 716 & n; "Her First Appearance" 716n; "The Marker" 98n; "P.N.C.C." 32n; "Segment's Shadows" 675n; *Some Literary Recollections* 672n, 674n, 716n; "The Two Janes" 456; "A Very Old Gentleman" 675n
Payn, Mrs James (Louisa Adelaide Edlin) 251n
Peabody, George 162
Peel, Captain Sir William 146n
Pelico, Silvio: *Francesca da Rimini* 171n
PEMBERTON, Robert 384n*; *The Infant Drama* 384
Pemberton, T. E.: *CD and the Stage* 397n
Pemble, John: *The Mediterranean Passion* 508n
Penny Pictorial Series 232n
Penny Post (journal) 651n
People's Concerts Committee, St Martin's Hall 182n, 677n
Persano, Countess Fanny di 164 & n
Perth, Scotland: CD reads at 676
Perthshire Journal and Constitutional 677n
Peter the Wild Boy 383
Peterborough Mechanics' Institute 14 & n
Peterloo massacre (1819) 272n
Peters, Catherine: *The King of Inventors* 95n, 361n, 700n
Peyreville, Becquier de 396n
Pfeiffer, Mrs J. E. (Emily Jane Davis): *Valisneria* 333n
PHELPS, Samuel: at Royal General Theatrical Fund Annual Festival 304 & n; and Jerrold memorial fund 350, 355–6; at Queen Victoria's night for *Frozen Deep* 363; plays in Jerrold's *Prisoner of War* 369n; daughter's schooling 649; CD's difficult negotiations with 690
PHELPS, Mrs Samuel (Sarah Cooper) 356n, 363
Phelps, W. May and John Forbes-Robertson: *The Life and Life-Work of Samuel Phelps* 305n
Phillips, F. L.: *Ambition, or The Throne and the Tomb* (*Catherine Howard*) 471n
Phillpotts, Rt Rev. Henry, Bishop of Exeter 272 & n
PHINN, Thomas 284n*
PHIPPS, Lieut.-Colonel the Hon. Charles Beaumont 356, 358–9, 366n, 540
Photographic Portraits of Living Celebrities 72n, 200n, 614n
Piccolomini, Mlle Marietta 639 & n
Pichot, Amédée 63 & n
Picken, Emma *see* Christian, Mrs Eleanor
Pickford, Thomas 18n, 115n
Pierri, Joseph 525n
PIESSE, Charles William Septimus: *The Art of Perfumery* 338n
PIGOTT, Edward Frederick Smyth: sails with Collins 27n, 95n, 214n; CD invites to Boulogne 162; leaves Boulogne with CD 180n; and rehearsals for *Frozen Deep* 214; CD invites to dine 300
Pigott, George 95n
PINNEY, Joel: *The Influence of Occupation on Health and Life* 386n
Pitcairn, Robert: *Criminal Trials in Scotland 1829–33* 7n
Planchén, James Robinson 547n; *The Discreet Princess* 71n; *The Loan of a Lover* 447n
Players, The (magazine) 571n
PLAYGROUND SOCIETY 584n, 586
Plouvier, M. E.: *Sang Melé* 76 & n
Plymouth: CD reads at 612n, 617–19, 621, 623
Plymouth, Devonport and Stonehouse Herald 618n
Plymouth Mail 618n
Pocock, Isaac 722n; *For England Ho!* 217n
Pollard, Rhena 127
Pollock, J. C.: *Way to Glory* 503n
Pollock, Sir Jonathan Frederick 260n
Pollock, Lady 254n
Pollock, William Frederick 270
Poole, John 7n, 24 & n, 87, 94, 522 & n; "A Pair of Razors" 418n, 419n, 481n, 490n; *Turning the Tables* 207 & n
Porter, Joseph 440
Porter, William Smith 726n
Portsea: CD reads at 697n
Portsmouth: CD reads at 697
Postans, Captain Thomas 117n
Potts, Mr & Mrs Charles 624
POWELL, Nathaniel 157, 285, 368n
Power, Ellen ('the Marchioness') 84n, 152, 252 & n
POWER, Marguerite 84n, 87, 152; CD submits Memorial for 242n; Monckton Milnes helps 252; support and appeals for 468, 486 & n, 497, 505; writings 468n; at Gad's Hill 614n, 697; "The Opal Ring" 159; "The Painter's Pet" 240n

Power, Tyrone 635n, 651
Pre-Raphaelite Brotherhood 543n
Preston, Lancashire 171; Theatre Royal 375
Preston Pilot (newspaper) 375n
Price, Ann 24n
Priestley, Eliza, Lady (*née* Chambers): *The Story of a Lifetime* 538n
Prince Imperial (of France) *see* Eugène Louis Jean Joseph Napoléon
Printers' Pension Fund Society 476n
Procter, Adelaide Anne ('Mary Berwick') 170 & n, 701n, 705n; "Beyond" 673 & n; *Legends and Lyrics* 723n; "The Old Sailor's Story" 195n; "Three Evenings in the House" 705n
PROCTER, Bryan Waller ('Barry Cornwall') 60n, 151n, 369n, 480 & n; "The Blacksmith" 723n; *Dramatic Scenes* 250 & n; "Hidden Chords" 723n; "Trade Songs" (series) 723n
Procter, Mrs Bryan Waller (Anne Skepper) 151 & n
Pryor, Richard 354n
Publishers' Circular 293n, 309n, 702n
Punch (magazine): and Miss Coutts's *Common Things* 160 & n; mocks Disraeli 466n; on 'Clemency' Canning 473n; on Deane and Manchester Art Treasures Exhibition 503n; and Lady Duff Gordon 510n; attacks Lord William Pitt Lennox 646n; rejects CD's 'Personal' statement 699n, 701n
Purkess, G. 650n
Pye, Thomas 429n
Pyne, Louisa 690n

Quarterly Review 160, 549 & n, 550n, 592n
Queenstown, Ireland 634
Quekett, Rev. William G. 235n

Rachel, Elisa (Elisabeth Rachel Félix) 61n
Railway Benevolent Society: Dinner (1867) 453n
RAMSBOTHAM, Dr Francis Henry 344n*, 684
Ranke, Leopold von 143n
Ray, Gordon N.: *Thackeray: the Age of Wisdom* 709n
Rayfield, George 698n
RAYNHAM, John Villiers Stuart Townshend, Viscount (*later* 5th Marquis Townshend) 106n*, 327 & n
Reade, Charles: *It is Never Too Late to Mend* 389n
Realf, Richard: *Guesses at the Beautiful* 378n
Record (newspaper) 288
Redgrave, Richard 19 & n
Reece, Mrs (Gladys Wharton Robinson) 687n
Reed, Dr Andrew 327n
REED, Thomas Allen 517n, 519n, 522n, 586n*
REED, Thomas German 352n, 408n*
Reed, Mrs Thomas German (Priscilla Horton) 352n, 408 & n*, 722
REEVES, John Sims 350n*, 352n
Reformatory and Refuge Union 551n
RÉGNIER, François Joseph Philoclès: and CD's article on Théâtre Français 37n; introduces CD to Legouvé 61n; CD invites to dine with Macready 82; and Marston's *Hard Struggle* 514, 519–22; children 519 & n
Régnier, Mme François Joseph Philoclès 83, 519, 521
Renton, Richard: *John Forster and his Friendships* 114n, 204n
Review 646n
Revue Britannique 63n, 131n
Reynolds, G. W. M. 597n, 650n, 651n, 745
Reynolds' Weekly Newspaper 365n, 597n, 745
Richards, Charles: *Algérie* 16n
Richardson, Sir John 66 & n*; *Journal* 265n
Richardson, Lady (Mary Booth; Sir John's second wife) 66n
Richardson, Lady (Mary Fletcher; Sir John's third wife) 66n
Richardson, Joseph 725n
Richardson, Mrs Joseph (Sarah) 725n
RICHARDSON, Sarah (daughter of above) 725n
'Richardson's Show' 571n
Richmond Enquirer, US Newspaper 5n
Richter, Jean Paul: *The Death of an Angel* 54n
RIEU, Charles Pierre Henri 376n*, 390
Ripon, 2nd Earl of *see* Goderich, Viscount
Ristori, Adelaide 61n, 85 & n*, 89, 156, 171, 374 & n, 396n
Ritchie, Thomas 5n
ROBERTS, David 263n, 586, 670–1
Robertson, Alex 607n
ROBERTSON, John: "Captain Doineau" 456n; "Coast Folk" (series) 98n; "The Self-made Potter" 410; "Sepoy Symbols of Mutiny" 410; "Unhappiness in the Elysian Fields" 101n
Robertson, Thomas William 722n
Robin Hood (pantomime) 690n
Robins, George Henry 601n
Robins, Joseph Henry (or Hulme) 601 & n*
Robinson, Gladys Wharton *see* Reece, Mrs
Robinson, William James 216n
ROBSON, Thomas Frederick 171, 352 & n, 387n, 418n, 419, 523n, 527; *Masaniello* 394n
Roche Abbey, near Doncaster 450n
Rochester, Kent 681, 721
Rochester and Chatham Mechanics' Institute

412, 476n, 489, 496, 498n, 501, 612n, 711–12
Rochester, Chatham and Strood Gazette 681 & n, 712n
Rockingham Castle, Northants 14 & n, 15n
Rodwell, George Herbert Buonaparte 141n; *Teddy the Tiler* (adapted from the French) 635n
Roebuck, John A. 72n
Rogers, Samuel 151 & n, 398; death and sale of pictures 213 & n, 215n; CD imitates 380; "Ginevra" 601 & n
Rolfe, Henry 605n
Romani, Pietro 606n
Romberg, Edouard 615n
Romer, Anne 207n
RONEY, James Edward 191n*, 203n, 236
Roney, R. C. 7n
Roney, Mrs R. C. *see* Hogarth, Helen Isabella
Ross, Henry 508n
Rossetti, Dante Gabriel 543n
Rossini, Gioachino Antonio: *La Gazza Ladra* (*The Thieving Magpie*) 722n
Roth, Dr Mathias: *Handbook of the Movement-Cure* 64n
Routledge, George 206n
ROYAL ACADEMY, London 45 & n, 94, 100, 109
Royal Female Philanthropic Society 235n
Royal General Theatrical Fund: anniversary dinner (1856) 32n, 45, 72; ~ CD's speech to 45n; CD declines to be examined by Committee 140; annual festival (1857) 304n, 316, 1850 dinner 453n; provision of relief 499; anniversary dinner (1858) 536n, 541n; gift of land and money from Dodd 609n; and proposed 'Dramatic College' 610n
Royal Geographical Society 330n
Royal Hospital for Incurables 52n, 129n, 300–1, 325, 327
ROYAL HUMANE SOCIETY 688
Royal Leamington Spa Courier 693n
ROYAL LITERARY FUND: CD consults Dilke on 44; 1855 meeting 60, 63; proposed administrative reforms 60 & n, 293n, 304, 324, 549–50, 551n, 554n; CD satirises 88n; helps Joseph Guy 206n; CD criticises Committee ('humbugs') 288n, 293 & n; 1857 Annual General Meeting 293n, 302; CD promotes reorganisation 302, 305n, 324; helps Julia Pardoe 419n; 1858 Annual General Meeting 529–30, 550n; CD criticises 544n; CD requests annual reports 549; article by W. M. Thomas on 591n, 592n; helps Haydn 707n; "The Case of the Reformers" (by CD, Dilke and Forster) 324n; *Summary of Facts* 550n; ~ *Answer* to 550n, 554n, 588n, 592n
ROYAL SCOTTISH ACADEMY, Edinburgh 670 & n, 671
Royal Society of Musicians 318n
Rudkin, Henry 201, 465
Ruge, Arnold: "The Russian Budget" 38 & n
Ruskin, John 108n, 111n, 443n, 506n, 543n, 729n
Russel, Alexander 645n
Russell, Lord John 137, 328, 329n, 504n
RUSSELL, Lady John (Frances Anna Maria Elliot) 137 & n*, 335
Russell, John Scott 47 & n
RUSSELL, William Howard 329n*; CD meets 330, 337; and Jerrold's death 344–7, 402n, 763; entertains Beale 402n; co-edits *Army and Navy Gazette* 529n; reports Indian Mutiny 599–600; *My Diary in India* 599n, 600n; "Personal Narrative of the Late Crimean War" (lecture) 345n, 763–4
Russell, Mrs William Howard (Mary Burrowes) 337 & n, 599–600
Ruston, Alan 571n
Rutherfurd, Andrew Lord 637n
Rutherfurd, Major James Hunter 637 & n, 640
RUTHERFURD, Mrs James Hunter (Elizabeth Young) 638n, 640
RYLAND, Arthur 354, 370 & n, 401

Sabine, Ellen 412n
Sadleir, John 79 & n*, 297n
ST ANN'S SOCIETY: School 302n; Anniversary Festival 318n
St Bernard Convent and Pass *see* Great St Bernard
St John, Bayle: "Tale of a Pocket Archipelago" 99 & n
Sainte-Beuve, Charles Auguste 603n
Sainton-Dolby, Charlotte Helen *see* Dolby
Sala, Charles Kerrison 20n
SALA, George Augustus: contributes to *Train* 5n, 20n; CD entertains 8; borrows from CD 20, 246 & n; contributes to *HW* 20 & n, 24; drinking 20n; trip to Russia 81, 94n, 187; intended visit to America 90 & n, 94n; ill-health 187, 190; quarrel and reconciliation with CD 246n; memoir of Robert Brough 582n; "All up with Everything" 88n, 98n; "Beef" 20n; "The Great Hotel Question" 32 & n, 59n; "A Journey Due North" 81n, 163n, 187, 190, 194, 246; *A Journey Due North* (book) 592n; *Life and Adventures of G. A. Sala* 81n, 246n, 592n; "Little Saint Zita" 20n; "Parisian Nights Entertainment" 20n; "Sunday Music" 121n; *Things I have Seen and People I have Known* 20n
Samee, Mrs Ramo 24 & n, 25
Sampson Low, publishers 515n

SAMS, William Raymond 387n
Samson, Joseph-Isidore 514 & n
Sand, George (Lucile Aurore Dupin; la baronne Dudevant): CD meets 13n, 29 & n*, 33; adapts *As You Like It* 86n; CD on 178
Sandwith, Dr Humphry 60 & n
Sartoris, Edward John 30n, 34
Sartoris, Mrs Edward John (Adelaide Kemble) 30 & n, 34
Saturday Review 389n, 600n, 643n
SAUNDERS, Charles Alexander 610n
Saunders, Detective Frederick White 148
Saunders, John: *Love's Martyrdom* 690n
S(awyer), C. J. and F. J. H. D(arton): *Dickens v. Barabbas, Forster intervening* 699n
Saxo Grammaticus 454
Scarborough: CD reads at 657–8, 661
Scarborough Mercury 657n
Scarlett, Mary 229n
Scheffer, Ary: paints portrait of CD 8 & n, 17, 26n, 28, 33, 45, 66, 79, 108, 326; and George Sand 34; Collins and 105; visits England 328
Scheffer, Mme Ary (Sophie Martin; *later* Baudrin) 34n
Scherzer, Carl: *Travels in the Free States of Central America* 470n
Scotsman (newspaper) 538n, 674n, 745
Scott, Dr J. 178
Scott, Jonathan 63n
Scott, Sir Walter 178, 254n, 492n, 618n; *Rob Roy* 281n
Scribe, Augustin Eugène 58, 61n, 63, 74, 77, 89
Scribe, Mme Augustin Eugène 63
Seaman, Miss 375n
Selby, Charles: *The Last of the Pigtails* 722n; *My Aunt's Husband* 722n
SERLE, Thomas James 724
Seymour, Alexander 395
"Shadow of George Herbert, A" (anon. poem) 20n
Shaftesbury, Anthony Ashley Cooper, 7th Earl of 707n
Shakespeare, William: Ternans play in 433n, 447n, 605n; Bellew reads 444n; Kean plays in Farewell Season 690n; *All's Well that Ends Well* 502n; *As You Like It* (adapted by G. Sand) 86 & n, 95; *Coriolanus* 502n; *Hamlet* 199n, 408n, 454n, 521n, 555n; *1 Henry IV* 265n, 303n; *2 Henry IV* 270n, 532n; *Henry V* 208n; *Julius Caesar* 701n; *King John* 605n, 690n; *King Lear* 408n; *Macbeth* 69n, 123n, 340n, 374n, 553n; *Measure for Measure* 541n; *The Merchant of Venice* 447n, 690n; *The Merry Wives of Windsor* 397n; *Much Ado about Nothing* 690n; *Richard III* 433n, 605n; *The Tempest* 408n; *The Winter's Tale* 605n
Sheepshanks, Rev Thomas 659n
Sheffield: CD reads at 663–4
SHEFFIELD LITERARY AND PHILOSOPHICAL SOCIETY 726
Sheffield Mechanics' Institute 3n, 14 & n, 18
Sheffield and Rotherham Independent 664n
Sheil, Edward: sketch of CD 646n
Shelley, Sir J. V. 121n
Shepherd, Richard 351 & n
Sherborne, Dorset: Evening School for the Industrious Classes 531n
Sheridan, Richard Brinsley 599 & n; *Pizarro* 433n
Shoolbred, James & Co. 510n
Shrewsbury: CD reads at 597n, 613, 621n, 626
Shrewsbury Chronicle 625n
Siddons, Joachim Heyward ('J. H. Stocqueler'): *Any Port in a Storm* 690n
Sidney, Samuel 21 & n
Simond, Louis 196; *Tour in Italy and Sicily* 196n
SIMPSON, John Palgrave 575n*, 596n, 611
Sir William Perkins Charity 225n
Skelton, Percival 266 & n
Skey, Dr Frederic Carpenter 109 & n, 110
Slater, Joseph: (ed.) *Correspondence of Emerson and Carlyle* 714n
Slater, Michael: *Dickens and Women* 559n, 632n
Slegg, James, plumber 366n, 381n
SLY, Joseph 443n*
Smedley, Frank 5n
Smiles, Samuel: *Life of George Stephenson* 339n
Smirke, Sir Robert 109n
Smith & Shepherd, solicitors 568n, 608n
Smith, Albert Richard: at Gallery of Illustration 333n; friendship with CD 334, 351n; speaks Prologue at Gallery of Illustration 384n; gives *Black-Eyed Susan* inter-Act address 387n; CD recommends to friends abroad 415–16, 472; helps Marguerite Power 497n; G. Eliot's *Scenes of Clerical Life* sent to 506n; in Hong Kong 599 & n, 662n; and Robins 601n; and CD's reading tour 661; and Arthur's illness 713, 717; return from China and marriage 713n; "The Ascent of Mont Blanc" (lecture) 16n; *The English Hotel Nuisance* 32 & n
Smith, Mrs Albert Richard (Mary Lucy Keeley) 713n
Smith, Alexander 291n
SMITH, Arthur: invited to Gad's Hill 334; and Jerrold's death and memorial fund concert 345–6, 351n, 354, 374n, 388, 424; and Manchester performance of *Frozen Deep* 407–8, 414; sends banknotes for Jerrold fund 448;

and CD's reading for Great Ormond Street Hospital 520n, 523; manages CD's public readings 533, 539, 541, 546, 549, 551–2, 558, 562–3, 599, 612, 617, 631, 689, 705, 720; and CD's 'violated letter' 568n, 648n, 705n; and Mrs Hogarth's scandal-mongering 568n, 572; and reading of *Little Dombey* 585; death 606n; and CD's requests for rail travel privileges 608–10; on tour with CD 611, 617–18, 621–6, 629, 631, 634–5, 637–8, 640–2, 644, 647, 651, 657–8, 660–1, 664, 669, 677, 685, 691, 694, 703; qualities 617, 624, 689; earnings 632, 643, 649; illness 642, 713, 717–18; buys Irish jaunting car 644, 646n; home 646n; CD retains 705; in Paris 711; and CD's reading at Chatham 712; recovers from illness and returns from Paris 724n; and Colin Rae Brown slander 755

SMITH, Charles Manby: *Curiosities of London Life* 362n

SMITH, Charles Roach 121n*; *Antiquities of Richborough, Reculver, and Lymne, in Kent* 121n

SMITH, ELDER & Co. publishers 80n, 710 & n

Smith, George 4n; "Recollections" 261n, 374n

Smith, George Frederick, of Smith & Shepherd, solicitors 568n, 579n, 648–9, 658, 742

Smith, Oswald 342

Smith, Payne & Smith's Bank 704n

Smith, Robert Vernon *see* Lyveden, Baron

Smith, Rev. Sydney 151n

Smith, Thomas Southwood 90 & n; *Epidemics Considered* 99n

Smithson, Charles 658 & n

Smithson, Elizabeth Dorothy (*née* Thompson) 474n

Smollett, Tobias 279; *Peregrine Pickle* 280n

Snow, William Parker 60 & n

Society for the Encouragement of Arts, Manufactures and Commerce (Society of Arts) 513 & n

Society for the Suppression of Vice 524n

Solly, H. S.: *Life of Henry Morley* 6n

Solomons, Edward 601n

SORRELL, William J. 435n*; *Like and Unlike* (with J. M. Langford) 112n

"Sorrow and My Heart" (anon. poem) 20n

Soulié, Frédéric: *Mémoires du Diable* 149n

Southampton: Walter sails from 379–82; CD reads at 695n, 697, 700

'South Coast Forger' 496n

Southgate & Barrett 403n

Spencer, Frederick, 4th Earl 516 & n

Spicer, Henry: "The New Boy at Styles's" 343n

Spofford, Dr Richard Smith 604n

Spofford, Mrs Richard Smith (Frances Maria Mills) 605 & n

SPOFFORD, Richard Smith, Jr. 604n*

Spofford, Mrs Richard Smith, Jr. (Harriet Elizabeth Prescott; 'Hally') 604n

Spottiswoode, G. A. 403n

Stafford, August Stafford O'Brien: death 489n

Stafford, Mrs Parnell 378n

Standard (newspaper) 286n

STANFIELD, Clarkson: exhibits at 1855 Paris Exhibition 12n; invited to birthday party 56; CD dines with 67–8, 115; exhibits at RA 68n, 108, 306n, 310; visits theatre with CD 70, 113; and Webster's proposals to rebuild Adelphi 109; and Charley's 20th birthday play 118; CD invites to Boulogne 135, 140, 142, 156; and Tavistock House theatre 136; sees *The Flying Dutchman* 141n; David Roberts on 185; in Wales 193; photograph of 200n; designs sets for *Frozen Deep* at Tavistock House 202, 208–9, 213–14, 217–18, 221, 223, 228, 230, 234–5, 238, 240, 249, 358, 380n, 401n; health 258; meets CD at *HW* office 304; CD dedicates *LD* to 327–8; 468n; at Wigan's farewell benefit 369n; death and funeral 603n; Walford writes on 614n; at Royal Scottish Academy dinner 670–1; *The Abandoned* (painting) 68n, 108n; *Calais Fishermen taking in their Nets* (painting) 306n; *Calm in the Gulf of Salerno* 306n; *A Dutch blazer coming out of Monnikendam, Zuyder Zee* (painting) 249n; *Fort Socoa, St Jean de Luz* (painting) 306n; *A guarda costa riding out a gale* (painting) 108n; *Port na Spania* (painting) 306n

Stanfield, Mrs Clarkson (Rebecca Adcock) 68n

Stanfield, George Clarkson 68n

Stanfield, Mrs George Clarkson (Maria Blackburn) 69 & n

Stanhope, Emily Harriet, Countess of (*née* Kerrison) 322 & n

STANHOPE, Philip Henry Stanhope, 5th Earl of 322n*

Stanley, Catherine 295–6

Stanley, Edward John, 2nd Baron Stanley of Alderley 551n

Stanley, Gerald 26n

Stark, Mrs 746

Stark, William 746n

Stark, Mrs William (Catherine Thomson) 746n

Stedman, John Gabriel 278n

Steel & Lawson, wholesale hardwaremen 677n

Steel, David: "CD, Lancaster and the Old King's Arms Royal Hotel, Lancaster" 443n

Stephen, James Fitzjames 389n
Stephenson, George 339
Stephenson, Robert 72n
Stereoscopic Views Warehouse, London 523n
Sterne, Laurence: *Tristram Shandy* 557n
Stevens, James 265n
Stevenson, Sir John 252n
Stiff, George 651n
Stirling, Mrs Edward (Fanny Kehl; *later* Lady Gregory) 523n
'Stocqueler, J. H.' *see* Siddons, Joachim Heyward
Stone, Arthur Paul 111 & n
STONE, Ellen (Nell) 285n, 339–41, 697; "Rather Low Company" 341n
STONE, Frank ('Pumpion'): acts in *Not so Bad as we Seem* 36n; nicknames (Pumpion, Middlesex) 36 & n; appearance 42; CD invites to Boulogne 158; plays in *Turning the Tables* 207; and Tavistock House theatre 225–6; and expenses for Tavistock Square houses 285, 289, 374, 510; CD invites to Gad's Hill 306; RA pictures 309–10; at Gallery of Illustration performance of *Frozen Deep* 377; CD offers part in *Uncle John* 404–5, 412; CD sends 1857 *HW* Christmas number to 483; stays at Sir John Falstaff Inn 557; *Bon Jour, Messieurs* (painting) 158n, 310n; *Doubt* (painting) 76n, 158n; *Margaret* (painting) 310n
Stone, Mrs Frank (Elizabeth) 285n
Stone, Marcus 405n
Stonehouse, J. H. (ed.): *Catalogue of the Library of CD* 122n, 132n, 196n, 316n, 389n, 391n, 481n; *Catalogue of the Pictures of CD* 347n
Stonehouse, near Plymouth: CD reads at 612n, 617n, 618
Storey, Gladys: *Dickens and Daughter* 372n, 472n, 560n
Storey, Graham: "An Unpublished Satirical Sketch by D" 76n
Stowe, Harriet Beecher 313n; *Uncle Tom's Cabin* 314n
STRACEY, Charlotte, Lady (*née* Denne) 5n*
Stracey, Sir Henry Josias, 5th Baronet 5n
Strange, William 650n
Stratheden, Mary, Baroness (*née* Scarlett) 229 & n
Strauss, David Friedrich: *Life of Jesus* 506n
STRUTT, George Henry 678n
Strutt, Mrs George Henry (Agnes Ann Ashton) 678n
Subterfuge (anon. play) 394n
Sucksmith, Harvey Peter 79n, 297n
Sumner, Charles 572n
Sumner, John Bird, Archbishop of Canterbury: *Commentary on the New Testament* 146n
Sunderland: CD reads at 668–9, 671–2
Super, R. H.: *W. S. Landor* 152n, 643n, 644n
Surrey Zoological Gardens 3n
Surtees, Robert 155n
Sutherland, Dr Alexander John 505 & n*
Sutherland, Harriet Elizabeth Georgiana Leveson-Gower, Duchess of 313n

TAGART, Rev. Edward 46n*, 587
Tagart, Mrs Edward (Helen Bourne) 46n
Talfourd, Francis: *Atalanta* 433n
Talfourd, Sir Thomas Noon 371 & n, 721 & n
Tanner, Harriet 127
Taparelli d'Azeglio, Marquis *see* Azeglio, Marquis Massimo Taparelli d'
TAUCHNITZ, Bernard 8n, 80, 81n, 237 & n, 501n
TAYLOR, Alice 691n
Taylor, Bridges 691n
Taylor, Jessie 247n, 334n
TAYLOR, Philip Meadows 640n
Taylor, T. J. 232n
TAYLOR, Tom 384, 387; *A Sheep in Wolf's Clothing* 369n; *Still Waters Run Deep* 70n; *Victims* 447n
TEBB, Robert Palmer 556n
Teignmouth, Devon 50
TELBIN, William: designs scenery for *Frozen Deep* 209 & n*, 218, 221, 228–9, 238, 240–2, 258, 358, 380n, 401n; ~ invited to performance of 228; receives Cheap Edition of CD's works 264 & n; visits Gad's Hill 380; and Manchester performance of *Frozen Deep* 395, 401n; CD declines photographic offer from 532
Telbin, Mrs William 380
Temple Bar (periodical) 175n
Templier, Emile 4n, 8n, 23n
Tennant, Rev. William 272n, 544–5
TENNENT, Sir James Emerson 114, 255–6, 272n
Tennent, Letitia, Lady 114 & n
Tennyson, Alfred (1st Baron): and Jerrold's death 365n; hears CD read in Manchester 399n; and Hulkes 494n; G. Eliot's *Scenes of Clerical Life* sent to 506n; "Charge of the Light Brigade" 526n; *Letters* (ed. Cecil Y. Lang and Edgar F. Shannon) 399n, 494n; *Maud* 319n; *Poems* (Moxon ed.) 543n
Tenterden, Charles Stuart Aubrey Abbott, 3rd Baron 45n, 134 & n
Ternan, Ellen Lawless (*later* Mrs George Wharton Robinson; 'Nelly') 433n*; plays in *Frozen Deep* and *Uncle John* 412n; CD's infatuation with 423n; in Doncaster 429n, 447n, 449n, 450n, 451n; in Kean's company 434n; engaged by Buckstone in London 465–6; CD quarrels with wife over 472n;

rumours of CD's relations with 565n, 573n, 577n, 580n, 597n, 632n, 745; schooling 605n; bracelet present from CD 632n; harassed by policeman 687; legacy in CD's will 750n

Ternan, Frances Eleanor (mother) *see* Ternan, Mrs Thomas Lawless

Ternan, Frances Eleanor (daughter; Fanny) 605 & n*; studies singing in Italy 606n, 666, 686; CD gives letter of recommendation to 666–7

Ternan, Maria Susanna ('Mia') 433n*; plays in *Prisoner of War* 369n; in *Uncle John* 412n; CD's infatuation with 423n; in Doncaster 429n, 447n, 449n, 451n; in *Frozen Deep* 432n, 488; in Kean's company 434n; plays in Hollingshead's *Birthplace of Podgers* 495n; rumours of relations with CD 605n; schooling 605n; harassed by policeman 687; at Strand Theatre 722n

Ternan, Michael 433n

Ternan, Susanna (*née* Lawless) 433n

Ternan, Thomas Lawless 433n*

Ternan, Mrs Thomas Lawless (Frances Eleanor Jarman; Ellen's mother) 433n*; plays in *Frozen Deep* 412n, 433; in Doncaster 447n, 450n, 451n, 500n; accompanies daughter Fanny to Florence 666–7, 687

Ternan, William 433n

Terry, Daniel 379n

Teston, near Maidstone 507n

Thackeray, Anne Isabella (Lady Ritchie) 33n, 300n, 461n; *Chapters from Some Memoirs* 33n

Thackeray, Harriet Marian ('Minnie') 300n

Thackeray, Richmond 461n

THACKERAY, William Makepeace: on CD's acting 261n; friendship with Phinn 284n; CD recommends valet to 285; Gurney praises 319n; speech at Royal Literary Fund meeting 324; and Jerrold's death 345–6; attends Jerrold's funeral 352n, 365n; at Queen Victoria's night for *Frozen Deep* performance 364; attachment to mother 461n; supports appeal for Marguerite Power 486, 497, 505; G. Eliot's *Scenes from Clerical Life* sent to 506n; chairs Royal General Theatrical Fund annual dinner 536n, 541n; praises Mrs Hogge 545n; hosts dinner party 551 & n; contradicts rumours about CD and Georgina Hogarth 573 & n; on CD's 'Personal' statement 580n; and dispute with Yates in 'Garrick Club affair' 588n, 591n, 595 & n, 596n, 600–1, 611n, 631; ~ CD mediates on 708, 709n; as Trustee of Royal General Theatrical Fund 610n; sends copy of CD letter to Garrick committee 711; *The Four Georges* (lectures) 688n, 726n; *Letters and Private Papers* (ed. Gordon N. Ray) 461n, 486n, 497n, 545n, 551n, 573n, 588n, 595n, 611n; *The Virginians* 601; "Week-day Preachers" 345 & n, 375n

Thames, river 598 & n

Theatrical Journal 610n, 649n

THOMAS, William Moy 22 & n, 492n, 652n; "Dr Graves of Warwick Street" 2n; "The Literary Fund" 591n, 592n

Thompson, Amelia 474n

THOMPSON, Caroline 119n, 122, 454

THOMPSON, John, CD's servant: duties for CD 20, 24, 65, 69, 109, 139, 172–3, 243n, 457, 561; pleasure at snowfall 70; and Mitchell 243n; and Tavistock House theatricals 254n; and Gad's Hill furnishing and alterations 284, 332; travels to Gad's Hill 338; takes stage props to Manchester 409–10; window-cleaning 541; on tour with CD 626, 629, 658, 660, 685, 693; ~ in Ireland 634–5, 639, 643

Thompson, Melville ('Mel') 584n

THOMPSON, Thomas James: CD meets 474; visit to Gad's Hill 583 & n, 614n, 617; and Frederick Dickens's marriage breakdown 690–1, 699, 706, 724–5

Thompson, Mrs Thomas James (Christiana Jane Weller) 472n, 474n, 583 & n, 584n, 614n

Thomson, George 749n

Thomson, Helen (Catherine's aunt): and CD–Catherine marriage breakdown 558n, 559n, 560n, 565n, 632n; and CD–Catherine Deed of Separation 578n, 579 & n; letter to Mrs Stark on CD–Catherine separation (text) 746–9 & nn

Ticknor, Reed & Fields, publishers of Boston, Mass. 298n, 589n

Times, The (newspaper): reviews *Jack and the Beanstalk* 11n; praises Webster's *Boots at the Holly Tree Inn* 46n; praises Miss Coutts for prize awards 160 & n; letter from Oaks Colliery miners 173 & n; on Crimean 'Salvage Medal' 174n; on A'Beckett's death 181n; on St Martin's Hall concerts 182n; reviews *Frozen Deep* 248n; reports British Workman's Association meeting on emigration 292n; reports meeting on reform of Royal Literary Fund 324n; reports Jerrold's funeral 352n; and Jerrold memorial fund 353n; on Geils–Dickinson divorce 361n; praises Jerrold Remembrance Night 379n; praises *The Lighthouse* 418n; CD and Smith write to on Jerrold fund 423–4; and Indian Mutiny 459n; prints CD's letter on result of Jerrold fund 463; on Canning's Indian policy 473n; prints letters from prostitutes 524n, 525n; on Massett's reading 526n; on CD's

Times, The (*cont.*):
readings 542n, 548n, 555n; attacks Pre-Raphaelite paintings 543n; publishes CD's 'Personal' statement 573n, 577n, 579n, 744n; on condition of Thames 598n; W. H. Russell reports Indian Mutiny for 599n, 600n; on Landor libel case 643n; on failure of Northumberland and Durham District Bank 668n; Harriet Martineau claims employs clairvoyant 674; prints Sydney Herbert address 702n; reports Winter's bankruptcy 703n; and Lowe sisters' appeal 729; *see also* Delane, John Thadeus
Tipperary Bank: collapse 79n
Todd, William B. and Ann Bowden: *Tauchnitz Editions in English 1841–1955* 8n, 501n
Tomalin, Claire: *The Invisible Woman* 433n, 605n
Toole, John Lawrence ('Johnny') 490 & n, 492n, 625
Torquay 50n, 331 & n, 479, 718n
TOWLE, George Makepeace 590n
Town Talk (periodical) 588n, 600, 708n
Townsend, E. 416n; "Indian Irregulars" 437n
Townshend, John Townshend, 4th Marquis 45n
TOWNSHEND, Rev. Chauncy Hare: in Paris 95–6; travels to Lausanne 177; at Nervi 265, 284; and Cerjat 265, 598; Hollingshead on 389n; at 1858 Royal General Theatrical Fund dinner 536; and reform of Royal Literary Fund 551; CD dines with 722; "Fly Leaves" 172n, 175n; "The Story of Mrs Bell" (unpublished) 176n
TRACEY, Lieut. Augustus Frederick 100n, 223n, 499, 611, 618
Tracey, Mrs Augustus Frederick (Marian Corydon) 101n
Tracey, Henry Elliott 100 & n
Train, The (periodical) 5n, 20n, 389n, 582n
Trollope, Anthony 40n; *Letters* (ed. N. John Hall) 40n; *The Three Clerks* 40n; *The Warden* 40n
TROLLOPE, Mrs Frances 667n
Trollope, Thomas Adolphus 667n; daughter 687n
TROOD, William Stocker 557n*
Truefitt, Henry Paul, hairdresser 619n
Tulloch, Col. Alexander 174n
Tunbridge Wells, Kent 53–4
Turgenev, Ivan Sergeevich 34n, 551n
Turner, Joseph Mallord William 729

Urquhart, Miss (?Mrs T. Whitford) 692n

Valetta, SS 256 & n
Vandenhoff, H. 375n
Varley, John 497n
Velasquez, Diego: *A Boar Hunt* (painting) 174n
Vermond, Paul (i.e. Eugène Grinot) 149n
Vestris, Madame Elizabeth Lucia (Mrs Charles J. Mathews) 73n, 394n, 691n
Viardot, Louis 34n
VIARDOT, Mme Louis (Michelle Ferdinand Pauline Garcia) 13 & n, 29, 33–4, 598
Vibart, H. M.: *Addiscombe* 461n
Victoria, Queen: string band 207 & n; wishes to see *Frozen Deep* 273, 275–6; attends performance of *Frozen Deep* 356–64, 366 & n, 368, 370n; on Indian Mutiny 473n; suggests Havelock's promotion 503n; wishes to hear CD read *Christmas Carol* 540–1; visits France 618n, 684n; visits Leeds 660n, 669n; cities give excessive welcomes to 669n; *Dearest Child* (ed. Roger Fulford) 275n
Vining, Frederick 394
Vining, Mrs George 412n
Voltaire, François Marie Arouet de: *Candide* 459n

Waggett, Dr John 129 & n*
Wailly, Armand François Leon De 508 & n
WALFORD, Edward 72n, 200n*, 612; *Men of the Time* 614n
Walker, Frederick 594n
Wallack, Henry 379n
Wallingford, Berkshire 303
Wallis, Henry: *Chatterton* (painting) 111n
Walpole, Miss, of St James's Theatre 24
Walpole, Horace 132n
"Wandering Willie" (traditional song) 82n
Wanostrocht, Nicholas 696n
WANOSTROCHT, Vincent 696n*
WARD, Edward Matthew 108
Warehousemen and Clerks' Schools anniversary dinner (1857) 477n
Warminster Athenaeum 702n
Warner, Mary Amelia 84n
Warner, Richard 261n, 273, 290
Warren, Samuel 79n, 133 & n*, 674n; "The Forger" 297n
WASHBOURNE, Henry: *The Book of Family Crests* 360n
Waterfield, Gordon: *Layard of Nineveh* 459n
Wates, James 311
WATKINS, Charles 620
Watkins, Emma ('The Coptic') 543n
WATKINS, Herbert 245n, 476, 669; photographs CD 576 & n, 602 & n, 607, 620n
Watkins, John 245n
Watson, Edward Spencer 146n*, 201–2
Watson, George 202 & n
Watson, Hon. Richard: death 14 & n
WATSON, Hon. Mrs Richard (Lavinia Jane

Quin): CD visits at Rockingham 14; children's illnesses 146, 266; visits Great St Bernard Convent 201n; CD sends *Frozen Deep* to 298–9; reads Collins's *Dead Secret* 298; absence abroad 487, 693; CD describes Maria Ternan to 488; invited to CD's Brighton reading 703
Watson, Dr Thomas 182, 410n
Watson, Rev. Wentworth 202 & n*, 693
Watts, Alan: *Dickens at Gad's Hill* 541n
WAUGH, Francis 593n
Waugh, Lieut.-Colonel William Petrie 593n
WEATHERLEY, Rev. Charles Thomas 557n*
Webb, Mrs 313
Webb, Charles: *Belphégor* 722n
Webb, R. K.: *Harriet Martineau, a Radical Victorian* 674n
WEBSTER, Benjamin Nottingham: attends theatre with CD 70; in Paris 77 & n; entertains CD 108; proposes rebuilding Adelphi 109; CD entertains 111, 113; plays in *Like and Unlike* 112n; CD invites to Boulogne 135, 140, 142; in *The Flying Dutchman* 141n, 163; as proprietor of *Field* 155n; invited to CD's Green Room supper 258; as Vice-President of Royal General Theatrical Fund 316n; performs for Jerrold memorial fund 350n, 369n, 379; and Wigan's farewell benefit 369; CD offers dramatisation of *Perils of Certain English Prisoners* to 481–2; speech at Royal General Theatrical Fund 610n; *Boots at the Holly Tree Inn* (adaptation) 32n, 46n; *Jack and the Beanstalk* 11 & n
Weedon, near Althorp 516n
Weekly Newspaper (Jerrold's) 463n
Weekly Record of the Temperance Movement, The 497n
Weidemann, of Leipzig (Andersen's friend) 372n
Weller, Christiana 472n *see* Thompson, Mrs Thomas James
Weller, Mary (*later* Mrs Gibson) 452n
Wellington House Academy, Hampstead 131n
WERNER, Carl Friedrich Heinrich 564n*
WEST, Dr Charles 720n*
West, Edward 584n
Westminster Review 506n
Wheatstone, Sir Charles 11n
White, Miss, of St Peter's Schools, Stepney 732
White, Charlotte ('Lotty') 142 & n
WHITE, Rev. James: CD makes payments to 7, 10n; contributes to *HW* 7 & n, 22, 38; leaves Paris 77; Kate and Mamey stay with 290n; invited to Gad's Hill 331; and 1858 *HW* Christmas number 673 & n; and CD's reading tour 697; "A King who *Could* Do Wrong" 7 & n; "The Scotch Boy's Story" 195n, 278n; "A Summer Night's Dream" 83n; "Two College Friends" 38n
White, Mrs James (Rose Hill) 77n, 97n
Whitehead, Charles: "Nemesis" 83 & n, 88, 98n
Whitelands Training Institution 79n, 128n, 146n, 160n, 272n, 288n, 295n; and Miss Coutts's prizes 731–4
Whitford, Thomas 692n
WHITFORD, Mrs Thomas (*née* Urquhart) 692n
Whittem, James Sibley 715
Whittingham, Paul B.: *Notes on the Late Expedition against the Russian Settlements in Eastern Siberia* 59n
Whitty, E. M.: "Post to Australia" 88n
Whitworth, H., baritone singer 354
Wickham, Helen 605n
Wickham, Rosalind 605n
Wieland, George 281
Wigan, Alfred Sydney 70 & n, 71, 368, 394n, 433n, 649 & n, 669
Wigan, Mrs Alfred Sydney (Leonora Pincott) 70n, 71, 649n
Wigton, Cumberland 439–40, 442–3
Wilby, Miss, of Christ Church Schools, Chelsea 732
Wilkes, J. E.: *How's Your Uncle?* 112n
Wilkie, Sir David 31n
WILKINSON, Rev. George 263n*
Wilkinson, James 6n
Willes, Sir James Shaw 243n, 260
Williams, Mrs 267
Williams, Barney (i.e. Bernard Flaherty) 142n, 143n, 490 & n*, 690n; *The Irish Tutor* 278n
Williams, Mrs Barney (Maria Pray) 115n*; acting parts 141n, 142 & n, 243n, 277n, 291n, 690n; wig 177; and Poole's "Pair of Razors" 490
Williamson, D.: (ed.) *The German Reeds and Corney Grain* 408n
Willmore, Graham 91n
WILLS, William Henry: editorial work at *HW* 2, 6, 16, 20–2, 32, 56–9, 63–4, 80–1, 83, 88, 93, 97–9, 139, 158, 163, 166, 172, 174–5, 193–5, 222, 253, 312, 397, 410, 437, 450, 454–6, 480, 620, 630, 673, 681, 694, 705–6; sends payment to White 10n; as part-time secretary to Miss Coutts 16 & n, 17, 19, 41, 49–50, 54; visits to Gad's Hill 48, 50, 54, 283, 523; and Forster's Agreement with *HW* 56, 730; and CD's purchase of Gad's Hill 71; eye trouble 166–7, 170; visits CD in Boulogne 167; takes holiday 170; lets house 172; and Collins's engagement at *HW* 188–9; invited to reading of *Frozen Deep* 208; mistakes *HW* audit day 218; and applicants to

Wills, William Henry (*cont.*):
see *Frozen Deep* 251, 252–3; and Frederick Dickens 255, 275, 277; and Emily Jolly 312; on storytelling 330; Hollingshead meets 389n; and Manchester performance of *Frozen Deep* 402, 407; pays Jerdan 417; on Jerrold fund committee 424n, 437; and CD's travels in North 438, 448–50; accompanies CD to Coventry 491; and requests for CD's readings 534; in Edinburgh with CD 538n; and publication of CD's 'Personal' statement 579n; named as Trustee and Executor for CD's will 581n, 750; and *Court Circular* article on CD 597n; and CD's reading tour 621, 647, 668, 674, 681, 686; CD dines with at Reform 623; family 664n; meets CD at Huddersfield 664; CD asks to help Maria and Ellen Ternan in London difficulty 686–7; share in *HW* 695n; negotiates with Bradbury & Evans over *HW* dissolution 699, 700n, 701–2, 723, 758, 761; toasted in Coventry 715n; in CD's will 751n; "The Manchester School of Art" 358n, 399n, 450n; "The Ninth of June" 93n, 98n; "Not Very Common Things" (with Morley) 146n

WILLS, Mrs William Henry (Janet Chambers): gives knife to CD 49; plays in *Frozen Deep* 82 & n, 87n, 217, 248n, 253, 254n, 412n; ~ invited to reading of 208; CD thanks for present 278; lameness 354; unwell 437, 451; at Sheffield 664

Wilson, Alexander Ball 498n

WILSON, Mrs Alexander Ball (Rebecca Mary Barrow) 498n

Wilson, Lieut.-General Sir Archdale 459n

WILSON, Professor George 219n*; *Five Gateways of Knowledge* 219 & n

Wilson, Dr James 64n

Wilson, James 573 & n

WILSON, William ('Doubleyou'): *Such is Life* 316n, 434n

Wilton, Emma 232n

Wilton, Marie Effie (*later* Lady Bancroft) 722 & n

Wimbledon School (*later* Roman Catholic Wimbledon College) 279 & n

WINTER, Ella Maria (*later* Barrell) 43 & n, 627, 720

WINTER, Henry Louis 43n, 627n, 703 & n

WINTER, Mrs Henry Louis (Maria Sarah Beadnell): CD presents books to 43 & n; CD's love for 82n; as Flora in *LD* 149 & n; in Liverpool 627 & n; and husband's bankruptcy 704

Wiseman, Cardinal Nicholas Patrick Stephen, Archbishop of Westminster 30n

Wolverhampton: CD reads at 597n, 625–6, 693–6

Wolverhampton Chronicle 625n, 694n

Wood & Co., Edinburgh 541n

Wood, J. M. & Co., Glasgow 541n

Wood, John Muir 541n

Woodford, General Sir Alexander 174n

Worcester: CD reads at 597n, 621

Wordsworth, William 209n; *The Excursion* 313n

Wright, W. M. 15n

Wrottesley, Hon. Mrs George 116 & n

Wrottesley, Sir John Wrottesley, 2nd Baron 116n

Wulff, Henriette 426n

Wynne, Rev. Charles James 279 & n

Wynter, Dr Andrew: "St George and the Dragon" 169n

Yardley, Charles 696

Yates, Charles Dickens Theodore 5n, 50, 379n

YATES, Edmund Hodgson 5n*; and Jerrold memorial fund 348n, 351, 353n, 374n; children 379n; visits Gad's Hill 380n; friendship with Bellew 444n; misquotes CD 513 & n; on Charles Dance 547n; praises CD's reading 555 & n; dispute with Thackeray in 'Garrick Club Affair' 588n, 591n, 595 & n, 600, 601n, 708; ~ loses Garrick membership 596n, 611n; in Thackeray's *Virginians* 601; CD recommends to Chapman 615; issues and abandons writ 631 & n; CD mediates for in Garrick Club affair 708, 709n; ~ CD sends copies of letters to 711; *After Office Hours* 615n; "A Fearful Night" 5n; "Gone Before" 253n; *Mr Thackeray, Mr Yates and the Garrick Club* 596n, 600n, 708n, 709n; *A Night at Nottingham* (with Harrington) 278n; *Recollections and Experiences* 20n, 380n, 479n, 513n, 547n, 553n, 555n, 588n, 596n, 601n, 707n, 708n; "Two in a Legion" 479n

YATES, Mrs Edmund Hodgson (Louisa Katharine Wilkinson) 6n, 48, 565n, 568n, 576n

Yates, Frank (Francis; Edmund's son) 379n

Yates, Frederick Henry (Edmund's father) 379n

Yates, Mrs Frederick Henry (Elizabeth Brunton) 379n, 564

Yates, Frederick Henry Albert (Edmund's son) 379n, 571n

Yescombe, Rev. Morris 643n

Yescombe, Mrs Morris 643n

Yonge, Charlotte M.: *The Heir of Redclyffe* 702n

York: CD reads at 621n, 656 & n, 657–8, 660, 685

York Herald 656n

Young, Alexander 638n

Young, Charles Mayne 164n
Young, H. 482n
Young, Rev. Julian Charles 164 & n, 693
Young, Mrs Marianne (*formerly* Postans) 117n*; *Aldershot and All about it* 117n; "Women at Aldershot" 83n, 117n
Young, Robert 219n
Young, William: *The History of Dulwich College* 136n
Young Man and the Young Woman, The (periodical) 26n

Zoological Gardens, London 281–2